BUTLER'S Lives of the Saints

COMPLETE EDITION

EDITED, REVISED AND SUPPLEMENTED BY

HERBERT J. THURSTON, S.J.
AND DONALD ATTWATER

VOLUME IV

OCTOBER • NOVEMBER • DECEMBER

General Index in This Volume

Christian Classics™
A DIVISION OF THOMAS MORE PUBLISHING

Allen, Texas

Nihil Obstat: Patricivs Morris, S.T.D., L.S.S.
Censor Depvtatvs
Imprimatvr: E. Morrogh Bernard
Vicarivs Generalis
WestmonasterII: die XXIII Febrvarii MCMLIII

Send all inquiries to:
Christian Classics™
a division of Thomas More Publishing
200 East Bethany Drive
Allen, Texas 75002

Lives of the Saints originally published 1756–9.
Revised edition by Herbert J. Thurston, S.J.,
published 1926–38. Copyright by Burns & Oates.
Second Edition, by Herbert J. Thurston, S.J. and
Donald Attwater, published 1956.
Copyright © Burns & Oates 1956.
Reprinted 1981, 1990, 1995, 1996

Library of Congress Catalog Card Number: 56–5383

ISBN:	Cloth Edition	Paperback Edition
Volume I	0–87061–046–5	0–87061–214–X
Volume II	0–87061–047–3	0–87061–215–8
Volume III	0–87061–048–1	0–87061–216–6
Volume IV	0–87061–049–X	0–87061–217–4
Complete Set	0–87061–045–7	0–87061–137–2

Printed in the United States of America

CONTENTS OF VOLUME IV

OCTOBER

NOVEMBER

DECEMBER

BIBLIOGRAPHICAL ABBREVIATIONS

Acta Sanctorum—This without qualification refers to the *Acta Sanctorum* of the Bollandists.

BHG.—The *Bibliotheca hagiographica graeca* of the Bollandists.

BHL.—The *Bibliotheca hagiographica latina* of the Bollandists.

BHO.—The *Bibliotheca hagiographica orientalis* of the Bollandists.

Burton and Pollen, LEM.—*Lives of the English Martyrs*, second series, ed. E. H. Burton and J. H. Pollen.

Camm, LEM.—*Lives of the English Martyrs*, first series, ed. Bede Camm.

CMH.—H. Delehaye's Commentary on the Hieronymian Martyrology, in the *Acta Sanctorum*, November, volume ii, part 2.

DAC.—*Dictionnaire d'Archéologie chrétienne et de Liturgie*, ed. F. Cabrol and H. Leclercq.

DCB.—*A Dictionary of Christian Biography*, ed. William Smith and Henry Wace.

DHG.—*Dictionnaire d'Histoire et de Géographie ecclésiastiques*, ed. A. Baudrillart *et al.*

DNB.—The *Dictionary of National Biography*, ed. Leslie Stephen *et al.*

DTC.—*Dictionnaire de Théologie catholique*, ed. A. Vacant *et al.*

KSS.—*Kalendars of Scottish Saints*, ed. A. P. Forbes.

LBS.—*Lives of the British Saints*, by S. Baring-Gould and John Fisher.

LIS.—*Lives of the Irish Saints*, by John O'Hanlon.

Mabillon—*Acta Sanctorum Ordinis Sancti Benedicti*, ed. J. Mabillon.

MGH.—*Monumenta Germaniae Historica*, ed. G. H. Pertz *et al.*

MMP.—*Memoirs of Missionary Priests*, by Richard Challoner, referred to in the edition of 1924, ed. J. H. Pollen.

PG.—*Patrologia graeca*, ed. J. P. Migne.

PL.—*Patrologia latina*, ed. J. P. Migne.

REPSJ.—*Records of the English Province of the Society of Jesus*, ed. Henry Foley.

Ruinart—*Acta primorum martyrum sincera et selecta*, ed. T. Ruinart.

Stanton's *Menology*—*A Menology of England and Wales*, by Richard Stanton.

VSH.—*Vitae Sanctorum Hiberniae*, ed. Charles Plummer.

Father H. Delehaye's *Les origines du culte des martyrs* is referred to in the " deuxième édition revue " of 1933.

There is an English translation by Mrs V. M. Crawford of Father Delehaye's *Les légendes hagiographiques* (" The Legends of the Saints "), made from the first edition. The third French edition (1927) is revised and is therefore sometimes referred to.

The English title of the work herein referred to as " Léon, *L'Auréole séraphique* (Eng. trans.) " is *Lives of the Saints and Blessed of the Three Orders of St Francis* (1885–87), by Father Léon (Vieu) de Clary. A corrected and enlarged edition of this work in Italian, by Father G. C. Guzzo, began publication in 1951 : *Aureola serafica*. By 1954 four volumes had appeared, covering January-August.

It has not been deemed necessary to give every reference to such standard works as the *Dictionary of Christian Biography*, the *Dictionnaires* published by Letouzey, and

A. Fliche and V. Martin's *Histoire de l'Église*, though these are often referred to in the bibliographical notes.   The first two volumes of Fliche and Martin, by J. Lebreton and J. Zeiller, have been translated into English by Dr E. C. Messenger (*The History of the Primitive Church*, 4 vols.), and the first two English volumes of the continuation, *The Church in the Christian Roman Empire*, are also published.

The reader may here be reminded once for all that for all modern saints and *beati* the surest source of information on the more strictly spiritual side is the *summarium de virtutibus* with the criticisms of the *Promotor fidei* which are printed in the process of beatification.   Copies of these are occasionally to be met with in national or private libraries, though they are not published or offered for sale to the general public. And for all saints named in the Roman Martyrology the standard short reference is in the *Acta Sanctorum, Decembris Propylaeum : Martyrologium Romanum ad formam editonis typicae scholiis historicis instructum* (1940).   This great work provides a running commentary on the entries in the Roman Martyrology, correcting where necessary conclusions expressed in the sixty-odd volumes of the *Acta Sanctorum*, and anticipating much that will be said at greater length in those volumes that have yet to appear ; and there are summary bibliographies throughout.   It is indispensable for all serious study and reference.

OCTOBER

1 : ST REMIGIUS, OR REMI, BISHOP OF RHEIMS   (*c.* A.D. 530)

S
T REMIGIUS, the great apostle of the Franks, was illustrious for his
learning, sanctity and miracles, which in his episcopacy of seventy and more
years rendered his name famous in the Church.   His father and his mother
were both descended from Gaulish families, and lived at Laon.   The boy made
great progress in learning, and in the opinion of St Sidonius Apollinaris, who was
acquainted with him in the earlier part of his life, he became the most eloquent
person in that age.   When only twenty-two, too young to be a priest, much less a
bishop, he was chosen in 459 to fill the vacant see of Rheims.   But he was ordained
and consecrated in spite of his youth, and amply made up for lack of experience by
his fervour and energy.   Sidonius, who had considerable practice in the use of
words of commendation, was at no loss to find terms to express his admiration of
the charity and purity with which this bishop offered at the altar a fragrant incense
to God, and of the zeal with which he subdued the wildest hearts and brought them
under the yoke of virtue.   Sidonius had a manuscript of his sermons from a man
at Clermont (" I do not know how he got hold of it.   Like a good citizen he gave
it to me, instead of selling it "), and wrote to tell Remigius how much he admired
them : the delicacy and beauty of thought and expression were so smooth that it
might be compared to ice or crystal upon which a nail runs without meeting the
least unevenness.   With this equipment of eloquence (of which unfortunately
there is no specimen extant for us to judge its quality for ourselves) allied to the
yet more valuable quality of personal holiness, St Remigius set out to spread
Christianity among the Franks.

Clovis, king of all northern Gaul, was himself yet a pagan, though not unfriendly
to the Church.   He had married St Clotildis, daughter of the Christian king of
the Burgundians, Chilperic, and she made repeated attempts to convert her husband.   He agreed to the baptism of their first-born, but when the child shortly
after died he harshly reproached Clotildis, and said, " If he had been consecrated
in the name of my gods, he had not died ; but having been baptized in the name of
yours, he could not live ".   The queen afterwards had another son, whom she
had baptized, and he also fell sick.   The king said in great anger, " It could not be
otherwise.   He will die as his brother did through having been baptized in the
name of your Christ."   This child recovered, but it required a more striking
manifestation of the might of the Christian God to convert the rough Clovis.   It
came apparently in 496, when the Alemanni crossed the Rhine and the Franks
marched out to drive them back.   One account says that St Clotildis had said to
him in taking leave, " My lord, to be victorious invoke the God of the Christians.
If you call on Him with confidence, nothing can resist you " ; and that the wary
Clovis had promised that he would be a Christian if he were victorious.   The

I

battle was going badly against him when the king, either reminded of these words or moved by desperation, shouted to the heavens, " O Christ, whom Clotildis invokes as son of the living God, I implore thy help ! I have called upon my gods, and they have no power. I therefore call on thee. I believe in thee ! Deliver me from my enemies and I will be baptized in thy name ! " The Franks rallied and turned the tide of battle ; the Alemanni were overcome.

It is said that Clovis, during his return from this expedition, passed by Toul, and there took with him St Vedast, that he might be instructed by him in the faith during his journey. But Queen St Clotildis was not trusting to any enthusiasm of victory, and sent for St Remigius, telling him to touch the heart of the king while he was well disposed. When Clovis saw her he cried out, " Clovis has vanquished the Alemanni and you have triumphed over Clovis. What you have so much at heart is done." The queen answered, " To the God of hosts is the glory of both these triumphs due ". Clovis suggested that perhaps the people would not be willing to forsake their gods, but said he would speak to them according to the bishop's instructions. He assembled the chiefs and warriors, but they prevented his speaking, and cried out, " We abjure mortal gods, and are ready to follow the immortal God whom Remigius preaches ". St Remigius and St Vedast therefore instructed and prepared them for baptism. To strike the senses of barbarous people and impress their minds, Queen Clotildis took care that the streets from the palace to the church should be adorned with hangings, and that the church and baptistery should be lighted with a great number of candles and scented with incense. The catechumens marched in procession, carrying crosses, and singing the litany ; St Remigius conducted the king by the hand, followed by the queen and the people. At the font the bishop is said to have addressed Clovis in words that are memorable, if not actually pronounced : " Humble yourself, Sicambrian ! Worship what you have burned, and burn what you have worshipped ! " Words which may be emphatically addressed to every penitent, to express the change of heart and conduct that is required of him.

St Remigius afterwards baptized the king's two sisters and three thousand men of his army, as well as women and children, with the help of the other bishops and priests present. Hincmar of Rheims, who wrote a Life of St Remigius in the ninth century, is the first to mention a legend that at the baptism of Clovis the chrism for the anointing was found to be missing, whereupon St Remigius prayed and a dove appeared from the heavens, bearing in its beak an *ampulla* of chrism. A phial of oil, fabled to be the same, was preserved at the abbey of Saint-Remi and used in the consecration of the kings of France until Charles X in 1825. It was broken up at the Revolution, but a piece of *la Sainte Ampoule* and its contents were saved and are kept in Rheims Cathedral. St Remigius is also supposed to have conferred on Clovis the power of touching for the " king's evil " (scrofula), which was exercised by the kings of France at their coronation, again up to Charles X. This power was confirmed by the relics of St Marculf, who died about 558.

Under the protection of Clovis, St Remigius spread the gospel of Christ among the Franks, in which work God endowed him with an extraordinary gift of miracles, if we may trust his biographers on this point. The bishops who were assembled in a conference that was held at Lyons against the Arians in his time declared they were stirred to exert their zeal in defence of the Catholic faith by the example of Remigius, " who ", say they, " has everywhere destroyed the altars of the idols by a multitude of miracles and signs ". He did his best to promote orthodoxy in

Arian Burgundy, and at a synod in 517 converted an Arian bishop who came to it to argue with him. But the actions of St Remigius did not always meet with the approval of his brother bishops. Sometime after the death of Clovis the bishops of Paris, Sens and Auxerre wrote to him concerning a priest called Claudius, whom he had ordained at the request of the king. They blamed Remigius for ordaining a man whom they thought to be fit only for degradation, hinted that he had been bribed to do it, and accused him of condoning the financial malpractices of Claudius. St Remigius thought these bishops were full of spite and told them so, but his reply was a model of patience and charity. To their sneer at his great age he answered, " Rather should you rejoice lovingly with me, who am neither accused before you nor suing for mercy at your hands ". Very different was his tone towards a bishop who had exercised jurisdiction outside his diocese. " If your Holiness was ignorant of the canons it was ill done of you to transgress the diocesan limits without learning them. . . . Be careful lest in meddling with the rights of others you lose your own."

St Remigius, whom St Gregory of Tours refers to as " a man of great learning, fond of rhetorical studies, and equal in his holiness to St Silvester ", died about the year 530.

Although the enthusiastic letter in which Sidonius Apollinaris (who has, not unfairly, been described as an " inveterate panegyrist ") commends the discourses of St Remigius is authentic, most of the sources from which we derive our knowledge of the saint are, to say the least, unsatisfactory. The short biography attributed to Venantius Fortunatus is not his, but of later date, and the *Vita Remigii*, written by Hincmar of Rheims three centuries after his death, is full of marvels and open to grave suspicion. We have therefore to depend for our facts upon the scanty references in St Gregory of Tours (who declares that he had before him a Life of St Remigius) and to supplement these by a phrase or two in letters of St Avitus of Vienne, St Nicetius of Trier, etc., together with three or four letters written by Remigius himself. The question in particular of the date, place and occasion of the baptism of Clovis has given rise to protracted discussion in which such scholars as B. Krusch, W. Levison, L. Levillain, A. Hauck, G. Kurth, and A. Poncelet have all taken part. A detailed summary of the controversy, with bibliographical references will be found, under " Clovis ", in DAC., vol. iii, cc. 2038–2052. It can safely be affirmed that no conclusive evidence has yet upset the traditional account given above, so far, at least, as regards the substantial fact that Clovis in 496, or soon after, after a victory over the Alemanni, was baptized at Rheims by St Remigius. As for more general matters, the principal texts, including the *Liber Historiae*, have been edited by B. Krusch ; see BHL., nn. 7150–7173. Consult also G. Kurth, *Clovis* (1901), especially vol. ii, pp. 262–265 ; and *cf.* A. Hauck, *Kirchengeschichte Deutschlands*, vol. i (1904), pp. 119, 148, 217, 595–599. There are popular but uncritical lives by Haudecœur, Avenay, Carlier and others. For " touching " see *Les rois thaumaturges* (1924), by M. Bloch ; and for the ampulla, F. Oppenheimer, *The Legend of the Sainte Ampoule* (1953).

ST ROMANUS THE MELODIST (Sixth Century)

The composition of liturgical poetry has naturally had an attraction for many holy men, and Romanus the Melodist, the greatest of the Greek hymn-writers, is recognized and venerated as a saint in the East. He was a Syrian of Emesa, who became a deacon in the church of Bairut. During the reign of the Emperor Anastasius I he came to Constantinople. Beyond the writing of many hymns (some in dialogue form), nothing else is known of his life, except a story in the Greek *Menaion* which professes to give an account of his receiving the gift of sacred poetry at Constantinople. One eve of Christmas our Lady appeared to Romanus in his sleep and gave him a roll of paper, saying, " Take this and eat it ". It

3

appeared to him that he did so, and then he awoke and in great exaltation of spirit went down to the church of the All-holy Mother of God to assist at the Christmas liturgy.   When the gospel-book was about to be carried solemnly into the sanctuary, he went up into the deacon's ambo and extemporized the hymn beginning ἡ παρθένος σήμερον τὸν ὑπερούσιον τίκτει : " On this day the Virgin gives birth to Him who is transcendent, and the earth offers a shelter to the Unattainable. Angels join with shepherds to glorify Him and the Magi follow the star.   For a new child is born to us, who was God before all ages."   This *kontakion* summarizing the day's feast is still sung in the Christmas offices of the Byzantine rite.

Some eighty other hymns of St Romanus survive, whole or in part.   They are vivid in feeling and dramatic in style, but sometimes spoiled by excessive length and too elaborate eloquence, like so much other Byzantine literary composition. They have a wide range of subjects, drawn from both Testaments and the feasts of the Church.

There has been discussion whether St Romanus lived under the Emperor Anastasius I (491–518) or under Anastasius II (713–715).   Krumbacher, who at first favoured the earlier date, later on inclined to the alternative view (see the *Sitzungsberichte* of the Munich Academy, 1899, vol. ii, pp. 3–156), but the more prevalent opinion connects Romanus with the sixth century.   If he lived two hundred years later it would be strange that we find in his *kontakia* no reference to iconoclasm.   Much interest has of late years been taken in St Romanus by Byzantinists.   See especially G. Cammelii, *Romano il Melode : Inni* (1930) ; E. Mioni, *Romano il Melode* (1937, with bibliography) ; and E. Wellesz, *A History of Byzantine Music and Hymnography* (1949).   In the *Byzantinische Zeitschrift*, vol. xi (1912), pp. 358–369, Father Petrides has printed a complete liturgical office of the Greek church composed in honour of St Romanus.   The thousand hymns he is said to have composed seems a large number, and it has been suggested by Father Bousquet, in *Échos d'Orient*, vol. iii (1900), pp. 339–342, that his output was not really a thousand hymns but a thousand strophes.   See also J. M. Neale, *Hymns of the Eastern Church* (1863) ; J. B. Pitra, *L'hymnographie de l'Église Grecque* (1867) and *Analecta sacra . . .*, vol. i (1876) ; and K. Krumbacher, *Geschichte der byzantinischen Literatur* (1897).

ST MELORUS, MELAR OR MYLOR, MARTYR   (DATE UNKNOWN)

THE church of the great nunnery at Amesbury in Wiltshire was dedicated in honour of our Lady and St Melorus, whose relics it claimed ; numerous places in the north and west of Brittany have St Mélar as their patron ; and a St Mylor was the patron of three churches in Cornwall, namely, Mylor, Linkinhorne and Merther Mylor in the parish of St Martin-in-Meneage.   The medieval Life of Melorus the Martyr, abridged from a French work and probably written at Amesbury, states that he was son of Melianus, Duke of Cornouaille (in Brittany).   When he was seven years old his uncle Rivoldus murdered Melianus, usurped his power, and maiming Melorus by cutting off his right hand and left foot, confined him in a monastery.   By the time the boy was fourteen his miracles earned him such honour that Rivoldus began to fear him, and bargained with his guardian Cerialtanus to get rid of him.   Accordingly Cerialtanus smote off his head.   The dead body of Melorus wrought several miracles, including the death of his murderers, and it was buried with honour.   After many years missionaries brought the relics to Amesbury, whence they were supernaturally prevented from removing them.   The legend current in Cornwall in the middle ages was substantially the same, but as written down by Grandisson, Bishop of Exeter, the events are staged in Devon and Cornwall.   The Breton legend, as it appears in the pages of Albert Le Grand in the seventeenth century, is longer and more detailed, many details being supplied out of the editor's head.   Abbé Duine regarded this story of the " martyred " prince as a " fable worked up out of bits of folk-lore and Celtic pseudo-genealogies, after the taste of the hagiographical romances of the eleventh and twelfth centuries " ; at the best it may have a quite forgotten foundation in fact in the murder of some innocent and noble youth.

During the reign of King Athelstan a number of relics of Breton saints were brought to churches in the south and west of England, and Canon G. H. Doble suggests that among them some of St Melorus came to Amesbury and so established the connexion between the saint and that place.   The same authority is of the opinion that the Mylor of Cornwall originally had reference not to Melorus the martyr but to St Melorius (Méloir), a Breton bishop.   He gives his name to Tréméloir and was a companion of St Samson of Dol, and the situation of the three Cornish Mylor dedications are favourable both to voyaging to and from Brittany and to association with St Samson.   The patronal feast of Mylor by Falmouth was on August 21 (and not October 1 or 3, St Mélar's days), while that of Tréméloir is on the last Sunday in August.   Both Mélar and Méloir must be distinguished from St Magloire (October 24) ; philologically the names are the same.   The death of St Melorus is localized by tradition at Lanmeur, in the diocese of Dol, and it is said that his severed members were replaced by a hand of silver and foot of brass, which were as useful as flesh and bone to him, even growing with the rest of his body.   The idea is met with elsewhere in Celtic folk-lore.   St Melorus was represented in the pictures on the walls of the English College chapel at Rome.

Canon Doble's booklet on *St Melor* in his series " Cornish Saints " provides undoubtedly the most careful study that has been made of this rather obscure legend.   He incorporates with his text a translation of an essay written by René Largillière.   Notices of less value may be found in LBS., vol. ii, p. 467 ; and in Stanton's *Menology*, p. 468.   See also the *Analecta Bollandiana*, vol. xlvi (1928), pp. 411–412.

ST BAVO   (*c.* A.D. 655)

THIS famous hermit, also called Allowin, was a nobleman, and native of that part of Brabant called Hesbaye.   After having led a very irregular life he was left a widower, and was moved to conversion to God by a sermon which he heard St Amand preach at Ghent.   Going home he distributed all his money among the poor, and went to the monastery at Ghent that was afterwards called by his name. Here Bavo received the tonsure at the hands of St Amand and was animated to advance daily in the fervour of his penance and the practice of virtue.   " It is a kind of apostasy ", said his director to him, " for a soul which has had the happiness to see the nothingness of this world and the depth of her spiritual miseries not to raise herself daily more and more above them and to make continual approaches to God."   St Bavo seems to have accompanied St Amand on his missionary journeys in France and Flanders, setting an example by the humiliation of his heart, the mortification of his will, and the rigour of his austerities.   St Amand after some time gave him leave to lead an eremitical life, and he is said first to have chosen for his abode a hollow trunk of a large tree, but afterwards built himself a cell at Mendonck, where vegetables and water were his chief subsistence.

St Bavo is said on one occasion to have done penance for selling a man into serfdom by making the man lead him by a chain to the common lock-up.   Bavo at length returned to the monastery at Ghent, where St Amand had appointed St Floribert abbot ; and with his approval Bavo built himself a new cell in a neighbouring wood, where he lived a recluse until the end of his life.   St Amand and St Floribert attended him on his deathbed and his peaceful passage made a deep impression on all who were present.   As in the diocese of Ghent so in that of Haarlem in Holland, St Bavo is titular of the cathedral and patron of the diocese.

The earliest life of St Bavo—there are two or three printed in the *Acta Sanctorum*, October, vol. i—has been re-edited by B. Krusch in MGH., *Scriptores merov.*, vol. iv, pp. 527–546. He assigns it to the latter part of the ninth century and deems it to be of little value as a historical source.   See also Van der Essen, *Étude . . . sur les saints mérov.* (1907), pp. 349–357 ; E. de Moreau, *St Amand* (1927), pp. 220 *seq.* ; R. Podevijn, *Bavo* (1945) ; and *Analecta Bollandiana*, vol. lxiii (1945), pp. 220–241, where Fr M. Coens discusses, *inter alia*, whether St Bavo was a bishop.

BD FRANCIS OF PESARO   (*c.* A.D. 1350)

THIS Francis, commonly called Bd Cecco, was born in Pesaro and, his parents having left him well off, he determined while still a young man to devote his wealth to the needy and himself to God.   Accordingly in the year 1300 he joined the third order of St Francis, and retired to a hermitage which he had built on the slope of Monte San Bartolo, by Pesaro.   Here he soon had a number of disciples, to help support whom he begged from place to place, and so became known and loved far and wide for his goodness and benevolence.   Bd Francis lived thus for some fifty years, and a number of remarkable occurrences were associated with his name. Having been with his disciples to Assisi to gain the Portiuncula indulgence, he was detained in Perugia and sent his companions on before him ; to their astonishment he was there waiting for them when they arrived at the hermitage.   However, this does not necessarily mean anything more than that he had a good knowledge of short-cuts across the country ; such simple incidents as this in the lives of the saints have been too easily magnified into miracles by enthusiastic biographers.

Bd Francis was not at all " stand-offish " and would sometimes accept invitations to dine with people in the world ; but on these occasions he took care not to give way to any excessive pleasure in unaccustomed good food, and dealt mercilessly with any sign of gluttony in himself : nor was he slow in rebuking this failing in others.   Once when he was ill he lost his appetite altogether, and his followers killed a cockerel, intending to cook it carefully in the hope of thereby coaxing him to eat.   But Francis missed the bird's crowing and enquired after it, and when he was told that it had been killed, he rebuked them.   " You ought ", he said, " to have been too grateful to it for its crowing at midnight and dawn to have taken its life away, even though it was out of your kind compassion to myself.   Its voice in the morning was a reproach to my laziness and stirred me to be up and about in the Lord's service."   His biographer goes on to say that he prayed over the cockerel, which was not only dead but plucked, and its life was restored, together with its plumage !   Bd Francis helped Bd Michelina Metelli to found the Confraternity of Mercy at Pesaro and to build a hospice for tramps and pilgrims at Almetero. His body was laid in the cathedral of Pesaro and his ancient *cultus* confirmed by Pope Pius IX.

There is a short medieval biography printed in the *Acta Sanctorum*, August, vol. i.   See also Mazzara, *Leggendario Francescano* (1679), vol. ii, pp. 199–202, and Léon, *Auréole Séraphique* (Eng. trans.), vol. ii, pp. 547 *seq.*

BD NICHOLAS OF FORCA PALENA   (A.D. 1449)

AFTER being a secular priest in his native town in the Abruzzi, this Nicholas went to Rome.   Finding that he was called to an eremitical life, he founded a society of hermits under the patronage of St Jerome and by the generous legacy of a friend was enabled to establish them at Naples.   Pope Eugenius IV gave him an empty monastery at Florence for a similar foundation there, and Bd Nicholas then returned to Rome and formed another community on the Janiculum, at the church of Sant' Onofrio, which is now a cardinalitial title.   At this time there was another congregation of hermits of St Jerome, with branches in Rome and elsewhere, recently founded by Bd Peter of Pisa, and with these Bd Nicholas amalgamated his religious. He died in 1449 at the age of a hundred, and his *cultus* among the Hieronymites was confirmed in 1771 ; Pope Benedict XIV would not agree to his solemn beatification.

The Bollandists could meet with no medieval life of this hermit, but under September 29 they compiled a fairly copious account from later sources, notably from the *Historica monumenta* of the Hieronymite Sajanello.   The evidence of *cultus* in the seventeenth century is good.

THE CANTERBURY MARTYRS AND OTHERS OF 1588

REFERENCE has been made under date August 28 to the London martyrs who suffered in the renewal of persecution which took place following the Armada scare in July 1588.   On October 1 there was a batch of executions in the provinces, seven *beati* being put to death, four at Canterbury and three elsewhere.   BD ROBERT WILCOX was born at Chester in 1558.   He was trained at the English College at Rheims, and sent on the mission in 1586.   He began to labour in Kent, but in the same year was taken up and imprisoned in the Marshalsea.   He was condemned to death and was hanged, drawn and quartered at Canterbury, on Oaten Hill, outside the city walls on the south side.   With him died BB. EDWARD CAMPION, CHRISTOPHER BUXTON and ROBERT WIDMERPOOL.   Campion (*vere* Edwards) was born at Ludlow in 1552 and was for two years at Jesus College, Oxford.   He was reconciled to the Church while in the service of Gregory, Lord Dacre, and went to Rheims in 1586, when he assumed the name of Campion.   He was ordained priest, " of the diocese of Canterbury ", early in the following year and was at once sent to England.   He was arrested at Sittingbourne and shut up first in Newgate and then the Marshalsea.   Mr Buxton was a Derbyshire man, born at Tideswell.   He was at school there under the venerable martyr Nicholas Garlick and was sent to study for the priesthood at Rheims and Rome.   He was arrested and condemned soon after his return to England.   These three secular priests all suffered for coming into the realm as seminary priests.   Bd Christopher was the youngest and it was thought that the sight of the barbarous execution of the others might frighten him into apostasy ; when offered his life on that condition, he replied that he would rather die a hundred times.   During his imprisonment in the Marshalsea he wrote out a *Rituale*, a relic which is still in existence.   The fourth Canterbury martyr, Mr Widmerpool, was a layman, born at Widmerpool in Nottinghamshire, educated at Gloucester Hall, Oxford, and a schoolmaster by profession.   He was for a time tutor to the sons of the Earl of Northumberland, and his offence was that he had helped a priest by getting him shelter in the house of the countess. Bd Robert was hanged, thanking God that he was privileged to die for the faith in the same city as St Thomas Becket.

On the same day were martyred, at Chichester, BD RALPH CROCKETT and BD EDWARD JAMES, and at Ipswich BD JOHN ROBINSON. They were secular priests, condemned for their priesthood. Crockett and James were captured on board ship at Littlehampton upon coming into England, in April 1586. The one was born at Barton-on-the-Hill in Cheshire, educated at Christ's College, Cambridge and Gloucester Hall, Oxford, and was a schoolmaster in East Anglia before going to the college at Rheims ; the other was born at Breaston in Derbyshire, brought up a Protestant, and educated at Derby Grammar School and St John's College, Oxford ; after his conversion he went to Rheims and then to Rome, where he was ordained by Goldwell of Saint Asaph. After their capture they were committed to prison in London and remained there two and a half years, till after the Armada, when they were sent for trial to Chichester to be made an example. The story of John Robinson was similar. He was born at Ferrensby, in Yorkshire, and after the death of his wife went to Rheims (he had a son, Francis, who also became a priest). He was ordained in 1585, was seized immediately on his arrival in England, and confined in the Clink in London. He was tried and condemned, and when the warrant for his execution at Ipswich arrived in September 1588, " the news did much to revive him, and to him that brought the warrant he gave his purse and all his money, and fell down on his knees and gave God thanks ".

In addition to MMP., pp. 146–150, consult Burton and Pollen, LEM., vol. i, pp. 447–507. For Buxton's *Rituale*, see the *Clergy Review* for February 1952.

2 : THE GUARDIAN ANGELS

ANGELS (ἄγγελος, messenger) are pure spirits, persons but bodiless, created by God with more acute intelligence and greater power than have human beings. Their office is to praise God, to be His messengers and to watch over man. That particular angels are appointed and commanded by God to guard each particular person that is born into the world is the general teaching of theologians, but the belief has not been defined by the Church and so is not of faith. These guardian angels lead the individual towards Heaven by defending him from evil, helping him in prayer, suggesting virtuous deeds, but acting upon the senses and imagination, not directly on the will, so that our co-operation is required. The psalmist assures us, " He hath given His angels charge over thee, to keep thee in all thy ways ". And in another place, " The angel of the Lord shall encamp round about them that fear Him, and shall deliver them ". The patriarch Jacob prayed his good angel to bless his two grandsons, Ephraim and Manasses, " The angel that delivereth me from all evils, bless these boys ". Judith said, " His angel hath been my keeper, both going hence, and abiding there, and returning from thence hither ". Christ deters us from scandalizing any of His little ones, because their angels always behold the face of God, and they will demand punishment of God against any by whose malice those who are their wards suffer harm. So certain and general was the belief of a guardian angel being assigned to every one by God, that when St Peter was miraculously delivered out of prison the disciples could not at first believe it, and said, " It is his angel ".

From early times liturgical honour was paid to all angels in the office of the dedication of the church of St Michael the Archangel *in Via Salaria* on September 29, and in the oldest extant Roman sacramentary, called Leonine, the prayers for the feast make indirect reference to them as individual guardians.   A votive Mass, *Missa ad suffragia angelorum postulanda*, has been in use at least from the time of Alcuin—he died in 804—who refers to the subject twice in his letters.   Whether the practice of celebrating such a Mass originated in England is not clear, but we find Alcuin's text in the Leofric Missal of the early tenth century.   This votive Mass of the Angels was commonly allotted to the second day of the week (Monday), as for example in the Westminster Missal, written about the year 1375.   In Spain it became customary to honour the Guardian Angels not only of persons, but of cities and provinces.   An office of this sort was composed for Valencia in 1411. Outside of Spain, Francis of Estaing, Bishop of Rodez, obtained from Pope Leo X a bull in 1518 which approved a special office for an annual commemoration of the Guardian Angels on March 1.   In England also there seems to have been much devotion to them.   Herbert Losinga, Bishop of Norwich, who died in 1119, speaks eloquently on the subject ; and the well-known invocation beginning *Angele Dei qui custos es mei* is apparently traceable to the verse-writer Reginald of Canterbury, at about the same period.   Pope Paul V authorized a special Mass and Office and at the request of Ferdinand II of Austria granted the feast to the whole empire. Pope Clement X extended it to the Western church at large as of obligation in 1670 and fixed it for the present date, being the first free day after the feast of St Michael.

An excellent article by Fr J. Duhr in the *Dictionnaire de spiritualité*, vol. i (1933), cc. 580–625, treats exhaustively of devotion to the Guardian Angels and its history.   On the general question of the veneration of angels see also DTC., vol. i, cc. 1222–1248 ; and on the liturgical aspect Kellner, *Heortology* (1908), pp. 328–332.   On the representation of angels in antiquity and art consult DAC., vol. i, cc. 2080–2161, and Künstle, *Ikonographie*, vol. i, pp. 239–264.

ST ELEUTHERIUS, Martyr   (Date Unknown)

" When the palace of Diocletian was burnt down at Nicomedia the holy soldier and martyr Eleutherius, with many others, was falsely accused of this crime.   All of them were summarily put to death by order of the said cruel emperor.   Some were cut down by the sword, others were burned, others thrown into the sea.   In turn Eleutherius, the chief among them, whose valour long torture only increased, achieved his victorious martyrdom as gold tried in the fire."   In these terms the Roman Martyrology refers to this martyr, but nothing certain is known about him except his name and the place of his passion.

The important fact is that on October 2 in the Syriac *breviarium* of the early fifth century we have the entry " at Nicomedia Eleutherius ".   From this the notice passed into the *Hieronymianum ;* see CMH., p. 537.   The association of the martyr with the incident of the burning of Diocletian's palace is, as Dom Quentin has shown (*Les Martyrologes historiques*, pp. 615–616), simply an invention of the martyrologist Ado.

ST LEODEGARIUS, or LEGER, Bishop of Autun, Martyr (A.D. 679)

St Leodegarius was born about the year 616.   His parents sent him to the court of King Clotaire II, who in turn sent him to Didon, his uncle and bishop of Poitiers, who appointed a priest to instruct him.   Leodegarius made great progress in learning and still more in the science of the saints, and in consideration of his abilities and merit his uncle ordained him deacon when he was only twenty years old, and soon after made him archdeacon.   When he had become a priest he was obliged to take upon himself the government of the abbey of Saint-Maxence, which he held six years.   Leodegarius was about thirty-five when he became abbot, and his biographer represents him as already a rather awe-inspiring person : " Being not uninformed in civil law he was a severe judge of lay people and, learned in the canons, an excellent teacher of the clergy.   Never having been softened by the joys of the flesh, he was strict in his treatment of sinners."   He is said to have introduced the Rule of St Benedict into his monastery, which was in need of his reforming hand.

St Leodegarius was called to court by the queen regent, St Bathildis, and in 663 nominated bishop of Autun.   That see had been vacant two years whilst the diocese was torn asunder by factions, of which one leader killed the other and so forfeited his claim to the see.   The arrival of Leodegarius quieted the disturbances and reconciled the parties.   He took care to relieve the poor, instructed his clergy, frequently preached to his people, adorned churches and fortified the town.   In a diocesan synod he enacted many canons for the reformation of manners and regarding the monastic order.   He says that if the monks were what they ought to be their prayers would preserve the world from public calamities.

The saint had been bishop ten years when King Clotaire III died in 673.   Upon this news he went at once to court, where he successfully supported Childeric against the schemes of the Neustrian mayor of the palace, Ebroin, who was exiled to Luxeuil.   King Childeric II governed well so long as he listened to the advice of St Leodegarius, who had so great a share in public affairs in the beginning of this reign that in some writings he is styled mayor of the palace.   But, being young and violent, the king at length abandoned himself to his own will and married his uncle's daughter without dispensation.   St Leodegarius admonished him, without effect ;   and certain nobles took the opportunity to render the saint's fidelity suspect when, at Easter 675, Childeric was at Autun.   Leodegarius was arrested and, barely escaping with his life, banished to Luxeuil, where his opponent Ebroin still was.   But Childeric, having caused a nobleman called Bodilo to be publicly scourged, was slain by him, and Theoderic III was put on the throne ;   St Leodegarius was restored to his see, and received at Autun with honour and rejoicing. Ebroin also left Luxeuil, however, and to deal with Leodegarius, his principal opponent, he sent an army into Burgundy which marched to Autun.   St Leodegarius would not fly, but ordered a fast and a procession, in which the relics of the saints were carried round the walls ;   at every gate the bishop prostrated himself, and besought God that, if He called him to martyrdom, his flock might not suffer. When the enemy came up, the people made a stout defence.   But after a few days St Leodegarius said to them, " Fight no longer.   It is on my account they are come.   Let us send one of our brethren to know what they demand."   Waimer, Duke of Champagne, answered the herald that Leodegarius was to be delivered up to them.   Leodegarius went boldly out of the town and offered himself to his enemies, who having seized him, put out his eyes.   This he endured without suffering his hands to be tied or emitting the least groan.   Waimer carried St Leodegarius to his own house in Champagne, where he returned him the money he had taken from the church of Autun, which St Leodegarius sent back to be distributed among the poor.

Ebroin became absolute master in Neustria and Burgundy.   He pretended a desire to revenge the death of King Childeric, and accused St Leodegarius and his brother Gerinus of having concurred in it. Gerinus was stoned to death in his brother's presence, and is named as a martyr in the Roman Martyrology on this same day. St Leodegarius could not be condemned till he had been deposed in a synod, but he was first treated with the utmost barbarity, his tongue mutilated and his lips cut off ; after which he was delivered into the hands of Count Waring, who placed him in the monastery of Fécamp in Normandy, where when his wounds healed he was able to speak, as it was thought, miraculously. When Gerinus was murdered he wrote a letter to his mother Sigradis, who was then a nun at Soissons. In it he congratulates with her upon her happy shelter from the world and comforts her for the death of Gerinus, saying that that ought not to be a grief to them which was an occasion of joy to the angels ; he speaks of himself with constancy and courage, and of the forgiveness of enemies with tenderness and charity.

Two years later Ebroin caused St Leodegarius to be brought to Marly, where he had assembled a few bishops that he might be deposed by their sentence. He was pressed to own himself privy to the death of Childeric, but constantly denied it. His accusers tore up his robe as a mark of deposition, and then he was delivered to Chrodobert, count of the palace, to be put to death. Ebroin, fearing lest he should be honoured as a martyr, ordered his body to be concealed in a well. Chrodobert disliked the task of executioner and left it to four servants, who led Leodegarius into a wood, where three of them fell at his feet, begging him to forgive them. He prayed for them and, when he said he was ready, the fourth cut off his head. In spite of Ebroin's order, the wife of Chrodobert had the body interred in a small oratory at a place called Sarcing in Artois, but three years after it was removed to the monastery of Saint-Maxence at Poitiers. The struggle between St Leodegarius and Ebroin is a famous incident in Merovingian history, and not all the right was on one side ; some good men, *e.g.* St Ouen, were supporters of the notorious Ebroin. It was inevitable in those days that bishops should take an active part in high politics, but, though the Roman Martyrology says St Leodegarius (whom it calls *beatus*) suffered *pro veritate*, it is not obvious why he should be venerated as a martyr.

In the *Acta Sanctorum* (October, vòl. i, published in 1765) Father C. de Bye devotes more than a hundred folio pages to the history of this saint. Two early lives are printed which, though they are by no means always in agreement, he believed to be the work of contemporaries. It was reserved for B. Krusch in the *Neues Archiv*, vol. xvi (1890), pp. 565–596, to explain more or less satisfactorily the problem presented by their textual identity in some passages and their divergences in many others. He holds that neither was of contemporary origin, but that there was a third life of which a considerable portion is preserved in a Paris MS. (Latin 17002), and that this was written some ten years after the death of Leodegarius by a monk of Saint-Symphorien who aimed at excusing the conduct of St Leodegarius's successor in the see. The lives published by the Bollandists were compiled from fifty to seventy years later, with this as a basis, but are still of historical importance. Krusch (in MGH., *Scriptores Merov.*, vol. v, pp. 249–362) has reconstituted the text of what he believes to have been the original life. Let us add that the letter of Leodegarius to his mother Sigradis is unquestionably an authentic document, whereas the will attributed to him is open to grave doubt. See further the *Analecta Bollandiana*, vol. xi (1890), pp. 104–110, and Leclercq in DAC., vol. viii, cc. 2460–2492. Pitra's *Histoire de S. Léger* (1890) is now out of date, though it called attention to some new texts. Father Camerlinck's life in the series " Les Saints " (1910), is inclined to panegyric and sometimes uncritical, but he gives an acceptable account of this tragic history. As the calendars show, Leodegarius was honoured in England from quite early times, mostly on October 2, but also on the 3rd.

3 : ST TERESA OF LISIEUX, Virgin   (A.D. 1897)

THE spread and enthusiasm of the *cultus* of St Teresa-of-the-Child-Jesus, a young Carmelite nun not exteriorly distinguished from hundreds of others, is one of the most impressive and significant religious phenomena of contemporary times. Within a few years of her death in 1897 she became known throughout the world ; her " little way " of simplicity and perfection in the doing of small things and discharge of daily duties has become a pattern to numberless " ordinary " folk ; her autobiography, written at the command of her superiors, is a famous book ; miracles and graces without number are attributed to her intercession. A contrast with a yet more famous Teresa forces itself : both were Carmelites and both were saints—and both have left long autobiographies in which may be traced the great external and temperamental and spiritual divergences and the inner common ground of their respective lives.

The parents of the saint-to-be were Louis Martin, a watchmaker of Alençon, son of an officer in the armies of Napoleon I, and Azélie-Marie Guérin, a maker of *point d'Alençon* in the same town, whose father had been a *gendarme* at Saint-Denis near Séez. Five of the children born to them survived to maturity, of whom Teresa was the youngest. She was born on January 2, 1873, and baptized Marie-Françoise-Thérèse. Her childhood was happy, ordinary and surrounded by good influences ; " my earliest memories are of smiles and tender caresses ". She had a quick intelligence and an open and impressionable mind, but there was no precocity or priggishness about the little Teresa ; when the older sister Léonie offered a doll and other playthings to Céline and Teresa, Céline chose some silk braid, but Teresa said, " I'll have the lot ". " My whole life could be summed up in this little incident. Later . . . I cried out, ' My God, I choose all ! I don't want to be a saint by halves.' "

In 1877 Mrs Martin died, and Mr Martin sold his business at Alençon and went to live at Lisieux (Calvados), where his children might be under the eye of their aunt, Mrs Guérin, an excellent woman. Mr Martin had a particular affection for Teresa, but it was an elder sister, Mary, who ran the household and the eldest, Pauline, who made herself responsible for the religious upbringing of her sisters. During the winter evenings she would read aloud to the family, and the staple was not some popular manual or effervescent " pious book " but the *Liturgical Year* of Dom Guéranger. When Teresa was nine this Pauline entered the Carmel at Lisieux and Teresa began to be drawn in the same direction. She had become rather quiet and sensitive, and her religion had really got hold of her. About this time she one day offered a penny to a lame beggar, and he refused it with a smile. Then she wanted to run after him with a cake her father had given her ; shyness held her back, but she said to herself, " I will pray for that poor old man on my first communion day "—and she remembered to do it, five years later : a day " of unclouded happiness ". For some years she had been going to the school kept by the Benedictine nuns of Notre-Dame-du-Pré, and among her remarks about it she says : "Observing that some of the girls were very devoted to one or other of the mistresses, I tried to imitate them, but I never succeeded in winning special favour. Happy failure, from how many evils have you saved me ! " When Teresa was nearly fourteen her sister Mary joined Pauline in the Carmel, and on Christmas eve of the same year Teresa underwent an experience which she ever after referred to as her " conversion ".   " On that blessed night the sweet child Jesus, scarcely an hour old, filled the darkness of my soul with floods of light.   By becoming weak and little, for love of me, He made me strong and brave ; He put His own weapons into my hands so that I went on from strength to strength, beginning, if I may say so, ' to run as a giant '." Characteristically, the occasion of this sudden accession of strength was a remark of her father about her child-like addiction to Christmas observances, not intended for her ears at all.

During the next year Teresa told her father her wish to become a Carmelite, and Mr Martin agreed ; but both the Carmelite authorities and the bishop of Bayeux refused to hear of it on account of her lack of age.   A few months later she was in Rome with her father and a French pilgrimage on the occasion of the sacerdotal jubilee of Pope Leo XIII.   At the public audience, when her turn came to kneel for the pope's blessing, Teresa boldly broke the rule of silence on such occasions and asked him, " In honour of your jubilee, allow me to enter Carmel at fifteen ".   Leo was clearly impressed by her appearance and manner, but he upheld the decision of the immediate superiors.   " You shall enter if it be God's will ", he said, and dismissed her with great kindness.   The pope's blessing and the earnest prayers made at many shrines during this pilgrimage bore their fruit in due season.   At the end of the year the bishop, Mgr Hugonin, gave his permission, and on April 9, 1888, Teresa Martin entered the Carmel at Lisieux whither her two sisters had preceded her.   " From her entrance ", deposed her novice mistress, " she surprised the community by her bearing, which was marked by a certain dignity that one would not expect in a child of fifteen."

During her noviciate Father Pichon, S.J., gave a retreat to the nuns and he testified in the cause of Teresa's beatification :   " It was easy to direct that child. The Holy Spirit was leading her and I do not think that I ever had, either then or later on, to warn her against illusions. . . . What struck me during that retreat were the spiritual trials through which God wished her to pass."   St Teresa was a most assiduous reader of the Bible and a ready interpreter of what she read (her *Histoire d'une âme* is full of scriptural texts), and, in view of the fact that her *cultus* has obtained the dimensions of a " popular devotion ", it is interesting to notice her love for liturgical prayer and her appreciation of its unsurpassed significance for the Christian.   When she was officiant for the week and had to recite the collects of the office in choir she reflected " that the priest said the same prayers at Mass and that, like him, I had the right to pray aloud before the Blessed Sacrament and to read the gospel [at Matins] when I was first chantress ".   In 1889 the three sisters in blood and in Carmel sustained a sad blow when their beloved father's mind gave way following two paralytic attacks and he had to be removed to a private asylum, where he remained for three years.   But " the three years of my father's martyrdom ", wrote St Teresa, " seem to me the dearest and most fruitful of our life.   I would not exchange them for the most sublime ecstasies."   She was professed on September 8, 1890.   A few days before she wrote to Mother Agnes-of-Jesus (Pauline) : " Before setting out my Betrothed asked me which way and through what country I would travel.   I replied that I had one only wish ; to reach the height of the mountain of Love. . . . Then our Saviour took me by the hand and led me into a subterranean way, where it is neither hot nor cold, where the sun never shines, where neither rain nor wind find entrance : a tunnel where I see nothing but a half-veiled light, the brightness shining from the eyes of Jesus looking down. . . . I wish at all costs to win the palm of St Agnes.   If it cannot be by blood it must be by love. . . ."

One of the principal duties of a Carmelite nun is to pray for priests, a duty which St Teresa discharged with great fervour at all times ; something she had seen or heard when visiting Italy had for the first time opened her eyes to the fact that the clergy need prayers as much as anybody else, and she never ceased in particular to pray for the good estate of the celebrated ex-Carmelite Hyacinth Loyson, who had apostatized from the faith.   Although she was delicate she carried out all the practices of the austere Carmelite rule from the first, except that she was not allowed to fast.   " A soul of such mettle ", said the prioress, " must not be treated like a child.   Dispensations are not meant for her."—" But it cost me a lot ", admitted Teresa, " during my postulancy to perform some of the customary exterior penances.   I did not yield to this repugnance because it seemed to me that the image of my crucified Lord looked at me with beseeching eyes, begging these sacrifices."   However, the physical mortification which she felt more than any other was the cold of the Carmel in winter, which nobody suspected until she admitted it on her death-bed.   " May Jesus grant me martyrdom either of the heart or of the body, or preferably of both " she had asked, and lived to say, " I have reached the point of not being able to suffer any more—because all suffering is sweet to me."

The autobiography which St Teresa wrote at the command of her prioress, *L'histoire d'une âme*, is an unique and engaging document, written with a delightful clarity and freshness, full of surprising turns of phrase, bits of unexpected know-ledge and unconscious self-revelation, and, above all, of deep spiritual wisdom and beauty.   She defines her prayer and thereby tells us more about herself than pages of formal explanation : " With me prayer is a lifting-up of the heart ; a look towards Heaven ; a cry of gratitude and love uttered equally in sorrow and in joy. In a word, something noble, supernatural, which enlarges my soul and unites it to God. . . . Except the Divine Office, which in spite of my unworthiness is a daily joy, I have not the courage to look through books for beautiful prayers. . . . I do as a child who has not learnt to read—I just tell our Lord all that I want and He understands."   Her psychological insight is keen : " Each time that my enemy would provoke me to fight I behave like a brave soldier.   I know that a duel is an act of cowardice, and so, without once looking him in the face, I turn my back on the foe, hasten to my Saviour, and vow that I am ready to shed my blood in witness of my belief in Heaven."   She passes over her own patience with a joke.   During meditation in choir one of the sisters continually fidgeted with a rosary, till Teresa was sweating with the irritation.   At last, " instead of trying not to hear it, which was impossible, I set myself to listen as though it had been some delightful music, and my meditation—which was *not* the ' prayer of quiet '—was passed in offering this music to our Lord."   The last chapter is a veritable paean of divine love, and concludes, " I entreat thee to let thy divine eyes rest upon a vast number of little souls ; I entreat thee to choose in this world a legion of little victims of thy love ". St Teresa numbered herself with these little souls : " I am a very little soul, who can only offer very little things to our Lord."

In 1893 Sister Teresa was appointed to assist the novice mistress and was in fact mistress in all but name.   On her experience in this capacity she comments, " From afar it seems easy to do good to souls, to make them love God more, to mould them according to our own ideas and views.   But coming closer we find, on the contrary, that to do good without God's help is as impossible as to make the sun shine at night. . . . What costs me most is being obliged to observe every fault and smallest imperfection and wage deadly war against them." She was only twenty years old. In 1894 Mr Martin died and soon after Céline, who had been looking after him, made the fourth Martin sister in the Lisieux Carmel. Eighteen months later, during the night between Maundy Thursday and Good Friday, St Teresa heard, " as it were, a far-off murmur announcing the coming of the Bridegroom " : it was a haemorrhage at the mouth. At the time she was inclined to respond to the appeal of the Carmelites at Hanoi in Indo-China, who wished to have her, but her disease took a turn for the worse and the last eighteen months of her life was a time of bodily suffering and spiritual trials. The spirit of prophecy seemed to come upon her, and it was now that she made those three utterances that have gone round the world. " I have never given the good God aught but love, and it is with love that He will repay. After my death I will let fall a shower of roses." " I will spend my Heaven in doing good upon earth." " My ' little way ' is the way of spiritual childhood, the way of trust and absolute self-surrender." In June 1897 she was removed to the infirmary of the convent and never left it again ; from August 16 on she could no longer receive holy communion because of frequent sickness. On September 30, with words of divine love on her lips, Sister Teresa of Lisieux died.

So unanimous, swift and impressive was the rise of the *cultus* of Teresa, miracles at whose intercession drew the eyes of the whole Catholic world upon her, that the Holy See, ever attentive to common convictions expressed by the acclamation of the whole visible Church, dispensed the period of fifty years which must ordinarily elapse before a cause of canonization is begun. She was beatified by Pope Pius XI in 1923, and in 1925 the same pope declared Teresa-of-the-Child-Jesus to have been a saint. Her feast was made obligatory for the whole Western church, and in 1927 she was named the heavenly patroness of all foreign missions, with St Francis Xavier, and of all works for Russia. These recognitions were gratefully received and acclaimed not only by Catholics but by many non-Catholics, whose attention had been called to her hidden life and who had read her autobiography. In appearance St Teresa was slight, with golden hair and grey-blue eyes, eyebrows very slightly arched, a small mouth, delicate and regular features. Something of her quality can be seen in prints taken from original photographic negatives, beside which the current composite pictures of her are insipid and lacking in character.

St Teresa quite definitely and consciously set out to be a saint. Undismayed by the apparent impossibility of attaining so great a height of disinterestedness, she said to herself : " ' The good God would not inspire unattainable desires. I may then, in spite of my littleness, aspire to holiness. I cannot make myself greater ; I must bear with myself just as I am with all my imperfections. But I want to seek a way to Heaven, a new way, very short, very straight, a little path. We live in an age of inventions. The trouble of walking upstairs no longer exists ; in the houses of the rich there is a lift instead. I would like to find a lift to raise me to Jesus, for I am too little to go up the steep steps of perfection.' Then I sought in the Holy Scriptures for some indication of this lift, the object of my desire, and I read these words from the mouth of the Eternal Wisdom : ' Whosoever is a *little one*, let him come to me ' " (Isaias lxvi 13).

The books and articles devoted to St Teresa of Lisieux are wellnigh countless, but they are all based upon her autobiography and her letters, supplemented in some cases by the evidence given in the process of her beatification and canonization. These last documents, printed for the use of the Congregation of Sacred Rites, are very important, for they let us see that, even among religious pledged to the austerities of the Carmelite rule, the frailties of human nature may still betray themselves, and that part of the work of this innocent child was to be, by force of example, the silent reformer and restorer of strict observance in her own convent.   Among the best biographies of the saint, though not by any means the longest, may be mentioned that of H. Petitot, *St Teresa of Lisieux : a Spiritual Renaissance* (1927) ; that of Baron Angot des Rotours in the series " Les Saints " ; F. Laudet, *L'enfant chérie du monde* (1927) ; and H. Ghéon, *The Secret of the Little Flower* (1934).   The more official publications, if one may so speak, are represented by the autobiography, *L'histoire d'une âme,* which has been translated into every civilized language, including Hebrew ; the first English translation was by Canon T. N. Taylor (reprinted 1947), and a new translation, by the Rev. A. M. Day, appeared in 1951 ; by Mgr Laveille's *Ste Thérèse . . . d'après les documents officiels du Carmel de Lisieux* (Eng. trans., 1929) ; and by the Abbé Combes's edition of the saint's *Collected Letters* (Eng. trans., 1950) ; see also *Le problème de l' " Histoire d'une âme " et des œuvres complètes de ste Thérèse de Lisieux* (1950).   Among more recent works are biographies or studies in French by M. M. Philipon, A. Combes (1946 ; Eng. trans. in 3 vols.), and M. van der Meersch (1947)—the last criticized at length in *La petite Ste Thérèse,* by A. Combes and others : V. Sackville West, *The Eagle and the Dove* (1943) ; and J. Beevers, *Storm of Glory* (1949).   As a curious demurrer to the enthusiasm evoked by the canonization mention may be made of the article in the Catalan journal *Estudis Franciscans,* vol. xxx, by Fr Ubald of Alençon ; but this should not be read without reference to the reply published in the same periodical by the Vicar General of Bayeux.   The latest book in English is H. Urs von Balthasar's *Thérèse of Lisieux* (1953), a theological study.   It is now announced that the *Histoire d'une âme* is to be published in its original unedited form.

ST HESYCHIUS   (FOURTH CENTURY)

MENTION of this holy monk is made in the Life of St Hilarion, whose faithful disciple he was.   He accompanied his master when he left Palestine for Egypt, and when Hilarion, being unwilling to return to Gaza, where he was so well known, fled secretly across the sea to Sicily, Hesychius sought him for three years.   He could hear no word of him either in the desert or the ports of Egypt, so he made his way into Greece, where at last a rumour reached him that a wonder-working prophet had arrived in Sicily.   He went thither, and tracked Hilarion to his retreat, where " he fell on his knees and watered his master's feet with tears ".   Continuing the vain search for complete solitude they went together to Dalmatia and then to Cyprus.   After two years St Hilarion sent Hesychius to Palestine to salute the brethren there, report on their progress, and visit the old monastery near Gaza. On his return in the spring he found that Hilarion, worried by the press of people, wanted to escape to yet another country, but he was now considerably advanced in age and Hesychius persuaded him to be content with a place of retreat deeper in the island which he had found for him.   Here Hilarion died.   St Hesychius was again in Palestine at the time and directly he heard the news he hurried back to Cyprus to watch over the body lest it be taken away by the people of Paphos.   He found that his beloved master had left a letter bequeathing to him all his worldly goods, namely a book of the gospels and some clothes.   To allay the suspicions of those who jealously guarded the hermitage he pretended that he was going to live there, but after ten months he was able, with great difficulty and risk, to carry off the body of St Hilarion and convey it back to Palestine.   It was met by crowds of monks and lay people who accompanied it for burial to the monastery which he had established at Majuma, and there some years later Hesychius himself died.

A sufficient account of St Hesychius is provided in the *Acta Sanctorum,* October, vol. ii. It is mainly derived from St Jerome ; but see later under Hilarion, October 21.

THE TWO EWALDS, Martyrs   (*c.* A.D. 695)

Soon after St Willibrord with eleven companions in the year 690 had opened the spiritual harvest in Friesland, two brothers, both priests from Northumbria, followed their example and went over into the country of the Old Saxons in Westphalia to preach the gospel.   They had previously been for some time in Ireland to improve themselves in sacred learning.   Both had the same name Ewald, or Hewald; for distinction the one was called the Dark, the other the Fair Ewald, from the colour of their hair.   The first was more learned in the Holy Scriptures, but both were equal in fervour of devotion and zeal.   The two brothers arrived in Germany about the year 694 and met a certain official, whom they desired to conduct them to his lord, because they had tidings for his advantage.   The man invited them into his house and kept them there for several days.   The missionaries passed the time in prayer, singing psalms and hymns, and every day offered the sacrifice of the Mass.

The barbarians observing this, and fearing lest the preachers might prevail upon their chief to forsake their gods for a new religion, resolved to murder them both. Fair Ewald they killed by the sword upon the spot, but inflicted on the Dark cruel torments before they tore him limb from limb.   The lord of the territory, when he heard of what had happened, was furious that the two strangers had not been brought to him : he put the murderers to the sword and burned their village.   The bodies of the martyrs, which had been thrown into the river, were discovered by a heavenly light which shone over them ; an English monk, Tilmon, was warned in a vision what this column of light portended and gave the bodies honourable burial.   St Bede says this river was the Rhine, but the traditional place of the Ewalds' martyrdom is at Aplerbeke on the Embscher, a tributary, near Dortmund. The Ewalds were at once honoured as martyrs, and Pepin had their bodies taken up and enshrined in the church of St Cunibert at Cologne, where they still are. They are named in the Roman Martyrology and venerated as the patrons of Westphalia ; their feast is also kept by the Premonstratensian canons regular, for whom St Norbert obtained some of their relics in 1121.

In the calendar known as St Willibrord's, which must have been written in the early years of the eighth century (probably before 710), we have under October 4 the entry, *natale sanctorum martyrum Heuualdi et Heualdi*.   The Fulda martyrology and that preserved in Anglo-Saxon both agree with Bede's *History* in naming October 3 as the proper day.   See also the notes of C. Plummer's edition of Bede, especially pp. 289–290 ; and H. A. Wilson in *The Calendar of St Willibrord* (1918), p. 41.

ST GERARD OF BROGNE, Abbot   (A.D. 959)

The county of Namur gave birth to this saint, towards the end of the ninth century. An engaging sweetness of temper gained him the esteem and affection of everyone, and his courtesy and beneficence gave charm to his virtue and made it shine.   One day as Gerard returned from hunting, whilst the rest went to take refreshment, he stole into a retired chapel at Brogne, which was part of his own estate, and remained there a long time in prayer.   He found so much sweetness therein that he rose from it with sadness and said to himself, " How happy are they who have no other obligation but to praise the Lord night and day, and who live always in His presence ".   To procure this happiness for others and their incessant tribute and honour to the supreme majesty of God was to be the work of his life.   He is alleged to have been told by St Peter in a vision to bring to Brogne the relics of St Eugenius, a companion of St Dionysius of Paris. Later the monks of Saint-Denis gave him what purported to be the relics of this martyr and St Gerard enshrined them at Brogne. Thereupon he was accused to the bishop of Liège of promoting the veneration of relics of doubtful authenticity. But the bishop was satisfied by the miraculous intervention of St Eugenius, and Gerard himself became a monk at Saint-Denis.

Gerard after his profession laboured every day with greater fervour to carry Christian virtues to their noblest heights, and in due course he received priestly orders, though his humility was not overcome in his promotion without difficulty. When he had lived eleven years in this monastery he was allowed in 919 to found an abbey of monks upon his estate at Brogne. This done, and finding the charge of a numerous community break in too much upon his retirement, he built himself a cell near the church and lived in it as a recluse. God some time after called him to an active life, and Gerard was obliged to undertake the reformation of the abbey of Saint-Ghislain, six miles from Mons, in which house he established the Rule of St Benedict and the most admirable discipline ; the religious had been in the habit of carrying the relics of their holy founder about the countryside, and exposing them for money which they put to bad uses. St Gerard carried out this difficult work with such prudence that the count of Flanders, Arnulf, whom the saint had miraculously cured of the stone and whom he had engaged to take up a better life, committed to him the general inspection and reformation of all the abbeys in Flanders. In the course of the next twenty years or so he introduced new and exact discipline in numerous monasteries, including some in Normandy, his reforms being carried out on the lines of the work of St Benedict of Aniane. But though St Gerard was widely honoured as a restorer of monastic discipline, not all monks were amenable to his efforts. Some of those of Saint-Bertin, for instance, migrated to England rather than follow a more austere life : they were welcomed by King Edmund, who in 944 accommodated them at the abbey of Bath.

No fatigues made the saint abate anything of his own austerities or interrupt the communication of his soul with God. When he had spent almost twenty years in these trying labours and was broken with age, he made a general visitation of all the monasteries that were under his direction, and when he had finished shut himself up in his cell at Brogne to prepare his soul to go to receive the reward of his labours, to which he was called on October 3 in 959.

The life (compiled a century after the death of St Gerard and printed by Mabillon and in the *Acta Sanctorum*, October, vol. ii), which Alban Butler summarized, has been the subject of much discussion. It depends no doubt upon some earlier account which has perished, but it is in many respects untrustworthy ; *e.g.* it is doubtful if he was ever a monk at Saint-Denis. But see Sackur, *Die Cluniacenser*, vol. i (1892), pp. 366–368 ; and, more especially, U. Berlière in the *Revue bénédictine*, vol. ix (1892), pp. 157–172. Cf. also the *Analecta Bollandiana*, vols. iii, pp. 29–57, and v, pp. 385–395 ; and M. Guérard, *Cartulaire de l'abbaye de Saint-Bertin*, p. 145.

ST FROILAN, BISHOP OF LEON, AND ST ATTILANUS, BISHOP OF ZAMORA   (TENTH CENTURY)

THESE two bishops were among the great figures of the early days of the reconquest of Spain from the Moors, and both find a place in the Roman Martyrology, Froilan today and Attilanus on the 5th. We are told that Froilan came from Lugo in

Galicia and at the age of eighteen went to live as a hermit in the wilderness ; among his disciples was Attilanus, who came to him when he was only fifteen. Together they organized their followers into a monastic community at Moreruela in Old Castile. They were promoted to the episcopate together, and consecrated to the adjoining sees of Leon and Zamora. St Froilan was a restorer of monasticism in Spain, and the martyrology speaks of his great charity to the poor. He died probably in 905.

The account of these saints in the *Acta Sanctorum*, October, vol. iii (under October 5), is mainly based upon Lobera, *Historia de las grandezas* . . . *de Leon y de su Obispo S. Froylan* (1596) ; though some mild satire is aimed at that writer's belief that when a wolf killed the donkey which carried the bishop's luggage, St Froilan compelled the wolf to do penance by serving him for many years in the same capacity of beast of burden. A Latin life (tenth century ?) is printed in Florez, *España Sagrada*, vol. xxxiv, pp. 422–425. See also J. Gonzalez, *St Froilan de Leon* (1947). It does not even seem certain that the main object of the *cultus* was not another Bishop Froilan who lived a century later.

ST THOMAS CANTELUPE, Bishop of Hereford   (A.D. 1282)

The Cantelupes were Normans, who came over with the Conqueror and received from him great estates and honours which they exceedingly increased, becoming by marriages kin of the Strongbows and Marshals, earls of Pembroke, of the FitzWalters, earls of Hereford, and of the Braoses, lords of Abergavenny. The father of St Thomas was steward of Henry III's household, and his mother, Millicent de Gournay, dowager Countess of Evreux and Gloucester. His parents had four other sons and three daughters, towards whom Thomas was not very friendly when he grew up. He was born about the year 1218 at Hambleden, near Great Marlow, and his education was entrusted to his uncle Walter, Bishop of Worcester, who sent Thomas to Oxford when he was nineteen ; but he did not stay there long, going on to Paris with his brother Hugh.* Here the young patricians lived in considerable state, and in 1245 accompanied their father, who was one of the English envoys, to the thirteenth general council, at Lyons. Here Thomas was probably ordained, and received from Pope Innocent IV dispensation to hold a plurality of benefices, a permission of which he afterwards freely availed himself.

After reading civil law at Orleans, Thomas returned to Paris, and after getting his licence he came back to Oxford to lecture there in canon law ; in 1262 he was chosen chancellor of the university. Thomas was always noted for his charity to poor students ; he was also a strict disciplinarian. There were large numbers of undergraduates in residence ; they were allowed to carry arms and were divided into opposing camps of northerners and southerners. Thomas had an armoury of weapons, confiscated for misuse. When Prince Edward camped near the city and the whole university was " gated ", the young gentlemen burned down the provost's house, wounded many of the townspeople, and emptied the mayor's cellar (he was a vintner). Unlike his grandfather, who had been a strong supporter of King John, Thomas the Chancellor was with the barons against Henry III, and was one of those sent to plead their cause before St Louis at Amiens in 1264. After the defeat

* The University of Oxford was turned upside down about this time, which may account for Thomas's short sojourn there. The brother of the papal legate, Cardinal Otto, had thrown soup over an Irish undergraduate who annoyed him, whereupon a Welsh undergraduate shot the legate's brother. The university protected its student and the cardinal put it under interdict and excommunicated the chancellor.

of the king at Lewes, Thomas was appointed chancellor of the kingdom. His prudence, courage, scrupulous justice, and disregard of human respect and of the least bribe which could be offered him completed the character of an accomplished magistrate. But he did not hold office long, being dismissed after the death of Simon de Montfort at Evesham. Thomas was then about forty-seven years old, and he retired to Paris.

Thomas came back to Oxford after some years, was perhaps re-appointed chancellor there, and took his D.D. in the church of the Dominicans : on which occasion Robert Kilwardby, then archbishop elect of Canterbury, declared in his public oration that the candidate had lived without reproach. But he continued to demonstrate that pluralism is not necessarily inconsistent with high character, for in addition to being archdeacon of Stafford and precentor of York he held four canonries and seven or eight parochial livings, especially in Herefordshire. These he administered by vicars, and he was in the habit of making unannounced visits to see how the souls and bodies of their flocks were being cared for. In 1275 he was chosen bishop of Hereford, and consecrated in Christ Church at Canterbury. On that occasion St Thomas commented on the fact that his episcopal brethren from across the Welsh border were not present ; he was not pleased.

Owing to the civil wars and the pusillanimity of his two predecessors the large and wealthy diocese of Hereford was in a bad state when St Thomas came to govern it. One after another he met, defied and overcame the lords, spiritual and temporal, who encroached on its rights and possessions : Baron Corbet, Llywelyn of Wales (whom he excommunicated), Lord Clifford (who had to do public penance in Hereford cathedral), the Bishop of Saint Asaph, the Bishop of Menevia (who tried by force to prevent him from consecrating the church of Abbey Dore in the Golden Valley), each in turn experienced the firmness of this feudal prelate, baron and bishop, who " was by nature careful and prudent in things pertaining to this world, and more so in those that pertained to God ". One of them said to him, " Either the Devil is in you, or you are very familiar with God ". There was a lively struggle with Gilbert de Clare, Earl of Gloucester, who insisted on hunting in the western side of Malvern chase, which the bishop claimed. Gilbert replied to his warning by calling him a " clergiaster " and threatening to beat him. The unseemly epithet (it has a horrid sound) not unnaturally annoyed St Thomas, and he began a suit against the earl of which one result can be seen to this day, in the " Earl's Ditch ", running along the top of the Malvern Hills. The original ditch is much older than Gilbert de Clare, but he repaired and palisaded it, to mark his boundary and to keep his deer from straying on to the episcopal lands. Among the numerous habits and traits of St Thomas recorded in the process of his canonization is that when he travelled in his diocese he asked every child he met if he had been confirmed, and if not the bishop at once supplied the omission. Public sinners he rebuked and excommunicated, equally publicly, particularly those who in high places set a bad example to those below them. Pluralism without the proper dispensation he would not permit, and among those whom he deprived of benefices in his diocese were the dean of Saint Paul's and the archdeacons of Northampton and Salop.

Unhappily, during the last years of his life there was dissension between St Thomas and John Peckham, Archbishop of Canterbury, first on some general questions of jurisdiction and then on particular cases arising in the diocese of Hereford. In a synod held at Reading in 1279 St Thomas was leader of the aggrieved suffragans, and in due course Rome gave them the reliefs they asked; but in his personal dispute he was excommunicated by the metropolitan.   Some bishops refused to publish the sentence, and St Thomas publicly announced his appeal to Pope Martin IV, whom he set out to see in person.   Some of Peckham's letters to his procurators at Rome are extant, but in spite of their fulminations St Thomas was very kindly received by the pope at Orvieto.   Pending the consideration of his cause he withdrew to Montefiascone, but the fatigues and heat of the journey had been too much for him and he was taken mortally sick.   It is related that, seeing his condition, one of his chaplains said to him, " My lord, would you not like to go to confession ? "   Thomas looked at him, and only replied, " Foolish man ".   Twice more he was invited, and each time he made the same reply.   The chaplain was not aware that his master went to confession every day.   Commending his soul to God, St Thomas died on August 25, 1282, and was buried at Orvieto ; soon his relics were conveyed to Hereford, where his shrine in the cathedral became the most frequented in the west of England (Peckham had refused to allow their interment until he had seen the certificate of absolution from the papal penitentiary).   Miracles were soon reported (four hundred and twenty-nine are given in the acts of canonization) and the process was begun at the request of King Edward I ; it was achieved in the year 1320.   He is named in the Roman Martyrology on the day of his death, but his feast is kept by the Canons Regular of the Lateran and the dioceses of Birmingham (commemoration only) and Shrewsbury on this October 3, by Cardiff and Salford on the 5th, and Westminster on the 22nd.

The Bollandists, who had access to the process of canonization, have given a very full account of St Thomas in the first volume of the *Acta Sanctorum* for October.   Father Strange, who published in 1674 his *Life and Gests of St Thomas of Cantelupe*, had to be content with such materials as Capgrave and Surius were able to furnish ; this account by Father Strange was reprinted in the Quarterly Series in 1879, but it is now quite inadequate.   An immense amount of fresh material has been rendered accessible through the publication of Cantelupe's episcopal register by the Canterbury and York Society, of *Bishop Swinfield's Household Expenses* (Camden Society), of Archbishop Peckham's correspondence (Rolls Series), etc., while nearly all the monastic chronicles of the period furnish more or less frequent references.   Professor Tout's article in the DNB., vol. viii, pp. 448–452, is not only thorough but admirable in tone.   The same, however, can hardly be said of the well-informed notice in A. T. Bannister, *The Cathedral Church of Hereford* (1924).   For the saint's relics, see an article by Abbot E. Horne in the *Clergy Review*, vol. xxviii (1947), pp. 99–104.   See also D. L. Dowie, *Archbishop Pecham* (1952).

BD DOMINIC SPADAFORA   (A.D. 1521)

HE was born at Messina of a family which had come from somewhere in the East to Sicily in the thirteenth century.   He received the habit of the Order of Preachers at Palermo and after his ordination was sent to the house of studies at Padua, where he took his degrees and spent some years teaching.   He was then sent back to Palermo, where he preached with much fruit, but was sent for to Rome to be on the staff of the master general, Father Joachim Torriano, who was soon to be in trouble over the affair of Savonarola.   But before this came to a head Bd Dominic had left Rome to take charge of a new foundation at the shrine of our Lady of Grace near Monte Cerignone.   He remained here for the rest of his life, twenty-eight years, undertaking long missionary journeys and winning many souls to Christ.   Bd Dominic died suddenly and without apparent illness.   After Vespers on December 21, 1521, he summoned his friars and gave them his last instructions, asked for the last sacraments, and quietly died.　His *cultus* was confirmed exactly four hundred years after.

The decree confirming the *cultus* is printed in the *Acta Apostolicae Sedis*, vol. xiii (1921), pp. 104–108 ; it contains a biographical summary.　A short life was published by R. Diaccini in 1921.

4 : ST FRANCIS OF ASSISI, Founder of the Friars Minor (A.D. 1226)

I T has been said of St Francis that he entered into glory in his lifetime, and that he is the one saint whom all succeeding generations have agreed in canonizing.　This over-statement has sufficient truth in it to provoke another, namely, that he is the one saint whom, in our day, all non-Catholics have agreed in canonizing.　Certainly no other has so appealed to Protestants and even to non-Christians.　He captured the imagination of his time by presenting poverty, chastity and obedience in the terms of the troubadours and courts of love, and that of a more complex age by his extraordinary simplicity.　Religious and social cranks of all sorts have appealed to him for justification, and he has completely won the hearts of the sentimental.　But the idylls that are associated with his name—the marriage with Lady Poverty, the listening birds, the hunted leveret, the falcon, and the nightingale in the ilex-grove, his " love of nature " (in the thirteenth century " nature " was still regarded as natural), his romance of speech and action, these were only, so to speak, " trimmings " of a character which was wholly imbued with the spiritual, inspired by Christian dogma, and devoted not simply to Christ but to the crucified Christ.　St Francis was born at Assisi in Umbria in 1181 or 1182. His father, Peter Bernardone, was a merchant, and his mother was called Pica ; some say she was gently born and of Provençal blood.　His parents were persons of probity, and were in good circumstances.　Much of Peter's trade was with France, and his son having been born while he was absent in that country, they called him *Francesco*, " the Frenchman ", though the name of John had been given him at his baptism.　In his youth he was devoted to the ideas of romantic chivalry propagated by the troubadours ; he had plenty of money and spent it lavishly, even ostentatiously.　He was uninterested alike in his father's business and in formal learning. He was bent on enjoying himself.　Nevertheless, he was not licentious, and would never refuse an alms to any poor man who asked it of him for the love of God.

When he was about twenty, strife broke out between the cities of Perugia and Assisi, and Francis was carried away prisoner by the Perugians.　This he bore a whole year with cheerfulness and good temper.　But as soon as he was released he was struck down by a long and dangerous sickness, which he suffered with so great patience that by the weakness of his body his spirit gathered greater strength and became more serious.　On his recovery he determined to join the forces of Walter de Brienne, who was fighting in southern Italy.　He bought himself expensive equipment and handsome outfit, but as he rode out one day in a new suit, meeting a gentleman reduced to poverty and very ill-clad, he was touched with compassion and changed clothes with him.　That night he seemed to see in his sleep a magnificent palace, filled with rich arms, all marked with the sign of the cross ; and he thought he heard one tell him that these arms belonged to him and his soldiers. He set out exultingly for Apulia, but never reached the front. At Spoleto he was taken ill again, and as he lay there a heavenly voice seemed to tell him to turn back, " to serve the master rather than the man ". Francis obeyed. At first he returned to his old life, but more quietly and with less enjoyment. His preoccupation was noticed, and he was told he was in love. " Yes ", he replied, " I am going to take a wife more beautiful and worthy than any you know." He began to give himself much to prayer and to have a desire to sell his goods and buy the precious jewel of the gospel. He knew not yet how he should do this, but certain strong inspirations made him understand that the spiritual warfare of Christ is begun by mortification and victory over one's self. Riding one day in the plain of Assisi he met a leper, whose sores were so loathsome that at the sight of them he was struck with horror. But he dismounted, and as the leper stretched out his hand to receive an alms, Francis, whilst he bestowed it, kissed the man.

Henceforward he often visited the hospitals and served the sick, and gave to the poor sometimes his clothes and sometimes money. One day as he was praying in the church of St Damian, outside the walls of Assisi, he seemed to hear a voice coming from the crucifix, which said to him three times, " Francis, go and repair my house, which you see is falling down ". The saint, seeing that church was old and ready to fall, thought our Lord commanded him to repair that. He therefore went home, and in the simplicity of his heart took a horseload of cloth out of his father's warehouse and sold it, with the horse. The price he brought to the poor priest of St Damian's, asking to be allowed to stay with him. The priest consented, but would not take the money, which Francis therefore left on a window-sill. His father, hearing what had been done, came in great indignation to St Damian's, but Francis had hid himself. After some days spent in prayer and fasting, he appeared again, though so disfigured and ill-clad that people pelted him and called him mad. Bernardone, more annoyed than ever, carried him home, beat him unmercifully (Francis was about twenty-five), put fetters on his feet, and locked him up, till his mother set him at liberty while his father was out. Francis returned to St Damian's. His father, following him thither, hit him about the head and insisted that he should either return home or renounce all his share in his inheritance and return the purchase-price of the goods he had taken. Francis had no objection to being disinherited, but said that the other money now belonged to God and the poor. He was therefore summoned before Guido, Bishop of Assisi, who told him to return it and have trust in God : " He does not wish His Church to profit by goods which may have been gotten unjustly." Francis did as he was told and, with his usual literalness, added, " The clothes I wear are also his. I'll give them back." He suited the action to the word, stripped himself of his clothes, and gave them to his father, saying cheerfully, " Hitherto I have called you father on earth ; but now I say, ' Our Father, who art in Heaven '." Peter Bernardone left the court, " burning with rage and with an exceeding sorrow ". The frock of a labourer, a servant of the bishop, was found, and Francis received this first alms with many thanks, made a cross on the garment with chalk, and put it on.

Francis went in search of some convenient shelter, singing the divine praises along the highways. He was met by a band of robbers, who asked him who he was. He answered, " I am the herald of the great King ". They beat him and threw him into a ditch full of snow. He went on singing the praises of God. He passed by a monastery, and there received alms and a job of work as an unknown poor man. In the city of Gubbio, one who knew him took him into his house, and gave him a tunic, belt and shoes, such as pilgrims wore, which were decent though poor and shabby. These he wore two years, and he walked with a staff in his hand like a hermit. He then returned to San Damiano at Assisi. For the repair of the church he gathered alms and begged in Assisi, where all had known him rich, bearing with joy the railleries and contempt with which he was treated by some. For the building he himself carried stones and served the masons and helped put the church in order. He next did the same for an old church which was dedicated in honour of St Peter. After this he went to a little chapel called Portiuncula, belonging to the abbey of Benedictine monks on Monte Subasio, who gave it that name probably because it was built on so small a parcel of land.* It stands in a plain two miles from Assisi, and was at that time forsaken and ruinous. The retiredness of this place appealed to St Francis, and he was delighted with the title which the church bore, it being dedicated in honour of our Lady of the Angels. He repaired it, and fixed his abode by it. Here, on the feast of St Matthias in the year 1209, his way of life was shown to St Francis. In those days the gospel of the Mass on this feast was Matt. x 7–19 : " And going, preach, saying : The kingdom of Heaven is at hand. . . . Freely have you received, freely give. . . . Do not possess gold . . . nor two coats nor shoes nor a staff. . . . Behold I send you as sheep in the midst of wolves. . . ." The words went straight to his heart and, applying them literally to himself, he gave away his shoes, staff and girdle, and left himself with one poor coat, which he girt about him with a cord. This was the dress which he gave to his friars the year following : the undyed woollen dress of the shepherds and peasants in those parts. Thus garbed, he began to exhort to repentance with such energy that his words pierced the hearts of his hearers. As he passed them on the road he saluted the people with the words, " Our Lord give you peace ". God had already given him the gifts of prophecy and miracles. When he was begging alms to repair the church of St Damian, he used to say, " Help me to finish this building. Here will one day be a monastery of nuns by whose good fame our Lord will be glorified over the whole Church." This was verified in St Clare five years after. A man in Spoleto was afflicted with a cancer, which had disfigured him hideously. He met St Francis and would have thrown himself at his feet ; but the saint prevented him and kissed his diseased face, which was instantly healed. " I know not ", says St Bonaventure, " which I ought most to wonder at, such a kiss or such a cure."

Many began to admire Francis, and some desired to be his companions and disciples. The first of these was Bernard da Quintavalle, a rich tradesman of Assisi. He watched the career of Francis with curiosity, invited him to his house, and had a bed made ready for him near his own. When Bernard seemed to be fallen asleep, the servant of God got up and passed a long time in prayer, frequently repeating aloud the words, *Deus meus et Omnia*, " My God and my All ". Bernard secretly watched, saying to himself, " This man is truly a servant of God ", and at length he asked the saint to make him his companion. They assisted at Mass together, and searched the Scriptures that they might learn the will of God. The *sortes biblicae* being favourable, Bernard sold all his effects and divided the sum among the poor. Peter of Cattaneo, a canon of the cathedral of Assisi, desired to be admitted with him, and Francis " gave his habit " to them both together on

---

* Porziuncola means the " little piece ". The tiny building is now entirely enclosed within the great church of Santa Maria degli Angeli.

April 16, 1209. The third person who joined them was the famous Brother Giles, a person of great simplicity and spiritual wisdom. When his followers had increased to a dozen, Francis drew up a short informal rule consisting chiefly of the gospel counsels of perfection. This he took to Rome in 1210 for the pope's approbation. Innocent III appeared at first averse, and many of the cardinals alleged that the orders already established ought to be reformed and their number not multiplied, and that the intended poverty of this new body was impracticable. Cardinal John Colonna pleaded in its favour that it was no more than the evangelical counsels of perfection. The pope afterwards told his nephew, from whom St Bonaventure heard it, that in a dream he saw a palm tree growing up at his feet, and in another he saw St Francis propping up the Lateran church, which seemed ready to fall (as he saw St Dominic in another vision five years after). He therefore sent again for St Francis, and approved his rule, but only by word of mouth, tonsuring him and his companions and giving them a general commission to preach repentance.

St Francis and his companions now lived together in a little cottage at Rivo Torto, outside the gates of Assisi, whence they sometimes went into the country to preach. After a time they had trouble with a peasant who wanted the cottage for the use of his donkey. " God has not called us to prepare a stable for an ass ", observed Francis, and went off to see the abbot of Monte Subasio. The abbot, in 1212, handed over the Portiuncula chapel to St Francis, upon condition that it should always continue the head church of his order. The saint refused to accept the property " in fee simple " but would only have the use of the place ; and in token that he held it of the monks, he sent them every year a basket of fish caught in a neighbouring river. The monks sent the friars in return a barrel of oil. This custom is now revived between the friars of Santa Maria degli Angeli and the Benedictines of San Pietro at Assisi. Round about the chapel the brothers built themselves huts of wood and clay. St Francis would not suffer any dominion or property of temporal goods to be vested in his order, or in any community or convent of it ; he called the spirit of holy poverty the foundation of the order, and in his dress, in everything that he used, and in all his actions he showed the reality of his love for it. Francis would call his body Brother Ass, because it was to carry burdens, to be beaten, and to eat little and coarsely. When he saw anyone idle, profiting by other men's labour, he called him Brother Fly, because he did no good, but spoiled the good which others did and was troublesome to them. As a man owes charity to his own body, the saint a few days before he died asked pardon of his for having treated it perhaps with too great rigour. Indiscreet or excessive austerities always displeased him. When a brother through immoderate abstinence was not able to sleep, Francis brought him food and, that he might eat it with less embarrassment, began himself to eat with him.

At the beginning of his conversion, finding himself assailed with violent temptations against purity he sometimes cast himself naked into ditches full of snow. Once, under a more grievous trial than ordinary, he began to discipline himself sharply, and when this failed of its effect threw himself into a briar-patch and rolled therein. The humility of Francis was no emotional self-depreciation, but grounded in the certainty that " what each one is in the eyes of God, that he is and no more ". He never proceeded in holy orders beyond the diaconate, not daring to be ordained priest. He had no use for singularity. In a certain house he was told that one of the friars was so great a lover of silence that he would only confess his faults by signs. The saint did not like it, and said, " This is not the spirit of God but of the

Devil. A temptation, not a virtue." God illuminated the understanding of His servant with a light and wisdom that is not taught in books. When a certain brother asked leave to study, Francis told him that if he would often repeat the *Gloria Patri* with devotion he would become very learned before God. He was himself an example of knowledge so attained. His love for and power over the lower animals were noted and often referred to by those who knew him : his rebuke to the swallows while he was preaching at Alviano, " My sisters the swallows, it is now my turn to speak. You have been talking enough all this time " ; the birds that perched around him while he told them to praise their Creator ; the rabbit that would not leave him at Lake Trasimene ; and the tamed wolf at Gubbio, which some maintain is an allegory and others a plain fact.

The early years at Santa Maria degli Angeli was a time of training in poverty and brotherly love. For their daily bread the brothers worked at their trades and in the fields for neighbouring farmers. When work was lacking, they begged from door to door, and even then were forbidden to accept money. They were always at the service of their neighbours, and particularly of lepers and similar sufferers. These, St Francis insisted, should be referred to and addressed as " my brother Christians ", with that same instinctive delicacy of mind which makes some country people in England and Wales today refer to tramps not as " tramps " but as " travellers ". Recruits continued to come, and among them the " renowned jester of the Lord ", Brother Juniper, of whom St Francis said, when he had been even more " simple " than usual, " I would that I had a forest of such junipers ! " He was the man who, when a crowd of people was waiting to receive him at Rome, was found playing seesaw with some children outside the walls. St Clare called him " God's plaything ". This young girl left her home in Assisi to be a follower of St Francis after hearing him preach, in the spring of 1212. He established her with other maidens at San Damiano, which soon became to the Franciscans what the nuns of Prouille were to the Dominicans : a tower of womanly strength and sense, an enclosed garden of supporting prayer. In the autumn of the same year, Francis, not content with all that he did and suffered for souls in Italy, resolved to go and preach to the Mohammedans. He embarked with one companion at Ancona for Syria, but they were driven straight on to the coast of Dalmatia and wrecked. The two friars could get no further and, having no money for their passage, travelled back to Ancona as stowaways. After preaching for a year in central Italy, during which the lord of Chiusi put at the disposal of the Franciscans as a place of retreat Mount Alvernia (La Verna) in the Tuscan Apennines, St Francis made another attempt to reach the Mohammedans, this time in Morocco by way of Spain. But again he was disappointed in his object, for somewhere in Spain he was taken ill, and when he recovered he returned into Italy, where again he laboured strenuously to advance the glory of God among all Christian people.

Out of humility St Francis gave to his order the name of Friars Minor, desiring that his brethren should really be below their fellows and seek the last and lowest places. He exhorts his brethren to manual labour, but will have them content to receive for it things necessary for life, not money. He bids them not to be ashamed to beg alms, remembering the poverty of Christ ; and he forbids them to preach in any place without the bishop's licence. Incidentally, it was provided that " should any one of them stray from the Catholic faith or life in word or in deed, and will not amend, he shall be altogether cast out of the brotherhood ". Many cities were now anxious to have the once-despised brothers in their midst, and small communities of them sprang up throughout Umbria, Tuscany, Lombardy and Ancona.   In 1216 Francis is said to have begged from Pope Honorius III the Portiuncula indulgence, or pardon of Assisi ;* and in the following year he was in Rome, where he probably met his fellow friar St Dominic, who had been preaching faith and penance in southern France while Francis was still a " young man about town " in Assisi.   St Francis also wanted to preach in France, but was dissuaded by Cardinal Ugolino (afterwards Pope Gregory IX) ; so he sent instead Brother Pacifico and Brother Agnello, who was afterwards to bring the Franciscans to England.   The development of the brotherhood was considerably influenced by the good and prudent Ugolino.   The members were so numerous that some organization and systematic control was imperatively necessary.   The order was therefore divided into provinces, each in charge of a minister to whom was committed " the care of the souls of the brethren, and should anyone be lost through the minister's fault and bad example, that minister will have to give an account before our Lord Jesus Christ ".   The friars now extended beyond the Alps, missions being sent to Spain, Germany and Hungary.

The first general chapter was held at the Portiuncula at Pentecost in 1217 ; and in 1219 was held the chapter called " of Mats ", because of the number of huts of wattles and matting hastily put up to shelter the brethren.   There were said to be five thousand of them present, and it was inevitable that among so many were some for whom the original spirit of Francis himself was already diluted.   He was too haphazard, that is, in this case, too trusting in God, for them ; they agitated for more " practicalness ".   Francis was moved to indignation.   " My brothers ", he replied, " the Lord has called me by the way of simplicity and humbleness, and this is the way He has pointed out to me for myself and for those who will believe and follow me. . . . The Lord told me that He would have me poor and foolish in this world, and that He willed not to lead us by any way other than by that.   May God confound you by your own wisdom and learning and, for all your fault-finding, send you back to your vocation whether you will or no."   And to those who wished him to obtain for them of the pope a licence to preach everywhere without the leave of the bishop of each diocese, he answered, " When the bishops see that you live holily, and attempt nothing against their authority, they will themselves entreat you to work for the salvation of the souls committed to their charge.   Let it be your singular privilege to have no privilege. . . ."   St Francis sent some of his friars from this chapter on their first missions to the infidels, to Tunis and Morocco, reserving to himself the Saracens of Egypt and Syria.   Innocent III's appeal at the Lateran Council in 1215 for a new crusade had resulted only in a desultory

---

* It is commonly held that, in accordance with a vision of Jesus Christ to St Francis in the Portiuncula chapel, Honorius III granted a plenary indulgence on one day in the year for visiting that chapel (now *toties quoties* on August 2).   Whether in fact this indulgence was originally granted to St Francis personally has been the subject of much discussion.   But whether the grant was made to him or not, it is quite certain that the gaining of the indulgence over and over again by going in at one door and out at another was not dreamed of in his day.   This would be *magis derisorium quam devotum*, wrote Nicholas de Lyra ; and other medieval theologians speak in the same sense.   It may be explained for non-Catholic readers that an *indulgence*, or *pardon*, is the remission, not of the guilt, but of the temporal punishment due to those sins of which the guilt has already been forgiven (normally by confession and absolution), granted by the Church and ratified by God ; the amount of the remission is expressed in terms of time, of which the significance is only relative.   A *plenary indulgence* is such a remission of *all* temporal punishment hitherto incurred.

attempt to bolster up the Latin kingdom in the East : Francis would wield the
sword of the word of God.

He set sail with twelve friars from Ancona in June 1219, and came to Damietta on
the Nile delta, before which the crusaders were sitting in siege. Francis was pro-
foundly shocked by the dissoluteness and self-seeking of the soldiers of the Cross.
Burning with zeal for the conversion of the Saracens, he desired to pass to their
camp, though he was warned that there was a price on the head of every Christian.
Permission was given him by the papal legate and he went with Brother Illuminato
among the infidels, crying out, " Sultan ! Sultan ! " Being brought before
Malek al-Kamil and asked his errand, he said boldly, " I am sent not by men but
by the most high God, to show you and your people the way of salvation by announcing to you the truths of the gospel ". Discussion followed, and other audi-
ences. The sultan was somewhat moved and invited him to stay with him.
Francis replied, " If you and your people will accept the word of God, I will with
joy stay with you. If you yet waver between Christ and Mohammed, cause a fire
to be kindled, and I will go into it with your priests that you may see which is the
true faith." The sultan answered that he did not believe any of the *imams* would
be willing to go into the fire, and that he could not accept his condition for fear of
upsetting the people. After some days Malek al-Kamil sent Francis back to the
camp before Damietta. Disappointed that he could do so little either with the
crusaders or their opponents, St Francis returned to Akka, whence he visited the
Holy Places. Then, summoned by an urgent message of distress, he returned to
Italy.

Francis found that in his absence his two vicars, Matthew of Narni and Gregory
of Naples, had introduced certain innovations whose tendency was to bring the
Franciscans into line with the other religious orders and to confine their proper
spirit within the more rigid framework of monastic observance and prescribed
asceticism. With the sisters at San Damiano this had taken the form of regular
constitutions, drawn up on the Benedictine model by Cardinal Ugolino. When
St Francis arrived at Bologna he was amazed and grieved to find his brethren there
housed in a fine convent : he refused to enter it, and lodged with the Friars
Preachers, from whence he sent for the guardian of his brethren, upbraided him
and ordered the friars to leave that house. St Francis saw these events as a be-
trayal : it was a crisis that might transform or destroy his followers. He went to
the Holy See, and obtained from Honorius III the appointment of Cardinal Ugolino
as official protector and adviser to the Franciscans, for he was a man who believed
in St Francis and his ideas while being at the same time an experienced man of
affairs. Then he set himself to revise the rule, and summoned another general
chapter, which met at the Portiuncula in 1221. To this assembly he presented the
revised rule, which abated nothing of the poverty, humbleness and evangelical
freedom which characterized the life he had always set before them : it was Francis's
challenge to the dissidents and legalists who now, beneath the surface, were definitely
threatening the peaceful development of the Franciscans. Chief among them was
Brother Elias of Cortona, who, as vicar of St Francis, who had resigned active
direction of the order, was in effect minister general of the brethren ; but he did
not dare too openly to oppose himself to the founder whom he sincerely respected.
The order had in fact become too big. " Would that there were fewer Friars
Minor ", cried Francis himself, " and that the world should so rarely see one as to
wonder at their fewness ! " At the end of two years, throughout which he had to

face the growing tendency to break away from his ideas and to expand in directions which seemed to him to compromise the Franciscan vocation, Francis once again revised his rule. This done, he handed it to Brother Elias for communication to the ministers. It was promptly lost, and St Francis had again to dictate it to Brother Leo, amid the protests of many of the brethren who maintained that the forbiddance of holding corporate property was impracticable. In the form in which it was eventually approved by Pope Honorius III in 1223, it represented substantially the spirit and manner of life for which St Francis had stood from the moment that he cast off his fine clothes in the bishop's court at Assisi. About two years earlier St Francis and Cardinal Ugolino may have drawn up a rule for the fraternity of lay people who associated themselves with the Friars Minor in the spirit of Francis's "Letter to all Christians", written in the early years of his mission—the Franciscan tertiaries of today. These congregations of lay penitents, bound to a life very different from that of their neighbours, grew to be a significant power in the religious life of the middle ages, and in canon law tertiaries, of whatever order, still have a status differing in kind from that of members of confraternities and sodalities.

St Francis spent the Christmas of 1223 at Grecchio in the valley of Rieti where, he told his friend John da Vellita, " I would make a memorial of that Child who was born in Bethlehem and in some sort behold with bodily eyes the hardships of His infant state, lying on hay in a manger with the ox and the ass standing by ". Accordingly a " crib " was set up at the hermitage, and the peasants crowded to the midnight Mass, at which Francis served as deacon and preached on the Christmas mystery. The custom of making a crib was probably not unknown before this time, but this use of it by St Francis is said to have begun its subsequent popularity. He remained for some months at Grecchio in prayer and quietness, and the graces which he received from God in contemplation he was careful to conceal from men. Brother Leo, his secretary and confessor, testified that he had seen him in prayer sometimes raised above the ground so high that he could only touch his feet, and that sometimes he was raised much higher. Towards the festival of the Assumption in 1224, St Francis retired to Mount Alvernia and there made a little cell. He kept Leo with him, but forbade any other person to come to him before the feast of St Michael. Here it was, on or about Holy Cross day 1224, that happened the miracle of the *stigmata*, of which an account has been given on September 17. Having been thus marked with the signs of our Lord's passion, Francis tried to conceal this favour of Heaven from the eyes of men, and for this purpose he ever after covered his hands with his habit, and wore shoes and stockings on his feet. Yet having first asked the advice of Brother Illuminato and others, he with fear disclosed to them this wonderful happening, and added that several things had been manifested to him which he never would disclose to anyone. To soothe him during illness he was one day asked to let someone read a book to him ; but he answered, " Nothing gives me so much consolation as to think of the life and passion of our Lord. Were I to live to the end of the world I should stand in need of no other book." It was in contemplation of Christ naked and crucified, and crucified again in the persons of his suffering poor, that Francis came to love poverty as his lady and mistress. And he extended his rule of poverty to what is interior and spiritual. Francis did not despise learning, but he feared it for his followers. Studies were good as a means to an end, if they spent still more time in prayer, and studied not so much how to speak to others as how to preach to themselves. Studies which feed vanity rather than piety be abhorred, because they extinguish charity and devotion, and drain and puff up the heart ; but above all he feared the Lady Learning as a rival of the Lady Poverty. " Wheedled by the evil spirits, these brethren of mine will leave the way of holy simplicity and most high poverty ", he groaned, as he watched their anxiety for books and schools. Before he left Alvernia St Francis composed that poem which has been called the " Praise of the Most High God ", then, after the feast of St Michael, he came down from the mountain bearing in his flesh the marks of the sacred wounds, and healed the sick who were brought to him in the plain below.

The two years that remained of his life were years of suffering and of happiness in God. His health was getting worse, the *stigmata* were a source of physical pain and weakness, and his sight was failing. He got so bad that in the summer of 1225 Cardinal Ugolino and the vicar Elias obliged him to put himself in the hands of the pope's physicians at Rieti. He complied with simplicity, and on his way thither paid his last visit to St Clare at San Damiano. Here, almost maddened with pain and discomfort, he made the " Canticle of Brother Sun ", which he set to a tune and taught the brethren to sing. He went to Monte Rainerio to undergo the agonizing treatment prescribed, and got but temporary relief. He was taken to Siena to see other physicians, but he was dying. He dictated a message to his brethren, to love one another, to love and observe the Lady Poverty, and to love and honour the clergy of the Church. Some time before his death he made a longer testament for his religious brethren, in which he recommends that they faithfully observe their rule and work with their hands, not out of a desire of gain but for the sake of good example and to avoid idleness. " If we receive nothing for our work, let us have recourse to the table of the Lord, begging alms from door to door." Then he went to Assisi and was lodged in the bishop's house. The doctors there, pressed to speak the truth, told him he could not live beyond a few weeks. " Welcome, Sister Death ! " he exclaimed, and asked to be taken to the Portiuncula. As they came on the way to a hill in sight of Assisi he asked for the stretcher to be put down, and turning his blind eyes towards the town called down the blessing of God upon it and upon his brethren. Then they carried him on to the Portiuncula. When he knew the end was close at hand, Francis asked that they would send to Rome for the Lady Giacoma di Settesoli, who had often befriended him, and ask her to come, bringing with her candles and a grey gown for his burial, and some of the cake that he liked so well. But the lady arrived before the messenger started. " Blessed be God ", said Francis, " who has sent our Brother Giacoma to us. Bring her in. The rule about women is not for Brother Giacoma." He sent a last message to St Clare and her nuns, and bade his brethren sing the verse of the song he had made to the Sun which praises Death. Then he called for bread and broke it and to each one present gave a piece in token of mutual love and peace, saying, " I have done my part ; may Christ teach you to do yours ". He was laid on the ground and covered with an old habit, which the guardian lent him. He exhorted his brethren to the love of God, of poverty, and of the gospel " before all other ordinances ", and gave his blessing to all his disciples, the absent as well as those that were present. The passion of our Lord in the gospel of St John was read aloud, and in the evening of Saturday, October 3, 1226, St Francis died.

He had asked to be buried in the criminals' cemetery on the Colle d'Inferno, but the next day his body was taken in solemn procession to the church of St

George in Assisi.   Here it remained until two years after his canonization when, in 1230, it was secretly removed to the great basilica built by .Brother Elias.   For six hundred years it was not seen by the eyes of man, till in 1818 after fifty-two days' search it was found deep down beneath the high altar in the lower church. St Francis was only forty-four or forty-five years old at the time of his death.   This is not the place to relate, even in outline, the chequered and glorious history of the order which he founded ; but in its three branches of Friars Minor, Friars Minor Capuchin and Friars Minor Conventual, together making the one Order of St Francis, it is the most numerous religious institute in the Church today.   And it is the opinion of Professor David Knowles that by the foundation of this brother-hood St Francis " did more than any other man to save the medieval Church from decay and revolution ".

So vast and ever-growing is the literature associated with the life of St Francis, and so intricate are the problems presented by some of the principal sources, that it would be impossible to enter into any detail in the space available here.   Let it be noted in the first place that we have certain small ascetical writings of the saint himself.   They have been critically edited by Fr Edouard d'Alençon, and have been translated into English, e.g. by Archbishop Paschal Robinson in America and by the Countess de la Warr in England. Secondly there is a series of *legendae* (a word which here implies no suggestion of a fabulous origin), in other words, the primitive biographies.   The most certainly attested are three documents attributed to Thomas of Celano, the *Vita prima*, written before 1229 ; the *Vita secunda*, a supplement composed between 1244 and 1247 ; and the *Miracula*, dating from about 1257.   Then we have the official life by St Bonaventure, c. 1263 (a critical text appeared first in vol. viii of his *Opera omnia*, edited at Quaracchi), from which the *legenda minor* was afterwards compiled for liturgical use.   This life by St Bonaventure was written with a view to pacification.   A heated controversy had broken out in the order between the *Zelanti*, or " Spiritual " friars, and those who favoured a mitigated observance.   The former appealed to acts and sayings of the founder which were on record in certain earlier writings.   Many of these incidents were suppressed in the Bonaventure life, and in order that such occasions of discord might not be revived, directions were issued that the older *legendae* should be destroyed.   The manuscripts representing this earlier tradition are therefore rare, and in many cases they have only been brought to light by modern research.   Brother Leo, the special confidant of St Francis, undoubtedly wrote certain *cedule* or *rotuli* about his seraphic father, and the great medievalist Paul Sabatier always maintained that the substance of these writings was preserved in a document known as the *Speculum perfectionis*.   His final revision of this work was edited by A. G. Little and brought out by the British Society of Franciscan Studies in 1931.   Its origin and date have been much controverted, and, on the other hand, a text discovered at Perugia by F. M. Delorme—he printed it in 1926 under the name *Legenda antiqua*— has, Delorme avers, a much better claim to be regarded as Brother Leo's long-lost work.   Among other primitive and important texts is the *Sacrum commercium*, " the Con-verse of Francis and his sons with holy Poverty ", which may well have been written, so it has been suggested, by John Parenti as early as 1227 ; an excellent translation was published by Montgomery Carmichael (1901).   Then we have the *Legenda trium sociorum*, the *Legenda Juliani de Spira* and other similar compositions, as well as the *Actus beati Francisci*, which last, under the name given in it in its Italian adaptation, the *Fioretti*, is familiar everywhere, and has been translated into every language.   Of the innumerable modern lives of St Francis it will be sufficient to mention a few best worthy of notice.   In the first place, there is the English life by Father Cuthbert, Capuchin, which in Sabatier's opinion is perhaps the best of all modern lives of Francis ; it has been supplemented by other books of the same author dealing with the early Franciscan history and spirit.   Another life is that of John Jörgensen which has appeared in many European languages ; unfortunately the English translation is not altogether satisfactory, and the same must be said of the English version of the biography by O. Englebert (1950) ; the French original should not be overlooked.   G. K. Chesterton's sketch, brief in compass, is admirably written and leaves a vivid impression.   Paul Sabatier was not a Catholic, but he wrote most sympathetically in his biography of St Francis.   It was first printed in 1894, but the *édition définitive* appeared only after the author's death in

1931. To these may be added Archbishop P. Robinson's *The Real St Francis ;* Bishop Felder's *The Knight-errant of Assisi* and *The Ideals of St Francis ; St Francis : the Legends and Lauds,* containing the contemporary writings, with commentary by O. Karrer ; and a good concise biography by J. R. H. Moorman (1950). The same writer produced *Sources for the Life of St Francis* (1940), and V. Facchinetti's *Guida bibliografica* (1928) is full and useful ; but it is hard to keep pace with Franciscan literature.

ST AMMON   (*c.* A.D. 350)

IT is often stated that St Ammon was the first of the Egyptian fathers to establish a monastery in Nitria ; this is by no means certain, but it is beyond doubt that he was one of the most famous hermit monks to live in that desert. After the death of his wealthy parents, his uncle and other relatives forced Ammon, when he was twenty-two years old, into matrimony. But he read to his wife what St Paul wrote in commendation of the state of virginity, by which she was persuaded to consent to their living together in perpetual continence. They thus lived eighteen years under the same roof. He was severe in his mortifications so as gradually to inure and prepare his body to bear the austerity of the desert. Having spent the day in hard labour tilling a large garden in which he planted and cultivated balsam, at evening he supped with his wife on vegetables or fruit, and afterwards retired to prayer in which he passed a great part of the night. When his uncle and others who opposed his retreat were dead, he retired to Nitria with his wife's consent, and she assembled in her house a number of religious women, who were visited and directed by St Ammon once every six months.

Nitria, now called the Wady Natrun, is about seventy miles south-east from Alexandria and has been described as " a poisonous marsh overgrown with weeds, full of reptiles and blood-sucking flies. There are good and evil oases. This was the marsh that gave its name to Nitria—the soda marsh. The hermits chose it because it was even worse than the desert." Palladius visited it fifty years after the time of St Ammon. He writes :

" On the mountain live some five thousand men with different modes of life, each living in accordance with his own powers and wishes, so that it is allowed to live alone or with another or with a number of others. There are seven bakeries in the mountain, which serve the needs both of these men and also of the anchorites of the great desert, six hundred in all. . . . In this mountain of Nitria there is a great church, by which stand three palm trees, each with a whip suspended from it. One is intended for the solitaries who transgress, one for robbers, if any pass that way, and one for chance comers ; so that all who transgress and are judged worthy of blows are tied to the palm tree and receive on the back the appointed number of stripes and are then released. Next to the church is a guest-house, where they receive the stranger who has arrived until he goes away of his own accord, without limit of time, even if he remains two or three years. Having allowed him to spend one week in idleness, the rest of his stay they occupy with work either in the garden or bakery or kitchen. If he should be an important person they give him a book, not allowing him to talk to anyone before the hour. In this mountain there also live doctors and confectioners. And they use wine and wine is on sale. All these men work with their hands at linen manufacture, so that all are self-supporting. And indeed at the ninth hour it is possible to stand and hear how the strains of psalmody rise from each habitation, so that one believes that one

is high above the world in Paradise.   They occupy the church only on Saturday
and Sunday.   There are eight priests who serve the church, in which so long
as the senior priest lives no one else celebrates or preaches or gives decisions,
but they all just sit quietly by his side " (*Lausiac History*, Lowther Clarke's
trans.).

Thus lived the monks and anchorites who, in the words of St Athanasius, " came
forth from their own people and enrolled themselves for citizenship in Heaven ".

St Ammon's first disciples lived dispersed in separate cells, till St Antony the
Great advised him to assemble the greater part of them under the eye of an attentive
superior, though even then the monastery was no more than a fortuitous aggregation
of private dwellings.   Antony himself selected the site for their group and set up
a cross there, and he and Ammon often exchanged visits.   St Ammon lived in great
austerity.   When he first retired into the desert he took a meal of bread and water
only once a day ; this he afterwards extended to two and sometimes to three or even
four days.   St Ammon wrought many miracles, one of which is recorded by St
Athanasius in his Life of St Antony and elsewhere.   He was going to cross a river
when the banks were overflowed, with Theodore his disciple, and they withdrew
from one another to undress.   But St Ammon even when alone was too shy to
swim across naked, and while he stood trying to make up his mind he found himself
on a sudden transported to the other side.   Theodore coming up and seeing he
had got over without being wet, asked him how it was done, and pressed him so
earnestly that Ammon confessed the miracle, making him first promise not to
mention it to anyone till after his death.   St Ammon died at the age of sixty-two
years ; and St Antony, at the distance of thirteen days' journey from him, knew the
exact time of his death, having seen in a vision his soul ascend to Heaven.

Our information comes mainly from the *Lausiac History* of Palladius, but one or two
miracles may be added from the document now commonly known as the *Historia monachorum*.
The Greek text of this last was edited by Preuschen in his book *Palladius und Rufinus* (1897).
See also the *Acta Sanctorum*, October, vol. ii, and Schiwietz, *Das morgenländische Mönchtum*,
vol. i, p. 94.

ST PETRONIUS, BISHOP OF BOLOGNA   (*c.* A.D. 445)

THERE was a Petronius who was prefect of the *praetorium* in Gaul at the beginning
of the fifth century, and this saint was perhaps his son.   A reference in a letter of
St Eucherius of Lyons suggests that the younger Petronius also at one time held
an important civil office, for he is said to have passed from a position of secular
rank to the service of the Church, and then became renowned in Italy for his virtues.
While a young man he is said to have made a journey to Palestine, " where he
passed many days collecting all the vestiges of Christian antiquity " and acquiring
information which he was afterwards to put to practical use.   About the year 432
he was appointed bishop of Bologna, and he devoted his attention first to the repair
of churches, which were in a ruined condition owing to the recent ravages of the
Goths.

We are told that " he built a monastery outside the city towards the east, in
honour of the protomartyr St Stephen : a spacious building with lofty walls, and
built with many columns of porphyry and precious marbles, having capitals carved
with the figures of men, animals and birds.   He devoted the greatest attention to
this building, and with special care in the reproduction of the Lord's sepulchre, of

which he set out the work himself with a measuring rod. . . . The buildings extended to the place which represented Golgotha, where the cross of Christ stood." In all there were seven churches and the system of buildings reproduced in general lines the Holy Places at Jerusalem. St Petronius made the church of San Stefano his cathedral, and it was so used by the bishops of Bologna until the tenth century, in the third year of which Emilia was ravaged by the Huns and the buildings of Petronius destroyed. They were rebuilt and restored at various times during the middle ages, and during the twelfth century San Stefano achieved great popularity as a place of pilgrimage for those who could not go to the East. In 1141 some new representations were set up which were probably fruitful in putting false relics into circulation. Rather conveniently, the relics of St Petronius himself were discovered at the same time, and a life of the saint was written in which fables and nonsense make up for lack of precise information. In a much-modified form the *Nuova Gerusalemme* of Bologna remains to this day : " it still possesses a singular air of the most profound antiquity."

The document printed in the *Acta Sanctorum*, October, vol. ii, as a life of St Petronius, is of no historical value ; it was fabricated only in the twelfth century. A compilation in Italian written one hundred and fifty years later is equally worthless. The whole question has been thoroughly investigated by Mgr Lanzoni in his monograph *S. Petronio, vescovo di Bologna nella storia e nella leggenda* (1907). See also Delehaye's review in *Analecta Bollandiana*, vol. xxvii (1908), pp. 104–106. In the periodical *Romagna*, vol. vii (1910), pp. 269–277, Mgr Lanzoni carries his investigation further. He seems very doubtful whether Petronius ever visited Palestine. For San Stefano, see G. Jeffery, *The Holy Sepulchre* (1919), pp. 195–211.

5 : ST PLACID, Martyr　　(Sixth Century)

IN consequence of the reputation of the great sanctity of St Benedict whilst he lived at Subiaco, the noble families in Rome brought their children to him to be brought up in his monastery. Equitius committed to his care his son Maurus, and the patrician Tertullus his son Placid, who was a boy of tender years. In his *Dialogues* St Gregory relates that Placid having fallen into the lake at Subiaco as he was fetching water in a pitcher, St Benedict, who was in the monastery, immediately knew of the accident, and calling Maurus said to him, " Brother, run ! Make haste ! The child has fallen into the water." Maurus ran to the lake and walked on the water a bow-shot from the bank to the place where Placid was struggling, and, taking hold of him by the hair, returned with the same speed. When he got to the shore and looked behind him he saw he had walked upon the water, which he had not noticed till then. St Benedict ascribed this miracle to the disciple's obedience, but St Maurus attributed it to the command and blessing of the abbot, which Placid confirmed. " When I was being pulled out of the water ", he said, " I saw the father's hood over my head, and I judged it was he who was getting me out." This miraculous corporal preservation of Placid may be regarded as a symbol of the preservation of his soul by divine grace from the spiritual shipwreck of sin. He advanced daily in wisdom and virtue so that his life seemed a true copy of that of his master and guide, St Benedict. He, seeing the progress which grace made in his heart, loved Placid as one of the dearest among his children and probably took him with him to Monte Cassino. This place is said to have been given to St Benedict by Tertullus, the father of Placid. This is all that is known of St Placid, who was venerated as a confessor till the twelfth century.

But the feast kept by the Western church today is of St Placid, " a monk and disciple of the blessed abbot Benedict, together with his brothers Eutychius and Victorinus, their sister the maiden Flavia, Donatus, Firmatus the deacon, Faustus, and thirty other monks ", who, we are told, were martyred by pirates at Messina. Of these it may be said that certain early martyrologies mention on this date the martyrdom in Sicily of SS. *Placidus*, Eutychius, and thirty companions. The present confusion in the liturgical books of the Benedictine Placid with a number of martyrs who died before he was born has its principal origin in a forgery of the middle twelfth century. At that time Peter the Deacon, a monk of Monte Cassino and archivist of that house, gave to the world an account of the life and passion of St Placid, whose martyrdom nobody had hitherto heard of. He claimed to have got his information from one Simeon, a priest of Constantinople, who had inherited a contemporary document. This purported to have been written by a companion of Placid called Gordian, who had escaped from the slaughter of Placid and his companions in Sicily, fled to Constantinople, and there written the account, which he gave to Simeon's ancestors. This story, like others of the same sort, gradually succeeded in imposing itself and was eventually accepted by the Benedictines and throughout the West. According to it St Placid was sent into Sicily where he founded the monastery of St John the Baptist at Messina. Some years later a fleet of Saracen pirates from Spain descended on the island, and when the abbot, his brothers and sister, and his monks would not worship the gods of the king, Abdallah, they were put to the sword. There were, of course, no Moors in Spain in the sixth century, and no Saracenic descents on Sicily from Syria or Africa are recorded before the middle of the seventh.

Additional evidence, of equally spurious sort, was duly forthcoming, including a deed of gift from Tertullus to St Benedict of lands in Italy and Sicily, but it was not till 1588 that the veneration of St Placid spread to the faithful at large. In that year the church of St John at Messina was rebuilt, and during the work a number of skeletons were found. These were hailed as the remains of St Placid and his martyred companions, and Pope Sixtus V approved their veneration as those of martyrs. The feast was given the rank of a double and inserted in the Roman Martyrology, which causes the Bollandists to question if the pope acted with sufficient prudence. Among the Benedictines the feast of St Placid and his Companions, Martyrs, is a double of the second class. When their calendar was undergoing revision in 1915 the editors proposed to suppress this feast entirely, and to join the commemoration of St Placid, as abbot and confessor, to that of St Maurus on January 15. The Congregation of Sacred Rites, however, directed that there was to be no innovation in respect of this feast until it could be brought into line with the decision of the historico-liturgical question involved which would be dealt with in the revision of the Roman Breviary (whose third lesson for the feast summarizes Peter the Deacon's story). The Benedictines accordingly retained the name and rank of the feast, but suppressed the proper office, replacing it by the common office of several martyrs, with a general collect that does not mention either St Placid or martyrs.

The whole story of this fabrication has been very carefully investigated by U. Berlière in the *Revue Bénédictine*, vol. xxxiii (1921), pp. 19–45 ; an article in which the liturgical as well as the historical aspects of the case have been taken into account. The spuriousness of the narrative attributed to " Gordian " had previously been convincingly demonstrated by E. Caspar, *Petrus Diaconus und die Monte Cassineser Fälschungen* (1909), see especially pp. 47–72. The text of the pseudo-Gordian *passio* will be found in the *Acta Sanctorum*, October, vol. iii. Consult also CMH., and see the summary in J. McCann, *Saint Benedict* (1938), pp. 282–291. The names of the martyrs in Peter the Deacon's forgery are all taken from the entry for October 5 in the Hieronymian martyrology, though Firmatus and Flaviana or Flavia are there expressly stated to have suffered at Auxerre in France.

ST APOLLINARIS, Bishop of Valence   (*c.* A.D. 520)

St Hesychius, Bishop of Vienne, had two sons, of whom the younger was the great St Avitus of Vienne and the elder was this Apollinaris of Valence. He was born about the year 453, educated under St Mamertus, and consecrated bishop by his brother before he was forty years old. Owing to the disorderly life of a previous prelate the see of Valence had been vacant for a number of years, and the diocese was in a deplorable state of ill-living and heresy. Soon after the year 517 a synod condemned an official of Sigismund, King of Burgundy, for having contracted an incestuous marriage. The culprit refused to yield, Sigismund supported him, and the bishops concerned were banished. St Apollinaris spent a year or more in exile. The occasion of his recall is said to have been the illness of Sigismund. The queen thought that her husband's malady was a divine punishment for his persecution of the bishops, and she sent to St Apollinaris to come to court. He refused. Then she asked for his prayers and the loan of his cloak, and this being laid upon the sick king he recovered. Thereupon, we are told, Sigismund sent a safe-conduct to the bishop and expressed contrition for his contumacy.

Some letters are extant which passed between St Apollinaris and St Avitus, which show mutual affection between the brothers and amusing touches of playfulness. In one of them Apollinaris reproves himself for having forgotten to observe the anniversary of the death of their sister Fuscina (whom Avitus praises in a poem) : and in another Avitus accepts an invitation to the dedication of a church, but suggests that on this occasion too much revelry should be avoided. Being forewarned of his death, St Apollinaris went to Arles to visit his friend St Caesarius and the tomb of St Genesius. His progress down and up the Rhône was marked by marvels of dispersing storms and exorcising demons, to which the Roman Martyrology refers, but the historicalness of this journey has been questioned. On his return to Valence he died, about the year 520. He is venerated as the principal patron of Valence, under the popular name of " Aplonay ".

The life printed in the *Acta Sanctorum*, October, vol. iii, is there attributed to a contemporary, but this does not seem very probable. See B. Krusch in *Mélanges Julien Havet* (1895), pp. 39–56, and in MGH., *Scriptores merov.*, vol. iii, pp. 194–203, where the text is critically edited. *Cf.* also Duchesne, *Fastes épiscopaux*, vol. i, pp. 154, 217–218, 223.

ST GALLA, Widow   (*c.* A.D. 550)

Among the victims of Theodoric the Goth in Italy was a noble patrician of Rome, Quintus Aurelius Symmachus, who had been consul in 485. He was put to death unjustly in 525 and left three daughters, Rusticiana (the wife of Boethius), Proba and Galla, who is mentioned in the Roman Martyrology today. A reference to her life and a brief account of her death are given in the *Dialogues* of St Gregory. Galla within a year of her marriage was left a widow and, though young and wealthy, she determined to become a bride of Christ rather than again enter into that natural matrimony which, as St Gregory says in a generalization that he would have found hard to substantiate, " always begins with joy and ends with sorrow ". She was not to be turned from her resolve even by the warning of her physicians that if she did not marry again she would grow a beard. She therefore joined a community of consecrated women who lived close by the basilica of St Peter, where she lived for many years a life of devotion to God and care of the poor and needy.

Eventually she was afflicted with cancer of the breast, and being one night unable to sleep for pain she saw standing between two candlesticks (for she disliked physical as well as spiritual darkness) the figure of St Peter. " How is it, master ? " she cried to him. " Are my sins forgiven ? " St Peter inclined his head. " They are forgiven ", he said. " Come, follow me." But Galla had a dear friend in the house named Benedicta, and she asked that she might come too. St Peter replied that Galla and another were called then, and that Benedicta should follow after thirty days. And accordingly three days later Galla and another were taken to God, and Benedicta after thirty days. St Gregory, writing fifty years after, says that " the nuns now in that monastery, receiving them by tradition from their predecessors, can tell every little detail as though they had been present at the time when the miracle happened ". The letter of St Fulgentius, Bishop of Ruspe, " Concerning the State of Widowhood ", is supposed to have been addressed to St Galla ; her relics are said to rest in the church of Santa Maria in Portico.

Little seems to be known beyond what is recorded in the *Acta Sanctorum*, October, vol. iii. It is probable that the church known as San Salvatore de Gallia in Rome really perpetuated the name of this saint. The French had a hospice at San Salvatore in Ossibus near the Vatican ; they had to move and settled close to San Salvatore de Galla, which consequently came to be known as de Gallia instead of Galla. See P. Spezi in *Bullettino della Com. archeolog. di Roma*, 1905, pp. 62–103 and 233–263.

ST MAGENULF, OR MEINULF   (c. A.D. 857)

MAGENULF was born of a noble Westphalian family, and on the death of his father his mother fled to the court of Charlemagne to escape the unwelcome attentions of her brother-in-law. Local tradition has it that Magenulf was a posthumous child, born while his mother was on the way to the king at Stadberg, beneath a lime tree shown near Bödeken. Charlemagne made him his godchild and sent the boy to the cathedral school at Paderborn. A conference of the bishop Badurad on the text, " The foxes have holes and the birds of the air nests : but the Son of Man hath not where to lay His head ", determined him to enter the ranks of the clergy, and on receiving minor orders he was presented to a canonry in the cathedral of Paderborn. He was ordained deacon and then made archdeacon.

It was the desire of St Magenulf to apply his riches to the foundation of a monastery for women on his own estate, and he chose as the site a spot where the deer came to drink at a brook. His choice was confirmed, it is said, by seeing a stag which displayed a cross between its antlers, like those of St Eustace and St Hubert. The monastery was duly founded at Bödeken and peopled with nuns from Aachen, for whose life he drew up a rule and constitutions. He made the monastery a centre from which he preached the gospel over the surrounding country, and he is accounted one of the apostles of Westphalia. St Magenulf died and was buried at Bödeken. A story, perhaps invented in view of some local dispute, says that while being carried to burial he sat up on the bier and exclaimed,

" Tell the bishop of Paderborn not to interfere in the election of a new superior ! " Other miracles were reported at his tomb, and these, with the memory of his humbleness and generosity, caused him soon to be venerated as a saint. Magenulf is called St Méen in France, and must be distinguished from the better-known St Méen (Mevennus, June 21).

A life of this saint seems to have been written about the year 895 when his remains were first exhumed for veneration, but this has not been preserved to us. It was, however, utilized by a certain Siegward who compiled a wordy but inadequate biography, *c.* 1035. Yet a third life was written from these materials and from his own acquaintance with the history of the period by Gobelinus Persona. It must have been produced, as Löffler has shown in the *Historisches Jahrbuch* for 1904 (pp. 190–192), between 1409 and 1416. The text of both Siegward and Gobelinus is printed in the *Acta Sanctorum*, October, vol. iii.

ST FLORA OF BEAULIEU, VIRGIN   (A.D. 1347)

THE " Hospitalières ", nuns of the Order of St John of Jerusalem, had a flourishing priory known as Beaulieu, between Figeac and the shrine of Rocamadour. Here about the year 1324 entered a very devout novice of good family, who is now venerated as St Flora. If we can trust the biography in the form we have it, she had passed a most innocent childhood, had resisted all her parents' attempts to find her a husband, but on dedicating herself to God at Beaulieu she was overwhelmed by every species of spiritual trial. At one time she was beset with misgivings that the life she was leading was too easy and comfortable, at another she had to struggle against endless temptations to go back to the world and enjoy its pleasures. She seems, in consequence, to have fallen into a state of intense depression which showed itself in her countenance and behaviour to a degree which the other sisters found intensely irritating. They gave her in consequence a very bad time. They declared that she was either a hypocrite or out of her mind. They not only treated her themselves as an object of ridicule, but they brought in outsiders to look at her and encouraged them to mimic and make fun of her as though she were crazy.

In all this time, obtaining help occasionally from some visiting confessor who seemed to understand her state, she was growing dearer to God and in the end was privileged to enjoy many unusual mystical favours. It is alleged that one year on the feast of All Saints she fell into an ecstasy in which she continued without taking any nourishment at all until St Cecilia's day, three weeks later. Again, we hear of a fragment of the Blessed Sacrament being brought to her by an angel from a church eight miles away. The priest who was celebrating there thought that through some carelessness of his this portion of the Host which he had broken off had slipped off the corporal and been lost. In great distress he came to ask Sister Flora about it, since her gift of spiritual discernment was widely known. But she smiled and comforted him, leaving him with the conviction that she herself had received what had disappeared from the altar. It must be confessed that this story bears a suspicious resemblance to a similar incident which occurs in the Life of St Catherine of Siena. Again, when meditating on the Holy Ghost, one Whit Sunday at Mass, Flora is said to have been raised four feet from the ground and to have hung suspended in the air for some time while all were looking on. But perhaps the most curious of her mystical experiences was her feeling that a rigid cross to which our Saviour's body was attached was inside her. The arms of the cross seemed to pierce her ribs and caused a copious flow of blood which sometimes flowed from her mouth, sometimes escaped through a wound in her side. Many instances were apparently reported of her inexplicable or prophetic knowledge of matters of which she could not naturally have learnt anything. She died in 1347 at the age of thirty-eight, and many miracles are believed to have been worked at her tomb.

The Bollandists were at first unable to procure any detailed information regarding St Flora, but eventually a Latin version was sent them, made in 1709, of a life which existed at Beaulieu in Old French. It is printed as an appendix in the *Acta Sanctorum*, June, vol. ii. The Old French text was printed in *Analecta Bollandiana*, vol. lxiv (1946), pp. 5–49. It was made before 1482 from a lost Latin original, said to have been written by the saint's confessor. See also C. Lacarrière, *Vie de Ste Flore ou Fleur* (1866); and *Analecta juris pontificii*, vol. xviii (1879), pp. 1–27. The cult of St Flora has received a sort of indirect confirmation in the fact that the Holy See has approved an office in her honour, used in the diocese of Cahors.

BD RAYMUND OF CAPUA (A.D. 1399)

THE family of delle Vigne was one of the noblest of Capua; Peter delle Vigne had been chancellor to the Emperor Frederick II (his conduct in that office is defended by Dante in the *Inferno*), and among his descendants was Raymund, born in 1330. While a student at Bologna he became a Dominican, and in spite of the continual handicap of bad health made steady progress in his order. When he was thirty-seven he was prior of the Minerva at Rome, and afterwards was lector at Santa Maria Novella in Florence and then, in 1374, at Siena. Here he met St Catherine who, assisting at his Mass on St John the Baptist's day, heard as it were a voice saying to her, " This is my beloved servant. This is he to whom I will entrust you." Father Raymund had already been chaplain to the Preacheresses at Monte-pulciano and so had experience of religious women, but he had never before met one like this young tertiary : she was twenty-seven, sixteen years younger than himself. He was a cautious, deliberate man, and did not allow himself either to be carried away by her vehemence or put off by her unusualness ; he did not at once recognize her mission, but he did recognize her goodness, and one of the first things he did on becoming her confessor was to allow her holy communion as often as she wished. For the six last and most important years of her life Raymund of Capua was the spiritual guide and right-hand man of Catherine of Siena, and would be remembered for that if he had done and been nothing else of note.

Their first work in common was to care for the sufferers from the plague by which Siena was then devastated. Father Raymund became a victim and had symptoms of death : Catherine prayed by him for an hour and a half without intermission, and on the morrow he was well. Thenceforward he began to believe in her miraculous powers and divine mission, and when the pestilence was stayed he co-operated in her efforts to launch a new crusade to the East, preaching it at Pisa and elsewhere and personally delivering Catherine's famous letter to that ferocious freebooter from Essex, John Hawkwood. This was interrupted by the revolt of Florence and the Tuscan League against the pope in France, and they turned their efforts to securing peace at home and working for Gregory's return to Rome. When in 1378 Gregory XI died, Urban VI succeeded him, the opposition party elected Clement VII, and the Schism of the West began. St Catherine and Bd Raymund had no doubt as to which was the legitimate pope, and Urban sent him to France to preach against Clement and to win over King Charles V. Catherine was in Rome and had a long farewell talk with this faithful friar who had been active in all her missions for God's glory and had sometimes sat from dawn till dark hearing the confessions of those whom she had brought to repentance ;

" We shall never again talk like that ", she said on the quayside, and fell on her knees in tears.

At the frontier Bd Raymund was stopped by Clementine soldiers and his life threatened. He returned to Genoa, where he received a letter from St Catherine, disappointed at his failure. Pope Urban wrote telling him to try and reach France through Spain, but this also was useless ; Catherine sent him another letter of stinging reproach for what she considered his faint-heartedness. But Raymund remained at Genoa, preaching against Clement and studying for his mastership in theology. While in Pisa, on April 28, 1380, he " heard a voice, which was not in the air, speaking words which reached my mind and not my ears ", and those words were, " Tell him never to lose courage. I will be with him in every danger : if he fails, I will help him up again." A few days later he heard that St Catherine was dead and that she had spoken those words of him to those who stood by. He succeeded to the charge of her *famiglia*, the little group of clerics and lay-people who had helped and hindered her in all her undertakings, and he continued all his life her labours for the ending of the schism.

But for the next nineteen years Bd Raymund was conspicuous also in a new sphere of activity. At the time of St Catherine's death he was elected master general of the Urbanist part of the Order of Preachers, and he set himself to restore its fervour, grievously impaired by the schism, the Black Death, and general debility. He particularly sought to revive the more specifically monastic side of the order, and established a number of houses of strict observance in several provinces, whose influence was intended to permeate the whole. The reform was not completely successful, and it has been made a reproach to Raymund that his provisions tended to modify and lessen the studies of the friars ; on the other hand they also formed many holy men, and it is not for nothing that the twenty-third master general has been popularly called the second founder of his order. To spread the third order in the world was also part of his scheme, in which he was particularly supported by Father Thomas Caffarini, to whose relentless urging-on we owe the fact that Raymund persevered with and completed his Life of St Catherine. He also wrote in his earlier and less burdened years a Life of St Agnes of Montepulciano. Bd Raymund of Capua died on October 5, 1399, at Nuremberg, while working for Dominican reform in Germany. He was beatified in 1899.

No formal biography of Bd Raymund is preserved to us from early times, but the sources for the life of St Catherine of Siena necessarily tell us a great deal about him (see April 30). There are also his writings, collected in the volume *Opuscula et Litterae* (1899) and the, unfortunately incomplete, *Registrum Litterarum* of the Dominican masters general edited by Fr Reichert. These official documents are of great importance for their bearing on the reform movement in the order which Raymund initiated. There is a good modern biography by H. Cormier, *Le bx Raymond de Capoue* (1899), and he occupies a conspicuous place in the third volume of Mortier's *Histoire des Maîtres Généraux O.P.* See further the article by Bliemetzrieder in the *Historisches Jahrbuch*, vol. xxx (1909), pp. 231–273.

6 : ST BRUNO, Founder of the Carthusian Order (A.D. 1101)

THE religious and learned Cardinal Bona, speaking of the Carthusian monks of whom St Bruno was the founder, calls them, " the great miracles of the world : men living in the flesh as out of the flesh ; the angels of the earth, representing John the Baptist in the wilderness ; the greatest ornament of the

Church ; eagles soaring up to Heaven whose state is justly preferred to the institutes of all other religious orders ". The originator of this remarkable body of men came of a good family and was born at Cologne about the year 1030. While still young he left home to finish his education at the cathedral school of Rheims, and returned to Cologne where he was ordained and was given a canonry in the collegiate church of St Cunibert (he may have held this even before he went to Rheims). In 1056 he was invited to go back to his school as professor of grammar and theology. The fact that he was appointed to such a post when only about twenty-seven years old shows that he was no ordinary man, but at the same time does not suggest the way in which he was to become really distinguished in the memory of Christians. He personally taught " the most advanced, the learned, not young clerics ", and in all his lessons and precepts he had chiefly in view to conduct men to God, and to make them know and respect his holy law. Many eminent scholars in philosophy and divinity did him honour by their proficiency and abilities, and carried his reputation into distant parts ; among these, Eudes de Châtillon became afterwards a beatified pope under the name of Urban II.

He taught in and maintained the reputation of the school of Rheims for eighteen years, when he was appointed chancellor of the diocese by Manasses, a man whose life made him unfit to be in holy orders at all, much less an archbishop. Bruno soon learned the truth about him, and Hugh of St Dié, the pope's legate, summoned Manasses to appear at a council at Autun in 1076, and upon his refusing to obey declared him suspended. St Bruno, another Manasses, the provost, and Pontius, a canon of Rheims, accused him in this council, and Bruno behaved with so much prudence and dignity that the legate, writing to the pope, extolled his virtue and wisdom. Manasses, exasperated against the three canons who had appeared against him, caused their houses to be broken open and plundered, and sold their prebends. The persecuted priests took refuge in the castle of Ebles de Roucy, and remained there till the simoniacal archbishop, by deceiving Pope St Gregory VII (no easy matter), had been restored to his see, when Bruno went to Cologne.

Some time before he had come to a decision to abandon the active ecclesiastical life, of which he himself gives an account in his letter to Raoul or Ralph, provost of Rheims. St Bruno, this Ralph, and another canon, in a conversation which they had one day together in the garden of Bruno's landlord, discoursed on the vanity and false ambitions of the world and on the joys of eternal life, and being strongly affected by their serious reflections, promised one another to forsake the world. They deferred the execution of this resolve till the third should return from Rome, whither he was going ; and he being detained there, Ralph slackened in his resolution and continued at Rheims. But Bruno persevered in his intention of embracing a state of religious retirement. He forsook the world in a time of flattering prosperity, when he enjoyed in it riches, honour and the favour of men, and when the church of Rheims was ready to choose him archbishop. He resigned his benefice and renounced whatever held him in the world, and persuaded some of his friends to accompany him into solitude. They first put themselves under the direction of St Robert, abbot of Molesmes (who was afterwards to help found Cîteaux), and lived in a hermitage at Sèche-Fontaine near by.* In this solitude

---

* The often repeated story of the conversion of St Bruno by being a witness of the declaration of the dead Raymond Diocrès that he was a lost soul is not mentioned by himself or any of his contemporaries, and indeed is not heard of till at least over a hundred years later. It was deleted from the Roman Breviary as apocryphal by Pope Urban VIII.

Bruno, with an earnest desire for true perfection in virtue, considered with himself and deliberated with his companions what it was best for them to do, seeking the will of God in solitude, penance and prayer. He at length decided that their present home was unsuitable and to apply to St Hugh, bishop of Grenoble, who was truly a servant of God and a person well qualified to assist him ; moreover, he was told that in the diocese of Grenoble there were woods and deserts most suitable to his desire of finding perfect solitude. Six of those who had accompanied him in his retreat attended him, including Landuin, who afterwards succeeded him as prior of the Grande Chartreuse.

St Bruno and these six arrived at Grenoble about midsummer in 1084, and came before St Hugh, begging of him some place where they might serve God, remote from worldly affairs and without being burdensome to men. Hugh received them with open arms, for these seven strangers had, it was said, been represented to him in a dream the night before : wherein he thought he saw God Himself building a church in the desert called the Chartreuse, and seven stars which went before him to that place as it were to show him the way. He embraced them very lovingly and assigned them that desert of Chartreuse for their retreat, promising his utmost assistance to establish them there. But that they might be armed against the difficulties they would meet with, lest they should enter upon so great an undertaking without having well considered it, he at the same time warned them of its situation, most difficult of access among the mountains, beset with high craggy rocks, almost all the year covered with snow. St Bruno accepted the offer with joy, St Hugh made over to them all the rights he had in that forest, and they had some spiritual tie with the abbot of Chaise-Dieu in Auvergne. Bruno and his companions immediately built an oratory there, and small cells at a little distance one from the other, like the ancient *lauras* of Palestine. Such was the origin of the order of the Carthusians, which took its name from this desert of Chartreuse.*

St Hugh forbade any woman to go into their lands or any person to fish, hunt or drive cattle that way. The monks first built a church on a summit and cells near it, in which they lived two together in each cell (soon after, alone), meeting in church at Matins and Vespers ; other hours they recited in their cells. They never took two meals in a day except on the great festivals, on which they ate together in a refectory. On other days they ate in their cells as hermits. Everything amongst them was extremely poor : even in their church they would have no gold or silver, except a silver chalice. Labour succeeded prayer. It was a chief work to copy books, by which they endeavoured to earn their subsistence, and, if all else was poor, the library was rich. The soil of their mountains was poor and its climate hard, so they had few cornfields, but they bred cattle. Bd Peter the Venerable, abbot of Cluny, some twenty-five years after St Bruno, writes of them : " Their dress is poorer than that of other monks ; so short and thin and rough that the very sight frightens one. They wear hair shirts next their skin and fast almost perpetually ; eat only bran-bread ; never touch flesh, either sick or well ; never buy fish, but eat it if given them as an alms. . . . Their constant occupation is praying, reading and manual work, which consists chiefly in transcribing books. They celebrate Mass only on Sundays and festivals." This

* As does each separate monastery of Carthusians, *e.g.* in Italian, *certosa*, in Spanish, *cartuja*, in English, *charterhouse*.

manner of life they followed without any written rule, though they conformed to that of St Benedict in some points which were compatible with an eremitical life. St Bruno made his disciples fervent observers of the customs and practices he had established, which Guigo, fifth prior of the Chartreuse, drew up in writing in 1127. Guigo made many changes in the rule, and his *Consuetudines* remained its foundation. The Carthusian is the only old religious order in the Church which never had any reform and has never stood in need of any, owing to the entire sequestration from the world and to the vigilance of superiors and visitors in never allowing a door to be opened for mitigations and dispensations to creep in. This institute has been regarded by the Church as the most perfect model of a penitential and contemplative state, and yet St Bruno when he established his hermit-monks had no intention of founding a new religious order. That they spread beyond the mountains of Dauphiné is due, under God, to a call which came to him only six years after he went to the Chartreuse and which was as unwelcome as it was unexpected. He had " to come down again to these prisoners and to have part in their toils and honours ".

St Hugh became so great an admirer of Bruno that he took him for his spiritual father, and without regard to the difficulty of the way often went from Grenoble to the Chartreuse to enjoy his conversation and improve himself by his advice and example. But his fame went beyond Grenoble and reached the ears of Eudes de Châtillon, his former pupil and now Pope Urban II. Hearing of the holy life which he led, and being from his own personal acquaintance fully convinced of his great prudence and learning, the pope sent him an order to come to Rome that he might assist him by his counsels in the government of the Church. Bruno could have scarcely met with a more severe trial of his obedience or made a greater sacrifice. Nevertheless he set out early in 1090, having nominated Landuin prior at the Chartreuse. The departure of the saint was an inexpressible grief to his disciples, and some of them went away. The rest, with Landuin, followed their master to Rome, but they were prevailed upon by Bruno to return to their former habitation, of which the monks of Chaise-Dieu had taken charge upon their leaving. They recovered their former cells, which were restored to them by the abbot of Chaise-Dieu.

St Bruno, meanwhile, had permission to occupy a hermitage among the ruins of the baths of Diocletian, where he would be close at hand when required by the pope. Exactly what part he played in the papal activities of the time we do not know. Work formerly attributed to him is now recognized as having been done by his namesake, St Bruno of Segni, but he certainly helped in the preparation of various synods in which Bd Urban aimed at the reformation of the clergy. That Bruno should efface himself and that his influence should be hidden is what is to be expected from so contemplative a spirit. Soon Urban pressed him to accept the archbishopric of Reggio in Calabria, but the saint excused himself with so great earnestness, and redoubled his importunities for the liberty of living in solitude, that the pope at length consented that he might retire into some wilderness in Calabria where he would be at hand, but not to the Chartreuse—that was too far off. Count Roger, brother of Robert Guiscard, gave him the beautiful and fertile valley of La Torre, in the diocese of Squillace, where he settled with some new disciples whom he had gained in Rome. Here he betook himself to a solitary life with more joy and fervour than ever. Remembering the resolve which his old friend Ralph of Rheims had made, he wrote him from this place a tender letter inviting him to his hermitage, putting him in mind of the obligation he had taken upon himself, and giving him an agreeable and cheerful description of his life, and of the joy and delight which he and his companions found in it. This letter shows how far the saint was from the least disposition of melancholy, moroseness or harsh severity. Gaiety of soul, which always attends true virtue, is particularly necessary in all who are called to a life of solitude, in which nothing is more pernicious than sadness, and to which nothing is more contrary than a tendency to morbid intro-spection.

In the year 1099 Landuin, prior of the Chartreuse, went into Calabria to consult St Bruno about the form of living which he had instituted, for the monks were desirous not to depart from the spirit and rule of their master. Bruno wrote them a letter full of tender charity and the spirit of God : in it he instructed them in all the practices of a solitary life, solved the difficulties which they proposed to him, comforted them in their troubles, and encouraged them to perseverance. In his two Calabrian hermitages, St Mary's and St Stephen's, Bruno fostered that spirit which guided the monks of the Grande Chartreuse, and on its temporal side he was generously helped by Count Roger, with whom he formed a close friendship. Bruno would visit Roger and his family at Mileto, when there was a baptism or some such matter toward, and Roger would go and stay at La Torre ; and they died within three months of one another. On one occasion, while besieging Capua, Roger was saved from the treachery of one of his officers by being warned by St Bruno in a dream. The treachery was verified and the man condemned to death, but he was pardoned at Bruno's request.

His last sickness came upon him towards the end of September 1101, and when he saw death near he gathered his monks about his bed, and in their presence made a public confession of his life and a profession of faith, which his disciples set down and preserved. He resigned his soul to God on Sunday, October 6, 1101. An account of his death was sent by his monks of La Torre to the chief churches and monasteries of Italy, France, Germany, England and Ireland according to custom to recommend the souls of persons deceased to their prayers. This mortuary-roll of St Bruno, with the *elogia* written thereon by the one hundred and seventy-eight recipients, is one of the fullest and most valuable of such documents extant. St Bruno has never been formally canonized, the Carthusians being averse from all occasions of publicity ; but in 1514 they obtained leave from Pope Leo X to keep his feast, and in 1674 Clement X extended it to the whole Western church. In Calabria he enjoys all the veneration of a " popular " saint ; the contrast of contemplative and active in his life is thus mirrored in the circumstances of his *cultus*.

Although there is nothing in the nature of a contemporary life of St Bruno, a good deal of information is available from other sources. The *Vita antiquior*, printed by the Bolland-ists, October, vol. iii, cannot have been written before the thirteenth century. But in Guibert de Nogent's autobiography, in Guido's account of St Hugh of Grenoble, and in contemporary chronicles and letters (including two letters of Bruno himself), etc., a vivid picture of the saint is presented. These materials have been collected and turned to account both in the *Acta Sanctorum* under this day, in the *Annales Ordinis Cartusiensis* of Dom Le Couteulx, vol. i, and in several modern lives. Mention in particular should be made of H. Löbbel, *Der Stifter des Karthäuserordens* (1899) ; and of the somewhat less critical *Vie de S. Bruno*, by a monk of the Grande Chartreuse (1888). See also the slighter sketches by M. Gorse and Boyer d'Argen, both published in 1902. St Bruno's authentic works, mostly scripture commentaries, were reprinted by the Carthusians at Montreuil-sur-Mer in 1891–92. On his relations with Archbishop Manasses in the earlier part of his life reference may be made to Wiedemann, *Gregor VII und Erzbischof Manasses I von Reims* (1885), together with Hefele-Leclercq, *Conciles*, vol. v, pp. 220–226. A tolerably full bibliography of writings concerning St Bruno is contained in the article " Chartreux " in DTC., vol. ii, cc. 2279–2282 ; and see *Dictionnaire de spiritualité*, vol. ii, cc. 705–776.

ST FAITH, Virgin and Martyr   (Third Century ?)

WHEN this maiden was summoned to answer for her Christianity before the procurator Dacian at Agen she signed herself with the cross and called to Heaven for help. Thus strengthened, she turned to Dacian, who asked her, " What is your name ? " She answered, " My name is Faith (*Fides*) and I endeavour to have that which I am named ". Then he asked, " What is your religion ? " and she said, " I have served Christ from my infancy, and to Him I have consecrated myself ". Dacian was disposed to be merciful, and appealed to her. " Come, child, remember your youth and beauty. Renounce the religion you profess and sacrifice to Diana ; she is a divinity of your own sex and will bestow on you all sorts of good things." But Faith replied, " The divinities of the Gentiles are evil. How then can you expect me to sacrifice to them ? "—" You presume to call our gods evil ! " exclaimed Dacian. " You must instantly offer sacrifice, or die in torment."—" No ! " she cried, " I am prepared to suffer everything for Christ. I long to die for Him." Dacian ordered a brazen bed to be produced and the saint to be bound on it. A fire was kindled under, the heat of which was made still more intolerable by the addition of oil. Some of the spectators, struck with pity and horror, exclaimed, " How can he thus torment an innocent girl only for worshipping God ! " Thereupon Dacian arrested certain of them, and as these refused to sacrifice they were beheaded with St Faith.

The legend of St Faith is untrustworthy and confused with that of St Caprasius (October 20), but her *cultus* was widespread in Europe during the middle ages. The chapel in the eastern part of the crypt of St Paul's Cathedral in London is still called St Faith's. Its predecessor before the Great Fire was the church of the parishioners of St Faith's parish in Faringdon Ward Within, their parish church having been pulled down when the choir of the cathedral was lengthened in the year 1240.

The legend of St Faith and of the miracles worked at her shrine was unusually popular in the middle ages. In BHL. thirty-eight distinct Latin texts, nn. 2928–2965, are enumerated, and these gave rise to a considerable literature in the vernacular which is of great philological interest. See, for example, Hoepfener and Alfaric, *La Chanson de Ste Foy* (2 vols., 1926), and the review of the same work in the *Analecta Bollandiana*, vol. xlv (1927), pp. 421–425. An early and relatively sober text of the *passio* (which does not mention St Caprasius by name) is printed in the *Acta Sanctorum*, October, vol. iii. *Cf.* also Bouillet-Servières, *Ste Foy* (1900) and Duchesne, *Fastes Épiscopaux*, vol. ii, pp. 144–146. The mention of St Faith in the *Hieronymianum* (CMH., p. 543) affords some presumption that she did actually suffer at Agen, but the date is problematical.

ST NICETAS OF CONSTANTINOPLE   (c. A.D. 838)

AMONG the courtiers of the Empress Irene, upholder of the doctrine and practice of the veneration of images of our Lord and the saints, was a young patrician named Nicetas. He came of a Paphlagonian family related to the empress, and is said to have been sent by her to the second oecumenical Council of Nicaea, in the acts of which, however, he is not mentioned as one of her two official representatives. In

45

the palace revolution which put Nicephorus on the throne Nicetas retained his office as prefect of Sicily (his feast is kept at Messina), perhaps at the cost of taking part against his patroness, but when Nicephorus was slain in 811 he entered the monastery of Khrysonike in Constantinople.   Here he remained until the Emperor Leo V began his attack on the holy images, when Nicetas and other monks retired to a country house, taking with them a very precious *eikon* of our Lord.   When the emperor heard of this he sent soldiers, who took away the picture by force, and Nicetas was forbidden to leave his place of refuge.   Nothing more is known of him for over a dozen years, when the Emperor Theophilus called on him to recognize the communion of the Iconoclast patriarch Antony.   This St Nicetas peremptorily refused to do, and with three other monks he was driven from his monastery.   As there was a penalty attached to giving shelter to defenders of the images they had great difficulty in finding another refuge ; they were pursued from place to place, till at last St Nicetas found peace and security on a farm at Katisia in his native Paphlagonia.   Here he lived for the rest of his life.

A brief account of this Nicetas, based mainly upon the Greek *Menaia*, is given in the *Acta Sanctorum*, October, vol. iii.   *Cf.* also the *Constantinople Synaxary*, ed. Delehaye, cc. 115, 137.

ST MARY FRANCES OF NAPLES, VIRGIN   (A.D. 1791)

BARBARA BASINSIN, mother of this saint, had much to suffer before the child's birth from the roughness and bad temper of her husband, Francis Gallo, and from horrible dreams and delusions.   In her distress she opened her heart to the Franciscan St John-Joseph-of-the-Cross and the Jesuit St Francis di Girolamo. They reassured and comforted her and are moreover said to have prophesied the future holiness of the unborn babe, who was born at Naples in 1715 and baptized Anne Mary Rose Nicolette.   When Anne was sixteen her father set his heart on her marrying a wealthy young man of rather better family, who was most anxious to have the virtuous and attractive girl as his wife.   But she had already made up her mind to give herself to Christ only, and therefore resolutely opposed her father, to his great indignation.   His brutal temper carried him away, and he beat the girl and locked her in her room with only bread and water.   She was glad enough to suffer thus for her faithfulness to God's call, while her mother tried to persuade Francis Gallo to let Anne have her wish of enrolling herself among the tertiaries of St Francis.   To help her she called in Father Theophilus, a friar of the Observance, who at length made Gallo see that his conduct was unjust and unreasonable, and got him to drop his insistence on the advantageous match.

Accordingly, on September 8, 1731, Anne received the habit of the third order in the Franciscan church of the Alcantarine reform at Naples.   As a testimony to her devotion to our Lord's passion she took the name of Mary-Frances-of-the-Five-Wounds.   In accordance with a practice then not entirely obsolete she continued to live at home, wearing the habit of her order and devoting herself to a religious life of piety and material usefulness ; during the last thirty-eight years she directed the household of a secular priest, Don John Pessiri.   Sister Mary Frances displayed in herself a number of the physical phenomena of mysticism in a marked degree. While making the stations of the cross, especially on the Fridays of Lent, she would experience pains corresponding to those of the Passion : of the agony in the garden, the scourging, the crowning with thorns, and so on week by week in order, culminating in an appearance of death. She is said to have received the *stigmata*. But the most remarkable occurrences were with reference to the Blessed Sacrament, which she was allowed to receive every day. It is alleged that three times the Host came to her mouth without visible agency : once from the celebrant's fingers as he said *Ecce Agnus Dei*, once from the ciborium, and once the piece which is broken off the larger Host to be put into the chalice. But the Barnabite St Francis Xavier Bianchi testifies to even more astonishing things concerning the Precious Blood. At the Christmas of 1741 Sister Mary Frances received the mystical espousals. While praying at the crib she seemed to see our Lord stretching out His right hand to her and to hear the words, " This night you shall be my bride ". The experience brought on a temporary loss of sight, which lasted till the next day. She was favoured with other visions and was very frequently rapt in ecstasy.

To the sufferings that have been referred to were added bodily ill-health and distress caused by the unkindness to her of her father and other members of her family. But St Mary Frances did not think these enough, and added to them severe voluntary austerities, at the same time asking God that she might take upon herself the pains of those in Purgatory (including, eventually, her father) and of her sick and sinful neighbours. Her confessor one day exclaimed that he wondered there were any souls left in Purgatory at all. Several times, it is said, dead persons appeared to her, asking for particular prayers to be said on their behalf. To the Theatine provincial, Father Gaetano Laviosa, she said that she had endured all that could be endured. Priests, religious and lay people came to her for help and direction. To Friar Peter Baptist, of the Alcantarines, she said, " Take care, father, not to let jealousies arise among your penitents. We poor women are very subject to it, as I know by experience ; I have suffered from it. I thank God for prompting my confessor to act in the way he did. He told me to come to confession after all his other penitents, and when I went in he often only said to me sharply, ' Go to communion.' Then the Devil whispered in my ear how little sympathy my confessor had for me, how he ignored what I suffered at home from my father and sisters when they complained angrily at my coming back from church so late. But what troubled me most were the remarks of the neighbours because I went to confession so often. I tell you this both that you may be careful and gentle, and also not spare those who need a little severity."

St Mary Frances lived till the early years of the French Revolution, and she clearly foresaw in a general way some of the events that were to come. " I can see nothing but disasters ", she said more than once. " Troubles in the present, greater troubles in the future. I pray God that I may not live to witness them." She died on October 6, 1791, and was buried in the church of Santa Lucia del Monte at Naples. She had promised St Francis Xavier Bianchi that she would appear to him three days before his death, and is said actually to have done so on January 28, 1815. St Mary Frances was canonized in 1867.

A short biography by Father Laviosa, who had known the saint personally, was published not long after her death, and this was revised and issued again in 1866, in anticipation of the canonization which took place next year ; it bears the title, *Vita di Santa Maria Francesca delle Cinque Piaghe di Gesù Cristo*. This life was also translated into French ; and from the same source was abbreviated the account in Léon, *Auréole Séraphique* (Eng. trans.), vol. iii, pp. 278–286. Another life, by L. Montella, was published in 1866. For the physical phenomena cf. H. Thurston, *The Physical Phenomena of Mysticism* (1952).

7 : OUR LADY OF THE ROSARY

THE rosary is a prayer, or series of prayers, in which, during the recitation of the Lord's Prayer and " Glory be to the Father . . ." fifteen times each, and of the Angelical Salutation one hundred and fifty times, divided into ones and tens, the faithful are taught to honour our divine Redeemer by meditating on the fifteen principal mysteries of His life and of His Mother.　It is therefore an epitome of the gospel, a history of the life, sufferings and triumphant victory of Jesus Christ, and an exposition of what He did in the flesh for our salvation.　The principal object of the devotion of every Christian ought to be always to bear in mind these mysteries, to return to God a perpetual homage of love, praise and thanksgiving for them, to implore His mercy through them, to make them the subject of meditation, and to mould his affections, regulate his life and form his spirit by the impressions which they make on his soul.　The rosary as a method of doing this is easy in itself and adapted to the slowest or feeblest capacity ; and at the same time sublime and faithful in the exercise of all the highest acts of prayer, contemplation and interior virtues.　These are best comprised in the prayer which our Lord Himself vouchsafed to teach us, which those who penetrate the spirit of each word can never weary in repeating ; and as well as the " Our Father ", the " Hail Mary " is often repeated in the rosary because, as it contains praise of the Incarnation, it best suits a devotion instituted to honour that mystery.　Though it be addressed to the Mother of God, with an invocation of her intercession, it is chiefly a praise and thanksgiving to the Son for the divine mercy therein.

As the Roman Martyrology today reminds us, Pope St Pius V in 1572 ordered an annual commemoration of our Lady of Victory to be made to implore God's mercy on His Church and all the faithful, and to thank Him for His protection and numberless benefits, particularly for His having delivered Christendom from the arms of the infidel Turks by the sea victory of Lepanto in the previous year, a victory which seemed a direct answer to the prayers and processions of the rosary confraternities at Rome made while the battle was actually being fought.　A year later Gregory XIII changed the name of the observance to that of the Rosary, fixing it for the first Sunday in October (the day of Lepanto).　On August 5, the feast of the dedication of St Mary Major, in the year 1716, again while Marian processions were taking place, the Turks were again signally defeated, by Prince Eugene at Peterwardein in Hungary.　In thanksgiving therefor, Pope Clement XI decreed that the feast of the Holy Rosary should be observed throughout the Western church.　The feast is now kept on the date of the battle of Lepanto, October 7 (except by the Dominicans, who observe the original first Sunday of the month).

According to the tradition of the Order of Preachers, recognized by many popes and accepted in the Roman Breviary, the rosary, just as we know it, was devised by St Dominic himself, and used by him in his missionary work among the Albigensians, in consequence of a vision in which our Lady revealed it to him.　No tradition of the kind has been more passionately supported and few have been more devastatingly attacked.　Its truth was first questioned some two hundred years ago, and the resulting controversy has been carried on at intervals ever since. It is well known that the use of beads or similar objects as a device for aiding the memory and keeping count is not only pre-Dominican but pre-Christian ; and the monks of the Eastern church use a rosary of ancient origin, having 100 or more beads, on a different plan from and entirely independent of the Western devotion. Nor is it now disputed that the custom of saying a number of *Paters* or *Aves* (often 150, corresponding to the number of the psalms), and keeping count of them by means of a string of beads, etc., was widespread in the West before the thirteenth century. The famous Lady Godiva of Coventry, who died about 1075, left by will to a certain statue of our Lady " the circlet of precious stones which she had threaded on a cord in order that by fingering them one after another she might count her prayers exactly " (William of Malmesbury). Moreover there seems to be no doubt that such strings of beads were used for long only for the counting of *Paters*. In the thirteenth century and throughout the middle ages such articles were called " paternosters " ; their makers were " paternosterers " ; and in London they worked in the street we still call Paternoster Row. A learned Dominican bishop, Thomas Esser, maintained that meditation while reciting numerous *Aves* was first practised by certain Carthusians in the fourteenth century. None of the stories about the origin of the rosary current before the fifteenth century mention St Dominic, and for another hundred years there was no uniformity in the way it was said, even among the Friars Preachers themselves. None of the early accounts of St Dominic make any mention of the rosary, either in referring to his methods of prayer or to anything else ; the early constitutions of his order are quite silent about it ; and there is little trace of a rosary in early Dominican iconography, from Fra Angelico's paintings down to St Dominic's sumptuous tomb at Bologna (finished in 1532).

Under stress of the facts just summarized recent opinion regarding the origin of the rosary has diverged considerably from the views which prevailed at the close of the sixteenth century. Writing in 1922, Dom Louis Gougaud states that " the various elements which enter into the composition of that Catholic devotion commonly called the rosary are the product of a long and gradual development which began before St Dominic's time, which continued without his having any share in it and which only attained its final shape several centuries after his death ". Father Getino, O.P., considers that St Dominic was the originator of the devotion on the ground that he presumably popularized the practice of reciting multiplied *Aves*, without, however, any special direction as to the number of repetitions or the systematic insertion of *Paters*. Father Bede Jarrett, O.P., on the other hand, considers that St Dominic's special contribution was the breaking up of the *Aves* into groups of ten by the insertion of *Paters ;* while Father Mortier, O.P., asserts with all the emphasis of italics that the rosary as conceived by St Dominic was not properly speaking *a devotion, a formula of prayer ; it was a method of preaching*. Father Petitot, O.P., regards the story of the vision of our Lady as true symbolically but not historically.

If it be necessary to abandon the idea of its invention and even the propagation of its use by St Dominic himself, the Western rosary is none the less properly distinguished as the Dominican rosary ; the friars of his order gave it the form it now has and for centuries have zealously spread its use throughout the world, bringing thereby unnumbered blessings to countless souls and sending up a ceaseless paean of worship before God. No Christian is too simple or unlettered to make use of the rosary ; it may be the vehicle of high contemplation as well as of the simplest petition or aspiration ; as a form of private prayer it comes only after the biblical psalms and those prayers with which the Church as Church praises almighty God and His Christ.   The idea is familiar to us that so great a means of good should be publicly celebrated in her liturgy ; nevertheless, such was the over-crowding of the calendar even in those days, this was one of the feasts that Pope Benedict XIV's commission wished to dispense with.

As to the origin of this feast consult Benedict XIV, *De festis*, bk ii, ch. 12, n. 16 ; and Esser, *Unseres Lieben Frauen Rosenkranz*, p. 354.   The case against the claim made for St Dominic in the matter of the institution of the rosary will be found most fully presented in the *Acta Sanctorum*, August, vol. i, pp. 422 *seq.* ; in *The Month*, October 1900 to April 1901 (by Fr Thurston ; summarized by him in the *Catholic Encyclopedia*, vol. xiii) ; and in Father Holzapfel, *S. Dominikus und der Rosenkranz* (1903).   There have, of course, been many attempted vindications of the Dominican tradition, but it is instructive to contrast the uncompromising tone of such books as that of Father Mézard, o.p., *Étude sur les Origines du Rosaire* (1912), or that of Father W. Lescher, o.p., *St Dominic and the Rosary* (1902), with the attitude of Father Mortier, o.p., *Histoire des Maîtres Généraux O.P.*, vol. i (1903), pp. 15–16 and vol. vii, p. 189 n., or of Father Bede Jarrett, o.p., *Life of St Dominic* (1924), p. 110.   See also *The Month*, October 1924 ; L. Gougaud in *La vie et les arts liturgiques*, October 1922, and July 1924 ; J. Guiraud in his *Life of St Dominic*, p. 11, and his *Cartulaire de Prouille*, pp. 328–330 ; F. M. Willam, *The Rosary, its History and Meaning* (1953) ; and Y. Gourdel in vol. ii of *Maria : Étude sur la Ste Vierge* (1951).

ST JUSTINA, Virgin and Martyr   (Date Unknown)

St Venantius Fortunatus, bishop of Poitiers early in the seventh century, ranks this Justina among the most illustrious virgins whose sanctity and triumph have adorned the Church, saying that her name makes Padua famous, as Euphemia does Chalcedon and Eulalia the city of Mérida.   And in his poem on the life of St Martin he bids those who visit Padua kiss the sacred sepulchre of the blessed Justina.   A church was built at Padua in her honour early in the sixth century, and herein in 1117 her alleged relics were found.   About the same time appeared a clumsily forged account of her passion, which pretends that St Justina was baptized by St Prosdocimus, " a disciple of the blessed Peter ", who gave this information to the writer.   This Prosdocimus, we are told, was the first bishop of Padua and a martyr under Nero, and St Justina was slain by the sword for her faithfulness to Christ, with a number of particulars for the truth of which there is no evidence.

The fifteenth-century Benedictine " reform " of St Justina (now the Italian Cassinese congregation) took its name from the abbey of this name at Padua, where it was inaugurated.

See the *Acta Sanctorum*, October, vol. iii, but there is an older text of the *Passio* printed in the *Analecta Bollandiana*, vol. x (1891), pp. 467–470 ; and *ibid.*, vol. xi (1892), pp. 354–358, an account of the alleged discovery of her relics in 1117.   See also Allard, *Histoire des persécutions*, vol. iv, pp. 430 *seq.*, and Trifone's three articles in the *Rivista Storica Benedettina*, 1910 and 1911.   As for Prosdocimus, of whom the first indication of *cultus* is in 860, his spurious twelfth-century biography has been printed in the *Acta Sanctorum* (November, vol. iii) with all necessary comments and cautions.   See also Lanzoni, *Le diocesi d'Italia*, vol. ii, pp. 911–915, and Leclercq in DAC., vol. xiii, cc. 238–239.

ST MARK, Pope   (A.D. 336)

St Mark was by birth a Roman and served God among the clergy of that church. He was the first pope to be elected after the freeing of Christianity by Constantine. He did not let the new conditions relax his watchfulness, but endeavoured rather to redouble his zeal during the peace of the Church ; knowing that, if men cease openly to persecute the faithful, the Devil never allows them any truce.   The saint contributed to advance the service of God during the pontificate of St Silvester ; after whose death he was himself placed in the apostolic chair on January 18, 336. He held the dignity only eight months and twenty days, dying on October 7 following.   St Mark perhaps founded the church that bears his name and built another at the cemetery of Balbina, and he possibly granted or confirmed the right of the bishop of Ostia to consecrate the bishop of Rome.   A fragmentary poem on a St Mark by Pope St Damasus is referred to this pope by some : it extols Mark's disinterestedness and spirit of prayer.

In the *Acta Sanctorum*, October, vol. iii, will be found what little is known of St Mark. See also the *Liber Pontificalis* (ed. Duchesne), vol. i, pp. 202–204.

ST OSYTH, Virgin and Martyr   (*c*. A.D. 675 ?)

According to her legend St Osyth was the daughter of a Mercian chief, Frithwald, and his wife Wilburga, said to have been a daughter of Penda of Mercia.   She was brought up in a nunnery, perhaps at Aylesbury, and wished herself to become a nun ; but her parents affianced her to Sighere, king of the East Saxons.   If this be the Sighere mentioned by St Bede, he apostatized from the faith during a pestilence about 665, but was, presumably, reconciled by the bishop Jaruman. This man had a passion for hunting, and when after the wedding he attempted to embrace his wife, against her will, his attention was distracted to a stray stag : he went off in pursuit, and on his return he found his bride had gone.   She made her way to the East Anglian bishops, Acca of Dunwich and Bedwin of Elmham, and Sighere, realizing that it was better to have no wife than an unwilling one, let them clothe her with the religious habit.   He himself gave to St Osyth some land at a place called Chich, on a creek of the Colne between Brightlingsea and Clacton, and here she established her monastery.   She governed it for some years with prudence and holiness, but it was situated in a dangerous place and disaster soon overtook it. In a piratical raid the marauders tried to carry St Osyth off, and when she fiercely resisted they smote off her head.

The body of St Osyth was taken to Aylesbury, but afterwards brought back to Chich, where a priory of Austin canons under her invocation was established in the twelfth century.   Near it grew up the present village of Saint Osyth, and the memory of the martyred abbess is preserved in several other local place-names, St Osyth Creek, St Osyth Marsh, St Osyth Wick, and St Osyth's Well.   Saint Osyth is locally pronounced " Toosey ".

There is a notice in the *Acta Sanctorum*, October, vol. iii, but the difficulties of the case are more clearly presented in Stanton, *Menology*, pp. 477 and 673, and in DNB., vol. xlii, p. 337.   The calendars collated by Edmund Bishop, which are noted in Stanton, point to the conclusion that there was a definite *cultus* in East Anglia.   This, however, was of late growth, for there seems to be little or no trace of it before the Norman Conquest.   In calendars and other references the name of this saint is frequently disguised under the form " Sythe " or some equivalent spelling.

ST ARTALDUS, or ARTHAUD, Bishop of Belley   (A.D. 1206)

Artaldus was born in the castle of Sothonod in Savoy.   At the age of eighteen he went to the court of Duke Amadeus III, but a year or two after he became a

Carthusian at Portes. After many years, being a priest and an experienced and holy religious, he was sent by the prior of the Grande Chartreuse to found a charterhouse near his home, in a valley in the Valromey significantly called " The Cemetery " ; here Artaldus established himself with six of his brethren from Portes. The community was no sooner well settled down than their buildings were destroyed by fire, and St Artaldus had to begin all over again. He chose a fresh site, on the Arvières river, and his second foundation was soon built and occupied. But a Carthusian cell could not contain the ever-increasing reputation of Artaldus : like his master St Bruno, he was consulted by the pope, and when he was well over eighty he was called from his monastery to be bishop of Belley, in spite of his vehement and reasonable protests. However, after less than two years of episcopate his resignation was accepted, and he thankfully returned to Arvières, where he lived in peace for the rest of his days. During his last years he was visited by St Hugh of Lincoln, who had come into France, and who, while he was prior of the charterhouse of Witham, had induced Henry II to become a benefactor of Arvières. The *Magna vita* of St Hugh records a gentle rebuke administered by Hugh when Artaldus asked him for political news in the presence of a community who had turned their backs upon the world to give themselves entirely to God. The *cultus* of St Artaldus, called simply Blessed by the Carthusians, was confirmed for the diocese of Belley in 1834. He was 105 years old when he died.

There is a short medieval life in the *Acta Sanctorum*, October, vol. iii, but a fuller account is obtainable from Dom Le Couteulx, *Annales Ordinis Cartusiensis*, vols. ii and iii.

BD MATTHEW OF MANTUA   (A.D. 1470)

JOHN FRANCIS CARRERI was a native of Mantua and received the name Matthew when he joined the Order of Preachers. He was a successful preacher, preparing himself for that ministry by long periods of recollection, and an upholder of strict observance in his order, but very few facts of external interest are recorded of his life, except the incident of his capture by pirates. This happened while on a voyage from Genoa to Pisa. The friar was set free, but when he saw that among the other prisoners were a woman and her young daughter, he went back to the pirate captain and offered himself in their place. The ruffian was so astonished at the request that he let all three of them go. Bd Matthew met Bd Stephana Quinzani, while she was still a child, and it is said that he promised her that she should be his heiress. Nobody knew what a mendicant friar could mean by this remark, but after Matthew's death she began regularly every Friday to have pain in her bosom, in exactly the same way as he had formerly done as a testimony of his devotion to the Passion. Bd Matthew died (after having asked his prior's permission so to do) at Vigevana on October 5, 1470, and twelve years later Pope Sixtus IV allowed his solemn translation and a liturgical commemoration.

An account of this *beatus* is furnished in the *Acta Sanctorum*, October, vol. iii ; but see further the *Monumenta O.P. Historica*, vol. xiv, pp. 115 *seq.* A brief sketch in English will be found in Procter, *Dominican Saints*, pp. 281–283.

8 : ST BRIDGET, Widow, Foundress of the Order of the Most Holy Saviour   (A.D. 1373)

S T BIRGITTA, more commonly called Bridget, was daughter of Birger, governor of Upland, the principal province of Sweden, and his second wife, Ingeborg, daughter to the governor of East Gothland. Ingeborg, who had several other children, died about the year 1315, some twelve years after the birth of Bridget, who thenceforward was brought up by an aunt at Aspenäs on lake Sommen. She had not begun to speak till she was three years old, and then she spoke quite clearly and unhesitatingly, rather than confusedly like a child ; her goodness and devotion matched her speech. But she tells us that in her youth she was inclined to be proud and overbearing. When she was seven she had a vision of being crowned by our Lady ; at ten she was deeply affected by a sermon on the passion of Christ, and the night following seemed to see Him hanging upon His cross and she thought she heard Him say to her, " Look upon me, my daughter ".— " Alas ", said she, " who has treated you thus ? " She seemed to herself to hear Him answer, " They who despise me, and spurn my love for them ". The impression made upon her mind was never effaced, and from that time the sufferings of her Redeemer became the centre of her spiritual life. Before she was fourteen, Bridget married Ulf Gudmarsson, who was himself only eighteen, and the marriage subsisted happily for twenty-eight years. They had eight children, four boys and four girls, of whom one is venerated as St Catherine of Sweden. For some years Bridget led the life of a feudal lady on her husband's estate at Ulfasa, with the difference that she cultivated the friendship of a number of learned and virtuous men.

About the year 1335 St Bridget was summoned to the court of the young king of Sweden, Magnus II, to be principal lady-in-waiting to his newly-wedded queen, Blanche of Namur. Before she had been long at court Bridget found that her responsibilities could not stop at the duties of her office. Magnus was weak and tended to be wicked ; Blanche was good-willed but irresponsible and luxury-loving. The saint bent all her energies to developing the better side of the queen's character and to establishing an influence for good over both of them. As so often happens in such cases, she earned the respect of the young sovereigns, but did not succeed in making much difference in their lives ; they could not or would not take her altogether seriously. The personal revelations which later were to make St Bridget so famous were already supporting her, and concerned matters so far apart as the necessity of washing and terms for peace between England and France, " which if the English king does not accept, he will prosper in none of his affairs, but will end his life in grief and leave his realm and children in tribulation and anguish ". But the court did not seem susceptible to these influences : " What was the Lady Bridget dreaming about last night ? " became a sort of byword. And St Bridget had troubles of her own. Her eldest daughter had married a riotous noble whom his mother-in-law refers to as " the Brigand " ; and about 1340 the youngest son, Gudmar, died. St Bridget thereupon made a pilgrimage to the shrine of St Olaf of Norway at Trondhjem, and on her return, fortified thereby, she made a further attempt to curb the excesses of Magnus and Blanche. Meeting with no more success than before, she got leave of absence from the court, and with Ulf went on pilgrimage to Compostela. On the way back Ulf was taken ill at Arras, where he received the last sacraments and all seemed over. But Bridget spared neither pains nor prayers for his recovery, and she received an assurance of it by a revelation of St Denis. He was in fact restored again to health, and husband and wife vowed henceforward to devote their lives to God in religious houses. But, apparently before this resolution could take effect, Ulf died in 1344, at the monastery of Alvastra of the Cistercian Order.

St Bridget continued to live at Alvastra for four years, having taken upon herself the state of a penitent, and from that day she seemed to forget what she had been in the world. She changed her manner of dress, using no more linen except for a veil to cover her head, wearing a rough hair-shift and cords full of knots for a girdle. Her visions and revelations now became so insistent that she was alarmed, fearing to be deluded by the Devil or by her own imagination. But a thrice-repeated vision told her to submit them to Master Matthias, a canon of Linköping and a priest of experience and learning, and he pronounced them to be of God. From now to her death she communicated them as they occurred to Peter, prior at Alvastra, who wrote them down in Latin. Those of this period culminated in a command of our Lord to go to the royal court and warn King Magnus of the judgement of God on his sins. She did so, and included the queen, the nobles and the bishops in her denunciation. For a time Magnus mended his ways, and liberally endowed the monastery which St Bridget now, in consequence of a further vision, planned to found at Vadstena, on Lake Vättern.

In this house St Bridget provided for sixty nuns, and in a separate enclosure monks, to the number of thirteen priests, in honour of the twelve Apostles and St Paul, four deacons, representing the Doctors of the Church, and eight choir-brothers not in orders, making the number of our Lord's apostles and disciples, eighty-five, in all. She prescribed them certain particular constitutions which are said to have been dictated to her by our Saviour in a vision. This circumstance is neither mentioned by Pope Boniface IX in the bull of her canonization, nor by Martin V when he ratified the privileges of Syon Abbey and reaffirmed the canonization ; and the popes when they speak of this rule mention only the approbation of the Holy See, without making reference to any such private revelation. In this institute, as in the Order of Fontevrault, the men were subject to the abbess of the nuns in temporals, but in spirituals the women were subject to the superior of the monks, because the order was principally instituted for women and the men were admitted only to afford them spiritual ministrations. The convents of the men and women were separated by an inviolable enclosure, but had the same church, in which the nuns' choir was above in a gallery, so they could not even see one another. There are now no men in the Order of the Most Holy Saviour, or Bridgettines as they are commonly called, and where formerly there were seventy houses of nuns there are today but about a dozen. All surplus income had every year to be given to the poor, and ostentatious buildings were forbidden ; but each religious could have as many books for study as he or she pleased.* During the fifteenth century Vadstena was the literary centre of Sweden.

---

* The Bridgettine community at South Brent in Devon has unbroken organic identity with a pre-Reformation community, and is the only English religious community of which this is true. It was founded by King Henry V in 1415, and settled in 1431 at Syon House, Isleworth. The nuns took refuge at Termonde in Flanders at the dissolution under Henry VIII, after various vicissitudes settled at Lisbon, and returned to England (Spettisbury in Dorset) in 1861. Building of the abbey at Vadstena was not finally begun till 1369.

In consequence of a vision St Bridget wrote a very outspoken letter to Pope Clement VI, urging him to abandon Avignon for Rome, and to bring about peace between Edward III of England and Philip IV of France.   The pope declined to leave Avignon, but sent Hemming, Bishop of Abö, to Philip's court, where, however, he could do nothing.   King Magnus, meanwhile, who valued Bridget's prayers if not her advice, asked for her interest in a projected crusade against the pagan Letts and Estonians, which was really a disguised plundering expedition. The saint saw through it, and tried to dissuade him.   She was now out of favour at the Swedish court, but was beloved by the people, among whom she went travelling about the country and looking after their temporal and spiritual welfare. Many of them were not long converted, and she enforced the preaching of her chaplains by miracles of healing.   In 1349, in spite of the Black Death that was ravaging Europe, she decided to go to popeless Rome for the year of jubilee in 1350. With her confessor, Peter of Skeninge, and others, she embarked at Stralsund, amid the tears of the people who were never to see her again : for at Rome she settled down, to work among the people and for the return of the popes to their City.   She lived by a rule, being present at Mass at five o'clock every morning ; it is said she went to confession every day and to communion several times a week.   The brightness of her virtue shone doubly in contrast to the degradedness of Rome in those days, where open robbery and violence were rife, vice no less open and unashamed, the churches falling through neglect, and the people uncared for except to be exploited.   The austerity of her way of living, the fervour of her devotion, her love of the holy shrines, her severity to herself and kindness to others, her tirelessness in serving the sick, the poor and pilgrims, made her loved by all in whom the light of Christianity was not entirely extinguished.   She made the care of her fellow-countrymen her particular charge, and every day she fed Swedish pilgrims in her house near St Laurence *in Damaso*.

Nor did St Bridget confine her good works and exhortations to holy living to the poor and humble.   She went to the great monastery of Farfa to remonstrate with the abbot, " a very worldly man, who did not trouble about souls at all " ; but it is to be feared that he did not mend his ways.   So Bridget turned her attention to another relaxed house, at Bologna, where she had more success.   It was probably at Bologna that she was joined by her daughter, St Catherine.   Bridget persuaded her not to return to Sweden, and Catherine remained her helper and dear companion throughout the remainder of her life.   Among the places particularly associated with St Bridget in Rome are the churches of St Paul's-outside-the-Walls and San Francesco a Ripa.   In the first is the most beautiful crucifix of Cavallini before which she prayed, which is said to have spoken to her, and in the second she had a vision of St Francis, who said to her, " Come, eat and drink with me in my cell ". She took this to be an invitation to go to Assisi, which she accordingly did.   Later she made a tour of shrines in Italy which lasted for two years.

The saint's prophecies and revelations had reference to most of the burning political and religious questions of her time, both of Sweden and Rome.   She prophesied that pope and emperor would shortly meet amicably in Rome (which Bd Urban V and Charles IV did in 1368), and the using of her by factions did somewhat to abate her popularity among the Romans.   Her prophecies that their iniquities would be visited with condign punishments had the same effect, and several times her ardour drew down persecution and slander upon her.   On the other hand, she was not sparing of her criticisms, and did not fear to denounce a pope as " a murderer of souls, more unjust than Pilate and more cruel than Judas ". Once she was turned out of her house at a month's notice, and more than once she and Catherine found themselves seriously in debt ; they sometimes even had to beg food at a convent of Poor Clares.   St Bridget's joy at the coming of Pope Urban V was short-lived, for he soon retired to Viterbo and Montefiascone, and it was rumoured he was going back to Avignon.   On her return from a pilgrimage to Amalfi she had a vision in which our Lord appeared to tell her to go to the pope, warn him that his death was near, and show him the rule of the religious at Vadstena.   This rule had already been submitted to Urban when he arrived in Rome, and he had done nothing about it.   So now Bridget set off to Montefiascone on her white mule, and as a result the pope gave a general approval to her religious foundation, prescribing for it the general Rule of St Augustine with the Bridgettine constitutions.   Four months later Urban was dead, and St Bridget three times wrote to his successor at Avignon, Gregory XI, warning him to come back to the apostolic see, which he eventually did four years after her death.

   In 1371, in consequence of another vision, St Bridget embarked on the last of her journeys, a pilgrimage to the Holy Places, taking with her St Catherine, her sons Charles and Birger, Alphonsus of Vadaterra and others.   The expedition started inauspiciously, for at Naples Charles got himself entangled with Queen Joanna I, of unenviable reputation.   Although his wife was still alive in Sweden, and her third husband in Spain, Joanna wanted to marry him, and he was far from unwilling.   His mother was horror-stricken, and set herself to ceaseless prayer for the resolution of the difficulty.   It came about in an unexpected and tragic way.   Charles was struck down by a fever, and after a fortnight's illness died in the arms of his mother.   He was, with St Catherine, her favourite child, and Bridget after his funeral went on in deepest grief to Palestine.   Here, after being nearly drowned in a wreck off Jaffa, her progress through the Holy Places was a succession of visions of the events that had happened there and other heavenly consolations.   On her way back, in the autumn of 1372, she landed at Cyprus where she denounced the wickedness of the royal family and the citizens of Famagusta, who had mocked at her warnings on her way out ; then she passed on to Naples, where her warnings were read by the clergy from the pulpit but with little effect on their uninstructed and erring congregations.   The party arrived back in Rome in March 1373.   Bridget had been ailing for some months, and now she got weaker every day till, having received the last sacraments from her faithful friend, Peter of Alvastra, she died on July 23 in her seventy-first year.   She was temporarily buried in the church of St Lawrence *in Panisperna ;* four months after, the body was taken up and, in the care of St Catherine and Peter of Alvastra, it was carried in triumphal progress by way of Dalmatia, Austria, Poland and Danzig to Vadstena, where it was laid to rest in the abbey.   St Bridget was canonized in 1391 and is the patron saint of the kingdom of Sweden.   Thirty-five or so years after her death, one of her maids in Rome told Margery Kempe of Lynn that Bridget " was kind and meek to every creature, and had a laughing face ".

   Nothing is more famous in the life of St Bridget than the many revelations with which she was favoured by God, chiefly concerning the sufferings of our Saviour and events which were to happen in certain kingdoms.   By order of the Council of Basle, the learned John Torquemada, afterwards cardinal, examined the book of St Bridget's revelations, and approved it as profitable for the instruction of the faithful, but this approbation met with not a little opposition.   It, however, amounts to no more than a declaration that the doctrine contained in that book is conformable to the orthodox faith, and that the revelations are credible upon a historical probability. Pope Benedict XIV referred specifically to the revelations of St Bridget, among others, when he wrote that, " Even though many of these revelations have been approved, we cannot and we ought not to give them the assent of divine faith, but only that of human faith, according to the dictates of prudence whenever these dictates enable us to decide that they are probable and worthy of pious credence ". St Bridget with true simplicity of heart always submitted her revelations to the judgement of the pastors of the Church ; and she was far from ever glorying in any extraordinary graces, which she never desired and on which she never relied except to be obedient thereto and to increase her love and humility. If her revelations have rendered her name famous, it is by her heroic virtue that it is venerable to the whole Church. To live according to the spirit of the mysteries of religion is something much greater and more sublime than to know hidden things or to be favoured with the most extraordinary visions. To have the knowledge of angels without charity is to be only a tinkling cymbal ; both to have charity and to speak the language of angels was the happy privilege of St Bridget. The book of her revelations was first printed at Lübeck in 1492, and has been translated into many languages. They were known in England soon after the saint's death, and part were translated by the Bridgettine Richard Whytford in 1531. The lessons at Matins in the Bridgettine office are taken from the revelations on the glories of our Lady, the *Sermo angelicus*, according to the alleged words of our Lord to St Bridget, " I will send my angel who will reveal to you the lesson that shall be read at Matins by the nuns of your monastery, and you shall write it as he tells you ". Alban Butler pertinently remarks that if we had the revelations as written down by St Bridget herself, instead of passing through the mind and translation of Peter of Alvastra and, in part, Alphonsus of Vadaterra, " it would have been compiled with more simplicity and with greater life and spirit, and would have received a higher degree of certainty ".

Owing to the immense interest which has been taken in St Bridget by Scandinavian scholars of all creeds, the materials formerly available in the various editions of the *Revelationes Stae Birgittae* and in the *Acta Sanctorum*, October, vol. iv, have to a large extent been superseded. The oldest life, which was compiled immediately after her death by her confessor Peter of Alvastra and Peter of Skeninge was only printed for the first time in 1871 in the collection *Scriptores rerum Suecicarum*, vol. iii, pt 2, pp. 185–206. Other lives, such as that by Birger, archbishop of Upsala, will be found in the Bollandists and in the publications of Swedish learned societies. A scholarly edition of the whole collection of the canonization documents has been compiled by Isak Collijn, *Acta et Processus canonizacionis Beate Birgitte* (1924–31). There are furthermore a number of biographies and of studies of special aspects of the saint's career, mostly in Swedish ; notably an account of the historical personages connected with her life in Sweden and in Rome. This, published under the title *Birgittinska Gestalter* (1929), is also by Collijn. One historically excellent Swedish life, by E. Fagelklou, has been translated into German (1929) by M. Loehr. Among French biographies that written by Countess de Flavigny, *Sainte Brigitte de Suède*, may be recommended as having made good use of Swedish sources. It seems rather doubtful whether the *Revelations* have not been to some extent coloured by the prepossessions of her confessors who copied them or translated them into Latin. The most reliable text is said to be that of G. E. Klemming in Swedish (1857–84), of which a modernized selection has been edited by R. Steffen (1900). An English life of St Bridget was contributed to the Quarterly Series in 1888 by F. Partridge ; *The Story of the English Bridgettines* (1933) has been briefly told by Canon J. R. Fletcher ; and in 1947 there was published in America *God's Ambassadress*, by Helen Redpath, an admirable biography, both scholarly and popular. *Cf.* also E. Graf, *Revelations and Prayers of St Bridget* (1928), which consists of the *Sermo angelicus ;* and *The Book of Margery Kempe* (1936), pp. 140–141. J. Jörgensen's *St. Bridget of Sweden* (2 vols.) appeared in English in 1954. St Bridget (and her daughter St Catherine) is commonly called " of Sweden ", but she was not of the royal house, either by birth or marriage ; nor did she ever found an order of knights.

SS. SERGIUS AND BACCHUS, MARTYRS   (A.D. 303 ?)

THESE martyrs were said to be officers of the Roman army on the Syrian frontier, Sergius being described as commandant of the recruits' school and Bacchus as his subaltern. They were personal favourites of the Emperor Maximian, until one day when he went into the temple of Jupiter to sacrifice he noticed that they stopped outside. They were ordered to come in and take part in the sacrifice. On their refusal, they were stripped of their arms and badges of rank, dressed up in women's clothes, and so paraded through the streets. They were then despatched to Rosafa in Mesopotamia, where the governor had them so severely scourged that St Bacchus died under the lash. His body was thrown out on to the highway, where vultures protected it from the attacks of dogs, an incident recorded of several other martyrs. St Sergius was made to walk a long distance in shoes with nails thrust through into his feet, and was beheaded. The martyrdom of these two officers is attested by the evidence of the martyrologies and early writers, but the particulars of their passion are far from trustworthy.

In the year 431 Alexander, Metropolitan of Hierapolis, restored and beautified the church over the grave of Sergius, whose walls in the middle of the sixth century were plated with silver. Alexander was very annoyed when, three years after he had spent so much money on it, Rosafa was taken from his jurisdiction and made a bishopric. Veneration for the martyr renamed the place Sergiopolis, and Justinian fortified it and greatly honoured the memory of the martyrs. The church at Rosafa was one of the most famous in the East, and Sergius and Bacchus became the heavenly protectors of the Byzantine army, with the two Theodores, Demetrius, Procopius and George.

If we may trust the *Voyage archéologique* of Le Bas and Waddington, vol. iii, n. 2124, a church in eastern Syria, dedicated to these two martyrs in 354, affords the earliest known example of this form of recognition of sanctity. Their " acts " are preserved in Latin, Greek and Syriac. See the *Analecta Bollandiana*, vol. xiv (1895), pp. 373–395, and, for a list of the various recensions, BHL., BHG. and BHO. Delehaye in his *Origines du culte des martyrs* (1933), pp. 210–211, calls attention to the extraordinary popularity of St Sergius in the East as evidenced not only by the number of churches and sanctuaries dedicated in his honour either alone or jointly with St Bacchus, but also by the prevalence of Sergius as a baptismal name (though in Russia this is now usually due to St Sergius of Radonezh). On Rosafa, consult Spanner and Guyer, *Rusafa* (1926), Herzfeld, *Archaeologische Reise* (1911–22) and Peeters in *Analecta Bollandiana*, xlv (1927), pp. 162–165. For the contribution of aviation to questions involved, see the same *Analecta*, vol. lxvii (1949), pp. 109–116.

SS. MARCELLUS AND APULEIUS, MARTYRS   (DATE UNKNOWN)

THESE martyrs are commemorated with SS. Sergius and Bacchus in the Roman liturgy on October 8. The Roman Martyrology says they were followers of Simon Magus (Acts viii 9–25), converted by St Peter and martyred in Rome after his passion. This is quite apocryphal, and the brief notice has been framed by the martyrologist Ado out of the mention of a Marcellus which occurs in the *Gesta SS. Nerei et Achillei*. There is, however, some likelihood that the first of them is a martyred Marcellus recorded at Capua ; but of Apuleius there is no trace.

See H. Quentin, *Les martyrologes historiques*, pp. 563, etc. ; and CMH., p. 544. The brief and very late *passio* of SS. Marcellus and Apuleius is printed in the *Acta Sanctorum*, October, vol. iii.

HOLY SIMEON   (First Century)

It is recorded in the Gospel of St Luke that Simeon was a citizen of Jerusalem, a righteous and devout man who awaited the consolation of Israel. And the Holy Ghost was in him, and had told him that he should not die before he had seen the Anointed of the Lord. When therefore Joseph and Mary brought the infant Jesus to be presented to God in the temple, Simeon also was moved by the Spirit to come in. And he took the Child in his arms and praised God in those words which are known after him as the Canticle of Simeon, the *Nunc Dimittis* sung by the Church at the office of Compline in the West and at Vespers in the East. And he pro- phesied of the Child and His mother, saying : " Behold ! this Child is set for the fall and for the resurrection of many in Israel, and for a sign which shall be con- tradicted. And thine own soul a sword shall pierce, that out of many hearts thoughts may be revealed." There are several apocryphal references and traditions about Holy Simeon, but nothing more is known of him than is stated above. He is named in the Roman Martyrology today and his feast is kept in several places in the West, but by the Byzantines on February 3.

There is a lengthy discussion in the *Acta Sanctorum*, October, vol. iv, but the modern commentators on St Luke's gospel have a fuller knowledge of the references to Simeon in early apocryphal literature. See *e.g.* Lagrange, *L'Évangile selon S. Luc* (1921), pp. 83–84.

ST PELAGIA THE PENITENT   (No Date)

Pelagia, more often called Margaret, on account of the magnificence of the pearls for which she had so often sold herself, was an actress of Antioch, equally celebrated for her beauty, her wealth and the disorder of her life. A synod having been called in that city by the patriarch, a group of bishops were sitting in the portico of the basilica of St Julian the Martyr, listening to the words of the greatly respected bishop from Edessa, St Nonnus. While he was speaking, Pelagia, surrounded by her admirers and attendants, rode by on a white donkey ; she was wearing her famous jewels, her face, arms and shoulders were bare as if she were a common courtesan, and she looked around her with bold and provoking glances. St Nonnus stopped speaking and his auditors turned away their eyes, but he watched her till she was out of sight, and then asked, " Did not that woman's beauty please you ? " The bishops were puzzled by the question and made no reply. And St Nonnus said, " I was well pleased to see her, for it seems to me God sent her as a lesson to us. She goes to an infinity of trouble to keep herself beautiful and to perfect her dancing, to please men, but we are considerably less zealous in the care of our dioceses and of our own souls."

That night Nonnus had a dream, in which he was celebrating the Liturgy but was much disturbed therein by an unclean and offensive bird that fluttered around the altar. When the deacon dismissed the catechumens the bird went away also, but came back again after the Liturgy and the dreamer caught it and threw it into the fountain in the atrium of the church. It came out of the water gleaming like snow and, flying up into the heavens, disappeared. The next day being Sunday, all the bishops assisted at the Liturgy of the patriarch, and St Nonnus was asked to preach. His words went straight to the heart of Pelagia, who had been moved to come to the basilica though she was not even a catechumen, and she wrote a note asking him to speak with her. St Nonnus agreed, on condition that the other bishops should be present, and coming in she threw herself on her knees before him and asked for baptism, beseeching him to come between her and her sins, which would otherwise recoil on his head. The patriarch was asked to provide a sponsor, and when he had appointed the senior deaconess, Romana, St Nonnus baptized the actress in her true name of Pelagia, confirmed her, and gave her holy communion. On the eighth day after her baptism, when she had given up her property to Nonnus for distribution to the poor, she laid aside her white garments, put on men's clothes, and disappeared from the city. She made her way to Jerusalem and there, in a cave on the Mount of Olives, lived as a solitary, being known and reverenced among the people as Pelagius, " the beardless monk ". Three or four years later, James, the deacon of St Nonnus, visited her, and while he was there St Pelagia died. When those who came to bury her discovered her sex, they cried out, " Glory be to thee, Lord Jesus, for thou hast many hidden treasures on earth, as well female as male ".

The original of this circumstantial narrative was written by one who claimed, falsely, to be the deacon James just mentioned, and the whole story as it stands must be set aside as a work of fiction, a religious romance. Father Delehaye detects in it two elements, the first and essential one of which comes from the sixty-seventh homily on St Matthew of St John Chrysostom. There he speaks of an Antiochene actress, whose infamy was known throughout Cilicia and Cappadocia, who underwent a sudden conversion ; after her baptism she lived for many years a life of extreme austerity as a recluse. Chrysostom does not mention her name and there is no reason to suppose that she was ever the object of a religious *cultus*. " James's " reliance on this story is obvious. Whether he deliberately adopted the second element also, or whether it is an accidental development, is not so certain. Pelagia the penitent has been confused with a real St Pelagia. She was a virgin martyr of Antioch who was celebrated in that city in the fourth century on October 8 (in the Roman Martyrology, June 9) ; she is mentioned both by St John Chrysostom and St Ambrose.*

" If there is any item of religious interest to be deduced from all this ", writes Father Delehaye after discussing the development of the tale at some length, " it is the fact that a traditional *cultus* may have the life crushed out of it by legend." He sees in this popular romance of the " Repentance of Pelagia " the starting-point of the tales of a whole group of imaginary saints, of whom a characteristic example is St Marina (February 12). The legend of the saint of Antioch " lost by degrees every vestige of historical fact ; even the account of the conversion became eliminated and the purely legendary residuum passed under various names . . . thanks to which we have the saints Mary and Marina, Apollinaria, Euphrosyne and Theodora, who are simply literary replicas of the Pelagia of the self-styled James ; or else, as in the case of St Eugenia, the theme of a woman hiding her sex was tacked

* A third Pelagia, of Tarsus, named in Eastern calendars also on October 8 (Roman Martyrology, May 4), seems to be a combination of the true and the false Pelagias of Antioch. The pseudo-Pelagia of Antioch is the only one of the three mentioned in the Roman Martyrology on October 8 ; her feast is celebrated liturgically not only by the Byzantines, but by the Latins of Jerusalem as well (on October 26).

on to other narratives having for their hero some historic personage " (*Legends of the Saints*, p. 203).

As Delehaye points out in the work just quoted (3rd French edition, 1927, p. 190), the historical Pelagia, who is commemorated on this day in the Syriac *breviarium* of the early fifth century, was not a penitent but an innocent maiden fifteen years of age ; her true story as known both to St Ambrose (PL., vol. xvi, cc. 229 and 1093) and to St John Chrysostom (PG., vol. l, cc. 579–585) is told herein under June 9.   It is curious that the original text of Alban Butler on October 8 completely ignores the true Pelagia and assumes the truth of the extravagant legend.   The text of the fictitious " acts " may be found in the *Acta Sanctorum*, October, vol. iv, but better in H. Usener, *Legenden der hl. Pelagia* (1897).   The attempt of the last-named scholar to explain the *cultus* of St Pelagia as a survival of the worship of Aphrodite has been dealt with by Delehaye in the book cited above.   " James's " story is pleasingly translated in Miss H. Waddell's *Desert Fathers* (1936), pp. 285–302.

ST THAÏS   (No Date)

ACCORDING to the legend there lived in Egypt during the fourth century a famous courtesan named Thaïs, who had been brought up a Christian.   Her infamy came to the ears of St Paphnutius at his hermitage in the Thebaïd, and he determined to try and redeem her.   He put off his penitential garb, dressed himself in such a manner as to disguise himself, and, going to her house (probably at Alexandria), was introduced to her room.   He told her he desired to talk with her, but wished it might be in some more private place.   " What is it you fear ? " said Thaïs.   " If men, no one can see us here ; but if you mean God, no place can hide us from His eye."   " What ! " replied Paphnutius, " do you know there is a God ? "   " Yes," said she, " and I moreover know that Heaven will be the portion of the good and everlasting Hell the punishment of the wicked."   " Is it possible ", mused aloud the hermit, " that you should know these truths and yet dare to sin and to draw so many after you, before Him who knows and will judge all things ? " Thaïs was overcome by the reproach of so venerable an old man, and at the same time the Holy Ghost who moved Paphnutius to speak enlightened her understanding to see the baseness of her sins, and softened her heart by the touch of His grace. Filled with confusion at her crimes and with bitter sorrow, detesting her ingratitude against God, she burst into tears and, throwing herself at the feet of Paphnutius, cried, " Father, tell me what to do.   Pray for me, that God may show me mercy. I want only three hours to settle my affairs, and then I am ready to do all you shall counsel me."   Paphnutius appointed a place to meet and went away.

Thaïs got together all her jewels, furniture, clothes and the rest of her ill-gotten wealth, and making a great pile in the street burnt it publicly, inviting all who had made her those presents and been the partners of her sin to join her in penance. Then she hastened to Paphnutius, and was by him conducted to a monastery of women.   There he shut her up in a cell, putting on the door a seal of lead as if that place had been her grave, nevermore to be opened.   He ordered the sisters to give her every day bread and water through the window, and she asked him, " Father, teach me how I am to pray ".   Paphnutius answered, " You are not worthy to call upon God by uttering His holy name, because your lips have been filled with iniquity ; nor to lift up your hands to Heaven, for they are defiled with impurities ; but turn yourself to the east, and repeat these words : ' Thou who hast created me, have pity on me.' "   Thus she continued to pray with continual tears, and when she had persevered with fervour in this life for three years, St Paphnutius went to St Antony to ask his advice whether this penitential course did not seem sufficient to prepare her for reconciliation and holy communion. St Antony and his monks passed the night together in prayer, and in the morning St Paul the Simple, his oldest disciple, said that God had prepared a place in Heaven for the penitent. Paphnutius therefore went to her cell to release her from her penance. Thaïs said that from the time of her coming thither she had never ceased bewailing her sins, which she had always weighing as a burden on her. " It is on that account ", said Paphnutius, " that God has blotted them out." She therefore left her prison to live with the rest of the sisters, but God withdrew her out of this world fifteen days after her release. She is honoured in the Greek menologies on October 8 ; and her story has long been known in the West. But St Thaïs is not named in the Roman Martyrology.

The texts vary in assigning the conversion of Thaïs to Paphnutius, Serapion or Bessarion ; but a sensation was caused when it was announced at the beginning of this century that the mummified remains of Serapion and Thaïs had been discovered at Antinoë in Egypt and were actually on view in the Musée Guimet at Paris. Undoubtedly those names are attached to the respective graves, but there are difficulties about the interpretation of the fragmentary inscriptions. Serapion was an ascetic, for iron instruments of penance were found on the body ; and the so-called Thaïs had with her an apparatus like a cribbage-board, pierced with holes, which has been explained as a *compte-prière*, a sort of rosary. But there is really nothing which would require us to connect these two interments, or identify them with the personages named in the legend.

The more important texts, Greek, Latin and Syriac, which refer to Thaïs, were brought together by the Abbé F. Nau in the *Annales du Musée Guimet*, vol. xxx, pt 3 (1903), pp. 51–112. The historical character of the narrative of her conversion is, however, extremely doubtful. To begin with, the identity of name with that of the famous courtesan who was associated with Alexander the Great is at least suspicious. Mgr Batiffol, after a careful discussion of all the available evidence, in the *Bulletin de littérature ecclésiastique*, 1903, pp. 207–217, came to the conclusion that the story was simply " une moralité ", a pious fable, and in this verdict Delehaye (*Analecta Bollandiana*, vol. xxiv, p. 400) and Dom Leclercq (DAC., vol. i, c. 2339) entirely concur. For the graves, see the account by A. Gayet in the *Annales du Musée Guimet*, vol. xxx, pt 2, pp. 35 *seq.* ; or better in his brochure, *Antinoë et les sépultures de Thaïs et de Sérapion* (1902).

ST REPARATA, Virgin and Martyr   (Date Unknown)

The Reparata mentioned in the Roman Martyrology today was said to be a virgin martyr at Caesarea in Palestine during the persecution of the Emperor Decius. Her spurious " acts " state that she was twelve years old and of a lively disposition. Being denounced as a Christian she was brought before the prefect, who was moved by her beauty and tried to win her over with fair words. Reparata argued with him and was therefore subjected to various tortures. As these failed to have any effect she was thrown into a furnace of fire where, like the three holy children of Juda, she stood unharmed and sang the praises of God. The prefect again tried to induce her to sacrifice to the gods, but Reparata only answered him back from within the furnace, till in desperation he commanded the guards, " Take the talkative and horrid creature and cut off her head, and don't let me set eyes on her again ". So she was led away, still singing, and as her head was smitten off " her soul was seen to go out from her body and ascend to Heaven in the form of a dove ".

Her alleged relics were translated to Italy, where the martyr is greatly venerated in several dioceses.

One text of the legendary *passio*, of which there are various recensions, is printed in the *Acta Sanctorum*, October, vol. iv.   It would seem that St Reparata's story was sometimes confused with that of St Pelagia or St Margaret.

ST DEMETRIUS, Martyr   (Date Unknown)

This Demetrius was probably a deacon martyred in an unknown year at Sirmium (Mitrovic in Yugoslavia).   During the fifth century Leontius, prefect of Illyricum, built two churches in honour of St Demetrius, one at Sirmium, the other at Thessalonika ; and in the second he deposited the bones of the martyr, *c.* 418, though in fact these may have been only lesser relics.   But from that time on Salonika was the great centre of the cult of St Demetrius : he was the local patron and heavenly protector, and huge crowds of pilgrims flocked to his tomb, where a miraculous oil was said to exude from the relics, whence he was called *Myrobletes*, but more commonly *Megalomartyr*, " the Great Martyr ".   His great church was burnt down in 1917.

According to the Salonika legend St Demetrius was a citizen of the place, who was arrested for preaching the gospel and speared, without trial, while shut up in a room of the public baths.   The earliest account, not older than the sixth century, says that the order for his murder was given by the Emperor Maximian in a fit of temper, consequent on the slaying of his favourite gladiator by an amateur called Nestor.   In subsequent fictitious accounts the deacon of Sirmium (if such he was) becomes a proconsul (so styled in the Roman Martyrology) and a warrior-saint, in which capacity his popularity was exceeded only by that of St George ; both were adopted by the Crusaders, being supposed to have been seen with St Mercurius in their ranks at the battle of Antioch in 1098.   The popular St Demetrius is an entirely imaginary character : like St Procopius, St Menas, St Mercurius and others, a genuine martyr of whom little or nothing was known was by a series of fabrications transformed into a literal warrior of Christ, a miliary martyr, and the patron and reinforcement of soldiers and chivalry.   His feast is kept with solemnity throughout the East on October 26 and he is named in the preparation of the Byzantine eucharistic liturgy.

An excellent account of this martyr, including Greek texts of the two principal families of the *passio*, is printed in the *Acta Sanctorum*, October, vol. iv ; but Delehaye, in his *Légendes grecques des saints militaires* (1909), pp. 103–109 and 259–263, has gone over the ground again and has furnished a critical revision of the earlier document.   He calls attention to the fact that Demetrius is commemorated in the Syriac *breviarium* and is there connected with Sirmium at a date previous to the building of the great basilica at Salonika by Leontius. At Ravenna, no doubt through Byzantine influence, the cult of St Demetrius seems to have established itself before it was known elsewhere in Italy ; the earliest chapel in Ravenna was dedicated in his honour.   The name *Dmitry*, so common among the Slavs, is from him.

ST KEYNE, Virgin   (Sixth Century ?)

The memory of St Keyne (Keyna or Cain) has been preserved in England by the verses which Robert Southey wrote about her holy well in the parish of Saint Keyne near Liskeard in Cornwall, the properties of which were known in the middle ages, though the story of the canny bride is probably a local joke of more recent date. St Keyne was very well known in parts of South Wales and the west of England,

but it is difficult, if not impossible, to find out anything authentic about her.   In
the Welsh lists (but not in the list which William of Worcester copied in Cornwall)
of the twenty-four children of Brychan of Brecknock, she appears as a daughter of
that liberal father of saints, and we learn that she was venerated " between the forks
of the Ogmore " river, in Morgannwg.

The account of her given in her *vita*, edited by John of Tynemouth in the fourteenth century probably from an earlier and longer life, is as follows.   The father
of the blessed Keyne was King Brychan Brycheiniog, who had twelve sons and
twelve daughters.   Keyne grew into a very beautiful young woman, but resolutely
refused all suitors and took a vow of virginity ; therefore she was called in Welsh
Cain Wyry, Keyne the Maiden.   Then she resolved to become a solitary and,
crossing the Severn, she took up her abode in the forests on the left bank.   The
place was infested with snakes, which she turned into stone, " for the stones in
the fields and villages there have the form of serpents, as if they had been carved
by mason's art, to this very day ".*   She lived there for years, making many
journeys and founding oratories, till at St Michael's Mount she met her nephew
St Cadoc, who persuaded her (with the help of an angel) to return to Wales.   " She
made for herself a habitation in a certain hillock at the roots of a certain great
mountain ", and there caused a healing well to spring up.   Just before her death
she told Cadoc that that place would fall into the hands of a sinful race, whom she
would root out and lead thither other men, who would find her forgotten tomb,
" and in this place the name of the Lord shall be blessed for ever ".

Camden records the tradition that the place of St Keyne's hermitage in England
was at Keynsham in Somerset, but there was no known *cultus* of the saint in that
county until, curiously enough, modern times : she is now commemorated throughout the diocese of Clifton on this day.   The site of her final resting-place in South
Wales has been the subject of much discussion.   For a time it was thought to be
Llangenny, near Crickhowell, where there is an old well, but this was through an
erroneous identification of St Keyne with St Ceneu.   Canon G. H. Doble has
made out a strong case for Llangeinor in Glamorgan.   The name is a corruption
of Llan-Gain-Wyry, the Church-place of the Virgin Cain ; topographically it meets
all the requirements ; and in a lonely place on Mynydd Llangeinor is a holy well
whose waters are still credited with salutary properties.   It is impossible to tell
how much (or little) of the *vita* of St Keyne is true.   Canon Doble concludes that
she was one of a band of missionaries who came from Brecknock into the parts of
Herefordshire east of the Black Mountains ; from there she visited and founded
churches in South Wales, Cornwall and perhaps Somerset : he has found her name
in one form or another in at least seven places.   But he ends up by querying if St
Keyne were not rather a man than a woman, seeing the amount of hard travel and
work this founder (if there were only one) must have got through.

The life attributed to John of Tynemouth is printed with a commentary in the *Acta
Sanctorum*, October, vol. iv, but Canon Doble, as an expert in Celtic topography and philology,
has been able to trace the slender clues to the saint's activities far more thoroughly than was
possible for any foreign scholar in the eighteenth century.   His account of St Keyne was
published in the *Downside Review* for January 1931, pp. 156–172, and the essay on " The
Children of Brychan ", of which this forms a part, was issued as no. 25 of the Cornish Saints
series, *St Nectan, St Keyne*. . . . But see further in *Analecta Bollandiana*, vol. lxxi (1953),
p. 398, and Introduction, pp. 381–382.

* And to this day.   There are plenty of the fossils called " ammonites " in the quarries
around Keynsham, and their mythical origin is remembered locally.

9 : ST JOHN LEONARDI, Founder of the Clerks Regular of the Mother of God (A.D. 1609)

JOHN LEONARDI was a young assistant to an apothecary in the city of Lucca in the middle of the sixteenth century. He was of a religious disposition, became a member of a confraternity founded by Bd John Colombini, and after a time began to study privately with the object of receiving holy orders. After he had been ordained he was very active in the works of the ministry, especially in hospitals and prisons, and he attracted several young laymen to assist 'him. Their headquarters was at the church of St Mary *della Rosa* in Lucca, and they lived in common in a house near by.

It was a time when the Council of Trent and the ravages of Protestantism had filled serious Catholics with a passion for reform, and John Leonardi and his followers, several of whom were studying for the priesthood, soon projected a new congregation of secular priests. When this scheme was spread abroad it at once provoked powerful opposition in the Lucchesan republic. This opposition was political, and rather difficult to understand, but was formidable enough to keep the founder an exile from Lucca for practically the rest of his life except when he was able to visit there under special papal protection. In 1580 he secretly acquired the church of Santa Maria Cortelandini (or Nera) for the use of his followers, who three years later were recognized officially by the bishop of Lucca, with the approval of Pope Gregory XIII, as an association of secular priests with simple vows (they were granted their present name and solemn vows in 1621). St John received the encouragement and help of St Philip Neri, who gave up to him his premises at San Girolamo della Carità, together with the care of his cat; and of St Joseph Calasanctius, with whose congregation his own was fused for a short time.

Father Leonardi and his priests became so great a power for good in Italy that their congregation was confirmed by Clement VIII in 1595. This pope had a very great regard for the character and capabilities of St John, and appointed him commissary apostolic to superintend the reform of the monks of Vallumbrosa and Monte Vergine. He obtained from Clement the church of Santa Maria in Portico, and Cardinal Baronius was made cardinal protector of the congregation. St John's miracles and his zeal for the spread of the faith are referred to by the Roman Martyrology, but the Clerks Regular of the Mother of God have had only one house outside of Italy; by the deliberate policy of their founder they never had more than fifteen churches, and they form today only a very small congregation. The saint was associated with Mgr J. B. Vives in the first planning of a seminary for foreign missions, instituted by Pope Urban VIII in 1627 as the College *de Propaganda Fide*.

John Leonardi died on October 9, 1609, from disease caught when tending the plague-stricken. He was canonized in 1938, and his feast was added to the general calendar in 1941.

More than one life of this saint has been published. See, for example, L. Marracci, *Vita del P. Giovanni Leonardi, Lucchese* (1673) ; A. Bianchini, *Vita del B. Giovanni Leonardi* (1861) ; and two works by F. Ferraironi (1938), on St John as a founder and in connection with the Urban College. His cause is frequently referred to by Prosper Lambertini (Benedict XIV) in bk ii of his great work, *De beatificatione*. . . .

ST DIONYSIUS THE AREOPAGITE   (FIRST CENTURY)

WHILE St Paul, having had to leave Berea, was waiting at Athens for Silas and Timothy, " his spirit was stirred within him, seeing the city wholly given to idolatry ". He therefore went into the market-place and the Jewish synagogue to talk with the people, and certain Epicurean and Stoic philosophers, hearing him, came to him and asked, " May we know what this new doctrine is, which thou speakest of ? " Paul therefore went with them to the Areopagus, or Hill of Mars, the meeting-place of the Athenian council, where, says St Luke, " all the Athenians and strangers that were there employed themselves in nothing else but either in telling or in hearing some new thing " ; or perhaps he was brought before the tribunal itself. Here he gave his famous discourse on the text of the Unknown God ; and among those who believed and followed him was a woman named Damaris and a man named Dionysius, who, being a member of the council, which was called after the hill whereon it assembled, was distinguished as " the Areopagite " (Acts xvii 13–34).

That is all that is known with complete certainty of St Dionysius the Areopagite. Eusebius gives the testimony of St Dionysius of Corinth that he became first bishop of Athens, and St Sophronius of Jerusalem and others call him a martyr, the Menology of Basil adding that he was burned alive at Athens under Domitian. In all ancient calendars the day of his feast is October 3, on which date it is still observed by the Byzantines and Syrians. Nowhere before the seventh century at the earliest is there any suggestion that St Dionysius the Areopagite ever left Greece, but afterwards his name is found connected with Cotrone in Calabria and Paris. His identification with St Dionysius (Denis) of France, referred to below, is still recorded in the Roman Martyrology and in the liturgy of the day ;* and the sixth lesson at Matins ends with the words : " He wrote admirable and truly heavenly books on the Divine Names, on the Celestial and Ecclesiastical Hierarchies, on Mystical Theology, and divers others." This is a reference to another error of the middle ages concerning St Dionysius the Areopagite, namely, that he was the author of four treatises and ten letters which, from the seventh until the fifteenth century, were among the most valued and admired theological and mystical writings, both in the East and West, and exercised an immense influence on the scholastics. The growing conviction that they were not the work of a disciple of St Paul, but written much later by one who falsely attributed them to the Areopagite, caused them to be long under a cloud ; but in modern times their own intrinsic worth and the strong evidence produced that they are genuine works, but of unknown date, have to a certain extent restored them to the honour and use which their value demands.

In the *Acta Sanctorum* a long dissertation of more than one hundred and sixty folio pages is mainly devoted to proving that the Dionysius converted by St Paul was not the writer of the book on the Divine Names and of other treatises attributed to the same authorship. There can be no question, however, that Pseudo-Dionysius wished to be identified with the Dionysius of the Acts of the Apostles. In the very earliest known mention of these writings, we find them brought forward (at the conference held at Constantinople in A.D. 533) as the

---

* Alban Butler could not bring himself to admit this openly. In a footnote he says, "Hilduin . . . upon the authority of spurious and fabulous records, pretends that St Dionysius, the first bishop of Paris, is the same person with the Areopagite ; of which mistake, *some traces are found in certain other writings* " (italics ours). Their identity was not questioned in the West from the ninth to the fifteenth century.

work of " Dionysius the Areopagite ", and rejected by Hypatius as forgeries.   An immense literature has grown up around them, but that hardly concerns us here ; the true author has never been identified.   The Pseudo-Dionysius claims that when at Heliopolis he witnessed the eclipse of the sun which occurred during the crucifixion of our Lord, and also that he was present at the death of the Blessed Virgin ; this is pure invention.   *Cf.* the article of P. Peeters in the *Analecta Bollandiana*, vol. xxix (1910), pp. 302–322, who there draws inferences very unfavourable to the literary honesty of Hilduin, Abbot of Saint-Denis, the first Latin translator of Pseudo-Dionysius, though not, it now seems, the first to proclaim his identity with Dionysius, Bishop of Paris ; see G. Théry, *Études dionysiennes* (2 vols., 1932–37) ; and R. J. Loenertz in *Analecta Bollandiana*, vol. lxix (1951), pp. 218–237.

ST DEMETRIUS, BISHOP OF ALEXANDRIA   (A.D. 231)

HE is said to have been the eleventh successor of St Mark, and is certainly the first bishop of Alexandria of whom anything is known, chiefly in his relations with Origen.   When Clement withdrew from the direction of the catechetical school of Alexandria Origen was raised to that post by St Demetrius, with whom he was then on terms of close friendship ; the bishop even defended him against those who had condemned the bodily mutilation to which he had voluntarily submitted himself. Later Origen went to Caesarea in Palestine and accepted an invitation to preach before the bishops there.   St Demetrius protested, for Origen was yet a layman, and recalled him to Alexandria.   Fifteen years later Origen set out for Athens, and on his way through Caesarea was ordained priest, without the leave of his own bishop.   Thereupon Demetrius convened a synod which sentenced him on several counts and forbade him to teach.

St Demetrius is said to have set up the first three suffragan sees of Alexandria and is often credited, on the authority of St Jerome, with having sent St Pantaenus on his mission to Yemen and Ethiopia.   But this probably took place before St Demetrius was bishop.   He governed the see of Alexandria for forty-two years and died in the year 231, at the age of 105, revered by his people and also feared, on account of the gift which was his of reading men's secret sins and thoughts.

There is little to add to the data collected in the *Acta Sanctorum*, October, vol. iv.   See also the articles on Demetrius and on Origen in DCB., and on the letters of Demetrius in DAC., vol. viii, cc. 2752–2753 ; and Abbot Chapman in the *Catholic Encyclopedia*, vol. iv.

SS. DIONYSIUS, OR DENIS, BISHOP OF PARIS, RUSTICUS AND ELEUTHERIUS, MARTYRS   (A.D. 258 ?)

ST GREGORY of Tours, writing in the sixth century, tells us that St Dionysius of Paris was born in Italy and sent in the year 250 with six other missionary bishops into Gaul, where he suffered martyrdom.   The " Martyrology of Jerome " mentions St Dionysius on October 9, joining with him St Rusticus and St Eleu-therius ; later writers make of these the bishop's priest and deacon, who with him penetrated to Lutetia Parisiorum and established Christian worship on an island in the Seine.   Their preaching was so effective that they were arrested and, after a long imprisonment, all three were beheaded.   The bodies of the martyrs were thrown into the Seine, from which they were rescued and given honourable burial. A chapel was later built over their tomb, around which arose the great abbey of Saint-Denis.

This monastery was founded by King Dagobert I (*d.* 638), and it is possible that some century or so later the identification of St Dionysius with Dionysius the

Areopagite began to gain currency, or at least the idea that he was sent by Pope Clement I in the first century. But it was not everywhere or even widely accepted until the time of Hilduin, abbot of Saint-Denis. In the year 827 the Emperor Michael II sent as a present to the emperor of the West, Louis the Pious, copies of the writings ascribed to St Dionysius the Areopagite (see above). By an unfortunate coincidence they arrived in Paris and were taken to Saint-Denis on the eve of the feast of the patron of the abbey. Hilduin translated them into Latin, and when some years later Louis asked him for a life of St Dionysius of Paris, the abbot produced a work which persuaded Christendom for the next seven hundred years that Dionysius of Paris, Dionysius of Athens, and the author of the " Dionysian " writings were one and the same person. In his " Areopagitica " Abbot Hilduin made use of spurious and worthless materials, and it is difficult to believe in his complete good faith : the life is a tissue of fables. The Areopagite comes to Rome where Pope St Clement I receives him and sends him to evangelize the Parisii. They try in vain to put him to death by wild beasts, fire and crucifixion ; then, together with Rusticus and Eleutherius, he is successfully beheaded on Montmartre. The dead body of St Dionysius rose on its feet and, led by an angel, walked the two miles from Montmartre to where the abbey church of Saint-Denis now stands, carrying its head in its hands and surrounded by singing angels, and so was there buried. Of which marvel the Roman Breviary makes mention.

The *cultus* of St Dionysius, better known, even in England, as Denis, was very strong during the middle ages ; already in the sixth century Fortunatus recognizes him as the saint of Paris *par excellence* (*Carmina*, viii, 3, 159), and he is popularly regarded as the patron saint of France.

Another long dissertation is devoted to St Dionysius, Bishop of Paris, in the *Acta Sanctorum*, October, vol. iv. The earliest *passio*, attributed of old, but erroneously, to Venantius Fortunatus, has been re-edited by B. Krusch, MGH., *Auctores Antiq.*, vol. iv, pt 2, pp. 101–105. This ascribes the sending of Dionysius into Gaul as bishop of Paris to Pope St Clement in the first century, but it does not identify him with the Areopagite. See also what has been said about the Areopagite above and consult J. Havet, *Œuvres*, vol. i, pp. 191–246 ; G. Kurth in *Études Franques*, vol. ii, pp. 297–317 ; L. Levillain in the *Bibliothèque de l'École des Chartes*, vol. lxxxii (1921), pp. 5–116 ; vol. lxxxvi (1925), pp. 5–97, with others more recent ; Leclercq in DAC., vol. iv, cc. 588–606 ; and E. Griffe, *La Gaule chrétienne* (1947), pp. 89–99. There is a good summary of the whole matter in Baudot and Chaussin, *Vies des saints* . . ., vol. x (1952), pp. 270–288.

ST PUBLIA, WIDOW   (c. A.D. 370)

ST PUBLIA, mentioned in the Roman Martyrology today as an " abbess ", is referred to by the historian Theodoret as a woman of good family in Antioch who was left a widow. She gathered together in her house a number of consecrated virgins and widows who wished to live a common life of devotion and charity. In the year 362 Julian the Apostate came to Antioch to prepare for his campaign against the Persians, and as he was passing by the house of Publia one day he stopped to listen to the inmates, who were singing the praises of God in their oratory. It so happened that they were singing the 115th psalm, and the emperor distinguished the words, " The idols of the Gentiles are silver and gold, the works of the hands of men : they have mouths and speak not ", and so on to the verse, " Let them that make them become like unto them, and all such as trust in them ". He was furious at what he took to be a personal insult, and bade the women be silent, then and in the future. They replied by singing, at the word of Publia, psalm 67 : " Let God arise and let His enemies be scattered." Thereupon Julian ordered her to be brought before him, and in spite of her sex and venerable appearance allowed her to be struck by his guards. Not thus could the choral prayer of the Christians be silenced, and it is said that the emperor intended to have put them all to death when he came back from Persia. But he was destined never to return alive and St Publia and her companions finished their course in peace.

See the *Acta Sanctorum*, October, vol. iv, where Theodoret's account (*Hist. Eccles.*, iii, 19) is quoted.

SS. ANDRONICUS AND ATHANASIA   (FIFTH CENTURY)

ANDRONICUS was a native of Alexandria who settled in Antioch to carry on the business of a silversmith. He was happily married to a young woman named Athanasia, they had two children, John and Mary, and their trade flourished ; but when they had been married twelve years both their children suddenly died on the same day, and Athanasia thereafter spent much of her time weeping at their grave and praying in a neighbouring church. She was here one day when suddenly a stranger stood before her, who assured her that John and Mary were happy in Heaven. Then he disappeared, and Athanasia knew that she had seen a vision of St Julian, the martyr in whose memory the church was dedicated. She went home rejoicing to her husband, and suggested to him that the time had come for them to renounce the world. Andronicus agreed ; and as they left their home, leaving the door standing open, St Athanasia called down the blessing of the God of Abraham and Sara upon herself and her husband, beseeching Him that, " as we leave this house door open for love of thee, so open to us the gates of thy kingdom ". They made their way into their native Egypt, where they sought out St Daniel, known as " of Many Miracles ", among the solitaries of Skete. He sent St Andronicus to the monastery of Tabenna, and St Athanasia to be an anchoress in the wilderness, dressed in the habit of a man. And so they lived for twelve years.

At the end of that time St Andronicus fell in with a beardless old monk, who said that his name was Athanasius and that he was going to Jerusalem. They travelled together, made their religious exercises together, and returned once more to the place where they had met. Then they realized that they had a great regard and affection one for another and were unwilling to be parted ; so they both went to the monastery called Eighteen, because it was so many miles from Alexandria, and a ce" was found there for Father Athanasius near to that of Andronicus. When the time came for Athanasius to die it was seen that he was weeping, and a monk asked him why he wept when he was about to go to God. " I am grieved for my father Andronicus ", was the reply, " for he will miss me. But when I am gone, give him the writing that you will find under my pillow." After he was dead the writing was found, and when he read it St Andronicus knew—what the other had known since they met on the way to Jerusalem—that Athanasius was his wife Athanasia. Then the monks came, dressed in white and carrying branches of palm and tamarisk, and bore the body of St Athanasia to burial. A monk stopped with St Andronicus until they had celebrated the seventh day of Athanasia, and then tried to persuade the old man to come away with him ; and he would not. So the monk departed alone, but he had not gone a day's journey when a messenger overtook him, saying that Father Andronicus was at the point of death. He hurried back, summoning the other monks, and St Andronicus died peacefully amid the prayers of his brethren.   They buried him beside his wife.

The Copts, Ethiops and some Byzantine churches commemorate " Our holy father Andronicus and his wife Athanasia ", and they were entered in the Roman Martyrology (with the place of death given as Jerusalem) by Cardinal Baronius.

Although a Greek version of this story is printed in the *Acta Sanctorum*, October, vol. iv, from the *Menaion*, the saints in question do not seem to have enjoyed any great popularity in Byzantine churches.   There is only the barest mention of them in the *Synax. Const*. (see Delehaye's edition, c. 501, under March 2).   On the other hand the whole story is told at length in the lectionaries of Abyssinia, and may be read in Budge's translation, *The Ethiopic Synaxarium*, p. 1167.   " Est ea pia fabella, plurimum lecta, saepius descripta et retractata (BHG., 120 ; BHO., 59), nec vera nec veri similis ", say the Bollandists.

ST SAVIN   (FIFTH CENTURY ?)

THIS saint is venerated as the apostle of the Lavedan, that district of the Pyrenees at one end of which is situated the town of Lourdes.   According to his legend he was born at Barcelona and brought up by his widowed mother, who when he became a young man sent him to the care of his uncle Eutilius at Poitiers.   Being appointed tutor to his young cousin, Savin (Sabinus) so impressed him by his religious example and inspiring words that the youth secretly left home and went to the great monastery at Ligugé.   Eutilius and his wife besought Savin to use his influence with their son to induce him to return home.   But he refused, quoting the words of our Lord that He must be loved even more than father and mother, and furthermore announced his intention of becoming a monk at Ligugé himself.

St Savin eventually left there with the object of becoming a solitary.   He walked to Tarbes and from thence made his way to the place in the Lavedan then called Palatium Aemilianum, where there was a monastery.   The abbot, Fronimius, showed him a place a little way off in the mountains well suited to his design. Here St Savin built himself a cell, which he afterwards exchanged for a pit in the ground, saying that everyone should expiate his sins in the way and the measure that seems to himself called for.   This in reply to Fronimius, who on one of his frequent visits to the hermit expressed the opinion that his austerities were becoming exaggerated.   Savin preached to the peasants of the neighbourhood by his mouth and by the example of his kindly and penitential spirit, and many and remarkable were the miracles with which they credited him.   For example, a farmer having roughly stopped him from crossing his land to reach a spring, he struck water from the rocks with his staff ; and one night, having no dry tinder, he lit his candle by the flames from his own heart !   He wore only one garment, summer and winter, and that lasted him for thirteen years.

St Savin was forewarned of his death and sent a message to the monastery, and he was surrounded by clergy, monks and devoted people when his peaceful end came.   His body was enshrined in the abbey church, which was afterwards called St Savin's, and the name extended to the adjacent village, Saint-Savin-de-Tarbes.

No reliance can be placed upon the short text of uncertain date printed in the *Acta Sanctorum*, October, vol. iv (*cf*. Mabillon, *Annales Benedictini*, vol. i, p. 575) ; even the century in which the hermit lived is a matter of pure conjecture : the above time-heading follows A. Poncelet.   It is characteristic of the methods of a certain type of hagiographer that out of these scanty materials a writer in the so-called *Petits Bollandistes* has evolved a biography of seven closely printed pages (over 4,500 words) in which he speaks with the same detail and definiteness of statement as he might have used in providing a summary of the career of Napoleon I.

ST GISLENUS, or GHISLAIN, Abbot (*c.* A.D. 680)

HAVING led for some time an eremitical life in a forest in Hainault this Frankish saint founded there a monastery in honour of SS. Peter and Paul. He governed it with great sanctity and prudence ; the abbey was long known as The Cell (now Saint-Ghislain, near Mons), but the original name of the place was Ursidongus, that is, " the bear's den ", whence arose the legend that a bear, hunted by King Dagobert I, took refuge with Gislenus and showed him the site of his future monastery. St Gislenus is said to have had great influence on St Vincent Madelgarius and his wife St Waldetrudis and their family ; with his encouragement Waldetrudis founded the convent at Castrilocus (Mons), where Gislenus had had his first hermitage, and St Aldegundis the convent of Maubeuge. With the last-named he was united in a very close friendship, and when they were both too old conveniently to make the journey to one another's monasteries, they built an oratory in between and would there meet to converse of God and matters connected with their respective communities.

The Roman Martyrology says that St Gislenus resigned a bishopric before becoming a hermit. This refers to the quite apocryphal legend that he was born in Attica, became a monk there, and was raised to the see of Athens. In consequence of a vision he resigned this office, went on pilgrimage to Rome with other Greek monks, and while there received divine direction to go on into Hainault, which he did with two companions. There he met St Amandus, and was encouraged by him to settle by the river Haine. The legend also explains why the eldest sons of a certain family at Roisin were all called Baldericus (Baudry). When the mysterious Greek stranger was on his way to give an account of himself to the bishop St Aubert at Cambrai, he received hospitality at Roisin, and during the night his host's wife was overtaken by a difficult labour. The husband appealed for his prayers to Gislenus, who handed him his belt, saying, " Put this round your wife like a baldric (*baudrei*), and she will safely give birth to a son ". The saint's promise was verified, and the grateful parents gave him two estates for the endowment of his monastery.

There is no very satisfactory account of the career of St Gislenus. An anonymous life is printed by Mabillon and the Bollandists ; and another, by Rainerus, a monk of Saint-Ghislain in the eleventh century, has been edited by Poncelet in the *Analecta Bollandiana*, vol. v (1887), pp. 212–239, with a third document, pp. 257–290. See also Van der Essen, *Étude critique sur les saints mérovingiens*, pp. 249–260 ; U. Berlière, *Monasticon Belge*, vol. i, pp. 244–246 ; and Berlière in *Revue liturgique et monastique*, vol. xiv (1929), pp. 438 *seq.* The story, as told in the early biographies, is very improbable.

BD GUNTHER (A.D. 1045)

THE first part of the life of Gunther, who was a cousin of St Stephen of Hungary and related to the Emperor St Henry, was by no means inspired by the holiness of his relatives, for until his fiftieth year he was a worldly and ambitious nobleman, and none too scrupulous at that. He then came under the influence of St Gothard of Hildesheim, at that time abbot of Niederaltaich and engaged in reforming the monastery of Hersfeld. This prelate succeeded also in reforming Gunther, who made up his mind to expiate his sins by becoming a monk. He devoted all his property to the endowment of Hersfeld, with the exception of an endowment for the abbey of Göllingen in Thuringia, of which house he retained the ownership in spite of the protests of St Gothard. Gunther then went on pilgrimage to Rome, and on his return entered Niederaltaich as a monk. But his conversion had not been complete, his humble position did not satisfy his ambition, and he insisted on being allowed to be made abbot of Göllingen. The experiment was not successful : there was friction between him and his monks, and the monastery began seriously to suffer. Aided perhaps by an illness which overtook Gunther, St Gothard succeeded by persuasion and rebuke in inducing him to resign his abbacy, and he returned to Niederaltaich. His turning to God was at last wholehearted, and whereas formerly the status of a simple monk had been too modest for him he now wished for an even more humble and retired life. Accordingly in 1008 he went to live as a hermit in the forest of Lalling, where a reputation of sanctity soon brought him disciples. Later he moved with them to the neighbourhood of Rinchnach on the Regen in Bavaria, where cells were built and a church ; this foundation developed into a regular monastery.

Bd Gunther in the meanwhile continued his eremitical existence, going from place to place to beg alms for the poor, and encouraging his cousin Stephen in the christianization of his realm. It is said that Gunther received the gift of infused knowledge and became a powerful preacher though deficient in ordinary ecclesiastical learning : he could probably neither read nor write. He atoned for the excesses of his earlier years by severe mortification, and he exercised a rigid discipline over his followers, to the extent of rationing the amount of water which each of his monks might have at disposal. Bd Gunther died at about the age of ninety, on October 9, 1045, at Hartmanice in Bohemia. He was buried at Brevnov, near Prague, and the reputation of the last thirty-five years of his life together with the wonders that were reported at his tomb led to a popular *cultus :* it is recognized liturgically at Passau and elsewhere.

The main facts in the Latin biography printed both by Mabillon and the Bollandists are probably reliable. This compilation seems to be based, at least in part, upon statements taken from the writings of Wolfher, a canon of Hildesheim, who was a contemporary. See also Grauert, in the *Historisches Jahrbuch*, vol. xix (1898), pp. 249–287 ; Oswald, *Das Kloster Rinchnach* (1902) ; MGH., *Scriptores*, vol. vi, p. 672, vol. xi, pp. 276–279 ; and the early lives of St Stephen of Hungary.

ST LOUIS BERTRAND (A.D. 1581)

LUIS BERTRÁN was born at Valencia in Spain in 1526. He was related through his father to St Vincent Ferrer and was baptized at the same font as that saint had been a hundred and seventy-five years before. Louis from his childhood seemed by his teachable disposition and humility of soul to have inherited the spirit of St Vincent : wanting to join the Dominicans, the celebrated Father John Mico, who had been brought up a shepherd in the mountains, gave the habit to young Bertrand when he was eighteen. Sacerdotal ordination was given to him by the archbishop of Valencia, St Thomas of Villanova, in 1547.

Louis was made master of novices five years after profession, and discharged that office for periods which totalled thirty years. He was very severe and strict, but both by his example and words taught them sincerely and perfectly to renounce the world and to unite their souls to God. St Louis Bertrand was not particularly learned, though a painstaking student, and he was lacking in humour, a characteristic not uncommon among Spaniards. Nor did his talents at first appear promising for the pulpit ; nevertheless he overcame all difficulties and his discourses produced very great results, for they were animated with charity and breathed a spirit of sincere religion and humility.   In 1557 a pestilence raged in Valencia and the saint knew no danger and spared no pains in comforting and assisting the sick.   He about this time made the acquaintance of St Teresa, who wrote and asked his advice about her projected convent of reformed Carmelites.   St Louis replied : " The matter about which you ask my advice is of such great importance to our Lord's service that I wished to recommend it to Him in my poor prayers and at the Holy Sacrifice : that is why I have been so long in replying.   Now I bid you, in the name of the same Lord, arm yourself with courage to undertake so great an enterprise.   He will help and support you in it and I assure you, as from Him, that before fifty years are out your order will be one of the most famous in the Church, who keeps you in her holy protection."

In 1562 St Louis left Spain to preach the gospel to the savages in America, and landed at Cartagena in New Granada (Colombia).   He spoke only Spanish and had to use an interpreter, but the gifts of tongues, of prophecy and of miracles were conferred by Heaven on this apostle, the bull of his canonization tells us.   In the isthmus of Panama and the province of Cartagena, in the space of three years, he converted to Christ many thousand souls.   The baptismal registers of Tubera, in St Louis's own handwriting, show that all the inhabitants of that place were converted, and he had a like success at Cipacoa.   The people of Paluato were more difficult, but in his next mission, among the inhabitants of the mountains of Santa Marta, he is said to have baptized about fifteen thousand persons ;* and also a tribe of fifteen hundred Indians who, having changed their minds, had followed him thither from Paluato.   He visited the Caribs of the Leeward Islands (whom Alban Butler considers " the most brutal, barbarous, and unteachable people of the human race "—they tried to poison St Louis), San Thomé in the Virgin Islands, and San Vincente in the Windwards, and then returned to Colombia.   He was pierced to the quick to see the avarice and cruelty of the Spanish adventurers in the Indies and not to be able to find any means of putting a stop to those evils.   He was desirous to seek redress in Spain, and about that time he was recalled thither, thus ending a marvellous mission of six years.

St Louis arrived at Seville in 1569, whence he returned to Valencia.   He trained up many excellent preachers, who succeeded him in the ministry of the word.   The first lesson he gave them was that humble and fervent prayer must always be the principal preparation of the preacher : for words without works never have power to touch or change hearts.   The two last years of his life he was afflicted with painful illness ; in 1580 he went to preach in the cathedral at Valencia, where he was carried from the pulpit to his bed, from which he never rose again, dying eighteen months later on October 9, 1581, being fifty-five years old.   St Louis Bertrand, who is the principal patron of Colombia, was canonized in 1671.

A very full and devout *Life of St Louis Bertrand* was published by Fr Bertrand Wilberforce in 1882 ; the book has been translated into German and French, and seemingly also into Spanish.   His narrative is founded on the biography of the saint, printed in 1582-83,

* These wholesale baptisms of Indians who could not possibly have an adequate idea of the faith and its obligations are tributes to the apostolic zeal rather than to the prudence of such great saints as St Louis Bertrand and St Francis Solano.   They were often a source of embarrassment to their successors.   When Father de Victoria, o.p., took over the vast diocese of Tucuman in 1581 he found there five secular priests and a few regulars, not one of whom could speak any of the local languages.

almost immediately after his death, by Fr V. J. Antist, his intimate friend and disciple. A Latin version of this, made from the Spanish original, is included in the *Acta Sanctorum*, October, vol. v, and it is there supplemented by a still longer biography which was compiled and published in 1623 by Fr B. Aviñone who was familiar with the evidence given in the process of beatification and had come to Rome as procurator of the cause. There were several other lives printed in Spain and Italy during the seventeenth and eighteenth centuries, but it does not seem that any new material of notable importance has so far been brought to light. Immense enthusiasm was aroused in Valencia when the decree of beatification was issued in 1608 ; a book describing these *Fiestas* was compiled by G. de Aguilar in 1608 and a modern edition of it was brought out in 1914. Another small work, by V. Gomez, dealing with the *Sermones y Fiestas* which marked the same occasion, appeared in 1609. Copies of both are in the British Museum.

10 : ST FRANCIS BORGIA (A.D. 1572)

THE family of Borja was one of the most noble of the kingdom of Aragon, but it was not till the fifteenth century that it became known outside Spain, when from 1455 to 1458 Alphonsus Borgia was pope under the name of Callistus III. At the end of that century there was another Borgia pope, Alexander VI, who at the time of his elevation to the papacy was the father of four children. As a provision for his son, Peter, he bought the dukedom of Gandia in Spain, and on Peter's death bestowed it upon another son, John. John was murdered soon after his marriage, and his son, the third duke of Gandia, married the daughter of a natural son of King Ferdinand V of Aragon. Of this union was born at Gandia in the year 1510 Francisco de Borja y Aragon, now known to us as St Francis Borgia, great-grandson of a pope and of a king and cousin of the Emperor Charles V. At the age of eighteen, his education completed,* young Francis was received at the imperial court. At this time occurred an incident of which the significance was not seen till long afterwards. At Alcalá de Henares Francis was impressed by the appearance of a man whom he saw being taken to the prison of the Inquisition. That man was Ignatius Loyola.

In the following year Francis Borgia, having been created marquis of Lombay, married Eleanor de Castro, and ten years later Charles V made him viceroy of Catalonia, whose capital was Barcelona. Francis afterwards said that " it was when I was viceroy of Catalonia that God prepared me to be general of the Society of Jesus. I then learned to decide important questions, to settle rival claims, to see both sides of an affair, in a way I could not otherwise have done." He was already a different man ; " he saw with other eyes and heard with other ears than before : he spoke with another tongue, because his heart also was not the same ". He devoted as much time to prayer as he could without prejudice to public affairs or the needs of his growing family, and the frequency of his sacramental communions caused comment, mostly unfavourable—the prevalent idea, contrary to the practice of the first Christians, was that it was presumptuous in a layman, concerned in the

---

* Here Alban Butler delivers a disquisition on humane studies, in which he says, " Many so learn these sciences as to put on in their thoughts and expressions a scholastic garb which they cannot lay aside, so that their minds may be said to be cast in Gothic moulds. . . . Nothing is more horrid than a mere scholar, that is, a pedant who appears in the world to have reaped from his studies scarce any other advantage than to be rendered by them absolutely unfit for civilized society." The association of " scholastic garb ", gothic, and unfitness for civilized society shows him a true child of the eighteenth century.

affairs of the world, to receive the Body of the Lord so often.   In 1543 St Francis became duke of Gandia by the death of his father, whereupon he retired with his family to his estates, following on the refusal of King John of Portugal to recognize him as master of the household to Prince Philip of Spain, who was about to marry the king's daughter.   This was a definite check to the public career of Francis Borgia and he proceeded to interest himself in more personal affairs.   He fortified Gandia that it might not be exposed to the Moors and pirates from Barbary, built a convent for the Dominicans at Lombay, and repaired the hospital.   The Bishop of Cartagena wrote to a friend at this time, " During my recent stay at Gandia I found Don Francis to be a model duke and a perfect Christian gentleman ; humble, truly good, a man of God in every sense of the term. . . . How carefully his children are brought up !   How thoroughly his dependents are looked after ! How great is his pleasure in the company of priests and religious ! . . ."

This happy and peaceful life at Gandia was brought suddenly to an end by the death in 1546 of Doña Eleanor.   For seventeen years she had been his beloved and faithful companion, and when she lay ill it took all Francis's determination to pray that not his will but God's should be done in her regard.   They had had eight children, of whom the youngest was eight at his mother's death.   Shortly afterwards Bd Peter Favre paid a brief visit to Gandia, and he left for Rome bearing a message to St Ignatius Loyola that Francis Borgia had resolved to ask to be received into the Society of Jesus—he had in fact made a vow to do so.   St Ignatius received his request with joy ; but in his answer advised the duke to defer the execution of his design till he had settled his children and finished the foundations he had begun, telling him in the meantime to study theology at Gandia in the university he had inaugurated there and to take the degree of doctor ; he was, moreover, to take every precaution to prevent this astonishing piece of news from being prematurely divulged—" the ears of the world are not ready for such an explosion ".   Francis punctually obeyed but was troubled in the following year by being summoned to assist at the *cortes* of Aragon.   He therefore wrote to St Ignatius and as a consequence was allowed to make his profession privately.   Three years were enough to see his children properly established and on August 31, 1550, St Francis Borgia set out for Rome.   He was yet only forty years old.

After less than four months in Rome, Francis went back to Spain, and retired to a hermitage at Oñate, near Loyola.   Here he received the emperor's permission to make over his titles and estates to his son Charles, whereupon he shaved his head and beard, assumed clerical dress, and was ordained priest in Whitsun week, 1551. " A duke turned Jesuit " was the sensation of the day, and when Francis celebrated his first public Mass, for assistance at which the pope granted a plenary indulgence, the crowd at Vergara was so great that the altar had to be set up in the open air. At Oñate the object of all this admiration was set by his superiors to serve the cook, fetch water and carry wood ; he made the fire and swept the kitchen ; and when he waited at table he had to kneel to beg pardon of the fathers and brothers for having served them with such clumsiness.   Directly after his ordination he was allowed to preach throughout Guipúzcoa, and he went through the villages with a bell, calling the children to catechism, instructing and preaching.   But within the house the superior treated Father Francis with such severity as he deemed the previous exalted position of his subject required.   The saint undoubtedly suffered much during this time, but the only signs of impatience he gave were when he was treated otherwise than as a religious.   Once he got a gash in his head, and the doctor who dressed it apologized, " I am afraid, my lord, that I cannot help hurting your grace ". " You can't hurt me more ", was the reply, " than you are doing by your unseemly manner of addressing me." St Francis's corporal mortifications after his " conversion " became excessive : he was an exceedingly fat man, and his girth decreased very notably ; his excesses were now curbed by religious obedience, but he was ingenious in the devising of physical discomforts. In after years he was of the opinion that he had been imprudent in his ways of mortifying his body, especially before he became a Jesuit. He left Oñate for several months to preach in other parts of Spain. Much success attended his labours ; many desired to regulate their affairs and their consciences by his advice, and he was one of the first to recognize the greatness of the Carmelite nun of Avila, Teresa. After doing wonders in Castile and Andalusia, he seemed to surpass himself in Portugal, and in 1554 St Ignatius made him commissary general of the Society of Jesus in Spain, an office which he discharged at times with something of the autocracy of a distinguished nobleman. He showed his real spirit when he said that he hoped the Society of Jesus would prosper for God's glory on three things, prayer and the sacraments, the opposition of the world, and perfect obedience. On those things flourished the soul of Francis Borgia.

During his years as commissary general St Francis Borgia was practically the founder of the Society in Spain, establishing in a short time houses and colleges at a score of places. But he did not neglect the immediate care of those whom he had left behind him in the world. He soothed and made sweet the last moments of the queen dowager, Joanna, who fifty years before had gone mad at the death of her husband and had shown a special aversion from the clergy. In the next year, soon after the death of St Ignatius, the Emperor Charles V abdicated, and sent for St Francis to visit him at Yuste. Charles had been prepossessed against the Society of Jesus and expressed his surprise that Francis should have preferred it to so many older orders. The saint removed his prejudices, and said, for the motives which had determined him in his choice, that God had called him to a state in which the active and contemplative life are joined together, and in which he was freed from the danger of being raised to dignities of which he had had enough in the world. He added that if the Society was a new order the fervour of those engaged in it answered that objection ; and in any case " Age is no guarantee of goodness ". St Francis was no friend of the Inquisition, nor that body of him ; and King Philip II listened to the calumnies which jealousy was raising against Francis. He remained on the work of the Society in Portugal till 1561, and was then summoned to Rome by Pope Pius IV, at the instance of the Jesuit general, Father Laynez.

St Francis was most warmly received in Rome and among those who regularly attended his sermons were Cardinal Charles Borromeo and Cardinal Ghislieri, afterwards St Pius V. Becoming acquainted with the work of the headquarters of the Jesuits, he filled high offices, and on the death of Father Laynez in 1565 was elected father general. During seven years he promoted the work of the Society of Jesus in all parts of the world with such success that he might be called a second founder, and the zeal with which he propagated the missions and animated the labourers in planting the gospel in remote countries entitles him to a great share in the conversion of those countries to the faith. He was not less active in directing his religious brethren in Europe for the reformation of the manners of Christians. St Francis's first care was to establish a properly regulated novitiate in Rome and to provide for the same in the provinces. When he first came to the city fifteen years before he had shown a strong interest in the project of a Roman college, and had given a large sum of money therefor.   He now concerned himself personally in the direction of the college and the arrangement of its curriculum.   In effect he was the founder of this college, but he always refused the title, which is given to Pope Gregory XIII who re-established it as the Gregorian University.   St Francis also built the church of Sant' Andrea on the Quirinal, with the adjoining residence, to house the novitiate, began the Gesù, and enlarged and improved the German college which was intended to send missioners to all those northern lands which had suffered from Protestantism.

Pope St Pius V had confidence in the Society of Jesus and a great trust and admiration for its general, so that he could proceed freely with the projects he had at heart.   St Francis provided for the extension of the Society of Jesus across the Alps, and established the province of Poland.   He used his influence with the French court to obtain a more favourable reception for the Jesuits in France, where he was able to set up colleges.   And he was engrossed by the foreign missions : those of the East Indies and the Far East were reformed and those of the Americas begun.   St Francis published a new edition of the rules of the Society and drew up regulations and directions for those members who were engaged in special work of various kinds.   The work he himself got through in seven years was amazing, and he never allowed it to distract him from the end to which it was directed or to affect adversely his own interior life.   Father Verjus wrote, a century later, " It may be truly said that the Society owes to St Francis Borgia its characteristic form and true perfection.   For if St Ignatius planned the building and laid the foundations, Father Laynez built the walls, and his successor St Francis roofed it and fitted up the inside, thus finishing the great work of which the design had been revealed to St Ignatius by God."   Nor was St Francis so immersed in the responsibilities of his office that he had no time to spare for matters outside.   This was shown when in 1566 a pestilence made great havoc in Rome, on which occasion he raised alms for the relief of the poor, and commissioned the fathers of his order, two and two, to attend the sick in all parts of the city, with imminent danger to their own lives.

In the year 1571 the pope sent Cardinal Bonelli on an embassy to Spain, Portugal and France, and St Francis accompanied him.   Though politically not a great success, it was a personal triumph for the Jesuit.   Everywhere crowds clamoured " to see the saint " and to hear him preach, old animosities were forgotten, and King Philip received him as gladly as did his people.   But the fatigues entailed were too much for St Francis.   He had been for some time in bad health ; his infirmities, inclination to retirement, and a deep sense of the weight of his post had worn him out, and at Ferrara on his return Duke Alfonso, who was his cousin, sent him from thence to Rome in a litter.   He lived for two days only after his arrival.   By his brother Thomas he sent his blessing to all his children and grandchildren, and as their names were rehearsed to him he prayed for each one.   When he had lost his speech a painter was, with peculiar insensibility, introduced to his bedside.   Francis saw him, expressed his displeasure with his dying hands and eyes, and turned away his face so that nothing could be done.   He died at the midnight of September 30–October 1, 1572, " one of the sweetest, dearest, noblest men our poor old world has known ", as Father James Brodrick observes.

From the time that he began to give himself totally to the divine service Francis Borgia, who was canonized in 1671, learned the importance and difficulty of attaining to humility, and he tried unremittingly to humble himself in the divine presence and within himself. Amidst the honours and respect that were shown him at Valladolid, his companion, Father Bustamante, noticed that he was not only quiet but more than ordinarily self-effacing, for which he asked the reason. " I considered ", said St Francis, " in my morning meditation that Hell is my due. I think that all men and even dumb creatures ought to cry out after me, ' Hell is your place '." He one day told the novices that in meditating on the actions of Christ he had for six years always placed himself in spirit at the feet of Judas ; but then he realized that Christ had washed the feet even of that traitor, so that he thenceforth felt unworthy to approach even him.

An immense amount of material is now available concerning the life of St Francis Borgia. But most of this, printed in five special volumes of the *Monumenta Historica Societatis Jesu* (1894–1911), has only been brought to light in modern times. There are over one thousand letters of the saint published *in extenso*, together with a spiritual diary of his later years and a number of miscellaneous documents relating to his family. These materials have been fully utilized by Father Suau, *Histoire de S. François de Borgia* (1910), and by Otto Karrer, *Der heilige Franz von Borja* (1921). Alban Butler had to be content with such earlier biographies as those of D. Vasquez (1585), still in manuscript but reproduced in substance by Father J. E. Nieremberg in 1644, and P. de Ribadeneira, *Vida del P. Francisco de Borja* (1598). Both Vasquez and Ribadeneira were contemporaries and friends of the saint, but for fear of giving scandal much was suppressed, more particularly concerning Francis Borgia's efforts as a layman to contend with grave abuses in the administration of justice by the grandees and magistrates of Spain. In these early biographies, and most conspicuously of all in that of Cardinal de Cienfuegos, the tone is one of extravagant panegyric, and fictitious anecdotes and marvels are accepted without any examination. The story, for example, that Francis, on viewing the corpse of the Empress Isabella, exclaimed, " Never more will I serve a master who can die ", is devoid of historical foundation (Suau, p. 68 ; Karrer, p. 281). An excellent shorter life of the saint by Suau appeared in the series " Les Saints " (1905), and in English by Mrs M. Yeo, *The Greatest of the Borgias* (1936). *Cf.* also Fr J. Brodrick's books on the *Origin* (1940) and the *Progress* (1946) of the Jesuits. A very complete bibliography is supplied by Karrer, pp. xi–xvi.

SS. GEREON AND HIS COMPANIONS, MARTYRS   (DATE UNKNOWN)

IN the Roman Martyrology there is entered on this day : " At Cologne, the passion of St Gereon the Martyr and his 318 Companions, who in the persecution of Maximian patiently gave their necks to the sword for the true religion. In the territory of the same city, the passion of St Victor and his fellow martyrs. At Bonn in Germany, the passion of the holy martyrs Cassius and Florentius with many others." The early medieval martyrologists refer to a number of martyrs near Cologne who were traditionally supposed to have been members of separated detachments of the Theban Legion (September 22), but it was not until the beginning of the thirteenth century that one Helinand, a Cistercian monk of Froimont, ventured to supply a *passio* for them. He averred that St Gereon and 318 others suffered at Cologne, St Victor and 330 more at Xanten, SS. Cassius, Florentius, and an unnamed number at Bonn. His forces being thus reduced, Maximian sent for reinforcements from North Africa, and when it was found that these also were Christians another massacre followed. Helinand says, absurdly enough, that the Empress St Helen found the relics of these martyrs and built churches to shelter them at Cologne and Bonn. There was a further finding of relics of the dead, at Cologne in 1121 and Xanten in 1284 ; these were hastily assumed to belong to the martyred Theban legionaries and were accordingly enshrined and venerated as such.

Whoever these martyrs of the Rhine were, they had nothing to do with those of

Agaunum and there is no reason to suppose that the relics found were authentic. But that there was a band of martyrs whose sepulchre was venerated at Cologne seems to be established by a fragmentary epitaph of the fifth century in which a certain Rudufula seems to be described as " *sociata martyribus* ", *i.e.*, buried in the neighbourhood of the martyrs.   Gregory of Tours further tells us that at Cologne " there was a basilica built in the place where fifty men of the sacred Theban legion had been put to death for Christ ".   He adds that, on account of the rich mosaics with which it was adorned, they were styled " the golden saints ".   It has been suggested that these *sancti aurei* may through some misconception have given rise to the idea of martyrs from Africa (*Mauri*) ; but the whole matter is very uncertain. The name Gereon is not mentioned by Gregory.

St Gereon is named in the Berne text of the *Hieronymianum* (see CMH., pp. 547–548, 550 and 557) and in Bede's Martyrology.   *Cf.* also Zilliken, *Der Kölnische Festkalender* (1901), pp. 104–107 ; Rathgen, *Die Kunstdenkmäler des Rheinprovinz*, vol. i, pp. 1–102 ; and Delehaye, *Origines du culte des martyrs* (1933), p. 360.

SS. EULAMPIUS AND EULAMPIA, MARTYRS   (*c.* A.D. 310 ?)

THESE two martyrs may have suffered at Nicomedia under Galerius.   Their unreliable *acta* relate that Eulampius was a youth among the Christians who fled from persecution in the city and took refuge in caves.   He was sent into the town to buy food and, seeing the decree against Christians posted up, he stopped to read it.   When a soldier spoke to him he was seized with panic, and took to his heels. Suspicion was thus aroused, he was pursued, caught, and brought before the prefect in chains.   This magistrate reproved the guards for their harshness, ordered the bonds of Eulampius to be removed, and began to question him.   When he had learned his name and honourable status the prefect suggested he should sacrifice to one or other of the gods, but this Eulampius stoutly refused to do, retorting that the gods were only idols.   This angered the prefect, who had the boy beaten and, when he showed himself yet more defiant, hung on the rack.   Thereupon the sister of Eulampius, Eulampia, ran out from the crowd and embraced him, so she too was arrested.   Both were then tortured in various ways but suffered no harm, coming unscathed even out of a bath of boiling oil.   This marvel and the constancy of the martyrs moved two hundred of the bystanders to confess Christ, and they were all beheaded together.

The Greek text of this *passio* with a full discussion will be found in the *Acta Sanctorum*, October, vol. v.   Another redaction is printed in Migne, PG., vol. cxv, cc. 1053–1065.

ST MAHARSAPOR, MARTYR   (A.D. 421)

THIS martyr was a Persian of noble birth, even more distinguished by his virtue and his zeal for the Christian faith.   On this account the persecution was no sooner begun by King Yezdigerd, precipitated by the destruction of a Mazdean temple, than Maharsapor was seized, the first of many, together with Narses and Sabutaka. The two latter after divers tortures finished their martyrdom by the sentence of a judge who had been raised to that dignity from a slave.   By this inhuman magistrate Maharsapor also was examined and put to the torture ; after which he was left to languish three years in prison in stench and darkness.   Then the same judge again examined the confessor and, finding him steadfast and invincible in confessing Christ, he condemned him to be thrown into a pit, there to perish with hunger.

Several days after this sentence had been executed, officers and soldiers opened the pit and found the martyr's body, without life indeed but in light and on his knees, as if he had been at prayer, in which attitude the saint, triumphing by such a death over his enemies, had breathed out his soul.

His *passio* may be found in S. E. Assemani, *Acta martyrum orientalium*, vol. i, pp. 234–236 ; but the Syriac text has also been more critically edited by P. Bedjan, *Acta martyrum et sanctorum*, vol. ii, no. 10.   St Mihrsabor (as the name is more scientifically transliterated) is not mentioned in the Martyrology of Rabban Sliba, but the name has been inserted in the margin of the manuscript ; see the *Analecta Bollandiana*, vol. xxvii (1908), p. 115.

ST CERBONIUS, BISHOP OF POPULONIA   (*c.* A.D. 575)

WHEN St Regulus and other bishops were driven out of Africa by the Vandals early in the sixth century, Cerbonius came with Regulus to Populonia (Piombino in Tuscany), and in due course was made bishop of the place.   St Gregory in his *Dialogues* (bk iii, ch. 11) says that because he had given shelter to some Roman soldiers Cerbonius was ordered by Totila, king of the invading Ostrogoths, to be exposed to a bear ; but the animal would do him no worse harm than to lick his feet.   Thereupon the bishop was set at liberty.   Under the Lombards he went into exile on Elba, where he died some thirty years later.   His body was brought back to Populonia for burial and he is venerated as the patron of the diocese of Massa Marittima.   The late and worthless life of St Cerbonius asserts that he was summoned before Pope Vigilius for insisting on celebrating Mass at dawn on Sundays, so that many in the city were unable to be present.   But because of the marvels which attended his journey to Rome the pope and his clergy came out to meet him as a saint, and sent him back with honour to his see.   The Roman Martyrology also mentions another St Cerbonius today, a bishop in Verona of whom nothing is known.   The feast of Cerbonius of Populonia is kept by the Canons Regular of the Lateran because he lived the common life with his clergy.

Two redactions are known of the legendary life of St Cerbonius ; one is printed in the *Acta Sanctorum*, October, vol. v, the other in Ughelli, *Italia Sacra*, vol. iii, pp. 703–709.

ST PAULINUS, BISHOP OF YORK   (A.D. 644)

ST PAULINUS is celebrated in the Roman Martyrology and in those of our country as the first apostle of the largest and at that time the most powerful of the kingdoms of the English ; he was one of the second group of missionaries sent to England by Pope St Gregory I.   When Edwin, King of Northumbria, demanded in marriage Ethelburga, sister of Edbald, King of Kent, promising liberty and protection with regard to her religion, no one was judged more proper to be her guardian and to undertake this new harvest than Paulinus.   He was ordained bishop by St Justus, Archbishop of Canterbury, in 625, and accompanied the young queen to her husband.

It was a continual affliction to his heart to live in the midst of a people who were strangers to the true worship of God, and all his preaching and endeavours to make Him known and served by them were at first unsuccessful.   But his prayers were at length heard.   King Edwin was brought over to the faith in a manner related in his life (October 12), and he was baptized by St Paulinus at York at Easter in 627. The king's two sons by his first wife and many of the nobles and people followed Edwin's example, and the crowds that flocked to receive baptism St Paulinus, when among the Deiri, baptized in the river Swale, near Catterick.   Edwin's residence among the Bernicians was at Yeavering in Glendale, and in that country St Paulinus baptized in the river Glen.   He once spent thirty-six days in this place, instructing and baptizing the people day and night.   The name Pallingsburn is said to preserve the memory of one of these baptizings (" Paulinus's Brook "), and tradition associates him also with Dewsbury, Easingwold and elsewhere.   The apostolate of St Paulinus was chiefly in the south of Northumbria, and he crossed the Humber and preached the faith to the inhabitants of Lindsey.   Here he baptized Blecca, the king's reeve, at Lincoln, and there built a church in which, after the death of St Justus, he consecrated St Honorius as archbishop of Canterbury.   Assisted by his deacon James he baptized a great number of people in the river Trent at Little-borough, as St Bede heard, through the abbot Deda, from one of the neophytes on that occasion.   From the same source he learned that St Paulinus was " a tall man, stooping a little, with black hair, thin face, and narrow aquiline nose, venerable and awe-inspiring in appearance ".

Pope Honorius I sent the *pallium* to St Paulinus as the northern metropolitan in England, and in his letter of congratulation to King Edwin upon his conversion he wrote, " We send *pallia* to the metropolitans Honorius and Paulinus, that whenever it shall please God to call either of them out of this world the other may ordain a successor for him by virtue of this letter ".   St Paulinus, however, never wore that *pallium* in his cathedral, and when the letter reached England Edwin was dead.   For, nearly two years before it was written (which shows the difficulties of communication), the pagan Mercians under Penda, reinforced by Christian Britons from Wales, invaded Northumbria, and at the battle of Hatfield Chase Edwin was slain.   Most of the work of Paulinus in Northumbria was undone and, leaving the deacon James in charge of the church of York, he conducted Queen St Ethelburga with her two children and Edwin's grandson by Osfrid into Kent by sea.   As the see of Rochester was at that time vacant, St Paulinus was asked to administer it, which he did for ten years, " until he departed to Heaven with the glorious fruits of his labours ".   He was probably at least sixty when he came south with St Ethelburga, and it was out of the question that he should return to the confusion and turmoil of Northumbria.   St Bede says that his *locum tenens*, the faithful James, was a holy man who, by long teaching and baptizing there, " rescued much prey from the power of the old Enemy of mankind " ;   when peace came again to his church " he began to teach many to sing according to the manner of the Romans ". St Paulinus died on October 10, 644, at Rochester, leaving his *pallium* to the cathedral and a golden cross and chalice he had brought from York to Christ Church at Canterbury.   His feast is observed in several English dioceses.

Our main authority is Bede's *Historia ecclesiastica* (see Plummer's edition and notes). Not much that is reliable can be gleaned from Alcuin's versified chronicle, or from Simeon of Durham and the other writers included in Raine's *Historians of the Church of York* (Rolls Series).   Canon Burton's excellent account in the *Catholic Encyclopedia* has a good bibliography, and see F. M. Stenton, *Anglo-Saxon England* (1943), pp. 113–116.   The widespread *cultus* of St Paulinus is proved by the insertion of his name in so many calendars (see Stanton's *Menology*, p. 485), as well as by the stone crosses in the north of England which tradition connects with him.

SS. DANIEL AND HIS COMPANIONS, MARTYRS   (A.D. 1227)

FIVE Franciscan missionaries having glorified God by martyrdom in Morocco in the year 1220, as has been related under January 16, seven years later six other friars of the same order received permission to go to Africa with the same object of announcing Christ to the Mohammedans. Their names were Samuel, Angelo, Leo, Domnus, Nicholas and Hugolino. On their way through Spain they were joined by Brother Daniel, minister provincial of Calabria, who became the superior of the band. On September 20, 1227, they reached Morocco, and spent ten days in preparation for their mission at a village near Ceuta which was inhabited by European merchants. On Saturday, October 2, they made their confessions and washed one another's feet, spent the night in prayer, and early on Sunday morning entered Ceuta and began to preach in the streets.

Their appearance provoked an uproar, they were badly hustled, and eventually taken before the *kadi*. When he saw their rough clothes and uncovered shaven heads he took them to be mad. They were imprisoned, freely exposed to the insults and ill-treatment of the Moors, whose religion the friars rejected with contempt. Daniel wrote a letter to the Christians of the village in which they had stayed, saying what had happened to them and adding, " Blessed be God, the Father of mercies, who comforts us in all our tribulations ! " The following Sunday, it having been ascertained that they were missionaries and not madmen, the seven friars were invited to renounce their faith, first corporately and then individually in private. Neither threats nor bribes could move them, they continued to affirm Christ and to deny Mohammed, so they were ordered to be put to death. Each one of the martyrs went up to Brother Daniel, knelt for his blessing, and asked permission to give his life for Christ ; and they were all beheaded outside the walls of Ceuta. Their bodies were mangled by the infuriated people, but the local Christians managed to rescue and bury them. Later on the relics were carried into Spain, and in 1516 Pope Leo X permitted the Friars Minor to observe the martyrs' feast liturgically.

These martyrs are commemorated in the Roman Martyrology on October 10, but in the *Acta Sanctorum* an account is given of them on October 13 (vol. vi), which seems to be the day they actually suffered. Nothing material has yet been added to the two texts printed by the Bollandists, *i.e.* a letter of a certain Friar Mariano, and a brief *passio* of later date. See *Analecta Franciscana*, vol. iii, pp. 32–33 and 613–616 ; A. Lopez, *La Provincia de España O.M. : Apuntes historico-criticas* (1915), pp. 61–65 and 329–330 ; and a not very critical essay of D. Zangari, *I sette Frati Minori martirizzati a Çeuta* (1926). An English account is furnished in Léon, *Auréole séraphique* (Eng. trans.), vol. iii pp. 296–299.

11 : THE MOTHERHOOD OF OUR LADY

THE celebration on this day throughout the Western church of a feast in honour of the Motherhood of the Blessed Virgin Mary, Mother of God, was enjoined by Pope Pius XI in the encyclical " *Lux veritatis* ", published on December 25, 1931, in view of the fifteenth centenary of the Council of Ephesus.

In the third lesson of the second nocturn of the office of the new feast mention is made of the arch in the basilica of St Mary Major, which Pope St Sixtus III (432–440) decorated with mosaics shortly after the council, and which has been restored in modern times by the care of Pius XI himself. This, we are taught, remains as a striking monument of the proclamation of our Lady's incomparable honour as Mother of God. But in the institution of the present festival, the pope, as his encyclical explains, had also other objects in view.

" One thing in particular ", he says, " and that indeed one of great importance, we specially desire that all should pray for, under the auspices of our heavenly Queen. That is, that she, who is loved and venerated with such ardent piety by the separated Christians of the East, would not suffer them to wander and be unhappily led further away from the unity of the Church, and therefore from her Son, whose vicar on earth We are. May they return to the common Father, whose judgement all the fathers of the synod of Ephesus most dutifully received, and whom they all saluted with concordant acclamations as the guardian of the faith ; may they all return to Us, who have indeed a fatherly affection for them all, and who gladly make our own those most loving words which Cyril used, when he earnestly exhorted Nestorius that ' the peace of the churches may be preserved, and that the bond of love and of concord among the priests of God may remain indissoluble '."

The text of the encyclical, *Lux veritatis*, is printed in the *Acta Apostolicae Sedis*, vol. xxiii (1931), pp. 493–517. Celebrations in honour of the motherhood of the Blessed Virgin were observed locally in many countries long before the present century, but there was no general usage and the dates selected for this commemoration differed widely. The earliest records of such a feast seem to be connected with Portugal and with the Portuguese overseas dominions. It was conceded to Portugal in 1751, but rapidly spread to other countries, *e.g.* to Venice and to Poland. See F. G. Holweck, *Calendarium festorum Dei et Dei Matris* (1925), pp. 368, 148, etc.

SS. TARACHUS, PROBUS AND ANDRONICUS, MARTYRS (A.D. 304)

THEIR *passio*, for long thought to be authentic, but judged by Father Delehaye to be a combination of a few facts with a lot of purely imaginative detail, states that the three martyrs were apprehended at Pompeiopolis in Cilicia during the persecution under Diocletian and Maximian ; they were presented to Numerian Maximus, governor of the province, and by his order were conducted to Tarsus, the metropolis. Maximus being arrived there, Demetrius the centurion brought them before him. Maximus addressed himself first to Tarachus, observing that he began with him because he was well on in years, and asked his name. Tarachus replied : " I am a Christian."

MAXIMUS : Speak not of your impiety but tell me your name.

TARACHUS : I am a Christian.

MAXIMUS : Strike him upon the mouth, and bid him not answer back.

TARACHUS : I tell you my true name. If you would know that which my parents gave me, it is Tarachus ; when I bore arms I went by the name of Victor.

MAXIMUS : What is your profession and country ?

TARACHUS : I am a Roman and was born at Claudiopolis in Isauria. I was a soldier, but left the service on account of my religion.

MAXIMUS : Your impiety rendered you unworthy to bear arms ; but how did you get your discharge ?

TARACHUS : I asked it of my captain, Publius, and he gave it me.

MAXIMUS : Consider your grey hairs. I will get you rewarded if you will obey the orders of our masters. Sacrifice to the gods, as the emperors themselves do who are masters of the world.

TARACHUS : They are deceived by the Devil in so doing.

MAXIMUS : Break his jaws for saying the emperors are deceived.

TARACHUS : I repeat it. As men, they are deluded.

MAXIMUS : Sacrifice to our gods and leave these subtleties.

TARACHUS : I cannot renounce the law of God.

After further exchanges Tarachus still remained firm, and Demetrius the centurion said to him, " Be advised by me ; sacrifice and save yourself ". But Tarachus told him to keep his advice to himself, whereupon Maximus ordered that he be taken back to prison in chains, and the next prisoner brought forward. Of him he asked, " What is your name ? "

PROBUS : My chief and most honourable name is Christian ; but the name I go by in the world is Probus.

MAXIMUS : Of what country and birth are you ?

PROBUS : My father was of Thrace. I am a plebeian, born at Side in Pamphylia, and I profess Christianity.

MAXIMUS : That will do you no good. Sacrifice to the gods, and enjoy my friendship.

PROBUS : I want nothing of that kind. I was once well off, but I gave up wealth to serve the living God.

MAXIMUS : Strip him and lash him with ox's sinews.

Demetrius the centurion said, whilst they were beating him, " Spare yourself. See how your blood runs in streams."

PROBUS : Do what you will with my body. Your torments are sweet to me.

MAXIMUS : Is your obstinate folly incurable, you foolish fellow ?

PROBUS : I am wiser than you are, because I do not worship devils.

MAXIMUS : Turn him, and strike him on the belly.

PROBUS : Lord, help thy servant !

MAXIMUS : Ask him at every stroke where is his helper.

PROBUS : He helps me, and will help me ; for I take so little notice of your torments that I do not obey you.

MAXIMUS : Look, fool, at your mangled body ; the ground is covered with blood.

PROBUS : The more my body suffers for Christ, the more my soul is strengthened.

Thereupon Maximus ordered him to the stocks and called up the third man, who said his name was Andronicus and that he was a patrician of Ephesus. He also refused to sacrifice, defied the judge, and ignored the good-natured hints of Demetrius. So he too was remanded to prison, and so ended the first examination. The second was held by Maximus at Mopsuestia, and the *acta* give *in extenso* similar interrogations and answers, the prisoners being submitted to various tortures. Andronicus draws attention to the fact that the wounds of his previous scourging are perfectly healed, and Maximus abuses the guards. " Rascals ! " he says. " Did I not strictly forbid you to let anyone see them or dress their wounds ? Yet see here ! " Pegasus the jailor replied, " I swear by your greatness that no one has applied anything whatever to his wounds, or even had admittance to him. He has been kept in chains in the innermost part of the prison. If you catch me in a lie, I'll forfeit my head."

MAXIMUS : How comes it then that there is nothing to be seen of his wounds ?

PEGASUS : I do not know.

ANDRONICUS : Foolish man, the physician our Saviour is powerful. He cures those who worship the Lord and hope in Him, not by the application of medicines, but by His word alone. Though He dwells in Heaven, He is present everywhere. But you know Him not.

MAXIMUS : This silly talk will not help you. Sacrifice, or you are a lost man.

ANDRONICUS : I will not change my answers. I am not a child to be wheedled or frightened.

The third examination was held at Anazarbus. In it Tarachus answered first, with his usual constancy, and when Maximus had him stretched on the rack he said, " I could plead the rescript which forbids judges to put military men to the rack. But I waive my privilege." Maximus had Probus also tortured, and ordered some of the wine and meat that had been offered on the altars of the gods to be forced down his throat. " There ! " he exclaimed. " Now you see that after suffering so much rather than sacrifice, you have nevertheless partaken of a sacrifice."

PROBUS : You have done no great feat in making me taste these accursed offerings against my will.

MAXIMUS : No matter ; it is done. Promise now to do it voluntarily and you shall be released.

PROBUS : If you should force into me all the offerings of all your altars, I should be in no way defiled. For God sees the violence which I suffer.

At length all three were sentenced to the wild beasts. Maximus sent for Terentian, who had care of the games and spectacles, and gave him orders to hold a public show the next day. In the morning a great multitude flocked to the amphitheatre, which was a mile distant from the town of Anazarbus. The author of the *acta* gives a circumstantial account of what followed, which he says he and two fellow Christians watched from a place of concealment on a neighbouring hill. No sooner were the martyrs led down than a deep silence followed at the sight of such pitiable objects, and the people began openly to murmur against the governor for his barbarous cruelty. Many even left the circus, which provoked the governor, and he ordered soldiers to guard all the ways to stop any from departing. A bear, a lioness and other animals were in turn loosed on the three Christians, but they all refused to harm them, fawning around them and licking their wounds. Maximus was furious, and called for the gladiators to dispatch the martyrs with their swords, which they did. He commanded the bodies to be mixed up with those of the gladiators who had been slain and also to be guarded that night by six soldiers, lest the Christians should carry them off. The night was very dark, and a violent storm of thunder and rain dispersed the guards. The searchers distinguished the three bodies by a miraculous star or ray of light which streamed on them, and they carried them on their backs and hid them in a cave on the neighbouring mountains. The Christians of Anazarbus, says the writer, sent this relation to the church of Iconium, desiring that it might be communicated to the faithful of Pisidia and Pamphylia for their encouragement.

The *Acta Sanctorum*, October, vol. v, with Ruinart, furnish Latin and Greek texts of the *passio*. Other recensions exist, and a Syriac version has been edited by Bedjan. There is also a panegyric by Severus of Antioch printed in the *Patrologia Orientalis*, vol. xx, pp. 277–295. Harnack (*Die Chronologie der altchrist. Litteratur*, vol. ii, 1904, pp. 479–480) in noticing these *acta*, gives reasons for thinking that they cannot be regarded as a transcript of any official document, but he seems to form a slightly better opinion of them than Delehaye expresses in *Les légendes hagiographiques* (1927), p. 114.

ST NECTARIUS, Archbishop of Constantinople   (A.D. 397)

When St Gregory Nazianzen resigned the see of Constantinople almost as soon as he was appointed in the year 381 he was succeeded by this Nectarius, a native of Tarsus in Cilicia and *praetor* of the imperial city. The peculiar and perhaps doubtful story of his election is as follows. While the second oecumenical council was in progress at Constantinople Nectarius, who was about to visit his home, called on Diodorus, Bishop of Tarsus, to ask if he could carry any letters for him. Greatly impressed by his looks and manner, Diodorus recommended him to the archbishop of Antioch as successor to St Gregory. Meletius laughed at the idea, but the name of Nectarius was nevertheless added to the list of candidates presented to the emperor. Theodosius chose Nectarius, much to everybody's astonishment, for he was not yet even baptized (he is also said to have been married, with one son). However, the choice was ratified by the council and Nectarius was duly baptized and ordained. On leaving Constantinople St Gregory Nazianzen wrote to the bishops : " You may have a throne and a lordly place then since you think that is the important thing. Rejoice, lift yourselves up, claim the title of patriarch, let broad lands be subject to you ", and the council gave some justification for the rebuke : for soon after the appointment of Nectarius it passed a canon giving Constantinople rank next after Rome. For this reason St Nectarius is often called the first patriarch of the city, though it was long before the Holy See recognized the precedence accorded against its judgement.

His episcopate lasted for sixteen years, but little is known of it or him. He consistently opposed the Arian heretics, with the result that, when in 388 there was a rumour that the emperor had died in Italy, they burnt his house over his head. St Nectarius is principally remembered for having abolished in his diocese the office of priest-penitentiary and the discipline of public penance, on account of an open scandal that had occurred. He died on September 27, 397, and was followed in his see by St John Chrysostom. St Nectarius figures in the Greek *Menaion* but not in the Roman Martyrology.

The more important passages of the church historians which bear upon the life and activities of Nectarius have been brought together in the *Acta Sanctorum*, October, vol. v. Regarding the abolition of the office of priest-penitentiary a convenient summary will be found in DTC., vol. xii, cc. 796–798.

ST CANICE, or KENNETH, Abbot   (*c.* A.D. 599)

Cainnech, also written Canice, Kenny and Kenneth, is a famous saint both in Ireland and Scotland, but in the traditions about him there is little upon which much reliance can be placed. He was an Irishman by birth, the son of a bard, born at Glengiven in Derry. It is said that when a youth he went over into Wales and became a monk under St Cadoc at Llancarfan, where he was ordained. His master's particular affection and the favour which he showed him earned for Canice the jealousy of some of his brethren. After an alleged visit to Rome St Canice went back to Ireland and came to study at the school of St Finnian at Clonard, whence he went with St Kieran, St Comgall and St Columba to St Mobhi at Glasnevin. For some time he preached in Ireland and made several monastic foundations, and then made his first visit to Scotland. There are many traces of him in place-name and legend in that country, notably at Cambuskenneth below

Stirling and at Kilchainnech on Iona itself. He went with St Columba on his mission to the Pictish King Brude at Inverness, and with the sign of the cross paralysed Brude's hand when he threatened the monks with his sword. He converted numerous pagans and was bound in close friendship with St Columba, who on one occasion when he was in great danger at sea said to his companions, " Don't be afraid ! God will listen to Kenneth, who is running to church with only one shoe on to pray for us." At the same time Canice in Ireland was aware of his friend's peril and jumped up from a meal to go to the church.

The best known of St Canice's foundations in Ireland was the monastery at Aghaboe in Ossory, but he probably also had an establishment at Kilkenny, whose old cathedral was dedicated in his honour. His zeal in preaching the gospel and practising Christian perfection have ranked him amongst the most glorious saints whose virtue has enlightened both Ireland and Scotland, and his feast is observed in both countries ; throughout the land in one and in the dioceses of Saint Andrews and of Argyll in the other.

There is a Latin biography which has been edited by C. Plummer in his VSH., vol. i, pp. 152–169, from a text in the Marsh Library in Dublin. Another text, from the *Codex Salmanticensis*, was printed by FF. De Smedt and De Backer. Consult also KSS., pp. 295–297. St Cainnech's intercourse with other Irish saints is noted in Kenney, *Sources for the Early History of Ireland*, vol. i, pp. 409, etc., and see the gloss on the *Félire* of Oengus, p. 223. The name Kenny usually corresponds, not with Cainnech, but with the old name contained in the patronymic Cinnéide (Kennedy).

ST AGILBERT, BISHOP OF PARIS (*c.* A.D. 685)

WHEN Coenwalh, King of the West Saxons, had received the Christian faith and baptism at the court of Anna, King of the East Angles, and been restored to his dominions, there came into Wessex a certain bishop called Agilbert. He was a Frank, but had been living in Ireland engaged in study. Coenwalh, impressed by his learning and zeal, asked him to stay there as bishop. To this St Agilbert agreed, and he showed himself an indefatigable pastor and missionary. When in Northumbria he ordained St Wilfrid priest ; and when it was decided to hold a council to decide the controversy between Roman and Celtic customs, he stayed on to assist at the Synod of Whitby. At this assembly he was looked on as leader of the " Roman " party and was called on by King Oswy to be the first to reply to St Colman of Lindisfarne. St Agilbert asked to be excused and named St Wilfrid to answer, because " he can explain our opinion better in English than I can by an interpreter ".

This language difficulty had already been a cause of serious trouble to Agilbert. After he had been bishop of the West Saxons for some years, King Coenwalh, " who ", says St Bede, " understood no tongue but that of the Saxons, grew weary of that bishop's barbarous speech ". He therefore divided his kingdom into two dioceses, and appointed to that which included the royal city of Winchester an English bishop named Wine. Agilbert was very vexed that the king should have done this without first consulting him (as he well might be) and, resigning his see, he eventually returned to France. In 668 he was made bishop of Paris. Wine in the meantime had become bishop of London by simony, Wessex was without a bishop again, and so Coenwalh asked St Agilbert to come back. He replied that he could not leave the see and flock of his own city, but sent instead his nephew Eleutherius, " whom he thought worthy to be made a bishop " ; he was consecrated by St Theodore of Canterbury. During St Agilbert's French episcopate he consecrated St Wilfrid bishop, as is narrated when treating of that saint. St Agilbert died before the year 691.

Here again Bede (see Plummer's text and notes) is our main authority, but we hear of Agilbert also in the *Liber historiae Francorum* and in the continuation of Fredegarius.

ST GUMMARUS, OR GOMMAIRE   (*c.* A.D. 774)

GUMMARUS was a son of the lord of Emblem, near Lierre in Brabant. He grew up without learning to read or write, but served at the court of Pepin, where from a spirit of religion he was faithful in every duty and liberal in works of mercy. Pepin raised him to a high post, and proposed a match between him and a lady of good birth named Guinimaria, and the marriage was solemnized with their mutual consent. This marriage, which seemed unhappy in the eyes of the world, was directed by God to perfect the virtue of His servant and exalt him to the glory of the saints : for Guinimaria was extravagant and perverse in her ways, cruel, capricious and altogether unteachable. Life became from that time a train of continual trials for Gummarus.

St Gummarus for several years endeavoured by all means which prudence and charity could suggest to encourage his wife to ways more agreeable to reason and religion. Then he was called upon by King Pepin to attend him in his wars, and he was absent eight years. Returning home, he found his wife had thrown all things into disorder, and that few among his servants, vassals or tenants had escaped her oppression. She was so mean that she even refused beer to the reapers at harvest. Gummarus made to every one of them full restitution and satisfaction ; and Guinimaria was so far overcome by his patience and kindness as to be ashamed of her past conduct, and to seem penitent. This change, however, was only exterior, and her wilfulness broke out again worse than ever. Gummarus tried to reclaim her : but at length he gave up the attempt and lived a retired life. With St Rumold he is said to have founded the abbey at Lierre which afterwards bore his name.

There is both a prose Latin Life of Gummarus and a metrical synopsis, for which see the *Acta Sanctorum*, October, vol. v. A very full discussion of the subject has also been printed in Flemish by P. G. Deckers, *Leven en eerdienst van den h. ridder Gummarus* (1872) ; and see T. Paaps, *De hl. Gummarus, . . . critische studie* (1944).

ST BRUNO THE GREAT, ARCHBISHOP OF COLOGNE   (A.D. 965)

OF the saints bearing the name of Bruno the founder of the Carthusians would seem most to deserve the epithet " the Great ", but traditionally it is given to the powerful prince-bishop who, eighty years before his namesake was born in his episcopal city of Cologne, co-operated so conspicuously with his own brother, the Emperor Otto I (also called " the Great "), in the religious and social building-up of Germany and the Empire. This Bruno was the youngest son of the Emperor Henry the Fowler and his wife St Matilda ; he was born in 925 and from early years showed that he shared the good dispositions of his parents. When only four he was sent to the cathedral-school at Utrecht, where he acquired a keen love of learning : Prudentius was said to be his favourite bedside book, and later on he learned Greek from some Byzantines at the imperial court. He was called thither by his brother Otto when he was fourteen, and in spite of his extreme youth he was given rapid preferment. In 940 he was made the emperor's confidential secretary, and soon after was ordained deacon and given the abbeys of Lorsch and Corvey. This irregular proceeding had a happy result in that he restored a stricter observance in both of them. Bruno was ordained priest when he was twenty-five, and went with Otto into Italy as chancellor, in which office he used all his power to bring about the emperor's ideal of a close union between church and state. The time was at hand when he would be in an even more favourable position to forward this unity. In the year 953 the archbishopric of Cologne became vacant, and Bruno was appointed to it.

Throughout the twelve years of his episcopate St Bruno played a leading part in imperial politics, in which ecclesiastical affairs were inextricably mixed up, but not for a moment did he slacken his attention to the spiritual requirements of the people and the purely religious responsibilities of his office. In the first place he set a high example of personal goodness and devotion, and kept clergy and laity on their mettle by frequent visitations. Sound learning and the monastic spirit were the means by which a high standard of pastoral care and spiritual life were to be maintained ; his cathedral-school was staffed by the best professors he could find, and he founded the abbey of St Pantaleon at Cologne. Nor was St Bruno's solicitude confined to his own diocese : he used his influence and authority to spread his reforms throughout the kingdom, and at the same time as he became archbishop this authority was further notably extended by the action of the emperor. While Otto was absent in Italy the duke of Lorraine, his son-in-law Conrad the Red, had risen in rebellion ; whereupon Otto deposed Conrad and put St Bruno in his place. The duchy was not made appurtenant to the bishopric, but this appointment of Bruno was the beginning of the temporal power formerly exercised by the archbishops of Cologne ; they were princes of the Holy Roman Empire. St Bruno was as capable a statesman as he was a good man. He had peculiar aptitude in settling the numerous political disputes of the Lorrainers, and he made German influence supreme over them. In this unifying task his highly trained and apostolic clergy played a large part, and such was the number and quality of the bishops that he appointed that St Bruno was called " the bishop-maker ". The recognition of his worth and ability reached its climax in 961 when, the emperor going to Rome to be crowned, Bruno was appointed with his half-brother William, archbishop of Mainz, co-regent of the empire and guardian of their nephew, the infant king of the Romans, during his father's absence.

Four years later, on October 11, 965, Bruno the Great died at Rheims ; he was only forty years old. His *cultus* in the diocese of Cologne was confirmed in 1870.

The Life of St Bruno by his devoted disciple Ruotger is reckoned one of the most reliable and satisfactory of medieval biographies. It may be read in the *Acta Sanctorum*, October, vol. v, or in MGH., *Scriptores*, new series, ed. Irene Ott (1951) ; there was a previous edition in vol. iv, pp. 224–275. It was written within three or four years of Bruno's death. For a careful study of this work see H. Schörs's series of papers in the *Annalen d. histor. Vereins f. d. Niederrhein*, 1910, 1911 and 1917. *Cf.* also Hauck, *Kirchengeschichte Deutschlands*, vol. iii, pp. 41 *seq.*

BD JAMES OF ULM   (A.D. 1491)

THE Griesingers were a respectable family of Ulm in Germany, where Bd James was born in the year 1407. He left home when he was twenty-five and went to

Italy. He was first a soldier at Naples, but the licence of military life shocked and frightened him, and when he found that his comrades took no notice of his better example and words he left the army and became secretary to a lawyer at Capua. He did his work so well that when, at the end of five years, he wanted to leave his master refused to let him go. So James slipped away and made for Germany, but when he got so far as Bologna he was induced again to enlist as a soldier. In that city he used often to go to the shrine of St Dominic, and presently he was moved to offer himself as a lay-brother to the friars there. He was accepted, and for fifty years he was a model of regular observance and virtue. His prior on one occasion wished to display the lay-brother's prompt obedience for the edification of a visiting prelate. He called for Brother James and gave him a letter, saying it was to be taken to Paris at once. The journey ordered was a long, toilsome and dangerous one, but James just pocketed the letter and asked permission first to go to his cell to get his hat and stick.

The works of the Friars Preachers hold a remarkable place in the history of Christian art, and Bd James, like his fellow Dominican William of Marcillat, was a master of the art of painting on glass. On such work he was principally engaged, and he prepared himself for it by assiduous prayer, whereat he was often rapt in ecstasy ; a number of miracles were attributed to him both before and after death. Bd James died on October 11, 1491, being eighty-four years old to a day, and was beatified in 1825.

A biographical memoir written by Fr Ambrosino of Saracino, a contemporary, has been translated from Italian into Latin in the *Acta Sanctorum*, October, vol. v. See also H Wilms, *Jakob Griesinger* (1922) in German, and Procter, *Dominican Saints*, pp. 287–291.

ST ALEXANDER SAULI, Bishop of Pavia　　(A.D. 1592)

It is recorded of Alexander Sauli that when he was a youth he one day burst into a crowd of people who were watching the antics of some acrobats and tumblers, and, waving a crucifix before the astonished eyes of audience and performers, he warned them solemnly against the dangers of frivolous amusements and pleasure-seeking. After allowance due to youth for the lack of proportion, this incident may be seen as prophetic of Alexander's career, of which the chief business was the restoration to order of Christians who had grown slack, feeble and worse in the enervating atmosphere of the mid-sixteenth century. He was born at Milan of a Genoese family in 1534, and after a good education became a Barnabite clerk regular at the age of seventeen. He was sent for his studies to their college at Pavia, to which he presented a library and for the enlargement of which he paid out of his own pocket. After his ordination to the priesthood in 1556 he taught philosophy and theology at the university, and was soon made theologian to the bishop, at the same time rapidly making a reputation as a preacher. He was so successful at Pavia that St Charles Borromeo invited him to preach in the cathedral of Milan, and St Charles and Cardinal Sfondrati (afterwards Pope Gregory XIV) were present. The burning words of the young Barnabite moved them to tears, and both became his penitents, Father Sauli continuing to direct and advise the archbishop for many years. In 1567 he was elected provost general of his congregation and, though only thirty-three years old, was sufficiently self-confident to withstand both Pope St Pius V and St Charles. Cardinal Borromeo was the protector of the small remnant of Humiliati friars and had a commission to reform them, for they had become both wealthy and, in some individual cases, wicked. It seemed to him, and the pope agreed, that it would be a good thing if these friars were united to the newly founded and zealous Barnabite congregation. But St Alexander, though willing to do all he might for the improvement of the Humiliati, did not feel called on to agree to any proceeding that might have a detrimental effect on his own spiritual children, and St Charles had to withdraw his proposal.

St Alexander had now shown himself unmistakenly to be the firm and zealous sort of priest required by St Pius's reforming activities, and in 1570 he was appointed bishop of Aleria in Corsica. He protested, in vain this time, was consecrated by St Charles, and proceeded to his diocese. It presented a formidable task. The clergy were ignorant and debased, the people barbarous and with hardly the rudiments of religion ; the island was overrun with brigands and family *vendette* were continual and ruthless. He took three clerks regular to help him and, when he had established himself at Tallona (his see city was a ruin), he summoned a synod at which he announced the reforms he proposed to carry out. He then proceeded to a visitation of the diocese, during which the new ways were inaugurated with considerable and necessary severity. He governed the unruly diocese for twenty years, and brought it to such a flourishing state that he was called the apostle of Corsica. In his third synod he promulgated the decrees of the Council of Trent, and his insistence on the observance of these did more than anything else for the restoration of religion. He had to cope not only with sullen opposition from within but with violence from without, from the raids of corsairs from the Barbary coast : three times on their account he had to move his residence and seminary, but eventually established his cathedral and chapter at Cervione.

During his episcopate Alexander Sauli had frequent occasion to visit Rome, where he became a close friend of St Philip Neri, who held him up as an example of a model bishop. He wrote a number of pastoral and catechetical works, and was a capable canonist. His success in Corsica caused him to be offered the sees of Tortona and Genoa, but he refused all preferment until Gregory XIV insisted on transferring him to Pavia. This was in 1591, but he died in the following year while on a visitation at Calozza in that diocese. During his life St Alexander had displayed the gift of prophecy, and the calming of storms and other miracles were attributed to his intercession. These were continued after his death, and his canonization took place in 1904.

A Latin life by J. A. Gabutius, who was a contemporary, is printed in the *Acta Sanctorum*, October, vol. v. The canonization gave rise to the publication of much important material in the *Rivista di Scienze Storiche* for 1905, 1907 and 1908 ; Fr O. Premoli was responsible for the more valuable part of these contributions, and he is also the author of an excellent work on the Barnabites, *Storia dei Barnabiti* (2 vols., 1914, 1922). Another full but less well documented account of St Alexander Sauli is that of F. T. Moltedo (1904), and there is a French life by A. Dubois (1904). On the saint's writings consult G. Boffito, *Scrittori Barnabiti* (1933–34).

BD MARY SOLEDAD, Virgin, Foundress of the Handmaids of Mary Serving the Sick   (A.D. 1887)

Bd Mary Soledad Torres-Acosta belongs to the company of St Mary Michaela Desmaisières, Bd Joachima de Mas and Bd Vincentia Lopez, nineteenth-century Spanish women who attained heroic sanctity in the service of their sick, suffering and needy neighbours. The parents of Mary Soledad were Francis Torres and Antonia Acosta, an exemplary couple living obscurely by a little business in Madrid ; she was the second of five children, born in 1826, and was christened Emanuela. She was a quiet child, who would hide food to give to her hungry playmates, and would rather teach them their prayers than play games. For a time it looked as if she would join the Dominican nuns, whose convent she frequented, but she was content to wait for a more clear indication of what was required of her.

This eventually came from the Chamberì quarter of Madrid, where the vicar was a Servite tertiary named Michael Martinez y Sanz, who had long been worried by the neglected state of so many of the sick in his parish. In 1851 he gathered together seven women, young and not so young, to devote themselves to their service in a religious community. The last of them was twenty-five-year-old Emanuela Torres-Acosta, who in the event was to become the real foundress of the new congregation. She took at her clothing the name Mary Soledad, Spanish for *Desolata*, " alone and grief-stricken ", a token of her love for our Lady of Sorrows.

The enterprise was beset with difficulties within and without—but not, it would seem, overwhelming difficulties ; nevertheless its early growth was very slow. Five years after the foundation Don Michael took half of the members with him to make a separate foundation in Fernando Po ; six were left in Madrid, with Sister Mary Soledad as superioress. For a moment the little group was threatened with dissolution by episcopal authority. But with the help of a new director, Father Gabino Sanchez, an Augustinian friar, it was able to struggle on ; and through the enterprise of Mother Mary support was obtained from the queen and from the local authorities.

The turning-point came in 1861, when the rule of the Handmaids of Mary received diocesan approval and another Augustinian, Father Angelo Barra, was appointed director. Beginning with the taking-over of an institution for young delinquents in Madrid, several new foundations were made, and in the cholera epidemic of 1865 all eyes were turned to the selfless work of Mother Mary Soledad and her nuns. A few years later there was a secession of some members to another congregation, with the usual complaints and accusations from which mother-foundresses have to suffer—as one of her nuns said, Mary Soledad was an anvil, something that was being continually hit. Heaven's reply to this was to bring about, in 1875, the first foundation overseas, at Santiago in Cuba. From that time on there was an accelerated spreading of the houses and hospitals of the congregation in every province of Spain, culminating in 1878 in the taking-over of the ancient hospital of St Charles in the Escorial itself.

The work involved and the increasing commitments continued to the end of Mother Mary's life, the last ten years of which were happily serene. Towards the end of September 1887 she was taken ill, and by October 8 the end was at hand. " Mother ", said her daughters, " bless us, like St Francis did." She shook her head. But one lifted her up in bed, and she raised her hand, saying slowly, " Children, live together in peace and unity ". She died tranquilly on October 11. For thirty-five years Mary Soledad had been the leader, the guide, the human inspiration of the Handmaids of Mary, fostering them from half-a-dozen aspirants to a flourishing, well-ordered, technically efficient body of devoted religious ; and since her death she has seen them spread to Italy, France, England, Portugal, the Americas. How much humbleness, how much charity, how much prudence and self-effacement is required for such a work of love it is given to few to know. But the Church knows : and in 1950 Mother Mary Soledad was declared Blessed.

The apostolic letter of beatification, with a biographical note, is in *Acta Apostolicae Sedis*, vol. xlii (1950), pp. 182–197. There is a life of the *beata* in Italian, by E. Federici (1950), reliable but very " long-winded " ; and at least one in Spanish, by J. A. Zugasti.

12 : ST MAXIMILIAN, BISHOP OF LORCH, MARTYR   (A.D. 284 ?)

MAXIMILIAN was an apostle of that part of the Roman empire formerly called Noricum, between Styria and Bavaria, where it is said he founded the church of Lorch, near Passau, and was martyred ; but the particulars depend on *acta* written so late as the thirteenth century and are quite unreliable. These state that he was born at Cilli (Steiermark) in Styria, and at the age of seven was entrusted to a priest to be educated. His parents were wealthy folk, and when he grew up he gave away his inheritance in charity and undertook a pilgrimage to Rome. Pope St Sixtus II sent him back to be a missionary in Noricum and he established his episcopal see at Lorch. Maximilian survived the persecutions under Valerian and Aurelian and ministered for over twenty years, making many conversions. But under Numerian the prefect of Noricum published an edict of persecution, in consequence of which St Maximilian was called on to sacrifice to the gods. He refused and was beheaded outside the walls of Cilli, at a spot still shown.

The legend is printed in the *Acta Sanctorum*, October, vol. vi, with the usual prolegomena. See also Ratzinger, *Forschungen z. bayr. Gesch.* (1898), pp. 325 *seq.*, and J. Zeiller, *Les origines chrétiennes dans les provinces danubiennes* (1914).

SS. FELIX AND CYPRIAN AND MANY OTHER MARTYRS   (*c.* A.D. 484)

THE second entry in the Roman Martyrology today runs : " In Africa, the passion of 4966 holy confessors and martyrs in the Vandal persecution under the Arian king, Huneric, some of whom were bishops of the churches of God and some priests and deacons, with the multitudes of the faithful associated with them. They were driven into exile in a horrible desert for defending Catholic truth. Many of them were cruelly treated by the Moors, being compelled to run by the points of spears and struck with stones ; others were dragged like corpses, with their legs tied together, over rough and stony ground, and torn limb from limb ; all of them, being tortured in various ways, at the last achieved martyrdom. Among them were those distinguished priests of the Lord, the bishops Felix and Cyprian." The persecution of orthodox Christians by the Arian Vandals thus summarized is described at length by Victor of Vita, an African bishop who was contemporary and an eye-witness.

Huneric exiled them by hundreds into the Libyan desert, where they perished under conditions of the greatest barbarity. Numbers were concentrated in a small building, where they were visited by Bishop Victor, who found prisoners and prison in a state reminiscent of the " black hole " of Calcutta. When at length the order was brought to lead the Catholics into the wilderness, they came out singing psalms and amid the lamentations of their fellow-Christians. Some even, including women and children, voluntarily followed the confessors to exile and death. St Felix, the bishop of Abbir, was very old and half paralysed, and it was represented to Huneric that he might just as well be left to die at home. But the brutal king replied that if he could not ride a horse he could be tied to a yoke of oxen and dragged. Eventually the old man made the terrible journey tied across the back of a mule. Many even of the young and strong did not reach their destination : stones were thrown at them and they were pricked with spears to make them keep up, till they collapsed by the wayside and perished of thirst and exhaustion. St Cyprian, another bishop, expended all his time, energy and property in caring for the confessors and encouraging them, till he too was apprehended and sent into banishment, where he died a martyr from the hardships he endured.

We know, practically speaking, no more of these martyrs than is told us by Victor of Vita. His text is quoted and discussed in the *Acta Sanctorum*, October, vol. vi. It is curious that no identifiable notice of the group seems to occur in the ancient calendar of Carthage or in the " Hieronymianum ".

ST EDWIN, Martyr   (A.D. 633)

In the year 616 King Ethelfrith of Bernicia was defeated and slain in battle, between Lincoln and Doncaster, by Redwald, King of the East Angles. By this victory Edwin of Deira was put in possession of the whole kingdom of Northumbria after being an exile for nearly thirty years ; and after the death of Redwald he had a certain lordship over the other English kings. He asked for the hand of Ethelburga, daughter of St Ethelbert, King of Kent, and was informed that " it is not lawful to marry a Christian maiden to a pagan husband ". However, he gave an assurance that she should be free in her religion, and that he would look into it himself, and thereupon the marriage was allowed, St Paulinus being sent north as chaplain to the queen and bishop for his converts. At Easter in 626 an assassin sent from the West Saxons attempted to stab King Edwin. He would have certainly killed him if Lilla, his thegn, had not interposed his own body and so saved the king's life with the loss of his own. Soon Queen Ethelburga gave birth of a daughter, and when the king gave thanks to his gods for her preservation St Paulinus told him it was the effect of the prayers of his queen and her bishop to the true God that she had had an easy and safe delivery. The king seemed pleased with this idea and was prevailed upon to consent that his daughter who was just born should be consecrated to God. She was baptized with twelve others on Whitsunday, and called Eanfleda, and they were the first-fruits of the Northumbrians.

Edwin being, as Bede says, a man of unusual wisdom, " sat much alone by himself, silent of tongue, deliberating in his heart how he should act and to which religion he should adhere ". Pope Boniface V sent him an encouraging letter, and a silver looking-glass and an ivory comb to the queen, admonishing her to press him upon that subject. Paulinus continued to instruct him and to pray for his conversion but without visible effect ; till one day the bishop came and apparently reminded him of some conditional promise of his early years, and said, " You see that God has delivered you from your enemies ; and He offers you His everlasting kingdom. Take care on your side to perform your promise, by receiving His faith and keeping His commandments." Edwin answered he would invite his chief counsellors to do the same with him, and assembled his nobles. Coifi, the chief priest, spoke first, declaring that by experience it was manifest their gods had no power. Another said that the short moment of this life is of no weight, if put in the balance with eternity : " like the swift flight of a sparrow through the warm room where we sit and sup in winter when there is snow without. It flies in at one door and out at the other, into the dark and cold from which it has just emerged." Others spoke to the like effect, and then St Paulinus addressed the assembly. Coifi applauded his discourse and advised the king to command fire to be set to the temples and altars of their false gods ; and then himself rode to a temple, which he profaned by casting his spear into it. " And the people beholding it, thought he was mad." Where this took place, says Bede, is shown not far from York, to the east beyond the Derwent, at Goodmanham, a mile from Market Weighton.

King Edwin was baptized at York at Easter in the year 627, on the site of the present York Minster, in the wooden church of St Peter which he had caused to be built. He afterwards began a large church of stone, which was finished by his successor, St Oswald. Both nobles and people flocked to be instructed and to receive the sacrament of baptism. People being converted in such numbers there were necessarily many who were unworthy of or dishonest in their new profession, but some became changed men, whose first thought now was to serve God in this world and enjoy Him for ever in the next. And of these Edwin was himself an example, being as zealous to spread the truth as to practise it.

Edwin imposed tribute on the north Welsh chieftains and took possession of the island of Môn, later called Anglesey ; and in the north consolidated his kingdom to the Forth. He provided that on the highways brass cups should be chained to stakes by springs for the convenience of travellers, nor dare any man touch them for any purpose but that for which they were put there. " There was then ", says St Bede in a well-known passage, " such perfect peace in Britain, wheresoever the rule of King Edwin extended, that, as is still proverbially said, a woman with her new-born babe might walk throughout the island from sea to sea unharmed." This good king had reigned seventeen years when the Welsh Cadwallon marched in arms against him with Penda of Mercia, a pagan. King Edwin met them at Hatfield Chase on October 12, 633, and in the ensuing battle he was slain.

St Edwin was certainly venerated in England as a martyr, but though his claims to sanctity are less doubtful than those of some other royal saints, English and other, he has had no liturgical *cultus* so far as is known. His relics were held in venera-tion ; Speed says that churches were dedicated in his honour in London and at Brean in Somerset ; and Pope Gregory XIII permitted him to be represented among the English martyrs on the walls of the chapel of the *Venerabile* at Rome.

The *Anglo-Saxon Chronicle* and other early sources add little or nothing to the account in Bede's *Historia ecclesiastica*. See Plummer's text and notes, and consult further the bibliography given above under St Paulinus, October 10.

ST ETHELBURGA, ABBESS OF BARKING, VIRGIN   (*c.* A.D. 678)

ETHELBURGA is said to have been born at Stallington in Lindsey, and she was the sister of St Erconwald, of whom it is said they were " bound together by a common love, one in heart and one in soul ". Fired doubtless by the example of her brother, St Ethelburga determined to become a nun, and nothing could shake her resolution, for the world loses all its influence upon a mind which is wholly taken up with the great truths of faith and eternal salvation. Erconwald, before he became bishop of London, founded a monastery at Chertsey and another for both monks and nuns at Barking in Essex. Over this he set Ethelburga as abbess, and as she and her sisters were quite inexperienced, St Hildelitha was fetched from a French abbey to train her. We are told there was somewhat of a competition in austerity between the two saints, and Ethelburga, when the rule of the house was entrusted to her, by her example and spirit sweetly led on all the other nuns in the path of virtue and Christian perfection. " She behaved in all respects as became the sister of such a brother, living according to the rule, devoutly and orderly, providing for those under her, as was also manifested by heavenly miracles ", of which St Bede relates several.

When an epidemic carried off some of the monks they were buried in the ground adjoining the church, and a discussion arose among the nuns as to where they should be buried when their time came, in the same part of the churchyard or another part. They could come to no decision, till one morning after Matins they were praying by the graves of the dead brothers, when suddenly a great light (which from Bede's description would certainly seem to have been summer lightning) fell first upon them and then upon another side of the church ; which light they understood " was intended to show the place in which their bodies were to rest and await the day of resurrection ". St Bede tells a touching story of a little boy of three years old, who was being brought up in the monastery and who died calling for one of the nuns, Edith, who shortly followed him ; and of another nun who, dying at midnight, asked for the candle to be put out, exclaiming, " I know you think I am mad, but I am not. I see this room so filled with light that your candle there looks dark to me." And when they left it, she said, " Very well ; let it burn. But it is not my light, for my light will come to me at daybreak." And at the dawn she died.

St Ethelburga's approaching end was foreseen in a vision by a nun called Theorigitha, who for nine years had been an invalid ; and Ethelburga's life " is known to have been such that no person who knew her ought to question but that the heavenly kingdom was opened to her directly she left this world ", says Bede. Three years later Theorigitha herself was dying, and had lost the use of her tongue. Suddenly she spoke and said, " Your coming is a great joy to me. You are welcome," and began to talk with an invisible person about how much longer she had to live. The bystanders asked whom she was talking to, and were told, " With my most dear mother, Ethelburga ". The feast of St Ethelburga is observed in the diocese of Brentwood.

There does not seem much to add to the account given in Bede, *Historia ecclesiastica*, bk iv (see Plummer's edition and notes) ; but the Bollandists have reprinted the short biography of Capgrave. Traces of liturgical *cultus* survive both in medieval calendars (noted in Stanton, *Menology*, p. 486), and in certain antiphons, etc. (Hardy, *Materials*, vol. i, p. 385). For the life by Goscelin of Canterbury in the Gotha MS., see *Analecta Bollandiana*, vol. lviii (1940), p. 101.

ST WILFRID, BISHOP OF YORK   (A.D. 709)

ST WILFRID stands out prominently among the early ecclesiastics of the Church in England as an upholder of the customs and discipline of the Roman church and for his own close contacts with the Holy See.* He was born in 634, son of a North-umbrian thegn ; Ripon claims to be his birthplace, but without producing any evidence. His mother died when he was a child, and the unkindness of his step-mother made him seek the court of Oswy, King of Northumbria, when he was thirteen. He was befriended by Queen Eanfleda, who sent him to the monastery of Lindisfarne that he might be trained in the study of the sacred sciences. A desire of greater improvement than he could attain to in that house, where he perceived the Celtic discipline that was practised to be imperfect, gave rise to a project of travelling into France and Italy. He made some stay at Canterbury, where he studied the Roman discipline under St Honorius, and learned the psalter according to the Roman version, instead of that which he had used before. In 654 St Benet Biscop, his countryman, passed through Kent on his first journey to Rome ; and St Wilfrid, who had set out with the same object, crossed the sea with him.

At Lyons Wilfrid was detained a whole year by St Annemund, bishop of that city, who took so great a liking to him that he offered him his niece in marriage, and promised him a considerable position ; but the youth continued steadfast in the resolution he had taken to devote himself to God. At Rome he put himself under Boniface the archdeacon, a pious and learned man ; he was secretary to Pope St Martin, and took much delight in instructing young Wilfrid. After this, Wilfrid returned to Lyons. He stayed three years there and received the tonsure after the Roman manner, thus adopting an outward and visible sign of his dissent from Celtic customs. St Annemund desired to make him his heir, but his own life was suddenly cut short by murder, and Wilfrid himself was spared only because he was a foreigner. He returned to England, where King Alcfrid of Deira, hearing that Wilfrid had been instructed in the discipline of the Roman church, asked him to instruct him and his people accordingly. Alcfrid had recently founded a monastery at Ripon and peopled it with monks from Melrose, among whom was St Cuthbert. These the king required to abandon their Celtic usages, whereupon the abbot Eata, Cuthbert and others, elected to return to Melrose. So St Wilfrid was made abbot of Ripon, where he introduced the Rule of St Benedict, and shortly after he was ordained priest by St Agilbert, the Frankish bishop of the West Saxons.

Wilfrid used all his influence to win over the clergy of the north to Roman ways. The principal trouble was that they followed an erroneous calculation of Easter ; and King Oswy and his Queen Eanfleda, who came from Kent, sometimes kept Lent and Easter at different times in the same court. To put an end to this dispute, in 663 or 664 a conference was held in the monastery of St Hilda at Streaneshalch, now Whitby, before Oswy and Alcfrid. As has been related in the account of St Colman (February 18), who was then bishop of Lindisfarne, the pro-Roman party triumphed, and Colman retired to Iona. Tuda was consecrated bishop of the Northumbrians in his room, but soon after died, and Alcfrid desired to have his own priest, Wilfrid, placed in the episcopal see. Wilfrid, quite unjustifiably, looked on the nonconforming northern bishops as schismatics, and so went to

* The *Life of St Wilfrid*, by F. W. Faber, published under Newman's editorship in 1844, caused a great outcry on account of its undisguisedly Roman sympathies. Some startling extracts were cited, years later, by Faber's biographer (pp. 224–225). His conversion followed quickly. He took the name of Wilfrid in confirmation, dedicated in honour of St Wilfrid the church he built at Cotton, and chose for himself the name of Brother Wilfrid in the congregation which he founded, the members of which were for the short time of its duration known as " Wilfridians ".

France to receive consecration, at Compiègne, at the hands of his old friend St Agilbert, who had returned to his native country. He was then in his thirtieth year. For some reason St Wilfrid did not come back at once, and when he did was delayed by shipwreck. In the meantime King Oswy sent St Chad, Abbot of Lastingham, south, where he was consecrated by Wine, Bishop of the West Saxons, and then appointed him to be bishop at York. Wilfrid on his return to England would not dispute the election of St Chad, but retired to Ripon monastery. He was often called into Mercia by King Wulfhere to ordain, and at the invitation of King Egbert he went to Kent for the same purpose. On his return he brought with him a monk named Eddius Stephanus, who became his friend and biographer.

In 669 St Theodore, the newly appointed archbishop of Canterbury, in his visitation found the election of St Chad to have been irregular, and removed him, and at the same time put St Wilfrid in possession of the see of York. With the help of Eddius, who had been precentor at Canterbury, he established in all the churches of the north the use of Roman chant, he restored the cathedral at York, and discharged all his episcopal duties in a most exemplary way. He made visitations of his large diocese on foot, and was deeply beloved and respected by all his people—but not by his prince, Egfrid, who had succeeded Oswy. Egfrid had in 659 married St Etheldreda, daughter of King Anna of the East Angles. For ten years she refused to consummate her marriage, and when he had appealed to the bishop, Wilfrid had taken Etheldreda's part and helped her to leave her husband's house and become a nun at Coldingham. In these circumstances Egfrid, not without reason, thought he had a grievance against the bishop, and had no intention of letting his resentment remain inactive. When therefore there was indication that St Theodore wanted as metropolitan to subdivide the great diocese of the Northumbrians, he encouraged the project, and moreover slandered St Wilfrid's administration and demanded his deposition. Theodore appears to have listened to Egfrid, the diocese of York was divided, and Theodore consecrated three bishops in Wilfrid's own cathedral. Wilfrid protested, and in 677 or 678 appealed to the judgement of the Holy See—the first example of such an appeal in the history of the Church in England. He set out for Rome, and being driven by contrary winds upon the coast of Friesland, during that winter and the following spring he stayed there and converted and baptized many. Thus he began that harvest which St Willibrord and others afterwards carried on.

After a stay in France, St Wilfrid reached Rome late in 679, and found Pope St Agatho already apprised of what had passed in England by a monk whom Theodore had despatched with letters. To discuss this cause the pope assembled a synod in the Lateran, which decided that Wilfrid was to be restored to his see, and that he himself should choose coadjutors or suffragans to assist him. St Wilfrid stayed over four months at Rome, and assisted at the Lateran council which condemned the monothelite heresy. When he arrived in England, he went to King Egfrid and showed him the decrees of the pope. The prince cried out that they had been obtained by bribery, and commanded Wilfrid to be taken to prison, where he was detained nine months. He then went by way of Wessex into Sussex. Here Wilfrid was among the still pagan South Saxons, but their King Ethelwalh, who had been lately baptized in Mercia, received him with open arms. The saint by his preaching converted nearly the whole people, and extended his activities to the Isle of Wight. In Sussex he manumitted 250 slaves, men and women. At his coming the country was oppressed with a dreadful famine and drought, but on the day on which St Wilfrid first administered baptism, with great solemnity, abundant rain fell. The saint also taught the people to fish, which was a great boon to them, for hitherto they had known only how to catch eels. The bishop's men collected a number of eel-nets and adapted them for sea-fishing ; in their first venture they caught three hundred fish, of which the saint gave one hundred to the poor and as many to those of whom they had borrowed the nets, keeping the rest for their own use. The king gave him land at Selsey, whereon he established a monastery ; this place became an episcopal see, which was afterwards removed to Chichester.

St Wilfrid chiefly resided in the peninsula of Selsey, and conducted his missions from thence for five years till, upon the death of King Egfrid, St Theodore, who was very old and ill, sent to him requesting that he would meet him at London with St Erconwald, bishop of that city. He confessed to them all the actions of his life, and said to St Wilfrid, " The greatest remorse that I feel is that I consented to your losing your see without any fault committed on your part. I confess this crime to God and St Peter, and I take them to witness that I will do all that lies in my power to make amends for my fault and to reconcile you to all the kings and lords who are my friends. I shall not live to the end of this year, and I wish to establish you in my lifetime archbishop of my see." St Wilfrid replied : " May God and St Peter pardon all our differences ; I will always pray for you. Send letters to your friends that they may restore to me my diocese, according to the decree of the Holy See. The choice of a successor in your see will be afterwards considered in a proper assembly." Accordingly, St Theodore wrote to Egfrid's successor, Aldfrid, to Ethelred, King of the Mercians, to St Elfleda, who had succeeded St Hilda in the abbey of Whitby, and others. Aldfrid recalled the bishop towards the end of the year 686, and restored to him his monastery of Ripon. How the complicated position in the north then developed is not altogether clear. But within five years there was disagreement between Aldfrid and Wilfrid, and he was again banished, in 691. He then retired to Ethelred of Mercia, who entreated him to take care of the vacant see of Lichfield, which he administered for some years. The new archbishop of Canterbury, St Berhtwald, was not sympathetic to St Wilfrid, and in 703 he called a synod which decreed, at the instigation of Aldfrid, that Wilfrid should resign his bishopric and retire to his abbey of Ripon. Wilfrid vindicated all he had done for the Church in the north in an impassioned speech, and again appealed to the Holy See. The synod broke up, and he started on his third journey to Rome. He was in his seventieth year.

St Wilfrid's opponents also sent representatives to Rome and many sessions were held over a period of four months to examine the cause. The synod was naturally impressed by the previous judgement of Pope St Agatho. Wilfrid's opponents had always acknowledged his life to be irreproachable, and a bishop cannot be deposed unless a canonical fault be proved against him. If it was necessary to divide his bishopric, this was not to be done without his concurrence and reserving to him his own see, and by the authority at least of a provincial council. Moreover, Wilfrid, being the best skilled in sacred learning and in the canons of the Church in all England, as St Theodore acknowledged him to be, was too great a disciplinarian for some at court. It is noteworthy too that, so far as is known, he never claimed metropolitan jurisdiction for the see of York and the *pallium* for himself, which had been granted to St Paulinus. St Wilfrid met at Rome with that protection and approval which were due to his heroic virtue. Pope

John VI sent letters to the kings of Mercia and Northumbria, charging Archbishop Berhtwald to call a synod which should do him justice : in default of which he ordered the parties to make their personal appearance at Rome.

St Wilfrid on his return found that King Aldfrid still made difficulties ; but he died in 705, and in his last sickness repented of the injustice he had done to St Wilfrid, as his sister St Elfleda gave testimony. Restitution, therefore, was agreed to. St Wilfrid, having vindicated the canons and the authority of the Holy See, consented to a compromise : he took possession of the diocese of Hexham, but chiefly resided in his monastery of Ripon, leaving York to St John of Beverley. " On that day ", writes Eddius, " all the bishops kissed and embraced one another, and, having broken bread, communicated. Then, giving thanks to the God of all this happiness, they returned to their own places in the peace of Christ." In 709 St Wilfrid made a visitation of the monasteries in Mercia of which he had been the founder, and he died at one of these, at Oundle in Northamptonshire, having divided his goods between his monasteries, churches and the former companions of his exile. His body was buried in his church of St Peter at Ripon. Dr T. Hodgkin in his *History of England to the Norman Conquest* avers that " the life of Wilfrid with all its strange vicissitudes of triumph and disgrace is confessedly one of the most difficult problems in early Anglo-Saxon history ", but further on he tells us : " With justice he (Wilfrid) exclaimed again and again, ' What are the crimes of which you accuse me ? ' They had, it would seem, no crimes to allege against him." Neither does Dr Hodgkin hesitate to describe him as " the brave old ·man " and " the greatest ecclesiastic " of Northumbria. St Wilfrid saw the clouds gather and burst over his head, yet was undismayed, and never reviled his persecutors. By his friend and biographer Eddius he was described as " courteous to everybody, active in body, a quick walker, eager for every good work, never cast down "‚. He is named in the Roman Martyrology and his feast is kept in most dioceses of England, the prayer of his office being taken from the old office of the church of York.

For materials, we have, beside the copious account given in Bede, a full biography by Wilfrid's companion and disciple Eddius (translated by B. Colgrave, 1927), as well as the somewhat turgid poem of Frithegod (*c.* 945), and some other sources of much later date, the principal of which is the life, or lives, by Eadmer. These biographical documents may most conveniently be consulted in the first volume of Raine's *Historians of the Church of York* (Rolls Series). To discuss the disputed episodes in the series of St Wilfrid's many conflicts would be impossible here. The account given above is substantially supported by the statements of Bede and Eddius, and though there is ground for suspecting the latter of a partiality which led him to suppress incidents which he deemed derogatory to his hero, there is no proof forthcoming that he was an unscrupulous falsifier of history. See also R. L. Poole, *Studies in Chronology and History* (1934), pp. 56–81 ; F. M. Stenton, *Anglo-Saxon England* (1943) ; W. Levison, *England and the Continent in the Eighth Century* (1946) ; E. S. Duckett, *Anglo-Saxon Saints and Scholars* (1947). Frithegod's poem has been edited by Alistair Campbell (1950).

13 : ST EDWARD THE CONFESSOR　　(A.D. 1066)

AFTER the neglect, quarrelling and oppression of the reigns of the two Danish sovereigns Harold Harefoot and Harthacanute, the people of England gladly welcomed the representative of the old English line of kings, known in history as Edward the Confessor. " All men took him as was his right ", and, for the peace and relief that prevailed during his reign, he was undoubtedly one of the most popular of English sovereigns, though his significance was much exaggerated later by the Normans, whose friend he had been. And the noble qualities for which Edward is venerated as a saint belonged to him rather as a man than as a king ; he was devout, gentle and peace-loving but with hardly sufficient force to stand up to some of the strong characters by whom he was surrounded. On the other hand he was not feeble and pietistic, as is now sometimes alleged : he was handicapped by lack of physical strength, but had a quiet determination which enabled him to cope successfully with opposing influences. Edward was the son of Ethelred the Redeless by his Norman wife Emma, and during the Danish supremacy was sent to Normandy for safety, with his brother Alfred, when he was ten years old. Alfred came to England in 1036 but was seized and mutilated, and died by the brutality of Earl Godwin. Thus Edward did not set foot again in his native land until he was called to be king in 1042 : he was then forty years old. Two years later he married Edith, the daughter of Godwin : a beautiful and religious girl, " whose mind was a school of all the liberal arts ". It is traditionally claimed as an aspect of Edward's sanctity that, for love of God and greater perfection, he lived with his wife in absolute continence. The fact is not certain, nor, if it were so, is his motive certain either. William of Malmesbury, eighty years later, says that the continency of the king and his wife was notorious, but adds, " I have not been able to discover whether he acted thus from dislike of her family or out of pure regard for chastity ". The chronicler Roger of Wendover says the same thing, but thinks that Edward was certainly unwilling " to beget successors of a traitor stock ", which seems rather far-fetched. However, the difficulty common to these cases—Why did they marry at all ?—perhaps does not arise in this one : Edward knew that his security was threatened by Earl Godwin more than by any other power.

Godwin for his part was the chief opponent of a certain Norman influence which had its centre at the royal court and made itself felt in appointments to bishoprics and offices as well as in lesser matters. After a series of " incidents ", things came to a crisis and Godwin and his family were banished ; even his daughter, Edward's queen, was confined to a convent for a time. In the same year, 1051, William of Normandy visited the English court, and it can hardly be doubted that Edward then offered him the succession to the crown : the Norman conquest began, not at the battle of Hastings, but at the accession of St Edward. It was not many months before Godwin returned, and as both sides were averse from a civil war the king restored him, and the council " outlawed all Frenchmen that aforetime disregarded the law, gave unjust judgements, and counselled ill counsel in the land ". The Norman archbishop of Canterbury and another bishop fled overseas " in a crazy ship ". Nothing is more praised at this time than the " laws and customs of good King Edward " and the realm's freedom from war. The only serious fighting was between Harold of Wessex (Godwin's son) and Gruffydd ap Llywelyn in the Welsh Marches, and the expeditions under Earl Siward to assist Malcolm III of Scotland against the usurper Macbeth. The king's religious and just administration caused him to reign in the hearts of his people. The love, harmony and agreement seen in retrospect between him and the great council of the nation became the traditional measure of the people's desires in all succeeding reigns, the law and government of King Edward being petitioned and strenuously contended for by English commons and Norman barons. Not the least popular of his acts was the remission of the *heregeld* or army-tax ; the amount of the tax in hand collected in his reign was handed over by Edward to the poor.

William of Malmesbury gives a personal picture of St Edward, in which he says that he was " a man by choice devoted to God, living the life of an angel in the administration of his kingdom, and therefore directed by Him. . . . He was so gentle that he would not say a word of reproach to the meanest person." He was generous to the poor and strangers, especially if they were from abroad, and a great encourager of monks. His favourite diversions were hunting and hawking, at which he would go out for days on end, but even then never omitted to be present at Mass every morning. In appearance he was tall and well built, with a ruddy face and white hair and beard.

St Edward during his exile in Normandy had made a vow to go on pilgrimage to St Peter's tomb at Rome if God should be pleased to put an end to the misfortunes of his family. When he was settled on the throne he held a council, in which he declared the obligation he lay under. The assembly commended his devotion, but represented that the kingdom would be left exposed to domestic divisions and to foreign enemies. The king was moved by their reasons, and consented that the matter should be referred to Pope St Leo IX. He, considering the impossibility of the king's leaving his dominions, dispensed his vow upon condition that by way of commutation he should give to the poor the sum he would have expended in his ourney and should build or repair and endow a monastery in honour of St Peter. King Edward selected for his benefaction an abbey already existing close to London, in a spot called Thorney. He rebuilt and endowed it in a magnificent manner out of his own patrimony, and obtained of Pope Nicholas II ample exemptions and privileges for it. From its situation it had come to be called West Minster in distinction from the church of St Paul in the east of the city. The new monastery was designed to house seventy monks, and, though the abbey was finally dissolved and its church made collegiate and a " royal peculiar " by Queen Elizabeth, the ancient community is now juridically represented by the monks of St Laurence's Abbey at Ampleforth. The present church called Westminster Abbey, on the site of St Edward's building, was built in the thirteenth century and later.

The last year of St Edward's life was disturbed by troubles between the Northumbrians and their earl, Tostig Godwinsson, whom eventually the king was constrained to banish. At the end of the year, when the nobles of the realm were gathered at the court for Christmas, the new choir of Westminster abbey-church was consecrated with great solemnity, on Holy Innocents' day, 1065. St Edward was too ill to be present ; he died a week later,* and was buried in his abbey.

---

* Alban Butler refers to his giving a ring to the abbot of Westminster, with the legend relating thereto and the fanciful derivation of the name of Havering-atte-Bower in Essex. At the time that the church of Havering was about to be consecrated, Edward, riding that way, alighted, to be present at the consecration. During the procession a fair old man came to the king and begged alms of him, in the name of God and St John the Evangelist. The king having nothing else to give, as his almoner was not at hand, took a ring from his finger and gave it to the poor man. Some years afterwards two English pilgrims, having lost their way as they were travelling in the Holy Land, " were succoured and put in the right way by an old man ", who at parting told them he was John the Evangelist, adding, as the legend proceeds, " Say ye unto Edwarde your Kying that I grete hym well by the token that he gaaf to me this Ryng wyth his own handes at the halowyng of my Chirche, whych Rynge ye shall deliver to hym agayn : and say ye to hym, that he dyspose his goodes, for wythin six monethes he shall be in the joye of Heven wyth me, where he shall have his rewarde for his

In 1161 he was canonized, and two years later his incorrupt body was translated to a shrine in the choir by St Thomas Becket, on October 13, the day now fixed for his feast ; the day of his death, January 5, is also mentioned in the Roman Martyrology.   There was a further translation, in the thirteenth century, to a shrine behind the high altar, and there the body of the Confessor still lies, the only relics of a saint (except those of the unidentified St Wite at Whitchurch Canonicorum in Dorsetshire) remaining *in situ* after the violence and impiety of Henry VIII and those who followed him.   To St Edward the Confessor was attributed the first exercise of the power of " touching for the King's Evil " (scrofula and allied affections), as was done subsequently by many others, and cures apparently obtained.   Alban Butler states that, " Since the revolution [of 1688] only Queen Anne has touched for this distemper ", but Cardinal Henry Stuart (*de iure* King Henry IX ; died 1807) also did so.   St Edward is the principal patron of the city of Westminster and a lesser patron of the archdiocese ; his feast is not only kept all over Great Britain but throughout the Western church since 1689.

A collection of *Lives of St Edward the Confessor* was edited for the Rolls Series by H. R. Luard in 1858.   This, besides a Norman-French poem and a Latin poem both of late date, includes an anonymous *Vita Æduuardi Regis* which is generally believed to have been written shortly after the king's death.   Another life, by Osbert of Clare, was compiled about 1141, and has been edited in the *Analecta Bollandiana* (vol. xli, 1923, pp. 5–131) by M. Bloch, who argues at length that the anonymous *vita* is not older than the twelfth century, between 1103 and 1120.   On this see H. Thurston in *The Month*, May 1923, pp. 448–451 ; and R. W. Southern in *Eng. Hist. Rev.*, vol. lviii (1943), pp. 385 *seq.*   Yet another biography is an adaptation of Osbert's by St Aelred, and it has been more than once printed among his works.   Besides this we have many briefer notices, *e.g.* in the *Anglo-Saxon Chronicle*, and in such writers as William of Malmesbury and Henry of Huntingdon.   The reign of Edward the Confessor is also, of course, discussed in numberless modern histories (notably in E. A. Freeman's *Norman Conquest*, vol. ii), often in a tone the reverse of sympathetic.   On the king's connection with Westminster, see Flete's *History of Westminster Abbey*, edited by Dean Armitage Robinson (1909).   As for the Confessor's reputation as a law-giver, it must be remembered, as F. Liebermann has shown in his *Gesetze der Angelsachsen*, that the code which at a later time was current under his name was not formulated until fifty years after the Conquest and cannot be traced to any enactments for which he was personally responsible.   For " touching ", see M. Bloch, *Les rois thaumaturges* (1924).

SS. FAUSTUS, JANUARIUS AND MARTIAL, MARTYRS   (A.D. 304 ?)

THESE saints are called by Prudentius " the Three Crowns of Cordova ", in which city they with undaunted constancy confessed Jesus Christ.   First Faustus, then Januarius, and lastly Martial, who was the youngest, was hoisted on to the instrument of torture called the " little horse ", and the judge charged the executioners to keep on increasing their pains till they should sacrifice to the gods.   Faustus cried out, " There is one only God, who created us all ".   The judge commanded his nose, ears, eye-lids and under-lip to be cut off.   At the cutting of each part, the martyr gave thanks to God.   Januarius was then treated in the same manner, and all the while Martial prayed earnestly for constancy as he lay on the rack.   The judge pressed him to comply with the imperial edicts, but he resolutely answered,

chastitie and his good lyvinge ".   At their return home, the two pilgrims waited upon the king, who was then at this Bower, and delivered to him the message and the ring ; from which circumstance this place is said to have received the name of Have-Ring.   Havering is really " Hæfer's people ".

" Jesus Christ is my comfort. There is one only God, Father, Son and Holy Ghost, to whom homage and praise are due." The three martyrs were condemned to be burnt alive and cheerfully finished their martyrdom by fire at Cordova in Spain.

Here again, as so frequently happens, we have a *passio* which is historically worthless, though the fact of the martyrdom and the locality where it occurred cannot be doubted ; the names of the martyrs are perpetuated in inscriptions of the fifth or sixth century, and also by an entry on this day in the *Hieronymianum* : see CMH., pp. 530, 554. The *passio* has been printed by Ruinart as well as in the *Acta Sanctorum*, October, vol. vi, but its details are quite untrustworthy.

ST COMGAN, ABBOT   (EIGHTH CENTURY)

THE diocese of Aberdeen today keeps the feast of the holy abbot Comgan. He was, it is said, son of Kelly, Prince of Leinster. Comgan succeeded to the authority of his father, which he wielded wisely until he was attacked by neighbouring rulers, defeated in battle, and wounded. He was forced to fly and, taking with him his sister and her children (of whom one became the abbot St Fillan), he crossed over to Scotland. He settled in Lochalsh, opposite Skye, and with seven men who had accompanied him made a monastic settlement there. St Comgan lived an austere life for many years, and after his death was buried on Iona by his nephew Fillan, who also built a church in his honour. This was the first of several which, in various forms, Cowan, Coan, etc., testify to the veneration in which the memory of St Comgan was formerly held in Scotland.

The lessons in the Aberdeen Breviary are reprinted in the *Acta Sanctorum*, October, vol. vi, in default of better material. A. P. Forbes in his KSS. (pp. 310–311) finds little to add, but he supplies a list of churches believed to have been dedicated in honour of St Comgan.

ST GERALD OF AURILLAC   (A.D. 909)

THIS nobleman was born in 855 ; and a lingering illness kept him a long time at home, during which he took so much delight in studies, prayer and meditation that he could never be drawn into the tumult of secular life. He became count of Aurillac after the death of his parents, and he gave a great part of the revenue of his estate to the poor ; he went modestly clad, in a manner suitable to the austere life he led, and kept always a very frugal table. He got up every morning at two o'clock, even on journeys, said the first part of the Divine Office, and then assisted at Mass ; he divided the whole day according to a rule, devoting a great part of it to prayer and reading. St Gerald made a pilgrimage to Rome, and after his return founded at Aurillac a church under the invocation of St Peter, in the place of that of St Clement which his father had built there, together with an abbey which he peopled with monks from Vabres. The monastery afterwards attained considerable fame. St Gerald had some thoughts of himself taking the monastic habit, but was dissuaded by St Gausbert, Bishop of Cahors, who assured him that he would be much more useful in the world, where he devoted himself to the welfare of his dependants and neighbours. For the last seven years of his life he was afflicted with blindness ; he died at Cézenac in Quercy in 909 and was buried at the abbey of Aurillac.

Although Butler has dealt rather summarily with the story of St Gerald, his life in the longer recension, printed in the *Acta Sanctorum*, October, vol. vi, is one of the freshest and most attractive character-sketches which have survived from the period in which he lived. He was the contemporary of another great layman, our own King Alfred, and he was more fortunate than the Anglo-Saxon monarch, in that he had for his biographer the famous St Odo of Cluny. The question of the authorship of the life and its relation to the shorter recension has been convincingly treated by A. Poncelet in the *Analecta Bollandiana*, vol. xiv (1895), pp. 88–107. See also E. Sackur, *Die Cluniacenser*, who shares Poncelet's views, though perhaps upon inadequate data. There is a detailed summary of the life by St Odo in Baudot and Chaussin, *Vies des saints* . . . vol. x (1952), pp. 413–426.

ST COLOMAN, Martyr (A.D. 1012)

IN the beginning of the eleventh century the neighbouring nations of Austria, Moravia and Bohemia were engaged against each other in dissensions and wars. Coloman, a Scot or Irishman who was going on a pilgrimage to Jerusalem, arrived by the Danube from the enemy's country at Stockerau, a town six miles above Vienna. The inhabitants, persuading themselves that he was a spy because, not knowing their language, he could not give a satisfactory account of himself, hanged him, on July 13 in 1012. His patience under unjust sufferings was taken as a proof of the sanctity of Coloman, and it was esteemed to be confirmed by the incorruption of his body, which was said to be the occasion of many miracles. Three years after his death his body was translated to the abbey of Melk. After a time St Coloman came to be venerated as a minor patron of Austria, and a quite imaginary royal ancestry was invented for him. He is the titular of many churches in Austria, Hungary and Bavaria, and is invoked for the help and healing of horses and horned cattle. On his feast the blessing of these animals takes place at Hohenschwangau, near Füssen.

The *vita*, attributed to Erchenfried, Abbot of Melk, has been printed in the *Acta Sanctorum*, October, vol. vi, and has also been edited for Pertz, MGH., *Scriptores*, vol. iv, pp. 675–677. See further Gougaud, *Gaelic Pioneers* (1923), pp. 143–145 and the *Lexikon für Theologie und Kirche*, vol. vi, c. 95. There is no evidence that St Coloman was in a strict sense martyred, and there has never been any formal canonization. On the folk-lore aspects of the case see Bächtold-Stäubli, *Handwörterbuch des deutschen Aberglaubens*, vol. ii, pp. 95–99.

ST MAURICE OF CARNOËT, Abbot (A.D. 1191)

THIS holy monk, who is venerated in the Cistercian Order and throughout Cornouailles, was brought up in the district of Loudéac in Brittany, and though his parents were of a modest state they contrived to get him well educated. He showed considerable ability and a distinguished career was open to him, but he was keenly conscious of the special dangers of life in the world to one of learning and sensibility, and he became a monk at the Cistercian abbey of Langonnet in his own country. He was then about twenty-five years old, the Cistercian reform was in its first fervour, and so wholeheartedly did he throw himself into the life that he surpassed all his fellows and was elected abbot, it is said, only three years after profession. His reputation for prudence and wisdom was not confined to his own monastery. It was with the encouragement of St Maurice that Duke Conan IV undertook to found a new Cistercian monastery and chose the forest of Carnoët for its site, which in accordance with monastic tradition was one which required to be broken into cultivation. Maurice was appointed the first abbot and had governed Carnoët for nearly fifteen years when he died, on September 29, 1191. St Maurice has always had a *cultus* in his order and in the dioceses of Quimper, Vannes and Saint-Brieuc, and Pope Clement XI permitted the Cistercians to observe his feast liturgically, as is done in those dioceses.

There is a longer Latin life which has been printed by Dom Plaine in the *Studien und Mittheilungen Ben. u Cist. Ord.*, vol. vii (1886), pt 1, pp. 380–393, and another more contracted in part 2 *ibid.*, pp. 157–164. A popular account was published by L. Le Cam, *St Maurice, abbé de Langonnet* (1924), and another by A. David (1936).

BD MAGDALEN PANATTIERI, Virgin (A.D. 1503)

MANY have seen in the dress of the Order of Preachers the emblem *par excellence* of loving-kindness and devotion to one's neighbour, and, in the days when such a course of action was common, many assumed the habit of the Dominican third order and lived in their homes a life of usefulness and charity in accordance with that dress. St Catherine of Siena is the outstanding example; Bd Magdalen Panattieri is another. She was born and spent all her life in the little town of Trino-Vercellese in the marquisate of Montferrat, between Piedmont and Lombardy, and before she was twenty bound herself by a vow of celibacy and became a Dominican tertiary in a local chapter of widows and maidens who engaged themselves in works of devotion and benevolence. The life of Bd Magdalen was notably lacking in eventfulness, and she seems to have been spared all external contradiction and persecution, soon becoming a force in her town of Trino. Her care for the poor and young children (in whose favour she seems several times to have acted miraculously) paved the way for her work for the conversion of sinners; she prayed and suffered for them and supplemented her austerities with exhortation and reprimands, especially against the sin of usury. She was a veritable Preacheress and was appointed to give conferences to women and children in a building called the chapel of the Marquis, adjoining the Dominican church; soon the men also, and priests and religious as well, attended and the young novices were taken to hear and profit by her words.

By her efforts the Dominicans were inspired to undertake a more strict observance, and in 1490 Bd Sebastian Maggi came from Milan to inaugurate it at her suggestion. These same friars were involved in a lawsuit with a Milanese councillor, who used his power so oppressively that he was excommunicated from Rome. In the resulting disorder a young man named Bartholomew Perduto publicly slapped Magdalen in the face, and she turned her other cheek and invited him to smack that also, which made him yet more angry. The people of Trino did not fail to attach significance to the fact that Bartholomew came to a violent end before the year was out, and that the Milanese was stricken with disease and died miserably : but to the gentle and forgiving Magdalen these unhappy deaths were an occasion only of sorrow. She seems to have foreseen the calamities that overtook northern Italy during the invasions of the sixteenth century and made several covert references to them; it was afterwards noticed and attributed to her prayers that, when all around was rapine and desolation, Trino was for no obvious reason spared; but not always, for in 1639 the town was bombarded by the Spaniards and Neapolitans and the relics of Bd Magdalen destroyed.

When she knew that she was dying she sent for all her tertiary sisters, and many others pressed into her room. She made her last loving exhortation to them, promising to intercede for them all in eternity, adding, " I could not be happy in

Heaven if you were not there too ". Then she peacefully made an end, while the bystanders were singing the thirtieth psalm. From before the day of her death, October 13, 1503, the grateful people of Trino had venerated Bd Magdalen Panattieri as a saint, a *cultus* that was confirmed by Pope Leo XII.

In the *Auctarium* for October, published as an appendix to the *Acta Sanctorum*, the Bollandists have given a full account of this *beata*, reprinting the life compiled by Marchese in his *Sagro Diario Domenicano*, vol. v. See also J. A. Iricus, *Rerum Patriae Tridinensis libri tres* (1745), and M. C. de Ganay, *Les Bienheureuses Dominicaines* (1924), pp. 355–368. There are other lives in Italian by S. M. Vallaro (1903) and by G. Cereghino (1927), and a summary in Procter, *Lives of the Dominican Saints*, pp. 291–294.

14 : ST CALLISTUS, OR CALIXTUS, I, POPE AND MARTYR (*c*. A.D. 222)

IT is unfortunate that most of what is known of St Callistus I is derived from an unfriendly source. The story of Hippolytus is that, when a young slave, Callistus was put in charge of a bank by his master, a Christian named Carpophorus, and lost the money deposited with him by other Christians : it may be assumed that it was not lost through dishonesty, or Hippolytus would have said so. However, he fled from Rome but was caught at Porto, after jumping into the sea in trying to escape, and was sentenced to the slave's punishment at the mill, a horrible penalty. From this he was released at the request of the creditors, who thought he might be able to recover some of the money, but was rearrested on a charge of brawling in a synagogue—presumably he had tried to collect debts owing by Jews and had carried his importunities into their place of worship. He was sentenced to work in the mines of Sardinia, and here he was when the Christians there were released at the instance of Marcia, a mistress of the Emperor Commodus. This story, and more of it, is doubtless founded on facts, but facts which Hippolytus presented in a very unfavourable light, *e.g.* that when Callistus jumped into the sea he was trying to kill himself.

When St Zephyrinus became pope about the year 199 he made Callistus, who was now enfranchised, superintendent of the public Christian burial-ground on the Via Appia, which is to this day called the cemetery of St Callistus : in a part of it known as the papal crypt all the popes from Zephyrinus to Eutychian were buried, except Cornelius and Callistus himself. He is said to have extended and unified the cemetery, bringing the isolated private portions into communal possession, perhaps the first property in land held by the Church. Zephyrinus also ordained Callistus deacon, and he became the pope's friend and counsellor.

After Callistus himself became pope by the election of a majority of the Roman clergy and people, he was bitterly attacked by St Hippolytus (who was the choice of a faction for the papal chair ; *cf.* August 13), both on doctrinal and disciplinary grounds, especially when, expressly basing himself on the power of binding and loosing, he admitted to communion those who had done public penance for murder, adultery and fornication. The critics of the pope were rigorists, and St Hippolytus is found complaining that St Callistus had ruled that commission of mortal sin was not in itself sufficient reason for deposing a bishop ; that he had admitted the twice or thrice married to the clergy ; that he recognized as legitimate marriages between free women and slaves, contrary to Roman civil law : matters of discipline, for his action in which, and for his opposition to his own theological views, Hippolytus calls Callistus a heretic—but he no longer speaks against his personal character. Actually Callistus condemned the very Sabellius of a modified version of whose heresy Hippolytus accused the pope. St Callistus was a firm upholder of true doctrine and good discipline and, as Abbot Chapman remarked, if more were known about him he would perhaps appear as one of the greatest of the popes.

Although he did not live at a time of persecution there is reason to think that St Callistus I was martyred, perhaps during a popular rising ; but his *acta*, which allege that he was flung down a well, have no authority. He was buried on the Aurelian Way. The chapel of St Callistus *in Trastevere* is possibly the successor of one built by the pope on a piece of ground adjudged to the Christians by Alexander Severus as against some inn-keepers : the emperor declared that any religious rites were better than a tavern.

In the assured faith of the resurrection of the body, the saints in all ages were careful to treat their dead with religious respect, and the practice of the primitive Christians in this respect was remarkable. Julian the Apostate, writing to a pagan pontiff, tells him to notice three things by which he thought Christianity had gained most upon the world, namely, " Their kindness and charity to strangers, their care for the burial of their dead, and the dignity of their carriage ". Their care of the dead did not consist in any extravagant pomp—in which the pagans far outdid them—but in a religious gravity and respect, which was most expressive of their firm hope of a future resurrection.

Very little can be learnt concerning the life of this pope from the *Liber Pontificalis* or from the quite worthless *passio* (in the *Acta Sanctorum*, October, vol. vi). A considerable literature, however, has gathered round those acts of his pontificate which have been mentioned above. It must suffice to indicate two or three notable authorities such as Duchesne, *History of the Early Church*, vol. i ; A. d'Alès, *L'édit de Calliste* (1913) ; and J. Galtier in the *Revue d'histoire ecclésiastique*, vol. xxiii (1927), pp. 465–488. A fuller bibliography may be found in J. P. Kirsch, *Kirchengeschichte*, vol. i (1930), pp. 797–799. On the burial and catacomb of St Callistus consult CMH., pp. 555–556, and DAC., vol. ii, cc. 1657–1754.

ST JUSTUS, BISHOP OF LYONS   (*c*. A.D. 390)

JUSTUS was born in the Vivarais, and whilst he served the church of Vienne as deacon he was advanced to the see of Lyons. His zeal made him severe in reproving everything that deserved reproof, and his attachment to discipline and good order was displayed at the Synod of Valence in the year 374. A council being assembled at Aquileia in 381, St Justus with two other bishops from Gaul assisted at it. The chief affairs there debated regarded the Arians, and St Ambrose, who was present, procured the deposition of two Arian bishops. He had a particular respect for St Justus, as appears from two letters which he addressed to him concerning certain biblical questions.

It happened that at Lyons a man, who had stabbed some persons in the street, took sanctuary in the church ; and St Justus delivered him into the hands of the magistrate's officer upon a promise that the prisoner's life should be spared. Notwithstanding this he was despatched by the populace. The good bishop was apprehensive that he had been accessory to his death and was by that disqualified for the ministry of the altar. Having long desired to serve God in retirement, it is said that he made use of this as a pretext to resign the pastoral charge. The opposition of his flock seemed an obstacle, but his journey to Aquileia afforded him an opportunity. On his return he stole from his friends in the night, and at Marseilles took ship with a lector of his church, named Viator, and sailed to Alexandria. He lived unknown in a monastery in Egypt, until he was discovered by one who came from Gaul to visit the monasteries in the Thebaid, and the church of Lyons sent a priest called Antiochus to urge him to return ; but he was not to be prevailed upon. Antiochus (who succeeded Justus in his see and is himself venerated as a saint, on October 15) determined to bear him company in his solitude, and the saint shortly after died in his arms about the year 390. His body was soon after translated to Lyons and buried in the church of the Machabees which afterwards bore his name. His minister St Viator survived him only a few weeks, and is named in the Roman Martyrology on October 21, and the translation of their bodies together on September 2.

Alban Butler states that the village of Saint Just in Cornwall takes its name from Justus of Lyons. This seems to be a guess, and a poor one : there are two Cornish Saint Justs, in Roseland and in Penwith, but their eponyms have not been identified.

An early Latin life of St Justus is printed in the *Acta Sanctorum*, September, vol. i (under September 2), and there seems no reason to doubt that it is in the main reliable. The fact that Justus is mentioned on five different days in the *Hieronymianum* (see CMH., pp. 566–567) may be taken as satisfactory proof of the interest which his *cultus* inspired. Sidonius Apollinaris in a letter gives a description of the enthusiasm with which crowds flocked to the shrine on his feast-day. Consult also Duchesne, *Fastes Épiscopaux*, vol. ii, p. 162 ; Coville, *Recherches sur l'histoire de Lyon* (1928), pp. 441–445 ; and Leclercq, DAC., vol. x, cc. 191–193.

ST MANECHILDIS, Virgin   (Sixth Century ?)

Sigmarus, *comes* in the Perthois, and his wife had seven daughters, all of whom are venerated as saints in different parts of Champagne ; they were Lintrudis, Amata (Amée), Pusinna, Hoildis, Francula, Libergis and Manechildis (Ménéhould), who was the youngest. They all received the veil of consecrated virgins from St Alpinus, Bishop of Châlons, and Manechildis in particular gave herself to all sorts of spiritual and temporal good works ; she would accompany her father on his visits to Château-sur-Aisne (now called Sainte-Ménéhould), one of the places in his jurisdiction, in order to tend the sick of that place. On the Côte-à-Vignes is a spring said to have been produced miraculously by the saint to quench the thirst of the people who came to her in large numbers when she was at her cell on the side of the mountain. After the death of her parents St Manechildis left her home and sisters to live as a solitary at Bienville on the Marne, and here she died amid the lamentations of the poor and sick whom she had tended.

There seems to be little or nothing to add to the account of the Bollandists who print and comment upon a very short and unconvincing Latin text which cannot be dated.

ST ANGADRISMA, Virgin   (*c.* A.D. 695)

Angadrisma (Angadrême) was brought up under the eye of St Omer, in whose diocese of Thérouanne she lived, and of her cousin St Lambert of Lyons, then a monk at Fontenelle. It was probably his influence and example that helped her to her resolution to become a nun, although her father had promised her in marriage to St Ansbert, the young lord of Chaussy. It is said that Angadrisma asked God to make her so physically repulsive as to put marriage out of the question, and that she was accordingly visited with leprosy. Be that as it may, Ansbert married someone else (later in life he was abbot of Fontenelle and then bishop of Rouen) and Angadrisma received the religious habit from the hands of St Ouen, on which occasion her disease disappeared, leaving her more beautiful than ever. She was an exemplary nun in the convent assigned to her, and was later transferred to a Benedictine monastery called Oroër near Beauvais, of which she became abbess. The prudence of her direction and holiness of life were rewarded by the gift of miracles, in one of which she is said to have stopped an outbreak of fire which threatened to devastate the whole house, by opposing to it the relics of St Ebrulfus, founder of the monastery. She died when over eighty years of age.

In the notice of this saint which appears in the *Acta Sanctorum*, October, vol. vi, the text of the Latin life from which Mabillon quoted (vol. ii, pp. 1016–1018) has not been printed at length. See also the *Vita Ansberti* in MGH., *Scriptores Merov.*, vol. v ; Vacandard, *Vie de S. Ouen*, pp. 191, 192, 204 ; and, for further references, DHG., vol. iii, cc. 3–4.

ST BURCHARD, Bishop of Würzburg   (A.D. 754)

THE priest Burchard left his home in Wessex to be a missionary in Germany, and offered his services to his fellow-countryman St Boniface about the year 732. Before long St Boniface consecrated St Burchard as the first bishop of Würzburg in Franconia, where St Kilian had preached the word of life and suffered martyrdom about fifty years before. This whole country profited by his apostolic labours. In 749 he was appointed by Pepin the Short to go with St Fulrad, Abbot of Saint-Denis, to lay before Pope St Zachary the question of the succession to the throne of the Franks, and brought back a reply favourable to the ambitions of Pepin. Burchard translated St Kilian's relics to the cathedral of St Saviour, to which he attached a school, and he founded the abbey of St Andrew in Würzburg, which afterwards bore his own name. Having exhausted his strength, he resigned his bishopric about 753. Retiring to Homburg on Main, he spent the remaining part of his life there, dying on February 2, probably in 754.

Two medieval Latin lives are preserved and, strange to say, the second, though two or three centuries later and abounding in fictitious incidents, preserves more data of historical value than the other. The former is printed in the *Acta Sanctorum*, October, vol. vi ; the latter, which seems to have been written by Engelhard, who later became abbot of the monastery of St Burchard, has been well edited in a brochure, *Vita sancti Burkardi* (1911), by F. J. Bendel, who has added an introduction and commentary in German. Several articles dealing with St Burchard have been published by Bendel and others in the *Archiv des hist. Vereins von Unterfranken*, notably a paper upon his death in vol. lxviii (1930), pp. 377–385.

ST DOMINIC LORICATUS   (A.D. 1060)

THE severity with which this young man condemned himself to penance for a misdeed which was not his own is a reproach to those who, after offending God with full knowledge and through malice, expect forgiveness without considering the conditions which true repentance requires. Dominic's parents aspired to an ecclesiastical state for their son, and his promotion to the priesthood was obtained by his father from the bishop by means of a present of a goatskin. When the young priest came to the knowledge of this, he was struck with remorse and could not, it is said, be induced again to approach the altar to celebrate Mass or exercise any other sacerdotal office. In Umbria at this time, amidst the Apennine mountains, a holy man called John of Montefeltro led a most austere life as a hermit, with whom in eighteen different cells lived as many disciples. Dominic repaired to this superior, and begged to be admitted into the company of these anchorites. He obtained his request, and by the austerity of his penance gave proof how deep the spirit of sorrow was with which his heart was pierced. After some years he changed his abode, about 1042, retiring to the hermitage of Fonte Avellana, which St Peter Damian then governed.

The abbot, who had been long accustomed to meet with examples of heroic penance, was astonished at this new recruit. Dominic wore next his skin a coat of mail (from which he was surnamed *Loricatus, i.e.* " the Mailed "), and further burdened his limbs with chains : his self-inflicted flagellations, moreover, were so frequent and violent that he seems to have exceeded all measure. He ate as little as was allowed, and then only bread and herbs, with water to drink ; and he slept kneeling on the ground. When he had loaded himself with his cuirass and chains and iron rings he would make numerous prostrations or stand with arms extended cross-wise, until the weight dragging on his limbs proved too much for him. And these practices he continued up to his death, which occurred some years after he had been appointed prior of a hermitage founded by St Peter Damian near San Severino. The last night of his life St Dominic recited Matins and Lauds with his brethren, and died whilst they sang Prime, on October 14, 1060.

Little or nothing is known of this saint beyond what we learn from St Peter Damian. All that is of value has been gathered up in the article devoted to St Dominic in the *Acta Sanctorum*, October, vol. vi. See also A. M. Zimmermann, *Kalendarium benedictinum*, vol. iii (1937), pp. 178–181, and *Annales Camaldulenses*, vol. ii.

15 : ST TERESA OF AVILA, Virgin, Foundress of the Discalced Carmelites (A.D. 1582)

ST TERESA, one of the greatest, most attractive and widely appreciated women whom the world has ever known, and the only one to whom the title doctor of the Church is popularly, though not officially, applied, speaks with loving appreciation of her parents. The one was Alonso Sanchez de Cepeda, the other Beatrice Davila y Ahumada, his second wife, who bore him nine children ; there were three children by his first marriage, and of this large family St Teresa says, " all, through the goodness of God, were like our parents in being virtuous, except myself ". She was born at or near Avila in Castile on March 28, 1515, and when only seven took great pleasure in the lives of the saints, in which she spent much time with a brother called Rodrigo, who was near the same age. They were much impressed by the thought of eternity, and they used to repeat often together, " For ever, for ever, for ever ", admiring the victories of the saints and the ever-lasting glory which they possess ; " For ever they shall see God." The martyrs seemed to them to have bought Heaven very cheaply by their torments, and they resolved to go into the country of the Moors, in hopes of dying for their faith. They set out secretly, praying as they went that they might lay down their lives for Christ. But when they had got as far as Adaja they were met by an uncle, and brought back to their frightened mother, who reprimanded them ; whereupon Rodrigo laid all the blame on his sister.

Teresa and the same little brother then wanted to become hermits at home, and built themselves hermitages with piles of stones in the garden, but could never finish them. Teresa sought to be much alone, and had in her room a picture of our Saviour discoursing with the Samaritan woman at the well, before which she often repeated the words, " Lord, give me of that water that I may not thirst ". Her mother died when she was fourteen, and " as soon as I began to understand how great a loss I had sustained I was very much afflicted ; and so I went before an image of our Blessed Lady and besought her with tears that she would be my mother ". Teresa and Rodrigo began to spend hours reading romances and trying to write them themselves. " These tales ", she says in the *Autobiography*, " did not fail to cool my good desires, and were the cause of my falling insensibly into other defects. I was so enchanted that I could not be content if I had not some new tale in my hands. I began to imitate the fashions, to take delight in being well dressed, to have great care of my hands, to make use of perfumes, and to affect all the vain trimmings which my position in the world allowed." The change in Teresa was sufficiently noticeable to disturb the mind of her father, and he placed his daughter, who was then fifteen, with a convent of Augustinian nuns in Avila where many young women of her rank were educated.

After a year and a half spent in this convent Teresa fell sick, and her father took her home, where she began to deliberate seriously about undertaking the religious life, in regard to which she was moved both by emotional attraction and repulsion. It was by the reading of a book that she was enabled to make up her mind and to fix her will, and this book was, very characteristically, the Letters of St Jerome, whose realism and fire found an answering echo in her Castilian spirit. She told her father that she wished to become a nun, but he would by no means give his consent : after his death she might dispose of herself as she pleased. Fearing she might relapse, though she felt a severe interior conflict in leaving her father, she went secretly to the convent of the Incarnation of the Carmelite nuns outside Avila, where her great friend, Sister Jane Suarez, lived.   " I remember . . . that whilst I was going out of my father's house, I believe the sharpness of sense will not be greater in the very instant or agony of my death than it was then. . . . There was no such love of God in me at that time as was able to quench that love which I bore to my father and my friends." She was then twenty years old and, the step being taken, Don Alonso ceased to oppose it. A year later she was professed. An illness, which seized her before her profession, increased very much after it, and her father got her removed out of her convent. Sister Jane Suarez bore her company, and she remained in the hands of physicians. Their treatment only made her worse (she seems to have been suffering from malignant malaria), and she could take no rest day or night. The doctors gave her up, and she got worse and worse. Under these afflictions she was helped by the prayer which she had then begun to use. Her devout uncle Peter had put into her hands a little book of Father Francis de Osuna, called the *Third Spiritual Alphabet*. Taking this book for her guide she applied herself to mental prayer, but for want of an experienced instructor she made little solid progress. But after three years' suffering Teresa was restored to bodily health.

Her prudence and charity and, not least, her personal charm, gained her the esteem of all that knew her, and an affectionate and grateful disposition inclined her to return the civilities which others showed her. By an irregular custom of her convent quite common in Spain in those days, visitors of all kinds were freely received and mixed with, and Teresa spent much time in conversing with seculars in the parlour of the monastery. She began to neglect mental prayer, and persuaded herself that this was a part of humility, as her unrecollected life rendered her unworthy to converse so much or so familiarly with God. She also said to herself that there could be no danger of sin in what so many others, more virtuous than she, did ; and for her neglect of meditation she alleged the infirmities to which she was subject. But she adds, " This reason of bodily weakness was not a sufficient cause to make me give up so good a thing, which requires not corporal strength, but only love and custom. In the midst of sickness the best of prayer may be made ; and it is a mistake to think that it can only be made in solitude." When her father died his confessor, a Dominican friar, pointed out to Teresa the dangerous state she was in. At his instance she returned to the practice of private prayer and never again abandoned it. But she had not yet the courage to follow God perfectly, or entirely to renounce dissipating her time and gifts. During all these years of wavering and yet of gradually increasing strength and growing purpose, St Teresa tells us she never tired of listening to sermons, " however bad they were " ; but in prayer her thoughts were " more busied about desiring that the hour resolved to be spent in prayer might come quickly to an end, still listening when the clock would strike, than upon better things ". Becoming more and more convinced of her own unworthiness, she had recourse to the two great penitents, St Mary Magdalen and St Augustine, and with them were associated two events decisive in fixing her will upon the pursuit of religious perfection. One was the reading of St Augustine's *Confessions* : the other was a movement to penitence before a picture of our suffering Lord, in which " I felt St Mary Magdalen come to my assistance . . . from that day I have gone on improving much ever since in my spiritual life ".

After she had finally withdrawn herself from the pleasures of social intercourse and other occasions of dissipation and faults (which she exceedingly exaggerated), St Teresa was favoured by God very frequently with the prayer of quiet, and also with that of union, which latter sometimes continued a long time with great increase of joy and love, and God began to visit her with intellectual visions and interior communications. The warning of certain women who had been miserably duped by imagination and the Devil much impressed her and, though she was persuaded her graces were from God, she was perplexed, and consulted so many persons that, though binding them to secrecy, the affair was divulged abroad, to her mortification and confusion. One to whom she spoke was Francis de Salsedo, a married man who was an example of virtue to the whole town. He introduced to her Dr Daza, a learned and virtuous priest, who judged her to be deluded by the Devil, saying that such divine favours were not consistent with a life so full of imperfections as she claimed hers to be. Teresa was alarmed and not satisfied, and Don Francis (to whom the saint says she owed her salvation and her comfort) bade her not to be discouraged. He recommended that she should consult one of the fathers of the newly-formed Society of Jesus, to whom she made a general confession in which, with her sins, she gave him an account of her manner of prayer and her extraordinary favours. The father assured her these were divine graces, but told her she had neglected to lay the true foundation of in interior life. On his advice, though he judged her experiences in prayer to be from God, she endeavoured for two months to resist and reject them. But her resistance was in vain.

Another Jesuit, Father Balthasar Alvarez, told her she would do well to beg of God that He would direct her to do what was most pleasing to Him, and for that purpose to recite every day the *Veni Creator Spiritus*. She did so, and one day whilst she was saying that hymn she was seized with a rapture, in which she heard these words spoken to her within her soul, " I will not have you hold conversation with men, but with angels ". The saint afterwards had frequent experience of such interior speeches and explains how they are even more distinct and clear than those which men hear with their bodily ears, and how they are also operative, producing in the soul the strongest impressions and sentiments of virtue, and filling her with an assurance of their truth, with joy and with peace. Whilst Father Alvarez was her director she suffered grievous persecutions for three years and, during two of them, extreme desolation of soul intermixed with gleams of spiritual comfort and enlightenment. It was her desire that all her heavenly communications should be kept secret, but they became a common subject in conversation and she was censured and ridiculed as deluded or an hypocrite. Father Alvarez, who was a good man but timorous, durst not oppose the tide of disapproval, though he continued to hear her confessions. In 1557 St Peter of Alcantara came to Avila, and of course visited the now famous, or notorious, Carmelite. He declared that nothing appeared to him more evident than that her soul was conducted by the Spirit of God ; but he foretold that she was not come to an end of her persecutions and sufferings. If the various proofs by which it pleased God to try Teresa served to purify her virtue, the heavenly communications with which she was favoured served to humble and fortify her soul, to give her a strong disrelish of the things of this life, and to fire her with the desire of possessing God. In raptures she was sometimes lifted in the air, of which she gives a careful description, and adds that God " seems not content with drawing the soul to Himself, but He must needs draw up the very body too, even whilst it is mortal and compounded of so unclean a clay as we have made it by our sins ". During these raptures or ecstasies the greatness and goodness of God, the excess of His love, the sweetness of His service, are placed in a great light and made sensibly manifest to the soul ; all which she understands with a clearness which can be in no way expressed. The desire of Heaven with which these visions inspired St Teresa could not be declared. " Hence also ", she says, " I lost the fear of death, of which I had formerly a great apprehension." During this time took place such extraordinary manifestations as spiritual espousals, mystical marriage, and the piercing (*transverberatio*) of the saint's heart.

Of this last she gives the following account : " I saw an angel close by me, on my left side, in bodily form. This I am not accustomed to see, unless very rarely. Though I have visions of angels frequently, yet I see them only by an intellectual vision, such as I have spoken of before. . . . He was not large, but small of stature, and most beautiful—his face burning, as if he were one of the highest angels, who seem to be all of fire : they must be those whom we call cherubim [*sic*]. . . . I saw in his hand a long spear of gold, and at the iron's point there seemed to be a little fire. He appeared to me to be thrusting it at times into my heart, and to pierce my very entrails ; when he drew it out, he seemed to draw them out also, and to leave me all on fire with a great love of God. The pain was so great that it made me moan ; and yet so surpassing was the sweetness of this excessive pain that I could not wish to be rid of it."* The saint's desire to die that she might be

---

* The proper of the Mass on August 27 in which the Carmelites commemorate this happening admirably illustrates the Church's attitude to mystical experiences of this sort, in striking contrast with the naturalism of Bernini's statue of the same subject in the church of Santa Maria della Vittoria at Rome.

speedily united to God was tempered by her desire to suffer for His love, and she writes, " It seems to me there is no reason why I should live but only to suffer, and accordingly this is the thing which I beg with most affection of God. Sometimes I say to Him · ıth my whole heart : Lord, either to die or to suffer ; I beg no other thing for myself." After the death of St Teresa her heart was found to bear a long and deep mark, as it were a scar ;* and her response to this remarkable happening was in the following year (1560) to make a vow that she would in everything do always that which seemed to be the most perfect and best pleasing to God. To bind oneself by vow to such an undertaking is an action so humanly rash that it can only be justified by the successful keeping of it. St Teresa kept her vow.

The account which this saint has given in her *Autobiography* of these visions, revelations and raptures carries with it the intrinsic marks of evidence. It is not possible attentively to peruse it and not be convinced of the sincerity of the author, by the genuine simplicity of the style, scrupulous care, and fear of exaggerating, characteristics which appear in all her writings. Her doctrine is called by the Church, in the prayer of her festival, *caelestis*, " heavenly ". In it secret places of the soul are laid open. The most elusive matters, which experience alone can teach but no words utter, are explained with greater perspicuity than the subject seems capable of bearing ; and this was done by a relatively uneducated woman, in the straightforward vernacular of Castile, which she had learnt " in her mother's womb ", the rough tongue of the folk of Avila ; a woman who wrote alone, without the assistance of books, without study or acquired abilities, who entered upon the recital of divine things with reluctance, submitting everything without reserve to the judgement of her confessor, and much more to that of the Church, and complaining that by this task she was hindered from spinning. She undertook to write about herself only out of obedience to her confessor : " Obedience is put to the test in different commands ", she said. And nothing seems a clearer proof how perfectly St Teresa was imbued with sincere humility than the artless manner in which she constantly, and not on certain occasions only, speaks of herself with depreciation. When she was attacked at Seville and someone asked her how she could hold her peace, she answered with a smile, " No music is so pleasing to my ears. They have reason for what they say, and speak the truth." Her patience under sickness, provocation and disappointment ; her firm confidence in God and in her crucified Redeemer under all storms and difficulties ; and her undaunted courage in bearing incredible hardship and persecution and dangers are a practical commentary on the words. The necessity of the spirit of prayer, the way it is practised, and the nature of its fruits are set out incomparably in her writings. These works were written during the years in which she was actively engaged in the most difficult business of founding convents of reformed Carmelite nuns and thus, quite apart from their nature and contents, are significant of St Teresa's vigour, industry and power of recollection. She wrote the *Way of Perfection* for the direction of her nuns, and the book of *Foundations* for their edification and encouragement, but the *Interior Castle* may be said to have been written for the instruction of the Church. In it she is a doctor of the spiritual life.

* " Je suis d'accord . . . que sainte Thérèse est bien morte d'un transport d'amour. Quant à la blessure indiquée à l'emplacement de l'artère coronaire . . . il est permis de penser que, tout en ayant été causée par l'élan d'amour surnaturel décrit par st Jean de la Croix, des symptômes réels de fatigue . . . ainsi qu'il est attesté, témoignent d'une disposition favorable à la dilatation du myocarde et à sa rupture."—Dr Jean Lhermitte, in *Études Carmélitaines*, 1936, vol. ii, p. 242.

The Carmelite nuns, and indeed those of other orders as well, were very much relaxed from their early austerity and enthusiasm in sixteenth-century Spain. We have seen how the parlour at Avila was a sort of social centre for the ladies and gentlemen of the town, and that the nuns went out of their enclosure on the slightest pretext ; those who wanted an easy and sheltered life without responsibilities could find it in a convent. The size of the communities was both a cause and an effect of this mitigation ; there were 140 nuns in the convent at Avila, and the result afterwards wrung from St Teresa the cry, " Experience has taught me what a house full of women is like. God preserve us from such a state ! " This state of things was taken for granted, there was no rebuking consciousness among religious at large that the nature of their daily life fell far short of what was required by their profession according to the mind of their founders, so that when a Carmelite of the Incarnation house at Avila, her niece, began to talk of the possibility of the foundation of a small community bound to a more perfect way of life the idea struck St Teresa not as a very natural one but as an inspiration from Heaven. She had been a nun for 25 years : she now determined to undertake the establishment of such a reformed convent, and received a promise of immediate help from a wealthy widow, Doña Guiomar de Ulloa. The project was approved by St Peter of Alcantara, St Louis Bertrand, and the Bishop of Avila, and Teresa procured the licence and approbation of Father Gregory Fernandez, prior provincial of the Carmelites ; but no sooner had the project taken shape than he was obliged by the objections which were raised to recall his licence. A storm fell upon Teresa through the violent opposition which was made by her fellow nuns, the nobility, the magistrates and the people. Father Ibañez, a Dominican, secretly encouraged her, and assisted Doña Guiomar to pursue the enterprise, together with Doña Juana de Ahumada, a married sister of the saint, who began with her husband to build a new convent at Avila in 1561, but in such a manner that the world took it for a house intended for herself and her family. Their son Gonzalez, a little child, was crushed by a wall which fell upon him while playing around this building, and he was carried without giving any signs of life to Teresa, who, taking him in her arms, prayed to God and after some minutes restored him perfectly sound to his mother, as was proved in the process of the saint's canonization. The child used afterwards often to tell his aunt that it was her duty to forward his salvation by her prayers, seeing it was owing to her that he was not long ago in Heaven.

Eventually a brief arrived from Rome authorizing the establishment of the new convent. St Peter of Alcantara, Don Francis de Salsedo and Dr Daza had persuaded the bishop to concur, the new monastery of St Joseph was set up by his authority, and on St Bartholomew's day in 1562 was made subject to him, Mass being celebrated in the chapel and the saint's niece and three other novices taking the habit. Hereupon great excitement broke out in the town. That very afternoon the prioress of the Incarnation sent for Teresa from St Joseph's, and she went in some trepidation, " thinking they would certainly put me in prison ". She had to give an explanation of her conduct before the prioress and Father Angel de Salazar, the prior provincial, in which, she admits, they had a certain case against her. However, Father Angel promised she should return to St Joseph's when the popular excitement had died down. The people of Avila looked on the new foundation as uncalled for, were nervous of suspicious novelties, and feared that an unendowed convent would be too heavy a burden on the town. The mayor and magistrates would have had the new monastery demolished, had not Father Bañez, a Dominican, dissuaded them from so hasty a resolution. Amidst slanders and persecution the saint remained calm, recommending to God His own work, and was comforted by our Lord in a vision. In the meantime Francis de Salsedo and other friends of the new establishment deputed a priest to go before the royal council to plead for the convent, the two Dominicans, Ibañez and Bañez, reasoned with the bishop and the provincial, the public clamour abated, and at the end of four months Father Angel sent Teresa to the new convent, whither she was followed by four other nuns from the old house.

Strict enclosure was established with almost perpetual silence, and the most austere poverty, at first without any settled revenues ; the nuns wore habits of coarse serge, sandals instead of shoes (whence they are called " discalced "), and were bound to perpetual abstinence. At first St Teresa would not admit more than thirteen nuns to a community, but in those which should be founded with revenues, and not to subsist solely on alms, she afterwards allowed twenty-one. The prior general of the Carmelites, John Baptist Rubeo (Rossi), came to Avila in 1567, and was charmed with the foundress and the wise regulations of the house. He gave St Teresa full authority to found other convents upon the same plan, in spite of the fact that St Joseph's had been established without his knowledge or leave, and she even received from him a licence for the foundation of two houses of reformed friars (" Contemplative Carmelites ") in Castile. St Teresa passed five years in her convent of St Joseph with thirteen nuns, being herself the first and most diligent, not only at prayer but also in spinning, sweeping the house or any other work. " I think that they were the most quiet years of my life ", she writes. " I there enjoyed the tranquillity and calmness which my soul has often since longed for. . . . His divine Majesty sent us what was necessary without asking, and if at any time we were in want (which was very seldom) the joy of these holy souls was so much the greater." She is not content with vague generalities, but records such enticing details as of the nun who obediently planted the cucumber horizontally and of the water which was piped into the house from a source that the plumbers said was too low.

In August 1567 Teresa went to Medina del Campo and, having conquered many difficulties, founded there a second convent. The Countess de la Cerda earnestly desired to found a convent of this order at her town of Malagon, and Teresa went to see her about it, incidentally paying a visit to Madrid which she describes as " boring ". When this convent was safely launched she went to Valladolid and there founded another. St Teresa made her next foundation at Toledo. She met great obstacles, and had no more than four or five ducats when she began. But she said, " Teresa and this money are indeed nothing : but God, Teresa and these ducats suffice ". Here a young woman who had gained a reputation of virtue petitioned to be admitted to the habit, and added, " I will bring my Bible with me."—" What ! " said the saint, " your Bible ? Do not come to us. We are poor women who know nothing but how to spin and to do as we are told." At Medina del Campo she had met with two Carmelite friars who were desirous to embrace her reform, Antony-of-Jesus (de Heredia), then prior there, and John Yepes (afterwards John-of-the-Cross). As soon, therefore, as an opportunity offered itself she founded a convent for men at a village called Duruelo in 1568, and in 1569 a second at Pastrana, both in extreme poverty and austerity. After these two foundations St Teresa left to St John-of-the-Cross the care of all other foundations that should be made for men. At Pastrana she also established a nunnery. When Don Ruy Gomez de Silva, who had founded these houses at Pastrana, died, his widow wished to make her religious profession there, but claimed many exemptions and would still maintain the dignity of princess. Teresa, finding she could not be brought to the humility of her profession, ordered the nuns, lest relaxations should be introduced, to leave that house to her and retire to a new one in Segovia. In 1570 St Teresa founded a convent at Salamanca where with another nun she took possession of a house which had been occupied by some students, who had had " little or no regard for cleanliness ". It was a large, rambling and eerie place, and when night fell the other nun became very nervous. As they lay down on their piles of straw (" the first furniture I provided when I founded monasteries, for having this I reckoned I had beds "), St Teresa asked her what she was looking about at. " I was wondering ", was the reply, " were I to die here now what would you do alone with a corpse ? " St Teresa admits the remark startled her, for, though she did not fear dead bodies, they always caused her " a pain at her heart ". But she only replied, " I will think about that when it happens, sister. For the present, let us go to sleep." In July of this year she had a revelation while at prayer of the martyrdom at sea of Bd Ignatius Azevedo and his companions of the Society of Jesus, among whom was her own relative, Francis Perez Godoy. She had a clear vision as it were both to her eyes and ears of what took place and she at once told it in detail to Father Balthasar Alvarez. When the news of the massacre reached Spain a month later, he recognized the minute accuracy of the account already given to him by St Teresa.

At this time Pope St Pius V appointed visitors apostolic to inquire into relaxations in religious orders with a view to reform, and he named a well-known Dominican, Peter Fernandez, to be visitor to the Carmelites of Castile. At Avila he not surprisingly found great fault with the convent of the Incarnation, and to remedy its abuses he sent for St Teresa and told her she was to take charge of it as prioress. It was doubly distasteful to her to be separated from her own daughters and to be put from outside at the head of a house which opposed her activities with jealousy and warmth. The nuns at first refused to obey her ; some of them went into hysterics at the very idea. She told them that she came not to coerce or instruct but to serve, and to learn from the least among them. " My mothers and sisters, our Lord has sent me to this house by the voice of obedience, to fill an office of which I was far from thinking and for which I am quite unfitted. . . . I come solely to serve you. . . . Do not fear my rule. Though I have lived among and exercised authority over those Carmelites who are discalced, by God's mercy I know how to rule those who are not of their number." Having won the sympathy and affection of the community, she had less difficulty in establishing discipline according to its rules. Too frequent callers were forbidden (to the annoyance of certain gentlemen of Avila), the finances of the house were put in order, and a more truly claustral spirit reigned—a characteristically Teresian performance. When making a foundation at Veas St Teresa met for the first time Father Jerome Gracián, and was easily persuaded by him to extend her activities to Seville ; he had just preached the Lent there, and was himself a friar of the reform. With the exception of the first, no one of her convents was so hard to establish as this. Among the difficulties was a disappointed novice who delated the new nuns to the Inquisition as *Illuminati*, and worse.

The Carmelite friars in Italy had, in the meantime, become afraid of the progress of the Spanish reform lest, as one of their number said, they should one day be compelled to set about reforming themselves, a fear which was shared by their mitigated brethren in Spain. The prior general, Father Rubeo, who had hitherto favoured St Teresa, now sided with the objectors and upheld a general chapter at Plasencia which passed several decrees gravely restricting the reform. The new nuncio apostolic, Philip de Sega, dismissed Father Gracián from his office of visitor to the Discalced Carmelites, and St John-of-the-Cross was imprisoned in a monastery ; St Teresa herself was told to choose one of her convents to which to retire and to abstain from further foundations. While recommending her undertaking to God, she did not disdain to avail herself of the help of her friends in the world. These interested the king, Philip II, on her behalf, and he warmly espoused her cause. The nuncio was called before him and sternly rebuked for his activities against the discalced friars and nuns, and in 1580 an order was obtained at Rome to exempt the Reformed from the jurisdiction of the mitigated Carmelites, so that each should have their own provincial. Father Gracián was elected for the Reformed. " The separation has given me one of the greatest pleasures and consolations I could receive in this life, for the order has had to endure more troubles, persecutions and trials in twenty-five years than I have space to tell. Now we are all at peace, Calced and Discalced, having no one to disturb us in the service of our Lord."

St Teresa was certainly endowed with great natural talents. The sweetness of her temperament, the affectionate tenderness of her heart, and the liveliness of her wit and imagination, poised by an uncommon maturity of judgement and what we should now call psychological insight, gained the respect of all and the love of most. It was no mere flight of fancy which caused the poet Crashaw to refer both to " the eagle " and to " the dove " in St Teresa. She stood up when need be to high authorities, ecclesiastical and civil, and would not bow her head under the blows of the world. It was no hysterical defiance when she bade the prior provincial, Father Angel, " Beware of fighting against the Holy Ghost " ; it was no authoritarian conceit that made her merciless to a prioress who had made herself unfit for her duties by her austerities. It is as the dove that she writes to her erring nephew, " God's mercy is great in that you have been enabled to make so good a choice and to marry so soon, for you began to be dissipated when you were so young that we might have had much sorrow on your account. From that you see how much I love you." She took charge of this young man's illegitimate daughter, and of his sister, who was seven years old : " We ought always to have a child of this age among us." Her wit and " forthrightness " were sublimely good-tempered, even when she used them, as sword or hammer, to drive in a rebuke. When an indiscreet man praised the beauty of her bare feet she laughed and told him to have a good look at them for he would never see them again. " You know what a number of women are when they get together ", or " My children, these are just women's fads ", she would say when her subjects were fussy and tiresome. In criticizing an essay by her good friend Francis de Salsedo she was quick to point out that " Señor de Salsedo keeps on repeating throughout his paper : ' As St Paul says ', ' As the Holy Ghost says ', and ends up by declaring he has written nothing but nonsense. I shall denounce him to the Inquisition." The quality of St Teresa is seen very clearly in her selection of novices for the new foundations. Her first requirement, even before any promise of a considerable degree of piety, was intelligence. A person can train herself to piety, but more hardly to intelligence, by which quality she meant neither cleverness nor imagination, but a power of good judgement. " An intelligent mind is simple and submissive ; it sees its faults and allows itself to be guided. A mind that is deficient and narrow never sees its faults, even when shown them. It is always pleased with itself and never learns to do right." " Even though our Lord should give this young girl devotion and teach her contemplation, if she has no sense she never will come to have any, and instead of being of use to the community she will be a burden." " May God preserve us from stupid nuns ! " Nobody was ever less sentimental.

By the time of the separation between the two observances of the Carmelite Order in 1580 St Teresa was sixty-five years old and quite broken in health. During her last two years she saw her final foundations, making them seventeen in all : foundations that had been made not only to provide homes of contemplation for individuals but as a work of reparation for the destruction of so many monasteries by Protestantism, notably in the British Isles and Germany. A cruel trial was reserved for her last days. The will of her brother Don Lorenzo, whose daughter was prioress at Valladolid, was in dispute and St Teresa was drawn unwillingly into the proceedings. A lawyer was rude to her, and to him she said, " Sir, may God return to you the courtesy you have shown to me ". But before the conduct of her niece she was speechless and impotent : for the prioress of Valladolid, hitherto an irreproachable religious, showed her aunt the door of the convent of which she was foundress and told her never more to return to it. St Teresa wrote to Mother Mary-of-St-Joseph, " I beseech you and your daughters not to wish or pray for me to live longer. Ask on the contrary that I may go to my eternal rest, for I can be of no more use to you." The last foundation, at Burgos, was made under difficulties, and when it was achieved in July 1582 St Teresa wished to return to Avila, but was induced to set out for Alba de Tormes, where the Duchess Maria Henriquez was expecting her. Bd Anne-of-St-Bartholomew describes the journey, not properly prepared for and the foundress so ill that she fainted on the road ; one night they could get no food but a few figs, and when they arrived at Alba St Teresa went straight to bed. Three days later she said to Bd Anne, " At last, my daughter, the hour of death has come ". She received the last sacraments from Father Antony de Heredia, who asked her where she wished to be buried. She only answered, " Is it for me to say ? Will they deny me a little ground for my body here ? " When the Blessed Sacrament was brought in she sat up in bed, helpless though she was, and exclaimed, " O my Lord, now is the time that we may see each other ! " Apparently in wonder at the things her Saviour was showing her, St Teresa-of-Jesus died in the arms of Bd Anne at nine in the evening of October 4, 1582. The very next day the Gregorian reform of the kalendar came into force and ten days were dropped, so that it was accounted October 15, the date on which her feast was ultimately fixed. Her body was buried at Alba de Tormes, and there it remains. She was canonized in 1622.

Although the history of St Teresa in the *Acta Sanctorum* occupies almost the whole of a very stout folio volume (October, vol. vii), and although it was compiled by Father Van der Moere less than a century ago, its contents have to a considerable extent been superseded by better edited texts and by fresh material which has since come to light. Amongst the most important sources of all must always be reckoned the *Autobiography* and the *Book of Foundations*. Both these have been printed in a photographic facsimile from St Teresa's own autograph (1873 and 1880). For scholarly use all her work and correspondence have now been critically edited in Spanish by Father Silverio, and occupy nine volumes ; six of Works (1915–19) and three of Letters (1922–24). Nearly all this material, though often translated from less accurate texts, had previously been accessible both in French and in English, David Lewis, Father Benedict Zimmerman, and the Benedictine nuns of Stanbrook having in this matter rendered great service to English readers. From Fr Silverio's edition Prof. E. Allison Peers made a new English translation of the Works (3 vols., 1946) and the Letters (2 vols., 1951). Lewis's version of the *Autobiography* was reissued in U.S.A. in 1943. For our knowledge of the character and activities of St Teresa we are also much indebted to her early biographers, notably to three who knew her intimately in her later years. The first was Father Francis de Ribera. The life he wrote was printed in 1590 ; the best edition is that of Father Jaime Pons (1908). Another biography was published (1599) by Diego de Yepes, who was also keenly interested in the sufferings of the English Catholics and became bishop of Tarragona. The third was written by St Teresa'a chaplain, Julian of Avila, but the manuscript having been lost sight of, it was only discovered and printed in 1881. Besides these, much information is obtainable from the writings and letters of such friends of the saint as Father Jerome Gracián, Bd Anne-of-St-Bartholomew, and many others. An English translation of the Autobiography by " W. M." was printed at Antwerp as early as 1611 ; but better from a literary point of view is Sir Tobie Mathew's version, which appeared in 1623 under the title of *The Flaming Heart ; or, The Life of the Glorious St Teresa*. A fuller account, which included some of the saint's writings, began to appear (1669) in more than one volume and was due to Abraham Woodhead. In more modern times we have the *Life and Letters of St Theresa* (3 vols.), by H. J. Coleridge ; G. Cunninghame Graham, *Santa Teresa* (1907) ; J. J. Burke, *St Teresa of Jesus* (1911 ; noteworthy for its illustrations of the saint's foundations) ; W. T. Walsh, *St Teresa of Avila* (1942) ; V. Sackville West, *The Eagle and the Dove* (1943) ; E. A. Peers, *Mother of Carmel* (1945) ; a short life by Fr Silverio (Eng. trans., 1947), and others by Kate O'Brien (1951) and M. Auclair (Eng. trans., 1952). Fr Gabriel's *St Teresa of Jesus* (Eng. trans., 1950) provides an introduction to her writings. To give a catalogue of the shorter biographies, or of those published in French, Spanish and Italian, would be endless. Reference, however, must be made to R. Hoornaert, *Ste Thérèse écrivain* (Eng. trans., 1931) and his *Ste Thérèse d'Avila* (1951), and to G. Etchegoyen, *L'amour divin . . .* (1953). See also the *Studies of the Spanish Mystics* and *St Teresa of Jesus and Other Essays* (1923) of Professor Peers.

ST LEONARD OF VANDŒUVRE, Abbot   (*c.* A.D. 570)

IN a footnote to his account of St Leonard of Noblac, Alban Butler refers to his contemporary and namesake of Vandœuvre, who introduced monastic life into the valley of the Sarthe. Wandering into Maine in search of solitude, he came to Vandœuvre on the banks of the river and settled at where is now Saint-Léonard-des-Bois. He was befriended by St Innocent, Bishop of Le Mans and a great encourager of monks, and soon Leonard had a number of followers under his direction. There were some who were ill-disposed towards the new monastery, and these reported to King Clotaire I that Leonard was persuading the king's subjects to alienate their goods and withdraw themselves from their service, claiming plenary authority over them himself. Clotaire sent commissioners to inquire into the matter, and at the very moment of their arrival they witnessed a young nobleman abandon his estate and receive the monastic habit. The commissioners pointed out that in this way the king was being deprived of valuable men-at-arms. St Leonard answered them by saying that he only taught people to put into practice the words of our Lord Himself, that all things and all earthly ties should be given up to follow Him. The envoys had nothing to say to this and went back to report to Clotaire, who in time withdrew his opposition and even became a patron of St Leonard and his abbey. Among the friends of this saint was Innocent's successor at Le Mans, St Domnolus, in whose arms Leonard died at a great age about the year 570.

In the *Acta Sanctorum*, October, vol. vii, a short life is printed with the usual commentary. See also DCB., vol. iii, pp. 686–687.

ST THECLA OF KITZINGEN, VIRGIN (*c.* A.D. 790)

ST THECLA, whom the Roman Martyrology names today, was one of the nuns sent by St Tetta, abbess of Wimborne, into Germany to help in the mission of St Boniface. She probably went at the same time as her kinswoman St Lioba, under whom she certainly was for a time at the abbey of Bischofsheim, until St Boniface made her abbess of Ochsenfurt. At the death of St Hadeloga, foundress and first abbess of the nunnery of Kitzingen on the Main, St Thecla was called to preside over that house as well, which she did for many years with conspicuous devotion and holiness. The name Thecla does not appear in the extant list of abbesses of Kitzingen, but it would seem that she is referred to under the name of Heilga, that is, " the Saint ". Both to her spiritual children and to the rough German women among whom they lived the holy abbess ever gave an example of humility, gentleness and charity. During the Peasants' War of the sixteenth century the relics of St Thecla and her predecessors in the abbey church were shamefully abused and scattered from their shrines.

The Bollandists in the *Acta Sanctorum*, October, vol. vii, have brought together a few scattered references to this abbess.

ST EUTHYMIUS THE YOUNGER, ABBOT (A.D. 898)

THIS holy monk was a Galatian, born at Opso, near Ancyra. He is called " the Thessalonian " because he was eventually buried at Salonika, or " the New " or " Younger ", apparently to distinguish him from St Euthymius the Great who lived four hundred years earlier. Euthymius at his baptism received the name of Nicetas. At an early age he married, and had a daughter Anastasia, but when he was still only eighteen, in the year 842, he left his wife and child (in circumstances that, as reported, look curiously like desertion) and entered a *laura* on Mount Olympus in Bithynia. For a time he put himself under the direction of St Joannicius, who was then a monk there, and afterwards of one John, who gave him the name of Euthymius. When he had trained him for a time, John sent him to lead the common life in the monastery of the Pissidion, where Euthymius advanced rapidly in the ways of holiness.

When the patriarch of Constantinople, St Ignatius, was removed from his see and Photius succeeded in 858, the abbot Nicholas was loyal to Ignatius and was deposed from his office ; Euthymius took the opportunity to seek a less troubled life in the solitudes of Mount Athos. Before leaving Olympus he asked for and received the " great habit ", the outward sign of the highest degree to which the Eastern monk can aspire, from an ascetic named Theodore. Euthymius was accompanied by one companion, but he was frightened away by the rigours of Athos, and Euthymius sought the company of a hermit already established there, one Joseph. He was a good and straightforward soul, in spite of the fact that he was an Armenian (says the biographer of St Euthymius), and soon the two hermits were engaged in a sort of competitive trial of asceticism. First they fasted for forty days on nothing but vegetables. Then Euthymius suggested that they should stop in their cells for three years, going outside only to gather their nuts and herbs, never speaking to the other hermits and only rarely to one another. At the end of the first year Joseph gave it up, but Euthymius persevered to the end of the period, and when he came out of his seclusion was warmly congratulated by the other brethren. In 863 he was at Salonika, visiting the tomb of Theodore, who before his death had made a vain attempt to join his disciple on Athos. While in Salonika St Euthymius lived for a time on a hollow tower, from whence he could preach to the crowds who came to him and use his power of exorcism over those who were possessed, while keeping something of the solitude which he loved. Before leaving the city he was ordained deacon. So many visitors came to him on Mount Athos that he fled with two other monks to the small island of Saint Eustratius ; when they were driven out of here by sea-rovers Euthymius rejoined his old friend Joseph and remained with him.

Some time after the death of Joseph St Euthymius was told in a vision that he had contended as a solitary long enough ; he was to move once more, this time to a mountain called Peristera on the east of Salonika. There he would find the ruins of a monastery dedicated in honour of St Andrew, now used for folding sheep : he was to restore and re-people it. Taking with him two monks, Ignatius and Ephrem, he went straight to the place and found as it had been said. At once he set about rebuilding the church and dwellings were also made for the monks, who rapidly increased in number and fervour, and St Euthymius was their abbot for fourteen years. Then he paid a visit to his home at Opso and gained there a number of recruits, male and female, including some of his own family. Another monastery was built for the women ; and when both houses were thoroughly established St Euthymius handed them over to the metropolitan of Salonika and went to pass the rest of his days in the solitude of Athos once more. When he knew that death was approaching he summoned his fellow-hermits to celebrate with him the feast of the translation of his patron St Euthymius the Great ; then, having said farewell to them, he departed with the monk George to Holy Island, where five months later he died peacefully on October 15 in the year 898.

The life of St Euthymius was written by one of his monks at Peristera, Basil by name, who became metropolitan of Salonika. He narrates several miracles of his master, of some of which he was himself a witness and even a beneficiary, and as an example of the saint's gift of prophecy he tells how, while he was in retreat after having been shorn a monk, Euthymius came to him and said, " Though I am utterly unworthy to receive enlightenment from on high, nevertheless, as I am responsible for your direction, God has shown me that love of learning will draw you from the monastery and you will be made an archbishop."—" And later ", says Basil, " the call of ambition made me choose the noisy and troubled life of a town before the peace of solitude."

The name of this St Euthymius does not seem to occur in the synaxaries and, except for a reference under October 15 in Martynov's *Annus ecclesiasticus graeco-slavicus*, his existence was hardly known in the West until Louis Petit published the Greek text of the life in the *Revue de l'Orient chrétien*, vol. vi (1903), pp. 155–205 and 503–536. The life, with the Greek office for the feast, was also published separately in 1904. The reference to the " hollow tower " which he occupied at Salonika shows, as Delehaye points out (*Les Saints Stylites*, pp. cxxix–cxxx), that Euthymius was at one time a " stylite ". See also E. von Dobschütz in the *Byzantinische Zeitschrift*, vol. xviii (1909), pp. 715–716.

16 : ST HEDWIG, Widow   (A.D. 1243)

HEDWIG (Jadwiga) was a daughter of Berthold, Count of Andechs, and was born at Andechs in Bavaria about the year 1174 ; through her sister Gertrude she was aunt to St Elizabeth of Hungary.   She was placed when very young in the monastery of Kitzingen in Franconia, and taken thence when twelve years old to marry Henry, Duke of Silesia, who was then eighteen.   They had seven children, of whom only one, Gertrude, survived her mother, and she became abbess of Trebnitz.   Her husband succeeded to his father's dukedom in 1202, and he at once at Hedwig's persuasion founded the great monastery of Cistercian nuns at Trebnitz, three miles from Breslau.   To construct the building it is said that all malefactors in Silesia, instead of other punishments, were condemned to work at it.   This was the first convent of women in Silesia,* and the first of a large number of monastic establishments by the foundation of which the duke and duchess both aided the religious life of their people and spread a Germanic culture over their territories.   Among them were houses of Augustinian canons, Cistercian monks, Dominican and Franciscan friars.   Henry established the hospital of the Holy Ghost in Breslau and Hedwig one for female lepers at Neumarkt, in which they took a close personal interest.   After the birth of her last child in 1209 Hedwig engaged her husband to agree to a mutual vow of continence, from which time they lived to a considerable extent in different places.   Her husband, we are told, for the thirty years that he lived afterwards, never wore gold, silver or purple, and never shaved his beard, from which he was named Henry the Bearded.

Their children were the occasions of a good deal of trouble for them.   For example, in 1212 Duke Henry made a partition of his estates between his sons Henry and Conrad, but on terms dissatisfying to them.   The two brothers with their factions came to an open rupture, and, notwithstanding their mother's efforts to reconcile them, a battle was fought, in which Henry routed his younger brother's army.   This was one of those crosses by which the duchess learned more bitterly to deplore the miseries and blindness of the world, and more perfectly to disengage her heart from its slavery.   After 1209 she made her principal residence near Trebnitz monastery, often retiring into that austere house, where she slept in the dormitory and complied with all the exercises of the community.   She wore the same cloak and tunic summer and winter, and underneath them a hair-shift, with sleeves of white serge that it might not be seen.   With going to church barefoot over ice and snow her feet were often blistered and chilblained, but she carried shoes under her arm, to put on if she met anyone.   An abbot once gave her a new pair, insisting that she should wear them, which she promised to do.   When he met her some time after she was still unshod, and he asked what had become of them.   Hedwig produced them from under her cloak, brand-new.   " I always wear them there ", she said.

In 1227 Duke Henry and Duke Ladislaus of Sandomir met to plan defence against Swatopluk of Pomerania.   They were unexpectedly attacked by Swatopluk, and Henry was surprised in his bath, barely escaping with his life.   St Hedwig

---

* It was suppressed and secularized in 1810, and the estate came to Prince Blücher after Waterloo.

hurried to nurse him, but he was soon in the field again, fighting with Conrad of Masovia for the territories of Ladislaus, who had been killed. Henry was successful and established himself at Cracow, but he was again surprised, this time while at Mass, and was carried off by Conrad to Plock. The faithful Hedwig followed, and induced the two dukes to come to terms, her two grand-daughters being promised in marriage to Conrad's sons. Thus the intervention of Henry's forces was rendered unnecessary, to the great joy of St Hedwig, who could never hear of bloodshed without doing all in her power to prevent it. In 1238 her husband died, and was succeeded by his son Henry, called " the Good ". When the news was brought, the nuns at Trebnitz shed many tears. Hedwig was the only person with dry eyes, and comforted the rest : " Would you oppose the will of God ? Our lives are His. Our will is whatever He is pleased to ordain, whether our own death or that of our friends." From that time she put on the religious habit at Trebnitz, but she did not take the corresponding vows, in order that she might be free to administer her own property in her own way for the relief of the suffering. Hedwig once got to know a poor old woman who could not say the Lord's Prayer, and was very slow at learning it. Hedwig went on patiently teaching her for ten weeks, and even had her into her own room to sleep, so that at every spare moment they could go through it together, until the woman could both repeat and understand it.

In 1240 the Mongol Tartars swept through the Ukraine and Poland. Duke Henry II led his army against them and a battle was fought near Wahlstadt, in which, it is said, the Tartars used a sort of poison-gas, for " a thick and nauseating smoke, issuing from long copper tubes shaped like serpents, stupefied the Polish forces ". Henry was killed, and his death was known to St Hedwig three days before the news was brought to her. " I have lost my son ", she told her companion Dermudis. " He has gone from me like a bird in flight, and I shall never see him again in this life." When the messenger arrived, it was she, the old woman, who comforted the younger ones, Henry's wife Anne and his sister Gertrude. The example of her faith and hope was honoured by God with the gift of miracles. A nun who was blind recovered her sight by the blessing of the saint with the sign of the cross, and her biographer gives an account of several other miraculous cures wrought by her and of several predictions, especially of her own death. In her last sickness she insisted on being anointed before any others could be persuaded that she was in danger. She died in October 1243, and was buried at Trebnitz. St Hedwig was canonized in 1267, and her feast added to the general Western calendar in 1706.

There is a Latin life or legend of St Hedwig which seems to have been compiled towards the close of the thirteenth century by an unknown writer who claims to have based his narrative in the main upon memoirs provided by a Cistercian, Engelbert of Leubus. There is a shorter as well as a longer form of the story, which is printed in the *Acta Sanctorum*, October, vol. viii, as well as elsewhere. A manuscript copy written in 1353 and preserved at Schlackenwert is of great interest on account of the miniatures with which it is decorated ; they have often been reproduced, as for example in the book of H. Riesch, *Die hl. Hedwig* (1926). There are several lives in German, *e.g.* by F. H. Görlich (1854), F. Becker (1872), E. Promnitz (1926), K. and F. Metzger (1927), and a few in French, notably that by G. Bazin (1886). See also G. Morin in the *Revue Bénédictine*, vol. vii (1890), pp. 465–469 ; and H. Quillus, *Königen Hedwig von Polen* (1938). There is a popular American account of St Hedwig, with a fancy title, *The Glowing Lily*, by E. Markowa (1946).

SS. MARTINIAN AND OTHER MARTYRS, AND MAXIMA   (A.D. 458)

AFTER referring to the passion of 270 martyrs who suffered together in Africa, the Roman Martyrology records the martyrdom in the same country of SS. Martinian and Saturian and their two brothers, " who, in the time of the Vandal persecution under the Arian King Genseric, were slaves of a certain Vandal and were converted to the faith of Christ by their fellow slave, the holy maiden Maxima. For their constancy in the Catholic faith they were first beaten with knotted whips, which bit to their very bones, by their heretical master. Then, when they had suffered such things for a long time and always appeared unhurt on the next day, they were forced into exile, where they converted many barbarians to the faith of Christ and obtained from the Roman pontiff a priest and other ministers who baptized them. Then lastly they were made to pass over thorny places in the woods, with their feet tied to the backs of moving chariots. Maxima, however, after triumphing in several contests, was set free by the power of God and made a good and peaceful end in a monastery, the mother of many virgins."

Victor of Vita in his history of the Vandal persecution gives an account of these confessors. Martinian, he says, was an armourer, and his master wanted to marry him to Maxima. She dared not refuse, though she had made a vow of virginity, but Martinian respected her vow and they all ran away to a monastery, from whence they were brought back and savagely beaten because they would not receive Arian baptism. On the death of their master they were given by his widow to another Vandal, who released Maxima and sent the three men to a Berber chief. It was here that they made converts and sent for a priest, and in consequence Genseric ordered them to be dragged to death.

This group of martyrs is dealt with in the *Acta Sanctorum* for October, vol. vii, pt 2. The only evidence of value is that of Victor of Vita.

ST GALL   (*c.* A.D. 635)

AMONG the eminent disciples which St Columban left to be imitators of his heroic life, none seems to have been more famous than this St Gall. He was born in Ireland and educated in the great monastery of Bangor under the direction of the holy abbot Comgall and of Columban. Studies, especially of sacred learning, flourished in this house, and St Gall was well versed in grammar, poetry and the Holy Scriptures, and was ordained priest there, according to some accounts. When St Columban left Ireland St Gall was one of those twelve who accompanied him into France, where they founded the monastery of Annegray and two years afterwards that of Luxeuil. St Gall lived here for twenty years, but the only incident recorded of that period is that, being sent to fish in one river, he went to another. On his return with an empty basket he was reproved for his disobedience, whereupon he went to the right river and made a big catch. When Columban was driven thence in 610 St Gall shared his exile and, after they had in vain tried to return to Ireland, they eventually found themselves in Austrasia, and preached around Tuggen, on Lake Zürich. The people did not receive their new teachers gladly, and they soon left " that stiff-necked and thankless crowd, lest in trying to fertilize their sterile hearts they should waste efforts that might be beneficial to well-disposed minds ", as St Gall's biographer says. Then one Willimar, priest of Arbon near the lake of Constance, afforded them a retreat. The servants of

God built themselves cells near Bregenz, converted many idolaters, and at the end of one of his sermons Gall broke their brazen statues and threw them into the lake. The bold action made as many enemies as it did converts, but they stayed there for two years, made a garden and planted fruit, and St Gall, who was evidently a keen fisherman, occupied his spare time in knotting nets and fishing the lake. But the people who remained obstinate persecuted the monks and slew two of them ; and on his opponent King Theoderic becoming master of Austrasia St Columban decided to retire into Italy, about 612. St Gall was unwilling to be separated from him, but was prevented from bearing him company by sickness. St Columban, however, says one legend, did not believe Gall was so ill as all that and thought he was malingering, wherefore he imposed on him never again to celebrate Mass during his (Columban's) lifetime. This unjust sentence St Gall obeyed. After his master and brethren had departed, Gall packed up his nets and went off by boat to stay with Willimar at Arbon, where he soon recovered his health. Then, directed by the deacon Hiltibod, he selected a suitable spot by the river Steinach (that it had a good fishing-pool is expressly mentioned ; also that they had trouble with water-sprites therein), and settled down there to be a hermit. He soon had disciples, who lived under his direction according to the Rule of St Columban, and the fame of Gall's holiness continued to grow year by year until his death, between 627 and 645, at Arbon, whither he had gone to preach.

St Gall's biographers give several more particulars of his life, some of doubtful authenticity, others certainly mistaken. The week after he established himself with the deacon Hiltibod he had to go, very unwillingly, to the duke Gunzo, whose demoniac daughter had been exorcized in vain by two bishops. Gall was successful, and the evil spirit went out of the girl in the form of a black bird issuing from her mouth. King Sigebert, the betrothed of this Fridiburga, offered Gall a bishopric in thankfulness, but he refused it and moreover induced Fridiburga to become a nun at Metz instead of marrying the king. However, this did not abate Sigebert's goodwill,* and it was afterwards claimed, erroneously, by the abbey of Saint-Gall that the king had given their land to Gall's community and exempted it from the jurisdiction of the bishop of Constance. This see was again offered to the saint, who again refused but nominated one of his own disciples, the deacon John, at whose consecration he preached. St Gall learned in a vision of the death of St Columban at Bobbio, whose monks at his direction sent Gall their dead abbot's pastoral staff as a token of his forgiveness for not accompanying his master into Italy. At the death of St Eustace, whom Columban had left abbot of Luxeuil, the monks chose St Gall ; but that house was then grown rich in lands and possessions, and the humble servant of God understood too well the advantages of poverty in a penitential life to suffer himself to be robbed of it. Instead he continued to be taken up in the apostolic labours of the ministry. He only left his cell to preach and instruct, chiefly the wildest and most abandoned among the inhabitants in the mountainous parts of the country : and returning to his hermitage he there often spent whole nights and days in prayer and contemplation before God.

Walafrid Strabo adds to his life of the saint a second book, of nearly equal length, relating the miracles which took place in connection with his tomb and relics. The same writer remarks that St Gall had " plenty of practical sense " and

---

* When he had himself handed his bride over to be the bride of Christ, he " went out of the church ", says Walafrid Strabo, " and wept secretly for his beloved ".

he was certainly a principal missionary of Switzerland (his feast is kept there as well as in Ireland), but his own fame has been exceeded by that of the monastery bearing his name which grew up on the site of his hermitage on the Steinach, where is now the town of Saint-Gall in the *canton* of the same name. In the eighth century it was organized by Otmar, and during the middle ages it rendered incalculable service to learning, literature, music and other arts ; its library and *scriptorium* were among the most famous of western Europe. It was secularized after the Revolution, but happily a large part of the library remains, adjoining the rebuilt abbey church, now the cathedral of the diocese of Saint-Gall.

Much painstaking research has been spent upon the history of St Gall. Apart from the casual references which occur in the Life of St Columban by Jonas, we have three main documents dealing with Gall in particular. The first, unfortunately preserved only in a fragmentary state, was written about a century after the saint's death, the second by Abbot Wetting dates from the early years of the ninth century, and the third by Walafrid Strabo must be another twenty years or so later. All three have been edited by B. Krusch in MGH., *Scriptores Merov.*, vol. iv, pp. 251–337. There is also a metrical life by Notker. See further J. F. Kenney, *The Sources for the Early History of Ireland*, vol. i, pp. 206–208 ; Gougaud, *Christianity in Celtic Lands* (1932), pp. 140–144, and *Les saints irlandais hors d'Irlande* (1936), pp. 114–119 ; and M. Joynt, *The Life of St Gall* (1927).

ST MOMMOLINUS, BISHOP OF NOYON   (*c.* A.D. 686)

HE was a native of the territory of Coutances, and became a monk at Luxeuil. He was sent with SS. Bertram and Bertinus to St Omer among the Morini in Artois, and was appointed superior whilst they lived in their first habitation, called the Old Monastery (now Saint-Momelin). Here he laboured tirelessly with his brethren for the conversion of the heathen, and removed with them to the New Monastery, St Peter's, at Sithiu. Upon the death of St Eligius in 660 he was consecrated bishop of Noyon, and constituted Bertram abbot of the monastery of Saint-Quentin, which he erected in that town. This abbey afterwards became a famous collegiate church. St Mommolinus governed his extensive see for twenty-six years ; his name occurs in the subscriptions to the Testament of St Amand and to several charters of that age.

There are two short Latin lives of this saint, the more important of the two being printed in the *Acta Sanctorum*, October, vol. vii, pt 2. See also Van der Essen, *Étude critique sur les Vitae des saints mérov.* (1907), pp. 375–384.

ST BERCHARIUS, ABBOT   (A.D. 696 ?)

WHEN St Nivard, Bishop of Rheims, was travelling in Aquitaine, some time just before the middle of the seventh century, he made the acquaintance of the parents of young Bercharius and, much impressed by the boy's openness and promise, urged them to do their best to have him educated for the priesthood. This they did, and in due course he was ordained and became a monk at Luxeuil. When St Nivard founded the monastery of Hautvillers St Bercharius was its first abbot. From it he established in the forest of Der a new monastery called thence Montier-en-Der, and he also founded a convent of women, known as Puellemontier, of which the first six nuns are said to have been slaves whom the abbot had ransomed.

There was in his monastery a young monk named Daguin, who was by no means a satisfactory religious. For some misdemeanour the abbot imposed a sharp penance on this Daguin who, furious at the continual reproofs that he brought on himself, slipped into the cell of Bercharius and stabbed him while he slept. Seized with remorse and fear immediately after, he rushed to the church and rang the bell, which brought the community running to the abbot's cell, where they found him dying. Daguin was found and miserably confessed his guilt. He was brought before Bercharius, who freely forgave him ; St Bercharius lingered for two days and died on March 26, Easter day, in 685 or 696. He is sometimes represented in art with a barrel. This has reference to a story told at Luxeuil, that, being called by the abbot while he was drawing wine or beer, Bercharius hurried off obediently but without turning off the tap. When he returned the liquid had not overflowed but was standing up in a column above the jug.

A Latin life of this " martyr " was written by Abbot Adso a hundred years after his death. It has been printed both by Mabillon and in the *Acta Sanctorum*, October, vol. vii, pt 2.

ST LULL, Bishop of Mainz   (A.D. 786)

Lull was an Englishman, doubtless a native of the kingdom of the West Saxons. The foundation of his education was laid in the monastery of Malmesbury, where he remained as a young man and was ordained deacon. Hearing the call of the foreign missions when he was about twenty years old, he passed into Germany, and was received with joy by St Boniface, who is thought to have been related to him. From this time Lull shared with that great saint the labours of his apostleship, and the persecutions which were raised against him. St Boniface promoted him to priest's orders and in 751 sent him to Rome to consult Pope St Zachary on certain matters which he did not care to commit to writing. Upon his return, St Boniface selected him for his successor ; he was consecrated as coadjutor, and when Boniface departed on his last missionary journey into Frisia St Lull took over the see of Mainz.

It is generally believed that the mission of St Lull to the Holy See had been to obtain exemption from episcopal jurisdiction for St Boniface's abbey of Fulda (where, in accordance with his wish, St Lull buried the body of the martyr, to the discontent of Mainz and Utrecht). A long dispute now began concerning this exemption between Lull, as bishop of Mainz, and St Sturmi, abbot of Fulda, in the course of which the abbot was deposed in favour of a nominee of the bishop. But King Pepin intervened and recognized the independence of Fulda, whereupon Sturmi was restored and St Lull refounded the monastery of Hersfeld. He was a most energetic pastor, and during the space of thirty years that he governed the diocese of Mainz he assisted at several councils in France and elsewhere.

It appears by the letters which were addressed to him from Rome, France and England that St Lull had a reputation for learning. His answers to these are lost, and only nine of his letters are published, among those of St Boniface. The contents are interesting. In the fourth, we notice his zeal to procure good books from foreign countries, and in the others we meet with examples of his firm attachment to his friends, his pastoral vigilance, and his zeal for the observance of the canons. One is an episcopal mandate to order prayers, fasts, and Masses, " those which are prescribed to be said against tempests ", to obtain of God that the rains might cease which were then ruining the harvest. St Lull announces in the same the death of the pope, for whom he orders the accustomed prayers to be said. Cuthbert, abbot of Wearmouth, in a letter to St Lull mentions that he had ordered ninety Masses to be offered for their deceased brethren in Germany, for they sent to each other the names of those that died among them, as also appears from several letters of St Boniface, *e.g.* in one to the abbot of Monte Cassino and several to his brethren in England. Towards the end of his life St Lull retired to his abbey at Hersfeld, where he died.

The main authority for the history of St Lull is the life by Lambert, Abbot of Hersfeld, though this, written two centuries after the death of Lull, is not very reliable. This document is printed in the *Acta Sanctorum*, October, vol. vii, pt 2, but the best text is that edited among the works of Lambert by Holder-Egger (1894), pp. 307–340. The letters of Lull should be consulted in the edition of M. Tangl, *Bonifatiusbriefe* (1915). See also H. Hahn, *Bonifaz und Lul* (1883); Hauck, *Kirchengeschichte Deutschlands*, vols. i and ii; and M. Stimming, *Mainzer Urkundenbuch* (1923), vol. i.

ST ANASTASIUS OF CLUNY   (*c.* A.D. 1085)

THIS Anastasius was a native of Venice and a man of considerable learning who, by the middle of the eleventh century, was a monk at Mont-Saint-Michel. The abbot there was not a satisfactory person—he was accused of simony—and Anastasius eventually left the monastery in order to live as a hermit on Tombelaine off Normandy. About the year 1066 St Hugh of Cluny induced him to join the community at Cluny. After seven years there he was ordered by Pope St Gregory VII to go into Spain, perhaps to help in inducing the Spaniards to give up their Mozarabic liturgy for the Roman, an undertaking begun by Cardinal Hugh of Remiremont (rather inappropriately called *Candidus*), who was then legate in France and Spain. St Anastasius was soon back at Cluny, where he lived quietly for another seven years, and then went to be a hermit in the neighbourhood of Toulouse. Here he preached to the people of the countryside (and is said to have shared his solitude with Hugh of Remiremont, who had been deposed and excommunicated for repeated acts of simony) and lived in contemplation until he was recalled to his monastery in 1085. On his way he died and was buried at Doydes.

His life by a certain Galterius is printed by Mabillon and in the *Acta Sanctorum*, October, vol. vii, pt 2. He may have been the author of an " Epistle to Geraldus " on the Real Presence : see DTC., vol. i, c. 1166.

ST BERTRAND, BISHOP OF COMMINGES   (A.D. 1123)

IN its more than a thousand years of existence before it was suppressed the see of Comminges (now included in Toulouse) was governed by several men well known in history, but no one of them is more famed locally than St Bertrand, who was bishop for fifty years in the eleventh–twelfth century. At first he had no other aim than to be a military lord like his father, but he soon turned to the ecclesiastical state, received a canonry at Toulouse, and became archdeacon : it was remarked that he owed his dignities neither to requests nor bribes. About 1075 he was called to govern the diocese of Comminges, and having rebuilt both the temporal and spiritual fortifications of his episcopal city he proceeded to a thorough reformation of the whole diocese, living with his canons under the Rule of St Augustine as an example for the secular clergy. His zeal was not always acceptable. When he went to preach in the Val d'Azun he met with a very hostile reception, and it required all his efforts to calm the people. However, they afterwards were so sorry for the way they had received their bishop that they promised to give in perpetuity to the see of Comminges all the butter that was made in Azun every year during the week before Whitsunday. This tribute was rendered, not always willingly, up to the time of the Revolution. St Bertrand several times had to face violent opposition even out of his own territory : in 1100 he was at the synod at Poitiers when King Philip I was excommunicated and the synodal fathers were stoned, and at the consecration of the cemetery of St Mary at Auch, when the aggrieved monks of Saint-Orens tried to set fire to the church.

A number of miracles are related of St Bertrand, one of which gave rise to the " Great Pardon " at his church in Comminges. In a feud between the counts of Comminges and Bigorre, Bertrand's diocese was overrun by the troops of Sans Parra of Oltia, who carried off all the cattle they could lay their hands on. To save his people from ruin the bishop implored their leader to restore the booty, but he refused unless he was paid its value. " All right ", said St Bertrand. " Bring them back. I'll pay you before you are dead." Some time after Bertrand himself was dead, Sans Parra was captured by the Moors in Spain. One night he had a dream in his dungeon of Bertrand, who said he had come to redeem his promise and led him out of prison to a spot near his home. This happening is commemorated locally on May 2 every year, and Pope Clement V, who had been bishop of Comminges, granted a plenary indulgence to be gained at the then cathedral church of St Bertrand every year that the feast of the finding of the Holy Cross falls on a Friday. St Bertrand was canonized some time before 1309, probably by Pope Honorius III.

In the *Acta Sanctorum*, October, vol. vii, pt 2, is printed a life said to be the work of Vitalis, a notary of Auch, who was a contemporary. See also P. Bedin, *St Bertrand de Comminges* (1912).

ST GERARD MAJELLA   (A.D. 1755)

ST GERARD, said Pope Pius IX, " was a perfect model for those of his own condition, the lay brothers " ; Leo XIII referred to him as " one of those angelic youths whom God has given to the world as models to men " ; and in his short life of twenty-nine years he became the most famous wonder-worker of the eighteenth century. He was born at Muro, fifty miles south of Naples, the son of a tailor. His mother testified after his death : " My child's only happiness was in church, on his knees before the Blessed Sacrament. He would stop there till he forgot it was dinner-time. In the house he prayed all day. He was born for Heaven." At the age of ten he was allowed to receive holy communion every other day, which at a time when the influence of Jansenism was yet not purged away argues that his confessor was sensible of what manner of child Gerard was. When his father died he was taken away from school and apprenticed to a tailor, Martin Pannuto, a worthy man who understood and respected his apprentice. Not so his journeyman, a rough fellow who ill-treated young Gerard and was only exasperated by the boy's patience. When he had learned his trade, which he did very efficiently, he offered himself to the local Capuchins, of whom his uncle was a member, but they refused him as too young and delicate. He then became a servant in the household of the Bishop of Lacedogna. Humanly speaking this was an unfortunate experience, for this prelate was a man of ungovernable temper who treated Gerard with a great lack of consideration and kindness. Nevertheless he served him faithfully and uncomplainingly till the bishop died in 1745, when he returned home to Muro and set up as a tailor on his own. He lived with his mother and three sisters, and one-third of his earnings he handed over to her, another third was given in alms to the poor, and the rest in stipends for Masses for the souls in Purgatory. He had already begun to discipline himself with severity and several hours of the night were passed in prayer in the cathedral.

When Gerard was twenty-three a mission was given in Muro by some fathers of the newly-founded Congregation of the Most Holy Redeemer. He offered himself to them as a lay-brother, but again his delicate appearance was against him and his mother and sisters were not at all anxious to let him go. But he persisted, and at length Father Cafaro sent him to the house of which he was rector at Deliceto, with the written message : " I send you a useless brother." When Father Cafaro returned thither he found he had been mistaken in his judgement, and at once admitted Gerard to the habit. Working first in the garden and then in the sacristy he was so industrious, punctual and self-effacing that it was said of him, " Either he is a fool or a great saint ". St Alphonsus Liguori, founder of the Redemptorists, knew which he was and deliberately shortened his novitiate for him. Brother Gerard was professed in 1752, adding to the usual vows one always to do that which should seem the more pleasing to God. Father Tannoia, who wrote the lives both of St Gerard and of St Alphonsus and who was healed by Gerard's intercession after his death, tells us that when Gerard was a novice he one day saw him praying before the tabernacle. Suddenly he cried aloud, " Lord, let me go, I pray thee ! I have work that I *must* do." ˙ Surely one of the most moving stories in the whole of hagiology.

During his three years as a professed lay-brother Gerard was engaged as the community tailor and infirmarian, in begging for the house, and in accompanying the fathers on their missions and retreats because of his gift of reading souls. There are over twenty examples of his having brought secret sinners to repentance by revealing their own wickedness to themselves. This was the period, too, of the principal supernatural phenomena : ecstatic flight (he is said to have been carried through the air a distance of half a mile), " bilocation ", and power over inanimate nature and the lower animals are recorded of him, as well as prophecy and infused knowledge. In his ecstasies an appeal to his obedience was the only force that could recall him to his surroundings before the appointed time. At Naples he knew of the murder of the Archpriest of Muro at the time it happened fifty miles away, and on several occasions he was apprised of and correctly acted on the mental wishes of persons at a distance. He read the bad conscience of the secretary of the Archbishop of Conza with such accuracy that the man completely changed his life and was reconciled to his wife, so that all Rome was talking of it. But it is for the phenomenon called bilocation that St Gerard is most famous in this connection. He was alleged to have been with a sick man in a cottage at Caposele at the same time as he talked with a friend in the monastery at the same place. Father Tannoia states, among other examples, that he was seen at Muro on a day when he certainly did not leave Caposele. Once the rector looked for him in his cell and he was apparently not there, so when he saw him in the church he asked where he had been. " In my cell ", was the reply. " What do you mean ? " asked the rector, " I have been there twice to look for you ". Pressed, Gerard explained that as he was in retreat he had asked God to make him invisible, lest he be disturbed. " I forgive you this time ", said the rector. " But don't make such prayers again."*

It is not, however, for these marvels that St Gerard Majella is canonized and revered ; they were simply an effect of his surpassing holiness which God in His wisdom could have withheld, without abating thereby one jot of that goodness, charity and devotion which made him that model which Pius and Leo declared him to be. One of the most surprising results of his reputation was that he was allowed to be, in effect, the spiritual director of several communities of nuns—an activity not usually associated with lay-brothers. He interviewed individuals and gave community conferences at the *grille*, and wrote letters of advice to superiors, religious and priests. Some of these are extant. There is nothing remarkable in them : plain, straightforward statements of a Christian's duty in whatever state it has pleased God to call him ; urging gentleness to a prioress, vigilance to a novice, tranquillity to a parish priest, conformity with the divine will to all. In 1753 the young divines at Deliceto went on an expedition to the shrine of St Michael at Monte Gargano. They had the equivalent of twelve shillings all told to cover their expenses, but they also had St Gerard with them, and he saw to it that they wanted nothing the whole time ; their nine days' holiday was a succession of marvels. But just a year later he was brought under suspicion, and underwent a terrible trial. A young woman whom he had befriended, Neria Caggiano, who was of wanton conduct, accused Gerard of lechery and he was sent for by St Alphonsus at Nocera. Believing it to be in accordance with his vow to do the more perfect thing, he did not deny the charge, and thereby placed his superior in a quandary, for it was difficult to believe that Gerard was really guilty. So he was forbidden to receive holy communion or to have any dealings with the outside world. " There is a God in Heaven. He will provide ", said Gerard. For some weeks suspicion rested on him, and then Neria and her accomplice voluntarily confessed that they had lied and trumped-up the charge. St Alphonsus asked St Gerard why he had not protested his innocence. " Father ", he replied, " does not our rule forbid us to excuse ourselves ? " A provision which, of course, was never intended to apply to circumstances such as these. Soon after this St Gerard was sent with Father Margotta to Naples, where his reputation and miracles caused the Redemptorist house to be beset day and night by people who wanted to see him ; so at the end of four months he was removed to the house at Caposele and made porter there.

This was a job after his own heart, and " our house at this time ", wrote Father Tannoia, " was besieged with beggars. Brother Gerard had the same concern for their good that a mother has for her children. He had the knack of always sending them away satisfied, and neither their unreasonableness nor cunning dodges ever made him lose patience." During the hard winter of that year two hundred men, women and children came daily to the door and received food, clothes and firing ; nobody but the porter knew where it all came from. In the spring he went again to Naples where, and at Calitri, Father Margotta's home, several miracles of healing were attributed to him. On returning to Caposele he was put in charge of the new buildings, and one Friday when there was not a penny in the house wherewith to pay the workmen his prayers brought an unexpected sum of money, sufficient for

---

* Examples of bilocation, when proved, are usually explained either by the imagination of the beholder being impressed by the image of a person not physically present, or by the production by God of a real external image of an absent person, or by the person being seen through all the intervening space as though he were present.

their immediate needs.   He spent the summer questing for funds for these build-ings, but the effort in the south Italian heat was too much for him, and in July and August his consumption made rapid advance.   He was a week in bed at Oliveto, where he cured (or as he put it, " gave effect to obedience ") a lay-brother who had been sent to look after him and was himself taken ill, and then dragged himself back to Caposele.   He was able to get up from bed again only for a few days in Septem-ber, and his last weeks were a compound of physical suffering and spiritual ecstasy, in which his gifts of infused knowledge and prevision seemed more powerful than ever before.   He died on the day and at the hour he had foretold, just before the midnight of October 15-16, in the year 1755.   St Gerard Majella was canonized in 1904.

The best authority for the story of St Gerard is the biography by Father Tannoia.   This was translated into English for the Oratorian Series and was printed in the volume *Lives of the Companions of St Alphonsus* (1849), pp. 243–453.   Besides this we have in English : O. Vassall-Phillips, *Life of St Gerard Majella* (1914) ; Saint-Omer, *Life, Virtues and Miracles of St Gerard Majella* (1907) ; and J. Carr, *To Heaven Through a Window* (1946).   The best German biography is that by Father Dilgskron (1923).

17 : ST MARGARET MARY, Virgin   (A.D. 1690)

NOTWITHSTANDING the great saints and many other holy people of the time, in France of the seventeenth century, love of God had gone cold, on the one hand because of widespread rebellion and sinfulness, on the other because of the numbing influence of Jansenism, which presented God as not loving all mankind alike.   And to rekindle that love there flourished, between 1625 and 1690, three saints, John Eudes, Claud La Colombière, and Margaret-Mary Alacoque, who between them brought and taught to the Church, in the form that we have had it ever since, devotion to our divine Lord in His Sacred Heart, " the symbol of that boundless love which moved the Word to take flesh, to institute the Holy Eucharist, to take our sins upon Himself, and, dying on the cross, to offer Himself as a victim and a sacrifice to the eternal Father."

The third and most prominent of these " saints of the Sacred Heart " was born in 1647 at Janots, the eastern quarter of L'Hautecour, a small town in Burgundy. Her father was a notary of some distinction, whose wife bore him seven children, of whom Margaret was the fifth.   She was a devout and good little girl, with a horror of " being naughty ".   When she was four she " made a vow of chastity ", though she admitted afterwards that, as one would expect at that age, she knew not what either a vow or chastity might be.   When she was about eight her father died and she was sent to school with the Poor Clares at Charolles ; she was at once attracted by what she could see and understand of the life of the nuns, and they on their side were so impressed by Margaret's piety that she was allowed to make her first communion when she was nine.   Two years later she was afflicted by a painful rheumatic affection that kept her to her bed till she was fifteen, and in the course of it she was taken back to her home at L'Hautecour.   Her father's house was now occupied by several other members of the family as well, and one sister and her husband had taken all domestic and business authority out of the hands of the widow Alacoque.   She and Margaret were treated almost as servants, and she recovered from her sickness only to be confronted by this persecution of her mother. " At this time ", she writes in her autobiography, " all my desire was to seek happiness and comfort in the Blessed Sacrament, but as I lived some way from the church I could not go without the leave of these persons, and sometimes one would give and another refuse her consent." They would say it was a pretext to meet some boy or other, and Margaret would go and hide herself in a corner of the garden, and stop there crying and praying for the rest of the day, without food or drink unless somebody from the village took pity on her. " The heaviest of my crosses was my powerlessness to lighten those laid upon my mother."

From the energy with which Margaret reproaches herself for worldliness, faithlessness and resistance to grace, it may reasonably be gathered that she was not averse from a reasonable participation in those opportunities for gaiety and amusement that came her way, and when her mother and other relatives wanted her to marry she considered the proposal not unfavourably for some time. In her uncertainty she inflicted cruel austerities on herself in punishment for her faults, and brought the further dislike of her relations upon herself by collecting neglected village children into the house or garden and giving them lessons. When she was twenty, more pressure was put on her to marry, but now, fortified by a vision of our Lord, she made up her mind once for all what she would do, and firmly refused. Not till she was twenty-two did she receive the sacrament of confirmation (it was then that she took the name of Mary), and thus armed she was able to withstand the final opposition of her family. Her brother Chrysostom furnished her dowry, and in June 1671 she entered the Visitation convent at Paray-le-Monial.

As a novice Margaret-Mary was humble, obedient, simple and frank, and she edified the community, testified a fellow-novice, " by her charity to her sisters, to whom she never uttered an irritating word, and by her patience under the sharp reproofs, scorn and ridicule to which she was often submitted ". But her novitiate was not an easy one. A Visitation nun must not " be extraordinary except by being ordinary ", and already God was leading Margaret-Mary by extraordinary paths. For example, she was quite unable to practice discursive meditation : " No matter how much I tried to follow the method taught me, I invariably had to return to my divine Master's way [*i.e.* ' prayer of simplicity '], although I did my best to give it up." In due course she was professed, and on that occasion our Lord was pleased to accept her as His bride, " but in a way that she felt herself incapable of describing ". From that time " my divine Master urged me incessantly to ask for humiliations and mortifications ", and they came unsought when she was appointed to assist in the infirmary. The infirmarian, Sister Catherine Marest, was temperamentally very different from her assistant : active, energetic, efficient, while Margaret-Mary was quiet, slow and clumsy. The result she summed up in her own words : " God alone knows what I had to suffer there, as much through my impulsive and sensitive disposition as from my fellow-creatures and the Devil." But, granted that Sister Marest was too vigorous in her methods, she on her side probably had something to suffer too. During these two and a half years our Lord continually made Himself sensibly present to Margaret-Mary, often as crowned with thorns, and on December 27, 1673, her devotion to His passion was rewarded with the first of the revelations.

She was kneeling alone at the *grille* before the Blessed Sacrament exposed on the altar, and all at once she felt herself, as she says, " invested " by the divine Presence, and heard our Lord inviting her to take the place which St John (it was his feast) had occupied at the Last Supper. He then went on speaking, " in so plain and effective a manner as to leave no room for doubt, such were the results that this grace produced in me, who am always afraid of deceiving myself about what I assert to take place interiorly ".   He told her that the love of His heart must needs spread and manifest itself to men by means of her, and that He would reveal the treasures of its graces through her, His chosen instrument and the disciple of His Sacred Heart.   Then it was as though our Lord took her heart and put it within His own, returning it burning with divine love into her breast.   During a period of eighteen months our Lord continued to appear to Margaret-Mary at intervals, explaining and amplifying the first revelation.   He told her that His heart was to be honoured under the form of a heart of flesh, represented in a way now familiar to Catholics throughout the world, and that, in consideration of the coldness and rebuffs given to Him by mankind in return for all His eagerness to do them good, she should make up for their ingratitude so far as she was able.   This was to be done by frequent loving communion, especially on the first Friday of each month and by an hour's vigil every Thursday night in memory of His agony and desertion in Gethsemane—practices which Catholics have made their own in the devotions of the Nine Fridays and the Holy Hour.   After a long interval a final revelation was made within the octave of Corpus Christi in 1675, when our Lord said to St Margaret-Mary, " Behold the heart which has so much loved men that it has spared nothing, even exhausting and consuming itself in testimony of its love. Instead of gratitude I receive from most only indifference, by irreverence and sacrilege and the coldness and scorn that men have for me in the sacrament of love." Then He asked that a feast of reparation be instituted for the Friday after the octave of Corpus Christi (now the feast of the Sacred Heart).   Thus through His chosen instrument God made known to the world His will concerning the reparation due for human ingratitude towards His goodness and mercy, by worship of the heart of flesh of His Son, considered as united to His divinity and as the symbol of His love in dying for our redemption.*

Our Lord had told St Margaret-Mary that she was to " do nothing without the approval of those who guide you, in order that, having the authority of obedience, you may not be misled by Satan, who has no power over those who are obedient ".   When she carried the matter to her superior, Mother de Saumaise, she " mortified and humiliated her with all her might, and allowed her to do none of the things that our Lord had asked of her, treating contemptuously all that the poor sister had said ".   " This ", adds St Margaret-Mary, " consoled me very much and I withdrew in great peace."   But she was seriously over-wrought by all that had happened, was taken ill, and her life was in danger.   Mother de Saumaise was looking for a sign to guide her in dealing with Sister Alacoque, and said to her, " If God cures you, I shall take it as a proof that all you experience comes from Him, and I will allow you to do what our Lord wishes in honour of His Sacred Heart ".   St Margaret-Mary prayed accordingly, she at once recovered, and Mother de Saumaise fulfilled her promise.   But there was a minority in the community definitely hostile to their sister and her spiritual experiences, and the superior ordered her to set them out for the opinion of certain theologians.   These men lacked experience in such matters, diagnosed them as delusions, and recommended

* It is interesting to note that just before this time, in 1651, Thomas Goodwin, Independent (Congregationalist) chaplain to Oliver Cromwell, wrote a book entitled *The Heart of Christ in Heaven towards Sinners on Earth* (vol. iv of his Complete Works, 1862).   It has remarkable affinities with the teaching of Bd Claud La Colombière.

that the visionary should take more food. Our Lord, however, had promised that an understanding director should come to St Margaret-Mary, and when Claud La Colombière arrived as confessor extraordinary to the nuns she knew at once that he was the man. He did not stay at Paray long, but long enough to be convinced of the genuineness of Margaret-Mary's experiences, to gain a deep respect and affection for her, and sincerely to adopt the teaching of the Sacred Heart while confirming the saint herself in it. Soon after Bd Claud had left for England (" where ", he complained, " there are no Daughters of Holy Mary, much less a Sister Alacoque "), Margaret-Mary underwent probably the most distressing trial of her life. She was asked in vision to become the sacrificial victim for the short-comings of the nuns of her community and for the ingratitude of some to the Sacred Heart. For long she demurred, asking that this cup might pass from her. Then our Lord asked her again that she would do this thing, not merely interiorly but in public. She accepted, not in desperation or defiance, but in an agony of fear at what she felt bound to do because God had asked her—and had had to ask her twice. On that very same day, November 20, 1677, this young nun of only five years' standing, having first told her superior and been told by her to obey God's voice, " said and did what her Lord required of her "—knelt before her sisters in religion and told them in the name of Christ that she was appointed to be the victim for their failings. They did not all take it in the same spirit of utter humility and obedience, and on that occasion, she says, our Lord, " chose to favour me with a little sample of the grievous night of His own passion ". It is a tradition at Paray that the next morning there were not enough priests available to hear all the nuns who wanted to go to confession, but unhappily there is reason to believe that for many years afterwards there were sisters who nursed resentment against St Margaret-Mary.

During the rule of Mother Greyfié, who succeeded Mother de Saumaise, St Margaret-Mary alternately received great graces and underwent great trials, both interiorly and from her fellow-creatures. She was tempted to despair, vain glory and self-indulgence, and had a good deal of sickness. In 1681 Claud La Colombiére came to Paray for the good of his health, and died there in February of the following year. St Margaret-Mary is said to have been supernaturally assured that his soul was in Heaven, as she was from time to time regarding the state of others who were dead. Two years later Mother Melin, who had known Margaret-Mary during all her religious life, was elected superior at Paray and she appointed the saint as her assistant, with the approval of the chapter. From henceforth any remaining opposition ceased, or at least was silenced. The secret of her divine revelations was made known to the community in a rather dramatic (and for her embarrassing) way, being read out, presumably by accident, in the refectory in the course of a book written by Bd Claud La Colombière. But the ultimate triumph made no difference, one way or another, to St Margaret-Mary. One of the duties of the assistant superior was to sweep out the choir, and one day while she was doing it she was asked to go and lend a hand in the kitchen. Without brushing up the dust under her hand she went off, and when the nuns assembled for office the heap of dust was still there in full view. That is the sort of thing that twelve years before had upset Sister Marest the infirmarian : she still lived and was to have Sister Alacoque to help her again, and doubtless she remembered it with a grim smile. St Margaret-Mary was also made mistress of the novices, with such success that professed nuns would ask leave to attend her conferences. Her secret being now known, she was less reticent in encouraging devotion to the Sacred Heart, and inculcated it among her novices, who privately observed the feast in 1685. In the following year the family of a dismissed novice caused trouble by denouncing the novice mistress as an impostor and unorthodox innovator, and for a time some of the old feeling was raised against her in the convent, but it soon subsided and on June 21 the whole house privately celebrated the feast so far as they were able. Two years later a chapel was built at Paray in honour of the Sacred Heart, and the devotion began to be accepted in other convents of the Visitandines, and to be propagated here and there throughout France.

While serving a second term as assistant superior St Margaret-Mary was taken ill in October 1690. " I shall not live ", she said, " for I have nothing left to suffer ", but the doctor did not think anything was very seriously wrong. A week later she asked for the last sacraments, saying, " I need nothing but God, and to lose myself in the heart of Jesus ". The priest came and began to administer the last rites ; at the fourth anointing, of the lips, she died. St Margaret-Mary Alacoque was canonized in 1920.

In the very complete *Vie de Ste Marguerite-Marie* by Fr A. Hamon, of which the first edition appeared in 1907, nearly thirty pages are devoted to an " étude des sources " and a full bibliography. It must suffice here to note, as most important of all, the autobiographical sketch (Eng. trans.) which was written by the saint at the bidding of her director five years before her death, as well as 133 letters of hers and a number of notes and spiritual memoranda in her own handwriting. Besides these we have a valuable *mémoire* by her superior, Mother Greyfié, with other letters concerning her, and the depositions of the sisters at Paray-le-Monial, who were examined on oath with a view to her ultimate beatification. The first printed summary of what was then known of the saint's history was published in 1691 as an appendix which Fr Croiset added to his little book on *Devotion to the Sacred Heart*. Upon this followed the very careful biography of Mgr Languet, Bishop of Soissons (1729). Since then we have a long succession of lives, among which it will be sufficient to mention those of Mgr Bougaud (Eng. trans., 1890), Mgr Léon Gauthey (3 vols., 1915), Abbé Demimuid (1912) in the series " Les Saints " (Eng. trans.), J. Rime (1947), and M. Yeo in *These Three Hearts*. There are many other short lives in every European language. For the text of the saint's own writings reference is generally made to the *Vie et Œuvres* which was published by the Visitation nuns of Paray-le-Monial in 1876. See further DTC., vol. iii, cc. 320–351. For the Nine Fridays, see Fr Thurston in *The Month*, June 1903, pp. 635–649 ; and J. B. O'Connell, *The Nine First Fridays* (1934).

ST JOHN THE DWARF   (FIFTH CENTURY)

ST JOHN, surnamed *Kolobos*, that is " the Little " or " the Dwarf ", was famous among the eminent saints that inhabited the deserts of Egypt. He retired when a young man into the wilderness of Skete and set himself with his whole heart to put on the spirit of Christ. The old hermit who was his director for his first lesson bade him plant in the ground a walking-stick, and water it every day till it should bring forth fruit. John did so with great simplicity, though the river was at a considerable distance. It is related that when he had continued his task, without speaking one word about it, into the third year the stick, which had taken root, pushed forth leaves and buds and produced fruit. The old hermit, gathering the fruit, carried it to the church, and giving it to some of the brethren, said, " Take, and eat the fruit of obedience ". Postumian, who was in Egypt in 402, assured Sulpicius Severus that he was shown this tree, which grew in the yard of the monastery and which he saw covered with shoots and green leaves.

St John believed that the perfection of a monk consists in his keeping to his cell, watching constantly over himself and having God continually present to his mind. He never discoursed on worldly affairs and never spoke of " news ", the ordinary amusement of the superficial. He was so intent on the things of God that he became very absent-minded. At his work he sometimes plaited into one basket the material which should have made two, and often went wrong through forgetting what he was doing. One day when a carrier knocked at his door to carry away his materials and tools to another place, St John thrice forgot what he went to fetch in returning from his door, till he repeated to himself, " The camel, my tools. The camel, my tools. The camel, my tools." The same happened to him when someone came to fetch the baskets he had made, and as often as he came back from his door he sat down again to his work, till at last he called the brother to come in, and take them himself. How St John tested the good dispositions of St Arsenius has already been related in the account of that saint on July 19. His own humility was the more remarkable because of his natural quick temper and good opinion of himself. But he knew his faults and he knew what provoked them, and therefore he avoided the ways of men and their discussions and so cultivated the things of peace that his words held the attention of all. It is said that a certain brother coming one day to speak to him for two or three minutes, so ardent and sweet was their conversation on spiritual things that they continued it the whole night till morning. Perceiving it was day, they went out, the one to return home, the other to go with him for a few steps, but their talk again turned to God and His kingdom and it lasted till midday. Then St John took him again into his cell to eat a little ; after which they really parted.

A certain charitable young woman, named Paesia, fell gradually into a disorderly life. The monks entreated St John to try to reclaim her, and he went to her house and sitting down by her he said with his accustomed sweetness, " What reason can you have to complain of Jesus that you should thus abandon Him ? " At these words she was struck silent, and seeing the saint in tears she said to him, " Why do you weep ? " St John replied, " How can I not weep whilst I see Satan in possession of your heart ? " She was moved by his gentleness and concern for her, and grace entered into her heart and she asked him, " Father, is the path of penitence still open to me ? " " It is," he replied. " Then show me the way." He rose up and she followed him without saying another word. As they slept in the desert, their heads pillowed on mounds of cold sand, St John dreamed he saw the soul of Paesia going up to Heaven and heard a voice telling him that her penitence was as perfect before God as it was short before man. And in the morning he found Paesia dead.

When the Berbers raided Skete, John went across the Nile towards the Red Sea, and there, in the place hallowed by St Antony, he died. When he drew near his end, his disciples entreated him to leave them some final lesson of Christian perfection. He sighed, and that he might shun the air of a teacher alleging his own doctrine and practice, he said, " I never followed my own will ; nor did I ever teach another what I had not first practised myself ".

The most reliable source of information seems to be the *Apophthegmata* (see Bousset, *Apophthegmata : Studien zur Geschichte des ältesten mönchtums*, 1923) ; but consult also the *Acta Sanctorum*, October, vol. viii, pp. 39–48. The panegyric of Bishop Zachary, published in Coptic by Amélineau (*Annales du Musée Guimet*, vol. xxv, 1894), and translated by Nau, from the Syriac, in the *Revue de l'Orient chrétien*, vols. vii to ix, is not very trustworthy. See also De L. O'Leary, *The Saints of Egypt* (1937), pp. 170–172.

ST ANSTRUDIS, or AUSTRUDE, Virgin　　(*c.* A.D. 700)

SHE was probably the daughter of St Salaberga, who founded an abbey at Laon, in which she, with the consent of her husband, took the religious veil. Anstrudis faithfully walked in her steps, and after her death succeeded her in the abbacy. The holiness of St Anstrudis was proved and made perfect by afflictions. Her brother Baldwin was treacherously assassinated, and she herself was accused to Ebroin, mayor of the palace, of taking side against his interest. When he came to Laon he burst into the convent and had the young abbess dragged before him, and would have led her to prison had he not been frightened off. The next day an attempt was made on the life of Anstrudis, but she escaped by clinging to the altar of the church. Attracted by her intrepid constancy and proved virtue and innocence, Bd Pepin of Landen declared himself her protector. When Madelgarius, Bishop of Laon, tried to lay hands on the income of the convent, St Anstrudis lodged a complaint and Pepin sent his son Grimoald to deal straitly with the unjust prelate. She died before 709.

> The Bollandists, following Mabillon, have printed a life of this saint in the *Acta Sanctorum*, October, vol. vii, pt 2. It purports to be of almost contemporary date, but Levison, in his critical edition, MGH., *Scriptores Merov.*, vol. vi, pp. 64 *seq.*, assigns it to the ninth century.

ST NOTHELM, Archbishop of Canterbury　　(*c.* A.D. 740)

NOTHELM, whom St Bede refers to as "a devout priest of the church of London ", succeeded St Tatwin in the see of Canterbury in the year 734. Two years later he received the *pallium* from Pope St Gregory III. He was consulted by St Boniface from Germany and furnished him with a copy of the famous letter of instruction from Pope St Gregory I to St Augustine of Canterbury about how to deal with the English converts. But St Nothelm's name is principally remembered for his part in the composition of St Bede's *Ecclesiastical History*. In the preface thereto, addressed to King Ceolwulf, Bede says that his chief aid and authority for his work had been the learned abbot Albinus at Canterbury, who transmitted to him " either by writing or by word of mouth of the same Nothelm, all that he thought worthy of memory that had been done in the province of Kent, or the adjacent parts, by the disciples of the blessed Pope Gregory, as he had learned them either from written records or the traditions of his ancestors. The said Nothelm afterwards went to Rome and, having with leave of the present Pope Gregory [III] searched into the archives of the holy Roman church, found there some letters of the blessed Pope Gregory and other popes. When he returned home he brought them to me, by the advice of the aforesaid most reverend father Albinus, to be inserted in my history. Thus . . . what was transacted in the church of Canterbury by the disciples of St Gregory or their successors, and under which kings they happened, has been conveyed to us by Nothelm through the industry of abbot Albinus. They also partly informed me by what bishops and under what kings the provinces of the East and West Saxons, as well as of the East Angles and the Northumbrians, received the faith of Christ." Nothelm also wrote some observations on St Bede's commentary on the books of Kings in the Bible, to which Bede replied in a personal letter.

> The saint is noticed in the *Acta Sanctorum*, October, vol. viii. We know little more than what Bede has told us : see Plummer's edition and notes. But since the publication

of the work of Dom S. Brechter, *Die Quellen zur Angelsachsenmission Gregors des Grossen* (1941), the authenticity of the alleged *Responsiones* of Pope Gregory to Augustine, and Nothelm's finding of them in the Roman archives, are subject to serious question : *cf.* Fr P. Grosjean in *Analecta Bollandiana*, vol. lx (1942), p. 287. But some scholars do not find Dom Brechter's arguments completely convincing.

ST SERAPHINO　　(A.D. 1604)

THE life of St Seraphino was of that uneventfulness which one associates with the vocation of a lay-brother, though spiritually he attained great heights and numerous miracles are related of him.　　He was born at Montegranaro in 1540, of very humble parentage, and like many another saint he began to earn his living as a shepherd boy.　　When he was left an orphan he was taken into the service of his elder brother, a bricklayer and a harsh master.　　Young Seraphino was treated rather brutally by him, and when he was sixteen he ran away and became a lay-brother with the Capuchins.　　He had always been very devout and good, and now he progressed rapidly on the path of heroic sanctity.　　Every night he spent three hours in prayer before the Blessed Sacrament, and did not go to bed again after Matins ; he won sinners by his kindness and moving words, and was beloved by all the poor.　　Had his superiors allowed, he would have emulated St Francis and gone to work among the infidels ; but he unmurmuringly accepted God's will that he should live and die in obscurity at home.　　The decree of his canonization (published in 1767) records two of his miracles : namely, that when on a pilgrimage to Loreto he passed the river Potenza in flood not merely unharmed but quite dry, and that when he was reproved for his reckless generosity to the poor the vegetables which he had cut for them overnight in the friary garden were grown up again the next day. With the sign of the cross he cured the sick and he received the gifts of discernment of spirits and reading the future, so that he was consulted by both civil and ecclesiastical dignitaries.　　St Seraphino died at Ascoli Piceno on October 12, 1604 ; his feast is kept on this day by the Capuchins in England, but on the 13th elsewhere.

　　The story of St Seraphino told in some detail is included in the *Annales Ordinis Capuccini* (1639) by Z. Boverio.　　This has been reprinted in the *Acta Sanctorum*, October, vol. vi, and with it the full text of the bull of canonization.　　There are other lives by C. de Harenberg (1642), P. B. Joannini (1709) and Cardinal Svampa (1904) ; and see Ernest de Beaulieu, *Deux émules de St Félix de Cantalice* (1919).　　Further bibliographical details may be gleaned from Giuseppe da Fermo, *Gli Scrittori Cappuccini delle Marche* (1928).

THE URSULINE MARTYRS OF VALENCIENNES　(A.D. 1794)

URSULINE nuns established themselves at Valenciennes in the year 1654 ; nearly a hundred and forty years later, after devoting themselves throughout that time to the interests of their fellow-citizens by teaching their children and looking after the poor, their convent was suppressed under the Revolution and the nuns took refuge in the house of their order at Mons.　　When Valenciennes was occupied by the Austrians in 1793 they returned, reopened their school, and remained in the town after it had been recaptured by the French.　　In September 1794 they were arrested at the instance of Citizen Lacoste's commission, on the charge of being *émigrées* who had unlawfully returned and reopened their convent, and confined in the public prison.　　On October 17 five of them were brought up for trial, and on their stating openly that they had come back to Valenciennes to teach the Catholic faith they were sentenced to death.   They were led to the guillotine in the great market-place amid the tears of their sisters.   " Mother, you taught us to be valiant, and now we are going to be crowned you weep ! " exclaimed Bd Mary Augustine (Mother Dejardin) to the mother superior.   Five days later the superior herself, Bd Mary Clotilde (Mother Paillot) and the other five nuns suffered in the same place, among the last victims of the Revolution.   " We die for the faith of the Catholic, Apostolic and Roman Church ", said Bd Mary Clotilde, and the truth of this statement was formally recognized by that same church when, in 1920, Pope Benedict XV solemnly beatified as martyrs the eleven Ursulines of Valenciennes. Among them were two, BB Lilvina (Lacroix) and Anne Mary (Erraux), who had been professed Bridgettines, and one, Bd Josephine (Leroux) who had been a Poor Clare ;   they joined the Ursulines when their own communities were expelled.

As vice-postulator of the cause of the Valenciennes martyrs, the Abbé J. Loridan in his little volume *Les bses Ursulines de Valenciennes* (in the series " Les Saints ") speaks with full authority and gives proof of exhaustive research.   See also Wallon, *Les Représentants du peuple* . . ., vol. v (1890), pp. 163–167 ;   and H. Leclercq, *Les Martyrs*, vol. xii.

18 : ST LUKE, Evangelist   (First Century)

IT is from St Paul himself that we learn that St Luke was a gentile, for he is not named among those of his helpers whom Paul mentions as Jews (Col. iv 10–11) ; that he was a fellow worker with the apostle, " Mark, Aristarchus, Demas and Luke, who share my labours " ;   and that he was a medical man, " Luke, the beloved physician " (or " the beloved Luke, the physician "), who doubtless had the care of Paul's much-tried health.   But nowhere does St Paul refer to Luke's writings ; if Luke be referred to in II Cor. viii 18–19 (as St Jerome thought), there is clearly here no question of a written gospel.   The first time in the history of the mission of St Paul that Luke speaks in his own name in the first person is when the apostle sailed from Troas into Macedonia (Acts xvi 10).   Before this he had doubtless been for some time a disciple of St Paul, and from this time seems never to have left him, unless by his order for the service of the churches he had planted ;   he was certainly with him not only during the first but also during the second imprisonment in Rome.   According to Eusebius, Luke's home was at Antioch, and he was almost certainly a Greek ; and his journeyings and tribulations with St Paul are, of course, set out by Luke himself in the Acts of the Apostles.

St Luke wrote his gospel, as he himself explains, that Christians might know the verity of those words in which they had been instructed : he was primarily a historian or recorder, writing for the information of Greeks.   And he indicates for us what were his sources : as many had written accounts of the things that had happened as they heard them from those " who from the beginning were eye-witnesses and ministers of the word ", it seemed good to him also, " having dili-gently attained to all things from the beginning ", to set them out in an ordered narrative.   It is only in the gospel of St Luke that we have a full account of the annunciation of the mystery of the Incarnation to the Blessed Virgin, of her visit to St Elizabeth, and of the journeys to Jerusalem (ix 51 ; xix 28).   He relates six miracles and eighteen parables not mentioned in the other gospels. He wrote the book called the Acts of the Apostles as an appendix to his gospel, to prevent false relations by leaving an authentic account of the wonderful works of God in planting His Church and of some of the miracles by which He confirmed it. Having related some general transactions of the principal apostles in the first establishment of the Church, beginning at our Lord's ascension, he from the thirteenth chapter almost confines himself to the actions and miracles of St Paul, to most of which he had been privy and an eye-witness.

Luke was with St Paul in his last days : after writing those famous words to Timothy, " The time of my dissolution is at hand. I have fought a good fight : I have finished my course : I have kept the faith . . .", the apostle goes on to say, " Only Luke is with me ". Of what happened to St Luke after St Paul's martyrdom we have no certain knowledge : the later statements about him are impossible to reconcile. But according to a fairly early and widespread tradition he was unmarried, wrote his gospel in Greece, and died at the age of 84 in Boeotia. St Gregory Nazianzen (d. 390), who speaks of Greece as the chief field of Luke's evangelism, is quoted as the first to say he was martyred ; but Gregory's words do not certainly mean that : the martyrdom seems more than doubtful. The Emperor Constantius II (d. 361) ordered the reputed relics of St Luke to be translated from the Boeotian Thebes to Constantinople.

As well as of physicians and surgeons, St Luke is the patron saint of painters of pictures. A writer of the earlier sixth century states that the Empress Eudokia had a century before sent to St Pulcheria from Jerusalem an eikon of our Lady painted by St Luke. Other pictures were afterwards attributed to him ; but St Augustine states clearly that nothing was known about the bodily appearance of the Virgin Mary. On the other hand there can be no question of the many subjects suggested to so many artists by St Luke's descriptions of events in his writings. In accommodating the four symbolical representations mentioned in Ezechiel to the four evangelists, the ox or calf was assigned to Luke ; St Irenaeus explains this by reference to the sacrificial element in the beginning of his gospel.

For a reliable appreciation of the author of the third gospel we must turn to such work of modern scholars as the admirable preface which Father Lagrange prefixed to his book, *L'Évangile selon St Luc* (1921). Of a proper biography there can of course be no question. Everything is uncertain beyond the little we find recorded in the New Testament itself, but Harnack, writing with the more persuasiveness as a non-Catholic at one time suspected of rationalizing tendencies, very solidly demonstrated that Luke the physician was the author both of the third gospel and of the whole of the Acts of the Apostles, despite the attempts which have been made, on the basis of the so-called " We " sections (*Wirstücke*) to prove that the text of this last was a conflation of at least two different documents. See Harnack, *Lukas der Arzt,* and subsequent publications of his written in support of the same thesis; all of which have been translated into English. For the history of St Luke, the Latin and Greek prefaces to early texts of the gospel are worthy of being taken into consideration (see the *Revue Bénédictine,* 1928, pp. 193 *seq.*), as also the short notice preserved in the Muratorian canon. See further the preface to E. Jacquier's great commentary, *Les Actes des Apôtres* (1926), and Theodore Zahn's *Die Apostelgeschichte des Lukas* (1919–21). On the portraits of our Lady supposed to have been painted by St Luke, see DAC., vol. ix, c. 2614. See also A. H. N. Green-Armytage, *Portrait of St Luke* (1955).

ST JUSTUS OF BEAUVAIS, Martyr   (Date Unknown)

" At Sinomovicus in the territory of Beauvais ", says the Roman Martyrology, " the passion of St Justus the martyr who, while still a boy, was beheaded by the governor Rictiovarus during the persecution of Diocletian." This young martyr was formerly famous all over north-western Europe, and the church of Beauvais even had his name in the canon of the Mass and accorded his feast a proper preface ; but the extension of his *cultus* was in some measure due to confusion with other saints of the same name. His legend as it has come down to us is worthless. According to it Justus lived at Auxerre, and when he was nine years old went with his father Justin to Amiens in order to ransom Justinian, Justin's brother, who was held a slave there. They called on his master, Lupus, who was ready to sell the slave if he could be identified, but when they were all paraded for inspection neither brother recognized the other. Whereupon Justus, who had never seen his uncle before, pointed out a man who was carrying a lamp, crying, " That is he ! " So it was, and Lupus handed him over.

A soldier who had witnessed the occurrence reported to Rictiovarus that there were some Christian magicians in the town, and the governor sent four men after them to bring them back, and if they would not come quietly they were to be killed on the spot. When the three Christians came to Sinomovicus (now Saint-Just-en-Chaussée), between Beauvais and Senlis, they sat down to eat by the side of a spring, when young Justus suddenly saw the four horsemen in the distance. Justin and Justinian at once hid themselves in a near-by cave, telling the boy to put the soldiers off if they came that way. When they rode up the pursuers saw Justus and asked him where were the two men they had seen with him and to what gods they were in the habit of sacrificing. He ignored one question, and replied to the other that he was a Christian. At once one of the soldiers smote off his head, and was about to pick it up to carry it back to Rictiovarus when the dead body stood upright and a voice was heard saying, " Lord of Heaven and earth, receive my soul, for I am sinless ! " At this prodigy the soldiers fled from the place, and when Justin and his brother came out of the cave there was the body of St Justus with its head in its hands ; and it is fabled to have directed them to bury the trunk in the cave and to take the head home to his mother, " who, if she wants to see me again, must look for me in Heaven ". A similar story is told of the St Justin venerated at Paris, for whom the " acts " of St Justus have been borrowed, " unde multiplex orta est in breviariis perturbatio ", observe the Bollandists.

Although this legend is entirely fabulous, we may infer from the fact that it is preserved in four recensions that it must have enjoyed a certain popularity. See the *Acta Sanctorum*, October, vol. viii, and BHL., nn. 4590–4594. There is no mention of this Justus in the *Hieronymianum*, and there seems grave reason to doubt whether Rictiovarus, the persecutor whose name occurs so frequently in the Roman Martyrology, ever existed. For an important comment and references, see *Analecta Bollandiana*, vol. lxxii (1954), p. 269.

19 : ST PETER OF ALCANTARA   (A.D. 1562)

PETER GARAVITA the younger was born at Alcantara, a small town in the province of Estremadura in Spain in 1499. His father was a lawyer and governor of that town ; his mother was of good family ; and both were eminent for their piety and personal merit. Peter was sent to school locally, and had not finished his philosophy when his father died. By his stepfather he was sent to Salamanca University, where he decided to become a Franciscan, and in the sixteenth year of his age he took the habit of that order in the convent of

Manjaretes, situated in the mountains which run between Castile and Portugal. An ardent spirit of penance determined his choice of this friary, for it was a house of those who, among the friars of the Observance, aimed at a yet stricter observance. During his novitiate he had first the care of the sacristy, then of the refectory, and afterwards of the gate, all which offices he discharged without prejudice to his recollection, but not always with exactitude ; he seems, indeed, to have been rather absent-minded. After having charge of the refectory for half a year he was chidden for never having given the friars any fruit. To which he answered that he had not seen any : he had never, in fact, lifted his eyes to the ceiling, where fruit was hanging in bunches. In time he seemed by long habits of mortification to have lost the sense of taste, for when vinegar and salt was thrown into a porringer of warm water, he took it for his usual bean soup. He had no other bed than a skin laid on the floor, on which he knelt a part of the night and slept sitting, leaning his head against a wall. His watchings were the most difficult and remarkable of all the austerities which he practised, and in consequence of them he has been regarded in after-ages as the patron saint of night-watchmen. He inured himself gradually to them, that they might not be prejudicial to his health.

A few years after his profession, Peter was sent to Badajoz to establish a small friary there, though he was at that time but twenty-two years old and not yet a priest. When the three years of his guardianship were elapsed he was promoted to the priesthood, in 1524, and soon after employed in preaching. The ensuing year he was made guardian of Robredillo and later of Plasencia. In all stations of superiority he set the strictest example by the literal acceptance of evangelical counsels, as in the matter of having only one coat : when his habit was being washed or mended he had to seek a warm retired spot in the garden, and wait there with nothing on. During this period he preached much throughout Estremadura, and great was the fruit which his sermons produced. Besides his natural talents and learning he was enriched by God with an experimental and infused knowledge and sense of spiritual things, which is the fruit only of divine grace gained by an eminent spirit of prayer and habits of virtue. His presence alone seemed a powerful sermon, and it was said that he had but to show himself to work conversions. He loved particularly to preach to the poor and from the words of the sapiential books and the prophets of the Old Law. The love of retirement was always St Peter's predominant inclination, and he made petition to his superiors that he might be placed in some remote convent, where he could give himself up to contemplation. Accordingly, he was sent to the friary at Lapa, a solitary place, but at the same time he was commanded to take up the charge of guardian. In that house he composed his book on prayer. This famous treatise was justly esteemed a masterpiece by St Teresa, Louis of Granada, St Francis of Sales and others, and has been translated into most European languages. St Peter was himself a proficient in the school of divine love, and his union with God was habitual ; his ecstasies in prayer were frequent, sometimes of long continuance and accompanied by remarkable phenomena. The reputation of St Peter reached the ears of John III, King of Portugal, who summoned him to the court at Lisbon and tried in vain to keep him there.

St Peter was in 1538 chosen minister provincial of the stricter observance friars' province of St Gabriel of Estremadura. Whilst he discharged this office he drew up even more severe rules, which he wished the whole province to accept in a chapter held at Plasencia in 1540, but his ideas met with strong opposition. He therefore resigned, and went to join Friar Martin-of-St-Mary, who interpreted the Rule of St Francis as an eremitical life, and was building his first hermitage upon a barren mountain called Arabida, at the mouth of the Tagus on the opposite bank to Lisbon. St Peter animated the fervour of these religious, and suggested many regulations which were adopted. They wore nothing on their feet, slept on vine-twigs or on the bare ground, never touched flesh or wine, and would have no library. A number of Spanish and Portuguese friars were attracted to this way of life, and other small communities were formed. That of Palhaes being appointed for the novitiate, St Peter was nominated guardian and charged with the direction of the novices.

Peter was greatly distressed at the trials which the Church was then undergoing, and to oppose prayer and penance to the effects of ill-living and false doctrine he in 1554 formed a design of establishing a congregation of friars upon a yet stricter plan. His project was disapproved by the minister provincial of Estremadura, but welcomed by the bishop of Coria, in whose diocese the saint, with one companion, made an essay of this manner of living in a hermitage. A short time after he went to Rome, travelling barefoot all the way, to obtain the support of Pope Julius III. He got no encouragement from the minister general of the Observance, but he prevailed on the pope to put him under the minister general of the Conventuals and was authorized to build a friary according to his plan. At his return a friend built such an one as he desired near Pedrosa, which is the beginning of the group of Franciscans called of the observance of St Peter of Alcantara. The cells were exceedingly small, and half of each was filled with a bed, consisting of three boards ; the church was of a piece with the rest. It was impossible for persons to forget their engagement in a penitential life while their habitations seemed rather to resemble graves than rooms. Among the supporters of this " reform " was a friend of St Peter to whom, when he one day bewailed the wickedness of the world, the saint replied, " The remedy is simple. You and I must first be what we ought to be : then we shall have cured what concerns ourselves. Let each one do the same, and all will be well. The trouble is that we all talk of reforming others without ever reforming ourselves."

Other houses received the new observance, and in the statutes which he drew up for them St Peter orders that each cell should be only seven feet long ; that the number of friars in a convent should never exceed eight ; that they should always go barefoot ; that they should employ three hours every day in mental prayer, and never receive any stipend for offering Mass ; and re-enacted the other extreme points of the observance of Arabida. In 1561 this new custody was made a province with the title of St Joseph, and Pope Pius IV removed it from the jurisdiction of the Conventuals to that of the Observants. (These " Alcantarines " disappeared as a separate body when Pope Leo XIII united the different branches of the Observants in 1897.) As is usual in affairs of this sort, the action of St Peter was not well received by those he had left, in this case, the province of St Gabriel. He was a hypocrite, traitor, disturber of peace, ambitious, and was sent for to be told so. " My fathers and brothers ", he replied, " make allowance for the good intention of my zeal in this matter, and if you are convinced it were better that it should not succeed, spare no pains to stop it." They did not spare them, but the " reform " nevertheless spread.

During the course of a visitation towards the year 1560, St Peter came to Avila, according to some in consequence of a direct instruction from Heaven. Here St

Teresa, still at the Incarnation convent, was suffering exterior and interior trials from scruples and anxiety, for many told her that she was deluded by an evil spirit. A friend of St Teresa got leave that she might pass eight days in her house, and arranged that St Peter should there talk with her at leisure. From his own experience and knowledge in heavenly communications he understood hers, cleared her perplexities, gave her strong assurances that her visions and prayer were from God, and spoke to her confessor in their favour. It is from St Teresa's autobiography that we learn much concerning St Peter's life and miraculous gifts, for he told her in confidence many things concerning the way in which he had lived for seven-and-forty years. " He told me ", says she, " that, to the best of my remembrance, he had slept but one hour and a half in twenty-four hours for forty years together ; and that in the beginning it was the greatest and most troublesome mortification of all to overcome himself against sleep, and that for this he was obliged to be always either kneeling or standing. . . . In all these years he never put up his hood, however hot the sun or heavy the rain ; nor did he ever wear anything upon his feet or any other garment than his habit of thick coarse cloth (without anything next his skin) and this short and scanty and as straight as possible, with a cloak of the same over it. He told me that when the weather was extremely cold, he was wont to put off his mantle and to leave the door and the window of his cell open, that when he put it on again and shut his door his body might be somewhat refreshed with this additional warmth. It was usual with him to eat but once in three days, and he asked me why I wondered at it : for it was quite possible to one who had accustomed himself to it. One of his companions told me that sometimes he ate nothing at all for eight days. But that perhaps might be when he was in prayer : for he used to have great raptures and vehement transports of divine love, of which I was once an eye-witness. His poverty was as extreme as his mortification, even from his youth. . . . When I came to know him he was very old, and his body so shrivelled and weak that it seemed to be composed as it were of the roots and dried bark of a tree rather than flesh. He was very pleasant but spoke little unless questions were asked him ; and he answered in a few words, but in these he was worth hearing, for he had an excellent understanding."

When St Teresa returned from Toledo to Avila in 1562 she found St Peter there, and he spent much of the last months of his life and what strength remained to him in helping her to carry through the foundation of her first house of reformed Carmelites, and her success was in good measure due to his encouragement and advice, and to the use which he made of his influence with the bishop of Avila and others. On August 24 he was present when the first Mass was celebrated in the chapel of the new convent of St Joseph. In the troublous times which followed St Teresa was strengthened and comforted by several visions of St Peter of Alcantara, who was by then dead. According to her testimony, quoted in the decree of his canonization, it was St Peter who did more for her nascent reform than anyone else. That he approached things in a way that would appeal to her may be judged from the opening of his letter to her defending absolute poverty for the new foundation : " I confess I am surprised that you have called in learned men to solve a question which they are not competent to judge. Litigation and cases of conscience belong to canonists and theologians, but questions of the perfect life must be left to those who lead it. To be able to deal with a matter one must know something about it, and it is not for a learned man to decide if you and I shall or shall not practise the evangelical counsels. . . . He who gives the counsel will provide the means. . . .

The abuses in monasteries which have given up revenues arise from this—that poverty in them is endured rather than desired."

Two months after the opening of St Joseph's St Peter was seized with a mortal sickness, and he was carried to the convent of Arenas that he might die in the arms of his brethren. In his last moments he repeated those words of the psalmist, " I rejoiced at the things that were said to me : We shall go into the house of the Lord ". Then he rose upon his knees, and in that posture calmly died. St Teresa wrote: "Since his departure our Lord has been pleased to let me enjoy more of him than I did when he was alive ; he has given me advice and counsel in many things, and I have frequently seen him in great glory. . . . Our Lord told me once that men should ask nothing in the name of St Peter of Alcantara wherein He would not hear them. I have recommended many things to him that he might beg them of our Lord, and I have always found them granted." St Peter of Alcantara was canonized in 1669.

As compared with such mystics as St Teresa of Avila and St John-of-the-Cross, the life of St Peter of Alcantara seems only to have aroused languid interest. The earliest printed biography which we now possess did not appear until 1615, fifty-three years after the saint's death. It was written by Fr John-of-St-Mary and a Latin version of it is printed in the *Acta Sanctorum*, October, vol. viii. With this the Bollandists have coupled a somewhat longer life by Fr Laurence-of-St-Paul, first published in 1669. In 1667 Fr Francis Marchese brought out a life in Italian in which he claims to have made use of the depositions of witnesses in the process of canonization. This has been translated into many languages, and an English version in two volumes was printed in the Oratorian Series in 1856. See also Léon, *Auréole séraphique* (Eng. trans.), vol. iv ; and S. J. Piat's short account in the " Profils franciscains " series (1942).

SS. PTOLEMAEUS, LUCIUS AND ANOTHER, MARTYRS (*c.* A.D. 161)

THE Roman Martyrology mentions today these three martyrs, the circumstances of whose passion at Rome are known from the evidence of a contemporary, St Justin Martyr. A certain married woman of dissolute life was converted to Christianity, and in turn tried to reform her husband and to induce him to become a catechumen. Her efforts failed, and the blasphemies and immoralities of her husband becoming unsupportable, she separated from him. He thereupon denounced her as a Christian, but the woman obtaining permission to delay her defence, the man instead informed against her instructor in the faith, Ptolemaeus. He was therefore arrested, and after being kept in prison for a long time was brought before the magistrate Urbicius. In reply to the question if he were a Christian, Ptolemaeus said that he was, and without more ado was sentenced to death. Thereupon a Christian named Lucius who was present protested to Urbicius, saying, " How is it that this man can be condemned when he is guilty of no crime whatever ? Your judgement does no credit to our wise emperor and the senate." Urbicius turned on him and exclaimed, "You also seem to be one of these Christians ", and when Lucius admitted that he was, he also was condemned. Another man, whose name is not recorded, suffered with the others.

In the *Acta Sanctorum*, October, vol. viii, the extract is printed which Eusebius has quoted from St Justin's *Apology*. See also Urbain, *Ein Martyrologium der christlichen Gemeinde zu Rom*, but it should be read in the light of Delehaye's comments in the *Analecta Bollandiana*, vol. xxi (1902), pp. 89–93.

ST VARUS, Martyr, and ST CLEOPATRA, Widow   (Fourth Century ?)

The circumstances of the passion of St Varus in Egypt are summarized thus by the Roman Martyrology : " Varus, a soldier, in the time of the Emperor Maximinus, visited and fed seven holy monks while they were kept in prison, and when one of them died offered himself as a substitute in his place.   And so, after suffering most cruel torments, he received the martyr's palm with them."

The mangled body of St Varus was secured by a Christian woman named Cleopatra, who hid it in a bale of wool and, so disguised, transported it to Adraha (Dera'a, east of Lake Tiberias), where she lived, and many Christians came to visit the martyr's tomb.   When Cleopatra's son, John, was about to become a soldier, she determined to build a basilica in honour of Varus and to translate his body thereto, and at the same time to put her son and his fortunes under the particular patronage of this martyr who had himself been a soldier.   She therefore built a church, and at its dedication she and John themselves carried the bones of St Varus to their new shrine under the altar.   That same evening John was taken suddenly ill, and during the night he died.   Cleopatra had his body carried into the new church and laid before the altar, and she gave way to her grief and reviled the saint in whose honour she had done so much.   She called on God to restore to life her only child whose body lay there, and so she remained till the following night, when she sank into a deep sleep, exhausted by weeping and sorrow.   While she slept she dreamed that St Varus appeared to her in glory, leading John by the hand, and that she laid hold of their feet in mute supplication.   And Varus looked down on ... and said, " Have I forgotten all the love you have shown for me ?   Did I not pray to God that He would give health and advancement to your son ?   And behold ! the prayer is answered.   He has given him health for evermore and raised him to be among the hosts who follow the Lamb whithersoever He goeth."   " I am satisfied ", replied Cleopatra, " but I pray you that I also may be taken, that I may be with my son and you."   But St Varus replied, " No.   Leave your son with me, and wait awhile, and then we will fetch you."   When Cleopatra awoke she did as she had been bidden in her dream and had the body of John laid beside that of Varus.   And she lived a life of devotion and penitence until, when seven years were passed, she also was called to God, and her body was buried with John and Varus in the basilica which she had built.

The Roman Martyrology does not mention either St Cleopatra or her son, but they are referred to in the Greek *Menaion* under the date October 19.

There is a Greek *passio* which is edited in the *Acta Sanctorum*, October, vol. viii, but in the absence of early *cultus* this pathetic story must be regarded with great suspicion.

ST ETHBIN   (Sixth Century)

His father dying when Ethbin was fifteen his mother entrusted him to the care of St Samson, and later he became a monk under St Winwaloe in Brittany.   He was one day walking with his master, when they saw a leper lying helpless at the side of the way.   " What shall we do with this poor fellow ? " asked Winwaloe.   " Do as the apostles of Christ did.   Bid him to rise up and walk ", replied St Ethbin promptly.   Winwaloe had faith both in his monk and in the power of God, and the sufferer was healed.   When the monastery was destroyed by the Franks,

Ethbin took refuge in Ireland, where he lived for twenty years, and there died, famous for his virtues and miracles. He is named in the Roman Martyrology, but is unknown to Irish calendars. The name Ethbin sounds Anglo-Saxon.

We cannot put trust in the short life which has been printed in the *Acta Sanctorum,* October, vol. viii. See also LBS., vol. ii, p. 466, and Duine, *St Samson* (1909).

ST AQUILINUS, BISHOP OF EVREUX   (*c.* A.D. 695)

LIKE many other Frankish saints of the Merovingian era, Aquilinus spent years in courts and camps before entering the clerical state and attaining the episcopate. He was a native of Bayeux, born there about the year 620. He fought in the wars of Clovis II, and on returning from a campaign against the Visigoths met his wife at Chartres, and they there determined to devote the rest of their days to the direct service of God and His poor, he being then about forty years old. They went to Evreux, where they lived quietly for ten years when, on the death of St Aeternus, St Aquilinus was considered the most worthy to succeed to the see. He was frightened of the distractions inseparable from the episcopate and sought to live rather as a hermit than a bishop ; he had a cell built near to his cathedral, whither he retired whenever opportunity offered to spend long hours in prayer and penance on behalf of the flock which he had been called on to govern. During his last years St Aquilinus was deprived of his sight, but it made no difference to his zeal, which God approved by the gift of miracles.

There is a late biography which is printed in the *Acta Sanctorum,* October, vol. viii. See also Mesnel, *Les saints du diocèse d'Évreux,* part v (1916) ; and Duchesne, *Fastes Épis-copaux,* vol. ii, p. 227.

ST FRIDESWIDE, VIRGIN   (A.D. 735 ?)

FRIDESWIDE is the patron saint of Oxford. Her legend in its simplest form is first told by William of Malmesbury, writing just before 1125. According to it Frideswide, having miraculously got rid of the unwelcome attentions of a king, founded a nunnery at Oxford and there spent the rest of her life. In its more developed form we are told that her kingly father was named Didan and her mother Safrida, and that her upbringing was entrusted to a governess called Algiva. Her inclinations early led her towards the religious state, for she had learned that " whatever is not God is nothing ". But Algar, another prince, smitten with her beauty, tried to carry her off. Frideswide thereupon fled down the Isis with two companions, and concealed herself for three years, using a pig's cote as her monastic cell. Algar continued to pursue her and eventually, on her invoking the aid of St Catherine and St Cecily, he was struck with blindness and only recovered on leaving the maiden in peace. From which circumstance it was said that the kings of England up to Henry II made a special point of avoiding Oxford ! In order to live more perfectly to God in closer retirement, St Frideswide built herself a cell in Thornbury wood (now Binsey), where by the fervour of her penance and heavenly contemplation she advanced towards God and His kingdom. The spring which the saint made use of at Binsey was said to have been obtained by her prayers, and was a place of pilgrimage in the middle ages. Her death is put in 735 ; her tomb at Oxford was honoured with many miracles and became one of the principal shrines of England.

The extant legend of St Frideswide seems to represent no real tradition, and little reliance can be put on it ; but she probably founded a monastery at Oxford in the eighth century, and after various vicissitudes it was refounded in the early twelfth century for canons regular of St Augustine.   In 1180 the relics of St Frideswide were solemnly translated to a new shrine in the church of her name ; and twice a year, at mid-Lent and on Ascension day, it was visited ceremonially by the chancellor and members of the university.   By permission of Pope Clement VII the priory of St Frideswide was dissolved by Cardinal Wolsey, who in 1525 founded Cardinal College on its site, the priory church becoming the college chapel.   In 1546 the college was re-established by King Henry VIII as Christ Church (*Aedes Christi :* " The House "), and the church which had been St Frideswide's became, as well as college chapel, the cathedral of the new diocese of Oxford (and was so recognized by the Holy See on the reconciliation in Mary's reign).   The relics of the saint had by this time been removed from their shrine, but apparently they were not scattered.   For in the year 1561 a certain canon of Christ Church, named Calfhill, went to such trouble to desecrate them that it would seem he must have been insane with fanaticism.   During the reign of Edward VI there had been buried in the church the body of an apostate nun, Catherine Cathie, who had been through a form of marriage with the friar Peter Martyr Vermigli.   Calfhill had Catherine's remains dug up (they had been removed from the church under Mary), mixed them with the alleged relics of St Frideswide, and thus reinterred them in the church.   In the following year an account of this performance was published in Latin (and another in German) which contained a number of pseudo-pious reflections on the text *Hic jacet religio cum superstitione :* " Here lies Religion with Superstition."   It does not appear that these words were actually inscribed on the tomb or coffin, though that they were is asserted by several writers, including Alban Butler, whose comment is, " the obvious meaning of which [epitaph] would lead us to think these men endeavoured to extinguish and bury all religion ".

St Frideswide is named in the Roman Martyrology, and her feast is observed in the archdiocese of Birmingham.   She is said also to have a *cultus* at Borny in Artois (under the name of Frévisse).

The legend of St Frideswide has been transmitted in several varying texts (see BHL., nn. 3162–3169).   The more important have been printed or summarized in the *Acta Sanctorum*, October, vol. viii, and have also been discussed by J. Parker, *The Early History of Oxford* (1885), pp. 95–101.   *Cf.* also Hardy, *Descriptive Catalogue* (Rolls Series), vol. i, pp. 459–462 ; DNB., vol. xx, pp. 275–276 ; an article by E. F. Jacob, in *The Times*, October 18, 1935, pp. 15–16 ; and another by F. M. Stenton in *Oxoniensia*, vol. i (1936), pp. 103–112 (both reprinted, O.U.P., 1953).   There is a popular account by Fr F. Goldie, *The Story of St Frideswide* (1881) ; see also E. W. Watson, *The Cathedral Church of Christ in Oxford* (1935).

BD THOMAS OF BIVILLE   (A.D. 1257)

AROUND the district of Biville in Normandy, where he was born about the year 1187, Thomas Hélye is known as " the Wonder-worker " and enjoys a widespread *cultus* which was confirmed in 1859.   His parents seem to have been people of some local importance and, particularly to please his mother, Thomas was sent to school.   When he was a young man he decided to put the fruits of this privilege at the disposal of other children, and he became a sort of village schoolmaster and catechist in his native place.   The good results of his teaching reached the ears of the citizens of Cherbourg, the nearest town, and he was invited to go and instruct the children there, which he did until sickness drove him home again.　When he was recovered he continued to live in his father's house, in a manner more like that of monk than of a layman, and he soon became known to the bishop of Coutances, who ordained him deacon.　Thomas then undertook pilgrimages to Rome and to Compostela, before going to Paris to complete his studies ; after four years he was made priest.　He increased his austerities, spending part of the night in prayer that he might have the more time in the day for pastoral care and preaching, for which he had a great gift.　Thomas was presented to the parochial benefice of Saint-Maurice, but he was by nature a missionary and, appointing a vicar for his cure, he took up his former work of preaching, catechizing, visiting the sick and sinners, encouraging the poor and oppressed, exhorting the lukewarm and in-different, wherever it seemed that God was calling him, not only in Coutances but in the neighbouring dioceses of Avranches, Bayeux and Lisieux as well.　In the midst of these missionary journeys Bd Thomas was taken ill at the castle of Vauville in La Manche, and died there on October 19, 1257 : the first miracle after his death was the healing of the withered hand of his hostess.

The relics of Bd Thomas Hélye have an interesting history.　His body was buried in the cemetery of Biville, and later translated to the church itself.　At the Revolution the church was profaned and the tomb of Thomas, left *in situ*, used as a desk, when M. Lemarié, vicar general of Coutances, determined to save the relics before it was too late.　At 10.15 in the evening of July 13, 1794, he, with the parish priest and several of the faithful, secretly opened the shrine.　The skeleton of the saint was found with nearly all the bones in place.　It was quickly wrapped in linen and transferred to a wooden coffin, together with an affidavit of the proceedings, sealed up, and conveyed to the church at Virandeville, where it was hidden.　The revolutionary authorities of Biville were unable to fix the responsibility for the " crime " and visited their annoyance on the " constitutional " *curé*, who was imprisoned for neglect of duty and for concealing the names of the delinquents, which he did not know.　The relics were returned to their proper shrine in 1803. There, seven hundred years after the death of Bd Thomas, they still rest.

There is a valuable medieval life by a certain Clement, a contemporary, who was an actual witness of much that he records.　Four years after the death of Bd Thomas an in-vestigation was held at which Clement assisted, and he quotes in his biography from the depositions made regarding the holy missionary's virtues and miracles.　The text has been edited both in the *Acta Sanctorum*, October, vol. viii, and by L. Delisle in the *Mémoires de la Soc. Acad. de Cherbourg*, 1861, pp. 203–238.　See also lives by L. Couppey (1903) and P. Pinel (1927).　There seems, however, as Fr Van Ortroy has pointed out, no adequate evidence for the statement that Bd Thomas was ever appointed chaplain to St Louis IX ; *cf*. the *Analecta Bollandiana*, vol. xxii (1903), p. 505.

BD PHILIP HOWARD, Martyr　　(A.D. 1595)

THOMAS HOWARD, fourth Duke of Norfolk, was beheaded by order of Queen Elizabeth in 1572, and in consequence of the attainder his son Philip did not succeed to the dukedom of Norfolk ; but he became earl of Arundel and Surrey by right of his mother.　His early education was partly under John Foxe and partly under Dr Gregory Martin, but the Protestant influence predominated and he went to Cambridge for two years, where " he received no small detriment ".　At the age of twelve he had been married to Anne, daughter of Thomas, Lord Dacre of Gillesland.　When he went to the court of Elizabeth, Philip suffered yet more detriment : he neglected his admirable wife, impoverished his estates, and earned the brief favour of the queen. But in 1581 he was deeply impressed by hearing a disputation in the Tower of London between Bd Edmund Campion and others and some Protestant divines ; he returned and became devoted to his wife, and in 1584 they were both reconciled to the Church by Father William Weston, s.j.

Before this event they had begun to be under suspicion, and Philip was for a time imprisoned in his own house in London. After it, the manifest change in his way of life gave a further handle for the intrigues of his enemies, and he determined, with his family and his brother William, to flee to Flanders. Philip wrote a long letter to the queen, explaining his conduct—he was come to the point " in which he must consent either to the certain destruction of his body or the manifest endangering of his soul "—and embarked in Sussex. But all his movements had been watched. He was captured at sea, brought back to London, and committed to the Tower. After twelve months, a charge of treason not being able to be substantiated, he was arraigned on lesser charges, vindictively fined £10,000, and sentenced to imprisonment during the royal pleasure. During the Armada scare he was again brought to trial, before his peers, for high treason in favouring the Queen's enemies. The evidence was partly fraudulent, partly worthless (extorted by fear of torture), but Philip was sentenced to death. The sentence was never executed ; why, is not known. He was instead held a prisoner in the Tower for another six years, and he died there on October 19, 1595 (not without suspicion of poison). His dying request that he might see his wife and son, born after his imprisonment, was refused because he would not comply with a condition of attending Protestant worship, which would have also bought his release.

Bd Philip Howard was thirty-eight years old at his death, and had been for ten years uninterruptedly in prison, wherein his patience and conduct were not merely exemplary but heroic. His conversion had been whole-hearted, and he spent much of his time in writing and translating works of devotion. As if close confinement were not sufficient mortification, until his health failed he fasted three days a week, and got up every day for morning prayers at five o'clock. He was particularly penitent for the way he had treated his faithful wife. To Bd Robert Southwell he wrote : " I call our Lord to witness that no sin grieves me anything so much as my offences to that party " ; and to her : " He that knows all things knows that which is past is a nail in my conscience and burden the greatest I feel there ; my will is to make satisfaction if my ability were able." He died " in a most sweet manner, without any sign of grief or groan, only turning his head a little aside, as one falling into a pleasing sleep ". In a declaration prepared for his expected execution he wrote : " The Catholic and Roman faith which I hold is the only cause (as far as I can any way imagine) why either I have been thus long imprisoned or why I am now ready to be executed."

In the Beauchamp tower of the Tower of London may be seen two inscriptions cut in the wall by the hand of Bd Philip in May and June 1587, and one referring to him after his death by another Catholic prisoner named Tucker. Philip Howard's relics are at Arundel.

Vol. xxi (1919) of the publications of the Catholic Record Society is entirely devoted to Philip Howard, and these documents, taken in conjunction with the narrative printed in 1857 from the original manuscript under the title *Lives of Philip Howard, Earl of Arundel, and of Anne Dacres his wife,* afford a more perfect insight into the career and character of the earl than is perhaps available in the case of any other of the Elizabethan martyrs.   The biography of the earl and countess, as Father Newdigate has shown in *The Month* (March 1931, p. 247), was written in 1635, five years after Lady Arundel's death ; the author was a Jesuit who acted as her chaplain but his name is not recorded.

20 : ST JOHN OF KANTI   (A.D. 1473)

JOHN CANTIUS receives his name from his birthplace, Kanti, near Oswiecim in Poland.   His parents were country folk of respectable position and, seeing that their son was as quick and intelligent as he was good, they sent him in due course to the University of Cracow.   He took good degrees, was ordained priest, and appointed to a lectureship or chair in the university.   He was known to lead a very strict life, and when he was warned to look after his health he replied by pointing out that the fathers of the desert were notably long-lived. There is a story told that once he was dining in hall, when a famished-looking beggar passed the door.   John jumped up and carried out all his commons to the man ;   when he returned to his seat he found his plate again full—miraculously. This, it is said, was long commemorated in the university by setting aside a special meal for a poor man every day ;   when dinner was ready the vice-president would cry out in Latin, " A poor man is coming ", to which the president replied, " Jesus Christ is coming ", and the man was then served.   But while he was yet alive John's success as a preacher and teacher raised up envy against him, and his rivals managed to get him removed and sent as parish priest to Olkusz.   St John turned to his new work with single-hearted energy, but his parishioners did not like him and he himself was afraid of the responsibilities of his position.   Nevertheless he persevered for some years, and by the time he was recalled to Cracow had so far won his people's hearts that they accompanied him on part of the road with such grief that he said to them, " This sadness does not please God.   If I have done any good for you in all these years, sing a song of joy."

St John's second appointment at the university was as professor of Sacred Scripture, and he held it to the end of his life.   He left such a reputation that his doctoral gown was for long used to vest each candidate at the conferring of degrees, but his fame was not at all confined to academic circles.   He was a welcome guest at the tables of the nobility (once his shabby cassock caused the servants to refuse him admission, so he went away and changed it.   During the meal a dish was upset over the new one.   " No matter," he said, " my clothes deserve some dinner because to them I owe the pleasure of being here at all "), and he was known to all the poor in Cracow.   His goods and money were always at their disposition, and time and again they literally " cleared him out ".   But his own needs were few ; he slept on the floor, never ate meat, and when he went to Rome he walked all the way and carried his luggage on his back.   He was never weary of telling his pupils to " fight all false opinions, but let your weapons be patience, sweetness and love. Roughness is bad for your own soul and spoils the best cause."   Several miracles were reported of St John, and when news got round the city that he was dying there was an outburst of sorrow.   " Never mind about this prison which is decaying ", he said to those who were looking after him, " but think of the soul that is going to leave it."   He died on Christmas eve, 1473, at the age of eighty-three. St John Cantius was canonized in 1767, and his feast extended to the whole Western church.   He is the only confessor not a bishop who has different hymns for Matins, Lauds and Vespers in the Roman Breviary.

The Bollandists in the *Acta Sanctorum*, October, vol. viii, were unable to discover any satisfactory medieval account of St John Cantius, and they reproduced a biography published in 1628 by Adam of Opatow.   This writer claims to have had access to materials preserved at Cracow, and in particular to have used notes compiled by a contemporary, Matthias of Miechow, who certainly drew up a record of miracles attributed to St John after his death. The latter document is also printed by the Bollandists.   A note upon the place and date of birth of St John will be found in the *Analecta Bollandiana*, vol. viii (1889), pp. 382–388. A French life by E. Benoît was published in 1862.   Lives in Polish are numerous.

ST CAPRASIUS, Martyr   (Third Century ?)

According to the legend of the church of Agen St Caprasius was the first bishop of that city, and when his flock dispersed and fled before persecution he followed them in their hiding-places to minister to them.   But from his place of refuge on Mont-Saint-Vincent he was a witness of the passion of St Faith (October 6), and when he saw the marvels with which God surrounded her martyrdom he went down to the place where her body still lay and confronted the prefect, Dacian. When asked his name he replied that he was a Christian and a bishop, and was called Caprasius.   Dacian remarked on his good looks and youth and offered him rewards and imperial favour if he would apostatize.   Caprasius replied that he wanted to live in no other palace than that of Him whom he worshipped or to have any other riches than those that were imperishable.   He was handed over to the torturers, and his constancy so impressed the bystanders that the prefect ordered him to prison.   The next day Caprasius was sentenced to death and on his way to execution met his mother, who encouraged him to remain firm.   Then he was joined by Alberta, sister of Faith, and by two young brothers called Primus and Felician, nor was the governor able to turn them from their determination to suffer with Caprasius.   So they were all led to the temple of Diana, to give them a last opportunity to sacrifice, and when they refused were beheaded.   Then followed a wholesale massacre, for many pagans professed Christianity on the spot and ere cut down by the soldiers or stoned by their neighbours.

This story is entirely fictitious, but there was a church at Agen dedicated in honour of St Caprasius in the sixth century and he was doubtless a real person. Alberta, Primus and Felician, on the other hand, probably never existed, though the feasts of all of them are kept at Agen ; the two last must be distinguished from the Roman martyrs of the same names on June 9.   The Roman Martyrology gives a long entry to St Caprasius, but does not call him a bishop and makes no mention of his companions.

In the *Acta Sanctorum*, October, vol. viii, two or three variants are printed of that form of the *passio* in which the story of St Caprasius and St Faith are fused into one.   See above under October 6.   Mgr Duchesne, *Fastes Épiscopaux*, vol. ii, pp. 144–146, is inclined to date this amalgamation of the legends as late as the ninth century.   See also Saltet, *Étude critique sur la Passion de Ste Foy et de St Caprais* (1899).

ST ARTEMIUS, Martyr   (A.D. 363)

Cardinal Baronius inserted the name of St Artemius in the Roman Martyrology, following the example of the Eastern church which had venerated him in spite of the fact that he was a supporter of the Arians.   We are told that he was a veteran of the army of Constantine the Great who was made imperial prefect of Egypt, and in discharging this office he had to be a persecutor as well as a heretic. George the Cappadocian had been intruded upon the episcopal throne of Alexandria by the Arian emperor, Constantius, St Athanasius had fled, and it was the duty of Artemius to find him, which he endeavoured to do with great zeal among the monasteries and hermitages of the Egyptian desert ; he also persecuted the orthodox in general. But Artemius was no less zealous against paganism, destroying temples and images, so that when Julian the Apostate became emperor the persecutor was in turn persecuted. Many accusations against Artemius were made to the emperor, among others, that of breaking up idols ; he was accordingly deprived of his property and beheaded.

Whether the Artemius whose healing shrine was a great centre of devotion at Constantinople was identical with this Artemius, the prefect of Alexandria put to death by Julian the Apostate, does not seem to be entirely clear. But the Greek life printed in the *Acta Sanctorum*, which is based ultimately upon the Arian chronicler Philostorgius, quite definitely assumes this. It also states that the Emperor Constantius II commissioned Artemius to convey the reputed relics of St Andrew the Apostle and St Luke the Evangelist from Achaia to Constantinople.

The special interest of this alleged martyr lies in the miracles wrought at his shrine, the detailed record of which has been edited by A. Papadopoulos-Kerameus in his *Varia Graeca Sacra* (1909), pp. 1–79. In these cures something analogous to the incubation, practised by the votaries of Aesculapius at Epidaurus and described by Aristides, seems to have been observed. See Delehaye, *Les recueils antiques des miracles des saints* in *Analecta Bollandiana*, vol. xliii (1925), pp. 32–38 ; and M. P. Maas ; " Artemioskult in Konstantinopel ", in *Byzantinisch-Neugriechische Jahrbücher*, vol. i (1920), pp. 377 *seq*. The Greek life is in the *Acta Sanctorum*, October, vol. viii. *Cf.* P. Allard, *Julien l'Apostat*, vol. iii (1903), pp. 21–32.

ST ACCA, BISHOP OF HEXHAM   (A.D. 740)

IN the household of St Bosa, who afterwards was bishop of Deira (York), was brought up a young Northumbrian named Acca, who profited greatly from the instruction and example of his master. After a time he attached himself to St Wilfrid, whom he served faithfully throughout his troubled life and accompanied on his last journey to Rome, where, says Bede, Acca " learned many useful things about the government of Holy Church which he could not have learned in his own country ". Wilfrid, when he was restored to the see of Hexham, made Acca abbot of the monastery of St Andrew there. St Wilfrid died in 709 and Acca succeeded to his bishopric. St Bede speaks highly of him : " He was ", he says, " a most active person and great in the sight of God and man . . . most orthodox in the profession of the Catholic faith and observant in the rules of ecclesiastical institution ; nor did he ever cease to be so till he received the reward of his religious devotion."

St Acca's activity was very varied. He decorated and enlarged his cathedral church. He was learned in the Scriptures and formed a library in which he deposited the histories of the confessors whose deeds as well as whose relics he was diligent in gathering, and he was a munificent patron of scholars and students. He obtained from Kent the services of a celebrated cantor, Maban or Mafa, who had been taught church chant according to the Roman manner by the successors of the monks sent to England by St Gregory. Both St Acca himself, who was a good singer, and his clergy profited by the tuition of Maban, learning many new chants and correcting those that were corrupt. In his encouragement of learning Acca caused Eddius to write the life of his beloved master St Wilfrid, and also assisted St Bede, who dedicated some of his works to him.

In the year 732, for some reason now unknown, St Acca had to leave his diocese, and is said to have lived in exile at Withern in Galloway. He died in 740 and was buried at Hexham.

For original sources we have Bede's *Ecclesiastical History*, and Richard of Hexham's *Brevis annotatio*, but this last is little more than a careful compilation from Eddius and other earlier authorities. Raine's *Memorials of Hexham*, vol. i, pp. xxx–xxxv and 31–36, supplies nearly all the information obtainable, but consult also the *Acta Sanctorum*, October, vol. viii ; and A. S. Cook in *Transactions of the Connecticut Academy of Arts and Sciences*, vol. xxvi (1924), pp. 245–332. A letter of St Acca to Bede has been printed in Bede's works and elsewhere.

ST ANDREW OF CRETE, MARTYR   (A.D. 766)

THIS martyr is sometimes distinguished as " the Calybite " or " in Krisi " from the other St Andrew of Crete (July 4), who died some twenty-five years earlier. During the aggravated campaign under the Emperor Constantine V against the veneration of holy images he made his way to Constantinople to take part in the struggle. He was present when the emperor himself was watching the torture of some orthodox Christians, and uttered a public and impassioned protest. He was dragged before the imperial throne, and when he had explained his action Constantine told him he was an idolater. St Andrew retorted by accusing the emperor of heresy. He was set on and beaten by the bystanders and was carried, bruised and bleeding, to prison, calling out to Constantine, " See how powerless you are against faith ! " The next day he repeated his defence of images before the emperor, who ordered him to be again scourged and then led through the streets as an example to the people. As he was being thus dragged along a fanatical iconoclast stabbed him with a fishing-spear, and at the Place of the Ox St Andrew fell dead from ill-usage and loss of blood. His body was thrown into a cesspit, but was retrieved and buried at a near-by place called Krisis, where the monastery of St Andrew was afterwards built.

The statement made by Theophanes (Confessor) that Andrew was at one time an anchorite seems to be erroneous. There are two apparently independent versions of the *passio*, both printed in the *Acta Sanctorum*, October, vol. viii. See also J. Pargoire in *Échos d'Orient*, vol. xiii (1910), pp. 84–86.

BD MARY TERESA DE SOUBIRAN, VIRGIN, FOUNDRESS OF THE SOCIETY OF MARY AUXILIATRIX   (A.D. 1889)

THE family of Soubiran is a very ancient and honourable one : its direct line has been traced so far back as the earliest years of the thirteenth century and is related, lineally or collaterally, to St Louis of France, St Elzear de Sabran and his wife Bd Delphina, Bd Rosaline of Villeneuve, St Elizabeth of Hungary, and half the royal families of Europe. In the second quarter of the nineteenth century the head of the family was Joseph de Soubiran la Louvière, who lived at Castelnaudary, near Carcassone. He married Noemi de Gélis de l'Isle d'Albi ; their second child was born on May 16, 1835, and was christened Sophia Teresa Augustina Mary.

The Soubirans worthily maintained the religious traditions of their family, if in a way that marked the sternness rather than the joy of Christianity. And Sophie, under the direction of her uncle, Canon Louis de Soubiran, early heard a call to the religious life in an order or congregation. There were others with like leanings in the sodality of our Lady which the canon directed, and when Sophie was nineteen he decided to form them into a community of béguines, that is, laywomen living in community under temporary vows of obedience and chastity. This was not at all what Sophie was looking for : béguines live a life of considerable freedom and ease, and can return entirely to the world at any time, whereas she felt drawn to the austerity and hiddenness of the Carmelites. However, after a period of considerable spiritual perturbation and after taking prudent advice, she decided to fall in with her uncle's wishes and went to the béguinage at Ghent to learn its rule and way of life. On her return the béguine house was opened at Castelnaudary, and she was appointed its superioress. This was in 1854-55.

During the years that followed the new foundation grew and made considerable progress, developing on rather different lines from those of the Belgian béguinages : the sisters gave up the free use of their own property, an orphanage was established and, after a disastrous fire, the practice of night-adoration of the Blessed Sacrament was instituted. Nevertheless it was a difficult time, both for the community and its superioress, and in the *langue d'oc* the Castelnaudary béguinage has been called the *coubent del patiment*, " convent of suffering ". In 1863 Mother Mary Teresa, as we may now call her, again consulted the superioress of the convent of our Lady of Charity at Toulouse and other trusted friends, and they advised her to make a retreat according to the Exercises of St Ignatius. This she did, under the direction of the famous Father Paul Ginhac, and during the retreat it was made clear to her that it was God's will that she should persevere with what was in her mind, which was to lead to the foundation of a new congregation, " de Marie Auxiliatrice ", our Lady of Help. Its aim was to be the following of the religious life in its fullness and work for " the most divine of all human objects, the saving of souls " ; no undertaking was to be too small or lowly for its members, especially if others were unwilling or unable to do it. In due course Canon de Soubiran agreed to these developments. The béguinage at Castelnaudary was not to be dissolved ; but in September 1864 Mother Mary Teresa with some of the sisters was to migrate to a convent in the Rue des Bûchers at Toulouse, which was to be the home of the new community. It is from the following year that the extant writings of Mother Mary Teresa date, which enable her inner life to be closely followed until her death a quarter of a century later.

At Toulouse the care of orphans and teaching of poor children was continued, but the great work inaugurated there was a hostel for working-girls, the first of its kind. It was called the *maison de famille*, " home ", a home for those who had none or were separated from it. The night-adoration also was continued, but from being monthly soon became daily. In drawing up the broad outlines of the constitutions of her society, Mother Mary Teresa based herself on the spirit of the rule of the Society of Jesus, and the final revision was made with the help of Father Ginhac, who associated himself closely with the new enterprise. It was approved in 1867 by the archbishop of Toulouse, at the end of 1868 the Holy See issued a brief of praise, and in the following year a second and a third house were opened, at Amiens and at Lyons. In these large cities, as at Toulouse, the sisters were principally engaged in the care of working-girls. Then came the Franco-Prussian war, and the members of the three houses took refuge for a time in Southwark and then Brompton, where they were befriended by the fathers of the Oratory ; later they established a hostel in Kennington. When they returned to France a community was left in the last-named convent, the beginning of the congregation in England.

In 1868 there had been admitted to the Society of Mary Auxiliatrix a novice who by 1871 was elected counsellor and assistant mother general by an almost unanimous vote of the chapter. She was known as Mother Mary Frances, a very capable and intelligent woman, five years older than the mother general, Mary Teresa de Soubiran. After the exile in England, Mother Mary Frances produced an ambitious scheme for the development of the society, and got it accepted by " the brilliance of her explanations, the force and clarity of her arguments, the justness of her estimates, her shrewdness, tact and skill in affairs . . . and the lively and warm faith that animated her ". Those are the words of Mother Mary Teresa, and they are a measure of the domination which the assistant general had over her ; she did not see for a long time, as was to become only too clear, that Mother Mary Frances was also " domineering, unstable and ambitious ". The result was that developments were allowed to go ahead far too quickly, new houses were opened without sufficient resources, and by the beginning of 1874 Mother Mary Frances announced (inaccurately, it now appears) that the financial position of the society was desperate.

At first Mother Mary Frances blamed herself : but soon she turned and reproached Mother Mary Teresa for what she alleged to be blundering, pride, weak hesitation and lack of religious spirit. The cry was taken up elsewhere, that the Society of Mary Auxiliatrix was in a bad way and that it was all the fault of the foundress. And Mother Mary Teresa remembered how a little time before our Lord had seemed to say to her, " Your mission is ended. There will soon be no place for you in the society. But I will do all with power and gentleness." She had replied, " So be it " then, and she replied " So be it " now ; but first Father Ginhac must be consulted. He, good man, was puzzled, and very properly sent for Mother Mary Frances too. She persuaded him of her view of the situation ; and he advised Mother Mary Teresa to resign. She did so ; and her counsellor took her place.

The mother house of the society was then at Bourges and the new mother general was anxious that her predecessor should return neither there nor to any other house of the society. So Mother Mary Teresa went to the Sisters of Charity at Clermont, ostensibly for a few weeks' rest ; in the event she was there for seven months, " seven months of anguish ", during which it was decided what should be done about her. There is no need to go into the painful details of how Mother Mary Frances sought to prevent any revival of the influence and authority of Mother Mary Teresa ; they were all steps leading to what eventually took place—the irrevocable dismissal of the foundress from the society she had founded. In September she had to leave the convent at Clermont, and she had now to discard her religious habit. By the end of 1874 Mother Mary Teresa, foundress of the Society of Mary Auxiliatrix, was again simply Sophie de Soubiran la Louvière.

She had to begin life all over again—an ordeal common among persons living " in the world " but rare after twenty years of conventual life. She applied for admission to the Visitation order, but they could not see their way to accept her ; nor would her " first love ", the Carmelites. So she turned to her old friends at the convent of our Lady of Charity in Toulouse, who were engaged in what is nowadays called rescue-work. These did not turn her away, and moreover agreed with her request that she should be received in their Paris house. After further delays due to canonical difficulties, and an illness that nearly cost her her life, Bd Mary Teresa made her profession in 1877, when she was forty-two years old. It is clear from her journal that she now entered upon a period of spiritual serenity, that our Lord was indeed doing all things with power and gentleness in her regard. " Mother de Soubiran carried self-abnegation so far ", wrote her director, Father Hamon, " that she was able to banish her first religious family from her mind and to leave it entirely to the will of divine Providence, thus as it were forcing the Good Shepherd to look after the poor orphans. The generosity with which she made this sacrifice seemed to me to partake of heroism."

In any case Mother Mary Frances allowed no contact, by correspondence or otherwise, between the Mary Auxiliatrix nuns and their foundress. Then, after eight years, contact was re-established in a dramatic and distressing way : Bd Mary Teresa's sister, Mother Mary Xavier, who had been one of the first to join the society, also was dismissed by the mother general, lest she should keep the memory of the foundress too much alive. She, too, found refuge in the Paris convent of our Lady of Charity, and the report she brought of the state of the Society of Mary Auxiliatrix was a sad one. " Now I am sure ", wrote Mother Mary Teresa, " that this little society, which God loves so much, which He has watched over so lovingly, in which there are so many fervent and deeply virtuous souls, I am sure, I say, that it is morally dead—that is, that its aims, its form, its methods have ceased to exist. That is and always will be a very deep and very bitter grief to me. I love God's plans, and I am as nothing before His holy and incomprehensible will."

Tuberculosis had got its hold on Bd Mary Teresa, and her last sickness was prolonged, the last seven months being passed in the infirmary. With the coming of June 1889 the end was clearly at hand, and on the 7th she died, with an unfinished sign of the cross, and the words " Come, Lord Jesus " on her lips. Her body was first buried in the convent vault in Montparnasse cemetery ; it is now enshrined in the chapel of the mother house of Mary Auxiliatrix in Paris. Bd Mary Teresa de Soubiran was beatified in 1946, and the spirit of her life is summed up in this passage from a letter written after her dismissal from the Society of Mary Auxilia-trix : " As you may imagine, all this did not happen without extreme suffering. Only God can measure its depth and intensity, as only He knows the graces of faith, hope and love that flow from it : the great truth that God is all, and the rest nothing, becomes the life of the soul, and upon it one can lean securely amid the incomprehensible mysteries of this world. And this is a good above all other good on earth, for it is on almighty love that we rely for time and eternity. And should I have learned this without such cruel anguish ? I do not think so. Time passes, and it passes quickly : we shall soon know the reason of so many things that surprise and shock our feeble, short-sighted reason." Her feast is celebrated on October 20.

The foundation is part of its founder, and a word must be added about the subsequent history of the society that Bd Mary Teresa de Soubiran founded. She had foretold that within a year of her own death everything would be changed in Mary Auxiliatrix. This came true. There was much discontent with the administration of Mother Mary Frances, several houses had to be closed, and from 1884 her arbitrary mismanagement became intolerable : for example, the seat of the novitiate was changed seven times in less than five years. The crisis came when the general chapter of 1889 refused to ratify yet more changes; and on February 13, 1890, sixteen years to the day from the expulsion of Bd Mary Teresa, Mother Mary Frances herself not only resigned her office but also left the society.

The archbishop of Paris, Cardinal Richard, nominated Mother Mary Elizabeth de Luppé to take her place. Under this nun the true story of Mother Mary Teresa came to light; her sister, Mother Mary Xavier, was recalled; and the Society of Mary Auxiliatrix picked up the threads of its true life and began again to move towards the honoured place that it has in the Catholic Church today.

These few pages are sufficient to show that the story of Bd Mary Teresa de Soubiran is a remarkable one.* But so, too, is the story of Mother Mary Frances— though it can have no place in the lives of the saints. It need simply be recorded that, after her death in 1921 (and so after the cause of Mary Teresa had been introduced) it was discovered that at the time she joined the Society of Mary Auxiliatrix, Mary Frances was a married woman who had deserted her husband; and he was then still alive and she knew it. She was therefore never validly a nun, much less a mother general, and accordingly all her actions in those capacities were invalid also and Mother Mary Teresa had canonically never ceased to be a member of the religious congregation that she founded. Nothing is known of the last thirty years of Mary Frances's life; she had private means and apparently lived alone in Paris.

The first life of Bd Mary Teresa de Soubiran, by Canon Théloz, was published in 1894, and in 1946 an admirable new one appeared by T. Delmas. *La Mère Marie-Thérèse de Soubiran d'après ses notes intimes*, in two volumes, by Father Monier-Vinard, consists mainly of the *beata's* own writings and notes on the spiritual life. Somewhat abridged, it was translated into English by Dom Theodore Baily in 1947, under the title *A Study in Failure*. See also the biography by Fr Wm. Lawson (1952) and Fr C. Hoare's excellent sketch in pamphlet form, *Life out of Death* (1946). Father Grivet's *Vie de la Mère Marie-Elisabeth de Luppé* may also be consulted. *Morte et Vivante* (1933) is an account of Bd Mary Teresa when at the convent of our Lady of Charity, and is said to be not entirely reliable.

ST BERTILLA BOSCARDIN, Virgin   (A.D. 1922)

St Bertilla was a follower of the " little way " of St Teresa of Lisieux: ailing in health, of slight intellectual capacity, lacking in initiative, but with a balanced practical judgement and firm will, she was sanctified in the unobtrusive carrying-out of daily duties, whatever they might be. She was born into a poor peasant family in 1888 at Brendola, between Vicenza and Verona, was christened Anne Frances, and was called Annetta. Her biographer, Don Emidio Federici, says of her childhood that it was " uneventful, hard-working and quiet ". The last epithet seems ill-chosen, for her father, Angelo Boscardin, a jealous man, was given to drink and accordingly there were rows and violence in the home—as Boscardin confessed in giving evidence for his daughter's beatification. Annetta went spasmodically to the village school, but had also from an early age to work in the house and as a domestic servant near by.

* Indeed, in its fullness it appears to be unique in the annals of religious congregations; but *cf.* St Alphonsus Liguori (August 2), St Joseph Calasanctius (August 27) and Bd Teresa Couderc (September 26). Not the least remarkable thing is that such men as Mgr de la Tour d'Auvergne, the archbishop of Bourges and Father Ginhac should have allowed to happen what did happen. In their anxiety to avoid a public scandal they contributed towards a worse one.

She was dubbed " the goose ", and the nickname does not seem to have been playful, so that when a local priest, Don Capovilla, recognized in her a religious vocation, her pastor, the Archpriest Gresele, laughed at the idea. Nevertheless, since, as he said, the girl could at any rate peel potatoes, Don Gresele proposed her to a convent, which refused to receive her. However, when she was sixteen Annetta was accepted by the Sisters of St Dorothy at Vicenza, and given the name Bertilla, after the abbess of Chelles.* " I can't do anything ", she said to the novice-mistress, " I'm a poor thing, a goose.† Teach me. I want to become a saint."

For a year Sister Bertilla worked in the scullery, the bakehouse and the laundry, and then was sent to learn nursing at Treviso, where the Sisters of St Dorothy had charge of the municipal hospital. But the local superioress used her as a kitchen-maid, and she remained among the pots and pans till after her profession in 1907, when she was promoted to help in the children's diphtheria ward. From then on Bertilla was the devoted servant of the sick ; but she soon became sick herself, and for the last twelve years of her life was in constant and severe pain from an internal malady that surgery failed to cure and which eventually killed her.

Early in 1915 the Treviso hospital was taken over for troops, and when two years later the disaster of Caporetto drove the Italians back to the Piave it was in the front line. When during air-raids some of the sisters were helpless with fear, Bertilla—no less frightened—saying her rosary, busied herself taking coffee and marsala to the patients who could not be moved to the basement. She was among those soon evacuated to a military hospital at Viggiù, near Como, and here it was that she came under the admiring notice of the chaplain Peter Savoldelli and of the officer Mario Lameri. The superioress, however, like other local superiors before her, failed to understand and appreciate Sister Bertilla : she thought she was overworking herself and getting too attached to her patients. And so Bertilla was banished to the laundry : here she remained uncomplainingly for four months, till she was rescued by the mother general, a remarkable woman named Azelia Farinea, who withdrew her from Viggiù. After the armistice she returned to the hospital at Treviso and was put in charge of the children's isolation ward.

Sister Bertilla's health had been getting worse and worse, and three years later a serious surgical operation was indicated. It was done ; but after three days, on October 20, 1922, Sister Bertilla died. On the first anniversary of her death a memorial plaque was put up in the hospital at Treviso, " To Sister Bertilla Boscardin, a chosen soul of heroic goodness, who for several years was a truly angelic alleviator of human suffering in this place. . . ." Crowds flocked to her first grave at Treviso and to her tomb at Vicenza ; miracles of healing were attributed to her intercession in Heaven ; and in 1952 Bd Bertilla was beatified, in the presence of members of her family and patients whom she had nursed.

See F. Talvacchia, *Suor Bertilla Boscardin* (1923) ; P. Savoldelli, *Soavi rimembranze* (1939) ; and E. Federici, *La b. M. Bertilla Boscardin* (1952). The last-named work makes full use of the documents of the beatification process.

* For information about St Bertilla, Don Federici refers his readers to the " *Vite dei Padri* ecc., dell' Abate Albano Butler ", quoting from an Italian translation published at Venice in 1825.

† The word used is the dialect *oco*, which seems actually to mean a gander.

21 : ST HILARION, Abbot   (*c.* A.D. 371)

HILARION was born in a village called Tabatha, to the south of Gaza, his parents being idolaters. He was sent by them to Alexandria to study, where, being brought to the knowledge of the Christian faith, he was baptized when he was about fifteen. Having heard of St Antony, he went into the desert to see him, and stayed with him two months, observing his manner of life. But Hilarion found the desert only less distracting than the town and, not being able to bear the concourse of those who resorted to Antony to be healed of diseases or delivered from devils, and being desirous to begin to serve God in perfect solitude, he returned into his own country. Finding his father and mother both dead, he gave part of his goods to his brethren and the rest to the poor, reserving nothing for himself (for he was mindful of Ananias and Sapphira, says St Jerome). He retired into the desert seven miles from Majuma, towards Egypt, between the seashore on one side and a swamp on the other. He was a comely and even delicate youth, affected by the least excess of heat or cold, yet his clothing consisted only of a sackcloth shirt, a leather tunic which St Antony gave him, and an ordinary short cloak. He never changed a tunic till it was worn out, and never washed the sackcloth which he had once put on, saying, " It is idle to look for cleanliness in a hair-shirt ", which mortifications, comments Alban Butler, " the respect we owe to our neighbour makes unseasonable in the world ".

For years together his food was fifteen figs a day, which he never took till sunset. When he felt any temptation of the flesh he would say to his body, " I will see to it, thou ass, that thou shalt not kick ", and then cut off part of his scanty meal. His occupation was tilling the earth and, in imitation of the Egyptian monks, making baskets, whereby he provided himself with the necessaries of life. During the first years he had no other shelter than a little arbour, which he made of woven reeds and rushes. Afterwards he built himself a cell, which was still to be seen in St Jerome's time ; it was four feet broad and five in height, and a little longer than his body, like a tomb rather than a house. Soon he found that figs alone were insufficient to support life properly and permitted himself to eat as well vegetables, bread and oil. But advancing age was not allowed to lessen his austerities. St Hilarion underwent many grievous trials. Sometimes his soul was covered with a dark cloud and his heart was dry and oppressed with bitter anguish ; but the deafer Heaven seemed to his cries on such occasions, the more earnestly he persevered in prayer. St Jerome mentions that though he lived so many years in Palestine Hilarion only once went up to visit the holy places at Jerusalem, and then stayed one day. He went once that he might not seem to despise what the Church honours, but did not go oftener lest he should seem persuaded that God or His worship is confined to any particular place.

St Hilarion had spent twenty years in the wilderness when he wrought his first miracle. A certain married woman of Eleutheropolis (Bait Jibrin, near Hebron) was in despair for her barrenness, and prevailed upon him to pray that God would bless her with fruitfulness ; and before the year's end she brought forth a son. Among other miraculous happenings, St Hilarion is said to have helped a citizen of Majuma, called Italicus, who kept horses to run in the circus against those of a *duumvir* of Gaza. Italicus, believing that his adversary had recourse to spells to stop his horses, came for aid to St Hilarion, by whose blessing and pouring water

over the chariot wheels his horses seemed to fly, while the others seemed fettered :
upon seeing which the people cried out that the god of the *duumvir* was vanquished
by Christ.   From the model which he set other settlements of hermits were founded
in Palestine, and St Hilarion visited them all on certain days before the vintage.
In one of these visits, watching the pagans assembled at Elusa, south of Beersheba,
for the worship of their gods, he shed tears to God for them.   Many of their sick
had been cured by him, so he was well known to them and they came to ask his
blessing.   He received them with gentleness, beseeching them to worship God
rather than stones.   His words had such effect that they would not suffer him to
leave them till he had traced the ground for the foundation of a church, and till
their priest, all dressed for his office as he was, had become a catechumen.

St Hilarion was informed by revelation in 356 of the death of St Antony.   He
was then about sixty-five years old, and had been long afflicted at the number of
people, especially women, who crowded to him ; moreover, the charge of his
disciples was a great burden.   " I have returned to the world ", he said, " and
received my reward in this life.   All Palestine regards me, and I even possess a
farm and household goods, under pretext of the brethren's needs."   So he resolved
to leave the country, and the people assembled in great numbers to stop him.   He
told them he would neither eat nor drink till they let him go ; and seeing him pass
seven days without taking anything, they left him.   He then chose some monks
who were able to walk without eating till after sunset, and with them he travelled
into Egypt and at length came to St Antony's mountain, near the Red Sea, where
they found two monks who had been his disciples.   St Hilarion walked all over
the place with them.   " Here it was ", said they, " that he sang, here he prayed ;
there he laboured and there he reposed when he was weary.   He himself planted
these vines, and these little trees ; he tilled this piece of ground with his own hands ;
he dug this pond to water his garden, and he used this hoe to work with for several
years."   On the top of the mountain (to which the ascent was very difficult,
twisting like a vine) they found two cells to which he often retired to avoid visitors
and even his own disciples ; and near by was the garden where the power of Antony
had made the wild asses respect his vegetables and young trees.   St Hilarion asked
to see the place where he was buried.   They led him aside, but it is unknown
whether they showed it him or no ; for they said that St Antony had given strict
charge that his grave should be concealed, lest a certain rich man in that country
should carry the body away and build a church for it.

St Hilarion returned to Aphroditopolis (Atfiah), and thence went into a neighbouring desert and gave himself with more earnestness than ever to abstinence and
silence.   It had not rained there for three years, ever since the death of St Antony,
and the people addressed themselves to Hilarion, whom they looked upon as
Antony's successor, imploring his prayers.   The saint lifted up his hands and eyes
to Heaven, and immediately obtained a plentiful downpour.   Many labourers and
herdsmen who were stung by serpents and insects were cured by anointing their
wounds with oil which he had blessed.   Hilarion, finding himself too popular also
in that place, spent a year in an oasis of the western desert.   But finding that he
was too well known ever to lie concealed in Egypt, he determined to seek some
remote island and embarked with one companion for Sicily.   From Cape Passaro
they travelled twenty miles up the country and stopped in an unfrequented place ;
here by gathering sticks Hilarion made every day a faggot, which he sent Zananas to
sell at the next village to buy bread.   St Hesychius, the saint's disciple, sought him

in the East and through Greece when, at Modon in Peloponnesus, he heard from a Jewish peddler that a prophet had appeared in Sicily who wrought many miracles. He arrived at Passaro and, inquiring for the holy man at the first village, found that everybody knew him : he was not more distinguished by his miracles than by his disinterestedness, for he could never be induced to accept anything from anyone.

He found that St Hilarion wanted to go into some country where not even his language should be understood, and so Hesychius took him to Epidaurus in Dalmatia (Ragusa). Miracles again defeated the saint's design of living unknown. St Jerome relates that a serpent of enormous size devoured both cattle and men, and that Hilarion induced this creature to come on to a pile of wood and then set fire to it so that it was burnt to ashes. He also tells us that when an earthquake happened the sea threatened to overwhelm the city. The affrighted inhabitants brought Hilarion to the shore, as it were to oppose him as a strong wall against the waves. He made three crosses in the sand, then stretched forth his arms towards the sea which, rising up like a mountain, returned back. St Hilarion, troubled over what he should do or whither he should turn, going alone over the world in his imagination, mourned that though his tongue was silent yet his miracles spake. At last he fled away in the night in a small vessel to Cyprus. Arrived there, he settled at a place two miles from Paphos. He had not been there long when his identity was discovered, so he went a dozen miles inland to an inaccessible but pleasant place, where he at last found peace and quietness. Here after a few years Hilarion died at the age of eighty ; among those who visited him in his last illness was St Epiphanius, Bishop of Salamis, who afterwards wrote about his life to St Jerome. He was buried near Paphos, but St Hesychius secretly removed the body to the saint's old home at Majuma.

The life by St Jerome is our primary source and there is no reason to doubt that much of his information was derived from St Epiphanius, who had had personal contact with Hilarion. The historian Sozomen also gives independent testimony, and there are other references elsewhere, which have all been carefully collected in the *Acta Sanctorum*, October, vol. ix. See especially Zöckler, " Hilarion von Gaza " in *Neue Jahrbücher für deutsche Theologie*, vol. iii (1894), pp. 146–178 ; Delehaye, " Saints de Chypre " in *Analecta Bollandiana*, vol. xxvi (1907), pp. 241–242 ; Schiwietz, *Das Morgenländische Mönchtum*, vol. ii, pp. 95–126 ; and H. Leclercq, " Cénobitisme " in DAC., vol. ii, cc. 3157–3158.

SS. URSULA AND HER MAIDENS, MARTYRS   (DATE UNKNOWN)

THE feast of St Ursula and the maiden martyrs of Cologne is now treated with considerable reserve in the Roman liturgy (it was a project of Pope Benedict XIV's commission to suppress it altogether). It is accorded only a commemoration, with no proper lesson at Matins ; the martyrology ventures to say that they suffered at the hands of the Huns on account of their constancy in religion and chastity, but gives no particulars of numbers or other circumstances.

There is in the church of St Ursula at Cologne a stone bearing a Latin inscription, probably cut during the second half of the fourth or early in the fifth century of our era. Its meaning is far from clear, but it seems certainly to record that one Clematius, a man of senatorial rank, rebuilt, in consequence of certain visions, a ruined basilica in honour of some virgins who had been martyred in that place. Nothing is said of the number, their names, or the time and circumstances of their passion. From this it may be inferred that at some time or other some maidens were martyred at Cologne, and that they were sufficiently well known to have had a church built in their honour at an early date, perhaps by the beginning of the fourth century.   And this is all that can be said with reasonable likelihood of the martyrs made famous by the great and ramified legend of St Ursula and her Eleven Thousand Virgins.

The earliest known form of that legend is a *sermo* composed at Cologne for their feast-day, probably during the earlier ninth century.   The author says that there was then no authentic written account of their passion and nothing certainly known of them, and professes himself to give the local tradition : they were numerous, even thousands ; their leader was called Vinnosa (Pinnosa) ; and they suffered in the persecution of Maximian.   He refers to the theory that the girls had come to Cologne in the wake of the Theban Legion, but himself inclines to the view that they were natives of Britain.   None of the classical martyrologies of this period mentions the martyrs, except that Usuard records the virgins Martha and Saula with several companions at Cologne on October 20 (these are given separately from St Ursula in the present Roman Martyrology) and Wandelbert of Prüm refers to the thousands of virgins of Christ who suffered on the Rhine on October 21.   The first mention by name of St Ursula, as one of eleven virgin-martyrs, occurs in a calendar of the end of the ninth century, and other liturgical sources of about that time give the name as one of five, eight or eleven, but in only one does Ursula come first.   In the early years of the tenth century the number was beginning to be fixed at " eleven thousand ", how or why is not known : the most favoured explanations are the abbreviation XI M.V. (*undecim martyres virgines*) misunderstood as *undecim milia virginum* or a combination of the " eleven " of some documents with the " thousands " of others.

The legend as it took shape in Cologne at the latter part of the tenth century is as follows.   Ursula, the daughter of a Christian king in Britain, was asked in marriage by the son of a pagan king.   She, desiring to remain unwed, got a delay of three years, which time she spent on shipboard, sailing about the seas ; she had ten noble ladies-in-waiting, each of whom, and Ursula, had a thousand companions, and they were accommodated in eleven vessels.*   At the end of the period of grace contrary winds drove them into the mouth of the Rhine, they sailed up to Cologne and then on to Bâle, where they disembarked and went over the Alps to visit the tombs of the apostles at Rome.   They returned by the same way to Cologne, where they were set upon and massacred for their Christianity by the heathen Huns, Ursula having refused to marry their chief.   Then the barbarians were dispersed by angels, the citizens buried the martyrs, and a church was built in their honour by Clematius.   Another and parallel story, of Gaulish provenance, interesting to Englishmen but no less fanciful, is given in a later version by Geoffrey of Monmouth.   He says that the Emperor Maximian (he means Magnus Clemens Maximus ; " Maxen Wledig "), having become master of Britain and Gaul (which Maximus did in 383), planted Armorica with British colonists and soldiers and put them under a prince called Cynan Meiriadog.   Cynan appealed to the king of Cornwall, curiously named Dionotus, to send out women as wives for his settlers. Dionotus responded very handsomely by despatching his own daughter Ursula, with 11,000 maidens of noble birth and 60,000 young women of the meaner sort. Ursula was very beautiful and was intended to be married to Cynan himself.   But

---

* There is a charming account of the mobilization of this company in the *Golden Legend.*

on its voyage to Brittany the fleet was scattered and blown north by a storm ; the women were cast away among strange islands and barbarous peoples, and suffered servitude and martyrdom at the hands of the Huns (and the Picts, adds Geoffrey).

The Cologne version represents the more or less official legend, the date 451 being assigned to the martyrdom, " when Attila and his Huns were retreating after their defeat in Gaul ; having captured Cologne, then a flourishing Christian city, the first victims of their fury were Ursula and her British followers " (lesson formerly read in England). But during the twelfth century it underwent incredible elaboration, chiefly by means of the " revelations " of St Elizabeth of Schönau and of a Premonstratensian canon, Bd Herman Joseph. It is not now questioned that these visionaries were deceived, but at the time they had the support of the " discovery " at Cologne in 1155 of numerous sham relics and forged inscriptions purporting to be the epitaphs of Pope St Cyriacus, St Marinus of Milan, St Papunius, King of Ireland, St Picmenius, King of England, and numerous other entirely imaginary people who were fabled to have suffered with St Ursula. The so-called revelations of Bd Herman (if indeed they were his and were meant to be taken seriously) are even more surprising than those of St Elizabeth. They profess to solve several problems presented by the ever-expanding legend, including the presence of the bones of men, children and even of babes among those of the martyrs. There is no doubt that the great finding of 1155 (there had been smaller ones previously) was due to the opening-up of a common burial-ground, and it is difficult to resist the conclusion that two abbots of Deutz engineered an impious fraud in which St Elizabeth and Bd Herman were inculpably implicated. There is a vast collection of these relics to this day in the church of St Ursula at Cologne, and portions of them have gone all over the world.

Quite apart from any other consideration, it may be emphasized that we learn from the inscription of Clematius that he restored a small basilica, or *cella memorialis* (which possibly had been laid waste by the Franks *circa* 353) ; the martyrs seem to have been buried there, and Clematius laid a ban upon other interments in that spot. The language is quite inconsistent with the idea of a vast cemetery in which thousands of bodies had been heaped together.

Through the later medieval activities names of individual Ursuline martyrs gained currency and are found in local calendars and martyrologies. Among them is St Cordula, named in the Roman Martyrology on the morrow. " She hid herself, being frightened by the sufferings and death of the others. But the next day she repented, gave herself up to the Huns, and was the last of all to receive the martyr's crown." This is a contribution of the nun Helentrudis of Heerse to the legend according to the *passio* " Fuit tempore ".

The long dissertation of Fr Victor de Buck which occupies 230 folio pages in the *Acta Sanctorum*, October, vol. ix (1858), was summarized by Cardinal Wiseman in an address which somehow seems to have escaped republication among his other writings. It may be read in a volume, *Essays on Religion and Literature*, edited by Manning (1865), where it bears the title " The Truth of Supposed Legends and Fables " (pp. 235–286) and is accompanied with a facsimile of the Clematius inscription. Father de Buck contributed much that was new and sound to the solution of the problem, reprinting most of the more vital texts, but his conclusions, more particularly his contention that the feast commemorates a great massacre of Christian virgins by the Huns in 451, have by no means been upheld by later research. The most important study of the subject which has since appeared is that of the eminently critical medievalist, W. Levison, *Das Werden der Ursula-Legende* (1928). He defends against all objections the authenticity of the Clematius inscription, but he agrees with other archaeologists in regarding it as definitely anterior to the Hun inroad of 451. After the Clematius inscription, the *Sermo in natali*, and the brief liturgical notices referred to above, the most important document is the earliest *passio*, " Fuit tempore ", which de Buck, not having seen the prologue, unfortunately disregarded.   It was first printed in the *Analecta Bollandiana*, vol. iii (1884), pp. 5–20.   From these origins the legend developed, but the evolution is too complicated and the literature too vast for more detailed notice. Consult, however, in particular, M. Coens in the *Analecta Bollandiana*, vol. xlvii (1929), pp. 80–110 ; G. Morin in *Études, Textes, Découvertes* (1913), pp. 206–219, who sagaciously calls attention to Procopius, *De Bello Gothico*, bk. iv, ch. 20 ; T. F. Tout, *Historical Essays* (1907), pp. 17–56 ; Albert Poncelet in the *Catholic Encyclopedia*, vol. xv, pp. 225–228 ; H. Leclercq in DAC., vol. iii, cc. 2172–2180 ; LBS., vol. iv (1913), pp. 312–347 ; and Neuss, *Die Anfänge des Christentums im Rheinlande* (1933).   One of the more recent contributions to the subject, dealing primarily with the representations of the legend in art, is that of Guy de Tervarent, *La légende de Ste Ursule* (2 vols., 1931).   The text of the Clematius inscription can be most readily found in LBS., DAC., or the *Catholic Encyclopedia* (*loc. cit.*).   The reference to Geoffrey of Monmouth is to his *History of the Kings of Britain*, bk. v, chs. 12–16.   As regards the statement that St Dunstan supplied the story which is recounted in the *passio* " Fuit tempore ", it is a curious fact that St Dunstan seems to have received episcopal consecration on October 21, and also that some of the few saints named in the Ursula legend were honoured at an early date at Glastonbury and in the west of England.   If Dunstan, as is now believed, was born in 910 and not in 925, some intercourse with Hoolf, the envoy of the Emperor Otto, would have been by no means impossible.

ST MALCHUS   (FOURTH CENTURY)

FOR the story of St Malchus, who is mentioned today in the Roman Martyrology, we are indebted to St Jerome, who says he had it from the lips of the man himself. When he was in Antioch about the year 375 he visited Maronia, some thirty miles away, where his attention was attracted to a very devout old man whose name, he discovered, was Malchus (Malek).   St Jerome was interested in what he heard about him, went to the old man for more information, and was told the following tale of his life.   Malchus was born in Nisibis, the only son of his parents, who when he had reached the requisite age wanted him to marry.   He, however, had already resolved to give himself wholly to the direct service of God, so he ran away and joined some hermits in the wilderness of Khalkis.   Some years later he learned of the death of his father, and he went to his superior and told him that he wished to go home in order to comfort and look after his mother.   The abbot was unsympathetic and represented the inclination to Malchus as a subtle temptation.   Malchus pointed out that he was now entitled to some property and that with it he would enlarge the monastic buildings, but the abbot was an honest man who had made up his mind, and it was not altered by a consideration of that sort.   He implored his young disciple to stay where he was, but Malchus was as persuaded of his duty as the abbot, and he started off without his permission.

Between Aleppo and Edessa the caravan to which Malchus had attached himself was attacked and plundered by Beduin, and Malchus and a young woman were carried off by one of the marauding chiefs.   They were carried on camels to the heart of the desert beyond the Euphrates, and Malchus was set to work as a sheep and goatherd.   He was not unhappy ; certainly he did not like living among heathens and in a greater heat than that to which he was accustomed, but " it seemed to me that my lot was very like that of holy Jacob, and I remembered Moses, both of whom had been shepherds in the wilderness.   I lived on dates and cheese and milk ; I prayed endlessly in my heart ; and I sang the psalms I had learned among the monks ."   No doubt his master was pleased with Malchus—

men carried off as slaves were rarely so obedient and contented—and he sought to arrange a marriage for him.   It is incredible to the wandering tribes of the desert that any man should choose to live alone, and the unmarried man must live as a servant in the tent of another, for none but women do what we should call domestic work, and much more.*   So Malchus was told to marry his fellow captive, and thereupon he was very alarmed : not only was he a monk and so had put marriage behind him, but he also knew that the girl was already married in her own country. It would seem, however, that she was not altogether unwilling.   But when Malchus threatened he would rather kill himself, the girl declared (over the centuries can be heard the note of wounded *amour propre* in her voice) that she was quite indifferent to him and that she was prepared to live with him under a mere appearance of matrimony, and so satisfy their master.   This they did, though neither of them found the arrangement completely satisfactory.   " I loved the woman as a sister " declared Malchus to St Jerome, " but I never entirely trusted her as a sister."

One day Malchus was watching a crowd of ants at work in their heap and the thought came to him how like the sight was to that of a busy and orderly company of monks.   Thereupon he suddenly became very homesick, the memory of his past happiness with the hermits was more than he could bear, and when he had driven in his flocks that evening he went and told his companion that he had made up his mind to escape.   She too was anxious to find her real husband again and was willing enough to adventure with Malchus, so they made their preparations secretly and ran away one night, carrying their provisions in two goatskins.   By means of these skins, which they inflated, they crossed the Euphrates in safety, but on the third day they saw their master and another man, on camels, coming up with them. They hid themselves near the mouth of a cave, and the chief, thinking he saw them go into the cave itself, sent his man in to fetch them out.   When he did not reappear, the chief himself approached and went in, but neither did he come out again. Instead there issued from the cave a lioness with a cub in her mouth, and she leaped off among the rocks, leaving the two Arab intruders dead on the floor of her den.   Malchus and the woman ran to the tethered camels, mounted them, and set off at a great pace.

After ten days' riding they came to a Roman station in Mesopotamia, where the officer in charge listened to their story and sent them on to Edessa.   From there St Malchus made his way back to the hermit colony by Khalkis and eventually went to end his days at Maronia, where St Jerome talked with him.   His companion never found her husband, and in her sorrow and disappointment her mind turned to the friend who had shared her captivity and helped her escape ; she went and settled down near him, giving her time to the service of God and her neighbour, and there she died at a great age.

The text of St Jerome is printed with a full commentary in the *Acta Sanctorum*, October, vol. ix.   Reginald, a monk of Canterbury (d. *c.* 1110), wrote several poems treating of St Malchus ; *cf. The Oxford Book of Medieval Latin Verse* (1928), pp. 73–75 and p. 221, n. 50. For the text with an English translation, see the *Classical Bulletin*, 1946 (Saint Louis, U.S.A.), pp. 31–60.   But the text is of little value, possibly a mere romance composed for purposes of edification : see *Comm. Mart. Rom.*, and P. Van den Ven, in *Le Muséon*, vol. xix (1900), pp. 413 *seq.* and xx, 208 *seq.*

* See C. M. Doughty's *Arabia Deserta*, vol. i, pp. 321–322.   The life described by Doughty is much the same as that lived fifteen hundred years ago by Malchus among the black tents.

ST FINTAN, or MUNNU, OF TAGHMON, Abbot   (*c.* a.d. 635)

Extreme austerity was an outstanding characteristic of the early Irish monks, and this St Fintan or Munnu was reported to be of them one of the most austere, and bodily sickness was added to his voluntary mortifications.   For eighteen years he was a monk under St Senell at Cluain Inis, and then crossed to Iona with the object of joining the community there.   Irish accounts say that St Columba was dead when Fintan arrived and that his successor, St Baithen, sent him back, saying that Columba had prophesied that he should found a monastery in his own country and be himself a father of monks.   The Scots tradition is that he lived on Iona for a time, and returned home on St Columba's death in the year 597.   Somewhere about the beginning of the seventh century Fintan founded the monastery of Taghmon (Tech Munnu) in county Wexford, and while governing this abbey was a zealous upholder of the Celtic method of computing Easter and other local customs.   At the synod held at Magh Lene in 630, and others, he strongly opposed on this matter St Laserian and those who wished to comply with the wish of Pope Honorius I that Ireland should come into line with the rest of Christendom.

The monastery of Taghmon soon became famous, and there are references to its founder in the Lives of St Canice, St Mochua and St Molua.   The last two state that St Fintan was for some time a leper, and there seems to have been a known rivalry between him and Molua : for when an angel who was supposed to visit Fintan twice a week missed a day, and explained subsequently that he had been detained by the necessity of receiving the soul of the recently dead Molua into Heaven, Fintan is represented as being distinctly " put out " about it.   His desire to emulate the merits of the abbot of Clonfert caused him to pray to be stricken with disease, that by his patient bearing of it he should deserve a similar welcome to the Celestial City.   Munnu is sometimes confused with St Mundus in Scotland.

Three Latin lives of this saint are available (see Plummer, *Miscellanea Hagiographica Hibernica*, p. 252).   The longest has been printed in the *Acta Sanctorum*, October, vol. ix, and the third has been edited by Plummer : see VSH., vol. ii, pp. 226–239, and also the introduction, pp. 84 *seq.*   J. F. Kenney, *Sources for the Early History of Ireland*, vol. i, p. 450, quotes with approval Plummer's comment : " Speaking generally the historical element in this life is larger than in some others, and we get an impression of Munnu as a real man and not merely a peg to hang miracles on, a man of somewhat harsh and hasty temper, but placable and conciliatory when the momentary irritation was over ".   There is considerable difficulty in identifying the Scottish St Mundus, and A. P. Forbes, in KSS., pp. 412–416, considers that he is no other than Fintan Munnu.   See, however, the *Acta Sanctorum*, April, vol. ii, and O'Hanlon, LIS., vol. iv, p. 173.

ST CONDEDUS   (*c.* a.d. 685)

Condedus, called in French Condé or Condède, is said to have been an Englishman who, wandering about in search of a place of complete seclusion, came to France and settled down at a spot called Fontaine-Saint-Valéry.   After some years he heard of the great reputation of the abbey of Fontenelle, which was at that time governed by St Lambert, and set out to visit it.   On his way Condedus came to a place where the inhabitants were so suspicious that they would not give him shelter for the night, although the weather was very threatening.   At last he found a woman who took pity on him, and we are told that her kindness was rewarded by a revelation of her guest's holiness.   For the storm broke during the night, and when the good woman got up to cover her window she saw a great column of light reaching from the sleeping-place of Condedus to the sky above.   That this was probably lightning or another phenomenon of the storm does not alter the significance that it had for the woman.   After being a monk at Fontenelle for a short time he returned to a solitary life on an island called Belcinac, in the Seine near Caudebec.   King Thierry III soon after made the acquaintance of the saint, and was so pleased with him that he gave the island and other land as endowment for the hermitage.   St Condedus built two chapels thereon, to which people came from all around to get his direction and listen to his preaching.   After his death he was buried on the island, but afterwards was translated to Fontenelle ; Belcinac has disappeared, swallowed by the waters of the Seine.

A short Latin life of St Condedus printed by Mabillon and in the *Acta Sanctorum*, October, vol. ix, has been re-edited by W. Levison in the MGH., *Scriptores Merov.*, vol. v, pp. 644–651.   As the writer lived more than a century after the subject of his biography, the narrative cannot claim any great authority.   Consult, on the other hand, Legris in the *Analecta Bollandiana*, vol. xvii (1898), pp. 282–287, and Vacandard, *St Ouen* (1902), pp. 198–201.   But Levison in the *Neues Archiv*, vol. xxv, vindicates his own earlier conclusions.

ST JOHN OF BRIDLINGTON   (A.D. 1379)

THOUGH it has been often said that St Thomas of Hereford was the last English saint of the middle ages to be formally canonized (Osmund, in 1457, was a Norman), there is a bull of Pope Boniface IX that canonized John of Bridlington in 1401 ; his feast is now celebrated in the diocese of Middlesbrough and by the Canons Regular of the Lateran (on October 10).   He was surnamed Thwing, from the place of his birth near Bridlington, on the coast of Yorkshire, and the little which is known of his life presents nothing of unusual interest.   At about the age of seventeen he went for two years to study at Oxford.   When he returned from the university he took the religious habit in the monastery of regular canons of St Augustine at Bridlington.   In this solitude he advanced daily in victory over himself and in the experimental knowledge of spiritual things.   John was successively precentor, cellarer, and prior of his monastery.   This last charge he had averted by his protests the first time he was chosen ; but upon a second vacancy his brethren obliged him to take up the office.   His application to prayer showed how much his conduct was regulated by the spirit of God, and a great spiritual prudence, peace of mind and meekness of temper were the fruits of his virtue. When he had been seventeen years prior and had earned a universal esteem and reverence he was called to God on October 10, 1379.

Many miracles wrought through his intercession are mentioned by the author of his *vita* and by Thomas of Walsingham, who testifies that by order of Pope Boniface IX, Richard Scrope, the greatly venerated archbishop of York, assisted by the bishops of Lincoln and Carlisle, translated his relics to a more worthy shrine. This took place on March 11, 1404.   The shrine attracted many pilgrims, among them King Henry V, who attributed his victory at Agincourt to the intercession in Heaven of two English Johns, of Bridlington and of Beverley.   The nave of the priory church in which St John Thwing presided is now the Anglican parish church of Bridlington.

See the *Acta Sanctorum*, October, vol. v, where a life by one Hugh, himself a canon regular, is printed.   There is also a shorter summary by Capgrave in his *Nova Legenda*

Angliae. But most important of all is the article of Fr Paul Grosjean in the *Analecta Bollandiana,* vol. liii (1935), pp. 101–129. He has gathered up much new material, while expressing his indebtedness to the book, *St John of Bridlington* (1924), and other papers by J. S. Purvis. Mr Purvis published the text of the canonization document from the Lateran *Regesta.*

BD JAMES STREPAR, Archbishop of Galich   (c. a.d. 1409)

The Friars Minor entered Poland not many years after their foundation and when they were well established extended their preaching to the reconciliation of dissident Orthodox and the conversion of pagans in Lithuania. Thus was inaugurated the Latin church in Galician Ukraine, which was organized into dioceses during the fourteenth century. Bd James Strepar was a member of a noble Polish family settled in Galicia. He joined the Franciscans and became guardian of their friary at Lvov, where he played a conspicuous part in very troubled ecclesiastical affairs, the city having been laid under an interdict. He was a zealous defender of the mendicant friars, who were bitterly attacked by the secular clergy, and at the same time keenly concerned about the dissident Orthodox. He worked among these for over ten years, making great use of the Company of Christ's Itinerants, a sort of missionary society of Franciscan and Dominican friars, and was put at the head of the Franciscan " mission " in western Russia.

As a missionary preacher and organizer Bd James had great success, and was in 1392 called to govern the see of Galich. He had himself evangelized a considerable part of his diocese, and was now in a position to consolidate his work. He built churches in remote districts and obtained experienced priests from Poland to take charge of them, founded religious houses, and established hospitals and schools. Though a senator of the realm as well as archbishop he sometimes carried out visitations on foot, and always wore the modest habit of his order at a time when prelates not infrequently copied the ostentatious clothes of lay lords. Bd James governed his large diocese till his death at Lvov on June 1, in 1409 or 1411. During his life he had been called " protector of the kingdom " and the miracles at his tomb showed that he was still mindful of his people. His *cultus* was confirmed in 1791.

There is more than one life in Polish, but only summaries seem to be available in languages more generally known. See, however, Scrobiszewski, *Vitae episcoporum Halicensium* (1628) ; Stadler, *Heiligen Lexikon,* vol. iii, pp. 111 *seq.* ; Léon, *Auréole séraphique* (Eng. trans.), vol. ii, pp. 312–315.

BD PETER OF TIFERNO   (a.d. 1445)

Very few particulars of the life of this confessor have been preserved, in part no doubt owing to the destruction by fire of the archives of the friary of Cortona, where he spent the greater part of his life. He belonged to the family of the Cappucci and was born at Tiferno (Città di Castello) in 1390. When he was fifteen he received the Dominican habit and was sent to Cortona, where he was trained under the direction of Bd Laurence of Ripafratta and in company of many other famous friars, including St Antoninus and Fra Angelico. Bd Laurence recommended him to devote himself to contemplation rather than to activity, but the lessons of his office note that he was as ready to minister to those who required his services outside his monastery as within it.   Several miracles are remembered of Bd Peter.   He once met a young man of bad character in the street, stopped him, and said, " What wickedness are you up to now ?   How much longer are you going on adding sin to sin ?   You have just twenty-four hours to live, and at this time tomorrow you'll have to give God an account of yourself."   The man was frightened but took not more notice, till that night he had a bad accident ; Peter was sent for, and he received the sinner's humble penitence before he died.   The *cultus* of Bd Peter, who used to hold a skull in his hands while preaching, was confirmed by Pope Pius VII.

Information regarding Bd Peter was certainly not widely disseminated.   In the vast collection of names which figure in the book of G. Michele Piò, printed at Bologna in 1607, *Delle vite degli huomini illustri di S. Domenico*, there is no mention of him.   We have to fall back upon the lessons of the Dominican breviary, the *Année Dominicaine*, and such summaries as Procter, *Lives of the Dominican Saints*, pp. 294–297.   Consult, however, Taurisano, *Catalogus hagiographicus O.P.*

BD MATTHEW, Bishop of Girgenti   (A.D. 1450)

BD MATTHEW was born at Girgenti in Sicily.   Renouncing riches and worldly hopes, he took the habit of St Francis amongst the Conventuals at the age of eighteen.   Some time after, he heard the fame of St Bernardino of Siena and he left the Conventuals to join the Observants, becoming one of St Bernardino's closest friends.   With him Matthew travelled about Italy and before long shared his fame as a preacher.   The disturbances of the time had led to a great slackening of discipline, and in Sicily in particular simony was rampant among the clergy and indifference among the laity.   Matthew, touched by the misery of his country, returned to Sicily and taught and preached up and down, rousing priests and people from their apathy and spreading everywhere devotion to the Holy Name.

The inhabitants of Girgenti desired to have Bd Matthew as their bishop and, although he himself was most unwilling, Pope Eugenius IV insisted upon his acceptance.   His first care was to restore discipline and check simony, but by so doing he aroused bitter opposition.   His enemies calumniated him, and he had to go to Rome to defend his cause before the pope, who recognized his innocence and restored him to his see.   Again he set about reforming scandals, but he was accused of being a firebrand and of disturbing the peace.   He concluded that he was incapable of governing and asked for his release, which the pope, after some demur, granted.   Matthew returned to the convent which he had founded, but the superior, who had been prejudiced against him, refused him admittance, saying that he had, through ambition, accepted a bishopric which he could not govern, that he would only destroy the harmony of the community and that he had better go elsewhere.   Matthew found a refuge with his old friends the Conventuals, but before long the minister provincial of the Observants begged him to return—which he did.   He lived several years longer ; but when he was afflicted by a malady which the Observants, owing to their poverty and distance from medical advice, were unable to tend, they took him back to the house of the Conventuals, where he died.   The *cultus* of Bd Matthew was confirmed in 1767.

See J. E. Stadler, *Heiligen-Lexikon*, and Léon, *Auréole séraphique* (Eng. trans.), vol. i.

22 : ST ABERCIUS, Bishop of Hieropolis (*c.* A.D. 200)

THERE lived in Phrygia Salutaris during the second century a certain Abercius Marcellus, who was bishop of Hieropolis and who, while in his seventy-second year, made a visit to Rome. His homeward journey was taken through Syria and Mesopotamia, he visited Nisibis, and everywhere he went he met Christians, whose foreheads bore the shining seal of baptism and whose souls were nourished with the body and blood of Christ, the virgin-born, under the forms of bread and wine. Abercius when he returned home prepared a tomb for himself and had carved thereon an epitaph which, in symbolical and to the non-Christian baffling terms, briefly described the journey which had made so deep an impression on the Greek disciple of the all-seeing and universal Shepherd, who had gone to Rome " to contemplate majesty ".

A Greek hagiographer made use of the epitaph as the basis of a fictitious account of the life of St Abercius. According to this ingenious narrative the bishop made so many converts by his preaching and miracles that he deserved to be called " equal to the Apostles " and his fame reached the ears of Marcus Aurelius. The expedition to Rome was made in consequence of a summons from the emperor, whose daughter Lucilla was afflicted by a devil (the symbolical gold-clad queen of the epitaph becomes the empress). St Abercius successfully exorcized this evil spirit and commanded it to transport a great stone altar from the Roman hippodrome to his episcopal city, where it should provide materials for his tomb. Other episodes were added from the legends of other saints, and the writer appended to his tale a transcription of the original genuine epitaph of Abercius.

This epitaph was formerly regarded with nearly as much suspicion as the *vita* of which it formed a part, until in 1882 the English archaeologist, W. M. Ramsay, discovered at Kelendres, near Synnada, an inscribed stone bearing the equivalent of the date A.D. 216. It was a memorial inscription to one Alexander, the son of Antony, which was found to correspond almost word for word with the first and last verses of the epitaph of Abercius. In the following year Ramsay found, built into the walls of the baths at Hieropolis, further fragments which supplied much of the part of the epitaph of Abercius missing from the other stone. With these two inscriptions and the text given in the life of the saint an authentic text of great value was restored. But the claim of Abercius to be a Christian was still not admitted by everyone to be established. On account of the symbolism with which it was expressed, interpreters of the inscription identified him as a priest of Cybele or of Attis or of some syncretistic cult, and it was only after long and lively controversies that it was generally admitted that the Abercius of the inscription was a Christian bishop. He has been venerated liturgically among the Greeks since the tenth century, and he is named today in the Roman Martyrology, but as bishop of Hierapolis (the see of St Papias) instead of Hieropolis, an error found in the bogus life.

A considerable literature has been created by the inscriptions which Sir W. M. Ramsay found at Hieropolis, and which now, by the gracious act of the discoverer, adorns the Christian Museum at the Lateran. All the discussion which has since arisen has added very little to the interpretation which the Anglican Bishop Lightfoot, with sure scholarly instinct, published in vol. i of his *Ignatius and Polycarp* (1885). Such sceptical critics as G. Ficker and A. Dieterich have not produced a fragment of evidence which would raise a doubt regarding the Christian character of the inscription.   The work of F. J. Dölger, *Ichthys* (see especially vol. ii, 1922, pp. 454–507), may be recommended as replying effectively, along with many other vindications, to the objections which have been urged.   Dom Leclercq's article in DAC. (vol. i, cc. 66–87), provides good illustrations and a full bibliography ; the same scholar's article in the *Catholic Encyclopedia*, vol. i, pp. 40–41, prints the Greek text of the inscription with an English translation.   With regard to the Life of Abercius, the two more ancient texts of this Greek fiction have been critically edited by T. Nissen, *S. Abercii Vita* (1912) ; though historically worthless, it contains geographical data of value, and its quotations from Bardesanes are of curious interest.   Writing in 1935 Father Thurston said he was inclined considerably to modify certain views expressed by him in the second of two articles on St Abercius in *The Month* for May and July 1890.

SS. PHILIP, BISHOP OF HERACLEA, AND HIS COMPANIONS, MARTYRS (A.D. 304)

PHILIP, Bishop of Heraclea, the metropolis of Thrace, was a martyr of Christ in the persecution of Diocletian.   Having discharged every duty of a faithful minister as deacon and priest, he was raised to the episcopal dignity and governed that church with virtue and prudence when it was shaken by persecution.   To extend and perpetuate the work of God he trained many disciples in sacred learning and solid piety.   Two of the most eminent among them had the happiness to be companions of his martyrdom, namely, Severus, a priest, and Hermes, a deacon, who was formerly the first magistrate of the city, but after he was engaged in the ministry earned his livelihood with his hands, and brought up his son to do the same.   When Diocletian's first edicts against the Christians were issued, many advised the bishop to leave the city ; but he would not stir, continuing to exhort the brethren to constancy and patience.   Aristomachus, an officer, came by the governor's order to seal up the door of the church.   Philip said to him, " Do you imagine that God dwells within walls, and not rather in the hearts of men ? " and continued to hold his assembly outside.   The next day officers came and set their seal upon the sacred vessels and books.   The faithful who beheld this were much grieved ; but the bishop stood leaning against the door of the church, encouraged them with burning words, and refused to leave his post.

Afterwards the governor, Bassus, finding Philip and many of his flock keeping the Lord's Day assembled before the church, gave orders that they should be brought before him.   " Which of you ", he asked, " is the teacher of the Christians ? "   Philip replied, " I am ".   Bassus said, " You know that the emperor has forbidden your assemblies.   Give up to me the vessels of gold and silver which you use and the books which you read."   The bishop answered, " The vessels we will give you, for it is not by precious metal but by charity that God is honoured. But the sacred books it becomes neither you to demand nor me to surrender." The governor ordered executioners to be called, and commanded one among them to torture Philip, who bore his torments with invincible courage.   Hermes told the governor that it was not in his power to destroy the word of God, even though he should take away all the writings in which the true doctrine is contained, and in reply Bassus had him scourged.   After this he was taken with Publius, the governor's assistant, to the place where the sacred writings and plate were hid. Publius would have taken away some of the vessels, but being hindered by Hermes he gave him such a blow on the face that blood flowed.   The governor was provoked at Publius for this action, and ordered the wound to be dressed.   He then ordered Philip and the other prisoners to be brought to the market-place, and the church roof to be stripped. In the meantime soldiers burned the sacred writings, the flames mounting so high as to frighten the bystanders. This being told to Philip in the market-place, he spoke at great length of the vengeance with which God threatens the wicked and told the people how their gods and temples had been often burned.

Then a pagan priest appeared in the market-place with his ministers, who brought with them the necessary preparations for a sacrifice, and the governor Bassus came, followed by a multitude, some of whom pitied the suffering Christians ; others, especially the Jews, clamoured loudly against them. Bassus pressed the bishop to sacrifice to the gods, to the emperors and to the fortune of the city. Pointing at a large and beautiful statue of Hercules, he bid him just to touch it : Philip replied by expounding the value of graven images to stone-carvers but their helplessness to worshippers. Then, turning to Hermes, Bassus asked if he, at least, would sacrifice. " I will not ", replied Hermes, " I am a Christian." Bassus asked, " If we can persuade Philip to offer sacrifice, will you follow his example ? " Hermes answered he would not ; neither could they persuade Philip. After many useless threats and pressing them to sacrifice at least to the emperors, Bassus ordered them to be carried to prison. As they went along, some of the rabble pushed Philip and threw him down ; he got up again with a smiling face. Many admired his patience, and the martyrs entered the prison joyfully, singing a psalm of thanksgiving to God. A few days after, they were allowed to stay at the house of one Pancras, near the prison, where many Christians and some neophytes came to them to be instructed, and later were removed to a prison near the theatre, which had a door into that building, with a secret entry. They there received at night the crowds that came to visit them.

In the meantime, Bassus went out of office at the end of his term and Justin succeeded him. The Christians were much disappointed at this change : for Bassus often yielded to reason and his wife had for some time been a Christian herself ; but Justin was a violent man. Zoilus, the magistrate of the city, brought Philip before him, and Justin declared once more what was the emperor's order, and pressed him to sacrifice. Philip answered, " I am a Christian, and cannot do what you require. You can punish our refusal, but you cannot force our compliance." Justin threatened him with torture, and the bishop replied, " You may torment, but will not conquer me ; no power can induce me to sacrifice ". He was told he would be dragged by the feet through the streets and thrown into prison to suffer anew. " God grant it may be so ", was Philip's comment. Then Justin told the soldiers to tie his feet and drag him along. They dashed him against the stones so roughly that he was torn and bruised all over, and the Christians carried him in their arms when he was brought back to his dungeon.

The persecutors had long been in quest of the priest Severus, who had hidden himself. Moved by the Holy Ghost, he at length surrendered and was committed to prison. Hermes was firm in his examination before Justin, and was treated in the same manner. The three martyrs were kept imprisoned in a bad place for seven months and then removed to Adrianople, where they were confined in a private house till the arrival of the governor. The next day, holding his court at the Baths, Justin had Philip brought before him and beaten till his flesh was a pulp. His endurance astonished the executioners and Justin himself, who remanded him to prison. Hermes was next examined. The officers of the court were favourable to him because he had been magistrate of Heraclea and a popular one. But he persisted in his profession, and was sent back to prison, where the martyrs joyfully gave thanks to Jesus Christ for this beginning of their victory. Three days after this, Justin brought them again before his tribunal, and having in vain pressed Philip to obey the emperors, said to Hermes, " If the approach of death makes this man think life not worth preserving, do not you be insensible to its blessings. Offer sacrifice." Hermes replied by denouncing idolatry, so that Justin, enraged, cried out, " You speak as if you wanted to make me a Christian ". Having then consulted his assessor and others, he pronounced sentence : " We order Philip and Hermes who, despising the commands of the emperor, have rendered themselves unworthy of the name and rights of Roman citizens, to be burned, that others may learn to obey."

They went joyfully to the stake. Philip's feet were so mutilated that he could not walk, and had to be carried. Hermes also walked with much difficulty, and said to him, ' Master, let us hasten to go to the Lord. Why should we be concerned about our feet, since we shall have no more use for them ? " Then he said to the crowds that followed, " The Lord revealed to me that I must suffer. While I was asleep, methought I saw a dove as white as snow, which rested on my head. Then it descended upon my breast and offered me food which was very sweet to the taste. I knew that it was the Lord that called me, and was pleased to honour me with martyrdom." At the place of punishment the executioners, according to custom, covered Philip's feet and legs with earth up to the knees, and tied his hands behind his back. They likewise made Hermes go down into the ditch whereat, having to support himself on a stick because of the weakness of his feet, he exclaimed laughing, " Well, demon, you don't help me even here ". Before the executioners lighted the fire Hermes called Velogius, a Christian, and said to him, " I implore you, by our Saviour Jesus Christ, tell my son Philip from me to restore whatever was committed to my charge, that I may incur no fault ; even the laws of this world ordain it. Tell him also, that he is young and must work for his living as he has seen me do ; and behave himself well to everybody." Then his hands were tied, and fire was set to the pile. The martyrs praised and gave thanks to God as long as they were able to speak. Their bodies were found entire : Philip, a venerable old man, seemed to have had his youth restored, and his hands were stretched out as in prayer ; Hermes with a clear countenance, only his ears a little livid. Justin ordered their bodies to be thrown into the river, but some citizens of Adrianople went in boats with nets, and fished them out. Severus the priest, who had been left alone in prison, when he was informed of their martyrdom, rejoiced at their glory, and earnestly besought God not to think him unworthy to partake in it, since he had confessed His name with them. He was heard, and suffered martyrdom the day following. The order for burning the Holy Scriptures and destroying the churches points out the time of their suffering to have been after the edicts of Diocletian. The Roman Martyrology erroneously puts it in the time of Julian the Apostate, and adds the name of a St Eusebius who does not belong to this group.

The martyrdom of SS. Philip, Hermes and Severus may be counted among the best attested of the episodes of the Diocletian persecution. It is commemorated on this same day in the Syriac *breviarium* of the early fourth century. There is, moreover, a certain indirect confirmation in the reference made to it in the *passio* of SS. Gurius and companions (see Gebhardt and Dobschütz in their edition of this last : *Texte und Untersuchungen*, vol. xxxvii, p. 6). The Latin text of the *acta* of Philip of Heraclea has been printed by

Ruinart, and by the Bollandists, October, vol. ix.   H. Leclercq provides a French translation in *Les Martyrs*, vol. ii, pp. 238–257.   *Cf.* also P. Franchi de' Cavalieri in *Studi e Testi*, no. 27, *Note agiografiche*, fascicule 5, and 175, 9.

ST MALLONUS, OR MELLON, BISHOP OF ROUEN   (FOURTH CENTURY ?)

THE name Mallonus (written Melanius in the Roman Martyrology) appears as that of the first bishop of Rouen in ancient lists and he lived perhaps in the earlier part of the fourth century, but nothing is known about him.   According to late and worthless legends he was a pagan Briton who was converted in Rome and sent by Pope St Stephen I to preach the gospel to the Gauls.   At the village near Cardiff called in Welsh Llanlleurog the church is dedicated in his honour and the place is now known as Saint Mellons.   Possibly this is the origin of the idea that he was a native of Cardiff.

There are three short Latin lives of St Mallonus, which are printed in the *Acta Sanctorum*, October, vol. ix, and in Sauvage (*Actes de S. Mellon*, 1884), but, as Vacandard maintains (*Vie de Saint Ouen*, p. 92), these biographies date only from the twelfth century and can deserve no confidence.   See also Duchesne, *Fastes Épiscopaux*, vol. ii, pp. 200–203 ; and LBS., vol. iii, p. 466.

SS. NUNILO AND ALODIA, VIRGINS AND MARTYRS   (A.D. 851)

THE great era of the martyrs in Spain began in the year 850, under the Moorish Abdur Rahman II, and these two maidens were among the numberless martyrs who in those days sealed their fidelity to God with their blood.   They were sisters, living at Huesca, their father being a Mohammedan and their mother a Christian. After the death of her first husband, she was so foolish as to take a second who also was a Mohammedan.   Her two daughters, who had been brought up in the Christian faith, had much to suffer from the brutality of their stepfather, who was a person of importance.   They were also pestered by many suitors to marry, but having decided to serve God in the state of virginity they obtained leave to go to the house of a Christian aunt.   When the laws of Abdur Rahman were published against the Christians, they were too well known by their family and the repute of their zeal and piety not to be soon arrested.   They appeared before the kadi not only undaunted but with a holy joy.   He employed flattery and promises to try to work them into compliance, and proceeded to threats.   When these failed him, he put them into the hands of wicked women, hoping these would be able to in-sinuate themselves into the hearts of the Christian women.   But Christ enlightened and protected them, and the temptresses were obliged to declare to the judge that nothing could conquer their resolution.   He therefore condemned them to be beheaded, which was accordingly done, and their passion is mentioned in the Roman Martyrology on this day.

Our information is all, practically speaking, derived from the *Memoriale Sanctorum* of St Eulogius.   The relevant passages are quoted and commented upon in the *Acta Sanctorum*, October, vol. ix.

ST DONATUS, BISHOP OF FIESOLE   (c. A.D. 876)

THE tradition of Fiesole is that Donatus was a man of Irish birth who in the early part of the ninth century made a pilgrimage to Rome.   On the return journey he arrived at Fiesole at a time when the clergy and people were gathered together to elect a new bishop, praying earnestly that the Holy Ghost would send them one who would be a true pastor in the manifold troubles with which they were beset. No one would have taken any notice of the stranger Donatus as he entered the cathedral, for he was an insignificant little man, but at the moment he crossed the threshold the bells began to ring and all the lamps and candles were kindled without human agency.   This was taken to be a sign from Heaven in favour of Donatus, and he was unanimously acclaimed bishop.

The life of St Donatus is interspersed with verses and an epitaph, supposed to have been written by himself, according to which he was an enthusiastic teacher of grammar and prosody and a trusted servant of King Lothair I and his son Louis II.   One of the poems describes the beauty of Ireland.   The feast of St Donatus of Fiesole is observed today throughout Ireland.

There is a biography—in fact more than one—printed in the *Acta Sanctorum*, October, vol. ix.   See further DNB., vol. xv, p. 216 ; M. Esposito in the *Journal of Theological Studies*, vol. xxxiii (1923), p. 129 ; L. Gougaud, *Les saints irlandais hors d'Irlande* (1936), p. 76 ; A. M. Tommasini, *Irish Saints in Italy* (1937), pp. 383–394 ; and J. F. Kenney, *Sources for the Early History of Ireland*, vol. i, pp. 601–602.

23 : ST ANTONY CLARET, ARCHBISHOP OF SANTIAGO DE CUBA, FOUNDER OF THE MISSIONARY SONS OF THE IMMACULATE HEART OF MARY (A.D. 1870)

DESPITE the imposing form in which his name is sometimes presented—Antonio Maria Claret y Clara—this holy archbishop was of relatively humble origin.   Born in 1807 at Sallent in the north of Spain, he practised his father's trade of cloth-weaving, and in his spare time learned Latin and printing.   When he was twenty-two he entered the seminary at Vich, where he was ordained priest in 1835.   After a few years he again began to entertain the idea of a Carthusian vocation, but as that seemed to be beyond his physical strength, he proceeded to Rome and eventually entered the Jesuit noviciate with the idea of consecrating his life to the foreign missions.   Here, however, his health broke down, and he was advised by the Jesuit father general to return to Spain and busy himself with the evangelization of his countrymen.   This course he adopted and for ten years he was engaged in giving missions and retreats throughout Catalonia ;   he was associated with Bd Joachima de Mas in the establishment of the Carmelites of Charity. His zeal inspired other priests to join in the same work, and in 1849 he was mainly instrumental in founding the congregation of Missionary Sons of the Immaculate Heart of Mary.   The institute, commonly known by his name as " The Claretians ", has spread and flourished, not only in Spain, but in the Americas and beyond.

Almost immediately after this great work had been inaugurated, Father Claret was appointed archbishop of Santiago de Cuba.   The task was one of exceptional difficulty, in which his efforts to bring about much-needed reforms were resisted by a powerful organization of disorderly and anti-Christian fanatics.   Several attempts were made upon his life, and in one instance a serious wound was inflicted by an assassin infuriated by the loss of his mistress who had been won back to an honest life.   It was the intercession of the archbishop himself which obtained the remission of the death sentence. In 1857 St Antony returned to Spain to become confessor to Queen Isabella II. He resigned his Cuban archbishopric, but avoided residence at the court for any longer than his official duties required, devoting himself to missionary work and the diffusion of good literature, especially in his native Catalan. To him Spain owes the foundation of the Libreria Religiosa in Barcelona, which has exerted immense influence in reviving a true Catholic spirit. In the course of his life St Antony is said to have preached 10,000 sermons and to have published 200 books or pamphlets for the instruction and edification of clergy and people. While rector of the Escorial he established a science laboratory, a museum of natural history, schools of music and languages, and other foundations. His continual union with God was rewarded by many supernatural graces not only in the way of ecstasies and the gift of prophecy, but also by the miraculous cure of bodily diseases.

Political conditions in Spain and the queen's attitude towards the Holy See made St Antony's position very difficult, and in the revolution of 1868 he was exiled together with the queen. He then went to Rome, where he made his influence felt in promoting the definition of papal infallibility. An attempt was made to bring him back to Spain, but it failed ; a fatal illness came upon him in France, and he went to his reward in the Cistercian monastery of Fontfroide, near Narbonne, on October 24, 1870. He was canonized in 1950.

See J. Echevarria, *Reminiscences of Antony Claret* (1938), and D. Sargent, *The Assignments of Antonio Claret* (1950), both published in U.S.A. There are many biographies in Spanish and Catalan ; those by L. Clotet (1882) and J. Blanch (1924) have been translated into French. The decree of canonization in the *Acta Apostolicae Sedis*, vol. xliv (1952), pp. 345–358, includes a sketch of his life.

ST THEODORET, Martyr   (A.D. 362)

JULIAN, uncle to the Emperor Julian and likewise an apostate, was made prefect of the East, of which Antioch was the capital city. Being informed that there was a quantity of gold and silver in the great church there, he ordered it to be brought to him, whereupon the clergy fled. But Theodoret, a zealous priest, refused to abandon his flock and continued to hold Christian assemblies. The prefect Julian commanded him to give up the sacred vessels, and when he refused charged him with having thrown down the statues of the gods and built churches in the previous reign. Theodoret owned he had built churches over the graves of the martyrs, and reproved the prefect because, after having known the true God, he had abandoned his service. So he was tormented in divers ways, during which the torturers were made helpless by a vision of angels about their victim. Julian in a rage ordered them to be drowned, whereat Theodoret said to them, " Go before, brethren. I will follow by vanquishing the Enemy."

The prefect asked him who that enemy was. " The Devil ", said the martyr, " for whom you fight. Jesus Christ, the Saviour of the world, is He who giveth victory." He then explained to his tormentor at some length the mysteries of the Incarnation and Redemption, and when Julian threatened him with instant death retorted by prophesying for him an early and painful end. He was then sentenced to be beheaded, which sentence was duly carried out. Julian then went to seize the church vessels, which he threw on the ground and profaned in a most outrageous manner.

When the prefect reported these happenings to his uncle, the emperor told him plainly that he did not approve his putting any Christian to death merely on account of his religion, and complained that this would afford an occasion to the Galileans to write against him and to make a martyr of Theodoret.   Julian the prefect, who little expected such a reception, was much upset, and that same evening was taken violently ill.   He was in great agony for over forty days, and then came to a miserable end.

Although the *passio* of this martyr is included by Ruinart amongst his *Acta Sincera* it is difficult to put confidence in the miraculous details recorded.   The text, with variations and a full commentary, may be read in the *Acta Sanctorum*, October, vol. x.   An earlier form of the *passio* has been discovered by P. Franchi de' Cavalieri ; see his *Note agiografiche*, vol. v, pp. 59–101.   Theodoret is called Theodore in the *Hieronymianum* and the Roman Martyrology, and it appears he must be identified with the young man Theodore who was tortured at Antioch under Julian the Apostate, with whom the prefect Sallust remonstrated on account thereof (Rufinus, *Eccl. hist.*, bk x).   There is ample evidence of the veneration in which he was held at Antioch : he was marvellously saved from death.

ST SEVERINUS, or SEURIN, Bishop of Bordeaux (*c*. A.D. 420)

THE Roman Martyrology, while putting his death at Bordeaux, calls Severinus " bishop of Cologne ".   This has reference to an identification, now abandoned, of Seurin with St Severinus of Cologne, also commemorated today.   He distinguished himself by his zeal against Arianism, and died at the beginning of the fifth century.   According to the legend Severinus while a priest was walking in the fields when he heard a voice say, " Severinus, you will be bishop of Cologne ".   " When will that happen ? " he asked.   " When your staff buds and flowers ", was the reply.   And his stick, stuck in the ground, took root and blossomed, and he was called to Cologne.   At Tongres, says Gregory of Tours, he knew by revelation the death and glory of St Martin at the time of his departure from this life.   In the midst of his labours against heresy he was again warned by a voice, this time that he was wanted in Bordeaux ; he went thither and was met by the bishop St Amand who, also instructed by Heaven, yielded up his office to him.

Modern research has clearly established that the only Life of St Severinus of any authority, and in fact the source from which the others have borrowed, is that written by Venantius Fortunatus.   Identified and printed for the first time by H. Quentin (*La plus ancienne Vie de S. Seurin*, 1902), it has been re-edited by W. Levison in the MGH., *Scriptores Merov.*, vol. vii, pp. 205–224.   Severinus before coming to Bordeaux had apparently been bishop of Trier ; but there is nothing to connect him with Cologne.   By a curious confusion, on which see the *Analecta Bollandiana*, vol. xxxviii (1920), pp. 427–428, Seurin seems to have been the original from which an imaginary bishop of Bordeaux " St Fort " was afterwards evolved.

ST SEVERINUS BOETHIUS, Martyr (A.D. 524)

ANICIUS MANLIUS SEVERINUS BOETHIUS was born about the year 480, a member of one of the most illustrious families of Rome, the *gens Anicia*, to which Pope St Gregory the Great probably belonged.   He was left an orphan while still very young, and came under the guardianship of Q. Aurelius Symmachus, to whom he became attached by the ties of closest friendship and whose daughter, Rusticiana, he eventually married.   Nothing else is known of his youth, but it must have been devoted to assiduous study, for before he was thirty Boethius was already reputed a very learned man.   He set himself to translate the whole of Plato and Aristotle into Latin and to show their fundamental agreement : this task he was not destined to finish, but Cassiodorus remarks that through his translations the people of Italy were able to know, as well as Plato and Aristotle, " Pythagoras the musician, Ptolemy the astronomer, Nichomachus the arithmetician, Euclid the geometer . . . and Archimedes the mechanician ".   This gives an idea of the many-sidedness of Boethius's interests, and he made his own contributions to logic, mathematics, geometry and music :   moreover he was skilled in practice as well, for a well-known letter of Cassiodorus asks him to make a water-clock and a sundial for the king of the Burgundians.   He was also a theological writer (the Anician family had been Christian since Constantine), and several of his treatises survive, including one on the Holy Trinity.   The works of Boethius were exceedingly influential in the middle ages, especially in the development of logic, and it is not for nothing that he has been called " the last of the Roman philosophers, and the first of the scholastic theologians ".   His translations were for long the only means for the study of Greek philosophy in the West.

Boethius was born very soon after the last of the Roman emperors in the West, Romulus " Augustulus ", had given up the remnants of his power to the barbarian Odoacer ;   he was about thirteen when Odoacer was murdered and the Ostrogoth Theodoric as *patricius* obtained mastery of the whole of Italy.   The father of Boethius had accepted the new state of things and been given high office by Odoacer, and his son followed the example thus set :   notwithstanding his devotion to scholarship he entered public life, and did so (as he tells us himself) as a deliberate response to Plato's teaching that " states would be happy either if philosophers ruled them, or if it chanced that their rulers turned philosophers ".   He was made consul by Theodoric in 510 ;   and twelve years later he reached what he called " the highest point of his good fortune ", when he saw his two sons installed as consuls and himself delivered an oration before them in praise of King Theodoric.   Soon after the king further honoured him with the post of " master of the offices ", which was one of the very highest importance and responsibility.   But his fall was at hand.

The aged Theodoric became suspicious that certain members of the Roman senate were conspiring with the Eastern emperor, Justin, at Constantinople to overthrow the Ostrogoth power in Italy.   Accordingly a charge was laid against the ex-consul Albinus, and Boethius rose in the court to defend him.   Whether or no there was such a plot, it may be taken as quite certain that Boethius had nothing to do with it.   But he also was arrested, and consigned to prison at Ticinum (now Pavia) ;   he was charged not only with treason but also with sacrilege, that is, in this case, the practice of mathematics and astronomy for impious ends. His condemnation followed, and Boethius spoke with bitter scorn of the senate, of which it seems only one member, his father-in-law Symmachus, had stood up for his innocence.

Boethius was in prison for about nine months, and during that time he wrote the best-known of his works, the *Consolation of Philosophy*.   It is in the form of a dialogue, with metrical interludes, between the writer and Philosophy, and she seeks to console him in his misfortune by showing the transitoriness and vanity of earthly success and the eternal value of the things of the mind : disaster is irrelevant to those who have learned to appreciate divine wisdom, and the governance of the universe is just and righteous despite appearances to the contrary.   Nothing is said about the Christian faith, but numerous problems of metaphysics and ethics are touched on, and the *Consolation of Philosophy* became one of the most popular books in the middle ages, not only among philosophers and theologians.   It was one of the works translated into Old English by King Alfred the Great.

The imprisonment of Boethius ended only with violent death, said to have been preceded by a brutal torture.   He was buried in the old cathedral of Ticinum, and his relics are now in the church of St Peter *in Ciel d'Oro* at Pavia.

That Boethius died a martyr seems to have been taken for granted, and the background of his medieval influence and popularity was that he had died for the faith and was Saint Severinus.*   But there is nothing reliable to suggest that he was executed for any but purely political reasons ; it is true that Theodoric was an Arian, but there is not the slightest evidence that this had any part in the prosecution of his hitherto trusted minister of state.   It is possible that the idea of Boethius's martyrdom may have originated in what may well have been the notorious fact that he was put to death *unjustly*, for death imposed on the innocent, without any necessary hatred of the faith, has often been the passport to a veneration for martyrdom in earlier times.

But since the eighteenth century a still more fundamental question has been raised, *viz.* Was Boethius at the time of his death a professing and practising Christian ?   That he was brought up and long remained a Christian admits of no doubt, especially since in 1877 a new piece of evidence confirms the authenticity of the theological writings with the authorship of which he had been credited for so long.   But the difficulty is this : How is it that a Christian man, who had written treatises in defence of the faith, should, in face of an unjust charge and of death, write a work for his own strengthening and solace which contains nothing distinctively Christian except one or two indirect quotations from the Bible ?   Or, as Boswell reports Dr Johnson as saying in 1770, " It was very surprising that, upon such a subject, and in such a situation, he should be *magis philosophus quam Christianus* ", " more of a philosopher than a Christian ".

The problem cannot be shrugged off, and the fact that nobody in the middle ages appeared to be worried by the anomaly does not help either way.   Here it is sufficient to say that, when the question had once been posed, some scholars of weight were all for " dechristianizing " Boethius ; but later on the opposite opinion strengthened, and the prevalent view is that he remained a Christian to the end.   Two scholars, a Protestant and a Catholic, may be quoted in support : " The old question as to the relation of Boethius to Christianity is meaningless . . . a Christian theologian may well have written such a work as the *Consolation*, not to express his own views but to give philosophy's answer to the chief problems of thought " (E. K. Rand in *Harvard Studies in Classical Philology*, vol. xv, p. 1) ; and the *Consolation of Philosophy* is " a masterpiece which, in spite of its deliberate reticence, is a perfect expression of the union of the Christian spirit with the classical tradition " (Christopher Dawson in *The Making of Europe*, p. 51).

* See, for example, the *Paradiso* of Dante, canto x, lines 125 *seq.*   References to and echoes of the *De consolatione* are frequent in Dante, though for some reason he thought that work was " not well known ".   How well known it in fact was, among lay people as well as clerics, is shown by the fact that in the later middle ages translations or adaptations of it were made into German, Provençal, Anglo-Norman, French, Polish, Magyar, Greek, Hebrew and English (by Chaucer and by John Walton).   It was one of the books with which the Benedictine martyr Bd Ambrose Barlow comforted himself when in prison.

The feast of St Severinus Boethius (as a martyr) is still kept at Pavia and in the church of St Mary *in Portico* in Rome. The confirmation of his *cultus* in these places by Pope Leo XIII in 1883 might be thought to settle the questions of Boethius's martyrdom and religion. But, though calling for the fullest respect, a confirmation of *cultus* is not an exercise of infallibility ; it is only permissive, and is not always and inevitably preceded by a full and exhaustive examination of the historical problems that may be involved.

H. F. Stewart's monograph on Boethius, published in 1891, is still a standard work ; more recent works of value are H. R. Patch, *The Tradition of Boethius* (1935) and H. Barrett, *Boethius : Some Aspects of His Times and Work* (1940). Patch provides a bibliography of twenty pages. The complete works, first published in Venice in 1497, are in Migne, PL., vols. lxiii and lxiv ; the theological treatises and the " Consolation " are in the Loeb Classical Library (Latin text and translation) ; King Alfred's version of the last-named is in the Oxford University Press Library of Translations (Alfred gives it a Christian colouring). In the Fortescue and Smith edition of *De consolatione philosophiae* (1925) the suggestion is made that it was written when Boethius was in exile but not yet in prison and under sentence of death ; but this explanation of its silence about Christianity is open to strong objections. In the Bodleian there is a manuscript of this work given by Bishop Leofric *c.* 1050 to the cathedral church of Exeter. In 1650 a book by Nicholas Caussin, *The Holy Court*, containing a rather extravagant life of Boethius, was translated into English by Sir Thomas Hawkins and other Catholics, and the story of Boethius was used to illustrate the position of Catholics in England under the penal laws. New translations of the *De consolatione*, by Fr G. G. Walsh, and of the theological tracts with selected other writings, by Dr A. C. Pegis, are promised in the series of patristic translations of the Cima Company, of New York. The church of St Mary *in Portico* (*in Campitelli*) stood on the site of the house of St Galla (October 5), who was sister-in-law to Boethius.

ST ROMANUS, Bishop of Rouen   (*c.* A.D. 640)

NOT much that is certainly authentic is known of this bishop. His father, alleged to be a convert of St Remigius, was born of a Frankish family, and Romanus was placed young in the court of Clotaire II. Upon the death of Hidulf, *c.* 630, he was chosen bishop of Rouen. The remains of idolatry exercised his zeal ; he converted the unbelievers and is said to have destroyed the remains of a temple of Venus. Amongst many miracles it is related that, the Seine having overflowed the city, the saint knelt to pray on the side of the water, with a crucifix in his hand, whereupon the floods retired gently within the banks of the river. The name of St Romanus is famous in France on account of a privilege which the metropolitical chapter of Rouen exercised until the Revolution, of releasing in his honour a prisoner under sentence of death every year on the feast of the Ascension of our Lord. The chapter sent notice to the *parlement* of Rouen two months before to stop the execution of criminals till that time ; and on that day chose the prisoner who, being first condemned to death, was then set at liberty to assist in carrying the shrine of St Romanus in the great procession. He heard two exhortations and then was told that in honour of St Romanus he was pardoned. The legend is that this privilege took its rise from St Romanus killing a great serpent, called Gargouille, with the assistance of a murderer whom he took out of his dungeon. No traces of this story are found in any life of this saint or in any writings before the end of the fourteenth century ; the deliverance of the condemned criminal was perhaps intended for a symbol of the redemption of mankind through Christ. The custom was called *Privilège de la Fierte* or of the *Châsse de St Romain*. St Romanus died about the year 640.

There are several short lives of St Romanus, but not of a date which would lend them any historical value. The texts for the most part are printed or summarized in the *Acta Sanctorum*, October, vol. x, but a useful note upon the lives and their authors is available in Vacandard, *Vie de St Ouen* (1902), pp. 356–358. Other references to St Romain occur *passim* in the text. See also Duchesne, *Fastes Épiscopaux*, vol. ii, p. 207 ; and L. Pillon in the *Gazette des Beaux-Arts*, vol. xxx (1903), pp. 441–454.

ST IGNATIUS, PATRIARCH OF CONSTANTINOPLE   (A.D. 877)

THE birth of this saint was illustrious : his mother was daughter to the Emperor Nicephorus I, and his father Michael, surnamed Rangabe, was himself raised to the imperial throne. Michael's reign was short. In the year 813 he was deposed in favour of Leo the Armenian, and his two sons were mutilated and shut up in a monastery. The younger of them became a monk and changed his former name, Nicetas, to Ignatius. He had much to suffer from the abbot of his monastery ; but upon the death of his persecutor he was himself chosen abbot, having already been ordained priest. In 846 Ignatius was taken from his monastery of Satyrus and made patriarch of Constantinople. His virtues shone brightly in this office, but the liberty which he used in opposing vice and reprimanding public offenders drew on him severe persecution. The *caesar* Bardas, uncle of the Emperor Michael III, was accused of incestuous sexual relations, and at Epiphany 857 Ignatius refused him communion in the Great Church. Bardas persuaded the young emperor, known ominously in history, but not altogether justly, as Michael the Drunkard, to get rid of the patriarch, and with the help of Bishop Gregory of Syracuse they trumped up charges and ordered Ignatius to be deposed and exiled.

This was not simply the revenge of an aggrieved individual. Behind it was the far-reaching tension and hostility between the dynasty and court clergy on the one hand, with some support from a large moderate party, and on the other the sometimes extreme rigorists, upholders of " the independence of the religious power ", led by the monks of the monastery of Studius. Of these last St Ignatius was an inflexible supporter. Accordingly he was banished to the island of Tere-binthos. Here, in spite of what was said afterwards, it appears certain that he resigned his see, though perhaps conditionally. In his place Bardas nominated his chief secretary, Photius, then a layman and a man of quite unusual talent, ability and learning. In the week before the Christmas of 858 Photius was made monk, reader, subdeacon, deacon, priest and bishop in as many days. When he wrote announcing his election to the pope, St Nicholas I sent legates to Constantinople to investigate the situation.

There followed a long " affair " that had most important results and is a matter of general church history. It must however be mentioned that researches carried on during the past fifty years have put a rather different complexion on it and changed some of the judgements that have been everywhere accepted, gladly or regretfully, for centuries. What had appeared to be a pertinacious and con-tumacious attempt of Constantinople to maintain complete independence of the Roman see, with Photius as the arch-schismatic, now appears rather as one aspect of a strife of parties, parties both political and ecclesiastical, in which the " die-hard " supporters of St Ignatius became as rebellious towards the Holy See as Photius at his most defiant.

Nine years later, in 867, the Emperor Michael, who in the previous year had connived at the murder of Bardas, was himself murdered by Basil the Macedonian, who now became emperor. Basil at once dismissed Michael's minister Photius from the patriarchal office (he was to return ten years later), and sought the support of Ignatius's intransigent followers by summoning Ignatius back to it. After his restoration the persecuted prelate asked Pope Adrian II, who had succeeded Nicholas I, to hold a general council. This, a small assembly, was convened in Constantinople in 869, nowadays called the eighth oecumenical council and the fourth of that city. It condemned Photius and his supporters, but treated them with leniency, though Photius himself was excommunicated.

For the remaining years of his life St Ignatius applied himself to the duties of his office with vigilance and energy, but unfortunately not with perfect prudence : ironically enough, he followed the policy of Photius towards the Holy See in respect of patriarchal jurisdiction over the Bulgars. He even went so far as to encourage their prince, Boris, to expel his Latin bishops and priests in favour of the Greeks whom Ignatius had sent. Pope John VIII was naturally indignant and sent legates with an ultimatum threatening excommunication. They arrived at Constantinople only to find that St Ignatius had died on the previous October 23, 877.

The personal holiness of the life of Ignatius, his fearlessness in rebuking wickedness in high places and his patience under unjust treatment caused his name to be added to the Roman Martyrology, and his feast is kept by the Latin Catholics of Constantinople as well as by the Byzantines, both Catholic and dissident.

In the *Acta Sanctorum*, October, vol. x, there is a Latin translation of the Greek life of St Ignatius by Nicetas the Paphlagonian : Dr Dvornik calls it " little better than a ' political tract ' and its veracity is highly questionable ". The Greek text is in Migne, PG., vol. cv. The diplomatic correspondence and documents of the period must be sought in Mansi or Hefele-Leclercq, *Conciles*, vol. iv. The modern work on Photius referred to above began with A. Lapôtre, *Le pape Jean VIII* (1895) and E. Amann in DTC. (articles on John VIII, John IX, Nicholas I and Photius) ; and was carried on by V. Laurent, V. Grumel, H. Grégoire and F. Dvornik : see especially his *Photian Schism* (1948). For a summary see Fliche and Martin, *Hist. de l'Église*, t. vi, pp. 465–475 and 483–490 for Ignatius, pp. 465–501 for Photius. There is a full article on St Ignatius in DTC., t. vii, but this, like Hergen-röther's monumental *Photius*, follows more conservative lines.

ST ALLUCIO   (A.D. 1134)

ALLUCIO, patron of Pescia in Tuscany, was a shepherd and herdman, who on account of the great interest he took in the almshouse of Val di Nievole was appointed master of it. He became in effect its second founder, and further devoted himself to the establishment of shelters at fords, mountain-passes, and so on, and to similar public works, such as the building of a bridge over the Arno ; he staffed the hospices with young men, who were afterwards known as the Brothers of St Allucio. A number of remarkable miracles were recorded of the saint and he was credited with bringing about a reconciliation between the warring cities of Ravenna and Faenza. In 1182, forty-eight years after his death, the relics of St Allucio were enshrined and the almshouse was given his name. The *cultus* was confirmed by Pope Pius IX by the granting of a new proper Mass for the saint.

The cult of St Allucio seems to be adequately attested by documents, one of which takes the form of a public instrument summarizing the principal episodes of his life. They are given in the *Acta Sanctorum*, October, vol. x. See also DHG., vol. ii, c. 627, and a popular account by D. Biagioti (1934).

BD JOHN BUONI   (A.D. 1249)

IN spite of his name, which he inherited from his family, the Buonomini, his earlier
life was not conspicuous for religion.   When his father died he left his home at
Mantua and made his living as an entertainer at the courts, palaces and wealthy
establishments of Italy, leading a licentious and debauched life, though ever
pursued by the prayers of his devoted mother.   In 1208, when he was about forty,
he had a serious illness which brought him near death, and when he had recovered
he took the warning to heart and was soon a changed man.   He had made a resolve
during his sickness to mend his ways and, a less common thing than such resolutions,
he kept it.   He opened his heart to the bishop of Mantua, who allowed him to
try a hermit's life, which he began near Cesena.   John set himself to conquer his
insurgent flesh in solitude and acquire habits of devotion and virtue with such
success that he soon had the reputation of a saint, and disciples began to gather
round him.   For a time they lived according to regulations which Bd John made
on the spot as need arose, but when a church had been built and the community
taken definite shape papal approval was sought and Innocent IV imposed the Rule
of St Augustine as their basis.

Bd John received many supernatural enlightenments in prayer, wrought a
number of most remarkable miracles, and did not allow advancing age to lessen
his austerities ; he kept three lents every year, wore only one light garment in the
coldest weather, and had three beds in his cell, one uncomfortable, another more
uncomfortable, and the third most uncomfortable.   He continued to suffer very
violent temptations, and was moreover slandered by malicious persons, calumnies
which he opposed merely by a simple denial.   The number of his penitents so
increased and so many people came to see him out of curiosity that John made up
his mind to go away secretly to a more quiet place ; but after having walked all
night he found himself at dawn once more before the door of his own cell, so he
concluded that it was God's will that he should stay where he was.   John died at
Mantua in 1249 and his tomb was illustrious for miracles.   His congregation of
penitents did not survive long as an independent organization.   Under the name
of *Boniti* they had eleven establishments within a few years of their founder's
death, but in 1256 they were united with the other congregations of which Pope
Alexander IV formed the order of Hermit-friars of St Augustine.   The feast of
Bd John Buoni is accordingly kept by the Augustinian friars and the Augustinians
of the Assumption ; his name was added to the Roman Martyrology, as *beatus*,
in 1672.

The Bollandists, in the *Acta Sanctorum*, October, vol. ix, fill nearly two hundred folio
pages with the documents which bear on the history of Bd John Bonus.   These comprise
a relatively lengthy biography written at the beginning of the sixteenth century by the
Augustinian, Ambrose Calepinus, and also the depositions of witnesses who in 1251, 1252
and 1254 gave evidence with a view to John's canonization.   They describe *inter alia* his
immunity from the effects of great heat, for he stood for several minutes shuffling his bare
feet about without injury in a heap of red-hot ashes ; see H. Thurston in *The Month* for
February 1932, pp. 146–147.

BD BARTHOLOMEW, BISHOP OF VICENZA   (A.D. 1271)

BARTHOLOMEW Breganza studied in his youth at Padua and about the year 1220
received the Dominican habit from the hands of the founder of the order himself,
in his native town of Vicenza.   He prudently directed a number of houses as

prior, and while preaching with Father John of Vicenza at Bologna in 1233 established a military order, called *Fratres Gaudentes*, for the preservation of peace and of public order ; it spread to other towns of Italy and existed till the eighteenth century. At this time the Near East was in particular need of holy bishops in view of the abuses of the Crusades, and Bartholomew was appointed to a see in the isle of Cyprus. From here he visited St Louis of France in Palestine and formed a deep friendship with the king, who urged him to visit him in France. This he was able to do a few years later when he was sent as papal legate to the king of England. Henry III was then in Aquitaine, where Bartholomew presented himself and accompanied the king to Paris. In 1256 Pope Alexander IV had translated Bartholomew to the see of Vicenza, wherein he was soon involved in troubles with the violent and evil Ghibelline leader, Ezzelino da Romano. For a time he was in exile from his diocese, but on his return devoted himself with increased energy to his flock, rebuilding the churches ruined by Ezzelino and striving for the peace of the distracted cities of the Veneto.

Four years before his death Bartholomew assisted at the second translation of the relics of St Dominic, and preached the panegyric on that occasion. He died on July 1, 1271. He was greatly venerated by the people and commonly called Blessed Bartholomew, a *cultus* that was confirmed in 1793.

A sufficient account will be found in the *Acta Sanctorum*, July, vol. i. See also G. T. Faccioli, *Vita e virtu del b. Bartolommeo* (1794) ; B. Altaner, *Dominikanermissionen des 13 Jahrhunderts* (1924), pp. 40 *seq.* ; M. de Waresquiel, *Le b. Barthélemy de Breganze* (1905) ; and Procter, *Lives of Dominican Saints*, pp. 297-301.

24 : ST RAPHAEL THE ARCHANGEL

OF the seven archangels, who in both Jewish and Christian tradition are venerated as pre-eminently standing before the throne of God, three only are mentioned by name in the Bible, Michael, Gabriel and Raphael. These have been venerated in the Church from early times, especially in the East, but it was not till the pontificate of Pope Benedict XV that the liturgical feasts of the two last were made obligatory throughout the Western church.

It is recorded in the sacred book of the history of Tobias that St Raphael was sent by God to minister to the old Tobias, who was blind and greatly afflicted, and to Sara, daughter of Raguel, whose seven bridegrooms had each perished on the night of their wedding. And when the young Tobias was sent into Media to collect money owing to his father, it was Raphael who, in the form of a man and under the name of Azarias, accompanied him on the journey, helped him in his difficulties, and taught him how safely to enter into wedlock with Sara. " He conducted me ", says Tobias, " and brought me safe again. He received the money of Gabelus. He caused me to have my wife, and he chased from her the evil spirit. He gave joy to her parents. Myself he delivered from being devoured by the fish ; thee also he hath made to see the light of Heaven ; and we are filled with all good things through him." The offices of healing performed by the angel in this story and the fact that his name signifies " God has healed " has caused Raphael to be identified with the angel who moved the waters of the healing sheep-pool (John v 1–4) ; this identity is recognized in the liturgy by the reading of that passage of the gospel in the Mass of St Raphael's feast. In Tobias xii 12 and 15, the archangel directly speaks of himself as " one of the seven who stand before the Lord ", and says that he continually offered the prayers of young Tobias up to God.

See the *Acta Apostolicae Sedis*, vol. xii (1922), and *cf.* note to St Michael on September 29. For the early mention of St Raphael in Christian documents and on the present commemoration, consult Cardinal Schuster, *The Sacramentary*, vol. v, pp. 189–191. In the *Ethiopic Synaxarium* (1928), vol. iv, pp. 1274–1278, is a curious account of the dedication of a church to St Raphael in an island off Alexandria early in the fifth century.

ST FELIX, BISHOP OF THIBIUCA, MARTYR   (A.D. 303)

IN the beginning of Diocletian's persecution numbers among the Christians delivered up the sacred books into the hands of the persecutors that they might be burnt. Many even sought for pretences to extenuate or excuse this crime, as if it ever could be lawful to concur in a sacrilegious or impious action. Felix, a bishop in proconsular Africa, was so far from being carried away by the falls of others that they were to him a spur to greater watchfulness and fortitude. Magnilian, magistrate of Thibiuca, ordered him to give up all books and writings belonging to his church, that they might be burnt. The martyr replied that the law of God must be preferred to the law of man, so Magnilian sent him to the proconsul at Carthage. This officer, the *passio* tells us, offended at his bold confession, commanded him to be loaded with irons and, after he had kept him nine days in a foul dungeon, to be put on board a vessel to be taken to stand his trial before Maximinus in Italy. The bishop lay under hatches in the ship, between the horses' feet, four days without eating or drinking. The vessel arrived at Agrigentum in Sicily, and the saint was treated with great honour by the Christians of that island and in all the cities through which he passed. When Felix had been brought as far as Venosa in Apulia, the prefect ordered his irons to be knocked off, and again put to him the questions whether he had the sacred writings and why he refused to deliver them up. Felix answered that he could not deny that he had the books, but that he would never give them up. The prefect without more ado condemned him to be beheaded. At the place of execution St Felix thanked God for all His mercies, and bowing down his head offered himself a sacrifice to Him who lives for ever and ever. He was fifty-six years old, and one of the first victims under Diocletian.

Nevertheless the story of the deportation of St Felix to Italy and his martyrdom there is no more than a hagiographer's fiction to make him an Italian saint : there seems no doubt at all that he suffered at Carthage by order of the proconsul there, and his relics were subsequently laid to rest in the well-known *basilica Fausti* in that city.

In the *Analecta Bollandiana*, vol. xxxix (1921), pp. 241–276, Fr Delehaye published a remarkable study of the text of this *passio*. The materials previously edited in the *Acta Sanctorum*, October, vol. x, were insufficient, and Delehaye, after printing representative forms of the two families into which the texts may be divided, supplies an admirable restoration of the primitive document which lies at the base of all. As stated above, the deportation of the martyr to Italy is a fiction of later hagiographers who unscrupulously embroidered the original text. Felix, as Delehaye very positively asserts (in agreement with M. Monceaux, *Revue archéologique*, 1905, vol. i, pp. 335–340), was put to death by the proconsul at Carthage. The proper day of the martyrdom of St Felix would seem to be the 15th or possibly the 16th of July. For the confusions which led to its transference, first to July 30, and finally to October 24, see Delehaye, and more fully Dom Quentin, *Les martyrologes historiques*, pp. 522–532 and 697–698.

ST PROCLUS, ARCHBISHOP OF CONSTANTINOPLE   (A.D. 446)

ST PROCLUS was a native of Constantinople, and was very young when he was made a lector. He was a disciple of St John Chrysostom, but nevertheless became secretary to St John's opponent, Atticus, archbishop of Constantinople, who ordained him deacon and priest. After his death many pitched upon Proclus as the fittest person to be placed in that important see ; but Sisinnius was chosen and he appointed Proclus bishop of Cyzicus. The inhabitants of that city refused to receive him and chose someone else. Proclus therefore continued at Constantinople, where he got a great reputation by his preaching. Upon the death of Sisinnius many again cast their eyes upon him as the most worthy of that dignity ; but Nestorius was chosen, who soon began to propagate his errors. St Proclus courageously maintained the truth against him, and in 429 preached a sermon to show that the Blessed Virgin ought to be styled the Mother of God ; in the course of it he made use of the memorable phrase, " We do not proclaim a deified man, but we confess an incarnate God ". When Nestorius was deposed Maximian was chosen to succeed him, but after his death in 434, as Proclus had never been able in fact to take possession of the see of Cyzicus, he was elected to that of Constantinople.

The mildness and tact with which he treated even the most obstinate among the Nestorians and other heretics was a distinguishing part of his character. The Armenian bishops consulted him about the doctrine and writings of Theodore of Mopsuestia, who was then dead, and whose name was in reputation in those parts. St Proclus answered by his *Tome to the Armenians*, the most famous of his writings. In it he condemned the doctrine mentioned as savouring of Nestorianism, and expounded the faith of the Incarnation ; without, however, naming Theodore, whose memory was revered by many and who had died in the communion of the Church. He exhorted them to adhere to the doctrine of St Basil and St Gregory Nazianzen, whose names and works were in particular veneration among them. Others carried on this contest with greater warmth. In concert with the Empress St Pulcheria, he translated the body of his old master St John Chrysostom from Comana Pontica to the church of the Apostles at Constantinople. The whole city went out to meet the procession, and the remaining intransigent followers of St John submitted themselves to his gentle and conciliatory successor.

During the episcopate of St Proclus Constantinople was visited by a disastrous earthquake, and amid the ruins men ran to and fro distracted with fear, not being able to find any place of security. The inhabitants wandered in the fields, and Proclus with his clergy followed his scattered flock, and ceased not to comfort them amidst their afflictions and to implore the divine mercy. The Greek Menology of Basil, on the authority of a chronicler who wrote three hundred and fifty years after the alleged event, refers to a legend that, as they thus prayed, crying out *Kyrie eleison*, a child was caught up out of sight into the air. When he came back to earth, the boy said he had heard the angelic choirs singing the words, " Holy God, holy Strong One, holy Deathless One " ; and straightway he died. The people repeated the words, adding, " Have mercy upon us ", and the earthquake ceased. In consequence St Proclus introduced this invocation, the *Trisagion*, into the liturgy. It is not known that he did this, but the first certain mention of the Trisagion is at the Council of Chalcedon, only a few years later, and it is possible that St Proclus and his people prayed in these famous words at the time of the earthquake.

Proclus is referred to by St Cyril of Alexandria as " a man full of religion, perfectly instructed in the discipline of the Church, and a careful observer of the canons ". " In moral excellence ", says the Greek historian Socrates, who knew him personally, " he had few equals. He was always gentle to everyone, for he was convinced that kindness advances the cause of truth better than severity. He therefore determined not to irritate and harass heretics, and so restored to the Church in his own person that mild and benignant dignity of character which had so often been unhappily violated. . . . He was a pattern of all true prelates." St Proclus died on July 24 in the year 446.

A number of the letters and sermons of St Proclus are extant. " The style of this father ", says Alban Butler, " is concise, sententious and full of lively witty turns, more proper to please and delight than to move the heart. This sort of composition requires much pains and study ; and though this father was mighty successful in this way, it is not to be compared to the easy natural gravity of St Basil or the sweet style of St Chrysostom."

A sufficiently full account of St Proclus, compiled from the church historians and other sources, is provided in the *Acta Sanctorum*, October, vol. x. But see also F. X. Bauer, *Proklos von Constantinopel* (1918), and Bardenhewer, *Geschichte der altkirchlichen Literatur*, vol. iv, pp. 202–208. Ever since the publication of the Syriac text of the *Bazaar of Heraclides*, the question of Nestorius's real teaching has been revived, and a large literature has resulted ; for details see the article " Nestorius " in DTC.

SS. ARETAS AND THE MARTYRS OF NAJRAN, AND ST ELESBAAN (A.D. 523)

EARLY in the sixth century the Aksumite Ethiopians extended their power over the Arabs and Jews of Himyar (Yemen), across the Red Sea, and imposed a viceroy upon this people. A member of the displaced Himyarite family, called Dunaan (Dhu Nowas), rose in revolt. He was a convert to Judaism, and he seized Zafar, massacred the garrison and clergy, turned the church into a synagogue, and then laid siege to Najran, a stronghold of Christianity. It put up a strong defence and Dunaan, in despair of taking it, offered an amnesty if it would surrender. The offer was accepted, but the terms were repudiated : the town was given over to Dunaan's soldiers to sack, and death was decreed for every Christian who would not apostatize. The leader in the defence had been the chief of the Banu Harith (whence he is called St *Aretas*), with many of his tribe ; these were all beheaded. All priests, deacons and consecrated virgins were thrown into pits filled with burning fuel. The wife of Aretas excited the desire of Dunaan. She repulsed him, and he had her daughters executed before her eyes and their blood poured into her mouth, before her own head was struck off. The Roman Martyrology mentions a boy of five years who jumped into the fire in which his mother was dying in agony. Four thousand men, women and children were slain.

An envoy of the Emperor Justin I, Bishop Simeon of Beth-Arsam, was at the camp of an Arab tribe on the Persian frontier when the tale of his achievement was brought from Dunaan, and he sent an account of it to another Simeon, abbot of Gabula. At the same time refugees from Najran spread the news over Egypt and Syria. It made a profound and awful impression, which lasted for many generations ; Mohammed mentions the massacre in the Koran and condemns its perpetrators to Hell (*sura* lxxxv). The patriarch of Alexandria wrote to the bishops of the East recommending a commemoration of the martyrs and prayers for the survivors, and urging that the Jewish elders of their school at Tiberias should be held responsible for what had happened : a suggestion more forcible than just. Both the emperor and the patriarch wrote urging immediate action upon the Aksumite king, Elesbaan (whom the Syrians call David and the Abyssinians Caleb).

He required no encouragement, and set off across the straits with a punitive force to avenge the slaughtered saints and to recover his power in Himyar. In the ensuing campaign Elesbaan was victorious, Dunaan being killed and his chief town occupied. Alban Butler says that Elesbaan, " having by the divine blessing defeated the tyrant, made use of his victory with great clemency and moderation ". This can hardly be maintained. He restored Najran and installed a bishop sent from Alexandria, but both in the field and in dealing with the Jews who had encouraged the massacre he conducted himself with that cruelty and rapacity which are only to be looked for in the barbarous prince of a semi-pagan nation. However, towards the end of his life he is said to have resigned his throne to his son, made a present of his crown to the church of the Holy Sepulchre in Jerusalem, and himself became an exemplary anchorite, as is stated by the eulogy accorded him in the Roman Martyrology on the 27th of this month.

The names of the Najran martyrs and of St Elesbaan were introduced into the Roman Martyrology by Baronius, in spite of the fact that all of them were perhaps, at least materially, monophysites.

The Greek text of the *passio* has been printed in the *Acta Sanctorum*, October, vol. x, and we have also the Syriac account written by Bishop Simeon. See further, Guidi in the *Atti della Accad. dei Lincei*, vol. vii (1881), pp. 471 *seq.* ; Deramey in the *Revue de l'histoire des religions*, vol. xxviii, pp. 14–42 ; the *Revue des études juives*, vols. xviii, xx and xxi, which contain papers by Halévy and Duchesne's reply ; Nöldeke in *Göttingen Gel. Anzeiger*, 1899, pp. 825 *seq.* ; and DCB., vol. ii, pp. 70–75.

ST SENOCH, ABBOT　　(A.D. 576)

THIS saint was a contemporary of St Gregory, Bishop of Tours, who knew him personally and wrote about him. Senoch (Senou) was born of barbarian parents in Poitou, and having been converted to Christ left his home with the intention of becoming a hermit. He wandered into Touraine, and found there a suitable place, where is now the village of Saint-Senou. He installed himself in some ruins, with the stones of which he built a dwelling for himself and a small chapel. Senoch was joined by three disciples, but he preferred to be quite alone and spent most of his time shut up in his own cell. The austerities of the new hermit earned him a great reputation for sanctity, and many visitors came to the place who insisted on making offerings, which St Senoch devoted to the relief of needy people.

When the bishop St Euphronius died in 573 Senoch went to Tours to pay his respects to his successor, St Gregory, with whom he exchanged the kiss of brotherhood and then returned quietly to his cell. But soon after he made another journey, to visit his friends and relatives at home, and met with such signs of respect and veneration while he was away that he came back rather proud of himself. Gregory noticed this and rebuked him sharply, reminding him of the words of St Paul, that he would glory in nothing but his infirmities in order that the power of Christ might dwell in him. Senoch humbly accepted the reprimand and agreed no longer to withdraw himself entirely from the company of his brethren. St Gregory narrates a number of miracles of healing vouchsafed by God at the prayer of St Senoch, who died in his arms. The bishop officiated at his funeral, for which an immense crowd gathered, and when he celebrated the Mass of the month's mind a paralytic was cured at St Senoch's grave.

Most of what we know concerning St Senoch comes from Gregory of Tours. All the relevant material will be found in the *Acta Sanctorum*, October, vol. x.

ST MARTIN, or MARK   (*c*. A.D. 580)

THE Roman Martyrology today mentions Mark, a solitary in Campania, and refers to his famous deeds chronicled by St Gregory the Great, who, however, calls him Martin.   In his *Dialogues* St Gregory says that many of his friends knew Martin personally and had been present at his miracles, and that he had heard much of him from his predecessor, Pope Pelagius II.   He lived alone in a small cave on Mount Marsicus (Mondragone), and after miraculously overcoming the lack of water had for three years the daily company of the Devil, in the form of a serpent (" his old friend ").   When he first took up his quarters in the cave the hermit fastened one end of a chain to his ankle and the other to the rock, so that he could not wander wantonly from his habitation.   Word of this came to St Benedict at Monte Cassino (where Martin is said to have been a monk), and he sent a message in which the authentic voice of Benedict can be heard speaking : " If you are God's servant, let yourself be held by the chain of Christ, not by any chain of iron."   St Martin accordingly loosed himself and later gave the chain to his followers when they complained that the bucket rope of the well kept on breaking.   There was a great rock overhanging Martin's cave and his neighbours were much afraid that it would fall and crush him.   Therefore one Mascator came with a number of people and offered to remove it.   Martin refused to budge from the cave while it was done, telling them nevertheless to do whatever they thought necessary, and they set to work in fear and trembling with him inside.   But when the rock was loosed it bounced harmlessly over the cave and rolled safely down the mountain-side.

The *Dialogues* of St Gregory (iii, 16) are our only source of information.

ST MAGLORIUS, or MAELOR, BISHOP OF DOL   (SIXTH CENTURY)

ST UMBRAFEL, who later became a monk under his nephew St Samson, was married to Afrella, daughter of Meurig of Morgannwg ; we are told they had a son, born in Glamorgan, whom they named Maelor, who is called in French Magloire and in Latin Maglorius.   According to his late lives, which contain much fabulous matter, he was entrusted while young to the care of St Illtyd at Llanilltyd Fawr, and became a monk and companion to St Samson, who ordained him deacon and took him into Brittany.   Here, we are told, Maglorius was given charge of a monastery at Kerfunt, shared the missionary labours of St Samson, and when he died succeeded him as abbot and bishop at Dol.   But he was getting an old man, and he resigned his responsibilities into the hands of St Budoc.

Maglorius then retired to a remote spot on the coast, but even here his life was soon made burdensome by the people who came to be cured of their ills or to see a miracle.   Among them was the chieftain of Sark, whom Maglorius healed of a skin disease, and in gratitude he gave the saint and his monks a part of his island, whither they went to live.   St Maglorius built a monastery where is now the *seigneurie* of Sark, and organized the people to resist raiders from the north.   The saint also visited Jersey, for the purpose of delivering that island from a " dragon ", in return for which service he was granted land there as well.   During plague and famine he worked heroically for the people, and God is said to have come to their help with miracles at the intercession of the saint. He died shortly after; for the last months of his life he had interpreted literally the words of the Psalmist, " This will I seek after, that I may dwell in the house of the Lord all the days of my life ", and never stirred out of the church except for necessity.

The feast of St Maglorius is observed in the Rennes diocese, and as the other chief centre of his *cultus* was the Channel Islands he has a commemoration today in the diocese of Portsmouth. He is referred to by Richard Rolle in *The Fire of Love* (ch. 13).

We have several short medieval biographies, on which see BHL., nn. 5139–5147. There is a full notice by Miss Bateson in DNB., vol. xxxv, pp. 323–324 ; and another in LBS., vol. iii, pp. 407 *seq.* ; but the most valuable contributions come from such continental scholars as A. de la Borderie and F. Duine. Consult the former's *Histoire de Bretagne*, vol. i (1896) and the latter's *Inventaire*, as well as his *Memento des sources hagiographiques de Bretagne*. It seems that Maglorius was never bishop of Dol, and his date is quite uncertain.

ST MARTIN OF VERTOU, Abbot   (Sixth Century)

VERY little beyond speculation is known of this saint, for his two extant lives were written some centuries after his death and consist chiefly of miracles, and there has been confusion between him and St Martin of Braga, who was abbot of Dumium in Portugal while this Martin was a hermit in the forest of Dumen in Brittany. He was born at Nantes, of a Frankish family, and was ordained deacon by St Felix, who sent him to preach in Poitou. The legend says that after much effort he had succeeded in converting only the master and mistress of the house wherein he dwelt, so, warning them to flee from the wrath to come, he left the town where he had laboured wallowing in its iniquities, and it was straightway visited by an earthquake which swallowed it up and waters flowed over its site. This place is now known as Lac de Grandlieu, and the village of Herbauges at its edge is the successor of the destroyed town. Moreover, near by is to be seen a *menhir*, which is the pillar of stone into which the fleeing woman was transformed because she looked back at the doomed town. Of which story may be said what Camden temperately remarks about a similar tale concerning Llyn Safaddan in Breconshire : " All which I suspect as fabulous, and not to be otherwise regarded."

After this failure as a missioner St Martin retired to a forest on the left bank of the Sèvre, and established the hermitage which grew into the abbey of Vertou. He evangelized this district, and other monastic foundations are attributed to him, including a nunnery at Durieu, where he died. The monks of Vertou are said to have stolen his body while it was awaiting burial in the church at Durieu and the nuns were singing the office for the dead at night. Among the stories told of St Martin (by confusion, in this case, with Martin of Braga) is that an unnamed British prince had a daughter who was fearfully tormented by evil spirits. One of them said through her mouth that they would be overcome by the prayers of a holy man called Martin, and the prince thereupon sent messengers in all directions to find such an one. At length they came to Vertou, told their errand, and the saint agreed to accompany them. He had hardly landed in Britain when the demons knew of his arrival and, unwilling to wait for him, tormented their victim for the last time and fled.   She of course received the nun's veil from her deliverer.

The Bollandists in the *Acta Sanctorum*, October, vol. x, seem to have printed all the texts which bear upon the life and miracles of this rather nebulous saint.

ST EVERGISLUS, BISHOP OF COLOGNE   (*c.* A.D. 600)

WHEN St Severinus of Cologne was making a visitation at the church of Tongres in Belgium a young child was presented to him to be consecrated to the service of God.   He saw in this boy, Evergislus (Ebregiselus), a chosen soul, took a personal interest in his education, and when he was grown up made him his archdeacon. Evergislus was present when St Severinus, as related by Gregory of Tours, had his vision of the entry of St Martin into Heaven, but the archdeacon himself saw and heard nothing, and sent a messenger to Tours to verify that Martin was dead. He succeeded his master as bishop of Cologne.   One day when visiting the church of the " Golden Saints " he greeted the martyrs with the verse, " Exultabunt sancti in gloria ", and at once the voice of an invisible choir responded, " Laetabuntur in cubilibus suis ! "   While at Tongres in the discharge of his pastoral duties St Evergislus went at night to the church of our Lady to pray ; here he was set upon by robbers, and met his death.

This is the legend of the church of Cologne, recognized in the Roman Martyrology today, but St Evergislus seems to have lived later, and not to have died a violent death.   St Gregory of Tours says he was among the bishops sent by Childebert II to restore observance in the nunnery at Poitiers.   He also records that Evergislus was freed from headaches after praying in the church of the " Golden Saints " at Cologne.

The data seem involved in hopeless confusion.   What purports to be a Life of Evergislus is printed in the *Analecta Bollandiana*, vol. vi (1887), pp. 193–198, and also elsewhere ; but it was written only in the eleventh century and is historically worthless.   See, however, the discussion of the problem by W. Levison in the *Festschrift für A. Brackman* (1931), pp. 40–63 ; and *cf.* Duchesne, *Fastes Épiscopaux*, vol. iii, p. 176.   For the " Golden Saints ", *cf.* St Gereon on October 10.

BD JOHN ANGELO PORRO   (A.D. 1506)

MILAN was the birthplace of this ornament of the order of the Servants of Mary, who soon after his profession and ordination was sent to the cradle of his order on Monte Senario as being more suited to a life of prayer and silence than to the works of the active ministry.   Having remained there in great holiness for some years he was drawn from his solitude to be master of novices at Florence, an office he fulfilled so well that he is venerated in his order as a patron of novice-masters. At various times he was at several other houses of his order, and wherever he was stationed he spent much time in giving instruction in Christian doctrine, especially to the poor and unlearned ; in Milan he went about the streets gathering in children for this purpose, a work which was to be organized in the same place by St Charles Borromeo in the next generation.   While at Cavacurta, Bd John Angelo learned in a vision of the death of his sister and that he too must go back home as his death was near.   Accordingly he returned to his native Milan, worn out with work and hardships, and died there in the Servite priory in 1506.   The *cultus* of Bd John Angelo Porro was approved in 1737.

A life by Philip Albericius has been reproduced in the *Acta Sanctorum*, October, vol. x, with the usual introduction and commentary ; but Fr Soulier, in the *Monumenta Ordinis Servorum B.M.V.*, vol. viii, pp. 121–211, and vol. ix, pp. 5–222, has been able to glean a few additional data.   It must be confessed, however, that the career and personality of the *beatus* still remain veiled in great obscurity.   A popular life in Italian by L. Raffaelli (1906), aims primarily at edification and can make no pretence to critical scholarship.

25 : SS. CHRYSANTHUS AND DARIA, MARTYRS   (DATE UNKNOWN)

In the United States of America the feast of St Isidore is celebrated on this day. See Vol. II, p. 323.

THAT these martyrs were actual persons who gave their lives for Christ is attested by the evidence of their early veneration at Rome, but their *passio* is a fanciful compilation of much later date.   It says that Chrysanthus was the son of a patrician named Polemius, who came with his father from Alexandria to Rome in the reign of Numerian.   He was instructed in the faith and baptized by a priest called Carpophorus.   On discovering this, Polemius was indignant and subjected his son to the blandishments of five young women, hoping that he would lose his chastity and with it his new religion.   When this device failed, Polemius proposed a marriage between Chrysanthus and a certain Daria, a priestess of Minerva.   How this was to be brought about is not explained, but Daria proved acceptable to Chrysanthus, he converted her, and they entered into a virginal union.   Between them they made a number of converts in Roman society, and were denounced and committed to the charge of the tribune Claudius. He handed Chrysanthus over to a company of soldiers, with instructions to make him sacrifice to Hercules by any means which they chose.   They subjected him to a number of torments, under which he remained so constant that the tribune himself was constrained to confess Christ, and with him his wife Hilaria and their two sons.   The soldiers likewise followed their example, and by order of the emperor all were slain together except Hilaria, who was seized later while praying at their tomb.   St Claudius and his companions are commemorated in the Roman Martyrology on December 3.   Daria in the meanwhile had been consigned to a brothel, where she was defended from harm by a lion, which escaped for the purpose from the amphitheatre.   To get rid of the beast the house had to be set on fire, and then the girl with her husband was taken before Numerian himself.   They were condemned to death, and were stoned and buried alive in an old sand-pit on the Via Salaria Nova.   On the anniversary of their passion some of the faithful met together in this pit, and while they were praying in the crypt where the martyrs were buried emissaries of the emperor closed up the entrance with rocks and earth, so that they were all entombed.   These are the SS. Diodorus the priest, Marianus the deacon and their fellows commemorated on December 1.

The statement that SS. Chrysanthus and Daria were stoned and buried in a sand-pit may be true.   Later their tomb, with the bones of the other martyrs, was said to be discovered, and St Gregory of Tours has left a hearsay description of the shrine that was made of it, but without naming the martyrs.   In the ninth century the alleged relics of SS. Chrysanthus and Daria were translated to Prüm in Rhenish Prussia and four years later to Münstereifel, where they still are.   The tomb was in the neighbourhood of the *Coemeterium Thrasonis* on the New Salarian Way, where are a number of ancient sand-pits.

There is both a Latin and a Greek text of this legend. Both are printed in the *Acta Sanctorum*, October, vol. xi. An exceptionally full discussion of the historical data will be found in Delehaye's CMH., under August 12, on which day these martyrs are there specially commemorated, but their names also recur on December 20, and in this connection Delehaye points out that the assignment of their feast in the Roman Martyrology to October 25 seems to be due to a statement made in an account of a translation of their relics that October 25 was not only the date of the translation but the actual day of their martyrdom. The marble calendar of Naples (*c.* 850) seems to confirm this. Pope St Damasus is recorded to have written an inscription for their tomb, but that which was at one time attributed to him must certainly be of later date. See further, J. P. Kirsch, *Festkalender* (1924), pp. 90–93 ; and DAC., vol. iii, cc. 1560–1568.

SS. CRISPIN AND CRISPINIAN, MARTYRS   (DATE UNKNOWN)

THE names of these two martyrs were famous throughout northern Europe in the middle ages, but are today known in England chiefly from the great speech which Shakespeare puts into the mouth of King Henry V on the eve of Agincourt (*Henry V*, act iv, scene 3). Their very late *passio* unfortunately cannot be relied on. It says that they came from Rome to preach the faith in Gaul toward the middle of the third century, together with St Quintinus and others. Fixing their residence at Soissons, they instructed many in the faith of Christ, which they preached during the day ; and, in imitation of St Paul, worked with their hands at night making shoes, though they are said to have been nobly born (and brothers). The infidels listened to their instructions and were astonished at the example of their lives, and the effect was the conversion of many to the Christian faith. They had continued this employment several years when, the Emperor Maximian coming into Gaul, a complaint was lodged against them. He, perhaps as much to gratify their accusers as to indulge his own superstition and cruelty, gave orders that they should be taken before Rictiovarus, an implacable enemy of Christians (if, in fact, he was an historical person). He subjected them to various torments and in vain tried to kill them by drowning and boiling ; this so infuriated him that he took his own life by jumping into the fire prepared for them. Thereupon Maximian commanded that they be beheaded, and this was done. Later a church was built over their tomb, and St Eligius the Smith embellished their shrine. SS. Crispin and Crispinian are supposed to have plied their trade without taking payment unless it was offered and thereby disposed men to listen to the gospel. They are the traditional patrons of shoemakers, cobblers and other workers in leather.

The Roman Martyrology says that the relics of these martyrs were translated from Soissons to the church of St Laurence *in Panisperna* at Rome. Nothing is certainly known about them, and it is possible—even more likely—that the reverse is the truth : that SS. Crispin and Crispinian were Roman martyrs whose relics were brought to Soissons and so started a local *cultus*.

The local tradition which associates these martyrs with the little port of Faversham in Kent is not mentioned by Alban Butler, though it must have been well known in his day, for it is still remembered. They are said to have fled thither to escape the persecution, and followed their trade of shoemaking at a house on the site of the Swan Inn, at the lower end of Preston Street, " near the Cross Well ". A Mr Southouse, writing about the year 1670, says that in his time this house had " considerable visits paid to it by the foreigners of that gentle calling ", so it looks as if the tradition was also known abroad. There was an altar dedicated in honour of SS. Crispin and Crispinian in the parish church of St Mary of Charity.

From the example of the saints it appears how foolish is the pretence of many Christians who imagine that the care of a family, the business of a farm or a shop, the attention which they are obliged to give to their secular profession, are impediments which excuse them from aiming at perfection. Such, indeed, they make them ; but this is altogether owing to their own sloth and weakness. Many saints have made these very occupations the means of their perfection. St Paul made tents ; SS. Crispin and Crispinian were shoemakers ; the Blessed Virgin was taken up with the care of her cottage ; Christ Himself worked with His reputed father ; and those who renounced all commerce with the world to devote themselves totally to the contemplation of heavenly things made mats and baskets, tilled the earth, or copied and bound books. Opportunities for every kind of good work never fail in any circumstances ; and the means of sanctification may be practised in every state of life.

The Bollandists in the *Acta Sanctorum*, October, vol. xi, print the *passio* and supply a very full commentary. The historical fact of the martyrdom seems sufficiently guaranteed by the entry on this day in the "Hieronymianum", "in Galiis civitate Sessionis Crispini et Crispiniani". *Cf.* Delehaye, *Étude sur le légendier romain*, pp. 126–129, 132–135, and CMH., pp. 337–338, 570–571 ; and Duchesne, *Fastes Épiscopaux*, vol. iii, pp. 141–152.

SS. FRONTO AND GEORGE, BISHOPS   (DATE UNKNOWN)

THOUGH no doubt these two saints really existed and were early apostles of Périgord, their legends seem to have been fabricated or altered with the object of giving an apostolic origin to the see of Périgueux. Fronto, it is said, was of the tribe of Juda and was born in Lycaonia. He was converted by the testimony of our Lord's miracles, was baptized by St Peter, and became one of the Seventy-two. He accompanied St Peter to Antioch and Rome, and was sent thence with the priest George to preach to the Gauls. On the way George died, but, like St Maternus of Trier and St Martial of Limoges, he was brought to life again by the touch of St Peter's staff. St Fronto preached with conspicuous success, and several fantastic miracles and inconsistent particulars are given of his mission. His centre was at Périgueux, whereof he is venerated as the first bishop. Later legends import into his life an incident recorded of quite another St Fronto, who was a hermit in the Nitrian desert. St George evangelized the Velay and is accounted the first bishop of Le Puy.

In the earliest known form of the legend, St Fronto is not described as born in Lycaonia, but at Leuquais in the Dordogne, not very far from the Périgueux he was destined to evangelize. The extravagances and anachronisms are much the same as those in the legend just summarized, but there are signs that the earlier compiler did use some historical material, and a seventh-century Life of St Géry undoubtedly speaks of a tomb of St Fronto venerated in Périgueux at that date.

The Benedictines of Paris in their *Vies des saints . . .*, vol. x (1952), have reprinted the following pleasing anecdote. It occurs in the prolegomena to André Lavertujon's edition of the Chronicle of Sulpicius Severus. Mr Lavertujon tells us that he learned to read from a *Histoire de S. Front*, and goes on : " What struck us most among the extraordinary happenings of St Fronto's life was this : Fronto was banished by the proconsul Squirius to a wilderness near Périgueux, and would there have died of hunger had not the fierce Roman been struck with remorse and sent him food, loaded on to seventy camels (for the holy man had companions). We were entranced and inflated by these camels walking about the banks of our Dordogne, and asked, ' Monsieur l'abbé, why aren't there any camels here now ? ' —' Because we no longer deserve them ', was the reply."

The pages devoted to this legend in the *Acta Sanctorum*, October, vol. xi, may be said to have been superseded by the very careful examination of the documents in the *Analecta Bollandiana*, vol. xlviii (1930), pp. 324–360, " La Vie ancienne de St Front ", by M. Coens. He there edits the text of an earlier legend of St Fronto, already recognized as more primitive by Mgr Duchesne (see *Fastes Épiscopaux*, vol. ii, pp. 130–134).

ST GAUDENTIUS, Bishop of Brescia   (*c.* A.D. 410)

GAUDENTIUS seems to have been educated under St Philastrius, Bishop of Brescia, whom he styles his " father ". His reputation was very high and he travelled to Jerusalem, partly on pilgrimage and partly hoping by his absence to be forgotten at home. In this, however, he was mistaken. At Caesarea in Cappadocia he met with the sisters and nieces of St Basil, who bestowed on him relics of the Forty Martyrs, knowing that he would honour those sacred pledges as they had honoured them. During his absence St Philastrius died, and the clergy and people of Brescia chose Gaudentius for their bishop : they bound themselves by an oath to receive no other for their pastor. St Gaudentius only yielded to the threat of refusal of communion by the Eastern bishops if he refused to obey. He was consecrated by St Ambrose about the year 387 ; the sermon which he preached on that occasion expresses the humility with which his youth and inexperience inspired him.

The church of Brescia soon found how great a treasure it possessed in so holy a pastor. A certain nobleman named Benevolus, who had been disgraced by the Empress Justina because he refused to draw up an edict in favour of the Arians, had retired to Brescia, and being hindered by sickness from attending the Easter sermons of Gaudentius, requested that he would commit them to writing for his use. By this means were preserved ten out of the twenty-one sermons of the saint which are extant. In the second, which he made for the neophytes at their coming from the font on Holy Saturday, he explained to them the mysteries which he could not expound in presence of the catechumens, especially the Blessed Eucharist, of which he says : " The Creator and Lord of Nature, who brings the bread out of the ground, makes also of bread His own body ; because He has promised, and is able to perform it. And He who made wine of water, converts wine into His own blood." Gaudentius in the preface to his discourses warns the reader against pirated editions of them. He built a church at Brescia which he named the " Assembly of the Saints ", and to the dedication of which he invited many bishops and in their presence made the seventeenth sermon of those which are extant. In it he says that he had deposited in this church relics of the Apostles and others, affirming that a portion of a martyr's relics is in virtue and efficacy the same as the whole. " Therefore ", he says, " that we may be succoured by the patronage of so many saints, let us come and supplicate with an entire confidence and earnest desire, that by their interceding we may deserve to obtain all things we ask, magnifying Christ our Lord, the giver of so great grace."

In 405, St Gaudentius was deputed with two others by Pope St Innocent I and the Emperor Honorius to go into the East to defend the cause of St John Chrysostom before Arcadius, for which Chrysostom sent him a letter of thanks.

The deputies were ill received, and imprisoned in Thrace; their papers were forcibly taken from them, and bribes were offered if they would declare themselves in communion with the bishop who had supplanted St John Chrysostom. St Paul is said to have appeared in a vision to one of their deacons to encourage them. They eventually arrived back safely in Italy, though it is supposed their enemies intended them to be cast away at sea, for they were put on a most unseaworthy vessel. St Gaudentius seems to have died about the year 410, and Rufinus styled him " the glory of the doctors of the age wherein he lives ". He is honoured on this day in the Roman Martyrology, which mentions on October 14 another St Gaudentius. He was the first bishop of Rimini, and may have been martyred by the Arians in the year 359. His feast is kept by the Canons Regular of the Lateran.

There seems to be no formal biography of St Gaudentius, but from contemporary allusions and letters a tolerably full account is furnished in the *Acta Sanctorum*, October, vol. xi. The activities of the saint have occasionally been made the subject of contributions to the local ecclesiastical journal, *Brixia sacra, e.g.* vol. vi and vol. vii (1915–16). See also Lanzoni, *Diocesi d'Italia* (1927), vol. ii, pp. 963–965 ; and the *Journal of Theological Studies*, vol. xii (1914), pp. 593–596. For the discourses, see A. Glueck, *Sti Gaudentii . . . tractatus* (1936).

BD CHRISTOPHER OF ROMAGNOLA　　(A.D. 1272)

Bd Christopher (often called " of Cahors ") was a personal disciple of St Francis of Assisi. He was a parish priest in the diocese of Cesena, and when about forty years of age he resigned his benefice and joined the newly-formed order of Friars Minor, among whom he was distinguished for his bodily austerities and his devotion to the lepers. He was eventually sent into France where he preached against the Albigensians and established his order at Cahors, among other places. He died here in 1272, at a great age, and his *cultus* was approved in 1905.

The Bollandists on October 31 relegate this holy friar among the *praetermissi* on the ground that no sufficient evidence had then been produced for his continued *cultus*. The decree of confirmation, which includes some biographical details, may be read in the *Analecta Ecclesiastica* for 1905, p. 206. There is a life by Bernard of Besse in the *Analecta Franciscana*, vol. iii, pp. 161–173. See also the biography by Léopold de Chérancé (1907).

BD THOMAS OF FLORENCE　　(A.D. 1447)

Thomas Bellacci, a native of Florence, was a Franciscan lay-brother, who as a young man had led a wild and disorderly life. Realization of the futility of it all and the wise words of a friend wrought a change in him and he was accepted—with some trepidation, for his excesses were notorious—by the friars of the Observance at Fiesole. But his penitence equalled his former sinfulness, and in time, for all he was a lay-brother, he was made master of novices, whom he trained in the strictest ways of the Observance. When in 1414 Friar John of Stroncone went to spread the reform in the kingdom of Naples he took Bd Thomas with him. He laboured there for some six years, strengthened with the gift of miracles, and then, authorized by Pope Martin V, he undertook, in company with Bd Antony of Stroncone, to oppose the heretical Fraticelli in Tuscany. While engaged in this campaign he made a number of new foundations, over which St Bernardino gave him authority, his own headquarters being at the friary of Scarlino. Here he established a custom of going in procession after the night office to a neighbouring wood, where each friar had a little shelter of boughs and shrubs wherein they remained for a time in prayer.

As a result of the "reunion council" at Florence in 1439, Friar Albert of Sarzana was sent as papal legate to the Syrian Jacobites and other dissidents of the East, and he took Thomas with him, although he was in his seventieth year. From Persia Albert commissioned him to go with three other friars into Ethiopia. Three times on their way they were seized by the Turks, who treated them with great cruelty. But Bd Thomas insisted on preaching to the Mohammedans, and eventually they had to be ransomed by Pope Eugenius IV, just before their captors were going to put them to death. Bd Thomas could not get over that God had refused the proffered sacrifice of his life, and in 1447, aged as he was, he set out for Rome to ask permission to go again to the East. But at Rieti he was taken ill, and died there on October 31. Many urged that he should be canonized with St Bernardino of Siena, whose cause was then in process. To prevent the delay that would have resulted, St John of Capistrano, it is said, went to Thomas's tomb at Rieti and commanded him in the name of holy obedience to cease his miracles until the canonization of Bernardino should be achieved. They stopped for three years, but Bd Thomas has never been canonized. His *cultus* was approved in 1771.

See Wadding, *Annales Minorum* ; Mazzara, *Leggendario francescano* ; and the summary in Léon, *Auréole Séraphique* (Eng. trans.), vol. iv.

BD BALTHASAR OF CHIAVARI (A.D. 1492)

BALTHASAR RAVASCHIERI was born at Chiavari on the Gulf of Genoa about the year 1420. He joined the Friars Minor of the Observance, and in due course was professed and ordained. Balthasar was a friend and fellow-preacher with Bd Bernardino of Feltre, and joined enthusiastically and successfully in his missions, but his activities were cut short by ill-health. When he could not walk he had himself carried into church in order to assist at Mass and the choir offices and to hear the confessions of the faithful who came to him in crowds. He also used to be taken into the woods and left there for long periods of meditation and reading, and here he had a vision of our Lady and was miraculously sheltered from a heavy fall of snow. This double marvel was commemorated in the sixteenth century by an inscription cut in stone, and in 1678 was recorded in the archives of the town of Chiavari. Bd Balthasar died on October 17, 1492, at Binasco, and his *cultus* was confirmed in 1930.

Though we have a certain amount of evidence regarding the later *cultus* of this *beatus*, very little can be stated with certainty about the facts of his life. See the *Archivum Franciscanum Historicum*, vol. ii (1909), p. 523. What little is known has been gathered together in the small volume of Fr Bernardino da Carasco, *Il b. Baldassare Ravaschieri* (1930).

BD THADDEUS, BISHOP OF CORK AND CLOYNE (A.D. 1497)

OF the early life of this bishop, the only Irishman beatified between the canonization of Lorcan O'Toole in 1228 and the beatification of Oliver Plunket in 1920, very little is known. He belonged to the royal MacCarthys in the part of Munster later known as the Desmond country, his father being lord of Muskerry and his mother a daughter of FitzMaurice, lord of Kerry ; Thaddeus (Tadhg) was a baptismal name in this house for seven hundred years. He is said to have begun his studies with the Friars Minor of Kilcrea and to have then gone abroad, and he seems to have been in Rome when, in 1482 at the age of twenty-seven, he was appointed bishop of Ross by Pope Sixtus IV. Three years later when Henry Tudor became ruler of the three kingdoms, the Yorkist Geraldines made a determined effort to have their own representative in the see of Ross. Ever since the appointment of Thaddeus MacCarthy there had been a rival claimant in the person of Hugh O'Driscoll, his predecessor's auxiliary, and it was now alleged that Thaddeus had intruded himself under false pretences, with other charges added. The earl of Desmond seized the temporalities of the see, and its bishop took refuge at the Cistercian abbey near Parma, which was given him *in commendam* by the bishop of Clogher. By the machinations of the FitzGeralds Thaddeus was in 1488 declared suspended by the Holy See, and he set off to Rome to plead his cause in person. After two years of investigation and delay Pope Innocent VIII confirmed the bishopric of Ross to Hugh, but nominated Thaddeus to the united dioceses of Cork and Cloyne, then vacant.

When Bd Thaddeus arrived, he found his cathedral closed against him and the see's endowments in the hands of the FitzGeralds, Barrys and others. In vain he endeavoured to assert his canonical rights and to obtain peaceful control of his charge : there was nothing for it but to go again to Rome and appeal to the Holy See. The pope condemned the tyrants and provided Thaddeus with letters to the earl of Kildare, then lord deputy of Ireland, to the heads of the bishop's own clan, and to others, exhorting them to protect and aid his just cause. With these Bd Thaddeus set out for home as a pilgrim on foot, and in the evening of October 24, 1497, reached Ivrea, at the foot of the Alps, where he stayed at the hospice of the canons regular of St Bernard of Montjoux. The next morning he was found dead in his bed.

When an examination of his luggage showed who the dead pilgrim was, the matter was reported to the bishop of Ivrea, who ordered that he should be buried with the utmost solemnity. The story of the episcopal pilgrim travelling *incognito* and on foot soon got around, and the cathedral was crowded with people from the neighbourhood who came to the funeral. They continued to visit the tomb, and the popular *cultus* of Bd Thaddeus, encouraged by many miracles, was thus begun. Bishops Richelmy of Ivrea and Cailaghan of Cork having co-operated in the forwarding of his cause, the *cultus* was confirmed in 1895. His feast is kept in the dioceses of Ivrea, Ross, Cork and Cloyne.

Not very much seems to be known concerning this *beatus*. In the *Irish Ecclesiastical Record* for 1896 the lessons sanctioned for the office of his festival are printed, pp. 859–861. The decree confirming the *cultus* may be read in the *Analecta Ecclesiastica*, vol. iii (1895), p. 456. It gives very little biographical detail, but dwells principally on the miracles worked at the shrine at Ivrea. *Cf.* V. Berardi, *Italy and Ireland in the Middle Ages* (1950).

BD RICHARD GWYN, MARTYR   (A.D. 1584)

FOR forty years after the dissolution of the monasteries Wales remained a stronghold of the Catholic faith ; many of the great families and most of the common people were faithful to it. But soon after the missionary priests began to arrive from the continent, Queen Elizabeth and her ministers set themselves to stamp out the religion by cutting off the channels of sacramental grace and closing the mouths of those who should preach the word of God. In Wales the first victim of this campaign was a layman, Richard Gwyn (*alias* White). He was born at Llanidloes in Montgomeryshire in 1537, and was brought up a Protestant. On leaving St

John's College, Cambridge, he went to Overton in Flintshire and opened a school. Some time after he became a Catholic, and his absence from Protestant worship drawing suspicion on himself, he left Overton with his family for Erbistock. In 1579, being in Wrexham, he was recognized by the vicar (an apostate), denounced, and arrested. He managed to escape. But in June 1580, the Privy Council directed the Protestant bishops to be more vigilant in their dealings with Catholic recusants, especially " all schoolmasters, public and private ". Accordingly, in the very next month, Richard Gwyn was seized and brought before a magistrate, who sent him to Ruthin gaol. At the Michaelmas assizes he was offered his liberty if he would conform, and on refusal was returned to prison, to be kept in irons. At the May assizes he was ordered to be taken by force to the Protestant church, where he interrupted the preacher by vigorously clanking his chains. He was then put in the stocks from 10 a.m. till 8 p.m., " vexed all the time with a rabble of ministers ". One of them claimed that he had the power of the keys as much as St Peter ; but he also had a conspicuously red nose, and Gwyn retorted in exasperation, " There is this difference, namely, that whereas St Peter received the keys of the kingdom of Heaven you appear to have received those of the beer-cellar ! " He was indicted for brawling in church and fined the equivalent of £800, and brought up again in September and fined £1680 in modern money for not having attended church during the seven months he had been in gaol. The judge asked him what means he had to pay these absurd fines. " I have somewhat towards it ", he replied. " How much ? " " Sixpence ", said Gwyn. He appeared at three more assizes and was then sent with three other recusants and a Jesuit, Father John Bennet, senior, before the Council of the Marches, which had them tortured at Bewdley, Ludlow and Bridgnorth to try and get the names of other Catholics.

In October 1584 Bd Richard appeared at his eighth assizes, at Wrexham, with two others, Hughes and Morris, and was indicted for treason, in that he was alleged to have tried to reconcile one Lewis Gronow to the Church of Rome and to have maintained the supremacy of the pope. He denied ever speaking with Gronow, and the man afterwards made a public declaration that his evidence and that of the other two witnesses was false and paid for at the instigation of the vicar of Wrexham and another zealot. The jury summoned had refused to appear, so another was impanelled on the spot. The members asked the judge whom they were to convict and whom to acquit ! Accordingly Gwyn and Hughes were sentenced to death (Hughes was afterwards reprieved) and Morris released. Mrs. Gwyn was brought into court with her baby and warned not to imitate her husband. She rounded on the sheriff. " If you lack blood ", she said, " you may take my life as well as my husband's. If you will give the witnesses a little bribe they will give evidence against me too ! " Bd Richard was executed on October 15, 1584, a very wet day, at Wrexham (now the see of the Catholic diocese of Menevia, Mynyw). The crowd called for him to be allowed to die before disembowelling, but the sheriff (himself an apostate) refused, and the martyr shrieked out in his agony, " O Duw gwyn, pa beth ydyw hwn ? " " Holy God, what is this ? " " An execution for the Queen's Majesty ", said an official. " Iesu, trugarha wrthyf ! " " Jesus, have mercy on me ! " exclaimed Bd Richard, and his head was struck off.

During his four years of imprisonment Gwyn wrote in Welsh a number of religious poems (not " carols ", as they are generally called), calling on his countrymen to keep to " yr hen Fam ", the old Mother Church, and describing with a bitterness that was unhappily excusable the new religion and its ministers. He was beatified in 1929, and his feast is kept in the diocese of Menevia on this date.

It is under the name of White (a translation of the Welsh " Gwyn ") that Challoner gives an account of this martyr in MMP., pp. 102–105. See also Burton and Pollen, LEM., vol. i, pp. 127–144 ; and T. P. Ellis, *The Catholic Martyrs of Wales* (1933), pp. 18–33. For his poetical compositions in Welsh, consult the publications of the Catholic Record Society, vol. v, pp. 90–99.

26 : ST EVARISTUS, Pope and Martyr   (*c.* a.d. 107)

ST EVARISTUS succeeded St Clement in the see of Rome in the reign of Trajan and governed the Church about eight years, being the fourth successor of St Peter. The *Liber Pontificalis* says that he was the son of a Hellenic Jew of Bethlehem, and, certainly incorrectly, that he divided Rome into several " titles " or parishes, assigning a priest to each and appointed seven deacons for the city. He is usually accorded the title of martyr, but his martyrdom is not proved ; it is probable that St Evaristus was buried near St Peter's tomb in the Vatican.

There is a notice in the *Acta Sanctorum*, October, vol. xi, but the text and notes of Duchesne's edition of the *Liber Pontificalis* tell us nearly all there is to be known. See, however, an interesting comment by Father von Nostiz-Rieneck on the " Brevierlektionen der Päpste Evaristos und Alexander I" in the *Zeitschrift für Katholische Theologie*, vol. xxix (1905), pp. 159–165.

SS. LUCIAN and MARCIAN, Martyrs   (a.d. 250 ?)

LUCIAN and Marcian, we are told in their *passio*, applied themselves to the study of black magic, but were converted to the faith by finding their charms lose their power against a Christian maiden. Their eyes being thus opened, they publicly burned their magical books in the city of Nicomedia ; and when they had effaced their crimes by baptism they distributed their possessions among the poor and retired together into solitude, that by mortification and prayer they might strengthen in their souls that grace which they had just received. After a time they made frequent excursions abroad to preach Christ to the Gentiles. The edicts of Decius against the Christians being published in Bithynia, they were apprehended and brought before the proconsul Sabinus, who asked Lucian by what authority he presumed to preach Jesus Christ. " Every man ", said the martyr, " does well to endeavour to draw his brother out of a dangerous error ", and Marcian likewise gloried in the power of Christ. The judge commanded them to be tortured, whereupon they reproached him that, whilst they worshipped idols, they had committed many crimes and made open profession of practising magic, without incurring any chastisement ; but when they were become Christians and good citizens they were barbarously punished. Sabinus threatened them with more torments. " We are ready to suffer ", said Marcian, " but we will not renounce the true God, lest we be cast into a fire which will never be quenched." At this Sabinus condemned them to be burned alive, and they went joyfully to the place of execution, singing hymns of praise and thanksgiving to God. This story is a romance woven round a group of genuine martyrs at Nicomedia.

The *passio* of these martyrs is preserved both in Latin and in Syriac ; the Greek text, which is probably the original, seems to have perished. The Latin *passio* is printed in the

Acta Sanctorum, October, vol. xi ; the Syriac was edited by S. E. Assemani (in his *Acta ss. mart. orientalium*, vol. ii, pp. 49 *seq.*) from a manuscript written in the sixth or possibly even the fifth century. The Syriac *breviarium* of the early fifth century also commemorates these martyrs on October 26, but assigns them to Antioch, and gives the name Silvanus in place of Lucianus. They are, however, correctly named (with Florus), and attributed to Nicomedia, in the " Hieronymianum ", and the question is discussed by Delehaye in CMH., p. 572.

ST RUSTICUS, BISHOP OF NARBONNE   (*c.* A.D. 461)

RUSTICUS was a native of southern Gaul and the son of a bishop named Bonosus. A letter written by St Jerome about the year 411 is supposed to be addressed to him : the recipient is given wise counsel about the solitary life. In 427 Rusticus was elevated to the bishopric of Narbonne. His diocese was in a very unsatis-factory state : the invading Goths were spreading Arianism and the orthodox were quarrelling among themselves, and eventually St Rusticus wrote to Pope St Leo I, setting forth his difficulties (which seem to have arisen out of a synod convoked by him in 458), and asking to be allowed to resign. The pope dissuaded him from this and sent him an important letter about the government of the diocese. St Rusticus built a cathedral at Narbonne and the inscription he put up recording its foundation is still in existence. He was held in high regard by his brother bishops, but of his activities little is known, except that he attended the synod at Arles which approved St Leo's " tome " condemning Monophysism.

A particular interest, however, attaches to this Gaulish bishop because his name appears in four different inscriptions discovered at Narbonne or in the immediate neighbourhood. The first and most complete tells us, incidentally that not only was he the son of Bishop Bonosus, but that an uncle, his mother's brother, was also a bishop called Arator. Another inscription, only discovered in quite recent years, contains the words *Orate pro me Rustico vestro* (Pray for me, your Rusticus).

There is no formal life of St Rusticus, but from scattered references the Bollandists have compiled a sufficient notice in the *Acta Sanctorum*, October, vol. xi. See on the inscriptions Leclercq, DAC., vol. xii (1935), cc. 828 and 847–854. *Cf.* also Duchesne, *Fastes Épiscopaux*, vol. i, p. 303.

ST CEDD, BISHOP OF THE EAST SAXONS   (A.D. 664)

ST CEDD was the brother of St Chad and long served God in the monastery of Lindisfarne. When Peada, King of the Middle Angles, became a Christian at the court of his father-in-law, Oswy of Northumbria, in 653, being baptized by St Finan of Lindisfarne, four priests were sent to preach the gospel to his people. Of these St Cedd was one. After labouring there for a time he was called to a new harvest. Sigebert, King of the East Saxons, was also persuaded to renounce heathenism and was baptized by St Finan, whereupon Cedd was called out of the midlands and sent with another priest into Essex. They travelled throughout the province to examine the situation, and then St Cedd revisited Lindisfarne to confer with Finan, who consecrated him bishop for the East Saxons. He returned among them to continue the work he had begun, building churches and ordaining priests and deacons.

Two monasteries were founded by St Cedd, which seem to have been destroyed by the Danes later and never restored. The first, where remains of Cedd's church still exist, was at Bradwell-on-Sea (Ythancaestir, Othona) ; the other was at

Tilbury. His visits to his native Northumbria were the occasion of a third foundation. Ethelwald, King of Deira, gave him a tract of land for a monastery in an
inaccessible spot among the fells of Yorkshire. Here Cedd spent forty days in
fasting and prayer, to consecrate the place to God according to the custom of
Lindisfarne, derived from St Columba. This monastery, founded in 658, was
called Laestingaeu, which has been identified with Lastingham in the North
Riding ; and it also came to be destroyed by the Danes.

In 664 St Cedd was present at the Synod of Whitby, being one of those who
agreed to forsake Celtic custom and to observe Easter by the Roman computation.
Very soon after this he died at Lastingham during a great pestilence. At the news
of his death thirty of his religious brethren among the East Saxons came to Lastingham to consecrate their lives where their holy father had ended his. But they too
were carried off by the same pestilence, all except one boy, who was afterwards
found not to have been baptized : he lived to become a priest and zealous missionary. Florence of Worcester tells us that St Cedd died on October 26, 664.

Practically all that is known of St Cedd is derived from Bede's *Ecclesiastical History*,
bk iii, caps. 22, 23.

ST EATA, Bishop of Hexham   (A.D. 686)

WHEN St Aidan came from Iona to his mission in Northumbria he selected twelve
English boys to be trained under himself to work in the service of Christ, and of
these twelve Eata was one. He became abbot of Melrose, and received St Cuthbert
there as a novice. When St Colman and some of his monks left Northumbria
after their defeat at the Synod of Whitby, Eata was put in charge of those who
remained at Lindisfarne. St Bede reports on hearsay that St Colman himself
asked King Oswy to make this appointment because Eata was a personal disciple
of St Aidan. When in 678 St Wilfrid was driven from his see and Northumbria
divided, St Eata was appointed bishop of the Bernicians in the north ; and as he
had the choice of Hexham or Lindisfarne for his see he chose Lindisfarne. Later
Tunbert was consecrated for Hexham, and when he was deposed St Cuthbert was
named in his place. He, however, preferred to be at Lindisfarne, whither he had
gone as a monk with St Eata, and so an exchange was made, Eata going to Hexham.
Here he remained for the short space of life that remained to him, and after his
death in 686 was revered as a saint by the grateful people among whom he had
laboured. Bede says of him that he was a most venerable man, meek and simple.
St Eata's feast is kept in the diocese of Lancaster.

There is a Life of St Eata which has been printed by Raine in his *Priory of Hexham*
and a summary by Capgrave in the *Acta Sanctorum*, October, vol. xi ; but there is little
to add to what may be gathered from the text and notes of Plummer's edition of Bede,
bk iii, cap. 26 and iv, 12, 26, 28.

ST BEAN, Bishop of Mortlach   (Eleventh Century)

ON December 16 there is named in the Roman Martyrology and in certain Irish
calendars a St Bean in Ireland, who has been confused with the St Bean whose
feast is still observed in the Scottish diocese of Aberdeen, but on October 26, as
founder of the bishopric of Mortlach in Banff which was the forerunner of that
of Aberdeen. Nothing else is known about him. The fourteenth-century
chronicler Fordun states that he was made bishop by Pope Benedict VIII, at the

request of Malcolm Canmore, who is said to have founded an episcopal monastery at Mortlach. If true, this would be between 1012 and 1024; but the see of Mortlach is generally said to date from 1063. St Bean's dwelling-place is supposed to have been at Balvanie, near Mortlach (Bal-beni-mor, " the dwelling of Bean the Great ").

See the *Acta Sanctorum*, October, vol. xi ; and KSS., p. 277.

BD DAMIAN OF FINARIO   (A.D. 1484)

DAMIAN FURCHERI was born towards the beginning of the fifteenth century at Perti, near Finario, which is now Finale Borgo, not far from Genoa. Writers much later than his time record that as an infant he was snatched away from his home by a lunatic, and only found after a lengthy search by the aid of a miraculous light showing where the child lay hidden. He entered the Dominican Order in his youth, and was renowned as a preacher in every part of Lombardy and Liguria. He died in 1484 at Reggio, near Modena, and was there buried. Bd Damian was famous for many miracles attributed to him after death. His *cultus* was confirmed in 1848.

See the *Acta Sanctorum*, October, vol. xiii ; *Année Dominicaine*, vol. x, p. 733 ; *Short Lives of Dominican Saints*, ed. Procter, pp. 301-302 ; Taurisano, *Catalogus hagiographicus O.P.*, p. 45.

BD BONAVENTURE OF POTENZA   (A.D. 1711)

HE was born at Potenza in the kingdom of Naples in 1651 and became a Conventual friar minor at Nocera. As an illustration of the exact obedience that he gave to his superiors it is related that, the key of the sacristy being lost, it was reported to be at the bottom of the cistern, and Brother Bonaventure was told to get hook and line and fish it out. This he did, and after angling for a time hauled up the key. This is recorded of him as a miracle, but whether the miracle lay in the key being transported into the cistern, or in the dexterity of Brother Bonaventure, does not appear. The eight years which he spent at Amalfi was the most fruitful period of his life and he worked there with great profit to the people and his own soul. Several times it was proposed to make him guardian, but at his own earnest wish he was never given any office of authority but that of master of novices. Bonaventure's devotion to our Lady was particularly directed towards her as conceived without original sin (he lived nearly two hundred years before that dogma was defined), and he would often express the wish that he were another Duns Scotus that he might as effectively defend the truth of the Immaculate Conception.

Bonaventure died at Ravello on October 26, 1711, and he is one of the saints of the Naples district whose blood is recorded to have flowed freely after he was dead. " It was the will of God that His servant should give an example of obedience even after death. Long after he had expired, the bishop's vicar general asked the surgeon to bleed him in the arm, and he said, ' Father Bonaventure, give us your arm '. The body remained motionless, so turning to the superior the vicar general said, ' Father Guardian, command him in the name of holy obedience to give us his arm '. No sooner had the guardian given the order than the blessed man raised his right arm and presented it to the surgeon. It may be imagined with what fear and admiration the bystanders beheld this action " (*Auréole Séraphique*). From the fuller evidence which was at their disposal the Bollandists have raised a disturbing doubt as to whether Bd Bonaventure was actually dead when these things happened. He was beatified in 1775.

In the *Acta Sanctorum*, October, vol. xii, Fr V. de Buck has compiled a life from the materials supplied in earlier biographies of this *beatus*, notably from the accounts published by G. M. Ruglio (1754) and G. L. Rossi (1775). See also Léon, *Auréole Séraphique* (Eng. trans.), vol. iii, pp. 423–429. In connection with the blood prodigy referred to above, it is noteworthy that Bd Bonaventure died at Ravello, a Neapolitan town, in which the annual liquefaction of the blood of St Pantaleon rouses intense popular enthusiasm. See that saint under July 27 herein. A popular account of Bd Bonaventure was published at Ravello in 1930.

27 : ST FRUMENTIUS, Bishop of Aksum   (*c.* A.D. 380)

SOMEWHERE about the year 330 a philosopher of Tyre, named Meropius, out of curiosity and a wish to see the world and improve his knowledge, undertook a voyage to the coasts of Arabia. He took with him two young men, Frumentius and Aedesius, with whose education he was entrusted. In the course of their voyage homeward the vessel touched at a certain port of Ethiopia, or as it is now often called, Abyssinia. The natives fell out with some of the sailors, attacked them, and put the whole crew and all the passengers to the sword, except the two boys, who were studying their lessons under a tree at some distance. When they were found they were carried to the king, who resided at Aksum in the Tigre country. He was attracted by the bearing and knowledge of the young Christians, and not long after made Aedesius his cupbearer and Frumentius, who was the elder, his secretary. This prince on his death-bed thanked them for their services and, in recompense, gave them their liberty. The queen, who was left regent for her eldest son, entreated them to remain and assist her, which they did.

Frumentius had the principal management of affairs and induced several Christian merchants who traded there to settle in the country. He procured them privileges and all conveniences for religious worship, and by his own fervour and example strongly recommended the true religion to the infidels. When the young king came of age and, with his brother, took the reins of government into his own hands, the Tyrians resigned their posts, though he urged them to stay. Aedesius went back to Tyre, where he was ordained priest and told his adventures to Rufinus, who incorporated them in his *Church History*. But Frumentius, having nothing so much at heart as the conversion of the whole nation, took the route to Alexandria, and entreated the bishop, St Athanasius, to send some pastor to that country. Whereupon Athanasius ordained Frumentius himself bishop of the Ethiopians, judging no one more proper to finish the work which he had begun. Thus began the association of the Christians of Abyssinia with the church of Alexandria which has continued to this day.

The consecration of St Frumentius took place probably just before the year 340 or just after 346 (or perhaps *c.* 355–356). He went back to Aksum and gained numbers to the faith by his preaching and miracles ; the two royal brothers are said to have themselves received baptism, and as Abreha and Asbeha are venerated as saints in the Ethiopic calendar. But the Arian emperor Constantius conceived an implacable suspicion against St Frumentius, because he was linked in faith and affection with St Athanasius ; and when he found that he was not even to be tempted, much less seduced by him, he wrote a letter to the two kings, in which he urged them to send Frumentius to George, the intruded bishop of Alexandria, who would be responsible for his " welfare ". The emperor also warned them against Athanasius as guilty " of many crimes ". The only result was that this letter was communicated to St Athanasius, who has inserted it in his *apologia* against the Arians. The conversion even of the Aksumite kingdom was far from completed during the lifetime of St Frumentius. After his death he was called *Abuna*, " Our father ", and *Aba salama*, " Father of peace ", and *abuna* is still the title of the primate of the dissident Church of Ethiopia.

The story told by Rufinus may be read with other matter in the *Acta Sanctorum*, October, vol. xii. This other matter includes a copy of a long Greek inscription found at Aksum, commemorating the exploits of Aïzanas, King of the Homeritae, and his brother Saïzanas. Now it was precisely to Aïzanas and Saïzanas that Constantius addressed his letter, of which St Athanasius has preserved the text, demanding the surrender of Frumentius. There can consequently be no doubt that the last-named really was at Aksum preaching the Christian faith. Although the earlier adventures of Frumentius, as Rufinus recounts them, may have been misunderstood or disfigured with legendary additions, his presence in Aksum, as a bishop, consecrated for this mission by St Athanasius, is a certain fact. See Professor Guidi in the *Enciclopedia italiana*, vol. xiv, pp. 480–481, and in DHG., vol. i, cc. 210–212 ; Leclercq in DAC., vol. v, cc. 586–594 ; Duchesne, *Histoire ancienne de l'Église*, vol. iii, pp. 576–578 ; and *cf.* the account given of St Frumentius in the *Ethiopic Synaxarium* (ed. Budge, 1928), vol. iv, pp. 1164–1165. According to F. G. Holweck, the old diocese of Louisiana, U.S.A. (erected 1787) observed the feast of St Frumentius ; was this a gesture towards the slaves of African origin in America ?

ST OTTERAN, OR ODHRAN, ABBOT   (A.D. 563)

OTTERAN, " noble and without sin ", was an abbot from Meath and one of the twelve who sailed with St Columba out of Loch Foyle to Iona ; Adamnan says he was a Briton. Soon after their arrival St Otteran felt death to be upon him, and he said, " I would be the first to die under the covenant of the kingdom of God in this place ". " I will give you that kingdom ", replied Columba, " and moreover this also, that whoever makes a request at my burial-place shall not get it until he prays to you as well." And Columba, unwilling to see his friend die, blessed him and went out of the house, and as he was walking in the yard he stopped, looking amazedly up to the heavens. Asked at what he gazed, Columba answered that he saw strife in the upper air between good and evil spirits, and angels carrying the soul of Otteran in triumph to Heaven. So he was the first by his death and burial there to seal Iona to the Irish monks, and the place of his burying, the only cemetery on the island, is still called *Reilig Orain*. This is said to be the Otteran who founded the monastery at Leitrioch Odrain (Latteragh in Tipperary). Although this is all that is known of St Otteran his feast (as a bishop) is kept today throughout Ireland.

How little is known concerning St Odhran appears clearly from the glosses to the *Félire* of Oengus, which suggest more than one alternative as to Odhran's identity. A notice in very vague terms is printed in the *Acta Sanctorum*, October, vol. xii. See also Forbes, KSS., p. 426. In the Annals of Ulster we are told that he died in the year 548. Odhran is the correct form of the name.

BD CONTARDO FERRINI   (A.D. 1902)

CONTARDO FERRINI was born in 1859 in a modest apartment in the Via Passerella at Milan. His father, Rinaldo Ferrini, was a teacher of mathematics and physics, who had married Louisa Buccellati in the previous year. Rinaldo had also graduated in civil engineering and architecture, and his son inherited both his intellectual ability and scientific spirit. Contardo indeed was a precocious lively child, and though he first went to school when he was six years old, his schooling had already begun with his father. According to a school-fellow, study and his religion were the only things that young Contardo was interested in ; as he grew up he was not free from the emotional disturbances common to adolescence—an echo of this can be detected in some verses he wrote for his mother's name-day when he was sixteen. But he weathered the storm, with the help of a wise and learned priest, Don Adalbert Catena, a friend of Manzoni and of Verdi. And while Don Catena guided him spiritually, another priest was watching over him intellectually : this was Mgr Antony Ceriani, prefect of the Ambrosian Library at Milan. Contardo wanted to read the Bible in its original languages, and it was to Mgr Ceriani that he turned to teach him Hebrew. Here, too, he found his father's insistence on a scientific approach reinforced : " Don't trust too much in second-hand information, even from the learned ", Mgr Ceriani would say. " Go directly to the sources of the truth." A third priest to whom Contardo owed much was a colleague of his father's, Don Antony Stoppani, whose geological and other learning chimed with that love of nature that distinguished Contardo throughout his life.

In 1876 Contardo entered the law school of the Borromeo College at Pavia. He was a very serious young man, and one gets the impression that at this time he was not altogether free from what in England is called " priggishness ". This might in a measure account for some of the ill-treatment he experienced at the hands of his fellow students. The patience with which he bore his trials and his general bearing gained him the nickname of " St Aloysius of the Borromeo ", used by some in respect and by others in derision. And an apostolic flame was kindled in him : " To preach by example is good ", he wrote, " and to preach by the word is good. But what is more effective than to preach by prayer ? " He became enthusiastic for the formation of a university-students' society, a thing then unheard of in Italy and of which he was a veritable pioneer. Nothing actually came of it till the year in which he left Pavia for Berlin ; the society was then given the name of St Severinus Boethius and it exists to this day. But the greater part of Ferrini's youthful apostolic ideals seem to have borne no fruit, at any rate visibly ; only the results of certain personal contacts were seen to be lasting. There was Ettore Cappa, who never forgot that it was Ferrini who introduced him to the writings of Cardinal Newman, and the life-long friendships with Count Paul Mapelli and his brother, Count Victor. The letters that he wrote to the last-named are one of the primary sources for Ferrini's life and thought.

Contardo Ferrini gained his doctorate in 1880 and was awarded a bursary for a year (later extended to two) in the University of Berlin. Before setting out for this centre of Protestantism he drew up a " Programme of Life " in the form of a letter to Victor Mapelli ; the document is a valuable testimony to his humble faith and the mystical trend of his spirit. He was somewhat depressed at leaving home, but his first impressions of Berlin cheered him : he found the Catholics there serious and observant, and the Catholic students of the university were organized and active.   In his little book *Un po' d'infinito* he notes how vividly the universality of the Church was brought home to him when he first went to confession in a foreign land.   At the local conference of the St Vincent de Paul Society (of which he had long been a member) he became friendly with Professor Maximilian Westermaier, the botanist, and he was in close contact with Alfred Pernice, Maurice Voigt and Zachary von Ligenthal.   It was the last-named he had in mind when he wrote that " Protestantism makes a man a very worthy person where our religion would make him a saint ".   As was to be expected, Ferrini was not among Theodore Mommsen's intimates, but over twenty years later, talking with Bartholomew Nogara, then director of the Etruscan Museum of the Vatican, Mommsen spoke of Ferrini with the greatest respect, saying that he had removed the primacy in Roman legal studies from Germany to Italy.   " Nor are we jealous ", he added. But there was another side to Berlin, and Ferrini was " nauseated by the sad sight of so corrupt a city ".   The proximity of wickedness deepened his own asceticism. Ferrini was then twenty-two, and concerned about what was his vocation in life. Marriage ?   The priesthood ?   The monastic state ?   He heard no call to any of them ; and towards the end of 1881 he made a vow of lifelong celibacy.*

Ferrini returned to Italy in the summer of 1883.   He was now engaged on a critical edition of the Greek paraphrase of the *Institutes* of Justinian.   In furtherance of this work he visited libraries at Copenhagen, Paris, Rome and Florence, and perfected that remarkable knowledge of languages that was so valuable to him in his studies.   German, Latin and Greek he spoke and wrote fluently, and with varying degrees of facility he knew French, Spanish, English, Dutch, Hebrew, Syriac, with a smattering of Coptic and Sanscrit.   Such qualifications could not be overlooked, and a year after returning home he was appointed to a readership in Roman criminal law at the University of Pavia.   Eighteen months later he was promoted to the chair of exegesis of the sources of Roman law.   One of his pupils remembers that the new professor was very strict but friendly, kind and encouraging with them, witty in private conversation and never sarcastic.   There was a distinction in his manner and bearing, quite free from hauteur, that well became the dignity of his position.   His life was indeed entirely devoted to his Maker, but in the natural order his work, as he used to tell his friends, was his wife ; Roman law was his passion, and he made of his research, his teaching and his erudition " a hymn of praise to the Lord of all learning ".   It was during this period that Ferrini became a Franciscan tertiary.

In 1887 he was appointed to the professorship of Roman law in the University of Messina, and for the next seven years he was teaching there and at Modena, always working with unremitting application and growing in reputation with each successive publication.   But though he was very happy in Sicily he wanted to get back permanently to the north, to be near his home and the Ambrosian Library. When therefore he was invited in 1894 to return to Pavia as successor to Professor

---

* He spoke to none, even of his intimates, about this vow.   This led to occasional embarrassments, from which Ferrini extricated himself by his wit, which could be mordant. On one occasion a woman was recommending a girl to his notice as a suitable wife, emphasizing her " expectations ".   " When her father dies, she will have so much.   When her mother dies, so much.   And when her uncle dies. . . ."   " Oh dear ", interrupted Ferrini, " What a lot of corpses ! "

Mariani, he accepted with joy.   Thus began the last and most fruitful period of his career.

Ferrini was concerned with the whole vast field of law, but it was above all in Roman law (and especially its Byzantine aspect) that he made his mark.   When Professor von Ligenthal died in 1894 Ferrini, his favourite pupil, inherited not only his master's manuscripts but also his acknowledged leadership in these studies ; and among those who in one way or another contributed to the success of his work were Don Achille Ratti, afterwards Pope Pius XI, and Dr John Mercati, later cardinal and librarian and archivist of the Holy Roman Church.   And his output was very large : during his short life he was responsible for over two hundred monographs, which make five stout volumes, as well as several text books.

But he found time to interest himself in public affairs too.   After the Piedmontese occupied Rome in 1870 the Holy See had decided that it was inexpedient for faithful Catholics to associate themselves publicly with the new régime, *e.g.* by voting in elections of deputies.   Ferrini loyally observed this ruling, while deploring that " our abstention from the legislative assembly leaves our legislation unprotected from the most deplorable influences."   This may have encouraged his own activity in social matters.   He was delighted when Pope Leo XIII published his encyclical letter " *Rerum novarum* ", on the condition of the working classes, and in 1895 he allowed himself to be elected to the municipal council of Milan ;* his duties upon which he took most seriously.   In the following years he continued his charitable and public work, doing all he could to combat the errors of materialistic socialism, to defend the Italian legal tradition of the indissolubility of marriage, and to uphold the religion of Christ wherever it was threatened.

Bd Contardo used to spend his vacations at Suna, on Lake Maggiore, where his father had a small house.   He was prostrated by his work in the heat of the summer of 1902, and in the early autumn sought to refresh himself with his favourite recreation, mountaineering.†   With a friend he climbed San Martino in Valle Anzasca, and came back to Suna feeling worse rather than better.   On October 5, a very wet Sunday, he went to Mass, and on his return he collapsed.   The doctor's report was grave, but not alarmingly so ; but Bd Contardo got worse, and after some days of delirium he died, of typhus, on October 17.   He was only forty-three years old.   At his bedside was his father, the first and greatest of his friends.‡

Dr Oggioni has recollected that he was once walking in Pavia with Ludovic Necchi when they passed Professor Ferrini, a wide-browed, bearded man in a frock-coat.   He returned their greeting with his usual courtesy and characteristic sweet smile.   Necchi stopped and exclaimed to his companion, " What *is* it about that man ?   He's a saint ! "   Father Augustine Gemelli records that many students frequented Ferrini's lectures not simply because of his reputation as a jurist but also because here, at the dawn of the twentieth century, was a professor who still believed in God.   " Learning is not the road to God ", he wrote in *Un po' d'infinito*,

* A member of the council drew caricatures of all his fellow members.   That of Ferrini he adorned with a halo of sainthood.   It would be interesting to know if the drawing is still in existence, for caricatures of saints must be rare—unless Bellarmine jugs can be considered such.   (Literary caricatures—unintended—are of course another matter ; they are only too common.)

† There has been argument among the experts about whether Ferrini was " an alpinist in the true sense of the word "—whatever that may be.   He certainly loved mountains and climbed them.

‡ They used to work at Suna both in the same bare room, their desks facing one another.

and " his letters and private papers all show a single purpose, the search for perfection, which he pursued with a serenity and simplicity of heart that was echoed
by all and sundry after his quiet spirit was carried away ".   Don Achille Ratti was
one of the first publicly to eulogize the dead professor, and he was one of the
promoters of the movement for introducing the cause of Contardo Ferrini, of which
the moving spirit was his old friend Professor Olivi.   In 1947 the beatification
took place, and his feast day has been assigned to October 27.

Addressing an audience of professors, lecturers and other pilgrims at this time,
Pope Pius XII referred to Bd Contardo as a man who " gave an emphatic ' Yes '
to the possibility of holiness in these days ".   " The history and development of
law and law-making ", he declared, " were for Ferrini simply an application of
the moral and divine law, without which human legislation is useless : for if they
are separated from God, it is only a matter of time before social organization and
its juridical enactments degenerate into tyranny and despotism. . . . It should
give us comfort that in Bd Contardo the Lord has given the Church a *beatus* who
was a master in the field of law and at the same time a man of God, one whose
exalted spirit and supremely righteous life is a model for us all."   Giving evidence
in the course of the process, the previous pope, Pius XI, had said, " My relations
with him were purely scientific or were concerned with the beauties of high mountains.   For him these were an inspiration to holiness and almost a natural revelation
of God."   Ferrini's appreciation of the material creation was indeed a salient
characteristic, and it was not confined to nature in her gentler aspects.   " God also
speaks to man in the clouds on the mountain tops ", he wrote, " in the roaring of
the torrents, in the stark awefulness of the cliffs, in the dazzling splendour of the
unmelting snow, in the sun that splashes the west with blood, in the wind that
strips the trees bare.   Nature lives by the breath of His omnipotence, smiles in
its joy of Him, hides from His wrath—yet greets Him, eternally young, with the
smile of its own youth.   For the spirit of God by which nature lives is a spirit for
ever young, incessantly renewing itself, happy in its snow and rain and mist, for
out of these come birth and life, spring ever renewed and undaunted hope, and all
the blessed prerogatives of youth a thousand times reborn."   Bd Contardo Ferrini
was in the true line of St Francis of Assisi.

A biography of Contardo Ferrini by J. Fanciulli was published in 1931, and another,
Contardo Ferrini : Santo d'Oggi, by C. Caminada, in 1947.   But the standard life is by
Mgr C. Pellegrini (1928), of which Father Bede Jarrett says, " The only criticism to be
made of it is that it is too monumental.   Still, the book is a perfect quarry from which to
hew stones for erecting a shrine to build in his memory."   And such a small shrine Father
Jarrett himself built in his short biographical study of Ferrini (1933).   Bd Contardo's
own *Pensieri e Preghiere* has been edited by Father Gemelli, himself " one of the most
striking examples of the influence of Ferrini in Milan and in Italy generally ".   See also
the *Miscellanea Contardo Ferrini*, published at Rome in 1947 and 1948.

28 : SS. SIMON AND JUDE, OR THADDEUS, APOSTLES   (FIRST CENTURY)

ST SIMON is surnamed the Cananean or Zelotes in the Holy Scriptures,
words which both mean " the Zealous ".   Some have mistakenly thought
that the first of these names was meant to imply that St Simon was born at
Cana in Galilee.   The name refers to his zeal for the Jewish law before his call,

and does not necessarily mean that he was one of that particular party among the Jews called Zealots. No mention of him appears in the gospels beyond that he was chosen among the apostles. With the rest he received the Holy Ghost, but of his life after Pentecost we have no information whatever ; it is not possible to reconcile the various traditions. The Menology of Basil says that St Simon died in peace at Edessa, but the Western tradition recognized in the Roman liturgy is that, after preaching in Egypt, he joined St Jude from Mesopotamia and that they went as missionaries for some years to Persia, suffering martyrdom there. They are accordingly commemorated together in the West on this day, but in the East separately and on various dates.

The apostle Jude (Judas), also called Thaddeus (or Lebbeus), " the brother of James ", is usually regarded as the brother of St James the Less. It is not known when and by what means he became a disciple of Christ, nothing having been said of him in the gospels before we find him enumerated among the apostles. After the Last Supper, when Christ promised to manifest Himself to His hearers, St Jude asked Him why He did not manifest Himself to the rest of the world ; and Christ answered that He and the Father would visit all those who love Him, " we will come to him, and will make our abode with him " (John xiv 22–23). The history of St Jude after our Lord's ascension and the descent of the Holy Ghost is as unknown as that of St Simon. Jude's name is borne by one of the canonical epistles, which has much in common with the second epistle of St Peter. It is not addressed to any particular church or person, and in it he urges the faithful to " contend earnestly for the faith once delivered to the saints. For certain men are secretly entered in . . . ungodly men, turning the grace of our Lord God into riotousness, and denying the only sovereign ruler and our Lord Jesus Christ."

St Jude Thaddeus has often been confounded with the St Thaddeus of the Abgar legend (see Addai and Mari, August 5), and made to die in peace at Bairut or Edessa. As has been said above, according to a Western tradition he was martyred with St Simon in Persia. Eusebius quotes a story that two grandsons of St Jude, Zoker and James, were brought before the Emperor Domitian, who had been alarmed by the report that they were of the royal house of David. But when he saw they were poor, hard-working peasants, and heard that the kingdom for which they looked was not of this world, he dismissed them with contempt.

There is what purports to be a *passio* of these two apostles, but in its Latin form it cannot be earlier than the latter part of the sixth century. It is attributed to a certain Abdias who is said to have been a disciple of Simon and Jude and to have been consecrated by them first bishop of Babylon. This no doubt explains the curious entry on this day in the *Félire* of Oengus : " Ample is their assembly : Babylon their burial ground : Thaddeus and Simon, huge is their host." On pseudo-Abdias see further R. A. Lipsius, *Die apocryphen Apostelgeschichten* . . ., vol. i, pp. 117 *seq.* ; and Batiffol in DTC., vol. i, c. 23. The mention of SS. Simon and Jude together is found in the *Hieronymianum* for this day, and the scene of their martyrdom is said to be " Suanis, civitate Persarum ", on which consult CMH., and Gutschmid, *Kleine Schriften*, vol. ii, pp. 368–369. On the invocation of St Jude as believed to have special efficacy in " desperate cases ", see the *Acta Sanctorum*, October, vol. xii, p. 449 ; and L. du Broc, *Les saints patrons des corporations et protecteurs* . . ., vol. ii, pp. 390 *seq.*

SS. ANASTASIA AND CYRIL, MARTYRS   (DATE UNKNOWN)

CARDINAL BARONIUS added the following entry to the Roman Martyrology under this date : " At Rome, the passion of the holy martyrs Anastasia the Elder, a virgin,

and Cyril.   This same virgin during the persecution of Valerian was bound with
fetters by the prefect Probus, smitten with blows and tortured with fire and scourges;
and as she continued unmoved in the confession of Christ her breasts were cut off,
her nails torn out, her teeth broken, her hands and feet hacked away.   Then she
was beheaded and, beautified with the jewels of so many sufferings, she passed to
her Bridegroom.   Cyril brought her water when she asked therefor, and received
martyrdom for his reward."   The traditions of the church of Rome know nothing
of these martyrs, who were first venerated in the East.   Their Greek *passio* says
that St Anastasia was a maiden of patrician birth, twenty years old, who lived in
a community of consecrated virgins.   The soldiers of the prefect broke into the
house, carried her off, and brought her before Probus, who ordered that she be
stripped naked.   On her protesting that this would shame him more than it would
her, she was maltreated as the martyrology sets out.   Her body was afterwards
translated to Constantinople.

> The *passio* exists both in Greek and in Latin.   Both texts are printed in the *Acta Sanc-
> torum*, October, vol. xii.   J. P. Kirsch seems inclined to think that the only historical martyr
> was the widow who suffered at Sirmium (December 25), but that, as her feast was kept on
> a different date in the East, some Greek hagiographer thought it well to invent a new story
> of a virgin bearing the same name, which he embellished with the fantastic details recounted
> above.   See *Lexikon für Theologie und Kirche*, vol. i (1930), c. 389.

ST FIDELIS OF COMO, Martyr   (A.D. 303 ?)

DURING the persecution of Maximian the imprisoned Christians of Milan were
visited and ministered to by an army officer named Fidelis, according to his legend
in which no trust can be placed.   He procured the freedom of five of them and,
with two soldiers, Carpophorus and Exanthus, they tried to make their escape into
the Alps.   They were overtaken near Como, and the two last-named with their
companions were executed on the spot, in a wood.   Fidelis got away and reached
Samolito, at the other side of the lake, but here he was captured by soldiers who
had followed him in a boat.   There they scourged and beheaded him.   There is
another version which says that SS. Fidelis, Carpophorus and Exanthus were
three Christian soldiers who when persecution began deserted the army and fled
to Como, where they were apprehended and put to death.   The *cultus* at Como is
ancient.

> The relatively sober text is printed in the *Acta Sanctorum*, vol. xii, from a fourteenth-
> century manuscript.   A tomb of St Fidelis at Como was known to Ennodius in the sixth
> century, and remains of a fourth-century basilica have been found by the lake.

ST SALVIUS, OR SAIRE   (SIXTH CENTURY ?)

THIS saint has been confused with St Salvius of Albi and St Salvius of Amiens (and
they with one another), but he seems to have been a distinct person and a hermit
in the forest of Bray in Normandy.   Nothing is known about him, but in a footnote
to his account of St Salvius of Albi, Alban Butler gives an extract from a manuscript
then preserved in the castle of Saint-Saire (Eure-et-Loir) of the counts of Boulain-
villiers.   It runs as follows :

> The titles of the metropolitan of Rouen prove that about the year 800,
> and near a century after, there was a place in the forest of Bray consecrated
> to the memory and honour of St Salvius. . . . There remain, however, formal

proofs of St Salvius being a solitary in an ancient MS. from five to six hundred years old, which contains the office of his feast.   He is also represented in a pane of glass in an ancient subterraneous chapel in the dress of a hermit, on his knees, praying with his hands extended.   The devotion of the people who visited the church or chapel which was built where his hermitage stood was supported by miracles and extraordinary cures which the divine power wrought there, insomuch that the reputation of it went very far. . . . The canons of Rouen were at the expense of clearing some of the more accessible lands for the subsistence of the priests who there performed the divine office ; and this is the first origin of the parish of Saint-Saire, and the foundation of the lordship which the chapter of Rouen possesses there.

A brief notice of St Salvius may be found in the *Acta Sanctorum*, October, vol. xii. There is no biography of any sort, except the lessons in breviaries.   Father Grosjean suggests that the breviary seen by Butler may be one of two now at Amiens, Bibliothèque municipale, MS. 111 or MS. 112 ; both were copied about 1250 and both have the lessons.

ST FARO, BISHOP OF MEAUX   *(c.* A.D. 672)

THE eminent sanctity of St Faro, one of the first known bishops of Meaux, has rendered his name the most illustrious of all the prelates of this see who are mentioned in the calendars of the Church.   He was the brother of St Chainoaldus of Laon and of St Burgundofara, first abbess of Faremoutier, and spent his youth in the court of King Theodebert II of Austrasia.   Later he married, and passed to the court of Clotaire II.   When that prince, provoked at the insolent speeches of certain Saxon ambassadors, had cast them into prison and sworn he would put them to death, St Faro prevailed on him by a stratagem to pardon them.   The life which he led was most edifying and holy, and when he was about thirty-five years old he determined, if his wife would agree, to enter the ecclesiastical state.   Blidechild was of the same disposition, and she retired to a place upon one of her own estates, where some years after she died, having persuaded her husband to persevere in his new vocation, which for a time he had wished to abandon and return to her.   St Faro received the tonsure among the clergy of Meaux, which episcopal see becoming vacant, he was chosen to fill it, about the year 628.   Under Dagobert I he became chancellor, and used his influence with his prince to protect the innocent, the orphan and the widow, and to relieve all that were in distress.

The holy prelate laboured for souls with unwearied zeal and attention, and promoted the conversion of those who had not yet forsaken idolatry.   The author of his life tells us that he restored sight to a blind man by conferring on him the sacrament of Confirmation, and wrought several other miracles.   Soon after Faro's episcopal consecration St Fiacre arrived at Meaux, and the bishop gave to Fiacre some land of his own patrimony at Breuil for a hermitage.   He founded in the suburbs of Meaux the monastery of the Holy Cross, which later bore his name. St Faro placed in it monks of St Columban from Luxeuil.   In 668 he gave hospitality to St Adrian, later of Canterbury, on his way to England.

The Life of St Faro, which was written 200 years after his death by another bishop of Meaux, Hildegar, is of no great historical value.   It has been critically edited after Mabillon by B. Krusch in MGH., *Scriptores Merov.*, vol. v, pp. 171–206.   This text is undoubtedly the original of the shorter narrative printed in the *Acta Sanctorum*.   There is reference in

Hildegar's compilation to a ballad which, we are told, was sung by the people in commemoration of Clotaire's victory over the Saxons, and which is known as the " Cantilène de St Faron ".   As a supposed specimen of the early Romance language it has given rise to a considerable literature, of which a full account, with bibliography, may be found in DAC., vol. v, cc. 1114–1124.   With regard to St Faro, see Beaumier-Besse, *Abbayes et prieurés de France*, vol. i, pp. 304 *seq.* ; Duchesne, *Fastes Épiscopaux*, vol. ii, p. 477 ; and in H. M. Delsart, *Sainte Fare* (1911).

29 : ST NARCISSUS, Bishop of Jerusalem   (*c.* A.D. 215)

ST NARCISSUS was already very old when he was placed at the head of the church of Jerusalem.   Eusebius says that the Christians there preserved in his time the remembrance of several miracles which God had wrought by this bishop, as when on one Easter-eve the deacons were unprovided with oil for the lamps in the church, Narcissus sent for water, offered prayer over it, and then bade them pour it into the lamps.   They did so, and it was immediately converted into oil.   The veneration of good men for this holy bishop could not shelter him from the malice of the wicked, and some, disliking his severity in the observance of discipline, laid to his charge a certain crime, which Eusebius does not specify.   They confirmed their calumny by fearful imprecations on themselves, but their accusation did not find credit.   However, St Narcissus made it an excuse for leaving Jerusalem and spending some time alone, as had long been his wish.   He spent several years undiscovered in his solitude and, that his church might not remain destitute of a pastor, the neighbouring bishops placed in it Dius, and after him Germanicus, who was succeeded by Gordius.   Whilst this last held the see, Narcissus appeared again like one from the dead.   The faithful, delighted at the recovery of their pastor, induced him to resume the administration of the diocese.   He acquiesced, but, under the weight of extreme old age, made St Alexander his coadjutor.   This Alexander has been noticed herein under March 18.   In a letter he wrote soon after the year 212 he refers to St Narcissus as being then 116 years old.

The Bollandists in the *Acta Sanctorum*, October, vol. xii, have brought together from Eusebius and other sources all that is known, or likely to be known, about St Narcissus of Jerusalem.

ST THEUDERIUS, or CHEF, Abbot   (*c.* A.D. 575)

ST THEUDERIUS was born at Arcisia (Saint-Chef-d'Arcisse) in Dauphiné.   Having exercised himself in monastic life at Lérins and been ordained priest by St Caesarius at Arles, he returned to his own country ; and, being joined by several disciples, built for them first cells and afterwards a monastery near the city of Vienne.   It was anciently a custom here that some monk of whose sanctity the people entertained a high opinion was chosen voluntarily to lead the life of a recluse ; he retired to a cell and spent his whole time in fasting and praying to implore the divine mercy in favour of himself and his country.   This practice would have been an abuse and superstition if any persons, relying on the prayers of others, were themselves remiss in prayer or penance.   St Theuderius was asked to undertake this penitential state, which obligation he willingly took upon himself, and discharged with much fervour at the church of St Laurence during the last twelve years of his life. An extraordinary gift of miracles made his name famous. He died about the year 575.

A life, first printed by Mabillon and the Bollandists, has been again edited by B. Krusch in MGH., *Scriptores Merov.*, vol. iii, pp. 526–530. As it was written by Ado in the ninth century, it merits no great confidence. It is not, however, true as was formerly believed that Ado inserted the name of Theuderius in his martyrology ; see Quentin, *Martyrologes historiques*, p. 477.

ST COLMAN OF KILMACDUAGH, BISHOP   (*c.* A.D. 632)

THE feast of this Colman is kept throughout Ireland on this day. He was born at Corker in Kiltartan about the middle of the sixth century and lived first on Aranmore and then, for greater solitude, at Burren among the mountains of County Clare. He is said to have hidden himself there because he had been made a bishop against his will ; he had one disciple, and they subsisted for many years on wild vegetables and water. He then founded a monastery at the place called after him Kilmacduagh (the cell of the son of Dui), and is venerated as the first bishop there. The land was given him by his near relation, King Guaire of Connacht, who had discovered Colman's retreat, according to the legend, through his Easter dinner being whisked away and carried by angels to the cell of the hermit at Burren. Among other fanciful stories about St Colman is that he was waited on by a cock, a mouse, and a fly : the cock woke him for the night office, the mouse prevented him from going to sleep again, and the fly acted as an indicator and book-marker.

In the Bollandists, October, vol. xii, there is a copious notice of Colman, borrowed for the most part from Colgan's *Acta Sanctorum Hiberniae*. See also O'Keeffe in *Ériu*, vol. i, pp. 43–48 ; and Whitley Stokes in the *Revue Celtique*, vol. xxvi, pp. 372–377. " Colman mac Duach " is entered first on February 3 in the Martyrology of Tallaght, in which there are twelve Colmans mentioned during the single month of October.

ST ABRAHAM OF ROSTOV, ABBOT   (TWELFTH CENTURY)

THIS holy monk and missionary seems to have lived during the earlier years of the twelfth century. He was born of heathen parents near Galich, and as a young man suffered from an obstinate disease, of which he was cured when he called upon the God of the Christians. Thereupon he received baptism, and soon after left his father's house to become a monk. Hearing a divine call to go to Rostov, where there were still many pagans, he obeyed and gave himself zealously to the preaching of the gospel there. Many of his hearers were converted, and Abraham built two churches for them. The first, in honour of St John the Divine, was in a place where he had beheld that apostle in a vision ; the other was at a place that was before given over to the worship of a well-known idol. At this second church, named from the Epiphany of our Saviour, Abraham founded a community of monks ; but he did not allow the direction of a monastery to lessen the energy and enthusiasm with which he sought to bring the light of Christ to the souls of unbelievers. The date of St Abraham's death is not known, but he was receiving public *cultus* by the end of the twelfth century.

See Martynov's *Annus ecclesiasticus Graeco-Slavicus*, in *Acta Sanctorum*, October, vol. xi. St Abraham of Rostov is a very uncertain figure ; he has sometimes, it would seem, been assigned to the tenth-eleventh century, as " the apostle of Rostov ".

THE MARTYRS OF DOUAY　(Sixteenth and Seventeenth Centuries)

In the year 1568 the English College at Douay was founded by William Allen (afterwards cardinal ; the anniversary of his death in 1594 is kept on the 16th of this month).　Its original object was to train young men for the priesthood with an eye to the needs of England when the faith should be re-established there, but within a short time these priests were being sent back to their country as missionaries—the " seminary priests " at whom legislation was aimed.　These began to arrive in 1574 and on November 29, 1577, their first martyr, Bd Cuthbert Mayne, suffered at Launceston.　During the next hundred years more than one hundred and sixty priests from the college (which from 1578 till 1594 was transferred to Rheims) were put to death in England and Wales, and of these over eighty have been beatified ; they are referred to under their respective dates in these volumes. For these martyrs from Douay a special collective feast is kept in the dioceses of Westminster today and of Hexham and Newcastle tomorrow.　When the Revolution made it impossible to carry on the college in France, it was re-established in 1794 at St Edmund's, Old Hall Green, for the south of England, and at Crook Hall, Durham (in 1808, St Cuthbert's, Ushaw), for the north, which colleges are respectively in the above dioceses.　" Kindle in us, Lord, the spirit to which the blessed martyrs of Douay ministered, that we too being filled therewith may strive to love what they loved and do as they taught " (collect for the feast).

The Douay Diaries, with the exception of the sixth volume which is lost, have now all been published.　The first two appeared as *Records of the English Catholics under the Penal Laws*, vol. i (1878), and were edited by Father T. F. Knox.　They extend from 1568 to 1593.　The third, fourth, fifth, and seventh diaries have been printed by the Catholic Record Society as vols. x, xi and xxviii of their publications.

30 : ST SERAPION, Bishop of Antioch　　(*c.* A.D. 212)

THE late fourth-century Syriac document called the *Doctrine of Addai* refers to Serapion as having been consecrated by Zephyrinus, Bishop of Rome, but he seems to have been bishop of Antioch for some years before the pontificate of St Zephyrinus began.　The Roman Martyrology says he was famous for his learning, and it is for his theological writings that he is remembered. Eusebius gives an extract from a private letter written to Caricus and Pontius, in which he condemns Montanism, which was being propagated by the pseudo-prophecies of two hysterical women.　He also wrote expostulating with a certain Domninus, who had apostatized under persecution and turned to Jewish " will-worship ".

During the episcopate of Serapion trouble arose in the church of Rhossos in Cilicia about the public reading of the so-called *Gospel of Peter*, an apocryphal work of gnostic provenance.　At first Serapion, not knowing its contents and trusting to the orthodoxy of his flock, permitted it to be read.　Then he borrowed a copy from the sect who used it, " whom we call Docetae " (that is, illusionists, because they affirmed that our Lord's manhood was not real but an illusion), and having read it wrote to the church at Rhossos to forbid its use ; for he found in it, he says, " some additions to the true teaching of the Saviour ", and tells them he will soon be visiting them to expound the true faith.

This Serapion has no *cultus* in the East ; but he is named in the Roman Martyrology, and his feast is kept by the Carmelites, who make the surprising claim that he belonged to their order.

All, practically speaking, that is known concerning St Serapion of Antioch is recounted and commented upon by the Bollandists in vol. xiii for October. The references to this name, however, contained in the *Doctrine of Addai*, had apparently not attracted their attention ; but these, as pointed out under St Addai (August 5), are quite unreliable. It is interesting to note that in the early Syriac *breviarium* we have mention on May 14 of " Serapion, Bishop of Antioch ".

ST MARCELLUS THE CENTURION, Martyr   (A.D. 298)

PARTICULARS of the passion of St Marcellus, one of the isolated martyrs before the outbreak of the great persecution of Diocletian, are preserved for us in a trustworthy account. Father Delehaye points out that the case of the centurion Marcellus is analogous to that of the conscript Maximilian (March 12). " Though they were not urged to sacrifice or to do some other act of idolatry, both of them judged—contrary to the opinion of most—that military service was incompatible with the practice of the Christian religion. Both of them were condemned to death for breach of discipline. Their contemporaries, without making subtle inquiries into the determining cause of the sentence, looked only to the religious motive that animated these heroes, and judged them worthy of the glorious name of martyr ". The brief document runs as follows.

In the city of Tingis [Tangier], during the administration of the president Fortunatus, when all were feasting on the emperor's birthday, a certain Marcellus, one of the centurions, condemning these banquets as heathen, cast away his soldier's belt in front of the standards of the legion which were there. And he testified in a loud voice, saying, " I serve Jesus Christ the eternal king. I will no longer serve your emperors, and I scorn to worship your gods of wood and stone, which are deaf and dumb idols."

The soldiers were dumbfounded at hearing such things ; they laid hold on him, and reported the matter to the president Fortunatus, who ordered him to be thrown into prison. When the feasting was over, he gave orders, sitting in council, that the man should be brought in. When this was done, Astasius Fortunatus the president said to Marcellus, " What did you mean by ungirding yourself contrary to military discipline, and casting away your belt and vine-switch ? " [The distinctive badge of the centurion].

MARCELLUS : On July 21, in the presence of the standards of your legion, when you celebrated the festival of the emperor, I made answer openly and clearly that I was a Christian and that I could not accept this allegiance, but could serve only Jesus Christ, the Son of God the Father Almighty.

FORTUNATUS : I cannot pass over your rash conduct, and therefore I shall report this matter to the emperors and *caesar*. You shall be sent to my lord Aurelius Agricolan, deputy for the praetorian prefects.

On October 30 at Tingis, the centurion Marcellus having been brought into court, it was officially reported : " Fortunatus the president has referred Marcellus, a centurion, to your authority. There is here a letter from him, which at your command I will read." Agricolan said, " Let it be read." The official report was read : " From Fortunatus to you, my lord ", *et reliqua.* Then Agricolan asked, " Did you say these things as set out in the president's official report ? "

MARCELLUS : I did.

AGRICOLAN : Were you serving as a regular centurion ?

MARCELLUS : I was.

AGRICOLAN : What madness possessed you to throw away the badges of your allegiance and to speak as you did ?

MARCELLUS : There is no madness in those who fear God.

AGRICOLAN : Did you say each of the things contained in the president's report ?

MARCELLUS : I did.

AGRICOLAN : Did you cast away your arms ?

MARCELLUS : I did. For it was not right for a Christian man, who serves the Lord Christ, to serve in the armies of the world.

" The doings of Marcellus are such as must be visited with disciplinary punishment ", said Agricolan, and he pronounced sentence : " Marcellus, who held the rank of a regular centurion, having admitted that he degraded himself by openly throwing off his allegiance, and having moreover used insane speech, as appears in the official report, it is our pleasure that he be put to death by the sword."

When he was being led to execution, Marcellus said, " May God be good to you, Agricolan ". In so seemly a way did the glorious martyr Marcellus pass out of this world.

It is generally admitted that the Acts of Marcellus are representative of the most trust-worthy class of such documents (*cf.* for example, Harnack, *Chronologie*, vol. ii, pp. 473–474). In *Analecta Bollandiana*, vol. xli (1923), pp. 257–287, Father Delehaye edited and commented the two texts, a setting which has been taken into account in G. Kruger's 3rd edition of Knopf's *Ausgewählte Martyrerakten* (1929). See also P. Franchi de' Cavalieri in *Nuovo Bullettino di Arch. Crist.*, 1906, pp. 237–267 ; and B. de Gaiffier, *Analecta Bollandiana*, vol. lxi (1943), pp. 116–139. *Cf.* St Cassian, December 3.

ST ASTERIUS, BISHOP OF AMASEA   (*c.* A.D. 410)

ALL that is known about the life of this saint, apart from his episcopate, is from his own statement that he was educated by a very able Scythian or Goth, who had himself been educated at Antioch, and that he was a rhetor before receiving holy orders. St Asterius was a preacher of considerable power, and twenty-one of his homilies are extant. In his panegyric of St Phocas he established the invocation of saints, the honouring of their relics, pilgrimages to pray before them, and miracles wrought through them. In the following sermon, on the holy martyrs, he says : " We keep their bodies decently enshrined as precious pledges : vessels of benediction, the organs of their blessed souls, the tabernacles of their holy minds. We put ourselves under their protection. The martyrs defend the Church as soldiers guard a citadel. The people flock from all quarters and keep great festivals to honour their tombs. All who labour under the heavy load of afflictions fly to them for refuge. We employ them as intercessors in our prayers. . . ." St Asterius describes with what magnificence and crowds of people the feasts of martyrs were celebrated. He says some people condemned the honours paid to them and their relics, and answers, " We by no means worship the martyrs, but we honour them as the true worshippers of God. We lay their bodies in rich sepulchres and put up stately shrines of their repose that we may be stirred to an emulation of their honours."

This St Asterius is not named in the Roman Martyrology, but there is another therein on October 21, who is said to have taken the body of St Callistus from the well into which it was thrown. He himself was cast into the Tiber and so gave his life.

There is no formal Life of St Asterius, but various references to him have been brought together in the *Acta Sanctorum*, October, vol. xiii. Some of his discourses have been made the subject of separate discussion. See, for example, A. Bretz, *Studien und Texte zu Asterius von Amasea*, and M. Richard in *Revue biblique*, 1935, pp. 538–548.

ST GERMANUS, BISHOP OF CAPUA   (*c.* A.D. 540)

THIS holy prelate was sent by Pope St Hormisdas with other legates to the Emperor Justin in 519 to persuade the Byzantines to put an end to the " Acacian schism " which had continued thirty-five years. The embassy was attended with success ; and the schism was ended by the signature of the pope's famous " Formula ". St Gregory the Great relates on the authority of " his elders " that Germanus saw Paschasius, deacon of Rome, in Purgatory long after his death for having adhered to the schism of Laurence against Pope St Symmachus, and that he was purging his fault as an attendant at the hot springs, whither Germanus had been sent to bathe for the good of his health. Within a few days Paschasius was released by the bishop's prayers. St Germanus was a personal friend of St Benedict who, again according to the account of St Gregory, when he was at Monte Cassino saw in a vision the soul of Germanus, at the hour of his departure, carried by the ministry of angels to eternal bliss. His death happened about the year 540.

A manuscript of the eleventh century at Monte Cassino preserves a short Life of St Germanus which has been printed in the *Acta Sanctorum*, October, vol. xiii. It is not entirely certain, though it is no doubt probable, that this Germanus is identical with the envoy sent to Constantinople by Pope Hormisdas. See, further, Lanzoni, *Diocesi d'Italia*, vol. i, p. 203.

ST ETHELNOTH, ARCHBISHOP OF CANTERBURY   (A.D. 1038)

WHILE dean of the cathedral church of Christ at Canterbury his learning and holiness caused Ethelnoth to be known as " the Good ", and on the death of the metropolitan Living in 1020 he was appointed in his place. Two years later Ethelnoth was in Rome, where Pope Benedict VIII received him " with great worship and very honourably hallowed him archbishop ", by which may be understood that he invested him with the *pallium*. In the following year Ethelnoth translated the relics of his predecessor St Alphege, martyred by the Danes in 1012, from London to Canterbury. The cost of a worthy shrine was defrayed by King Canute, at the instance of his wife and the archbishop, his father's men having been guilty of the murder. St Ethelnoth enjoyed the favour of Canute, and he encouraged the king's liberality to promote several other religious undertakings, among them the rebuilding of Chartres cathedral.

Ethelnoth is one of those Anglo-Saxon ecclesiastics whose claim to saintship is very contestable. His name does not seem to occur in any medieval calendar, and there is no other evidence of *cultus*. The Bollandists, however, following the example of Mabillon (vol. vi, pt 1, pp. 394–397), have devoted a notice to him (under the spelling " Ædelnodus "), October, vol. xiii.   In the absence of any early biography they have pieced together an account from contemporary and later chroniclers.   See further DNB., vol. xvii, p. 25 ; and Stanton's *Menology*, pp. 517–518.

BD BENVENUTA OF CIVIDALE, Virgin   (A.D. 1292)

It has been said that the life of Benvenuta Bojani was " a poem of praise to our Blessed Lady, a hymn of light, purity and joy, which was lived rather than sung in her honour ".   This life began in the year 1254, at Cividale in Friuli, and there were already six young Bojani, all girls.   Her father naturally hoped for a boy this time, and when he learned he had yet another daughter he is said to have exclaimed, " Very well !   Since it is so, let her too be welcome."   And so she was called Benvenuta.   Her devotion to our Lady was noticeable from very early years, and she would repeat the Hail Mary, in the short form ending at " Jesus ", as then used, many times in the day, accompanying each repetition with a profound inclination such as she saw the Dominican friars make so often in their church. Like Bd Magdalen Panattieri, commemorated this month (13th), Benvenuta was happy in belonging to a family whose members were as truly religious as herself, rejoicing in her goodness and devotion, and who, when she wished to bind herself to perfect chastity and become a tertiary of the Dominicans, put no obstacles in her way.

But unlike Bd Magdalen she took no part in the public life of her town, emphasizing the contemplative rather than the active side of the Dominican vocation. Her spirit of penitence, in particular, made her inflict most severe austerities on herself.   She would sometimes discipline herself three times in a night, and when she was only twelve she tied a rope (the " cord of St Thomas " ?) so tightly round her loins that the flesh grew around it.   The suffering it caused became intolerable, and she feared that the only way to remove it was by a surgical operation, till one day when she was asking God to help her about it she found the rope lying unbroken at her feet.   Benvenuta confided this miracle to her confessor, Friar Conrad, who mitigated her penances and forbade her to undertake any without his approval. For five years she suffered from serious bad health and could scarcely leave her room, during which time she was furiously tempted to despair, and in other ways ; but the worst trial was being unable to assist at Mass, except when occasionally carried, and at Compline with its daily singing of *Salve Regina*.   Eventually she was suddenly and publicly cured in church on the feast of the Annunciation, having vowed to make a pilgrimage to the shrine of St Dominic at Bologna if she recovered. This she carried out with her sister Mary and her youngest brother.

Benvenuta's patience and perseverance in sickness and temptation were rewarded by numerous graces, visions and raptures in prayer.   A delightful story is told (though belonging to her youth) that she went into a church one day just after her mother had died, and saw there a child, to whom she said, " Have you got a mother ? "   He said he had.   " I haven't now ", said she, " But since you have, perhaps you can already say the Hail Mary ? "   " Oh yes ", replied the child, " can you ? "—" Yes, I can."—" Very well then, say it to me."   Benvenuta began the Hail Mary in Latin, and as she ended on the name Jesus, " It is I ", interrupted the child, and disappeared from sight.   Cheerfulness and confidence were the marks of the life of Bd Benvenuta, but she had to go through one more assault of the Devil, tempting her to despair and infidelity as she lay dying.   She overcame triumphantly, and died peacefully on October 30, 1292. Her *cultus* was approved in 1765, but her burial-place at Cividale is lost.

As we may learn from the full account in the *Acta Sanctorum*, October, vol. xiii, a life of this *beata*, written in Latin shortly after her death, was translated into Italian and published in 1589. This biography figured largely in the process which ended in the formal *confirmatio cultus*, and the original Latin is printed in full by the Bollandists. See also M. C. de Ganay, *Les Bienheureuses Dominicaines* (1913), pp. 91–108 ; and Procter, *Lives of Dominican Saints*, pp. 302–306.

BD DOROTHY OF MONTAU, Widow   (A.D. 1394)

SHE takes her name from Montau (Marienburg) in Prussia, where she was born in 1347. At the age of seventeen Dorothy married one Albert, a swordsmith of Danzig, by whom she had nine children, of whom only the youngest survived. Albert was an ill-tempered and overbearing man, and during their twenty-five years of married life his wife suffered much on this account ; but her own kindliness and courage modified his disposition considerably, and in 1384 she induced him to take her on a pilgrimage to Aachen. Thenceforward they often went on pilgrimage together, to Einsiedeln, Cologne and elsewhere, and they were planning to go to Rome when Albert fell ill. Dorothy therefore went alone, and at her return her husband had just died. Thus left a widow at the age of forty-three, she went to live at Marienwerder, and in 1393 became a recluse in a cell by the church of the Teutonic Knights. She was there only a year before her death, on May 25, 1394, but long enough to gain a great repute for holiness and supernatural enlightenment. Numerous visitors sought her cell, to ask advice or in hope of obtaining a miraculous cure of their ills.

Her life, in Latin and German, with an account of her visions and revelations, was written by her confessor, from whom we learn that Dorothy had a very intense devotion to the Blessed Sacrament, and was often supernaturally enabled to look upon it, which she greatly desired to do. In the middle ages great importance was attached to seeing the Body of the Lord, especially at the elevation at Mass, and the " life " of Bd Dorothy shows that in her time it was exposed all day for this purpose in some churches of Prussia and Pomerania. She was greatly revered by the people and soon after her death the cause of canonization was begun, but as soon dropped. Nevertheless the *cultus* spread, and Dorothy was popularly regarded as the patroness of Prussia.

Regarding this interesting mystic a good deal of information is available. In the *Acta Sanctorum*, October, vol. xiii, more than a hundred folio pages are devoted to her, and this was supplemented by the publication in the *Analecta Bollandiana* of the work called the *Septililium*, compiled from the revelations and utterances of Bd Dorothy by her confessor John of Marienwerder. This was printed by instalments in vols. ii, iii and iv of the *Analecta* (1883–85). More than one biographical sketch seems to have survived, for the most part written shortly after her death, and compiled with a view to the process of her canonization. See also F. Hipler, *Johannes Marienwerder und die Klauserin Dorothea* (1865) ; Ringholtz, *Geschichte von Einsiedeln* (1906), pp. 268 *seq.*, and 689 *seq.* ; and a sketch by H. Westpfahl, *Dorothea von Montau* (1949). For bibliography of recent work, see Westpfahl in *Geist und Leben*, vol. xxvi (1953), pp. 231–236.

BD JOHN SLADE, Martyr   (A.D. 1583)

JOHN SLADE was born in Dorsetshire, educated at New College, Oxford, and became a schoolmaster. His zeal in upholding the faith led to his arrest on a charge of denying the royal supremacy in spirituals, and he was brought up for trial at Winchester, together with Bd John Bodey, in April 1583. They were both condemned, but there was a re-trial on the same indictment at Andover four months later, which Cardinal Allen imputed to a consciousness in their prosecutors of the first sentence having been unjust and illegal. But the result was the same, the sentence was repeated, and Bd John Slade was hanged, drawn and quartered at Winchester on this day in the year 1583.

   See MMP., pp. 83–85 ; and Burton and Pollen, LEM., vol. i, pp. 1–7.

ST ALPHONSUS RODRIGUEZ   (A.D. 1617)

THERE are two well-known canonized lay brothers commemorated this month, but in other external circumstances there were considerable differences between St Gerard Majella and St Alphonsus Rodriguez. For instance, at the age when Gerard was dead, Alphonsus was still a married man, living with his family ; while the one died before he was thirty, the other lived to be nearly ninety ; during his three years of profession Gerard served in several houses of his congregation and was employed in a variety of ways, but Alphonsus was porter at the same college for forty-five years. Diego Rodriguez was a well-to-do wool-merchant in Segovia, and Alphonsus, born about 1533, was his third child in a big family. When Bd Peter Favre and another Jesuit came to preach a mission at Segovia they stayed with Diego, and at the end accepted his offer of a few days' holiday at his country house. Young Alphonsus, then about ten, went with them and was prepared for his first communion by Bd Peter. When he was fourteen he was sent with his elder brother to study under the Jesuits at Alcala, but before the first year was out their father died, and it was decided that Alphonsus must go into the business, which his mother was going to carry on. She retired and left him in sole charge when he was twenty-three, and three years later he married a girl called Mary Suarez.

   The business had been doing badly and his wife's dowry did not do much to improve it ; Alphonsus was not an incapable business man, but " times were bad ". Then he lost his little daughter, and, after a long illness following the birth of a boy, his wife too. Two years later his mother died, and this succession of misfortunes and losses made Alphonsus give very serious thought to what God was calling him to do in the world. He had always been a man of devout and righteous life, but he began to realize that he was meant to be something different from the numerous commercial men who led exemplary but unheroic lives in Segovia. If he sold his business he would have enough for himself and his little son to live on, so he did this and went to live with his two maiden sisters. These two, Antonia and Juliana, were a pious couple and taught their brother the rudiments of mental prayer, so that he was soon meditating two hours every morning and evening on the mysteries of the rosary. Alphonsus began to see his past life as very imperfect when regarded in the light of Christ and, following a vision of the glories of Heaven, he made a general confession and set himself to practise considerable austerities, as well as going to confession and communion every week. After some years his son died, and the edge of Alphonsus's sorrow was turned by the consideration that the boy had been saved from the danger and misery of ever offending God.

   He now contemplated, not for the first time, the possibility of becoming a religious and applied to the Jesuits at Segovia. They unhesitatingly refused him :

he was nearly forty, his health was not good, and he had not finished an education good enough to make him fit for sacerdotal studies. Undaunted, he went off to see his old friend Father Louis Santander, s.j., at Valencia. Father Santander recommended him to get ordained as soon as possible, and as a first step to learn Latin. So, like St Ignatius Loyola before him, and with like mortifications, he put himself to school with the little boys. As he had given nearly all his money to his sisters and to the poor before leaving Segovia, he had to take a post as a servant and supplement his earnings by begging to support himself. He met at the school a man of his own age and inclinations, who induced him to consider giving up all idea of becoming a Jesuit and to be instead a hermit. Alphonsus went to visit this man at his hermitage in the mountains, but suddenly seeing the suggestion as a temptation to desert his real vocation, he returned to Valencia and confessed his weakness to Father Santander, saying, " I will never again follow my own will for the rest of my life. Do with me as you think best." In 1571 the Jesuit provincial, over-ruling his official consultors, accepted Alphonsus Rodriguez as a lay-brother, or temporal coadjutor, as such is called in the Society. Six months later he was sent from Spain to the College of Montesione in the island of Majorca, and soon after his arrival was made hall-porter.

St Alphonsus carried out the duties of this post till he became too old and infirm, and the reputation he had in it was summed up once for all by Father Michael Julian in his exclamation, " That brother is not a man—he is an angel ! " Every minute left free by his work and what it entailed was given to prayer, but though he achieved a marvellous habitual recollection and union with God his spiritual path was far from an easy one. Especially in his later years he suffered from long periods of desolation and aridity, and with terrifying regularity he was seized with pain and sickness whenever he set himself formally to meditate. Added to this, he was beset with violent temptations, just as though for years he had not curbed his body by fierce austerities, which now had to be made even more rigorous. But he never despaired, carrying out every duty with exact regularity, knowing that in God's own time he would be seized again in an ecstasy of love and spiritual delight. Priests who had known him for forty years used to say that they had never noticed a word or action of Brother Alphonsus which could justly receive adverse criticism. In 1585, when he was fifty-four years old, he made his final vows, which he used to renew every day at Mass. A hall-porter is not to be envied at the best of times, and when a boys' school is part of the establishment he needs to have a firm hand and an extra fund of patience ; but the job has its compensations ; the porter meets a variety of people and is a link between the public world without and the private world within. At Montesione, in addition to the students, there was a constant coming and going of clergy of all sorts, of nobles and professional men and members of their families having business with the Jesuit fathers, of the poor wanting help and merchants and tradesmen from Palma wanting orders. All these people got to know, to respect and to love Brother Alphonsus, whose opinions and advice were sought and valued as well by the learned and holy as by the simple, and his reputation was known far beyond the boundaries of the college. The most famous of his " pupils " was St Peter Claver, who was studying at the college in 1605. For three years he put himself under the direction of St Alphonsus who, enlightened by Heaven, fired his enthusiasm for and urged him on to that work in America which was eventually to gain for St Peter the title of " Apostle of the Negroes ".

St Alphonsus had always a very deep devotion towards the Mother of God as conceived free from original sin, a truth that had been defended in Majorca three hundred years before by Bd Raymund Lull.   For a time it was believed by many that the Little Office of the Immaculate Conception had been composed by Alphonsus ; he had a great regard for this office and popularized its use among others, from which arose the mistake that he was its author.   Nor did he write the famous treatise on the *Practice of Perfection and Christian Virtues :* this was the work of another Jesuit of the same name, who has not been canonized.   But St Alphonsus left some fugitive writings, set down at the command of his superiors, full of the simple, solid doctrine and exhortation that one would look for from such a man, showing too that he was indeed a mystic favoured of Heaven.   When he was over seventy and very infirm, his rector told him one day, just to see what he would do, to go on duty to the Indies.   St Alphonsus went straight down to the gate and asked for it to be opened for him.   " I am ordered to the Indies ", he said, and was going there and then to look for a ship at Palma, but was told to go back to the rector. That during the later part of his life he suffered from spiritual dereliction and diabolical assaults has been mentioned above, and to these were added the trials of ill-health and physical suffering ; at last he was practically confined to his bed. But his invincible perseverance and patience brought consolations " to such a degree that he could not raise his eyes in spirit to Jesus and Mary without their being at once before him ".

In May of 1617 the rector of Montesione, Father Julian, was down with rheumatic fever, and asked for the prayers of St Alphonsus.   He spent the night interceding for him, and in the morning Father Julian was able to celebrate Mass. In October Alphonsus knew that his end was at hand, and after receiving holy communion on the 29th all pain of mind and body ceased.   He lay as it were in an unbroken ecstasy until, at midnight of the 31st, a terrible agony began. At the end of half an hour composure returned, he looked around lovingly at his brethren, kissed the crucifix, uttered the Holy Name in a loud voice, and died. His funeral was attended by the Spanish viceroy and nobility of Majorca, by the bishop, and by crowds of the poor, sick and afflicted whose love and faith were rewarded by miracles.   He was canonized in 1888 with St Peter Claver.

The documents printed for the Congregation of Sacred Rites in view of the beatification and canonization of St Alphonsus are very copious owing to the objections raised by the *promotor fidei* in connection with the saint's early occupations and his writings.   These documents, with the autobiographical notes, which he wrote down by order of obedience between the years 1601 and 1616, supply the most valuable materials for his life.   The notes in question are printed at the beginning of his *Obras Espirituales*, which were edited in three volumes by Fr J. Nonell at Barcelona in 1885–1887.   The same Fr Nonell wrote in Spanish what is still perhaps the best biography of the saint, *Vida de San Alonso Rodriguez* (1888) ; and this was largely used by Father Goldie in the English life which he published in 1889. In the *Acta Sanctorum*, October, vol. xiii, is reprinted the earliest published life of Alphonsus, that by Father Janin which appeared in 1644 and was written in Latin.   On the saint's connection with the Little Office of the Immaculate Conception, often erroneously printed under his name, see Uriarte, *Obras anonimas y seudonimas*, S.J., vol. i, pp. 512–515 ; and on his ascetical teaching see Viller, *Dictionnaire de Spiritualité*, vol. i (1933), cc. 395–402.   The latest biographies seem to be that of M. Dietz, *Der hl. Alfons Rodriguez* (1925), and a popular account by M. Farnum, *The Wool Merchant of Segovia* (1945).

BD ANGELO OF ACRI   (A.D. 1739)

THE fame of St Leonard of Port Maurice as a mission-preacher in Tuscany and northern Italy during the first half of the eighteenth century has gone far beyond the boundaries of his own order and country, but his contemporary preacher in Calabria, Angelo of Acri, also a Franciscan, is not so well known, though he was as famous in the south as St Leonard in the north.   He was born at Acri in the diocese of Bisignano in 1669, and when he was eighteen was accepted as a postulant by the Capuchins, but the austerity of their life was too much for him and he left.   But he was not satisfied, and after a time was permitted again to try his vocation in the same order.   And again he failed to persevere.   Thereupon his uncle, a priest, pointed out to him that he was obviously intended by God for a secular life and had better marry.   Angelo was still unconvinced : he had a strong attraction to the religious life and a corresponding aversion from trying to settle down " in the world ", and in 1690 he made a third attempt with the Capuchins.   This time he overcame his difficulties by the aid of urgent prayer, and after a rather stormy novitiate was professed and began his studies for the priesthood.

His superiors saw that he still stood in need of strict discipline and treated Angelo with considerable severity, and at the same time he was greatly tried by temptations against chastity ; he overcame both trials and so profited by them that it is said that during the celebration of his first Mass he was rapt in ecstasy.   It was not till 1702 that he was first entrusted with public preaching, when he was sent to preach the Lent at San Giorgio.   He prepared his course with great care, but in the pulpit his confidence and memory deserted him and he failed so lament- ably that he gave up and returned to his friary before it was over.   Meditating on his failure and asking God's help in his trouble, he one day seemed to hear a voice saying, " Be not afraid.   The gift of preaching shall be yours."   " Who art thou ? " asked Father Angelo, and the reply came, " I am who I am.   For the future preach simply and colloquially, so that all may understand you."   Father Angelo did as he was told ; he laid aside all his books of oratory and with them the flowers of speech and flights of learning, and prepared his discourses only with the help of his Bible and crucifix.

His new manner was immediately successful with the common people ; but these were the days before St Alphonsus Liguori and his Redemptorists had simplified the style of preaching prevalent in Italy, and more refined people were contemptuous of the straightforwardness and familiar phrasing of Father Angelo. The attention of these was won in a rather dramatic way when, in 1711, Cardinal Pignatelli invited him to preach the Lent at Naples.   His first sermon there provoked the usual superior amusement among the gentry, and the two following days the church was almost empty.   The parish priest asked him to discontinue the course, but Cardinal Pignatelli said he was to continue, and this " incident " stimulated curiosity, so that the church was crowded next day.   At the end of his sermon Father Angelo asked the congregation to pray for the soul of somebody in the church who was about to die.   As they left the building, speculating about the prophecy, a well-known lawyer, who had made himself conspicuous by his raillery at the preacher, fell dead from a stroke.   This happening, which was followed by others equally remarkable, made Father Angelo's reputation in Naples ; for the future there were more listeners than the church could hold, and many who came merely from curiosity received the grace of God and were brought to their knees.

For the next twenty-eight years Bd Angelo preached as a missioner in the kingdom of Naples and particularly up and down his own province of Calabria, where he brought thousands to penance and amendment of life. His mission was emphasized by many miracles, especially of healing the sick, and examples of seeming supernatural agility or of bilocation are recorded of him. He had insight into the souls of men, reminding them of forgotten or concealed sins, and several times, as at Naples, predicted future events with exactness. He continued his labours to within six months of his death, when he became blind, but was able to celebrate Mass daily till the end, which came peacefully at the friary of Acri on October 30, 1739. A flow of blood in the veins and movement of an arm at the word of the father guardian, similar to the phenomena reported of Bd Bonaventure of Potenza (October 26), are stated to have taken place three days after death. Bd Angelo of Acri was beatified in 1825.

The Bollandists have supplied a full account in the *Acta Sanctorum*, October, vol. xiii, drawing almost entirely upon the evidence presented in the beatification process. See, however, also the lives written by Ernest de Beaulieu (1899) and Giacinto da Belmonte (1894). A summary in English may be read in Léon, *Auréole Séraphique* (Eng. trans.), vol. iv, pp. 1–7.

31 : ST QUINTINUS, OR QUENTIN, MARTYR   (DATE UNKNOWN)

ST QUINTINUS was a Roman who, his legend tells us, left his country and, attended by St Lucian of Beauvais, made his way to Gaul. They preached the faith together in that country till they reached Amiens in Picardy, where they parted. St Quintinus stayed at Amiens, endeavouring by his prayers and labours to make that country a portion of the Lord's vineyard, and the reward of his labours was the crown of martyrdom. The prefect Rictiovarus heard what great progress the Christian faith had made at Amiens, and he ordered Quintinus to be thrown into prison. The next day the holy preacher was brought before the prefect, who tried to win him over with promises and threats ; finding him proof against both, he ordered him to be whipped and confined to a dungeon without the liberty of receiving assistance from the faithful. The *passio* of St Quintinus is a worthless recital of tortures and marvels. It says that his limbs were stretched with pulleys on the rack till his joints were dislocated, his body torn with iron wire, boiled pitch and oil were poured on his back and lighted torches applied to his sides. By the ministry of an angel he escaped from prison but was taken again while preaching in the market-place. When Rictiovarus left Amiens he commanded Quintinus to be conducted to Augusta Veromanduorum (now Saint-Quentin), where he made fresh attacks upon the confessor of Christ. Ashamed to see himself vanquished by his courage, Rictiovarus ordered him to be tortured anew, and at last his head to be cut off, whereupon a dove issued from the gaping neck and flew away into the heavens. The martyr's body was thrown into the river Somme ; but it was recovered by the Christians and buried near the town.

Since St Gregory of Tours already speaks of a church dedicated in honour of St Quintinus, there can be little reason for questioning the fact that he was an authentic martyr. But the story has been embellished with all sorts of legendary excrescences and is preserved to us in a great variety of forms, of which a list is given in BHL., nn. 6999–7021. Several of these texts, including accounts of the translations of relics, are reproduced in the long article devoted to St Quintinus in the *Acta Sanctorum*, October, vol. xiii. Others have since been discovered, notably a number of Carolingian metrical effusions which have been printed in the *Analecta Bollandiana*, vol. xx (1901), pp. 1–44. It is interesting to note that the legend of Quintinus was already known to Bede ; for his notice, see the *Martyrologes historiques* of Dom Quentin, who believes it to be authentic.

ST FOILLAN, ABBOT   (*c.* A.D. 655)

ST FOILLAN was the brother of St Fursey, of whom an account is given herein under January 16. They came to England, together with another brother, St Ultan, after the year 630 and established a monastery at Burgh Castle, near Yarmouth, from which they did missionary work among the East Angles. After a time Fursey crossed over to Gaul, where he died about the year 648. East Anglia was overrun by the Mercians under Penda, when the monastery at Burgh Castle had been pillaged by the invaders, and Foillan and Ultan determined to follow the example of their brother. They came into Neustria where, like Fursey before them, they were well received by Clovis II. From Péronne St Foillan went to Nivelles, where he was given land at Fosses by Bd Itta, widow of Bd Pepin of Landen, who had founded the monastery at Nivelles of which their daughter St Gertrude was abbess. Here he established a monastery, and was in close contact with the abbey of Nivelles, where he exercised a great influence. St Foillan also engaged himself in missionary work among the Brabanters, and left a strong impression upon the religious life of the place and time ; he is one of the best remembered of the lesser Irish missionary monks on the continent.

About the year 655, on the eve of the feast of St Quintinus, St Foillan sang Mass at Nivelles and then set out with three companions. While passing through the forest of Seneffe they were set upon by outlaws, robbed, murdered, and their bodies left lying. These were not found till the following January 16, when St Gertrude ordered them to be buried at the abbey which St Foillan had founded. As he was slain while journeying on the business of the Church, St Foillan is commemorated as a martyr in several places of Belgium ; he is said also to have been a bishop, though there appears to be no good authority for this.

A number of texts have been printed in the *Acta Sanctorum* bearing on the history of St Foillan, but one still more valuable is a short document which appears in some manuscripts as an appendix to the earliest Life of St Fursey. B. Krusch who has edited it in MGH., *Scriptores Merov.*, vol. iv, pp. 449–451, believes it to have been written by an eye-witness, probably an Irish monk in the service of the nuns at Nivelles. It describes the death and burial of St Foillan. See also Kenney, *Sources for the Early History of Ireland*, vol. i, pp. 503–504 ; Crépin, " Le Monastère des Scots de Fosses " in *La Terre Wallonne*, vols. viii (1923), pp. 357–385, and ix (1923), pp. 16–26 ; and L. Gougaud, *Christianity in Celtic Lands*, pp. 147–148.

ST WOLFGANG, BISHOP OF REGENSBURG   (A.D. 994)

ST WOLFGANG came of a Swabian family and was born about the year 930. In his youth he was sent to the abbey of Reichenau, on an island in Lake Constance, which was at that time a flourishing school of learning ; here he became friendly with a young nobleman called Henry, brother to Poppo, Bishop of Würzburg, who had set up a school in that city. This Henry persuaded Wolfgang to bear him company to this new school at Würzburg, where the ability of the young Swabian soon provoked jealousy as well as admiration. In 956 Henry was elected archbishop of Trier, and took Wolfgang with him, making him a teacher in the cathedral school. At Trier he came under the influence of the reforming monk Ramuold, and entered wholeheartedly into Henry's efforts for the improvement of religion in his diocese. Upon the death of the archbishop in 964 Wolfgang became a Benedictine in the monastery of Einsiedeln, governed at that time by Gregory, an Englishman. The abbot soon found the reputation of Wolfgang to be less than his merit, and appointed him director of the school of the monastery. St Ulric, Bishop of Augsburg, now ordained St Wolfgang priest ; and with his ordination he received an apostolic missionary spirit, and was sent to preach the gospel to the Magyars in Pannonia. The results of this undertaking did not correspond to his zeal, and he was recommended to the Emperor Otto II as a person qualified to fill the see of Regensburg (Ratisbon) which was then vacant. He was conducted to the emperor at Frankfurt, who gave him the investiture of the temporalities, though Wolfgang entreated him to allow him to return to his monastery. Being sent back to Regensburg, at Christmas 972 he was consecrated.

St Wolfgang never quitted the monastic habit, and practised all the austerities of conventual life when in the episcopal dignity. The first thing he did after regulation of his own household was to settle a thorough reformation among all his clergy, and in all the monasteries of his diocese, especially two disorderly nunneries. One of the sources of revenue of the see was the abbey of St Emmeram at Regensburg, which the bishops held *in commendam*, with the usual bad results. Wolfgang restored its autonomy and called Ramuold from Trier to be its abbot. He was indefatigable in preaching and, being a man of prayer, possessed the art of touching the hearts of his hearers. Every duty of his office he discharged with vigilance and fidelity during twenty-two years' administration. Several miracles are recorded of him and his generosity to the poor was proverbial. Once when the vintage had failed, some ignorant priests took to using water in the chalice at Mass. The bishop was naturally horrified, and distributed wine from his household stocks throughout the diocese.

At one time St Wolfgang deserted his see and retired to a solitary place, where he was found by some huntsmen and brought back. But his desire for a monastic quiet did not prevent him from a careful discharge of his secular duties, and he attended several imperial diets as well as accompanying the emperor on a campaign into France. The territory of Bohemia being part of his vast diocese, he gave up a part of it for a bishopric in that country, the see being set up at Prague. Henry, Duke of Bavaria, held St Wolfgang in the highest veneration, and entrusted to him the education of his son Henry, afterwards emperor and canonized saint. Wolfgang was taken ill while travelling down the Danube into Lower Austria and died at a little place called Puppingen, not far from Linz. He was canonized in 1052; his feast is kept in many dioceses of central Europe, and also by the Canons Regular of the Lateran because he restored the canonical life for his clergy.

We are well informed regarding St Wolfgang. The book of Arnold the monk concerning St Emmeram and the biography of Wolfgang by Othlo, with some other supplementary materials, are reliable sources, and they have been edited very carefully in the *Acta Sanctorum*, November, vol. ii, pt 1. See also a popular, but not uncritical, volume by Otto Häfner *Der hl. Wolfgang, ein Stern des X. Jahrhunderts* (1930) ; and also the archaeological study of J. A. Endres, *Beiträge zur Kunst- und Kulturgeschichte des mittelalterlichen Regensburgs*, as well as I. Zibermayr, *Die St Wolfganslegende in ihrem Entstehen und Einflusse auf die österreichische Kunst* (1924).

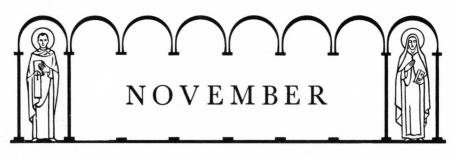

NOVEMBER

1 : ALL SAINTS

IN those churches in which the Divine Office is recited in choir the hour of Prime is followed by the reading of the martyrology for the day, and this reading always ends with the words *Et alibi aliorum plurimorum sanctorum martyrum et confessorum atque sanctarum virginum:* " And in other places [the commemoration] of many other holy martyrs, confessors and virgins." On the feast of All Saints the Church celebrates in the most solemn fashion, as well as all those whom she has formally beatified and canonized and those whose names are entered in the various martyrologies or whose *cultus* is of local observance, these " many others " : and not only the martyrs, confessors and virgins in the technical sense of those words, but all, known to man or known only to God, who, in whatever circumstances and whatever states of life, have contended manfully in this life and now enjoy the blissful vision of God for ever in Heaven. The Church thus honours all the saints reigning together in glory to give thanks to God for the graces and crowns of His servants ; to move ourselves to strive after their virtues by considering their example ; to implore the divine mercy through this multitude of powerful intercessors ; and to repair any failure or insufficiency in not having duly honoured God in His saints on their particular festivals, and to glorify Him in those saints who are unknown to us or for whom no particular festivals are appointed. Therefore our fervour on this day ought to be a reparation for our lukewarmness in all the other feasts of the year ; they being all comprised in this one solemn commemoration, which is an image of that eternal great feast which God continually celebrates in Heaven with all the righteous, whom we humbly join in praising His goodness and mercies. In this, as in all other feasts of the saints, God is our only object of supreme worship, and the whole of that lesser and different veneration which is paid to them is directed to give sovereign honour to Him alone, whose gifts their graces are ; and our prayers to them are only petitions to holy fellow-creatures for the assistance of their prayers to God for us. When therefore we honour the saints, in them and through them we honour God, and Christ, true God and true man, the redeemer and saviour of mankind, the king of all the saints, the source of their holiness and glory.

These glorious citizens of the heavenly Jerusalem God has chosen out of all peoples and nations without any distinction ; persons of all ages, showing there is no age which is not ripe for Heaven, and out of all states and conditions : amidst the pomp of worldly grandeur, in the cottage, in the army, in trade, in the magistracy ; clergy, monks, nuns, married persons and widows, slaves and freemen. There is no state that has not been honoured with its saints. And they were all made saints by the very occupations of their state and by the ordinary occurrences of life : prosperity and adversity, health and sickness, honour and contempt, riches and poverty—all these they made the means of their sanctification. God does not require, then, that men abandon their employments in the world, but that they hallow them by disengagement of heart and religious motive or intention. Thus has every station in the world been adorned with saints.

It is sometimes objected against the ideal of holiness held up by the Church before all men indiscriminately that it is incompatible with that secular life in which the overwhelming majority of men and women are, and are meant to be, engaged. And in support of this objection it is alleged that more clergy and members of religious orders of both sexes become saints than do lay people, more not only relatively but absolutely. This is not known to be so, and is impossible of proof. If it be a question of *canonized* and *beatified* saints, then it is true that there are far more religious than lay people, and also far more bishops than priests, and men than women. But canonization and beatification are exterior marks, " certificates ", if the expression may be allowed, by which the Church honours certain individuals, a selection from among those many holy ones who contribute to her sanctity. And in the making of that selection some purely natural factors necessarily come into play. A religious order has the means and the motive for forwarding the " cause " of an individual who in other circumstances would have never been heard of outside his own circle ; the episcopal office brings its holder into greater prominence, lends of itself a weight to his name, and carries with it the means and influence to prosecute his cause ; and men, as distinct from women, have by their very sex greater opportunities of notable achievement and of the fame of their virtues becoming widespread in this world. But even so a modification is taking place. Among those saints or candidates for canonization in our own day whose cause, where it has been introduced, was or is the interest of so many diverse people that it could almost be said to be proposed by the Church herself, and not by a particular country, order or diocese, a greater variety of " states of life " is exhibited : a pope, Pius X, and a country parson, St John Vianney ; St Teresa of Lisieux, a simple nun ; Frederic Ozanam, Bd Contardo Ferrini, Ludovic Necchi, Matt Talbot, laymen ; Bd Anne Mary Taigi was the wife of an obscure man-servant, but her recognition is probably due, under God, to the interest of the Trinitarians, of which she was a tertiary. And in reading the full-length biographies of the many recently canonized or beatified foundresses of religious congregations it is noticeable how much space is taken up by accounts of the spiritual and corporal works of mercy which the subjects undertook or of which they were the cause ; full information about their " inner life " often seems to be lacking (Bd Mary Teresa de Soubiran is a notable exception) and is dealt with in general, or even common-form, terms. These people attained holiness in the course of lives which were full, " pressed down and running over ", with activities directed immediately to the good of others, lives that were in a sense as much " in the world " as those of lay people. This circumstance—no new one, of course—must be of encouragement to those who are tempted to think that " a really Christian life " can hardly be led outside a cloister, or at any rate outside some ecclesiastical state. There is but one Gospel, one Sacrifice, one Redeemer, one Heaven and one way to Heaven ; it has been traced out by Jesus Christ, the rule of salvation laid down by Him is invariable and the same for all. It is an entirely false idea that Christians in the world are not bound to aim at perfection, or that they may be saved in a different path from that of the saints.

The saints are far from having simply ethical significance only, as patterns of virtuous life ; they have also immense religious significance, not only as living and functioning members of the mystical Body of Christ who by intercession with Him are in vital contact with the Church militant and suffering, but also as fruits of the Redemption who have attained their last end in the vision of God : " they who are come out of great tribulation and have washed their robes and have made them white in the blood of the Lamb. Therefore they are before the throne of God...." " The feast of All Saints ", said the holy J. J. Olier, founder of Saint-Sulpice, " seems to me to be in some sort a greater than that of Easter or the Ascension. Our Lord is perfected in this mystery, because, as our head, He is only perfectly fulfilled when He is united to all His members, the saints. [The feast] is glorious because it manifests exteriorly the hidden life of Jesus Christ. The greatness and perfection of the saints is entirely the work of His spirit dwelling in them."

There are considerable indications of the celebration in quite early times of a collective feast of the martyrs—martyrs in those days being alone reckoned as saints. Although certain passages which have been appealed to in Tertullian and in St Gregory of Nyssa's Life of St Gregory Thaumaturgus are too vague to be of much service, we are on firmer ground when, in the *Carmina Nisibena* of St Ephraem (d. *c.* 373), we find mention of a feast kept in honour of " the martyrs of all the earth ". This was apparently fixed for May 13, a fact which suggests the intervention of some oriental influence in the choice of precisely May 13 for the dedication of the Pantheon in Rome, mentioned below. Throughout the Syrian church in general, however, we know that already in 411, or earlier, a feast of " all the martyrs " was celebrated on the Friday of Easter week, for the Syriac *Breviarium* expressly records this. Easter Friday is still thus distinguished by the Catholics of the Chaldean rite and by the Nestorians. On the other hand the Byzantine churches kept and still keep a feast of all the saints on the Sunday after Pentecost, our Trinity Sunday ; Chrysostom at Constantinople tells his hearers, in a sermon entitled " A Panegyric of all the Martyrs that have suffered throughout the world ", that seven days have hardly passed since the feast of Pentecost.

How the celebration of All Saints began in the West still remains somewhat of a problem. In both the *Félire* of Oengus and the Martyrology of Tallaght we find on April 17 a commemoration of all the martyrs, and on April 20 a feast " of all the Saints of the whole of Europe ". As the Tallaght text phrases it, this day is the " communis sollemnitas omnium sanctorum et virginum Hiberniae et Britanniae et totius Europae ". Turning to England, we note that the primitive text of Bede's Martyrology contained no mention of All Saints, but in copies dating from the close of the eighth century or the beginning of the ninth, we find on November 1 the entry : " Natale sancti Caesarii et festivitas omnium sanctorum." Dom Quentin has suggested that the idea that Pope St Boniface IV intended by the dedication of the Pantheon (in honour of our Lady and all martyrs, on May 13, *c.* 609 ; still commemorated in the Roman Martyrology) to establish something in the nature of a feast of All Saints may have been deduced by Ado and others from a phrase used by Bede, who has spoken of this dedication both in his *Ecclesiastical History* and in his *De temporum ratione*. Bede says—what was not stated in the *Liber Pontificalis* which he had before him—that the pope designed that "the memory of all the saints might in future be honoured in the place which had formerly been devoted to the worship, not of gods, but of demons". In any case it is certain that Alcuin in the year 800 was in the habit of keeping the *solemnitas sanctissima* of All Saints on November 1, with a previous three days' fast. He knew that his friend Arno, Bishop of Salzburg, shared his interest in the festival, since Arno had a short time before presided over a Bavarian council which included that day in its list of holy days. We also hear of a certain Cathwulf who about the year 775 besought Charlemagne to institute a feast, with a fasting vigil preceding, "in honour of the Trinity, the Unity, the angels and all the saints". In the calendar in Bodley MS. Digby 63, ninth century, northern English, All Saints is marked on November 1 as a principal feast. Rome seems finally to have adopted that date under Gallican influence.

In support of the above observations on the beginnings of this feast, see Tertullian, *De corona*, cap. 3 ; Gregory of Nyssa in Migne, PG., vol. xlvi, c. 953 ; Ephraem Syrus, *Carmina Nisibena*, ed. Bicknell, pp. 23, 84 ; Chrysostom in Migne PG., vol. l, c. 705 ; D. Quentin, *Martyrologes historiques*, pp. 637–641 ; and the *Revue bénédictine*, 1910, p. 58, and 1913, p. 44. On the general question consult Abbot Cabrol in DAC., vol. v, cc. 1418–1419 ; and particularly the *Acta Sanctorum, Propylaeum decembris*, pp. 488–489, from which it appears that a supposed reference of Oengus to November 1 as All Saints' day is a mistake. *Cf.* also Duchesne, *Liber pontificalis*, vol. i, pp. 417, 422–423 ; and, for the oriental tradition, Nilles, *Calendarium utriusque ecclesiae*, especially vol. i, p. 314, and vol. ii, pp. 334 and 424. The folk-lore aspects of the feast are discussed by Bächtold-Stäubli, *Handwörterbuch des deutschen Aberglaubens*, vol. i, pp. 263 *seq.* A number of religious orders have the privilege of a feast of all the saints of their respective orders. Many dioceses, especially in France, formerly observed a collective feast of their local diocesan saints ; such feasts have now been abolished, though All Saints of Ireland is kept in that country on November 6. In England the feast was formerly often called All Hallows.

SS. CAESARIUS AND JULIAN, MARTYRS   (DATE UNKNOWN)

THE "acts" of these martyrs are not authentic. Stripped of some common-form marvels they are summarized by Alban Butler as follows :

At Terracina in Italy it was a barbarous custom on certain solemn occasions for a young man to make himself a voluntary sacrifice to Apollo, the tutelar deity of the city. After having been pampered for some months by the citizens, he offered sacrifice to Apollo, and then threw himself headlong from a precipice into the sea. Caesarius, a deacon from Africa, happened once to be present at this impious scene and, not being able to contain his indignation, spoke openly against so abominable a superstition. The priest of the temple caused him to be apprehended, and accused him before the governor, by whose sentence the deacon was, after nearly two years' imprisonment, put into a sack and cast into the sea, together with a Christian priest named Julian. Whatever their true story, SS. Caesarius and Julian are mentioned in the early martyrologies ; and in Rome there has been since the sixth century a church of San Cesareo, which is now a cardinalitial title.

See the *Acta Sanctorum*, November, vol. i, where four separate texts of the *passio* are printed, together with a paraphrase of one of them in Greek. The church of San Cesareo is on the Palatine and it has been suggested that the adoption of this dedication in the imperial quarter was due to the form of the saint's name suggesting a connection with emperors. Consult Delehaye, *Origines du culte des martyrs*, pp. 308, 409 ; Lanzoni in *Rivista di archeologia cristiana*, vol. i, pp. 146–148 ; Duchesne in *Nuovo bullettino di arch. crist.*, 1900, pp. 17 *seq.* ; and J. P. Kirsch, *Der stadtrömische Fest-Kalender*, p. 208.

ST BENIGNUS OF DIJON, Martyr   (Third Century ?)

Although the Roman Martyrology lends its authority to the statement that St Benignus was a disciple of St Polycarp at Smyrna and was martyred at Dijon in the reign of Marcus Aurelius, Alban Butler only ventures that he was a Roman missionary who suffered near Dijon, " probably in the reign of Aurelian ". Even this is going too far, as his nationality is not known, and the suggested date is perhaps too late : he may have been a disciple of St Irenaeus of Lyons, martyred at Épagny. He came to be venerated in the neighbourhood of Dijon, but at the beginning of the sixth century nothing was known about him locally.

St Gregory of Tours says that at this time the people of Dijon honoured a certain tomb, which his great-grandfather, St Gregory, Bishop of Langres, believed to be the grave of a pagan. He was warned in a dream and by a miracle that it was actually the resting-place of the martyred St Benignus. Gregory of Langres accordingly restored the tomb and built a basilica over it. He had no particulars of the life and death of the martyr, but in due course some pilgrims returning from Italy put him in possession of a *passio Sancti Benigni ;* that this document had its origin in Rome is not likely, and it is manifest that in its present form (which seems to be contemporaneous with St Gregory of Langres) it has at the very least been edited in Dijon and is completely spurious.

This *passio* relates that St Polycarp of Smyrna had a vision of St Irenaeus, then dead (in fact he did not die until some fifty years after Polycarp), in consequence of which he sent two priests, Benignus and Andochius, and the deacon Thyrsus to preach the gospel in Gaul. After being wrecked on Corsica, where they picked up St Andeolus, they landed at Marseilles and made their way to the Côte d'Or. At Autun they were received into the house of one Faustus, whose son St Symphorian was baptized by St Benignus. The missionaries then separated and at Langres Benignus converted St Leonilla and her three twin grandsons (*see* St Speusippus, etc., on January 17). He went on to Dijon and there preached with great effect, and wrought many miracles. Persecution of Christians having broken out, the judge Terence denounced Benignus to the Emperor Aurelian, who was in Gaul (so he was, about a hundred years after the death of St Polycarp). The missionary was arrested at Épagny, near Dijon, and after many trials and torments, which he opposed by no less startling miracles, his head was crushed with an iron bar and his heart pierced. The body was buried in a tomb which was made to look like a pagan monument in order to deceive the persecutors. Mgr Duchesne has shown that this tale is the first link in a chain of religious romances written during the early part of the sixth century to describe the beginnings of the churches of Autun, Besançon, Langres and Valence (SS. Andochius and Thyrsus, Ferreolus and Ferrutio, Benignus, Felix, Achilleus and Fortunatus) ; no reliance whatever can be placed on them and the very existence of some of these martyrs is doubtful.

Here again five separate texts of the *passio* will be found in the *Acta Sanctorum*, November, vol. i. Besides the commentary of the Bollandists, see also Duchesne, *Fastes Épiscopaux*, vol. i, pp. 51–62, and Leclercq in DAC., vol. iv, cc. 835–849.

ST AUSTREMONIUS, Bishop of Clermont   (Fourth Century ?)

Nothing very certain is known of this saint except that he was a missionary in Auvergne where, as St Stremoine, he is venerated as the apostle and first bishop of

Clermont. Even the time during which he flourished is a matter of some discussion. According to St Gregory of Tours he was one of the seven bishops sent from Rome into Gaul about the middle of the third century. His *cultus* having become popular owing to a vision seen by a deacon of his reputed tomb at Issoire, a legendary account of St Austremonius evolved during the sixth and following centuries. This made him one of the seventy-two disciples of our Lord, and attributed his death to a Jewish rabbi whose son the saint had converted : the rabbi killed him and cut off his head, throwing it down a well to which it was afterwards traced by the trail of blood. St Austremonius was (and is, at Clermont) accordingly revered as a martyr. His body was first buried at Issoire. There is no reason to suppose that St Austremonius was a martyr, and he is not recognized as such in the Roman Martyrology.

Three legendary lives of St Austremonius, the third of which has been attributed without reason to St Praejectus, are printed in the *Acta Sanctorum*, November, vol. i. With these the Bollandists have edited other texts relating to the translations of the saint's supposed relics and his miracles. See further Duchesne, *Fastes Épiscopaux*, vol. ii, pp. 119–122 ; Poncelet in *Analecta Bollandiana*, vol. xiii (1894), pp. 33–46 ; Leclercq in DAC., vol. iii, cc. 1906–1914 ; and L. Levillain in *Le Moyen-Age* (on the translations) for 1904, pp. 281–337. It seems true that St Praejectus (Prix) did complete an account of his predecessor Austremonius, but it has perished.

ST MARY, VIRGIN AND MARTYR   (FOURTH CENTURY ?)

MARY was slave to Tertullus, a Roman official, and a Christian from her cradle, the only one in the household. She prayed much and fasted frequently, especially on idolatrous festivals. This devotion displeased her mistress, but her fidelity and diligence were appreciated. When persecution broke out Tertullus tried to induce Mary to renounce her faith, but he could not shake her constancy. Fearing to lose her if she fell into the hands of the prefect, he had her unmercifully whipped and then hidden in a dark room. The matter became known, and the prefect made a charge against Tertullus that he had concealed a Christian in his house ; the slave was forthwith delivered up. The mob in the court, hearing her confess the name of Christ, demanded that she should be burnt alive. Mary stood praying that God would give her constancy, and said to the judge, " The God whom I serve is with me. I fear not your torments, which can only take away a life that I am ready to lay down for Jesus Christ." The judge commanded her to be tortured, which was done with such cruelty that the bystanders now cried out that they could not bear so horrible a sight and entreated that she might be released. The judge handed her over to a soldier, who, however, respected her helplessness and allowed her to escape. St Mary eventually died a natural death, but she is called a martyr in the Roman Martyrology on account of her sufferings for Christ.

The Bollandist Father Van Hooff, in agreement with E. Le Blant, was inclined to believe that some traces of an authentic story are preserved in the *passio* of this martyr. It is printed in the *Acta Sanctorum*, November, vol. i. But the text, as we possess it, has certainly been rewritten to suit the taste of later times. It contains extravagances borrowed from other hagiographical fictions, and the writer, moreover, assigns the martyrdom to the time of Marcus Aurelius, which is quite unlikely. There is a doubtful mention of Maria in the *Hieronymianum*, and in this manner, as Dom Quentin (*Les Martyrologes historiques*, p. 180) explains, Mary, the *ancilla*, has, by way of Ado and Usuard, found a place in the Roman Martyrology.

ST MATURINUS, OR MATHURIN   (FOURTH CENTURY ?)

THE entirely legendary Life of St Maturinus says he was the son of pagan parents at Larchant in the territory of Sens.   Unlike his father, who was a persecutor, Maturinus listened to the Christian gospel, and at the age of twelve was judged worthy to receive baptism.   His first converts were his own parents.   He became a priest at twenty, with a great gift of casting out evil spirits, and was so trusted by his bishop that when he had to go to Rome he left Maturinus in charge.   The saint preached in the Gâtinais and made many converts, until, his reputation as an exorcist having travelled, he also was sent for to Rome, to deliver a noble maiden who was grievously tormented.   There, says the legend, he died.   His body was brought back to Sens and then to his native place, where the Huguenots destroyed the relics.   The *cultus* seems never to have been extensive, and his name is most familiar, in " Mathurins ", as the colloquial name in France of the Trinitarian friars, to whom was given a church in Paris dedicated in honour of St Mathurin.

See the *Acta Sanctorum*, November, vol. i, where the Latin texts of the legend are printed with a commentary.   The local bearings of the cult have been fully studied by E. Thoison in a series of articles contributed to the *Annales de la Société hist.-archéol. Gâtinais* from 1886 to 1888.   *Cf.* also H. Gaidoz in *Mélusine*, vol. v (1890), pp. 151–152.

ST MARCELLUS, BISHOP OF PARIS   (*c.* A.D. 410 ?)

IT is stated that this Marcellus was born at Paris of parents not conspicuous for rank in the world but on whom his holiness reflected the greatest honour : he gave himself entirely to the discipline of virtue and prayer, so as to seem disengaged both from the world and the flesh, says the author of his life.   The uncommon gravity of his character and his progress in sacred learning recommended him to Prudentius, Bishop of Paris, who ordained him reader and later made him his archdeacon. From this time the saint is said to have given frequent proofs of a wonderful gift of miracles, and upon the decease of Prudentius was unanimously chosen bishop of Paris.   It is related that by his prayers and authority he defended his flock from the raids of barbarians, and some surprising marvels (including victory over a great serpent or dragon) are attributed to him by his biographer.   " But ", as Alban Butler remarks, " the circumstances depend upon the authority of one who wrote over a hundred years after the time, and who, being a foreigner, took them upon trust and probably upon popular reports."   The saint died early in the fifth century. His body was buried in the catacomb known by his name on the left bank of the Seine, a district now joined to the city and called the suburb of Saint-Marceau.

Modern criticism seems agreed that the Life of this saint may without hesitation be assigned to the authorship of St Venantius Fortunatus, who, *pace* Alban Butler, can hardly be regarded as a foreigner in Gaul, except technically.   It has been critically edited both by B. Krusch in MGH., *Auctores antiquissimi*, vol. iv, pt 2, pp. 49–54, and in the *Acta Sanctorum*, November, vol. i.   See also Duchesne, *Fastes Épiscopaux*, vol. ii, p. 470.

ST VIGOR, BISHOP OF BAYEUX   (*c.* A.D. 537)

VIGOR was born in Artois and was active during the reign of King Childebert I. His education was entrusted to St Vedast at Arras, but Vigor feared his father would not approve of his desire to be a priest, so he ran away with a companion and concealed himself at the village of Ravière, near Bayeux.   Here they preached and instructed the people, and after he had been ordained Vigor extended his missionary labours.   In 513 the bishop of Bayeux died and St Vigor was put in his place. He found that some people still gave religious worship to a stone figure on a hill near the city.   He therefore threw down the idol, and built a church in its place, renaming it the Hill of Anointing.   When Count Bertulf fell from his horse and broke his neck, it was regarded as a judgement on him for having laid claim to this newly sanctified hill.   Saint-Vigeur-le-Grand, near Bayeux, takes its name from this bishop, who founded a monastery there ; two or three churches in England were dedicated in his honour by the Normans.

See the *Acta Sanctorum*, November, vol. i, where a short Latin life, probably of the eighth century, has been critically edited from a variety of manuscripts.   See also Corblet, *Hagiographie d'Amiens*, vol. iv, pp. 657–664, and Duchesne, *Fastes Épiscopaux*, vol. ii, p 220.

ST CADFAN, ABBOT   (SIXTH CENTURY)

DURING the second half of the fifth century settlements were made in north and west Wales by emigrants from Letavia, which is commonly understood to be Brittany ; but there is not wanting some evidence that it was a district somewhere in south-east Wales.   One of the companies was led by Cadfan, grandson of Emyr Llydaw.   Among those with him was his cousin St Padarn, who went to Cardigan-shire, while Cadfan founded the church at Towyn in Merioneth.   His monastery there persisted into the middle ages as a college of priests (the prebendaries were often laymen), which helped to keep his memory green when British saints became of little account.   A twelfth-century bard speaks of " Cadfan's high church near the shore of the blue sea ", wherein were " three magnificent altars, famous for miracles ", dedicated in honour of our Lady, St Peter and St Cadfan himself.   It was " the glory of Merioneth ", and was a place of sanctuary whither many fled for protection.   His holy well there was a place of resort—but apparently on purely natural grounds—until into the nineteenth century, but is now enclosed within a stable.   But St Cadfan's name is at least as well known in connection with the monastic island of Bardsey (Ynys Enlli), to which he later went, according to tradition, and became the first abbot there.   He was venerated as the founder of this resort of " 20,000 monks ", which even in the time of Pennant, the third quarter of the eighteenth century, was still regarded with such reverence that the local fishermen as they approached it " made a full stop, pulled off their hats, and offered up a short prayer ".

In the medieval poem just referred to St Cadfan is called the " protector in battle ", he was a patron of warriors, and in a chapel near Quimper is a statue, said to be of him, dressed as a soldier, with a sword.   From this it may be inferred that before he was a missionary and monk he had distinguished himself as a fighting-man ; but it may all be a misunderstanding, as his cousin and fellow-missionary in Powysland, St Tydecho, is referred to as " one of Heaven's warriors " in a poem of the fifteenth century ; or it is possible that the tendency to regard St Cadfan as a military patron may be due to some confusion with Cadfan, King of Gwynedd, who was a Welsh leader in the wars against Ethelfrith, King of Northumbria. St Cadfan is usually said to have died and been buried on Bardsey, but his

burying-place is claimed for Towyn as well.   His other principal foundation is
Llangadfan in Montgomeryshire.

There is no formal life of St Cadfan, and we have to be content with casual references
as they have been gathered up in R. Rees, *Essay on the Welsh Saints* (1836), pp. 213–214 ;
LBS., vol. ii, pp. 1–9 ; and A. W. Wade-Evans, *Welsh Christian Origins* (1934), pp. 161–164.
For Bardsey, see G. H. Jones, *Celtic Britain and the Pilgrim Movement*, pp. 354–362 ; and
for the Cadfan stone at Towyn, V. E. Nash-Williams, *Early Christian Monuments of Wales*
(1950).   Bardsey seems to have survived until the dissolution of the monasteries as a Celtic
settlement outside the normal later medieval monastic patterns.   See E. G. Bowen, *Settlements of the Celtic Saints in Wales* (1954).

2 : THE COMMEMORATION OF ALL THE FAITHFUL DE-
PARTED, COMMONLY CALLED ALL SOULS' DAY

THE Church of Christ is composed of three parts : the Triumphant in
Heaven, the Militant on earth, and the Patient, or suffering, in Purgatory.*
Our charity embraces all the members of Christ.   Our love for Him
engages and binds us to His whole Body, and teaches us to share both the afflictions
and the blessings of all that are comprised in it.   The communion of saints which
we profess implies a communication of certain good works and a mutual intercourse
among all the members of Christ.   This we maintain with the saints in Heaven by
thanking and praising God for their triumphs and crowns, imploring their intercession, and receiving the help of their prayers for us.   All Saints' day is set apart
in a special way for this purpose, and on the following day the Church on earth
particularly emphasizes her relations with the souls in Purgatory by soliciting the
divine mercy in their favour.   Nor does it seem to be doubtful that they pray also
for us ; though the Church never addresses public suffrages to them, not being
warranted by primitive practice and tradition so to do.   It is certainly a " holy and
wholesome thought to pray for the dead " (2 Mach. xii 46).   Holy because most
acceptable to God, to whom no sacrifices are more honourable and pleasing than
those of charity and mercy, especially spiritual.   The souls in Purgatory are heirs
of Heaven, the eternal possession of the Kingdom is secured to them, and their
names are written there.   But they must first be wholly cleansed by patient
suffering of punishment incurred.   Such is God's hatred of the least sin, and such
is the opposition which the stain of sin bears to His infinite justice and holiness.
His mercy recommends them to the charitable aid which we, as their fellow-
members in Christ, have in our power to afford them.   If a compassionate charity
towards all that are in any distress, even towards the most undeserving, be an essential ingredient of a Christian spirit and one in which the very soul of religion and
piety towards God consists, how much more should we exert our charity for those
in spiritual need, no longer able to help themselves, and perhaps bound to us by
ties of blood or friendship ?

* It may be explained to the non-Catholic reader that Purgatory is the place or state
in which souls, who deserve not the punishment of eternal loss but nevertheless are yet
unfit for the vision of God, suffer for a while and are cleansed after death before they go
to Heaven.   The suffering of Purgatory consists in the pain of intense longing for God,
whose blissful vision is delayed, and also, as is commonly taught, in some pain of sense.
That this last is inflicted through the medium of material fire is not part of the official teaching
of the Church.

The custom of offering the Holy Sacrifice for an individual deceased person on a particular day was, of course, firmly established long before a special day was set aside for the memorial of all the dead in general.   The first formal testimony to a collective day of the dead is found in the first half of the ninth century, when it was the custom in monasteries to commemorate their own dead and their benefactors all together on one day, the date varying.   The earliest definite suggestion of a connection between the feast of All Saints and a commemoration of All Souls seems to be supplied by Amalarius early in the ninth century.   In his *De ordine antiphonarii* he writes : " After the office of the Saints I have inserted the office for the dead ; for many pass out of this world without at once being admitted into the company of the blessed."   It is quite possible that this passage may have been before the mind of St Odilo of Cluny two hundred years later, when he directed the congregation of which he was supreme head to observe November 2 as a day of commemoration of all the faithful departed, on which the office of the dead was to be said and Masses of requiem celebrated.   In any case, as stated above, the idea of a collective memory of the departed was already familiar.   For example, in the year 800 a compact was drawn up between the monasteries of Saint Gall and Reichenau concerning their mutual suffrages for each other's deceased members. Besides praying for every monk when his death was announced, both communities agreed to observe November 14 in every year as a day of commemoration of the religious who had passed away in either abbey.   On that occasion each priest would offer Mass three times and the rest recite the whole psalter for the souls of the departed of both houses.   It is noteworthy that November 14 was the beginning of what was known in Ireland as the " Moses Lent " in preparation for Christmas, and Saint Gall was, of course, an Irish foundation.

For the rather extravagant story of the hermit who had heard the cries of rage of the demons complaining that the souls of those whom they were torturing were rescued from them by the prayers said at Cluny, we have the contemporary authority of Ralph Glaber and of others later.   We are told that St Odilo, on this being reported to him, was moved to issue his famous decree.   But the text of the ordinance says nothing of this tale of the hermit ; it merely states that " as the feast of all the blessed saints was already celebrated throughout the Church of God, so it seemed desirable that at Cluny they should also keep with joyous affection the memory of all the faithful departed who have lived from the beginning of the world until the end ".   We have a detailed account of how in St Odilo's own lifetime this observance was carried out at the monastery of Farfa, near Spoleto, in Italy.   It seems to have spread widely and rather rapidly, though there is no trace of any papal enactment extending it to the Church in general.   On the other hand two or three centuries passed before we find the entry *Commemoratio animarum* commonly occurring under November 2 in calendars or martyrologies.   A striking illustration of this may be noted at Canterbury.   Somewhere about 1075 the archbishop, Lanfranc, promulgated certain decrees for the Benedictine monks.   In these much is made of the high Mass for the dead on November 2 before which, on the eve, all the bells were to be rung and other solemnities observed.   None the less, though we have four or five Canterbury calendars of the twelfth and thirteenth centuries, no one of them at that date makes mention of any such celebration.   There is, however, a definite mention of All Souls' day in the so-called Protadius martyrology, compiled at Besançon in the middle of the eleventh century.

It seems clear that the privilege long enjoyed only in Spain and its dominions permitting priests to celebrate Mass thrice on All Souls' day originated in the practice of the Dominican priory at Valencia, where it can be traced to the early fifteenth century.   The number of influential people buried there in and around the church was considerable, and so many demands were made for special Masses on November 2 that these claims could only be satisfied by allowing the friars of that community to offer two or even three Masses each on that day.   This irregularity was apparently tolerated by local authority and grew into an established custom.   It was eventually sanctioned and extended to the whole kingdom by Pope Benedict XIV in 1748 ; and during the first world war, in 1915, Pope Benedict XV further extended the privilege to the whole Western church.   With a certain nice appropriateness the Armenians make a special commemoration of the dead on Easter Monday.

On the general question of observance of the *Commemoratio omnium fidelium defunctorum*, consult Cabrol in DAC., vol. v, cc. 1419–1420 ; and Leclercq in the same, vol. iv, cc. 427–456, with vol. xii, cc. 34–38 ; also Kellner, *Heortology*, pp. 326–328 ; Schuster, *The Sacramentary*, vol. v, pp. 213–231 ; and H. Thurston, *The Memory of our Dead*, pp. 101–134 and 224–241.   For further illustrations of folk-lore customs *cf.* Bächtold-Stäubli, *Handwörterbuch des deutschen Aberglaubens*, vol. i, pp. 267–273 ; for the Canterbury calendars, E. Bishop, *The Bosworth Psalter*, pp. 68–69, 113 ; and for Spain, Villanueva, *Viage literario*, vol. ii, pp. 5 *seq.*   For the " Moses Lent ", see *Analecta Bollandiana*, vol. lix (1941), p. 234, n. 3 ; and J. Ryan, *Irish Monasticism* (1931), pp. 392–393.

ST VICTORINUS, Bishop of Pettau, Martyr   (*c.* A.D. 303)

St Jerome speaks well of this early exegete and tells us, in the words of Alban Butler, " that his works were sublime in sense though the Latin style was low, the author being by birth a Grecian ".   From being a rhetorician he became bishop at Pettau in Upper Pannonia and he wrote commentaries on a number of books of the Old and New Testaments St Jerome quotes from these, but he sometimes qualifies his good opinion of the bishop.   Victorinus opposed certain heresies of his time but was himself reputed to be inclined to Millenarianism, *i.e.* expectation of a temporal reign of Christ on earth for a thousand years.   St Victorinus is believed to have died a martyr in the persecution under Diocletian.   He was at one time supposed to have been the first bishop of Poitiers, owing to an erroneous latinization of the name of his see.

The *passio* of St. Victorinus having perished, we know little concerning him beyond what can be gleaned from casual references in the writings of St Jerome, Optatus of Milevis and Cassiodorus.   See the *Acta Sanctorum*, November, vol. i.   This Victorinus does not seem to have been commemorated in the *Hieronymianum*, but Florus of Lyons assumed that a St Victor, whose name does occur on November 2, referred to him.   See Quentin, *Martyrologes historiques*, pp. 310 and 380 ; and Bardenhewer, *Geschichte der altkirchlichen Literatur*, 2nd ed., vol. ii, pp. 657–663.

ST MARCIAN   (*c.* A.D. 387)

The city of Cyrrhus in Syria was the birthplace of St Marcian ; his father was of a patrician family.   Marcian himself left his friends and country and, that he might not do things by halves, retired into the desert of Chalcis, between Antioch and the Euphrates.   He chose in it the most remote part and shut himself up in a small enclosure, wherein he built himself a cell so narrow and low that he could neither stand nor lie in it without bending his body.   This solitude was to him a paradise, and his whole employment was to sing psalms, read, pray and work.   Bread was all his food and this in a small quantity ; but he never went a day without taking some, lest he should not have strength to do what God required of him.   The supernatural light which he received in contemplation gave him a wonderful knowledge of the great truths and mysteries of faith ; and notwithstanding his care to live unknown to men, the reputation of his holiness spread abroad and he was prevailed upon to admit two first disciples, Eusebius and Agapitus.   In time St Marcian had a considerable body of followers, over whom he appointed Eusebius abbot.   Once St Flavian, Patriarch of Antioch, and other bishops paid him a visit together, and begged he would give them a spiritual conference according to his custom.   The dignity of this company alarmed Marcian and he stood some time silent.   Being urged to speak, he said, " God speaks to us every day by His creatures and by this universe which we behold.   He speaks to us by His gospel, wherein He teaches us what we ought to do both for ourselves and others.   What more can Marcian say that can be of use ? "

St Marcian wrought several miracles and was greatly humiliated by the reputa-tion of a wonder-worker which consequently attached to him.   He would not listen to requests for any miraculous intercession, and when a certain hermit came on behalf of a man of Beroea to get some oil blessed for his sick daughter, St Marcian refused peremptorily.   But at the same hour the girl recovered.   Marcian lived to a considerable age, and during his last years was troubled by the indecent importunity of those who looked forward to having the custody of his dead body. Several people went so far as to build chapels in different places wherein to bury it, among them being his nephew Alipius.   St Marcian therefore made Eusebius promise to bury him secretly.   This accordingly was done and it was not till fifty years after the saint's death that the place of burial was disclosed, when the relics were solemnly translated and became an object of pilgrimage.

We are entirely indebted to Theodoret's *Religious History* for our knowledge of St Marcian.   The Bollandists have reprinted his Greek text with Latin translations and com-ments in the *Acta Sanctorum*, November, vol. i.

BD THOMAS OF WALDEN   (A.D. 1430)

THIS holy and learned man has enjoyed a certain local *cultus* in the Carmelite Order which has, however, not yet been formally confirmed by the Holy See.   He was an Essex man, born at Saffron Walden about 1375, his family name being Netter. He joined the Carmelites in London, studied at Oxford, where he took his doctorate in theology, and was ordained priest about 1400.   He made a name for himself as a professor, and in 1409 was sent to the Council of Pisa, where he is said to have supported the election of Pope Alexander V.   On his return to England Friar Thomas entered whole-heartedly into the opposition to the Lollards and other followers of the errors of John Wyclif, and he is regarded as the most able of the controversialists against them and their brethren on the continent—" never was there such a *netter* of heretics ".   He took part in the trials of their leaders, notably Sir John Oldcastle, and his chief writings were directed against their errors, notably his *Doctrinale fidei*.   At this time the Carmelites were popular among the nobility as confessors, and Thomas was appointed to that office for King Henry V, being at the same time prior provincial of his order in England, though probably not yet forty years old. He was among the English representatives at the Council of Constance, which condemned the teachings of Wyclif and Hus, and immediately after was a member of an embassy to Poland on behalf of the pope and the emperor. He is said to have established friaries of his order in Lithuania and Prussia.

Friar Thomas was with Henry V in France in 1422, and the king died in his arms at Vincennes. The guardians of the infant Henry VI later appointed Thomas to be his tutor, so that in some degree he may have been responsible for that king's subsequent holiness. Though Thomas was engaged so much in conflict with stubborn and sometimes violent heretics, he was himself of a kindly disposition and affectionate in his relations with others. He went to France with the boy king in 1430, and died at Rouen on November 2, leaving a reputation of holiness which was confirmed by miracles at his tomb. Friar Thomas's numerous written works, which received the praise of Pope Martin V, earned for him the title of *Doctor praestantissimus*, "the Pre-eminent Teacher", and *Doctor authenticus*, "the Authoritative Teacher". His treatise *De sacramentalibus* includes a discussion of canonization which is of much interest in the history of the subject.

Thomas Netter is not included by the Bollandists even among the *praetermissi* on this day. Neither is he mentioned in Stanton's *Menology*, or in the martyrologies of Whitford or Wilson. The sources available have been indicated by B. Zimmerman in his *Monumenta historica Carmelitana* (1907), pp. 442–482 ; and also by the same learned writer in the *Catholic Encyclopedia*, vol. x, pp. 764–765. *Cf.* R. L. Hine, *History of Hitchin* (1927), vol. i, pp. 133–138 ; Netter was a young friar at Hitchin.

BD JOHN BODEY, Martyr   (A.D. 1583)

JOHN BODEY was born at Wells in 1549, the son of a merchant ; he was at school at Winchester and then went to New College, Oxford, of which he became a fellow at the age of nineteen. In 1576 he was deprived with seven other fellows, by the bishop of Winchester, and in the following year went over to Douay to read law. On his return to England he probably married ; Bd William Hart, of Wells, in a letter to his mother before his execution in March 1583, mentions that " John Body " is in prison and a little further on asks to be recommended to " Mrs Body and all the rest ". On account of his zeal for the faith, John Bodey was imprisoned at Winchester in 1580 and brought up at the spring assizes of 1583, with Bd John Slade, charged with denying the royal supremacy. There was a retrial at Andover in August, but conviction and sentence were repeated. On September 16 he wrote to Dr Humphrey Ely expressing the firmness of himself and his fellow prisoner and asking " the good prayers of you all for our strength, our joy, and our perseverance unto the end ". He suffered at Andover on November 2, professing his innocence of all treason. It is said that his mother celebrated the glory of her son's martyrdom by giving a dinner to their friends.

Apart from Challoner's MMP., fuller details concerning the history of Bd John Bodey were first published by J. H. Pollen in his *Acts of English Martyrs* (1891), pp. 49–65, and in the *Publications* of the Catholic Record Society, vol. v, pp. 39–50. See also Burton and Pollen, LEM., vol. i, pp. 8–21.

3 : ST WINIFRED, OR GWENFREWI, Virgin and Martyr   (*c*. A.D. 650)

WINIFRED * was and is venerated outside her own country more than any other of the numerous Welsh saints, but we have no written record of the traditions concerning her until some five hundred years after her death.   These legends are set out by Alban Butler as follows :

Her father was a wealthy man of Tegeingl in Flintshire, and her mother a sister of St Beuno, and this saint came to settle for a time near his relatives.   Winifred eagerly listened to his teaching and was deeply affected with the great truths which God addressed to her by his mouth.   We are informed that young Caradog, a chieftain from Hawarden, had fallen in love with her, and finding it impossible to extort her consent to gratify his desires, in his rage he one day pursued her and cut off her head as she was flying from him to take refuge in the church which St Beuno had built.   Robert of Shrewsbury's life of the saint tells us that Caradog was swallowed up by the earth upon the spot ; that in the place where Winifred's head fell the stream which is seen there sprang up, with pebbles and parts of the rock in the bottom stained with red streaks, and with moss growing on the sides which has a fragrant smell ; and that the maiden was raised to life by the prayers of St Beuno, who set the severed head upon the shoulders, where it regrew at once, showing only a scar.   This beheading of St Winifred took place and was commemorated on June 22, and on account of it she was regarded as a martyr.   Soon after St Beuno went to found his church at Clynnog Fawr in Arfon, and some time after his departure or death Winifred also left home and entered the nunnery of Gwytherin in Denbighshire.   A holy abbot called Eleri governed a double monastery there, and on the death of the abbess Tenoi, St Winifred was chosen to succeed her.   Here she died and was buried by St Eleri fifteen years after her miraculous resuscitation.   Her relics remained enshrined at Gwytherin until 1138, when they were translated with much pomp to the Benedictine abbey of Shrewsbury. The life of the saint by Robert, prior of that house, was written just after this event.   In 1398 her feast was ordered to be kept throughout the province of Canterbury.

Though those have gone too far who assert that St Winifred never existed at all, it must be admitted that all our information about her is far too late to enable any certainties to be established, as Father De Smedt points out in his examination of the case.   But there are subsequent events connected with her name that can be more easily checked.   The miraculous spring above referred to (a commonplace in Celtic and other ancient legends) has given its name to the place called in English Holywell and in Welsh Tre Ffynnon (Welltown).   The writers of both the medieval lives speak of the miracles associated with the relics and sanctuaries of St Winifred, and Alban Butler gives particulars of five individual cures at Holywell in the seventeenth century (two at least in favour of Protestants), selected from several detailed, with certain evidence, by Father Philip Metcalf, s.j., in his book based on Prior Robert's Life, published in 1712.   It would seem that pilgrimages and cures have taken place at St Winifred's Well for a thousand years and more almost without interruption, and references to them in public and private records

---

* In Welsh *Gwenfrewi* ; the two names are unconnected philologically.

are frequent.   On the feast of the saint in 1629, for example, in the midst of the penal times, over 14,000 people and 150 priests were estimated to have been present, and Dr Johnson saw people bathing there on August 3, 1774.   At Holywell the faith has never died out, and early in the penal times it became a centre for Jesuit missionaries, who handed the parish over to the diocesan clergy in 1930.   The Catholic authorities hold the well on lease from the town of Holywell ; the buildings which enclose it were built by Margaret, Countess of Richmond and Derby, mother of King Henry VII, and others of the Welsh nobility.   When the Jesuits became guardians of this ancient sanctuary, Catholics were encouraged to resort thereto in yet greater numbers (especially from Lancashire), and cases of healing, some of them *prima facie* of a miraculous nature, take place in the waters of the well up to our own day.   Alban Butler justly remarks that " If these authors [of the Lives of St Winifred] were by some of their guides led into any mistakes in any of the circumstances they relate, neither the sanctity of the martyr nor the devotion of the place can be hereby made liable to censure " ; and after quoting the recommendation by one Dr Linden of St Winifred's Well as a natural cold bath, " the source of innumerable authentic cures ", he adds, " Nevertheless, in the use of natural remedies we ought by prayer always to have recourse to God, the almighty physician.   And it is undoubted that God is pleased often to display also a miraculous power in certain places of public devotion."

The feast of St Winifred is observed in the dioceses of Menevia and Shrewsbury, and she is named, as a virgin-martyr in England, in the Roman Martyrology ; she is one of the few Welsh saints so honoured (Asaph, Samson, Maglorius, but not David, are the others).   Owing to mining operations in the neighbourhood of Holywell, the spring which, as the poet Michael Drayton and others attest, had been celebrated for centuries as conspicuous among the natural wonders of Great Britain, ran dry in the year 1917.   An arrangement, however, has since been made by which a portion of the water from the original subterranean reservoir now again flows into the well.   The danger that the water might be drained away had for some time been foreseen, and, at the instance of Lady Mostyn of Talacre and others, restrictions had been placed by Parliament in 1904 upon the tunnelling projected by the mining engineers ; but the limitations proved insufficient.

Father De Smedt, in the first November volume of the *Acta Sanctorum*, has devoted sixty-seven folio pages to an account of St Winifred, her well and her miracles.   In this the Latin life by pseudo-Elerius, as well as that by Robert of Shrewsbury, are critically edited from the surviving manuscript sources.   The text of the *vita prima*, from Cotton MS. Claudius A. v, may also be found, with a translation, in A. W. Wade-Evans, *Vitae sanctorum Britanniae* (1944).   The Life of St Winifred written by Father Philip Metcalf in 1712 was reprinted, with an introduction and notes by Father Thurston, in 1917.   An earlier English life had been printed by Caxton about 1485, and there was also a translation from the Latin by Father Falconer in 1635.   Metcalf's little book excited more attention because it was rather violently assailed, the year after it appeared, by Wm. Fleetwood, Bishop of St Asaph.   On later developments of interest in St Winifred and her well see *The Month* (November 1893, pp. 421–437 ; February 1895, pp. 153–182 ; and July 1916, pp. 38–51).   An interesting collection of " miracles " recorded at Holywell in the seventeenth century has been printed in the *Analecta Bollandiana*, vol. vi (1887), pp. 305–352.   It is curious to note that two of the sufferers who were healed had met with accidents in playing football.   See also LBS., vol. iii, pp. 185–196 ; and on Welsh devotion to St Winifred as manifested in native sources, consult G. Hartwell-Jones, *Celtic Britain and the Pilgrim Movement*, pp. 19–21 and 399–409.

ST RUMWALD (Seventh Century ?)

Alban Butler devotes a few lines to the birth, death and burial of St Rumwald, without adverting to the legend that makes his story an English hagiological curiosity. He is said to have belonged to the royal house of Northumbria, generally as a son of King Alchfrid and St Cyneburga. He was born at King's Sutton, six miles from Brackley in Northamptonshire, and was baptized by a bishop called Widerin. Whereupon, says the legend, the baby pronounced his own profession of faith in a clear voice, and died on the third day after his birth after addressing a sermon to his parents. He was buried at King's Sutton and in consequence of the prodigy attributed to him a *cultus* sprang up locally. His relics were translated a few months after his death to Brackley and two years later to Buckingham. The feast of St Rumwald was formerly observed at these two places, on August 28, and in the hamlet of Astrop there is a well bearing his name : " St Rumoaldes Welle, wher they say that, within a fewe dayes of his birth, he prechid ", says Leland. November 3 is alleged to be the date of St Rumwald's death and August 28 of his translation to Brackley.

All the available materials which bear upon this childish story have been gathered up in the *Acta Sanctorum*, November, vol. i. It seems that John of Tynemouth and Capgrave have only reproduced a legend of which the earliest text is found in an eleventh-century manuscript at Corpus, Cambridge. St Rumwald is entered under November 2 in the calendar of the *Bosworth Psalter*, dating from about the year 1000, but few, if any, other calendars contain any mention of him, and his story seems to have been practically unknown to the rest of Europe outside England. For the so-called *rumbal* feast of the Folkestone fishermen, see the *Victoria County History of Kent*, vol. iii (1932), p. 428.

ST HUBERT, Bishop of Liège (A.D. 727)

" God called St Hubert from a worldly life to his service in an extraordinary manner ; though the circumstances of this event are so obscured by popular inconsistent relations that we have no authentic account of his actions before he was engaged in the service of the church under the discipline of St Lambert, Bishop of Maestricht ". The " extraordinary manner " referred to in Alban Butler's commendably guarded statement is related to have been as follows : Hubert was very fond of hunting and one Good Friday went out after a stag when everybody else was going to church. In a clearing of the wood the beast turned, displaying a crucifix between its horns. Hubert stopped in astonishment, and a voice came from the stag, saying, " Unless you turn to the Lord, Hubert, you shall fall into Hell ". He cast himself on his knees, asking what he should do, and the voice told him to seek out Lambert, the bishop of Maestricht, who would guide him. This, of course, is the same as the legend of the conversion of St Eustace (September 20).

However the retirement of Hubert from the world came about, he entered the service of St Lambert and was ordained priest. When the bishop was murdered at Liège about the year 705 Hubert was selected to govern the see in his place. Some years later he translated Lambert's bones from Maestricht to Liège, then only a village upon the banks of the Meuse, which from this grew into a flourishing city. St Hubert placed the relics of the martyr in a church which he built upon the spot where he had suffered and made it his cathedral, removing thither the episcopal see from Maestricht. Hence St Lambert is honoured at Liège as principal patron of the diocese and St Hubert as founder of the city and church, and its first bishop.

In those days the forest of Ardenne stretched from the Meuse to the Rhine and in several parts the gospel of Christ had not yet taken root. St Hubert penetrated into the most remote and barbarous places of this country and abolished the worship of idols ; and as he performed the office of the apostles, God bestowed on him a like gift of miracles. Amongst others, the author of his life relates as an eye-witness that on the rogation-days the holy bishop went out of Maestricht in procession through the fields and villages, with his clergy and people according to custom, following the standard of the cross and the relics of the saints, and singing the litany. This procession was disturbed by a woman possessed by an evil spirit ; but St Hubert silenced her and restored her to her health by signing her with the cross. Before his death he is said to have been warned of it in a vision and given as it were a sight of the place prepared for him in glory. Twelve months later he went into Brabant to consecrate a new church. He was taken ill immediately after at Tervueren, near Brussels. On the sixth day of his sickness he quietly died, on May 30, in 727. His body was conveyed to Liège and laid in the church of St Peter. It was translated in 825 to the abbey of Andain, since called Saint-Hubert, in Ardenne, on the frontiers of the duchy of Luxemburg. November 3, the date of St Hubert's feast, is probably the day of the enshrining of his relics at Liège sixteen years after his death. St Hubert is, with St Eustace, patron saint of hunting-men, and is invoked against hydrophobia.

St Hubert was formerly, and perhaps is still, greatly venerated by the people of Belgium. It is therefore not altogether surprising that Fr Charles De Smedt, writing in 1887, devoted 171 pages of the *Acta Sanctorum* (November, vol. i) to do him honour. But the one short primitive memoir by a contemporary tells us nothing of his origin, of his alleged time at the court of Austrasia, or of his wife ; and the " son ", Floribert, who became bishop, seems to have been his son only in a spiritual sense. It is clearly manifest from the succession of lives printed by Father De Smedt, and from his introduction, that the details of St Hubert's early career and conversion were not heard of before the fourteenth century. But the story of the stag and the other miracles attributed to the saint made his cult popular far beyond the confines of the Netherlands. Two orders of chivalry, one in Lorraine and one in Bavaria, were founded under his patronage, and there is a considerable literature, dealing especially with his relics and the folk-lore aspects of the case. On this last subject see Bächtold-Stäubli, *Handwörterbuch des deutschen Aberglaubens*, vol. iv, pp. 425–434 ; E. Van Heurck, *Saint Hubert et son culte en Belgique* (1925) ; and L. Huyghebaert, *Sint Hubertus, patroon van de jagers . . .* (1949). Consult also A. Poncelet in the *Revue Charlemagne*, vol. i (1911), pp. 129–145 ; the *Analecta Bollandiana*, vol. xlv (1927), pp. 84–92 and 345–362 ; H. Leclercq, in DAC., vol. ix (1930), cc. 630–631 and 655–656. A useful handbook is that of Dom Réjalot, *Le culte et les reliques de S. Hubert* (1928). The best work from an historical point of view is by F. Baix in *La Terre Wallonne*, vol. xvi (1927), *et seq.;* see also " Une relation inédite de la conversion de S. Hubert ", ed. M. Coens, in *Analecta Bollandiana*, vol. xlv (1927), pp. 84–92.

ST PIRMINUS, Bishop   (A.D. 753)

THE early evangelization of what was formerly the grand-duchy of Baden was principally the work of several monasteries, and St Pirminus was a prominent figure among their founders. He probably came from southern Gaul or Spain, a refugee from the Moors, and he rebuilt the abbey of Dissentis in the Grisons, it having been destroyed by the Avars. But he is best known as the first abbot of Reichenau, on an island in Lake Constance, which he founded—the oldest Benedictine house on German soil, it is said—in 724 ; Reichenau for a time was a rival of Saint Gall in influence.   But for political reasons the founder was subsequently exiled and went to Alsace, where he founded the monastery of Murbach, between Trier and Metz.   He also founded the Benedictine house at Amorbach in Lower Franconia, and to him is attributed a summary manual of popular instruction, known as the *Dicta Pirmini* or *Scarapsus*, which was very widely circulated in Carolingian times.   St Pirminus was a regionary bishop, but never bishop of Meaux, as stated in the Roman Martyrology.   He died in 753.

There is a Latin Life of Pirminus, written in the ninth century, which has been edited from a number of early manuscript copies both in MGH., *Scriptores*, vol. xv, and in the *Acta Sanctorum*, November, vol. ii.   Though very short and jejune, this memoir, written by an unknown monk of Hornbach, was the principal source of a later more diffuse biography and of a metrical life, both of which with a full introduction are also printed in the *Acta Sanctorum*.   See further E. Egli, *Kirchengeschichte Schweiz* (1893), pp. 72–82 ; J. Clauss, *Die Heiligen des Elsass* (1935), pp. 246–247 ; G. Jecker in *Die Kultur der Abtei Reichenau*, vol. i (1925), pp. 19–36, and his *Die Heimat des hl. Pirmin* (1927).

ST AMICUS   (*c.* A.D. 1045)

HE came of a good family of the neighbourhood of Camerino, and was a secular priest in that town.   Then he became a hermit and afterwards a monk, his example inducing, it is said, his father and mother, brothers and nephews also to embrace the religious life.   But St Amicus found the discipline of his monastery insufficiently austere, and he again became a solitary, this time in the Abruzzi.   He lived here completely alone for three years, when disciples began to gather round him.   On one occasion he miraculously relieved a famine.   The last years of his life were passed at the monastery of Fonteavellana, recently founded by St Dominic of Sora, where he died, it is said at the age of 120 years.   He is not the same person as the monk Amicus of whom St Peter Damian writes in one of his letters.

Two medieval Latin lives of St Amicus are printed in the *Acta Sanctorum*, November, vol. ii, one of which was seemingly written by a contemporary.   The contents, however, are mainly taken up with the saint's miracles.

ST MALACHY, ARCHBISHOP OF ARMAGH   (A.D. 1148)

DURING the ninth century Ireland began to feel the effects which had followed invasion in other countries.   It was infested in its turn by heathen barbarians who, under the general name of Ostmen, ravaged the maritime districts, the Danes in particular making permanent settlements at Dublin and elsewhere.   Wherever their power prevailed they massacred, demolished monasteries and burned their libraries.   In these confusions the civil power was weakened ; local kings contending with a foreign enemy and among themselves lost much of their authority. Through long and unavoidable intercourse between the natives and the oppressors of religion and law, relaxation of religion and morals gradually took place ; and Ireland, though doubtless not sunk in iniquity to the degree which English and other foreign churchmen (including St Bernard) supposed, had definitely become a very distressful country by the time of the civil war which succeeded the final defeat of the Danes at Clontarf in 1014.

It was in this state of the nation that was born, in 1095, Mael Maedoc Ua Morgair, whose name is anglicized as Malachy O'More.   The boy was brought up at Armagh, where his father taught in the school.   Throughout his school-days

Malachy was quiet and religious, and after the death of his parents he put himself under a hermit, Eimar.   St Celsus (Cellach), Archbishop of Armagh, judged him worthy of holy orders and obliged him to receive the priesthood when he was twenty-five.   At the same time the archbishop commissioned him to preach the word of God to the people and to extirpate evil customs, which were many and grievous in that church.   It was a case of " setting fire to brambles and thorns and laying the axe to the root of worthless trees ", says St Bernard in his life of the saint, and great was the zeal with which St Malachy discharged this commission. But fearing lest he was not sufficiently instructed in the canons of the Church to carry on a thorough reformation of discipline and worship, he went to St Malchus, Bishop of Lismore, who had been educated in England, at Winchester, and was known for his learning and sanctity.   Malachy was courteously received by this good old man and diligently instructed by him in all things belonging to the divine service and to the care of souls, and at the same time he employed his ministry in that church.

The great abbey of Bangor in county Down lay at that time desolate, held with its revenues by an uncle of St Malachy as lay-abbot and *coarb* of St Comgall.   This uncle in 1123 resigned it to his nephew that he might restore and settle it in regular observance.   But the lands of the abbey St Malachy resigned to another, in spite of protests.   St Bernard praises his spirit of poverty herein shown, but observes that he " carried his disinterestedness or spirit of holy poverty too far, as subsequent events proved ".   With ten members of Eimar's community Malachy rebuilt the house, of wood in the Irish manner, and governed it for a year ; " a living rule and a bright mirror, or as it were a book laid open, in which all might learn the true precepts of the religious life ".   Several miraculous cures, some of which St Bernard recounts, added to his reputation.   St Malachy in his thirtieth year was chosen bishop of Connor, where he found that his flock were Christians in not much more than name (they had been right in the line of the Danish raids).   He spared no pains to turn these wolves into sheep.   With his monks he preached with an apostolic vigour, mingling sweetness with a wholesome severity ; and when the people would not come to church to hear him, he sought them in the fields and in their houses.   Some of the most savage hearts were softened into humanity and a sense of religion ; the saint restored the frequent use of the sacraments, filled the diocese with zealous pastors, and settled the regular celebration of the canonical hours, which since the Danish invasion had been omitted even in cities, in which it was of service to him that from his youth he had applied himself to the study of church music.   But in 1127 a chief from the north swept over Antrim and Down, driving the community from Bangor, where the bishop still lived.   So St Malachy with some of his monks withdrew first to Lismore and then to Iveragh in Kerry, and there settled down again to their monastic life.

In 1129 St Celsus of Armagh died.   The metropolitan see had been hereditary in his family for generations, and to break so bad a custom he ordained on his death-bed that he should be succeeded by Malachy of Connor, sending him his pastoral staff.   But the kinsmen of Celsus proceeded to install his cousin Murtagh and for three years Malachy refused to try and occupy the see.   His objections were then overruled by St Malchus, by the papal legate, Gilbert of Limerick, and others, and protesting that when he had restored order he would at once resign, he went from Iveragh to Armagh.   So far as he could he took over the government of the diocese, but he would not enter his city and cathedral lest he should cause disorder and bloodshed by so doing.   Murtagh died in 1134, after naming Niall, brother of St Celsus, to succeed him.   Both sides were backed by armed force, and Malachy's determined to see him enthroned in his metropolitan church.   A gathering held for this purpose was surprised by a band of Niall's supporters, but they were scattered by a thunderstorm so violent that twelve of his men were killed by lightning.   But though he took possession of his see, St Malachy could still not rule it in peace, for Niall when he had to leave Armagh carried with him two relics held in great veneration ; the common people believed that he was true archbishop who had them in his possession.   These were a book (probably the " Book of Armagh ") and a crozier, called the Staff of Jesus, both supposed to have belonged to St Patrick.   Therefore some still adhered to him, and his kindred violently persecuted Malachy.   One of the chief among them invited him to a conference, with a design to murder him.   The saint, against the advice of his friends, went thither, offering himself to martyrdom for the sake of peace ; but his courage and calm dignity disarmed his enemies, and a peace was concluded.   Nevertheless it continued to be necessary for St Malachy to have an armed bodyguard, until he recovered the Staff and the Book and was acknowledged as archbishop by all. Having broken the tradition of hereditary succession to the see and restored discipline and peace, he insisted upon resigning the archiepiscopal dignity, and ordained Gelasius (Gilla), the abbot of Derry, in his place.   He then returned to his former see in 1137.

Here Malachy divided the diocese, consecrated another bishop for Connor, and reserved to himself that of Down.   Either at Downpatrick or, more probably, on the ruins of the Bangor monastery he established a community of regular canons, with whom he lived as much as the external duties of his charge would permit him. Two years later, to obtain the confirmation of many things which he had done, he undertook a journey to Rome.   One of his motives was to procure the *pallium* for the two archbishops : namely, for Armagh and for another metropolitical see which St Celsus had settled at Cashel.   St Malachy crossed to Scotland, made his way to York, where he met St Waltheof of Kirkham (who gave him a horse), then came into France and by way of Burgundy reached the abbey of Clairvaux.   Here he met St Bernard, who became his devoted friend and admirer and afterwards wrote his life.   Malachy was so edified with the spirit which he discovered in the Cistercian monks that he desired to join them in their penance and contemplation and to end his days in their company.   At Ivrea in Piedmont he restored to health the child of his host, who was at the point of death.   Pope Innocent II would not hear of his resigning his see.   He confirmed all Malachy had done in Ireland, made him his legate there, and promised the *pallia* if they were applied for in solemn form. On his way home he called again at Clairvaux, where, says St Bernard, " he gave us his blessing a second time ".   Not being able to remain himself with those servants of God, he left there four of his companions who, taking the Cistercian habit, came back to Ireland in 1142 and instituted the abbey of Mellifont of that order, the parent of many others.   St Malachy went home through Scotland, where King David entreated him to heal his son Henry, who lay dangerously ill. The saint said to the sick prince, " Be of good courage ; you will not die this time ". Then he sprinkled him with holy water, and the next day Henry was perfectly recovered.

At a great synod of bishops and other clergy held on Inishpatrick, off Skerries, in 1148, it was resolved to make formal application for *pallia* for the two metropolitans, and St Malachy himself set off to find Pope Eugenius III, who was then in France. He was delayed by the political suspicions of King Stephen in England, and when he reached France the pope had returned to Rome. So he turned aside to visit Clairvaux, where he was greeted with joy by St Bernard and his monks. Having celebrated Mass on the feast of St Luke, he was seized with a fever and took to his bed. The monks were active in waiting on him ; but he assured them that all the pains they took were to no purpose, because he would not recover. He insisted that he should go downstairs into the church that he might there receive the last sacraments. He begged that all would continue their prayers for him after his death, promising to remember them before God, and he commended also to their prayers all the souls which had been committed to his charge ; then, on All Souls' day, in the year 1148, he died in St Bernard's arms. He was buried at Clairvaux. St Bernard, in his second discourse on this saint, says to his monks, " May he protect us by his merits, whom he has instructed by his example and confirmed by his miracles " ; and in the requiem Mass at his funeral he boldly sang the post-communion prayer from the Mass of a confessor-bishop. This " canonization by a saint of a saint " was confirmed by Pope Clement III in 1190, the first papal canonization of an Irishman. His feast is kept by the Cistercians, the Canons Regular of the Lateran, and throughout Ireland ; St Malachy did for the unification of the Church in his own land something of what St Theodore did for England 500 years earlier.

An account of St Malachy would not be complete without a reference to the so-called prophecies about the popes, attributed to him. They consist of the attribution of certain conditions and characteristics to the popes, from the time of Celestine II (1143–44) until the end of the world under " Peter the Roman ", under the form of symbolical titles or mottoes. They were first heard of, and given to the world by Dom Arnold de Wyon, o.s.b., in 1595, who attributed them to St Malachy but did not say on what grounds or even where they had been found. A Jesuit in the seventeenth century maintained they had been forged by a supporter of Cardinal Simoncelli during the conclave of 1590, but in 1871 Abbé Cucherat wrote a book in which he said that they had been revealed to St Malachy at Rome, who had communicated them in writing to Pope Innocent II, and they had lain forgotten in the papal archives for 450 years till they were found by Dom de Wyon. There can be no doubt that these " prophecies " are in themselves spurious, and had nothing to do with St Malachy. Even a cursory examination shows that the mottoes for the popes up to Gregory XIV (1590) are precise in wording and unmistakably " fulfilled ", often by reference to their Italian family names ; while for the succeeding popes they are vague and general, and cannot always be made to fit even by ingenuity and distortion of words. The motto corresponding to Pope Pius XII is *Pastor angelicus*, " angelic shepherd ", which is sufficiently general; but St Pius V was a " woodland angel " and Benedict XIV a " rustic animal ".

Apart from the panegyrical and perhaps at times rather misleading life written by St Bernard—a critical text is printed in the *Acta Sanctorum*, November, vol. ii—not much information regarding Malachy is obtainable from other sources. There are, however, some letters of St Bernard addressed to him, others describing his death, and two sermons of the same saint. An excellent translation of the life, with valuable notes, was published by the Anglican dean of St Patrick's, Dublin, H. J. Lawlor, in 1920 ; J. F. Kenney in his *Sources for the Early History of Ireland* describes this book as probably the best study of the organization of the early church in that country. See also the lives of St Malachy by

O'Hanlon (1854), O'Laverty (1899), A. J. Luddy (1930) and J. O'Boyle (1931), as well as L. Gougaud, *Christianity in Celtic Lands*, pp. 401–408. On the alleged prophetic pope-mottoes, now completely discredited, see Vacandard in the *Revue apologétique* (1922), pp. 657–671, and Thurston, *The War and the Prophets* (1915), pp. 120–161. Other spurious prophecies have also been fathered upon St Malachy; see in particular P. Grosjean in the *Analecta Bollandiana*, vol. li (1933), pp. 318–324, and vol. liv (1936), pp. 254–257. The best work on St Malachy is Fr A. Gwynn's study in the *Irish Ecclesiastical Record*, 5th series, vol. lxx (1948), pp. 961–978, and following issues.

BD ALPAIS, Virgin   (A.D. 1211)

Alpais was a peasant-girl, born about 1150 at Cudot, now in the diocese of Orleans. She worked in the fields, until she was stricken by a disease, which may have been leprosy. Her biographer, a Cistercian monk of Les Echarlis, who knew her personally, avers that she was perfectly cured during a vision of our Lady which was granted her. But Alpais lost the use of her limbs and was confined helpless to her bed, though otherwise perfectly well. Nothing in the way of food or drink, except the Blessed Sacrament, passed her lips for a long period. When this was brought to the notice of Archbishop William of Sens, he appointed a commission which examined and confirmed the truth of this fast. By his order a church was built adjoining the lodging of Bd Alpais at Cudot, in order that by means of a window she could assist at the religious offices celebrated by a community of canons regular therein. The holiness of the maiden and her reputation for miracles and ecstatic states made it a place of pilgrimage, and prelates and nobles came from all parts to see her. Queen Adela, wife of Louis VII of France, in 1180 made a benefaction to the canons " for love of Alpais ". The *cultus* rendered to her from the time of her death in 1211 was confirmed in 1874.

What lends great interest to the account preserved of this maiden is the fact that it was written, while she was yet living, by one who knew her well, and that it finds confirmation in contemporary chronicles and in some still existing public records. The text of the biography is printed in the *Acta Sanctorum* (November, vol. ii) from a collation of four manuscripts, and the editor has cited in full the passages referring to Bd Alpais which occur in the chronicles of Robert of Auxerre and Ralph Coggeshall. Alpais seems to be the earliest person of whom it is recorded on reliable evidence that she lived for years upon the Blessed Eucharist alone. A careful and sober study was written by L. H. Tridon, *La vie merveilleuse de Ste Alpais de Cudot* (1886). See also the *Analecta Juris Pontificii* for 1874, pp. 1029–1076, and two works by M. Blanchon (1893 and 1896).

BD IDA OF TOGGENBURG, Matron   (A.D. 1226)

The fictitious romance of Bd Ida is a story of innocence maligned and patiently suffering undeserved punishment. She is presented as the childless wife of a Count Henry of Toggenburg (who is unknown to history), a man of violent temper whose anger and impatience made him as much feared and disliked as his gentle wife was loved. There was in his household an Italian named Dominic who shared the general admiration for Countess Ida, but did not confine it within the limits of virtue, and on one occasion he waylaid her as she was passing through a wood. She cried for help, and was delivered from Dominic's attentions by a man-servant, Cuno, who heard her call. She bound him to silence about the incident, out of kindness to the Italian, but Dominic was furious at his disappointment and revengefully hinted to Count Henry that all was not as it should be between his wife and Cuno. Henry kept his eyes open and said nothing. It so happened that Ida lost one of her rings, which was picked up and carried off by a jackdaw, and this ring was found in its nest by Cuno when he was catching young birds. Not knowing whose it was, he slipped it on his little finger and returned to the castle. Count Henry saw the ring, recognized it as his wife's, and, without waiting for any explanations, had Cuno dragged at the tail of an unbroken horse till life was dashed out of him. The count meanwhile, bursting with fury, ran upstairs to his wife's parlour and, seizing her round the middle, threw her out of the window on to the rocks below. But Ida was not killed. Thick bushes broke her fall, and when she recovered herself she determined to run away under cover of night and hide in the mountains.

When Count Henry cooled down his remorse was as strong as his anger. He looked in vain for his wife's mangled body, and found no comfort in the treacherous Dominic's assurance that Ida was a guilty woman, justly put to death. She in the meantime was living in a cave, furnishing it with moss and branches, and eating wild fruit and nuts. Seventeen years passed thus, when one day one of Henry's foresters stumbled across the cave, saw Ida, and recognized her. When she learned that her husband was so contrite that everybody knew of it, she told the man to go back and tell him where she was. Henry hastened to the place and threw himself at Ida's feet, swearing that he knew her innocent, begging forgiveness, and entreating her to return to him. She assured him of her forgiveness, but she would not come back as his wife, for she had learned to love her solitude. Instead she asked him to build her a cell near the castle chapel, and there she lived until the crowds that flocked to see her drove her to seek refuge in a nunnery at Fischingen. There she died in the year 1226. The popular *cultus* of Bd Ida was confirmed in 1724, and her feast is kept in Switzerland, though nothing is known of her except her existence and veneration.

From the point of view of historical evidence the legend of Bd Ida presents a striking contrast to the Life of Alpais which here precedes it. The story of this Ida as recounted above is pure fiction, an echo of the type of saga of which the best-known example is perhaps the tale of Geneviève de Brabant. The fifteenth-century liturgical material (lessons and hymns), which here does duty for sources, has been printed in the *Acta Sanctorum*, November, vol. ii. The best study of the subject is that of Leo M. Kern in *Thurgauische Beiträge zur vaterlandische Geschichte*, parts 64–65 (1928), pp. 1–136. Reviewing this in the *Analecta Bollandiana*, vol. xlvii (1929), pp. 444–446, Delehaye says that we know only this much— that there was a holy woman named Ida who was buried at Fischingen and whose anniversary was kept there on November 3. See also Fr Delehaye's article on Ida in *Nova et Vetera*, vol. iv (1929), pp. 359–365.

BD SIMON OF RIMINI (A.D. 1319)

SIMON BALLACHI at the age of twenty-seven offered himself to God as a lay-brother in the Dominican friary of Rimini, his native place. Not content with this humble position he still further mortified himself by volunteering to do all the most lowly tasks, and he disciplined his body with an iron chain, offering his pain for the conversion of sinners. He is said to have suffered greatly from diabolical visitations. Simon was principally employed in the garden, but he was also entrusted with the cultivation of young human plants, and would go through the streets with a cross in his hand calling the children to catechism. When he was fifty-seven he was stricken with blindness, and so lived for twelve years, during the last few of which he had to keep to his bed entirely. Bd Simon bore these afflictions with courage and cheerfulness, and was rewarded with the gift of miracles,

so that from the day of his death he was venerated as a saint.   This *cultus* was
confirmed in 1821.

See the *Acta Sanctorum*, November, vol. ii, where a brief account has been compiled
from the very slender materials available ; and *cf.* Procter, *Lives of Dominican Saints*, pp.
306–309.

4 : ST CHARLES BORROMEO, ARCHBISHOP OF MILAN AND CARDINAL (A.D. 1584)

O F the great and holy churchmen who in the troubled days of the sixteenth
century worked for a true and much-needed reformation within the
Church, and sought by the correction of real abuses and evil living to
remove the basic excuses for the destructive and false reformation which was
working such havoc in Europe, none was greater and holier than Cardinal Charles
Borromeo ; with Pope St Pius V, St Philip Neri and St Ignatius Loyola he is one
of the four outstanding public men of the so-called Counter-reformation.   He
was an aristocrat by birth, his father being Count Gilbert Borromeo, himself a man
of talent and sanctity.   His mother, Margaret, was a Medici, of the newly risen
house of that name at Milan, whose younger brother became Pope Pius IV.
Charles, the second of two sons in a family of six, was born in the castle of Arona
on Lake Maggiore on October 2, 1538, and from his earliest years showed himself
to be of a grave and devout disposition.   At the age of twelve he received the
clerical tonsure, and his uncle, Julius Caesar Borromeo, resigned to him the rich
Benedictine abbey of SS. Gratinian and Felinus, at Arona, which had been long
enjoyed by members of his family *in commendam*.   It is said that Charles, young
as he was, reminded his father that the revenue, except what was expended on his
necessary education for the service of the Church, was the patrimony of the poor
and could not be applied to any secular uses.   Charles learned Latin at Milan and
was afterwards sent to the university of Pavia, where he studied under Francis
Alciati, who was later promoted cardinal by St Charles's interest.   On account of
an impediment in his speech and a lack of brilliance he was esteemed slow, yet he
made good progress.   The prudence and strictness of his conduct made him a
model to the youth in the university, who had an evil reputation for vice.   Count
Gilbert made his son a strictly limited allowance from the income of his abbey, and
we learn from his letters that young Charles was continually short of cash, owing
to the necessity in his position of keeping up a household.   It was not till after the
death of both his parents that he took his doctor's degree, in his twenty-second year.
He then returned to Milan, where he soon after received news that his uncle,
Cardinal de Medici, was chosen pope, in 1559, at the conclave held after the death
of Paul IV.

Early in 1560 the new pope created his nephew cardinal-deacon and on February
8 following nominated him administrator of the vacant see of Milan.   Pius IV,
however, detained him at Rome and intrusted him with many duties.   In quick
succession Charles was named legate of Bologna, Romagna and the March of
Ancona, and protector of Portugal, the Low Countries, the Catholic cantons of
Switzerland, and the orders of St Francis, the Carmelites, the Knights of Malta,
and others.   The recipient of all these honours and responsibilities was not yet

twenty-three years old and still in minor orders.   It is marvellous how much business Charles despatched without ever being in a hurry, by dint of unwearied application and being regular and methodical in all that he did.   He found time to look after his family affairs, and took recreation in music and physical exercise. He was a patron of learning, and promoted it among the clergy ; and, among other establishments for this end, having also in view the amenities of the pope's court, he instituted in the Vatican a literary academy of clergy and laymen, some of whose conferences and studies appear among the saint's works as *Noctes Vaticanae*.   He judged it so far necessary to conform to the custom of the renaissance papal court as to have a magnificent palace, to keep a large household and a table suitable to his secular rank, and to give entertainments.   Yet he was in his heart disengaged from these things, mortified in his senses, humble and patient in his conduct. Many are converted to God by adversity ; but St Charles, in the full tide of prosperity, by t: king a near view of its emptiness, became more and more disentangled from it.   He had provided for the diocese of Milan, for its government and the remedying of its disorders, in the best manner he was able, but the command of the pope by which he was obliged to attend in Rome did not make him entirely easy on that head.   It happened that the Venerable Bartholomew de Martyribus, Archbishop of Braga, came to Rome, and to him as to a faithful servant of God St Charles opened his heart.   " You see my position ", he said.   " You know what it is to be a pope's nephew, and a nephew beloved by him ; nor are you ignorant what it is to live in the court of Rome.   The dangers are infinite.   What ought I to do, young as I am, and without experience ?   God has given me ardour for penance ; and I have some thoughts of going into a monastery, to live as if there were only God and myself in the world."   Whereupon Archbishop Bartholomew cleared his doubts, assuring him that he ought not to quit his hold of the plough which God had put into his hands for the service of the Church, but that he ought to contrive means to attend to his own diocese as soon as God should open him a way.   When Borromeo discovered that the archbishop himself was in Rome because he wanted to resign his see he required an explanation of the advice that had been given him, and Bartholomew had to use all his tact.

Pope Pius IV had announced soon after his election his intention of reassembling the council of Trent, which had been suspended in 1552.   St Charles used all his influence and energy to bring this about, amid the most difficult and adverse ecclesiastical and political conditions.   He was successful, and in January 1562 the council was reopened.   But as much work, diplomacy and vigilance were required of Charles during the two years it sat as during the negotiations for its assembly.   Several times it nearly broke up with its work unfinished, but St Charles's never-failing attention and his support of the papal legates kept it together, and in nine sessions and numerous meetings for discussion many of the most important dogmatic and disciplinary decrees of the great reforming council were passed.   To the efforts of St Charles more than of any other single man this result was due ; he was the master-mind and the ruling spirit of the third and last period of the Council of Trent.

During its assembly Count Frederick Borromeo died, so that St Charles found himself the head of this noble family, and in a more disturbing position than ever. Many took it for granted that he would leave the clerical state and marry.   But Charles would have none of it.   He resigned his family position to his uncle Julius and received the priesthood in 1563.   Two months later he was consecrated bishop.

He was not allowed to go to his diocese, and, in addition to his other duties, he had to supervise the drawing-up of the Catechism of the Council of Trent and the reform of liturgical books and church-music ; to his commission we owe the composition of Palestrina's mass called " Papae Marcelli ".   Milan had been without a resident bishop for eighty years, and was in a deplorable state.   St Charles's vicar there had done his best to carry out a programme of reform, assisted by a number of Jesuits specially sent, but he was far from successful and at length St Charles was given permission to go and hold a provincial council and make a visitation.   The pope, before his departure, created him legate *a latere* for all Italy. The saint was received at Milan with the utmost joy, and he preached in his cathedral from the text, " With desire I have desired to eat this pasch with you ". Ten suffragans attended the provincial council, and the excellence of its regulations for the observance of the decrees of the Council of Trent for the discipline and training of the clergy, the celebration of divine service, the administration of the sacraments, the giving of catechism on Sundays, and many other points, caused the pope to write to St Charles a letter of congratulation.   But while discharging legatine duties in Tuscany he was summoned to Rome to assist Pius IV on his death-bed, where St Philip Neri was also present.   The new pope, St Pius V, induced St Charles to stay on at Rome for a time in the same offices which he had discharged under his predecessor.   But Charles saw the opportunity for which he had been waiting, and pressed his return to his people with such zeal that the pope presently dismissed him with his blessing.

St Charles arrived at Milan in April 1566 and went vigorously to work for the reformation of his diocese.   He began by the regulation of his household, and, the episcopal character being a state of perfection, he was most severe towards himself. Yet his austerities were always discreet, lest his strength should fail him for his duties ; it seemed to redouble when extraordinary fatigues presented themselves. He enjoyed a very considerable income from one source and another, but he allotted a large part of it to charity and was uncompromisingly opposed to all ostentation and luxury.   When someone would have had a bed warmed for him, he said with a smile, " The best way not to find a bed cold is to go colder to bed than the bed is ".   Francis Panigarola, Bishop of Asti, said in his funeral oration, " Out of his income he expended nothing for his own use except what was absolutely necessary. When I attended him in making a visitation in the valley of Mesolcina, a very cold place, I found him studying at night in a single tattered old cassock.   I entreated him, if he would not perish with cold, to put on some better garment.   He answered me smiling, ' What if I have no other ?   I am obliged to wear a cardinal's robes in the day ; but this cassock is my own and I have no other, either for winter or summer.' "   When St Charles came first to reside at Milan he sold plate and other effects to the value of thirty thousand crowns, and applied the whole sum for the relief of distressed families.   His almoner was ordered to give the poor two hundred crowns a month, besides whatever extra sums he should call upon the stewards for, which were very many.   His liberality appears too in many monuments, and his help to the English College at Douay was such that Cardinal Allen called St Charles its founder.   He arranged retreats for his clergy and himself went into retreat twice a year, and it was his rule to confess himself every morning before celebrating Mass. His ordinary confessor was Dr Griffith Roberts, of the diocese of Bangor, author of a famous Welsh grammar.   St Charles appointed another Welshman, Dr Owen Lewis (afterwards a bishop in Calabria), to be one of his vicars general, and he always had with him a little picture of St John Fisher.*   He had a great regard for the Church's liturgy, and never said any prayer or carried out any religious rite with haste, however much he was pressed for time or however long the rite continued.

From this spirit of prayer and the love of God which burned within him, his words infused a spiritual joy into others, gained their hearts, and kindled a desire of persevering in virtue and cheerfully suffering all things for its sake.   And in this spirit St Charles, who laboured so strenuously for the sanctification of his own soul, began the reformation of his diocese by the regulation of his own large household :   it consisted of about a hundred persons, the greater part being clergy, who were allowed good salaries and were strictly forbidden to receive presents from anyone. Throughout the diocese religion was little known or understood and religious practices were profaned by gross abuses and disgraced by superstition.   The sacraments were neglected, for many of the clergy scarcely knew how to administer them and were lazy, ignorant and debauched ; monasteries were full of disorder. St Charles, in provincial councils, diocesan synods and by many pastoral instructions, made regulations for the reform both of clergy and people which pastors have ever since regarded as a model and studied to emulate.   He was one of the foremost of the great pastoral theologians who arose in the Church to remedy the disorders engendered by the decay of medieval life and the excesses of Protestant reformers. Partly by tender entreaties and zealous remonstrances and partly by inflexible firmness in the execution of these decrees, without favour, distinction of persons or regard to rank or pretended privileges, the saint in time overcame the obstinate and broke down difficulties which would have daunted the most courageous.   He had even to contend with a handicap to his own preaching.   An impediment in his speech seemed to disqualify him :   this too he overcame by much patience and attention.   " I have often wondered ", says his friend Achille Gagliardi, " how it was that, without any natural eloquence or anything attractive in his manner, he was able to work such changes in the hearts of his hearers.   He spoke but little, gravely, and in a voice barely audible—but his words always had effect."   St Charles directed that children in particular should be properly instructed in Christian doctrine.   Not content with enjoining parish-priests to give public catechism every Sunday and holyday, he established the Confraternity of Christian Doctrine, whose schools are said to have numbered 740, with 3000 catechists and 40,000 pupils.   Thus St Charles was an originator of " Sunday-schools ", two hundred years before Robert Raikes, whose great work for Protestant children has naturally been better known in England.   Among religious congregations St Charles made special use of the Clerks Regular of St Paul (" Barnabites ") whose constitutions he had helped to revise, and he instituted in 1578 the society of secular priests called Oblates of St Ambrose, who voluntarily offer themselves to the bishop, making a simple vow of obedience to him, as ready at his discretion to be employed in any manner whatever for the salvation of souls.†

But the saint's reforms were far from being well received everywhere, and some

---

* Thomas Goldwell, Bishop of Saint Asaph, the last survivor of the old English hierarchy, was also a vicar of St Charles for a while.

† Pope Pius XI was a member of this society, now known as the Oblates of St Ambrose and St Charles.   The Oblates of St Charles in London were founded by H. E. Manning (afterwards cardinal), at the direction of Cardinal Wiseman, on the model of St Charles Borromeo's society.

were carried through only in the face of violent and unscrupulous opposition.* In 1567 he had a contest with the senate. Certain lay persons who lived notoriously evil lives, and could not be reclaimed by remonstrances, were imprisoned by his order. The senate threatened the officers of the archiepiscopal court for this action ; and the matter was referred to the king, Philip II of Spain, and the pope. Meanwhile the episcopal sheriff was seized, beaten and driven from the city, and St Charles, after much deliberation, declared the civil officers concerned excommunicated for having assaulted an officer of the ecclesiastical court. Eventually this conflict of jurisdiction was settled in favour of the archbishop, who had some civil executive authority by ancient right, but the governor of Milan nevertheless issued a decree against it. In the meantime St Charles set out on the visitation of the three Alpine valleys of Levantina, Bregno and La Riviera, which had been as it were abandoned by former archbishops and were full of disorders, the clergy there more corrupt even than the laity. He preached and catechized everywhere, displaced the unworthy clergy, and put in their room others who were capable of restoring the faith and morals of the people and resisting the inroads of Zwinglian Protestantism. But his enemies at Milan were soon at work again. The conduct of some of the canons of the collegiate church of Santa Maria della Scala (which claimed exemption from the jurisdiction of the ordinary) not being conformable to their state, St Charles consulted St Pius V, who answered him that he had a right to make the visitation of this church and to proceed against any of its clergy. The archbishop therefore went to make a canonical visitation, but the church door was shut in his face by the canons, and the cross, which in the tumult he had taken into his own hand, was shot at. The senate took up the cause of these canons, and sent the most virulent charges against the archbishop to Philip of Spain, accusing him of invading the king's rights, this church being under the royal patronage, and the governor of Milan wrote to Pope Pius threatening to banish Cardinal Borromeo as a traitor. At length the king wrote to the governor, ordering him to support the archbishop. The canons persisted for a time in their obstinacy, but eventually submitted.

Before this affair was over the life of St Charles was again, and more seriously, in danger. The religious order called Humiliati having been reduced to a few members, but having many monasteries and great possessions, had submitted to reform at the hands of the archbishop, but the order was thoroughly degenerate and the submission was unwilling and only apparent. They tried every means to prevail upon the pope to annul the regulations which had been made, and when these failed three priors of the order hatched a plot to assassinate St Charles. One of the Humiliati themselves, a priest called Jerome Donati Farina, agreed to do the deed for forty gold pieces, which sum was raised by selling the ornaments from a church. On October 26, 1569, Farina posted himself at the door of the chapel in the archbishop's house, whilst St Charles was at evening prayers with his household. An anthem by Orlando di Lasso was being sung, and at the words " It is time therefore that I return to Him that sent me ", Charles being on his knees before the altar, the assassin discharged a gun at him. Farina made good his escape

* One of the strongly opposed regulations of St Charles was that all his clergy should be clean-shaven. This aroused as much surprise and indignation in sixteenth-century Italy as would a direction in the opposite sense in the United States of America today. If to the archbishop a well-kept beard savoured too much of worldliness, to his opponents a smooth chin was decadent and effeminate.

during the ensuing confusion, and St Charles, imagining himself mortally wounded, commended himself to God.   But it was found that the bullet had only struck his clothes in the back, raising a bruise, and fallen harmlessly to the floor.   After a solemn thanksgiving and procession, he shut himself up for some days in a Carthusian monastery to consecrate his life anew to God.*

St Charles then returned to the three valleys of his diocese in the Alps, and took that opportunity of visiting each of the Catholic cantons, wherein he converted a number of Zwinglians and restored discipline in the monasteries.   The harvest having failed, Milan was afflicted the following year with a great famine.   St Charles by his care and appeals procured supplies for the relief of the poor, and himself fed 3000 people daily for three months.   He had been very unwell for some time and at doctors' orders he modified his way of life, but without getting any relief.   After visiting Rome for the conclave which elected Pope Gregory XIII he returned to his normal habits, and soon recovered his health.   He now again came into collision with the civil power at Milan, where a new governor, Don Luis de Requesens, was trying to curtail the local jurisdiction of the Church and to embroil the archbishop with the king.   St Charles fearlessly excommunicated Requesens, who retorted by patrolling the neighbourhood of the episcopal residence with soldiers and forbidding the meeting of confraternities except in the presence of a civil official.   The governor was eventually removed by King Philip.   But such public triumphs were not the most important part of the " pastoral care " to which the prayer of the office of St Charles alludes as having made him glorious.   Above all it was to form a virtuous and capable clergy that he directed his energies.   When a certain exemplary priest was sick and likely to die, the great concern shown by the archbishop was a subject of comment.   " Ah," he said, " you do not realize the worth of the life of one good priest."   The successful institution of the Oblates of St Ambrose has already been mentioned, and during his episcopate of eighteen years he held five provincial councils and eleven diocesan synods.   He was indefatigable in parochial visitations, and when one of his suffragans said he had nothing to do, wrote out for him a long list of episcopal duties, adding the comment to each one, " Can a bishop ever say that he has nothing to do ? "   The archdiocese of Milan owed three seminaries to the zeal of St Charles, for the requirements of three different classes of clerical student, and everywhere he urged that the Tridentine directions for sacerdotal training should be put into effect.   In 1575 he went to Rome to gain the jubilee indulgence and in the following year published it at Milan. Huge crowds of penitents and others flocked to the city, and they brought with them the plague, which broke out with great virulence.

The governor fled and many of the rest of the nobility left the town.   St Charles gave himself up completely to the care of the stricken.   The number of priests of his own clergy to attend the sick not being sufficient, he assembled the superiors of the religious communities and begged their help.   The effect of this appeal was that a number of religious at once volunteered, and were lodged by Charles in his own house.   He then wrote to the governor, Don Antony de Guzman, upbraiding him for his cowardice, and induced him and other magistrates to return to their posts and try to cope with the disaster.   The hospital of St Gregory was entirely

* The attempt was traced to its true authors, and Farina and two others were, in spite of St Charles's plea for leniency, tortured and executed.   In the following year Pope St Pius V abolished the order of Humiliati entirely.   In its earlier days it had given many holy men to the Church.

inadequate, overflowing with dead, dying, sick and suspects, having nobody to care for them.   The sight of their terrible state reduced St Charles to tears, but he had to send for priests and lay helpers to the Alpine valleys, for at first the Milanese clergy would not go near the place.   With the coming of the plague commerce was at an end and want began.   It is said that food had to be found daily for sixty or seventy thousand persons.   St Charles literally exhausted all his resources in relief and incurred large debts on behalf of the sufferers.   He even made use of the coloured fabrics that hung up from his house to the cathedral during processions, having it made up into clothes for the needy.   Empty houses for the sick were taken outside the walls and temporary shelters built, lay helpers were organized for the clergy, and a score of altars set up in the streets so that the sick could assist at public worship from their windows.   But the archbishop was not content with prayer and penance, organization and distribution ; he personally ministered to the dying, waited on the sick and helped those in want.   The pestilence lasted with varying degrees of intensity from the summer of 1576 until the beginning of 1578.   Even during its continuance the magistrates of Milan tried to make mischief between St Charles and the pope.   It is possible that some of their complaints were not altogether ill-founded, but the matters complained of were ultimately due to their own supineness and inefficiency.   When it was over St Charles wanted to reorganize his cathedral chapter on a basis of common life, and it was the canons' refusal which finally decided him to organize his Oblates.

In the spring of 1580 he entertained at Milan for a week a dozen young Englishmen, who were going on the English mission, and one of them preached before him. This was Bd Ralph Sherwin, who in some eighteen months' time was to give his life for the faith at Tyburn.   In the same way he met his fellow martyr, Bd Edmund Campion, and talked with him.   A little later in the same year St Charles met St Aloysius Gonzaga, then twelve years old, to whom he gave his first communion. At this time he was doing much travelling and the strain of work and worry was beginning to tell on him ; moreover, he curtailed his sleep too much and Pope Gregory personally had to warn him not to overdo his Lenten fasting.   At the end of 1583 he was sent as visitor apostolic to Switzerland, and in the Grisons he had to deal not only with Protestantism but with an outbreak of alleged witchcraft and sorcery.   At Roveredo the parish-priest himself was denounced by his flock as a wizard, and St Charles judged it necessary to degrade him and hand him over to the secular arm.   He did not disdain patiently to discuss points of theology with Protestant peasant-women, and on one occasion refused to leave an ignorant little herd-boy till he had taught him the Lord's Prayer and Hail Mary.   Hearing that Duke Charles of Savoy was fallen sick at Vercelli, he went thither and found him, as was thought, at the last gasp.   But the duke, seeing him come into his room, cried out, " I am cured ".   The saint gave him holy communion the next day, and Charles of Savoy was restored to health, as he was persuaded, by the prayers of St Charles, and after the saint's death sent a silver lamp to be hung up at his tomb.

During 1584 his own health got worse and, after arranging for the establishment of a convalescent home in Milan, St Charles went in October to Monte Varallo to make his annual retreat, having with him Father Adorno, s.j.   He had clearly foretold to several persons that he should not remain long with them, and on the 24th he was taken ill.   On the 29th he started off for Milan, where he arrived on All Souls', having celebrated Mass for the last time on the previous day at his birth-place, Arona.   He went straight to bed and asked for the last sacraments,

" At once ".　He received them from the archpriest of his cathedral ; and with the words *Ecce venio*, " Behold I come ", St Charles quietly died in the first part of the night between the 3rd and 4th of November.　He was only forty-six years old.　Devotion to the dead cardinal spread rapidly, and in 1601 Cardinal Baronius, who called him " a second Ambrose ", sent to the clergy of Milan an order of Clement VIII to change the anniversary mass *de requiem* into a solemn mass of the day ; and St Charles was formally canonized by Paul V in 1610.

The Bollandists have up to the present published no biography of St Charles Borromeo. When in 1894 they issued the second volume of the *Acta Sanctorum* for November, which should have included all the saints honoured on the fourth day of that month, it was seen that the sources for the history of the great archbishop, especially those still unprinted, could not be adequately investigated and utilized without a delay which would have held up indefinitely the further progress of the main work.　It was accordingly decided to send to press vol. ii, part 1, reserving part 2 for an exhaustive treatment of St Charles's life which had been undertaken by Fr F. Van Ortroy.　Unfortunately that very able scholar, though he had collected an immense mass of materials, procrastinated, and eventually died before he had done anything to reduce his notes to order.　See on this the *Analecta Bollandiana*, vol. xxxix (1921), p. 15.　To this same periodical, however, Fr Van Ortroy had contributed many valuable reviews of books bearing on the saint's activities.　He had pointed out, for example (vol. xiv, p. 346), how mistaken was the idea that the young cardinal got himself ordained priest by stealth ; and he had called attention to the fact that the holy archbishop, in his zeal to secure the most apostolic labourers for his own diocese, came from time to time to write rather intemperate letters to the superiors general of religious orders (*ibid.*, vol. xxix, p. 373).　Still more important, perhaps, is the long review of Borromean literature contributed by Fr Van Ortroy to the same periodical, vol. xxxix (1921), pp. 338–345.　It must be said in truth that no quite adequate life of St Charles, based as it needs to be upon the vast materials available in private, diplomatic and ecclesiastical archives, has yet appeared. The saint is known to modern readers principally through the life by Giussano (1610), annotated in the Latin edition of 1751 by Oltrocchi, and that by the Abbé Sylvain, *Histoire de St Charles Borromée* (3 vols., 1884).　An English translation of Giussano appeared also in 1884.　Perhaps the most valuable source of all, as being the work of a friend who knew the saint intimately, was the essay of the Barnabite, Father Bascapè, *De vita et rebus gestis Caroli cardinalis*, first printed in 1592.　But for the last half-century or more a constant succession of historical studies has been appearing, which, while dealing with different phases of the ecclesiastical changes which resulted from the Council of Trent, all throw some measure of light upon the activities and interests of St Charles.　It would be possible to draw up an immensely long list, but only a few can be mentioned here.　Apart from such general works as Pastor's *History of the Popes* and the vast collection of documents begun by Merkle and Ehses to illustrate the proceedings of the Tridentine assembly, may be named Aristide Sala, *Documenti circa la vita e le gesta di San Carlo* (3 vols., 1857–1861) ; the *Acta ecclesiae Mediolanensis*, 4 vols. in folio, edited by Achille Ratti (later Pope Pius XI), 1890 *seq.* ; S. Steinherz, *Nuntiaturberichte aus Deutschland*, vol. i (1897) ; Steffens und Reinhardt, *Nuntiaturberichte aus der Schweiz*, vol. i (1906) ; D. Tamilia, *Monte di Pietà di Roma* (1900) ; the series of essays and documents published in quasi-periodical form from 1908 to 1910 under the title *San Carlo Borromeo nel terzo centenario della canonizazione ;* G. Boffito, *Scrittori Barnabiti . . .*, 3 vols. (1933–1935) ; Levati e Clerici, *Menologia dei Barnabiti*, 8 vols. (1932–1935) ; A. Bernareggi, *Le origini della Congregazione degli Oblati di S. Ambrogio* (1931) ; A. Sara, *Federico Borromeo e i mistici del suo tempo* (1933).　There is a convenient and on the whole reliable sketch, *St Charles Borromée*, by L. Celier in the series " Les Saints ", and a rather fuller Italian life in two volumes by R. Orsenigo : this is perhaps the most satisfactory work now available and was translated into English (1943).　There are also biographies by E. H. Thompson and by M. Yeo (*A Prince of Pastors*, 1938), and an exceptionally full account in French in DHG.　The writings of St Charles were edited by J. A. Sassi in 1747 in five volumes, but much of his vast correspondence was then unknown or inaccessible.　On an accusation of ruthless heresy-hunting levelled against St Charles see *The Tablet*, July 29, 1905 ; and on certain criticisms upon the lack of proper sanitary precautions during the great plague consult the very important study by Fr A. Gemelli in the *Scuola Cattolica* for 1910.

SS. VITALIS AND AGRICOLA, Martyrs   (Date Unknown)

WE are told that in the year 393 it was revealed to Eusebius, Bishop of Bologna, that the bodies of two Christian martyrs, Vitalis and Agricola, rested in the Jewish cemetery of that city.   Their remains were duly found and removed, and St Ambrose of Milan was present on that occasion.   Ambrose refers to the martyrs in a discourse on virginity, bidding his hearers receive with respect the presents of salvation—relics—which were laid under the altar.   This mention by St Ambrose is the sole authority for the passion of SS. Vitalis and Agricola, who were formerly much more celebrated in the West than they are today.

But although nobody had heard of these martyrs before attention was supernaturally drawn to them, accounts of their confession were in due course forthcoming.   It is said by these that Agricola was a resident of Bologna, greatly beloved for his gentleness and virtue by the people amongst whom he lived.   Vitalis was his slave, learned the Christian religion from him, and first received the crown of martyrdom.   He was put to death in the amphitheatre, no part of his body being left unwounded.   His master's execution was deferred out of a cruel compassion, that delay and the sight of the sufferings of his faithful servant might daunt his resolution.   But he was fortified and encouraged by such an example, whereupon the affection of the judges and people was turned to anger.   Agricola was hung on a cross and his body pierced with so many nails that he had more wounds than limbs.

St Gregory of Tours complains that no proper *passio* of these martyrs was to be found in his day.   This omission was supplied at a later period by two fictitious accounts unwarrantably fathered upon St Ambrose.   In the *Acta Sanctorum*, November, vol. ii, are printed both the authentic statement of St Ambrose, with much illustrative matter, as well as the text of the pseudo-Ambrosian " acts ".   On the widespread early *cultus* of these saints, see Delehaye in his *Origines du culte des martyrs*, and in CMH., pp. 623–624.   This last note is attached to November 27, on which day " Agricola and Vitalis ", in that order, appear in the *Hieronymianum*, but the observance of their feast on November 4 at Bologna seems to go back to the eighth century or earlier, as is proved by the ancient calendar described by Dom G. Morin in the *Revue Bénédictine*, vol. xix (1902), p. 355.   Consult further Dom Quentin, *Martyrologes historiques*, pp. 251 and 627.

ST PIERIUS   (*c*. A.D. 310)

AT the time that St Theonas was bishop at Alexandria the priest Pierius was head of the catechetical school there, and was the master of St Pamphilus, a defender of Origen, who was afterwards martyred.   Pierius himself was so distinguished for love of work and learning, and his discourses to the people were so popular and instructive, that he was called the " Younger Origen ".   Both Eusebius and St Jerome praise him, and we know from the last named that he survived the persecution of Diocletian and spent his last years at Rome.   Photius speaks of his temperance and poverty, and the clear, brilliant and spontaneous qualities of his writings.   The Roman Martyrology has a long *elogium* of St Pierius.

All the texts bearing on St Pierius are quoted and fully discussed in the *Acta Sanctorum*, November, vol. ii.   See also L. B. Radford, *Three Teachers of Alexandria* (1908), and DTC., vol. xii, cc. 1744–1746.

SS. JOHN ZEDAZNELI AND HIS COMPANIONS   (*c.* 580)

THOUGH the title Apostle of Iberia (Georgia) is accorded to St Nino (December 15), the evangelization of that country came from more than one direction and over a considerable period of time.   About the middle of the sixth century a band of thirteen Syrian monks came into the Caucasus country, led by John Zedazneli, and made the beginning of that intense monastic life for which the early Christian centuries in Georgia were notable.   One of St John's disciples, St Scio Mghvimeli, is reputed to have had two thousand monks under his direction, and St David Garejeli also had a large community in the mountains above Tiflis, where for a time he had lived as a solitary in a cave.   St Antony the Recluse, said to have been a disciple of the younger St Simeon Stylites, himself became a stylite, living on, or in, a column, while two of the missionaries became bishops.   One of them, St Abibus of Nekressi, was a martyr, being stoned to death by Persians for opposing " fire-worshipping " Mazdaism.   So well did these monks do their work that soon monasteries of native Georgians were founded not only in their own land, but in Palestine, Syria and Sinai, and so far west as Salonika and Crete.   Each of the thirteen is venerated individually as a saint in Georgia, and on this day they have as well a common feast under the name of the " Fathers of the Iberian Church ".

A sufficient account of St John of Zedazen and his companions may be found in M. Tamarati, *L'Église Géorgienne des origines jusqu'à nos jours* (1910), especially pp. 211–220. There is something in the nature of a legendary history of St John incorporated in the Georgian text of the Life of St Scio Mghvimeli, as is pointed out by Fr Peeters in his article " L'Église Géorgienne du Clibanion " in the *Analecta Bollandiana*, vol. xlvi (1928), pp. 254 and 283.   He there calls attention to the anachronisms and inconsistencies which render these records unsatisfactory, besides indicating the printed sources where orientalists may consult the texts.   See further DTC., in the article " Géorgie " (vol. v, especially c. 1255), and Brosset, *Histoire de la Géorgie*, vol. i.

ST CLARUS, MARTYR   (EIGHTH CENTURY ?)

THE name of St Clarus, priest and martyr, was introduced into the Roman Martyrology from that of the French Benedictine Usuard ; in his time (ninth century) St Clarus was greatly honoured in France and his feast is still observed in several French dioceses.   He was said to be an Englishman by birth, a native of Rochester, who crossed over to Normandy and there led a hermit's life, teaching true religion by word and example to those among whom he lived.   Eventually he settled in the Vexin, at Naqueville, near Rouen, and here he had the misfortune to attract the attention of an uncontrolled woman of rank, whose advances he repulsed and hid himself in a neighbouring forest.   The woman in revenge had him ferreted out by two ruffians, who killed him and cut off his head.   St Clarus was among the English saints represented in the wall-paintings in the chapel of the Venerabile at Rome, and he has given his name to Saint-Clair-sur-Epte, near the place of his martyrdom.

At the 8th of this month the Roman Martyrology mentions another ST CLARUS, " whose epitaph St Paulinus wrote ".   He was a priest at Tours, who died a few days before his master, St Martin.

A full account of the rather unsatisfactory sources available for this notice is given in the *Acta Sanctorum*, November, vol. ii.   Apart from the brief mention in Usuard we are in fact thrown back upon a Latin life, hardly longer than would suffice for three breviary lessons, which certainly was not written earlier than the twelfth century. Several suspicious features suggest that it cannot be relied on as a record of historical fact. But there can be no doubt that St Clarus enjoyed a considerable cult.

ST JOANNICIUS (A.D. 846)

THIS saint, by long penance after a dissolute youth, arrived at so high a degree of sanctity as to be ranked by the Greek church amongst the illustrious saints of the monastic order and honoured with the title of " the Great " ; and his name occurs in the Roman Martyrology on this day. He was a native of Bithynia, and when a boy was a swineherd. At the age of nineteen he became a soldier in the guard of Constantine Copronymus ; he was carried away with the torrent of the times, and became a supporter of the persecutors of holy images. By the conversation of a holy monk he was reclaimed from his errors and dissolute ways, and led an exemplary life for six years. At forty he quitted the service, and retired to Mount Olympus in Bithynia, where he was instructed in the rudiments of monastic life till he had learned to read and to recite the psalter by heart, and had exercised himself in all the duties of his new state. Joannicius called this process the " seasoning of his heart ". He afterwards led an eremitical life and became famous for gifts of miracles and prophecy and for his prudence in directing souls. Among his miracles were the release of a number of prisoners taken by the Bulgarians and the freeing of St Daniel of Thasion from an evil spirit.

St Joannicius became a monk at Eraste, near Brusa, and zealously defended orthodoxy against the Emperor Leo V and other iconoclasts, being closely associated with the great confessors St Theodore Studites and St Methodius of Constantinople. On the advice of Joannicius, the last named restrained the over-zealous ones among his followers, who were for treating as invalid the orders of those ordained by iconoclastic bishops. " They are erring brethren ", said the monk, " Treat them as such while they persist in their errors, but when they repent receive them into their proper rank, unless they have been notoriously violent heretics and persecutors ". He was particularly fearless in rebuking the Emperor Theophilus, who had added to the prohibition of sacred images an order that the word " holy " should be erased before the names of saints ; but the prophecy of St Joannicius that Theophilus would eventually restore images to the churches was only fulfilled in the person of his widow, Theodora, who throughout had remained orthodox. Among the monks who were trained by St Joannicius in his old age was St Euthymius the Thessalonian. At length, after having for long been one of the most prominent ascetics and prophetical figures of his age, Joannicius retired to a hermitage, and there died on November 3, 846. He was ninety-two years old and had lived to see the second triumph of orthodoxy over that iconoclast heresy which he had himself once professed and then so vigorously opposed.

The Bollandists in their second volume for November have printed at length two detailed Greek lives of this saint, each with a Latin translation. The authors, Peter and Sabas, were both monks who had lived under the rule of St Joannicius. The life by Peter seems to have been the earlier written, but that by Sabas is better executed and on the whole more complete. On the question of the date of his death see Pargoire in *Échos d'Orient*, vol. iv (1900), pp. 75–80. A short sketch of Joannicius is included in *Verborgene Heilige des griech. Ostens*, by Dom Hermann (1931).

BD EMERIC   (A.D. 1031)

THE ninth centenary of the death of Bd Emeric (Imre) was kept with solemnity in Hungary in 1931, but not many reliable particulars of his short life are available. He was the only son of St Stephen, King of Hungary, born in the year 1007, and was educated by St Gerard Sagredo.   When the Emperor Conrad II planned to disendow the diocese of Bamberg he proposed to give the young prince Emeric an interest in the spoliation, but this St Stephen would not allow.   The authenticity of Stephen's " instructions " to his son is denied, but he was desirous of handing over some of his responsibilities to Emeric (it is not true that he resigned his crown to him) ;   before this could be done Emeric was killed while hunting.   " God loved him, and so He took him away soon ", exclaimed St Stephen when the news was brought to him.   The prince was buried in the church at Szekesfehervar, and many marvels were wrought at his tomb.   The bodies of father and son were " elevated " together in 1083, and he is generally referred to as Saint Emeric, but he is called only *beatus* in the Roman Martyrology.

There is a Latin life which was written by some ecclesiastic whose name is not recorded, but who compiled it when Emeric had been dead for nearly a century.   The text has been critically edited by Father Poncelet in the *Acta Sanctorum*, November, vol. ii.   As a historical document this life is not very reliable, but it may be supplemented by information derived from such sources as the *Annales Hildesheimenses*, the Life of St Stephen, etc.   *Cf.* C. A. Macartney, *The Medieval Hungarian Historians* (1953).

BD FRANCES D'AMBOISE, WIDOW   (A.D. 1485)

IN 1431 John V, Duke of Brittany, arranged a matrimonial alliance between his house and that of Thouars, and Louis d'Amboise sent his four-year-old daughter Frances to be brought up at the ducal court.   When she was fifteen she married Duke John's second son, Peter, and found she had a rather troublesome husband : he was jealous, sulky and sometimes violent.   She put up with her troubles uncomplainingly, did her best to compose incessant family quarrels, and by her patience and prayers wrought a considerable improvement in her husband.   They had no children.   In 1450 Peter succeeded as duke, and Frances took full advantage of her position to forward the work of God.   She founded a convent at Nantes for Poor Clares, interested herself in the canonization of St Vincent Ferrer, and spent large sums in relief of the poor and other benefactions.   In 1457 her husband died, and his successors did not relish the popularity and influence of the dowager duchess (who was still only thirty), so that she withdrew herself more and more from public affairs, resisting the attempts of Louis XI of France to entice her into another marriage.   She spent much time at the Nantes convent and afterwards with the Carmelite nuns at Vannes.   These she established and endowed there in 1463, with the help and encouragement of Bd John Soreth, prior general of the order.

That she was not free from the tendency of foundresses to interest themselves too closely in the affairs of their foundations is illustrated by the story that she once obtained the services of an extraordinary confessor for a nun, without referring the matter to the prioress.   But when she was rebuked for her interference Duchess Frances humbly apologized and asked the prioress to impose on her a suitable penance.   In 1468 she became a nun herself at the Vannes convent, being clothed by John Soreth.   She filled the office of infirmarian, and four years after profession was elected prioress for life.   Under her rule the Vannes house became too small, and she opened another at Couëts, near Nantes.   Here she died in 1485.   Bd Frances was the means of Bd John Soreth introducing Carmelite nuns into France, and was in some measure the co-founder of the women's branch of the order.   Her virtues and the miracles wrought at her tomb caused her to be venerated as a saint, but the *cultus* was not confirmed until 1863.

No early biography of Bd Frances is known, and the Bollandists put the reader on his guard against accepting as historical such narratives as were published at a later date by Albert Le Grand of Morlaix and other enthusiastic panegyrists.   In the second volume of the *Acta Sanctorum* for November will be found only a general discussion of doubtful points, and an abstract of the more prominent happenings connected with the life of the *beata*.   The approval of her *cultus* in 1863 was conceded upon the presentment of the case submitted by the Abbé F. Richard, who afterwards became archbishop of Paris and cardinal ; in 1865 Mgr Richard published in two volumes a *Vie de la bse Françoise d'Amboise*.   There are also other French lives, for the most part uncritical, notably that by the Vicomte Sioc'han de Kersabiec (1865).   See also B. Zimmerman, *Monumenta historica Carmelitana* (1907), pp. 520–521.

5 : SS. ZACHARY AND ELIZABETH   (First Century)

SS. ZACHARY and Elizabeth were the parents of St John the Baptist. Zachary was a priest of the Old Covenant, and his wife was of the family of Aaron : both were " well approved in God's sight, following all the commandments and observances of the law without reproach ".   They were without children, and perhaps beyond the normal age of generation, when Zachary, while officiating in the Temple, had a vision of an angel, who told him that in response to their prayers they should have a son, " to whom thou shalt give the name John ", who should be filled with the Holy Ghost even in his mother's womb, and who should bring back many of the sons of Israel to the Lord their God.

The coming to pass of these things and their circumstances ; the visit of our Lady to her kinswoman Elizabeth, when she too was filled with the Holy Ghost and greeted Mary as blessed among women ; Mary's hymn of praise, " My soul doth magnify the Lord " ; after John's birth the return of speech, of which he had been deprived, to Zachary's lips, so that he spoke in prophecy, " Blessed be the Lord, the God of Israel, who hath visited and redeemed his people " : these things are all set out in the first chapter of St Luke's Gospel.   After that nothing more is heard of Zachary and his wife.   But it was a common opinion among the fathers, *e.g.* Epiphanius, Basil, Cyril of Alexandria, that St Zachary died a martyr, and according to an apocryphal writing he was killed in the Temple, " between the porch and the altar ", by command of Herod because he refused to disclose the whereabouts of his son.   But the Roman Martyrology makes no mention of martyrdom when it names Zachary and Elizabeth on November 5, the day on which their feast is kept in Palestine.   St Zachary is named in the commemoration of the saints at Mass according to the Mozarabic rite.

As has been said, all that is known about SS. Zachary and Elizabeth is to be found in St Luke's Gospel, chap. i, and it was St Peter Damian's opinion that to inquire about things the evangelists did not choose to tell us shows an improper and superfluous curiosity (in his third sermon on the birth of our Lady).   But those who disagree with him may refer also to Bardenhewer's *Biblische Studien*, vi, 187 (1901) and the various biblical dictionaries and encyclopaedias.

SS. GALATION AND EPISTEME　　(No Date)

IT is disconcerting to find that Galation's parents were called Clitophon and Leucippe, and it must be said at once that the story of Galation and Episteme is nothing but a Christian continuation of the romance of Tatius.　Unfortunately Cardinal Baronius, following the example of the Eastern church, inserted their names in the Roman Martyrology, and a brief notice is therefore not out of place here.　We are introduced to Clitophon and Leucippe as married and living at Emesa (Homs) in Syria, but unhappy on account of their childlessness.　Leucippe having kindly entertained a Christian hermit, Onuphrius, who was hiding from persecution, she was rewarded with the gift of faith, and in answer to her prayers she conceived.　Thereupon Clitophon also became a Christian.　A son was born to them, who because of his milk-white complexion was baptized Galation (Galakteon).　He grew up into a very handsome and accomplished man, and his father married him to a beautiful pagan girl named Episteme (" Knowledge ").　But, Clitophon being so well known as a hero of natural love, the continuator of Tatius presents his son as an example of virginity chosen from love of God.　After his marriage Galation declared to Episteme his desire to live with her in a state of virginity, and she, to whom such an idea was sufficiently strange and unwelcome, tried her best to break down his resolution.　She of course failed, and when Galation had explained his religion to her she consented to be baptized by him.　Then they sold all their goods for the benefit of the poor and retired, Galation to the hermitage of Publion in the desert of Sinai, Episteme to a community of consecrated virgins.　After three years Galation was arrested and brought before the magistrate at Emesa.　When Episteme heard of it she gave herself up to suffer with her husband ; when her clothes were torn off to shame her the fifty-three officers who were looking on were struck blind.　After they had been beaten and otherwise tortured, their tongues, hands and feet were cut off, and they were put to death by beheading.

In their scrupulous regard for what scholarship now demands the Bollandists have critically edited in their third volume for November the two Greek recensions of this pious fable.　The earlier is attributed to the authorship of a certain Eutolmius, the latter in date has long ago been printed among the works which pass under the name of Simeon Metaphrastes.　It is noteworthy that in neither text is there any indication of the particular persecution in which these martyrs suffered.　Neither Decius nor Diocletian are mentioned, though the former is now named in the Roman Martyrology.

ST BERTILLA, VIRGIN　　(A.D. 705 ?)

ST BERTILLA (Bertila is the more correct form) was born in the territory of Soissons. As she grew up she learned the deceits of the world, and earnestly desired to renounce it.　She was encouraged in her resolution by St Ouen, Bishop of Rouen, and her parents sent her to Jouarre, a monastery near Meaux, founded not long before under the Rule of St Columban.　St Bertilla was received with joy in this community and trained up in the strictest practice of monastic perfection.　Though yet young, her prudence and tact were remarkable, and the care of strangers, of the sick, and of the children that were educated in the monastery was successively committed to her.

When St Bathildis, the English wife of Clovis II, refounded the abbey of Chelles, she asked the abbess of Jouarre to furnish this community with a small colony of her most experienced and virtuous nuns.   Bertilla was sent at the head of this company, and was appointed first abbess of Chelles.   The reputation of the saint and the discipline which she established in this house attracted a number of foreign vocations, among them Hereswitha, widow of Ethelhere, King of the East Angles and sister to St Hilda.   The widowed Queen Bathildis herself, as soon as her son Clotaire was of age to govern, retired hither.   She took the religious habit from the hands of St Bertilla *c.* 665 and obeyed her as if she had been the last sister in the house, rather than its sovereign and foundress.   But the holy abbess, who saw two queens every day at her feet, seemed the most humble and the most fervent among her sisters, and showed by her conduct that no one commands well who has not first learned, and is not always ready, to obey well.   In her old age, far from abating her fervour, St Bertilla strove to redouble it both in her penances and in her devotions, and she died beloved by all, after having governed Chelles for forty-six years.

There is a short Latin life, probably compiled about the year 800, but based upon authentic materials of earlier date.   It has been critically edited both by A. Poncelet in the *Acta Sanctorum*, November, vol. iii, and by W. Levison in MGH., *Scriptores Merov.*, vol. vi.   Something is also said of St Bertilla in the exceptionally trustworthy Merovingian Life of St Bathildis.   Father Poncelet shows that, owing to a mistake of Bede, certain erroneous deductions have been drawn regarding the chronology.

ST MARTIN DE PORRES   (A.D. 1639)

AMONG the people to whom the epithet " half-caste " is often given as a term of contempt, the first of whom it is recorded that he practised Christian virtue in an heroic degree is this Dominican lay-brother.   He was born in Lima in Peru in 1579, the natural child of John de Porres (Porras), a Spanish knight, and a coloured freed-woman from Panama, Anna by baptism.   Young Martin inherited the features and dark complexion of his mother, which was a matter of vexation to the noble Porres, who nevertheless acknowledged the boy and his sister as his children, but eventually left Martin to the care of his mother.   When he was twelve she apprenticed him to a barber-surgeon ; but three years later, having received the habit of the third order of St Dominic, he was admitted to the Rosary convent of the Friars Preachers at Lima, eventually becoming a professed lay-brother.

" Many were the offices to which the servant of God, Brother Martin de Porres, attended, being barber, surgeon, wardrobe-keeper and infirmarian.   Each of these jobs was enough for any one man, but alone he filled them all with great liberality, promptness and carefulness, without being weighed down by any of them.   It was most striking, and it made me [Brother Fernando de Aragones] realize that, in that he clung to God in his soul, all these things were effects of divine grace."   Martin extended his care of the sick to those of the city, and was instrumental in establishing an orphanage and foundling-hospital, with other charitable institutions attached ;   he was given the office of distributing the convent's daily alms of food to the poor (which he is said sometimes to have increased miraculously) ;   and he took upon himself to care for the miserable slaves who were brought to Peru from Africa.   He was greatly desirous of going to some foreign mission where he might earn the crown of martyrdom, but this was impossible, so he made a martyr of his own body ;   and as well as of his penances much is said of his aerial flights, bilocations and other supernatural gifts.   Brother Martin's charity embraced the lower animals (which seems to have surprised the Spaniards) and even vermin, excusing the depredations of rats and mice on the ground that the poor little things were insufficiently fed, and he kept a " cats' and dogs' home " at his sister's house.

St Martin's protégé, Juan Vasquez Parra, shows the lay-brother as eminently practical in his charities, using carefully and methodically the money and goods he collected, raising a dowry for his niece in three days (at the same time getting as much and more for the poor), putting up the banns, showing Parra how to sow camomile in the well-manured hoof-prints of cattle, buying a Negro servant to work in the laundry, looking after those who needed blankets, shirts, candles, sweets, miracles or prayers—the procurator apparently both of the priory and the public.   Don Balthasar Carasco, a jurist, wanted to be Brother Martin's " adopted son " and to call him " father ".   Martin objected : " Why do you want a mulatto for a father ?   That would not look well ".—" Why not ?   It would rather be said that you have a Spaniard for a son ", retorted Don Balthasar.   On one occasion when his priory was being dunned for a debt, Martin offered himself in payment : " I am only a poor mulatto ; I'm the property of the order : sell me."

St Martin was a close friend of St Rose of Lima as well as of Bd John Massias, who was a lay-brother at the Dominican priory of St Mary Magdalen in the same town.   Martin was at the Rosary priory, and he died there on November 3, 1639 : he was carried to his grave by prelates and noblemen.   He was beatified in 1837, after long delays, and canonized on May 6, 1962.   He is patron of social justice.

Fr Van Ortroy adopted in this case a course unprecedented in earlier volumes of the *Acta Sanctorum*, for he printed a tolerably full account of the servant of God in a modern language.   Fr B. de Medina gave testimony regarding Martin de Porres before the apostolic commission in 1683 ; his evidence was translated into Italian for the benefit of the C.R.S. in Rome, and this version Fr Van Ortroy reproduced.   But see also *With Bd Martin* (1945), pp. 132–168, and the *Fifteenth Anniversary Book* (1950), pp. 130–158, publications of the Blessed Martin Guild, New York, edited by Fr Norbert Georges, where are printed translations of the evidence of ten witnesses at the apostolic process.   The appropriate adoption of Bd Martin in America and elsewhere as patron of work for inter-racial justice and harmony has led to the publication of several popular and devotional works on him, such as that of J. C. Kearns (1950).   There is a life in French by S. Fumet (1933), rather uncritical.   See Fr C. C. Martindale in *The Month*, April 1920, pp. 300–313 ; and M. C. de Ganay in *Vie spirituelle*, vol. ix (1923–24), notably pp. 54–61.

BD GOMIDAS KEUMURGIAN, Martyr   (A.D. 1707)

At the end of the seventeenth and the beginning of the eighteenth centuries Constantinople was a seething pot of secular and ecclesiastical politics, from which emerged many reunions of dissident Christians, some opportunist, some truly religious, with the Catholic Church.   Unfortunately the ambassador of France, Charles de Ferréol, was a man who did not mix discretion with his political and religious zeal and played far too active a part in ecclesiastical affairs, wherein he was encouraged by not a few western clerics.   Accordingly, it was simplicity itself for anti-Catholic dissidents to point out to the Porte the dangerous French activity in Turkey, and persecution followed.   Among its victims was Gomidas Keumurgian.   That he was a martyr is quite certain (even if the Church had not officially proclaimed it by his beatification), for he chose death rather than apostasy to schism or to Islam.   That the pretext and occasion of his death were provided by the imprudence—if no worse—of some Catholics is also certain : though no doubt his enemies would have found another excuse if that had failed them.

Gomidas was born in Constantinople about 1656, the son of a dissident Armenian priest, and was educated by a learned prelate of the same communion.   He married when he was about twenty, continued his studies with competence, was ordained priest and was appointed assistant in the great Armenian parish of St George in the south of Constantinople.   Here his eloquence, his disinterestedness, and his deep religious spirit soon brought him to the fore, he was caught up in the reunion movement within his church, and, when he was forty, with his wife and children, he abjured schism and error.   According to the custom of the place and time Father Gomidas continued to minister at St George's, using his influence to bring his people into union with Rome.   He worked in harmony with the Venerable Abbot Mekhitar and the *vartapet* Khatchatur, and within a few years five more of the twelve priests at St George's had followed his example.   From 1695 the dissident Armenians got more and more alarmed and stirred up the Turkish authorities against their Catholic brethren ; these had to proceed very warily, and it was judged wise for the leaders to disperse for a time : Mekhitar transferred his nascent religious order first to the Morea and then to Venice, and Father Gomidas went to Jerusalem.   Here, in supporting the Catholic party in the great Armenian monastery of St James, he had the misfortune to provoke the enmity of a certain John of Smyrna, and on the death of the persecuting Armenian patriarch in 1702 Gomidas was glad to return to Constantinople.   The succeeding patriarch, Avedik, proved to be no better ; moreover, he made John of Smyrna his vicar, and Gomidas had to lie hidden in the house of a friend.   Here he remained, writing a metrical paraphrase of the Acts of the Apostles, till at the end of nine months a political upheaval caused Avedik to be exiled.

For a time there was peace.   Then the patriarch Avedik came back, but fell into disgrace again (as " a Frank ") and was deported to Cyprus, whence M. de Ferréol " conveyed " him to France.   The anti-Catholic " Frank " was in fact kidnapped by the Frankish ambassador.   This folly roused the dissidents of Constantinople, who soon induced the Turkish authorities to proceed against the Catholics.   Father Gomidas, physically impressive, energetic and fearless, was not a man who could be long hid.   During the Lent of 1707 he was arrested, charged before Ali Pasha, and condemned to the galleys.   A few days later his friends bought his freedom for 500 piastres, and on Good Friday Bd Gomidas returned to his parish, where he continued to preach reunion, under the noses of the priests who had betrayed him. He would neither flee nor accept the shelter of the French embassy, in spite of the fact that his old opponent, John of Smyrna, was now patriarch of the Armenians in Constantinople.   On November 3, 1707, Gomidas was again arrested and brought up.   The complaint was simply that he was a Frank * and had stirred up trouble in the Armenian nation within the Turkish realm.   Ali Pasha referred the case to the chief kadi, Mustafa Kamal, at Galata.   He was a Mohammedan canonist, knew perfectly well that Gomidas was an Armenian priest, and was moreover suspicious of the prosecutors.   He therefore solemnly adjured the witnesses by Jesus and His mother Mary not to deviate from the truth ; but thirteen out of fourteen swore that the prisoner was a Frank, an enemy of the sultan, and a subverter of public order.   A crowd of Armenians, incited by their patriarch, clamoured for his death, and eventually Mustafa Kamal informed the vizir that Gomidas

* This meant either a Latin Catholic or a foreigner, less ordinarily a Catholic of any rite. But in those days the Turks did not take civil cognizance of any Catholics other than Latins, and Bd Gomidas was justified in denying the charge, as he did.

had embraced the religion of the Franks and had led others to do the same. " But blood will flow from the pen that draws up the sentence ", he added to the bystanders.

Bd Gomidas was taken to prison, where he would neither eat nor drink. " He had forgotten hunger and thirst in remembering the passion of his Saviour ", says Gregory of Tokat, " and in his love of the Crucified he had no thought for what was about to befall him." He received the sacraments and said farewell to his wife, giving her his ring and his watch, and to a friend ten piastres for the executioner. The next morning he was taken before Ali Pasha in the divan of the Old Seraglio, still to be seen at Constantinople, to hear his sentence. Gomidas again protested his innocence and challenged the right of the vizir to condemn him for a religious cause. " His blood is on your head, if you have lied ", Ali warned John of Smyrna and his clergy. " So be it ", replied the patriarch, " on our heads—and on those of the Frankish priests who have perverted so many of our church."—" You hear they say you have deserted your religion," said Ali to Bd Gomidas. " Which seems to you the best among the faiths of the Christians ? " asked the martyr in reply. " They are all equally disgusting to me," answered the Mohammedan. " Very well. Then what does it matter to you which one I choose ? " Impressed by his demeanour, and perhaps liking his candour, Ali was willing to save him and, remembering an unhappy Armenian bishop who had apostatized, he invited him to embrace Islam. When this failed, sentence of death was pronounced and Bd Gomidas was led away, with two other confessors. Twice on the way to the place of execution he was stopped by messengers, who offered him freedom in exchange for apostasy to Islam, and the second time his sister Irene burst through the crowd, imploring him to feign compliance. At the four-went-way called Parmak-Kapu, in the Psamatia quarter, he was bidden to kneel. He did so, facing towards the east. "Face the south " , he was told, but he would not budge. The executioner offered him life for the last time and then, while he was reciting the profession of faith of Nicaea, struck off his head with one stroke.

The heroic bearing of Blessed Gomidas made a profound impression, especially among the dissident Greeks and Armenians. So much so indeed that in another hundred year's time the Catholic Armenians of Constantinople were so numerous that the name " Catholic " was ordinarily understood to mean one of the Armenian rite. The body of the martyr was buried by Greek Orthodox clergy— no Catholic priest came forward to do so. Bd Gomidas Keumurgian was beatified in 1929, the most illustrious martyr at Constantinople since the days of the Iconoclast persecution, and probably the first recorded priest martyr since the days of the early persecutions who was followed to the place of execution by his wife and children. One of his sons, also Gomidas, entered the service of the kingdom of Naples and called himself Cosimo di Carbognano, a name that was adopted by his descendants and is sometimes given to the martyr himself.

The best available life seems to be that of H. Riondel, *Une page tragique de l'histoire religieuse du Levant* (1929), on which *cf.* the *Analecta Bollandiana*, vol. xlviii (1930), pp. 450–451. Some further sidelights may be gleaned from Vahan Inglisian, *Der Diener Gottes Mechitar von Sebaste* (1929), and D. Attwater, *Book of Eastern Saints* (1938), pp. 109–121.

6 : ST LEONARD OF NOBLAC (Sixth Century ?)

ALTHOUGH he was one of the most " popular " saints of western Europe in the later middle ages, nothing is heard of this St Leonard before the eleventh century, when a life of him was written, upon which, however, no reliance at all can be put. According to it he was a Frankish nobleman who was converted to the faith by St Remigius. Clovis I was his godfather, and offered St Leonard a bishopric, which he refused. He went into the country of Orleans, to the monastery of Micy, where he took the religious habit and lived until, aspiring after a closer solitude, he chose for his retirement a forest not far from Limoges. Here he built himself a cell, lived on vegetables and fruit, and had for some time no witness of his penance and virtues but God alone. One day Clovis came hunting in that forest and his queen was there brought to bed by a difficult labour. By the prayers of St Leonard she was safely delivered, and the king in gratitude gave him as much land as he could ride round in a night on his donkey. Leonard formed a community, which in succeeding times became a flourishing monastery, first called the abbey of Noblac and now identified as the town of Saint-Léonard. From it the saint evangelized the surrounding neighbourhood, and died there, it is said, about the middle of the sixth century, revered for his holiness and miracles.

From the eleventh century devotion to St Leonard flourished remarkably, especially in north-west and central Europe. In England his name occurs in calendars and churches were dedicated in his honour : there is a St Leonard's chapel so far west as Saint Ives ; at Worcester in the thirteenth century his feast was kept as a half-holyday, on which Mass was to be heard and only certain work (*e.g.* ploughing) might be done. The church at Noblac became a great pilgrimage shrine and the saint was invoked, on the one hand, by women in labour, and on the other, by prisoners of war (because, according to the legend, Clovis promised to release every captive Leonard visited) ; in one Bavarian town alone 4000 cures and other answers to prayer were attributed to his intercession from the fourteenth to the eighteenth centuries. Of this great *cultus* there now remains only a certain amount of local popular devotion and the observance of his feast at Limoges, Munich and in a few other places.

The account of St Leonard furnished in the *Acta Sanctorum*, November, vol. iii, is exceptionally thorough and authoritative, for it was written in 1910 by Fr Albert Poncelet, an expert in Merovingian and Carolingian hagiography. The text of the Latin life, which had already been critically edited by B. Krusch in MGH., *Scriptores Merov.*, vol. iii, is printed again by the Bollandist, with a long series of narratives of later miracles. Poncelet agrees with Krusch that the life was compiled somewhere about the year 1025, certainly not before 1017, and that of itself it does not provide evidence even that such a person as St Leonard ever existed. It seems that no trace of any *cultus* of the saint is to be found either in church-dedications, inscriptions, martyrologies or calendars earlier than the eleventh century. The special devotion to St Leonard as a liberator of prisoners of war probably gained popularity from the story of the release of Bohemund, Prince of Antioch, in 1103 after he had been taken captive by the Moslems. It is historically certain that he paid a visit to Noblac and there presented an *ex-voto* in gratitude ; on which see the *Analecta Bollandiana*, vol. xxxi (1912), pp. 24–44. A French Life was published in 1863 by Canon Arbellot, and there are others, mostly uncritical. The anachronisms of the life of St Leonard are discussed by G. Kurth, *Clovis*, vol. ii, pp. 167 and 259–260. Much has been written on the popular practices of devotion and on the folk-lore associated with the St

Leonard cult : consult, *e.g.* W. Hay, *Volkstumliche Heiligentage* (1932), pp. 264–269. Curiously enough this French saint was nowhere more honoured than in Bavaria, as has been shown by G. Schierghofer, *Alt-Bayerns Umritte und Leonhardifahrten* (1913), and in his *Umrittbrauch* (1922) ; also by Rudolf Kriss, *Volkskundliches aus alt-bayerischen Gnaden-statten* (1930), and Max Rumpf, *Religiöse Volkskunde* (1933), p. 166.

ST MELAINE, BISHOP OF RENNES   (*c.* A.D. 530)

MELAINE (Melanius) was a native of Placet in the parish of Brain, in Brittany. He had served God with great fervour in a monastery for some years when, upon the death of St Amand, Bishop of Rennes, he was constrained by the clergy and people to fill that see.   As a bishop he played a leading part in drawing up the canons of the Council of Orleans in 511 (see *Neues Archiv*, xiv, 50), and with others wrote a letter of rebuke to two Breton priests who were wandering from place to place and behaving very irregularly.   His virtue was chiefly enhanced by a sincere humility, and a spirit of continual prayer, and the author of his life tells us that he performed many miracles.   King Clovis after his conversion held him in great esteem.   St Melaine died in a monastery which he had built at Placet, some time before 549.   He was buried at Rennes, where his feast is kept to-day, as it was formerly at Mullion in Cornwall, where he had come to be regarded as the local patron, supplanting an earlier St Mollien or Moellien.   He must not be confused with the St Mellon venerated in Normandy, who gave his name to Saint Mellons between Newport and Cardiff.

See his life in the *Acta Sanctorum*, January 6, of which other, and probably older, re-dactions may be found in the *Catalogus Cod. Hagiog. Lat. Paris*, i, 71 and ii, 531.   *Cf.* also MGH., *Scriptores Merov.*, vol. iii ; Duchesne, *Fastes Épiscopaux*, vol. ii, pp. 340–341 ; and G. H. Doble, *St Melaine* (1935).

ST ILLTUD, OR ILLTYD, ABBOT   (SIXTH CENTURY)

THE first information we have about Illtud, one of the most celebrated of the Welsh saints, is in the perhaps early seventh-century Life of St Samson.   Here it is said that he was a disciple of St Germanus (of Auxerre), who ordained him priest, and that he presided over the monastic school at Llantwit in Glamorgan ; much stress is laid on his learning and wisdom : " This Illtud was the most learned of all the Britons both in the Old Testament and the New, and in all kinds of philosophy—poetry and rhetoric, grammar and arithmetic . . . were I to begin to relate all his wondrous works I should be led to excess ".   There are further references in the ninth-century Life of St Paul Aurelian : there it is stated that the saint's monastery was established on a certain island " within the borders of Dyfed, called Pyr ", which is usually identified with Caldey, off Tenby.   This statement has given rise to the baseless conjecture that there was an original Llanilltud on Caldey, and that a later and bigger foundation in Glamorgan was distinguished from it as Llanilltud *Fawr*, that is " the Great ".   Illtud is said to have increased the size of this " very limited area hemmed in by the sea ", at the suggestion of his pupils Paul, David, Samson, and Gildas.*   Illtud took the young men into the church to pray for that marvel, and when they had all answered

* Little credence can be attached to the statement that St David was a pupil of St Illtud : *cf.* A. W. Wade-Evans, *Life of St David*, p. 73.   The same scholar sought to identify the *insula* with Manorbier on the mainland of Pembrokeshire (*Notes and Queries*, 1950).

" Amen " they came out and " behold the island made bigger on every side and bright flowers blossoming everywhere ", says the Life of Gildas ; the Life of Paul gives a more circumstantial account.

The only life we have of St Illtud himself is a Latin composition dating from about 1140. This tells us that his father was a Briton who lived in Letavia with his wife ; it has been suggested that Letavia here really means a district in central Brecknock rather than Brittany. When he grew up Illtud went by water to visit " his cousin King Arthur ", and married a lady called Trynihid. Leaving Arthur, he entered the military service of a chieftain in Glamorgan, whence he is sometimes called Illtud the Knight. The story goes that he was startled into taking up the monastic life by a hunting accident in which some of his friends lost their lives, and that he was recommended to leave the world by St Cadoc (who was hardly born at this time). Illtud went to live with Trynihid in a reed hut by the river Nadafan, but was warned by an angel, in peculiar circumstances, to leave his wife. This he did, very roughly, early in the morning, and went to St Dubricius to receive the tonsure of a monk. Then he made his abode by a stream called the Hodnant, and lived austerely there as a solitary until disciples began to flock around. They flourished materially and spiritually, their land was good and they worked hard, and St Illtud's monastery became the first great monastic school of Wales, known as Llanilltud Fawr (now Llantwit Major in Glamorgan).

Once Trynihid came to see her husband, whom she found working in the fields, but he was offended and would not speak to her (The narrator here attributes a similar discourtesy to Almighty God). When Illtud was driven from his monastery by the oppression of a local chieftain he had to take refuge for a time in a cave by the river Ewenny, where he was fed from Heaven ; their lands were threatened by the collapse of the sea-wall, which the monks built up again, but finally it had to be made good miraculously by the saint. He is said to have gone with corn-ships to relieve a famine in Brittany, and places and churches bearing his name are found there as well as many in Wales. Illtud was honoured as having introduced to his monks, and so to the people, an improved method of ploughing. The life is largely taken up with anecdotes of wonders, which provoked Dom Serenus Cressy in the seventeenth century to complain of " fables and unsavoury miracles ", when he met them in Capgrave's *Nova legenda Angliae*. It states that in his old age Illtud again crossed the sea, and died at Dol ; but the Life of Samson gives a moving account of his last days at Llantwit.

A local tradition of Breconshire says he died at Defynock and was buried at the place still called Bedd Gwyl Illtud, the Grave of Illtud's Feast. In one of the Welsh triads Illtud is named, with Cadoc and Peredur, as one of the three knights of Arthur who had charge of the Holy Grail, and attempts have been made to identify him with the Galahad of the Arthurian legends. No mention of Illtud seems to be found in calendars, martyrologies or litanies earlier than the eleventh century. In a ninth-century inscription on a cross at Llantwit there is mention of " Iltet, Samson and Ebisar ", and this is probably the earliest surviving notice of the saint. His feast is observed in the archdiocese of Cardiff and on Caldey.

The best texts of the Latin life of St Illtud are those edited by Father De Smedt in the *Acta Sanctorum*, November, vol. iii, and by A. W. Wade-Evans in *Vitae sanctorum Britanniae* (1944), with a translation (both correct many errors which occur in the transcript of W. J. Rees, *Lives of the Cambro-British Saints*, pp. 158–182). The best and handiest general work in English is G. H. Doble's *St Illtut* (1944). See also A. W. Wade-Evans, *Welsh*

Christian Origins (1934), pp. 132–137 and *passim ;* and especially F. Duine, *Memento des sources hagiographiques . . . de Bretagne* (1918), pp. 129–131.   The saint's name appears in many forms, Iltutus, Eltut, Hildutus, etc.

ST WINNOC, Abbot   (A.D. 717 ?)

WINNOC was probably of British origin.   When a young man he, with three companions, came to the newly founded monastery of St Peter at Sithiu (Saint-Omer).   He was so edified with the fervour of the monks and the wisdom of their abbot, St Bertin, that he and his companions agreed to take the habit together. Soon, as the chronicler of the monastery testifies, St Winnoc shone like a morning star among the hundred and fifty monks who inhabited that sanctuary.

When it was judged proper to found a new monastery in a remoter part of the country of the Morini, for the instruction and example of the inhabitants of that part, Heremar, a man who had lately embraced the faith, bestowed on St Bertin some land at Wormhout, near Dunkirk, very convenient for that purpose.   Bertin sent thither his four British monks to found the new monastery.   St Winnoc and his brethren worked tirelessly in building their church and cells, together with a hospital for the sick, and the place soon became an important missionary centre. Many miracles were attributed to Winnoc, who was always foremost in the service of his monastic brethren and his heathen neighbours.   Even in his old age he ground corn for the poor of his community, turning the hand-mill himself without any assistance.   When others were astonished that he should have strength enough to do constantly such hard labour, they looked through a chink into the barn and saw the quern turning without being touched, which they ascribed to a miracle.

St Winnoc died on November 6, the year, according to the fourteenth-century tradition, being 717.   Count Baldwin IV built and founded at Bergues an abbey which he peopled with a colony from Sithiu and enriched with the relics of St Winnoc ; the lands of the monastery of Wormhout were settled upon this house, and the town bears the name of Bergues-Saint-Winnoc.

In curious contrast to St Illtud, St Winnoc, though his direct connection with Great Britain is very slight, is commemorated in nearly all the English calendars of the tenth and eleventh centuries (see those edited for the Henry Bradshaw Society by F. Wormald in 1934).   What is more, his name is mentioned and the miracle of the corn-grinding described in detail in the Old-English martyrology of *c.* 850.   Three Latin lives of St Winnoc have been printed in the *Acta Sanctorum*, November, vol. iii, but only the first, which may have been written as early as the eighth century, is of much account, the other two being obviously based upon this.   This first life has also been edited by Levison in MGH., *Scriptores Merov.*, vol. v.   See also Van der Essen, *Étude critique sur les Saints méroving.*, pp. 402 *seq.* ; Flahault, *Le culte de St Winnoc à Wormhout* (1903) ; and Duine, *Memento*, p. 64.   St Winnoc is apparently the titular of Saint Winnow in Cornwall, and in an excellent monograph (1940) Canon Doble gives reasons for thinking he was a Welshman who founded this Cornish church, and subsequently came to Sithiu, no doubt via Brittany.

ST DEMETRIAN, Bishop of Khytri   (*c.* A.D. 912)

HE was born at Sika, a village in Cyprus, his father being a venerated priest of that place.   Demetrian himself was married at an early age, but three months later his wife died and he took the angelical habit in the monastery of St Antony.   He soon became well known for his piety and powers of healing, and was ordained priest. He was elected abbot and governed in wisdom and holiness until the see of Khytri (now Kyrka ; the ancient Kythereia) became vacant and he was appointed to it.

Demetrian had now been a monk for nearly forty years, and was loath to involve himself in the responsibilities and distractions of the episcopate.   He therefore ran away to a friend, one Paul, who hid him in a cave.   But Paul had scruples about this, informed the authorities where the fugitive was, and Demetrian had to submit to consecration.   Near the end of an episcopate of some twenty-five years Cyprus was ravaged by the Saracens and many Christian Cypriots carried off into slavery. St Demetrian is said to have followed and interceded with the raiders, who, impressed by his venerable age and selflessness, let the prisoners return to their homes.   He is accounted one of the greatest bishops and saints of Cyprus.

There is one early Life of St Demetrian, written in Greek, which, so far as is known, has been preserved to us only in a single manuscript, somewhat mutilated at the end.   From this codex it was edited by H. Grégoire in the *Byzantinische Zeitschrift*, vol. xvi (1907), pp. 217–237, and again more accurately by Fr Delehaye in the *Acta Sanctorum*, November, vol. iii.   Delehaye thinks that the life was written about the middle of the tenth century.

ST BARLAAM OF KHUTYN, Abbot   (A.D. 1193)

He was born into a wealthy family at Novgorod and was christened Alexis.   On the death of his parents he sold his property, giving away much to the poor, and went to live as a solitary at a place called Khutyn on the banks of the river Volga. The fame of his virtues in time brought companions to him, and these he organized as a monastic community, ruling over them as abbot, with the name of Barlaam (Varlaam).   His wooden chapel was rebuilt in stone, and dedicated in honour of the Transfiguration.   Pilgrims and other visitors flocked to the new monastery, among them the Duke Yaroslav, who became its benefactor.   St Barlaam did not live long after the final establishment of this community ; after having provided for its continuance and upkeep, and having nominated the monk Antony to succeed him, he died on November 6, 1193.   His burying-place was the scene of miracles, and his relics were solemnly enshrined in 1452.

The life of St Barlaam of Khutyn was written by a Serbian monk named Pachomius ; in the Russian use of the Byzantine Mass he is commemorated at the preparation of the holy things.

See Martynov's *Annus ecclesiasticus Graeco-Slavicus* in *Acta Sanctorum*, October, vol. xi ; and *cf.* note under St Sergius on September 25 herein.

BD CHRISTINA OF STOMMELN, Virgin   (A.D. 1312)

During her life and from the time of her death until to-day Christina Bruso was venerated as a saint in her native village of Stommeln, near Cologne, and at Jülich, where she was eventually buried ; and on account of this uninterrupted local veneration Pope Pius X confirmed the *cultus* in 1908, just on 600 years after her death.   Were it not for the large amount of contemporary, eye-witnesses', and personal testimony to the phenomena which make her one of the most extraordinary cases in all hagiology, she would have to be dismissed as a devout but mentally diseased young woman who suffered from hallucinations on a very large scale indeed or whose biographers were either hopelessly deceived or unscrupulous liars.   Even as it is, some of the Catholic scholars who have studied the documents are of the opinion that many statements of experiences were made by her when she was not mistress of herself ; and, as one of them has put it, it is " easier to believe that the whole story was a romance concocted, letters and all, by Peter of Dacia and that no such person as Christina ever existed " than to believe the extravagances recorded in her letters written by the hand of the village schoolmaster.

Christina's father was a prosperous peasant, and the girl had some sort of school-ing, for she learned to read the psalter, but not to write. In the short account of her early life that she dictated to her parish priest, John, she says that she affianced herself to our Lord when He appeared to her in vision at the age of ten. When she was thirteen she ran away from home and became a *béguine* at Cologne. She lived with such austerity and extravagance of devotion that the *béguines* thought her mad, and already she thought herself singled out for attention by supernatural powers, both divine and diabolical : Satan, for example, disguised as St Bartholo-mew, tempted her to suicide. After some time she left the *béguinage*, where she had been treated with scant sympathy as an hysterical subject, and returned home. When she was twenty-five Christina made the acquaintance of Father Peter of Dacia (*i.e.* Scandinavia and Denmark), a pious and capable young Dominican, and at their first meeting she was, in the presence of others as well, thrown about the room and pierced with wounds in her feet by invisible agency. For the next two years or so Father Peter kept a record of what he saw in connection with Christina, between whom and the Swedish friar there was a warm personal friend-ship. The numerous remarkable happenings which he narrates include long ecstasies and temporary *stigmata* which bled copiously during Holy Week. On one occasion Christina was found up to her neck in mud in a pit without knowing how she got there, and on another Satan tormented her by fixing to her body hot stones, which the bystanders could see and touch. But the manifestation of which Father Peter gives the most careful and detailed account was of so repulsive a nature that no particulars of it can be given here. It is sufficient to say that on numerous occasions for weeks on end Christina and those who visited her, Father Peter himself and other Dominicans, other clergy, and lay people of both sexes, were covered with showers of filth that came apparently from nowhere.

After Father Peter left Cologne in 1269 Christina corresponded with him through the parish priest, John, who sometimes added to her dictation comments of his own. From these letters it appears that the visitations which Christina attributes to the malice of the Evil One continued unabated, though in ever-varying forms. These violent happenings were not confined to Christina herself. Her father was hit with stones on the head and arms, her friend the Benedictine prior of Brauweiler was badly bitten by invisible teeth, and a skull, after moving about in the air, tied itself about the neck of the Brusos' servant. A Dominican wrote to Father Peter from Cologne that " [The devil] gnaws her [Christina's] flesh like a dog, and bites out great pieces ; he burns her clothes next her skin while she is wearing them, and shows himself to her in horrible forms." Thrice, says John the Priest, she was dragged from her bed, once on to the roof of her house and twice to a tree in the garden to which she was left bound. John himself untied her, in the presence of her mother and others. In 1277 John the Priest died and his place as amanuensis was taken by Master John, a young schoolmaster at Stommeln. He filled this office over a period of eight years, and the contents of the letters exceed anything previously reported by or of Christina. " The accounts of Christina's experiences between 1279 and 1287 ", says the writer quoted at the beginning of this article, " which reached her Dominican friend through the intermediary of Magister Johannes are so preposterous that, if they really emanated from herself, one can only regard them as the hallucinations of a brain which, for the time being at least, was completely unhinged." All the paraphernalia used by the medieval artist in depicting Hell and its denizens is brought into play, and Christina over and over again is physically tormented in corresponding ways. Sometimes the powers of Heaven come to her aid, our Lord or His Mother or angels, and restore her from the harms which she has suffered. For what is related in these letters there is no shred of corroborative evidence, and from two very significant passages therein it is argued that their incredible extravagances were communicated by Christina (if Master John did not deliberately invent, which in all the circumstances he seems unlikely to have done) when in trance or other abnormal states, and were filled out and rounded off by the schoolmaster.

Father Peter of Dacia died about 1288 and Christina's known history ends at that time, but she lived for another twenty-four years, dying at the age of seventy, in 1312, with a great reputation of sanctity. Thirty years after her relics were translated to Niedeggen in the Eifel, and again in 1569 to Jülich, where they still repose and receive the veneration of the people. Nor does anything which has been said above reflect on the credit of Bd Christina or suggest that that veneration is misplaced ; for heroic virtue, which is the condition of holiness, is entirely independent of abnormal physical phenomena or extraordinary divine favours, and the first of these are not inconsistent with a life far from holy. The Holy See has recognized that the evidence touching the personal virtue of Bd Christina justifies the continuation of her age-long local *cultus*.

The material collected by Peter of Dacia for his projected book on " The Virtues of the Bride of Christ Christina " were printed for the first time in the *Acta Sanctorum*, June, vol. iv ; but Father Papebroch had to use a copy which was in places becoming illegible. A better text, which, however, does not include all the documents, is provided in the *Scriptores latini medii aevi Suecani*, vol. i, pt 2, pp. 1–257, by J. Paulson. See also Th. Wollersheim, *Das Leben der ekstatischen und stigmatisirten Jungfrau Christina von Stommeln* (1859) ; E. Renan, *Nouvelles études d'histoire religieuse* (Eng. trans.), pp. 353–396 ; H. Thurston in *The Month*, October and November, 1928, pp. 289–301 and 425–437 ; *Douleur et stigmatisation* (1936), pp. 44–49, in the series " Études Carmélitaines " ; and *Analecta Bollandiana*, vol. lvii (1939), pp. 187–189.

BD JOAN MARY DE MAILLÉ, Widow   (A.D. 1414)

On April 14, 1332, at Roche-Saint-Quentin in Touraine, there was born to Baron Hardouin VI of Maillé or Maillac, and his wife Joan de Montbazon, a girl, who received at her baptism the name of Joan and at her confirmation that of Mary. She showed great piety from infancy, and once, when playing with other children of her age, she is said to have saved by her prayers the life of a little neighbour, Robert de Sillé, who had fallen into a pond. The boy himself became deeply attached to her, and when they grew up a marriage was arranged between them by Mary's grandfather, her father being dead. The girl had proposed to consecrate herself to God, and her intention had been intensified after her recovery from a serious illness, but she was obliged to obey the old man, who, however, died on the wedding day. The young couple agreed to live together as brother and sister, and this they did for sixteen years. No gambling or bad language was permitted in their *château*, which became the asylum of the poor of the neighbourhood ; and they adopted and educated three orphans.

Their holy and happy existence was disturbed by war : the Baron de Sillé followed the king to defend his country against the English, and in the disastrous battle of Poitiers he was wounded and left for dead.   The capture of King John put Touraine at the mercy of the enemy troops, who overran the land and pillaged the *château* of Sillé.   Robert himself having been made prisoner, the large sum of 3000 florins was demanded for his ransom, and his wife sold her jewels and horses and borrowed what more was required to make up the sum.   This entailed delay, and to hasten payment Robert's gaolers are said to have kept him practically without food for nine days.   His eventual liberation he ascribed to the interposition of our Lady, who appeared to him in a vision to break his chains and enable him to escape.   To their former charities they now added donations for the ransom of prisoners, and lived if possible a more holy and self-denying life than ever until Robert's death in 1362.   The grief of the widow at the loss of her husband was intensified by the unkindness of his family, who reproached her bitterly for the impoverishment of the estate through the alms which she had encouraged Robert to give.   They went so far as to deprive her of her marriage portion and to drive her from her home.   She took refuge at first with an old servant, who, however, finding that she had arrived empty-handed, received her grudgingly and treated her with contempt.   Afterwards she returned to her mother at Luynes and learnt to make up medicines and salves.   Joan was still young, and her peace of mind was soon disturbed by suitors, who were encouraged by her mother and brother. To escape from them, she withdrew to a little house in Tours, adjacent to the church of St Martin, and devoted herself to prayer, to attendance at the canonical offices and to the care of the sick and poor.

Once while Joan Mary was praying in church a madwoman threw a stone which injured her back so severely that the surgeon whom Anne of Brittany sent to her relief declared that he could do nothing.   But God Himself cured her miraculously, and although she carried the mark of the blow until her death, she was able to resume her former way of life.   Her austerities were extreme, and she became a Franciscan tertiary, whose habit she always wore.   After one of the several grave illnesses which she had to bear, she determined to strip herself of all earthly possessions, including the Château des Roches, which had been restored to her by her husband's family.   She gave everything to the Carthusians of Liget, and made a declaration of renunciation of any property which might accrue to her in the future.   By so doing she alienated her own relations, and when she returned to Tours, completely destitute, no one would house her : she had to beg her bread from door to door and sometimes she slept in disused pigstyes and dog-kennels. At one time she was admitted among the servants of the hospital of St Martin, but her very holiness aroused jealousy, and she was calumniated and expelled.   At last she found peace in the solitude of Planche-de-Vaux, near Cléry : there she lived for a long time, almost hidden from the world.   Nevertheless she was able to bring about the restoration of a ruined chapel which was called after her the chapel of the Good Anchoress and became a favourite place of pilgrimage.   Later she returned to Tours, and at the age of fifty-seven took up her abode in a tiny room near the Minorite church.   Some people still regarded her as a madwoman or a witch, but there were others who recognized that they had a saint living amongst them.   Many were the conversions and miracles of healing worked by her, but perhaps what finally won her the fame and recognition which she was far from desiring was her gift of prophecy ; she had remarkable revelations about the future, some of which she felt constrained to impart to the king.   In memory perhaps of the sufferings of her husband, Joan Mary had a great compassion for prisoners, whether they were criminals or war captives. She visited them in prison, assisted and instructed them, and once obtained from the king liberation of all the prisoners in Tours. On March 28, 1414, Bd Joan Mary de Maillé died. Her *cultus* was approved in 1871, and the Friars Minor keep her feast today.

See the *Acta Sanctorum*, March, vol. iii ; and Léon, *Auréole Séraphique* (Eng. trans.), vol. ii, 106–130. There are also lives in French, the most recent by A. de Crisenoy (1948).

BD NONIUS   (A.D. 1431)

NONIUS (Nuñes) Alvares de Pereira, son of a grand-master of the Knights of Rhodes, was born near Lisbon in 1360. At the age of seventeen he married, and when twenty-three was made constable in command of the armed forces of Portugal by the grand-master of the Knights of Aviz, who became king as John I. Together they overcame the armies of Castile and established their country as a sovereign state. Thus Bd Nonius is one of the national heroes of Portugal, whose story is told in the sixteenth-century *Chronica do Condestavel*. In 1422, his wife being dead, he entered a Carmelite friary which he had founded at Lisbon as a lay-brother, and remained there for the rest of his life. He died on All Saints' day in 1431, while reading the Passion according to St John, just as he came to the words, " Behold thy mother ! " His popular *cultus* was approved for Portugal and the Carmelite Order in 1918. By the marriage of his daughter Beatrice with the eldest son of King John, first duke of Braganza, he is looked on as the founder of that Serene House ; King Manuel II, the last king of Portugal, long familiar in England after his abdication in 1910, was a descendant of Bd Nonius.

Apart from the *Chronica do Condestavel* (1526), highly praised as a classic of early Portuguese literature, we have an excellent modern biography, J. P. de Oliveira Martins, *A Vida de Nun' Alvares* (1893), and others by Ruy Chianca (1914), E. Battaglia (1918) and V. A. Cordeiro (1919). There is a popular account in English by J. M. Haffert, *The Peacemaker* (1945).

BD MARGARET OF LORRAINE, WIDOW   (A.D. 1521)

MARGARET OF ANJOU, daughter of " good King René ", married the holy Henry VI of England ; her sister, Yolande, married Ferri of Lorraine and of their union was born the Margaret whose ancient *cultus* was confirmed in 1921. When she was twenty-five she married René, Duke of Alençon. The duke died four years later, and Margaret was left with three babies, and the estates of Alençon to be looked after for them. The first thing she did was to ensure the guardianship of her children, which Charles VIII of France wanted to take from her, and then settled down to bring them up at her castle of Mauves. Bd Margaret was as solicitous for the spiritual and temporal welfare of her vassals as for that of her sons ; and she proved herself a most capable administrator, so that when her son Charles came of age and married, he received his inheritance in a good deal better state than it had been left by his father.

Margaret had come under the influence of St Francis of Paula, and during her years of widowhood had been leading a life of considerable asceticism. About 1513, when her responsibility for her children was at an end, she withdrew to Mortagne, where there was a convent and she could unostentatiously look after the poor and the sick. From there she took some of the nuns and established them, under the rule of the Poor Clares, at Argentan. In this convent Bd Margaret herself took the habit in 1519.   She refused the office of abbess, and died, a simple nun, on November 2, 1521.   Her body was taken from its tomb by the Jacobins in 1793 and thrown into the common burying-ground.   It was a dastardly act, but there is a certain fitness in the ashes of this holy Duchess of Alençon mingling with those of the nameless poor and obscure people to whom she had been so devoted.

In the *Acta Sanctorum* (November, vol. i, pp. 418–419) Bd Margaret is mentioned among the *praetermissi*, and the writer describes the evidences of a still fervent *cultus* which he witnessed on a visit to Argentan in 1878.   He also refers to a catalogue of miracles at the shrine, drawn up by Fr Marin de Proverre, but at that date unprinted.   Several lives of this servant of God were published in the seventeenth century ; for example, one by P. de Hameau in 1628.   In more modern times we have biographies by E. Laurent (1854) and R. Guérin (1926).   The decree confirming the *cultus* is printed in the *Acta Apostolicae Sedis*, vol. xiii (1921), pp. 231–233.

THE MARTYRS OF INDO-CHINA, II   (A.D. 1851–1862)

THERE is often so much of extravagance and even of pure invention in the accounts handed down to us of the early martyrs that the doubt may suggest itself whether there is any truth at all in the descriptions of the refined cruelties to which they are said to have been subjected.   But the brutality latent in human nature is everywhere much the same, and the torments which we know upon indisputable evidence to have been inflicted on modern missionaries in the Far East enable us, as nothing else can, to realize what a tyrannical magistrate in pagan Rome, Alexandria or Antioch is likely to have been capable of.   The story of BD THEOPHANES VÉNARD, a young Frenchman who even from childhood had dreamed of martyrdom, and who laid down his life in Tongking at the age of thirty-one, is harrowing in the details it supplies of the diabolical cruelty which prevailed in those regions and of the hardships which he and his companions encountered joyously for Christ's sake. In his tender affection for all the family circle he was a prolific letter-writer, and not only does every word of his bear the stamp of sincerity, but his statements are confirmed in the fullest detail by the correspondence of those who lived with him.

Theophanes was ordained subdeacon in December 1850, and then sought admission into the college of the Missions Étrangères at Paris, *en route*, as it proved, for martyrdom.   In a letter to his sister, just after making his decision, he begins thus :

> MY DARLING SISTER,
>   How I cried when I read your letter !   Yes, I knew well the sorrow I was going to bring upon my family, and especially upon you, my dear little sister. But don't you think it cost me tears of blood, too, to take such a step, and give you all such pain ?   Whoever cared more for home and a home life than I ? All my happiness here below was centred there.   But God, who had united us all in links of the tenderest affection, wished to wean me from it.

Theophanes was always delicate and a severe illness nearly postponed his ordination, but after being admitted to the priesthood he started in September 1852 for Hongkong.   Fifteen months were spent there in studying languages, and thence he passed in 1854 to Western Tongking.   The new missionary with an elder companion reached his destination in safety, but he had to contend both with almost uninterrupted attacks of illness and with a violent outbreak of persecution. For more than five years he struggled on, labouring unremittingly in a district which numbered 10,000 fervent native Christians.   Of the climax of this spell of fanaticism he writes :

> The order has come to seize all the Christians, and to put them to death by what is called *lang-tri* ; that is, by slow torture, cutting off first the ankles, then the knees, then the fingers, then the elbows, and so on until the victim is nothing but a mutilated trunk.   Mgr Melchior, the Dominican vicar apostolic of the eastern district of Tongking, was seized and suffered this horrible death in August last.

Of the desperate straits to which he and the other fathers were reduced he gives many pictures.   " What do you think of our position ? " he writes ; " three missionaries, of whom one is a bishop, lying side by side, day and night, in a space of about a yard and a half square, our only light and means of breathing being three holes, the size of a little finger made in the mud wall, which our poor old woman is bound to conceal by means of faggots thrown down outside ".   On November 30, 1860, Theophanes was taken, and for two months was kept chained in a cage ; but the sweetness of his character impressed even his captors and he was not too cruelly used.   He managed to write letters from his cage, and in one he says : " These last days in my prison pass quietly ; all those who surround me are civil and respectful, and a good many love me.   From the great mandarin down to the humblest private soldier, everyone regrets that the laws of the country condemn me to death.   I have not been put to the torture like my brethren."   His decapitation, however, owing to the brutality of the executioner, was a gruesome spectacle, but it is interesting to read in the account of an eyewitness : " No sooner had the soldiers left than the crowd threw themselves upon the spot to soak their linen cloths and paper handkerchiefs in the martyr's blood ; and such ardour did they show that not a blade of grass was left in the place."   He suffered martyrdom on February 2, 1861.

Ten years before two other alumni of the Paris Society for Foreign Missions, BD AUGUSTUS SCHÖFFLER and BD JOHN LOUIS BONNARD, had been put to death by beheading.   Schöffler was a native of Lorraine, who had come to Tongking in 1848 and soon learned enough of the language to hear confessions and give simple instruction.   In 1851 owing to political disturbances a persecution of Christians broke out.   Father Schöffler was rearrested on March 1, and, although he was not tortured, he must have suffered terribly from the great wooden frame (*cang*) round his neck, and the fetters which confined his limbs, not to speak of the vermin and of the company in the common prison into which he was thrown.   His execution was attended with much parade, but the martyr's courage and bearing impressed even his enemies.

Father Bonnard reached Tongking in 1850, at the crisis of the cholera epidemic then raging, but laboured strenuously among the plague-stricken while continuing his study of the language.   The vicar apostolic under whose orders he served wrote of him with the tenderest affection and admiration.   A very beautiful letter of Father Bonnard is preserved in which, when under sentence of death, he took leave of his family in France.   His head was struck off on May 1, 1852, and, as was usual, his remains, heavily weighted, were thrown into the river.   In the case of the martyr last named the native Christians succeeded in recovering the body.

Among the other martyrs who suffered at this time, BD STEPHEN THEODORE CUÉNOT, in virtue of his episcopal dignity and of his many years of labour under conditions which would daunt the stoutest heart, must claim a place.   He was born in 1802, and after making his studies at the seminary of the Missions Étrangères in Paris came to Annam in 1829.   A violent persecution broke out in 1833, and Cuénot was directed by his superiors to seek refuge in Siam with some of the native students for the priesthood.   Sad discouragements and reverses met him everywhere, but his courage and resourcefulness were so manifest that in 1835 at Singapore he was consecrated episcopal coadjutor to Mgr Taberd.   The persecution still raged in Annam, but Mgr Cuénot managed to effect an entrance, and though terribly hampered in his work by having to remain continually in hiding, he performed marvels in reorganizing the scattered Christian communities and in giving fresh courage to the old native priests and catechists.   His zeal was contagious in spite of the adverse conditions, and many converts were made.

In fifteen years Mgr Cuénot had established three separate vicariates in Cochin-China, each served by some twenty priests, though, on his arrival as vicar apostolic, there had hardly been more than a dozen priests, most of them aged and decrepit, in the whole country.   After an episcopate of more than twenty-five years, during which there had at no time been immunity from persecution, a very violent outbreak of fanaticism occurred which affected even the province of Binh-Dinh, where the Christians had hitherto been left in comparative peace.   The bishop took refuge in the house of a pagan, " who concealed him in a narrow cell adroitly built in the thickness of a double wall ".   The searchers failed to discover his hiding-place, but finding traces of his belongings, kept watch in the same spot.   After two days the bishop, exhausted and ill, could no longer endure the thirst which consumed him, and ventured to show himself.   He was at once seized, thrust into a narrow cage, in which the prisoner could only squat, bent almost double, and was in this conveyed to the chief town of the district.   Though he was then given some measure of liberty within the fortress, he died a few days later as the result of a violent attack of dysentery.   He had scarcely breathed his last when orders arrived from the capital that he should be beheaded.   One of the mandarins proposed to execute the sentence on the corpse, but the two others prevented this last barbarity.

> Half the clerical students, all the pupils of the junior college, all the nuns, altogether a band of 250, have fallen into the hands of the persecutors and are branded on the face with the letters *ta dao* (false religion) as a badge of infamy. They either have a cang or a chain around their necks, some have both ; they are divided into small parties and distributed among the different villages where they are crowded into wretched hovels. . . . The rumour has now spread that two villages have burnt the Christians in order to save their guards the trouble of watching them, and when called to account by the mandarins, they pretended that the fire was accidental.

So wrote the pro-vicar from Saigon in January 1862.   Bd Stephen Cuénot had died on November 14 in the previous year, and two other bishops were martyred during the same month.   BD JEROME HERMOSILLA, a Spanish Dominican, succeeded Bd Ignatius Delgado as vicar apostolic of Eastern Tongking, and when persecution began again he was captured by the mandarin Nguyen.   Mgr Hermosilla managed to escape and continued secretly to minister to the people till he was betrayed by a soldier.   He was imprisoned with two other Dominican missionaries, BD VALENTINE BERRIO-OCHOA, vicar apostolic of Central Tongking, and BD PETER ALMATO. Mgr Berrio-Ochoa was brought up in the Biscayan province, and was apprenticed to a joiner, his noble family having come down in the world.   He left his trade to enter a seminary, and then joined the Friars Preachers with the expressed object of becoming a missionary.   He left for Tongking in 1856, and became vicar apostolic of the central district on the martyrdom of Mgr Sampedro eighteen months later.   During the persecution his hiding-place was revealed by an apostate. Father Peter Almato was a Catalan, who had worked as a missionary for six years under the handicap of ill-health.   Mgr Hermosilla tried to get him over the frontier into China, but the attempt was too late.   These three were beheaded together on November 1, 1861.   It was Bd Peter's thirty-first birthday.   Five weeks later a native secular tertiary, BD JOSEPH KHANG, was put to death at the same place.

The methods of the persecutors were such as have become only too familiar in later days and much nearer home : " All Christians shall be scattered among the non-Christian villages, wives separated from their husbands, and children from their parents.   Christian villages must be destroyed and their possessions distributed elsewhere.   Every Christian shall be marked on his face with the words, ' False religion '."   Other Indo-Chinese who suffered were the priests BB. LAURENCE HUNG (1856), PAUL LOK (1859) and JOHN HOAN (1861) ; BD ANDREW NAM-THUNG (1855), a catechist ; BD MICHAEL HO-DINH-HY (1857), an important official ; and BD MARTHA WANG (1861), who was taken while carrying letters from the imprisoned seminarists BB. JOSEPH SHANG and PAUL CHENG.   The above and their many fellow martyrs were beatified in 1900, 1906 and 1909 ; to-day, November 6, is the feast of BB. Jerome Hermosilla and his Dominican companions.

In 1951 Pope Pius XII beatified a further twenty-five martyrs who suffered in Tongking (now Viet-Nam) between 1857 and 1862 in the persecution of Yu-Duk. Their leaders were the Spanish bishops BD JOSEPH SANJURJO and BD MELCHIOR SAMPEDRO.   Just before his execution Bishop Sanjurjo wrote : " I am without house, books, clothes, anything.   But I am quiet and cheerful, and happy to be able to be a little like our Blessed Lord who said that the Son of man had nowhere to lay His head ".   All the others of this group were Indo-Chinese, and all laymen except four.   They ranged from a judge, BD VINCENT TUONG, to two fishermen, BB. PETER THUAN and DOMINIC TOAI, who with BD PETER DA were burned alive in their bamboo hut.   Other martyrs in Indo-China are mentioned herein under July 11.

The principal source of information about Theophanes Vénard is his own letters and those of his friends, *Vie et Correspondance de J. T. Vénard* (1864).   There is a full life by Mgr F. Trochu (1929), and a less satisfactory anonymous biography translated into English by Lady Herbert.   A full account of the martyrdom of Fathers Schöffler and Bonnard will be found in the *Annals of the Propagation of the Faith* for 1852 and 1853, and of Stephen Cuénot in the same for 1862, pp. 250–260.   There is a life of J. L. Bonnard by Mgr Vindry (1876).   An account of the Dominicans is given in G. Clementi, *Gli otto martiri Tonchinesi O.P.* (1906) and A. Bianconi, *Vita e martirio dei beati Domenicani* (1906).   See also the letter of Father Estavez in the above-mentioned *Annals*, 1863, pp. 178–204.   Several of the references given for the first group of Indo-Chinese martyrs (July 11) are relevant.

7 : ST HERCULANUS, BISHOP OF PERUGIA, MARTYR   (*c.* A.D. 547)

WHEN the Goths took the city of Perugia after beleaguering it off and on for seven years King Totila ordered that the bishop, Herculanus, should be put to death in most barbarous fashion : a strip of skin was to be pulled off him from his crown to his heels before he was beheaded.   The officer entrusted with the execution had the humanity to cut off his head before flaying him, and the body was then thrown off the walls into the fosse.   Christians hastily buried it there with the severed head, but when they disinterred it forty days later for translation to the church of St Peter, the head, St Gregory the Great says, was found attached to the trunk with no sign of separation.   When the Goths captured Tifernum (Città di Castello) a young deacon had taken refuge in Perugia and was there made priest by St Herculanus.   He was afterwards bishop of Tifernum, and as St Floridus he is commemorated on the 13th of this month.   The Perugians venerate also another St Herculanus, bishop of their city, who, they say, was a Syrian who came to Rome and was sent to evangelize Perugia, where he was put to death for the faith.   This Herculanus is probably a duplication of the one mentioned above.

The Bollandists hold that there was only one St Herculanus connected with Perugia, and they discuss the matter primarily on March 1, quoting the notice in the dialogues of St Gregory the Great.   They have also a brief reference to the same matter in their third volume for November, p. 322.   The story of the miracle, and Bonfigli's frescoes in the Palazzo del Municipio, have helped to perpetuate the memory of Herculanus.

ST FLORENTIUS, Bishop of Strasburg   (Seventh Century)

St Florentius is said to have been an Irishman, who came to Alsace (of which he is venerated as an apostle) and settled as a hermit in a valley at the foot of the Ringelberg.   From thence he preached to the neighbouring people, and, having healed King Dagobert's daughter, who was a blind-mute, the king enabled him to found a monastery near by, at Haslach.   After he had become bishop, about 678, many Irish monks and others came to St Florentius at Strasburg.   For these he built a house outside the walls, dedicated in honour of St Thomas the Apostle, which became a monastery under the Irish rule and later a collegiate chapter of canons.

The twelfth-century Life of St Florentius, which is printed in the *Acta Sanctorum*, November, vol. iii, with a full discussion of the difficulties involved, is of no historical value. The date of the saint's death, whether towards the close of the seventh or the beginning of the eighth century must be left quite indeterminate.   As Dom Gougaud makes no mention of Florentius either in his *Gaelic Pioneers of Christianity* (1923) or in his *Saints irlandais hors d'Irlande* (1936) it may be assumed that he discredits the saint's supposed Irish origin. See also Duchesne, *Fastes Épiscopaux*, vol. iii, p. 171 ; and M. Barth, *Der hl. Florentius von Strassburg* (1952).

ST WILLIBRORD, Bishop of Utrecht   (A.D. 739)

St Willibrord was born in Northumbria in the year 658, and placed before he was seven years old in the monastery of Ripon, which was at that time governed by St Wilfrid.   In his twentieth year he went over to Ireland, where he joined St Egbert and St Wigbert who had gone thither to study in the monastic schools and lead a more perfect life among their monks.   In their company he spent twelve years in the study of the sacred sciences.   St Egbert was anxious to preach the gospel in northern Germany but was prevented, and his companion Wigbert came back to Ireland after spending two fruitless years on this mission.   Thereupon Willibrord, who was then thirty-one, and had been ordained priest a year before, expressed a desire to be allowed to undertake this laborious and dangerous task, and was accordingly sent out with eleven other monks, Englishmen, among whom was St Swithbert.

They landed in 690 at the mouth of the Rhine, made their way to Utrecht, and then to the court of Pepin of Herstal, who encouraged them to preach in Lower Friesland, between the Meuse and the sea, which he had conquered from the heathen Radbod. Willibrord set out for Rome and cast himself at the feet of Pope St Sergius I, begging his authority to preach the gospel to idolatrous nations. The pope granted him ample jurisdiction and gave him relics for the consecration of churches. He then returned and with his companions preached the gospel with success in that part of Friesland that had been conquered by the Franks. St Swithbert was consecrated as bishop by St Wilfrid in England, but perhaps Pepin did not approve of this, for Swithbert soon went off up the Rhine to preach to the Boructvari ; and Pepin soon sent St Willibrord to Rome, with letters of recommendation that he might be ordained bishop. Pope Sergius still sat in St Peter's chair and he received him with honour, changed his name to Clement and ordained him bishop of the Frisians in St Cecilia's basilica on her feast-day in the year 695. St Willibrord stayed only fourteen days in Rome, and coming back to Utrecht built there the church of our Saviour, in which he fixed his see. The bishop's indefatigable application to the conversion of souls seemed to prove that, with the new obligation he had received at his consecration of labouring to enlarge the kingdom of his Master, he had acquired fresh strength and zeal. Some years after his consecration, assisted by the liberality of Pepin and the abbess St Irmina, he founded the abbey of Echternach in Luxemburg, which soon became an important centre of his influence.

Willibrord extended his labours into Upper Friesland, which still obeyed Radbod, and penetrated into Denmark, but with no more success than to purchase thirty young Danish boys, whom he instructed, baptized and brought back with him. In his return, according to Alcuin, he was driven by stress of weather upon the island of Heligoland, revered as a holy place by the Danes and Frisians. It was looked upon as a sacrilege for anyone to kill any living creature on that island, to eat anything that grew on it, or to draw water out of a spring there without observing strict silence. St Willibrord, to undeceive the inhabitants, killed some of the beasts for his companions to eat and baptized three persons in the fountain, pronouncing the words very loudly. The idolaters expected to see them go mad or drop down dead, and when no such judgement befell could not determine whether this was to be attributed to the patience of their god or to his want of power. They informed Radbod, who ordered lots to be cast for the person who should appease the god, so that one of Willibrord's company was sacrificed to the superstition of the people and died a martyr for Jesus Christ. The saint, upon leaving Heligoland, went ashore on Walcheren and his charity and patience made considerable conquests to the Christian religion there. He overthrew and destroyed an idol, whereupon he was attacked by its outraged priest who tried to kill the missionary, but he escaped and returned in safety to Utrecht. In 714 Charles Martel's son Pepin the Short, afterwards king of the Franks, was born, and baptized by St Willibrord, who on that occasion is related by Alcuin to have prophesied that the child would surpass in glory all his ancestors.

In 715 Radbod regained the parts of Frisia he had lost, and undid much of Willibrord's work, destroying churches, killing missionaries and inducing many apostasies. For a time Willibrord retired, but after the death of Radbod in 719 he was at full liberty to preach in every part of the country. He was joined in his apostolical labours by St Boniface, who spent three years in Friesland before he went into Germany. Bede says, when he wrote his history in 731, " Willibrord, surnamed Clement, is still living, venerable in his old age, having been bishop thirty-six years, and sighing after the rewards of the heavenly life after many spiritual conflicts ". He was, says Bd Alcuin, of a becoming stature, venerable in his aspect, comely in his person, graceful and always cheerful in his speech and countenance, wise in his counsel, unwearied in preaching and all apostolic works, amidst which he was careful to nourish the interior life of his soul by public prayer, meditation and reading. By the prayers and labours of this apostle and his colleagues the faith was planted in many parts of Holland, Zeeland, and the Netherlands, whither St Amand and St Lebwin had never penetrated ; and the Frisians, till then a rough and barbarous people, became more civilized and virtuous. He is commonly called the Apostle of the Frisians, a title to which he has every claim ; but it must not be lost sight of that in the earlier days of the mission St Swithbert also played a very considerable part and seems in some degree to have been its leader. And the Frisians, like other nations, were not converted with the speed and in the numbers that medieval hagiographers would have us believe. " Willibrord was to England what Columbanus had been to Ireland. He inaugurated a century of English spiritual influence on the continent " (W. Levison).

It had always been St Willibrord's habit to go from time to time to his monastery at Echternach for periods of retreat, and in his old age he made it his place of permanent retirement. There he died at the age of eighty-one on November 7, 739, and was buried in the abbey church, which has ever since been a place of pilgrimage. In connection with the shrine there takes place every Whit-Tuesday a curious observance called the *Springende Heiligen*, the Dancing Saints. Its true origin is unknown, but it is known to have taken place regularly (except from 1786 till 1802) from at least 1553 until the present day. It consists of a procession from a bridge over the Sure to St Willibrord's shrine. The participants, four or five abreast and hand-fasted or arm-in-arm, proceed with a hopping or dancing motion, in which for every three steps forward they take two back, in time to a traditional tune played by bands. Priests, religious, and even bishops take part, and the ceremony ends with benediction of the Blessed Sacrament. Whatever its origin, the procession is now penitential in character and intercessory on behalf of those suffering from epilepsy and similar maladies. St Willibrord's feast is kept in the diocese of Hexham as well as in Holland.

The account of St Willibrord contributed to the *Acta Sanctorum*, November, vol. iii, by Fr A. Poncelet, is worthy of all praise, not only for its clear statement, but for its complete mastery of the facts and of the whole period. He recalls the tributes paid to St Willibrord by his contemporaries St Bede, St Boniface, etc., and prints entire a critically revised text of the life by Alcuin as also of that by Theofrid, abbot of Echternach, though this last adds very little to our reliable historical data. A point of special interest is the fact that in what is known as the " Epternach MS." of the *Hieronymianum* (now MS. Paris Latin 10837) a calendar is prefixed which contains a note written by Willibrord himself in 728, stating that he, " Clement ", came over the sea in 690 and was consecrated bishop by Pope Sergius at Rome in 695. See on this and other points of detail the *Calendar of St Willibrord* edited for the Henry Bradshaw Society by H. A. Wilson (1918). There are also good notices of St Willibrord in DNB. (by Mrs Tout) and DCB. On the dancing procession at Echternach consult Fr John Morris in *The Month*, December, 1892, pp. 495–513, and Krier, *Die Springprozession in Echternach* (1870). A Life of St Willibrord in English, prepared originally for J. H. Newman's Anglican series (? by Fr T. Meyrick), was published anonymously in

1877. The more important texts concerned with the saint have also been edited by W. Levison, whose conclusions in nearly all cases agree with those of Fr Poncelet, notably in his acceptance of the genuineness of the so-called " will " of St Willibrord.. As recently as 1934 Levison has included in the continuation of the MGH., *Scriptores*, vol. xxx (pp. 1368–1371), a collection of the miracles attributed to him. Some of the reputed relics of the saint have come to light in the church of St Gertrude at Utrecht, and have been described by W. J. A. Visser, on which see the *Analecta Bollandiana*, vol. lii (1934), pp. 436–437. See also G. H. Verbist, *St Willibrord, apôtre des Pays-Bas* (1939) ; and W. Levison, *England and the Continent* . . . (1946), especially pp. 53–69. The life by Alcuin is translated by C. H. Talbot in *Anglo-Saxon Missionaries in Germany* (1954).

ST ENGELBERT, Archbishop of Cologne, Martyr   (A.D. 1225)

Among the ecclesiastical abuses rife in the middle ages was the presentation of youths, and even children, to church benefices, and often more than one at a time. This Engelbert, who doubtless owed his preferment to the fact that his father was the powerful count of Berg, provides a characteristic example. While still a boy at the Cologne cathedral-school he was provost of St Mary's at Aachen and of St George's, of St Severinus, and of the cathedral at Cologne itself. His youthful life was not at all in accordance with his obligations and he was excommunicated for taking up arms against the Emperor Otto IV. For a short time he joined the crusade against the Albigensians ; and then, playing his cards skilfully between two claimants, was himself consecrated to the see of Cologne in 1217. He was only about thirty years old and the great diocese had suffered severely from political and ecclesiastical upheavals. Nevertheless, Engelbert was well endowed with the natural qualities necessary for his task, a keen judgement, regard for justice, strong will and commanding presence. And after his excommunication was raised his personal life was blameless, though had it not been for his violent end in defence of a religious house it is doubtful if his *cultus* would have ever arisen or been officially recognized.

Engelbert welcomed both the Friars Minor and the Dominicans to the diocese, and held synods for the maintenance of discipline among the clergy, both secular and regular. He was popular with the people, for he was affable, generous to the poor, and peace-loving in spite of his firmness. But his time was in the main taken up by affairs of state. He supported the Hohenstaufen emperor, Frederick II, and when in 1220 Frederick went to Sicily he appointed Engelbert regent during the minority of his son, Henry. This boy of twelve was crowned king of the Romans by his guardian at Aachen in 1222. St Engelbert discharged his duties with vigour and determination, but, while earning the love and respect of King Henry, his firm justice raised up many powerful enemies, especially among his own kinsfolk.

St Engelbert's cousin, Count Frederick of Isenberg, took advantage of his position as administrator for the nuns of Essen to steal their property and oppress their vassals. Engelbert called him to order and restitution, and Frederick laid a plot to murder his cousin. St Engelbert was warned of his danger, and he took precautions, but on November 7, 1225, he set out to go from Soest to Schwelm with an inadequate escort. At the Gevelsberg he was set upon by Frederick of Isenberg, with other aggrieved nobles and half a hundred soldiers, and was left dead with forty-seven wounds in his body. Young King Henry had Count Frederick brought to justice, and the papal legate, Cardinal von Urach, declared that Engelbert was a martyr. He has never been formally canonized, but his feast was instituted at Cologne and his name admitted to the Roman Martyrology.

There is a life by Caesarius of Heisterbach, a contemporary, which has been edited in the *Acta Sanctorum* for November, vol. iii. The *Regesta* of the diocese of Cologne also supply useful information ; the relevant texts were published in 1909 by R. Knipping, forming vol. iii of the series. Two or three dispatches from the English envoy, Walter, Bishop of Carlisle, printed in the *Letters of Henry III* (Rolls Series), show that Engelbert of Cologne just before his death was on very friendly terms with England. See also the German biographies by J. Ficker (1853) and H. Foerster (1925).

BD HELEN OF ARCELLA, Virgin　　(A.D. 1242)

About the year 1220 St Francis of Assisi came to Arcella, near Padua, to make a foundation of Poor Clare nuns there. On that occasion he gave the habit to Bd Helen, of the noble Enselmini family. When she had been six years in religion she was visited with a painful malady which persisted all her life, but she bore her sufferings with the greatest patience, and was the recipient of some very remarkable heavenly consolations. She is said, on the one hand, to have been permitted a sight of the glory of the elect, especially of St Francis and his faithful followers, and, on the other, to have as it were visited Purgatory, where she saw the holy souls relieved and liberated by the prayers and good works of the faithful on earth. She is said to have lived several months with no other bodily nourishment than that provided by the sacred Host. Towards the end of his life St Antony of Padua was the spiritual guide of Bd Helen. Though only thirty-four years old when she died, she had already added to her other physical trials the loss of both sight and speech. Bd Helen died on November 4, 1242, and her *cultus* was approved in 1695.

We have no detailed account of this *beata* from a contemporary, or indeed from anyone who wrote within a century of her death. Bartholomew of Pisa (*c.* 1385), in his *De conformitatibus*, part viii, speaks of her in some detail but supplies no dates ; other writers affirm that she died in 1230 or 1231, but Mariano of Florence and Wadding seem to be unquestionably right in holding that she lived on until 1242. Fr Van Ortroy in the *Acta Sanctorum*, November, vol. ii, has printed a short biography compiled in 1437 by Sicco Polentono, a legal official of Padua. The patience and sufferings of Bd Helen are also described in such popular summaries as that of Fr Léon, *Auréole Séraphique* (Eng. trans.), vol. iv, pp. 36–38.

BD MARGARET COLONNA, Virgin　　(A.D. 1280)

Margaret was daughter of Prince Odo Colonna, but losing both her parents when a child she was brought up under the care of her two brothers. She refused the marriage arranged for her, and lived a retired life with two attendants in a villa at Palestrina, devoting her time and her goods to the relief of the sick and poor. It was her intention to join the Poor Clares in their house at Assisi, but sickness prevented this, and she conceived the idea of establishing a convent at Palestrina. Her younger brother, James, who had been created cardinal (and so is distinguished as *dignior frater* from her *senior frater*, John, who wrote her life), obtained the pope's permission and the community was given the rule of the Poor Clare nuns as modified by Urban IV. But it would seem that, on account of ill-health, Bd Margaret herself neither governed nor was professed in this convent ; for the last seven years of her life she suffered from a malignant growth, bearing continual pain with the greatest courage and patience. She had the gift of miracles, and other unusual graces are recorded of her. After her death at an early age the nuns of Palestrina removed into the City to San Silvestro in Capite, taking the body of their foundress with them. When this monastery was turned into a general post office seven hundred years later the relics were translated to the nuns' new home at St Cecilia in Trastevere. Pope Pius IX confirmed the *cultus* of Bd Margaret Colonna in 1847.

The Franciscan Chroniclers, such as Wadding and Mark of Lisbon, have published full accounts of Bd Margaret ; the story is told in detail in, *e.g.* Mazzara, *Leggendario Francescano* (1680), vol. ii, pt. 2, pp. 775–780. In *B. Margherita Colonna* (1935) Fr L. Oliger edited and introduced an unpublished MS. of the fourteenth century, which combines parts of *vitae* by John Colonna (d. *c.* 1292) and by a Poor Clare of San Silvestro (*fl.* 1290). For English readers there is an account available in Léon, *Auréole Séraphique* (Eng. trans.), vol. iv, pp. 170–173.

BD MATTHIA OF MATELICA, Virgin   (A.D. 1300)

At the town of Matelica in the March of Ancona there is a monastery of Poor Clare nuns whose origin is said to go back to about the year 1233, when St Clare was still living; this ancient convent was dedicated in honour of St Mary Magdalene, but since 1758 has been known as Bd Matthia's. This *beata* was born in Matelica about the same time as the convent was founded, the only child of Count Gentile Nazzarei, who naturally wished his daughter to marry and perpetuate his house. She, however, was called to be a nun and offered herself to the abbess of Santa Maria Maddalena, who was related to Count Gentile and refused to receive her without her father's consent. According to an old tradition Matthia thereupon went into the convent chapel, changed her secular clothes for a religious habit, cut off her hair, and there offered herself to Christ before a crucifix. Count Gentile found her thus, and was reluctantly persuaded to give his permission. Nothing is known of the life in religion of Bd Matthia except vague generalities. She filled the office of abbess for forty years, and died on December 28, 1300. Miracles became so frequent at her grave that the body was soon moved to a tomb beside the high altar of the chapel, where her veneration was continued without interruption. In 1756 the tomb had to be moved on account of repairs, and the Bishop of Camerino took the opportunity to examine the relics ; the body was found to be incorrupt and giving off a pleasant smell. It was re-enshrined under the altar of St Cecilia, and since then miracles have again been reported there. In particular, the body is said to have exuded from time to time a sweet-smelling, blood-like liquid, especially when a member of the community is going to die.

The *cultus* of Bd Matthia was confirmed in 1765. It must be added that it is said by some that the Matelica convent was founded for Benedictine nuns and became Franciscan only after the lifetime of Bd Matthia, which is put earlier.

Full accounts of the *beata* are available in nearly all the Franciscan chroniclers. Mazzara commemorates her in June ; see the *Leggendario Francescano*, pt 1 (1676), pp. 875–876. There are Italian lives by G. Baldassini (1852), and by Vincent de Porto San Giorgio (1877). See also Léon, *Auréole Séraphique* (Eng. trans.), vol. i, pp. 332–338 ; and *cf.* A. M. Zimmermann, *Kalendarium Benedictinum*, vol. iii (1937).

BD PETER OF RUFFIA, Martyr   (A.D. 1365)

The Friars Preachers, especially during the mastership of Humbert of Romans, were very reluctant to accept offices in the Inquisition, and particularly after the murder of St Peter of Verona in 1242 urged the Holy See to relieve them from this service. Their request was not granted, and during the second half of the four-teenth century these duties brought more martyrs to the order. Bd Peter of Ruffia, a member of the Piedmontese family of the Cambiani, joined the Dominicans, and in 1351 was nominated inquisitor general for Piedmont, Upper Lombardy and Liguria. Several sects were active in northern Italy at that time, particularly the Waldensians, and for fourteen years Bd Peter laboured among them. The measure of his success was also the measure of the hatred which the more stubborn heretics had for him. While he was staying at Susa in 1365 some sectaries attacked him and put him to death. Peter was at once venerated as a martyr, and this *cultus* was confirmed in 1856.

The Bollandists in the *Acta Sanctorum*, November, vol. iii, complain that little was to be learnt of the history of this martyr, but they were able to print a contemporary legal instrument, issued by the bishop of Turin, which authorized another bishop to reconcile and reconsecrate the Franciscan cloister which had been the scene of the violent death of Bd Peter. See also Procter, *Lives of the Dominican Saints*, pp. 313–314.

BD ANTONY BALDINUCCI   (A.D. 1717)

ON this day the Society of Jesus and several Italian dioceses that profited by his labours keep the feast of this Bd Antony, the fifth son of Philip Baldinucci and Catherine Scolari, of Florence. His father, painter and writer by profession, after recovery from an illness, which he attributed to the intercession of St Antony of Padua, vowed his next child to that saint; and when a boy was born in 1665, appropriately within the octave of his feast, he had him baptized Antony and brought up with the idea of becoming a priest. The Baldinucci family lived in the same house in the via degli Angeli at Florence in which St Aloysius Gonzaga had lived for a time when a child, and the intimate memory of this young saint had much influence on the growing Antony. When he was sixteen he offered himself to the Society of Jesus and was accepted, in spite of his rather uncertain health.

Antony hoped to be sent as a missionary to the Indies, but instead he was set to teach young men and give instructions to confraternities, first at Terni and then in Rome. A bout of seizures and bad headaches caused him to be sent back to Florence, and then to several country colleges, where his health improved and he began to preach, very successfully. When he was thirty he was ordained priest, and after he had completed his tertianship he asked if he might now go to the Indies. He was refused and sent to minister in Viterbo and Frascati, in whose neighbourhood he spent the remaining twenty years of his life, working principally among the poorer and uninstructed people. To attract them he adopted missionary methods that were, to put it mildly, demonstrative and startling, modelled on those of St Peter Claver among the Negroes and Bd Julian Maunoir among the Bretons. Bd Antony organized imposing processions from different places to the centre where the mission was being held, in which penitents walked wearing crowns of thorns and beating themselves with a discipline; he himself often preached carrying a heavy cross or wearing chains, and would strike the hearts of the people by going along the streets scourging himself violently. After a due impression had been made and he had got the people of a place to come and listen to him, he would modify his methods to a more usual pattern. To keep order in the crowds that flocked to his preaching he appointed lay marshals, often men of notoriously bad lives, who were thus flattered and brought to a more amenable frame of mind. Among the exterior results of his missions was generally a public burning of cards, dice, obscene pictures and other occasions of sin and excess. He found particularly widespread the evils of reckless gambling, violence arising from revenge, and lewdness of speech and action, and his zeal did not end in bonfires but brought about many real conversions and the establishment of organized good works.

Although he was incessantly engaged in preaching missions and the work ancillary thereto, Bd Antony wrote down numerous sermons and instructions and kept up a wide correspondence. He rarely slept more than three hours in a night, and then on a bed of planks, and fasted three days of every week ; in view of his tremendous activity Pope Clement XI dispensed him from the daily recitation of the Divine Office, but Antony did not make use of the dispensation. In all he gave in twenty years 448 missions in thirteen dioceses of the Abruzzi and Romagna. In 1708 he was called to preach the Lent at Leghorn by order of Duke Cosimo III. Antony arrived bare-footed, in a tattered cassock, with his luggage on his back, and at first the gentry would not come to his sermons. But he won them in the end, and every Lent after he had to preach in some principal city. The year 1716 saw a terrible famine in central Italy, and Bd Antony was indefatigable in the work of relief. He was still only just over fifty, but he was literally worn out with work and hardly survived the strain of this additional effort. He died on November 7 in the following year. During a mission at Carpineto in 1710 he had stayed in the house of the Pecci, a family which afterwards gave a pope to the Church in the person of Leo XIII. By this pope Bd Antony Baldinucci was beatified in 1893.

The details of the history of Bd Antony are very fully known from the testimony of the witnesses in the process of beatification as well as from his own letters and other contemporary documents. There is a satisfactory, if summary, account of these sources in the *Acta Sanctorum*, November, vol. iii. Within two and a half years of the missioner's death a substantial biography had been published by Father F. M. Galluzzi. The best modern life is probably that by Father Vannucci (1893), but there are several others, *e.g.* by Father Goldie in English (1894). See also DHG., vol. iii, cc. 756–760. A large collection of Bd Antony's letters was edited and published by Father L. Rosa in 1899.

8 : THE FOUR CROWNED ONES, MARTYRS   (A.D. 306 ?)

THE Roman Martyrology has to-day : " At Rome, three miles from the City on the Via Lavicana, the passion of the holy martyrs Claudius, Nicostratus, Symphorian, Castorius and Simplicius, who were first cast into prison, then terribly beaten with loaded whips, and finally, since they could not be turned from Christ's faith, thrown headlong into the river by order of Diocletian. Likewise on the Via Lavicana the birthday of the four holy crowned brothers, namely, Severus, Severian, Carpophorus and Victorinus, who, under the same emperor, were beaten to death with blows from leaden scourges. Since their names, which in after years were made known by divine revelation, could not be discovered it was appointed that their anniversary, together with that of the other five, should be kept under the name of the Four Holy Crowned Ones ; and this has continued to be done in the Church even after their names were revealed."

These two entries and the *passio* upon which they are founded provide a puzzle which has not yet been solved with complete certainty. Severus, Severian, Carpophorus and Victorinus, names which the Roman Martyrology and Breviary say were revealed as those of the Four Crowned Martyrs, were borrowed from the martyrology of the diocese of Albano, where their feast is kept on August 8.   On the other hand, the Four Crowned Martyrs were sometimes referred to as Claudius, Nicostratus, Symphorian and Castorius.   These, with the addition of Simplicius, so far from being the names of Roman martyrs (as stated above), belonged to five martyrs under Diocletian in Pannonia.

The legend falls into two distinct parts, the conventional and vague " Roman *passio* ", preceded by the vivid and interesting " Pannonian *passio* " wherein, as Father Delehaye points out, we have a striking picture of the imperial quarries and workshops at Sirmium (Mitrovica in Yugoslavia), and Diocletian appears not simply as a commonplace blood-stained monster but as the emperor of rather unstable temperament with a passion for building.   His attention is drawn by the work of four specially skilled carvers, Claudius, Nicostratus, Simpronian and Castorius, all Christians, and a fifth, Simplicius, who also has become a Christian, because it seems to him that the skill of the others is due to their religion.   Diocletian orders them to do a number of carvings, which are duly executed with the exception of a statue of Aesculapius, which they will not make because they are Christians (though their other commissions have already included a large statue of the Sun-god).   " If their religion enables them to do such good work, all the better ", says the emperor, and confides Aesculapius to some heathen workmen.

But public opinion was aroused against Claudius and his comrades, and they were jailed for refusing to sacrifice to the gods.   Both Diocletian and his officer Lampadius treated them with moderation at first ; but Lampadius dying suddenly, his relatives furiously blamed the five Christians, and the emperor was induced to order their death.   Thereupon each was enclosed in a leaden box, and thrown into the river to drown.   Three weeks later the bodies were retrieved by one Nicodemus.

A year later Diocletian was in Rome, where he built a temple to Aesculapius in the baths of Trajan, and ordered all his troops to sacrifice to the god.   Four *cornicularii* refused : whereupon they were beaten to death with leaded scourges and their bodies cast into the common sewer.   They were taken up and buried on the Via Lavicana by St Sebastian * and Pope Miltiades, who later directed, their names having been forgotten, that they should be commemorated under the names of Claudius, Nicostratus, Simpronian and Castorius.

A basilica was built and dedicated in honour of the Four Crowned Ones on the Coelian hill at Rome, probably during the first half of the fifth century : it became, and its successor still is, one of the titular churches of the cardinal-priests of the City.   There is evidence that those thus commemorated were four of the Pannonian martyrs (why Simplicius was omitted does not appear), and that their relics were later translated to Rome.   Then, it has been suggested, their names and history became known, and there emerged the difficulty that they were five, not four ; and accordingly a hagiographer produced the second story outlined above, showing that the *Quatuor Coronati* were four Romans, not five Pannonians, and soldiers, not stone-masons.   Of which convenient fiction Father Delehaye remarks that it is " l'opprobre de l'hagiographie ".

It was natural that in the medieval organizations of " operative " masonry the Four Crowned Ones should be held in great honour.   A poem of the early fifteenth

* The names Claudius, Nicostratus, Symphorian and Castorius, with Victorinus, also occur in the legend of St Sebastian, among the converts of St Polycarp the Priest who were cast into the sea, and have as such separate mention in the Roman Martyrology on July 7.

century setting out the articles of one of these stone-mason gilds is preserved in MS. Royal XVII. A. 1 at the British Museum.   It has a section headed *Ars quatuor coronatorum*, beginning :

> Pray we now to God almyght
> And to hys moder Mary bryght ;

and it then goes on to tell briefly the story " of these martyres fowre, that in thys craft were of gret honoure ".   It is stated that those who want to know more about them may find—

> In the legent of sanctorum
> [*i.e.* the book *Legenda Sanctorum*]
> The names of quatuor coronatorum.
> Their fest wol be, withoute nay,
> After Alle Halwen the eyght day.

The English Freemasons of modern times have in a sense clung to the tradition, and the most scholarly organ of the craft in this country has for many years past been published under the name *Ars Quatuor Coronatorum*.   Bede refers to a church at Canterbury dedicated in honour of the Four Crowned Martyrs so early as *c.* 620.

Any detailed discussion of the problems outlined above would be out of place here.   In the *Acta Sanctorum*, November, vol. iii, Delehaye in 1910 devoted thirty-six folio pages to the question, editing the text of the *passio* of the Pannonian group, written, it is believed, by a certain Porphyry, and also the tenth-century recension of the same, due to one Peter of Naples.   The *Depositio martyrum* of the fourth century, confirmed by the Leonine and other sacramentaries, leaves no doubt that this group of martyrs was honoured in Rome at an early date, and Delehaye, in the *Analecta Bollandiana*, vol. xxxii (1913), pp. 63–71, as well as in his *Les passions des martyrs . . .* (1921), pp. 328–344, his *Étude sur le légendier romain* (1936), pp. 65–73, and the CMH., pp. 590–591, adheres firmly to the view that there ·was only one group of martyrs, the stone-masons of Pannonia, whose relics were brought to Rome and interred in the catacomb on the Via Labicana.   Other theories, however, have been propounded, notably by Mgr Duchesne in *Mélanges d'archéologie et d'histoire*, vol. xxxi (1911), pp. 231–246 ; by P. Franchi de' Cavalieri in *Studi e Testi*, vol. xxiv (1912), pp. 57–66 ; and J. P. Kirsch in the *Historisches Jahrbuch*, vol. xxxviii (1917), pp. 72–97.

ST CYBI, or CUBY, Abbot   (Sixth Century)

Of the numerous Celtic saints whose feasts occur this month Cybi was probably one of the most important, but information about him is dependent chiefly on a very unreliable Latin *vita* of the thirteenth century and whatever can be gleaned from the evidence of place-names and local traditions.   He was born in Cornwall, we are told, the son of Selyf (" St Levan "), and two old churches in his native county are dedicated in his honour, at Duloe, near Liskeard, and at Cuby, in Tregony.   The life says he learned to read at seven, and twenty years later, after the common imaginary pilgrimage to Jerusalem, became a disciple of St Hilary, by whom he was made bishop at Poitiers.   This is chronologically impossible. Cybi is supposed to have left Cornwall because he would not consent to be king there, and gone into what is now Monmouthshire ; there is a place there called Llangibby, on the Usk.   Then, by way of St David's Menevia, he visited Ireland and spent four years on Aranmore with St Enda.   He had to leave there because of a dispute with another monk, called Fintan the Priest, about a straying cow, and he went to the south of Meath where he founded a church.   But Fintan followed him and turned him out and drove him eastward across Ireland and over the sea. The crossing was made in a coracle which had the usual framework, but no hides to cover it.

There is no necessity to suppose that St Cybi was ever in Ireland, for probably the writer of his life knew the traditions about St Enda, and by a confusion of names took Cybi to Aran and associated him with various incidents in the life of Enda. But when St Cybi lands in Anglesey we are on more solid ground, for this island was the chief centre of his *cultus*. Here he founded a monastery, and around that monastery rose the town called in English Holyhead but in Welsh Caer Gybi (" Cybi's Fort "), as the smaller island on which it stands, Holy Island, is called Ynys Gybi. From it Cybi evangelized the neighbourhood, where his name appears in places and local legends, as elsewhere in Wales ; and there he died and was buried, and his shrine was a place of pilgrimage. Throughout the middle ages his monastic community was represented by a college of secular canons, and on a gable of the fifteenth-century church of Holyhead may still be read the invocation, *Sancte Kebie, ora pro nobis.*

It is probable that St Cybi, like so many other Celtic saints, journeyed by water whenever he could ; all the chief places bearing his name are on or near the sea. An old Welsh proverb is attributed to him, in conversation with " the son of Gwrgi "—" There is no misfortune like wickedness." November 8 for his feast is taken from the Latin life ; Welsh calendars and other sources give several other dates.

The Latin life spoken of above has been printed in the *Acta Sanctorum*, November, vol. iii, and the tangled story which it tells has been discussed very completely by Canon Doble in his booklet *St Cuby* (1929), no. 22, in his Cornish Saints Series. See also A. W. Wade-Evans, *The Life of St David* (1923), pp. 98–100 ; and LBS., vol. ii, pp. 202–215. In his *Vitae Sanctorum Brittaniae* (1944) Wade-Evans gives the text and translation of the two versions of the *Vita Kebii*. *Cf.* E. G. Bowen, *Settlements of the Celtic Saints in Wales* (1954), pp. 118–120.

ST DEUSDEDIT, POPE (A.D. 618)

VERY little is known of the life and three-year pontificate of Pope Deusdedit (Adeodatus I), who was a Roman by birth and son of a subdeacon named Stephen. The times were troubled by civil disorder, war, and by an epidemic of skin disease following an earthquake ; St Deusdedit was foremost in caring for the suffering (the Roman Martyrology mentions the tradition of his having healed a " leper " by a kiss), and encouraged his impoverished clergy to do the same. He is said to have been the first pope to have used the leaden seals called *bullae*, from which papal " bulls " get their name : one such seal dating from his time still exists. Pope St Deusdedit is called a Benedictine in ancient Benedictine calendars, but there is no certain evidence for the statement.

See Duchesne, *Liber Pontificalis*, vol. i, pp. 319–320 ; H. K. Mann, *Lives of the Popes*, vol. i, pp. 280–293.

ST TYSILIO, OR SULIAU, ABBOT (SEVENTH CENTURY ?)

ACCORDING to the Breton account and the few surviving Welsh references, Tysilio was son of Brochwel Ysgythrog, prince of Powys in North Wales. When a young man he ran away to be a monk under the abbot Gwyddfarch at Meifod in

Montgomeryshire. His father sent to fetch him back, but Tysilio refused to go and fled for greater security to an islet in the Menai Straits, Ynys Suliau. At the end of seven years he came back to Meifod, where he found Gwyddfarch in spite of his great age contemplating a pilgrimage to Rome. " I know what that means ", was Tysilio's comment. " You want to see the churches and palaces there. Dream about them, instead of going all that way." He took the old man a long walk over the mountains and tired him out, and Tysilio did not fail to point out that Rome was a much longer journey than they had been. Then they sat down and Gwydd-farch went to sleep, and dreamed he saw all the glory of Rome, and he was satisfied. When he died, Tysilio became abbot in his place.

When his elder brother, the prince of Powys, died, his widow Haiarnwedd wished to marry Tysilio and make him prince. To this he would not agree, for he had no taste for war and secular pursuits or for marriage, least of all within the prohibited degrees. His sister-in-law took this refusal as a personal insult, drove him from Meifod, and he took refuge at Builth in Breconshire. As her anger still pursued him, he left Wales altogether and sailed for Armorica with some of his monks. They landed at the mouth of the Rance, established contact with St Malo, and settled at the place still called Saint-Suliac. When Haiarnwedd died, a deputa-tion came to fetch Tysilio back to Meifod ; he did not go, but sent a book of the gospels and his staff as an indication of goodwill and blessing. He died and was buried in Brittany. As well as Ynys Suliau, Tysilio's name is associated with other places in Wales ; it is an element of the Anglesey (faked) place-name which has the distinction of having twenty-four syllables in it. A twelfth-century bard, Cynddelw, wrote of Tysilio, " the royal saint of Powys " :

> A lord magnificent . . .
> A prince with princes holding intercourse.
> Whoso loves cruelty he sorely hates,
> Whilst all whose ends are loveable he loves ;
> To chastisement he charity prefers.

See LBS., vol. iv, pp. 296–305 ; the *Myvyrian Archaiology of Wales*, vol. iii (1807) ; A., W. Wade-Evans, *Welsh Christian Origins* (1934), pp. 200–201 ; and especially G. H. Doble, *St Sulian and St Tysilio* (1936) ; they seem to have been two (or three) different people, one Breton and one Welsh. See E. G. Bowen, *Settlements of the Celtic Saints in Wales* (1954).

ST WILLEHAD, BISHOP OF BREMEN   (A.D. 789)

WILLEHAD was an Englishman, a native of Northumbria, and was educated probably at York, for he became a friend of Alcuin. After his ordination the spiritual conquests which many of his countrymen had made for Christ, with St Willibrord in Friesland and St Boniface in Germany, seemed a reproach to him, and he also desired to carry the saving knowledge of the true God to some of those barbarous nations. He landed in Friesland about the year 766 and began his mission at Dokkum, the place near which St Boniface and his companions had received the crown of martyrdom in 754. (The Roman Martyrology mistakenly calls St Wille-had a disciple of St Boniface.) After baptizing some, he made his way through the country now called Overyssel, preaching as he went. In Humsterland the mission-aries were all put in peril of their lives, for the inhabitants cast lots whether he and his companions should be put to death ; Providence determined the lots for their preservation. Having escaped out of their hands, St Willehad thought it prudent to go back to Drenthe, in the more favourable neighbourhood of Utrecht. Here, in spite of the labours of St Willibrord and his successors, there was still plenty of heathens to convert, but the promising field was spoiled by imprudent zeal. Some of Willehad's fellow missionaries venturing to demolish the places dedicated to idolatry, the pagans were so angered that they resolved to massacre them. One struck at St Willehad with such force that the sword would have severed his head but that the force of the blow, as his biographer assures us, was entirely broken by cutting a string about the saint's neck by which hung a little box of relics which he always carried with him. The whole incident bears a suspicious resemblance to that recorded of St Willibrord on the island of Walcheren.

Having made so little progress among the Frisians St Willehad went to the court of Charlemagne, who in 780 sent him to evangelize the Saxons, whom he had recently subdued. The saint thence proceeded into the country where Bremen now stands, and was the first missionary who passed the Weser ; some of his companions got beyond the Elbe. For a short time all went well, but in 782 the Saxons rose in revolt against the Franks. They put to death all missionaries that fell into their hands, and St Willehad escaped by sea into Friesland, whence he took an opportunity of going to Rome and laying before Pope Adrian I the state of his mission. He then passed two years in the monastery of Echternach, founded by St Willibrord, and assembled his fellow labourers whom the war had dispersed ; here, too, he made a copy of the letters of St Paul.

Charlemagne put down the Saxon rebellion in ruthless fashion, and Willehad was able to return to the country between the Weser and the Elbe.* When the saint had founded many churches, Charlemagne in 787 had him ordained bishop of the Saxons, and he fixed his see at Bremen, which city seems to have been founded about that time. St Willehad redoubled his zeal and his solicitude in preaching. His cathedral church he built of wood and consecrated it on November 1, 789, in honour of St Peter. A few days later he was taken ill, and it was seen that he was very bad. One of his disciples said to him, weeping, " Do not so soon forsake your flock exposed to the fury of wolves ". He answered, " Withhold me not from going to God. My sheep I recommend to Him who intrusted them to me and whose mercy is able to protect them." And so he died, and his successor buried his body in the new stone church at Bremen. St Willehad was the last of the great English missionaries of the eighth century.

Our knowledge of St Willehad is almost entirely derived from a Latin life written about the year 856 by some ecclesiastic of Bremen. It was formerly attributed to the authorship of St Anskar, but this view has now been abandoned, though Anskar seems to be responsible for the book of miracles attached to the life. The best text of both is that edited by A. Poncelet in the *Acta Sanctorum*, November, vol. iii ; but they have been printed several times before, *e.g.* by Mabillon, and in Pertz, MGH., *Scriptores*, vol. ii. See also H. Timerding, *Die christliche Frühzeit Deutschlands*, vol. ii (1929) ; Louis Halphen, *Études critiques sur l'histoire de Charlemagne* (1921) ; and Hauck, *Kirchengeschichte Deutschlands*, vol. ii. *Cf.* W. Levison, *England and the Continent* . . . (1946).

ST GODFREY, BISHOP OF AMIENS (A.D. 1115)

AT the age of five Godfrey was entrusted to the care of the abbot of Mont-Saint-Quentin and, having in due course decided to become a monk, he was ordained priest. He was chosen abbot of Nogent, in Champagne, a house whose community

---

* Charlemagne's dealings with the barbarous Saxons were not such as to make solid missionary work any easier.

was reduced to half a dozen monks, whose discipline was, like their buildings, neglected and dilapidated. Under his direction this house began again to flourish ; but when in consequence of this the archbishop of Rheims and his council pressed the saint to take upon him the government of the great abbey of Saint-Remi, he started up in the assembly and alleged contrary canons with vehemence, adding, " God forbid I should ever desert a poor bride by preferring a rich one ! " Nevertheless, in 1104 he was appointed bishop of Amiens. His residence was truly the house of a disciple of Christ, for he never allowed himself to forget that he was a monk. He lived in the simplest fashion, and when he thought the cook was treating him too well he took the best food from the kitchen and gave it away to the poor and sick.

But in his episcopal capacity St Godfrey was unbending, severe, and inflexibly just. One Christmas when singing Mass before the count of Artois at Saint-Omer he refused to accept the offerings of the court until the nobles had modified the ostentation of their dress and deportment ; the abbess of St Michael's at Doullens had to go ón foot to Amiens and back to receive a rebuke and warning for her ill-treatment of a nun (she is said to have been kept there all day looking for the missing nun, whom the bishop had concealed in his house) ; and the claim of his see to jurisdiction over the abbey of Saint-Valéry was vigorously pursued. The refusal of the monks to allow him to bless altar-linen for their church was the occasion of a long dispute. St Godfrey had a bitter struggle in his own diocese against simony and for the celibacy of the clergy, in the course of which it is said an attempt was made on his life by a disgruntled woman. His rigid discipline made him very unpopular among the less worthy, and he became so discouraged that he wanted to resign and join the Carthusians. St Godfrey's severity seems in some things to have been excessive, *e.g.* he forbade the eating of meat on Sundays in Lent. He set out in November 1115 to discuss affairs with his metropolitan and died on the way at Soissons, where he was buried.

What Guibert of Nogent in his autobiography tells us concerning Godfrey is our most reliable source of information. The Latin life by Nicholas, a monk of Soissons, is much more detailed and in many respects valuable, but it is written in a tone of undiscriminating panegyric, and certain statements made in it are demonstrably incorrect. It was compiled about 1138, and it is printed, with the relevant passages of Guibert and an illuminating introduction, by A. Poncelet in the *Acta Sanctorum*, November, vol. iii. See also A. de Calonne, *Histoire de la ville d'Amiens* (1899), vol. i, pp. 123-142 ; C. Brunel in *Le moyen âge*, vol. xxii (1909), pp. 176-196 ; and J. Corblet, *Hagiographie d'Amiens* (1870), vol. ii, pp. 373-445.

9 : THE DEDICATION OF THE ARCHBASILICA OF THE MOST HOLY SAVIOUR, COMMONLY CALLED ST JOHN LATERAN

THE whole Western church celebrates to-day the anniversary of the consecration to divine worship of the basilica of St John Lateran, on whose façade is carved the proud title OMNIUM URBIS ET ORBIS ECCLESIARUM MATER ET CAPUT : The Mother and Head of all churches of the City and of the World ; for this church is the cathedral of Rome and the pope's permanent *cathedra* stands in its apse. It is senior in dignity to St Peter's itself, and is in some sort the cathedral of the world.

In the earliest days of Christianity worship was carried out in private houses and the Holy Sacrifice was offered at an ordinary table (doubtless a special one was often kept for the purpose) ; but so early as the first quarter of the third century we hear of a building in Rome specially set apart as a Christian church, at the beginning of the fourth century there are said to have been many there, and Constantine's decree of freedom was naturally followed by great activity in the building of new churches.   Following the example of the Jews with their Temple (and indeed of the pagans with theirs), these places of worship were set apart for their purpose by a dedication of them to the service of Almighty God.   Eusebius in his *Ecclesiastical History* speaks of the solemn dedication of the church at Tyre in the year 314, and several historians make reference to the magnificence with which Constantine's basilica at Jerusalem was dedicated in 335, on the anniversary of the finding of the true cross.   For long the dedicatory rite consisted simply in the consecration of the altar by the solemn celebration of Mass thereat, to which the deposition of relics was added when there were any, and later certain prayers, sprinklings and anointings, modifications which arose in respect of buildings that had formerly been used for pagan worship and had to be purified.   But the developments which went to form the long, complex and imposing ceremony that is now found in the *Pontificale Romanum* hardly began before the eighth century.

The annual celebration of the anniversary of a church's dedication is a practice probably as old as that of the dedication itself, and certainly far older than our present rite of consecration.   It was undeniably a custom of the Jews, for such a feast was instituted by Judas Machabeus in 164 B.C., when the Temple had been purified after its pollution by Antiochus Epiphanes ; St John in his gospel (x 22) speaks of our Lord walking in Solomon's porch at the time of this feast.   This Jewish festival was, and is, kept with an octave and was celebrated not only in the Temple at Jerusalem but in every synagogue as well, somewhat as every Western Catholic church observes the dedication of St John Lateran.   These things are referred to in the sixth lesson at Matins in the common office of the octave-day of a dedication anniversary, which is said in the Roman Breviary to be taken from a letter to Pope St Felix IV (III), who died in the year 530.   Actually the piece belongs only to the ninth century, but its words represent a much older discipline. In Sozomen's time, the early part of the fifth century, the anniversary of the dedication of the Martyrion at Jerusalem, referred to above, was observed with an octave and other solemnities.   This custom of commemorating the dedication of a church is responsible for the existence of several feasts in the Church's calendar, and determines the date of others, *e.g.* St John before the Latin Gate (May 6), St Peter in Chains (August 1), and St Michael the Archangel (September 29).

The mansion of the Laterani at Rome came into the hands of the Emperor Constantine through his second wife, Fausta, and by him it was given to the Church.   It was the principal residence of the popes from that time until the exile to Avignon at the beginning of the fourteenth century, a period of a thousand years. The church made there was in all likelihood an adaptation of the great hall of the house, but the famous baptistery was founded and newly built, in its main lines as we see it today.   The basilica was dedicated to our Most Holy Saviour and the baptistery in honour of St John the Baptist.*   The now universal practice of

---

* It may be here noted that all churches and ecclesiastical buildings are dedicated to God and to God only.   Other names by which they may be known are those of saints or mysteries of religion in whose honour or under whose patronage they are dedicated.   Nevertheless, custom allows the loose expression " dedicated to such-and-such a saint ".

calling the church itself St John Lateran arose at a time when it was served by monks from an adjoining monastery of St John the Baptist and St John the Divine.* In its fifteen hundred years of Christian history the basilica has undergone numerous vicissitudes, from pillage by the barbarians, from earthquakes, from fire ; but it retained its ancient basilican form till the seventeenth century, when Francesco Borromini made of it the church that we see today.   The apse was enlarged into a choir, in more happy fashion, in 1878.   The high altar of St John Lateran, encased in marble, is the only altar in the Western church made not of stone but of wood.   It is a relic of the days of persecution, and is believed by some to have been used by St Peter himself.   In the *ciborium* over the altar are enshrined the reputed heads of SS. Peter and Paul.

" As often as we celebrate the dedication festival of an altar or church," says St Augustine, " if we assist with faith and attention, living holily and righteously, that which is done in temples made with hands is done also in us by a spiritual building.   For he lied not who said, ' The temple of God, which you are, is holy ' ; and again, ' Do you not know that your bodies are the temple of the Holy Ghost, who is in you ? '   Therefore, since we are made worthy to become the temple of God—not by any foregoing worth of our own but by His grace—let us work, as hard as we are able with His help, that our Lord find not in His temple, that is, in us, anything whereby the eyes of His majesty may be offended. . . . If no one in dirty garments would dare to approach the table of an earthly ruler, how much the more ought one who is infected with the poison of envy or hate, or full of unrighteous anger, reverently and humbly to draw back from the table of the eternal King, that is, from the altar of God ?   For it is written, ' Go first and be reconciled with thy brother, and then come and offer thy gift '; and again, ' Friend, how camest thou in hither not having on a wedding-garment ? ' "

Much has been written about the Lateran basilica and its history, as well as upon the rite of the consecration of churches.   Concerning this last topic the reader may be conveniently referred to Duchesne, *Christian Worship* (1919), pp. 399–418 ; *cf.* also *The Month*, June 1910, pp. 621–631.   Among the many works dealing with the Lateran that of P. Lauer, *Le palais du Latran, Étude historique et archéologique* (1911) is perhaps the most comprehensive ; and in special relation with the subject of this notice consult also Lauer on the " Date de la dédicace de la basilique du Latran " in the *Bulletin de la Soc. nat. des antiquaires de France* for 1924, pp. 261–265.   A very long article on the Lateran with a vast bibliography has been contributed by H. Leclercq to DAC., vol. viii, cc. 1529–1887, in which see especially cc. 1551–1553.

ST THEODORE TIRO, Martyr   (*c.* A.D. 306 ?)

AN early panegyric, attributed to St Gregory of Nyssa, pronounced upon this martyr on his festival, begins by ascribing to his intercession the preservation of Pontus from the inroads of the Scythians, who had laid waste all the neighbouring provinces.   Imploring his patronage, it says, " As a soldier defend us ; as a martyr speak for us—ask peace.   If we need stronger intercession, gather together your brother martyrs, and with them all pray for us.   Stir up Peter, Paul and John, that they be solicitous for the churches which they founded.   May no heresies

* The Canons Regular of the Lateran are so called because they represent a reformed congregation of Augustinian canons which originated at the Lateran in the eleventh century, when the basilica was served by canons regular.

sprout up, but may the Christian commonwealth become, by your and your companions' prayers, a fruitful field." The panegyric says that by St Theodore's intercession devils were expelled and distempers cured; that many resorted to his church and admired the actions of the saint painted on the wall; then approached the tomb, whose touch, they believed, imparted a blessing, and carried away the dust of the sepulchre as a treasure; if any were allowed to touch the sacred relics, they reverently applied them to their eyes, mouth and ears. " Then they address themselves to the martyr as if he were present, and pray and invoke him, who is before God and obtains gifts as he pleases." The panegyrist then refers to St Theodore's life and passion.

The martyr whose shrine at Euchaïta was so great a centre of devotion was a young man, newly enlisted in the Roman army, whence he was surnamed Tiro, " the Recruit " (or more probably because he belonged to the *Cohors tironum*). According to his earliest legend his legion was sent into winter quarters in Pontus, and he was at Amasea when he refused to join his comrades in idolatrous observances. He was presented to the governor of the province and the tribune of his legion and asked how he dare to profess a religion which the emperors punished with death. He boldly replied, " I know not your gods. Jesus Christ, the only Son of God, is my God. If my words offend you, cut out my tongue; every part of my body is ready when God calls for it as a sacrifice." They dismissed him for the present, but Theodore, being resolved to convince his judges that his resolution was inflexible, set fire to a pagan temple which stood in the city. When he was carried a second time before the governor and his assistant he was ready to anticipate their questions by his confession. They endeavoured to terrify him with threats, and allure him by promises, but he refused to be seduced. He was therefore unmercifully torn with whips, but under all manner of torments maintained his tranquillity. The martyr was remanded to prison, where in the night he was wonderfully comforted by angels. After a third examination, Theodore was condemned to be burnt alive in a furnace and was so executed. His ashes were begged by a lady named Eusebia, who gave them burial at Euchaïta.

This account of St Theodore Tiro cannot be relied on, but it has reference to a real martyr who may or may not have been a soldier. In the course of time his " acts " were embellished by further fictitious and fantastic additions, until he became one of the best known of the " warrior-saints " and included in the East among the Great Martyrs. So complicated and contradictory did his story become that, in order to make it less inconsistent, a second soldier St Theodore had to be posited and so we have the St Theodore Stratelates of February 7. St Theodore Tiro's former popularity in the West is illustrated by thirty-eight of the famous thirteenth-century windows of Chartres cathedral, those in the choir, which depict scenes from his legend. The church of San Teodoro (" Toto ") at the foot of the Palatine hill in Rome is named after him. When in 971, on February 17 (Theodore's feast-day in the East), the Emperor John Zimiskes gained a great victory over the Russians at Dorystolon, it was attributed to the personal leadership of the martyr; the emperor rebuilt his church at Euchaïta and renamed the city Theodoropolis. St Theodore Tiro is still greatly venerated in the East and is mentioned in the " preparation " of the Byzantine Liturgy, together with his fellow dragon-slayer, St George, and a third " warrior ", St Demetrius.

Father Delehaye devoted great attention to this martyr. In 1909, in his book *Les légendes grecques des saints militaires*, he edited five different texts of the *passio* and miracles of St

Theodore with a long preliminary discussion. The most ancient evidence of the *cultus* of the saint is to be found in the sermon attributed to St Gregory of Nyssa. We cannot be quite sure that Gregory was really the author, but it is unquestionably of early date. It is printed in Migne, PG., vol. xlvi, pp. 736–748, as well as in the *Acta Sanctorum*, November, vol. iv, where Delehaye has again dealt at length with the story of both Theodore the recruit and Theodore the general, editing also as much of these varied " acts ", partly in Greek, partly in ancient Latin versions, as would serve best to illustrate how the fictitious developments have diverged as they multiplied. Theodore the general has already been noticed separately herein under February 7, which see. Doubt has been cast upon Mgr Wilpert's identification of the two figures in the mosaic of the church of St Theodore in Rome, which he holds to represent separately the recruit and the general. Consult on this the *Analecta Bollandiana*, vol. xlii (1925), p. 389, and see in the same volume, pp. 41–45, an account of further miracles of St Theodore. In *Anatolian Studies presented to Sir W. M. Ramsay* (1923) is another paper by Delehaye, on " Euchaïta et St Théodore " (pp. 129–134). Künstle, *Ikonographie* (vol. ii, pp. 551–552), discusses St Theodore in art, but much might be added from the fuller study of oriental mosaics, etc., by Diehl, Bréhier, Fr de Jerphanion, and other experts.

ST BENIGNUS, or BENEN, Bishop   (A.D. 467)

WHILST St Patrick was on his way to Tara from Saul it is said he passed some days at the house of a chieftain named Sechnan, in Meath. This man and his family were converted by the teaching of Patrick, and the gospel made a particular impression on his son Benen (latinized as Benignus). The boy, we are told, would scatter flowers over Patrick as he slept, and when the apostle would continue his journey clung to his feet and implored to be allowed to go too. So he was taken, and became Patrick's dearest disciple and eventually his successor. St Benen was noted for gentleness and charm of disposition and for his good singing, wherefore he was known as " Patrick's psalmodist ". The first evangelization of Clare and Kerry is attributed to him, and from thence he went north into Connaught. It is also claimed that St Patrick founded a church at Drumlease, in Kilmore diocese, of which Benen was given charge, and that he ruled it for twenty years. It seems certain that Benen was St Patrick's right-hand man, their names are coupled in the composition of the code of law called *Senchus Mor*, and after Patrick's death he became the chief bishop of the Irish church.

William of Malmesbury relates that St Benen resigned his office in the year 460, and came to Glastonbury, where he found St Patrick, who had preceded him thither. His old master sent him out to live as a hermit, telling him to build his cell at the spot where his staff should burst into leaf and bud. This happened at a swampy place called Feringmere, and there St Benen died and was buried, till in 1091 his relics were removed to Glastonbury Abbey. No doubt somebody's relics were translated on that occasion, but there is no truth in the legend of the association of St Patrick and St Benen with Glastonbury.

It may be said that in the *Acta Sanctorum*, November, vol. iv, pp. 145–188, a serious attempt has for the first time been made (by Fr Paul Grosjean) to piece together a consistent account of the history of St Benignus. He has printed the previously inedited life in Irish, the only manuscript copy of which, made by Michael O'Clery, is preserved in Brussels. This, which is rather a panegyric than a biography, is interspersed with fragments of verse and consists mainly of extravagant miracles. It is consequently not very informative. The facts of St Benignus's career have mainly to be learnt from the Patrician documents published in such collections as Whitley Stokes, *The Tripartite Life* (Rolls Series). The contributions made to the subject by William of Malmesbury and John of Tynemouth are plainly of little value ; they are based largely on the Glastonbury fictions, now completely discredited, as Dean Armitage Robinson has shown in his book, *Two Glastonbury Legends*. On *The Book of Rights*, attributed to St Benignus, see Eoin MacNeill, *Celtic Ireland*, pp. 73–95 ; on the *Senchus Mor*, Haddan and Stubbs, *Councils*, vol. ii, pp. 339 *seq.* ; and Bury, *Life of St Patrick*, pp. 355–357. It is curious that there seems to be no mention of St Benignus in the *Félire* of Oengus. See Fr P. Grosjean, " An Early Fragment on St Patrick . . . in the Life of St Benén ", in *Seanchas Ardmhacha*, vol. i, no. 1 (Armagh, 1954), pp. 31–44.

ST VITONUS, OR VANNE, BISHOP OF VERDUN   (*c.* A.D. 525)

ST FIRMINUS having died while his episcopal city was being besieged by Clovis, it is said that the king, on taking Verdun, nominated an old priest, St Euspicius, to the vacant see. Euspicius refused the office because he wanted to be a monk, and suggested his nephew Vitonus, who was found acceptable. His episcopate lasted over twenty-five years, during which he is said to have converted the remaining pagans of his diocese, but all the information that we have about his life is legendary : as, for example, that he destroyed a dragon by drowning it in the Meuse. St Vitonus is now chiefly remembered by the great congregation of Benedictines which bore his name. The foundation of a college of clergy outside the walls of Verdun is attributed to St Vitonus, whose buildings in the year 952 were handed over to Benedictine monks and re-dedicated in honour of the founder as the abbaye de Saint-Vanne. In 1600 the prior, Dom Didier de la Cour, began a thorough-going reformation of the monastery, which with Moyenmoutier became the centre of a group of reformed houses in Lorraine, Champagne and Burgundy. They were united officially as a new congregation, " de Saint-Vanne et Saint-Hydulphe ", in 1604, the French monasteries withdrawing to form the congregation of St Maur fourteen years later. They were both suppressed at the Revolution, but were nominally revived (with Cluny) in 1837 to form the new congregation of Solesmes. The feast of St Vitonus is therefore observed by that congregation as well as at Verdun.

There is a Latin life, still in manuscript, of which Mabillon speaks in the *Acta Sanctorum O.S.B.* (vol. vi, pt 1, pp. 496–500) ; but, written as it was five hundred years after the death of Vitonus, he apparently deemed it not worth printing, though he has published a short collection of miracles worked at the shrine. A compendium of this life was, however, printed by Surius. See also Duchesne, *Fastes Épiscopaux*, vol. iii, p. 70. On Moyenmoutier and its reform, consult *Gallia Christiana*, vol. xiii, pp. 1165 *seq.*, and L. Jérôme, *L'Abbaye de Moyenmoutier* (1902).

BD GEORGE NAPPER, MARTYR   (A.D. 1610)

THE history of the passion of this martyr has been preserved in a letter written by a fellow prisoner in Oxford jail. George Napper (Napier) was born in 1550 at Holywell manor, Oxford, his mother being a niece of Cardinal William Peto. He was entered at Corpus Christi College when he was fifteen and three years later was ejected as a recusant. At the end of 1580 he was imprisoned and remained so for nearly nine years, when he obtained his release by recognizing the royal supremacy. He repented of this weakness and entered the English College at Douay, where he was ordained in 1596. He was not sent on the mission till 1603, and then worked for seven years in Oxfordshire. Early in the morning of July 19, 1610, he was arrested in the fields at Kirtlington. He had on him at the time a pyx containing two consecrated Hosts and a small reliquary ; these in an extraordinary way escaped the notice of his searchers, but a breviary and oil-stocks were found, and these were sufficient evidence to secure his condemnation as a priest at the next assizes.

His friends obtained a stay of execution and it is likely that he would have been reprieved altogether, but for the fact that in jail he ministered to a condemned felon, who died declaring himself a Catholic. " The people stormed ; the ministers threw all the blame upon the condemned priest, made a heavy rout, called for justice, and went straight away to Abingdon to make complaint to the judges." When he was examined on the matter by the high sheriff and the vice-chancellor of the university, Mr Napper agreed he had reconciled the man and offered " to do as much for their lordships ". There was a further reprieve, but the prisoner strenuously refused to take the oath of allegiance in the form stigmatizing the pope's deposing power as " impious, heretical and damnable " (the treatise of the Arch-priest Blackwell approving it was given him to read), and his execution took place on November 9 at Oxford. Before he died he prayed publicly for the king, James I. " His charity was great, for if any poor prisoner wanted either meat to fill him or clothes to cover him he would rather be cold himself than they should " ; while on the mission " he was remarkably laborious in gaining souls to God ".

A rather full account of this martyr is preserved by Challoner in MMP., pp. 307–317. It is based upon the letter of a fellow prisoner, who goes into much detail. See also Stapleton, *Oxfordshire Missions ;* J. Morris, *Troubles . . .,* p. 302 ; and especially Bede Camm, *Forgotten Shrines,* pp. 149–182.

10 : ST ANDREW AVELLINO   (A.D. 1608)

ST ANDREW AVELLINO was a native of Castronuovo, a small town in the kingdom of Naples, and born in 1521. His parents gave him the name of Lancelot at baptism. He determined to enter the clerical state, and was sent to Naples to study civil and canon law. Being there promoted to the degree of doctor and to the priesthood, he began to practise in the ecclesiastical courts. This employment, however, too much engrossed his thoughts and dissipated his mind ; and, having while pleading a cause caught himself in a lie, and reading that same evening the words of Holy Scripture, " The mouth that belieth killeth the soul," he resolved to give himself up entirely to the spiritual care of souls. This he did, and with such prudence and ability that in 1556 Cardinal Scipio Ribiba entrusted to him the task of trying to reform the nuns of Sant' Arcangelo at Baiano. This convent had an evil reputation, and the efforts of the young priest were ill received both by some of the nuns and certain men who used to visit them. These did not stop short of physical violence, but Don Lancelot's strivings and willingness to give his life for the good of souls met with little success, for eventually the convent had to be suppressed.

Don Lancelot in the meantime determined to put himself under a rule, and joined the congregation of clerks regular called Theatines, which had been founded at Naples by St Cajetan thirty years before ; his novice-master was Bd John Marinoni. Lancelot himself was now thirty-five, and on changing his way of life he also changed his name, to Andrew. He remained in the Theatine house at Naples for fourteen years, his goodness, spiritual fervour and exactness in discipline causing him to be employed as master of novices, and then elected superior. Among those whom he trained was Father Lorenzo Scupoli, author of the *Spiritual Combat,* who became a clerk regular when he was forty. The fine qualities of St Andrew Avellino and his zeal for a better priesthood were recognized by many reforming prelates in Italy, particularly Cardinal Paul Aresio and St Charles Borromeo.   The last-named in 1570 asked the provost general of the Theatines to send St Andrew into Lombardy, where he founded a house of his congregation at Milan and became a close friend and counsellor of St Charles.   He then founded another house, at Piacenza, where his preaching converted several noble ladies, induced others to enter the religious life, and generally " turned the city upside down ", so that complaints were made to the Duke of Parma, who sent for him.   St Andrew was able to satisfy the duke, and so impressed his wife that she asked him to be her spiritual director.   In 1582 St Andrew returned to Naples, and preached with great fruit in the conversion of sinners and the disabusing of the minds of the people of the beginnings of Protestant error which had penetrated even into southern Italy.   A number of miraculous happenings are recorded in his life, including the case of a man who denied the real presence of our Lord in the Blessed Sacrament.   This man is said to have gone to holy communion out of human respect and fear, but removed the Host from his mouth and wrapped It up in a handkerchief, which he subsequently found stained with blood.   In remorse and terror he went to St Andrew, who published the story but refused to divulge the penitent man's name lest he should be proceeded against for sacrilege.

On November 10, 1608, being in his eighty-eighth year, St Andrew Avellino had an attack of apoplexy just as he was beginning to celebrate Mass, and died that same afternoon.   His body was laid out in the crypt of the church of St Paul, where it was visited by large crowds of the faithful, many of whom snipped off locks of his hair to be carried away as relics.   In so doing they seem to have made cuts in the skin of his face.   The next morning, thirty-six hours after death, these cuts were seen to have exuded blood, and as the body of the saint was still warm it is natural to suppose that he was not really dead.   Further incisions were made by physicians, and for another thirty-six hours blood continued to trickle from them.   This blood was, of course, carefully kept, and four days later it was seen to be bubbling ; in subsequent years it is recorded that, on the anniversary of St Andrew's death, the solidified blood liquefied, after the manner of that of St Januarius in the same city of Naples.   St Andrew was canonized in 1712.   During the process the phenomena connected with his blood were proposed as a miracle, but the evidence was regarded as inadequate.   Mgr Pamphili (afterwards Pope Innocent X) deposed that a phial of the solid blood in his care failed to liquefy on any occasion.

The Bollandists, in the *Acta Sanctorum*, November, vol. iv, virtually apologize for the limited space allotted to this saint, but, as they point out, the large numbers of lives published in the seventeenth and eighteenth centuries have made him very well known, and have left no particular problems to elucidate.   Besides a clear but concise summary of the principal incidents of his career and a very full bibliography of the printed literature, they have edited a valuable manuscript memoir in Italian by Father Valerio Pagani, the intimate friend of St Andrew, dealing more particularly with the saint's connection with the Theatines.   In the *Analecta Bollandiana*, vol. xli (1923), pp. 139–148, there had previously been printed some interesting details regarding the " conversion " of St Andrew.   Most of the information that comes to us is contributed by contemporaries.   In 1609 Bishop del Tufo published a *Historia della Religione de' Padri Cherici Regolari* in which he included a narrative of the saint's early days ; while a formal biography by Father Castaldo appeared in 1613.   Other Italian lives, *e.g.* by Baggatta, Bolvito, de Maria, are easily met with.   On the blood pheno-mena mentioned above see *The Month* for May 1926, pp. 437–443.   In the *Dictionnaire de Spiritualité*, vol. i (1937), cc. 551–554, G. de Luca has contributed an article dealing mainly with St Andrew's devotional writings.   Five volumes of these were published at Naples in 1733–1734, but there are others still unprinted.

ST THEOCTISTA, Virgin   (No Date)

THE Roman Martyrology today mentions the death on the island of Paros of St Theoctista, but it is the conclusion of the Bollandists that her story is an empty fable, imitated from the last days of St Mary of Egypt : " a pious tale fabricated by a man of leisure for the gratification of simple religious people ".   It tells that in the year 902 a certain Nicetas accompanied the expedition under the admiral Himerius sent against the Arabs of Crete.   While there he visited the ruined church of our Lady at Paros, and met an old priest who had been a hermit on the island for thirty years.   He told Nicetas all about the Arab devastations and finally of what he had heard from a man called Simon some years before about a certain Theoctista.   This Simon came with some friends to Paros to hunt, and as they approached the middle of the island they heard a voice calling to them, " Don't come any nearer.   I am a woman and I should be ashamed to be seen by you, for I am naked."   They were astounded, but threw a cloak among the bushes in the direction of the voice, and soon a woman emerged.   She told them that her name was Theoctista and that she and her family had lived on Lesbos, until she was carried off by Arabs.   They took her to Paros, where she escaped into the woods and remained in hiding until the marauders withdrew.   That was thirty years before, and she had lived there ever since as an ankress, feeding herself on vegetables and fruit ; her clothes had become so worn out that the rags fell from her body.   Never in all that time had she been able to assist at the Eucharist or receive the body of the Lord, and she implored Simon the next time he came that way to bring her holy communion.   This they did in the following year, bringing the Blessed Sacrament in a pyx, which Theoctista received with the *Nunc dimittis*. Afterwards they called on her again to say good-bye, and found her at the point of death.   Before she was buried Simon severed one of her hands to take away as a relic, but his ship was miraculously prevented from putting to sea until he had restored it, when it grew again on to the wrist.   When the others went to look into this marvel, the body had entirely disappeared.

It was formerly supposed that the man who went to Paros and heard this story from the mouth of the hermit was Simeon Metaphrastes himself, the great Byzantine compiler of saints' legends, in whose collection the tale of Theoctista is found. But in fact he transcribed the legend just as it was written down by Nicetas, only adding thereto a preface, expressed in general terms of edification which did not make it clear that the events narrated in the first person did not happen to himself. Metaphrastes, who figures in the Greek *Menaia* on the 28th of this month, lived some fifty years after the expedition of Himerius.

In the *Acta Sanctorum*, November, vol. iv (under November 9), Delehaye has dealt with the question exhaustively, editing the original Greek narrative of Nicetas from a variety of manuscripts, and recording the variations of the Metaphrast.   See also his *Legends of the Saints*, p. 88.

SS. TRYPHO, RESPICIUS AND NYMPHA, Martyrs   (Dates Unknown)

THESE saints are named together today in the Roman Martyrology because what purported to be the relics of all three were preserved in the church of the hospital of the Holy Ghost *in Sassia* at Rome.   Trypho is said to have been a native of

Phrygia who was a goose-herd when a boy; of Respicius too nothing whatever is known: he is first joined with Trypho in an early eleventh-century *passio*, compiled from older ones by a monk of Fleury.   The legend is an historical romance woven around a martyrdom said to have taken place at Nicaea during the persecution of Decius.   St Nympha, according to one account, was a Panormitan maiden who fled to Italy and was put to death at Porto in the fourth century. Another says that when the Goths regained Sicily in the sixth century she went from Palermo to Tuscany, where she served God in holiness and died in peace at Savona.

Although Ruinart included Trypho and Respicius in his *Acta Sincera*, Delehaye, in the *Acta Sanctorum*, November, vol. iv, speaks of this *passio*, together with the life and miracles, in all their variants, as belonging to the most unsatisfactory class of martyr acts, a view which Harnack, *Chronologie der altchristlichen Litteratur*, vol. ii, p. 470, fully ehdorses.   All the principal texts in Greek and Latin have been edited by Delehaye in the article referred to.   Tryphon was a very popular martyr in the Greek church, where his feast is kept on February 1.   Consult further Franchi de' Cavalieri in *Studi e Testi*, vol. xix, pp. 45–74, and Arnauld in *Échos d'Orient*, 1900, pp. 201–205.

ST AEDH MAC BRICC, BISHOP   (A.D. 589)

THE birth of this St Aedh, a son of Brecc of the Hy Neill, was marked by marvels and the prediction of a stranger that he would be great in the eyes of God and man. He received no schooling in his youth, being intended for the lay state, but worked on his father's land, where one day St Brendan of Birr and St Canice helped him to find the pigs that had strayed.   After the death of Brecc, Aedh's brothers withheld his patrimony from him, and he tried to coerce them into yielding his share by carrying off a girl from their household.   Coming to Rathlihen in Offaly he was persuaded by St Illathan, bishop in that place, to renounce his claim and to send the girl back again.   This Aedh accordingly did, and remained with the bishop till, in consequence of a sign of God's favour given while his disciple was ploughing, Illathan sent him to establish a monastery in his own district.   His chief settlement is said to have been at Cill-áir in Westmeath, but he was active over a wide area.

Many miracles are recorded of St Aedh, some of them extravagant enough: healing, transportation through the air (with or without his car), turning water into wine, and resuscitating three people who had had their throats cut by robbers are among them.   It is said that St Brigid herself (alternatively, " a certain man ") came to him to be cured of a chronic headache, which he took upon himself.   There is a story told of St Odo of Cluny which is paralleled by the following told of St Aedh: that he one day saw a girl washing her head after Saturday Vespers (*i.e.* when, ecclesiastically, Sunday had begun), and that at his word all her hair fell out until she had repented of doing servile work on the Lord's day.   When he came to die, St Aedh said to one of his monks, " Prepare to take the road to Heaven with me ".   The man was not willing to die, but a country fellow standing by exclaimed, " Would to God you would ask me to come with you ".   " Very well," said St Aedh, " go and wash yourself and get ready."   So the peasant did, and lay down on the saint's bed, and together they died.   At the same moment, St Columba in far Iona knew of Aedh's departure to Heaven, and told the news to his brethren.

There are three Latin lives of this saint, but no text is known to have been preserved in Irish.   The Latin recensions have all been printed in full by Fr P. Grosjean in the *Acta*

Sanctorum, November, vol. iv, the second being here edited for the first time, though C.
Plummer had quoted fragments of it when he published the third life in his VSH., vol. i,
pp. 34–45.   In any case the second differs little from the first, which is preserved to us in
the Codex Salmanticensis and had been previously printed in 1888.   Fr Grosjean has
greatly added to the value of his article by copious annotations.   See also Plummer's preface
to VSH., vol. i, pp. xxvi–xxviii, and G. Stokes in *Journal* of R. Soc. of Antiq., Ireland,
vol. xxvi (1896), pp. 325–335.   St Aedh seems to have been popularly invoked to cure
headaches ; *cf.* J. F. Kenney, *Sources*, vol. i, p. 393.

ST JUSTUS, ARCHBISHOP OF CANTERBURY   (*c.* A.D. 627)

WHEN in the year 601 Pope St Gregory the Great sent more missionaries to help
St Augustine in England, Justus was of their number.   Three years later St
Augustine consecrated him to be bishop of Rochester, the first of that see, where
King Ethelbert built a church dedicated in honour of St Andrew, from whose
church on the Coelian the Roman missionaries had set out.   When Augustine
was succeeded at Canterbury by St Laurence, Justus joined with him and St
Mellitus of London in addressing a letter to the Irish bishops and abbots inviting them to conform certain of their ecclesiastical usages to those of Rome.
A similar letter was sent to the clergy of the Christian Britons ; " what was
gained by so doing ", St Bede caustically observes, " the present times still
declare ".

After the death of King Ethelbert in 616 a pagan reaction set in in Kent and
the same happened among the East Saxons.   In face of it the three bishops,
Laurence, Justus and Mellitus, decided to retire for a while as they could do no
good where they were in opposition to the pagan princes.   Accordingly Justus
and Mellitus crossed over into Gaul.   Within a year Justus was recalled,
for St Laurence, spurred on by a vision of St Peter, had succeeded in converting
King Edbald of Kent.   St Justus himself became archbishop of Canterbury
in 624, and Pope Boniface V sent him the *pallium*, together with a letter
delegating the patriarchal right to consecrate bishops in England.   In the
course of his letter the pope shows what he thinks of Justus : he refers to " the
perfection which your work has obtained ", to God's promise to be with His
servants, " which promise His mercy has particularly manifested in your ministry ",
and to Justus's " hope of patience and virtue of endurance ".   " You must therefore endeavour, my brother ", he concludes, " to preserve with unblemished
sincerity of mind that which you have received through the favour of the Apostolic
See, as an emblem whereof you have obtained so principal an ornament [*i.e.* the
pallium] to be borne on your shoulders. . . . God keep you in safety, most dear
brother."   St Justus did not long survive his promotion but before his death he
consecrated St Paulinus, to accompany Ethelburga of Kent when she went north
to marry the heathen Edwin, King of Northumbria, an alliance which was " the
occasion of that nation's embracing the faith ", as St Bede remarks.   The feast of
St Justus is kept in the diocese of Southwark.

Our knowledge of the doings of St Justus depends mainly upon the *Ecclesiastical History*
of Bede (see C. Plummer's edition and notes).   In the *Acta Sanctorum*, November, vol. iv,
Delehaye has also printed the eleventh-century life by Goscelin.   With regard to the relics
of the early archbishops of Canterbury see W. St John Hope, *Recent Discoveries in the Abbey
Church of St Austin at Canterbury* (1916).   It is noteworthy that Justus with Mellitus and
Laurence, but not Augustine, is inscribed in the diptychs of the Irish sacramentary known
as the Stowe Missal.

11 : ST MARTIN, Bishop of Tours (A.D. 397)

THE great St Martin, the glory of Gaul and a light to the Western church in the fourth century, was a native of Sabaria, a town of Pannonia. From thence his parents, who were pagans, had to remove to Pavia in Italy, for his father was an officer in the army, who had risen from the ranks. Martin himself has, rather curiously, come to be looked on as a " soldier saint ". At the age of fifteen he was, as the son of a veteran, forced into the army against his will and for some years, though not yet formally a Christian, he lived more like a monk than a soldier. It was while stationed at Amiens that is said to have occurred the incident which tradition and image have made famous. One day in a very hard winter, during a severe frost, he met at the gate of the city a poor man, almost naked, trembling and shaking with cold, and begging alms of those that passed by. Martin, seeing those that went before take no notice of this miserable creature, thought he was reserved for himself, but he had nothing with him but his arms and clothes. So, drawing his sword, he cut his cloak into two pieces, gave one to the beggar and wrapped himself in the other half. Some of the bystanders laughed at the figure he cut, but others were ashamed not to have relieved the poor man. That night Martin in his sleep saw Jesus Christ, dressed in that half of the garment which he had given away, and heard Jesus say, " Martin, yet a catechumen, has covered me with this garment ".* His disciple and biographer Sulpicius Severus states that he had become a catechumen on his own initiative at the age of ten, and that as a consequence of this vision he " flew to be baptized ".

Martin did not at once leave the army, and when he was about twenty there was a barbarian invasion of Gaul. With his comrades he appeared before Julian Caesar to receive a war-bounty, and Martin refused to accept it. " Hitherto ", he said to Julian, " I have served you as a soldier ; let me now serve Christ. Give the bounty to these others who are going to fight, but I am a soldier of Christ and it is not lawful for me to fight." Julian stormed and accused Martin of cowardice, who retorted that he was prepared to stand in the battle-line unarmed the next day and to advance alone against the enemy in the name of Christ. He was thrust into prison, but the conclusion of an armistice stopped further developments and Martin was soon after discharged. He went to Poitiers, where St Hilary was bishop, and this doctor of the Church gladly received the young " conscientious objector " among his disciples.†

Martin had in a dream a call to visit his home and, crossing the Alps where he had a remarkable escape from robbers, he went into Pannonia, and converted his mother and others ; but his father remained in his infidelity. In Illyricum he opposed the triumphant Arians with so much zeal that he was publicly scourged and had to leave the country. In Italy he heard that the church of Gaul also was oppressed by those heretics and St Hilary banished, so he remained quietly at Milan. But Auxentius, the Arian bishop, soon drove him away. He then retired with a priest to the island of Gallinaria in the gulf of Genoa, and remained there till St Hilary was allowed to return to Poitiers in 360. It being Martin's earnest

---

* Our familiar word " chapel " is said to be derived from this incident. The oratory in which the alleged cloak of St Martin was preserved was called in Latin the *cappella* (diminutive of *cappa*, a cloak), in Old French *chapele*.

† The narrative of Sulpicius Severus here presents considerable chronological difficulties.

desire to pursue his vocation in solitude, St Hilary gave him a piece of land, now called Ligugé, where he was soon joined by a number of other hermits. This community—traditionally the first monastic community founded in Gaul—grew into a great monastery which continued till the year 1607, and was revived by the Solesmes Benedictines in 1852. St Martin lived here for ten years, directing his disciples and preaching throughout the countryside, where many miracles were attributed to him. About 371 the people of Tours demanded Martin for their bishop. He was unwilling to accept the office, so a stratagem was made use of to call him to the city to visit a sick person, where he was conveyed to the church. Some of the neighbouring bishops, called to assist at the election, urged that the meanness of his appearance and his unkempt air showed him to be unfit for such a dignity. But such objections were overcome by the acclamations of the local clergy and people.

St Martin continued the same manner of life. He lived at first in a cell near the church, but not being able to endure the interruptions of the many visitors he retired from the city to where was soon the famous abbey of Marmoutier. The place was then a desert, enclosed by a steep cliff on one side and by a tributary of the river Loire on the other ; but he had here in a short time eighty monks, with many persons of rank amongst them. A very great decrease of paganism in the district of Tours and all that part of Gaul was the fruit of the piety, miracles and zealous instruction of St Martin. He destroyed many temples of idols and felled trees and other objects that were held sacred by the pagans. Having demolished a certain temple, he would also have cut down a pine that stood near it. The chief priest and others agreed that they themselves would fell it, upon condition that he who trusted so strongly in the God whom he preached would stand under it where they should place him. Martin consented, and let himself be tied on that side of the tree to which it leaned. When it seemed about to fall on him he made a sign of the cross and it fell to one side. Another time, as he was pulling down a temple in the territory of Autun, a man attacked him sword in hand. The saint bared his breast to him ; but the pagan lost his balance, fell backwards, and was so terrified that he begged for forgiveness. These and many other marvels are narrated by Sulpicius Severus ; some are so extraordinary that, he tells us himself, there were not wanting " wretched, degenerate and slothful men " in his own day who denied their truth. He also recounts several instances of revelations, visions and the spirit of prophecy with which the saint was favoured by God. Every year St Martin visited each of his outlying " parishes ", travelling on foot, on a donkey, or by boat. According to his biographer he extended his apostolate from Touraine to Chartres, Paris, Autun, Sens and Vienne, where he cured St Paulinus of Nola of an eye trouble. When a tyrannical imperial officer, Avitian, had come to Tours with a batch of prisoners and was going to put them to death with torture on the following day, St Martin hurried from Marmoutier to intercede for them. He did not arrive till nearly midnight, but went straight to Avitian and would not go away until mercy was extended to the captives.

Whilst St Martin was employed in making spiritual conquests, and in peaceably spreading the kingdom of Jesus Christ, the churches in Spain and Gaul were disturbed by the Priscillianists, a gnostic-manichean sect named after their leader. Priscillian appealed to the Emperor Maximus from a synod held at Bordeaux in 384, but Ithacius, Bishop of Ossanova, attacked him furiously and urged the emperor to put him to death. Neither St Ambrose at Milan nor St Martin would countenance Ithacius or those who supported him, because they sought to put heretics to death and allowed the emperor's jurisdiction in an ecclesiastical matter. Martin besought Maximus not to spill the blood of the guilty, saying it was sufficient that they be declared heretics and excommunicated by the bishops.   Ithacius, far from listening to his advice, presumed to accuse him of the heresy involved, as he generally did those whose lives were too ascetic for his taste, says Sulpicius Severus. Maximus, out of regard to St Martin's remonstrances, promised that the blood of the accused should not be spilt.   But after the saint had left Trier, the emperor was prevailed upon, and committed the case of the Priscillianists to the prefect Evodius.   He found Priscillian and others guilty of certain charges, and they were beheaded.   St Martin came back to Trier to intercede both for the Spanish Priscillianists, who were threatened with a bloody persecution, and for two adherents of the late emperor, Gratian ; he found himself in a very difficult position, in which he seemed to be justified in maintaining communion with the party of Ithacius, which he did : but he was afterwards greatly troubled in conscience as to whether he had been too complaisant in this matter.*

St Martin had a knowledge of his approaching death, which he foretold to his disciples, and with tears they besought him not to leave them.   " Lord ", he prayed, " if thy people still need me I will not draw back from the work.   Thy will be done."   He was at a remote part of his diocese when his last sickness came on him.   He died on November 8, 397, today being the day of his burial at Tours, where his successor St Britius built a chapel over his grave, which was later replaced by a magnificent basilica.   Its successor was swept away at the Revolution, but a modern church now stands over the site of the shrine, which was rifled by the Huguenots in 1562.   Till that date the pilgrimage to Tours was one of the most popular in Europe, and a very large number of French churches are dedicated in St Martin's honour.   And not only in France.   The oldest existing church in England bears his name, that one outside the eastern walls of Canterbury which St Bede says was first built during the Roman occupation.   If this be so, it doubtless at first had another dedication, but was called St Martin's by the time St Augustine and his monks came to use it.   By the end of the eighth century there were at least five other Martin dedications in Great Britain, including of course St Ninian's church at Whithorn.   St Martin was named in the canon of the Mass in the Bobbio Missal.

In the BHL. no less than fifty-six medieval Latin texts are indicated as in some sense sources for the life of St Martin, and the literature arising out of these is of course immense. But the fundamental narrative comes to us from Sulpicius Severus, who had visited the saint at Tours and whose successive contributions to the subject are immensely more important than any later materials.   At the time of St Martin's death Sulpicius had already compiled his biography.   A little later he revised it, supplementing the text with three long letters he had written in the interval, the last of these describing the saint's death and funeral. Sulpicius meanwhile had been busy in writing a general chronicle, and in this Book II, ch. 50 is devoted to St Martin's share in the Priscillianist controversy.   Finally in 404 Sulpicius threw into dialogue form some further materials, comparing Martin with earlier ascetics, and gathering up a number of new anecdotes.   The text edited by C. Halm in the Vienna *Corpus* (vol. i, pp. 107–216) has not yet been superseded.   *Cf.* however, the Sulpicius section of the Book of Armagh, edited by Professor John Gwynn (1913).   More than a

---

* For their parts in the affair of Priscillian both the emperor and Ithacius were censured by Pope St Siricius.   It was the first judicial death-sentence for heresy, and it was followed by a spread of Priscillianism in Spain.   Sulpicius Severus says that two of Priscillian's followers were exiled " to the Scilly island that lies beyond Britain ".

century and a half elapsed before St Gregory at Tours itself made another notable contribution to the history of his venerated predecessor.   Unfortunately the chronology of Sulpicius and Gregory is often at variance, and these inconsistencies formed the basis of an essay in destructive criticism by E. Babut (*St Martin de Tours*, 1912) which created a considerable sensation when it appeared.   A detailed reply by Fr Delehaye in the *Analecta Bollandiana* (vol. xxxviii, 1920, pp. 1–136) may count as perhaps the most up-to-date contribution to the subject, and another high authority, C. Jullian, in the *Revue des Études anciennes* (vols. xxiv and xxv) and in his *Histoire de la Gaule* (vol. viii) has written in general agreement with Delehaye.   Biographies and studies of the different aspects of St Martin's history are numerous.   See especially the books of A. Lecoy de la Marche, C. H. van Rhijn, P. Ladoué and, most useful of all, the little volume of Paul Monceaux (Eng. trans., 1928).   On St Martin in art consult Künstle, *Ikonographie*, vol. ii, pp. 438–444 ; and the volume by H. Martin, in the series *L'art et les saints*.   St Martin has also played a great part in the traditions of the people ; many popular phrases in French recall his name.   Much of this folk-lore has been gathered up by Lecoy de la Marche, and for Germany see Bächtold-Stäubli, *Handwörterbuch des deutschen Aberglaubens*, vol. v, cc. 1708–1725.   For Martin's influence in Ireland, see J. Ryan, *Irish Monasticism* (1931) ; and Fr Grosjean in *Analecta Bollandiana*, vol. lv (1942), pp. 300–348 ; for the early English dedications, W. Levison, *England and the Continent* . . . (1946), p. 259.   The great veneration for St Martin in medieval England is witnessed by the fact that the calendar of the Book of Common Prayer not only retains his *dies natalis* but also the fesat of the translation of his relics on July 4.   The life by Sulpicius Severus is translated in the Fathers of the Church series, vol. vii (1949), and again in F. R. Hoare, *The Western Fathers* (1954), together with his three letters on St Martin and the dialogues with Postumianus and Gallus.

ST MENNAS, Martyr   (Date Unknown)

THE outline of the legend of St Mennas (Menas) is that he was an Egyptian by birth and a soldier in the Roman army.   He was at Cotyaeum in Phrygia when the persecution of Diocletian began, whereupon he deserted and hid himself in the mountains, where he led a life of prayer and austerity.   On the occasion of some games at Cotyaeum he left his hiding-place and displayed himself in the amphitheatre, announcing that he also was a Christian.   He was arrested and brought before the president who, after having him beaten and tortured, ordered him to be beheaded.   His remains were recovered and brought back to Egypt, where the miracles reported at his tomb soon made it a great centre of devotion. The *cultus* of St Mennas spread far and wide in the East, his true history was overlaid and distorted by fictions and embellishments which brought him into the ranks of the " warrior saints ", and he was credited with absurd wonders, one of them (which, however, he shares with SS. Cosmas and Damian) being, in the words of Tillemont, " in the highest degree scandalous ".   Father Delehaye is of the opinion that all that can be fairly certainly known about St Mennas is that he was an Egyptian who was martyred and buried in his native place.   Churches were built in his honour at, among other places, Cotyaeum, and these gave rise to mythical duplicates of the martyr connected with those cities.

The great shrine of St Mennas, built over his tomb, was at Bumma (Karm Abu-Mina), south-west from Alexandria, which was a principal pilgrimage sanctuary until the Arab invasion in the seventh century.   Its ruins, basilica, monastery, baths, secular buildings, were excavated by Mgr K. M. Kaufmann in 1905–08, who found innumerable traces of the former popular *cultus* of the martyr.   Among them were numerous phials bearing such inscriptions as " Souvenir of St Mennas ", which were shown to have been made to contain water from a well near the shrine. Such phials had been long previously found elsewhere in Africa and in Europe, and had hitherto been supposed to have contained " oil of St Mennas " taken from the lamps in the church. In 1943 the Orthodox patriarch of Alexandria, Christopher II, issued an encyclical letter in which he attributed the saving of Egypt from invasion at the battle of Alamein to " the prayers to God of the holy and glorious great martyr Mennas, the wonder-worker of Egypt " ; and he put forward a project for restoring the saint's ruined sanctuary near Alamein as a memorial to the fallen.

The Roman Martyrology mentions to-day another St Mennas, who was a solitary in the Abruzzi. He was a Greek from Asia Minor whose holiness and zeal are spoken of by Pope St Gregory in his *Dialogues*.

As in the case of the great St George, we have here to do with a martyr of whose historical existence, owing to his localized, wide-spread and early cult, we can hardly entertain a doubt, but whose story has been lost and supplied at a later date by deliberate fabrication. Starting from this primitive fiction it has been transmitted to subsequent generations with endless varieties of detail, and translated into many languages, oriental and western. The Greek *passio* is known to us in three distinct families, but the kernel recognizable in all of them has been obtained by the simple process of borrowing the story of another martyr and giving him a new name. The martyr in this case was St Gordius, whose conflict is described to us in a panegyric preached by St Basil. An immense amount of research has been lavished upon St Mennas by such scholars as Krumbacher, Delehaye, P. Franchi de' Cavalieri, K. M. Kaufmann and others. What is of main interest is that the cradle of the *cultus* of this Egyptian martyr was brought to light in the present century through the excavations of Mgr Kaufmann. It has been described in his folio volume, *Die Menas-stadt und das Nationalheiligtum der altchristlichen Aegypter* (1910). Father Delehaye in particular has written very fully on the subject. See the *Analecta Bollandiana*, vol. xxix (1910), pp. 117–150 ; and vol. xliii, pp. 46–49 ; *Origines du culte des martyrs* (1933), pp. 222–223 and *passim ; Les passions des martyrs et les genres littéraires*, pp. 388–389 ; and CMH., pp. 595–596. See also Budge, *Texts relating to St Mena of Egypt* (1909) ; P. Franchi de' Cavalieri in *Studi e Testi*, vol. xix (1908), pp. 42–108 ; and H. Leclercq in DAC., vol. xi, cc. 324–397, where also is a full bibliography.

ST THEODORE THE STUDITE, Abbot   (A.D. 826)

St Plato, abbot of Symboleon upon Mount Olympus in Bithynia, had a brother-in-law who with his three sons went to their estate at Sakkoudion, also near Olympus, and there began to lead a monastic life. Among these novices no one was more fervent than Theodore, the eldest son, then in his twenty-second year. St Plato was prevailed upon to resign his abbacy and to undertake the government of this new monastery, and in due course he sent Theodore to Constantinople to be ordained priest. He made so great progress in virtue and learning that in 794 his uncle abdicated the government of the house and, by the consent of the community, confided it to Theodore.

The young emperor Constantine VI having put away his wife and taken Theodota, a relation of SS. Plato and Theodore, they protested against his conduct. Constantine desired to gain Theodore to his side and used his utmost endeavours, by promises and by the consideration of their kindred. When these failed, the emperor went to take the waters at Brusa, near Sakkoudion, expecting St Theodore to pay him a ceremonial visit ; but neither the abbot nor any of his monks were there to receive him. The prince returned to his palace in a rage, and sent officers with an order to deport Theodore and those monks who were his most resolute adherents. They were banished to Thessalonika, and a strict order was published forbidding anyone to receive or entertain them, so that even the monks of that country durst not help them. The aged Plato was confined in a solitary cell in Constantinople. St Theodore wrote to him from Thessalonika an account of the journey and hardships of himself and his companions, a letter full of courage and of admiration for his old master. But the exile lasted only a few months, being brought to an end by a characteristic example of the brutal ambitions of the time and place. In 797 the emperor's mother, Irene, dethroned her son, and ordered his eyes to be put out. She reigned five years and recalled the exiles. St Theodore returned to Sakkoudion, and reassembled his scattered flock; but finding this monastery exposed to the raids of the Arabs they in 799 took shelter within the walls of the city. Theodore was given charge of the famous monastery of Studius, so called from its founder, the consul Studius who, coming from Rome to Constantinople, had built it in the year 463. Constantine Copronymus had expelled the monks and Theodore found the place a desert, with a bare dozen inmates; under his rule the community and its dependants came to number a thousand. As a legislator St Theodore takes the first place in the development of monasticism deriving from St Basil. St Athanasius the Lauriote brought his regulations to Mount Athos, and they spread to Russia, Bulgaria and Serbia, where and elsewhere they still form the basis of cenobitical monastic life.* He especially fostered learned studies and the practice of the fine arts, and the school of calligraphy that he established was long famous. St Theodore's own written works were chiefly instructions and sermons, liturgical hymns, and treatises on monastic asceticism, in which, compared with many orientals, he was notably moderate. He told a hermit, " Don't cultivate a self-satisfied austerity. Eat bread, drink wine occasionally, wear shoes, especially in winter, and take meat when you need it." For eight years St Theodore governed his monastery in peace amid the turmoil of imperial politics, and then the affair of Constantine's adultery was brought up again.

To fill the vacant patriarchal throne of Constantinople the Emperor Nicephorus I chose his namesake, afterwards St Nicephorus, who was a layman at the time. For this reason St Theodore, St Plato, and other monks opposed the appointment, and were imprisoned for twenty-four days in consequence. Then, at the request of the emperor, Nicephorus and a small synod of bishops reinstated the priest Joseph, who had been degraded for blessing the marriage between Constantine VI and Theodota. St Theodore and others refused to hold communion with Joseph or to accept the decision of a second synod that the marriage had been valid, and he, his brother Joseph, Archbishop of Thessalonika, and St Plato were relegated to Princes' Island and shut up in separate prisons. Theodore wrote explaining matters to the pope and St Leo III replied, commending his prudence and constancy, but the other side had spread rumours in Rome that Theodore was heretical and was annoyed at not having been made patriarch, and Leo made no formal judgement. The Studite monks were dispersed among other monasteries and grievously ill-treated, and the imprisonment of the leaders lasted nearly two years, until the death of the Emperor Nicephorus in 811.

A reconciliation was brought about between Theodore and Patriarch Nicephorus, which was cemented by their unity on the vexed question of the veneration of images. Particulars of the outbreak of the second Iconoclast persecution, under

---

* There was a revival of Studite monasticism among Catholic Byzantines in our own day. In 1901 Andrew Szepticky, Archbishop of Lvov, founded a monastery in then Austrian Galicia, which prospered and gave off affiliations; but the monks were suppressed by the Soviet government after 1945. A group of refugee monks have made a fresh start in Canada.

Leo V the Armenian, have been given in the account of St Nicephorus (March 13). St Theodore openly denied any right of the emperor to interfere in ecclesiastical affairs, and on the Palm Sunday after the banishment of St Nicephorus he ordered all his monks to take images in their hands and to carry them solemnly in public procession, singing a hymn which begins, " We reverence thy holy image, O blessed one ".   From this moment St Theodore was recognized as the leader of the orthodox, and he continued to encourage all to honour holy images, for which the emperor banished him into Mysia, where he continued to animate the faithful by letters, of which a number are extant.   His correspondence being discovered, the emperor ordered him to Bonita, at a greater distance in Anatolia, with instruction to his gaoler to have the confessor scourged.   This man, Nicetas, seeing the cheer-fulness with which St Theodore put off his tunic and offered his naked body, wasted with fasting, to the blows, was moved with compassion.   He therefore contrived to send all others out of the dungeon ; then, throwing a sheep-skin over Theodore's bed, he discharged upon it a number of blows, which were heard by those without ; then, pricking his arm to stain the whip with blood, he showed it when he came out and seemed out of breath with the pains he had taken.   St Theodore was still able to write letters, and among them those which he sent to all the patriarchs and to Pope St Paschal I.   To him he writes, " Give ear, apostolic bishop, shepherd appointed by God over the flock of Jesus Christ.   You have received the keys of the kingdom of Heaven ; you are the rock on which the Church is built ; you are Peter, since you fill his see.   Come to our assistance."   The pope having sent legates to Constantinople (who, however, achieved nothing), St Theódore wrote a letter of thanks, in which he said, " You are from the beginning the pure source of the orthodox faith.   You are the secure harbour of the universal Church, her shelter against the storms of heretics, and the city of refuge chosen by God."

For three more years St Theodore and his faithful attendant Nicholas were imprisoned at Bonita with extreme rigour ; enduring great cold in winter and almost stifled in summer and tormented with hunger and thirst, for their guards threw them in at a window only a little bread every other day.   St Theodore says that he expected they would soon perish with hunger, adding, " God is yet but too merciful to us ", and they probably would have, had not a court official who passed that way been shocked by their condition and ordered them to be properly fed. The Emperor Leo, having intercepted another letter in which the saint encouraged the faithful to defy " the infamous sect of image-burners ", gave order to the prefect of the East to punish its author.   This officer was not won over as Nicetas had been, and caused Nicholas, the monk who had written the letter, to be cruelly scourged and then a hundred stripes to be given to Theodore, who was left lying on the ground exposed to the cold of February.   He was a long time unable to take any rest or food, and was only saved by the care of Nicholas who, forgetting his own sufferings, fed him drop by drop with a little broth, and after he had thus strength-ened him, endeavoured to dress his wounds, from which he had to cut away the mortified flesh.   Theodore was for three months in excessive pain, and before he was recovered an officer arrived to conduct him and Nicholas to Smyrna.   They had to walk in the day-time and at night were put in irons.

At Smyrna the archbishop, who was a bitter Iconoclast, kept Theodore confined closely, and said he would ask the emperor to send an officer to cut off his head, or at least to cut out his tongue.   But the persecution ended in 820, with the murder of him who had raised it.   Leo was succeeded by Michael the Stammerer, who at first affected great moderation : the exiles were restored, and St Theodore the Studite came out after seven years of imprisonment.   He wrote a letter of thanks to Michael, exhorting him to be united with Rome, the first of the churches, and freely to permit the veneration of images.   But the new emperor refused to allow any images in the imperial city, or to restore the patriarch, the abbot of the " Studium " or any other orthodox prelates to their offices unless they agreed.   St Theodore, after making fruitless remonstrances, left Constantinople—in effect an exile—and visited the monasteries of Bithynia to encourage and strengthen his followers.   " The winter is over ", he said, " but spring is not yet come.   The sky is clearer and there is hope of a good passage.   The fire is out—but there is still smoke."   The influence of Theodore was so great that monks in general and Studites in particular were regarded as synonymous with orthodoxy ; and some of his monks gathered round him in a monastery on the peninsula of Akrita.   He was here taken ill in the beginning of November 826, yet walked to church on the fourth day and celebrated the Holy Sacrifice.   His sickness increasing, he dictated to a secretary his last instructions ; and died on the following Sunday, November 11.   His body was translated to the monastery of Studius eighteen years after his death.

St Theodore the Studite is greatly venerated in the East and is named in the Roman Martyrology as " famous throughout the Church ", as indeed he well deserves to be, as a monastic legislator, an upholder of the supreme authority of the see of Rome, and a spirited defender of and sufferer for the veneration of holy images.   He opposed the Iconoclasts essentially on theological grounds.   He did not regard sacred pictures as a necessary artistic adornment of a church ; he definitely discouraged the pictorial representation of the Virtues and Vices and any other " unauthorized flights of the religious fancy ".   Nor did he deem their veneration a *necessary* devotional exercise ; he seems to have used it but little himself, regarding it simply as an aid to devotion for the " weaker brethren ".   In his own instructions on prayer he sees the heart and mind in direct communion with God without reference to any exterior helps or intermediaries.   But he saw clearly that to deny the lawfulness of the display and veneration of holy images was to deny the validity of certain theological principles which are essential to the Christian faith.   Many of his writings have come down to us, including numerous letters, treatises on monastic life and the veneration of images, sermons, and a number of hymns.   Like the life of the saint they are marked with that rigorism and uncompromising detachment from the world, almost amounting to " puritanism ", which was characteristic of many of his followers and in some of their successors was so exaggerated as gravely to disturb the peace of the Church.

In volume xcix of Migne's Greek Patrology are printed two biographies with some other documents referring to St Theodore as well as his own writings.   His life was so completely identified with the controversies of the period that for a fuller understanding we must turn to the exponents of general ecclesiastical history.   Pargoire, *L'Église Byzantine de 527 à 847* (1923), is very valuable ; as is also Hefele-Leclercq, *Histoire des Conciles* (especially bk 18 in vol. iii, pt 2) ; Mgr Mann's *Lives of the Popes*, vol. ii, pp. 795–858 ; and Bréhier, *La Querelle des Images* (1904).   Among works more directly relating to St Theodore may be mentioned : J. Hausherr, *St Théodore . . . d'après ses catéchèses* (1926) in the series " Orientalia Christiana ", no. 22 ; Alice Gardner, *Theodore of Studium* (1905) ; H. Martin, *St Théodore* (1906) ; Dobschütz, " Methodius und die Studiten " in the *Byzantinische Zeitschrift*, vol. xviii (1909), pp. 41–105 ; and G. A. Schneider, *Der hl. Theodor von Studion* (1900).   Several articles bearing on St Theodore have been published in the *Analecta Bollandiana*.   In vol. xxxi (1912) Fr C. Van de Vorst published for the first time Theodore's eulogy of St Theophanes, and in vol. xxxii another Greek text describing the translation of Theodore's relics, as well as a paper on his relations with Rome, and in vol xxxiii a discussion of his " smaller catechism ".   See also in DAC. the account of St Theodore's activities in the Iconoclasm controversy (vol. vii, 1926, cc. 272–284).   There is an excellent popular sketch by Prince Max of Saxony, *Der hl. Theodor* (1929) ; and *cf.* N. H. Baynes and C. L. B. Moss, *Byzantium* (1948).

ST BARTHOLOMEW OF GROTTAFERRATA, ABBOT   (*c.* A.D. 1050)

THE founder of the Greek abbey of Grottaferrata in the Tuscan plain, St Nilus, died in the year 1004, and was succeeded as abbot in quick succession by Paul, Cyril and Bartholomew.   They were all personal disciples of Nilus, the last named being venerated as the lesser founder of the monastery ; for St Nilus and his first two successors were able only to clear the land and begin building, while St Bartholomew carried the work to its conclusion and firmly established his monks, who had been driven from southern Italy and Sicily by Saracen invasions.   He made his monastery a centre for learned studies and the copying of manuscripts, himself being skilled in the art of calligraphy, and he composed a number of liturgical hymns.

A *kanon* in the liturgical office of St Bartholomew contains these words : " When, O father, thou didst see the Roman Pontiff rejected, thou didst persuade him by wise words to give up his throne and to end his days in the happy life of a monk." This refers to the Grottaferrata tradition—perhaps a true one—concerning the last years of Pope Benedict IX, whose grandfather, Count Gregory of Tusculum, had given the land on which the abbey is built.   When Benedict, after a stormy and scandalous reign of twelve years, having first resigned the papacy for a money payment and then tried to regain it, was finally driven from Rome in 1048, he came to Grottaferrata in a state of remorse.   Abbot Bartholomew was quite definite as to what was Benedict's duty : by his disorders he had made himself unfit to be a priest, much less a pope ; he must definitely resign all claim to that dignity and fulfil the rest of his life in penance (he was still only about thirty-six years old). The influence of the abbot gradually changed Benedict's remorse into true penitence ;   he remained at Grottaferrata as a simple monk and died there.   This account of the saint's part in the career of Benedict IX is first found in the Life of St Bartholomew, perhaps written by his third successor, Abbot Luke I, and is supported by monuments at the abbey ; but it appears that in 1055, the year of his death, Benedict was still calling himself pope.   The vigorous government of St Bartholomew was responsible for raising his monastery to that position of importance from which it played a part in the history of the medieval papal states, a position which ultimately led to its decline as a religious house until its restoration in the nineteenth century.

Two Greek texts giving some account of St Bartholomew will be found printed in Migne, PG., vol. cxxvii, cc. 476–516.   Some of the manuscripts copied by his hand are believed still to survive in the library of Grottaferrata ; and an ancient mosaic representing SS. Nilus and Bartholomew is still visible in the sanctuary of the abbey church.   The resignation of Pope Benedict IX is discussed in Mgr Mann's *Lives of the Popes*, vol. v, p. 292.   See also S. G. Mercati in *Enciclopedia italiana*, vol. vi, p. 254 ; L. Bréhier in DHG., vol. vi, cc. 1006–1007 ; and F. Halkin in *Analecta Bollandiana*, vol. lxi (1943), pp. 202–210, who points out that, of the two Greek texts just referred to, one, the Encomium, refers to another St Bartholomew.

12 : ST MARTIN I, POPE AND MARTYR   (A.D. 656 ?)

ST MARTIN was a native of Todi in Umbria, renowned among the clergy
of Rome for his learning and holiness. Whilst he was deacon he was sent
by Pope Theodore I as *apocrisiarius* or nuncio to Constantinople, and upon
the death of Theodore Martin himself was elected pope in July 649. In the
October following he held a council at the Lateran against Monothelism (the denial
that Christ had a human will), in which the orthodox doctrine of the two wills was
affirmed and the leaders of the heresy anathematized. Two imperial edicts, the
" Ekthesis " of Heraclius and the " Typos " of Constans, were likewise censured :
the first because it contained an exposition of faith entirely favourable to the
monothelites, the second because it was a formulary by which silence was imposed
on both parties and it was forbidden to mention either one or two wills and energies
in Christ. " The Lord ", said the Lateran fathers, " has commanded us to shun
evil and do good, but not to reject the good with the evil. We are not to deny
at the same time both error and truth "—which sounds like a reference to
Pope Honorius I, though he is not mentioned. These decrees were published
throughout the West, Martin invoking the energy of the bishops of Africa,
Spain and England for the putting down of Monothelism, and in the East he
appointed a vicar to enforce the synodal decisions in the patriarchates of Antioch
and Jerusalem.

The emperor, Constans II, was infuriated. He had already sent an exarch to
Rome who had failed in his mission of sowing dissension among the bishops at
the synod, and he now sent another, Theodore Kalliopes, with orders to bring the
pope to Constantinople. Martin, who was sick, took refuge in the Lateran basilica,
where he was lying on a couch in front of the altar when Kalliopes and his soldiers
broke in ; he refused to make any resistance, and was taken secretly out of Rome
to be put on board ship at Porto. The voyage was long and Martin suffered
greatly from dysentery. He arrived in Constantinople in the autumn of 653 and
was there left in jail for three months ; he wrote in a letter : " I have not been
allowed to wash, even in cold water, for forty-seven days. I am wasted away and
frozen through, and have had no respite from dysentery. . . . The food that is
given me makes me feel sick. I hope that God, who knows all things, will bring
my persecutors to repentance after He will have taken me out of this world ".
The pope was eventually arraigned before the senate on a charge of treason and
condemned unheard (His real offence, as St Martin pointed out to his accusers,
was his refusal to sign the theological " Typos ") ; then, after shameful public
indignities and ill-treatment, which aroused the indignation of the people, he was
returned to prison for another three months. His life, however, was spared (at
the intercession of the dying patriarch Paul) and in April 654 he was taken into
exile at Kherson in the Crimea.

From there St Martin wrote an account of the famine, his own difficulty in
getting food, the barbarism of the inhabitants, and the neglect with which he
was treated.

> I am surprised at the indifference of all those who, though they once knew
> me, have now so entirely forgotten me that they do not even seem to know
> whether I am in the world. I wonder still more at those who belong to the

church of St Peter for the little concern they show for one of their body.   If
that church has no money, it wants not corn, oil or other provisions out of
which they might send us a small supply.   What fear has seized all these
men that it hinders them from fulfilling the commands of God in relieving
the distressed ?   Have I appeared such an enemy to the whole Church, or
to them in particular ?   However, I pray God, by the intercession of St
Peter, to preserve them steadfast and immovable in the orthodox faith.
As to this wretched body, God will have care of it.   He is at hand ;   why
should I trouble myself ?   I hope in His mercy that He will not prolong my
course.

St Martin was not disappointed in his hope, for he died perhaps about two
years later, the last of the popes so far to be venerated as a martyr.   His feast is
celebrated in the West on November 12 and in the East on various dates, the
Byzantine liturgy acclaiming him as a " glorious defender of the true faith " and
an " ornament of the divine see of Peter ".   A contemporary wrote of Pope St
Martin I as being a man of great intelligence, learning and charity.

For sources we have in this case the letters of the pope, though these have not always
come to us in a very satisfactory form.   There is also a contemporary account in the *Liber
Pontificalis*—see Duchesne's edition, vol. i, pp. 336 *seq.* with his admirable notes—and the
Commemoratio, a narrative written by an ecclesiastic who had accompanied St Martin in
his exile.   This, with the letters, may be found in Migne, PL., vols. lxxxvii and cxxix.   The
Life of St Eligius by St Ouen, and the Greek biography of St Maximus the Confessor,
supply some further details.   From these materials Mgr Mann compiled a tolerably complete
history of the pontificate : *Lives of the Popes*, vol. i, pt 1, pp. 385–405.   But since he wrote
in 1902 other valuable contributions have been made to the subject, notably the publication
by Fr P. Peeters in the *Analecta Bollandiana*, vol. li (1933), pp. 225–262, of a previously
unknown Greek life of St Martin.   See also R. Devreesse, " La Vie de St Maxime le Con-
fesseur ", in *Analecta Bollandiana*, vol. xlvi (1928), pp. 5–49, and in vol. liii (1935), pp.
49 *seq.* ;   W. Peitz in the *Historisches Jahrbuch*, vol. xxxviii (1917), pp. 213–236 and 428–458 ;
Duchesne, *L'Église au VI*ᵉᵐᵉ *siècle* (1925), pp. 445–453 ;   E. Amann in DTC., vol. x, cc.
182–194, etc.

ST NILUS THE ELDER   (*c.* A.D. 430)

AMONG the disciples of St John Chrysostom was a certain Nilus, who was an official
at Constantinople and is said even to have been prefect of the city.   He was
married and had two children, some years after the birth of whom Nilus was seized
by a great craving after solitude.   He eventually agreed with his wife that they
should withdraw from the world, he taking his son Theodulus with him.   They
went to reside with the monks of Mount Sinai, from whence Nilus wrote two letters
of protest and rebuke to the Emperor Arcadius after the banishment of Chrysostom
from Constantinople.   After a few years the monastery suffered a raid from Arabs,
when many monks were slaughtered and the young Theodulus was carried
off.   His father followed up the raiders with the intention of ransoming the boy,
and at last traced him to Eleusa, south of Beersheba, where Theodulus had been
bought by the local bishop out of charity and given employment in the church.
Before sending them back to Sinai this bishop ordained both Nilus and his son
priests.

By the letters and other writings attributed to him Nilus was well known as a
writer, theological, Biblical and especially ascetic.   In his treatise on prayer he
recommends that we beg of God in the first place the gift of prayer, and entreat

the Holy Ghost to form in our hearts those desires which He has promised always to hear, and continually to ask of God that His will may be done in the most perfect manner.   To persons in the world he inculcates temperance, meditation on death and the obligation of giving alms, and he was always ready to communicate to others his spiritual science.   What proficiency he had attained in an interior life and in the study of the Holy Scriptures, and how much he was consulted by persons of all ranks, appear from the number of his letters which are still in existence.   One of these was in reply to the prefect Olympiodorus, who had built a church and wanted to know if he might adorn its walls with mosaics not only of sacred subjects but also of hunting scenes, birds, beasts and the like.   St Nilus makes short work of this suggestion, and then says that the walls should be painted with scenes from the Old and New Testaments for the instruction of those who could not read, but only one cross should be displayed, and that in the sanctuary.   St Nilus wrote a special treatise to show the life of hermits to be preferable to that of religious who live in communities in cities, but that hermits have their particular difficulties and trials.   These he himself had experienced by violent temptations, troubles of mind and assaults of evil spirits.   To a certain monk living on a pillar he writes that his lofty position is due to pride : " Every one that exalteth himself shall be humbled."

It would seem, however, that the story of St Nilus, accepted by Tillemont and Alban Butler on the authority of the *Narrationes* (printed in Migne, PG., vol. lxxix, pp. 583–694), is open to the gravest doubt.   We have no reason to believe that Nilus was a high court official, that he was married, betook himself to Sinai and underwent alarming experiences in the search for his captive son.   This is, no doubt, the tale perpetuated in the synaxaries, but it cannot be made to agree with the data furnished in Nilus's authentic letters.   Nilus the writer would appear to have been another person, a monk of Ancyra in Galatia (modern Ankara), and the two contemporaries seem to have been confused into one.

See the reference in Migne, PG., given above ; K. Heussi, *Untersuchungen zu Nilus dem Asketen* in *Texte und Untersuchungen* (1917) ; F. Degenhart, *Der hl. Nilus Sinaita* (1915) and *Neue Beiträge zur Nilusforschung* (1918) ; and also DTC., vol. xi (1931), cc. 661–674, which includes a full bibliography.

ST EMILIAN CUCULLATUS, ABBOT   (A.D. 574)

THIS St Emilian, under the name of San Millán de la Cogolla, *i.e.* " with the Hood ", was a famous early saint of Spain and is regarded as a patron of that country.   The Roman Martyrology refers to the fact that his life was written by St Braulio, Bishop of Saragossa, about fifty years after his death.   Emilian's birthplace has for centuries been a matter in dispute between Aragon and Castile.   As a youth he was a shepherd.   At the age of twenty he heard a call from God to His direct service, and for a time he attached himself to a hermit.   Then he returned to his home, but so many people importuned him that he wandered off into the mountains above Burgos.   He lived there for forty years—according to tradition on the mountain where the abbey of San Millán was afterwards built—till the bishop of Tarazona insisted on his receiving holy orders and becoming a parish priest. But the heroic virtues that the hermit had learned in the wilderness were not understood by his fellow clergy, and he was accused to the bishop of wasting the goods of the church, which he had given away in charity.   He was therefore

deprived of his cure, and with some disciples returned to solitude and contempla-
tion, and so spent the rest of his life.   St Emilian is sometimes called the first
Spanish Benedictine, but the monastery of La Cogolla of course did not have the
Benedictine Rule till long after his time.

The Latin biography by Braulio is printed by Mabillon, vol. i, pp. 198–207.   In Florez,
España Sagrada, vol. l, will also be found an account of the saint's translation and of the
miracles wrought at his shrine.   See further T. Minguella, *S. Millán de la Cogolla, estudios
historicos* (1883), and V. de la Fuente, *San Millán, presbitero secular* (1883).   A new critical
edition of the *vita*, ed. L. Vazquez de Parga, was published at Madrid in 1943.

ST MACHAR, BISHOP   (SIXTH CENTURY)

THE diocese of Aberdeen today keeps the feast of St Machar (Mochumma), but
nothing certain is known about him except that he was an Irish missionary who
came to Scotland with St Columba.   He is said to have evangelized the isle of
Mull, and to have been consecrated bishop before being sent to preach to the
Picts in what is now Aberdeenshire.   It is likely that he was a missionary in that
neighbourhood, and the establishment of what became the see of Aberdeen is
attributed to him.   Water from St Machar's well at Old Aberdeen used always
to be used for baptisms in the cathedral.

Little is known of St Machar beyond what we find in the Aberdeen Breviary.   Forbes
in KSS., treats of him (pp. 393–394) under the heading " Mauritius, Machar or Mocumma ".
In the Aberdeen Martyrology he is described as " Archbishop of Tours ".   We are further
told that " Mr Bradshaw has discovered in the University Library at Cambridge a metrical
Life of this saint, which he supposes to have been composed by Barbour in his extreme old
age ".   This metrical life, written about 1390, has since been printed by Horstmann in his
Altenglische Legenden (1881).   And *cf.* an article by Professor A. S. Ferguson in *Scottish
Gaelic Studies*, vol. vi, pp. 58 *seq.*

ST CUNIBERT, BISHOP OF COLOGNE   (*c.* A.D. 663)

THE fine church of St Cunibert at Cologne was founded by this bishop, who
dedicated it in honour of St Clement ; when his own relics were enshrined therein
it was renamed after its founder.   He was undoubtedly a great and holy prelate,
but the authorities for details of his life are not very reliable or full.   He is said
to have been brought up at the court of Clotaire II, received holy orders, and was
made archdeacon of the church of Trier.   About 625 he was advanced to the
bishopric of Cologne, and wielded such influence that he is commonly referred to
as archbishop, though there was no actual metropolitan of that city till the end of
the eighth century.   He was a royal counsellor and assisted at several important
synods, and when Dagobert I made his four-year-old son Sigebert king of Austrasia,
Cunibert was appointed one of his two guardians.   St Cunibert was concerned for
the evangelization of the Frisians, as we learn from a letter of St Boniface ; and in
his later years he left the court to devote himself entirely to his diocese.   He died
in an uncertain year, leaving a great reputation for holiness.

Medieval lives of St Cunibert are numerous, belonging to two different types.   Fr M.
Coens in the *Analecta Bollandiana*, vol. xlvii (1929), pp. 338–367, has discussed the whole
question very thoroughly, and published one particular text, adding abundant references
to the more recent literature of the subject.   On the church of St Cunibert see the *Festschrift
Anton Ditges gewidmet* (1911), and also P. Clemen in *Kunstdenkmäler der Rheinprovinz*,
vol. vi, pt 4 (1916), pp. 231–313 ; the relics of The Two Ewalds (October 3) are preserved
there.

ST CUMIAN, Abbot   (*c.* A.D. 665)

CUIMINE FOTA, that is to say " the Tall ", was born about the year 590, a son of Fiachna, King of West Munster.   While he was young he became a monk, and later presided over the school and district of Clonfert, where he is said to have been bishop.   He is often identified with the Cumian who founded a house at Kil-cummin in Offaly, where he introduced the Roman computation of Easter.   This gave offence in many quarters and the abbot of Iona rebuked Cumian for abandoning the Celtic computation, which had been hallowed by the observance of St Colum-cille.   Cumian replied in a letter known as the Paschal Epistle, in which he learnedly defends the Roman reckoning, citing synods, Western fathers and the paschal cycles of antiquity.   This epistle, as Alban Butler remarks, alone suffices to give us a high idea of the learning, eloquence and virtue of the writer.   But the eloquence and learning of St Cumian had no effect on the intransigent monks of Iona.   He also wrote a hymn, the last three stanzas of which are found as part of a liturgical office in the Book of Mulling in Trinity College, Dublin.

There seems to be no proper life of St Cumian in either Latin or Irish.   The *Félire* of Oengus, however, under November 12 has the entry : " There has been given with wisdom, science and much prudence, to my Cumian of beautiful warfare, the fair tall (*Fota*) son of Fiachna ".   See especially Kenney, *Sources for the Early History of Ireland*, vol. i, pp. 220–221, and 324–325.   Whether this Cumian was the author of a penitential sometimes attributed to him seems very doubtful.   On this consult J. T. McNeill in the *Revue Celtique* for 1922 and 1923, and other authorities referred to by L. Gougaud, *Christianity in Celtic Lands*, p. 285 and *passim*.   Forbes in his KSS. states (p. 317) that " Fort Augustus is in the vulgar language called Killchuimin ", *i.e.* the church of Cumian ; but Cumians were numerous and their identities are very tangled.

ST LIVINUS, Bishop and Martyr   (No Date)

THE Church in Ireland today keeps the feast of St Livinus, who is mentioned in the Roman Martyrology as having been martyred in Belgium and who, like several other Irish missionaries on the continent, is credited with having been bishop in Dublin.   His medieval life states that he was the son of a noble Scottish father and a royal Irish mother, and that he was baptized by St Augustine of Canterbury, who also ordained him.   He later became a bishop and with three companions left Ireland for Flanders, where they were received by the abbot St Floribert at Ghent.   Then he went preaching among the heathen in Brabant, was hospitably received by a lady, and eventually killed by pagans, who cut off his head at Eschen, near Alost.   His relics finally found a resting-place at the abbey of St Peter in Ghent.

The Life of St Livinus professes to have been written from information received from his personal disciples, but it is not heard of before the eleventh century, and the resemblance of the above story to that of St Lebuin (see below) is obvious.   It is now generally received among scholars that this bishop had no independent existence, that the St Livinus commemorated in the Roman Martyrology, in Ireland and at Ghent is the same as the St Lebuin who was certainly a missionary in Holland and is venerated in that country.

A medieval life, purporting to have been written by a certain " Bonifacius peccator ", and at one time ascribed to the great St Boniface, is printed in Mabillon, vol. ii, pp. 449–461. Its worthlessness has been demonstrated by O. Holder-Egger in *Historische Aufsätze an G. Waitz gewidmet* (1886), pp. 622–665.   J. Kenney, *Sources for the Early History of Ireland*, says, p. 509 : " It is probable that Livinus is a doublet of the English St Liafwin or Lebuin of Deventer in Holland " ; on which *cf. Analecta Bollandiana*, vol. lxx (1952), pp. 285–308.

ST LEBUIN, OR LIAFWINE   (*c.* A.D. 773)

THIS saint was by birth an Englishman, called in his own tongue Liafwine, and became a monk in the monastery of Ripon where he was promoted to priest's orders.   That he might employ his talent for the salvation of souls, he went over into lower Germany sometime after 754, where several English missionaries were planting the gospel, and he addressed himself to St Gregory, vicar at Utrecht for that diocese.   This holy man received him with joy, and sent him with St Marchelm (Marculf) to carry the gospel into the country now called Overyssel.   St Lebuin was joyfully received by a lady named Abachilda and, many being converted, they built a chapel on the west bank of the river near Deventer ; later a church and residence were built on the other bank, at Deventer itself.   But many shut their ears to the truth, from whom the saint had much to suffer ; he seemed to gather greater courage from persecutions and continued his work until his enemies allied themselves with the Westphalian Saxons, burned down his church, and scattered his Frisian converts.

These Saxons used to hold a yearly assembly at Marklo, upon the river Weser, to deliberate on the affairs of their nation, and St Lebuin determined to brave them thereat.   Clothed in his priestly vestments, he entered the assembly, holding a cross and a gospel-book.   And he cried out to them with a loud voice, saying, " Hear me, all of you !   Listen to God who speaks to you by my mouth.   Know that the Lord, the Maker of the heavens, the earth and all things, is the only true God."   They stopped to listen, and he went on, affirming that their gods were powerless dead things and that he had been sent by the Lord of Heaven to promise them His peace and His salvation if they would acknowledge Him and receive baptism.   But if they refused he threatened (perhaps a little tactlessly) that they should be speedily destroyed by a prince whom God in His wrath would raise up against them.   Whereupon many of the Saxons ran to the hedges and plucked up sharp stakes to murder him.   But one in authority cried out that they had often received with respect ambassadors from men ; much more ought they to honour an ambassador from a god who was so powerful that his messenger had escaped from their hands, as Lebuin had done.   This impressed the barbarians and it was agreed that he should be permitted to travel and preach where he pleased.   St Lebuin after this heroic venture returned to Deventer and continued his work till he died.

The paper contributed in 1916 by Hofmeister to the volume *Geschichtliche Studien Albert Hauck dargebracht*, pp. 85–107, is of special importance.   Besides the life by Hucbald of Elnone (in Migne, PL., vol. cxxxii, cc. 877–894) see that edited by Hofmeister in MGH., *Scriptores*, vol. xxx, pt 2, pp. 789–795.   This had been previously printed by Fr M. Coens in the *Analecta Bollandiana*, vol. xxxix (1921), pp. 306–330.   There is an account by F. Hesterman, *Der hl. Lebuin* (1935).   The second life mentioned above is translated by C. H. Talbot in *Anglo-Saxon Missionaries in Germany* (1954).

SS. BENEDICT AND HIS COMPANIONS, MARTYRS   (A.D. 1003)

ST BENEDICT of Benevento was a friend of St Bruno of Querfurt, they having shared a cell at a monastery near Ravenna, under the direction of St Romuald. When the Emperor Otto III wished to evangelize the Slavs of Pomerania, Benedict and other monks were sent to engage in the work.   They first went into western Poland, where they were well received at the court of Duke Boleslaus I and teachers were appointed to instruct them in the Slavonic speech.   The monks established themselves at Kazimierz, near Gniezno, where on November 11, 1003, St Benedict and four others were murdered by pagan robbers.   They were venerated as martyrs, their relics solemnly translated to Olomuc, and their names added to the Roman Martyrology: " the holy martyred hermits Benedict, John, Matthew, Isaac and Christian who, intent upon the service of God, were grievously troubled by robbers and by them slain with the sword ", as their notice now runs.   These martyrs, who are venerated in Poland as the Five Polish Brothers, although they were neither Poles nor (apart from Matthew and Isaac), other than spiritually, brothers, are accounted to the glory of the Camaldolese Order, though in fact they were dead some years before St Romuald founded Camaldoli.   When St Bruno of Querfurt learned of the fate of his friend Benedict and his four fellows, he collected evidence from Poland and wrote down an account of what had happened.

There are two main sources for the history of these martyrs.   The first is the narrative of St Bruno of Querfurt, of which the text may be read in MGH., *Scriptores*, vol. xv, pp. 716–738, and in the German annotated translation of H. G. Voigt, *Bruno von Querfurt* (1907).   The second account, of later date, is that of Cosmas of Prague.   It is printed in Migne, PL., vol. clxvi, cc. 109–113.   See also the *Neues Archiv*, vol. viii, pp. 365 *seq.*

ST ASTRIK, OR ANASTASIUS, ARCHBISHOP OF THE HUNGARIANS (c. A.D. 1040)

IT is agreed that the first archbishop in Hungary was called Astrik, but there is a great deal of uncertainty about his identity.   There are three " candidates ", all associated with St Adalbert of Prague : *viz.* Anastasius, the first abbot of Brevnov in Bohemia, Astericus, one of Adalbert's clergy, and Radla, Adalbert's fellow student at Magdeburg and his close friend.   The first two of these may be really one person.

On the whole it seems likely to have been Radla, a Czech or Croat from Bohemia who is known to have been a monk in Hungary.   He probably received the habit at Brevnov, taking the name of Anastasius, of. which Astrik seems to be an equivalent.   Then, when St Adalbert failed to consolidate his position in Bohemia, and left Prague, Astrik Radla went to help the missionaries among the Magyars. He is known to have been in the service of the wife of Duke Geza in 997 ; and he was almost certainly the first abbot of St Martin's (Pannonhalma), the first ecclesiastical institution of Hungary, founded by Geza.   On the duke's death and the accession of his son St Stephen I the evangelization of the Magyars was taken seriously in hand, and St Astrik was active in the work of preaching the gospel and establishing an ecclesiastical organization.   In connection with this Stephen sent him to Rome to confer with Pope Silvester II, and soon after his return the sovereign was crowned with a royal crown, granted no doubt at the instance of the Emperor Otto III, in 1001.   There is a good case for Radla being the Astrik who was now promoted to be archbishop of the new Hungarian church.

When Astrik attended a synod at Frankfurt in 1006 he was styled simply *Ungarorum episcopus*, and it seems that his seat was not at Esztergom, which before long became the primatial see ; Vesprem is the first Hungarian diocese for which there is documentary evidence, but Astrik's see may have been at Kalocsa. Throughout the remainder of his long life he worked hand in hand with King St Stephen for the proper settlement of the Church in his dominions and for the conversion of the fierce Magyars to the faith of Christ. He died soon after his royal master, about the year 1040.

Of the personality and personal life of St Astrik nothing is known ; but it is significant that St Adalbert of Prague had so much affection for and trust in him : Adalbert wrote to Geza's wife asking her to send " his master " back to him in Poland ; and to Astrik Radla himself he wrote saying that if the duchess would not release him, he should slip away secretly and rejoin " your Adalbert ". But to Astrik his duty was clear that he must stay among the Magyars.

The best examination of the problem is doubtless that of F. Dvornik in his *Making of Central and Eastern Europe* (1949), pp. 159–166, which shows clearly how confused and uncertain is the history of the conversion of Hungary, even for scholars who are natives of eastern Europe. *Cf.* C. Kadlec in the *Cambridge Medieval History*, vol. iv, p. 214. See also St Bruno's Life of St Adalbert in *Fontes rerum Bohemicarum* (1871), vol. i ; the Life of St Stephen in MGH., *Scriptores*, vol. xi, and *cf.* vol. iv, pp. 547, 563 ; and *Lexikon für Theologie und Kirche*, vol. i (1930), c. 394.

## BD RAINERIUS OF AREZZO	(A.D. 1304)

INFORMATION is lacking about the details of the life of this early Franciscan *beatus*. He was born at Arezzo, of the Mariani family, and gave up a secular career to join the Friars Minor. He was a companion of Bd Benedict of Arezzo, who had been received into the order by St Francis himself. Miracles were attributed to Bd Rainerius during his life, and immediately after his death, at Borgo San Sepolcro on November 1, 1304, the municipality of the town had an altar set up in his honour and record kept of his miracles. His *cultus* was confirmed in 1802.

Bd Rainerius is dealt with by the Bollandists on November 1. They found no record of his life beyond such brief notices as were supplied by Wadding and other annalists, but they print from manuscript sources a record of miracles worked at his tomb. See further Mazzara, *Leggendario Francescano* (1680), vol. iii, pp. 295–296 ; and Léon, *Auréole Séraphique* (Eng. trans.), vol. iv, pp. 34–35.

## BD JOHN DELLA PACE	(*c.* A.D. 1332)

A *confirmatio cultus* may, or at any rate used, in former days, to be accorded with very little knowledge of the life of the servant of God to whom honour was paid. When Pope Pius IX in 1856 approved the celebration of this feast for the Franciscan Order, it was supposed that Bd John died in the first half of the fifteenth century. Since then it has come to light, through the indefatigable researches of the archivist S. Barsotti, that there were two Johns at Pisa who have become confused. He who died in 1433 was a furrier who lived in matrimony all his days ; but the founder of the Fraticelli della Penitenza at Pisa was at one time a hermit, and his death took place about 1332.

See the two books of S. Barsotti, *Pro memoria sul B. Giovanni della Pace* (1901) and *Un nuovo fiore serafico* (1906) ; and the notice of the confirmation of cult in the *Analecta Juris Pontificii*, vol. iii (1858), cc. 378–380. The confusion has been perpetuated in other works, *e.g.* Léon, *Auréole Séraphique* (Eng. trans.), vol. iv, p. 60.

## BD GABRIEL OF ANCONA	(A.D. 1456)

ST JAMES DELLA MARCA, whose feast is kept on the 28th of this month, was instructed by Pope Callistus III to draw up an account of the life of this holy Franciscan.

Unfortunately the document could not be found when his *cultus* came up for confirmation in 1753, and particulars of his career are few. He belonged to the Ferretti of Ancona and became a friar minor of the Observance when he was eighteen. He was a missioner for fifteen years in the March of Ancona, where he was conspicuous by his holiness and miracles, and was then appointed guardian of the Observants in his native town. It is said that he greatly encouraged among his young friars the use of the devotion called the Franciscan or Seraphic Crown, a rosary in honour of the joys of our Lady, and that her approval of this was marvellously demonstrated. On one occasion Bd Gabriel was reported to St James for some small dereliction of duty. St James, looking rather to the quality of the doer than the smallness of the fault, ordered him to accuse and discipline himself before his community. This Gabriel did cheerfully, and sent a sugar-loaf and a carpet for his church to St James as a token of goodwill. He died at Ancona on November 12, 1456. Pope Pius IX (Mastai-Ferretti) belonged to another branch of Bd Gabriel's family.

Most of the older collections of Franciscan lives provide some account of Bd Gabriel; for example, we find a tolerably full notice in Mazzara, *Leggendario Francescano* (1680), vol. ii, pt 2, pp. 425–427. In particular a certain authority attaches to the information furnished by Wadding, *Annales Ordinis Minorum*, vol. xii, nn. 206–214. Short sketches were published separately by V. M. Ferretti in 1754, and by S. Melchiori in 1846. See also Léon, *Auréole Séraphique* (Eng. trans.), vol. iv, pp. 61–66.

13 : ST DIDACUS, OR DIEGO   (A.D. 1463)

In the United States of America the feast of St Frances Xavier Cabrini is celebrated on this date. See Vol. IV, p. 593ff.

DIDACUS was a native of the little town of San Nicolas del Puerto in the diocese of Seville, and his parents were poor folk. Near that town a holy priest led an eremitical life. Didacus obtained his consent to live with him and, though very young, he imitated the austerities and devotions of his master. They cultivated together a little garden, and also employed themselves in making wooden spoons, trenchers and such-like utensils. After having lived thus a recluse for some years he was obliged to return to his home, but he soon after went to a convent of the Observant Friar Minors at Arrizafa, and there took the habit among the lay-brothers. After his profession he was sent to the mission of his order in the Canary Islands, where he did a great work in instructing and converting the people. Eventually, in 1445, he, though a lay-brother, was appointed guardian of the chief convent in those islands, called Fuerteventura. After four years he was recalled to Spain, and lived in several friaries about Seville with great fervour and recollection. In the year 1450 a jubilee was celebrated at Rome and, St Bernardino of Siena being canonized at the same time, very many religious of the Order of St Francis were assembled there. Didacus went thither with Father Alonzo de Castro, and at Rome he had to attend his companion during a dangerous illness. His devotion in this duty attracted the notice of his superiors and he was put in charge of the many sick friars who were accommodated in the infirmary of the convent of Ara Caeli. St Didacus was thus engaged for three months, and is said to have miraculously restored some of his patients. He lived for another thirteen years after his return to Spain, chiefly at the friaries of Salcedo and Alcala in Castile.

In 1463 he was taken ill at Alcalá, and in his last moments asked for a cord (such as the friars wear) ; he put it about his neck and, holding a cross in his hands, begged the pardon of all his brethren assembled about his bed.   Then, fixing his eyes on the crucifix, he repeated with great tenderness the words of the hymn on the cross, " Dulce lignum, dulces clavos, dulce pondus sustinet ", and peacefully died on November 12.   Several miracles were attributed to him in his lifetime, and many more through his intercession after his death.   King Philip II, out of gratitude for one in favour of his son, solicited the saint's canonization, which was decreed in 1588.

There is apparently no medieval life of St Didacus, but the various Franciscan chronicles of later date supply copious information.   For example, Father Mark of Lisbon (d. 1591) devotes a long section to San Diego : see the Italian translation (1591), vol. iii, fol. 155 *seq.* Among separate biographies may be mentioned Moreno de la Rea, *Vida del S. Fray Diego* (1602) and two slight sketches in more modern times, by Berguin and Chappuis in French (1901) and by A. Gioia in Italian (1907).   The canonization of St Didacus (1588) was an occasion for rejoicing in Spain : one or two of the booklets with panegyrics delivered at the time are in the British Museum.

SS. ARCADIUS AND HIS COMPANIONS, MARTYRS   (A.D. 437)

" IN Africa ", says the Roman Martyrology, " the passion of the holy Spanish martyrs Arcadius, Paschasius, Probus and Eutychian who, in the Vandal perse- cution, when they absolutely refused to enter into the Arian perfidy, were first proscribed by the Arian king, Genseric, then exiled and treated with atrocious cruelty, and finally slain in various ways.   At that time, too, was seen the constancy of Paulillus, the little brother of SS. Paschasius and Eutychian, who, since he could in no way be turned from the Catholic faith, was long beaten with sticks and con- demned to the lowest slavery."   The boy afterwards died of exposure.   In a letter to St Arcadius in captivity, Antoninus Honoratus, Bishop of Constantine, calls him " the standard-bearer of the faith ", and we learn from it—if indeed it was addressed to this Arcadius—that the martyr was married and had a family.

There seems to be no independent *passio* of this group of martyrs, but there is a summary account in the Chronicle of Prosper of Aquitaine.   The letter of Bishop Antoninus Honoratus is printed in Migne, PL., vol. l, cc. 567–570.

ST BRICE, BISHOP OF TOURS   (A.D. 444)

BRICE (Britius, Brictio) was brought up by St Martin of Tours at Marmoutier but for long was no credit to his master.   He was badly-behaved, and contemptuous towards St Martin, who refrained from degrading and dismissing Brice only lest he should thereby be avoiding a trial sent from God.   Moreover, if the story be true, he had already foreseen that the troublesome cleric would be his successor. For while Brice was yet a deacon he had characterized his master as crazy ; and when St Martin asked why he thought he was mad, denied his words.   But St Martin replied that he had heard them.   " Nevertheless ", he said, " I have prayed for you and you shall be bishop of Tours.   But you will suffer many adversities in your office."   And Brice went away grumbling that he had always said the bishop was a fool.   In one of the dialogues of Sulpicius Severus, Brice is represented as holding himself up as a model because he had been brought up at Marmoutier, while St Martin had been bred in camps and was falling into superstition and folly in his old age.   Then suddenly he threw himself at St Martin's feet and begged his pardon and Martin, whose pardon it was never difficult to get, forgave him, saying, " If Christ could tolerate Judas, surely I can put up with Brice ".

St Martin died in 397 and Brice was in fact elected to his place. He did not give satisfaction as a bishop and several unsuccessful attempts were made to get him condemned, until in the thirty-third year of his episcopate a happening was alleged with a woman. St Gregory of Tours asserts that Brice cleared himself by a very astonishing miracle, but he was driven from his see and went to Rome to protest his innocence. He remained in exile for seven years, during which he became a reformed character, and when Armentius, who had administered Tours in his place, died, he returned to his see. Brice lived to govern it for some years and by his exemplary life made such amends for his past that when he died he was venerated as a saint, considerable evangelical activity being attributed to him.

Within twenty-five years of his death the feast of St Brice was kept at Tours with a vigil, and his *cultus* soon spread. He was very popular in England (the Anglican calendar still retains his name), but nowadays he is only associated with the Massacre of St Brice's Day in 1002, when Ethelred the Redeless ordered the wholesale murder of Danes which provoked Sweyn's invasion of this country.

What we know of St Brice is almost entirely derived from Sulpicius Severus's writings on St Martin and from the popular traditions retailed by St Gregory of Tours. There is, no doubt, much that is perplexing in the story of St Brice, but the matter should be considered in the light of what two specialists have written on the subject : see Poncelet in the *Analecta Bollandiana*, vol. xxx (1911), pp. 88–89, and Delehaye in the same, vol. xxxviii (1920), pp. 5–136, especially pp. 105 and 135. The letters of Pope Zosimus will be found summarized in Jaffé-Kaltenbrunner, *Regesta Pontificum*, nn. 330–331, and the full text in Migne, PL., vol. xx, cc. 650 and 663. In the second of these he expressly declares that Lazarus, the accuser of Brice, was " pro calumniatore damnatus, cum Bricii innocentis episcopi vitam falsis objectionibus appetisset ". It was probably his close connection with St Martin which made St Brice a popular saint both in England and in Italy ; in nearly every one of the early English calendars printed by F. Wormald for the Henry Bradshaw Society his name is entered under November 13.

ST EUGENIUS, Archbishop of Toledo   (A.D. 657)

It is said there was an Eugenius who occupied the see of Toledo and was an astronomer and mathematician ; his successor, St Eugenius, was a musician and poet. He was a Spanish Goth, a monk at Saragossa, and to avoid ecclesiastical promotion he hid himself in a cemetery. But he was forced to return and receive episcopal consecration. Some of the writings of St Eugenius, in prose and in verse, are extant ; and we are told that he was a good musician, who tried to improve the poor singing of which he heard so much. He governed his see with great edification, and was followed therein by his nephew, St Ildephonsus. Alban Butler refers to another St Eugenius, called " of Toledo ", who is mentioned in the Roman Martyrology on November 15. He is said to have been a martyred associate of St Dionysius of Paris, but he had nothing to do with Spain. The martyrology also names, on the 17th, a third St Eugenius, deacon to St Zenobius of Florence and a disciple of St Ambrose.

There has been confusion in the early episcopal lists of Toledo, and the existence of Eugenius I is questionable. The story printed in the *Analecta Bollandiana*, vol. ii, is probably a myth.   But there can be no question about the real existence and the literary activities of the Eugenius who died in 657.   St Ildephonsus gives a short account of him in his *De viris illustribus*, cap. xiv (Migne, PL., vol. xcvi, c. 204).   His poetical writings, with notes, etc., have been edited in MGH., *Auctores Antiquissimi*, vol. xiv.   See on this the *Analecta Bollandiana*, vol. xxiv (1905), pp. 297–298.   See also J. Madoz in *Revue d'histoire ecclésiastique*, vol. xxxv (1939), pp. 530–533.

ST MAXELLENDIS, Virgin and Martyr   (*c.* A.D. 670)

THE diocese of Cambrai observes today the feast of St Maxellendis, the maiden daughter of the noble Humolin and Ameltrudis of the town of Caudry.   Her hand in marriage was sought by many young men, among whom her parents favoured a certain Harduin of Solesmes, but Maxellendis said she did not wish to be married. When her father pointed out that God could be served well in the married state and that many saints had been wives as well, she asked for time to think it over. During the night she dreamed that her resolution was confirmed by an angel, and the next day she told Humolin that she was quite determined to take no other bridegroom but Christ.   But her parents were equally determined that she should be the bride of Harduin, and when preparations for the wedding were going forward Maxellendis fled from the house.   She took refuge with her nurse near Cateau-Cambrésis, but her hiding-place was discovered and Harduin and his friends broke into the house.   Maxellendis could not be seen anywhere, but in ransacking the place a large clothes-chest was thrown open, and the girl found therein.   Disregarding her cries and struggles they carried her off, but she broke loose and tried to run away, so that Harduin in his anger drew his sword and struck her with such force that she was killed on the spot.   The men ran away in horror, all except Harduin himself, who was seized with blindness.   St Maxellendis was buried in a neighbouring church, where she was the occasion of many marvels, so that St Vindician, Bishop of Cambrai, about the year 673 translated her body solemnly to Caudry.   On this occasion the repentant Harduin asked to be led out to meet the procession.   When he was brought near the coffin he fell on his knees, loudly accusing himself of his crime and asking God for pardon : and at once his sight was restored.

The *passio* of the saint has been printed in Ghesquière, *Acta Sanctorum Belgii*, vol. iii, pp. 580–589.   The details are quite untrustworthy, but there were translations of her relics and an active *cultus*, especially at Cambrai where the greater part were eventually enshrined. See C. J. Destombes, *Vies des Saints de Cambrai et Arras* (1887), vol. iv, pp. 177–187.

ST KILIAN   (Seventh Century)

THIS Kilian (Chilianus), a native of Ireland, was said to be related to St Fiacre whom, returning from a pilgrimage to Rome, he visited at his hermitage in Brie, staying some time with him there.   St Aubert having asked for some missionaries for Artois, St Faro of Meaux induced St Kilian to leave his solitude and undertake the work.   It is related that, coming to the house of a nobleman near the banks of the Aisne, the weary traveller asked for something to drink, and was told by the mistress of the house that the river was just behind him, whereat he could quench his thirst at his leisure : she had nothing for him to drink.   " May it be to you as you have said ", replied Kilian, and walked off.   When the nobleman came home from hunting, he also called for a drink, and was annoyed to find that all his barrels, full in the morning, were now empty.   There was a hue and cry for Kilian, and when he was found profuse apologies were made to him, and the barrels were found again to be full.   This nobleman had another house at Aubigny, and here St Kilian eventually made his headquarters, building a church on a piece of land given him near the Scarpe and preaching the gospel zealously throughout Artois until the day of his death.

There is a Latin life of late date which was printed for the first time in the *Analecta Bollandiana*, vol. xx (1901), pp. 431–444.   It has since been edited by B. Krusch in MGH., *Scriptores Merov.*, vol. v.   On this Kenney (*Sources*, vol. i, pp. 494–495) remarks " the extant life contains much that is absurd " ; but Hildegaire (*c.* 889) speaks of a Life of Kilian in his possession, so that it is possible that there may have been some foundation in authentic materials.   See also A. Perret, *Histoire de S. Kilien d'Aubigny* (1920), and L. Gougaud, *Les Saints irlandais hors d'Irlande* (1936).

ST NICHOLAS I, POPE   (A.D. 867)

WHEN Nicholas I died on this day in the year 867 after a pontificate of nine years all men of goodwill bewailed his loss, and heavy rains at that time were looked on by the Romans as testimony to the grief of the very heavens, for the dead pope had well deserved the titles " Saint " and " the Great " which succeeding ages bestowed on him.   " Since the time of Blessed Gregory [the Great] ", writes a contemporary, " no one comparable with him has been raised to the papal dignity.   He gave orders to kings and rulers as though he were lord of the world.   To good bishops and priests, to religious lay-people, he was kind and gentle and modest ; to evil-doers he was terrible and stern.   It is rightly said that in him God raised up a second Elias ", and the greatest pope between Gregory I and Hildebrand.

He was a scion of a good Roman house, and Sergius II attached him to the papal household.   His talents were used by St Leo IV and Benedict III, and on the death of the last-named in 858 Nicholas, then a deacon, was elected to the supreme pontificate.   The new pope was at once confronted with the troubled state of affairs in the second see of Christendom, Constantinople.   It has been related in the notice of St Ignatius, Patriarch of Constantinople (October 23), how that hierarch was removed from his see by Bardas Caesar and the Emperor Michael III, and Photius put in his place.   Other important matters were soon involved, and St Nicholas was engaged in very difficult and delicate relations with Constantinople throughout his pontificate.   During the course of them he received a letter from the newly-baptized ruler of the Bulgars, Boris, asking a number of questions : Nicholas's reply was " a masterpiece of pastoral wisdom and one of the finest documents of the history of the papacy ".   It also reproved Boris for his cruelty to pagans, forbidding their " conversion " by force, and told the Bulgars to be less superstitious, less ferocious in war, and not to use torture.   Naturally St Nicholas wished these new Christians to belong to his patriarchate, but Boris eventually submitted his people to Constantinople.

St Nicholas I stands out as a firm defender of the integrity of marriage, of the weak and oppressed, and of the equality of all before the divine law.   He had to uphold the matrimonial sacrament not only against King Lothair of Lorraine but also against the complaisant bishops who had approved his divorce and remarriage ; and when Charles the Bald of Burgundy obtained from the Frankish bishops the excommunication of his daughter Judith for having married Baldwin of Flanders without her father's consent, Nicholas intervened in favour of freedom of marriage, recommending less severity and urging Hincmar of Rheims to try and reconcile Charles with his daughter.*

This Hincmar was a prominent figure among early medieval bishops, but he was proud and ambitious, and Nicholas, like other popes, had to force him to acknowledge the right of the Holy See to take cognizance of all important causes, one of Hincmar's suffragans having appealed to Rome against the sentence of his metropolitan.   St Nicholas also twice excommunicated Archbishop John of Ravenna, for his intolerance towards his suffragans and other clergy and open defiance of the pope.   People turned to this strong and just judge from all over Europe and beyond.

The Church in the West was in a bad way at the time when St Nicholas was called to govern it after the collapse of Charlemagne's empire.   Young, inexperienced and even vicious bishops received and lost sees at the will of secular nobles ; excommunication was used (and for long after) as a daily weapon in the most unsuitable circumstances ; contempt for the persons of the clergy led to disrespect for their office ; evil-living had followed on the degeneration and disuse of canonical penance.   The great pope did his utmost against thronging ills during a short reign : injustice and wickedness he denounced unsparingly, whether in high or low, clergy or laity.   Certainly he did not lack ambition, but it was the ambition to consolidate for the Apostolic See a position in which the maximum amount of good could be done for souls.†   " If ", wrote the Anglican Dean Milman, " he treated the royal dignity of France with contempt, it had already become contemptible in the eyes of mankind ; if he annulled by his own authority the decree of a national council, composed of the most distinguished prelates of Gaul, that council had already been condemned by all who had natural sympathies with justice and with innocence."   When any scandal or disorder arose, " he gave no rest to his frame or repose to his limbs " till he had tried to remedy it.

Though his responsibilities were conterminous with Christendom, Nicholas had a deep personal solicitude for his own episcopal flock.   For example, he had drawn up a list of all the disabled poor in Rome, who were fed daily in their homes, while the able-bodied were given food at the papal residence.   Each person on the register had a particular day of the week on which to fetch it, and was provided with a sort of tally to remind him which was his day.   St Nicholas was worn down by ill-health, as well as by his own ceaseless energy.   " Our heavenly Father ", he wrote, " has seen good to send me such pain that not only am I unable to write proper replies to your questions, but I cannot even dictate them, so intensely do I suffer."   He died at Rome on November 13, 867.   Pope St Nicholas the Great, whose feast is kept each year by the Romans, " was patient and temperate, humble and chaste, beautiful in face and graceful in body.   His speech was both learned and modest, illustrious though he was by great deeds.   He was devoted to penance and the Holy Mysteries, the friend of widows and orphans, and the champion of all the people " (*Liber Pontificalis*).   Yet whilst he lay dying he was robbed by one of his officials of money that he had set aside for the poor.

* The lady was a widow, having been the wife of Ethelwulf of Wessex and also united to her stepson Ethelbald.   From her marriage with Baldwin was descended Matilda, the wife of William the Conqueror.

† He has been accused of deliberately making use of those documents known as the False Decretals, knowing them to be false.   Whatever limited use he may have made of them he certainly did not know they were forged : nobody did before the fifteenth century. They were brought into Italy from France.

St Nicholas I belongs to general church history and there is nothing which can be regarded as an early hagiographical life of this great pope.   The account in the *Liber Pontificalis* (see Duchesne's edition, vol. ii, pp. 151–172) is somewhat less of an inventory than other preceding notices and is probably due to Anastasius the Librarian himself.   A very good biography is provided in Mann, *Lives of the Popes*, vol. iii (1906), pp. 1–148, and in the little volume of Jules Roy, *St Nicholas I* (Eng. trans., 1901) ; both these furnish a full list of sources and works to be consulted.   But since they wrote additions have been made.   The important correspondence of Pope Nicholas is accessible not only in Migne, PL., vol. cxix, but in MGH., *Epistolae*, vol. vi, on which see E. Perels in the *Neues Archiv*, vol. xxxvii (1912) and vol. xxxix (1914), as well as the book of the same scholar, *Papst Nicolaus I und Anastasius Bibliothecarius* (1920).   See also Duchesne, *Les Premiers Temps de l'État pontifical* (1911) ;   F. Dvornik, *Les Slaves, Byzance et Rome au IXeme siècle* (1926), and *The Photian Schism* (1948) ;   F. X. Seppelt, *Das Papsttum im Früh-Mittelalter* (1934), pp. 241–284.   On the question of the Forged Decretals, see especially P. Fournier and G. Le Bras, *Histoire des Collections caroniques en Occident*, vol. i (1931), pp. 127–233, and J. Haller, *Nikolaus I und Pseudo-Isidor* (1936).

ST ABBO OF FLEURY, ABBOT   (A.D. 1004)

ABBO OF FLEURY was a monk among the most conspicuous for learning in his time and one, moreover, associated for a short period with our own country.   About the year 971 St Oswald of York, then bishop of Worcester, founded a monastery at Ramsey in Huntingdonshire.   Oswald had received the Benedictine habit at Fleury-sur-Loire, and about 986 he received from that monastery the services of Abbo as director of the school at Ramsey.   He filled this office for two years, having himself studied in the schools of Paris, Rheims and Orleans, and then returned to Fleury to resume his own studies in philosophy, mathematics and astronomy.   He was not allowed to pursue these in quietness, for on the death of the governing abbot he was elected to take his place.   But the election was disputed, and a contest ensued which spread far beyond the walls of the monastery.   It was eventually decided in favour of Abbo, with the help of Gerbert, who a few years later was to become pope as Silvester II.

Abbo's career as a prelate was very lively, for he threw himself into the affairs of his time with great energy :   he strove for the exemption of monasteries from episcopal control ;   he made himself conspicuous at synods, and failed to get King Robert II's very irregular second marriage recognized at Rome.   He is perhaps better remembered for his writings, notably a collection of canons and, in England, his Life of St Edmund, king and martyr.

We learn from Abbo's letters that he was much in request for restoring peace in disturbed monastic communities, and it was his zeal for discipline that brought about his violent death, for which he was venerated as a martyr.   In 1004 he set out to restore order in the monastery at La Réole in Gascony.   A brawl broke out between some monks and their servants, and Abbo in trying to pacify them was stabbed.   He staggered to his cell, and there died in the arms of one of his monks. A feast of St Abbo is kept in one or two French dioceses, but it has been questioned whether this recognition is altogether appropriate on the evidence available.

There is a reliable life of Abbo by his contemporary Aimoin. This and the circular letter, sent round to announce the tragedy of his death and to ask prayers for his soul, are printed in Mabillon, vol. vi, pt 1, pp. 32–52. Some of Abbo's writings and a collection of his letters will be found in Migne, PL., vol. cxxxix, but no complete edition of his works exists.   His interest in mathematics and science has attracted attention, see, *e.g.* M. Cantor, *Vorlesungen über d. Geschichte der Mathematik* (1907), vol. i, pp. 845–847.   Abbo, despite statements to the contrary, had no connection with the forged decretals ; see Sackur, *Die*

Cluniacenser, vol. i, pp. 270–299, and *cf.* the work of Fournier and Le Bras mentioned in the preceding note. Dom P. Cousin published *S. Abbon de Fleury, un savant, un pasteur, un martyr*, in 1954.

ST HOMOBONUS   (A.D. 1197)

COMMERCE, as Alban Butler justly remarks, is often looked upon as an occasion of too great attachment to the things of this world and of too eager a desire of gain, as well as of lying, fraud and injustice. That these are the vices of men, not the faults of the profession, is clear from the example of this and other saints. Homobonus was son of a merchant at Cremona in Lombardy, who gave him this name (which signifies " good man ") at baptism. Whilst he trained his son up to his own mercantile business without any school education, he inspired in him both by example and instruction a love of probity, integrity and virtue. The saint from his childhood abhorred the very shadow of untruth or injustice. To honesty Homobonus added economy, care and industry. His business he looked upon as an employment given him by God, and he pursued it with diligence and a proper regard to himself, his family and the commonwealth of which he was a member. `If a tradesman's books are not well kept, if there is not order and regularity in the conduct of his business, if he does not give his mind seriously to it, he neglects an essential and Christian duty. Homobonus was a saint by acquitting himself diligently and uprightly, for supernatural motives, of all the obligations of his profession.

In due course St Homobonus married, and his wife was a prudent and faithful assistant in the government of his household. Ambition, vanity and ostentation are no less preposterous than destructive vices in the middle classes of society, whose characteristics should be modesty, moderation and simplicity. Whatever exceeds this in dress, housekeeping or other expenses is unnatural and affected, offensive to others, and uneasy and painful to the persons themselves. A man of low stature only becomes frightful by strutting upon stilts. The merchant may be an honour and support of society, but an ostentatious parade least of all suits his character or conduces to the happiness of his state. St Homobonus avoided such common rocks on which so many traders dash. And, moreover, not content with giving his tenths to the distressed members of Christ, he seemed to set no bounds to his alms ; he sought out the poor in their homes and, whilst he relieved their corporal necessities, he exhorted them to a good life. The author of his life assures us that God often recognized his charity by miracles in favour of those whom he relieved. It was his custom every night to go to the church of St Giles, for prayer accompanied all his actions and it was in its exercise that he gave up his soul to God. For, on November 13, 1197, during Mass, at the *Gloria in excelsis* he stretched out his arms in the figure of a cross and fell on his face to the ground, which those who saw him thought he had done out of devotion. When he did not stand up at the gospel they took more notice and, coming to him, found he was dead. Sicard, Bishop of Cremona, went himself to Rome to solicit his canonization, which Pope Innocent III decreed in 1199.

A short medieval Latin life was printed in 1857 by A. Maini under the title *S. Homoboni civis Cremonensis Vita antiquior*, but besides this we have little more information than is provided by a few breviary lessons. St Homobonus is, however, mentioned by Sicard of Cremona, his contemporary, and he was canonized (Potthast, *Regesta*, vol. i, p. 55) less than two years after his death. As patron of tailors and clothworkers his fame spread not only over Italy, but into Germany (under the name " Gutman ") and into France. A volume of quite imposing dimensions was published about him in 1674 by G. Belladori under the title of *Il trafficante celeste, oceano di santità e tresoriero del cielo, Huomobuono il santo, cittadino Cremonese*. More modern popular booklets have been written by F. Camozzi (1898), D. Bergamaschi (1899), R. Saccani (1938) and others. Marco Vida, the sixteenth-century neo-classical poet (who disapproved the "low style" of Homer), was a native of Cremona and honoured St Homobonus with a hymn, of which Alban Butler quotes four stanzas. He greatly admired Vida and here calls him "the Christian Virgil".

ST STANISLAUS KOSTKA   (A.D. 1568)

THE Roman Martyrology, in referring to him on August 15, the day of his death, truly says of St Stanislaus Kostka that he "was made perfect in a short while and fulfilled many times by the angelic innocence of his life". He was the second son of John Kostka, senator of Poland, and Margaret Kryska, and was born in the castle of Rostkovo in 1550. The first elements of letters he learned at home under a private tutor, Dr John Bilinsky, who attended him and his elder brother, Paul, to the college of the Jesuits at Vienna when the saint was fourteen years old. From the first Stanislaus gave as much of his time as possible to prayer and study, and he was notably sensitive to any coarseness of talk. " Don't tell that story before Stanislaus ", his father would say to his free-spoken guests, " he would faint." When he arrived at Vienna and was lodged among the pupils of the Jesuits, everyone was struck by the recollection and devotion with which he lived and prayed. Eight months after their arrival the Emperor Maximilian II took from the Jesuits the house which Ferdinand I had lent them for their students. Paul Kostka, two years older than his brother, was a high-spirited youth, fond of amusement, and he prevailed on Bilinsky to take lodgings in a Lutheran's house in the city. This did not at all please Stanislaus, but Paul treated his brother's devotion and reserve with contemptuous amusement. One day when Paul had been ill-treating him Stanislaus rounded on him with the boyish taunt, " This will end in my running away and not coming back. And then you'll have to explain to father and mother." Meanwhile he communicated every Sunday and holy day, always fasted the day before his communion, and when he was not at church or college he was always to be found at his devotions or studies in his own room. He dressed quietly, practised bodily mortifications, and particularly disliked having to attend dancing classes. Paul's lack of sympathy became downright bullying and Dr Bilinsky himself, though not unreasonable, was far from being sufficiently sympathetic.

After nearly two years of this Stanislaus was taken ill and wished to receive viaticum ; but the Lutheran landlord would not allow the Blessed Sacrament to be brought to his house. The boy in extreme affliction recommended himself to the intercession of St Barbara (to whose confraternity he belonged), and he seemed in a vision to be communicated by two angels. The Blessed Virgin is said to have appeared to him in another vision, told him that the hour of his death was not yet come, and bade him devote himself to God in the Society of Jesus. He had already entertained such a thought, and after his recovery petitioned to be admitted. At Vienna the provincial, Father Maggi, dared not receive him, for fear of incurring the anger of his father. Stanislaus therefore determined to walk if necessary to Rome itself to ask the father general of the Society in person. He stole away on foot to Augsburg and thence to Dillingen, to make the same request first to St Peter Canisius, provincial of Upper Germany. He set out on his 350-mile walk, dressed in coarse clothes, and immediately his flight was discovered Paul Kostka and Bilinsky rode off in pursuit.   Various reasons are given to account for their failure to overtake or recognize him.   St Peter Canisius received him encouragingly and set him to wait on the students of the college at table and clean out their rooms, which he did with such respect and humility that the students were astonished, though he was utterly unknown to them.   Canisius, after having kept him three weeks, sent him with two companions to Rome, where he went to St Francis Borgia, then general of the Society, and earnestly renewed his petition.   St Francis granted it, and Stanislaus was admitted in 1567, when he was seventeen years old.   He had received from his father a most angry letter, threatening that he would procure the banishment of the Jesuits out of Poland and abusing Stanislaus for putting on " contemptible dress and following a profession unworthy of his birth ".   Stanislaus answered it in the most dutiful manner, but expressed a firm purpose of serving God according to his vocation.   Without disturbance or trouble of mind he applied himself to his duties, recommending all things to God.

It was the saint's utmost endeavour, declared his novice-master, Father Fazio, to sanctify in the most perfect manner all his ordinary actions, and he set no bounds to his mortifications except what obedience to his director prescribed.   His faults he exaggerated with unfeigned simplicity, and the whole life of this novice seemed a continual prayer.   The love which he had for Jesus Christ in the Holy Sacrament was so ardent that his face appeared on fire as soon as he entered the church, and he was often seen in a kind of ecstasy at Mass and after receiving communion.   But his model novitiate was not destined to last more than nine months.   The summer heat of Rome was too much for St Stanislaus, he had frequent fainting-fits, and he knew that he had not long to live.   On the feast of the dedication of St Mary Major, talking with Father Emmanuel de Sa about the Assumption of our Lady, he said : " How happy a day for all the saints was that on which the Blessed Virgin was received into Heaven !   Perhaps the blessed celebrate it with special joy, as we do on earth.   I hope myself to be there for the next feast they will keep of it." No particular significance was attached to this remark at the time, but ten days later it was remembered.   On St Laurence's day he found himself ill and two days later, when taken to a better bedroom, he made the sign of the cross upon his bed, saying he should never more rise from it.   Father Fazio jokingly rallied him on his physical weakness.   " O man of little heart ! " he said.   " Do you give up for so slight a thing ? "   " I am a man of little heart ", replied Stanislaus, " but it is not so slight a matter, for I shall die of it."   Early in the morning of the Assumption he whispered to Father Ruiz that he saw the Blessed Virgin accompanied with many angels, and quietly died a little after three o'clock in the morning.   A month later Paul Kostka arrived in Rome with instructions from his father to bring back Stanislaus to Poland at all costs.   The shock of finding him dead made Paul carefully consider his own behaviour with regard to his brother, and during the process of beatification he was one of the principal witnesses.   Dr Bilinsky was another. He said among other things that, " The blessed boy never had a good word from Paul.   And we both knew all the time the holiness and devotion of all that he did." Paul was bitterly remorseful all his life, and at the age of sixty himself asked for admission to the Society of Jesus.   St Stanislaus was canonized in 1726, and is venerated as a lesser patron of his native country.

    The depositions of witnesses and other documents presented in the cause of the beatifica-
tion have been in great measure utilized by the saint's biographers, but some of these materials

have only been printed entire in recent times.   An account by S. Varsevicki, who lived in the same Jesuit house with the saint, only saw the light in 1895 ; and perhaps the fullest early narrative, that of Father Ubaldini, after remaining in manuscript for more than two centuries, was published in instalments in the *Analecta Bollandiana*, vol. ix (1890), and following volumes.   But St Stanislaus had long before found many biographers to recount from their different points of view the story of his short life, beginning with the Latin booklet of Father Sacchini in 1609.   Father Bartoli and Father d'Orléans in the seventeenth century wrote lives which went through many editions ; Fathers Michel, Grüber and Goldie have presented the same facts in a more modern setting.   From a literary point of view the booklet of Fr C. C. Martindale, *Christ's Cadets* (1913), and that of Mother Maud Monahan, *On the King's Highway* (1927), make a great appeal.   *Cf.* also the *Life of St Peter Canisius*, by Fr James Brodrick (1935), pp. 674–676.

14 : ST JOSAPHAT, ARCHBISHOP OF POLOTSK, MARTYR   (A.D. 1623)

IN the month of October 1595, at Brest-Litovsk in Lithuania (a town which three hundred and twenty-two years later again became talked of throughout Europe but in a quite different connection), the dissident Orthodox metropolitan of Kiev and five bishops, representing millions of Ruthenians (to-day called Byelorussians and Ukrainians), decided to seek communion with the Holy See of Rome.   The controversies which followed this event were disfigured by deplorable excesses and violence, and the great upholder of Christian unity whose feast is kept today was called on to shed his blood for the cause, whence he is venerated as the protomartyr of the reunion of Christendom.   At the time of the Union of Brest he was still a boy, having been born at Vladimir in Volhynia in 1580 or 1584, and baptized John.   His father, a Catholic, was a burgess of a good family called Kunsevich, who sent John to school in his native town and then apprenticed him to a merchant of Vilna.   John was not particularly interested in trade, and employed his spare time in mastering Church Slavonic in order that he might assist more intelligently at divine worship and recite some of the long Byzantine office every day ; and he got to know Peter Arcudius, who was then rector of the oriental college at Vilna, and the two Jesuits, Valentine Fabricius and Gregory Gruzevsky, who took an interest in him and gave him every encouragement.   At first his master was not favourably disposed towards John's religious preoccupations, but he did his work so well that eventually the merchant offered him a partnership and one of his daughters in marriage.   Both offers were refused, for John had decided to be a monk and in 1604 he entered the monastery of the Holy Trinity at Vilna.   He induced to join him there Joseph Benjamin Rutsky, a learned convert from Calvinism who had been ordered by Pope Clement VIII to join the Byzantine rite against his personal wishes, and together the two young monks concerted schemes for promoting union and reforming Ruthenian monastic observance.

John Kunsevich, who had now taken the name of Josaphat, was ordained deacon and priest and speedily had a great reputation as a preacher, especially on behalf of reunion with Rome.   He led a most austere personal life and added to a careful observance of the austerities of eastern monastic life such extreme voluntary mortifications that he was often remonstrated with by the most ascetic.   At his beatification the burgomaster of Vilna testified that " there was not a better religious in the town than Father Josaphat ".   Meanwhile, the abbot of Holy Trinity having developed separatist views, Rutsky was promoted in his place and the monastery was soon full, so Father Josaphat was taken away from his study of the Eastern fathers to help in the foundation of new houses in Poland. In 1614 Rutsky was made metropolitan of Kiev and Josaphat succeeded him as abbot at Vilna. When the new metropolitan went to take possession of his cathedral Josaphat accompanied him and took the opportunity of visiting the great monastery of The Caves at Kiev. The community of two hundred monks was relaxed, and they threatened to throw the Catholic reformer into the river Dnieper. He was not successful in his efforts to bring them to unity, but his personality and exhortations brought about a somewhat changed attitude and a notable increase of good-will.

The archbishop of Polotsk at this time was a very old man and a favourer of the dissidents, and in 1617 Abbot Josaphat was ordained bishop of Vitebsk with right of succession to Polotsk. A few months later the old archbishop died and Josaphat was confronted with an eparchy which was as large in extent as it was degraded in life. The more religious people were inclined to schism through fear of arbitrary Roman interference with their worship and customs ; churches were in ruins and benefices in the hands of laymen ; many of the secular clergy had been married two and three times * and the monks were decadent. Josaphat sent for some of his brethren from Vilna to help him and got to work. He held synods in the central towns, published a catechism and imposed its use, issued rules of conduct for the clergy, and fought the interference of the " squires " in the affairs of the local churches, at the same time setting a personal example of assiduous instructing and preaching, administration of the sacraments and visiting of the poor, the sick, prisoners and the most remote hamlets. By 1620 the eparchy was practically solidly Catholic, order had been restored, and the example of a few good men had brought about a real concern for Christian life. But in that year a dissident hierarchy of bishops was set up in the territory affected by the Union of Brest, side by side with the Catholic one ; and one Meletius Smotritsky was sent as archbishop to Polotsk, who began with great vigour to undo the work of the Catholic archbishop. He zealously spread a report that St Josaphat had " turned Latin ", that all his flock would have to do the same, and that Catholicism was not the traditional Christianity of the Ruthenian people. St Josaphat was at Warsaw when this began and on his return he found that, though his episcopal city was firm for him, some other parts of the eparchy had begun to waver ; a monk called Silvester had managed to draw nearly all the people of Vitebsk, Mogilev and Orcha to the side of Smotritsky. The nobility and many of the people adhered strongly to the union, but St Josaphat could do little with these three towns ; and not only at Vitebsk but even at Vilna, when the proclamation of the King of Poland that Josaphat was the only legitimate archbishop of Polotsk was publicly read in his presence, there were riots and the life of St Josaphat was threatened.

Leo Sapieha, the chancellor of Lithuania and a Catholic, was fearful of the possible political results of the general unrest, and lent too willing an ear to the heated charges of dissidents outside of Poland that Josaphat had caused it by his policy. Accordingly in 1622 Sapieha wrote accusing him of violence in the maintenance of the union, of putting the kingdom in peril from the Zaporozhsky Cossacks by making discord among the people, of forcibly shutting-up non-Catholic churches, and so on. These and similar accusations were made in general

---

* Though according to Eastern canon law a married man may be ordained to the priest-hood, if his wife dies he cannot marry another ; and if ordained a bachelor he must remain single.

terms, and their unjustifiability was amply demonstrated by contemporary *ad hoc* testimony from both sides : the only actual fact of the sort is the admitted one that Josaphat invoked the aid of the civil power to recover the church at Mogilev from the dissidents.   Thus the archbishop had to face misunderstanding, misrepresentation and opposition from Catholics as well.   There is no doubt that some of the easy reversion to schism was due to the firm discipline and reform of morals that had been inaugurated under Catholic auspices, and St Josaphat did not receive the support he was entitled to from the Latin bishops of Poland because of the uncompromising way in which he maintained the right of the Byzantine clergy and customs to equal treatment with those of Rome.   He continued doggedly and fearlessly on his way and, Vitebsk continuing to be a hot-bed of trouble, he determined in October 1623 to go there in person again.   He could neither be dissuaded nor would he take a military escort.   " If I am accounted so worthy as to deserve martyrdom, then I am not afraid to die ", he said.   He went accordingly, and for a fortnight preached in the churches and visited the houses of all without distinction. He was continually threatened in the streets, and his opponents tried to pick quarrels with his attendants in order that he might be killed in the ensuing fracas.   On the feast of St Demetrius the Martyr he was surrounded by an angry mob, and exclaimed : " You people of Vitebsk want to put me to death.   You make ambushes for me everywhere, in the streets, on the bridges, on the highways, in the market-place.   I am here among you as your shepherd and you ought to know that I should be happy to give my life for you.   I am ready to die for the holy union, for the supremacy of St Peter and of his successor the Supreme Pontiff."

Smotritsky was fomenting this agitation, his object doubtless being no worse than to drive his rival from the diocese.   But his followers got out of hand, and a plot was laid to murder St Josaphat on November 12, if he could not be induced to give excuse for violence before then.   A priest named Elias was put up to go into the courtyard of the archbishop's house and to use insulting words to his servants about their master and their religion, and after several complaints St Josaphat gave permission for him to be seized if it happened again.   On the morning of the 12th, as the archbishop came to the church for the office of Daybreak, he was met by Elias, who began to abuse him to his face ; he therefore allowed his deacon to have the man taken and shut up in a room of the house.   This was just what his enemies were waiting for : the bells of the town-hall were rung and a mob assembled, demanding the release of Elias and the punishment of the archbishop.   After office St Josaphat returned to his house unharmed, and let Elias go with a warning, but the people broke in, calling for their victim and striking his attendants.   St Josaphat went out to them.   " My children ", he asked, " what are you doing with my servants ?   If you have anything against me, here I am : but leave them alone "—words remarkably reminiscent of those of another archbishop, St Thomas Becket, on a similar occasion.   Amid cries of " Kill the papist ! " he was brained with a halberd and pierced by a bullet.   The mangled body was dragged out and contemptuously cast into the river Dvina.

St Josaphat Kunsevich was canonized in 1867, the first saint of the Eastern churches to be formally canonized after process in the Congregation of Sacred Rites.   Fifteen years later Pope Leo XIII gave his feast to the whole Western church for this date ; the Ukrainians and others keep it on November 12, or the Sunday following, according to the Julian calendar.   An immediate result of the

martyrdom was a revulsion in favour of Catholicity and unity ; but the controversy continued to be carried on with an unholy bitterness, and the dissidents too
had their martyr, Abbot Athanasius of Brest, who was put to death in 1648.   On
the other hand, Archbishop Meletius Smotritsky himself eventually was reconciled
with the Holy See, and the great Ruthenian reunion persisted, with varying fortunes,
until after the partition of Poland the Russian sovereigns forcibly aggregated a
majority of the Ruthenian Catholics to the Orthodox Church of Russia.   To the
afflictions with which a repetition of history has visited the remainder in our own
time Pope Pius XII bore sufficient witness, in his encyclical letter " *Orientales
omnes* " issued at the 350th anniversary of the Union of Brest in 1946.

In 1874 Dom Alphonse Guépin published two stout octavo volumes, amounting altogather
to more than a thousand pages, under the title *Saint Josaphat, archevêque martyr, et l'Église
grecque unie en Pologne*.   In the preface he speaks of'the sources upon which his work is
based.   He thanks Father J. Martynov in particular for placing at his disposition a copy
of the beatification process and a number of other papers transcribed from the Roman
archives.   He also makes appeal to a vast collection of documents formed by the Basilian
hieromonk Paul Szymansky, and to another great manuscript library of similar character
which Bishop Naruszewicz had accumulated with a view to his own work as a historian.   All
these had been entrusted to Dom Guépin, and they were put to such good use that most of
the Western writers who have since then touched upon the subject have been largely dependent upon his researches.   Attention should, however, be called to the very useful little books
of Father G. Hofmann, nos. 6 and 12 of the series " Orientalia Christiana ".   When St
Josaphat was put to death the news spread quickly throughout Europe, and the British
Museum possesses a copy of a tract, *Relacion verdadera de la Muerte y Martirio de . . .
Josafat* ;   it was printed at Seville in 1625.   See also O. Kozanewyc, *Leben des hl. Josaphat*
(1931) ;   and the periodical *Roma e l'Oriente*, vol. x (1920), pp. 27–34.   The background of
the events narrated above may be read in the *Cambridge History of Poland*, vol. i (1950),
pp. 507 *seq*.   St Josaphat and the Metropolitan Rutsky were the initiators of that movement
in Ruthenian monasticism which eventually became the organized Order of St Basil, and
accordingly these monks have been officially known since 1932 as the Basilians of St Josaphat.
In 1952 they published at Rome the first volume of the Latin text of the beatification
documents of St Josaphat.

ST DUBRICIUS, OR DYFRIG, BISHOP   (SIXTH CENTURY)

MANY legends have grown up around the figure of St Dubricius, who was undoubtedly an important person in the Welsh church of the fifth-sixth century.
Among them, it is said that he was a pupil of St Germanus of Auxerre, which is
chronologically unlikely, and that he was the first bishop of Llandaff, an error or
invention of the twelfth century.   Geoffrey of Monmouth makes him archbishop
of Caerleon-on-Usk and the prelate who confers the traditional crown of Britain
on King Arthur at Colchester (Dubricius is " the high saint " of Tennyson's
" Idylls ").   The original and chief centre of his influence was undoubtedly in
what is now called western Herefordshire, and he may have been born at Madley,
some six miles from Hereford.   He became a monk and made the first foundation
of his own at Henllan, near Ross, where he had many disciples.   Then he moved
up the Wye to Moccas, and from these two centres he and his disciples are said to
have founded numerous churches and monastic settlements of which many have
been identified.   Some of them, such as Abbey Dore, carried their monastic
tradition on into the middle ages.   St Illtyd came to St Dubricius to be shorn a
monk, and SS. Samson and Deiniol to be consecrated bishops ; and with the last
named he induced St David to attend the synod of Llandewi Frefi and resigned to
him the " metropolitanship " of Wales.   But this last is another medieval invention.

It is stated in the Life of St Samson—a less unreliable source—that St Dubricius used to go and spend Lent on Caldey.   He made Samson abbot of that ancient monastic island, in one of whose two old churches (now restored to Catholic worship) is an inscribed stone whose inscription seems to contain a reference to him, or to another Dubricius.   Near the end of his life, we are told, he retired to Ynys Enlli (Bardsey), and there he died and was buried.   His reputed relics were translated to the cathedral of Llandaff in 1120, and he was made one of the four titulars of that church.   The feast of St Dubricius is now observed only in the archdiocese of Cardiff and on Caldey.

The so-called life of St Dubricius in the Book of Llandaff may be best consulted in the edition of Evans (1893).   Kenney describes it as " a liturgical composition posterior to 1120 which deserves no trust ".   The life by Benedict of Gloucester is printed in Wharton's *Anglia Sacra*, vol. ii, pp. 654–661.   The fact that it has incorporated various details from the developed legend of Geoffrey of Monmouth shows that it was written late in the twelfth century.   See Hardy, *Descriptive Catalogue* (Rolls Series), vol. i, pp. 40–44 ; Lloyd, *History of Wales*, vol. i, pp. 147–148 ; LBS., vol. ii, pp. 359–382 ; but principally Canon Doble's *St Dubricius* (1943), where all the evidence is expertly examined.   The latest examination of the Dubrician church dedications is by E. G. Bowen in his *Settlements of the Celtic Saints in Wales* (1954).

ST LAURENCE O'TOOLE, ARCHBISHOP OF DUBLIN   (A.D. 1180)

LORCAN UA TUATHAIL was born in 1128, probably near Castledermot in co. Kildare, son of Murtagh, chieftain of the Murrays.   When Laurence O'Toole (as his name is commonly anglicized) was ten years old, the king of Leinster, Dermot McMurrogh, made a raid on his neighbour's territory, and Murtagh was forced to deliver up his son as a hostage.   For two years Laurence was badly treated, in a stony and barren region near Ferns, till his father heard of it and by threats of reprisals forced Dermot to give the boy up to the bishop of Glendalough.   Murtagh hurried thither and asked the bishop to cast lots which of his four sons he should destine to the service of the Church.   Laurence cried out with laughter, " There is no need to cast lots.   It is my desire to have for my inheritance the service of God in the Church."   Hereupon his father, taking him by the hand, offered him to God by delivering him to the bishop, in whose hands he left him.

Laurence when but twenty-five years old was chosen abbot of Glendalough and soon after avoided episcopal dignity only by alleging the canons that require in a bishop thirty years of age.   He governed his community with virtue and prudence, and in a great famine which raged during the first four months of his administration was the saviour of the countryside by his boundless charities.   Outside the ecclesiastical enclosure he had to cope with the outlaws and robbers who infested the Wicklow hills, and within it there were false brethren, who could not bear the regularity of his conduct and the zeal with which he condemned their disorders, and attacked his reputation by slander, to which he opposed no other arms than silence and patience.   In 1161 died Gregory, the first archbishop of Dublin.   Laurence was elected in his place, and consecrated in Holy Trinity (later Christ Church) cathedral by Gelasius, archbishop of Armagh.   This was significant of the new unity of the Irish church since the Synod of Kells in 1152, before which the bishops of Dublin had depended on Canterbury.   But the new state of affairs was not fully to outlast St Laurence's own lifetime.

His first care was to reform his clergy and to furnish his church with worthy ministers.   He bound the canons of his cathedral to receive the rule of the regular

canons of Arrouaise, an abbey which was founded in the diocese of Arras in 1090
and had such reputation for sanctity and discipline that it became the pattern of
numerous other houses.   Laurence himself took the religious habit, ate with the
religious in the refectory, observed their hours of silence and assisted with them
at the midnight office.   Every day he entertained at table thirty poor persons, and
often many more, besides those which he maintained in private houses.   All found
him a father both in their temporal and spiritual necessities, and he was indefatigable in preaching and the due ordering of public worship.   King Dermot had
preferred to the church of Glendalough one so unworthy that he was in a short
time expelled, and Thomas, a nephew of the saint, was canonically elected.   By
the care of this young abbot-bishop discipline and piety again flourished and from
that time St Laurence frequently made choice of Glendalough for his retreats from
the noise and turmoil of Dublin, staying in a rock-hewn cell in the cliff above the
Upper Lake.

The enormities of Dermot McMurrogh caused him at length to be driven from
Ireland, and in order to regain his position he asked the help of Henry II of England,
who was only too glad to permit any of his nobles to join an expedition that jumped
with his own ambitions.   The chief of these volunteers was Richard de Clare,
Earl of Pembroke (" Strongbow "), who in 1170 landed at Waterford, overran part
of Leinster, and marched on Dublin.   St Laurence was sent to negotiate with the
invaders, but during the discussions Dermot's Anglo-Norman allies seized the
city and gave themselves over to massacre and rapine.   Laurence returned to
succour the sufferers and defend the survivors, and to be a centre of strength in
the new danger.   Dermot died in his moment of success, and Strongbow claimed
Leinster, as Dermot's heir and husband of his daughter Eva (who was St Laurence's niece).   Thereupon King Henry recalled his vassal to England, the Irish
united under the high king, Rory O'Conor, and Strongbow shut himself up in
Dublin.   Again Laurence conducted negotiations : they failed, but Strongbow
made a sudden rally of desperation and unexpectedly routed the Irish forces.   St
Laurence saw the end of his patriotic hopes, and the " Irish problem " had begun.

Some fifteen years earlier King Henry II had obtained from Pope Adrian IV a
bull (" *Laudabiliter* ") authorizing him to proceed to Ireland in order " to subject
its people to the rule of law and to root out therefrom the weeds of vice ".*   Henry
now went to Ireland for this beneficent purpose, and in 1171 received at Dublin
the submission of all the Irish chiefs, except those of Connaught, Tyrconnel and
Tyrone.   In the following year he convened a synod at Cashel.   Here for the first
time the Irish bishops were confronted by the bull of Adrian IV, provision was
made for clerical discipline, the English form of the Roman liturgy (*i.e.* the use
of Sarum) was adopted, and Pope Alexander III was asked to confirm their decisions,
which in due course he did.   At this meeting St Laurence accepted the papal bull,
concurred in the synodal proceedings, and from that time on was in frequent
request as a go-between and peacemaker between King Henry and the Irish princes.
In 1175 he travelled to Windsor and successfully negotiated a treaty between the
English sovereign and the high king, Rory O'Conor.   While in England he

* And also to provide for the collection of " Peter's pence ".   The authenticity of this
bull has been contested, but not very convincingly.   Among those who favour its authenticity
is Dom Gougaud, who writes in his *Christianity in Celtic Lands*, p. 408 : " Although the
bull is not drawn up in strict conformity with the rules followed at the time by the papal
chancery, it can nevertheless be proved that in substance it is in accord with other contemporary and uncontested witnesses."

visited Canterbury and was received by the monks at Christ Church with the honour due to his repute and rank, and that whole night he spent in prayer before the shrine of St Thomas Becket.   On the day following, as he was going up to the altar to officiate, a madman who had heard much of his sanctity and had a wild idea of making so holy a man a martyr and another St Thomas, gave him a violent blow on the head with a staff.   He fell senseless, but quickly recovered, asked for the wound to be bathed, and proceeded to sing the Mass.*   The king ordered the would-be assassin to be hanged, but Laurence interceded in his favour and obtained his pardon.

The third general council of the Lateran was held at Rome in 1179, and St Laurence went to Rome, with five other Irish bishops.   Before they were allowed to leave England, King Henry extracted an oath that they would make no representations to the Holy See likely to prejudice his position in Ireland.   Laurence explained to Alexander the state of the Irish church, and begged that effectual remedies might be applied to many disorders in the country and care taken for preserving the liberties of its church.   The pope was pleased with his proposals, confirmed all the rights of his see, adding to them jurisdiction over five suffragan dioceses, and appointed him his legate in Ireland.   As soon as the saint was returned home he began vigorously to execute his legatine powers.   But King Henry remembered Becket, and he was nervous at the authority which had been given Laurence in Rome ; and accordingly when in 1180 the archbishop had met him in England to negotiate further on behalf of Rory O'Conor, the king afterwards forbade him to return home.   After waiting for three weeks at Abingdon Laurence determined again to seek Henry, who was in Normandy.   He got a passage across the Channel and landed near Le Tréport, at a spot still called Saint-Laurent.   The king gave him permission to go back to Ireland, but on the way he was taken very ill. As he approached the abbey of the canons regular of St Victor at Eu, he murmured, " Haec requies mea in saeculum saeculi " : St Laurence was ready for death.   To the abbot who put him in mind to make a will, he answered with a smile, " God knows I have not a penny in the world ".   Then, his last thoughts on his flock, he exclaimed in Irish, " Alas ! you stupid, foolish people, what will you do now ? Who will look after you in your misfortunes ?   Who will help you ? "

St Laurence O'Toole died on Friday, November 14, 1180, and he was canonized in 1225.   His relics still rest principally in the crypt of the church of our Lady at Eu.   The feast of St Laurence is observed throughout Ireland, by the Canons Regular of the Lateran, and in the diocese of Rouen, in which Eu is situated.

By far the most important of the ancient lives of St Laurence is that edited from the Codex Kilkenniensis in Dublin, forming part of the Marsh library, by C. Plummer.   The text, with a valuable introduction, appeared in the *Analecta Bollandiana*, vol. xxxiii (1914), pp. 121–186.   There are other Latin lives, notably one printed by the Bollandists in their *Catalogus Cod. Hagiogr. Latin. Paris.*, vol. iii, pp. 236–248, but this, while probably based upon the same materials as the former, has recounted the incidents in a different order and expanded them with rather tedious moral reflections.   It does not make so good an impression of trustworthy history.   Some useful comments on the manuscript sources which have contributed to our knowledge of the saint will also be found in the preface of Plummer's VSH., pp. xv–xxiii.   The life printed in Surius, so far as regards its first portion, is in close agreement with that which Plummer has edited, but Surius, according to his wont, has amended the Latin phraseology.   A certain amount of information regarding St Laurence

* When Cardinal de Bonnechose, archbishop of Rouen, examined the saint's relics at Eu in 1876 he found that the effects of this blow were observable on the skull.

is also obtainable from the chroniclers of the period. There is a good short life in French by A. Legris (1914) ; that by O'Hanlon (1857) is perhaps now hardly adequate. See further, J. F. O'Doherty, *Laurentius von Dublin und das irische Normannentum* (1933), and Dom Gougaud, *Les Saints irlandais hors d'Irlande* (1936), pp. 130–131. A Life in Irish was published by Fr Benedict, o.d.c., in 1929. *Cf.* also M. V. Ronan in the *Irish Ecclesiastical Record*, 1926 and 1936 ; and Fr A. Gwynn on the saint as legate in *Analecta Bollandiana*, vol. lxviii (1950), pp. 223–240. P. Carpentier's *S. Laurent O'Toole* (1953) is a shortened rewriting of Legris, above ; unfortunately it has not been brought up to date.

BD SERAPION, Martyr   (A.D. 1240)

In 1728 Pope Benedict XIII approved the *cultus* of this little-known martyr, who is said to have been born in England. The story goes that he became a soldier in the service of Alfonso IX of Castile, and then joined the newly founded Mercedarian Order for the redemption of captives. He is supposed to have visited the British Isles to gain recruits for it, but without much success. He went among the Moors of Murcia and obtained the release of some Christian slaves, and then went to Algiers to negotiate for more. Here he was kept as hostage for the payment of the balance of the ransom, and employed his time in preaching to the Mohammedans, among whom he made several conversions. This angered the Moors, and after cruel ill-treatment Bd Serapion was nailed to a cross and cut to pieces. Pope Benedict XIV added his name to the Roman Martyrology, wherein is also mentioned on this day, " The passion at Alexandria of St Serapion, martyr, whom the persecutors under the Emperor Decius . . . threw off the roof of his own house and so he became a glorious witness for Christ ".

It has been pointed out more than once in these pages that both for the Mercedarian and the Trinitarian Orders the historical records of their early years are very scanty and of most unsatisfactory quality : *cf.* for example, St Peter Nolasco on January 28. The story of Bd Serapion's connection with England, etc., cannot be depended on, but there seems to have been a *cultus* of long-standing date. The case and documents are cited by Prosper Lambertini (Pope Benedict XIV) in his *De beatificatione et canonizatione*, bk 2, ch. 24, § 42.

BD JOHN LICCIO   (A.D. 1511)

John's mother died in giving him birth, and his father, whether through poverty or malice against the innocent child, provided no proper care, so that he would have died had not a kind woman made herself responsible for him. John was eventually brought up by an aunt and the boy soon showed signs of unusual devotion. When he was about fifteen he met Bd Peter Geremia at Palermo, and was fired by him to take the habit of St Dominic ; in due course he became a good preacher. Bd John was sent to establish a house of his order at Caccamo, his native town, which he did under great difficulties. It was built on the foundations of an unfinished and forgotten building, which, as nobody remembered them, were attributed to supernatural provision. John became prior there in 1494, his administration being marked by great virtue and many marvels. The lessons of his office state that he was one hundred and eleven years old when he died, but even if he were a personal disciple of Bd Peter Geremia he was probably not much more than seventy-five. The *cultus* of Bd John Liccio was approved in 1753.

See the *Monumenta Ord. Praedic. Historica*, vol. xiv, pp. 229–230 ; Procter, *Dominican Saints*, pp. 318–321 ; and lives by M. Ponte (1853) and G. Barreca (1926). For a fuller bibliography consult Taurisano, *Catalogus Hagiographicus O.P.*

15 : ST ALBERT THE GREAT, Bishop of Regensburg, Doctor of the Church   (A.D. 1280)

IT was his contemporaries who dubbed St Albert " the Great " ; they also, referring to the depth and scope of his learning, called him " the Universal Doctor ", and said that he was " a man no less than godlike in all knowledge, so that he may fitly be called the wonder and miracle of our age ".   Even Friar Roger Bacon regarded him, more modestly, as " an authority ", and his works as " original sources".   That he was the master of St Thomas Aquinas has added to his fame, but his contemporaries recognized that he was great in his own right as certainly as posterity has done.   He was a Swabian by descent, born of the family of Bollstädt at the castle of Lauingen on the Danube in 1206.   Little is known of his youth or the age at which he went to the University of Padua, but in 1222 Bd Jordan of Saxony, second master general of the Friars Preachers, wrote from that city to Bd Diana de Andelo at Bologna that he had received ten postulants for the order, " and two of them are the sons of great lords, counts in Germany ".   One of them was Albert, whose uncle in Padua had tried to keep him away from the Dominican church, but had failed before the influence of Bd Jordan.   When he heard that his son was clothed as a mendicant the Count of Bollstädt was most indignant, and there was talk of retrieving him by force, but nothing came of it for Albert was discreetly removed to another friary.   This was probably Cologne, where he was teaching in 1228 ; afterwards he supervised the studies and taught at Hildesheim, Freiburg-im-Breisgau, Regensburg, Strasburg and back again at Cologne, making for himself a great reputation throughout the German province. He was instructed to go to Paris, then as always the intellectual centre of western Europe, and he was there some years, lecturing under a master until he himself took his master's degree.   At the end of this time the Dominicans decided to open four new *studia generalia*, and in 1248 St Albert was sent to be regent of that at Cologne, where until 1252 he had among his students a young friar called Thomas Aquinas.

In those days philosophy was understood as the totality of the main branches of knowledge which could be known by the natural powers of the mind : logic, metaphysics, mathematics, ethics and what we now call physical science ; and the writings of St Albert, which fill thirty-eight quarto volumes in print, include works on all these subjects as well as biblical and theological treatises and sermons.   He stands beside Roger Bacon as a great natural scientist, whose aim, he says, " is to investigate the causes that are at work in nature ", and some scholars have claimed that he did even more than Bacon himself for the advancement of scientific study. He was an authority on physics, geography, astronomy, mineralogy, alchemy (*i.e.* chemistry) and biology, so that it is not surprising that legends grew up that he had and used magical powers.   He wrote a treatise on botany and another on human and animal physiology, in the course of which he disposed, from personal observation, of various fables current at that time, as that of Pliny that eagles wrap their eggs in a fox-skin and leave them to hatch in the sun.   As a geographer he has received especial praise in later times ; he traced the chief mountain ranges of Europe, explained the influence of latitude on climate, and gave an excellent physical description of the earth, which he demonstrated by an elaborate argument to be spherical in shape.   But the principal fame of St Albert as a doctor resides not in these achievements, but in the fact that, realizing the autonomy of philosophy and seeing the use that could be made of the philosophy of Aristotle in ordering the science of theology, he re-wrote the works of the Philosopher so as to make them acceptable to Christian critics, and by the application of Aristotelean methods and principles to the study of theology inaugurated (with the Englishman Alexander of Hales) the scholastic system which was to be brought to perfection by his pupil St Thomas Aquinas. He was the principal pioneer and forerunner of the " preferred system of the Church " : he collected and selected the materials, even laid the foundations ; St Thomas built the edifice.

Throughout his long years of teaching Albert was writing as well, and he continued the work throughout his otherwise busy life. While directing the Cologne *studium* his practical abilities became widely recognized, he was in request to adjust administrative and other disputes, and in 1254 he was made prior provincial of his order in Germany. Two years later he attended in that capacity the chapter general in Paris which forbade Friars Preachers at the universities to be called " master " or " doctor ", or anything but their right name. He himself had already been dubbed " the Universal Doctor " and his prestige had helped to provoke the jealousy against the friars of the secular professors. On account of this, which had led to delay in granting degrees to St Thomas and St Bonaventure, Albert went to Italy to defend the mendicant orders against the attacks being made on them at Paris and elsewhere, especially as voiced by William of Saint-Amour in a tract " on the Dangers of these Present Times ". While he was in Rome, St Albert filled the office of master of the sacred palace (*i.e.* the pope's personal theologian and canonist, always a Dominican friar) and preached in the churches of the City. In 1260 he received an order from the Holy See to undertake the government of the diocese of Regensburg, a church, he was informed, that was " turned upside-down in spiritual as well as temporal matters ". He was bishop for under two years, Pope Urban IV then accepting his resignation ; he did much to remedy the distresses of the diocese, but the scheming of powerful interests and the stubbornness of entrenched abuses made the task too much for him. To the great joy of his master general, Bd Humbert of Romans, who had in vain tried to induce Alexander IV not to make him a bishop, St Albert returned to the *studium* at Cologne. But the next year he was called away again, this time to help the Franciscan Berthold of Ratisbon to preach the crusade in Germany. This over, he went back again to Cologne and taught and wrote there in peace till 1274, when he was bidden to attend the fourteenth general council at Lyons. Just before he set out he heard of the death of his beloved disciple, Thomas Aquinas (it is said to have been revealed directly to him by God), but in spite of this shock and his advancing age St Albert took an active part in the assembly ; he worked with Bd Peter of Tarentaise (Innocent X) and William of Moerbeke for the reunion of the Greeks, throwing all his influence to the side of peace and reconciliation.

St Albert probably made his last public appearance three years later, when some of the writings of St Thomas were seriously attacked by Stephen Tempier, Bishop of Paris, and other theologians. He hurried to Paris to defend the teaching of his dead disciple, teaching that was in great measure his own as well ; he challenged the university to examine himself personally upon it, but he could not avert the local condemnation of certain points. In 1278, during a lecture, his memory suddenly failed ; there is a story, insufficiently attested, that he related to his auditors how when he was a young friar he had been very discouraged and strongly inclined to return to secular life, how our Lady had appeared to him in a prophetic dream and promised to ask for him illuminating grace in his studies if he would persevere, but that his powers would fail again in old age, and that this lapse was a warning of the end.   The loss of memory became acute, the strength of his mind failed, and after two years St Albert died, peacefully and without illness, sitting in his chair among his brethren at Cologne, on November 15, 1280.

It has been said that, " Throughout Albert's writings there are frequent signs that his whole life was one of remarkable holiness, but there are also signs that as long as he wielded a pen he fell short of the saintly suppression of self that distinguished St Thomas.   It is not until Albert has laid aside his pen and taken to expressing his profoundest thought in tears that we feel ourselves in the presence of a candidate for canonization."   This gradual attainment of the heights of sanctity is paralleled by the slow journey of Albert to the altars of the Church.   He was not beatified till the year 1622 and, though there was considerable increase in devotion to him, especially in Germany, canonization did not follow.   In 1872 and again in 1927 the German bishops petitioned the Holy See to canonize him, without apparent effect.   Then, on December 16, 1931, Pope Pius XI by a decretal letter proclaimed Albert the Great a doctor of the Church, thereby equivalently declaring him to be a saint and, moreover, one whose feast should be observed throughout the Western church.   St Albert had, said the pope, " that rare and divine gift, scientific instinct, in the highest degree . . . he is exactly the saint whose example should inspire the present age, which so ardently seeks peace and is so full of hope in its scientific discoveries ".   He is the patron saint of students of the natural sciences.

Especially since the canonization, a number of excellent lives of St Albert have been published, and in nearly all of them a careful account is given of the sources.   Of medieval biographies the most important is that of Peter of Prussia, though it was not written until towards the close of the fifteenth century.   An earlier sketch was produced in the middle of the fourteenth century by Henry of Herford (Herford in Westphalia ; by some perversity many translators from the German present the name as Hereford, which is quite a different place), and before this we have sundry short appreciations in the *Vitae fratrum* of Gerard de Fracheto, the *Bonum universale* of Thomas of Cantimpré, and the *De viris illustribus* by John of Cologne.   Modern investigators, who have set about their task in a more scientific spirit, point out that a considerable amount of biographical material is latent in St Albert's own writings.   His commentaries on the gospels and his sermons contain not infrequent references to incidents of his childhood or to his experiences as bishop.   Further, we may obtain light from documents of a more or less official character, for example, the *Acta capitulorum generalium O.P.* (ed. Reichert, vol. i, 1898), or such a collection as H. Finke's *Ungedruckte Dominicaner Briefe des XIII Jahrhunderts* (1891).   Using these or similar materials, Quétif and Echard in their *Scriptores Ordinis Praedicatorum*, vol. i (1719), had already compiled a reliable literary portrait of the saint ; to which a valuable supplement was provided in the series of articles by P. von Loë in the *Analecta Bollandiana*, vols. xix to xxi (1900–2), and in his *Kritische Streifzüge auf dem Gebiete der Albertus-Magnus-Forschung* (1904). Another notable contribution to the understanding of St Albert's influence on medieval culture was that of Emil Michael, *Geschichte des deutschen Volkes*, vol. iii (1903), pp. 69–128, and also M. Grabmann's articles in the *Zeitschrift für Kath. Theologie*, vol. lii (1928).   Among recent lives may be mentioned H. Wilms, *Albert the Great* (1933) ; T. M. Schwertner, *Saint Albert the Great* (1933) ; A. Garreau, *Saint Albert le Grand* (1932) ; H. C. Scheeben, *Albert der Grosse* (1931) ; and a good general sketch by Sister M. Albert (1948).   Other aspects of St Albert's work have been dealt with by A. R. Bachiller, *Alberto Magno y las Ciencias empiricas* (1933) ; Bonné, *Die Erkenntnislehre Alberts der Grossen* (1935) ; H. Fleckenstein,

Die theologische Lehre von der materiellen Welt (1933) ; M. M. Gorce, *L'Essor de la pensée au moyen âge, Albert le Grand* (1933) ; R. Liertz, *Die Naturkunde von der menschlichen Seele nach Albert dem Grossen* (1933), etc. There is a good bibliography in the life by Wilms, to supplement which consult the *Analecta Bollandiana*, vol. li (1933), pp. 183–190.

SS. GURIAS, SAMONAS AND ABIBUS, MARTYRS (FOURTH CENTURY)

ONE of the two principal sanctuaries at Edessa in Syria enshrined the bodies of these martyrs. Their legends relate that, during the persecution of Diocletian, Gurias and Samonas were arrested and imprisoned, and on their refusal to sacrifice were hung up by one hand with weights tied to their feet. Then they were thrown into a foul dungeon and left without food or light for three days. When they were taken out Gurias was already nearly dead, but Samonas was submitted to a horrible torture, which failed to shake his resolution. They were therefore both beheaded. Later, Abibus, a deacon of Edessa, hid himself from the persecution of Licinius, but eventually gave himself up that he might earn the martyr's crown. The officer to whom he surrendered gave him the opportunity to change his mind and escape, but Abibus would not avail himself of it. He was sentenced to be burnt, and was accompanied to the place of execution by his mother and other relatives, to whom he was allowed to give the kiss of peace before he was thrown to the flames. Afterwards they took his body, which had not been destroyed in the fire, and buried it near those of his friends Gurias and Samonas.

All three martyrs are mentioned in the Roman Martyrology today, but in two separate entries. They had the curious distinction of being venerated as the " avengers of unfulfilled contracts ".

There are several Greek variants of the *passio* of St Gurias and companions ; they will be found enumerated in BHG., nn. 731–736. But besides these there are oriental texts in Syriac (of which another fragment of earlier date was afterwards discovered by Mar Ephrem Rahmani), and a version in Armenian. It seems that the language of the original account was unquestionably Syriac. The matter has been very fully treated by E. von Dobschütz in vol. xxxvii, pt. 2, of *Texte und Untersuchungen;* on which also see the review in *Analecta Bollandiana*, vol. xxxi (1912), pp. 332–334. The later Syriac text in its sophisticated form, purporting to be written by an eye-witness, has been translated into English by Professor Burkitt in his *Euphemia and the Goth* (1913). The Armenian version was translated by F. C. Conybeare and printed in *The Guardian* for 1897. The fact of the martyrdom is not open to doubt, for in the Syriac *breviarium* we have the entry on November 15, " in the city of Edessa, Shamona and Guria the confessors ". There is also a homily preached in their honour by James of Sarug.

ST DESIDERIUS, OR DIDIER, BISHOP OF CAHORS (A.D. 655)

THIS Desiderius is one of several saints honoured in France under the name of Didier (he is also called Géry). His father was a noble with large estates around Albi, and the religious dispositions of his mother are mentioned in the saint's life with reference to letters written by her to him. Desiderius became a high official at the court of King Clotaire II of Neustria, where he met St Arnulf of Metz, St Eligius and other holy men, as well as less desirable acquaintances. His brother Rusticus became a priest and then bishop of Cahors ; but he soon after was murdered (he is venerated as a martyr at Cahors) and Desiderius was elected to fill his see in 630, though still a layman. He proved a zealous and effective bishop, and his extant correspondence gives some idea of the scope of his activities, which were directed towards the temporal as well as the spiritual welfare of his diocese. He encouraged the nobles to endow religious foundations, and was a strong promoter of monasticism both for men and women.   He directed a convent of his own foundation, built the monastery of St Amantius and endowed it, and built three large churches.   Cahors also benefited by the provision of an aqueduct and the repair of its fortifications.   But the first concern of St Desiderius was always the Christian life of his flock, which he knew to be best forwarded by a virtuous and well-instructed clergy, among whom he maintained a strict discipline.   He died in 655 near Albi, and was buried at Cahors, where miracles took place at his tomb.

There is a Latin life of the better class, written towards the close of the eighth or the beginning of the ninth century, which incorpoates the text of certain letters and documents of some historical value.   The best edition is that of B. Krusch, with an important introduction, in MGH., *Scriptores Merov.*, vol. iv, pp. 547–602 ; the text is also in Migne, PL., vol. lxxxvii, cc. 219–239.

ST MALO, Bishop   (Seventh Century)

Machutus, Maclovius, Maclou (and other forms) is best known to English-speaking people, by association with the Breton port, as Malo.   Medieval hagiographers say that he was born in South Wales, near Llancarfan, and was educated in the monastery there.   When he grew up his parents wanted him to leave the monks, but he refused and, after hiding for a time in one of the islands of the Severn Sea, he was ordained priest and determined to leave Britain, perhaps on account of the great pestilence in the middle of the sixth century.   He landed in Brittany, and began to evangelize the neighbourhood of Aleth (Saint-Servan), having his headquarters on an island where now stands the town of Saint-Malo. He built churches and made monastic settlements, tried to protect the weak from the violence of the local chiefs, and made many converts ; as he rode from place to place on his missionary journeys he recited psalms in a loud voice.   But St Malo made enemies as well as converts, and after the death of the chief who had first persecuted and then protected him, and whom Malo is said to have converted, they began to get the upper hand.   St Malo decided to leave ; and, going on board ship with thirty-three monks, he solemnly anathematized the malcontents and sailed off down the coast.   He settled near Saintes and stayed there for some years until a deputation from Aleth came and asked him to return : his flock was suffering from a bad drought, which was attributed to their treatment of their bishop.   He visited them as requested, and immediately on his arrival there was a heavy fall of rain.   Malo, however, did not stay at Aleth long ; he set out again for Saintes, but died just before he arrived there.

In the Lives of St Malo there is narrated a number of stories and miracles of a highly unconvincing kind.   In particular it is stated that he emulated St Brendan in his fabulous voyages of quest for the Isle of the Blessed, and celebrated Easter on the back of a whale.

There are four or five medieval lives of St Malo duly enumerated in BHL., nn. 5116–5124. The best known is that attributed to the deacon Bili, who wrote in the latter part of the ninth century.   There probably was a primitive life which has perished, from which the' Bili version and the anonymous text (BHL. 5117) have both been elaborated.   The texts may be conveniently consulted in Plaine and La Borderie, *Deux vies inédites de S. Malo* (1884). The matter is too complicated to discuss here, but see especially F. Lot, *Mélanges d'histoire bretonne* (1907), pp. 97–206 ; Duine, *Memento*, pp. 53–57 ; Duchesne in the *Revue Celtique*, vol. xi (1890), pp. 1–22 ; Poncelet in *Analecta Bollandiana*, vol. xxiv (1905), pp. 483–486.

ST FINTAN OF RHEINAU   (A.D. 879)

THIS Fintan (Findan) is said to have been a native of Leinster, born there at the beginning of the ninth century.   In a Norse raid he was carried off as a slave to the Orkneys, from whence he managed to make his escape and spent two years under the protection of a bishop in Scotland.   He then went on pilgrimage to Rome ; on his way back he stopped with some hermits at Rheinau in the Black Forest, and spent the rest of his life there.   His holiness was a great edification to the community, and for the last twenty-two years of his life he was allowed to live as a solitary, always refusing to have any fire in his lonely cell.   The relics of St Fintan were enshrined at Rheinau in 1446, and his feast is still observed in the town.

The text of the only Latin life of the saint may be read in Mabillon, vol. iv, pt 1, pp. 356–360 ; or better in MGH., *Scriptores*, vol. xv, pp. 503–506.   See also Gougaud, *Les Saints irlandais hors d'Irlande* (1936), pp. 95–96.

ST LEOPOLD OF AUSTRIA   (A.D. 1136)

THIS prince, known as " the Good ", was canonized three hundred and fifty years after his death by Pope Innocent VIII, but only a few reliable particulars of his life have survived.   He was born at Melk in 1073, brought up under the influence of the reforming bishop St Altman of Passau, and succeeded his father when he was twenty-three years old.   In 1106 he married Agnes, daughter of the Emperor Henry IV and a widow.   She had had two sons by her first husband, and she now gave eighteen children to Leopold.   Of the eleven who survived childhood, one was the historian, Otto of Freising, and it was at the request of this Otto, then Cistercian abbot of Morimond in Burgundy, that St Leopold founded the still existing abbey of Heiligenkreuz in the Wienerwald.   Another great foundation of his was Klosterneuburg, near Vienna, for Augustinian canons.   This abbey is also still in being, and is a most influential centre of the " liturgical movement " among German-speaking peoples.   The Benedictine monastery of Mariazell, in Styria, whose church is now a popular place of pilgrimage, was also founded by St Leopold. By these benefactions he forwarded the cause of true religion in his country, setting before the people examples of charity, self-abnegation and devotion to the worship of God.

In the tortuous and difficult politics, ecclesiastical and secular, of his time Leopold IV played an inconspicuous part, but no doubt an important one, for when his brother-in-law Henry V died in 1125 the Bavarians wished the imperial crown to be offered to him.   But in any case Leopold refused to be nominated. After a reign of forty years St Leopold died in 1136, and was buried at Klosterneuburg amid the lamentations of his people.

Surius and Pez (*Scriptores rerum Austriacarum*, vol. i, pp. 577–592) print the only known medieval life of St Leopold.   A short German biography by B. A. Egger (1885), was translated into French in 1891.   See also V. O. Ludwig, *Die Legende von milden Markgraf Leopold* (1925) ; and the volume of essays on the saint (ed. S. Wintermayr) published at Klosterneuburg in 1936.

16* : SS. GERTRUDE THE GREAT AND MECHTILDIS, VIRGINS
(A.D. 1302 AND 1298)

THE date of the death and of the feast of St Mechtildis is November 19, but it is convenient and suitable to speak of her here with her pupil St Gertrude. Mechtildis when she was seven years old was confided to the care of the nuns of Rossdorf, who shortly after elected her elder sister, Gertrude von Hackeborn, to be their abbess. It is by confusion with this Abbess Gertrude that St Gertrude the Great is herself often erroneously referred to as an abbess. Mechtildis herself became a nun of Rossdorf ; she was chief chantress of the house and mistress of the children who were sent there to be trained. In 1258 the nuns moved to a monastery at Helfta in Saxony, the home of the noble Hackeborn family, and three years later they were joined by St Gertrude, then a child of five. Nothing is known either of her parentage or the place of her birth. She came under the charge of St Mechtildis, and mistress and pupil took to one another ; Gertrude was personally very attractive and of great intellectual ability ; she became a good Latin scholar and in due course was professed a nun, probably never having left the cloister which she entered as a little girl.

When Gertrude was nearly twenty-six years old she received the first of the revelations which have made her famous. In the dormitory, as she was about to go to bed, she seemed to see our Lord, in the form of a young man. When He had spoken to her, " although I was certain of my bodily presence in that place, nevertheless it seemed to me that I was in choir, in that corner where I was accustomed to make my lukewarm prayers, and that there I heard these words, ' I will save and deliver you. Fear not.' When He had said this I saw His fine and delicate hand take mine as though solemnly to ratify this promise, and He went on, ' You have licked the dust with my enemies and sucked honey from thorns. Now come back to me, and my divine delights shall be as wine to you.' " Then a thorn-covered hedge seemed to stretch between them, but Gertrude found herself as it were lifted and placed by our Lord's side, and " I then recognized, in the hand that had just been given me as a pledge, the radiant jewels of those sacred wounds which have made of no effect the handwriting that was against us ". Thus she received that experience which even in the purest and most faultless souls is called conversion ; she applied herself consciously and deliberately to the attainment of perfection and ever closer union with God. Hitherto her delight had been in profane studies, but now she turned to the Bible and the works of the fathers, especially St Augustine, St Gregory and the not-long-dead St Bernard : " from being a grammarian she became a theologian ", and her own writings show clearly the influence both of the Church's liturgy and her private reading.

Exteriorly the life of St Gertrude was like that of any other contemplative nun and therefore deficient in incident. We hear of the copies of scriptural passages and the little biblical treatises she made for her sisters in religion, her charity towards the dead, and the liberty of spirit which informed her. The last is well

---

* The feast of St Margaret is kept throughout Scotland on this day, the anniversary of her death. But an account is given of her herein under June 10, the day on which her feast is observed by the rest of the Western church. It was finally fixed for this date in 1693 at the request of King James II and VII, being the birthday (in 1688) of his son James (*de iure* III and VIII) ; but November 16 was restored for Scotland by Pope Leo XIII in 1898.

illustrated by her attitude towards sudden or unattended death. " I wish with my whole heart to be strengthened by those health-giving last sacraments ; nevertheless, the will and appointment of God seem to be the best and surest preparation. I am certain that, whatever the manner of my death, sudden or foreseen, I shall never lack His mercy, without which I cannot possibly be saved in either case." After her first vision of our Lord she continued to see Him " indistinctly " at the time of communion, until the vigil of the Annunciation, when He visited her at the morning chapter-meeting and " henceforth He gave me a more clear knowledge of Himself, so that I was led to correct my faults by the sweetness of His love far rather than by fear of His just anger ". The five books of the *Herald of God's Loving-kindness* (commonly called the Revelations of St Gertrude), of which only the second book was actually written by the saint, contain a succession of visions, communications and mystical experiences which have received the approval of a number of holy mystics and distinguished theologians. She speaks of a ray of light like an arrow coming from the wound in the right side of a crucifix ; of beholding her soul, in the likeness of wax softened at a fire, presented to the bosom of our Lord as though to receive the impress of a seal ; and of a spiritual marriage in which she was as it were drawn into the heart of Jesus : but " adversity is the spiritual ring with which the soul is betrothed to God ". St Gertrude anticipated the later revival of frequent communion, as well as devotion to St Joseph and, particularly, to the Sacred Heart. With both St Mechtildis and St Gertrude the love of the Sacred Heart was a frequently recurring theme, and it is stated that Gertrude in vision twice reposed her head upon the breast of our Lord and heard the beating of His heart.

In the meantime, St Mechtildis, fifteen years older than Gertrude and still by her singing a " nightingale of Christ," had been following the same mystical way ; but it was not till she was fifty that she learned that her pupil had been assiduously writing down all she had been told of her mistress's experiences and teaching. Mechtildis was at first alarmed at this, but our Lord assured her that all had been committed to writing by His will and inspiration, and so she was reassured and herself corrected the manuscript. This is the work called the *Book of Special Grace*, or the Revelations of St Mechtildis. Seven years later, on November 19, 1298, Christ called her to Himself ; " she offered Him her heart, plunging it into His ; and our Lord touched it with His own, giving to her eternal glory, wherein we hope she will obtain grace for us by her intercession." St Mechtildis has never been canonized, but her feast is permitted to numerous houses of Benedictine nuns. By some she is identified with the " Donna Matelda " in cantos 27 and 28 of the *Purgatorio* of Dante.

These two saints are probably best known to the Catholic public today by a series of prayers attributed to them. They were first published at Cologne at the end of the seventeenth century and, whatever their merits as prayers, they were certainly not written by Gertrude and Mechtildis. Prayers extracted from their genuine works were first published by Dom Castel in French, and in English by Canon John Gray in 1927. St Gertrude's book is called by Alban Butler " perhaps the most useful production, next to the writings of St Teresa, with which any female saint has enriched the Church for the nourishing of piety in a contemplative state ". St Gertrude died on November 17 in the year 1301 or 1302, at the age of about forty-five, after suffering much ill-health for a decade. She was never formally canonized, but in 1677 Pope Innocent XI added her name to the Roman Martyrology, and Clement XII directed that her feast be observed throughout the Western church. She is greatly venerated by the Benedictines and the Cistercians, by both of which orders the monastery of Helfta has been claimed.

There are no materials for the life of either of these saints beyond what is found in their own writings. These were first collected and adequately edited in the two Latin volumes published in 1875 by the Benedictines of Solesmes under the general title *Revelationes Gertrudianae et Mechtildianae*, but the contents were made up of several separate treatises. In that called *Legatus divinae pietatis*, which is divided into five books, the second book was certainly written by Gertrude herself, books 3, 4 and 5 were composed under her guidance, and book 1 was compiled by her intimates shortly after her death. This work is the principal source of the little we know concerning her history and literary activities, but we also obtain some further information from the *Liber specialis gratiae* which has mainly to do with St Mechtildis and is printed in the second volume of the *Revelationes*. There is an excellent English life by Dom G. Dolan, *St Gertrude the Great* (1912), and one in French by G. Ledos (1901). St Gertrude's influence upon the devotional feeling of her age has been well treated by E. Michael, *Geschichte des deutschen Volkes vom dreizehnten Jahrhundert*, vol. iii, pp. 174–211. Many articles and books have been written on this mystic's anticipation of the special *cultus* of the Sacred Heart. See amongst the rest A. Hamon, *Histoire de dévotion au Sacré Cœur*, vol. ii ; U. Berlière, *La dévotion au Sacré Cœur dans l'Ordre de St Benoît* (1920) ; K. Richstätter, *Herz-Jesu-Verehrung des deutsch. Mittelalters* (1924). The question whether St Gertrude was a Benedictine or a Cistercian has been much debated. See Dom U. Berlière in the *Revue Bénédictine*, vol. xvi (1899), pp. 457–461 ; E. Michael in the *Zeitschrift f. Kath. Theol.*, vol. xxiii (1899), pp. 548–552 ; and the *Cistercienser Chronik* for 1913, pp. 257–268. That she was much influenced by contact with the Franciscans has been shown in the *Archivum Franciscanum Historicum*, vol. xix (1926), pp. 733–752. On Donna Matelda consult E. Gardner, *Dante and the Mystics*, p. 269.

ST EUCHERIUS, Bishop of Lyons (A.D. 449)

NEXT to Irenaeus, no name has done so great honour to the church of Lyons as that of Eucherius. By birth he was a Gallo-Roman of good position, and he married one called Galla, by whom he had two sons, Salonius and Veranus, whom he placed in the monastery of Lérins ; they both became bishops and both were venerated as saints. After a time Eucherius himself retired to Lérins. St John Cassian called Eucherius and Honoratus, Abbot of Lérins, the two models of that house of saints. Out of a desire of closer solitude St Eucherius left Lérins to settle in the neighbouring island now called Sainte-Marguerite. There he wrote his book in praise of the solitary life, which he addressed to St Hilary of Arles, and to his cousin Valerian his incomparable exhortation which no one can read without being inspired with a contempt of the world and quickened to a strong resolution of making the service of God our only concern. Of the illusion of the world and the transitoriness of all its enjoyments he paints so striking a picture that it seems to pass like a flash of lightning before the eyes of the reader, making its appearance only to sink away in a moment. " I have seen ", he says, " men raised to the highest point of worldly honour and riches. Fortune seemed to be in their pay, throwing everything to them without their having the trouble of asking or seeking. Their prosperity in all things outdid their very desires. But in a moment they disappeared. Their vast possessions were fled, and the masters themselves were no more."

Eucherius who, as Cassian says, shone as a bright star in the world by the perfection of his virtue, was a model to the monastic order by the example of his life therein. At length he was forced from his retirement, and placed in the see of Lyons, probably in the year 434, in which he proved himself a faithful pastor, humble in mind, rich in good works, powerful in eloquence and accomplished in knowledge.   The foundation of several churches and religious establishments at Lyons is ascribed to him.   He ended an excellent life by a holy death about 449. St Paulinus of Nola, St Honoratus, St Hilary of Arles, St Sidonius and other great men of that age sought his friendship and commend his virtue.   He was a copious writer, and Salvian wrote to him, " I have read the letters you sent me.   They are sparing in words but full of doctrine, easy to read but perfect in their instruction. In short, they are worthy of your abilities and of your piety."   But not all the works attributed to St Eucherius were from his pen, and some others are doubtful.   A letter of his is an important document in the history of the legend of St Maurice and the Theban Legion (September 22).

There is no formal biography, but Gennadius in his *De viris illustribus* devotes a brief notice to St Eucherius.   His activities are discussed in some detail by Tillemont, *Mémoires*, vol. xv, pp. 126–136 and 848–857, who convincingly disposes of the legend of a second Bishop Eucherius at Lyons.   His works are printed in Migne, PL., vol. l, and some of them have been re-edited in the Vienna *Corpus scrip. eccles. lat.*   On his literary activities see DTC., vol. v, cc. 1452–1454 ; and Bardenhewer, *Geschichte der altkirchlichen Literatur*, vol. iv, pp. 561–570.   The *Laterculus* of Polemius Silvius or Salvius, the best text of which is that of Mommsen in the *Corpus inscrip. lat.*, vol. i (2nd edn.), pp. 254 *seq.*, is dedicated to Eucherius.

ST AFAN, Bishop   (Sixth Century ?)

In the churchyard of Llanafan Fawr (*i.e.* Great Avanchurch), in the hills a few miles north-west of Builth Wells in the county of Brecknock, is an ancient tomb-stone bearing the inscription *Hic Iacet Sanctus Avanus Episcopus :* " Here lies Saint Avan the Bishop."   The existence of this stone, which naturally arouses the interest of the visitor or reader, is the sole reason for mentioning St Afan here, since nothing whatever is known about his life.   The lettering is said to be not older than the end of the thirteenth century, but St Afan certainly lived long before that : by some he has been identified with a holy Afan, of the house of Cunedda and a kinsman of St David, who lived during the early part of the sixth century and was the leading holy man of his district, being known as Afan Buellt, *i.e.* of Builth.   According to the local legend he was put to death by Irish raiders.

The following is related by Gerald the Welshman in the first chapter of the first book of his *Itinerary through Wales :* " In the reign of King Henry I, the lord of the castle of Radnor, the territory adjoining Builth, went into the church of St Afan (called Llanafan in the British tongue) and rashly and irreverently spent the night there with his hounds.   When he got up early the next morning (as hunting men do), he found his hounds mad and himself blind.   After living for years in darkness and misery he was taken on pilgrimage to Jerusalem, for he took care that his inward sight should not similarly be put out.   And there, being armed and led to the field on horseback, he spurred upon the enemies of the faith, was mortally wounded, and so ended his life with honour."   An anecdote which tells us some-thing about the religious ideas of the twelfth century, but unfortunately nothing about St Afan.

See LBS., vol. i, s.v., and T. Jones's *History of Brecknock*, vol. ii, pp. 225–226 (1908 edn.).

ST EDMUND OF ABINGDON, Archbishop of Canterbury
(A.D. 1240)

EDMUND was the eldest son of Reynold (or Edward) Rich of Abingdon in Berkshire and his wife Mabel, who were but slenderly provided with the goods of this world but were abundant in virtue and grace. Reynold in his middle years, having provided for his family, with his wife's free consent made his religious profession in the monastery of Eynsham, where he soon died. Mabel lived in a very austere way, and brought up her children both religiously and strictly. When Edmund was about twelve he went to school at Oxford,* and some three years later, accompanied by his brother Robert, to Paris to continue their studies there. The two boys were not unnaturally shy and nervous at leaving home and going so far on their own. The austere Mabel urged them to trust in God, and to encourage them gave each a hair-shirt, which they promised to wear. Edmund was recalled to England by the mortal sickness of his mother, and before she died she gave him her last blessing. Edmund begged the same for his brother and sisters, but she answered, " I have given them my blessing in you, for through you they will share abundantly in the blessings of Heaven ", and she confided them to his care. The two girls wished to be nuns, and he placed them in the Benedictine nunnery of Catesby in Northamptonshire, where both were eminent for the sanctity of their lives, and died successively prioresses. Then Edmund went back to Paris to pursue his studies. Whilst he lived at Oxford he had consecrated himself to God by a vow of chastity, and this vow he observed with the utmost fidelity, sometimes in trying circumstances, as his biographer ·narrates. His life as a student was exemplary and he was assiduous in his attendance at the Church's offices. He became regent in arts at Oxford, and was deeply immersed in the study and teaching of mathematics, until he seemed one night to see his mother in a dream, who, pointing to certain geometrical figures before him, asked him what all that signified ? When he explained they represented the subject of his lectures, she told him rather to make the worshipful Trinity the object of his studies.

From that time he gave himself up to theology, took his doctorate, and was ordained, either in Oxford or Paris. For eight years he was a lecturer in theology at Oxford and is said to have been the first to teach the logic of Aristotle in that university. He was a successful professor and preacher, and a number of his pupils attained distinction. He took a personal interest in them, especially were they poor or sick, but for himself carried on his mother's severe asceticism ; an abbot of Reading noticed that he did not relax even in vacation time. About 1222 Edmund accepted a canonry, as treasurer, in the cathedral of Salisbury, with the prebend of Calne, in Wiltshire, where he had to reside three months out of the twelve. One quarter of his income he gave to the building fund of the cathedral, and most of the rest to the poor, leaving himself destitute the greater part of the year, so that he had to seek the hospitality of Stanley Abbey, near Calne. The abbot more than once rebuked him for his extravagance and lack of foresight. In 1227 Pope Gregory IX sent him an order to preach the crusade against the Saracens, with the right to receive a stipend from each church in which he should do so.

---

* It was at this time he was said to have had a vision of the boy Jesus in the fields, who told him that whoever should before sleeping trace the words *Jesus of Nazareth* on his forehead should be preserved that night from sudden and unprepared death. Whence the custom of tracing the initials I.N.R.I., with a prayer to the same end.

Edmund executed the commission with great zeal, but would accept no stipend. When he preached his words were words of fire, which powerfully moved souls, and miracles were reported to attend his preaching at Worcester, Leominster and elsewhere. William Longsword, Earl of Salisbury, who had lived a long time neglectful of the duties of a Christian, was converted by hearing a sermon which the saint preached and by conversing with him. St Edmund was one of the most experienced doctors of the interior life in the Church at that time, and he was solicitous to teach Christians to pray in affection and spirit. " A hundred thousand persons ", he writes, " are deceived in multiplying prayers. I would rather say five words devoutly with my heart, than five thousand which my soul does not relish with affection and intelligence. Sing to the Lord with understanding : what a man repeats by his mouth, that let him feel in his soul." He so well united in himself the science of the soul with that of the schools, mystical theology with speculative, that he became a perfect contemplative.

The see of Canterbury had been long vacant, when, after three annulled elections, St Edmund was chosen to fill it. A deputation was sent to Calne to give notice of his election, and to conduct him to his see. Edmund, who was till then, it is said, ignorant of these proceedings, protested against the office that was offered him. The deputies then applied to Bishop Robert of Salisbury, who exerted his authority to compel him to acquiesce. Edmund submitted, after much resistance, and was consecrated on April 2, 1234. A few days later he took part in a parliament at Westminster which solemnly warned the king, Henry III, of the state of his realm and called on him to dismiss his unworthy ministers. This Henry did, and sent St Edmund with other bishops to the west to negotiate a truce with Llewelyn of Wales and the disaffected nobles. He further acted as mediator in the king's dealings with the disgraced ministers, Peter des Roches, Bishop of Winchester, and others. About this time St Edmund appointed as his diocesan chancellor St Richard of Wych, afterwards bishop of Chichester, and he, together with Robert Rich the archbishop's brother, seem to have been by his side for the rest of his life. In 1237 St Edmund presided at King Henry's solemn ratification of the Great Charter in Westminster Abbey ; but his marriage with Eleanor of Provence had opened the way to more ministers and favourites from abroad and, to strengthen his hand against his own barons, Henry obtained the appointment of a papal legate, Cardinal Otto. St Edmund went to the king and protested at what he had done, foretelling that the appointment of a legate would be the cause of more trouble in the kingdom. Cardinal Otto duly arrived, creating a good impression by refusing the presents which were offered him on all sides, and presided at a council in St Paul's at which were promulgated a number of canons concerning the discipline of the clergy and the holding of benefices ; but some of them favoured foreign incumbents at the expense of Englishmen and were received with protests. Soon Henry was playing the legate off against St Edmund and the English bishops and barons.

Love of peace and work for that end stand out prominently in the life and character of Edmund Rich, yet he chose to see his friends break with him and turn his persecutors, rather than approve or tolerate deviation from justice and right. Their bitterness against him never altered the peace of his mind or his charity and tenderness towards them ; and he seemed indifferent to any injuries or injustices that were done him. He used to say that tribulations were a food which God prepared for the nourishment of his soul, and that their bitterness was mixed with much sweetness, as it were a wild honey, with which his soul had need to be fed in the desert of this world, like John the Baptist in the wilderness. Nicholas Trivet, the English Dominican annalist, records that St Edmund had always some learned Dominican with him wherever he went, and that one of them, who lived to be very old, assured him that one day, when the saint had invited several persons to dine with him, he kept them waiting a long while before he came out. When dinner had been ready some time, Richard, his chancellor, went to call him, and found him in the chapel, raised a considerable height above the ground in prayer. St Edmund was of a friendly and affectionate disposition, and like other innocent people suffered from the censoriousness of others. When a lady whom he had befriended came from Catesby to pass Holy Week at Canterbury he said to her, " You are indeed welcome. And, if the world's judgements were not too harsh for the purity of our intentions, nothing should be allowed ever to part us from each other."

St Edmund's troubles were far from being confined to resisting the encroachments and injustices of the king in matters of church and state. The monks of Christ Church at Canterbury, who served the metropolitan cathedral, in defence of certain alleged rights and liberties, raised what was in effect a revolt against their archbishop. Though he offered a compromise, and the papal legate counselled them to submit, they carried on the controversy till it was a scandal throughout the land, and St Edmund took the matter to Rome in person in 1237. One evening while he was there he was summoned to the pope after Compline, and said the pope's message had come while he was at prayer. " You would make a good monk ", said Gregory laughing. " Would that I could be a good monk and free from all these troubles ", replied St Edmund. " How happy and peaceful is the state of a monk ! " But the Canterbury monks were not at all peaceful, and after he got back the archbishop had to excommunicate seventeen of them by name. Then King Henry openly opposed himself to St Edmund and his suffragans, and Cardinal Otto did likewise, absolving those whom he had excommunicated, reversing decisions he had given in various high matters, and even usurping personal rights of the English primate. Then at a council at Reading the legate asked for a levy of one-fifth on the goods of the bishops and clergy to help the pope in his struggle with the Emperor Frederick II. Already there was bitter resentment against the holding of so many wealthy English benefices by non-resident papal nominees, generally Italians, and the consequent material and spiritual harm (the great opponent of this abuse was the holy Robert Grosseteste, whom St Edmund consecrated bishop of Lincoln), and the bishops turned to their primate for counsel. " My brethren ", said Edmund, " you know that we are in such difficult times that we would all rather be dead. We must make a virtue of necessity. For, while the pope drags us one way and the king the other, I do not see how we can resist."

Henry, in order to have the benefit of the revenues during vacancy, was in the habit of leaving offices and benefices in his gift unoccupied and of hindering the elections to others, with obvious hurt to the faithful. With great trouble and expense St Edmund had obtained a brief from Gregory IX that after six months' vacancy the metropolitan could present to any cathedral or monastic church. Henry induced the pope to withdraw this brief, and it is not surprising that at this grave reverse St Edmund began to see himself as possibly another Thomas Becket. It had become almost impossible for him to administer his office, for whatever steps he took Cardinal Otto was liable to reverse them, and he decided to leave the country.   After taking leave of the king and blessing the land, " standing on a hill [Shooters Hill ?] near the city of London ", he sailed from Thanet ; and " looking back on England he wept bitterly, knowing in spirit that he would never see it again."

St Edmund went to the Cistercian abbey of Pontigny, " where a refuge had been found by all prelates who had been exiled from England for justice's sake. . . . Blessed Thomas the Martyr before the time of his martyrdom had awaited there for [two] years the reward of his life."   During the few months he was there Edmund lived as one of the community, writing in the *scriptorium* and preaching in the neighbouring villages.   In the summer of 1240 he went for his health to a priory of canons regular at Soissy.   Here he died at dawn on Friday, November 16, after raising the excommunication on the Canterbury monks, and sending his hair-shirt to his brother Robert and his camlet cloak and a holy image to his sisters at Catesby.   He was buried in the great church at Pontigny, where his body is still enshrined and venerated.   St Edmund was canonized six years later, and his feast is kept in nearly every diocese of England and by the Cistercians, as well as at Meaux and Sens.

We are on the whole very well informed regarding the history of St Edmund.   Besides the abundant notices in Matthew Paris and several other contemporary chroniclers, there are at least four independent biographies of serious value.   Unfortunately we have no certain knowledge as to their respective authors, and though there is good reason to suppose that Robert Rich, St Edmund's brother, Bertrand, a Cistercian who was prior of Pontigny, Matthew Paris, Eustace, a monk of Canterbury, and Robert Bacon the Dominican, an uncle or brother of the more celebrated Roger Bacon the Franciscan, all wrote lives of the archbishop, there is no agreement as to which writer is responsible for which life.   The longest and perhaps the most satisfactory of these texts is that printed in the *Thesaurus novus anecdotorum* of Martène and Durand, vol. iii, pp. 1775–1826.   The second has been edited by W. Wallace in his *Life of St Edmund of Canterbury* (1893), pp. 543–583, and with this two others, pp. 589–624.   Besides this excellent work we have lives by the Baroness de Paravicini (1898), by Bishop Bernard Ward (1903), and by M. R. Newbolt (1928).   See also an article by H. W. C. Davis in the *English Historical Review*, vol. xxii (1907), pp. 84–92 ; the *Dublin Review* for October, 1904, pp. 229–237, and a criticism of this last in the preface to the *Eynsham Cartulary* edited by H. E. Salter (1907–1908) ; and A. B. Emden, *An Oxford Hall in Medieval Times* (1927).   Some theological treatises written by St Edmund seem to have remained in manuscript unrecognized, as has been shown by Mgr Lacombe in *Mélanges Mandonnet* (1930), vol. ii, pp. 163–191, under the title of " Quaestiones Aberdonenses."   Edmund's sisters, Alice and Margaret, are mentioned by the Bollandists among the *praetermissi* ; and *cf.* B. Camm in *Revue bénédictine*, vol. x (1893), p. 314.

ST AGNES OF ASSISI, Virgin   (A.D. 1253)

IN the account of St Clare (August 12) it has been told how she left her parents' house at Assisi in order to become a nun under the direction of St Francis ; and it was mentioned that when she was placed temporarily at the Benedictine convent of Sant' Angelo di Panzo she was there joined by her sister Agnes, who was then about fifteen years old.   In the *Chronicle of the Twenty-four Generals* there is a circumstantial account of the brutal violence with which her relatives tried to get St Agnes away again and the miracles by which they were thwarted and her determination upheld ; but no mention of any such occurrences is made in Pope Alexander IV's bull of canonization of St Clare.   St Francis gave Agnes the habit as she desired, and sent her with her sister to San Damiano.   Eight years later, when St Francis established the convent of Monticelli at Florence, Agnes was made its abbess, and from there she is said to have supervised the foundations at Mantua, Venice, Padua and other places.   Under her wise direction Monticelli became hardly less famous than San Damiano itself, and St Agnes firmly upheld her sister in her long struggle for the privilege of complete poverty.   In August 1253 she was summoned to Assisi to be with St Clare during her last hours, when it is said that the dying saint declared her sister would soon follow her.   In fact, St Agnes died on November 16 following, and was buried at San Damiano till 1260, when her body joined that of her sister in the new church of Santa Chiara at Assisi.   The tomb of St Agnes was made glorious by miracles, and her feast was granted to the Franciscans by Pope Benedict XIV.   A touching letter written by St Agnes to St Clare, after having to leave San Damiano for Monticelli in 1219, is still extant.

For the account devoted to her in the *Chronica XXIV Generalium*, see the *Analecta Franciscana*, vol. iii (1897), pp. 173–182.   She is also several times spoken of in the early volumes of Wadding's *Annales Ordinis Minorum*.   Naturally St Agnes figures in all lives of her sister, *e.g.* that by Locatelli.   Consult also the bibliography under August 12, St Clare, and Léon, *Auréole Séraphique* (Eng. trans.), vol. iv, pp. 66–70.

BD LOUIS MORBIOLI   (A.D. 1485)

A METRICAL life of this *beatus*, adorned with classical allusions and figures after the manner then fashionable, was written a few years after his death by the Carmelite friar Baptist of Mantua.   Louis belonged to a *bourgeois* family of Bologna where he was born in 1433.   He was a handsome young man, who soon married, but led a careless and at times sinful life.   But in 1462, while he was staying in the monastery of the canons regular of St Saviour at Venice, Louis was taken very ill, and the threat to his life, aided by the exhortations of his hosts, brought about a complete change in him.   From being a scandal, he became an example to Bologna and his inward conversion was manifested by his outward appearance : the man of fashion now wore the same thin, plain garments summer and winter, and no longer curled and dressed his hair.   After he had made provision for her, the wife of Louis agreed to a separation, and he then began to go from place to place preaching repentance.   He begged alms for the poor, taught Christian doctrine to the young and ignorant, and did not care how ridiculous he seemed to make himself to the eyes of his former associates.   In his moments of leisure he amused himself by carving images in bone and wood.   During the last years of his life his lodging was below the staircase of a Bolognese mansion, and when his last illness began he resolutely refused to see a doctor.   Instead, he asked for the sacraments, and when he had received them with great devotion he died, on November 9, 1485.   He was buried in the cemetery of the cathedral, but so many miracles were attributed to his intercession that the body was soon translated to within the building.   During alterations and rebuilding in the cathedral a hundred years later the site of his grave was lost and has never been recovered ; but this did not interrupt the *cultus* of Bd Louis Morbioli, which was confirmed in 1843.   The Carmelites claim that Bd Louis became a secular tertiary of their order after his conversion, and they keep his feast today.

The metrical life by Baptista Mantuanus is printed in the *Acta Sanctorum*, November, vol. iv, pp. 288–297, where it is remarked that the author does not indulge in poetic licence and depends on his own or eye-witnesses' knowledge.   The Bollandists refer also to other works. There seems to be some little doubt about the chronology. There is an account in the *Analecta Juris Pontificii*, vol. xix (1880), pp. 1043 *seq.* ; and in R. McCaffrey, *The White Friars* (1926), pp. 62–63.

BD GRATIA OF CATTARO   (A.D. 1508)

ACCORDING to tradition Gratia was a native of Cattaro (Kotor) in Dalmatia who followed the trade of the sea till he was thirty years old.   Coming one day into a church at Venice he was deeply impressed by a sermon from an Augustinian friar, Father Simon of Camerino.   Gratia determined to enter that order and was accepted as a lay-brother at Monte Ortono, near Padua.   Here Brother Gratia was employed in the gardens, and soon earned the respect and veneration of the whole convent.   When he was transferred to the friary of St Christopher at Venice a mysterious light was seen above his cell, and miracles took place at his intercession. When the church was being repaired and he was working on the building, a cistern was marvellously supplied with water all through a dry summer, and the water remained fresh even when the sea got into it.   In his seventy-first year Gratia was taken seriously ill, and insisted on getting out of bed to receive the last sacraments on his knees ; he died on November 9, 1508.   The *cultus* of Bd Gratia was confirmed in 1889, and his feast is kept by the Augustinians on this day.

See the *Acta Sanctorum*, November, vol. iv, pp. 297–304.   The earliest accounts (S. Lazarini, in Italian, 1643 ; Eliseus Polonus, in Latin, 1677) were not compiled till over a century after Gratia's death ; all writings on him seem to go back to a common source. A more recent Italian life is by N. Mattioli (1890) ; and there is one in Serbo-Croat by I. Matović (1910).

BD LUCY OF NARNI, VIRGIN   (A.D. 1544)

THE treasurer of the commune of Narni in Umbria during the second half of the fifteenth century was a certain Nicholas Brocadelli, who married Gentilina Cassio and became by her the father of eleven children.   The eldest of these was Lucy, who was born at Narni in 1476.   At an early age she determined to consecrate herself to God, but, her father being dead, her guardians had other views for her, and when she was fourteen tried to betroth her by force.   Lucy threw the ring to the floor, slapped the suitor's face, and ran out of the room.   In the following year another young man was brought forward, a certain Count Peter, and Lucy, after resisting at first, agreed to marry him, having been recommended to do so by a vision of our Lady and by the advice of her confessor.   The Congregation of Sacred Rites in granting to Bd Lucy in 1729 the Mass and Office of a virgin has accepted the evidence for the union of her and Peter being only nominally marital, and after about three years her husband told her she was free to do whatever she liked.   Whereupon she withdrew to her mother's house, received the habit of the Dominican third order, and joined a community of regular tertiaries in Rome.   A little later she went to a similar convent at Viterbo.   Here Bd Lucy received the *stigmata*, and when to these were added a sensible participation in the sufferings of the Passion, which happened, accompanied by loss of blood, every Wednesday and Friday for the three years that she remained at Viterbo, her state could not be concealed.   She was examined, sceptically enough, by the local inquisitor, by the Master of the Sacred Palace, by a Franciscan bishop, and by the physician of the pope himself, Alexander VI.   They were all convinced of the genuineness of the phenomena.   Finally Count Peter came to see ; he was convinced too, and is said in consequence to have joined the Friars Minor.

The fame of Bd Lucy came to Ercole I, Duke of Ferrara, who had a deep admiration for the memory of St Catherine of Siena and was a sincere friend of such contemporary holy women as Bd Stephana Quinzani, Bd Columba of Rieti and Bd Osanna of Mantua.   He obtained the pope's permission and her agreement to found a convent for Lucy at Ferrara.   Great difficulties were put in the way of her leaving Viterbo, and in the end she had to be smuggled out of the town in a clothes-basket strapped to the back of a mule.   But Bd Lucy was only twenty-three years old and she had not the natural qualities necessary to a superior ; moreover, Ercole d'Este was a man of large ideas and wanted his new convent (on whose building and decoration he spent large sums of money) to house not less than a hundred sisters, so he invited none other than Lucretia Borgia (who had just become his daughter-in-law) to help him in his quest for subjects.   These came from several quarters, some of them were not at all suitable, and Lucy's task became more and more difficult.   She was deposed from office and her place taken by Sister Mary of Parma, who was not a tertiary at all but a Dominican nun of the so-called second order, to which she wanted to affiliate the whole community.   In 1505 Bd Lucy's ducal protector died, and from being a " fashionable mystic " and the *protégée* of d'Este she sank into complete obscurity and so remained for thirty-nine years.   Moreover, the new prioress treated her with a severity that was not short of persecution : the parlour was closed to her, she might speak to nobody except the confessor who was appointed for her, a sister was told off to be always in charge of her.   It was during these weary years, unjustly condemned by the sisters of the house she had been brought with so much trouble from Viterbo to found, that Bd Lucy became a saint.   Not a word of impatience or complaint is heard, even when she is ill and left unattended.   So completely did she allow herself to be effaced that when she died on November 15, 1544, the people of Ferrara were astonished to hear that she had been still alive : they thought she was dead years ago.   Immediately popular veneration was aroused, soon her body had to be translated to a more public resting-place, and many miracles were claimed.   This *cultus* of Bd Lucy of Narni was confirmed in 1710.

There is plenty of evidence available concerning the early mystical life of this *beata*. Edmund Gardner in his book *Dukes and Poets in Ferrara* (1904), has left us a graphic account of the more memorable incidents connected with her ; see pp. 366–381, 401–404 and 465–467.   His description is largely based upon the work of L. A. Gandini, *Sulla venuta in Ferrara della beata Lucia da Narni* (1901), and upon the *Vita della beata Lucia di Narni* of Domenico Ponsi (1711).   In connection with this last there is a curious supplement printed in 1740, *Aggiunta al libro della Vita della B. Lucia*.   In this we have a bibliography of earlier publications concerning Lucy, but the substance of the book is taken up with the attempt made by the Franciscans of Majorca to suppress a printed picture of her in which she was represented with the stigmata.   The Franciscans contended that by a decree of Sixtus IV (a Franciscan) it had been forbidden under pain of excommunication to represent anyone except St Francis himself as marked with the stigmata.   The case was referred to Rome and by a decree of 1740 the matter was decided in favour of the Dominicans.   The question of the reality of Lucy's stigmata had been very thoroughly investigated by Duke Hercules of Ferrara himself, and his letter on the subject printed in the booklet *Spiritualium personarum facta admiratione digna* (1501)—there is a copy in the British Museum—is a document of great interest.   See also another letter of his in G. Marcianese, *Narratione della nascita, etc., della b. Lucia di Narni* (1616).

17 : ST GREGORY THE WONDERWORKER, Bishop of Neocaesarea
(A.D. 268)

THEODORE, afterwards called Gregory, and from his miracles surnamed Thaumaturgus or Worker of Wonders, was of Neocaesarea in Pontus, born of parents eminent in rank and pagan in religion.　At fourteen years of age he lost his father, but continued his education, which was directed towards a career in the law.　His sister going to join her husband, an official at Caesarea in Palestine, Gregory accompanied her with his brother Athenodorus, who was afterwards a bishop and suffered much for the faith of Jesus Christ.　Origen had arrived at Caesarea a little before and opened a school there, and at the first meeting with Gregory and his brother discerned in them capacity for learning and dispositions to virtue which encouraged him to inspire them with a love of truth and an eager desire of attaining the sovereign good of man.　Fascinated with his discourse, they entered his school and laid aside all thoughts of going to the law-school of Bairut, as they had originally intended.　Gregory does justice to Origen by assuring us that he excited them to virtue no less by his example than by his words ; and tells us that he inculcated that in all things the most valuable knowledge is that of the first cause, and thus he led them on to theology.　He opened to their view all that the philosophers and poets had written concerning God, showing what was true and what was erroneous in the doctrines of each and demonstrating the incompetence of human reason alone for attaining to certain knowledge in the most important of all points, that of religion.　The conversion of the brothers to Christianity was complete and they continued their studies under their master for some years, going back home about the year 238.　Before he took leave of Origen, Gregory thanked him publicly in an oration before a large audience, in which he extols the method and wisdom by which his great master conducted him through his studies, and gives interesting particulars of the way in which Origen taught.　A letter also is extant from the master to the disciple : he calls Gregory his respected son and exhorts him to employ for the service of religion all the talents which he had received from God and to borrow from the heathen philosophy what might serve that purpose, as the Jews converted the spoils of the Egyptians to the building of the tabernacle of the true God.

On his return to Neocaesarea St Gregory intended to practice law, but within a short time, although there were only seventeen Christians in the town, he was appointed to be its bishop ; but of his long episcopate few certain particulars have come down to us.　St Gregory of Nyssa gives a good deal of information in his panegyric of the saint with regard to the deeds which earned him the title of Wonderworker, but there is little doubt that a good deal of it is legendary.　However, it is known that Neocaesarea was rich and populous, deeply buried in vice and idolatry, that St Gregory, animated with zeal and charity, applied himself vigorously to the charge committed to him, and that God was pleased to confer upon him an extraordinary power of working miracles.　St Basil tells us that " through the co-operation of the Spirit, Gregory had a formidable power over evil spirits ; he altered the course of rivers in the name of Christ ; he dried up a lake that was a cause of dissension between two brothers ; and his foretelling of the future made him equal with the other prophets. . . . Such were his signs and wonders that both friends and enemies of the truth looked on him as another Moses." *

When he first took possession of his see Gregory accepted the invitation of Musonius, a person of importance in the city, and lodged with him. ⟂ That very day he began to preach and before night had converted a number sufficient to form a little church. Early next morning the doors were crowded with sick persons, whom he cured at the same time that he wrought the conversion of their souls. Christians soon became so numerous that the saint was enabled to build a church for their use, to which all contributed either money or labour. The circumstances in which St Gregory caused Alexander the Charcoal-burner to be chosen bishop of Comana have been narrated in the notice of that saint on August 11 ; and his wisdom and tact caused him to be referred to in civil as well as religious causes, and then his interrupted legal studies came in useful. Gregory of Nyssa and his brother Basil learned much of what was currently said about the Wonderworker from their grandmother, St Macrina, who was born in Neocaesarea about the time of his death. St Basil says that the whole tenor of his life expressed the height of evangelical fervour. In his devotion he showed the greatest reverence and re-collection and never covered his head at prayer, and he loved simplicity and modesty of speech : " yea " and " nay " were the measure of his ordinary conversation. He abhorred lies and falsehood ; no anger or bitterness ever appeared in his words or behaviour.

The persecution of Decius breaking out in 250, St Gregory advised his flock rather to hide than to expose themselves to the danger of losing their faith ; he himself withdrew into the desert, accompanied only by a pagan priest whom he had converted and who was then his deacon. The persecutors were informed that he was concealed upon a certain mountain and sent soldiers to apprehend him. They returned, saying they had seen nothing but two trees ; upon which the informer went to the place and, finding the bishop and his deacon at their prayers, whom the soldiers had mistaken for two trees, judged their escape to have been miraculous and became a Christian. The persecution was followed by a plague, and the plague by an irruption of Goths into Asia Minor, so that it is not surprising to find that, with these added to the ordinary cares and duties of the episcopate, St Gregory was not a voluminous writer. What these cares and duties were he sets out in his " Canonical Letter ", occasioned by problems arising from the barbarian raids. It is stated that St Gregory organized secular amusements in connection with the annual commemorations of the martyrs, which attracted pagans as well as popularizing the religious gatherings among Christians : doubtless, too, he had it in mind that the martyrs were honoured by happy recreation in addition to formally religious observances. But he " is the sole missionary we know of, during these first three centuries, who employed such methods ; and he was a highly-educated Greek ".

A little before his death St Gregory Thaumaturgus inquired how many infidels yet remained in the city, and being told there were seventeen he thankfully acknow-ledged as a great mercy that, having found but seventeen Christians at his coming

* Alban Butler narrates the famous miraculous removal of a great stone, which in the *Dialogues* of St Gregory the Great becomes a mountain. When the feast of St Gertrude was to be added to the Western calendar in 1738 it was found that her *dies natalis* coincided with that of St Gregory. Clement XII thought that a saint who moved mountains should not himself be moved, even by a pope, and St Gertrude's feast was assigned to the 15th.

thither, he left but seventeen idolaters. Having then prayed for their conversion, and the confirmation and sanctification of those that believed in the true God, he enjoined his friends not to procure him any special place of burial but that, as he lived as a pilgrim in the world claiming nothing for himself, so after death he might enjoy the common lot. His body is said to have been ultimately transferred to a Byzantine monastery in Calabria, and there is considerable local *cultus* of St Gregory in southern Italy and Sicily, where he is invoked in times of earthquake and, on account of his miracle of stopping the flooding of the River Lycus, against inundations.

Apart from what Gregory himself tells us about his relations with Origen, and sundry casual allusions which we find in the writings of St Basil, St Jerome and Eusebius, the information which we possess concerning this saint is of a very unsatisfactory character. The panegyric by St Gregory of Nyssa recounts many marvels, but says little of his history, and even less confidence can be placed in the Syriac life (the best text is in Bedjan, *Acta Martyrum*, vol. vi, 1896, pp. 83–106). Besides this there is an Armenian life and one in Latin, both of little value. See also Ryssel, *Gregorius Thaumaturgus, sein Leben und seine Schriften* (1880) ; Funk in the *Theologische Quartalschrift* for 1898, pp. 81 *seq.* ; *Journal of Theological Studies* for 1930, pp. 142–155. A valuable article by M. Jugie on the sermons attributed to St Gregory is in the *Analecta Bollandiana*, vol. xliii (1925), pp. 86–95. Here it is clearly shown that most of these attributions are unreliable, but Fr Jugie inclines to accept the authenticity of one of those preserved in Armenian, though he rejects that which F. C. Conybeare translated into English in the *Expositor* for 1896, pt 1, pp. 161–173. Critics, however, seem generally agreed in admitting the genuineness of the panegyric of Origen, the treatise on the Creed, the canonical epistle, and the dissertation addressed to Theopompus ; this last only exists in Syriac. The greater part of the writings printed under the name of St Gregory Thaumaturgus in Migne, PG., vol. x, are either gravely suspect or certainly spurious. See Bardenhewer, *Geschichte der altkirchlichen Literatur*, vol. ii, pp. 315–332.

ST DIONYSIUS, Bishop of Alexandria   (A.D. 265)

St Basil and other Greek writers honour this prelate with the epithet of " the Great ", and he is called by St Athanasius the " Teacher of the Catholic Church ". Alexandria, which was the place of his education, was then the centre of the sciences, and Dionysius whilst yet a heathen gave himself to learning. He assures us that he was converted to the Christian faith by a vision and a voice which spake to him, as well as by diligent reading and an impartial examination. He became a scholar in the catechetical school of Origen, and made such progress that when Heraclas was made bishop the care of that school was committed to Dionysius, who conducted it for fifteen years. In 247 he was himself chosen bishop. Soon after the populace, stirred up by a certain heathen prophet at Alexandria, raised a fierce persecution, of which St Dionysius wrote an account to Fabius, Bishop of Antioch ; then the edict of Decius put arms into the hands of the enemies of the Christians, and directly the decree reached Alexandria the governor sent a troop to arrest the bishop. They looked everywhere for him except in his house, where he was all the time, but at the end of four days he left it with his household to try and get away. They were seen and arrested, except one servant, who told a peasant whom he met going to a wedding what had happened. The peasant was not a Christian but seemed glad of an excuse to fight the police, for he rushed off and told the wedding party, who " with a single impulse " as if by agreement, ran to the rescue and drove off the guards. St Dionysius thought the wedding-guests were robbers and offered them his clothes. Then when it was explained that he was free he was grieved at losing a martyr's crown and refused to budge. The Egyptians did not understand this idea at all, so they seized him, put him on a donkey, and drove him to a place of refuge in the Libyan desert.   Here Dionysius remained with two companions, governing the church of Alexandria from thence, until the persecution ceased.

Then the Church was rent by the schism formed by Novatian against Pope St Cornelius.   The antipope sent him a request for his support, and St Dionysius answered, " You ought to have suffered all things rather than have caused a schism in the Church.   To die in defence of its unity would be as glorious as laying down one's life for its faith ; in my opinion, more glorious : because here the safety of the whole Church is concerned.   If you bring your brethren back to union your fault will be forgotten.   If you cannot gain others, at least save your own soul." In opposition to the heresy of Novatian, who denied to the Church the power of remitting certain sins, he ordered that communion should be refused to no one that asked it in the right dispositions at the hour of death.   When Fabius of Antioch seemed inclined to favour the rigorism of Novatian towards the lapsed, Dionysius wrote him several letters against that principle.   In one he relates that an old man called Serapion, of hitherto blameless life, had offered pagan sacrifice and had therefore been refused communion.   In his last sickness he could get absolution from no one, till he cried out, " Why am I detained here ?   I beg to be delivered."   Then he sent his little grandson to a priest who, being sick and not able to come, sent the Holy Eucharist by the child (for during persecutions the Blessed Sacrament is allowed to be so carried and received in domestic communion). So the aged man died in peace.   St Dionysius contends that his life was miraculously preserved that he might receive communion.   At this time a pestilence began to rage and made great havoc for several years.   St Dionysius left an account of its terrors, in which he contrasts the behaviour of the Christians, many of whom died martyrs of charity, with the selfishness—and greater mortality—of the pagans. In opposing the false opinion that Christ will reign on earth with his elect a thousand years before the day of judgement Dionysius showed himself a keen scriptural critic, and in his enthusiasm against dogmatic error used arguments against St John's authorship of the Apocalypse which seventeen hundred years later were revived by " higher critics ".   St Dionysius took part also in the controversy about baptisms by heretics, in which he seems to have inclined to the view that such baptisms were invalid but followed the practice directed by Pope St Stephen I. This indefatigable bishop also had to proceed against some of his brethren in the Pentapolis who professed Sabellianism.   In writing against them he vented opinions which caused him to be delated to his namesake, Pope St Dionysius.   The pope wrote expounding the bishop's errors, whereupon he published an explanation of his teaching.

Persecution being renewed by Valerian in 257, Emilian, prefect of Egypt, had St Dionysius with some of his clergy brought before him and pressed them to sacrifice to the gods, the protectors of the empire.   St Dionysius replied, " All men do not worship the same deities.   We worship one only God, the creator of all things, who has bestowed the empire on Valerian and Gallienus.   We offer up prayers to Him for the peace and prosperity of their reign."   The prefect tried to persuade them to worship the Roman deities with their own God, and then sent them into banishment to Kephro in Libya.

The exile of St Dionysius this time lasted for two years, but when he was allowed to return to his see in 260 it was to a distracted city.   A political upheaval brought on Alexandria all the evils of civil war, and it was a prey to violence of all sorts. Trifling incidents caused riots. The town ran to arms, the streets were filled with dead bodies, and the gutters ran with blood. The peaceable demeanour of the Christians could not protect them from violence, as St Dionysius complains, and a man could neither keep at home nor stir out of doors without danger. He even had to communicate with his people by letter, for it was easier, he wrote, to go from East to West than from Alexandria to Alexandria. Plague again added its havoc, and, whilst the Christians attended the sick with care and charity, the heathen threw putrid carcases into the highways, and often put their dying friends out of doors and left them to perish in the streets. Towards the end of the year 265 St Dionysius died at Alexandria, after he had governed that church with great wisdom and sanctity about seventeen years. His memory, says St Epiphanius, was preserved there by a church dedicated in his honour, but much more by his virtues and writings, of which only a few fragments have survived.

St Dionysius of Alexandria is mentioned in the Roman Martyrology on this day, and also on October 3, where he is erroneously named as a martyr together with his companions in his first exile and others. He is commemorated in the canon of the Syrian and Maronite Mass.

Almost all we know of St Dionysius is derived from Eusebius and from the extracts from the saint's letters which Eusebius has preserved for us. There are a few references to him in the writings of St Athanasius and other early fathers, but they do not amount to much. The best edition of Dionysius's literary remains is that of C. L. Feltoe (1904), who has also produced (1918) another book of translations and comments. There is an exhaustive article devoted to this Dionysius by Abbot Chapman in the *Catholic Encyclopedia*. See also Bardenhewer, *Geschichte der altkirchlichen Literatur*, vol. ii, pp. 206–237 ; DTC., vol. iv (1911), cc. 425–427 ; the *Journal of Theological Studies*, vol. xxv (1924), pp. 364–377 ; the *Zeitschrift f. N.-T. Wissenschaft*, 1924, pp. 235–247; the monographs of F. Dittrich (1867) and J. Burel (1910) ; and H. Delehaye, *Les passions des martyrs* . . . (1921), pp. 429–435.

SS. ALPHAEUS AND ZACHAEUS, MARTYRS　　(A.D. 303)

IN the first year of Diocletian's general persecution, upon the approach of the games for celebrating the twentieth year of his reign, the governor of Palestine obtained the emperor's pardon for all criminals, Christians only excepted. At that very time, Zachaeus, deacon at Gadara beyond the Jordan, was apprehended. He was inhumanly scourged, then torn with iron combs, and afterwards thrown into prison, where his feet were stretched to the fourth hole of the stocks, by which his body was almost rent asunder : yet he lay in this condition very cheerfully, praising God night and day. Here he was soon joined by Alphaeus, a native of Eleutheropolis, of a good family, and lector in the church of Caesarea. In the persecution he boldly encouraged the faithful to constancy and, being seized, baffled the prefect at his first examination and was committed to prison. At a second appearance in court, his flesh was torn first with whips, then with hooks ; after which he was cast into the dungeon with Zachaeus and put in like manner in the stocks. In a third examination they were both condemned to die, and were beheaded together on November 17, 303.

We know nothing of these martyrs beyond what Eusebius has recorded in his *Martyrs of Palestine*, bk 1, ch. 5. See CMH., pp. 604–605.

SS. ACISCLUS AND VICTORIA, MARTYRS   (FOURTH CENTURY ?)

THESE martyrs were considered of sufficient importance to warrant their being accorded a proper office in the Mozarabic liturgy, and it is often said that they suffered under Diocletian ; but there is no agreement within a hundred years or more as to when they lived and died.   In his *Memorial of the Saints* St Eulogius says they belonged to Cordova and were brother and sister.   Having been denounced as Christians they were committed to prison, and beaten and tortured to induce them to apostatize.   They were eventually put to death in the amphitheatre, Acisclus by beheading and Victoria by piercing with arrows.   Their bodies were buried by the matron Minciana at her country-house, where later a church was built, at which many martyrs under the Arab persecution were buried.

Although the medieval *passio* (printed in Florez, *España sagrada*, vol. x, pp. 485–491) is no better than a pious fiction, and there seems to be no warrant for the existence of any such person as Victoria, Acisclus was an unquestionably genuine martyr.   He is mentioned by Prudentius, and entered in the *Hieronymianum* (see CMH., pp. 606–607) under November 18, with the curious addition that " on this day roses are gathered ".   His name also occurs in a Spanish inscription of the early sixth century referring to relics, as noted in J. Vives, *Inscripciones cristianas de la España romana y visigoda* (1942), no. 316.

ST ANIANUS, OR AIGNAN, BISHOP OF ORLEANS   (*c.* A.D. 453)

ANIANUS was born in Vienne and, after living a hermit's life there for some time, went to Orleans, attracted by the reputation of its holy bishop, Evurtius.   By him Anianus was ordained priest.   Towards the end of his life St Evurtius determined to resign his bishopric, and summoned an assembly to appoint a successor.   According to a legend the names of the candidates were put in a vessel and, the lot having been drawn by a child, it fell upon St Anianus ; lest this should be but chance, the choice was confirmed by the *sortes biblicae*.   When he came to take possession of his cathedral, Anianus asked the governor of the city according to custom to release all the prisoners who were in gaol.   The governor refused until, having had a near escape from death, he took this to be a warning from Heaven and did as the new bishop had requested.

In the year 451 Orleans was threatened by Attila and his Huns and, as in many other examples at this time, the credit of saving the city was given to its bishop. St Anianus helped to organize the defences and encourage the people, and appealed urgently to the Roman general Aetius to come to their help.   Aetius was slow in moving, the town was taken, and the Huns had already begun to carry off their booty and captives, when they had to turn and defend themselves against the troops of Aetius, who drove them from Orleans and across the Seine.   St Anianus died two years later at a great age.

The two Latin lives of this saint are late in date and unreliable.   The better of the two has been edited by B. Krusch in MGH., *Scriptores Merov.*, vol. iii, pp. 104–117.   St Gregory of Tours also describes in some detail the relief of Orleans when attacked by Attila, and attributes it to St Aignan.   See further C. Duhan, *Vie de St Aignan* (1877), and L. Duchesne, *Fastes Épiscopaux*, vol. ii, p. 460.

ST GREGORY, BISHOP OF TOURS   (A.D. 594)

THE best-known bishop of the early church of Tours after St Martin was Georgius Florentius, who afterwards took the name of Gregory.   He was born in 538 at

Clermont-Ferrand of a distinguished family of Auvergne : he was a great-grandson of St Gregory of Langres and a nephew of St Gallus of Clermont, to whom he was entrusted as a boy on the death of his father.   Gallus died when Gregory was sixteen and, a serious illness having turned his mind to God's service, he began the study of the Scriptures under St Avitus I, then a priest at Clermont.   In 573, in accordance with the wishes of King Sigebert I and the people of Tours, Gregory was appointed to succeed St Euphronius as bishop there.

It was a much-troubled age in Gaul, and Tours was a particularly troubled diocese.   After three years of war at the beginning of St Gregory's episcopate it came into the hands of King Chilperic, who was very averse from the new bishop, and Gregory consequently had to deal with powerful enemies.   He gave sanctuary to Chilperic's son Meroveus, in defiance of the step-mother Fredegund, and firmly supported St Praetextatus of Rouen whom Chilperic summoned on a charge of having blessed the marriage of Meroveus with his step-aunt Brunhilda.   Then one Leudastis, whom Gregory had caused to be removed from the countship of Tours as unworthy, accused him to the king of political disloyalty and of having slandered Queen Fredegund.   He was accordingly arraigned before a council, wherein he purged himself of the charge on oath and behaved with such propriety that the bishops acquitted him and ordered Leudastis to be punished as a false witness. Chilperic, like many another monarch of those times, fancied himself as a theologian, and here again St Gregory came into conflict with him, for he could not dissimulate that the royal theology was bad and the manner in which it was set out even worse. Chilperic, however, died in 584 and Tours was held first by Guntram of Burgundy and then by Childebert II ; these sovereigns were friendly to Gregory and he was able to go on unhampered with the varied work of his diocese and with his writings.

Faith and good works were much increased in Tours under Gregory's adminis- tration.   He rebuilt his cathedral and several other churches, and a number of heretics were brought over to unity of faith by him, though he was no great theologian.   St Odo of Cluny extols his humility, zeal for religion and charity towards all, especially his enemies.   Several miracles are ascribed to St Gregory of Tours, which he attributed to the intercession of St Martin and other saints whose relics he always carried about him.

Though Gregory was one of the most effective of the Merovingian bishops, he is best remembered today as a historian and hagiographer.   His *History of the Franks* is an original source for the early history of the French monarchy and gives a great deal of information about himself.   His books " of the Glory of the Mar- tyrs " and of other saints, " of the Glory of the Confessors ", and " of the Lives of the Fathers " are less valuable as history.   He was writing according to the taste of his day, and an excessive preponderance is given to legends and marvels, marvels of which he was only occasionally critical.   As Alban Butler moderately puts it, " In his ample collections of miracles he seems often to have given credit to popular reports ".

What we know of the life of St Gregory of Tours is mainly derived from his own works, with some little supplementary information which comes to us from Venantius Fortunatus or contemporary records.   There is a life (it is printed in Migne, PL., vol. lxxi, cc. 115–128), but it was compiled only in the tenth century, and is of little independent value.   A great deal has been written about Gregory of Tours, but less from a hagiographical point of view than as a study of his writings.   One of the most notable contributions to this aspect of the subject is that of G. Kurth, *Histoire poétique des Mérovingiens* (1893) ; but see also the *Études Franques* (1919), pp. 1–29 of the same author ; L. Halphen in *Mélanges Lot* (1925), pp. 235–244 ; B. Krusch in *Mittheilungen Inst. Oester. Geschichte* (1931), pp. 486–490 ; DAC., vol. vi, cc. 1711–1753 ; and Delehaye, " Les Recueils des Miracles des Saints " in *Analecta Bollandiana*, vol. xliii (1925), pp. 305–325. The most satisfactory edition of the historical works of Gregory is that of Krusch and Levison in MGH., *Scriptores Merov.*, vol. i, pt i (1937–51). There is an interesting article on the saint by Harman Grisewood in *Saints and Ourselves* (1953), pp. 25–40.

ST HILDA, Abbess of Whitby, Virgin   (A.D. 680)

THE *cultus* of this great abbess must have been recognized almost at once after her death, for her name appears in the calendar of St Willibrord, written at the beginning of the eighth century.   Hilda (Hild) was the daughter of Hereric, nephew of St Edwin, King of Northumbria, and she was baptized by St Paulinus together with that prince, when she was thirteen years old.   The first thirty-three years of her life, says St Bede, " she spent living most nobly in the secular state ; and more nobly dedicated the remaining half to the Lord as a nun ".   She went into the kingdom of the East Angles, where her cousin, King Anna, reigned ; her idea was to retire to the monastery of Chelles in France, where her sister Hereswitha served God.   But St Aidan prevailed upon Hilda to return to Northumberland, where he settled her in a small nunnery upon the River Wear.   Then she was made abbess of Heiu's double monastery at Hartlepool.   Here her first business was to bring better order to the house, in accordance with " her innate wisdom and love for the service of God ".

Some years later St Hilda was transferred to Streaneshalch (afterwards called Whitby), either to found a new abbey or to reform an old one.   This again was a double monastery of monks and nuns, who lived entirely apart but sang the office together in church ; as was usual in such houses, the abbess was in supreme charge, except where strictly spiritual matters were concerned.   St Hilda filled this office so well, writes Bede, " that not only ordinary people, but even kings and princes sometimes asked and accepted her advice.   And she obliged those who were under her direction to attend much to reading the Holy Scriptures and to exercise themselves freely in works of righteousness in order that many there might be found fit for ecclesiastical duties and to minister at the altar."   Several of her monks became bishops, including St John of Beverley.   The poet Caedmon was a servant of the monastery, and took the habit there at Hilda's suggestion ; he also was locally commemorated as a saint, and she was followed in her office by St Elfleda, her pupil.   The success of St Hilda's rule and the love which she inspired in her subjects may be clearly seen in the pages of Bede's *Ecclesiastical History*.   Probably, too, it was the reputation of the house as well as the convenience of its situation that caused Whitby Abbey to be selected as the place for the great synod of 664, summoned to decide on what day Easter should be observed and other vexed questions.   St Hilda and her religious sided with the Scots in favour of the Celtic customs, but St Wilfrid and the other party triumphed and King Oswy ordered the Roman customs to be observed in Northumbria.   Doubtless St Hilda obeyed this decision of the synod, but perhaps was vexed by St Wilfrid's part in it, for later she strongly supported St Theodore of Canterbury against him in the matter of the northern dioceses.

Seven years before her death St Hilda contracted a sickness which never again left her ; but all the time " she never failed either to return thanks to her Maker or publicly and privately to instruct those under her care.   By her own example she admonished all to serve God dutifully when in health and to remain grateful to Him in adversity or bodily infirmity." She died at dawn, presumably on November 17, in the year 680. A nun who, says St Bede, " loved her most passionately," but being in charge of the postulants was not present at her death, nevertheless saw it in vision and told her charges thereof. And at the daughter-house at Hackness, thirteen miles away, a nun called Begu heard in her sleep the passing-bell and saw as it were the soul of her abbess departing to Heaven. She called her sisters and they remained praying in the church until daylight, " when the brothers came with news of her death from the place where she had died ". The monastery of Whitby * was destroyed by the Danes, when the relics of St Hilda were either lost or translated to a place unknown. Her feast is now kept in the diocese of Middlesbrough.

We know little more of St Hilda than what is told us in Bede's *Ecclesiastical History ;* but see the notes in C. Plummer's edition, and also Howorth, *The Golden Days of the Early English Church*, vol. iii, pp. 186–195 and *passim. Cf.* Stanton, *Menology*, pp. 551–552.

ST HUGH, BISHOP OF LINCOLN   (A.D. 1200)

THE foundations of an interior life are most surely laid in solitude, which is the best preparation for the works of the active life and the support of a spirit of religion amidst its distractions. It was in the desert of Chartreuse that St Hugh learned first to govern himself and stored up in his heart habits of virtue, the most essential qualification of a minister of Christ. He was born of a good family in Burgundy in 1140, his father being William, Lord of Avalon, a good soldier and an even better Christian. Hugh's mother, Anne, died when he was eight years old, and he was educated from that age in a convent of regular canons at Villard-Benoît. William of Avalon at the same time retired himself to the same place and there ended his days in the exercises of a devout and penitential religious life. Hugh when he was fifteen was allowed to make his religious profession and at nineteen was ordained deacon, at once beginning to distinguish himself as a preacher. He was put in charge of a small dependency of his monastery at Saint-Maximin, and from thence accompanied his prior on a visit to the Grande Char-treuse. The retirement and silence of the place, and the contemplation and saintly deportment of the monks who inhabited it, kindled in Hugh's breast a strong desire of embracing that life. The Carthusian prior painted an alarming picture of its hardships, and Hugh's own superior extorted from him a vow that he would not leave Villard-Benoît. After more mature reflection Hugh decided that this vow had been made too hastily and under stress of emotion, and, now being per-suaded that God called him to this state, he went back to the Chartreuse and was admitted to the habit. A Carthusian cottage provides little outward matter for the biographer but we know that St Hugh in his little garden was a special attraction to squirrels and birds, of whom he was very fond and over whom he had consider-able power.†

* Alban Butler says in a footnote : " The common people formerly imagined that St Hilda changed serpents into stones in this place, because on the face of the cliff were found abundance of stones, which have the appearance of serpents or snakes rolled up, or in their coil, but without heads ; which are natural stones called Ammonites, and are still plentiful there." *Cf.* St Keyne at Keynsham (October 8).

† In pictorial representations of St Hugh his emblem is generally a swan. His chaplain and biographer assures us that when a bishop he had a pet wild swan at Stow, one of his

He had passed ten years in his solitary cell when the office of procurator of the monastery was committed to him, which charge he had held for about seven years when, at the age of forty, his life took an abrupt turn.

King Henry II of England founded, as part of his penance for the murder of St Thomas Becket, the first house of Carthusian monks in England, at Witham in Somersetshire; but so great difficulties occurred in the undertaking under the two first priors that the monastery could not be settled. The king, therefore, sent Reginald, Bishop of Bath, to the Grande Chartreuse, to desire that the holy monk Hugh, who had been recommended by a French nobleman, might be sent over to take upon him the government of this monastery. After much debating in the house it was determined that it became not Christian charity so to confine their solicitude to one family as to refuse what was required for the benefit of others, and, though the saint protested that he was most unfit for the charge, he was ordered by the chapter to accompany the deputies to England. At Witham he found that the monastic buildings had not even been begun, and that no provision had been made for the compensation of those who had been, or would have to be, evicted from their lands and tenements to make room for the monks. St Hugh refused to undertake his office until the king had compensated these people, " down to the last penny ". The work was then carried on successfully till it was nearing completion, and then was held up again because Henry had not paid the bills, except in promises. St Hugh's tact overcame this difficulty and the first English charterhouse was at last in being. Hugh by his humility and meekness of manner and the sanctity of his life gained the hearts of the enemies of the foundation; and men began to relish their close solitude and to consecrate themselves to God under the discipline of the saint. As with many another exemplary monk, the reputation of Hugh's goodness and abilities spread far beyond the cloister walls, and in particular King Henry never went hunting in his forest of Frome-Selwood without visiting the prior of Witham. The extent to which he trusted in Hugh is thus illustrated. As the king returned with his army from Normandy to England he was in great danger at sea in a furious storm. Their safety seemed despaired of, when the king cried aloud, " O God whom the prior of Witham so truly serves, through his merits and intercession look with pity on our distress, in spite of our sins which deserve thy judgements ". Almost at once the wind abated and the voyage was completed without mishap, the king's confidence in St Hugh being naturally confirmed and increased.

St Hugh did not hesitate to remonstrate with his royal patron upon matters which required amendment, among which was his habit of keeping sees vacant in order to draw their revenues. A scandalous example was Lincoln which, with an interval of eighteen months, had no bishop for nearly eighteen years. At a council held at Eynsham Abbey in 1186 order was given to the dean and chapter to elect a pastor, and the election fell upon St Hugh—under pressure from king and primate. His objections were not admitted, and he was obliged by the authority of the prior of the Grande Chartreuse to drop the strong opposition which he had made and to receive episcopal consecration. After so long a vacancy the diocese of Lincoln was naturally in dire need of reform, and St Hugh at once engaged several priests of learning and piety to be his assistants; and he employed all the

manors, which would feed from his hand, follow him about, and keep guard over his bed, so that " it was impossible for anyone to approach the bishop without being attacked by it ". Giraldus Cambrensis confirms these statements.

authority which his office gave him in restoring ecclesiastical discipline amongst his clergy.   By sermons and private exhortations he laboured to quicken in all men the spirit of faith, and in ordinary conversation equally incited others to divine love ; but he was full of talk and fun (which often took the form of puns), cheerful, enthusiastic and easily roused, as Giraldus Cambrensis tells us.   In administering the sacraments or consecrating churches he sometimes spent whole days, beginning before daybreak and persevering into the night, without allowing himself rest or food.   He was particularly strict against the exaction of improper fees by the clergy, following his own example at his enthronization when he refused an honor- arium to the archdeacon of Canterbury who had performed the office.   He was deeply devoted to his poor and sick children, and would visit the leper-houses and wait upon the inmates.   When his chancellor pointed out to him that St Martin had cured leprosy by his touch, St Hugh answered, " St Martin's kiss healed the leper's flesh ; but their kiss heals my soul ".   He took great pleasure in children and babies, and his biographer (who was the bishop's chaplain) tells several charming stories illustrative of this trait, as well as miracles done in favour of little ones.

In the epidemic of Jew-baiting which broke out in England at the time of the Third Crusade St Hugh was conspicuous in defence of those persecuted.   In his own cathedral at Lincoln, at Stamford, and again at Northampton, he single- handed faced armed and angry mobs, and cowed and cajoled them into sparing their hated victims.   His concern for justice on behalf of his own people is illus- trated by his actions in regard to the royal forest-laws.   The foresters and their agents " hunt the poor as if they were wild animals and devour them as their prey ", wrote Peter of Blois, a contemporary.   Hugh had had trouble with them at Witham, and so soon as a company of these rangers had, upon a slight occasion, laid hands on a subject of the church of Lincoln, he, after due summons, excommunicated the head of them.   This action King Henry took very ill.   However, he dissembled his resentment, and soon after by letter requested of the bishop a prebend, then vacant in the church of Lincoln, in favour of one of his courtiers.   St Hugh, having read the petition, returned answer by the messenger, " These places are to be conferred upon clerics, not upon courtiers.   The king does not lack means to reward his servants."   The king of course was more furious than ever, and sent for St Hugh, who found him sitting with his court in the grounds of Woodstock castle.   By Henry's order nobody took any notice of the bishop, and he went on sewing a bandage round a cut finger.   St Hugh watched him for a time and then said sweetly, " Now, you know, you look exactly like your kinsfolk at Falaise ! "*   This bold sally broke down the king's ill-humour, and he listened quietly while Hugh demonstrated how in the whole affair he had regard purely to the service of God and to his episcopal duty.   The king was, or pretended to be, perfectly satisfied.   The ranger showed himself penitent and was absolved by the bishop, and from that time became his steady friend.   St Hugh had found his cathedral in ruins, and soon began its rebuilding, on which he sometimes worked with his own hands.   Some of the actual magnificent building there is due to Hugh, and on his deathbed he gave final instructions to the master-builder, Geoffrey de Noiers.   All St Hugh's great achievements in activity were grounded in contem- plation, and it was his custom to retire once a year to his beloved cloister at Witham,

---

* Henry's great-grandfather, William the Conqueror, was the natural son of Robert of Normandy and the daughter of a furrier and glove-maker of Falaise.

and there pass some time observing the common rule, without any difference but that of wearing the episcopal ring on his finger.

St Hugh had such a reputation for justice in his judicial capacity that two poor orphans in a cause appealed to Rome and asked that the Bishop of Lincoln might judge the case, and he exercised this quality in great things and in small.   When in 1197 King Richard I wanted the bishops as well as the barons to subsidize his war with Philip Augustus for twelve months, St Hugh maintained that his see was only liable to assist in home-defence.   Only Bishop Herbert of Salisbury supported him, and he at once had all his goods confiscated.   Hugh stood out, rebuked the king to his face for his unjust oppression and other ill deeds, and triumphed.   But whereas he calmed Henry's rage with a joke, he overcame Richard by a kiss. Stubbs, the constitutional historian, says that this " is the first clear case of the refusal of a money-grant demanded directly by the Crown, and a most valuable precedent for future times ".   Just before his contest with the king, St Hugh had been strengthened in his faith and duty by a vision granted to a young cleric of our Lord, in the likeness of a tiny child, held in the saint's hands at the consecration at Mass.   This youth had previously been supernaturally warned to go to the Bishop of Lincoln and tell him to draw the attention of the Archbishop of Canterbury to the lamentable laxity of many of the English clergy ; a vision at Mass was promised in confirmation.   This was by no means the only time that St Hugh was encouraged and consoled in his difficult labours by clear marks of the help of Heaven, whether by the healing of the sick, the driving out of evil spirits or the conversion of hardened sinners.

After the death of Richard I, who had said of Hugh that " if all the prelates of the Church were like him, there is not a king in Christendom who would dare to raise his head in the presence of a bishop," and the coronation of his successor, King John sent St Hugh into France on affairs of state.   He visited, among other places, his old home at the Grande Chartreuse and the great abbeys of Cluny and Cîteaux, and was everywhere received with joy and veneration, for he was known by reputation all over France as well as England.   But his last sickness was now upon him, and on his return he went to pray at St Thomas's shrine in Canterbury. However, he got worse, and when he was summoned to a national council in London he had to take to his bed at his house in the Old Temple, Holborn (whence " Lincoln's Inn "), receiving the last anointing on the vigil of the nineteenth anniversary of his episcopal consecration.   He lingered on in pain and patience for nearly two months, dying in the evening of November 16, 1200.   The body was taken in a sort of triumphal progress to Lincoln, where it was buried in the cathedral amidst universal grief on November 24.   There were present beside the primate of all England, fourteen bishops and a hundred abbots, an archbishop from Ireland and another from Dalmatia, a prince, Gruffydd ap Rhys, from South Wales, King William the Lion of Scotland and King John of England—and the Lincoln ghetto was there, bewailing the loss of its protector and a " true servant of the great God ".   Twenty years later St Hugh was canonized by Pope Honorius III.   His feast is now observed by the Carthusian Order and in several English dioceses ;   the great charterhouse at Parkminster in Sussex is dedicated in his honour.

The biography known as the *Magna Vita*, which was written by Adam, a monk of Eynsham who was St Hugh's chaplain, is a life which for fullness of detail and reliability of statement has hardly a parallel in medieval literature.   It was edited by Mr Dimock for the Rolls

Series in 1864.   But besides this we have an important memoir by Giraldus Cambrensis, printed in vol. vii of his works (also in the Rolls Series), as well as a metrical life of unknown authorship which was the first to be published by Mr Dimock at Lincoln in 1860.   There are, moreover, a number of references to St Hugh in such contemporary chroniclers as Hoveden, Benedict, etc., and not a few charters and papal documents in which his name figures.   The fullest modern life is that published under Carthusian auspices at Montreuil-sur-Mer in 1890 ; this was translated into English and edited with copious additional notes by Fr H. Thurston in 1898.   Two excellent popular lives of less compass are those of F. A. Forbes (1917) and Joseph Clayton (1931).   A concise Anglican biography of merit is that by Canon R. M. Woolley (1927).   Miss Margaret Thompson has published two admirable books, the fruit of years of research, in which St Hugh plays a prominent part—*The Somerset Carthusians* (1895) and *The Carthusian Order in England* (1930).   St Hugh's tomb and his translation, etc., have been much discussed : see particularly the *Archaeological Journal*, vol. l and vol. li, but these matters are noted in almost every book on Lincoln Cathedral ; *cf.* also Bramley, *St Hugh's Day at Lincoln* (1900).

BD SALOME, Widow   (A.D. 1268)

SOME time about the year 1205 Bd Vincent Kadlubek, Bishop of Cracow, was commissioned to take a child of three years old to the court of King Andrew II of Hungary.   She was Salome, daughter of Leszek the Fair of Poland, who had arranged a marriage for her with Andrew's son, Koloman.   Ten years later the marriage was solemnized.   But Salome lived more like a nun than a princess ; she became a tertiary of the Franciscan Order, and did her best to make her court a model of Christian life.   About 1225 Koloman was killed in battle.   Salome continued to live in the world for some years, being a liberal benefactress of the Friars Minor and founding a convent of Poor Clares, to which she herself retired eventually.   She was a nun for twenty-eight years, and was elected abbess of the community.   Bd Salome died on November 17, 1268, and her *cultus* was approved by Pope Clement X.

There is a medieval Latin life printed in the *Monumenta Poloniae Historica*, vol. iv, pp. 776–796 ; and some account in Wadding, *Annales Ord. Min.*, vol. iii, pp. 353–355 and vol. iv, pp. 284–285.   See also Léon, *Auréole Séraphique* (Eng. trans.), vol. iv, pp. 71–74.

BD JOAN OF SIGNA, Virgin   (A.D. 1307)

A NUMBER of miracles are related of this Franciscan tertiary, but very few particulars of her life are available.   Signa is a village on the Arno, near Florence, and Joan was born there about the year 1245.   Her parents were very poor peasants, and at an early age she was sent out to look after sheep and goats.   She would collect other herdsfolk round her and talk to them of the truths of faith, and urge them to live a Christian life, to which her own example was an even better inducement than her simple heart-felt words.   Her ability to keep dry in wet weather was much talked of, but this seems to have been due to the simple expedient of sheltering under a large and thick tree when it rained.   At the age of twenty-three Bd Joan, possibly inspired by the tales she had heard of St Verdiana of Castelfiorentino, who died about the time Joan was born, became a solitary in a cell on the banks of the Arno, not far from her native place.   Here she lived for forty years.   Her reputation for miracles was great, and people came from all the surrounding country to consult her and bring their sick and afflicted.   Immediately after her death on November 9, 1307, a *cultus* sprang up, which was greatly enhanced in 1348 by the attribution of a sudden cessation of an epidemic to her intercession.   This *cultus* was confirmed in 1798.

An anonymous Latin life is in existence which must have been written about the year 1390.   It has been printed by Fr Mencherini in the *Archivum Franciscanum Historicum*, vol. x (1917), pp. 367–386, and also in the *Acta Sanctorum*, November, vol. iv.   Two other accounts of later date in Italian verse add nothing to our knowledge.   Not only the Franciscans, but the Vallombrosan monks, the Carmelites and the Augustinians have claimed that the recluse was attached to their respective orders.   On the Vallombrosan case see F. Soldani, *Ragguaglio istorico della B. Giovanna da Signa* (1741).   The Franciscan claim can be gathered from Mencherini as above, who supplies a bibliography.   In the opinion of the Bollandists evidence is lacking that the recluse had a definite connection with any order.   An account of Bd Joan is given by Léon, *Auréole Séraphique* (Eng. trans.), vol. iv, pp. 160–164.

BD ELIZABETH THE GOOD, Virgin   (A.D. 1420)

THERE was born in 1386 at Waldsee in Würtemberg, to a couple in humble circumstances called John and Anne Achler, a child who because of her sweetness and innocence was known from very early years as *die gute Betha*, " the good Bessie ". When she was fourteen her confessor, Father Conrad Kügelin, a canon regular, who directed her all her life and wrote an account of her soon after her death, recommended her to become a Franciscan tertiary ; this she did, and went to lodge with a woman weaver to learn her trade.   Elizabeth remained there three years and was then put by Father Conrad with four other tertiaries, for whom she did the cooking.   She seems to have been more expert at this than at the loom. This little community was at Reute, near Waldsee, and there Elizabeth lived for the rest of her life.   She was one of the last of the medieval women mystics, mostly connected with one or other of the mendicant orders, who were remarkable for their extreme austerities, visions and visitations, and abnormal physical phenomena : Bd Christina of Stommeln, mentioned on the 6th of this month, is a better known example.

Elizabeth the Good is notable for the frequent supposedly diabolical manifestations of which she was the object and for the reputed length of time during which she would abstain completely from food.   Once she is said to have done this for three years on end, and to have then broken her fast only at the command of the Devil disguised as her confessor.   Later, many things were missing from the house, which were at last found under Elizabeth's bed.   She had not put them there and believed that the Devil had ; but she patiently accepted the severe rebuke and penance imposed on her and the natural distrust of her sisters.   At other times she sustained supernatural physical attacks and other bodily ills, but she was also said to be granted visions of Heaven and Purgatory, frequent ecstasies, and on one occasion a miraculous communion.   She received the *stigmata* of the Passion from time to time, including marks resembling those of the crown of thorns and of the scourging ; these bled copiously on Fridays and in Lent, and the pain was almost unceasing.   For years and years Bd Elizabeth lived on an amount of food far short of the minimum normally required to keep a human being alive, and eventually died attended by the faithful priest, Father Conrad Kügelin, who had been the witness of her extraordinary life.   Her *cultus* was approved in 1766, and her shrine at Reute is still a place of resort.

We are well informed regarding Bd Elizabeth, for Conrad Kügelin, her confessor, wrote a life of her in German, the original of which is still preserved.   The text was reprinted in the periodical *Alemannia* for 1881 and 1882, from a scarce early edition which had appeared in 1624.   Another life is that of Nidermayer, *Die selige gute Betha von Reute* (1766).   See also Lechner, *Leben der sel. Elisabetha Bona von Reuthe* (1854) ; and A. Baier, *Die sel. gute Betha von Reute* (1920).

BB. ROQUE GONZALEZ AND HIS COMPANIONS, THE MARTYRS OF PARAGUAY   (A.D. 1628)

THE earliest martyrs of the Americas who have been raised to the altars of the Church suffered in 1628.   They were not of course the first martyrs of the New World : three Franciscans were killed by Caribs in the Antilles in 1516 ; massacres on the mainland of South America soon followed ; and in 1544 Friar Juan de Padilla was slain, the first martyr of North America.   Where he suffered is not certain—eastern Colorado, western Kansas, Texas have all been suggested.   But these and others have not been beatified, for lack of sufficient certain evidence about the circumstances of their death : such evidence may turn up one day. Meanwhile the earliest beatified martyrs of America are three Jesuits of Paraguay, and one of them was American-born.

Roque Gonzalez y de Santa-Cruz was the son of noble Spanish parents, and he came into this world at Asunción, the capital of Paraguay, in 1576.   He was an unusually good and religious boy, and everybody took it for granted that young Roque would become a priest.   He was in fact ordained, when he was twenty-three : but unwillingly, for he felt very strongly that he was unworthy of priesthood. At once he began to take an interest in the Indians of Paraguay, seeking them out in remote places to preach to and instruct them in Christianity ; and after ten years, to avoid ecclesiastical promotion and to get more opportunity for missionary work, he joined the Society of Jesus.

These were the days of the beginnings of the famous " reductions " of Paraguay, in the formation of which Father Roque Gonzalez played an important part. These remarkable institutions were settlements of Christian Indians run by the Jesuit missionaries, who looked on themselves, not like so many other Spaniards did as the conquerors and " bosses " of the Indians, but as the guardians and trustees of their welfare.   To the Jesuits the Indians were not a subject or " lower " people, but simple untutored children of God ; they had no contempt for their civilization and life, in so far as these were not at variance with the gospel of Christ ; the missionaries sought to make them Christian Indians and not imitation Spaniards. The Jesuits' opposition to Spanish imperialism, to slavery by the colonists, and to the methods of the Inquisition eventually brought about their own downfall in Spanish America and the dissolution of the reductions, over a century after Father Roque's death.   Even the scoffing Voltaire had been impressed, and he wrote that, " When the Paraguayan missions left the hands of the Jesuits in 1768 they had arrived at what is perhaps the highest degree of civilization to which it is possible to lead a young people. . . . In those missions law was respected, morals were pure, a happy brotherliness bound men together, the useful arts and even some of the more graceful sciences flourished, and there was abundance everywhere."

It was to bring about such a happy state of things that Father Roque laboured for nearly twenty years, grappling patiently and without discouragement with hardships, dangers and reverses of all kinds, with intractable and fierce tribes and with the open opposition of the European colonists.   He threw himself heart and soul into the work. For three years he was in charge of the Reduction of St Ignatius, the first of them, and then spent the rest of his life establishing other reductions, half-a-dozen in all, east of the Paraná and Uruguay rivers ; he was the first European known to have penetrated into some districts of South America. A contemporary Spaniard, the governor of Corrientes, testified from his knowledge of the country that " he was able to appreciate how much the life which Father Roque led must have cost him—hunger, cold, exhaustion from travelling on foot, swimming across rivers, wading through bogs, not to mention plaguing insects and the discomforts which no man but a true apostle, who was holy as this priest was, could have borne with such fortitude ". Father Roque attained an extraordinary influence among the Indians, but his work was hampered in his last years by the attempt of the civil authorities to use this influence for their own ends. They insisted on having their representatives at the new reductions ; and the brutality of these Europeans aroused in the Indians bitter resentment and suspicion of all Europeans. It is a situation that in one form or another is only too common in missionary history—the work of devoted missionaries being undone by the behaviour of less worthy Christians.

In 1628 Father Roque was joined by two young Spanish Jesuits, Alonso (Alphonsus) Rodriguez and Juan (John) de Castillo, and together they founded a new reduction near the Ijuhi river, dedicated in honour of our Lady's Assumption. Father Castillo was left in charge there, while the other two pushed on to Caaró (in the southern tip of what is now Brazil), where they established the All Saints' reduction.

Here they were faced with the hostility of a powerful " medicine-man ", and at his instigation the mission was soon attacked. Father Roque was getting ready to hang a small church-bell, when the raiding party arrived : one man stole up from behind and killed him with blows on the head from a tomahawk. Father Rodriguez heard the noise and, coming to the door of his hut to see what it was about, met the blood-stained savages, who knocked him down. " What are you doing, my sons ? " he exclaimed. But he was silenced by further blows. The wooden chapel was set on fire, and the two bodies thrown into the flames. It was November 15, 1628. Two days later the mission at Ijuhi was attacked : Father Castillo was seized and bound, barbarously beaten, and stoned to death.

The first steps towards the beatification of these missionaries were taken within six months of their martyrdom, by the writing down of evidence about what had happened. But these precious documents were lost, apparently on their way to Rome, and for two hundred years no progress could be made : it seemed that their cause must fail. Then copies of the originals turned up in the Argentine, and in 1934, Roque Gonzalez, Alonso Rodriguez and Juan de Castillo were solemnly declared blessed. Among these ancient documents was the evidence of an Indian chief, Guarecupi, that " all the Christians among my countrymen loved the Father [Roque] and grieved for his death, because he was the father of us all, and so he was called by all the Indians of the Paraná ".

Nearly all the available evidence has been brought together in the book of Fr J. M. Blanco, _Historia documentada de la Vida y gloriosa Muerte de los PP. Roque Gonzalez . . ._ (1929). See also Fr H. Thurston's article in _The Catholic Historical Review_, vol. xx (Baltimore, 1935), pp. 371–383. R. B. Cunninghame Graham wrote a very readable account of the Reductions of Paraguay, _A Vanished Arcadia_ (1924).

BD PHILIPPINE DUCHESNE, Virgin   (A.D. 1852)

UNDER May 25 herein there is printed an account of St Madeleine Sophie Barat and the foundation of the Society of the Sacred Heart.   In the course of it there are references to a certain Mother Duchesne, who introduced the newly-established congregation to North America ; and this Mother Duchesne was beatified in 1940.   She was born in 1769, at Grenoble in Dauphiny, her father being the head of a prosperous mercantile family.   At her christening she was given the names Rose Philippine, of which the first was a veritable augury, for St Rose of Lima, on the eve of whose feast she was born, was the first canonized saint of the New World.   There was nothing specially remarkable about her childhood : she had a strong and rather imperious nature (characteristic of her father's family), she was of a serious disposition, and she early showed interest in history.   At the age of eight her first enthusiasm for missionary life and the American land was kindled by a Jesuit who had worked in Louisiana and told the Duchesnes stories about the Indians.   Philippine went to school with the Visitation nuns of Sainte-Marie-d'En-haut and also was taught by a tutor with her cousins the Périers, and she became uncommonly well-educated.   Then when she was seventeen, and her parents were looking around for a husband for her, she announced her intention of being a nun ; and after some opposition she was allowed to join the community with which she had been at school.   Eighteen months later, however, her father forbade her profession—and for a sound reason : he did not like the outlook for the future in France.   And sure enough, in 1791, the Visitandines of Grenoble were expelled, and Philippine returned to her family, who were now living in the country.

Throughout the years of revolution Philippine did her best to live in a way in all respects befitting a religious.   She looked after her family, she tended the sick and confessors of the faith and others in prison, and above all was concerned for the education of children.   And then, when the Holy See concluded its concordat with Napoleon in 1801, she was enabled to acquire the buildings of her old convent of Sainte-Marie-d'En-haut.   Philippine had always hoped to be instrumental in re-establishing the Visitandine community of which she had been a member, but now she found the undertaking even more difficult than she had expected : indeed, it proved to be impossible.   On a day in August, 1802—it was in fact the 21st, the feast day of the foundress of the Visitation nuns, St Jane Frances de Chantal—it was decided to abandon the venture ; and a few days later Philippine and another sister were left alone in the convent.   Unkind outsiders were not slow to say that it was another example of the " stiffness " of the Duchesne character, that Sister Philippine made things difficult in community life.   Philippine decided to offer Sainte-Marie-d'En-haut to Mother Barat, who not long before had begun the first house of the Society of the Sacred Heart, at Amiens.   The proposal was agreed, and on December 31, 1804, Philippine and four others were admitted as postulants at Sainte-Marie.   Thus were brought together, as novice-mistress and as novice, these two souls, " one of marble, the other of bronze ", St Madeleine Sophie Barat and Bd Philippine Duchesne.   Less than a year later the novice was professed.   The months of preparation had seen a growing-together of foundress and aspirant, a better understanding of discipline on the part of the young nun who had been so much " on her own "—perhaps her hardest struggle was to give up personal mortifications and penances at the word of her mother in religion.

Early in 1806 Sainte-Marie-d'En-haut was visited by the abbot of La Trappe, Dom Augustine de Lestrange, who three years before had sent the first Cistercian monks to North America ; and this visit served to inflame Bd Philippine's desire to be a missionary in that land.   Nowadays we do not think of the United States as mission territory ; but a hundred and forty years ago far the greater part of that huge country was still unsettled by Europeans, or indeed by anybody ; the frontier was only gradually moving west, and the Indians were still a notable proportion of the population.   But though Mother Barat approved in principle, it was still to be another twelve years before Mother Duchesne achieved her ambition, years during which the instrument was to be prepared and tempered, both spiritually and in the handling of affairs.   At last the appointed time came.   Mgr Dubourg, Bishop of Louisiana, called on Mother Barat and asked her to let him have some of her religious as soon as they could be spared from France.   She promised to do so, but would perhaps have put the enterprise off indefinitely had it not been for the direct and impetuous intervention of Mother Duchesne.   And so, in March 1818, five religious of the Sacred Heart left Bordeaux for the New World.   Mother Duchesne, to her great regret, had been appointed their superioress.

After a trying voyage (" Seasickness is really evil ", wrote Bd Philippine, " It affects the head as well as the stomach, and makes one useless for anything ") the little party landed at New Orleans on May 29, the feast of the Sacred Heart.   They went up the Mississippi to Saint Louis, then a town of about 6,000 inhabitants, in what is now Missouri.   Here they were welcomed by Mgr Dubourg, who found them a house for their first establishment at Saint Charles : it was a small log cabin.   And here, among the children of the poor, was started the first free school west of the Mississippi.   The white population was in majority Catholic, and composed of French, Creole, English and others, many of them bi-lingual ; the nuns had been studying English ever since they were assigned to America, but Bd Philippine never really mastered the language.   Two passing remarks of hers throw light on the sort of people they had to work among : " Some of our pupils have more gowns than chemises or, above all, pocket-handkerchiefs ", and " At Portage-des-Sioux the walls [of the church] were adorned with representations of Bacchus and Venus.   . . . put up out of sheer ignorance ".   As for the Indians, " We used to entertain the pleasing thought of teaching docile and innocent savages, but the women are idle and given to drink as much as the men ".   After a hard winter the bishop decided to move the community to Florissant, nearer Saint Louis.   A three-storied brick building was provided, and into this the nuns moved on the two days before Christmas, 1819 ; Mother Duchesne wrote a vivid account of the bitterly cold rigours of the move, complicated by a cow that ran away.   The more commodious residence raised the possibility of starting a novitiate, about which Mgr Dubourg was not too sanguine in view of the independent American character.   But the ground was broken when a postulant presented herself to be a lay-sister, and the first American to receive the habit of the Society of the Sacred Heart was clothed on November 22, 1820 : her name was Mary Layton.

The opening of the novitiate and the progress of the school were more encouraging signs for the future, and Bd Philippine herself was getting to understand better the strange people of a strange land.   It must be remembered that she was in her fiftieth year when she crossed the Atlantic—and she was very much of a Frenchwoman.   The Americans baffled her both in their faults and their virtues, and it has been well said that " she probably never attained, in its perfection, ' tact in dealing with those whose customs are not European ' ". In any case she underwent some of that " mellowing " that increasing age so often brings, but without losing the old enthusiasm : she could write to Mother Barat in 1821, " I thought I had reached the height of my ambition—but I am burning with desire to go to Peru. However, I am more reasonable than I was in France when I used to pester you with my vain aspirations." In the same year the second house was opened, at Grand Côteau, about one hundred and fifty miles from New Orleans. Mother Duchesne's visit to this new foundation involved probably the worst journey she ever undertook : it took four weeks out and nine weeks in, and the return trip was partly made on a boat on which yellow fever broke out—a horrible experience of the neglected sick and of the callous fear of the rest. She devoted herself to the care of one stricken man, whom she baptized before he died ; and it nearly cost her own life, for she too sickened and had to be put ashore at Natchez, where she could find no shelter but the bed of a woman who had herself just died of the fever.

Back at Florissant, Bd Philippine found it was a case of one grim trial after another. Temporal difficulties and the jealousy and slanders of outsiders were ruining the school—" They say everything about us, except that we poison the children ", she wrote to Mother Barat. At length there were only five pupils left ; but when things were looking their worst improvement came through help from a new quarter. The difficulties had been partly caused by the withdrawal of Mgr Dubourg to Lower Louisiana ; but in 1823 he was able to arrange for the establishment at Florissant of the novitiate of the Jesuits in Maryland. It is difficult to tell whether in the ensuing period the Society of the Sacred Heart owed more to the Society of Jesus or the fathers to the nuns. In 1826 and the following year two more houses were opened, St Michael's near New Orleans and in Saint Louis itself ; and the house at Saint Charles was refounded in 1828. With Bayou-la-Fourche there were now six houses of the society in the valley of the Mississippi. The next ten years continued to be full of trials and hardships, disappointment and ill-health, borne by Bd Philippine with trust in God but with ever-mounting fatigue. However, it was not till 1840 that her wish to resign her responsible office was granted, and then not by St Madeleine Sophie. The assistant general of the Society of the Sacred Heart came on a visitation of the American houses. She was Mother Elizabeth Galitsin, a woman of strong and imperious character, not unlike Mother Duchesne in her earlier years, and she caused a certain amount of upheaval among the nuns in America. Bd Philippine did not resist the autocratic methods of the visitor (who was twenty-eight years younger than herself) ; but she was made to fear that perhaps she had failed in the trust assigned to her, and she asked to be allowed to resign. Mother Galitsin agreed without demur, and Mother Duchesne returned to the Saint Louis house as a simple religious.

And now, when she was seventy-one years old, she was able to turn her attention to those people for whose sake she had originally wanted to come to America—the Indians. The famous Jesuit Father De Smet had asked Mother Galitsin to send nuns to set up a school in the mission among the Potawatomi at Sugar Creek in Kansas. Four religious were nominated to go, including Mother Duchesne " if able to travel ". She was able to travel. But she was with her beloved Indians for only about twelve months : she could not master their language, the hardships of the life were too much for her failing strength. Her heart spoke of Indians among the Rocky mountains to be converted to Christ ; but her superiors spoke of the need for her to come away. " God knows the reason for this recall," she said, " and that is enough."

Bd Philippine's last years were spent at Saint Charles, but the tide of her life went out on no gentle ebb. The fortunes of the Society of the Sacred Heart in America did not rise in one unwavering curve of progress ; houses that Mother Duchesne had founded and nursed were threatened with dissolution ; and for nearly two years correspondence between herself and her deeply loved Mother Barat was not delivered—a mystery never properly cleared up. So, during a prolonged old age of suffering and prayer, Mother Duchesne completed her life of apostleship and self-sacrifice. She died on November 18, 1852. She was eighty-three years old. It was said of her by a contemporary : " She was the St Francis of Assisi of the Society. Everything in and about her was stamped with the seal of a crucified life. She would have liked to disappear from the sight of men, and it may indeed be said that no one occupied less space in the world than Madame Duchesne. Her room was a miserable hole with a single window, in which paper supplied the place of some of the panes ; her bed was a mattress two inches thick, laid on the ground by night and put away in the day in a cupboard ; her only covering at night was an old piece of black stuff with a cross like a pall." While she lay dead a daguerreotype was taken of Philippine Duchesne, " in case ", as was said, " she may one day be canonized ". Less than a century later that day is within sight. This missionary of the American frontier was beatified in 1940, and her feast is kept on November 17.

On the death of Mother Duchesne, Father De Smet wrote, " You should publish a beautiful biography. . . . No greater saint ever died in Missouri, or perhaps in the whole Union." This was first most adequately done by Mgr Baunard, whose *Life of Mother Duchesne* was translated into English in 1879. Then in 1926 appeared *Mother Philippine Duchesne* by Marjory Erskine. This is a full-length work that depends of necessity largely on Baunard, but corrected in certain points and with fresh matter added. See also *The Society of the Sacred Heart in North America*, by Louise Callan (1937), and *Redskin Trail*, by M. K. Richardson (1952).

18 : THE DEDICATION OF THE BASILICAS OF ST PETER AND OF ST PAUL

AS the commemorative feast of the dedication of the archbasilica of the Lateran is kept by the whole Western church, so also is that of the other greater patriarchal basilicas at Rome, St Mary Major on August 5, and St Peter's and St Paul's together on this day. Amongst all the places which the blood of martyrs has rendered illustrious, that part of the Vatican Hill which was consecrated with the blood and enriched with the relics of the Prince of the Apostles has always been the most venerable. " The sepulchres of those who have served Christ crucified ", says St John Chrysostom, " surpass the palaces of kings ; not so much in the greatness and beauty of the buildings (though in this also they go beyond them) as in other things of more importance, such as the multitude of those who with devotion and joy repair to them. For the emperor himself, clothed in purple, goes to the tombs of the saints and kisses them ; humbly prostrate on the ground he beseeches the same saints to pray to God for him ; and he who wears a royal crown looks on it as a great privilege from God that a tentmaker and a fisherman, and these dead, should be his protectors and defenders, and for this he begs with great earnestness." The martyrdom of St Peter took place according to tradition at the circus of Caligula in Nero's gardens on the Vatican Hill, and he was buried nearby. It is held by some that in the year 258, to avoid desecration during the persecution of Valerian, the relics of St Peter, together with those of St Paul, were translated for a time to the obscure catacomb now called St Sebastian's; but they came back to their original resting-place, and in 323 the Emperor Constantine began the building of the basilica of St Peter over the tomb of the Apostle. For nearly twelve hundred years this magnificent church remained substantially the same, a great papal establishment gradually growing up between it and the Vatican Hill. This was made the permanent residence of the popes on their return from the exile at Avignon, and by the middle of the fifteenth century the old church was found to be inadequate. In 1506 Pope Julius II inaugurated a new building, designed by Bramante, whose erection was carried on over a period of a hundred and twenty years, undergoing many alterations, additions and modifications at the hands of various popes and architects, especially Paul V and Michelangelo. The new basilica of St Peter, as we see it today, was consecrated by Pope Urban VIII on November 18, 1626, the day of its original dedication. The high altar was set up over the Apostle's resting-place, which until 1942 had been inaccessible for many centuries. Though St Peter's must always yield in dignity to the cathedral of St John Lateran, it has nevertheless for long been the most important church of the world, both in fact and in the hearts of Catholic Christians.

The martyrdom of St Paul took place some seven miles from that of St Peter at Aquae Salviae (now called Tre Fontane) on the Ostian Way. He was buried about two miles therefrom, on the property of a lady named Lucina, in a small vault. Early in the third century, according to Eusebius (*Hist. eccl.*, ii, 25, 7), a Roman priest, Caius, refers to the tombs of SS. Peter and Paul: " I can show you the trophies [tombs] of the apostles. If you go to the Vatican or on the road to Ostia you will see the trophies of those who founded this church." Constantine is said to have begun a basilica here too, but the great church of St Paul-outside-the-Walls was principally the work of the Emperor Theodosius'I and Pope St Leo the Great. It remained in its primitive beauty and simplicity till the year 1823, when it was consumed by fire. The whole world contributed to its restoration, non-Christians as well as non-Catholics sending gifts and contributions. During the course of the work the fourth-century tomb was found, with the inscription PAULO APOST MART: To Paul, apostle and martyr; it was not opened. The new basilica, on the lines of the old one, was consecrated by Pope Pius IX on December 10, 1854, but the annual commemoration was appointed for this day, as the Roman Martyrology records.

" We do not ", says St Augustine, " build churches or appoint priesthoods, sacred rites and sacrifices *to* the martyrs, because, not the martyrs, but the God of the martyrs, is our God. Who among the faithful ever heard a priest, standing at the altar set up over the body of a martyr to the honour and worship of God, say in praying: We offer up sacrifices to thee, Peter, or Paul, or Cyprian? . . . We do not build churches to martyrs as to gods, but as memorials to men departed this life, whose souls live with God. Nor do we make altars to sacrifice on them to the martyrs, but to their God and our God."

The reader may be referred to Cardinal Schuster, *The Sacramentary* (Eng. trans.), vol. v, pp. 280-287; to O. Marucchi, *Basiliques et églises de Rome* (1902), and Ch. Hülsen,

Le chiese di Roma (1927).   The martyrdom and burial-places of SS. Peter and Paul have already been touched upon, with further references, herein under June 29 ; and *cf.* the first entry under November 9.

ST ROMANUS OF ANTIOCH, MARTYR   (A.D. 304)

THE passion of Romanus, a deacon of the church of Caesarea, is related by Eusebius in his account of the martyrs of Palestine because, though he suffered at Antioch, he was a native of Palestine.   We have also a panegyric of St John Chrysostom on this saint, and a poem in his honour by Prudentius.   When the persecution of Diocletian broke out he went about exhorting the faithful to stand firm ; and at Antioch, in the very court of the judge, observing certain Christian prisoners about to sacrifice through fear, he cried out in rebuke and warning.   At once hands were laid on him and, after he had been scourged, the judge condemned him to be burnt alive.   The fire was put out by a heavy rainstorm, and the emperor, who was in the city, ordered the martyr's tongue to be plucked out by the roots.   This was done, yet Romanus still spoke, urging his hearers to love and worship the true and only God.   The emperor had him sent back to prison, his legs to be stretched in the stocks to the fifth hole and his body raised off the ground.   He suffered this torture a long time, and finished his martyrdom by being strangled in prison. Prudentius (who begs that, as he stood amongst the goats, he might by the prayers of Romanus pass to the right hand and be placed amongst the sheep) mentions an unnamed boy of seven who, encouraged by St Romanus, confessed one God, and was scourged and beheaded.   Under the name of Barula he is mentioned with St Romanus in the Roman Martyrology, but Eusebius says nothing about him.

In CMH. (pp. 605–606) Delehaye points out that besides the account in Eusebius, the panegyric of St John Chrysostom and the poem of Prudentius, we have a very reliable testimony to the cult of St Romanus in the mention made of him in the Syriac *breviarium* of the early fifth century.   Furthermore, Severus, Patriarch of Antioch, at the beginning of the sixth century was consecrated in a church dedicated to him and preached several sermons in his honour.   Prudentius seems to have been the first to mention the boy companion.   The tangle is too complicated to discuss here, but Delehaye shows that Barula almost certainly represents an authentic Syrian martyr, Baralaha or Barlaam, whose name by some juxtaposition in the ancient lists became attached to that of Romanus.   See also the *Analecta Bollandiana*, vol. xxii (1903), pp. 129–145 ; vol. xxxviii (1920), pp. 241–284 ; and especially vol. l (1932), pp. 241–283.   In this last article Delehaye lays stress upon the important part played in this development by the " Homilia de Resurrectione ", which A. Wilmart proved to be the work of Eusebius of Emesa (d. 359).

ST MAWES, OR MAUDEZ, ABBOT   (SIXTH CENTURY ?)

IF we may judge from the number of churches dedicated in his honour St Maudez (Maudetus) was the most popular of the saints of Brittany after St Ivo, but very little is known about him.   Although his name is British, he is said to have been an Irishman who went to Brittany in the days of Childebert I.   With a few disciples he settled off the coast of Léon, on an island, Île Modez, which he cleared of snakes and vermin by firing the grass : earth from this island is still supposed to be useful for the same and similar purposes.   Both in Cornwall and Brittany St Maudez was traditionally regarded as a monk who spent much time teaching his pupils in the open air.   Except for this, recorded by Leland, there are no other traditions whatever of St Maudez in Cornwall, or any indication of how the village chapel and well of St Mawes in Roseland came to bear his name.   No doubt he was a zealous missionary throughout Armorica as the number of his dedications suggests ; and there is topographical evidence that he and St Budoc were monks and missionaries from Wales, or elsewhere in Britain, who founded churches and monasteries in Cornwall and Brittany and were in some way connected with Dol.

There are two medieval lives of this saint, both of which have been printed by A. de la Borderie in his volume *Saint Maudez* (1891). From a historical point of view they are of little value. Canon Doble has included St Mawes in his series of monographs on Cornish saints (1938), and this is probably the most thorough investigation which has been attempted. See, however, F. Duine, *Memento* (1918), pp. 97–99 ; L. Gougaud, *Les saints irlandais hors d'Irlande* (1936), pp. 135–139 ; and LBS., vol. iii, pp. 441–449. Dom Gougaud, in the book just mentioned, tells us something of the popular devotion to St Maudez in Brittany and the folklore practices associated with it.

ST ODO OF CLUNY, ABBOT   (A.D. 942)

FROM the middle of the tenth century until the beginning of the twelfth the abbey of Cluny in Burgundy was the most powerful influence in the monasticism of western Europe and played a part in religious affairs second only to that of the papacy itself ; as the centre and directing authority of a vast monastic " reform " it affected the life and spirit of the monks of St Benedict for a far longer period, and its influence can be traced even till today. Cluny owed its driving-power and achievements principally to seven of its eight first abbots, of whom St Odo was the second. He was brought up in the family of Fulk II, Count of Anjou, and afterwards in that of William, Duke of Aquitaine, who founded the abbey of Cluny. At nineteen Odo received the tonsure, and was instituted to a canonry in St Martin's church at Tours, and he spent some years studying in Paris. Here he gave much time to music, an enthusiasm which was shared by his master, Remigius of Auxerre. One day, in reading the Rule of St Benedict, Odo was shocked to see how much his life fell short of the rules of perfection there laid down, and he determined to embrace the monastic state. He some time after went to the monastery of Baume-les-Messieurs in the diocese of Besançon, where the abbot, Berno, admitted him to the habit in 909.

The abbey of Cluny was founded in the following year by Duke William, and was committed to the care of St Berno, who put St Odo in charge of the monastery school at Baume. It is recorded that on one occasion while Odo was on a journey the daughter of his host for the night appealed to him secretly to help her : she was going shortly to be married, against her will. He could not resist her tears and entreaties, and enabled the girl to escape from her home, taking her with him to Baume. Not unnaturally, the abbot was indignant at his subject's rashness, and ordered Odo to look carefully after the girl and make proper provision for her safety. Accordingly, after taking her meals to her daily and instructing her in the religious life, he found a place for her in a convent of nuns. With age came more prudence and, when he was about forty-eight, St Odo was appointed to succeed St Berno as abbot of Cluny.

Berno had already undertaken the reformation of a number of monasteries from Cluny, and under Odo the number grew apace, among them being the famous house of Fleury on the Loire, which was destined to have a considerable influence in England. Of Odo's school at Cluny it was said that, " A boy is brought up as well there as a prince in his father's castle ". But it was no life of ease. A monk had once complained to St Odo that St Berno ruled Baume with a rod of iron, but a hard and rigid discipline was required to keep order among the vigorous spirits of the tenth century, and Cluny was no exception.   Odo also ruled with a rod of iron, and would intimidate refractory monks with stories yet more terrific than his own discipline.   But not always.   In exhorting them to deeds of charity he told one day of a young student who, while entering the church for Matins early one cold winter's morning, saw a half-naked beggar, freezing under the porch.   The student took off his cloak and wrapped it round him, and went into the cold church for the long office.   After Lauds he lay down on his bed to get warm, and as he rolled the blankets round himself found a gold piece, more than sufficient to buy a new cloak.   " I did not then know the name of the hero of this incident ", says the biographer, " but I have found it out since."   It was, of course, Odo himself who at Tours had learned the spirit of St Martin.

In 936 St Odo made his first visit to Rome, called thither by Pope Leo VII. The city was being besieged by Hugh of Provence, who called himself king of Italy and who had considerable respect for St Odo, and it was to try to conclude a peace between him and Alberic, " Patrician of the Romans ", that Odo had been summoned.   His first, temporary success was the negotiation of a marriage between Alberic and Hugh's daughter.   At the abbey of St Paul-outside-the-Walls he " regulated the spiritual life of the monastery in an apostolical way and by his words kindled faith, piety and love of truth in all hearts."   The spirit of Cluny had been carried beyond the borders of France, and the influence of St Odo was felt in the monasteries of Monte Cassino, Pavia, Naples, Salerno and elsewhere in Italy.   Once an attempt was made on his life, a peasant, who said the monks of St Paul's owed him some money, attempting to brain him with a stone.   Odo paid the man and thought no more about it, till he heard that Alberic had sentenced him to lose his right hand for his intended crime.   Thereupon the saint went to the prince and got the sentence annulled, and the man set free.   Twice more within six years Odo had to go to Rome to try and keep the peace between Hugh and Alberic for the distracted pope, and on each occasion he extended the sphere of his reforming zeal.   Meanwhile in France the work went on, secular nobles handing over to him monasteries over which they had exercised an uncanonical control and superiors inviting him to visit their abbeys and prescribe for their communities.   As usual there were plenty of monks who resented being jolted out of their easy-going ways, and put every obstacle in the way of the reformer.   At one house it was made a grievance against the Cluny monks that they washed their underclothes after Vespers on Saturday.   When they made no reply but went on with their washing, the critic exclaimed, " I was not made a snake to hiss or an ox to low, but a man with a human voice.   Is this how you come to teach us the Rule of St Benedict ? " and departed in indignation to complain to the abbot.   At Fleury St Odo was received at first with swords and stones, some monks even threatening his life if he entered the monastery.   He talked gently to them, gave them three days to cool down, and then rode up to the entrance on his donkey as if nothing had happened.   " They received him like a father and his escort had nothing to do but to go away."

In the year 942 St Odo went to Rome for the last time, and on his return called at the monastery of St Julian at Tours.   After assisting at the solemnities of the feast of his patron, St Martin, he took to his bed, and died on November 18.   One of his last actions was to compose a hymn, still extant, in honour of St Martin. In spite of his full and very active life St Odo found time to write, as well as another hymn and twelve metrical antiphons for St Martin, three books of moral essays, a Life of St Gerald of Aurillac, and a long epic poem on the Redemption.   There is also a tradition, mentioned by all his biographers, that he wrote several works on ecclesiastical music ; but they have not come down to us, though some falsely bear his name.

John, a monk of Cluny, and another monk named Nalgodus both wrote lives of Abbot Odo.   These are printed in Mabillon, vol. v, and in Migne, PL., vol. cxxxiii.   E. Sackur in *Neues Archiv*, vol. xv, pp. 105–112, has called attention to another recension of the life by John, but it is later in date.   There is a good modern biography by O. Ringholz (1885), and an attractive, but rather inaccurate, account, *Saint Odon*, by Dom du Bourg in the series " Les Saints ".   See also Sackur, *Die Cluniacenser*, vol. i, pp. 36–120 ; A. Hessel in the *Historische Zeitschrift*, vol. 128 (1923), pp. 1–25 ; and for the relations of Cluny with England, L. M. Smith, *The Early History of the Movement of Cluny* (1925) and D. Knowles, *The Monastic Order in England* (1949), cap. viii ; Watkin Williams, *Monastic Studies* (1938), pp. 24–36.

19 : ST ELIZABETH OF HUNGARY, WIDOW   (A.D. 1231)

IT is related by Dietrich of Apolda in his life of this saint* that on an evening in the summer of the year 1207 the minnesinger Klingsohr from Transylvania announced to the Landgrave Herman of Thuringia that that night a daughter had been born to the king of Hungary, who should be exalted in holiness and become the wife of Herman's son ; and that in fact at that time the child Elizabeth was born, in Pressburg (Bratislava) or Saros-Patak, to Andrew II of Hungary and his wife, Gertrude of Andechs-Meran.   Such an alliance as that " foretold " by Klingsohr had substantial political advantages to recommend it, and the baby Elizabeth was promised to Herman's eldest son.   At about four years of age she was brought to the Thuringian court at the castle of the Wartburg, near Eisenach, there to be brought up with her future husband.   As she grew up she underwent much unkindness from some members of the court, who did not appreciate her goodness, but on the other hand the young man Louis (Ludwig) became more and more enamoured of her.   We are told that when he had visited a city he would always bring back a present for her, a knife or a bag or gloves or a coral rosary. " When it was time for him to be back she would run out to meet him and he would take her lovingly on his arm and give her what he had brought."   In 1221, Louis being now twenty-one and landgrave in his father's place, and Elizabeth fourteen, their marriage was solemnized, in spite of attempts to persuade him to send her back to Hungary as an unsuitable bride ; he declared he would rather cast away a mountain of gold than give her up.   She, we are told, was " perfect in body, handsome, of a dark complexion ; serious in her ways, and modest, of kindly speech, fervent in prayer and most generous to the poor, always full of goodness and divine love " ; he also was handsome and " modest as a young maid ", wise, patient and truthful, trusted by his men and loved by his people.   Their wedded life lasted only six years and has been called by an English writer " an idyll of

* Alban Butler's own comment, under the 16th of this month, on the *De contemptu mundi* of St Eucherius of Lyons, " in this piece certain superfluities might have been spared and the full sense more closely expressed with equal strength and perspicuity in fewer words ", is true also of his account of St Elizabeth of Hungary in an even greater degree than usual in his lives.   His long notice of her has therefore been almost entirely discarded.

enthralling fondness, of mystic ardour, of almost childish happiness, the like of which I do not remember in all I have read of romance or of human experience ". They had three children, Herman, who was born in 1222 and died when he was nineteen, Sophia, who became duchess of Brabant, and Bd Gertrude of Aldenburg. Louis, unlike some husbands of saints, put no obstacles in the way of his wife's charity, her simple and mortified life, and her long prayers. " My lady ", says one of her ladies-in-waiting, " would get up at night to pray, and my lord would implore her to spare herself and come back to rest, all the while holding her hand in his for fear she should come to some harm. She would tell her maids to wake her gently when he was asleep—and sometimes when they thought him sleeping he was only pretending." *

Elizabeth's material benefactions were so great that they sometimes provoked adverse criticism. In 1225 that part of Germany was severely visited by a famine and she exhausted her own treasury and distributed her whole store of corn amongst those who felt the calamity heaviest. The landgrave was then away, and at his return the officers of his household complained to him of her profusion to the poor. But Louis, without examining into the matter, asked if she had alienated any of his dominions. They answered, " No ". " As for her charities ", said he, " they will bring upon us the divine blessings. We shall not want so long as we let her relieve the poor as she does." The castle of the Wartburg was built on a steep rock, which the infirm and weak were not able to climb (the path was called " the knee-smasher "). St Elizabeth therefore built a hospital at the foot of the rock for their reception, where she often fed them with her own hands, made their beds, and attended them even in the heat of summer when the place seemed insupportable. Helpless children, especially orphans, were provided for at her expense. She was the foundress of another hospital in which twenty-eight persons were constantly relieved, and she fed nine hundred daily at her gate, besides numbers in different parts of the dominions, so that the revenue in her hands was truly the patrimony of the distressed. But Elizabeth's charity was tempered with discretion ; and instead of encouraging in idleness such as were able to work, she employed them in ways suitable to their strength and ability. There is a story about St Elizabeth so well known that it would hardly need repeating here but that Father Delehaye picks it out as an example of the way in which hagiographers so often embellish a tale to make a greater impression on their readers.

> Everyone is familiar with the beautiful incident in the life of St Elizabeth of Hungary when, in the very bed she shared with her husband, she laid a miserable leper. . . . The indignant landgrave rushed into the room and dragged off the bedclothes. " But ", in the noble words of the historian, " at that instant Almighty God opened the eyes of his soul, and instead of a leper he saw the figure of Christ crucified stretched upon the bed." This admirable account by Dietrich of Apolda was considered too simple by later biographers, who consequently transformed the sublime vision of faith into a material apparition. *Tunc aperuit Deus interiores principis oculos*, wrote the historian.

* " She had ordained that one of her women, which was more familiar with her than another, that if peradventure she were overtaken with sleep, that she should take her by the foot for to awake her ; and on a time she supposed to have taken her lady by the foot and took her husband's foot, which suddenly awoke and would know wherefore she did so ; and then she told him all the case, and when he knew it he let it pass and suffered it peaceably " (*Golden Legend*).

On the spot where the leper had slept, say the modern hagiographers, " there lay a bleeding crucifix with out-stretched arms " (*The Legends of the Saints*, p. 90).

At this time strenuous efforts were being made to launch another crusade, and Louis of Thuringia took the cross.   On St John the Baptist's day he parted from St Elizabeth and went to join the Emperor Frederick II in Apulia ; on September 11 following he was dead of the plague at Otranto.   The news did not reach Germany until October, just after the birth of Elizabeth's second daughter.   Her mother-in-law broke the news to her, speaking of " what had befallen " her husband, and the " dispensation of God ".   Elizabeth misunderstood.   " Since he is a prisoner ", she said, " with the help of God and our friends he shall be set free."   When she was told he was not a prisoner but dead, she cried, " The world is dead to me, and all that was joyous in the world ", and ran to and fro about the castle shrieking like one crazed.

What happened next is a matter of some uncertainty.   According to the testimony of one of her ladies-in-waiting, Isentrude, St Elizabeth's brother-in-law, Henry, who was regent for her infant son, drove her and her children and two attendants from the Wartburg during that same winter that he might seize power himself ; and there are shocking particulars of the hardship and contempt which she suffered until she was fetched away from Eisenach by her aunt, Matilda, Abbess of Kitzingen.   It is alternatively claimed that she was dispossessed of her dower-house at Marburg, in Hesse, or even that she left the Wartburg of her own free will. From Kitzingen she visited her uncle, Eckembert, Bishop of Bamberg, who put his castle of Pottenstein at her disposal, whither she went with her son Herman and the baby, leaving the little Sophia with the nuns of Kitzingen.   Eckembert had ambitious plans for another marriage for Elizabeth, but she refused to listen to them : before his departure on the crusade she and her husband had exchanged promises never to marry again.   Early in 1228 the body of Louis was brought home and solemnly buried in the abbey church at Reinhardsbrunn ;* provision was made for Elizabeth by her relatives ; and on Good Friday in the church of the Franciscan friars at Eisenach she formally renounced the world, later taking the unbleached gown and cord which was the habit of the third order of St Francis.

An influential part was played in all these developments by Master Conrad of Marburg, who henceforward was the determining human influence in St Elizabeth's life.   This priest had played a considerable part therein for some time, having succeeded the Franciscan Father Rodinger as her confessor in 1225.   The Landgrave Louis, in common with Pope Gregory IX and many others, had a high opinion of Conrad, and had allowed his wife to make a promise of obedience to him, saving of course his own husbandly authority.   But the conclusion can hardly be avoided that Conrad's experience as a successful inquisitor of heretics and his domineering and severe, if not brutal, personality made him an unsuitable person to be the director of St Elizabeth.   Some of his later critics have been moved in their adverse criticism by emotion rather than thought and knowledge ; on the other hand, his defenders and apologists have not always been free from special pleading.   Subjectively, it is true that Conrad, by giving to Elizabeth obstacles which she overcame, helped her on her road to sanctity (though we cannot know that a director of more sensibility would not have led her to yet greater heights) ;

* He is popularly venerated in Germany as " St Ludwig ".   See September 11.

objectively, his methods were offensive.   From the Friars Minor St Elizabeth had acquired a love of poverty which she could put into action only to a limited extent all the time she was landgravine of Thuringia.   Now, her children having been provided for, she went to Marburg, but was forced to leave there and lived for a time in a cottage at Wehrda, by the side of the River Lahn.   Then she built a small house just outside Marburg and attached to it a hospice for the relief of the sick, the aged and the poor, to whose service she entirely devoted herself.

In some respects Conrad acted as a prudent and necessary brake on her enthusiasm at this time : he would not allow her to beg from door to door or to divest herself definitely of all her goods or to give more than a certain amount at a time in alms or to risk infection from leprosy and other diseases.   In such matters he acted with care and wisdom.   But " Master Conrad tried her constancy in many ways, striving to break her own will in all things.   That he might afflict her still more he deprived her of those of her household who were particularly dear to her, including me, Isentrude, whom she loved ; she sent me away in great distress and with many tears.   Last of all he turned off Jutta, my companion, who had been with her from her childhood, and whom she loved with a special love. With tears and sighs the blessed Elizabeth saw her go.   Master Conrad, of pious memory, did this in his zeal with good intentions, lest we should talk to her of past greatness and she be tempted to regret.   Moreover, he thus took away from her any comfort she might have in us because he wished her to cling to God alone." For her devoted waiting-women he substituted two " harsh females ", who reported to him on her words and actions when these infringed his detailed commands in the smallest degree.   He punished her with slaps in the face and blows with a " long, thick rod " whose marks remained for three weeks.   No plea of " other times, other manners " can take the sting from Elizabeth's bitter cry to Isentrude, " If I am so afraid of a mortal man, how awe-inspiring must be the Lord and Judge of the world ! " *

Conrad's policy of breaking rather than directing the will was not completely successful.   With reference to him and his disciplinary methods St Elizabeth compares herself to sedge in a stream during flood-time : the water bears it down flat, but when the rains have gone it springs up again, straight, strong and unhurt. Once when she went off to pay a visit of which Conrad did not approve, he sent to fetch her back.   " We are like the snail ", she observed, " which withdraws into its shell when it is going to rain.   So we obey and withdraw from the way we were going."   She had that good self-confidence so often seen when a sense of humour serves submission to God.

One day a Magyar noble arrived at Marburg and asked to be directed to the residence of his sovereign's daughter, of whose troubles he had been informed.

---

* Alban Butler's treatment of Conrad of Marburg is an excellent example of a defect of his method in writing of the saints.   He says : " Conrad, a most holy and learned priest and an eloquent pathetic preacher, whose disinterestedness and love of holy poverty, mortified life, and extraordinary devotion and spirit of prayer rendered him a model to the clergy of that age, was the person whom she chose for her spiritual director, and to his advice she submitted herself in all things relating to her spiritual concerns.   This holy and experienced guide, observing how deep root the seeds of virtue had taken in her soul, applied himself by cultivating them to conduct her to the summit of Christian perfection, and encouraged her in the path of mortification and penance, but was obliged often to moderate her corporal austerities by the precept of obedience."   True in substance, if exaggerated in expression : but . . .

Arrived at the hospital, he saw Elizabeth in her plain grey gown, sitting at her spinning-wheel. The magnificent fellow started back, crossing himself in alarm : " Whoever has seen a king's daughter spinning before ? " He would have taken her back to the court of Hungary, but Elizabeth would not go. Her children, her poor, the grave of her husband were all in Thuringia, and she would stay there for the rest of her life. It was not for long. She lived with great austerity and worked continually, in her hospice, in the homes of the poor, fishing in the streams to earn a little more money to help sufferers ; even when she was sick herself she would try to spin or card wool. She had not been at Marburg two years when her health finally gave way. As she lay abed her attendant heard her singing softly. " You sing sweetly, madam," she said. " I will tell you why," replied Elizabeth. " Between me and the wall there was a little bird singing so gaily to me, and it was so sweet that I had to sing too." At midnight before the day of her death she stirred from her quietness and said, " It is near the hour when the Lord was born and lay in the manger and by His all-mighty power made a new star. He came to redeem the world, and He will redeem me." And at cock-crow, " It is now the time when He rose from the grave and broke the doors of hell, and he will release me." St Elizabeth died in the evening of November 17, 1231, being then not yet twenty-four years old.

For three days her body lay in state in the chapel of the hospice, where she was buried and where many miracles were seen at her intercession. Master Conrad began collecting depositions touching her sanctity, but he did not live to see her canonization, which was proclaimed in 1235. In the following year her relics were translated to the church of St Elizabeth at Marburg, built by her brother-in-law Conrad, in the presence of the Emperor Frederick II, and " so great a concourse of divers nations, peoples and tongues as in these German lands scarcely ever was gathered before or will ever be again ". There the relics of St Elizabeth of Hungary rested, an object of pilgrimage to all Germany and beyond, till in 1539 a Protestant landgrave of Hesse, Philip, removed them to a place unknown.

A glance at the BHL., nn. 2488–2514, suffices to reveal how much was written about St Elizabeth within a relatively short time of her death. For a somewhat more detailed bibliography of sources, consult A. Huyskens, *Quellenstudien zur Geschichte der hl. Elizabeth* (1908), and also the introduction and notes to the text printed by D. Henniges in the *Archivum Franciscanum Historicum*, vol. ii (1909), pp. 240–268. It must suffice to say here that the most important materials are supplied by the *Libellus de dictis IV ancillarum* (a summary of the depositions of the saint's four handmaidens) ; by the letters of Conrad to the pope ; the accounts of miracles and other documents sent to Rome in view of her canonization ; the life written by Caesarius of Heisterbach with a discourse of his concerning the translation (both before 1240) ; and the life by Dietrich of Apolda, composed as late as 1297, but important on account of its wide diffusion. Some of the most notable of these texts were edited by Karl Wenck, and others by Huyskens, in view of the seventh centenary of the saint's birth. A detailed criticism is provided in the *Analecta Bollandiana*, vols. xxvii, pp. 493–497 and xxviii, pp. 333–335. Of modern biographies the work of Count de Montalembert (1836 ; best English translation by F. D. Hoyt, 1904) for more than half a century held the field, but unfortunately the author's charm of style and deep religious feeling are handicapped by a lack of historical criticism. The attitude of Conrad of Marburg towards his penitent has been in some measure vindicated by P. Braun in his articles in the *Beiträge zur Hessische Kirchengeschichte*, vol. iv (1910), pp. 248–300 and 331–364. There are French lives of the saint of moderate compass by E. Horn (1902), Leopold de Chérancé (1927), and J. Ancelet-Hustache (1947), and German ones by A. Stolz (1898) and E. Busse-Wilson (1931). There is a sensitive simple sketch in English by William Canton ; but the book called *Saint Elizabeth of Hungary*, by F. J. von Weinrich (Eng. trans., 1933), is a mere work of fiction based upon the story of St Elizabeth. She has sometimes been credited with the writings called the *Revelationes B. Elisabeth*, but these contain nothing of hers, as F. Oliger has proved : neither did they spring from the fertile imagination of St Elizabeth of Schönau ; *cf. Analecta Bollandiana*, vol. lxxi (1953), pp. 494–496.

ST PONTIAN, POPE AND MARTYR   (*c.* A.D. 236)

PONTIAN, who is said to have been a Roman, followed St Urban I as bishop of Rome about the year 230.   The only known event of his pontificate is the synod held at Rome which confirmed the condemnation already pronounced at Alexandria of certain doctrines attributed to Origen.   At the beginning of the persecution by the Emperor Maximinus the pope was exiled to Sardinia, an island described as *nociva*, " unhealthy ", whereby perhaps the mines were meant ; here he resigned his office.   How much longer he lived and the manner of his death are not known : traditionally life was beaten out of him with sticks.   Some years later Pope St Fabian translated his body to the cemetery of St Callistus in Rome, where in 1909 his original epitaph was found : *ΠONTIANOC EΠICK MPT*, the last word having been added later.

In the fourth-century *Depositio Martyrum* the name of St Pontian is coupled with that of Hippolytus, and August 13 is the day assigned for the commemoration : " Idus Aug. Ypoliti in Tiburtina et Pontiani in Callisti." Fr Delehaye has discussed the whole matter very fully in his CMH., pp. 439–440. See also Marucchi in *Nuovo Bullettino* for 1909, pp. 35–50 ; Wilpert, *Die Papstgräber und die Cäciliengruft* (1909), pp. 17–18 ; and E. Caspar, *Geschichte des Papsttums*, vol. i (1930), pp. 44 *seq.*

ST NERSES I, KATHOLIKOS OF THE ARMENIANS, MARTYR   (*c.* A.D. 373)

THIS bishop, the first of several Armenian saints of his name, was a strong reformer and began the work which was carried on by his son St Isaac.   He was brought up at Caesarea in Cappadocia, where he married.   After the death of his wife he became an official at the court of the Armenian king, Arshak, received holy orders, and in 363 was made chief bishop of Armenia, much against his will.   At Caesarea he had come under the influence of St Basil, and accordingly about the year 365 he convened the first national synod at Astishat, in order to bring better discipline and efficiency to his church.   He encouraged monasticism, established hospitals, and promulgated canonical legislation imitated from the Greeks.   This embroiled him with the king, and worse followed when Arshak murdered his wife, Olympia. St Nerses condemned him and refused to attend the court, whereupon he was banished and another bishop intruded in his office.   Arshak was killed in battle with the Persians shortly after and St Nerses returned, only to find that the new king, Pap, was even worse than his predecessor : a contemporary Armenian chronicler says he was possessed by the Devil.   His life was so atrocious that St Nerses refused him entrance to the church until he mended his ways.   Pap meditated revenge.   Pretending penitence he invited Nerses to dine at his table, and there poisoned him.   St Nerses has ever since been venerated as a martyr, his name occurs in the canon of the Armenian Mass, and he is referred to as " the Great ".

A very full account of St Nerses will be found in Tournebize, *Histoire politique et religieuse de l'Arménie* (1901), especially pp. 469–489.   See also S. Weber, *Die Katholische Kirche in Armenien* (1903), pp. 287–316 ; the *Analecta Bollandiana*, vol. xxxix (1921), pp. 65–69 ; and Messina and Markwart in *Orientalia christiana*, vol. xxvii (1932), pp. 141–236.

ST BARLAAM, Martyr   (Fourth Century ?)

THERE is a panegyric of this martyr by St John Chrysostom, but his *acta* as we have them are spurious.   This legend says that Barlaam was a labourer in a village near Antioch, where his confession of Christ provoked the persecutors, who detained him a long time in jail before he was brought to trial.   When he was arraigned the judge laughed at his uncouth language and appearance, but was forced to admire his virtue and constancy.   He was nevertheless cruelly scourged, but no word of complaint was extorted from him.   He was then put on the rack and his bones dislocated.   When this failed to move him, the prefect threatened him with death and had swords and axes fresh stained with the blood of martyrs displayed before him.   Barlaam beheld them without a word.   He was therefore re- manded to prison, and the judge, who was ashamed to see himself beaten by an illiterate peasant, tried to invent some new torment.   At length he flattered himself that he had found a method by which Barlaam should be compelled, in spite of his resolution, to offer sacrifice.   He was brought out of prison, and an altar with burning coals upon it was made ready.   The martyr's hand was then forcibly held over the flames and incense with red-hot embers was laid upon it, so that, if he shook them off his hand, he might be said to offer sacrifice by throwing the incense into the fire upon the altar.   Barlaam, fearing scandal and the very shadow of idolatry (though by throwing off the fire to save his hand he could not be esteemed to have meant to sacrifice), kept his hand steady whilst the fire burnt into it and so dropped his flesh, with the incense, upon the altar.   The martyrdom of St Barlaam, whenever and in whatever circumstances it took place, hap- pened at Antioch, and not at Caesarea in Cappadocia as stated in the Roman Martyrology.

This Barlaam, it may be said with confidence, is none other than the " Barula " whom we find on November 18 associated with St Romanus.   See the article of Delehaye in the *Analecta Bollandiana*, vol. xxii, pp. 129–145, and other references given above under Romanus.

20 : ST FELIX OF VALOIS, Co-founder of the Order of the Most Holy Trinity   (A.D. 1212)

THE surname of Valois was given to this saint according to later writers of his order because he was of the royal family of Valois in France, but it was originally because he lived in the province of Valois.   He lived, we are told, as a hermit in the wood of Gandelu in the diocese of Soissons, at a spot called Cerfroid ; and he had no thoughts but of dying in the obscurity of this retreat when God called him thence.   This was by means of his disciple, St John of Matha, who made the suggestion of establishing a religious order for the redemp- tion of captives.   Felix, though said to be then seventy years of age, readily offered himself to do and suffer whatever it should please God in the carrying-out of so charitable a work, and together they set out in the winter of 1197 to obtain the approval of the Holy See.

From henceforward, indeed from the beginning, the life of St Felix of Valois shares the legends and uncertainties of that of St John of Matha and of the early history of the Trinitarian Order.   These have already been set out herein in the account of St John of Matha under the date of his feast, February 8.   According to the traditional account, while St John was working for the Christian slaves in Spain and Barbary, St Felix propagated the new order in Italy and France, founding the convent of St Maturinus (Mathurin) in Paris.   When John finally returned to Rome, St Felix, in spite of his great age, administered the French province and the mother-house of the order at Cerfroid, where he died in his eighty-sixth year on November 4, 1212.   Alban Butler notes that it is the tradition of the Trinitarians that the two founders were canonized by Pope Urban IV in 1262, but that " the bull is nowhere extant ".   Alexander VII recognized their *cultus* in 1666, and twenty-eight years later the feast of St Felix of Valois was extended to the whole Western church.

Materials for the life of St Felix are practically non-existent, though Fr Calixte-de-la-Providence compiled a *Vie de St Félix de Valois* of which a third edition appeared in 1878. The reader must be referred to the note on St John of Matha herein under February 8. See also Mann, *History of the Popes*, vol. xii, pp. 84 and 272 ; and *cf.* the observations in Baudot and Chaussin, *Vies des saints*, vol. xi (1954), pp. 669–670.

ST DASIUS, Martyr   (A.D. 303 ?)

THIRTY days before the winter festival called Saturnalia it was the custom in the Roman army to elect a " lord of misrule " whose office it was to be a leader in the revels, which did not stop short of excess and debauchery, and ended with the sacrifice of the leader to Kronos.   At Durostorum (Silistria in Bulgaria) in the year 303 the garrison chose one of their number called Dasius.   He knew well enough what was expected of him and, being a Christian, refused to play the part, arguing that he had to die in either case, and had better die in a good cause than a bad one.   He was brought before the legate Bassus, who pressed him to renounce his faith or at least to go through the form of sacrificing before images of the emperors, reminding him of his obligation as a soldier to obey.   But Dasius remained firm in his refusal, and was put to death by beheading.   His alleged relics are preserved at Ancona, to which place they are supposed to have been taken, perhaps to save them from the Avars, in the second half of the sixth century.

The Greek Acts of St Dasius, first published from a unique text by Franz Cumont in the *Analecta Bollandiana*, vol. xvi (1897), pp. 5–11, have excited great interest but have met with very divergent judgements.   By some the story has been received as an absolutely authentic narrative, in the eyes of others it is a tale with a moral purpose which has been elaborated upon the simple theme of a martyr's decapitation.   Delehaye, both in his CMH. (pp. 609–610) and his *Les passions des martyrs* . . . (1921), pp. 321–328, has dealt with the matter very fully, and has paid due regard to opinions differing from his own.   In his view we cannot be certain that the martyr was a soldier, or that he suffered at Durostorum rather than at Heraclea.   On the Ancona inscription see G. Mercati in the *Rendiconti dell' accademia pontificia di archeologia*, vol. iv, pp. 59–71.

SS. NERSES, Bishop of Sahgerd, and Other Martyrs   (A.D. 343)

IN the fourth year of the great persecution raised by Sapor II in Persia were apprehended Nerses, Bishop of Sahgerd, and his disciple Joseph, whilst the king happened to be in that city.   When they were brought before him he said to Nerses, " Your grey hairs and your pupil's youth incline me in your favour.   Consider your own safety.   Worship the sun and I will confer honours upon you." Nerses answered, " Your flattery does not deceive us.   I am now over eighty years old and have served God from my infancy.   I pray Him that I may be preserved from so grievous an evil and may never betray Him by worshipping the work of His hands."   He was threatened with death, and Nerses replied, " If you had power to put us to death seven times over we should never yield ".   The martyrs were led out of the tents, followed by a multitude of people.   At the place of execution Joseph said to the bishop, " See how the people gaze at you.   They are waiting for you to dismiss them and go to your own home."   Nerses embracing him replied, " You are happy, my blessed Joseph, to have broken the snares of the world and entered the narrow path of the kingdom of Heaven ".   Their heads were then struck off.

In the same acts, the martyrdom of several others about the same time is recorded.   Among them a eunuch in the royal palace refused to sacrifice, whereupon Vardan, an apostate priest who had shrunk at his trial and renounced his faith, was ordered to kill him with his own hand.   He advanced, but at first sight of the martyr trembled and stopped, not daring.   The martyr said to him, " Can you, who are a priest, come to kill me ?   I certainly am wrong when I call you a priest. Do your work, but remember the apostasy and end of Judas."   The impious Vardan made a trembling thrust and stabbed.

A very full account of this martyr, with the Syriac text, a Latin translation, and an immense array of bibliographical references, has been printed by P. Peeters in the *Acta Sanctorum* for November, vol. iv, under November 10.   The text had previously been edited by E. Assemani in his *Acta martyrum orientalium*, vol. i, pp. 99 *seq.*, and also by Bedjan and Hoffmann.

ST MAXENTIA, Virgin and Martyr   (No Date)

According to the legend of the church of Beauvais this maiden was of Irish birth daughter of a prince.   She dedicated herself to God at an early age, and when her father wished to give her in marriage to a pagan chief she fled from home.   Taking with her two servants, a man and a woman, she crossed the sea to Gaul and settled at the place on the Oise that is now called Pont-Sainte-Maxence, near Senlis.   One day she was surprised by the arrival of a number of horsemen outside her cottage : it was the disappointed suitor, who had tracked her down.   He asked her to return with him, but Maxentia refused indignantly.   Then, when threats were of no avail, the man, carried away with fury, seized her by the hair and cut off her head. Her faithful servants suffered a like fate.

Two variant texts of this worthless *passio* have been printed in Renet, *S. Lucien et les autres saints du Beauvaisis*, vol. iii, pt 2 (1895), pp. 543–548.   Capgrave has summarized the legend, but it is ignored, very rightly, by Dom Gougaud in his *Saints irlandais hors d'Irlande*.

ST EDMUND THE MARTYR   (A.D. 870)

During the ninth century the Northmen or Danes with increasing frequency raided the coasts of England, till in the middle of the century " the heathen first began to winter in our land ".   At this time, on Christmas Day, 855, the nobles and clergy of Norfolk, assembled at Attleborough, acknowledged as their king Edmund, a youth of fourteen, who in the following year was accepted by Suffolk as well.   He is said to have been as talented and successful as a ruler as he was virtuous as a man, learning the Psalter by heart in order that he might join in the Church's worship and emulate the good deeds of King David. He was, wrote the Benedictine Lydgate in the fifteenth century, " In his estate most godly and benign, heavenly of cheer, of counsel provident, showing of grace full many a blessed sign. . . ." Then came the biggest Danish invasion that had yet been. " In the year 866," says the *Anglo-Saxon Chronicle*, " a great army [of Danes] came to the land of the Angle kin and took up winter quarters among the East Angles, and there they were provided with horses. And the East Angles made peace with them." Then the invaders crossed the Humber and took York, and marched south into Mercia as far as Nottingham, plundering, burning and enslaving as they went. In 870 the host rode across Mercia into East Anglia, and took up winter quarters at Thetford. " And that winter Edmund fought against them, and the Danish men got the victory and slew the king, and subdued all that land and destroyed all the monasteries that they came to."

That brief and unadorned statement tells us all that is historically certain about the death of St Edmund. The traditions related by Abbo of Fleury, in his *passio* of the martyr, and other chroniclers are summed up by Alban Butler as follows. The barbarians poured down upon St Edmund's dominions, burning Thetford, which they took by surprise, and laying waste all before them. The king raised what forces he could, met a part of the Danes' army near Thetford, and discomfited them. But seeing them soon after reinforced with fresh numbers, against which his small body was not able to make any stand, he retired towards his castle of Framlingham in Suffolk. The barbarian leader, Ingvar, had sent him proposals which were inconsistent both with religion and with the justice which he owed to his people. These the saint rejected. In his flight he was overtaken and surrounded at Hoxne, upon the Waveney (alternatively, he allowed himself to be taken in the church). Terms were again offered him prejudicial to religion and to his people, which he refused, declaring that religion was dearer to him than his life, which he would never purchase by offending God. Ingvar had him tied to a tree and torn with whips, which he bore with patience, calling upon the name of Jesus. Then his tormentors shot at him with arrows, cunningly, so as not to kill him, till his body was " like a hedgehog whose skin is closely set with quills, or a thistle covered with thorns ". At last Ingvar cut his bonds, dragged him from the tree to which he was nailed by the arrows, and his head was hacked off.

The body of the king was buried at Hoxne, and about the year 903 translated to Beodricsworth, the town now known as Bury St Edmund's (*i.e.* St Edmund's Borough). In 1010, during the Danish ravages it was taken to the church of St Gregory by St Paul's, in London, and three years later brought back to Bury.* During the reign of Canute the great Benedictine abbey of St Edmundsbury was founded, and the body of St Edmund was the principal relic in the abbey church.

---

* The " station " for the second night on this return journey was at Greensted in the parish of Chipping Ongar, and an existing church is said to have been hastily put up to shelter the relics. The nave walls (the only original parts of the building) are exactly as Alban Butler describes the first church built for St Edmund at Bury : " Trunks of large trees were sawn lengthways in the middle, and reared up with one end fixed in the ground, with the bark or rough side outermost. These trunks being made of an equal height, and set up close to one another and the interstices filled up with mud or mortar, formed the four walls, upon which was raised a thatched roof." Almost so remains the church of Greensted today.

Thomas Carlyle's comments (in *Past and Present*) on the chronicle of Jocelin of Brakelond, wherein is described the translation of the body to a new shrine in 1198, by Abbot Samson, have made the name of St Edmund and his abbey more familiar to many than they otherwise would be.   The subsequent history of the relics is a matter of dispute.   Devotion to St Edmund the Martyr was formerly very wide-spread and popular in England, numerous churches were dedicated in his honour, and in the thirteenth century and later his feast was a holiday of obligation.   It is now observed in the dioceses of Westminster and Northampton, and by the English Benedictines.

One *passio* by Abbo of Fleury, and a second by Gaufridus de Fontibus, together with Archdeacon Herman's collection of miracles and another similar collection made by Abbot Samson, have all been edited by Thomas Arnold for the *Memorials of St Edmund's Abbey*, vol. i, in the Rolls Series.   The editor in his introduction points out that William of Malmesbury and the chroniclers purport to supply further information, though this is probably of little value.   The same must be said of *La Vie Seint Edmund le Rey*, a French poem of the thirteenth century printed by Mr Arnold in his second volume, and also of the English poem of Dan Lydgate, himself a monk of Bury.   There is a modern life by J. B. Mackinlay (1893) which is unfortunately quite uncritical (see *The Month*, October, 1893, pp. 275–280). On the other hand, Lord Francis Hervey in his *Corolla Sti Eadmundi* (1907) and his *History of King Eadmund* (1929) has given proof of a very careful and scholarly study of the subject. The supposed transference of the remains of St Edmund to the church of St Sernin at Toulouse and the return of part of them to England in 1901 have been the occasion of much animated discussion.   See also Stanton's *Menology*, pp. 559–561.   *La Vie Seint Edmund* was published again in 1935, by H. Kjellman at Göteborg, and Jocelin's Chronicle in 1949, by H. E. Butler.   *Cf.* also R. M. Wilson, *The Lost Literature of Medieval England* (1952).

ST BERNWARD, BISHOP OF HILDESHEIM   (A.D. 1022)

HE came of a Saxon family and, being left an orphan at an early age, was taken charge of by his uncle, Bishop Volkmar of Utrecht, who sent him to the cathedral-school of Heidelberg.   To complete his studies he was sent to Mainz, where he was ordained priest by St Willigis, but he refused any preferment until after the death of his grandfather, to whose care he devoted himself.   The old man died in 987 and Bernward was made an imperial chaplain and tutor to the child-emperor, Otto III, over whose subsequent career the influence of Bernward had a strong though insufficient effect.   Six years later he was elected bishop of Hildesheim, where he built the great church and monastery of St Michael and ruled his see with prudence and ability.   St Bernward had always been a great amateur of ecclesiastical art and his name is particularly remembered in connection with all kinds of metal-work ; as bishop of a wealthy see he had ample opportunity and means of promoting good work and encouraging good workmen.   Moreover his biographer, Thangmar, who had formerly been his preceptor, states that St Bernward himself was a painter and metal-worker and spent much time in the exercise of these arts.   Several very beautiful pieces of metal-work at Hildesheim are attributed to his hands.

St Bernward's episcopate of thirty years was unhappily disturbed by a dispute with St Willigis, Archbishop of Mainz, who made claim to episcopal rights in the great nunnery of Gandersheim.   This dispute had begun during the episcopate of Bernward's predecessor, and was revived by the bad conduct of a nun called Sophia, who " egged on " the Archbishop of Mainz, when the Bishop of Hildesheim called her to order.   The conflict went on for over seven years, even after the

Holy See had pronounced in favour of St Bernward, whose behaviour throughout
was irreproachable.   At length St Willigis submitted publicly and made full
amends for his lack of prudence and his headstrong conduct.   St Bernward died
on November 20, 1022, after having assumed the habit of St Benedict.   He was
canonized in 1193.

The best text of the life by Thangmar is that in MGH., *Scriptores*, vol. iv, pp. 754–782 ;
it is also printed in Migne, PL., vol. cxl, cc. 393–436.   See further the *Neues Archiv*, vol.
xxv, pp. 427 *seq.* ;   V. C. Habicht, *Der hl. Berwards von Hildesheim Kunstwerke* (1922) ;
the *Archiv für Kulturgeschichte*, vol. xvii (1921), pp. 273–285 ;   and F. J. Tschan, *St Bernward
of Hildesheim : his Life and Times* (2 vols. and plates, 1942–52 ;   University of Notre Dame
Press, U.S.A.).

BD AMBROSE OF CAMALDOLI, Abbot   (A.D. 1439)

Ambrose Traversari was a conspicuous and engaging figure in the religious and
literary life of the early fifteenth century in Italy : he was a characteristic " all-
round " man of the Renaissance, humanist, monk and man of affairs.   He came
of a noble Tuscan family, and was born at Portico in 1386.   At the age of fourteen
he became a Camaldolese monk in the monastery of our Lady of the Angels at
Florence, and lived there for thirty years.   During this time he became a thorough
master of Greek and Latin, learned Hebrew, read deeply, especially in Greek, and
collected a fine library ;   he made many valuable translations from the writings of
the Greek fathers, including the *Spiritual Meadow* of John Moschus and the
Ladder of Perfection of St John Climacus, some of which still appear in Migne's
Greek Patrology.   His great scholarship earned him a profound respect in Florence.
He was patronized by Cosimo de' Medici, and was asked to give lectures on theology
and history to the sons of the nobility.   There gathered in his cell such diverse
characters as St Laurence Giustiniani, Niccolò Niccoli and Poggio Bracciolini,
Manuel Chrysoloras (of whom it could be said, as it has been said of Bd Ambrose
himself, that " the careful niceness of his conscience as a humanist has not been
maintained by all his followers "), and his pupil Leonard Bruni.   Ambrose went
out of his way to protect and help the last-named, who rewarded his benefactor
by slandering him.

In 1431 this long and undisturbed period of worship, study and intellectual
activity was brought to a sudden end, when Pope Eugenius IV appointed Bd
Ambrose abbot general of the Camaldolese Order, with instructions to carry out
certain reforms of urgent necessity.   This he did with considerable vigour, and
his own diary survives as evidence of the need for reform and the extraordinary
difficulties with which the abbot visitor had to contend, not always successfully.
Later the Holy See entrusted to him similar duties in respect of the Vallumbrosan
monks.   The researches which Bd Ambrose carried out in the libraries of the
monasteries he had to visit still further commended him to the pope, and when
in 1434 Eugenius fled from Rome and took refuge at Florence he attached Ambrose
to his person.   In the following year he was one of the papal envoys to the troublesome council at Basle, where he strongly defended the rights of the Holy See and
warned the extremists against the sin of schism.   Bd Ambrose showed himself an
admirable minister, particularly efficient in keeping the pope supplied with accurate
information about persons and events.

In 1438 he was the papal representative at Venice to meet the emperor of the
East, John VII, and his brother Joseph, Patriarch of Constantinople, coming to

the Council of Ferrara.   Because of his expert knowledge of the Greek tongue
and of Eastern theology, Ambrose was called on to play a very active part in the
negotiations which led to the short-lived reunion of the Western and Eastern
churches ; the emperor said that Ambrose knew Greek better than anyone else
among the Latins.   With Bessarion he was commissioned to draw up the decree
of union, beginning, " Let the heavens rejoice and the earth be glad ", which was
solemnly proclaimed at Florence in July 1439.   Less than five months later, on
October 20, Ambrose Traversari was dead, at the age of fifty-three.   He has never
been officially beatified, but a popular *cultus* is extended to him at Florence and
among the Camaldolese monks, and he is commemorated on this day.

Much of his history can be gathered from his letters, which have been printed in Martène,
Veterum scriptorum amplissima collectio, vol. iii, supplemented by L. Bertalot, in the *Römische
Quartalschrift*, vol. xxix (1915), pp. 91 *seq.*   There is also the account which Ambrose
wrote of his visitations of the Camaldolese houses in 1431.   It was edited by Bertholini,
Beati Ambrosii Hodoeporicon (1680), but a better text is that of A. Dini-Traversari in the
book *Ambrogio Traversari e i suoi tempi* (1912).   See also Pastor, *History of the Popes*, vol. i,
pp. 140–142, 306, 318 ; and G. G. Coulton, *Five Centuries of Religion*, vol. iv (1950), caps.
xxvi–xxxi.

21 : THE PRESENTATION OF THE BLESSED VIRGIN MARY

THIS feast is popularly associated with a story that the parents of our Lady
brought her to the Temple at Jeruselem when she was three years old and
left her there to be brought up, related in several of the apocryphal gospels,
e.g. in the *Protevangelium of James.*

And the child was two years old, and Joachim said, " Let us take her up
to the Temple of the Lord, that we may pay the vow that we have vowed, lest
perchance the Lord send to us and our offering be not received ".   And Anne
said, " Let us wait for the third year, in order that the child may not seek for
father or mother ".   And Joachim said, " Let us so wait ".   And the child
was three years old . . . and they went up into the Temple of the Lord, and
the priest received her and kissed her and blessed her, saying, " The Lord
has magnified thy name in all generations.   In thee, on the last of the days,
the Lord will manifest His redemption to the sons of Israel."   And he set
her down upon the third step of the altar, and the Lord God sent grace upon
her ; and she danced with her feet and all the house of Israel loved her.
And her parents went down marvelling, and praising the Lord God because
the child had not turned back.   And Mary was in the Temple of the Lord
as if she were a dove that dwelt there. . . .

It is not stated anywhere in the liturgy of the Roman church that this is the
occasion of the presentation eelebrated in today's feast.   The festival is not a
very ancient one, even in the East where it originated : the Entrance of the All-holy
Mother of God into the Temple.   It seems probable that its origin was in the
commemoration of the dedication of New St Mary's church at Jerusalem in 543.
In the West the first, and sporadic, observance of it was in the eleventh century,
in England.   Here it was, to quote Edmund Bishop,

a real liturgical feast and was actually observed in practice.   Assurance of
the fact is supplied by the Canterbury Cathedral Benedictional.   In its proper

place in this Benedictional (*i.e.* between the feasts of St Martin, November 11, and St Cecily, November 22) is a " Benedictio de præsentatione sancte Marie ".   This is that feast of the Presentation which after appearing in our English books of Winchester and Canterbury only to disappear again, was started in Latin Christendom in the later decades of the fourteenth century ; our English essay of 350 years earlier being forgotten by all the world *usque in hodiernum diem* (*Liturgica Historica*, p. 257).

The feast won general acceptance only gradually and was not finally admitted to the Western calendar till the pontificate of Sixtus V (1585).

See Kellner, *Heortology*, pp. 265–266 ; Schuster, *The Sacramentary*, vol. v, pp. 290–291 ; Holweck, *Calendarium Liturgicum* (1925), p. 386 ; S. Beissel, *Verehrung Marias in Deutschland*, vol. i, p. 306 ; vol. ii, p. 281.   It is curious that in none of these sources is any mention made of the fact that as early as the eleventh century the feast of the Presentation of our Lady was liturgically celebrated in England, and that at Canterbury itself : see the Henry Bradshaw Society's edition of the Canterbury Benedictional, p. 116.   This celebration seems to have had some diffusion in England.   It is found in the calendar of an East Anglian *Horae* (Christ's Coll. Camb., MS. 6, early thirteenth century) in the form " Oblacio B.M.V.".   In this form also it occurs in two Worcester books of the same date : see *The Leofric Collectar*, vol. ii, p. 599.   That the feast was somehow introduced from the East may be inferred from the fact that we find it attached to this same day (November 21) in the Greek synaxaries (the text is printed in Delehaye's edition, cc. 243–244) and these synaxaries certainly date from the tenth century.   In the Henry Bradshaw Society's reprint of the *Missale Romanum* of 1474 (vol. ii, pp. 251–253) is an interesting note which, while pointing out that the Presentation feast does not occur in the calendar or text of the 1474 edition, prints a Mass for the feast from a Roman missal of 1505.   This includes a long sequence so barbarously worded that one can readily believe that St Pius V thought it better to suppress the feast altogether— as he did—rather than tolerate the continued recitation of such doggerel.   For later references to the feast's origins, see M. J. Kishpaugh, *The Feast of the Presentation* (1941) ; E. Campana, *Maria nel culto cattolico*, vol. i (1943), pp. 207–214 ; and N. Chirat, *Mélanges* (1945), pp. 127–143.

ST GELASIUS I, POPE   (A.D. 496)

THE successor of Pope St Felix II in 492 was a capable and vigorous pontiff, " famous all over the world ", says a contemporary, " for his learning and holiness ". Gelasius maintained the firm attitude of his predecessor to the " Acacian schism " arising out of the monophysite troubles ; at Constantinople the Patriarch Euphemius, Acacius being dead, was anxious to heal the breach, but the emperor, Anastasius I, upheld the condemned Henotikon, and, till this document was repudiated and the condemnation of Acacius recognized, communion could not be restored.   " We shall certainly come to the great judgement-seat of Christ, brother Euphemius ", wrote the pope, " surrounded by those by whom the faith has been defended.   It will there be proved whether the glorious confession of St Peter has been lacking in anything for the salvation of those given him to rule, or whether there has been rebellion and obstinacy in those who were unwilling to obey him."

On several other occasions, especially in his letters, St Gelasius emphasized the supremacy of the see of Peter, notably in a passage of a letter to the Emperor Anastasius wherein he expounds the right relation between religious and secular authority.   But when he referred to the bishop of Constantinople as " an unimportant suffragan of Heraclea " the pope displayed a better sense of past history than of actuality.   He was emphatic on the duty of bishops to devote a quarter of their revenue to charity, and strongly opposed an attempt to revive the pagan

Lupercalia festival. An interesting declaration of St Gelasius was when he insisted on communion in both kinds : this was aimed at the Manicheans, who regarded wine as an unlawful drink and therefore abstained from the eucharistic cup. Gelasius is believed to have been a prolific writer, but little has survived. A contemporary priest, Gennadius, informs us that he compiled a sacramentary ; but the Gelasian Sacramentary so called today belongs later. A decree upon which writings are canonical books of Holy Scripture has often been attributed to St Gelasius, but is now recognized not to be his.

Our chief sources of information are the *Liber Pontificalis* (Duchesne's edition), vol. i, pp. 254–257, and the pope's letters, which may be found in Thiel, *Epistolae Romanorum Pontificum*, supplemented by Löwenfeld, *Epistolae Pontificum Romanorum ineditae* (1885). See also A. Roux, *Le Pape St. Gélase* (1880) ; Grisar, *Geschichte Roms und der Päpste*, vol. i, pp. 452–457 ; and Hefele-Leclercq, *Conciles*, vol. ii, pp. 940 *seq.* As for the famous *Decretum de libris recipiendis et non recipiendis* it is now generally admitted that this cannot be attributed to Pope St Gelasius : the form in which it is preserved to us dates from the sixth century, and is a compilation of pieces of varied origin, some perhaps emanating from Pope Damasus, others from Hormisdas, etc. See the monograph of E. von Dobschütz, in *Texte und Untersuchungen*, vol. xxxviii, pt 3 ; Abbot Chapman in the *Revue Bénédictine*, vol. xxx (1913), pp. 187–207 and 315–333 ; and DAC., vol. vi, cc. 722–747. The standard edition of the " Gelasian " Sacramentary is that edited by H. A. Wilson (1894), but see also Mohlberg and Baumstark, *Die älteste erreichbare Gestalt des Liber Sacramentorum* (1927), and E. Bishop in *Liturgica Historica*, pp. 39–61.

ST ALBERT OF LOUVAIN, BISHOP OF LIÈGE, MARTYR (A.D. 1192)

DURING the twelfth century there was strong competition between the noble houses of Brabant and Hainault for possession of the extensive and powerful see of Liège, whose occupant was necessarily of great weight in the politics of the time, and it was this improper—but in those days very common—use of a bishopric as a political " strong-point " which led to the violent death of Albert of Louvain. He was born about the year 1166, son of Godfrey III, Duke of Brabant, and his wife Margaret of Limburg, and was brought up in his father's castle on that hill of Louvain which is now called Mont-César and whereon is now a well-known Benedictine abbey. Albert was early destined for the clerical state and while still a school-boy of twelve was made a canon of Liège, but when he was twenty-one he renounced his benefice and asked Baldwin V, Count of Hainault (his own bitter enemy), to receive him as a knight. Baldwin agreed, and attached him to his own entourage. In view of what happened afterwards it seems a reasonable speculation that Albert wished to go crusading. For when a few months later the papal legate, Cardinal Henry of Albano, preached the crusade in Liège (and incidentally received the resignation of seventy simoniacal prelates), among those who " took the cross " was Albert—but he at the same time rejoined the ranks of the clergy and received back his canonry. The inner history of this curious episode is not known, but certainly Albert never went to the East, either as soldier or churchman, and in the following year he was archdeacon of Brabant. Other dignities followed, but, though he was archdeacon and provost by office, Albert was still only subdeacon by orders.

In 1191 the bishop of Liège died and two candidates were put forward to fill the vacancy : both were named Albert, both were archdeacons, and neither of them was a priest. Albert of Rethel was a deacon, cousin of Baldwin of Hainault, and uncle of the Empress Constance, wife of Henry VI. A contemporary chronicler says that at the election Liège was full of dukes, counts and men-at-arms. But there was no doubt that Albert of Louvain was the more suitable candidate and the chapter appointed him by an overwhelming majority. Thereupon Albert of Rethel appealed to his relative the emperor, who was an enemy of Albert of Louvain's brother, Henry of Brabant, and the cause was appointed to be heard at Worms. St Albert was supported by practically all the clergy of Liège, Albert of Rethel by his minority of canons, but the emperor would pronounce in favour of neither of them. He announced that he had disposed of the see of Liège to Lothaire, provost of Bonn, whom he had just made imperial chancellor in return for three thousand marks. St Albert quietly told Henry that his own election was canonically valid, rebuked the interference with the Church's liberties, and gave notice of his appeal to the Holy See. He set out for Rome in person and, as the emperor was trying to intercept him, travelled by a devious route and disguised as a servant. He groomed his own horse at night, helped in the kitchen, and was once told to dry and clean an inn-keeper's shoes for him. Pope Celestine III after due deliberation pronounced the election of St Albert to be valid and confirmed it.

On his return, however, Albert was unable to take possession of his see, held by the intruded Lothaire, and Archbishop Bruno of Cologne would not ordain and consecrate him for fear of the emperor (he was, moreover, old and ill). Pope Celestine had foreseen this and had authorized Archbishop William of Rheims to carry out these duties and St Albert was made priest and bishop at Rheims. At the same time news was brought that the Emperor Henry was in Liège, vowing to exterminate Albert and his followers. Albert's uncle would have set off at once with a following of nobles to assert his nephew's rights, but St Albert had a better idea of the duties of a Christian and preferred to remain in exile rather than to precipitate war. The emperor meanwhile took strong measures with the faithful clergy of Liège, forced the submission of Albert's supporters, and left the city for Maestricht, where a further plot was hatched. On November 24, 1192, when St Albert had been nearly ten weeks at Rheims, he went on a visit to the abbey of Saint-Remi, outside the walls. In a narrow part of the way German knights set upon and murdered him. The whole city was horrified, and St Albert was buried with honour in the cathedral. The Emperor Henry had to do penance, and his creature, Lothaire, excommunicated, took refuge in flight.

The history of the relics of St Albert is a matter of some interest. What purported to be these relics were in 1612 translated from Rheims to the church of the Carmelite convent in Brussels, and on that occasion Pope Paul V granted a Mass and Office of St Albert, bishop and martyr, to all the churches of that city and the cathedral of Rheims. When during 1919 the choir of the cathedral at Rheims was being cleared of the *débris* from the German bombardment, a tomb was opened which was supposed to be that of Odalric, a tenth-century archbishop. An examination of its contents aroused the suspicions of the authorities, and a commission of clergy, archaeologists and medical men was appointed to go into the matter. In 1921 this commission reported its unanimous agreement that the skeleton found in " Odalric's " tomb was that of St Albert of Louvain, and that the relics taken to Brussels in 1612 were those of Odalric.* In reply to the hope

* There was no suggestion of fraud on the part of the seventeenth-century canons of Rheims. The proceedings of the commission make it quite clear how such a mistake could easily have been made at that time, the inscriptions on the tombs being obliterated.

expressed by a Belgian member of the commission that the metropolitan chapter of Rheims would honour its promise of three hundred years before and send the relics of St Albert to Belgium, Mgr Neveux, auxiliary bishop in Rheims, said that he could not then give a definite answer, but that in his opinion " solemn engagements were not scraps of paper ".   In the event, the bones of Odalric, detached portions having been called in by Cardinal Mercier, archbishop of Malines, were sent back from Brussels ; and on November 18, 1921, the true relics of St Albert were solemnly handed over by Cardinal Luçon, archbishop of Rheims, to Mgr Van Cauwenbergh and Dom Sebastian Braun, o.s.b., deputed by the Primate of Belgium to receive them.   A considerable relic was subsequently detached and returned to Rheims.

A reliable life by a contemporary has been printed by Heller in MGH., *Scriptores*, vol. xxv, pp. 137–168.   For an account of the identification of the true relics at Rheims, see the *Analecta Bollandiana*, vol. xl (1922), pp. 155–170 ; and *cf.* L. Demaison, *Reims à la fin du xii⁰ siècle* (1925).   Consult further David, *Histoire de St Albert de Louvain* (1848) ; B. del Marmol, *St Albert de Louvain* (1922) in the series " Les Saints " ; and E. de Moreau, *St Albert de Louvain* (1946).

22 : ST CECILIA, OR CECILY, VIRGIN AND MARTYR   (DATE UNKNOWN)

FOR over a thousand years St Cecilia (the more traditional English form of her name is Cecily) has been one of the most greatly venerated of the maiden martyrs of the early Church and is one of those named in the canon of the Mass.   Her " acts " state that she was a patrician girl of Rome and that she was brought up a Christian.   She wore a coarse garment beneath the clothes of her rank, fasted from food several days a week, and determined to remain a maiden for the love of God.   But her father had other views, and gave her in marriage to a young patrician named Valerian.   On the day of the marriage, amid the music and rejoicing of the guests, Cecilia sat apart, singing to God in her heart and praying for help in her predicament.   When they retired to their room, she took her courage in both hands and said to her husband gently, " I have a secret to tell you.   You must know that I have an angel of God watching over me.   If you touch me in the way of marriage he will be angry and you will suffer ; but if you respect my maidenhood he will love you as he loves me."   " Show me this angel," Valerian replied.   " If he be of God, I will refrain as you wish."   And Cecilia said, " If you believe in the living and one true God and receive the water of baptism, then you shall see the angel ".   Valerian agreed and was sent to find Bishop Urban among the poor near the third milestone of the Appian Way.   He was received with joy and there appeared a venerable old man bearing a writing : " One Lord, one faith, one baptism, one God and father of all, above all, and in us all."   " Do you believe this ? " Valerian was asked, and he assented and was baptized by Urban.   Then he returned to Cecilia, and found standing by her side an angel, who put upon the head of each a chaplet of roses and lilies.   Then appeared his brother, Tiburtius, and he, too, was offered a deathless crown if he would renounce his false gods.   At first he was incredulous.   " Who ", he asked, " has returned from beyond the grave to tell us of this other life ? "   Cecilia talked long to him, until he was convinced by what she told him of Jesus, and he, too, was baptized and at once experienced many marvels.

From that time forth the two young men gave themselves up to good works. Because of their zeal in burying the bodies of martyrs they were both arrested. Almachius, the prefect before whom they were brought, began to cross-examine them.   The answers he received from Tiburtius he set down as the ravings of a madman, and, turning to Valerian, he remarked that he hoped to hear more sense from him than from his crazy brother.   Valerian replied that he and his brother were under the charge of one and the same physician, Jesus Christ, the Son of God, who could impart to them His own wisdom.   He then proceeded at some length to compare the joys of Heaven with those of earth, but Almachius told him to cease prating and to tell the court if he would sacrifice to the gods and go forth free. Tiburtius and Valerian both replied : " No, not to the gods, but to the one God to whom we offer sacrifice daily."   The prefect asked whether Jupiter were the name of their god.   " No, indeed ", said Valerian.   " Jupiter was a corrupt libertine and, according to the testimony of your own writers, a murderer as well as a criminal."

Valerian rejoiced when they were delivered over to be scourged, and cried out to the Christians present : " Roman citizens, do not let my sufferings frighten you away from the truth, but cling to the one holy God, and trample under your feet the idols of wood and stone which Almachius worships."   Even then the prefect was disposed to allow them a respite in which to reconsider their refusal, but his assessor assured him that they would only use the time to distribute their possessions, thus preventing the state from confiscating their property.   They were accordingly condemned to death and were beheaded in a place called Pagus Triopius, four miles from Rome.   With them perished one of the officials, a man called Maximus, who had declared himself a Christian after witnessing their fortitude.

Cecilia gave burial to the three bodies, and then she in turn was called on to repudiate her faith.   Instead she converted those who came to induce her to sacrifice ; and when Pope Urban visited her at home he baptized over 400 persons there : one of them, Gordian, a man of rank, established a church in her house, which Urban later dedicated in her name.   When she was eventually brought into court, Almachius argued with Cecilia at some length, and was not a little provoked by her attitude : she laughed in his face and tripped him up in his words.   At length she was sentenced to be suffocated to death in the bathroom of her own house.   But though the furnace was fed with seven times its normal amount of fuel, Cecilia remained for a day and a night without receiving any harm, and a soldier was sent to behead her.   He struck at her neck three times, and then left her lying.   She was not dead and lingered three days, during which the Christians flocked to her side and she formally made over her house to Urban and committed her household to his care.   She was buried next to the papal crypt in the catacomb of St Callistus.

This well-known story, familiar to and loved by Christians for many ages, dates back to about the end of the fifth century, but unfortunately can by no means be regarded as trustworthy or even founded upon authentic materials.   It must be regretfully admitted that of St Valerian and St Tiburtius nothing beyond the fact of their martyrdom, place of burial (the cemetery of Praetextatus) and date of commemoration (April 14) is certainly known ; St Cecilia perhaps owed her original *cultus* to her specially honourable place of burial as foundress of a church, the *titulus Caeciliae*.   Nor are we any better informed about when she lived.   The dates suggested for her martyrdom vary from 177 (de Rossi) to the middle of the fourth century (Kellner).

Pope St Paschal I (817–824) translated the supposed relics of St Cecilia (found, in consequence of a vision or dream, not in the cemetery of Callistus but in that of Praetextatus), together with those of SS. Valerian, Tiburtius and Maximus, to the church of Santa Cecilia in Trastevere. In 1599 Cardinal Sfondrati in repairing this church reinterred the relics of the four martyrs, the body of Cecilia being alleged to be then still incorrupt and complete, although Pope Paschal had enshrined the head separately, and between 847 and 855 it was mentioned among the relics at the church of the Four Crowned Ones. The story goes that in 1599 the sculptor Maderna was allowed to see the body and made a life-size statue of what he is said to have seen, naturalistic and very moving : " not lying upon her back like a body in a tomb, but upon the right side, as a maiden in her bed, her knees drawn together, and seeming to be asleep." This statue is in the church of St Cecilia, under the altar contiguous to the place where the relics were reburied in a silver coffin ; it bears the sculptor's inscription : " Behold the most holy virgin Cecilia, whom I myself saw lying incorrupt in her tomb. I have made for you in this marble an image of that saint in the very posture of her body." De Rossi located the original burying-place of Cecilia in the cemetery of Callistus, and a replica of Maderna's statue now occupies the recess.

However, Father Delehaye and others are not satisfied that there is any justification for the common belief that the body of the saint was found entire in 1599 just as Maderna has sculptured it. Both he and Dom Quentin call attention to the inconsistencies in the accounts which such contemporaries as Baronius and Bosio have left us of the discovery. Another difficulty is caused by the fact that no mention is made of a Roman virgin martyr named Cecilia in the period immediately following the persecutions. There is no reference to her in the poems of Damasus or Prudentius, in the writings of Jerome or Ambrose, and her name does not occur in the *Depositio martyrum* (fourth century). Moreover, what was later called the *titulus Sanctae Caeciliae* was originally known simply as the *titulus Caeciliae, i.e.* the church founded by a lady named Cecilia.

Today perhaps St Cecilia is most generally known as the patron-saint of music and musicians. At her wedding, the *acta* tell us, while the musicians played, Cecilia sang to the Lord in her heart. In the later middle ages she was represented as actually playing the organ and singing aloud ; and in the first antiphon of Lauds on her feast, referring to this incident, the words " in her heart " are omitted.

The legendary *passio* is printed at full length in Mombritius and summarized by Delehaye in his book cited below, while those portions of the text which are of more practical interest may be found in Dom Quentin's article in DAC., vol. ii, cc. 2712–2738. There is a considerable literature, and in particular the whole matter has been very fully discussed by H. Delehaye in his book *Étude sur le légendier romain* (1936), pp. 73–96. He mentions, besides Quentin's article just referred to, the following authorities as particularly worth consulting : De Rossi, *Roma sotterranea,* vol. ii, pp. xxxii–xliii ; Erbes, *Die heilige Caecilia in Zusammenhang mit der Papstcrypta,* in the *Zeitschrift für Kirchengeschichte,* 1888, pp. 1–66 ; J. P. Kirsch, *Die heilige Caecilia in der römischen Kirche* (1910), and *Die römischen Titelkirchen im Altertum* (1918), pp. 113–116 and 155–156 ; P. Franchi de' Cavalieri, *Recenti studi intorno a S. Cecilia* in *Note agiografiche,* vol. iv (1912), pp. 3–38 ; F. Lanzoni in *Rivista di archeologia cristiana,* vol. ii, pp. 220–224 ; Duchesne, *Liber Pontificalis,* vol. i, p. 297, and vol. ii, pp. 52–68 ; P. Styger, *Römische Märtyrergrüfte* (1935), pp. 83–84 and 88 ; and L. de Lacger in *Bulletin de littérature ecclésiastique* (1923), pp. 21–29. There is a full summary of Mgr J. P. Kirsch's views, written by himself, in the *Catholic Encyclopedia,* vol. iii, pp. 471–473.

Upon the representations of St Cecilia in art, see Künstle, *Ikonographie*, vol. ii, pp. 146–150. The case and cult of St Cecilia is examined at some length in Baudot and Chaussin, *Vies des saints*, vol. xi (1954), pp. 731–759.

SS. PHILEMON AND APPHIA, MARTYRS   (FIRST CENTURY)

PHILEMON, a citizen of Colossae in Phrygia, a man of rank and wealth, was probably converted by St Paul, whose personal friend he was, when he preached at Ephesus. His house was notable for the devotion and piety of those who composed it, and the assemblies of the faithful seem to have been kept there. But Onesimus, a slave of Philemon, so far from profiting by the good example before his eyes, robbed his master, and fled to Rome, where he met St Paul, who was then prisoner there ; and the spirit of charity and religion with which the apostle treated him wrought an entire change in his heart, so that he became his spiritual son. St Paul would have liked to have kept the converted Onesimus as an assistant, but Philemon had the prior claim on his services and so he sent him back to Colossae, with a letter that appears in the Bible as the Epistle to Philemon. Therein St Paul writes with much tenderness and power of persuasion. He calls Philemon his beloved fellow labourer, commending his charity and faith. He also names Apphia, " our dearest sister ", presumably Philemon's wife, and Archippus, " our fellow soldier ". He then prefers a request, modestly putting Philemon in mind that, as an apostle, he could command him in Christ : but he is content to ask that the obligation which Philemon had to him, the writer, might acquit Onesimus of the wrong he had done : that he might be received " not now as a servant, but instead of a servant a most dear brother, especially to me : but how much more to thee, both in the flesh and in the Lord ? " The result of St Paul's appeal is not known, but Christian tradition says that Philemon granted Onesimus his liberty, forgave him his crime, and made him a worthy fellow labourer in the gospel.

So much about St Philemon can be gleaned from St Paul's letter to him, and nothing else is known. But there are several legends, as that he became bishop of Colossae, or of Gaza, that he was martyred at Ephesus, or again at Colossae. The story accepted in the East is thus summarized in the Roman Martyrology : " When, under the Emperor Nero, the gentiles broke into the church on the feast of Diana at Colossae in Phrygia and the rest fled, the holy Philemon and Apphia were taken. By command of the governor Artoclis they were scourged and then buried in a pit up to the waist, where they were overwhelmed with stones."

A commemoration of these saints occurs in the Greek synaxaries and *menaia*, though November 23 is the date to which it is commonly assigned, and a third martyr, Archippus, is associated with them. See Delehaye's edition of the *Synaxarium Constantinopolitanum*, cc. 247–248.

23*: ST CLEMENT I, POPE AND MARTYR   (*c.* A.D 99)

THE third successor of St Peter—as he seems to have been—is believed also to have been a contemporary of SS. Peter and Paul ; he " saw the blessed apostles and talked with them; their preaching was still in his ears and their tradition before his eyes ", wrote St Irenaeus during the second part of the

* A commemoration is made of St Felicity in the Mass and Office of St Clement today, but she is referred to herein under July 10, the feast of the Seven Brothers, her reputed sons.

second century.   Origen and others identified him with the Clement whom St
Paul refers to as a fellow labourer (Phil. iv 3), an identity accepted in the proper
of his Mass and Office, but it is doubtful.   He was certainly not the same as the
consul Clement, of the Flavii, put to death in the year 95, but may have been a
freed-man of the imperial household, perhaps of Jewish descent.   Particulars of
his life we have none.   The entirely apocryphal *acta* of the fourth century state
that, having converted a patrician named Theodora and her husband Sisinnius
and four hundred and twenty-three others, and an outcry being raised against him
among the people, he was banished by Trajan to the Crimea, where he had to work
in the quarries.   As the nearest drinking-water was six miles away Clement
miraculously found a nearer spring for the use of the numerous Christian captives,
and preached among the people with such success that soon seventy-five churches
were required.   He was therefore thrown into the sea with an anchor tied round
his neck, and angels came and built him a tomb beneath the waves, which once a
year was revealed by a miraculous ebbing of the tide.

" Under this Clement ", says St Irenaeus, " no small sedition took place among
the brethren at Corinth, and the church of Rome sent a most sufficient letter to
the Corinthians, establishing them in peace and renewing their faith, and announcing the tradition it had recently received from the apostles."   It is this letter that
has made the name of Pope Clement I famous.   It was so highly esteemed in the
early Church that it took rank next to the canonical books of the Holy Scriptures
(or even among them), and was with them read in the churches.   A copy of it was
found in the fifth-century manuscript copy of the Bible (Codex Alexandrinus)
which Cyril Lukaris, Patriarch of Constantinople, sent to King James I, from which
Patrick Young, the keeper of the king's library, published it at Oxford in 1633.

St Clement begins his letter by explaining that his delay in writing was due to
the trials the Church was undergoing at Rome (Domitian's persecution).   He then
reminds the Corinthians how edifying their behaviour was when they were all
humble-minded, desiring rather to be subject than to govern, to give than to
receive, content with the portion God had dispensed to them, listening diligently
to His word.   At that time they were sincere, without offence, not mindful of
injuries, and all sedition and schism was an abomination to them.   He laments
that they had then forsaken the fear of the Lord and were fallen into pride, jealousy,
and strife, and exhorts them to lay aside pride and anger, for Christ is theirs who
are humble and not theirs who exalt themselves.   The sceptre of the majesty of
God, our Lord Jesus Christ, came not in the show of power, but with humility.
He bids them look up to the order of the world, and think how it all obeys God's
will and the heavens, earth, ocean, and worlds beyond are governed by His commands.   Considering how near God is to us and that none of our thoughts are hid
from Him, we ought never to do anything contrary to His will, and should honour
them who are set over us ; bishops and deacons had been instituted from a necessity
of discipline and to them obedience is due.   Disputes must arise and the just must
suffer persecution, but a few Corinthians were disgracing their church.   " Let
every one ", he says, " be subject to another according to the order in which he is
placed by the gift of God.   Let not the strong man neglect the care of the weak ;
let the weak see that he respect the strong.   Let the rich man distribute to the
necessity of the poor, and let the poor bless God who gives him one to supply his
want.   Let the wise man show forth his wisdom not in words but in works. . . .
They who are great cannot yet subsist without those that are little, nor the little

without the great. In our body, the head without the feet is nothing, neither the feet without the head. And the smallest members of our body are useful and necessary to the whole." Thus the saint teaches that the lowest in the Church may be the greatest before God, if they are more faithful in the discharge of their respective duties. He urges the Corinthians to send his two messengers " back to us again with all speed in peace and joy, that they may the sooner acquaint us with your peace and concord, so much prayed for and desired by us, that we may rejoice in your good order."

In the course of this letter occurs a well-known passage, which the great Anglican scholar Dr Lightfoot referred to as a " noble remonstrance ", but " the first step towards papal domination ". " If certain persons ", wrote Pope Clement, " should be disobedient to the words spoken by Him through us, let them understand that they will involve themselves in no trifling transgression and danger ; but we shall be guiltless of this sin." The letter is not only important for its beautiful passages, its evidence of Roman prestige and authority at the end of the first century, and its incidental historical allusions : it is " a model of a pastoral letter . . . a homily on Christian life ". There are other writings, now known as the " Pseudo-Clementines ", which were formerly wrongly attributed to this pope. One of them is another letter to the Corinthians and it also is included in the Alexandrine *codex* of the Bible.

St Clement is venerated as a martyr, but the earliest references to him make no mention of this. Nor is the place of his death known. It may well have been in exile, even in the Crimea, but the relics which St Cyril brought from thence to Rome towards the end of the ninth century are most unlikely to have been really those of Pope St Clement. They were deposited below the altar of San Clemente on the Coelian. Below this church and the fourth-century basilica on which it was built are the remains of rooms, of the imperial age, which de Rossi believed were those of the actual house of Pope Clement himself ; but it is not known who was the Clement who gave his name to this church originally, the *titulus Clementis*. The pope is named in the canon of the Mass and is accounted the first of those early writers who are called the Apostolic Fathers because they came under the direct or very close influence of the apostles of the Lord. He is the titular and patron saint of the Gild, Fraternity and Brotherhood of the Most Glorious and Undivided Trinity, of London, *i.e.* " Trinity House ".

The various references made to Pope St Clement in early Christian literature have nowhere perhaps been more painstakingly brought together than by J. B. Lightfoot, Anglican Bishop of Durham, in his *Apostolic Fathers*, pt 1, vol. i, pp. 148–200. The more important, notably the *De viris illustribus* of St Jerome, the *Liber Pontificalis*, and the entries in sacramentaries and calendars are also cited in CMH., pp. 615–616. There is a *passio*, whieh exists both in Latin and Greek (the Latin, according to Franchi de' Cavalieri and Delehaye, being the original), and it is from this that the legend (perpetuated in the lessons of the Roman Breviary) of the tomb beneath the sea with the anchor used to sink the body has been derived. See for the texts F. Diekamp, *Patres apostolici*, vol. ii (1913), pp. 50–81. The apocryphal literature known as the " Clementines ", existing in two forms, the " Homilies " and the " Recognitions ", did much to give prominence to the name of St Clement, but these of course add absolutely nothing to our knowledge from the point of view of either history or hagiography. The subject of St Clement has been much discussed of late years, most recently and very thoroughly by H. Delehaye in his *Étude sur le légendier romain* (1936), pp. 96–116. As in the case of St Cecilia, he draws attention to the development of the *titulus Clementis* into that of *sancti Clementis*. Consult also P. Franchi de' Cavalieri, *Note agiografiche*, vol. v, pp. 3–40 ; I. Franko, *St Klemens in Chersonesus* (1906);

J. P. Kirsch, *Die römischen Titelkirchen* (1918). The Greek text of Clement's letter to the Corinthians, with a translation by Kirsopp Lake, is in the Loeb Classical Library, *The Apostolic Fathers* (1930) ; and a new translation by J. A. Kleist in vol. i of the American Ancient Christian Writers series, *The Epistles of St Clement . . . and St Ignatius . . .* (1946).

ST AMPHILOCHIUS, Bishop of Iconium　　(c. A.D. 400)

THIS saint was an intimate friend of St Gregory Nazianzen (his cousin) and of St Basil, though rather younger than they were, and their letters to him are the principal source of information about his life. He was a native of Cappadocia and in his earlier years was a rhetor at Constantinople, where he seems to have got into money difficulties. He was still young when he withdrew to a life of retirement at a place not far from Nazianzus, where also he took care of his aged father. St Gregory supplied his friend with corn in return for vegetables from his garden, and in a letter complains playfully that he gets the worst of the bargain. In the year 374, when he was only some thirty-five years old, Amphilochius was appointed bishop of Iconium. He accepted the office very reluctantly, and his old father complained to St Gregory at being deprived of his son's care ; in his reply Gregory disclaims responsibility and says that he too will suffer by the loss of the company of Amphilochius. St Basil, who probably was ultimately responsible for the episcopal appointment, wrote to compliment the new bishop, exhorting him never to be drawn into connivance at what is evil because it is become fashionable or precedented by the example of others : he must guide others, not be led by them. Immediately after his consecration St Amphilochius paid a visit to St Basil at Caesarea, and preached before the people, who relished his sermons more than those of any stranger they had heard. Amphilochius often consulted St Basil upon difficult points of doctrine and discipline, and it was in response to his friend's request that Basil wrote his treatise on the Holy Ghost. Amphilochius delivered the panegyric at the funeral of St Basil.

St Amphilochius held a council at Iconium against the Macedonian heretics, who denied the divinity of the Holy Ghost, and assisted at the general council of Constantinople against the same heretics in 381, when he met St Jerome, to whom he read his own work on the Holy Ghost. Amphilochius petitioned the Emperor Theodosius I that he would forbid the Arians to hold their assemblies, which the emperor judged too rigorous and refused to do. Amphilochius came some time after to the palace and, seeing Arcadius, the emperor's son (who had been already proclaimed emperor), close by his father, saluted the father but took no notice of the son ; and when Theodosius pointed out this omission, he simply greeted the boy and patted his cheek. Theodosius lost his temper, whereupon the bishop said to him, " You cannot bear a slight to your son. How, then, can you suffer those who dishonour the Son of God ? " The emperor, struck by his reply, soon made a law whereby he forbade Arian heretics to hold their meetings, whether publicly or in private. St Amphilochius also zealously opposed the rising heresy of the Messalians, an illuminist and Manichean sect which put the essence of religion in prayer alone ; against these he presided over a synod held at Sida in Pamphylia. St Gregory Nazianzen calls St Amphilochius a bishop without reproach, an angel and herald of truth, and his father averred that he healed the sick by his prayers.

St Amphilochius is fairly well known to us from the references in contemporary Christian literature, and there are two short Greek biographies, printed in Migne, PG., vol. xxxix, pp. 13–26, and vol. cxvi, pp. 956–970. The collection of the surviving fragments of his writings in Migne is not complete. Other supplementary matter has been printed by K. Holl, *Amphilochius von Ikonium* (1904), and by G. Ficker, *Amphilochiana* (1906). See also Bardenhewer, *Altkirchliche Literatur*, vol. iii, pp. 220–228 ; DHG., vol. ii, pp. 1346–1348 ; and DCB., vol. i, pp. 103–107.

ST GREGORY, BISHOP OF GIRGENTI   (*c.* A.D. 603)

ACCORDING to an unreliable life purporting to be written soon after his death by Leontius, a monk of St Sabas at Rome, this Gregory was born near Girgenti (Agrigentum) in Sicily, and brought up under the eye of St Potamion, bishop of that place. He went on a pilgrimage to Palestine, where he spent four years studying in different monasteries and was ordained deacon at Jerusalem. He then went to Antioch and Constantinople, where, says Nicephorus Callistus, he was looked upon as one of the most holy and wisest men of the age. Ultimately he came to Rome, and was appointed to the see of Girgenti ; but almost immediately his zeal for discipline gave offence and he was the victim of a scurvy plot. A woman of bad character was secretly introduced into his house, duly " discovered ", and the bishop denounced. He was summoned to Rome, where he soon cleared himself and was sent back to his see. St Gregory is usually identified with the Gregorius Agrigentinus to whom allusions are made in letters written by Pope St Gregory the Great, but the chronology of the life of St Gregory of Girgenti has been the subject of considerable discussion. He is now best remembered as the author of a commentary in Greek on the book of Ecclesiastes. He is named in the Roman Martyrology and his feast is kept in Greek churches of the Byzantine rite, to which he belonged.

A long Greek life by one Leontius is printed in Migne, PG., vol. xcviii, cc. 549–716, and there is another in PG., vol. cxvi, cc. 190–269. See further DCB., vol. ii, pp. 776–777 ; Bardenhewer, *Geschichte der altkirchlichen Literatur*, vol. v, pp. 105–107 ; and L. T. White in the *American Historical Review*, vol. xlii (1936), pp. 1–21.

ST COLUMBAN, ABBOT OF LUXEUIL AND BOBBIO   (A.D. 615)

THE date of the birth of the greatest of the Irish missionary-monks on the continent of Europe must have been very near the year which saw the death of St Benedict, that patriarch of Western monks whose rule all monasteries of St Columban eventually adopted. Columban was born in west Leinster and had a good education, which was interrupted when he was a young man by a sharp struggle with the insurgent flesh. Certain *lascivae puellae*, as his biographer Jonas calls them, made advances to him, and Columban was grievously tempted to yield. In his distress he asked the advice of a religious woman who had lived solitary from the world for years, and she told him to flee the temptation even to the extent of leaving the land of his birth : " You think you can freely avoid women. Do you remember Eve coaxing and Adam yielding ? Samson made weak by Dalila ? David lured from his former righteousness by the beauty of Bathsheba ? The wise Solomon deceived by love of women ? Go away, turn from the river into which so many have fallen." Columban heard her words as more than just sensible counsel to a youth distracted by an ordinary trial of adolescence ; it was to him a call to renounce the world, definitely to choose the cloistered rather than secular life. He left his mother, grievously against her will, and fled to Sinell, a monk who lived on Cluain Inis, an island in Lough Erne, and from thence in time he went on to the great monastic seat of learning at Bangor, opposite Carrickfergus on Belfast Lough.   How long he lived here is not known ; Jonas speaks of " many years ", and he was probably about forty-five when he obtained St Comgall's permission to leave the monastery and adventure in foreign lands.   With twelve companions Columban passed over into Gaul, where barbarian invasions, civil strife and clerical slackness had reduced religion to a low ebb.

The Irish monks at once set about preaching to the people by showing an example of charity, penance and devotion, and their reputation reached the king of Burgundy, Guntramnus, who *c.* 590 offered St Columban ground for building at Annegray in the mountains of the Vosges, which became his first monastery. His biographer relates several incidents reminiscent of others in the life of St Francis of Assisi, which took place here.   This house soon became too small to contain the numbers that desired to live under the discipline of the saint.   He therefore built a second monastery called Luxeuil, not far from the former, and a third, which on account of its springs was called Fontes, now Fontaine.   These, with Bobbio later, were the foundations of Columban himself ; his followers established numerous monasteries in France, Germany, Switzerland and Italy, centres of religion and industry in Europe throughout the dark ages.   St Columban lays down for the foundation of his rule the love of God and of our neighbour, as a general precept upon which the superstructure of all the rest is raised.   He appointed that monks shall eat only the simplest food, which is to be proportioned in amount to their labour.   He will have them eat every day that they may be able to perform all duties ; and he prescribes the time to be spent in prayer, reading and manual labour.   St Columban says that he received these rules from his fathers, that is, the monks of Ireland.   He mentions the obligation of every one's praying privately in his own cell, and adds that the essential parts are prayer of the heart and the continual application of the mind to God.   After the rule follows a penitential, containing prescriptions of penances to be imposed upon monks for every fault, however light.   It is in the harshness of its discipline, characteristic of much Celtic Christianity, the imposition of fasts on bread and water, and beatings, for the smallest transgressions, and the great length of the Divine Office (there was a maximum of seventy-five psalms a day in winter), that the Rule of St Columban most obviously differs from that of St Benedict.   In austerity the Celtic monks rivalled those of the East.

After the Columban monks had pursued their strenuous life in peace for twelve years a certain hostility manifested itself among the Frankish bishops, and St Columban was summoned before a synod to give an account of his Celtic usages (computation of Easter, etc.).   He refused to go, " lest he might contend in words ", but addressed a letter to the assembly in which he, " a poor stranger in these parts for the cause of Christ ", asks humbly to be left in peace, but also more than hints that there are more important matters than the date of Easter which they ought to attend to.   As the bishops pressed him he appealed to the Holy See, and addressed letters to two popes in which he protests the orthodoxy of himself and his monks, explains the Irish customs, and asks that they be confirmed.*   He writes freely and respectfully apologises for seeming to argue with the Supreme Pontiff, and

* In the first letter, to Pope St Gregory the Great, Columban, referring to the directions of Pope St Leo I quoted by his opponents, makes a famous pun : " Is not a live dog [*i.e.* Gregory] better than a dead lion [*leo*] ? "

says, " Forgive, I beseech you, O blessed Pope, my boldness in writing so pre-
sumptuously.   I beg that you will, once at least in your holy prayers to our common
Lord, pray for me, a most unworthy sinner."   But soon Columban was involved
in worse trouble.   King Theodoric II of Burgundy had respect for St Columban
and the abbot reproved him for keeping concubines instead of marrying a queen.
His grandmother, Queen Brunhilda, who had been regent, fearing lest a queen
should ruin her power, was much provoked against Columban.   Her resentment
was increased by his refusing to bless at her request the king's four natural children,
saying, " They shall not inherit the kingdom ; they are a bad breed ! "   St
Columban also denied her entrance into his monastery, as he did to all women
and even to lay men, and this, being contrary to Frankish custom, Brunhilda
made a pretext for stirring up Theodoric against Columban.   The upshot was that
he was in 610 ordered to be deported to Ireland, with all his Irish brethren
but none others : there may probably be seen the hidden influence of Frankish
court bishops behind all this.   At Nantes he wrote a famous letter to the monks
left at Luxeuil, of which Montalembert says it contains " some of the finest and
grandest words which the Christian genius has ever produced ", and then embarked.

But the ship at once met bad weather and ran aground, and the next we hear
of Columban is that he made his way through Paris and Meaux to the court of
Theodebert II of Austrasia at Metz, by whom he was well received.   Under his
protection he went with some of his disciples to preach to the infidels near the lake
of Zurich, but the zeal of the missionaries was not well received and they went on
to the neighbourhood of Lake Constance, to a fruitful pleasant valley amidst the
mountains (now Bregenz), where they found an abandoned oratory dedicated in
honour of St Aurelia, near which they built themselves cells.   But here too the
vigorous methods of some of the missionaries (especially of St Gall) provoked the
people against them, and danger arose as well from another quarter.   Austrasia
and Burgundy were at war, and Theodebert, being defeated, was delivered
up by his own men and sent by his brother Theoderic to their grandmother
Brunhilda.

St Columban, seeing his enemy was master of the country where he lived and
that he could no longer remain there with safety, went across the Alps (he was
about seventy years old by now) and came to Milan, where he met with a kind
reception from the Arian Agilulf, King of the Lombards, and his wife Theodelinda.
He at once began to oppose the Arians, against whom he wrote a treatise, and
became involved in the affair of the Three Chapters (writings which were condemned by the fifth general council at Constantinople as favouring Nestorianism).
The bishops of Istria and some of Lombardy defended these writings with such
warmth as to break off communion with the pope, and the king and queen induced
St Columban to write very outspokenly to Pope St Boniface IV in defence of them,
urging him to take steps that orthodoxy might prevail.   The subject at issue was
one upon which St Columban was badly informed indeed ; on the other hand, he
makes clear his burning desire for unity in the faith and his own intense devotion
to the Holy See and belief that " the pillar of the Church is always at Rome ".
" All we Irish ", he says, " living in the furthest parts of the earth are followers of
St Peter and St Paul and of the disciples who wrote the sacred canon under the
Holy Ghost.   We accept nothing outside this evangelical and apostolic teaching.
. . . I confess that I am grieved by the bad repute of the chair of St Peter in this

country. . . . We are, as I have said, bound to the chair of St Peter. For, thongh Rome is great and known afar, she is great and honoured with us only because of this chair." Realizing that he has spoken very boldly, not hesitating to refer to Pope Vigilius as a " cause of scandal ", he writes in the same letter : " If in this or any other letter . . . you find any expressions as of excessive zeal, put them down to my indiscretion, not to self-sufficiency. . . . Look after the peace of the Church . . . use the calls and the familiar voice of the true shepherd, and stand between your sheep and the wolves " ; and he refers to the pope as " pastor of pastors ", " leader of the leaders ", and " the only hope, mighty through the honour of Peter the Apostle ".

Agilulf gave to Columban a ruined church and some land at Ebovium (Bobbio), in a valley of the Apennines between Genoa and Piacenza, and here he began the establishment of the abbey of St Peter. In spite of his age he himself was active in the work of building, but for the rest Columban now wanted only retirement to prepare for death. When he had visited King Clotaire II of Neustria on his way back from Nantes he had prophesied the fall of Theoderic within three years. This had been verified : Theoderic was dead, old Brunhilda brutally murdered, and Clotaire was master of Austrasia and Burgundy as well. He remembered the prophecy of St Columban, and invited him to come back to France. He would not go, but asked the king to look kindly on the monks of Luxeuil. Soon after, on November 23 in 615, St Columban died.

Alban Butler, writing in the middle of the eighteenth century, could say that " Luxeuil is still in a flourishing condition ", as a monastery of the Benedictine congregation of Saint-Vanne. But within fifty years the French Revolution brought to an end its long, chequered and glorious history. Bobbio, whose library was one of the greatest of the middle ages, declined from the fifteenth century, and was finally suppressed by the French in 1803 ; the library had begun to be dispersed nearly three hundred years before. But the feast of St Columban is still observed in the small diocese of Bobbio, he is mentioned in the Roman Martyrology on November 21, on which day the Benedictines commemorate him, and his feast is kept throughout Ireland on the 23rd, while numerous traces of his former wide *cultus* exist in northern Italy.

A life, written very soon after the saint's death by Jonas, who was a monk of Bobbio, supplies the greater part of the information we possess concerning Columban. It has been critically edited by B. Krusch in MGH., *Scriptores Merov.*, vol. iv, pp. 1–156. A good deal has been written about St Columban of late years, much of which will be found indicated in the excellent notice devoted to the saint by Dom Gougaud in *Les Saints irlandais hors d'Irlande* (1936), pp. 51–62, or in his *Christianity in Celtic Lands* (1932). See also E. Martin, *St Colomban* (1905) ; G. Metlake, *The Life and Writings of St Columban* (1914) ; H. Concannon, *Life of St Columban* (1915) ; J. J. Laux, *Der hl. Kolumban* (1919) ; J. F. Kenney, *The Sources for the Early History of Ireland*, vol. i (1929), pp. 186–191 ; M. Stokes, *Six Months in the Appenines* . . . (1892) ; J. M. Clauss, *Die Heiligen des Elsasses* (1935) ; A. M. Tommasini, *Irish Saints in Italy* (1937) ; L. Gougaud, " Le culte de St Colomban " in the *Revue Mabillon*, vol. xxv (1935), pp. 169–178 ; and M. M. Dubois, *St Colomban* (1950). The pertinent section of Montalembert's *Monks of the West* was reprinted separately in America in 1928. The letters of Columban should be read in the text provided by the MGH., *Epistolae*, vol. iii, pp. 154–190. The Penitential ascribed to him is of doubtful authenticity, but his Rule for monks seems authentic and has been widely discussed. The text is in Migne, PL., vol. lxxx, cc. 209 *seq.*, or better in the *Zeitschrift f. Kirchengeschichte* for 1895 and 1897 ; and a translation of the Penitential in McNeill and Gaymer, *Medieval Handbooks of Penance* (1938). He has also been credited with a commentary on the psalms, but this is certainly not his ; see Dom Morin in the *Revue Bénédictine*, vol. xxxviii (1926), pp. 164–177. It is curious that no notice of St Columban appears in the *Félire* of Oengus, despite a mention in the *Hieronymianum*. The very difficult chronology of this saint's life has been investigated anew by Fr P. Grosjean in *Analecta Bollandiana*, vol. lxiv (1946), pp. 200–215.

ST TRUDO, OR TROND   (*c.* A.D. 690)

THE province of Brabant was by no means free of paganism by the seventh century, and on account of his missionary zeal this saint is venerated as the apostle of that part of it called Hasbaye. His parents were Franks, and he gave himself to the service of the Church. St Remaclus sent Trudo to the cathedral school of Metz, where he was eventually ordained by St Clodulf. He then returned to his native district, where he preached among the heathen and built a church on his own estate, with a monastery attached which gave its name to the present Saint-Trond, between Louvain and Tongres. He also founded a nunnery near Bruges.

A life, compiled by the deacon Donatus less than a century after the death of the saint, may be accepted as fairly reliable. It was printed by Mabillon, and more critically by Levison in MGH., *Scriptores Merov.*, vol. vi. Another life, by Theoderic, is of little value. See also Van der Essen, *Étude critique sur les saints mérovingiens* (1907), pp. 91–96. The early Wissenburg text of the *Hieronymianum* mentions St Trudo. See Fr M. Coens in *Analecta Bollandiana*, vol. lxxii (1954), pp. 90–94, 98–100.

24 : ST JOHN OF THE CROSS, DOCTOR OF THE CHURCH   (A.D. 1591)

GONZALO DE YEPES belonged to a good Toledan family, but having married " beneath him " he was disinherited and had to earn his living as a silk-weaver. On his death his wife, Catherine Alvarez, was left destitute with three children, of whom John, born at Fontiveros in Old Castile in 1542, was the youngest. He went to a poor-school at Medina del Campo and was then apprenticed to a weaver, but he showed no aptitude for the trade and was taken on as a servant by the governor of the hospital at Medina. He stopped there for seven years, already practising bodily austerities, and continuing his studies in the college of the Jesuits. At twenty-one years of age he took the religious habit among the Carmelite friars at Medina, receiving the name of John-of-St-Matthias. After his profession he asked for and was granted permission to follow the original Carmelite rule, without the mitigations approved by various popes and then accepted in all the friaries. It was John's desire to be a lay-brother, but this was refused him. He had given satisfaction in his course of theological studies, and in 1567 he was promoted to the priesthood. The graces which he received from the holy Mysteries gave him a desire of greater retirement, for which purpose he deliberated with himself about entering the order of the Carthusians.

St Teresa was then establishing her reformation of the Carmelites and, coming to Medina del Campo, heard of Brother John. Whereupon she desired to see him, admired his spirit, and told him that God had called him to sanctify himself in the Order of Our Lady of Mount Carmel ; that she had received authority from the prior general to found two reformed houses of men ; and that he himself

413

should be the first instrument of so great a work.   Soon after the first monastery of discalced (*i.e.* barefooted) Carmelite friars was established in a small and dilapidated house at Duruelo.   St John entered this new Bethlehem in a perfect spirit of sacrifice, and about two months after was joined by two others, who renewed their profession on Advent Sunday, 1568, St John taking the new religious name of John-of-the-Cross.   It was a prophetic choice.   The fame of the sanctity of this obscure house spread, and St Teresa soon established a second at Pastrana, a third at Mancera, whither she translated that from Duruelo, and in 1570 a fourth, at Alcalá, a college of the university, of which John was made rector.   His example inspired the religious with a perfect spirit of solitude, humility and mortification, but Almighty God, to purify his heart from all natural weaknesses and attachments, made him pass through the most severe interior and exterior trials.   St John, after tasting the first joys of contemplation, found himself deprived of all sensible devotion.   This spiritual dryness was followed by interior trouble of mind, scruples and a disrelish of spiritual exercises, and, while the Devil assaulted him with violent temptations, men persecuted him by calumnies.   The most terrible of all these pains was that of scrupulosity and interior desolation, which he describes in his book called *The Dark Night of the Soul*.   This again was succeeded by another more grievous trial of spiritual darkness, accompanied with interior pain and temptations in which God seemed to have forsaken him.   But in the calm which followed this terrible tempest he was wonderfully repaid with divine love and new light.   On one occasion St John was subjected to a bare-faced attempt by an unrestrained young woman of considerable attraction.   Instead of the burning brand that St Thomas Aquinas used on a like occasion, John used gentle words to persuade her of the error of her ways.   By like means but in other circumstances he got the better of another lady, whose temper was so fierce that she was known as Robert the Devil.

In 1571 St Teresa undertook, under obedience, the office of prioress of the unreformed convent of the Incarnation at Avila, and she sent for St John to be its spiritual director and confessor.   " He is doing great things here ", she wrote to her sister, and to Philip II, " The people take him for a saint ; in my opinion he is one, and has been all his life ".   He was sought out by seculars as well as religious, and God confirmed his ministry by evident miracles.   But grave troubles were arising between the Discalced and the Mitigated Carmelites.   The old friars looked on this reformation, though undertaken with the licence and approbation of the prior general given to St Teresa, as a rebellion against their order ; on the other hand, some of the Discalced were tactless and exceeded their powers and rights.   Moreover, confusing and contradictory policies were pursued by the prior general, the general chapter and the papal nuncios respectively.   At length, in 1577, the provincial of Castile ordered St John to return to his original friary at Medina.   He refused, on the ground that he held his office from the papal nuncio and not from the order.   Whereupon armed men were sent, who broke open his door and carried him off.   Knowing the veneration which the people at Avila had for him, they removed him to Toledo, where he was pressed to abandon the reform.   When he refused he was locked up in a small cell that had practically no light, and treated in a way that shows only too clearly how little, nearly sixteen hundred years after the Incarnation, the spirit of Jesus Christ had penetrated into the hearts of many who claimed His name.

St John's cell measured some ten feet by six, and the one window was so small and high up that he had to stand on a stool by it to see to read his office.   He was bloodily beaten—he bore the marks to his dying day—publicly in chapter, by order of Jerome Tostado, vicar general of the Carmelites in Spain and a consultor of the Inquisition.   St John's were all those sufferings described in St Teresa's " Sixth Mansion "—insults, slanders, physical pain, agony of soul and temptation to give in.   But, " Do not be surprised ", he said in after years, " if I show a great love of suffering ; God gave me a high idea of its value when I was in prison at Toledo ".   And his immediate answer was his earliest poems, a voice crying in the wilderness :

> Ah ! Where art thou gone hiding
> My Love, and leavest me alone with moaning ?
> Fleet as the deer thou fleddest
> When thou hadst me sore stricken,
> And thou art gone.   I follow thee with outcry.

In the intolerable atmosphere of the cell, stinking in the summer heat, the prior Maldonato visited Brother John on the eve of the Assumption, stirring him up with his foot as he lay prostrate.   John apologized for the weakness that did not allow him to get up more promptly when his superior entered.

"You were very absorbed," said Maldonato, " What were you thinking about?"

" I was thinking," replied John, " that it is our Lady's feast tomorrow, and what a happiness it would be to say Mass."

" Not in my time," retorted the prior.

On the night of the feast-day the Mother of God appeared to her suffering servant.   " Be patient, my son," she seemed to say, " Your trials will soon be over."   A few days later she appeared again, and showed him in vision a window overlooking the river Tagus.   " You will go out that way ", she said, " and I will help you."   And so it happened, nine months after his imprisonment began, that John had his opportunity when he was allowed a few minutes exercise.   He walked through the building, looking for that window ; he recognized it, and went back to his cell.   He had already begun to loosen the screws of the door lock ; that night he broke if off and, though two visiting friars were sleeping close by the window, he let himself down from it on a rope of twisted coverlets and clothes. The rope was too short, he fell down the ramparts to the river bank, picked himself up unhurt, and followed a dog which jumped into an adjoining courtyard.   And so he got away, with attendant circumstances that on the face of it appear miraculous.*

John made his way to the reformed friary of Beas de Segura and then to the near-by hermitage of Monte Calvario ; in 1579 he became head of the college at Baeza, and in 1581 he was chosen prior of Los Martires, near Granada.   Though the male founder and spiritual leader of the Discalced friars he took little part during these years, when their continued existence hung in the balance, in the negotiations and events which led up to the establishment of a separate province for the Discalced in 1580.   Instead he began those writings which have made him

* Prescinding from the methods used, it should be borne in mind that juridically the opponents of St John had a case.   There was a conflict of jurisdiction, but from their point of view Friar John came within the provision in Bd John Soreth's constitutions concerning rebels, fugitives and the like.

a doctor of the Church in mystical theology.   In his teaching he was a faithful follower of ancient tradition : human life on earth is ordered to an end which is the perfection of charity and transformation in God by love ; contemplation is not an end in itself, it does not stop at understanding, but it is for love and for union with God by love, and ultimately involves the experience itself of that union towards which everything is ordered.   " There is no better or more necessary work than love ", he says.   " We have been created for love."   " God uses nothing but love."   " As love is the union of the Father with the Son, so it is of the human soul with God."   It is by love that contemplation is attained, and since this love is produced by faith—which alone can bridge the gulf between our understanding and the infinity of God—it is a living and lived faith that is the principle of mystical experience.   Such traditional doctrine St John was never wearied of inculcating in his own lofty way and burning words ; but that he was at the same time a characteristic son of his age and country a glance at his own design for a " crucifixion " (now preserved in the Carmelite convent at Avila) at once shows.   Sometimes the austerities which he practised seemed to exceed bounds ; he only slept two or three hours in a night, employing the rest in prayer before the Blessed Sacrament.   Three things he frequently asked of God : that he might not pass one day of his life without suffering something, that he might not die in office, and that he might end his life in humiliation and contempt.   His confidence in God earned miraculous supplies for his monasteries, which firm confidence in divine providence he called the patrimony of the poor.   He was frequently so absorbed in God that he was obliged to do violence to himself to treat of temporal affairs.   This love appeared in a certain brightness which was seen in his countenance on many occasions, especially when he came from the altar.   His heart seemed a fire of love which could not be contained within his breast, but showed itself by these exterior marks.   By experience in spiritual things and an extraordinary light of the Holy Ghost he had the gift of discerning spirits, and could not be easily imposed upon in what came from God.

After the death of St Teresa in 1582 a disagreement within the ranks of the Discalced friars themselves became more pronounced, St John favouring the moderate policy of the prior provincial, Father Jerome Gracián, against the extremist Father Nicholas Doria, who aimed at separating the Discalced completely from the old stock.   After Father Nicholas himself became provincial, the chapter made St John vicar for Andalusia and he applied himself to the correction of certain abuses, especially those arising from the necessity of religious going out of their monasteries for the purpose of preaching.   It was his opinion that their vocation and life was primarily contemplative.   Thus opposition was raised against him.   He founded more friaries, and on the expiry of his term of office went as prior to Granada.   The policy of Father Nicholas had so prospered that a chapter held at Madrid in 1588 received a brief from the Holy See authorizing a further separation of the Discalced Carmelites from the Mitigated.   In spite of protests the venerable Father Jerome Gracián was deprived of all authority ; Father Nicholas Doria was made vicar general ; and the one province was divided into six, with a consultor for each (St John himself was one) to help him in the government of the new congregation.   This innovation caused grave discontent, especially among the nuns, and the Venerable Anne-of-Jesus, then prioress at Madrid, obtained from the Holy See a brief confirming their constitutions, without reference to the vicar general.   The consequent troubles were eventually composed, but at a chapter held at Whitsun 1591, St John spoke in defence both of Father Jerome Gracián and of the nuns.   Father Nicholas Doria had suspected him all along of being in league with them, and he now took the opportunity of reducing St John from all offices to the status of a simple friar and sending him to the remote friary of La Peñuela.   Here he spent some months, passing his days in meditation and prayer among the mountains, " for I have less to confess when I am among these rocks than when I am among men ".

But there were those who would not leave St John alone even here.   When visiting Seville as vicar provincial he had had occasion to restrict the preaching activities of two friars and to recall them to the observance of their rule.   They submitted at the time, but the rebuke had rankled, and now one of them, Father Diego, who had become a consultor of the congregation, went about over the whole province making inquiries about St John's life and conduct, trumping up accusations, and boasting that he had sufficient proofs to have him expelled from the order.   Many at that time forsook him, afraid of seeming to have any dealings with him, and burnt his letters lest they might be involved in his disgrace.   St John in the midst of all this was taken ill, and the provincial ordered him to leave out-of-the-way Peñuela and gave him the choice to go either to Baeza or Ubeda. The first was a convenient convent and had for prior a friend of the saint.   At the other Father Francis was prior, the other person whom he had corrected with Father Diego.   St John chose this house of Ubeda.   The fatigue of his journey made him worse, he suffered great pain, and submitted cheerfully to several operations.   But the unworthy prior treated him with inhumanity, forbade any one to see him, changed the infirmarian because he served him with tenderness, and would not allow him any but the ordinary food, refusing him even what seculars sent in for him.   This state of affairs was brought to the notice of the provincial who came to Ubeda, did all he could for the saint, and reprimanded Father Francis so sharply that he was brought to repentance for his malice.   After suffering acutely for nearly three months, St John died on December 14, 1591, still under the cloud which the ambition of Father Nicholas and the revengefulness of Father Diego had raised against him in the congregation of which he was co-founder and whose life he had been the first to take up.

Immediately after his death there was an outburst of recognition on all hands, and clergy and laity flocked to his funeral.   His body was removed to Segovia, the last house of which he had been prior.   He was canonized in 1726.   St John-of-the-Cross was not learned when compared with some learned doctors, but St Teresa saw in him a most pure soul to whom God had communicated great treasures of light and whose understanding was filled from on high.   Her judgement is amply borne out by his writings, principally the poems and their accompanying commentaries, the *Ascent of Mount Carmel*, the *Dark Night of the Soul*, the *Living Flame of Love* and a *Spiritual Canticle ;* and its rightness was superlatively recognized by the Church when, in 1926, he was proclaimed a doctor of the Church for his mystical works.   St John's doctrine was one of ever more suffering and complete abandonment of the soul to God, and that made him harsh and hard to himself ; but to others he could be kind, gentle, and forbearing, nor did he pass by or fear material things : " Natural things ", he said, " are always lovely ; they are the crumbs that fall from God's table ".   He lived the complete renunciation which he preached so powerfully, but, unlike so many lesser ones, he was " free as the spirit of God is free " : not tending to reiterated negation and emptiness but positive and full with the fullness of divine love, God and the soul in substantial communion. He " united in himself the ecstatic light of the Divine Wisdom with the shattering folly of the despised Christ ".

Whoever wishes to arrive at an understanding of the facts which so long impeded an adequate setting out of the history of St John-of-the-Cross may be recommended to read the Postscript with which Father Benedict Zimmerman has enriched the translation of Father Bruno's *St Jean de la Croix* (1932). The depositions taken in view of the beatification of the saint still exist at Rome in manuscript. The lives published in the first half of the seventeenth century, notably those by Joseph Quiroga and Jerome-of-St-Joseph, together with the *Reforma de los Descalzos*, vols. i and ii, written by Francis-of-St-Mary, tell us a great deal, but leave many points obscure. Besides these we have St Teresa's correspondence and spiritual works, as well as the records of the Carmelites, and even state-papers and diplomatic despatches, for the administration of Philip II was greatly interested in all that affected the reform of the religious orders. The most authoritative edition of the writings of St John himself in the original Spanish is that edited by Father Silverio (5 vols., 1929–31) ; Eng. trans. from this text by E. A. Peers (3 vols., new edn., 1953). Most of the works have also been translated into English by David Lewis, revised by Fr B. Zimmerman. Besides the excellent life by Father Bruno which has been based upon a very wide study of the sources, we have also an earlier life in English by D. Lewis (1897), that in Spanish by M. M. Garnica, *San Juan de la Cruz* (1875), and the shorter work of Mgr Demimuid, *St Jean de la Croix* (1916) in the collection " Les Saints ". See also J. Baruzi, *Saint Jean de la Croix et le problème de l'expérience mystique* (1931) ; and Father Wenceslaus, *Fisonomia de un Doctor* (1913) ; as well as a number of articles which since 1932 have appeared in *Études Carmélitaines*. See also FF. Crisogono and Lucinio, *Vida y Obras de San Juan de la Cruz* (1946) ; Father Gabriel, *St John of the Cross* (1946), an introduction to his works and doctrine ; E. A. Peers, *St John of the Cross* (essays ; 1946) ; and the translations of the poems by Roy Campbell (1951) and by Peers (1948). The best popular introduction is perhaps *Spirit of Flame* (1943), also by Professor Peers. See also his *Studies of the Spanish Mystics* (2 vols. 1927–30), an important essay in his *St Teresa of Jesus and Other Essays and Addresses* (1953), examining the second edition (1950) of the Spanish life of St John by Fr Crisogono Garrachón, and *A Handbook to the Life and Times of St Teresa and St John of the Cross* (1954).

ST CHRYSOGONUS, MARTYR   (*c.* A.D. 304 ?)

ALTHOUGH this martyr is one of those who has the distinction of being named in the canon of the Roman Mass nothing is known of him, except that he appears to have suffered at Aquileia, and he was venerated in northern Italy. His *cultus* was introduced at Rome ; the titular church of Chrysogonus in the Trastevere is mentioned in 499, and it is called *titulus Sancti Crisogoni* in an inscription of 521. According to the *passio* of St Anastasia (December 25) St Chrysogonus was a Roman official, who became her spiritual father. When he was imprisoned under Diocletian he continued to direct her by letter until he was sent for by the emperor at Aquileia, condemned and beheaded. His body was cast into the sea, whence it was recovered and buried by the priest St Zoilus, who lived close by in the house of SS. Agape, Chionia and Irene.

The story of St Chrysogonus forms the first part of the *Passio S. Anastasiae*. The Latin text has been re-edited in Delehaye's *Étude sur le légendier romain* (1936), pp. 221–249, but it seems to belong to the class of hagiographical fictions (*op. cit.*, pp. 151 *seq.*). It may be that the owner of the house in Rome, which was converted into a church (the *titulus Chrysogoni*) in the fourth century, was named Chrysogonus, and that when this was mistaken for a dedication to a *Saint* Chrysogonus, a legend was invented which identified him with a real martyr who suffered at Aquileia. But all the sacramentaries and calendars give the date November 24, and this does not seem to have been the day assigned to the

Aquileian martyr. See CMH., pp. 618–619; and also J. P. Kirsch, *Die römischen Titelkirchen im Altertum*, pp. 108–113; M. Mesnard, *La basilique de Saint-Chrysogone à Rome* (1935).

ST COLMAN OF CLOYNE, Bishop   (Sixth Century)

Colman of Cloyne, the " sun-bright bard ", was son of Lenin, born in Munster near the beginning of the sixth century. He was a poet of great skill and became royal bard (that is, chronicler and genealogist as well as poet laureate) at Cashel. He was nearly fifty years old before he became a Christian, and the circumstances of his conversion are said to have been as follows. St Brendan came to Cashel to help in the settlement of a dispute about the succession, and while he was there the grave and relics of St Ailbhe were found. Colman took part in this discovery, and St Brendan observed that hands which had been hallowed by the touch of such holy remains should not remain the hands of a pagan. So the bard was baptized by Brendan, and received from him the name of Colman, which was extraordinarily common in the early Irish church. In the Life of St Columba of Terryglass we hear that the boy Columba was given to the care of this Colman, who taught him to read. Having been ordained priest and afterwards consecrated bishop, St Colman preached in Limerick and the eastern parts of Cork, where he was granted land for a church at Cloyne, of which he is venerated as the first bishop. The feast of this St Colman is kept throughout Ireland.

There seems to be an absolute dearth of biographical material. An article by " J. C." in the *Journal of the Cork Historical and Archaeol. Soc.*, vol. xvi (1910), pp. 132–140, serves only to reveal the penury of data. But St Colman is mentioned in the *Félire* of Oengus under November 24, and there is a good paper on him by R. Thurneysen, " Colman mac Lenene und Senchan Torpeist ", in *Zeitschrift für celtische Philologie*, vol. xix (1933), pp. 193–209.

SS. FLORA and MARY, Virgins and Martyrs   (A.D. 851)

In the reign of Abdur Rahman II, king of the Moors at Cordova in Spain, Flora, being of Mohammedan birth by her father but secretly brought up in the Christian faith by her mother, was impeached by her own brother before the judge of the city. This magistrate had her scourged brutally, and then put her into the hands of her brother that he might overcome her resolution. After some time she made her escape and took shelter with a sister. Having lain concealed some time, she ventured back to Cordova and prayed publicly in the church of St Acisclus the martyr. There she met with Mary, sister to a deacon who had lately received the crown of martyrdom, and they agreed to give themselves up as Christians to the magistrate, by whose order they were confined where no one had access to them but some loose women. St Eulogius, who was at that time detained in another prison, wrote them an exhortation to martyrdom, in which he told them that no involuntary infamy could harm their souls and that to yield temporarily in hope of better things must not be considered. The two girls were eventually beheaded together, declaring they would intercede in Heaven for the release of St Eulogius and the other brethren; and they were in fact set free a week later.

These Spanish martyrs belong to the group of whom we know practically nothing but what has been recorded in the narrative of St Eulogius, which may be most conveniently consulted in Migne, PL., vol. cxv, cc. 835–845.

25 : ST CATHERINE OF ALEXANDRIA, Virgin and Martyr
(Date Unknown)

SINCE about the tenth century or earlier veneration for St Catherine of Alexandria has been marked in the East, but from the time of the Crusades until the eighteenth century her popularity was even greater in the West. Numerous churches were dedicated in her honour and her feast was kept with great solemnity ; she was included among the Fourteen Holy Helpers and venerated as the patroness of maidens and women students, of philosophers, preachers and apologists, of wheelwrights, millers and others.   Adam of Saint-Victor wrote a poem in her honour ; hers was one of the heavenly voices claimed to have been heard by St Joan of Arc ; and to her Bossuet devoted one of his most celebrated panegyrics.   But not a single fact about the life or death of Catherine of Alexandria has been established.

It is said in her completely worthless *acta* that she belonged to a patrician family of Alexandria and devoted herself to learned studies, in the course of which she learnt about Christianity.   She was converted by a vision of our Lady and the Holy Child.   When Maxentius began persecuting, Catherine, still only eighteen years old and of great beauty, went to him and rebuked him for his tyranny.   He could not answer her arguments against his gods, so summoned fifty philosophers to oppose her.   These confessed themselves convinced by the learning of the Christian girl, and were therefore burned to death by the infuriated emperor.   Then he tried to seduce Catherine with an offer of a consort's crown, and on her indignant refusal she was beaten and imprisoned, and Maxentius went off to inspect a camp. On his return he discovered that his wife and an officer had gone to see Catherine out of curiosity and had both been converted, together with two hundred soldiers of the guard.   They accordingly were all slain and Catherine was sentenced to be killed on a spiked wheel (whence our " catherine-wheel ").   When she was placed on it, her bonds were miraculously loosed and the wheel broke, its spikes flying off and killing many of the onlookers.   Then she was beheaded, and there flowed from her severed veins a white milk-like liquid.   There are variations of the story, including Catherine's conversion in Armenia, and the details introduced by the Cypriots when they claimed the saint for their island in the middle ages.

All the texts of the " acts " of St Catherine state that her body was carried by angels to Mount Sinai, where a church and monastery were afterwards built, but the legend was not known to the earliest pilgrims to the mountain.   In 527 the Emperor Justinian built a fortified monastery for the hermits of this place, and the supposed body of St Catherine was said to have been taken there in the eighth or ninth century, since when it has borne her name.   The great monastery of Mount Sinai, once a famous pilgrim-shrine, is now only a shadow of what it was.   But the alleged relics of St Catherine still repose there, in the care of monks of the Eastern Orthodox Church.   Alban Butler quotes Archbishop Falconio of Santa Severina as saying, " As to what is said, that the body of this saint was conveyed by angels to Mount Sinai, the meaning is that it was carried by the monks of Sinai to their monastery, that they might devoutly enrich their dwelling with such a treasure.   It is well known that the name of angelical habit was often used for a monastic habit, and that monks on account of their heavenly purity and functions were anciently called *angels.*" " Angelical life " and " angelical habit " are still current and usual expressions in Eastern monasticism.

" The female sex is not less capable of the sublime sciences nor less remarkable for liveliness of genius " than the male, comments Alban Butler elsewhere ; and St Catherine because of her traditional erudition is still regarded as the patroness of Christian philosophers and students of philosophy.

The story of St Catherine is perpetuated in many texts, oriental as well as Greek and Latin, and so far as regards the outstanding features of the narrative there is not much variation.   The Greek of Simeon the Metaphrast dating from the latter part of the tenth century may be read in Migne, PG., vol. cxvi, pp. 276–301 ; there is also a somewhat earlier Greek text ; see BHG., n. 31.   That the long-standing opinion among scholars as to the unreliability of the legend summarized above is general may be illustrated by the tone of the notice in Cardinal Schuster's book, *The Sacramentary* (1930), vol. v, p. 302.   He tells us that the story of St Catherine " is unfortunately unsupported by any authority.   The ancient Eastern and Egyptian calendars do not mention her name.   In the West the *cultus* of the saint began only about the eleventh century."   *Cf.* H. Delehaye, *Les martyrs d'Égypte* (1923), pp. 35–36, 123–124, and his *Legends of the Saints*, p. 57 ; and W. L. Schreiber, *Die Legende des hl. Catherine von Alexandria* (1931).   St Catherine in art is dealt with in Künstle, *Ikonographie*, vol. ii, pp. 369–374, and in Drake, *Saints and their Emblems* (1916), p. 24.   For the folklore aspects consult Bächtold-Stäubli, *Handwörterbuch des deutschen Aberglaubens*, vol. iv, pp. 1074–1084.   There is a good account of the whole matter in Baudot and Chaussin, *Vies des saints*, vol. xi (1954), pp. 854–872.   Katharine, rather than the French Catherine, seems the preferable spelling in English.

ST MERCURIUS, Martyr   (Date Unknown)

This martyr is one of the so-called warrior-saints so popular in the East, and he doubtless was a real person who died for the faith, but his various *acta* are all versions of a pious romance.   These relate that he was the son of a Scythian officer at Rome, and himself a successful soldier, who attained the rank of *primicerius*.   When the City was threatened by barbarians and the Emperor Decius in great fear, Mercurius encouraged him and himself led the imperial troops, armed with a sword which had been given him by an angel.   After a great victory Decius noticed that Mercurius was absent from the sacrifices to the gods, and sent for him to know the reason.   Whereupon Mercurius threw his military cloak and belt in the emperor's face, saying, " I will not deny my Lord Jesus ".   Fearing the anger of the people of Rome, Decius sent him to Caesarea in Cappadocia to be grievously tortured and then beheaded.   According to the Eastern legend, one hundred and thirteen years later St Basil invoked the aid of St Mercurius against Julian the Apostate, and he was made the instrument of divine wrath.   For Mercurius appeared from the heavens, girded with a sword and brandishing a spear, with which he transfixed and killed the infidel emperor.   St Mercurius is called in Egypt Abu Saifain, " the Father of Swords ", on account of the weapons with which he is always represented and his alleged military prowess, and many churches are dedicated in his honour in that country.   St Mercurius was said to have appeared with St George and St Demetrius to the soldiers of the First Crusade at Antioch.

Fr Delehaye has dealt very fully with the legend of St Mercurius.   In his book, *Les légendes grecques des saints militaires* (1909) he has not only discussed (pp. 91–101) the incidents of this quite unreliable narrative, but in an appendix (pp. 234–258) he has edited the two Greek texts which are of more notable interest.   The statement of the pilgrim Theodosius (*c.* 525) that the martyr Mercurius reposes at Caesarea seems to be the earliest sure attestation we possess of the saint's real existence.   As might be expected from the popularity of his cult in Egypt, we find his name constantly recurring in the Ethiopic synaxaries.   Sir E. Wallis Budge's translation of these last (4 vols., 1928) has a full index in which the references to St Mercurius are numerous.   Budge has also published a Coptic version of the *passio* in his *Miscellaneous Coptic Texts* (1915).   See also S. Binon, *Essai sur le cycle de St Mercure* (1937), and *Documents grecs inédits relatifs . . .* (1937).

ST MOSES, MARTYR   (A.D. 251)

MOSES, perhaps of Jewish origin, was a priest at Rome and leader of a group of clergy who, according to St Cyprian, were the first confessors in the Decian persecution.   They exchanged letters of encouragement with St Cyprian and the clergy of Carthage, and withdrew themselves from communion with Novatian, the danger of whose rigorism St Moses perceived.   After he had been in prison with his companions for eleven months and eleven days, that is to say, about January 1, 251, Moses died and was accounted a martyr : made illustrious, says the Roman Martyrology, by an excellent and wonderful martyrdom after he had stood with undaunted spirit as well against schismatics and Novatianist heretics as against the heathen.

It is from the letters of St Cyprian that our information is principally derived, but we also find Moses spoken of in Eusebius, bk VI, ch. 43, n. 20, and in the *Liber Pontificalis* (ed. Duchesne), vol. i, pp. 148 and 150.   The question is discussed by Tillemont, *Mémoires* vols. iii and iv ; and there is a good article in DCB., vol. iii, pp. 948–949.

26 : ST SILVESTER GOZZOLINI, ABBOT, FOUNDER OF THE SILVESTRINE BENEDICTINES   (A.D. 1267)

THE Gozzolini were a noble family of Osimo, where St Silvester was born in 1177.   He was sent to read law at Bologna and Padua, but soon abandoned his legal studies for theology and the Holy Scriptures, greatly to the anger of his father, who is said to have refused to speak to him for ten years on that account.   Silvester was presented to a canonry at Osimo, where he laboured until his zeal involved him in difficulties with his bishop.   This prelate was a man of disedifying life, and Silvester took it upon himself to rebuke him, respectfully but firmly.   The bishop was moved only to anger, and threatened to relieve the saint of his benefice, which would not have troubled him much for he had long been strongly drawn to the contemplative life.   This inclination is said to have strengthened into resolve when Silvester saw the decaying corpse of a man who had been famous for his physical beauty, a story told also of St Francis Borgia (untruly) and several other saints.   In 1227, being fifty years old, St Silvester resigned his rich benefice and retired to a lonely spot some thirty miles from Osimo, where he lived in great poverty and discomfort till the lord of the place gave him a better hermitage.   But this proved to be too damp, and he moved to Grotta Fucile where he stayed, living an extremely penitential life, till 1231, when he decided to establish a monastery for the disciples who now surrounded him.   This he did at Monte Fano, near Fabriano, building it partly from the ruins of a pagan temple.

St Silvester chose for his monks the Rule of St Benedict in its most austere interpretation, but owing to his extreme stress on certain points, particularly poverty, and to the nature of the organization of his institute, it has remained separate from the other congregations of Benedictines and does not form part of their confederation. Silvester governed his congregation with great wisdom and holiness for thirty-six years, and when he died at the age of ninety eleven monasteries, either new or reformed, recognized his leadership. His tomb was the scene of many miracles, and in 1275 his relics were enshrined in the abbey church at Monte Fano (where they still are). Clement VIII in 1598 ordered the name of Silvester Gozzolini to be added to the Roman Martyrology and Leo XIII gave his feast to the whole Western church. The Silvestrines are now a very small order, whose monks are distinguished by a dark blue habit.

The Life of St Silvester was written by a contemporary, Andrew de Giacomo of Fabriano, who must have penned his narrative between 1275 and 1280, some ten years after the founder's death. His account is full and seemingly reliable. The Latin text was first printed by C. S. Franceschini, in his *Vita di S. Silvestro Abate* (1772). Full use was made of this valuable source in the work of Amadeo Bolzonetti, *Il Monte Fano e un grande anacoreta; Ricordi storici* (1906), which discusses in detail the history of the *cultus* of the saint.

ST PETER, Bishop of Alexandria, Martyr   (A.D. 311)

EUSEBIUS calls this prelate an excellent teacher of the Christian religion and a great bishop, being admirable for his virtue and for his knowledge of the Holy Scriptures. In the year 300 he succeeded St Theonas in the see of Alexandria and he governed that church for twelve years, for the nine last of which he sustained the persecution carried on by Diocletian and his successors. He never ceased begging of God for himself and his flock necessary grace and courage, exhorting them to die daily to their own wills that they might be prepared to die for Christ. The confessors he comforted and encouraged by word and example, and was the father of many martyrs who sealed their faith with their blood. His watchfulness and care were extended to all the churches of Egypt, the Thebaid and Libya, and in this large district there were numbers of Christians who apostatized in one way or another. St Peter published fourteen canons of instruction as to how such *lapsi* who wished to be reconciled were to be treated, and these canons were later adopted by the whole Eastern church.

Eventually St Peter himself had to seek concealment away from Alexandria, and during his absence the Meletian Schism was formed (not to be confused with the more important Meletian Schism at Antioch, fifty years later). The exact circumstances are uncertain, but it would appear that Meletius, Bishop of Lycopolis, began uncanonically to exercise St Peter's metropolitan functions, and held ordinations in sees whose occupants were living but in hiding. To justify his actions and to impose upon men by a zeal for discipline he published calumnies against St Peter and had the assurance to say that Peter was indulgent to the lapsed in receiving them too easily to communion. Thus he formed a schism and succeeded in disturbing the whole church of Egypt when all the energy and strength of Christians was required to stand up against the persecution. Meletius being contumacious, there was nothing for St Peter to do but to excommunicate him.

From his place of hiding St Peter was able to continue to administer his church and care for the suffering faithful, and eventually he could return to his see ; but almost at once Maximinus Daia, *caesar* in the East, renewed persecution, and Peter was seized, when no one expected it, and hurried to execution without charge or trial. The Roman Martyrology also names the four other bishops who with over 600 others " were raised to Heaven by the sword of persecution " in Egypt at this time.

In Egypt St Peter is called " the Seal and Complement of the Persecution ", because he was the last martyr put to death by public authority at Alexandria, and also sometimes, " He who passed out through the wall ". The reason for this curious designation is explained in his Greek *passio*, which, however, lacks all authority. It is said therein that when St Peter was arrested his prison was completely surrounded by Christians who interceded for him with Heaven and would not go away, and when the order came for his execution the crowd was so great that the officers could not approach the building. It was therefore decided to massacre them all. St Peter foresaw this and, not wishing to be the occasion of such slaughter, secretly sent a message to the commandant that if a breach was made in the wall of the prison at night, he could be taken without anybody knowing. This was accordingly done, and there was such heavy rain and wind that nobody heard the noise made by the masons. St Peter urged the guards to make haste lest someone should awake, and he was executed before any of his faithful friends knew what had happened.

Various texts exist both in Greek and Latin of a supposed *passio* of St Peter, but they contain nothing which deserves credit ; see CMH., pp. 620–621. On the other hand Eusebius in his *Ecclesiastical History* (bks VII, VIII and IX) several times makes mention of this martyr, and in the early Syriac *breviarium* we have an entry under November 24 : " At Alexandria the Great, the bishop Peter, an ancient confessor." Although the saint displayed great literary activity, only fragments of his works remain. There is evidence of a widespread cult of St Peter : for example, he early found a place in the *Typikon* of Jerusalem. Consult also Tillemont, *Mémoires*, vol. v, pp. 755–757 ; Bardenhewer, *Geschichte der altkirchlichen Literatur*, vol. ii, pp. 203–211 ; DTC., vol. xii, cc. 1802–1804 ; *Analecta Bollandiana*, vol. lxvii (1949), pp. 117–130 ; and for a summary of the canons for the *lapsi*, DCB., vol. iv, pp. 331–332.

ST SIRICIUS, POPE   (A.D. 399)

THE name of St Siricius was added to the Roman Martyrology by Pope Benedict XIV, with the statement that he was " distinguished for his learning, piety and zeal for religion, condemning various heretics and strengthening ecclesiastical discipline by very salutary decrees ". The heretics referred to were principally the monk Jovinian, who denied the perpetual virginity of our Lady and the merit of virginity, and Bonosus, Bishop of Sardica, who shared these errors. Discipline was strengthened by a letter in which he replies to certain questions asked by Himerius, Bishop of Tarragona. This general instruction, which he ordered Himerius to publish to other bishops, is the earliest papal decretal extant in its entirety. Among its provisions it required that priests and deacons who were married should cease to cohabit with their wives, and this is the earliest known enforcement of clerical celibacy by the Roman see. Siricius sent this letter also to the church of Africa. It was this pope who supported St Martin of Tours, and excommunicated Felix of Trier for taking part with Ithacius to bring about the execution by the emperor's order of the heretic Priscillian.

In 390 Pope Siricius consecrated the basilica of St Paul (" outside the walls "), which had been enlarged by the Emperor Theodosius I, and his name is still to be seen on a pillar salvaged from the fire of 1823. St Siricius governed for fifteen years and was buried in the cemetery of Priscilla.

We know very little of St Siricius as an individual, though the *Liber Pontificalis* (ed. Duchesne), vol. i, pp. 217–218, tells us something of his action as a pontiff and administrator. See also Hefele-Leclercq, *Histoire des Conciles*, vol. ii, pp. 68–80 ; Tillemont, *Mémoires*, vol. x ; and E. Caspar, *Geschichte des Papsttums*, vol. i (1930), pp. 257 *seq.*   There is also a long notice in DCB., vol. iv, pp. 696–702.

ST BASOLUS, OR BASLE   (*c.* A.D. 620)

BASOLUS was born at Limoges in the middle of the sixth century, and after living some time as a soldier, heard the call of God to become a monk.   He went on pilgrimage to the shrine of St Remigius at Rheims, and was sent by the archbishop to the monastery of Verzy.   He was an exemplary monk, but he needed a life of more solitude, so his abbot allowed him to inhabit a cell alone, near the top of a neighbouring hill.   He remained there for the rest of his life.   Numerous miracles were attributed to St Basolus.   Among them, it is said that the count of Champagne, hunting nearby, ran a boar in the direction of the saint's cell.   The animal took refuge under the skirt of his habit, and the hounds stopped dead some yards away, refusing to come any nearer.*   The count was so impressed by this manifestation of the sacredness of the hermit's home that he made him a present of a large tract of land.   St Basolus had several disciples in the solitary life, one of them being St Sindulf.   Both these holy hermits are named in the Roman Martyrology.

Three short Latin lives of this religious have been printed ; the first was edited by Mabillon, vol. ii, pp. 60–62 ; the second may most conveniently be found in MGH., *Scriptores*, vol. xiii, pp. 449–451 ; the third is in Migne, PL., vol. cxxxvii, cc. 643–658.   See also E. Quentelot, *St Basle et le monastère de Verzy* (1892).

ST CONRAD, BISHOP OF CONSTANCE   (A.D. 975)

THIS saint belonged to the great Guelf family, being the second son of Henry, Count of Altdorf, founder of the existing abbey of Weingarten in Würtemberg. The boy was sent to the cathedral-school of Constance to make his clerical studies ; and soon after he was ordained priest the provostship of the cathedral was conferred upon him.   The bishop himself dying in 934, Conrad was chosen to fill the episcopal chair.   St Ulric, Bishop of Augsburg, who had promoted his election, frequently visited him and the friendship in which these two great prelates were linked together was very close.   St Conrad, having dedicated himself with all that he possessed to God, made an exchange of his estates with his brother for other lands situated nearer Constance, and settled them all upon that church and the poor, having first built and endowed three stately churches at Constance in honour of St Maurice, St John the Evangelist and St Paul, and renovated many old ones.

Pilgrimages to Jerusalem were already frequent in those days, and St Conrad thrice visited those holy places, making his journeys truly pilgrimages of penance and devotion.   Practically nothing else reliable is recorded in the lives of the saint, all of which were written a long time after his death.   In pictures and statues he is usually represented with a chalice and spider, for this reason : It happened that a large spider dropped into the chalice whilst he was celebrating Mass one Easter-day ; it was the common belief of his time that all or most spiders were poisonous, but Conrad, out of devotion and respect for the holy mysteries, deliberately swallowed the spider, without receiving any harm.   After an episcopate of over forty years St Conrad died in 975, and was canonized in 1123.   Considering the time in which

* This story with variations is, of course, a commonplace of hagiology.   It is told in Wales of St Melangell, the animal in her case being a hare.   She, like Basolus, received a grant of land from the astonished hunter (May 27).

he lived, he seems to have kept somewhat aloof from secular politics, but it is recorded that he accompanied the Emperor Otto I to Italy in the year 962.

A biography of Conrad written more than a century after his death by Udalschalk of Maissach is an unsatisfactory composition, full of legendary matter. It is printed by Pertz in MGH., *Scriptores*, vol. iv, pp. 430–460, and is followed by another setting of what is practically the same story. Some further material is contained in the *Historia Welforum Weingartensis*, also printed in Pertz, *Scriptores*, vol. xxi, pp. 454–477, and there are a few official documents belonging to Conrad's episcopate in Ladewig, *Regesta episcoporum Constantiensium*, vol. i (1886), pp. 44–48. There was a considerable later *cultus*, and this was probably responsible for the violence of the Reformers who in 1526 threw his relics into the lake, though the head was hidden and preserved. See also the Freiburg *Diöcesan-Archiv*, vol. xi, pp. 255–272, and vol. xxiii (1893), pp. 49–60 ; J. Mayer, *Der hl. Konrad* (1898) ; Gröber und Merk, *Das St Konrads Jubiläum* (1923) ; and Künstle, *Ikonographie*, vol. ii, pp. 385–388.

ST NIKON "METANOEITE" (A.D. 998)

NIKON, a native of Pontus, in his youth fled from his friends to a monastery called Khrysopetro, where he lived twelve years in the practice of the most austere penance and prayer. The spiritual fruit which his conferences and exhortations produced induced his superiors to employ him in preaching the word of God to the people. He therefore went as a missionary to Crete, which island had recently been recovered from the hands of the Saracens. Here Nikon reconverted many who had apostatized to Islam. He began all his sermons with the word *Metanoeite*, that is, " Repent ! " whence this surname was given him. By teaching penitents to lay the axe to the very root of sin, St Nikon had the comfort of seeing many wonderful conversions wrought. After having preached in Crete almost twenty years, he passed to the continent of Europe, and announced the divine word in Sparta and other parts of Greece, confirming his doctrine with miracles. He died in a monastery in Peloponnesus in 998, and is honoured both in the Greek and Roman martyrologies.

The long Greek Life of St Nikon has been known since Martène and Durand published Sirmond's Latin translation of it in their *Amplissima collectio*, vol. vi, pp. 837–887. In 1906 S. Lambros edited the Greek text from another manuscript at Mount Athos. The document is of considerable historic interest and we also possess what purports to be the spiritual will and testament of the saint. See also Prince Max of Saxony, *Das christliche Hellas* (1919), pp. 129–133, and DTC., vol. xi, cc. 655–657.

BD PONTIUS OF FAUCIGNY, ABBOT (A.D. 1178)

IN the year 1896 Pope Leo XIII confirmed the *cultus* of this holy abbot ; he had been greatly venerated by St Francis de Sales, who opened his tomb in 1620 to examine the relics and took away several small pieces of bone, which are said to have been the occasion of miracles. Pontius belonged to a noble Savoyard family, and at twenty became a canon regular at the abbey of Abondance in Chablais. He was entrusted with the revision of the constitutions of his house and the foundation in 1144 of a new monastery at Sixt, of which he was made abbot. After ruling it with great distinction for twenty-eight years he went to fulfil the same office at Abondance, but relinquished it soon after and died a holy death in retirement at Sixt.

Not much reliable information seems to be available regarding this abbot. Jean de Passier published in 1666 *La vie du bx Ponce de Faucigny*, but ancient records were then little studied. See, however, Mercier, " L'abbaye et la vallée d'Abondance " in the *Mémoires et documents de l'Académie salésienne*, vol. viii (1885), pp. 1–308, and DHG., vol. i, cc. 147 and 151. The best attempt to trace the career of Bd Pontius is that of Canon L. Albert, *Le bx Ponce de Faucigny* (1903).

BD JAMES, Bishop of Mantua   (A.D. 1338)

Nicholas Boccasini, while he was master general of the Dominicans, saw and appreciated the goodness and talents of Friar James Benefatti, and called him to his side to be his companion and adviser. He retained his services when he was created cardinal in 1298, and when five years later Nicholas became pope (Bd Benedict XI) one of the first acts of his brief pontificate was to appoint James Benefatti to the see of Mantua. This was James's native town, and he discharged the duties of its pastor for many years with heroic energy and prudence. After his death on November 19, 1338, he was at once venerated as a saint, but devotion cooled until, in 1483, his tomb was accidentally broken up, when the body was found to be incorrupt. This fact, and the report of miracles, caused it to be solemnly enshrined, but again Bd James was almost forgotten. Then in 1604 his tomb was again opened and the body found still entire ; whereupon Bishop Annibale of Mantua bore public testimony to the veneration in which Bd James had been and should be held. This *cultus* was confirmed in 1859.

Not much seems to be known of this *beatus*, but when the confirmation of his *cultus* was being proceeded with at Rome a summary account was published in the *Analecta Juris Pontificii*, vol. iv (1860), cc. 1896–1897. See also A. Touron, *Hommes illustres O.P.*, vol. ii, pp. 134–136 ; Ughelli, *Italia Sacra*, vol. i, c. 938 ; and Procter, *Dominican Saints*, pp. 337–339.

ST JOHN BERCHMANS   (A.D. 1621)

" If I do not become a saint when I am young ", said John Berchmans, " I shall never become one." He died when he was twenty-two and he was a saint, one of the three notable young saints of the Society of Jesus. He differed from the other two, St Aloysius and St Stanislaus Kostka, in his origins, for while they belonged to aristocratic families John was the eldest son of a master-shoemaker, a burgess of the town of Diest in Brabant. John was born in 1599, at his father's shop at the sign of the Big and Little Moon in Diest, and seems to have been a good and attractive child. He was most devoted to his mother, who suffered very bad health. His early education was in the hands first of a lay schoolmaster and then of Father Peter Emmerich, a Premonstratensian canon from the abbey of Tongerloo, who taught him Latin versification and took the boy with him when he visited the shrines or clergy of the neighbourhood. This rather encouraged John's tendency to prefer his own and his elders' company to that of other boys, but he entered whole-heartedly with them in their festival mystery-plays, and particularly distinguished himself in the part of Daniel defending Susanna. By the time he was thirteen his father's affairs had become straitened and there were growing brothers and sisters to be considered, so John was told that he must leave school and learn a trade. He protested that he wished to be a priest, and at length his father compromised by sending him as a servant in the household of one of the cathedral canons, John Froymont, at Malines, where he could also attend the classes at the archiepiscopal seminary.

The secular canon Froymont was a different sort of man from the regular canon Emmerich, and with him young John went duck-shooting rather than visiting shrines ; he is said to have learned the difficult art of teaching a dog to retrieve, and his particular duty in the house was waiting at table. In 1615 the Jesuits opened a college at Malines and John Berchmans was one of the first to enter himself thereat, " not without a good deal of feeling on the part of his former master and rector, on account of which ' there was a great gulf fixed ' between them and us ", wrote his confessor and tutor in Greek, Father De Greeff. He studied with earnest application, continued to be an enthusiastic player of sacred dramas, and was sometimes found kneeling at the foot of his bed after midnight when sleep had overtaken him at his prayers. A year later, after some objection from his father, he joined the novitiate. He wrote home a week before, " I humbly pray you, honoured father and dearest mother, by your parental affection for me and by my filial love for you, to be so good as to come here on Wednesday evening at the latest, either by the Malines coach from Montaigu or by Stephen's wagon, so that I may say ' Welcome and good-bye ' to you, and you to me when you give me, your son, back to the Lord God who gave me to you ".

As was expected by those who knew him best, John Berchmans was an admirable novice, and throughout his ascetical notes and other writings of that time it appears that, like another holy young religious three hundred and fifty years later, he kept before himself a way of perfection which he expressed in the phrase " Set great store on little things ". His industry in writing down his reflections was remarkable, and it extended to making an analysis of Father Alphonsus Rodriguez's book on Christian perfection, which had been published less than ten years. Soon after his novitiate began his mother died (there is extant a touching letter from him to her during her last illness), and within eighteen months his father had been ordained priest and presented to a canonry in his native town. On September 2, 1618, Brother John wrote to Canon Berchmans announcing that he was about to take his first vows, and asking in a postscript, " Please send me by his reverence the precentor, eleven ells of cloth, six ells of flannel, three ells of linen, and two calf-skins to make my clothes ". Canon Berchmans died the day before his son's profession, but John did not hear of this until he wrote to make an appointment to meet him at Malines before he set out for Rome where he was to begin his philosophy. Before leaving he wrote to his relatives expressing his astonishment and displeasure at their not having told him of his father's death, and another to his old master Canon Froymont asking him to keep an eye on his younger brothers, Charles and Bartholomew, " whom perhaps I shall never see again ".

St John arrived in Rome on new year's eve 1618, after having walked with one companion from Antwerp in ten weeks, and began his studies at the Roman College under Father Cepari, who afterwards wrote his biography. A professor there, Father Piccolomini, testified that, " Berchmans had good talent, capable of taking in several different subjects at the same time, and in my opinion his enthusiasm and application to work have been rarely equalled and never surpassed. . . . He spared himself no labour or weariness thoroughly to master the various languages and branches of knowledge that go to make a learned and scholarly man." Father Massucci, the spiritual director of the senior students, declared that, " After Blessed Aloysius Gonzaga, with whom I lived in the Roman College during the last year of his life, I have never known a young man of more exemplary life, of purer conscience, or of greater perfection than John ". And withal " his brethren loved and revered him as an angel from Heaven ". Among these brethren was a number of students from England, of whom the martyr Bd Henry Morse was one. For two and a half years St John continued his " little way ", without singularity or excess ; " my penance ", he would say, " is to live the common life ", and he jotted down, " I like letting myself be ruled like a baby a day old ".

St John's success at his examination in May 1621, caused him to be selected to defend a thesis against all comers in a public debate. But the strain of prolonged study during the heat of a Roman summer had been too much for him, and he began rapidly to fail. On August 6, though feeling unwell, he took a prominent part in a public disputation at the Greek College, but the next afternoon he had to be sent off to the infirmary. He was cheerful as usual—Father Cepari records there was always a smile playing about his mouth. When he had drunk a peculiarly nasty dose of medicine he asked the attendant father to say the grace after meals, and he told the rector that he hoped the death of another Flemish Jesuit in Rome would not cause friction between the two provinces of the Society ; when the doctor ordered his temples to be bathed with old wine he observed that it was lucky such an expensive illness would not last long. After four days Father Cornelius a Lapide, the great Biblical exegete, asked if aught were on his conscience. " *Nihil omnino.* Nothing at all ", replied St John, and he received the last sacraments with great devotion. He lingered two more days (the doctors were at a loss to diagnose what it was that had brought him so low), and died peacefully on the morning of August 13, 1621.

There were extraordinary scenes at the funeral, numerous miracles were attributed to John's intercession, and the recognition of his holiness was spread so rapidly that within a few years Father Bauters, s.j., wrote from Flanders, " Though he died in Rome, and but few of his countrymen knew him by sight, ten of our best engravers have already published his portrait and at least 24,000 copies have been struck off. This is not including the works of lesser artists and numbers of paintings." Nevertheless, though his cause was begun in the very year of his death, the beatification of St John Berchmans did not take place till 1865, and his canonization till 1888.

By far the most valuable contribution to our knowledge of St John Berchmans is that of A. Poncelet, printed in the *Analecta Bollandiana*, vol. xxxiv (1921), pp. 1–227. The whole question of sources is there discussed, and attention is drawn to the work of his more accredited biographers. Among these are specially mentioned V. Cepari (1627), L. J. M. Cros (1894), H. P. Vanderspecten (1886), and N. Angelini (1888). Fr Poncelet's article also includes copies of unpublished documents and letters—many of them submitted to St John's first biographer, Father Cepari. See further, in the series " Les Saints ", the life by Fr H. Delehaye (Eng. trans., 1921). There is also an English life by Father Goldie (1873), another by J. Daly (1921), and a sketch by Fr C. C. Martindale in his *Christ's Cadets* (1913).

ST LEONARD OF PORT MAURICE   (A.D. 1751)

DOUBTLESS while Alban Butler was writing these *Lives of the Saints* the fame often reached his ears of a Franciscan Father Leonard Casanova, whose missionary labours in Italy were at their height in the second quarter of the eighteenth century and who died five years before the publication of Butler's work. The name by which that friar is now known is taken from his native town, Porto Maurizio on the Italian Riviera, where he was born in 1676, and baptized Paul Jerome. His father, Dominic Casanova, was a master-mariner and a good Christian man, and when his eldest son was thirteen he entrusted him to the care of his wealthy uncle Augustine at Rome, who sent the boy to the Roman College of the Jesuits. Paul soon realized that he had a religious vocation and his own inclination was towards the Friars Minor.   But his uncle, who wanted him to be a physician, objected and eventually turned him out of his house ; but Paul found shelter with another relative, Leonard Ponzetti, with whom he stayed until he received his father's ready permission to become a friar.   He was clothed, when he was twenty-one, at the Franciscan novitiate at Ponticelli, taking the name of Leonard in gratitude for the kindness of Ponzetti, and completed his studies at St Bonaventure's on the Palatine, where he was ordained in 1703.   This friary was the principal house of an off-shoot of the strict *Riformati* branch of the Franciscans, called *Riformella*, and throughout his life St Leonard, both for himself and for others, combined active missionary work with a severely ascetic monastic observance and much solitude : the first that he might live *for* God and the last that he might live *in* God, as he himself expressed it.

In 1709 St Leonard was sent with other friars, under Father Pius, to take over the monastery of San Francesco del Monte at Florence, which the Grand Duke Cosimo III de' Medici had presented to the *Riformella*.   These friars lived according to the austerest principles of St Francis, refusing to accept endowments from Cosimo, or Mass and preaching stipends from the clergy and people, depending solely for material support on what they could beg as required.   The community flourished and increased in numbers, and became a great religious centre whence Leonard and his companions preached with great fruit throughout Tuscany.   A parish-priest at Pistoia wrote to the guardian, " Blessed be the hour in which I first thought of asking for Father Leonard.   God alone knows all the good he has done here.   His preaching has touched everybody's heart. . . . All the confessors in the town have had to work hard."   The saint himself was appointed guardian of del Monte, and he established the hermitage of St Mary at Incontro in the neighbouring mountains, where individual religious might retire for a space twice in every year.   "We will make a novitiate for Paradise ", he said, " I have given many missions to others, and now I am going to give one to Brother Leonard."   The regulations which he drew up for this retreat-house provided for strict enclosure, almost perpetual silence, fasting on bread, vegetables and fruit, and a daily discipline, with nine hours of the day devoted to the Divine Office and other spiritual exercises, and the rest to manual work.

For many years St Leonard laboured in Tuscany, but after a time he was frequently called to preach further afield, and at his first preaching visit to Rome his services were so long in request that Duke Cosimo sent a ship to the Tiber to fetch him back.   For six years he was conducting missions around Rome, and in 1736, when he was sixty years old, he had to take up the office of guardian at St Bonaventure's there.   From thence he preached for three weeks at Civita Vecchia, particularly to the soldiers and sailors, convicts and galley-slaves, and including a " visit to an English skipper, who wanted to see me on his ship.   We found three or four of them who had been present at the sermons [he had preached from the bridge of a vessel] and seemed inclined to abandon their errors.   The poor fellows had been more touched by what they saw than what they heard, for they hardly understood the language at all—which only shows that grace is the prime mover in stirring the heart."   After a year he was released from office, and preached in Umbria, Genoa and the Marches, where such crowds assembled that he had often to leave the churches, and speak in the open air.   To command the attention of those who were too hard-hearted and stiff-necked to take any notice of him otherwise, St Leonard would sometimes discipline himself in public, but the " devotion " which he principally used was the Way of the Cross, and it is to him that its popularity today is largely due.   He often gave it as a penance and preached it continually, and the setting up of the stations became a part in every mission he undertook.   It is said that he set them up in 571 places in Italy.   He also encouraged the exposition of the Blessed Sacrament and devotion to the Sacred Heart and to our Lady as conceived free from original sin, all of which were very far less wide-spread than they are to-day.   In particular did he make zealous efforts to get the Immaculate Conception defined as a dogma of faith and he was the first to suggest, what was done a century later, that the mind of the Church should be sounded on the matter without summoning a general council.

St Leonard was for a time the spiritual director of Clementina Sobieska of Poland, the wife of him who was recognized in Italy as King James III of England. All his letters to her were destroyed,* but there are extant one written by James to St Leonard a month after the queen's death in 1735, thanking him for his prayers and asking to see him, and several of direction written by the saint to one of the queen's ladies.   Pope Benedict XIV had a great regard for Leonard and his capabilities and in 1744, in concert with the Genoese Republic, the sovereign of the island, he sent him to Corsica to try and bring the people there to peace and order.   He was not well received, being regarded as an agent of the doge disguised as a missioner.   Admittedly there was a political aspect to his mission, for the troubles in Corsica were mainly due to discontent with the domination of Genoa. What with the political situation, the turbulent temperament of the Corsicans (they came to his sermons with weapons in their hands), and the mountainousness of the country, this was the most arduous of all St Leonard's missionary tasks.   He wrote numerous letters from the island, in one of which he says, " In every parish we meet with the most formidable feuds, but peace and quietness generally come to the top at last.   But unless the administration of justice gets strong enough to stamp out these vendettas, the good we are doing can be only transitory. . . . During these years of war the people have had no instruction whatever.   The young men are dissolute, wild, and don't come near the sacraments.   Many of them don't trouble even to make their Easter duties, and, what is worse, nobody thinks of reminding or rebuking them.   When I have an opportunity to meet the bishops I shall tell them what I think. . . . However, though the work is so exacting, the harvest is abundant. . . ."

But the fatigue, the intrigues, the strain of constant vigilance were too much for St Leonard, who was now sixty-eight, and at the end of six months he was so ill that a ship was sent from Genoa to bring him back.   He had gauged the state of Corsican affairs correctly, for the pope wrote to him soon after, " The Corsicans have got worse than ever since the mission, and so it is not thought advisable that you should go back there ".   Side by side with his public missions St Leonard gave retreats to nuns and lay-people, especially at Rome in preparation for the year of Jubilee 1750.   That year saw one of his ambitions realized, when Benedict XIV permitted him to set up the stations of the cross in the Colosseum, Leonard preaching to a large and fervent crowd a sermon which is still preserved.   " I am getting old ", he wrote, " My voice carried as it did two years ago, but I felt worn out.

* One was found under her pillow when she was dead.   St Leonard used to write to the most distinguished correspondents on any old piece of paper.   " They know Leonard is a poor man ", he would say, " so they won't bother to stand on ceremony."

However, it is a consolation to see this Colosseum no longer a common resort but a real sanctuary. . . ."

In the spring of the following year, when St Leonard went off to give missions at Lucca and elsewhere, the pope told him to give up travelling on foot and to go by carriage. He had been a missioner of the most powerful energy for forty-three years, and was beginning to fail. Owing to this and to the hostility and indifference of certain places, some of these last missions were relatively unsuccessful. At length, at the beginning of November, he turned south, and he knew his work was done. His carriage broke down and he had to walk part of the way through rain to Spoleto, where the friars tried in vain to detain him. On the evening of November 26 he arrived in Rome and was carried to bed at St Bonaventure's, and while they prepared to give him the last sacraments he sent a message to Pope Benedict that he had kept his promise—to come to Rome to die. At nine o'clock Mgr Belmonte arrived from the Vatican with an affectionate message from the pope. Before midnight St Leonard was dead.

In spite of his amazing activity St Leonard found time during the intervals of solitude and contemplation which he prized so much to write many letters, sermons and devotional treatises. His *Resolutions*, for the better attainment of Christian perfection, is a work valuable both in itself and for what it tells us about its author. The cause of his beatification in 1796 was furthered by Cardinal Henry of York, son of that Queen Clementina whose director St Leonard had been sixty years before. He was canonized in 1867.

As might be expected from St Leonard's comparatively recent date, his great reputation and his active life as a preacher, abundant materials are available for his biography. That by Fr Giuseppe da Masserano, the postulator of the cause of his beatification, was published in 1796, and has since been translated into most European languages. An English version was included in the Oratorian series in 1852. Another well-known life, by Salvatore di Ormea, appeared in 1851, and perhaps the most popular of all, that written by Fr Leopold de Chérancé in French, in 1903. As materials for an understanding of the activities and spirit of the great missioner, St Leonard's writings and letters have considerable importance. The collection published in Rome in 1853–1854 was far from complete. Eighty-six letters addressed to his penitent Elena Colonna were first printed in 1872, under the title *Soavità di spirito di S. Leonardo ;* and since then Fr B. Innocenti in 1925 and 1929, and Fr Ciro Ortolani da Pesaro in 1927 have found fresh material to publish. Many articles and notices in the *Archivum Franciscanum Historicum* have added to our knowledge of St Leonard. There is a good article by Fr M. Bihl in the *Catholic Encyclopedia ;* and a short life by Fr Dominic Devas, as well as a notice in Léon, *Auréole Séraphique* (Eng. trans.), vol. iv, pp. 98–112.

27 : SS. BARLAAM AND JOSAPHAT (NO DATE)

"I N the Indies bordering upon Persia, the birthday of the holy Barlaam and Josaphat, of whose wonderful deeds St John Damascene has written." This entry was added to the Roman Martyrology by Cardinal Baronius, but the document upon which he relied is now known not to have been written by St John. The story it tells is that an Indian king persecuted those of his subjects who were Christians, and when it was foretold that his son Josaphat (Joasaph) would become a Christian he had him brought up in the closest confinement. But the young man was nevertheless converted by an ascetic, disguised as a merchant carrying a " pearl of great price ", called Barlaam. The king, Abenner, tried to undo the work but, when he failed, himself became a Christian and eventually a hermit. Josaphat, too, resigned his throne, joined his old master Barlaam in the desert, and there passed the rest of his days.

Not only is this a purely imaginative romance about two saints who never existed, but its source is now recognized as being the legend of Siddartha Buddha, who was kept in confinement by the raja his father to prevent his becoming a professional ascetic. The Christian version of this legend spread in both East and West, and was translated into numerous languages. By this means was preserved a valuable piece of Christian apologetic, written by an Athenian philosopher called Aristides in the second century, which the compiler of the Barlaam legend incorporated in his text. This was not recognized as what it is till towards the end of the nineteenth century, when a Syriac version of the " Apology " of Aristides was found in the library of the monastery of Mount Sinai (an Armenian translation had been found by the Mekhitarist monks at Venice a few years before). Thus a story of the Buddha was spread over Christendom in a Christian disguise, and carrying on its back a vindication of the Church's teaching on the One God.

A very considerable literature has grown up around this story in modern times. It will be sufficient here to call attention to the article " Joasaph " by H. Leclercq in DAC., vol. vii, cc. 2359–2554, in which abundant references are given. The text and English translation of the Greek novel, ed. G. R. Woodward and H. Mattingly, is in the Loeb Classical Library (1914). It is now argued that the adapter, or rather translator, " John the Monk " of Mar Saba, was St Euthymius the Hagiorite (May 13) ; it was translated into Latin at Constantinople about 1048 : see P. Peeters in *Analecta Bollandiana*, vol. xlix (1931), pp. 276–312 ; and *Byzantion*, vol. vii, p. 692. See also J. Sonet, *Le roman de Barlaam et Josaphat* (1949). There was of course a genuine St Barlaam, a martyr at Antioch (November 19).

ST JAMES INTERCISUS, Martyr   (*c.* A.D. 421)

THE second great persecution of Christians in Persia began about the year 420, provoked by the intemperate zeal of the bishop Abdias, and the best known of its victims was this James. He was in high favour with King Yezdigerd I, and when that prince declared war against the Christian religion he had not the courage to renounce his master's friendship ; so he abandoned, or at least dissimulated, the worship of the true God which he before professed. His mother and wife were extremely grieved, and upon the death of King Yezdigerd they wrote to James, rebuking and warning him. He was strongly affected by this letter, and began to repent of what he had done. He appeared no more at court, renounced the honours which had occasioned his fall, and openly condemned himself for it. The new king sent for him. James confessed himself a Christian. Bahram reproached him for ingratitude, enumerating the honours he had received from his father. James calmly said, " Where is he now ? What is become of him ? " These words annoyed King Bahram, who threatened that his punishment should be a lingering death. " Any kind of death is no more than a sleep," replied St James. " May my soul die the death of the just." " Death ", retorted Bahram, " is not a sleep ; it is the terror of kings." James answered, " It indeed terrifies kings, and all others who ignore God, because the hope of the wicked shall perish ". The king took him up at these words : " Do you then call us wicked, you who worship neither sun nor moon nor fire nor water, the offspring of the god ? " " I accuse you not ", replied James, " but I say that you give the incommunicable name of God to creatures."

The council came to a resolution that, unless the criminal renounced Christ, he should be hung up and his limbs cut off one after another, joint by joint : the whole city flocked to see this new form of execution, and the Christians poured forth their prayers to God for the martyr's perseverance.   James was brought out, the executioners violently stretched out his arms, and in that posture explained to him the death he was to suffer, and pressed him to avert so terrible a punishment by obeying the king.   They urged him to dissemble his religion just for the present, saying he could immediately return to it again.   St James answered that, " This death which appears so dreadful is very little for the purchase of eternal life. " Then turning to the executioners, he said, " Why do you stand looking on ?   Begin your work."   They therefore cut off his right thumb, at which he prayed aloud, " Saviour of Christians, receive a branch of the tree.   It will putrefy, but will bud again and be clothed with glory.   The vine dies in winter, yet revives in spring. Shall not the body when cut down sprout up again ? "   When his first finger was cut off, he cried out, " My heart hath rejoiced in the Lord, and my soul hath exulted in His salvation !   Receive another branch, O Lord."   And at the lopping of every finger he exulted and thanked God afresh.   When his fingers and toes had all been cut off, he said cheerfully to the executioner, " Now the boughs are gone, cut down the trunk ".   Then his other limbs were hacked away and his thighs were torn from the hips.   Lying a naked trunk, having lost half his body, St James still continued to pray and praise God till a soldier by severing his head from his body completed his martyrdom.   The author of these " acts ", who says he was an eye-witness, adds, " We all implored the intercession of the blessed James ", who on account of the manner of his passion was named *Intercisus*, that is, " the Chopped-to-pieces ".

The Syriac text of this *passio* has been edited by P. Bedjan, *Acta martyrum et sanctorum* (1890–1897), vol. ii, pp. 539–558 ; and there is a German translation in the *Bibliothek der Kirchenväter*, vol. xxii, pp. 150–162.   The story became very popular, though much of it is clearly fabulous.   There are adaptations in Greek, Latin, Coptic, etc.   See also S. E. Assemani, *Acta sanctorum martyrum orientalium et occidentalium*, vol. i, pp. 242–258.   This martyr was much honoured in Cyprus, and some of his relics were believed to have been conveyed to Braga in Portugal.   Fr. P. Devos gives the martyr's *dossier* in *Analecta Bollandiana*, vol. lxxi (1953), pp. 157–210, and lxxii, 213–256.

ST SECUNDINUS, OR SECHNALL, BISHOP   (A.D. 447)

SECUNDINUS, the Irish translation of whose name is Sechnall, was one of the three *seniores* sent from Gaul to help St Patrick.   The Annals state that he came to Ireland in 439, together with Auxilius and Iserninus, Secundinus being named first ; according to the same source he died there in 447.   The Annals of Ulster add that he was then aged seventy-two, a particular that does not go back to the original Irish annals of the fifth century.

Secundinus is remembered as a hymn-writer.   He is the author of *Audite, omnes amantes Deum*, the earliest known Latin hymn written in Ireland.   It has twenty-three stanzas, the initial letters being alphabetical, and was composed in honour of St Patrick.   It was regarded as a " preserver ", to be recited in emergency, and the last three stanzas, which were particularly valued, appear liturgically in the Book of Mulling.   The beautiful communion hymn of the Irish church, *Sancti, venite, Christi corpus sumite*, is also attributed to St Sechnall, but in the Bangor Antiphonary, in which it is found, it is referred to only as

" The hymn when the priests communicate " ; the Tripartite Life of St Patrick speaks of Patrick and Sechnall hearing it sung by angelic voices.

The text of a Latin *vita* of medieval origin in the Royal Library of Belgium is printed in *Analecta Bollandiana*, vol. lx (1942), pp. 26–34. A good many allusions to him may be collected from such sources as the Tripartite Life of St Patrick, the *Lebar Brecc*, the additions to Tirechan's Collections, etc. See in particular Bernard and Atkinson, *The Irish Liber Hymnorum*, vol. ii, p. 96, etc. ; F. E. Warren, *The Antiphonary of Bangor*, pt II, p. 44, etc. ; Plummer, *Miscellanea Hagiographica Hibernica*, p. 223 ; Kenney, *Sources for the Early History of Ireland*, vol. i, pp. 250–260 ; and E. MacNeill, *St Patrick* (1934). The name of St Secundinus came next after St Patrick's in the diptychs at Armagh ; he is mentioned in the *Félire* of Oengus and reference is made there to his hymn on St Patrick. See also G. F. Hamilton, *In St Patrick's Praise* (1920).

ST MAXIMUS, Bishop of Riez   (*c.* A.D. 460)

St Maximus was born in Provence, near Digne. His Christian parents brought him up in the love of virtue, and no one was surprised when as a young man he retired to the monastery of Lérins, where he was received by St Honoratus, its founder. When the last named was made bishop of Arles in 426, Maximus was chosen the second abbot of Lérins. St Sidonius assures us that the monastery seemed to acquire a new lustre by his prudent example ; and the gift of miracles and the reputation of his sanctity drew crowds to his monastery from the mainland. At one time he felt obliged to quit the house and conceal himself in a forest and we are assured that the reason why he thus lay hid, in a very rainy season, was that the clergy and people of Fréjus had demanded him for bishop. However, not long after, the see of Riez in Provence became vacant and he was compelled to fill it, although he tried to get away in a boat. His parents were originally of that city so the saint was looked upon as already a citizen and on account of his holiness received with great joy. As a bishop he continued to observe the monastic rule so far as was compatible with his duties ; he retained the same love of poverty, the same spirit of penance and prayer, the same indifference to the world, and the same humility for which he had been so conspicuous in the cloister.

A laudatory oration printed among the works of Eusebius of Emesa was probably written by Faustus, the successor of Maximus. Besides this we have a life by one Dynamius, who was a patrician of the period. It is printed in Migne, PL., vol. lxxx, cc. 31–40. See also Duchesne, *Fastes Épiscopaux*, vol. i, pp. 283–284.

ST CUNGAR, Abbot   (Sixth Century)

There is very little satisfactory information to be found about St Cungar (Congar, Cyngar), but it is desirable to mention him here as his feast is observed today in the diocese of Clifton (November 7 is the traditional date in Wales). He is said to have established a monastery at a marshy place near Yatton in Somerset, now called after him Congresbury, and later, perhaps flying before the Saxons, went into South Wales and founded a church near Cardiff. According to Welsh legend he accompanied his " cousin " St Cybi to Ireland. St Cungar " was now an old man, and St Cybi bought for him a cow with her calf, because his age prevented him from taking any food but milk ". It was this calf which aggravated the feeling between Cybi and Fintan, as a consequence of which he and St Cungar left Aran and eventually came to Anglesey, where Cungar is said to have founded the church of Llangefni. According to a Breton tradition he died at Saint-Congard in

Morbihan.   The medieval *vita* identifies St Cungar with St Docco (Doccuin), who founded a monastery at St Kew in Cornwall and other churches in Wales.

The whole question of the life and identity of St Cungar is a hopeless tangle : there may have been two or three St Cungars.   We can only give an indication of some of the attempts to throw light on the subject.   See, for example, P. Grosjean in the *Analecta Bollandiana*, vol. xlii (1924), pp. 100–120 ; Armitage Robinson in the *Journal of Theological Studies*, vol. xx (1918), pp. 97–108 ; vol. xxiii (1921), pp. 15–22 ; and vol. xxix (1928), pp. 137–140 ; and G. H. Doble in *Antiquity*, vol. xix (1945), pp. 32–43, 85–95.   *Cf.* also *Analecta Bollandiana*, vol. xlvii (1929), pp. 430–431 ; LBS., vol. ii, pp. 248–253 ; and Schofield on the Muchelney Calendar in the *Proceedings of the Somerset Record Society*, vol. xlii.

ST FERGUS, Bishop   (Eighth Century ?)

This Fergus was an Irishman and distinguished in his own country as " the Pict ". According to the tradition of the church of Aberdeen he was already a bishop when he left Ireland for Scotland, and settled in Strathearn in Perthshire, where he founded three churches and dedicated them all in honour of St Patrick.   He was a missionary also in Caithness, Buchan and finally, Forfarshire, where at Glamis he founded the church and died.   St Fergus may be identical with the " Fergustus, Bishop of the Scots ", who assisted at a synod held by Pope St Gregory II in Rome in 721.   His feast was restored to the diocese of Aberdeen in 1898, and is also observed by Dunkeld.

We know little of this saint beyond what is contained in the lessons of the Aberdeen Breviary.   It would seem, however, that the statements made therein are borne out in large measure by local dedications which can be traced.   See A. P. Forbes in KSS., pp. 336–338, who has dealt with the matter very fully ; and *cf.* DCB., vol. ii, pp. 505–506.

ST VIRGIL, Bishop of Salzburg   (A.D. 784)

St Virgil was an Irishman, Feargal or Ferghil by name, and in the *Annals of the Four Masters* and the *Annals of Ulster* he is identified with an abbot of Aghaboe. About the year 743 he started out on a pilgrimage to the Holy Land, but after spending two years in France got no further than Bavaria.   Here Duke Odilo appointed him abbot of St Peter's at Salzburg and administrator of the diocese. St Virgil had a bishop, an Irishman like himself, to perform episcopal acts, reserving to himself the office of preaching and ruling, till he was compelled by his colleagues to receive episcopal consecration.   In the course of his duties he came across a priest who was so ignorant of Latin that he did not pronounce the words of baptism properly (*Ego te baptizo in nomine patria et filia et spiritu sancta*, is what he is said to have made of them).   St Virgil decided that as the error was an accidental one of language, with no religious significance, baptisms that this priest had administered were valid and need not be repeated.   St Boniface, then archbishop of Mainz, strongly disapproved of the verdict of Virgil, and appeal was made to Pope St Zachary.   He confirmed the ruling of Virgil, and expressed surprise that Boniface had questioned it.

Some time after this incident, Virgil was denounced to the Holy See, again by St Boniface, for teaching that—if his doctrine be accurately represented—there is beneath the earth another world and other men and also a sun and moon.   St Zachary answered that this was a " perverse and wicked doctrine, offensive alike to God and to his own soul " : and that if it were proved that Virgil did in fact

hold it he should be excommunicated by a synod.   This has been taken hold and
made ùse of for controversial purposes, but without reason.   For it is not known
exactly what Virgil did hold about the earth and other races of men ; and it is
clear that what brought him under suspicion was the idea that he taught something
which involved a denial of the unity of the human race and the universality both
of original sin and the Redemption.   If he in fact taught that the earth is a sphere
and that the antipodes were inhabited by humans, such *prima-facie* suspicion was
not entirely unreasonable in the middle of the eighth century.   There is not a tittle
of evidence for supposing that Virgil was tried, condemned and made to retract ;
but he must have satisfied his critics that he believed nothing " against God and
his own soul ", for about 767 (or earlier) he was consecrated bishop.

St Virgil rebuilt the cathedral of Salzburg on a grand scale, and translated
thereto the body of St Rupert, founder of the see.   He baptized at Salzburg two
successive Slav dukes of Carinthis, and at their request sent thither four preachers
under the bishop St Modestus ; other missionaries followed.   Virgil himself
preached in Carinthis as far as the borders of Hungary, where the Drava falls into
the Danube.   Soon after his return home he was taken ill, and cheerfully departed
to the Lord on November 27, 784.   St Virgil was canonized in 1233, and his feast
is kept throughout Ireland as well as in several parts of central Europe, where he
is venerated as the apostle of the Slovenes.

The Life of St Virgil printed in MGH., *Scriptores*, vol. xi, pp. 86–95, is a late production
and not wholly reliable ; what speaks more convincingly is the laudatory epitaph written
by Alcuin (in MGH., *Poetae Latini*, vol. i, p. 340).   See more particularly the valuable
notice of L. Gougaud, *Les saints irlandais hors d'Irlande* (1936), pp. 170–172 ; and *cf.* J.
Ryan, *Early Irish Missionaries . . . and St Vergil* (1924) ; H. Frank, *Die Klosterbischöfe
des Frankenreiches* (1932) ; and B. Krusch, in MGH., *Scriptores Merov.*, vol. vi, pp. 517 *seq.*
For the cosmological dispute see H. Krabbo in *Mitteilungen des Instituts für Österreichische
Geschichtsforschung*, vol. xxiv (1903), pp. 1–28 ; and H. Van der Linden in *Bulletins de
l'Acad. royale de Belg., Classe des lettres*, 1914, pp. 163–187.   *Cf.* also *Analecta Bollandiana*,
vol. xlvi (1928), p. 203.

BD BERNARDINO OF FOSSA   (A.D. 1503)

THE great Franciscan apostle St Bernardino of Siena was buried at Aquila in the
Abruzzi, where Bernardino Amici had his early education and took his namesake
as his model and heavenly patron, and afterwards wrote his life.   He had been
born near by, at Fossa in 1420, and was sent from Aquila to Perugia to study law.
Like another Bd Bernardino, " of Feltre ", a few years later, he was attracted to
the Friars Minor of the Observance at a Lenten mission preached by St James of
the March, and received the habit from him at Perugia in 1445.   After his ordination he became a well-known and successful preacher in Italy.   In 1464 he was
sent as peace-maker into Dalmatia and Bosnia, where differences of nationality
had caused difficulties among the friars, and he successfully united the diverse
elements into one province.   On his return he would have been promoted to the
see of Aquila had not the Holy See accepted his plea to be allowed to continue his
work as a simple friar.   Among his writings is a historical *Chronicle of the Friars
Minor of the Observance*.   Bd Bernardino of Fossa died at the friary of St Julian
near Aquila in 1503, and his *cultus* was approved in 1828.

A full account of Bd Bernardino is provided by Fr Van Ortroy in the *Acta Sanctorum*,
November, vol. iii, though he has to fall back for the details of the life upon the printed

narrative of Mark of Lisbon.   This is supplemented by a memoir which Antony Amici, a grand-nephew of the *beatus*, contributed to a volume of Bernardino's sermons.   See also a short biography by Ugo de Pescocostanza (1872), and Léon, *Auréole Séraphique* (Eng. trans.), vol. iv, pp. 42–44.

BD HUMILIS OF BISIGNANO   (A.D. 1637)

THIS *beatus* was a native of Bisignano in Calabria, where he received the name of Luke at baptism.   He earned his living as a farm-labourer, and when he was eighteen determined to become a Franciscan.   But it was not till nine years later, in 1609, that he was accepted as a lay-brother by the Observant friars at his birth-place.   At his clothing he was given the name of Humilis, a most appropriate choice as it turned out, for he maintained real humility in circumstances wherein that virtue must be greatly tried.   He in fact became so celebrated for miracles and the prudence of his opinions that not only did learned men come to consult him, but he was sent for to Rome by Pope Gregory XV.   While Bd Humilis was there, Gregory died, and his successor Urban VIII continued to keep the lay-brother at his side.   But the climate of Rome did not suit him ; he was taken ill, and it was deemed advisable to send him back to Bisignano.   Here he continued to lead a most holy and mortified life till his death, on November 26, 1637, at the age of fifty-five.   Bd Humilis was beatified in 1882.

There is useful material in the *Acta Ordinis Fratrum Minorum ad ordinem quoquo modo pertinentia*, vol. xxix (1910).   A very full account of Bd Humilis may be found in Mazzara, *Leggendario Francescano* (1680), vol. ii, pt 2, pp. 554–572, and there is a life in Italian by Fr Antony da Vicenza (1872).   See also Léon, *Auréole Séraphique* (Eng. trans.), vol. iv, pp. 154–156.

28 : ST STEPHEN THE YOUNGER, MARTYR   (A.D. 764)

ST STEPHEN, surnamed the Younger, one of the most renowned martyrs in the persecution by the Iconoclasts, was born at Constantinople, and his parents placed him when he was fifteen years old in the monastery of St Auxentius, not far from Chalcedon.   Stephen's employment was to fetch the provisions daily for the monastery.   The death of his father obliged him to make a journey to Constantinople, where he sold his share of the estate and distributed the price among the poor.   He had two sisters, one of whom was already a nun ; the other he took with his mother into Bithynia, where he found them a home in a monastery.   When John the abbot died, Stephen, though but thirty years of age, was placed at the head of the monastery.   This was a number of small cells scattered up and down a mountain, and the new abbot succeeded his predecessor in a cave on the summit, where he joined labour with prayer, copying books and making nets.   After some years Stephen resigned his abbacy, and built himself a remoter cell, so narrow that it was impossible for him to lie or stand up in it at ease.   He shut himself up in this sepulchre in his forty-second year.

The Emperor Constantine Copronymus carried on the war which his father Leo had begun against holy images, his efforts being chiefly levelled against the monks, from whom he expected and received the most resolute opposition.   Knowing the influence of Stephen, he was particularly anxious to get his subscription to the decree passed by the Iconoclast bishops at the council of 754.   Callistus, a patrician, tried to persuade the saint to consent, but he had to report failure. Constantine, incensed at St Stephen's resolute answer, sent Callistus back with soldiers and an order to drag him out of his cell. They found him so weak in body that they were obliged to carry him to the bottom of the mountain. Witnesses were suborned to accuse the saint, and he was charged with having criminally conversed with his spiritual daughter, the holy widow Anne. She protested he was innocent, and because she would not say as the emperor wished she was whipped and then confined to a monastery, where she died soon after of the hard usage she suffered.

The emperor, seeking a new excuse to put Stephen to death, trapped him into clothing a novice, which had been forbidden ; whereupon armed men dispersed his monks and burnt down the monastery and church. They took St Stephen, put him roughly on board a vessel, and carried him to a monastery at Chrysopolis, where Callistus and several court bishops came to examine him. They treated him first with civility, and afterwards with extreme harshness. He asked them how they could call a general council one which was not approved by the other patriarchs, and stoutly defended the honour due to holy images, insomuch that Stephen was condemned to banishment to the island of Proconnesus, in the Propontis. Two years after Copronymus ordered him to be removed to a prison in Constantinople, where some days later he was carried before the emperor, who asked him whether he believed that men trampled on Christ by trampling on His image. " God forbid ", said Stephen ; but then, taking a piece of money, he asked what treatment was deserved by one who should stamp upon that image of the emperor. The suggestion was received with indignation. " Is it then ", asked St Stephen, " so great a crime to insult the image of the king of the earth, and none to cast into the fire that of the King of Heaven ? " The emperor commanded that he should be scourged. This was done with brutal violence, and Copronymus when he heard that Stephen was nevertheless yet alive cried out, " Will no one rid me of this monk ? " Whereupon some of his hearers ran to the jail, seized the martyr and dragged him through the streets by his feet. Many of the mob struck him with stones and staves, till one dashed out his brains with a club. The Roman Martyrology mentions with St Stephen other monks who suffered in the same cause about the same time.

A Greek life, written by another Stephen, " deacon of Constantinople ", is printed in Migne, PG., vol. c, pp. 1069–1086. It has been pointed out that the text contains passages borrowed from the Life of St. Euthymius by Cyril of Scythopolis. A short account of the martyrdom will be found in B. Hermann's *Verborgene Heilige des griechischen Ostens* (1931).

ST SIMEON METAPHRASTES (*c.* A.D. 1000)

SIMEON METAPHRASTES, that is, " the Reteller ", requires a brief notice in a book of this kind for the same reason as do Bd Ado of Vienne and Bd James of Voragine, for he was the principal compiler of the legends of the saints found in the menologies of the Byzantine church. Though his life was written by Michael Psellos (d. 1078), little is known of him for certain. Unlike the other two hagiographers mentioned he was not a prelate ; Psellos says he was a *logothete*, a sort of secretary of state, and that he undertook his work on the saints at the command of an emperor, probably Constantine VII Porphyrogenitus. He is now generally identified with the tenth-century Simeon the Logothete who wrote a chronicle.

Simeon's collection of legends has made him one of the best-known of medieval Greek writers ; but there is still some uncertainty about his sources and where he got some of his material. He has been accused of wholesale fabrication and childish credulity, but his reputation has been vindicated by Ehrhard, Delehaye and others : the numerous ridiculous stories which he retails were not invented by him but were current, in writing or oral tradition, in his time, and he simply wrote them down. To what extent he believed them himself is another matter. He was the principal compiler of Greek legends of the saints, and has not inaptly been likened to Bd James of Voragine : his collection was translated into Latin and printed at Venice in the mid-sixteenth century.

The feast day of St Simeon Metaphrastes is on November 28 in the Byzantine church, but there has been no *cultus* of him in the West, as the Latins remarked in the seventh session of the Council of Florence.

See A. Ehrhard, *Die Legendensammlung des Symeon Metaphrastes* . . . (1897) ; H. Delehaye in *Analecta Bollandiana*, vol. xvi (1897), pp. 312–329 and vol. xvii (1898), pp. 448–452, in the *American Ecclesiastical Review*, vol. xxiii (1900), pp. 113–120, and in the *Encyclopaedia Britannica*, 11th edition, vol. xxvi, p. 285 ; A. Fortescue in the *Catholic Encyclopaedia*, vol. x, pp. 225–226 ; and H. Leclercq in DAC., t. xi, cc. 420–426. The collection of legends is in Migne, PG., vols. cxiv–cxvi : vol. cxiv contains the life by Psellos and the office for St Simeon's feast ; and in *Analecta Bollandiana*, vol. lxviii (1950), pp. 126–134 is printed the text of verses on Simeon's death by Nikephoros Ouranos (*fl.* 996). For a criticism of the attempt to date the Metaphrast in the middle of the eleventh century see A. Ehrhard, *Überlieferung und Bestand der hagiographischen und homiletischen Literatur der griechischen Kirche*, in *Texte und Untersuchungen zur Gesch. der altchristlichen Literatur*, vol. li, pp. 307 *seq*.

ST JAMES OF THE MARCH (A.D. 1476)

THE native town of this saint was Montebrandone in the March of Ancona, whence his appellation *della Marca ;* his family name was Gangala and his parents were humble folk. He was born in 1394, and in 1416 asked to be received among the Friars Minor at Assisi. He was sent for his novitiate to the small convent near Assisi called the Carceri, and afterwards studied under St Bernardino of Siena at Fiesole. He was ordained priest when he was twenty-nine, and at once began to preach in Tuscany, Umbria and the March. St James regularly inflicted severe penances on himself, and is said to have allowed only three hours for sleep. He copied for himself most of the books he required to have with him, and he always wore a most threadbare habit. His zeal for souls was boundless and throughout his long active life he was continually engaged in preaching, which he did with great vehemence and effect whether he addressed himself to heretics or to sinful Catholics : his missions took him to Germany, Bohemia, Poland and Hungary.

James worked in concert with St John Capistrano, who had been his fellow student under St Bernardino, and in 1426 they were named together by Pope Martin V as inquisitors against the Fraticelli, the name given to a number of rigorist and heretical sects then rampant in Italy. The two friars proceeded with such severity that some bishops and others were moved to protest : not only were thirty-six houses of the Fraticelli dispersed and destroyed, but some of the members themselves were burned at the stake. But James took part in less violent measures as well, both as regards them and other schismatics : at the Council of Basle he helped in the conciliation of the moderate Hussites by the concession of communion in both kinds, and when the council moved to Florence he took part in the reunion of the dissident orientals.   In 1445 St James preached the Lent at Perugia, and there clothed with the Franciscan habit Bd Bernardino of Fossa.   Four years later he was again commissioned to deal with the Fraticelli, and wrote a " Dialogue " which was published against them.   St James belonged to the Observants among the Friars Minor, whose marked success at that time had excited a deal of envy and jealousy ; in a letter to St John Capistrano he sets out his own difficulties and sufferings because of this.   He took part in the efforts to settle the matters at issue between Observants and Conventuals, but the compromise which James recommended to the Holy See satisfied neither party.   In 1456 there was an interesting coincidence in his career.   He was again preaching a series of Lenten sermons, this time at Padua, and again he attracted a young saint named Bernardino to the Friars Minor, Bd Bernardino of Feltre.   St James himself was a favourer of those *montes pietatis* which it was to be this Bernardino's work to reorganize and popularize.   Later in the same year St John Capistrano died and St James was sent to take his place in Austria and Hungary, where he carried on his work against the extreme Hussites.

On his return to Italy St James was offered the see of Milan, which he refused, preferring to serve souls by continuing to preach up and down the country ; but two years later, in 1462, he got himself into trouble.   Preaching at Brescia on Easter Monday he gave voice to a theological opinion which caused him to be cited before the local Inquisition.   He refused to appear, and when the matter was pursued appealed to Rome.   The subject was one upon which Friars Minor and Friars Preachers had already taken sides (the inquisitor was a Dominican), and this incident precipitated a full-length disputation before Pope Pius II.   No decision was given and eventually silence was imposed on both parties.

St James of the March passed the last three years of his life at Naples and died there on November 28, 1476.   He was canonized in 1726.

It is only of recent years that the most authentic testimony concerning St James has seen the light.   This is the life or memoir written in Italian by Fr Vincent da Fabriano, who was his companion and intimate friend.   It was edited in the *Archivum Franciscanum Historicum*, vol. xvii (1924), pp. 378–414, by Fr Teodosio Somigli.   In the same article is contained a full bibliography, which dispenses us from any but a brief notice of other lives of the saint.   Wadding, Mark of Lisbon, Tossignano and Mazzara in their chronicles all give full accounts.   The principal separate biographies are those of G. B. Barberio (1702), Giuseppe-Arcangelo di Fratta Maggiore (1830), and G. Rocco (1909).   See also Léon, *Auréole Séraphique* (Eng. trans.), vol. iv, pp. 125–154 ; and G. Caselli, *Studi su S. Giacomo della Marca* (2 vols., 1926).

BD JAMES THOMPSON, Martyr   (A.D. 1582)

This martyr was a native of York and spent most of his life in that city.   He went to Rheims to study for the priesthood in 1580, where his health broke down, and within a year he had returned to England.   But not before he had been ordained priest by virtue of a special dispensation.   He worked on the mission, under the name of Hudson, for just a year before he was arrested and brought before the Council of the North.   He at once admitted that he was a priest, which caused considerable surprise, for his short absence from the city had not been noticed. Some details of his examination, trial and passion are extant.   Among the questions asked was whether he would take arms against the pope should he invade the realm. To which he replied, "When that time shall come I will show myself a true patriot ". But when asked if he would fight against the pope now, he answered " No ".

After three months' confinement, for a time in irons and among common criminals, Bd James was hanged, but not drawn or quartered, in the Knavesmire at York on November 28, 1582. He addressed the people, protested his loyalty to the queen, and as he was mounting the scaffold turned and said, " I have forgotten one thing. I pray you all to bear witness that I die in the Catholic faith." As he hung, swinging and choking, he was seen, " to the great astonishment of the spectators ", to make the sign of the cross.

The fullest account obtainable is that given in Camm and Pollen, LEM., vol. ii, pp. 589–599. See also MMP., pp. 70–72 ; and J. Morris, *Troubles* . . ., pp. 39–40.

ST JOSEPH PIGNATELLI   (A.D. 1811)

THE Pignatelli to whom this saint belonged was the Spanish branch of a noble family of Naples, and he was born at Saragossa in 1737. He became a Jesuit at Tarragona when he was sixteen, and after his ordination returned to work in his native city. Four years later, in 1767, the persecution which had already driven the Society of Jesus from Portugal and France spread to Spain, and Charles III banished it from his dominions, " for reasons which were kept locked up in the royal bosom ". As grandees of Spain, Father Joseph and his brother, Father Nicholas, were offered permission to stay if they would abandon their order ; they refused. For a time the Aragonese Jesuits found a home in Corsica, but when the French occupied that island they were expelled from there, and eventually Father Pignatelli helped to arrange a centre for them, as well as their brothers from Peru and Mexico, at Ferrara. Pope Clement XIII, a great defender of the Jesuits, died in 1769, and four years later his successor, Clement XIV, yielded to the ever-growing pressure of the Bourbon princes and suppressed the Society altogether. It was a purely administrative measure and the papal brief was careful not to state that the charges brought were proved. When this brief was read to the assembled fathers at Ferrara and the vicar general asked if they submitted themselves to it, they were true to their special fidelity as Jesuits to the Holy See and replied at once, " Yes, willingly ". The effect of the decree was to secularize 23,000 religious : " It is a sad page of history, as everybody agrees ", said Pope Pius XI at the beatification of Father Joseph, " sad to read even after so many years. What then must it have been for Father Pignatelli and his numerous brethren ! "

In the twenty years which followed he lived principally at Bologna, devoting himself to study, collecting books and manuscripts bearing on the history of the Society, and aiding his brethren spiritually and materially : many of them were in grave want and the Spaniards among them were not even allowed to fulfil their priestly office. It is recorded that once, when on a visit to Turin, a stranger pointed out to Father Pignatelli a new church and cemetery as having been built with funds taken from the Jesuits. " It ought to be called Haceldama ! "* he observed grimly.

As the Empress Catherine had refused to allow the bishops to promulgate the brief of suppression, the continued existence of the Society was tolerated in White Russia by the Holy See, and in 1792 the Duke of Parma invited three Italian fathers from there to establish themselves in his state. Father Pignatelli wished to associate himself with this venture, but was not willing to act without authority. When, however, Duke Ferdinand obtained a guarded approval from Pope Pius VI,

* " The field of blood." (See Matt. xxvii 8.)

Pignatelli renewed his vows privately and was put in charge, and two years later (1799), having received verbal permission from the pope, he organized a quasi-novitiate at Colorno. The students had to go to Russia to make their profession, and this proceeding was recognized as canonical when, in 1801, Pope Pius VII gave formal approbation to the Jesuit province in Russia. Father Pignatelli worked unceasingly by prayer and secular activity for the further revival of the Society, and his efforts were rewarded in 1804 when it was re-established in the kingdom of Naples, he himself being named provincial. In the following year the French invasion again brought dispersion. Most of the fathers, however, were able to retire to Palermo (the resulting Sicilian province became the mother of the modern Jesuit province in Ireland), but Joseph Pignatelli went to Rome and was there made provincial for Italy. With the help of the generous alms of his sister, he was able to restore the Society in Sardinia and re-lay its foundations in Rome, Tivoli and Orvieto ; while during the critical period of the French occupation and the exile of Pius VII his prudence conserved safely all that he had gained towards his ultimate object—the complete restoration of the Society of Jesus. This took place in 1814, three years after his death ; nevertheless, St Joseph Pignatelli fully deserves to be regarded as what Pope Pius XI called him, " the chief link between the Society that had been and the Society that was to be . . . the restorer of the Jesuits ".

This " example of manly and vigorous holiness "—we again quote Pius XI—died at Rome on November 11, 1811, and was canonized in 1954.

A sketch of the life of this servant of God seems first to have been published in Italian by Fr A. Monçon in 1833, but a fuller and better-informed biography is that of Fr G. Boero, *Istoria della Vita del V Padre Giuseppe M. Pignatelli* (1856), and on this was based the French life which Fr G. Bouffier brought out in 1868. The most complete work seems to be that of Fr Nonell in Spanish, *El V. P. José M. Pignatelli* . . . (3 vols., 1893–94) ; this includes many of his letters. Since then several other lives have been produced, *e.g.* by P. Zurbitu (Spanish, 1933), by C. Beccari (Italian, 1933), by J. March (Spanish, 1935), and by D. A. Hanly (English, 1938).

ST CATHERINE LABOURÉ, Virgin (A.D. 1876)

Zoé Labouré was the daughter of a yeoman-farmer at Fain-les-Moutiers in the Côte d'Or, where she was born in 1806. She was the only one of a large family not to go to school and did not learn to read and write. Her mother died when Zoé was eight, and when her elder sister, Louisa, left home to become a Sister of Charity the duties of housekeeper and helper to her father devolved upon her. From the age of fourteen or so she also heard a call to the religious life, and after some opposition M. Labouré allowed her to join the Sisters of Charity of St Vincent de Paul at Châtillon-sur-Seine in 1830. She took the name of Catherine, and after her postulancy was sent to the convent in the rue du Bac at Paris, where she arrived four days before the translation of the relics of St Vincent from Notre-Dame to the Lazarist church in the rue de Sèvres. On the evening of the day of those festivities began the series of visions which were to make the name of Catherine Labouré famous. The first of the three principal ones took place three months later, on the night of July 18, when at about 11.30 p.m. she was woken up suddenly by the appearance of a " shining child ", who led her down to the sisters' chapel. There our Lady appeared and talked with her for over two hours, telling her that she would have to undertake a difficult task and also, it is said, speaking of the future and the violent death of an archbishop of Paris forty years later (Mgr Darboy, in the Commune of 1871). On November 27 following, our Lady appeared to Sister Catherine in the same chapel, in the form of a picture and as it were standing on a globe with shafts of light streaming from her hands towards it, surrounded by the words : " O Mary, conceived free from sin, pray for us who turn to thee ! " Then the picture turned about, and Sister Catherine saw on the reverse side a capital M, with a cross above it and two hearts, one thorn-crowned and the other pierced with a sword, below. And she seemed to herself to hear a voice telling her to have a medal struck representing these things, and promising that all who wore it with devotion should receive great graces by the intercession of the Mother of God. This or a similar vision was repeated in the following month and on several other occasions up to September 1831.

Sister Catherine confided in her confessor, M. Aladel, and he, after making very careful investigations, was given permission by the archbishop of Paris, Mgr de Quélen, to have the medal struck. In June 1832 the first 1500 were issued— the medal now known to Catholics throughout the world as " miraculous ". This epithet seems to be due to the circumstances of its origin rather than, as is commonly supposed, to miracles connected with its pious use. In 1834 M. Aladel published a *Notice historique sur l'origine et l'effets de la Médaille Miraculeuse*, of which 130,000 copies were sold in six years. It was translated into seven languages, including Chinese. The archbishop of Paris instituted a canonical inquiry into the alleged visions in 1836, before which, however, Sister Catherine could not be induced to appear. The precautions she had taken to keep herself unknown, the promise she had wrung from M. Aladel not to tell anybody who she was, the secrecy she had kept towards everyone except her confessor, her constant unwillingness to appear before an ecclesiastical authority, account for this inquiry not being extended to the young sister herself. The tribunal decided in favour of the authenticity of the visions, taking into consideration the circumstances, the character of the sister concerned, and the prudence and level-headedness of M. Aladel. The popularity of the medal increased daily, especially after the conversion of Alphonse Ratisbonne in 1842. He was an Alsatian Jew who, having reluctantly agreed to wear the medal, received a vision of our Lady in that form in the church of Sant' Andrea delle Frate at Rome, whereupon he became a Christian and was later a priest and founder of a religious congregation, the Fathers and Sisters of Zion.

This vision of Ratisbonne also was the subject of a canonical inquiry, and the reports of this and of the archbishop of Paris's were extensively used in the process of beatification of Catherine Labouré, of whose personal life very little is recorded. Her superiors speak of her as " rather insignificant ", " matter-of-fact and un-excitable ", " cold, almost apathetic ". From 1831 until her death on December 31, 1876, she lived unobtrusively among the community at Enghien-Reuilly, as portress, in charge of the poultry, and looking after the aged who were supported in the hospice. Not until eight months before her death did she speak to anyone except her confessor of the extraordinary graces she had received, and then she revealed them only to her superior, Sister Dufès. Her funeral was the occasion of an outburst of popular veneration, and a child of twelve, crippled from birth, was instantaneously cured at her grave soon after. St Catherine Labouré was canonized in 1947, and this day appointed for her feast.

A good deal has been written about St Catherine and " the miraculous medal ". The best-known biography is probably that of Fr E. Crapez, of which an English abbreviation was published in 1920.   Another life is that by Fr E. Cassinari, and this also has been issued in English, in 1934.   An earlier account is that of Lady Georgiana Fullerton, *Life and Visions of a Sister of Charity* (1880).   Among other books are a popular life in English by Mrs P. Boyne (1948), and *La vie secrète de Catherine Labouré* (1948), by C. Yves.

29 : ST SATURNINUS, Martyr   (*c.* A.D. 309)

THE Western church makes a commemoration of this martyr in today's liturgy, but particulars of him are known only from the unauthentic *passio* of Pope St Marcellus I.   The Roman Martyrology says : " At Rome on the Salarian Way the birthday of the holy martyrs, the aged Saturninus and Sisinnius, the deacon, under the Emperor Maximian.   After they had been weakened by a long imprisonment the prefect of the city ordered them to be put on the rack and stretched, beaten with rods and scourges, scorched with fire, and then taken down from the rack and beheaded."   St Saturninus is said in an epitaph by Pope St Damasus to have been a priest who came to Rome from Carthage ;   he was certainly buried in the cemetery of Thraso on the Via Salaria Nova.

The *passio* of Pope Marcellus, from which the legend of Saturninus and Sisinnius is derived, has been printed in the *Acta Sanctorum*, January, vol. ii, as well as in Surius, etc. The whole question has been fully discussed in CMH., pp. 626–627.   A basilica on the Salarian Way which was seemingly dedicated to this St Saturninus was burnt down in the time of Pope Felix III (IV) *c.* 528, but was rebuilt and again restored by Popes Hadrian and Gregory IV in the eighth and ninth centuries, which facts are duly recorded in the *Liber Pontificalis*.

ST SATURNINUS, OR SERNIN, BISHOP OF TOULOUSE, MARTYR (THIRD CENTURY ?)

ST SATURNINUS is venerated as a missionary who was the first bishop of Toulouse, and Fortunatus tells us that he converted a great number of idolaters by his preaching and miracles.   He is supposed to have preached on both sides of the Pyrenees. The·author of his *passio*, who wrote before the seventh century, relates that he assembled his flock in a small church in Toulouse, and that the chief temple in the city stood between that church and the saint's house.   In this temple oracles were given, but they had been long silent, which was attributed to the presence of the Christian bishop.   Accordingly the priests seized him one day going by and dragged him into the temple, declaring that he should either appease the offended deities by offering sacrifice to them or propitiate them with his blood.   Saturninus replied, " I worship one only God and to Him I am ready to offer a sacrifice of praise. Your gods are evil and are more pleased with the sacrifice of your souls than with those of your bullocks.   How can I fear them who, as you acknowledge, tremble before a Christian ? "   The infidels, enraged at this reply, tied his feet to a bull, which was brought thither to be sacrificed, and the beast was goaded to run violently down the hill, so that the martyr's skull was broken and his brains dashed out. The bull continued to drag the body until, the cord breaking, what remained of it was left outside the gates of the city till it was taken up by two women and hidden in a ditch.   Later the relics were enshrined in what is now the great church of St Sernin.   A church built at the place where the bull stopped is still called the *Taur*.

445

Later other legends, that he was sent to Gaul by Pope St Clement or even by the apostles, were woven round St Saturninus.

The *passio* of St Saturninus of Toulouse figures, strangely enough, among the *Acta sincera* of Ruinart. Here again Delehaye's CMH. supplies references to all details of importance. St Gregory of Tours refers more than once to St Saturninus and his basilica at Toulouse, and he clearly had before him the text of the *passio*. Both Sidonius Apollinaris and Venantius Fortunatus pay honour to the holy bishop, and echo the same legendary account of his martyrdom. Saturninus of Toulouse is also commemorated on this day in all the Mozarabic calendars. See further, Duchesne, *Fastes Épiscopaux*, vol. i, p. 26 and pp. 306–307.

ST RADBOD, Bishop of Utrecht   (A.D. 918)

RADBOD, the last pagan king of the Frisians (who said he preferred to be in Hell with his ancestors rather than in Heaven without them), was great-grandfather of this saint, whose father was a Frank. The young Radbod received his first schooling under the tuition of Gunther, Bishop of Cologne, his maternal uncle. Little is known of St Radbod's life, but he wrote hymns and an office of St Martin, an eclogue and sermon on St Lebwin, a hymn on St Swithbert and other poems which are extant. In a short chronicle which he compiled he says, under the year 900, " I, Radbod, a sinner, have been taken, though unworthy, into the company of the ministers of the church of Utrecht ; with whom I pray that I may attain to eternal life ". Before the end of that year he was chosen bishop of that church, when he put on the monastic habit, his predecessors having been monks because the church of Utrecht had been founded by priests of the monastic order. After he had received the episcopal consecration he never tasted flesh meat, often fasted two or three days together, and was renowned for his kindness to the poor. During a Danish invasion St Radbod removed his see to Deventer, and there died in peace.

There is a medieval Life of St Radbod, written not long after his death, but it is a poor piece of biography. It is edited in MGH., *Scriptores*, vol. xv, pp. 569–571 ; and has also been printed with Radbod's literary works in Migne, PL., vol. cxxxii. A better edition of his verse compositions is in MGH., *Poetae latini*, vol. iv, pp. 160–173. Text and translation of two lyrics in Helen Waddell, *Mediaeval Latin Lyrics* (1935), pp. 130–135, and *cf.* pp. 323–324.

BD FREDERICK OF REGENSBURG   (A.D. 1329)

PRACTICALLY nothing is known of the life of this servant of God, whose uninterrupted *cultus* from the time of his death was confirmed in 1909. He was born of poor parents at Regensburg (Ratisbon) and was received as a lay-brother in the friary of Augustinian hermits in that city. He was employed by the community principally as a carpenter and to chop wood for fuel, and he used to thank God that there was any job that he was found capable of doing. Among the marvels related of him is that he received holy communion at the hands of an angel. The inscription of his name in calendars, the title Blessed given to him, and the special place of his tomb show the veneration with which he was regarded by his contemporaries. Bd Frederick died on November 30, 1329, but his feast is observed by the Augustinian friars and at Regensburg on the previous day.

A short biography, largely made up of miracles of a very conventional type, together with an imposing folio page engraving of the holy brother, stands in M. Rader's *Bavaria Sancta* (1702), vol. i, p. 298. As the book was first published in 1615, it at least serves as evidence of a *cultus* which in some sense goes back to time immemorial.   The decree of *confirmatio cultus* will be found in the *Acta Apostolicae Sedis*, vol. i (1909), pp. 496–498.

BD CUTHBERT MAYNE, Martyr   (A.D. 1577)

THE English College at Douay was founded in 1568 and in the early days of the penal laws a legal distinction was made between those priests trained in this and other seminaries abroad and those " Marian priests " who had been ordained in England.   The first " seminary priest " to pay for his mission with his life was Bd Cuthbert Mayne.   He was a Devon man, born at Youlston, near Barnstaple, in 1544, and brought up a Protestant by his uncle, a schismatic priest.   He went to Barnstaple Grammar School and at eighteen or nineteen was ordained a minister, with neither inclination nor preparation.   His uncle then sent him to Oxford, where at St John's College he got to know Dr Gregory Martin and Bd Edmund Campion, who was still a Protestant, and he was soon inwardly persuaded of the truth of Catholicism ; but he held back for fear of losing his appointments and falling into poverty.   When Martin and Campion had gone over to Douay they wrote several times to Mayne urging him to join them, and in 1570, soon after he had taken his M.A., one of these letters fell into the hands of the bishop of London, who sent a pursuivant to Oxford to arrest all those named therein.   Mayne was away at the time, and this narrow escape decided him : he abjured Protestantism and in 1573 was accepted at Douay.   During the next three years he was ordained priest and took his bachelor's degree in theology, and in April 1576 was sent back to England with Bd John Payne.   Mayne was the fifteenth missionary priest sent out from Douay.

He took up his residence at the mansion of Francis Tregian at Golden in the parish of Probus in Cornwall, where he passed as the estate-steward.   Few particulars are known of his ministry from this centre, but suspicions were excited and a year later the high sheriff, Richard Grenville,* searched Tregian's house.   Mayne was found to have an *agnus Dei* round his neck, and was accordingly arrested, together with Mr Tregian.   Cuthbert was carried by the sheriff from one gentleman's house to another till they came to Launceston, where he was confined in a filthy cell of the prison, chained to the bedpost.   At the Michaelmas assizes he was indicted for having obtained from Rome and published at Golden a " faculty containing matter of absolution " of the Queen's subjects (actually they had found a printed announcement, from Douay, of the jubilee indulgence of 1575, two years out of date) ; for having taught, in Launceston jail, the ecclesiastical power of the Bishop of Rome (on the uncertain evidence of three illiterate witnesses) ; that he had brought into the kingdom and delivered to Mr Tregian " a vain and superstitious thing, commonly called an *agnus Dei* " (no evidence was offered of importation or delivery) ; and for having celebrated Mass (on the strength of finding a missal, chalice and vestments at Golden).   All these things contrary to statutes of 1 and 13 Elizabeth.

On the direction of Mr Justice Manwood (and after prolonged consultation with Mr Sheriff Grenville) the jury found a verdict of guilty ; Bd Cuthbert was sentenced to death, and three of the four gentlemen and their three yeomen, charged with him as abettors, to perpetual imprisonment and forfeiture.   But the second judge, Mr Justice Jeffrey, had qualms about these proceedings and procured a

* Of *Revenge* fame.   He got his knighthood for his part in Mayne's condemnation.

reconsideration of the case by the whole judicial bench, at Serjeants' Inn.   These judges could not agree and, though the weight of opinion favoured Jeffrey's opinion, the Privy Council directed that the conviction should stand as a warning to priests coming from beyond the seas.   The day before his execution Bd Cuthbert was offered his liberty if he would swear to the queen's ecclesiastical supremacy.   He asked for a Bible, kissed it, and said, " The queen neither ever was nor is nor ever shall be the head of the Church of England ".   He was drawn to Launceston market-place on a sledge, but was not allowed to address the crowd from the scaffold.   When invited to implicate Mr Tregian and his brother-in-law, Sir John Arundell, Mayne replied, " I know nothing of them except that they are good and pious men ; and of the things laid to my charge no one but myself has any know-ledge ".   He was cut down alive but was probably unconscious before the butchery of disembowelling began.

Cuthbert Mayne was among those whose beatification was declared by Pope Leo XIII, and his feast is observed in Plymouth and several other English dioceses. The Carmelite nuns of Lanherne possess a considerable relic of the martyr's skull, recovered from Launceston , where it was displayed.   The noble confessor Francis Tregian was deprived of his lands and was in various prisons for nearly thirty years, for harbouring Bd Cuthbert.   After his death, at Lisbon in 1608, it was claimed that miracles were wrought by his relics.   " It is particularly remarked that not one of those whom Mr Maine reconciled to the Church could ever be induced to renounce the Catholic truth, which they had learned from so good a master."

The most reliable account of this martyr is that written by E. S. Knox for Camm, LEM., vol. ii, pp. 204–221 and 656.   See also MMP., pp. 1–6 and 601 ; R. A. McElroy, *Bd Cuthbert Mayne* (1929) ; A. L. Rowse, *Tudor Cornwall* (1941), cap. xiv ; and P. A. Boyan and G. R. Lamb, *Francis Tregian* (1955).

BB. DIONYSIUS and REDEMPTUS, Martyrs   (A.D. 1638)

THERE was born at Honfleur in Normandy in the year 1600 to the family of Ber-thelot the first of ten children, and he was baptized Peter.   When he was nineteen he sailed to the East Indies in the French ship *Espérance*, which was captured and burnt by Dutch privateers.   Young Berthelot made his escape from Java and for some years traded on his own.   Then he entered the Portuguese service at Malacca, became first a pilot and then cartographer, and took part in several expeditions. In 1635 he met at Goa the prior of the Discalced Carmelites, and was induced by him to join that order, taking the name of Dionysius.   Soon after his profession the Portuguese viceroy asked for his services as pilot to the embassy which he was sending to Sumatra.   The Carmelite authorities agreed, and ordained Friar Dionysius priest so that he could act as chaplain as well ; he was accompanied by a lay-brother, Redemptus.   His name in the world was Thomas Rodriguez da Cunha, and he had been a soldier in India before he joined the Carmelites.   No sooner had they arrived at Achin (Koetaraja) than the ambassador and his suite were seized by the Sumatrans and put in prison.   A number of them were mas-sacred, including the two friars.   Dionysius, refusing to apostatize, was to be trampled by elephants, but the impatient pagans cut him down ; Redemptus was killed a few days later.   Directly the news reached Goa the prior, Friar Philip, collected evidence and prepared to introduce the cause of beatification of his two subjects ; but Dionysius and Redemptus were not in fact beatified until 1900.

An account of these martyrs is given in considerable detail by Frey João do Sacramento in his *Chronica de Carmelitas Descalços*, vol. ii (1721), pp. 798–813. He informs us that Father Philip induced Archbishop Francis of Goa to institute a formal process with a view to the beatification of the martyrs and that the same Father Philip published a relation of the events which attended their death. This seems to be contained in his books, *Itinerarium Orientale* (1649) and *Decor Carmeli* (1665). We have in modern times Thomas de Jésus, *Les bx Denis de la Nativité et Rédempt de la Croix* (1900) ; P. Gonthier, *Vie admirable de Pierre Berthelot* (1917) ; and a series of articles in *Études Carmélitaines*, 1912, pp. 426–442, and 1913, pp. 215–227 and pp. 387–397. Some maps drawn by Bd Dionysius are said to be in the British Museum.

BD FRANCIS ANTONY OF LUCERA   (A.D. 1742)

IN the later part of the seventeenth century there was living at Lucera in Apulia a poor family—the man was a farm-labourer—called Fasani, into which was born in 1681 a boy who was christened Donato Antony John Nicholas, commonly called Johnnie. It was a good and respectable household, but before little John was ten his father died, and his mother married again. However, her second choice was good too, and it was due to the step-father, Francis Farinacci, that John Fasani was sent to be educated by the Conventual Friars Minor at Lucera. He also heard a call to that order, and in his fifteenth year was clothed at the provincial novitiate on Monte Gargano. Brother Francis Antony made his studies in various colleges, and in 1705 was ordained priest at Assisi. He gained his doctorate in theology soon after, and in 1707 was sent as lector in philosophy to the Conventual college at Lucera.

Father Francis's headquarters was in his home-town for the rest of his life. From the time that he received his mastership in theology he was known as " Padre Maestro ", Father Master, in Lucera (as he still is familiarly called there), although he fulfilled a succession of offices, including that of minister provincial of the province of Sant' Angelo. He had made his mark as a teacher and as a preacher throughout Apulia and the Molise : as a superior it was said of him, " He measures our spirit by his own—he wants us all to be as holy as he is ". Like St Joseph Cafasso at the other end of Italy a century later, Father Francis was particularly concerned for the inmates of prisons, of whom those condemned to death were perhaps the more fortunate : as an indication of their condition one of his Italian biographers quotes Gladstone's denouncement of Neapolitan prisons one hundred years after. But the Franciscan's love embraced all : it was he who started in Italy a Christmas custom of collecting gifts for the poor, and people continually came to him with their wants, whether possible or impossible. And sometimes the seemingly impossible ones were fulfilled too, notably where shortages of water were concerned.

It was currently said in Lucera, " If you want to see St Francis, watch Father Master " ; and his first superior said of him that he had reached such a degree of mystical union with God that he was filled with Him. One of his characteristics was an intense devotion to the Mother of God as conceived free from original sin, and every year he celebrated a solemn public novena before the feast of the Conception (Lucera still observes it). It was on the first day of this novena, November 29, in 1742, that Father Francis died. Some time before, when he seemed to be in good health, he had foretold that his earthly end was at hand to one of his penitents, and to Father Ludovic Gioca who, he suggested, would accompany him. Father Ludovic was rather upset. " Listen, Father Master ", he said, " If you want to die, that is your affair.   But I am in no hurry."   " We must both make the journey : I first, you later ", was the reply.   Father Ludovic survived Father Master by only two months.   Bd Francis Antony Fasani was beatified in 1951.

There are Italian biographies by Canon T. M. Vigilanti (1848), Fr L. Berardini (1951) and Fr G. Stano (1951).   The last, a short life, has been translated into English by Fr R. Huber in America (1951) ; it includes two interesting portraits of the *beatus*.

30 : ST ANDREW, APOSTLE, PATRON OF SCOTLAND   (FIRST CENTURY)

ST ANDREW was a native of Bethsaida, a town in Galilee upon the banks of the lake of Genesareth.   He was the son of Jona, a fisherman of that town, and brother to Simon Peter, but whether older or younger the Holy Scriptures do not say.   They had a house at Capharnaum, where Jesus lodged when he preached in that city.   When St John Baptist began to preach penance, Andrew became his disciple, and he was with his master when St John, seeing Jesus pass by the way after He had been baptized by him, said, " Behold the Lamb of God ! " Andrew was so far enlightened as to comprehend this mysterious saying, and without delay he and another disciple of the Baptist went after Jesus, who saw them with the eyes of His spirit before He beheld them with His corporal eyes.   Turning back as he walked, he said, " What seek ye ? "   They said they wanted to know where He dwelt, and He bade them come and see.   There remained but two hours of that day, which they spent with him, and Andrew clearly learned that Jesus was the Messias and resolved from that moment to follow Him ; he was thus the first of His disciples, and therefore is styled by the Greeks the " Protoclete " or First-called.   He then fetched his brother, that he might also know Him, and Simon was no sooner come to Jesus than the Saviour admitted him also as a disciple, and gave him the name of Peter.   From this time they were his followers, not constantly attending Him as they afterwards did, but hearing Him as frequently as their business would permit and returning to their trade and family affairs again.   When Jesus, going up to Jerusalem to celebrate the Passover, stayed some days in Judaea and baptized in the Jordan, Peter and Andrew also baptized by His authority and in His name.   Our Saviour, being come back into Galilee and meeting Peter and Andrew fishing in the lake, He called them permanently to the ministry of the gospel, saying that He would make them fishers of men.   Whereupon they immediately left their nets to follow Him, and never went from Him again.   The year following our Lord chose twelve to be His apostles, and St Andrew is named among the first four in all the biblical lists.   He is also mentioned in connection with the feeding of the five thousand (John vi 8, 9) and the Gentiles who would see Jesus (John xii 20–22).

Apart from a few words in Eusebius, who informs us that St Andrew preached in Scythia and that certain spurious " acts " bearing his name were made use of by heretics, we have practically nothing but apocryphal writings which profess to tell us anything of the later history of St Andrew.   There is, however, one curious mention in the ancient document known as the Muratorian Fragment.   This dates from the very beginning of the third century and therein it is stated : " The fourth gospel [was written by] John one of the disciples [*i.e.* apostles].   When his fellow disciples and bishops urgently pressed him, he said, ' Fast with me from today, for three days, and let us tell one another what revelation may be made to us, either for or against [the plan of writing].' On the same night it was revealed to Andrew, one of the apostles, that John should relate all in his own name, and that all should review his writing." Theodoret tells us that Andrew passed into Greece; St Gregory Nazianzen mentions particularly Epirus, and St Jerome Achaia. St Philastrius says that he came out of Pontus into Greece, and that in his time (fourth century) people at Sinope believed that they had his true picture and the *ambo* from which he preached in that city. Though there is agreement among these as to the direction of St Andrew's apostolate there is no certainty about it. The favourite view of the middle ages was that he eventually came to Byzantium and there left his disciple Stachys (Romans xvi 9) as bishop. This tradition is due to a document forged at a time when it was a great help to the ecclesiastical position of Constantinople apparently to have an apostolic origin for their church, like Rome, Alexandria and Antioch. (The first historically certain bishop of Byzantium was St Metrophanes, early in the fourth century.) The place and manner of the death of St Andrew are equally in doubt. His apocryphal *passio* says that he was crucified at Patras in Achaia, being not nailed but bound to a cross, on which he suffered and preached to the people for two days before he died. The idea that his cross was of the kind called saltire or decussate (X-shaped) was apparently not known before the fourteenth century. Under the Emperor Constantius II (d. 361) what purported to be the relics of St Andrew were translated from Patras to the church of the Apostles at Constantinople; after the seizure of that city by the Crusaders in 1204 they were stolen and given to the cathedral of Amalfi in Italy.

St Andrew is the patron saint of Russia, on account of a valueless tradition that he preached in that country so far as Kiev, and of Scotland. It is not claimed that he preached in Scotland, but the legend preserved by John of Fordun and in the Aberdeen Breviary is no less undeserving of credence. According to this a certain St Rule (Regulus), who was a native of Patras and had charge of the relics of St Andrew in the fourth century, was warned by an angel in a dream to take a part of those relics and convey them to a place that would be indicated. He did as he was told, going forth in a north-westerly direction "towards the ends of the earth", until by a sign the angel stopped him at the place we call Saint Andrews, where he built a church to shelter them, was made its first bishop, and evangelized the people for thirty years. This story may have originated in the eighth century. A feast of the translation is observed in the archdiocese of Saint Andrews on May 9.

The name of St Andrew appears in the canon of the Mass with those of the other apostles, and he is also named with our Lady and SS. Peter and Paul in the embolism after the Lord's Prayer. This is generally attributed to the personal devotion of Pope St Gregory the Great for the saint, but the usage may antedate his time.

Although Duchesne, Delehaye and others regard St Andrew's connection with Patras as unreliable, some are inclined to affirm it very positively. " More certain ", says Kellner (*Heortology*, p. 289), " is his martyrdom at Patras, of which we have a trustworthy account." [He means the *passio* printed by Max Bonnet, *Analecta Bollandiana*, vol. xiii, pp. 373–378.] " Besides this, there is a well-known encyclical letter from the priests and deacons of Achaia, which in all essential points agrees with the account of the martyrdom, although in some other respects it is open to criticism." This is putting the matter rather strongly, but it is certainly worthy of remark that there is almost perfect uniformity in Latin and Greek calendars at all periods in assigning St Andrew's feast to November 30, and also that the " *Hieronymianum* " under February 5 has the entry *Patras in Achaia ordinatio episcopatus sancti Andraeae apostoli*. The letter of the Achaia clergy is printed in Migne, PG., vol. ii, pp. 1217–1248, but the best of the apocryphal material regarding St Andrew can be most conveniently studied in the contributions of M. Bonnet to the *Analecta Bollandiana*, vol. xiii (1894), afterwards separately reprinted.   There are also Ethiopic, Coptic and other oriental texts. 'See further the *Dictionnaire de la Bible : Supplément*, vol. i, cc. 504–509 ; Flamion, *Les actes apocryphes de l'apôtre André* (1911) ; Hennecke, *Neutestamentliche Apocryphen* (1904), pp. 459–473, and *Handbuch* (1904), pp. 544–562.   The legend of St Andrew must have excited interest in England at an early date ; the Anglo-Saxon poem, *Andreas*, based upon it is probably the work of Cynewulf, who wrote about the year 800.   On St Andrew's connection with Scotland see W. Skene, *Celtic Scotland*, vol. i, pp. 296–299 ; for Eusebius's reference, his *Eccl. Hist.*, bk iii ; and for the Muratorian reference, DAC., vol. xii, c. 552, a facsimile of the original manuscript.

SS. SAPOR AND ISAAC, BISHOPS AND MARTYRS   (A.D. 339)

THE long and shocking persecution of the Christians of Persia under Sapor II was due to a suspicion that they were intriguing with the Roman emperors against their own country, and profession of the national religion, Mazdeism, was made the test of loyalty.   Mahanes, Abraham and Simeon were the first who fell into the hands of the officers, and soon after Sapor and Isaac, both bishops, were taken up for building churches and making converts.   All five were presented to the king, who said to them, " Have you not heard that I am descended from the god ?   Yet I sacrifice to the sun and pay divine honours to the moon.   Who are you to resist my laws ? "   The martyrs answered, " We acknowledge one God, and Him alone we worship ", and Sapor the bishop said, " We confess one only God, who made all things, and Jesus Christ, born of Him ".   The king commanded that he should be struck on the mouth, which was done with such cruelty that his teeth were knocked out, and he was beaten with clubs till his whole body was bruised and bones broken.   Isaac appeared next, and Sapor the king reproached him for having presumed to build churches.   He maintained Christ with inflexible constancy, so several apostates were sent for and by threats made to carry off Isaac and stone him to death.   At the news of his martyrdom, St Sapor exulted and himself died of his wounds two days after, in prison.   The barbarous king, to be sure of his death, caused his head to be cut off, and brought to him.   The other three were then called up and the king, finding them no less invincible, ordered the skin of Mahanes to be flayed from the top of his head to the navel ; under which torture he died.   Abraham's eyes were bored out with a hot iron, and Simeon was buried in the earth up to his breast and shot to death with arrows.

The story of the martyrdom of these bishops, written in Syriac, was published in the eighteenth century by S. E. Assemani in his *Acta sanctorum martyrum orientalium et occidentalium*, vol. i, pp. 225–230.   A better text has since been edited from a collation of other manuscripts by P. Bedjan in his *Acta martyrum et sanctorum*, vol. ii (1891).   It would seem that this Sapor must be the same who is mentioned in the early Syriac *breviarium* amongst " the bishops of Persia ".   The notice, to which no day of the month is attached, simply names " John and Shabur (Sapor), bishops of the city of Beth-Seleucia ".

BD ANDREW OF ANTIOCH   (*c.* A.D. 1348)

THIS Andrew, Norman by blood, was born at Antioch about 1268, the year in which the Sultan Bibars finally broke the Crusaders' power in Syria ; he was descended from Bohemund III, Prince of Antioch in the Latin kingdom, and so from Robert Guiscard.   Andrew joined the community of Augustinian canons regular which had been formed to serve the basilica of the Holy Sepulchre at

Jerusalem, and was appointed by the Latin patriarch to be the key-bearer ; that is, he had charge of the key of the Holy Sepulchre, a purely honorary office, since the Saracens had retaken possession of Jerusalem twenty-five years before Andrew was born.* Few particulars of his life are known, but towards its end he was sent on a mission to visit the houses of his order in Europe and to collect funds for the maintenance of the canons who had shared the ruin of the Crusaders' kingdom. He visited Sicily, Italy, Poland and France, and in 1347 he was at Annecy in Savoy, where he received a contribution for the funds of the local priory of the Holy Sepulchre. He died in that place, with a great reputation for holiness, and in 1360 his *cultus* was recognized and spread by the elevation of his relics to a shrine. St Francis of Sales had a devotion to Bd Andrew, and testified to the miracles that took place at his tomb. His feast was celebrated annually at Annecy on this date until the Revolution.

Information is very defective. See, however, DHG., vol. ii, c. 1632.

* The Latin canons were not driven out, but the keys of the church were handed over to the Mohammedan families of Judah and Nussaibah, to whom they had probably been entrusted by Saladin in 1187. It is said that descendants of those families are still the official door-keepers and hold the keys, though they are also still Mohammedans.

DECEMBER

1 : ST ANSANUS, Martyr   (A.D. 304 ?)

ST ANSANUS, a Roman by birth, is venerated as the first apostle of Siena, where he made so many converts that he was named " the Baptizer ". During the persecution under Diocletian he was imprisoned, and after torture his head was cut off at a place outside the walls still marked by a church. In the year 1170 his relics were translated to the cathedral ; miracles marked the occasion, and these were written down, together with a fanciful life of the martyr. This states that Ansanus was a youth who was denounced as a Christian by his own father. He confessed the faith, but managed to escape from Rome and fled towards Tuscany. On the way he preached at Bagnorea and was imprisoned where the church of our Lady *delle Carceri* now stands. In Siena the memory of the boy saint is still devoutly cherished : " In the vaults under the Spedale are the meeting-places of several devout confraternities, which are said to trace back their origin from the first Sienese Christians, the converts of St Ansanus, who met in secret on this spot in the days of the Roman persecutions."

Evidence seems to be entirely lacking for any early *cultus* of St Ansanus. His so-called *passio*, two different texts of which have been printed in Baluze-Mansi, *Miscellanea* (vol. iv, pp. 60–63), amounts to no more than a double set of breviary lessons which betray their date by their very form. *Cf.* also the Bollandist *Catalogus cod. hagiog. Bruxel.*, vol. i, pp. 129–132. See E. G. Gardner, *Story of Siena,* p. 187 and *passim* ; and V. Lusini, *Il San Giovanni di Siena*, who states that a little church, the remains of which still exist, can be shown by documents to have been dedicated to St Ansanus as early as 881. It is supposed to have served as the first baptistery of Siena.

ST AGERICUS, or AIRY, Bishop of Verdun   (A.D. 588)

ST AGERICUS was born at or near Verdun, perhaps at Harville, about the year 521. He became one of the clergy of the church of SS. Peter and Paul at Verdun, and when he was thirty-three was appointed bishop of that city in succession to St Desiderius. He was visited there by St Gregory of Tours and St Venantius Fortunatus, both of whom write in his praise : " The poor receive relief, the despairing hope, the naked clothing ; whatever you have, all have ", says Fortunatus. St Agericus enjoyed the favour also of King Sigebert I, whose son, Childebert, he baptized, and counselled after he came to the throne. But he was not able to obtain mercy for Bertefroi and other revolting nobles who came to him for sanctuary and protection. Bertefroi was murdered in the bishop's own chapel by the royal officers. A more pleasing association between Agericus and Childebert was when the whole of the court was billeted on the bishop ; there were so many of them and they were so thirsty that the supply of drink was stretched to its limit. St Agericus had the last cask of wine set in the hall, blessed it, and it proved to have a miraculous and never-ending flow.   Another miracle attributed to him was the delivery of a condemned malefactor at Laon, for whom he obtained pardon.   St Agericus died in 588, it is said of a broken heart because he had failed to save Bertefroi.   He was buried in the church of SS. Andrew and Martin which he had built at Verdun.   Here an abbey was established early in the eleventh century and dedicated in his honour.

Besides the information furnished by St Gregory of Tours and St Venantius Fortunatus, Hugh of Flavigny in his chronicle has gathered up the data scattered in these same sources and produced some sort of biography (see Migne, PL., vol. cliv, cc. 126-131).   Two Latin lives of late date are printed in the Bollandist *Catalogus cod. hagiog. Lat. Bib. Nat. Paris,* vol. i, pp. 479-482 ; and vol. iii, pp. 78-92 ; neither, however, contains any material of value.   See also DHG., vol. i, cc. 1223-1224.

ST TUDWAL, Bishop   (Sixth Century)

ACCORDING to Breton tradition St Tudwal (Tutwal, Tugdual) was a Briton from Wales who crossed over to Brittany with his mother, his sister, some monks, and others, where the king of Dumnonia, Deroc, was his cousin.   He settled at Lan Pabu in Léon (Tudwal was called *Pabu, i.e.* Father, in Brittany) and made several other monastic foundations.   He went to Paris to have his grants of land confirmed by King Childebert I and was consecrated bishop, and ended his days in the monastery of Treher, now Tréguier, of which city he is accounted the first bishop. His appellation, Pabu, led to the legend that he became pope under the name of Leo, a fable that has been richly embroidered by Breton hagiographers.   St Tudwal does not figure in any Welsh calendars, but the name occurs in three places in the Lleyn peninsula, the northern arm of Cardigan Bay.   The chief of these, a small uninhabited island off Abersoch, is called Ynys Tudwal, and has ruins of an ancient chapel.   It was here that, from May to December 1887, the holy Henry Hughes, a Welsh priest of the diocese of Shrewsbury and tertiary of the Order of Preachers, began to lead a heroic missionary life cut short by an untimely death.   The feast of St Tudwal is kept in Brittany, and the Catholic church at Barmouth is dedicated in his honour.

The three separate accounts of St Tudwal which have been preserved to us are late (one may be of the ninth century), conflicting and unreliable.   The Latin texts may best be consulted in A. de la Borderie, *Les trois anciennes Vies de S. Tudwal* (1887), pp. 12-45 ; and *cf.* the *Analecta Bollandiana,* vol. viii (1889), pp. 158-163.   St Tudwal is invoked in the tenth-century Breton litany originally printed by Mabillon and reproduced by Haddan and Stubbs, *Councils,* vol. ii, p. 82.   See also LBS., vol. iv, pp. 271-274 ; Duine, *Memento,* p. 61 ; A. Oheix, *Études hagiographiques* (1919), no. 8 ; Mgr Duchesne in the *Bulletin Critique,* vol. x (1889), pp. 228-229 ; and, regarding the reputed relics of the saint, A. de Barthélemy in the *Revue de Bretagne,* vol. xxv (1901), pp. 401-413.   Dom Gougaud was of the opinion that Tudwal was a native of insular Dumnonia, *i.e.* Devon or Cornwall.

ST ELIGIUS, OR ELOI, Bishop of Noyon   (A.D. 660)

THE name of Eligius, and those of his father, Eucherius, and his mother, Terrigia, show him to have been of Roman Gaulish extraction.   He was born at Chaptelat, near Limoges, about the year 588, the son of an artisan.   His father, seeing in due course that the boy had a remarkable talent for engraving and smithing, placed him with a goldsmith named Abbo, who was master of the mint at Limoges. When the time of his apprenticeship was finished Eligius went into France, that is, across the Loire, and became known to Bobbo, treasurer to Clotaire II at Paris. This king gave Eligius an order to make him a chair of state, adorned with gold and precious stones. Out of the materials furnished he made two such thrones instead of one. Clotaire admired the skill and honesty of the workman, and finding that he was a man of parts and intelligence took him into his household and made him master of the mint. His name is still to be seen on several gold coins struck at Paris and Marseilles in the reigns of Dagobert I and his son, Clovis II. His *vita* states that among other works the reliquaries of St Martin at Tours, of St Dionysius at Saint-Denis, of St Quintinus, SS. Crispin and Crispinian at Soissons, St Lucian, St Germanus of Paris, St Genevieve, and others, were made by Eligius. His skill as a workman, his official position and the friendship of the king soon made him a person of consideration. He did not let the corruption of a court infect his soul or impair his virtue, but he conformed to his state and was magnificently dressed, sometimes wearing nothing but silk (a rare material in France in those days), his clothes embroidered with gold and adorned with precious stones. But he also gave large sums in alms. When a stranger asked for his house he was told, " Go to such a street, and it's where you see a crowd of poor people ".

A curious incident occurred when Clotaire tendered him the oath of allegiance. Eligius having a scruple lest this would be to swear without sufficient necessity, or fearing what he might be called upon to do or approve, excused himself with an obstinacy which for some time displeased the king. Still he persisted in his resolution and repeated his excuses as often as the king pressed him. Clotaire, at length perceiving that the motive of his reluctance was really a tenderness of conscience, assured him that his conscientious spirit was a more secure pledge of fidelity than the oaths of others. St Eligius ransomed a number of slaves, some of whom remained in his service and were his faithful assistants throughout his life. One of them, a Saxon named Tillo, is numbered among the saints and commemorated on January 7 ; he was first among the seven disciples of St Eligius who followed him from the workshop to the *évêché*. At the court he sought the company of such men as Sulpicius, Bertharius, Desiderius and his brother, Rusticus, and in particular Audoenus, all of whom became not only bishops but saints as well. Of these Audoenus (St Ouen) must have been a boy when St Eligius first knew him ; to him was long attributed the authorship of the *Vita Eligii*, which is now commonly regarded as the work of a later monk of Noyon. By it St Eligius is described as having been at this time, " tall, with a fresh complexion, his hair and beard curling without artifice ; his hands were shapely and long-fingered, his face full of angelic kindness and its expression grave and unaffected ".

King Clotaire's regard for and trust in Eligius was shared by his son, Dagobert I, though, like many monarchs, he valued and took the advice of a holy man more willingly in public than in private affairs. He gave to the saint the estate of Solignac in his native Limousin for the foundation of a monastery, which in 632 was peopled with monks who followed the Rules of St Columban and St Benedict combined. These, under the eye of their founder, became noted for their good work in various arts.* Dagobert also gave to St Eligius a house at Paris, which he converted into a nunnery and placed under the direction of St Aurea. Eligius

---

* The original charter of Solignac is preserved in the archives of Limoges. It is signed by, among others, Eligius, Adeodatus of Mâcon, Lupus of Limoges, Audoenus and Vincent " the least of all the deacons of Christ ".

asked for an additional piece of land to complete the buildings, and it was granted
him.   But he found that he had somewhat exceeded the measure of the land which
had been specified.   Upon which he immediately went to the king and asked his
pardon.   Dagobert, surprised at his careful honesty, said to his courtiers, " Some
of my officers do not scruple to rob me of whole estates ; whereas Eligius is afraid
of having one inch of ground which is not his ".   So trustworthy a man was
valuable as an ambassador, and Dagobert is said to have sent him to treat with
Judicaël, the prince of the turbulent Bretons.

St Eligius was chosen to be bishop of Noyon and Tournai, at the same time as
his friend St Audoenus was made bishop of Rouen.   They were consecrated
together in the year 641.   Eligius proved as good a bishop as he had been layman,
and his pastoral solicitude, zeal and watchfulness were most admirable.   Soon he
turned his thoughts to the conversion of the infidels, who were a large majority in
the Tournai part of his diocese, and a great part of Flanders was chiefly indebted
to St Eligius for receiving the gospel.   He preached in the territories of Antwerp,
Ghent and Courtrai, and the inhabitants, who were as untamed as wild beasts,
reviled him as a foreigner, " a Roman " ; yet he persevered.   He took care of their
sick, protected them from oppression, and employed every means that charity
could suggest to overcome their obstinacy.   The barbarians were gradually
softened, and some were converted ; every year at Easter he baptized those whom
he had brought to the knowledge of God during the twelve preceding months.
The author of the Life tells us that St Eligius preached to the people every Sunday
and feast-day and instructed them with indefatigable zeal ; an abstract is given of
several of his discourses united in one, by which it appears that he often borrowed
whole passages from the sermons of St Caesarius of Arles.   It would perhaps be
more correct to say that the writer of the Life has borrowed from St Caesarius,
though there are similar borrowings in the sixteen homilies attributed to St Eligius.
One of these may possibly be authentic, a very interesting discourse in which the
preacher warns his hearers against superstitions and pagan practices : observances
of January 1 and also of June 24 are mentioned, work must not be abstained from
out of respect for Thursday (*dies Jovis*) or May month, charms, biblical and other,
fortune-telling, watching the omens, and many other superstitions (some of them
still used in Great Britain today) are forbidden.   In their place he urges prayer,
the partaking of the body and blood of Christ, anointing in time of sickness, and
the sign of the cross, with the recitation of the creed and the Lord's Prayer.

At Noyon St Eligius established a house of nuns, to govern which he fetched
his *protégée*, St Godeberta, from Paris, and one of monks, outside the city on the
road to Soissons.   He was very active in promoting the *cultus* of local saints, and
it was during his episcopate that several of the reliquaries mentioned above were
made, either by himself or under his direction.   He took a leading part in the
ecclesiastical life of his day, and for a short time immediately before his death was
a valued counsellor of the queen-regent, St Bathildis.   His biographer gives
several illustrations of the regard which she had for him, and they had in common
not only political views but also a deep solicitude for slaves (she had been carried
off from England and sold when a child).   The effect of this is seen at the Council
of Chalon (*c.* 647), which forbade their sale out of the kingdom and decreed that
they must be free to rest on Sundays and holidays.   The only certainly authentic
writing of St Eligius is a charming letter to his friend St Desiderius of Cahors.
" Remember your Eligius ", he says in the course of it, " O my Desiderius, who

art dear to me as mine own self, when your soul pours itself out in prayer to the Lord. . . . I greet you with all my heart and the most sincere affection. Our faithful companion, Dado, greets you also." Dado is St Audoenus. When he had governed his flock nineteen years Eligius was visited with a foresight of his death, and foretold it to his clergy. Falling ill of a fever, he on the sixth day called together his household and took leave of them. They all burst into tears and he was not able to refrain from weeping with them; he commended them to God, and died a few hours later, on December 1, 660. At the news of his sickness St Bathildis set out from Paris, but arrived only the morning after his death. She had preparations made for carrying the body to her monastery at Chelles. Others were anxious that it should be taken to Paris, but the people of Noyon so strenuously opposed it that the remains of their pastor were left with them. They were afterwards translated into the cathedral, where a great part of them remain. St Eligius was for long one of the most popular saints of France, and his feast was universal in north-western Europe during the later middle ages. In addition to being the patron saint of all kinds of smiths and metalworkers, he is invoked by farriers and on behalf of horses : this on account of legendary tales about horses that have become attached to his name. He practised his art all his life, and a number of existing " pieces " are attributed to him.

Of all the Merovingian saints, the history of St Eloi possibly brings us most nearly into touch with Christian practice at that period. It is therefore not surprising that his life has given rise to a relatively abundant literature. Everything centres round the *Vita S. Eligii*, an unusually lengthy document, of which, as stated above, St Ouen is the reputed author. The best text is that edited by B. Krusch in MGH., *Scriptores Merov.*, vol. iv, pp. 635–742 ; it is also to be found in Migne, PL., vol. lxxxvii, cc. 477–658. It seems certain that St Ouen did write some account of his friend, but the life now preserved to us was compiled at Noyon a half-century or more later ; and though it probably incorporates a good deal of what St Ouen wrote, it has been recast and supplemented in many places. An excellent account of St Eligius is given by E. Vacandard in DTC., vol. iv, cc. 2340–2350, and there are several articles of the same author bearing on the subject, notably in the *Revue des questions historiques* for 1898 and 1899, where the question of the authenticity of the homilies attributed to the saint is very fully discussed. See also Van der Essen, *Étude critique sur les saints mérovingiens* (1904), pp. 324–336 ; H. Timerding, *Die christ. Frühzeit Deutschlands*, vol. i (1929), pp. 125–149 ; S. R. Maitland, *The Dark Ages* (1889), pp. 101–140 ; and P. Parsy, *Saint Eloi* (1904) in the series " Les Saints ". In the long article by H. Leclercq in DAC., vol. iv, cc. 2674–2687, a detailed account is given of the different works of art attributed to the saint's craftsmanship. On " missionary sermons " and the homiletic influence of St Caesarius, see W. Levison, *England and the Continent* . . . (1946), appendix x, pp. 302–314, " Venus, a Man ".

BD BENTIVOGLIA (A.D. 1232)

BENTIVOGLIA, a native of San Severino in the Marches, joined the Franciscan Order in the lifetime of the founder, and though his family was well-to-do a number of his near relatives subsequently followed his example. The imperfect records preserved to us do not seem to supply anything very characteristic or personal regarding this *beatus*. He, no doubt, shared in full measure the love of poverty and simplicity which was so conspicuous in the first generation of the Friars Minor. We are told of his great charity, his zeal for souls and of the inspiring earnestness of his sermons. The parish priest of San Severino is said in the *Fioretti* to have been brought to the order by witnessing a rapture of Bd Bentivoglia when praying in a wood, in the course of which he saw this holy brother raised for a long time high above the ground.   In the same source we read how, " while sojourning once alone at Trave Bonanti in order to take charge of and serve a certain leper, he (Bentivoglia) received commandment from his superior to depart thence and go unto another place, which was about fifteen miles distant, and, not willing to abandon the leper, he took him with him with great fervour of charity, and placed him on his shoulders, and carried him from the dawn till the rising of the sun all the fifteen miles of the way, even to the place where he was sent, which was called Monte San Vicino, which journey, if he had been an eagle, he could not have flown in so short a time, and this divine miracle put the whole country round in amazement and admiration ".   He died, where he was born, at San Severino on Christmas day, 1232.

See Mazzara, *Leggendario Francescano* (1680), vol. i, pp. 239–240 ; Léon, *Auréole Séraphique* (Eng. trans.), vol. ii, pp. 31–33 ; and *Actus B. Francisci et sociorum ejus*, edited by Paul Sabatier, p. 160.   In deference to the reading of Sabatier's manuscripts I have spelt the name Bentivoglia rather than Bentivoglio.

BD JOHN OF VERCELLI   (A.D. 1283)

THIS John was born near Vercelli about the year 1205, but he is not first certainly heard of till forty years later, when he was prior of the Dominicans at Vercelli and a marked man for his abilities and character.   After filling various offices and missions he was elected sixth master general of the Order of Preachers in 1264, an office which he held with great distinction for nineteen years.   John was rather short of stature—in his first letter to his brethren he refers to himself as a " poor little man "—and so amiable of expression that he is said to have required of his *socius* that he should be of a severe and awe-inspiring countenance.   But he made up for lack of size by sufficiency of energy and was tireless in his visitation and correction of the Dominican houses up and down Europe ; nor would he on these journeys dispense himself from the fasts either of the Church or of his order. Immediately on his election to the see of Rome, Bd Gregory X imposed on John of Vercelli and his friars the task of again pacifying the quarrelling states of Italy, and three years later he was ordered to draw up a *schema* for the second oecumenical Council of Lyons.   At the council he met Jerome of Ascoli (afterwards Pope Nicholas IV), who had succeeded St Bonaventure as minister general of the Franciscans, and the two addressed a joint letter to the whole body of friars.   Later on they were sent together by the Holy See to mediate between Philip III of France and Alfonso X of Castile, continuing the work of peace-maker, in which John excelled.

Bd John of Vercelli was one of the early propagators of devotion to the name of Jesus, which the Council of Lyons prescribed in reparation for Albigensian blasphemies.   Bd Gregory X selected John particularly, as head of a great body of preachers, to spread this devotion, and the master general at once addressed all his provincial priors accordingly.   It was decided that there should be an altar of the Holy Name in every Dominican church and that confraternities against blasphemy and profanity should be formed.   In 1278 Bd John sent a visitor into England, where some friars had been attacking the teaching of St Thomas Aquinas, then lately dead, whom John had reappointed to the chair of theology at Paris after the refusal of St Albert the Great.   Two years later John came himself to Oxford, where a general chapter was held.   Like Humbert of Romans, his predecessor, he refused episcopacy and a curial office at Rome ; but he was induced to withdraw his resignation of the generalate, which he retained until his death at Montpellier on November 30, 1283. The *cultus* of Bd John of Vercelli was approved in 1903.

A very full life was composed in French by P. Mothon and it has been translated into Italian, *Vita del B. Giovanni da Vercelli* (1903) ; naturally also Fr Mortier in his *Histoire des Maîtres généraux O.P.*, vol. ii, pp. 1–170, gives much space to this important generalate. A careful account in briefer compass is that of M. de Waresquiel, *Le bx Jean de Verceil* (1903). See also Taurisano, *Catalogus Hagiographicus O.P.*

BD GERARD CAGNOLI   (A.D. 1345)

THE cult which from time immemorial has been paid at Palermo and elsewhere to this follower of St Francis was confirmed in 1908. Gerard, born about 1270, was the only son of noble parents in the north of Italy. He lost his father at the age of ten, and his mother not many years afterwards. Resisting the persuasions of his relatives to marry, he distributed his goods to the poor and led, until he was forty, the life of a pilgrim and hermit, spending most of his time in the wilder parts of Sicily. In the early years of the fourteenth century, the holiness and miracles of St Louis of Anjou, who though heir to a throne had become a Franciscan, were much talked about. Gerard took him for his patron, and about the year 1310 ended by joining the same order. Whilst he discharged the duties of a lay-brother, his simplicity and devotion were the admiration of all. On one great feast-day, when he was acting as cook, being absorbed in prayer, he seemed to have forgotten all about the dinner ; when, late in the morning, the father guardian, apprised that even the fire had not yet been lighted, remonstrated with the brother on his neglect, Gerard, quite unperturbed, betook himself to the kitchen, where, assisted, it is said, by an unknown youth of radiant beauty, he produced, punctually to the moment, a more delicious meal than the community had ever before eaten. Many miracles were attributed to the intercession of the holy brother. For example, it was said that, finding a child crying because it had dropped and broken the glass beaker it was carrying home to its mother, he collected the fragments, blessed them and restored the vessel to the child as sound as it had been before. His miracles of healing were commonly performed by anointing the sick with the oil which burned in a lamp before a little shrine of his patron St Louis. His diet was bread and water, he slept upon a plank, he scourged himself to blood, and there were many stories told of ecstasies in which he was seen surrounded with light and raised from the ground. He died on December 30, 1345.

See the decree of the Congregation of Rites in *Analecta Ecclesiastica* (1908), vol. xvi, pp. 293–295 ; B. Mazzara, *Leggendario Francescano* (1680), vol. iii, pp. 767–773 ; and *Analecta Franciscana* (1897), vol. iii, pp. 489–497.

BD ANTONY BONFADINI   (A.D. 1482)

THE Bonfadini were a good family of Ferrara, where Antony was born in the year 1400. When he was thirty-nine he became a friar minor of the Observance at the friary of the Holy Ghost in his native town, and soon distinguished himself as a teacher and preacher. He was sent on the Franciscan mission in the Holy Land, and on a journey from there, in his old age, he died and was buried at the village of Cotignola in the Romagna. A year later his body was found to be still incorrupt, and miracles were reported at his tomb. Accordingly, when some years later the

Friars Minor made a foundation at Cotignola, they were given permission to translate the body to their church.   The *cultus* of Bd Antony was approved in 1901.

Although the continued *cultus* is well attested, we know little detail of the life of this holy friar.   Some account is furnished by such chroniclers as Mazzara in *Leggendario Francescano*, vol. iii (1680), pp. 601–602.   See also the *Acta Ord. Fratrum Minorum*, vol. xx (1901), pp. 105 *seq.* ; and DHG., vol. iii, c. 763.

BB. RICHARD WHITING, ABBOT OF GLASTONBURY, AND HIS COMPANIONS, MARTYRS   (A.D. 1539)

THE prestige conferred both by legend and history gives Glastonbury a literally unique place among the numerous great monasteries of ancient England, and, if it be impossible to accept the story of its foundation by St Joseph of Arimathaea (and several other stories about it), the very existence of such a legend testifies to the veneration in which our ancestors held the place.   It is therefore fitting that, at a time when many ecclesiastics, secular and regular, and distinguished lay-people fell away lamentably from their calling as Catholic Christians, the last abbot of Glastonbury should have died for his faith at the hands of the civil power.   Richard Whiting was born at Wrington in Somerset, probably soon after 1460, and was educated at Cambridge (Magdalene ?), where he took his M.A., in 1483, and returned for his S.T.D., in 1505.   In all likelihood he was a monk before the first date.   He was ordained priest at Wells in 1501, and for some years held the office of chamberlain in the monastery.   Upon the death of Abbot Bere, in 1525, the community requested Cardinal Wolsey to name a successor.   He chose Dom Richard Whiting : " an upright and religious monk, a provident and discreet man, and a priest commendable for his life, virtues, and learning ".   Among those who signed the commission was St Thomas More.

For ten years his rule was quiet and uneventful, till in 1534 came the summons to take the oath of supremacy, that the king was head of the Church in England. With the exception of More, Fisher, the Carthusian monks and the Franciscan Observants, there were few who stood out from the first against this ; Abbot Whiting and his monks took the oath when it was tendered to them.   In the following year the royal commissioners visited Glastonbury, and reported (with regret) that the brethren were kept in such good order that they could not offend ; and assured the monks that nothing was intended against them.   A year later the lesser monasteries were suppressed, and by the time the greater ones were condemned, in 1539, Glastonbury was the only religious house left in Somerset. Three commissioners arrived there in September.   They impounded various incriminating documents (a book against the king's divorce, copies of papal bulls, and a Life of St Thomas Becket) and questioned Abbot Whiting.   But now he refused to surrender his charge and showed " his cankerous and traitorous mind against the King's Majesty and his succession ".   So they carried him off to London, to the Tower.   Mr Commissioner Layton sent after him to Cromwell a " book of evidences " of " divers and sundry treasons " committed by the abbot, which is not extant and the contents are unknown.   But in consequence of it Cromwell noted in his *Remembrances* :   " Item, the Abbot of Glaston to be tried at Glaston, and also executed there "—a pretty anticipation of the course of injustice.   There is a good deal of uncertainty as to what actually took place : whether Abbot Whiting was tried in London or in Wells or at both places ; but he was condemned to death.   The indictment was not allowed to survive, or even, apparently, to be made public, but there is general agreement that it was for high treason (in which case the abbot was entitled to be tried by his peers in the House of Lords), and the available evidence points to denial of the royal supremacy as having been the specific offence.

Bd Richard arrived at Wells with his escort on Friday, November 14, 1539. The next day he was hurried to Glastonbury, was refused leave to make a farewell visit to his abbey (he apparently did not know it was deserted, the community scattered), and was dragged on a hurdle to the top of the Tor, a hill some 500 feet high overlooking the town.   There, beneath the tower of St Michael's chapel, the aged man, "very weak and sickly", sustained the barbarities of hanging and disembowelling.   Before the evening his head was displayed above the gate of his monastery, and his quarters had been sent off to Wells, Bridgewater, Ilchester and Bath.*   After the abbot had been despatched, two of his monks suffered in a like manner.   These were BD JOHN THORNE, treasurer of the abbey church, and BD ROGER JAMES, its sacristan.   Their offence was called *sacrilege*, in that they had hidden various treasures of their church to save them from the king's hands.   It is likely that this was also one of the charges against Whiting.   The memory of the martyred abbot was long held in benediction by the people of Somerset, and he is not forgotten in Glastonbury and its neighbourhood today.   It was probably on the evidence of Father William Good, s.j., a contemporary and a native of Glastonbury, that Pope Gregory XVI permitted his representation among the martyrs on the walls of the chapel of the *Venerabile*, and so led to his equipollent beatification with the others in 1895.

The feast of these three martyrs is observed in the diocese of Clifton on the day of their death, and in the archdiocese of Westminster and by the English Bene-dictine Congregation on December 1, together with the other two martyred abbots, Hugh Faringdon and John Beche.

The principal materials for this and the two following notices are to be found in the calendar of *Letters and Papers, Foreign and Domestic, of the reign of Henry VIII*, edited for the Record Office by J. S. Brewer, James Gairdner and R. H. Brodie.   The story of Richard Whiting is told in some detail by F. A. Gasquet in *The Last Abbot of Glastonbury* (1895), on which also consult Canon Dixon's notice in the *English Historical Review*, vol. xii (1897), pp. 781–785.   The most accurate account of the martyr is that furnished by Bede Camm in LEM., vol. i (1904), pp. 327–412.

BB. HUGH FARINGDON, ABBOT OF READING, AND HIS COMPANIONS, MARTYRS   (A.D. 1539)

BD HUGH was commonly called Faringdon probably after his birthplace in Berk-shire, but his true surname was Cook and he bore (or assumed) the arms of Cook of Kent.   He became a monk of Reading, and while discharging the office of sub-chamberlain was elected abbot in 1520.   It was an important abbacy, carrying a seat in the House of Lords and in Convocation, and the holder was a county magistrate.   Dom Hugh took an active part in the duties involved, though hostile chroniclers have called him "utterly without learning".   This was not the opinion of Leonard Cox, master of Reading Grammar School, who dedicated to

* The Catholic church of St John is said to be built on the place where his limbs were exposed at Bath.

him a book on rhetoric.   He maintained an excellent discipline in his monastery, and " could not abide " the preachers of the new doctrines, whom he called " heretics and knaves ".   But at first he was on good terms with Henry VIII—too good terms.   The king visited him and called him " my own abbot " ; the abbot sent presents of hunting-knives and of trout netted in the Kennet.   He went further, for he signed the petition to Pope Clement VII for the nullity of Henry's marriage and supplied him with a list of books likely to help his case.   And in 1536 he signed Convocation's articles of faith which virtually acknowledged the royal supremacy over the English church.   At the end of 1537 he still enjoyed the royal favour, and took a prominent part in the funeral of Queen Jane Seymour at Windsor.   A few weeks later he offended the king by reporting to Cromwell and to the neighbouring abbot of Abingdon the rumour that Henry was dead.   He was examined by a commission, but released.

In 1539 the greater abbeys were suppressed.   It was known that the abbot of Reading would not surrender his, and in the late summer he was consigned to the Tower of London, charged with treason.   With him were tried BD JOHN EYNON and BD JOHN RUGG.   Eynon was a priest of St Giles's church at Reading, who had already been in trouble for writing and distributing a copy of Robert Aske's proclamation of the Pilgrimage of Grace in 1536.   Rugg was a prebendary of Chichester living in retirement at Reading Abbey.   Among the charges against him was that he had preserved a relic of the hand of St Anastasius, " knowing that his Majesty had sent visitors to the said abbey to put down such idolatry ".*   These two priests are generally accounted to have been monks, but it is not certain that they were.   As in the case of Bd Richard Whiting, the terms of the indictment are not known, but it was not doubted at the time that it was primarily for denying the royal supremacy, and Bd Hugh spoke clearly on the scaffold.   The supremacy of the Holy See in spiritual matters was, he said, " the common faith of those who had the best right to declare the true teaching of the English church ".   The execution of all three took place outside Reading Abbey gateway, on the same day as that of the Glastonbury monks.

These martyrs were beatified by equipollence in 1895.   Their feast is kept in the diocese of Portsmouth on November 14, and by Westminster and the English Benedictines with BB. Richard Whiting and John Beche on December 1.

The books mentioned in the notice of Bd Richard Whiting also contain whatever information is available concerning the Abbot of Reading ; see in particular pp. 121–158 of Cardinal Gasquet's book, and pp. 358–387 in that of Bede Camm.

BD JOHN BECHE, ABBOT OF COLCHESTER, MARTYR   (A.D. 1539)

THE martyr who was equivalently beatified in 1895 as John Beche was also known as Thomas Marshall ; the last seems to have been his proper surname, and Thomas was perhaps his name " in religion ". His birthplace and parentage are not known ; he took his D.D. at Oxford in 1515 and for some years was abbot of St Werburgh's at Chester.   In 1533 he was elected abbot of St John's, Colchester. He was a friend of More and Fisher and his new community was opposed to the ecclesiastical policy of Henry VIII, but in the following year the abbot and sixteen

* It has been suggested by Dom Bede Camm that the hand preserved at the Catholic church of St Peter at Marlow, known to have been found in Reading, is this very relic. See LEM., vol. i, p. 376, note.

monks, like their fellows throughout the land, took the oath of royal supremacy. The writer of an early Life of St John Fisher, who refers to Dom John Beche as "excelling many of the abbots of his day in devotion, piety and learning", states that he first came under suspicion owing to a "traitorous guest", who encouraged him to speak against the execution of More and Fisher and then reported his words to the king's advisers. In November 1538 commissioners were sent to dissolve Colchester Abbey, to whom Bd John said : "The king shall never have my house but against my will and my heart, for I know by my learning that he cannot take it by right and law. Wherefore in my conscience I cannot be content, nor shall he have it with my heart and will." Within a year the abbot was in the Tower, charged with treason, in the same way and for the same reason as his fellow-abbots, Richard Whiting and Hugh Faringdon.

During the first four days of November 1539 two commissioners were at Brentwood, in Essex, examining witnesses against Beche, and evidence was given that he had spoken against the suppression of the monasteries, against the king's marriage with Anne Boleyn, against the royal supremacy, and in favour of the full prerogatives of the Holy See. When interrogated on these accusations the abbot, under duress of captivity and fear, tried to explain them away and affirmed the king's supremacy as against the pope's "usurped authority", and asked Henry "to be good to me for the love of God".* He was nevertheless sent back to Colchester to be tried. There is no record of the proceedings, but one of the judges reported to Cromwell that the prisoner "acknowledged himself in substance to be guilty according to the effect of the indictment". He was duly sentenced, and was hanged, drawn and quartered at Colchester on December 1, 1539.

The feast of Bd John Beche is kept in the diocese of Brentwood and, with the other two martyred abbots, by Westminster and the English Benedictines. An anonymous pamphleteer, of the king's party, gave valuable testimony to the cause for which these martyrs died when he wrote scornfully : "It is not to be doubted but his Holiness will look upon their pains as upon Thomas Becket's, seeing it is for like matter."

Here again the authorities are the same as in the two previous notices. See Gasquet, pp. 159–176, and Camm, pp. 388–407.

BD RALPH SHERWIN, Martyr   (A.D. 1581)

Sir William Petre, secretary of state to Henry VIII and the three following sovereigns and founder of the fortunes of his house, founded eight fellowships in Exeter College, Oxford, to one of which he nominated, in 1568, Ralph Sherwin, a young gentleman of Rodsley in Derbyshire. He took his M.A. in 1574, "being then accounted", says Anthony à Wood, "an acute philosopher and an excellent Grecian and Hebrician". The next year he was reconciled to the Church, went to Douay, and was there ordained priest in 1577. A few months later he went to the English College at Rome, where he took a leading part in the deplorable dissensions between the English and Welsh students, and was one of the four who petitioned Pope Gregory XIII to entrust the direction of the college to the Society

* The document to this effect, in Abbot Beche's own handwriting, came to light only after his case had been examined at Rome. When his cause of canonization is brought forward it will be taken into consideration. A decree of equipollent beatification is only *permissive*. But he seems to have retracted all schismatical admissions at his trial.

of Jesus. This was eventually done, and Sherwin's name stands first in the register under the new régime of those who declared their willingness to go on the English mission at any time. He was one of the party which, under the leadership of Bishop Goldwell, set out in 1580. At Milan they were the guests of St Charles Borromeo for a week, and Mr Sherwin preached before him. From Paris he wrote to a friend in Rome, Ralph Bickley, telling particularly of their adventures at Geneva, and broke off the letter because Mr Paschal had come in " with the frip to frenchify me ", *i.e.* the secular clothes for his disguise, which he much disliked wearing. He ends : " My loving Ralph, I request thee once in thy greatest fervour to say over thy beads for me, and procure as many of my friends as you can to do the same there, and let your petition be this : that in humility and constancy with perseverance to the end, I may honour God in this vocation, whereunto though unworthy I am called."

At Rheims the missionaries separated, and on August 1 Ralph Sherwin set out for England. In November he was arrested while preaching in the house of Nicholas Roscarrock in London, and was chained in the Marshalsea. Of his brief apostolate Father Persons wrote that he spent it preaching in various parts of the kingdom, in which work " he enjoyed a very special grace and ascendancy ". From the prison he managed to write a cheerful note to Persons, referring to the bells, *i.e.* fetters, on his ankles, and after a month was removed to the Tower. Here he was severely racked on December 15, with the object of getting information about his fellow-missionaries, about a feared invasion of Ireland, etc. Afterwards he was left to lie out in the snow, and next day was tortured again. He told his brother that after he had been twice racked he lay five days and nights without any food or speaking to anybody, " as he thought in a sleep, before our Saviour on the cross. After which time he came to himself, not finding any distemper in his joints by the extremity of the torture." He was offered a bishopric if he would apostatize. After more than a year's imprisonment he was brought to trial with Edmund Campion and others, and convicted on the charge of entering the realm in order to raise a rebellion. " The plain reason of our standing here ", he observed, " is religion, not treason."

While awaiting death Ralph wrote several letters to friends, including one to his uncle in Rouen, who had formerly been rector of Ingatestone. In it he says : " Innocency is my only comfort against all the forged villainy which is fathered on my fellow priests and me. . . . God forgive all injustice, and if it be His blessed will to convert our persecutors, that they may become professors of His truth. . . . And so, my good old John, farewell." On December 1, 1581, he was dragged to Tyburn on the same hurdle as Alexander Briant, and suffered immediately after Campion. On the scaffold he again protested his innocence of treason, professed the whole Catholic faith, and prayed for the Queen, and died amid the open prayers of the crowd. He was thirty-one years old.

Bd Ralph Sherwin was among the martyrs beatified in 1886, and his feast is observed in the diocese of Nottingham ; he was the protomartyr of the English College at Rome.

A full account of this martyr has been contributed by E. S. Keogh to the second volume of Camm's LEM., pp. 358–396. See also MMP., pp. 30–35. The earlier sources of information are indicated by Father Keogh on p. 396 of the first book, but to these should be added Cardinal Allen's account of Fr Campion and his companions edited by J. H. Pollen in 1908, pp. 34–46.

BD EDMUND CAMPION, Martyr   (A.D. 1581)

EDMUND CAMPION, senior, was a bookseller in the city of London, and he and his wife were Catholics until the time of Queen Elizabeth. Edmund junior was born about 1540, and when he was ten was admitted to the " Bluecoat School " by the interest of the Grocers' Company. He was an extraordinarily promising boy, and when fifteen was given a scholarship in St John's College, Oxford, then newly founded by Sir Thomas White. Two years later Campion was appointed a junior fellow, and he made a great reputation as an orator ; he was chosen to speak at the re-burial of Lady Amy Dudley (Robsart), at the funeral of Sir Thomas White, and before Elizabeth when she visited Oxford in 1566 : as a bluecoat boy he had been selected to make a speech of welcome to her predecessor at St Paul's thirteen years before. His talents and personality earned him the goodwill and patronage of the queen, of Cecil and of Leicester ; to the last-named he dedicated his *History of Ireland,* and Cecil later referred to him as " one of the diamonds of England ". He had taken the oath of royal supremacy and, although his allegiance to Protestantism was much shaken by his reading in the fathers, he was persuaded by Dr Cheney, Bishop of Gloucester, to receive the diaconate of the Anglican Church. At Oxford he was very popular (Dr Gregory Martin, with whom he was friendly, wrote from Rome warning him against ambition) and was the centre of a group of personal disciples, rather like Newman two hundred and fifty years later. But the taking of orders in a church about which he was doubtful began to trouble him and, at the end of his term as junior proctor of the university in 1569, the Grocers' Company (whose exhibitioner he was) being restive about his papistical tendencies, he went to Dublin, where an attempt was being made to revive its university. While there he wrote a short history of the country.*

Campion had left Oxford " full of remorse of conscience and detestation of mind " for himself as an Anglican minister, and he took no pains to conceal his sentiments. Accordingly, after the publication of Pope St Pius's bull against Elizabeth, he was in danger as a suspected person. In 1571 he returned to England in disguise, was present at the trial of Bd John Storey in Westminster Hall, and then made for Douay. He was stopped on the way for having no passport, but was allowed to escape on giving up his luggage and money. One of his first actions at Douay was to send a long and striking letter, a " vehement epistle ", to Dr Cheney, who had strong Catholic leanings.† Campion took his B.D. and was ordained subdeacon at Douay, and then, in 1573, went to Rome and was admitted to the Society of Jesus. As there was yet no English province he was sent to that of Bohemia, and after his novitiate at Brno went to the college of Prague to teach.

In view of the great success of the Society among the Protestants of Germany, Bohemia and Poland, Dr Allen persuaded Pope Gregory XIII to send some

---

* He said of the Irish : " The people are thus inclined : religious, franke, amorous, irefull, sufferable of paines infinite, very glorious, many sorcerers, excellent horsemen, delighted with warres, great almes-givers, passing in hospitalitie : the lewder sort both clarkes and laymen are sensuall and loose to leachery above measure. The same being vertuously bred up or reformed are such mirrours of holinesse and austeritie, that other nations retaine but a shewe or shadow of devotion in comparison of them." The work was not well received in Ireland.

† Cheney may have been reconciled secretly before his death, though Campion knew nothing of it. The only other Protestant bishop in England who may have died a Catholic was also of Gloucester : Dr Godfrey Goodman (1582–1655).

Jesuits to England, and at the end of 1579 Father Edmund Campion and Father Robert Persons were chosen as the first to be sent. The night before he left Prague one of the fathers, by an irresistible impulse, wrote over the door of his cell the words : *P. Edmundus Campianus, Martyr.* He left Rome in the spring of 1580, one of the party whose adventures are so well described in Bd Ralph Sherwin's letter to Ralph Bickley. When they got to the Protestant stronghold of Geneva Campion pretended to be an Irish serving-man called Patrick, and they all seem to have behaved with that reckless cheerfulness that makes more serious-minded people think the English mad. At the gate on leaving, after having had a discussion with Beza, Campion disputed with a minister, and then left the " poor shackerel " to be ragged by the rest.* From Saint-Omer Persons set out for England disguised as a returning soldier from the Lowlands, followed by Campion as a jewel merchant, with his servant, a coadjutor-brother, Ralph Emerson.

The Jesuits were not welcomed by all the Catholics, many of whom feared what new troubles the arrival of representatives of the redoubtable Society might bring on their heads ; and it was necessary for the two to declare on oath that " their coming was only apostolical, to treat of matters of religion in truth and simplicity, and to attend to the gaining of souls without any pretence or knowledge of matters of state ". Their coming was known to the government, and they soon had to leave London, Campion going to work in Berkshire, Oxfordshire and Northamptonshire, where he made some notable converts. He wrote to the father general in Rome : " I ride about some piece of the country every day. The harvest is wonderful great. . . . I cannot long escape the hands of the heretics. . . . I am in apparel to myself very ridiculous ; I often change it and my name also. I read letters sometimes myself that, in the first front, tell news that Campion is taken, which roused in every place where I come so filleth my ears with the sound thereof that fear itself hath taken away all fear." After meeting Persons in London, where persecution was very hot, he went to Lancashire, where he preached almost daily and with conspicuous success, pursued always by spies and several times nearly taken : fifty years later his sermons were still remembered by those who had heard them. All this time he was writing a Latin treatise, which was called *Decem Rationes* because in it he expounded ten reasons why he had challenged the most learned Protestants openly to discuss religion with him. The greatest difficulty was found in getting this work printed, but eventually it was achieved on a secret press at the house of Dame Cecilia Stonor, in Stonor Park, Berkshire, and on " Commemoration ", June 27, 1581, four hundred copies of it were found distributed on the benches of the university church at Oxford. It made a tremendous sensation,† and efforts to capture the writer were redoubled. Three weeks later he was taken.

---

* When someone asked " Mr Patrick " : " Cujas es ? " he replied, " Signor, no." The questioner tried again : " Potesne loqui latine ? " Whereupon the Latin orator and professor of rhetoric shrugged his shoulders with a puzzled expression and walked away.

† This book, *Libellus aureus, vere digito Dei scriptus,* has gone through forty-eight editions, printed in all parts of Europe, of which five have been English translations. Of the original edition only four copies are known. Owing to shortage of type it had to be set and printed one sheet at a time, and it took half a dozen men nine weeks. " Campion's Challenge ", or " Brag ", addressed to the Privy Council, had been written for publication in case he were captured, to try and ensure him a fair hearing ; but the document got spread abroad prematurely and directed the attention of the whole country to him.

After the publication of *Decem Rationes* it was judged prudent that Bd Edmund should retire to Norfolk, and on the way he stayed at the house of Mrs Yate at Lyford, near Wantage. On Sunday, July 16, some forty people assembled there to assist at Mass and hear him preach, but among them was a traitor. Within the next twelve hours the house was searched three times, and at the last Bd Edmund was found with two other priests concealed above the gateway. They were taken to the Tower, from Colnbrook onward being pinioned and Edmund labelled : " Campion, the seditious Jesuit." After three days in the " little-ease " he was interviewed by the Earls of Bedford and Leicester and, it is said, the queen herself, who tried to bribe him into apostasy. Other attempts of the same sort having failed he was racked ; and arrests were then made of some who had sheltered him, whose names had already been known to the government but which, it was lyingly said, Campion had betrayed. While still broken by torture he was four times confronted by Protestant dignitaries, whose questions, objections and insults he answered with spirit and effectiveness.* He was then racked again, so fiercely that when asked the next day how he felt he could reply, " Not ill, because not at all ". No handle could be found against him, so on November 14 he was indicted in Westminster Hall, with Ralph Sherwin, Thomas Cottam, Luke Kirby and others, on the fabricated charge of having plotted at Rome and Rheims to raise a rebellion in England and coming into the realm for that purpose. When told to plead to the charge he was too weak to move his arms, and one of his companions, kissing his hand, held it up for him. Campion conducted the defence both of himself and the others with much ability, protesting their loyalty to the queen, demolishing the evidence, discrediting the witnesses, and showing that their only offence was their religion. The packed jury brought them in " guilty ", but it took them an hour to make up their minds to do it. Before sentence of death Bd Edmund addressed the court : " . . . In condemning us you condemn all your own ancestors. . . . To be condemned with these old lights—not of England only, but of the world—by their degenerate descendants is both gladness and glory to us. God lives. Posterity will live. Their judgement is not so liable to corruption as that of those who now sentence us to death."

Campion's sister came to him with a message from Hopton, offering him a good benefice as the price of apostasy, and he also had a visit from Eliot, who had both betrayed and given evidence against him, and now went in fear of his life. Bd Edmund freely forgave him and gave him a letter of recommendation to a nobleman in Germany, where he would be safe. On December 1, a wet, muddy day, Campion, Sherwin, and Briant were drawn to Tyburn together, and there executed with the usual barbarities. On the scaffold Bd Edmund again refused to give an opinion of the pope's bull against Elizabeth, and publicly prayed for her : " your queen and my queen, unto whom I wish a long reign with all prosperity ". Some of the blood of this man, " admirable, subtle, exact and of sweet disposition ", splashed on to a young gentleman, one Henry Walpole, who was present : he too became a Jesuit and a beatified martyr.†

---

   * Among those present who were permanently affected by his words and bearing was Philip Howard, Earl of Arundel, afterwards himself a martyr and now beatified.

   † Among the poems of Walpole on the life and death of Bd Edmund one lyric, " Why do I use my paper, ink and pen ", was beautifully set to music by William Byrd, who was himself frequently " presented " for recusancy. It was first published in his *Psalms, Sonnets and Songs in Five Parts* in 1588, among the " Songs of Sadness and Piety ".

The feast of Bd Edmund Campion is kept not only by the Society of Jesus but as well by the dioceses of Northampton, Portsmouth, Brno and Prague.

We are very fully informed concerning the mission of Bd Edmund Campion and Father Persons to England, though the sources from which we learn the details are too numerous and scattered to be enumerated here. In the articles which Richard Simpson contributed to *The Rambler* from 1856 to 1858, and in the full biography which he published in 1867, there is very adequate documentation and this is further supplemented in the account of Campion which fills pp. 266–357 in Camm, LEM., vol. ii. Special mention, however, should be made of the *Vita et martyrium Edmundi Campiani*, by P. Bombino, printed at Antwerp in 1618 ; of Father Persons' account of the journey to England in vol. ii of the Catholic Record Society's *Publications* (1906), pp. 186–201 ; of Cardinal Allen's *Martyrdom of Father Campion* . . . (ed. Pollen, 1908) ; and of Fr J. H. Pollen's numerous articles in *The Month* (notably September 1897, January and December 1905, and January 1910). A very attractive life of Bd Edmund, free from the ' Cisalpine pleading " which prejudices Richard Simpson's work, was published by Evelyn Waugh in 1935. It contains on pp. 224–225 a useful bibliography of relevant literature, to which may now be added A. C. Southern, *Elizabethan Recusant Prose* (1950), cap. iii. On Campion's relics see especially Bede Camm, *Forgotten Shrines* (1911), pp. 377–378.

BD ALEXANDER BRIANT, Martyr   (A.D. 1581)

WHEN after the appearance of the publications of Fathers Campion and Persons the authorities were making frenzied efforts to lay the two Jesuits by the heels, several other active Catholics were arrested *en passant*, and among them Alexander Briant. He was a young secular priest, born in Somerset and distinguished for his good looks as well as his zeal, who, while at Hart Hall, Oxford, had been reconciled to the Church and gone abroad to the Douay seminary. He was ordained and came back to England in 1579, where he at first ministered in the west and brought the father of Father Persons back to the Church. Mr Briant was taken in London on April 28, 1581, being in an adjoining house when Persons' house was fruitlessly searched by order of the Privy Council. It was determined to extract from him information as to the whereabouts of Persons, whatever methods should have to be used, and after six days of almost complete starvation in the Counter prison he was removed to the Tower. Needles were thrust under his finger-nails (he is the only martyr of the time of whom this torture is recorded) to make him betray Persons or compromise himself. When this was not successful he was left in an unlit underground cell for a week, and then racked to the limit on two successive days. The rack-master, Norton, himself admits that Briant was " racked more than any of the rest ", and a public outcry caused Norton to be imprisoned for a few days for his cruelty on this occasion, to save the face of the authorities. From the Tower Bd Alexander contrived to write a long letter to the Jesuits in England, in the course of which he says that the first time he was racked, towards the end : " I was without sense and feeling wellnigh of all grief and pain ; and not so only, but as it were comforted, eased, and refreshed of the griefs of the torture bypast." " Whether this that I say be miraculous or no, God he knoweth ; but true it is, and thereof my conscience is a witness before God." On the testimony of Norton (for what that is worth), after the torture Bd Alexander experienced pain of a more than usual sharpness. In the same letter he asked that he might be admitted into the Society of Jesus, even in his absence, having made a vow to offer himself if he should be released from jail, and he is in consequence numbered among the martyrs of the Society.

Bd Alexander was tried in Westminster Hall with Bd Thomas Ford and others, the day after Campion, Sherwin and Cottam, and on the same indictment. He came into court carrying a small crucifix drawn in charcoal on a piece of wooden trencher and with his head tonsured to show he was a priest ; and in spite of his sufferings his appearance was still of " a serenity, innocency and amiability almost angelic ". He suffered at Tyburn on December 1, 1581, after BB. Edmund Campion and Ralph Sherwin. On this day also is commemorated the martyrdom of BD RICHARD LANGLEY, a gentleman of Ousethorpe and Grimthorpe, who was hanged at York on December 1, 1586, for harbouring priests at his mansions.

The archdiocese of Birmingham observes today the feast of all those members of the University of Oxford, over forty in number, who have been beatified for giving their lives as martyrs for the faith during the persecutions of the sixteenth and seventeenth centuries.

Many of the publications noticed in connection with Edmund Campion have also some bearing on the story of his companion martyr. But see especially Camm, LEM., vol. ii, pp. 397–423 ; and REPSJ., vol. iv, pp. 343–367. Briant seems to have been of good yeoman birth and the will of his father, which mentions him, is preserved. For Mr Langley, *cf.* Gillow, *Biog. Dict. Eng. Caths.*, Pollen, *Acts of Eng. Marts.*, and REPSJ., vols. iii and vi.

2 : ST BIBIANA, or VIVIANA, VIRGIN AND MARTYR   (DATE UNKNOWN)

THE church of St Bibiana in the city of Rome existed in the fifth century and is said by the *Liber Pontificalis* to have been dedicated by Pope St Simplicius and to have contained her body. But of the time at which she suffered and the circumstances of her passion nothing certain is known. The notices of her and her family in the Roman Martyrology, and the lessons of her feast in the Roman Breviary, are taken from a late legend which is a quite untrustworthy compilation. According to it St Bibiana suffered under the Emperor Julian the Apostate. She was a native of Rome, and daughter to Flavian, ex-prefect of the city, and his wife, Dafrosa, who were both zealous Christians. Flavian was apprehended, burned in the face with a hot iron, and banished to Acquapendente, as the Roman Martyrology asserts on the twenty-second of this month. After his death his wife, Dafrosa, being equally faithful to Christ, was on the same account confined to her house for some time, and at length beheaded. Bibiana and her sister, Demetria, were stripped of all they had in the world and suffered much from poverty for five months, but spent that time in their own house in fasting and prayer. At length, brought into court, Demetria fell down dead in the presence of the judge, who gave orders that Bibiana should be put into the hands of a woman named Rufina, who was extremely artful and undertook to bring her to another way of thinking. But Rufina's blandishments were tried in vain on St Bibiana, and when they failed to tempt her from the way of faith and chastity blows were found to be just as fruitless. She was tied to a pillar and whipped with scourges loaded with lead : and so she died. Her body was left in the open air that it might be eaten by scavenging dogs. But they would not touch it, and, having lain exposed two days, it was buried in the night near the palace of Licinius by a priest called John, in the same house where lay her mother and sister.

This John is associated with St Pimenius who was the tutor of the Emperor Julian before he apostatized. When Julian began persecuting, Pimenius escaped to Persia and thus survived all the other personages in the story. Returning at length to Rome he met Julian in the street, whereupon the emperor said, " Glory be to my gods and goddesses because I see you ". To which the saint replied, " Glory be to my Lord Jesus Christ, the Nazarene who was crucified, because I see you not ". Whereupon Julian ordered him to be thrown off the bridge into the Tiber. But the whole legend, as Delehaye shows, has been evolved from slightly older hagiographical fictions of the same character, particularly those connected with the story of SS. John and Paul. It is possible that the name Pimenius is simply an adaptation of the Greek word ποιμήν, which means " shepherd ", and that thus we get into touch with " St Pastor ".

The story of St Bibiana has been very fully discussed by Delehaye in his *Étude sur le légendier romain* (1936), pp. 124–143 ; and in an appendix (pp. 259–268) he has edited the two texts which are of particular importance. These respectively bear the headings *Passio Sancti Pygmenii* and *Vita Sancti Pastoris*. Pimenius or Pygmenius is in fact the central figure of this setting of the legend, and it is his name, not that of Bibiana, which is commemorated in the *Hieronymianum*. See further M. E. Donckel's article " Studien über den Kultus der hl. Bibiana " in the *Römische Quartalschrift*, vol. xliii (1935), pp. 23–33, and Quentin, *Les martyrologes historiques*, pp. 494–495. Because St Bibiana is represented in her story as having been locked up with mad people she was widely honoured as a patron of the insane and epileptics.

ST CHROMATIUS, BISHOP OF AQUILEIA   (c. A.D. 407)

CHROMATIUS was brought up in the city of Aquileia, of which he was probably a native, and lived there with his widowed mother (of whom St Jerome's good opinion is seen in a letter written to her in the year 374), his brother, who also became a bishop, and unmarried sisters. After his ordination to the priesthood St Chromatius took part in the synod of Aquileia against Arianism in 381, baptized Rufinus in his early manhood, and soon acquired a great reputation. On the death of St Valerian in 388 he was elected bishop of Aquileia, and in that office became one of the most distinguished prelates of his time. He was a friend and correspondent of St Jerome (who dedicated several of his works to him), at the same time preserving his association with Rufinus, and trying to act as peace-maker and moderator in the Origenistic dispute. It was owing to the encouragement of St Chromatius that Rufinus undertook the translation of the *Ecclesiastical History* of Eusebius and other works, and at his suggestion St Ambrose commented on the prophecy of Balaam ; he helped St Heliodorus of Altino to finance St Jerome's translation of the Bible. Chromatius was an energetic and valued supporter of St John Chrysostom, who had a high opinion of him ; he wrote to the Emperor Honorius protesting against the persecution of Chrysostom, and Honorius forwarded the protest to his brother, Arcadius, at Constantinople. But the efforts of Chromatius were without effect. He was himself a capable commentator of the Holy Scriptures ; seventeen of his treatises on parts of St Matthew's gospel are extant and a homily on the Beatitudes. St Chromatius died about the year 407, and is named in the Roman Martyrology ; his feast is observed in the churches of Gorizia and Istria, formerly parts of the Aquileian province.

There seems to be no formal biography ; but some attention has been directed to St Chromatius of late years on account of the writings attributed to him. See Bardenhewer, *Geschichte der altkirchlichen Literatur*, vol. iii, pp. 548–551 ; P. de Puniet in the *Revue d'histoire ecclésiastique*, vol. vi (1905), pp. 15–32, 304–318 ; P. Paschini in the *Revue Bénédictine*, vol. xxvi (1909), pp. 469–475. The works attributed to Chromatius are printed in

Migne, PL., vol. xx, cc. 247–436, but the state of the text is very unsatisfactory.   To him must probably be attributed the " Expositio de oratione dominica " printed by M. Andrieu in *Les Ordines romani du haut moyen âge*, vol. ii (1948), pp. 417–447.

BD JOHN RUYSBROECK   (A.D. 1381)

JAN VAN RUYSBROECK, Joannes Rusbrochius, or as he is generally called in English, John Ruysbroeck, was born at the place of that name near Brussels in 1293.   In those days it was a small village, and John was certainly of humble birth, though of his father nothing is known, and of his mother only her goodness and love for her son.   At the age of eleven he went to live with his uncle, John Hinckaert, who was a minor canon of the collegiate church of St Gudula at Brussels, and attended the schools of the city.   Some years later his mother joined him there, living in a *béguinage*, and soon after her death John was ordained priest at the age of twenty-four.   Subsequently, in consequence of a sermon preached in St Gudula's, Canon Hinckaert's way of life underwent considerable modification. He gave away his superfluous goods and income and, in company with another canon, Franco van Coudenberg, a younger man, undertook to join a life of contemplation to his canonical activities.   Bd John associated himself with these two. Between 1330 and 1335 he wrote some polemical pamphlets which have perished, but soon after he wrote the *Book of the Kingdom of God's Lovers*.   This work like all his others was written in Flemish that it might reach people at large, and is a refutation of false mysticism and an exposition of the true way to God.   It was followed by the *Spiritual Espousals*, and several other mystical works of a practical kind.   Some commentators have claimed that John was illiterate and ignorant, thus adding an adventitious interest and merit to his writings.   But in fact there is every evidence that he was a capable philosopher and theologian, well read both in the works of the contemporary scholastics and of the masters of the past.   The claim was made in his own time and answered by Gerson at Paris, who accused him of pantheistic ideas in the third book of the *Spiritual Espousals* : " It has been said that the man who wrote this book was illiterate and uneducated, and consequently an attempt has been made to regard it as inspired by the Holy Ghost. But it gives evidence rather of human scholarship than of divine inspiration . . . and the style is somewhat laboured.   Besides, in order to deal with such a subject, piety is not enough : one must be a scholar as well."

Between 1340 and 1343 John was writing the first part of the *Book of the Spiritual Tabernacle*, an allegory of the mystical life, and in the spring of the latter year the three priests left Brussels.   They were called to a complete dedication of themselves to God in a life of uninterrupted contemplation ; in the city they were hampered by a clergy many of whom were debased and worldly, and, moreover, while John had raised hostility by his vigour against heresy, Canon van Coudenberg had got into trouble with his prince.   With the permission of this John III, Duke of Brabant, they received an assignment from the hermit Lambert of the hermitage of Groenendael in the forest of Soignes, where they built a larger chapel and established themselves.   But their first six years were not peaceful, troubled in particular on the one hand by the criticism of the chapter of Sainte-Gudule and of neighbouring monks, and on the other by the ducal hunt and its followers : not being associated with any religious order they had no protection against these nuisances.   Accordingly, in 1349, being then increased by five disciples, they formed themselves into a community of canons regular of St Augustine and made their vows before the bishop of Cambrai.   The aged Hinckaert dying the following year, Franco van Coudenberg was nominated to govern the new monastery as provost, aided by John Ruysbroeck as prior.   It was Franco who "made" Groenendael in a material and administrative sense, and John's presence there was a great attraction to the numerous aspirants who offered themselves to the community.   He was an exemplary religious, docile, patient, obedient, fond of manual labour (at which he was rather clumsy), and a better subject than superior.

Gerard Naghel, a Carthusian of Hérinnes, speaks of Ruysbroeck making a visit to that monastery : "How much might be said of his strong manly face, alight with joy, of his humble and affectionate speech, of the spirituality radiating from him, of a religious bearing that showed itself even in his way of wearing his clothes. . . . Though we wanted to hear him talk about himself he never would, but just drew lessons from the sacred epistles. . . . He showed himself as free from conceit as if he had never written his own books."   Bd John would spend hours in the forest which surrounded the monastery, listening, as it were, where no human distractions came between his ear and the voice of God.   He made notes on waxed tablets, and elaborated and arranged them at his leisure in his cell.   Once when he was missing at supper a canon went out to look, and found him sitting in ecstasy under a lime tree, surrounded by unearthly light.   Thus he completed the *Spiritual Tabernacle* and undertook the other books which have given him an assured place among the greater contemplatives of the middle ages.*   It is often urged that Ruysbroeck said nothing that had not been said by other mystics before him, that his originality lay in the way the matter was presented.   But to say something in a new way is emphatically to say something new, and, standing between the thirteenth century and the Renaissance, he effected a combination between philosophical elements drawn from Scholasticism on the one hand and Neoplatonism on the other.   It has been well said that if Ruysbroeck's voice had not possessed an altogether new accent, if his doctrine had contained nothing original, his extraordinary influence would be unexplainable.   The attraction of personal sanctity is sufficient to account for the heterogeneous crowds that made pilgrimages to see him at Groenendael.   But there were others, *doctores ac clerici non mediocres*, on whom he is known to have had a strong direct influence.   Chief among them was Gerard Groote, founder of the Brothers of the Common Life, through whom Bd John's teaching had its effect on the school of Windesheim and on Thomas a Kempis ; while the pattern of monastic life at Groenendael was responsible for Windesheim becoming not Carthusian or Cistercian but Augustinian.

The last few years of his life Bd John was unable to leave the cell which he shared with Provost Franco, who was even older than himself.   One night he dreamed that his mother came to him and said that God would call him before Advent.   The next day he asked to be taken to the common infirmary, where, wasted by a fever, he prepared for death with devotion and a ready mind.   It came on December 2, 1381, in his eighty-eighth year.   Once a year, on the second Sunday after Pentecost, the chapter of Sainte-Gudule came in procession to

---

* It is curious that in Ruysbroeck, as in other mystics of that age, notably the Englishman Richard Rolle of Hampole, there was a marked tendency to pass from ordinary prose into a rhythmical cadence, and even into whatever was then the prevailing form of poetic diction whether it was rhyme or alliteration.   The tendency is noticeable even in the Latin of Thomas a Kempis's "Imitation of Christ", which was sometimes known for this reason as the *Musica ecclesiastica*.

Groenendael in honour of John Ruysbroeck ; and when the monastery was suppressed in 1783 his relics were translated to Brussels, only to be lost at the Revolution. The often interrupted efforts to secure his beatification were successful only in 1908, when St Pius X confirmed his *cultus* and allowed his feast to the Canons Regular of the Lateran and the diocese of Malines. In Abbot Cuthbert Butler's opinion there has probably been no greater contemplative than Ruysbroeck, " and certainly there has been no greater mystical writer ".

What we know of the history of John Ruysbroeck is almost entirely derived from a Latin biography written by a certain Henry Pomerius (the name is a latinization of *Bogaerts, Van den Bogaerde*). This biography seems certainly to have been composed between 1429 and 1431 and consequently some fifty years after the death of Bd John. But the biographer had before him an earlier life by John van Schoonhoven which has perished. The text of Pomerius may be found printed with a valuable introduction in the *Analecta Bollandiana*, vol. iv (1885), pp. 257–334. See also A. Auger, *Étude sur les mystiques des Pays-Bas au moyen âge* (1892) ; W. De Vreese in the *Biographie nationale* de Belgique, vol. xx, cc. 507–591 ; J. Van Mierlo in *Dietsche Warande en Belfort* (1910), vols. i and ii ; C. S. Durrant, *Flemish Mystics and English Martyrs* (1925), pp. 3–14 ; F. Van Ortroy in the *Analecta Bollandiana*, vol. xxxi (1912), pp. 384–387 ; J. Kuckhoff, *Johannes von Ruysbroeck* (1938) ; and S. Axters, *Spiritualité des Pays-Bas* (1948). Although Ruysbroeck undoubtedly knew Latin, all his works were written in the Flemish of the period. This, we are told, readily lends itself to misinterpretation by those who are not experts, and translations are often unreliable. The Latin version of his works made by Surius is in many cases no better than a loose paraphrase. On the other hand a very scholarly and careful rendering of all the authentic writings into French, under the general title of *Œuvres de Ruysbroeck l'Admirable*, has been brought out by the Benedictines of Saint-Paul de Wisques (6 vols., 1912–38). A life of the *beatus* was written in English by D. Vincent Scully (1910) ; Evelyn Underhill wrote a study, *Ruysbroeck* (1915) ; R. F. Sherwood Taylor translated the *Seven Steps of the Ladder of Spiritual Love* (1944), and E. Colledge *The Spiritual Espousals* (1952), previously known in English as " The Adornment of the Spiritual Marriage ". The book by Fr Axters, above, was published in English in 1954.

3 : ST FRANCIS XAVIER (A.D. 1552)

A CHARGE to go and preach to all nations was given by Christ to His apostles, and in every age men have been raised up by God and filled with His holy Spirit for the discharge of this arduous duty, men who, being sent by the authority of Christ and in His name by those who have succeeded the apostles in the government of His Church, have brought new nations to the fold of Christ for the filling up the number of the saints. Among those who have laboured most successfully in this great work is the illustrious St Francis Xavier, who was named by Pope Pius X the official patron of foreign missions and of all works for the spreading of the faith. He was one of the greatest of all missionaries, and among numerous eulogies that of Sir Walter Scott is striking : " The most rigid Protestant, and the most indifferent philosopher, cannot deny to him the courage and patience of a martyr, with the good sense, resolution, ready wit and address of the best negotiator that ever went upon a temporal embassy." He was born in Spanish Navarre, at the castle of Xavier, near Pamplona, in 1506 (his mother-tongue was Basque), the youngest of a large family, and he went to the University of Paris in his eighteenth year. He entered the college of St Barbara and in 1528 gained the degree of licentiate. Here it was that he met Ignatius Loyola and, though he did not at once submit himself to his influence, he was one of the band of seven, the first Jesuits, who vowed themselves to the service of God at Montmartre in 1534. With them he received the priesthood at Venice three years later and shared the vicissitudes of the nascent society until, in 1540, St Ignatius appcinted him to join Father Simon Rodriguez on the first missionary expedition it sent out, to the East Indies.

They arrived at Lisbon about the end of June, and Francis went immediately to Father Rodriguez, who was lodged in a hospital in order to attend and instruct the sick. They made this place their ordinary dwelling, but catechized and instructed in the town, and were taken up all Sundays and holidays in hearing confessions at court, for the king, John III, had a high regard for these religious ; so much so that eventually Rodriguez was retained by him at Lisbon. St Francis was obliged to stay there eight months : " the king has not yet made up his mind whether he will send us to India, because he thinks we should serve our Lord as well in Portugal as there ", he wrote to St Ignatius at Rome. Before he at last sailed, on his thirty-fifth birthday, April 7, 1541, the king delivered to him briefs from the pope in which Francis Xavier was constituted apostolic nuncio in the East. The king could not prevail on him to accept any gifts except some clothes and a few books. Nor would he consent to have a servant, saying that " the best means to acquire true dignity is to wash one's own clothes and boil one's own pot, unbeholden to anyone ". He had two companions to the Indies, Father Paul of Camerino, an Italian, and Francis Mansilhas, a Portuguese who was not yet in orders, of whom St Francis wrote that he had " a larger store of zeal, virtue and simplicity than of any extraordinary learning ", in his lively farewell letter to St Ignatius.

St Francis was accommodated on the ship which carried Don Martin Alfonso de Sousa, a governor of the Indies who went with five ships to take up his post. The admiral's vessel contained crew, passengers, soldiers, slaves and convicts, whom Francis considered as committed to his care. He catechized, preached every Sunday before the mast, took care of the sick, converted his cabin into an infirmary, and all this though suffering at first seriously from sea-sickness. There were all sorts among the ship's company and passengers ; Xavier had to compose quarrels, quell complaints, check swearing and gaming, and remedy other disorders. Scurvy broke out, and there was no one but the three Jesuits to nurse the sick. It took them five months to get round the Cape of Good Hope and arrive at Mozambique, where they wintered. They continued to hug the east coast of Africa and called at Malindi and Socotra, from whence it took them two months to reach Goa, where they arrived on May 6, 1542, after a voyage of thirteen months (twice the then usual time). St Francis took up his quarters at the hospital to await the arrival of his companions, who were following in another ship.

The Portuguese had been established in Goa since 1510 and there was a considerable Christian population, with churches, clergy, secular and regular, and a bishop. But among very many of these Portuguese, ambition, avarice, usury and debauchery had extinguished their religion : the sacraments were neglected, there were not four preachers and no priests outside the walls of Goa ; when slaves were atrociously beaten, their masters counted the blows on the beads of their rosaries.*

* Fr H. J. Coleridge, s.j., in his biography of Xavier, remarks justly that : " There has probably never yet been a zealous European missionary in any part of the heathen world in which Christians from his own country have been settled, or which they have occasionally visited for purposes of commerce, who has not found among them the worst enemies to his

The scandalous behaviour of the Christians, who lived in direct opposition to the gospel which they professed and by their lives alienated the infidels from the faith, was like a challenge to Francis Xavier and he opened his mission with them, instructing them in the principles of religion and forming the young to the practice of virtue. Having spent the morning in assisting and comforting the distressed in the hospitals and prisons—both alike filthy and foul—he walked through the streets ringing a bell to summon the children and slaves to catechism. They gathered in crowds about him, and he taught them the creed and prayers and Christian conduct. He offered Mass with the lepers every Sunday, preached in public and to the Indians, and visited private houses : the sweetness of his character and his charitable concern for his neighbours were irresistible to many. One of the most troublesome disorders was the open concubinage of Portuguese of all ranks with Indian women, which was aggravated by the fewness of women of their own religion and race in Goa. Tursellini, who wrote the first published Life of St Francis in 1594, gives a vivid account of his combating this by methods which commend themselves alike to Christian morality, common sense, human instincts and tactful dealing. For the instruction of the very ignorant or simple he versified the truths of religion to fit popular tunes, and this was so successful that the practice spread till these songs were being sung everywhere, in the streets and houses and fields and workshops.

After five months of this St Francis was told that on the Pearl Fishery coast, which extends from Cape Comorin to the isle of Manar, opposite Ceylon, there were people called Paravas, who to get the protection of the Portuguese against the Arabs and others had been baptized, but for want of instruction still retained their superstitions and vices. Xavier went to the help of these people, who " just knew that they were Christians and nothing more "—the first of thirteen repetitions of this torrid and dangerous journey. Under every difficulty he set himself to learn the native language and to instruct and confirm those who had been already baptized, especially concentrating on teaching the rudiments of religion to the children. Then he preached to those Paravas to whom the name of Christ was till that time unknown. So great were the multitudes he baptized that sometimes by the bare fatigue of administering the sacrament he was scarcely able to move his arms, according to the account which he gave to his brethren in Europe.* The Paravas were a low-caste people, and St Francis had a different reception and very little success among the Brahmans ; at the end of twelve months he had converted only one. It seems certain that at this time God wrought a number of miracles of healing through him.

St Francis, as always, came before the people as one of themselves. His food was that of the poorest, rice and water ; he slept on the ground in a hut. And God

work. No exception can be made as to this lamentable truth in favour of Catholic nations : Spaniards, Frenchmen, Portuguese have as much to answer for in this respect as Dutchmen and Englishmen." In a note on this subject, quoting an illustrative complaint by a Protestant writer about converts to his religion in North America, Alban Butler says with his usual courteous charity : " It is hoped that there is more exaggeration than truth in [this complaint] ", and adds of the quotation, " This remark is meant not as a reproach to any, but as a caution to all."

* From a very long letter of January 15, 1544, of great importance in waking Europeans up to foreign missions and their needs. It was indeed outspoken, written from the depths of Xavier's great heart.

visited him with interior delights : " I am accustomed ", he says, " often to hear one labouring in this vineyard cry out to God, ' Lord, give me not so much joy in this life ; or, if in thy mercy thou must heap it upon me, take me all together to thyself '." Soon he was obliged to return to Goa to get help, and returned to the Paravas with two Indian priests and a lay-catechist, and Francis Mansilhas, whom he stationed in different centres. To Mansilhas he wrote a series of letters that are some of the most revealing of all he ever wrote for the understanding of his spirit amid the difficulties with which he had to contend. The sufferings of native people at the hands both of heathen and Portuguese became " a permanent bruise on my soul ". When an Indian servant was abducted he wrote, " Would the Portuguese be pleased if one of the Hindus were to take a Portuguese by force and carry him up country ? The Indians must have the same feelings." St Francis was able to extend his activities to Travancore ; here his achievements have been rather exaggerated by some writers, but village after village received him with joy, and after baptizing the inhabitants he wrote to Father Mansilhas telling him to come and organize the convers.* As elsewhere, he enlisted the help in this of the children (who doubtless thought it great fun), and used them as auxiliaries to the catechists to teach to others what they had just learned themselves. His difficulties were increased by the misfortunes of the Christians of Comorin and Tuticorin, who were set upon by the Badagas from the north, who robbed, massacred and carried them into slavery. Xavier is said on one occasion to have held off the raiders by facing them alone, crucifix in hand. He was again handicapped by the Portuguese, their local commandant having his own secret dealings with the Badagas. But when this man had himself to take refuge from them, St Francis wrote in haste to Mansilhas, " Go at once to his help, I beseech you, for the love of God ". But for the tireless efforts of St Francis it looks as if the Paravas would have been exterminated. They for their part received the Catholic faith so firmly that no oppression or persuasion has ever been able to remove it.

The ruler of Jaffna, in northern Ceylon, hearing of the progress of the faith in his island of Manar, slew six hundred Christians there.† The governor, Martin de Sousa, ordered an expedition to punish this massacre and it was to fit out at Negapatam, whither St Francis went to join it ; but the officers were diverted from their purpose and so Francis instead made a journey on foot to the shrine of St Thomas at Mylapore, where there was a small Portuguese settlement to be visited. Many incidents are related of him during these travels, especially of his conversion of notorious sinners among the Europeans by the gentle and courteous way in which he dealt with them ; other miracles too were ascribed to him. From Cochin in 1545 he sent a long and very outspoken letter to the King of Portugal giving an account of his mission. He speaks of the danger of those who had already been gathered into the Church falling back into their former state, " scandalized and scared away by the many grievous injuries and vexations which they suffer—especially from your Highness's own servants. . . . For there is danger that when our Lord God calls your Highness to His judgement that your Highness may hear angry words from Him : ' Why did you not punish those who were your subjects and owned your authority, and who were enemies to me in India ? ' "

* There had, of course, been some Christians on the Malabar coast of India for perhaps a thousand years. *Cf.* December 21, St Thomas.

† It is said that some of the converts had destroyed the shrines of idols and so incurred the wrath of the raja.

He speaks in the highest terms of Don Miguel Vaz, vicar general of Goa, and implores the king to send him back to India with plenary powers when he shall have made his report in Lisbon. " As I expect to die in these Indian regions and never to see your Highness again in this life, I beg you, my lord, to help me with your prayers, that we may meet again in the next world, where we shall certainly have more rest than here." He repeats his praise of Miguel in a letter to Father Simon Rodriguez, and is more explicit about the Europeans : " People scarcely hesitate to think that it cannot be wrong to do that which can be done easily. . . . I am terrified at the number of new inflexions which have been added to the conjugation of that miserable verb ' to rob '."

In the spring of 1545 St Francis set out for Malacca, on the Malay peninsula, where he spent four months. It was then a large and prosperous city, which Albuquerque had captured for the Portuguese in 1511, and its life was peculiarly licentious. Anticipating the manners of a later age adult girls went about the place in men's clothes, without the excuse of being engaged on men's work. Francis was received with great reverence and cordiality, and his efforts at reform met with some success. For the next eighteen months his movements are difficult to follow, but they were a time of great activity and interest, for he was in a largely unknown world, visiting islands, which he refers to in general as the Moluccas, not all of which are now identifiable. He preached and ministered at Amboina, Ternate, Gilolo, and other places, in some of which there were Portuguese merchants and settlements. In this mission he suffered much, but from it wrote to St Ignatius : " The dangers to which I am exposed and the tasks I undertake for God are springs of spiritual joy, so much so that these islands are the places in all the world for a man to lose his sight by excess of weeping : but they are tears of joy. I do not remember ever to have tasted such interior delight and these consolations take from me all sense of bodily hardships and of troubles from open enemies and not too trustworthy friends." When he got back to Malacca he passed another four months there, ministering to a very unsatisfactory flock, and then departed for India again. But before he left he heard about Japan for the first time, from Portuguese merchants and from a fugitive Japanese named Anjiro. Xavier arrived back in India in January 1548.

The next fifteen months were spent in endless travelling between Goa, Ceylon and Cape Comorin, consolidating his work (notably the " international college " of St Paul at Goa) and preparing for an attempt on that Japan into which no European had yet penetrated. He wrote a final letter to King John III, on behalf of an Armenian bishop and a Franciscan friar ; but also saying, " Experience has taught me that your Highness has no power in India to spread the faith of Christ, while you have power to take away and enjoy all the country's temporal riches ", and more to the like effect. In April 1549, St Francis set out, accompanied by a Jesuit priest and a lay-brother, by Anjiro—now Paul—and by two other Japanese converts. On the feast of the Assumption following they landed in Japan, at Kagoshima on Kyushu.

At Kagoshima they were not molested, and St Francis set himself to learn Japanese (so far from having the gift of tongues with which he is so often credited, he seems to have had difficulty in learning new languages). A translation was made of a simple account of Christian teaching, and recited to all who would listen. The fruit of twelve months' labour was a hundred converts, and then the authorities began to get suspicious and forbade further preaching. So, leaving Paul in charge of the neophytes, Francis decided to push on further with his other companions and went by sea to Hirado, north of Nagasaki. Before leaving Kagoshima he visited the fortress of Ichiku, where the " baron's " wife, her steward and others accepted Christianity. To the steward's care Xavier recommended the rest at departure ; and twelve years later the Jesuit lay-brother and physician, Luis de Almeida, found these isolated converts still retaining their first fervour and faithfulness. At Hirado the missionaries were well received by the ruler (*daimyō*), and they had more success in a few weeks than they had had at Kagoshima in a year. These converts St Francis left to Father de Torres and went on with Brother Fernandez and a Japanese to Yamaguchi in Honshu. Francis preached here, in public and before the *daimyō*, but the missionaries made no impression and were treated with scorn.

Xavier's objective was Miyako (Kyoto), then the chief city of Japan, and having made a month's stay at Yamaguchi and gathered small fruit of his labours except affronts, he continued his journey with his two companions. It was towards the end of December, and they suffered much on the road from heavy rains, snow and the difficult country, and did not reach their destination till February. Here Francis found that he could not procure an audience of the mikado (who in any case was but a puppet) without paying a sum of money far beyond his resources ; moreover, civil strife filled the city with such tumult that he saw it to be impossible to do any good there at that time and, after a fortnight's stay, they returned to Yamaguchi. Seeing that evangelical poverty had not the appeal in Japan that it had in India, St Francis changed his methods. Decently dressed and with his companions as attendants he presented himself before the *daimyō* as the representative of Portugal, giving him the letters and presents (a musical-box, a clock and a pair of spectacles among them) which the authorities in India had provided for the mikado. The *daimyō* received the gifts with delight, gave Francis leave to teach, and provided an empty Buddhist monastery for a residence. When thus he obtained protection, Francis preached with such fruit that he baptized many in that city.

Hearing that a Portuguese ship had arrived at Funai (Oita) in Kyushu St Francis set out thither. Among those on board was the traveller Fernão Mendez Pinto, who left a full and amusing account of the ceremony and display with which the Portuguese surrounded the visit of their admired Xavier to the local *daimyō;* unfortunately Mendez Pinto was a highly fanciful writer, and no reliance can be put on what he tells us of Xavier's activities and adventures at Funai. Francis had decided to make use of this Portuguese ship to revisit his charge in India, from whence he now hoped to extend his mission to China. The Japanese Christians were left in charge of Father Cosmas de Torres and Brother Fernandez : they numbered perhaps 2000 in all, the seed of many martyrs in time to come. In spite of some unhappy experiences in their country, it was the opinion of St Francis Xavier that " among all unbelievers, no finer people will be found than the Japanese ".

Francis found that good progress had been made in India, but there were also many difficulties and abuses, both among the missionaries and the Portuguese authorities, that urgently needed his attention. These matters he dealt with, lovingly and very firmly and thoroughly. At the end of four months, on April 25, 1552, with a Jesuit priest and a scholastic, an Indian servant and a young Chinese to interpret (but he had forgotten his own language), he sailed eastward again ; he was awaited at Malacca by Diogo Pereira, whom the viceroy in India had appointed ambassador to the court of China.

At Malacca St Francis had to treat about this embassy with Don Alvaro da Ataíde da Gama (a son of Vasco da Gama), the maritime authority there. This Alvaro had a personal grudge against Diogo Pereira, whom he flatly refused to let sail either as envoy or as private trader. Nothing could move him, even when St Francis informed him of the brief of Pope Paul III by which he was appointed apostolic nuncio. By impeding a papal legate Alvaro incurred excommunication, but Francis had unfortunately left the original document behind at Goa. At length Don Alvaro conceded that Xavier should go to China in Pereira's ship, but without its owner ; and to this Pereira most nobly agreed. When the project of the embassy thus failed Francis sent his priest companion to Japan, and eventually was left with only the Chinese youth, Antony. With him he hoped to find means to land secretly in China, the country closed to foreigners. In the last week of August 1552 the convoy reached the desolate island of Sancian (Shang-chwan), half-a-dozen miles off the coast and a hundred miles south-west of Hong Kong.

From here by one of the ships St Francis sent off letters, including one to Pereira, to whom he says : " If there is one man in the whole of this undertaking who deserves reward from divine Providence it is undoubtedly you ; and you will have the whole credit of it." Then he goes on to tell the arrangements he has made : he had with great difficulty hired a Chinese merchant to land him by night in some part of Canton, for which Xavier had engaged to pay him, and bound himself by oath that nothing should ever bring him to confess the name of him who had set him on shore. Whilst waiting for his plans to mature, Xavier fell sick and, when the Portuguese vessels were all gone except one, was reduced to extreme want : in his last letter he wrote, " It is a long time since I felt so little inclined to go on living as I do now ". The Chinese merchant did not turn up. A fever seized the saint on November 21, and he took shelter on the ship ; but the motion of the sea was too much for him, so the day following he requested that he might be set on shore again, which was done. The vessel was manned chiefly by Don Alvaro's men who, fearing to offend their master by common kindness to Xavier, left him exposed on the sands to a piercing north wind, till a friendly Portuguese merchant led him into his hut, which afforded only a very poor shelter. He lay thus in a high fever, being bled with distressing results, praying ceaselessly between spasms of delirium. He got weaker and weaker till at last, in the early morning of December 3, which fell on a Saturday, " I [Antony] could see that he was dying and put a lighted candle in his hand. Then, with the name of Jesus on his lips, he rendered his soul to his Creator and Lord with great repose and quietude ". St Francis was only forty-six years old, of which he had passed eleven in the East. His body was laid in the earth on the Sunday evening : four people were present, the Chinese Antony, a Portuguese and two slaves.*

At the suggestion of somebody from the ship the coffin had been packed with lime around the body in case it should later be desired to move the remains. Ten weeks and more later the grave and the coffin were opened. The lime being removed from the face, it was found quite incorrupt and fresh-coloured, the rest of the body in like manner whole and smelling only of lime. The body was accordingly carried into the ship and brought to Malacca, where it was received

---

* Details of the saint's last days were given by the faithful Antony in a letter to Manuel Teixeira, who printed it in his biography of Xavier.

with great honour by all, except Don Alvaro.   At the end of the year it was taken away to Goa, where its continued incorruption was verified by physicians ; there it still lies enshrined in the church of the Good Jesus.   St Francis Xavier was canonized in 1622, at the same time as Ignatius Loyola, Teresa of Avila, Philip Neri and Isidore the Husbandman—indeed a noble company.

It was long believed that the letters and other biographical materials, collected in two bulky volumes under the title *Monumenta Xaveriana* (1899–1912), left nothing more to be discovered about St Francis Xavier.   Certainly these documents, critically edited at Madrid in the *Monumenta historica Societatis Jesu*, are of supreme importance.   They supply a much more reliable text than any previously available of the letters written by the saint, as well as a faithful transcript of the depositions of the witnesses in the process of beatification, with other early materials of value.   But Father George Schurhammer, working in the archives at Lisbon, and making use at Tokyo of native Japanese sources previously unexplored, has been able to collect a good deal more information, which supplements and sometimes corrects the data hitherto accepted as reliable.   His definitive edition, with Fr J. Wicki, of the invaluable letters appeared in two volumes in 1943–44.   Fr Schurhammer issued a short life of the saint, *Der heilige Franz Xaver* (1925), of which a free translation was published in America, and he supplemented this with a number of important articles and monographs, dealing with various special aspects of the great missionary's career.   Most of these contributions will be found noticed in the *Analecta Bollandiana ;* see especially vol. xl (1922), pp. 171–178, vol. xliv (1926), pp. 445–446, vol. xlvi (1928), pp. 455–456, vol. xlviii (1930), pp. 441–445, vol. l (1932), pp. 453–454, vol. liv (1936), pp. 247–249, and vol. lxix (1951), pp. 438-441.   Under the first of these references will be found a valuable article of Fr Schurhammer himself dealing with the relics of St Francis Xavier, and in the fourth a notice of his brochure *Das kirchliche Sprachproblem in der japanischen Jesuitenmission* (1928).   In this it is shown that the belief that St Francis was able to converse and hold disputations in the Japanese tongue is quite unfounded.   The legend grew up out of the imagination and ignorance of two unreliable witnesses in the beatification process.   Unfortunately, as Fr Astrain in his official *Historia de la Compañia de Jesús* was among the first to point out, many of the miraculous incidents recorded in early biographies of the saint must now be rejected as mythical.   For this reason no great reliance can be placed on the life by O. Tursellini, or on that by Bouhours, which last was translated into English by the poet John Dryden.   In modern times much critical material concerning the family of Xavier, etc., was collected by Fr L. J. M. Cros before the publication of the *Monumenta Xaveriana.* This appeared as *Documents nouveaux* (1894) and also in his *S. François Xavier, sa vie et ses lettres*, 2 vols. (1900) ; but the most trustworthy French life is that by Father A. Brou, 2 vols. (1912).   In English, Fr H. J. Coleridge published a very sympathetic biography in 2 vols. (1886), though unfortunately he had not access to a critical text of the saint's letters.   For this reason the more compendious life by Mrs Yeo (1933) is preferable from the point of view of accuracy.   In the opinion of Fr James Brodrick, Edith A. Stewart's *Life of St Francis Xavier* (1917), " except for occasional small ebullitions of Protestant sentiment, is more scholarly and satisfying than any English Catholic biography of the saint " ; that may have been so in 1940 when he wrote, but the definitive life in English is now Fr Brodrick's own splendid work, *St Francis Xavier* (1952).   The work of St Francis in Japan and India is discussed by Fr Thurston in *The Month* for February and March 1905 and December 1912.   For the key-note and spirit of Xavier's apostolate see the sketch by Fr C. C. Martindale, *In God's Army*, vol. i (1915) ; and on his reputed miracles the *Analecta Bollandiana*, vol. xvi (1897), pp. 52–63.

ST LUCIUS   (No Date)

IN the earliest part of the *Liber Pontificalis*, compiled about the year 530, it is stated under the name of Pope St Eleutherius (*c.* 174–*c.* 189) that : " He received a letter from Lucius, a British king, to the effect that he might be made a Christian by his order ", *i.e.* asking that the pope would send missionaries.   This statement was copied by St Bede the Venerable into his *Chronicon* in almost the same words.   In his *Ecclesiastical History* he writes : " In the year of our Lord's incarnation 156, Marcus Antoninus Verus [*i.e.* Marcus Aurelius], the fourteenth from Augustus, was made emperor, together with his brother, Aurelius Commodus [*i.e.* Lucius Verus]. In their time, while the holy man Eleuther presided over the Roman church, Lucius, King of Britain, sent a letter to him asking that by his mandate he might be made a Christian. He soon obtained his religious request, and the Britons kept the faith as they had received it, pure and in its fullness, in peace and quietness until the time of the Emperor Diocletian." Bede makes a third reference to the conversion of Lucius in the recapitulation at the end of the *Ecclesiastical History*, the three references being inconsistent only in the chronology, which he tries to adjust.

The original simple statement underwent amplification and embroidery in the course of time. Nennius retells the story with improvements in the ninth century, celticizing Lucius into Lleufer Mawr (" Great Splendour ") and calling the pope " Eucharistus " ; the *Liber Landavensis* gives the names of Lucius's envoys to Rome as Elvinus and Meduinus, an editor of William of Malmesbury adding those of the missionaries sent, Faganus and Deruvianus. Geoffrey of Monmouth adds more : the whole country having been converted to the faith, Lucius divided it into provinces and bishoprics ; he says he died and was buried at Gloucester. John Stow, in his survey of sixteenth-century London, writes of St Peter's on Cornhill : " There remaineth in this church a table whereon it is written, I know not by what authority, but of a late hand, that King Lucius founded the same church to be an archbishop's see metropolitan and chief church of his kingdom, and that it so endured the space of four hundred years unto the coming of Augustine the monk." In another place he quotes from Jocelin of Furness the names of the apocryphal archbishops, fourteen in number, up to 587. " Thus much out of Jocelin of the archbishops, the credit whereof I leave to the judgement of the learned ", he observes.

The Welsh version of the Lucius legend is that Lleufer Mawr (Lleirwg, etc.) sent Elfan and Medwy (Elvinus and Meduinus) to Pope St Eleutherius, who baptized them, made Elfan a bishop, and sent them back with two missionaries, Dyfan and Ffagan (Deruvianus and Faganus). Lleufer Mawr thereupon founded the church of Llandaff, " which was the first in the isle of Britain ", and gave legal privileges to all who should become Christians. He put a bishop at Llandaff and also there founded schools.* The legend of the church of Chur in the Grisons claims that Lucius of Britain was an apostle of the Rhaetian Alps, and a bishop and martyr to boot. A further Swiss extravagance about him is that he was baptized by St Timothy, the disciple of St Paul, who is represented as coming into Britain from Gaul. The Roman Martyrology records his death at Chur on this day and says he was the first king of the Britons to accept the Christian faith, in the time of the holy Pope Eleutherius, but calls him neither bishop nor martyr.

The only point of importance about St Lucius is the fundamental one, whether the statement of the *Liber Pontificalis* copied by St Bede is a record of historical fact or not. For long it was unquestioned ; by the time Alban Butler wrote there were already some objections raised, but in his opinion they did not deserve notice.

* Lleirwg, Dyfan, Ffagan and Medwy are all found in church dedications and place-names around Llandaff. To travellers on the W.R. South Wales line Saint Fagans is a familiar station just beyond Cardiff. They presumably were church-founders who flourished some time during the first six centuries, but nothing whatever is known about them.

It is not antecedently impossible that a local British chief (Lucius was certainly not a king) of the late second century should want to be a Christian and should send all the way to Rome for the purpose ; but it is extremely improbable, and considerably better evidence than a single unsupported statement of three hundred and fifty years later is required to substantiate it. Moreover, we have not the slightest indication that the mission of Pope Eleutherius to Lucius was known to Gildas, Gregory the Great, Augustine of Canterbury, Colman of Lindisfarne, Aldhelm or others, to all of whom in one way or another such a fact of history would have had a practical use and importance. " The judgement of the learned ", to which Stow deferred, as represented by such scholars as Mgr Duchesne, Dr Plummer, Mgr Kirsch and Dom Leclercq, strongly supports the view that the story is a fable ; if it be such, the very existence of our St Lucius remains to be proved.

The genesis of the legend is another matter. It has been asserted that it was deliberately invented to demonstrate the Roman origin of British Christianity and the submission of the Britons to the discipline of the Holy See, in view of the controversies between the old British church and the new English church. But in Rome the story first appears before these dissensions began, and in England we first hear of it, in the pages of Bede, after they were for all practical purposes finished ; there is no evidence that the Lucius legend was used in controversy by a pro-Roman side until after the Reformation. Its continued use by controversialists on either side is to be deplored. A solution of the problem, by no means certain but plausible and interesting, has been advanced by Harnack. He points out that King Abgar IX of Edessa was named *Lucius* Aelius Septimius Megas Abgarus, and that he is known to have become a Christian about the time St Eleutherius was pope. Moreover, Birtha (*i.e.* the fortress) of Edessa is found latinized in ancient documents as *Britium* Edessenorum. In transcribing a record of the conversion of Lucius Abgar, " Hic accepit epistulam a Lucio, in *Britio* rege . . ." might easily be misread as, or wrongly emended to, " a Lucio, *Brittanio* rege ".

The story of Lucius and Pope Eleutherius has been discussed in some detail by Duchesne, *Liber Pontificalis*, pp. ccxxii *seq.* ; by Haddan and Stubbs, *Councils*, vol. i, pp. 25–26 ; by C. Plummer in Bede's *Ecclesiastical History*, vol. ii, p. 14 ; J. P. Kirsch in *Catholic Encyclopedia*, vol. v, p. 379 ; A. Harnack in the *Sitzungsberichte* of the Berlin Academy for 1904, pp. 906–916, and *cf. Eng. Hist. Rev.*, vol. xxii, pp. 767–770 ; and by H. Leclercq in DAC., vol. ix, cc. 2661–2663. No one of these shows any disposition to regard the episode as historically trustworthy. On the supposed Deruvianus and Faganus see J. Armitage Robinson, *Two Glastonbury Legends* (1926). *Cf.* also V. Berther in *Zeitschrift für Schweizerische Kirchengeschichte*, vol. xxxii (1938), pp. 20–38, 103–124.

SS. CLAUDIUS, HILARIA AND THEIR COMPANIONS, MARTYRS
(DATE UNKNOWN)

" AT Rome ", says the Roman Martyrology, " the passion of the holy martyrs, Claudius the tribune, Hilaria his wife, their sons Jason and Maurus, and seventy soldiers. Of these, the Emperor Numerian ordered Claudius to be tied to a huge stone and flung headlong into the river, and his sons with the soldiers to be punished by the capital sentence. The blessed Hilaria, however, a little while after burying the bodies of her sons, was taken by the heathen while praying at their tomb, cast into prison, and passed to the Lord." This Claudius was the tribune of that name who, according to the legend of SS. Chrysanthus and Daria, was converted by the sight of their constancy under torture, as has been related herein under October 25. Other figures in the same legend, namely, SS. Diodorus the priest, Marian the deacon and their companions, who were slain while commemorating the martyrs Chrysanthus and Daria, are named in the martyrology on December 1.

Nothing whatever is known of these martyrs beyond the casual and quite untrustworthy reference in the *passio* of Chrysanthus and Daria. There was indeed an Hilaria whose resting-place on the Via Salaria is mentioned by pilgrims of the seventh century, but she seems to belong more properly to December 31, and she is not there associated with any Claudius. See Delehaye, *Étude sur le légendier romain*, pp. 53–54, and also his CMH., p. 17.

ST CASSIAN, Martyr (A.D. 298 ?)

WE are told that when St Marcellus the Centurion (October 30) was tried before Aurelius Agricolan at Tangier, the proceedings were being taken down by a shorthand-writer named Cassian. But when he heard Agricolan reply to the devotion of Marcellus by a sentence of death, he vowed with an imprecation he would go no further, and threw his *stilus* and tablets to the ground. Amid the astonishment of the staff and the laughter of Marcellus, Aurelius Agricolan trembling leapt from the bench and demanded why he had thrown down his tablets with an oath. St Cassian answered that Agricolan had given an unjust sentence. To avoid further contradiction, Agricolan ordered him to be at once removed and cast into prison.

" Now the blessed martyr Marcellus had laughed because, having knowledge of the future through the Holy Spirit, he rejoiced that Cassian would be his companion in martyrdom. On that very day amid the eager expectation of the city blessed Marcellus obtained his desire. After no long interval, namely, on December 3, the worshipful Cassian was brought to the same place in which Marcellus had been tried and, by almost the same replies and statements as holy Marcellus had made, merited to obtain the victory of martyrdom, through the help of our Lord Jesus Christ, to whom belong honour and glory, excellency and power for ever and ever. Amen."

On the writer's explanation of the laughter of St Marcellus it may be permitted to comment that the fate of the bold Cassian could be anticipated by the natural powers, without any *charisma* of prophecy ; it is more likely that the prisoner laughed at the spectacle, amusing enough, of the deputy-prefect leaping from his bench in rage at being openly defied by his own clerk in his own court.

Although the story of the martyrdom of SS. Marcellus and Cassian is included by Ruinart among his *Acta sincera*, Father Delehaye, in *Analecta Bollandiana*, vol. xli (1923), pp. 257–287, gives no countenance to the idea that what we now read is a shorthand report of what happened. The substance of the account, however, may be accepted. But as regards Cassian, while the fact that a martyr of that name was honoured at Tangier in Mauretania is confirmed by Prudentius, who in his *Peristephanon* (iv, 45) writes, " Ingeret Tingis sua Cassianum ", nevertheless Delehaye gives (*loc. cit.* pp. 276–278) strong reasons for thinking that ignorance about him was made up for by associating him with Marcellus, whose *acta* were known. See further Monceaux, *Hist. litt. de l'Afrique chrétienne*, vol iii, pp. 119–121 ; Leclercq in DAC., vol. xi, c. 1140 ; and the note under St Marcellus on October 30 herein, to which a further reference to *Analecta Bollandiana* must be added, vol. lxiv (1946), pp. 281–282.

ST SOLA   (A.D. 794)

THIS saint was an Englishman who, following St Boniface into Germany, became his disciple and was ordained priest by him.   Called by the Holy Ghost to a solitary life, by the advice of his master he retired to a lonely place first at Fulda and then on the banks of the River Altmuhl, near Eichstätt, where in a little cell he passed his days in penance and prayer.   After the martyrdom of St Boniface, the holy brothers Willibald the bishop and Winebald the priest encouraged him to make his cell the religious centre of the surrounding country.   For this purpose there was bestowed on him a piece of land, and here later grew up the abbey of Solnhofen, which was a dependency of Fulda.   St Sola departed to the Lord on December 3, 794, and a chapel was built where his oratory had stood.   The name Sola (Sualo) is still preserved in that of the village of Solnhofen, west of Eichstätt.

There is a Latin life of St Sola which was written in 835, forty years after his death, by Ermanrich, a monk of Ellwangen, who obtained his information from a servant of the saint and other surviving contemporaries.   The Latin of this biography was revised in the following year by a certain Master Roland.   The best text is that printed in MGH., *Scriptores*, vol. xv, pt 1, pp. 151–163, but it is also to be found in Mabillon, vol. iii, pt 2, pp. 429–438.   The saint's curious name has led to his cult being popularly identified with certain carvings and inscriptions which are really monuments of an ancient sun-worship. See E. Jung, *German. Götter* (1922), pp. 218–231 ; and *Kunstdenkmäler d. Bez. Weissenburg* (1932), pp. 426–437.

4 : ST PETER CHRYSOLOGUS, ARCHBISHOP OF RAVENNA, DOCTOR OF THE CHURCH   (c. A.D. 450)

ST PETER was a native of Imola, a town in eastern Emilia.   He was taught the sacred sciences and ordained deacon by Cornelius, bishop of that city, of whom he speaks with veneration and gratitude.   Under his prudent direction Peter was formed to virtue from his youth and understood that to command his passions and govern himself was true greatness and the only means of learning to put on the spirit of Christ.   The raising of this holy man to the episcopate was, according to his legend, in the following circumstances.   Archbishop John of Ravenna dying about the year 433, the clergy of that church, with the people, chose a successor, and entreated Bishop Cornelius of Imola to go at the head of their deputies to Rome to obtain the confirmation of Pope St Sixtus III. Cornelius took with him his deacon, Peter, but the pope (who, it is said, had been commanded so to do by a vision the foregoing night of St Peter and St Apollinaris, the martyred first bishop of Ravenna) refused to ratify the election already made, and proposed Peter, as the person designed by Heaven in his vision, for that post ; after some opposition the deputies acquiesced.   The new bishop, after receiving episcopal consecration, was conducted to Ravenna and there received with some unwillingness.   It is very unlikely that St Peter became archbishop of Ravenna in any such fashion.   The Emperor Valentinian III and his mother, Galla Placidia, then resided in that city, and St Peter enjoyed their regard and confidence, as well as the trust of the successor of Sixtus, St Leo the Great.   When he entered on his charge he found large remains of paganism in his diocese, and abuses had crept in among the faithful ; the total extirpation of the one and the reformation of the other were the fruit of his labours.   At the town of Classis, then the port of

Ravenna, St Peter built a baptistery, and a church dedicated in honour of St Andrew. He employed an extensive charity and unwearied vigilance on behalf of his flock, which he fed assiduously with the bread of life, the word of God. We have many of his discourses still extant : they are all very short, for he was afraid of fatiguing the attention of his hearers.

A life of St Peter was written in the ninth century, but it tells little about him, and Alban Butler made up for lack of information by quoting from the saint's sermons. These are, he says, "rather instructive than pathetic ; and though the doctrine is explained in them at large we meet with little that quickens or affects much. Neither can these discourses be regarded as models of true eloquence, though his reputation as a preacher ran so high as to procure him the surname of Chrysologus, which is as much as to say, that his speeches were of gold, or excellent." Nevertheless, if the manner is not all that it might be (though elsewhere Butler says his words are "fit, simple and natural"), the matter of the discourses of St Peter Chrysologus caused him to be declared a doctor of the Church by Pope Benedict XIII in 1729 : a fact which Butler does not mention. St Peter is said to have preached with such vehemence that he sometimes became speechless from excitement. In his sermons he strongly recommends frequent communion, that the Eucharist, the body of Christ, may be the daily bread of our souls. Eutyches, the heresiarch, having been condemned by St Flavian in 448, addressed a circular letter to the most distinguished prelates in the Church in his own justification. St Peter, in the answer which he sent, told him that he had read his letter with sorrow, for if the peace of the Church causes joy in Heaven, divisions beget grief; that the mystery of the Incarnation, though inexplicable, is delivered to us by divine revelation and is to be believed in the simplicity of faith. He therefore exhorted him to acquiesce and not dispute. In the same year St Peter received St Germanus of Auxerre with great honour at Ravenna, and after his death there on July 31 officiated at his funeral and kept his hood and sackcloth shirt as relics. St Peter Chrysologus did not long survive him. Being forewarned of approaching death, he returned to Imola, his own country, and there gave to the church of St Cassian some precious altar vessels. After counselling great care in the choice of his successor, he died at Imola on December 2, probably in 450, and was buried in St Cassian's church.

The unsatisfactory Latin life, which is the only source of information we possess regarding the personal activities of this doctor of the Church, was written as late as the year 836 by Abbot Agnellus : it forms a section of his history of the archbishops of Ravenna. The text has been twice over printed by Migne, PL., vol. lii, cc. 13–20 and vol. cvi, cc. 553–559, but by far the most satisfactory edition is that of Testi Rasponi, *Codex pontificalis ecclesiae Ravennatis*, vol. i (1924). A short biographical sketch of value is that of D. L. Baldisserri, *San Pier Crisologo* (1920) ; and there are German monographs by H. Dapper (1867) and G. Böhmer (1919). The question of the sermons attributed to Chrysologus has been much discussed. See in particular Mgr Lanzoni, *I sermoni di S. Pier Crisologo* (1909) ; F. J. Peters, *Petrus Chrysologus als Homilet* (1918) ; Baxter in *Journal of Theol. Studies*, vol. xxii (1921), pp. 250–258 ; and D. De Bruyne in the same, vol. xxix (1928), pp. 362–368 ; as also C. Jenkins in *Church Quarterly Review*, vol. ciii (1927), pp. 233–259. In the *Revue Bénédictine*, vol. xxiii (1906), pp. 489–500, Abbot Cabrol gives reasons for attributing the *Rotulus* of Ravenna to St Peter Chrysologus, but this is doubtful. The sermons which have been edited under the name of Chrysologus may most conveniently be consulted in Migne, PL., vol. lii, but in the volume *Spicilegium Liberianum* published by F. Liverani in 1863, pp. 125–203, will be found some further sermons and collations of new manuscripts. Consult also Bardenhewer, *Geschichte der altkirchlichen Literatur*, vol. iv, pp. 604–610.

ST BARBARA, Virgin and Martyr   (Date Unknown)

" In the time that Maximian reigned there was a rich man, a paynim, which adored and worshipped idols, which man was named Dioscorus. This Dioscorus had a young daughter which was named Barbara, for whom he did make a high and strong tower in which he did keep and close this Barbara to the end that no man should see her because of her great beauty. Then came many princes unto the same Dioscorus for to treat with him for the marriage of his daughter, which went anon unto her and said : ' My daughter, certain princes be come to me which require me for to have thee in marriage, wherefore tell to me thine intent and what will ye have to do.' Then St Barbara returned all angry towards her father and said : ' My father, I pray you that ye will not constrain me to marry, for thereto I have no will nor thought.' . . . After this he departed thence and went into a far country where he long sojourned.

" Then St Barbara, the handmaid of our Lord Jesu Christ, descended from the tower for to come to see [a bath-house which her father was having built] and anon she perceived that there were but two windows only, that one against the south, and that other against the north, whereof she was much abashed and amarvelled, and demanded of the workmen why they had not made no more windows, and they answered that her father had so commanded and ordained. Then St Barbara said to them : ' Make me here another window.' . . . In this same bath-house was this holy maid baptized of a holy man, and lived there a certain space of time, taking only for her refection honeysuckles and locusts, following the holy precursor of our Lord, St John Baptist. This bath-house is like to the fountain of Siloe, in which he that was born blind recovered there his sight. . . . On a time this blessed maid went upon the tower and there she beheld the idols to which her father sacrificed and worshipped, and suddenly she received the Holy Ghost and became marvellously subtle and clear in the love of Jesu Christ, for she was environed with the grace of God Almighty, of sovereign glory and pure chastity. This holy maid Barbara, adorned with faith, surmounted the Devil, for when she beheld the idols she scratched them in their visages, despising them all and saying : ' All they be made like unto you which have made you to err, and all them that have faith in you ' ; and then she went into the tower and worshipped our Lord.

" And when the work was full performed her father returned from his voyage, and when he saw there three windows he demanded of the workmen : ' Wherefore have ye made three windows ? ' And they answered : ' Your daughter hath commanded so.' Then he made his daughter to come afore him and demanded her why she had do make three windows, and she answered to him and said : ' I have done them to be made because three windows lighten all the world and all creatures, but two make darkness.' Then her father took her and went down into the bath-house, demanding her how three windows give more light than two. And St Barbara answered : ' These three windows betoken clearly the Father, the Son and the Holy Ghost, the which be three persons and one very God, on whom we ought to believe and worship.' Then he, being replenished with fury, incontinent drew his sword to have slain her, but the holy virgin made her prayer and then marvellously she was taken in a stone and borne into a mountain on which two shepherds kept their sheep, the which saw her fly. . . . And then her father took her by the hair and drew her down from the mountain and shut her fast in prison. . . . Then sat the judge in judgement, and when he saw the great beauty of Barbara he said to her : ' Now choose whether ye will spare yourself and offer to the gods, or else die by cruel torments.' St Barbara answered to him : ' I offer myself to my God, Jesu Christ, the which hath created Heaven and earth and all other things. . . .' "

When she had been beaten, and comforted by a vision of our Lord in her prison, and again scourged and tortured, " the judge commanded to slay her with the sword. And then her father, all enraged, took her out of the hands of the judge and led her up on a mountain, and St Barbara rejoiced in hastening to receive the salary of her victory. And then when she was drawn thither she made her orison, saying : ' Lord Jesu Christ, which hast formed Heaven and earth, I beseech thee to grant me thy grace and hear my prayer for all they that have memory of thy name and my passion ; I pray thee, that thou wilt not remember their sins, for thou knowest our fragility.' Then came there a voice down from Heaven saying unto her : ' Come, my spouse Barbara, and rest in the chamber of God my Father which is in Heaven, and I grant to thee that thou hast required of me.' And when this was said, she came to her father and received the end of her martyrdom, with St Juliana. But when her father descended from the mountain, a fire from Heaven descended on him, and consumed him in such wise that there could not be found only ashes of all his body. This blessed virgin, St Barbara, received martyrdom with St Juliana the second nones of December. A noble man called Valentine buried the bodies of these two martyrs, and laid them in a little town in which many miracles were showed in praise and glory of God Almighty."

So is told in Caxton's version of the *Golden Legend* the story of one of the most popular saints of the middle ages. There is, however, considerable doubt of the existence of a virgin martyr called Barbara and it is quite certain that her legend is spurious. There is no mention of her in the earlier martyrologies, her legend is not older than the seventh century, and her *cultus* did not spread till the ninth. Various versions differ both as to the time and place of her martyrdom : it is located in Tuscany, Rome, Antioch, Heliopolis and Nicomedia. St Barbara is one of the Fourteen Holy Helpers and that she is invoked against lightning and fire and, by association, as patroness of gunners,* military architects, and miners is attributed to the nature of the fate that overtook her father. The tower represented in her pictures and her directions to the builders of the bath-house have caused her to be regarded as a patroness of architects, builders and stonemasons ; and her prayer before her execution accounts for the belief that she is an especial protectress of those in danger of dying without the sacraments.

There seems to be general agreement that the story of St Barbara was first written in Greek, but there is no evidence of any early local *cultus* which would rescue it from being classed in the category of pure romance. We have numerous versions in Latin, Syriac and other languages. See, for the Syriac, Mrs Agnes Smith-Lewis, *Studia Sinaitica*, vols. ix and x (1900), where an English translation is available. *Cf.* also W. Weyh, *Die syrische Barbara Legende* (1912). The Latin texts are pretty fully represented in N. Müller, *Acta S. Barbarae* (1703), and in P. Paschini, *Santa Barbara, note agiografiche* (1927). The oldest Greek recension is perhaps that printed by A. Wirth, *Danae in christlichen Legenden* (1892), pp. 105–111, though the editor is disposed to exaggerate the dependence of such legends

* During the war of 1914–18 there was a tendency among gunners to put themselves under the patronage of St Joan of Arc. Somebody noticed that during the process of her rehabilitation the Duke of Alençon stated that she excelled in the tactical disposition of artillery.

as that of St Barbara on pagan mythology. A good deal has been written concerning her inclusion among the fourteen *Nothelfer* and the very wide range of interests for which her patronage is invoked. See, for example, T. Marchesi, *Santa Barbara protectrice dei cannonieri* (1895) ; Peine, *St Barbara, die Schutzheilige der Bergleute und der Artillerie* (1896) ; J. Moret, *Ste Barbe, patronne des mineurs* (1876) ; but no very satisfactory explanation has ever been suggested. In an English calendar (Bodleian MS., Digby 63) of the late ninth century St Barbara's name is already found under December 4. In art her most distinctive emblem is a tower ; see Künstle, *Ikonographie*, vol. ii, pp. 112–115. The folk-lore connected with St Barbara has been dealt with by Bächtold-Stäubli, *Handwörterbuch des deutschen Aberglaubens*, vol. i, cc. 905–910.

CLEMENT OF ALEXANDRIA   (*c.* A.D. 215)

AFTER devoting several pages to the life and writings of this eminent father of the Church, Alban Butler says : " Pope Benedict XIV in his learned dissertation, addressed in the form of a brief to the King of Portugal, prefixed to the edition of the Roman Martyrology made in 1748, excellently shows that there is not sufficient reason for ever inserting his name in the Roman Martyrology. The authority of certain private calendars and the custom of sacred biographers suffices for giving his life in this place." The title Saint is still sometimes accorded to Clement in popular usage, but the deliberate and formal exclusion of his name from the Roman Martyrology is a decisive reason for omitting him from any ordinary collection of saints' lives.

ST MARUTHAS, BISHOP OF MAIFERKAT   (*c.* A.D. 415)

THIS holy prelate was an illustrious father of the Syrian church at the end of the fourth century, and was bishop of Maiferkat, between the Tigris and Lake Van near the border of Persia. He compiled the " acts " of the martyrs who suffered in that kingdom during Sapor's persecution, and brought the relics of so many to his episcopal city that it came to be called Martyropolis. Under that name it is still a titular see. St Maruthas wrote several hymns in praise of the martyrs, which are sung by those who use Syriac in the church offices. Yezdigerd having ascended the Persian throne in 399, St Maruthas made a journey to Constantinople in order to induce the Emperor Arcadius to use his interest with the new king in favour of the distressed Christians. He found the court much occupied with the affairs of St John Chrysostom, and we learn incidentally that Maruthas was very fat : so much so that when at a meeting of bishops he accidentally trod on the foot of Cyrinus of Chalcedon the skin was broken ; the wound gangrened and eventually Cyrinus died of it. In a letter to St Olympias, Chrysostom in exile speaks of writing twice to Maruthas and asks her to see the bishop for him. " I need him badly for Persian affairs. Try and find out from him what success he has had in his mission. If he is afraid to write himself, let him tell me the result through you. Do not delay a day in trying to see him about this."

While at the Persian court on behalf of Theodosius the Younger, St Maruthas endeavoured to get the king's good will towards his Christian subjects. The historian Socrates says that his knowledge of medicine enabled him to cure Yezdigerd of violent headaches, and that the king from that time called him " the friend of God ". The Mazdeans, fearing that the prince would be brought over to the Christian faith, had recourse to a trick. They hid a man underground in the temple, who, when the king came to worship, cried out, " Drive from this holy place him who impiously believes a priest of the Christians ". Yezdigerd hereupon was going to dismiss the bishop, but Maruthas persuaded him to go again to the temple, assuring him that by opening the floor he would discover the imposture. The king did so, and the result was that he gave Maruthas leave to build churches wherever he pleased. Whatever the circumstances may have been, Yezdigerd certainly favoured St Maruthas, and the bishop set himself to restore order among the Persian Christians.

The organization then established lasted until the Mohammedan invasion in the seventh century, but the Christian hope—and Mazdean fear—that Yezdigerd I would be the " Constantine of Persia " was not fulfilled. St Maruthas's work of pacification was undone by the violence of Abdas, Bishop of Susa, who towards the end of his reign provoked the king to a renewal of persecution. By this time Maruthas was probably dead, for he predeceased Yezdigerd, who died in 420. The Roman Martyrology says of St Maruthas that he was " renowned for miracles and earned honour even from his adversaries ". He is accounted one of the chief Syrian doctors after St Ephraem because of the writings with which he is credited.

A certain amount of information regarding this saint is furnished by the historian Socrates, as also by Bar Hebraeus, and in the *Liber Turris* of Mari ibn Sulaiman. There is a later biography preserved in Armenian, which was printed with a Latin translation by the Mekhitarists at Venice in 1874, and has been translated into English, with valuable comments, in the *Harvard Theological Review* for 1932, pp. 47–71. See also Bardenhewer, *Geschichte d. altkirchl. Literatur*, vol. iv, pp. 381–382 ; Labourt, *Le Christianisme dans l'Empire perse* (1904), pp. 87–90 ; W. Wright, *Syriac Literature* (1894), pp. 44–46 ; *Oriens Christianus* for 1903, pp. 384 *seq.* ; Harnack in *Texte und Untersuchungen*, vol. xix (1899), and the long footnote in Hefele-Leclercq, *Histoire des Conciles*, vol. ii, pp. 159–166. A doubt exists whether Maruthas was really the author of several of the works attributed to him.

ST ANNO, ARCHBISHOP OF COLOGNE   (A.D. 1075)

ANNO's father was a Swabian nobleman whose family had seen better days, and he hoped that in a secular career his very capable son would be able to restore the fortunes of the house. But a relative who was a canon of Bamberg induced Count Walter to entrust Anno to him, and the young man was set to learn in the episcopal school of Bamberg, of which he ultimately became master. Anno had good looks and manner as well as learning and eloquence, and came to the notice of the Emperor Henry III, who made him one of his chaplains and in 1056, when he was forty-six years old, promoted him to be the archbishop of Cologne and chancellor of the empire. The appointment did not give general satisfaction, especially to the citizens of Cologne, who did not think that Anno's family was good enough : but the magnificence of his consecration ceremonies was beyond criticism. In the same year Henry III died and the government passed nominally into the hands of his widow, Agnes of Poitou, as regent for the minor Henry IV. She was a gentle woman without political acumen and incapable of vigorous action, her policy alienated the greater nobles, and at Whitsuntide in 1062, Henry was kidnapped and taken up the Rhine to Cologne. Anno now became guardian and regent, but had to join with himself Adalbert, Archbishop of Bremen, and when the young king came of age he got rid of Anno altogether and gave Adalbert a free hand. In the schism raised against Pope Alexander II by the antipope Cadalus of Parma, Anno was the leader of the German bishops who supported Alexander ; but this did not save him from being summoned to Rome for the alleged holding of relations with

Cadalus, and again, two years later, to answer a charge of simony. Of this he cleared himself; but he was not free from that favouring of his relatives which was a fault of bishops of his time, and benefices were freely given to his nephews and partisans, on one occasion with disastrous results for the beneficiary.

This was when Anno nominated his nephew Conrad, or Cuno, to the see of Trier. The appointment caused great dissatisfaction among the clergy and people of Trier; they had a canonical right to elect their own bishop, and valued the privilege. To their remonstrances Anno turned a deaf ear, although he must have realized that his power was waning. He sent Conrad with the Bishop of Speyer and an armed escort to take possession of his see. The malcontents had found a strong and unscrupulous leader in Count Theodoric, who though a layman claimed a prescriptive title to bestow investiture upon the archbishop of Trier. As Conrad and his party were passing through Biedburg, they were set upon by the count's men-at-arms. The Bishop of Speyer, after being plundered, was allowed to escape with his life, but Conrad was hurried off amid many indignities to a castle where he was imprisoned, and then thrown over the battlements. As he was found to be still breathing, he was stabbed to death. His body was found by a peasant hidden under leaves in a wood, and it was subsequently translated to the abbey of Tholey, where Conrad received *cultus* as a martyr.

Nearly the whole of the life of Anno is a record of events belonging to the troubled political history of the age, much of it rather disedifying now that great prelates no longer have *ex officio* to take an active part in civil government and all sorts of public affairs. Nevertheless he did not allow secular duties and activities to make him neglect the welfare of the diocese that was his first charge; and, particularly when the emperor's dislike of him was in the ascendant and he was driven from public life, he prosecuted its reform with something of the energy and thoroughness of his contemporaries St Peter Damian and Cardinal Hildebrand, and by the same means. The monasteries were rigorously reformed and new ones were established by St Anno himself; he rebuilt or enlarged a number of churches; he purged public morals; and he distributed large sums in alms. But, though he built up the position of his see and was a generous benefactor of its flock, St Anno never succeeded in overcoming the opposition of Cologne itself, which grievously disturbed his closing years. At length he retired to the abbey of Siegburg which he had founded, and spent the last twelve months of his life there in rigorous penance, dying on December 4, 1075. It is known that, moving among many of most corrupt morals, St Anno was notable for his purity and austere standards, and it is for the virtue of his private life that he is numbered among the saints.

There is a long but unsatisfactory Life of St Anno compiled by a monk of Siegburg in the twelfth century. It has been edited with useful annotations by R. Köpke in MGH., *Scriptores*, vol. xi, pp. 463–514. The text in Migne, PL., vol. cxliii, is in many ways inadequate. The early German metrical life, known as the *Annolied*, is interesting as a monument of vernacular speech in the early twelfth century, but it is of no value as an historical source. See also Hauck, *Kirchengeschichte Deutschlands*, vol. iii, pp. 712 seq.; A. Stonner, *Heilige der deutschen Frühzeit* (1935), vol. ii; and DHG., vol. iii, cc. 395–396. On the canonization of St Anno consult Brackman in the *Neues Archiv*, vol. xxxii (1906), pp. 151–165. An account of his nephew St Conrad was written by Theodoric of Verdun before 1089; it is edited by G. Waitz in MGH., *Scriptores*, vol. viii, pp. 212–219. The life printed in the *Acta Sanctorum*, June, vol. i, has been interpolated with sundry mythical incidents.

ST OSMUND, BISHOP OF SALISBURY   (A.D. 1099)

A DOCUMENT of the late fifteenth century states that Osmund was the son of Henry, Count of Séez, and Isabella, a half-sister of William the Conqueror.   He certainly came to England with the Normans, and succeeded Herfast as chancellor of the realm.   In 1078 King William nominated him bishop of Salisbury, and he was consecrated by Lanfranc of Canterbury.   Salisbury at this time was no more than a fortress built over the hill which we now call Old Sarum.* Osmund's predecessor, Herman, had begun the building of a cathedral, which was finished by Osmund and consecrated in 1092.   Five days later it was struck by lightning and very badly damaged.   The foundations of Osmund's church are clearly marked on the hill, which is now a playground for the children of the suburbs of New Sarum.   He constituted a cathedral chapter on the Norman model, with a clergy school presided over by the chancellor, and the canons were bound to residence and the choral celebration of the Divine Office.   This example had considerable importance, for some of the most important cathedrals of England were at that time served by monks and not by the secular clergy.   St Osmund was one of the royal commissioners for the Domesday survey, and he was one of the principal ecclesiastical lords present at Old Sarum in 1086 when the Domesday Book was received and the nobles swore that they would be faithful to the king against all other men.   In the struggle between William Rufus and St Anselm concerning investitures St Osmund considered Anselm unnecessarily intransigent.   At the Council of Rockingham, when Anselm made so moving an appeal to his fellow bishops, he openly sided with the king.   But just before his death he submitted his judgement, and asked pardon of St Anselm for his opposition.

St Osmund's name is commonly associated with work in the field of divine worship.   In his time, and for long after, very many dioceses of western Christendom had their own liturgical " uses ", variations from that of Rome, and the liturgical books of the church of Salisbury were in a state of considerable confusion. Osmund reduced them to order, and drew up regulations for the celebration of Mass and the Divine Office and the administration of the sacraments uniformly throughout his diocese.   Within a hundred years these revised offices—" according to the use of the Distinguished and Noble Church of Sarum "—had been adopted in most of the English and Welsh dioceses ; they were introduced into Ireland in 1172, and into Scotland about 1250.   They remained the ordinary use in England till after the reign of Queen Mary, when they were gradually superseded by the reformed Roman rite of Pope St Pius V ; this change was made at the Douay college in 1577.†   For this work of liturgical revision a considerable collation of manuscripts was necessary, and St Osmund collected together an extensive library at his cathedral.   He is said to have written a Life of St Aldhelm, his predecessor in the ecclesiastical government of west Wessex, for whose memory he had a great reverence ; he assisted at the enshrining of his relics at Malmesbury.

* Peter of Blois called the church and castle the " ark of God shut up in the temple of Baal ".   Centuries later William Cobbett, for other reasons, refers to the deserted site as the " Accursed Hill ".

† There was even some talk of reviving the Sarum use after the re-establishment of an ordinary hierarchy in England in 1850.   At the present day the Mass and offices proper to the Dominicans most resemble those used in this country up to the end of the sixteenth century.   The distinctive customs in the English Catholic marriage service are a survival from the Sarum *rituale*.

For all his public activities St Osmund seemed to have spent a good deal of time quietly in his cathedral city, where he liked both to copy and to bind books in the library.   William of Malmesbury praises the purity of his life, and remarks that he was neither ambitious nor avaricious, the besetting temptations of great prelates in those days.   He was known for his rigour and severity towards penitents, but was no harder to others than he was to himself.   He died in the night of December 3–4, 1099, and was buried in his cathedral.   Though Richard Poore, Bishop of Salisbury, petitioned for his canonization in 1228 it was not until 1457 that it took place—the last canonization of a saint from England before More and Fisher in 1935.   In the same year his relics were translated from Old Sarum to the Lady-chapel of the new cathedral in the new city of Salisbury.   The shrine was destroyed by Henry VIII (Alban Butler says the relics were re-interred in the same chapel) ;   a slab from the tomb, inscribed with the date MXCIX, now lies in one of the bays of the nave.*   St Osmund is named in the Roman Martyrology, and his feast is observed in the dioceses of Westminster, Clifton and Plymouth.

There is no early life of St Osmund, though a fragment of some such biography seems to be preserved in MS. Cotton, Titus, F. III at the British Museum.   For what we know of the saint we are dependent mainly on William of Malmesbury and Simeon of Durham. A number of documents connected with the canonization are still in existence ; they consist mostly of accounts of miracles and they were published from the originals in the muniment-room of Salisbury Cathedral by the Wiltshire Record Society in 1901, under the editorship of H. R. Malden.   See also W. H. Frere, *The Sarum Use*, 2 vols. (1898 and 1901) ; W. H. R. Jones, *The Register of St Osmund*, 2 vols. (1883–84), in the Rolls Series ; Bradshaw and Wordsworth, *Lincoln Cathedral Statutes*, vol. iii, pp. 869 seq. ; the DNB., vol. xlii, pp 313–315 ; and the *Dict. of Eng. Church History*, pp. 427–428.   A short life, written from the Anglican standpoint, was published by W. J. Torrance in 1920.

ST BERNARD, Bishop of Parma and Cardinal   (A.D. 1133)

BERNARD was a member of the great Uberti family at Florence and gave up brilliant secular prospects to become a monk with the Vallumbrosans, an austere congregation founded not long before by St John Gualbert.   Bernard became in time abbot of the monastery of San Salvio, then abbot general of the whole order, and Bd Urban II created him cardinal and entrusted him with legatine duties.   Parma at this time was shockingly disturbed by schisms, caused first by Bishop Cadalus, who set himself up as antipope, and then by other bishops who supported another antipope, Guibert of Ravenna, himself a Parmesan.   In the midst of these disorders St Bernard was appointed bishop of Parma and consecrated by Pope Paschal II. He was a zealous supporter of the true pope and upholder of the reforms of St Gregory VII, especially in the matter of simony, which was rampant in his diocese. He was consequently driven from his see in 1104 by the followers of the antipope Maginulf, who laid hands upon him at the very altar, and was in exile for two years.

At a time when many bishops not only accepted but sought temporal power, St Bernard was distinguished by resigning that which had been received by his predecessors in the see of Parma, and he never forgot, or allowed others to forget, that he had been trained as a monk in the school of perfection ; and so far as was compatible with his duties he retained all his monastic observances.   When in

* Here on a summer's day in 1924 the present writer heard a verger inform a group of visitors that : " This is all that remains of the tomb of Bishop Osmund, who compiled the first English Prayer Book."   While appreciating that people must be addressed in terms that they can understand, it is pardonable to think that this statement was somewhat misleading.

1127 the leaders of the Hohenstaufens proclaimed Conrad as German king against Lothair II, St Bernard protested and was again obliged to flee from Parma. Lothair came to Rome to be crowned emperor in 1133 and St Bernard died at Parma in the same year on December 4.

In the supplement to MGH., vol. xxx, pt II, fasc. 2 (1929), the two more important Latin Lives of St Bernard of Parma, formerly printed is the *Chronica Parmensia*, have been re-edited by P. E. Schramm from better texts ; see on this the *Analecta Bollandiana*, vol. xlviii (1930), p. 414. A biography on popular lines is that of M. Ercolani, *S. Bernardo degli Uberti* (1933). Of the older biographies the best is that of I. Affò (1788) ; but see also D. Munerati in *Rivista di scienze storiche,* vol. iii (1906), pp. 79–86 and 257–264 ; the *Dictionnaire de Spiritualité*, vol. i, c. 1512 ; and DHG., vol. ix, c. 718. The general political situation is well set out by R. Davidsohn in vol. i, pp. 289 *seq.* of his *Geschichte von Florenz* and in pp. 66 *seq.* of his *Forschungen zur alt. Gesch. Florenz.*

5 : ST SABAS, Abbot   (A.D. 532)

ST SABAS, one of the most renowned patriarchs of the monks of Palestine, was born at Mutalaska in Cappadocia, not far from Caesarea, in 439. His father was an officer in the army and, being obliged to go to Alexandria, took his wife with him and recommended his son Sabas, with the care of his estate, to his brother-in-law. This uncle's wife used the child so harshly that, when he was eight, he ran away, went to another uncle, called Gregory, brother to his father, hoping there to live more happily. Gregory, having the care of the child, demanded also the administration of the property, whence lawsuits and animosity arose between the two uncles. Sabas, who was of a quiet disposition, was upset at these discords and ran away again, this time to a monastery near Mutalaska. His uncles, after some years, ashamed of their conduct, agreed together to take him out of his monastery, restore him his property, and persuade him to marry. But young Sabas had tasted the bitterness of the world and the sweetness of the yoke of Christ, and his heart was so united to God that nothing could draw him from his new home. Though he was the youngest in the house he surpassed the rest in fervour and virtue. Once, when he was serving the baker, this monk put his wet clothes into the oven to dry, and then, forgetting them, put in fire. Seeing him much troubled for his clothes Sabas crawled into the oven and fetched them out through the flames, without hurt. When Sabas had been ten years in this monastery, being eighteen years old, he went to Jerusalem to learn from the example of the solitaries of that country. He passed the winter in a monastery governed by the holy abbot Elpidius, whose monks desired earnestly that he would fix his abode among them. But his love of silence and retirement made him prefer the manner of life practised by St Euthymius, who even when a monastery was built for him refused to abandon his complete solitude. When Sabas asked to be accepted as his disciple St Euthymius judged him too young for an absolutely solitary life, and therefore recommended him to his monastery below the hill, about three miles distant, which was under the conduct of St Theoctistus.

Sabas consecrated himself to God with new fervour, working all day and watching in prayer a good part of the night. As he was very energetic and strong he assisted his brethern in their heavier work, and himself prepared the wood and water for the house. Once he was sent by his abbot as companion to another monk on business to Alexandria. There his parents met him and desired him to accept his father's profession and influence in the world. When he refused they pressed him at least to accept money for his necessaries; but he would only take three pieces of gold, and those he gave to his abbot on his return. When he was thirty years of age he obtained leave of St Euthymius to spend five days a week in a remote cave, which time he passed in prayer and manual labour. He left his monastery on Sunday evening carrying wtih him bundles of palm-twigs, and came back on Saturday morning with fifty baskets which he had made, imposing upon himself a task of ten a day. St Euthymius chose him and one Domitian for his companions in his yearly retreat in the desert of Jebel Quarantal, where Christ is said to have made His forty-days' fast. They entered this solitude together on the octave-day of the Epiphany and returned to their monastery on Palm Sunday. In the first retreat Sabas collapsed in the wilderness, almost dead with thirst. St Euthymius, moved with compassion, prayed to Christ that He would take pity on His fervent soldier, and it is said that, striking his staff into the earth, a spring gushed forth; of which Sabas. drinking a little, he recovered his strength. After the death of Euthymius, St Sabas retired further into the desert towards Jericho. Four years he spent in this wilderness in total separation from intercourse with men, when he chose a new dwelling in a cave on the face of a cliff, at the bottom of which ran the brook Cedron. He was obliged to hang a rope down the descent to hold on by when going up and down. Wild herbs which grew on the rocks were his food, till certain countrymen brought him sometimes a little bread, cheese, dates and other things which he might want. Water he had to fetch from a considerable distance.

After Sabas had lived here some time many came to him, desiring to serve God under his direction. He was at first unwilling to consent, but eventually founded a new *laura*.* One of the first difficulties was shortage of water. But having noticed a wild ass pawing and nosing at the ground, Sabas caused a pit to be dug at the spot, where a spring was discovered which subsisted to succeeding ages. The number of his disciples was increased to one hundred and fifty, but he had no priest in his community, for he thought no religious man could aspire to that dignity without presumption. This provoked some of the monks to complain of him to Sallust, Patriarch of Jerusalem. The bishop found their grievances groundless, except that the want of a priest was a trouble in the community. He therefore compelled Sabas to receive ordination at his hands in 491. The abbot was then fifty-three years old. The reputation of his sanctity drew persons from remote countries to his *laura*, and among the monks were Egyptians and Armenians, for whom special arrangements were made so that they could celebrate the offices in their own tongues. After the death of the saint's father, his mother came to Palestine and served God under his direction. With the money which she brought he built two hospitals, one for strangers and another for the sick; and also a hospital at Jericho and another monastery on a neighbouring hill. In 493 the patriarch of Jerusalem established St Sabas as archimandrite over all the monks of Palestine who lived in separate cells (hermits), and St Theodosius of Bethlehem over all who lived in community (cenobites).

St Sabas, after the example of St Euthymius, left his disciples every year, or oftener, and at least passed Lent without being seen by anyone, and this was

* A *laura* was a monastery in which the monks lived in separate huts or cells, grouped around the church without any definite plan. The maximum of solitude possible in such circumstances was aimed at.

one of the things complained of by some of his monks. As they got no sympathy from the patriarch some sixty of them left the *laura*, and settled themselves in a ruined monastery at Thecua, where the prophet Amos was born. When he heard that these malcontents were in sore straits, St Sabas gave them supplies and repaired their church. He himself had been driven for a time from his own monastery by the factions therein, but returned at the command of St Elias, the successor of Sallust at Jerusalem. Among the stories told of St Sabas is that he once lay down to sleep in a cave that happened to be the den of a lion. When the beast came in it clawed hold of the monk's clothes and dragged him outside. Nothing perturbed, Sabas returned to the cave and eventually reduced the lion to a considerable degree of friendliness. But it was still a rather troublesome companion, and at length Sabas told it that if it could not live with him in peace it had better go away. So the lion went away.

At this time the Emperor Anastasius was supporting the Eutychian heresy, and banished many orthodox bishops. In 511 the Patriarch Elias sent to him as deputies St Sabas, with other abbots, to endeavour to stop this persecution. Sabas was seventy years old when he undertook this journey to Constantinople. As he looked like some beggar the officers at the gate of the palace admitted the rest but stopped him. Sabas said nothing, but withdrew. When the emperor had read the letter of the patriarch, in which great commendations were bestowed on Sabas, he asked where he was. The saint was sought, and at length found in a corner saying his prayers. Anastasius gave the abbots liberty to ask what they wanted for themselves ; they presented their petitions, but Sabas had no request to make in his own name. Being pressed, he only begged that Anastasius would restore peace to the Church and not disturb the clergy. Sabas stayed the winter in Constantinople, and often visited the emperor to argue against heresy. But Anastasius for all that procured the banishment of Elias of Jerusalem and put one John into his place. Whereupon St Sabas and other monks hastened to Jerusalem and persuaded the intruder at least not to repudiate the Council of Chalcedon. Sabas is said to have been with the exiled Elias at his death at Aïla on the Red Sea ; in the following years he went to Caesarea, Scythopolis and other places, preaching the true faith, and bringing back many to orthodoxy and right living.

In his ninety-first year, at the request of Patriarch Peter of Jerusalem, St Sabas undertook a second journey to Constantinople, in connection with troubles arising out of the Samaritan revolt and its violent repression by the emperor. Justinian received him with honour and offered to endow his monasteries. Sabas gratefully replied that they stood not in need of such revenues so long as the monks should faithfully serve God. But he begged a remission of taxes in favour of the people of Palestine in consideration of what they had suffered on account of the Samaritans ; that he would build a hospital at Jerusalem for pilgrims and a fortress for the protection of the hermits and monks against raiders ; and that he would authorize further strong measures for the putting down of the Samaritans. All which things were granted. It happened one day, the emperor being busy despatching certain affairs of St Sabas, who was himself present, that when it was the third hour the abbot went out to his prayers. His companion, Jeremy, said it was not well done to leave the emperor in this way. " My son ", replied Sabas, " the emperor does his duty, and we must do ours." Very shortly after his return to his *laura* he fell sick, and the patriarch persuaded him to let himself be taken to a neighbouring church, where he served him with his own hands. The sufferings of Sabas were very sharp, but God supported him under them in perfect patience and resignation. Finding his last hour approach, he begged the patriarch that he might be carried back to his *laura*. He appointed his successor, gave him instructions, and then lay four days in silence without seeing anyone, that he might concern himself with God alone. On December 5, 532, in the evening, he departed to the Lord, being ninety-four years old. His relics were venerated at his chief monastery until they were carried off by the Venetians.

St Sabas is one of the outstanding figures of early monasticism, and his feast today is kept throughout the Church both in the East and the West ; he is named at the preparation in the Byzantine Mass. The Typikon of Jerusalem, setting out the rules for the recitation of the Divine Office and carrying out of ceremonies, which is the norm in nearly all churches of the Byzantine rite, bears his name, as does a monastic rule ; but his part in their composition is a matter of doubt. His chief monastery, called after him Mar Saba and sometimes distinguished as the Great Laura, still exists in a gorge of the Cedron, ten miles south-east of Jerusalem in the desert country towards the Dead Sea. Among its monks were St John Damascene, St John the Silent, St Aphrodisius, St Theophanes of Nicaea, St Cosmas of Majuma and St Theodore of Edessa. After a period of ruin it was restored by the Russian government in 1840 and is now inhabited by monks of the Eastern Orthodox Church, whose life is not unworthy of the example of the holy founder. After St Catherine's on Mount Sinai (and perhaps Dair Antonios and Dair Boulos in Egypt) Mar Saba is the oldest inhabited monastery in the world, and the most remarkable ; the wildness of its situation and grandeur of its fortress-like buildings at least equal those of St Catherine's. St Sabas's spring still flows there, his palm-tree still bears stoneless dates, and the dark blue grackles that abound are called " his blackbirds ", and are daily fed by the monks.

The Life of St Sabas, written in Greek by Cyril of Scythopolis, is one of the most famous and trustworthy of early hagiographical documents. The full text has to be sought either in Cotelerius, *Ecclesiae Graecae Monumenta*, vol. iii, pp. 220–376 ; or in *Kyrillos von Skythopolis*, ed. E. Schwartz (1939). Another biography, an adaptation attributed to the Metaphrast, has been printed by Kleopas Koikylides as an appendix to the two first volumes of the Greek review, *Nea Sion* (1906). The Life of St Sabas at a relatively early date was also translated into Arabic. On the chronology of the life see Loofs in *Texte und Untersuchungen*, vol. iii (dealing with Leontius of Byzantium), pp. 274–297 ; and on the literary and liturgical work ascribed to Sabas consult A. Ehrhard in the *Kirchenlexikon*, vol. x (1897), cc. 1434–1437, or his fuller article in the *Römische Quartalschrift*, vol. vii (1893), pp. 31–79. An exhaustive and satisfactory account of Sabas himself and of his monastery was published in Greek by J. Phokylides at Alexandria in 1927. Cyril of Scythopolis had been impressed even as a boy by a casual meeting with St Sabas ; he seems to have entered the monastery of St Euthymios in 544 and to have passed on to Mar Saba not long before his death in 558.

ST CRISPINA, MARTYR   (A.D. 304)

ST AUGUSTINE frequently mentions St Crispina as one well known in Africa in his time, and we learn from him that she was a woman of rank, native of Thagara in Numidia, married, with several children, and worthy of estimation with such famous martyrs as St Agnes and St Thecla. During the persecution of Diocletian she was brought before the proconsul Anulinus at Theveste, charged with ignoring the imperial commands. When she came into court Anulinus asked : " Have you understood the meaning of the decree ? " Crispina replied : " I do not know what that decree is."

ANULINUS : It is that you should sacrifice to all our gods for the welfare of the emperors, according to the law given by our lords Diocletian and Maximian, the pious *Augusti*, and Constantius, the most illustrious *Caesar*.

CRISPINA : I will never sacrifice to any but the one God and to our Lord Jesus Christ His Son, who was born and suffered for us.

ANULINUS : Give up this superstition and bow your head before our sacred gods.

CRISPINA : I worship my God every day, and I know no other.

ANULINUS : You are obstinate and disrespectful and you will bring upon yourself the severity of the law.

CRISPINA : If necessary I will suffer for the faith that I hold.

ANULINUS : Are you so vain a creature that you will not put away your folly and worship the sacred deities ?

CRISPINA : I worship my God every day, and I know no other.

ANULINUS : I put the sacred edict before you for your observance.

CRISPINA : I observe an edict, but it is that of my Lord Jesus Christ.

ANULINUS : You will lose your head if you do not obey the emperors' commands. All Africa has submitted to them and you will be made to do the same.

CRISPINA : I will sacrifice to the Lord who made the heavens and the earth, the sea and all things that are in them. But I will never be forced to sacrifice to evil spirits.

ANULINUS : Then you will not accept those gods to whom you must give honour if you would save your life ?

CRISPINA : That is no true religion that forces the unwilling.

ANULINUS : But will you not comply, and with bent head offer a little incense in the sacred temples ?

CRISPINA : I have never done such a thing since I was born, and I will not do it so long as I live.

ANULINUS : Do it, however, just to escape the penalty of the law.

CRISPINA : I do not fear what you threaten, but I fear the God who is in Heaven. If I defy Him then shall I be sacrilegious and He will cast me off, and I shall not be found in the day that He comes.

ANULINUS : You cannot be sacrilegious if you obey the law.

CRISPINA : Would you have me sacrilegious before God that I may not be so before the emperors ? No indeed ! God is great and almighty : He made the sea and the green plants and the dry land. How can I consider men, the work of His hands, before Himself ?

ANULINUS : Profess the Roman religion of our lords the unconquerable emperors, as we ourselves observe it.

CRISPINA : I know one only God. Those gods of yours are stones, things carved by the hands of men.

ANULINUS : You utter blasphemy. That is not the way to look after your own safety.

Then Anulinus ordered her hair to be cut off and her head shaved, exposing her to the derision of the mob, and when she still remained firm asked her : " Do you want to live ? Or to die in agony like your fellows Maxima, Donatilla and Secunda ? "

CRISPINA : If I wanted to die and abandon my soul to loss and endless fire I should treat your demons in the way you wish.

ANULINUS : I will have you beheaded if you persist in mocking at our venerable gods.

CRISPINA : Thank God for that. I should certainly lose my head if I took to worshipping them.

ANULINUS : Do you then persist in your folly ?

CRISPINA : My God, who was and who is, willed that I be born. He brought me to salvation through the waters of baptism. And He is with me to stay my soul from committing the sacrilege that you require.

ANULINUS : Can we endure this impious Crispina any longer ?

The proconsul ordered the proceedings that had taken place to be read over aloud, and he then sentenced Crispina to death by the sword. At which she exclaimed : " Praise to God who has looked down and delivered me out of your hands ! " She suffered at Theveste on December 5, in the year 304.

The *passio* of this martyr is printed in Ruinart's *Acta sincera*, but a more critical text has been edited by P. Franchi de' Cavalieri in *Studi e Testi*, vol. ix (1902), pp. 23–31. Among similar records which are so often overlaid with wordy declamations and extravagant miracles, the document ranks high. Still, as Delehaye has pointed out, it cannot in its entirety be accepted as a faithful transcript of an official *procès verbal* preserved as a legal record of the trial. See the valuable comments in his *Les passions des martyrs* . . . (1921), pp. 110–114. Consult also P. Monceaux in *Mélanges Boissier* (1903), pp. 383–389. From the Calendar of Carthage and the *Hieronymianum*, it seems probable that Crispina was one of a group of other martyrs. There was a great basilica at Theveste (Tabessa) which probably contained her shrine ; see Gsell, *Les monuments antiques de l'Algérie*, vol. ii, pp. 265–291.

ST NICETIUS, BISHOP OF TRIER   (c. A.D. 566)

SEVERAL distinguished men of his age, among them St Gregory of Tours and St Venantius Fortunatus, bear witness to the merits and deeds of Nicetius of Trier, who was the last Gallo-Roman bishop of Trier in the early days of Frankish domination in Gaul. He was born in Auvergne, with a *corona* of hair around his head, which was taken to be an omen of his future ecclesiastical state. He did in fact become a monk, and abbot of his monastery, apparently at Limoges, and attracted the notice of King Theoderic I. When the bishop of Trier, St Aprunculus, died, the clergy and people sent a deputation to the king asking him to appoint St Gallus of Clermont. Theoderic refused, and named Nicetius. Already while the royal officers were escorting the bishop elect to Trier, he showed what sort of a prelate he was going to be. When they halted for the night the escort turned their horses out in the fields of the neighbouring peasants. Nicetius ordered them to be removed, and the officers laughed at him. So Nicetius, threatening excommunication for those who oppressed the poor, drove the horses out himself. He had often preached to his monks from the text that " a man may fall in three ways—by thought, word and deed ", and he did not fear to rebuke the irregularities of Theoderic and his son Theodebert. These princes perhaps profited by his reproofs, but Clotaire I was less tractable and, when St Nicetius excommunicated him for his crimes, unjustly banished him. The exile continued but a very short time, for Clotaire soon died and Sigebert, one of his sons who succeeded him in that part of his dominions, saw that Nicetius was restored.

The bishop assisted at several important synods at Clermont and elsewhere, and was indefatigable in restoring discipline to a diocese that had suffered much from civil disorders. He called in Italian workmen to rebuild his cathedral and fortified the city on the side of the Moselle. He founded a clergy-school, but himself was the best lesson to clerics and laity alike. Though he enjoyed the favour and protection of King Sigebert his zeal did not fail to raise more persecution, but no human respect or fear could make him abandon the cause of God. The extirpation of incestuous marriages cost him many difficulties, and he freely excommunicated the offenders. Several letters of St Nicetius have been preserved. One, written about the year 561, was to Clodesindis, daughter to Clotaire I and married to Alboin, the Arian king of the Lombards. He tells her to endeavour to convert her husband to the orthodox faith, pointing out the miracles which were wrought in the Catholic Church through the relics of saints which the Arians themselves venerated. " Let the king ", he says, " send messengers to the church of St Martin. If they dare enter it they will see the blind enlightened, the deaf recover their hearing, and the dumb their speech : the lepers and sick are cured and return home sound, as we see. . . . What shall I say of the relics of the holy bishops Germanus, Hilary and Lupus at which so many miracles are wrought that we cannot recount them all ? The very demoniacs are forced to confess their virtue. Do they do so in the churches of the Arians ? They do not. One devil never exorcises another." Another letter is addressed to the Emperor Justinian, who had been led by his wife into a semi-Monophysism. In it Nicetius tells him that his lapse was bewailed throughout Italy, Africa, Spain and Gaul, and that did he not repudiate his errors he would be lost. St Nicetius died about the year 566, perhaps on October 1, the day on which his feast is kept at Trier (today in the Roman Martyrology).

Most of what we know of St Nicetius comes to us from the *Vitae Patrum* of Gregory of Tours. The saint's correspondence, or what survives of it, may best be studied in MGH., *Epistolae*, vol. iii, pp. 116, etc. See also Duchesne, *Fastes Épiscopaux*, vol. iii, pp. 37–38.

ST BIRINUS, BISHOP OF DORCHESTER   (*c.* A.D. 650)

BIRINUS was a priest at Rome, probably of Germanic stock, who heard God's call to offer himself for the foreign missions and was recommended by Pope Honorius I to go to the island of Britain. In preparation for his mission he was consecrated to the episcopate by Asterius, Bishop of Genoa. There is a story told that after he had gone aboard ship he found he had left behind a sort of pyx, given to him by Honorius, containing the Corpus Domini. Though they were well out to sea he jumped overboard, waded ashore, recovered the pyx, and returned to the vessel— without getting wet and to the great admiration of the sailors. St Birinus had announced to the pope that he intended to preach the gospel " in the inner parts, beyond the dominions of the English, where no other teacher had been before " ; perhaps he meant by this the midlands, or even the Britons of Wales and the marches, for he may well have been ignorant of the fact that they were Christians already. But on his arrival in England in 634 he found the West Saxons so sunk in idolatry that " he thought it better to preach the word of God there, rather than to go further looking for others to evangelize ". One of the first fruits of his labours was the king himself of the West Saxons, Cynegils, at whose baptism St Oswald, King of Northumbria, was sponsor. The presence of Oswald in Wessex must have been a great help to St Birinus, and the two kings gave him the town of Dorchester* for his see. From thence he is said to have converted large numbers

* The Dorchester in Oxfordshire, on the borders of Mercia and Wessex, which had been an important Roman centre. It remained a bishopric till 1085, when it was merged in Lincoln.

of people, so earning for himself the title of Apostle of Wessex.   St Birinus died
on December 3, about the year 650, and was buried at Dorchester ; but thirty
years later St Hedda translated his relics to Winchester.   The Roman Martyrology
mentions St Birinus on the day of his death ; his feast is kept in the dioceses of
Birmingham and Portsmouth today.

Although there are several manuscript lives of St Birinus, telling substantially the same
story with slight variations, we know little for certain of his history beyond what we learn
from Bede and the Anglo-Saxon Chronicle.   On these manuscript lives, of which the earliest
is not older than the eleventh century, consult Hardy, *Descriptive Catalogue* (Rolls Series)
vol. i, pp. 235–239.   See also the notes in Plummer's edition of Bede ; Howorth, *The Golden
Days of Eng. Church Hist.*, vol. i, pp. 35–46 ; DCB., vol. i, p. 318 ; and Bright, *Chapters of
Eng. Church Hist.*   There is also a short Anglican life by J. E. Field, and another by T.
Varley, *St Birinus and Wessex* (1934).

ST SIGIRAMNUS, OR CYRAN, ABBOT   (c. A.D. 655)

SIGIRAMNUS belonged to a noble Frankish family of Berry, and went to the court
of Clotaire II, whose cupbearer he became.   He was drawn to the religious rather
than secular life, but his father insisted on his being betrothed to the daughter of
an influential nobleman and paid no attention to his son's wishes.   At length
Sigiramnus broke his engagement, withdrew from the court, and went to the
church of St Martin at Tours where he received the tonsure and vowed himself to
God.   But his father was now bishop of Tours, and so Sigiramnus could not
escape preferment even in his new state.   He was a great friend of the poor, and
distributed alms with such recklessness when he inherited his father's estate (and
his father was no longer there to protect him) that he was for a time put under
restraint as a lunatic.   Sigiramnus then joined a bishop, an Irishman called Falvius
(Failbe), who was on a pilgrimage to Rome.   They travelled during the vintage,
and Sigiramnus would stop and do a day's work with the peasants and serfs in the
vineyards, and in the evening gather them round him to hear the word of God.
On his return to France he received a piece of land at Méobecq, amid the forests
of Brenne, whereon he first built himself a wooden cell and then founded a monastery.   This prospered, and St Sigiramnus was able to found another, on the royal
estate of Longoretum, whither he removed himself.   Several striking stories are
told of his sympathy with the hard-working peasants and with poor criminals ; and
his later years were darkened by the misfortunes of his former guardian and close
friend.   This man lived a more and more careless life, till at last he killed an innocent man.   Eleven days later he was dead himself, to the great grief of St Sigiramnus
who had so often tried to bring him to his own way of life.

There is a Latin life, written seemingly in the ninth or tenth century, but compiled, so
the author insists, from an earlier text which had become almost illegible through age.   It
was printed by Mabillon from an incomplete copy, but the whole has since been recovered,
and it has been edited by the Bollandists in their *Analecta*, vol. iii (1884), pp. 378–407.   The
abbey at Longoretum, which later took the name of Saint-Cyran (du-Jambot) after its founder,
was dissolved in 1712.   John Duvergier de Hauranne, famous as one of the authors of the
Jansenist faction, took his name " Abbé de Saint-Cyran " from this monastery, which he held
in commendam.

BD NICHOLAS OF SIBENIK, MARTYR   (A.D. 1391)

NICHOLAS TAVILIĆ was born at Sibenik in Dalmatia during the first half of the
fourteenth century and became a friar minor at Rivotorto, near Assisi.   At this

time, and for long before, Bosnia and the Dalmatian coast was the prey of the
mischievous sect of Bogomili or Paterines. Even bishops became infected, and the
task of restoring Christian faith and life was entrusted to the Dominican and
Franciscan friars. The last-named were particularly successful, and among their
foremost missioners was Bd Nicholas, who laboured for twenty years in Bosnia.
At the end of that time he was sent to the Franciscan mission in Palestine, where
he was thrown into prison and afterwards hacked to pieces, with three other friars,
for publicly preaching to the Mohammedans. He has ever since been venerated
as a martyr and this *cultus* was confirmed in 1888.

> The surname of this martyr appears in several forms, *e.g.* Tavigli ; Mazzara (*Leggendario
> Francescano*, 1680, vol. iii, p. 413) and others give it as Taulici. The Franciscan annalists
> with Wadding speak of this group of martyrs under the year 1391. See also an article by
> P. Durrien in the *Archiv. Soc. Orient-latin* for 1881, vol. i, pp. 539–546 ; but especially G.
> Golubovich, *Biblioteca bio-bibliografica della Terra Santa*, vol. v (1927), pp. 282–295. There
> seems to be a reference to these martyrs in the almost contemporary Kirkstall Chronicle ;
> *cf.* the *Bulletin of the John Rylands Library*, vol. xv (1931), pp. 118–119.

BD BARTHOLOMEW OF MANTUA   (A.D. 1495)

NOT much is known of the life of Bartholomew Fanti, who was one of several
notably holy Carmelites who adorned the city of Mantua during the fifteenth
century. He was born there in 1443, and joined the order when he was seventeen
years old. After his ordination he showed himself a preacher of great power, with
a burning devotion to our Lord in the Blessed Sacrament : it was by anointing
with oil taken from the lamp burning before the Most Holy that Bd Bartholomew
brought about several among his miracles of healing. At Mantua he instituted
for lay-people the confraternity of our Lady of Mount Carmel, whose statutes
and devotional exercises he drew up himself. Bartholomew is generally said to
have been novice-master of the Carmelite poet, Bd Baptist Spagnuolo ; Baptist
speaks of him as a " most holy guide and spiritual master ". Bd Bartholomew
died on December 5, 1495, and his *cultus* was confirmed in 1909.

> See C. de Villiers, *Bibliotheca Carmelitana*, vol. i, p. 243 ; *Il Monte Carmelo*, vol. i (1915),
> pp. 362–365 ; and *Il Mosé Novello ossia il B. Bartolomeo Fanti* (1909).

BD JOHN ALMOND, MARTYR   (A.D. 1612)

JOHN ALMOND was a Lancashire man, born at Allerton, near Liverpool, and he
went to school at Much Woolton. While still a boy he went to Ireland and
remained there till he entered the English College at Rheims and from thence was
sent to Rome, where he completed his training by a brilliant disputation which
called forth the praise of Cardinal Baronius, who presided. Mr Almond was
ordained in 1598 and four years later was sent on the English mission. During
his ten years' apostolate he " exercised a holy life with all sincerity, and a singular
good content to those that knew him, and worthily deserved both a good opinion
of his learning and sanctity of life ; a reprover of sin, a good example to follow ;
of an ingenious and acute understanding, sharp and apprehensive in his conceits
and answers, yet complete with modesty, full of courage, and ready to suffer for
Christ that suffered for him ".

Mr Almond was arrested in March 1612, and examined by Dr John King,
Bishop of London, upon which occasion he demonstrated very forcibly in several

passages with his inquisitor the " acute understanding, sharp and apprehensive answers " of which the just-quoted panegyrist speaks.   He was tendered the oath of allegiance in an impossible form and refused it, offering to swear, " I do bear in my heart and soul so much allegiance to King James (whom I pray God to bless now and evermore) as he, or any Christian king, could expect by the law of nature, the law of God, or the positive law of the true Church, be it which it will, ours or yours ".   This was not accepted, and he was committed to Newgate.   Nine months later he was tried for high treason as a seminary priest, and sentenced to death.   He was drawn to Tyburn on December 5, 1612, and, after addressing the people, publicly answered the objections of a minister who stood by.   Then he emptied his pockets, throwing their contents to the crowd, including three or four pounds in silver, complaining the while that the keeper of Newgate had not left him much.   " One hour overtaketh another ", he said, " and though never so long at last cometh death.   And yet not death ; for death is the gate of life unto us whereby we enter into everlasting blessedness.   And life is death to those who do not provide for death, for they are ever tossed and troubled with vexations, miseries, and wickedness.   To use this life well is the pathway through death to everlasting life."   He asked for a handkerchief from among the crowd, wherewith to cover his eyes, and he died with the name of Jesus on his lips.

A good account is furnished in MMP., pp. 329–338.   See also Pollen, *Acts of English Martyrs* (1891), pp. 170–194 ; and Bede Camm, *Forgotten Shrines* (1910), pp. 164, 357, 378.

6 : ST NICHOLAS, called " of Bari ", Bishop of Myra   (Fourth Century)

THE great veneration with which this saint has been honoured for many ages and the number of altars and churches which have been everywhere dedicated in his memory are testimonials to his holiness and of the glory which he enjoys with God.   He is said to have been born at Patara in Lycia, a province of Asia Minor.   Myra, the capital, not far from the sea, was an episcopal see, and this church falling vacant, the holy Nicholas was chosen bishop, and in that station became famous by his extraordinary piety and zeal and many astonishing miracles.   The Greek histories of his life agree that he suffered imprisonment for the faith and made a glorious confession in the latter part of the persecution raised by Diocletian, and that he was present at the Council of Nicaea and there condemned Arianism.   The silence of other authors makes many justly suspect these circumstances.   He died at Myra, and was buried in his cathedral.

This summary account by Alban Butler tells us all that is known about the life of the famous St Nicholas, and even a little more : for his episcopate at Myra during the fourth century is really all that seems indubitably authentic.   This is not for lack of material, beginning with the life attributed to the monk who died in 847 as St Methodius, Patriarch of Constantinople.   But he warns us that " Up to the present the life of this distinguished shepherd has been unknown to the majority of the faithful ", and sets about enlightening their ignorance nearly five hundred years after the saint's death.   This is the least unreliable of the " biographical " sources available, and a vast amount of literature, critical and expository, has grown up around them.   Nevertheless, the universal popularity of the saint for so many centuries requires that some account of these legends should be given here.

We are assured that from his earliest days Nicholas would take nourishment only once on Wednesdays and Fridays, and that in the evening according to the canons. " He was exceedingly well brought up by his parents and trod piously in their footsteps. The child, watched over by the Church with the care of the turtle-dove for her chicks, kept untarnished the innocence of his heart." At five years old he began to study the sacred sciences, and " day by day the teaching of the Church enlightened his mind and encouraged his thirst for sincere and true religion ". His parents died when he was a young man, leaving him well off, and he determined to devote his inheritance to works of charity. An opportunity soon arose. A citizen of Patara had lost all his money, and had moreover to support three daughters who could not find husbands because of their poverty ; so the wretched man was going to give them over to prostitution. This came to the ears of Nicholas, who thereupon took a bag of gold and, under cover of darkness, threw it in at the open window of the man's house. Here was a dowry for the eldest girl, and she was soon duly married. At intervals Nicholas did the same for the second and third ; at the last time the father was on the watch, recognized his benefactor, and overwhelmed him with his gratitude. It would appear that the three purses, represented in pictures, came to be mistaken for the heads of three children, and so they gave rise to the absurd story of the children, resuscitated by the saint, who had been killed by an innkeeper and pickled in a brine-tub.*

Coming to the city of Myra when the clergy and people of the province were in session to elect a new bishop, St Nicholas was indicated by God as the man they should choose. This was at the time of the persecutions at the beginning of the fourth century, and, " As he was the chief priest of the Christians of this town and preached the truths of faith with a holy liberty, the divine Nicholas was seized by the magistrates, tortured, then chained and thrown into prison with many other Christians. But when the great and religious Constantine, chosen by God, assumed the imperial diadem of the Romans, the prisoners were released from their bonds and with them the illustrious Nicholas, who when he was set at liberty returned to Myra." St Methodius asserts that " thanks to the teaching of St Nicholas the metropolis of Myra alone was untouched by the filth of the Arian heresy, which it firmly rejected as death-dealing poison ", but says nothing of his presence at the Council of Nicaea in 325. According to other traditions he was not only there but so far forgot himself as to give the heresiarch Arius a slap in the face. Whereupon the conciliar fathers deprived him of his episcopal insignia and committed him to prison : but our Lord and His Mother appeared there and restored to him both his liberty and his office. As against Arianism so against paganism, St Nicholas was tireless and took strong measures : among other temples he destroyed was that of Artemis, the principal in the district, and the evil spirits fled howling before him. He was the guardian of his people as well in temporal affairs. The governor Eustathius had taken a bribe to condemn to death three

* The alleged visit of St Nicholas to Jerusalem and other incidents are importations from the life of another Nicholas, bishop of Pinara during the sixth century. The confusion between the two was perpetuated by the Metaphrast, when he collected the legends in the tenth century. In 1751 a learned archbishop of Santa Severina, Falconi, volubly maintained that Nicholas of Myra and Nicholas of Pinara (or " the Zionite ") were identical, as Butler notes and refutes.

innocent men. At the time fixed for their execution Nicholas came to the place, stayed the hand of the executioner, and released the prisoners. Then he turned to Eustathius and did not cease to reproach him until he admitted his crime and expressed his penitence. There were present on this occasion three imperial officers who were on their way to duty in Phrygia. Later, when they were back again in Constantinople, the jealousy of the prefect Ablavius caused them to be imprisoned on false charges and an order for their death was procured from the Emperor Constantine. When the officers heard this they remembered the example they had witnessed of the powerful love of justice of the Bishop of Myra and they prayed to God that through his merits and by his instrumentality they might yet be saved. That night St Nicholas appeared in a dream to Constantine, and told him with threats to release the three innocent men, and Ablavius experienced the same thing. In the morning the emperor and the prefect compared notes, and the condemned men were sent for and questioned. When he heard that they had called on the name of the Nicholas of Myra who had appeared to him, Constantine set them free and sent them to the bishop with a letter asking him not to threaten him any more but to pray for the peace of the world. For long this was the most famous miracle of St Nicholas, and at the time of St Methodius was the only thing generally known about him.

The accounts are unanimous that St Nicholas died and was buried in his episcopal city of Myra, and by the time of Justinian there was a basilica built in his honour at Constantinople. An anonymous Greek wrote in the tenth century that, " the West as well as the East acclaims and glorifies him. Wherever there are people, in the country and the town, in the villages, in the isles, in the furthest parts of the earth, his name is revered and churches are built in his honour. Images of him are set up, panegyrics preached and festivals celebrated. All Christians, young and old, men and women, boys and girls, reverence his memory and call upon his protection. And his favours, which know no limit of time and continue from age to age, are poured out over all the earth : the Scythians know them, as do the Indians and the barbarians, the Africans as well as the Italians." When Myra and its great shrine finally passed into the hands of the Saracens, several Italian cities saw this as an opportunity to acquire the relics of St Nicholas for themselves. There was great competition for them between Venice and Bari. The last-named won, the relics were carried off under the noses of the lawful Greek custodians and their Mohammedan masters, and on May 9, 1087 were safely landed at Bari, a not inappropriate home seeing that Apulia in those days still had large Greek colonies. A new church was built to shelter them and the pope, Bd Urban II, was present at their enshrining. Devotion to St Nicholas was known in the West long before his relics were brought to Italy, but this happening naturally greatly increased his veneration among the people, and miracles were as freely attributed to his intercession in Europe as they had been in Asia. At Myra " the venerable body of the bishop, embalmed as it was in the good ointments of virtue, exuded a sweet-smelling ' myrrh ', which kept it from corruption and proved a health-giving remedy against sickness, to the glory of him who had glorified Jesus Christ, our true God." The translation of the relics did not interrupt this phenomenon, and the " manna of St Nicholas " is said to flow to this day. It was one of the great attractions which drew pilgrims to his tomb from all parts of Europe

It is the image of St Nicholas more often than that of any other that is found on Byzantine seals ; in the later middle ages nearly four hundred churches were dedicated in his honour in England alone ; and he is said to have been represented by Christian artists more frequently than any saint except our Lady. St Nicholas is venerated as the patron-saint of several classes of people, especially, in the East, of sailors and, in the West, of children. The first of these patronages is probably due to the legend that, during his life-time, he appeared to storm-tossed mariners who invoked his aid off the coast of Lycia, and brought them safely to port. Sailors in the Aegean and Ionian seas, following a common Eastern custom, had their " star of St Nicholas " and wished one another a good voyage in the phrase " May St Nicholas hold the tiller ". The legend of the " three children " gave rise to his patronage of children and various observances, ecclesiastical and secular, connected therewith ; such were the boy-bishop and, especially in Germany, Switzerland and the Netherlands, the giving of presents in his name at Christmas time. This custom in England is not a survival from Catholic times. It was popularized in America by the Dutch Protestants of New Amsterdam, who had converted the popish saint into a nordic magician (Santa Claus = Sint Klaes = Saint Nicholas) and was apparently introduced into this country by Bret Harte. It is not the only " good old English custom " which, however good, is not " old English ", at any rate in its present form. The deliverance of the three imperial officers naturally caused St Nicholas to be invoked by and on behalf of prisoners and captives, and many miracles of his intervention are recorded in the middle ages.

Curiously enough, the greatest popularity of St Nicholas is found neither in the eastern Mediterranean nor north-western Europe, great as that was, but in Russia. With St Andrew the Apostle he is patron of the nation, and the Russian Orthodox Church even observes the feast of his translation ; so many Russian pilgrims came to Bari before the revolution that their government supported a church, hospital and hospice there. He is a patron-saint also of Greece, Apulia, Sicily and Lorraine, and of many cities and dioceses (including Galway) and churches innumerable. At Rome the basilica of St Nicholas in the Jail of Tully (*in Carcere*) was founded between the end of the sixth and the beginning of the seventh centuries. He is named in the preparation of the Byzantine Mass. ˙

Two very able studies of St Nicholas and his cult have been published since 1900. The earlier is that of G. Anrich, *Hagios Nikolaos . . . in der griechischen Kirche* (2 vols., 1917). In this will be found all the Greek texts of any interest, much better edited than those in Falconius or Migne, as well as a full introduction and notes. The second work is that of K. Meisen, *Nikolauskult und Nikolausbrauch im Abendlande* (1931), with many pictorial illustrations. See on this the *Analecta Bollandiana*, vol. 1 (1932), pp. 178–181, where attention is drawn to the fact that one Latin text printed by Meisen is taken from a manuscript written in the ninth century, thus proving that the story of St Nicholas was already known in the West two hundred years before the translation of his relics to Bari. An imposing *Vie de S. Nicolas* by Jules Laroche should be read in the light of the criticisms in the *Analecta Bollandiana*, vol. xii, p. 459. On the folk-lore of St Nicholas among the Hellenes see further the book of N. G. Politis (in modern Greek) *Laographika symmikta* (1931), and on other aspects of the legend J. Dorn in *Archiv f. Kulturgeschichte*, vol. xiii (1917), especially p. 243 ; R. B. Yewdale, *Bohemond I, Prince of Antioch*, p. 31 ; Karl Young, *The Drama of the Medieval Church* (1933), *passim*. On the emblems of St Nicholas and his treatment in art, consult, besides Künstle, *Ikonographie*, vol. ii, and Drake, *Saints and their Emblems*, the monograph of D. van Adrichem, published both in Italian and in Dutch in 1928. The miraculous " manna " of St Nicholas still finds ardent champions ; *e.g.* in P. Scognamilio, *La Manna di San Nicola* (1925).

SS. DIONYSIA, MAJORICUS, AND OTHER MARTYRS   (A.D. 484)

IN the year 484 the Arian king, Huneric, banished the Catholic bishops from their African sees, and began a violent persecution of orthodox Christians, many of whom were put to death. Dionysia, a woman remarkable for beauty, zeal and piety, was scourged in the forum till her body was covered with blood. Seeing Majoricus, her young son, tremble at the sight, she said to him, " My son, do not forget that we have been baptized in the name of the Holy Trinity. We must not lose the garment of our salvation, lest the Master of the feast find us without wedding-raiment and cast us into outer darkness." The boy, strengthened by her words, suffered a most cruel martyrdom with constancy. St Dionysia's sister Dativa, her cousin Emilian, a physician, Leontia, Tertius and Boniface also suffered horrible torments for the faith, so that the Roman Martyrology says that they deserved to be joined to the number of Christ's holy confessors. SS. Dionysia, Majoricus and Dativa died at the stake and SS. Emilian and Tertius were flayed alive.

St Servus, who is commemorated on the following day, a man of Thuburbo, was tortured by the persecutors wit hthe utmost fury : he was hoisted in the air by pulleys and then pulled up and down so that he fell with all his weight on the pavement. Then he was dragged along the streets till his flesh and skin hung in strips from his body. At Cucusa there was among the martyrs and confessors a woman named Victoria, who was hung in the air whilst a fire was kindled under her. Her husband, who had apostatized from the Catholic faith, appealed to her in the most moving manner, urging her at least to have pity on her innocent babes and save herself by obeying the king. She would not listen, and turned her eyes away from her children. The executioners thought she was dead, and took her down ; but she came to herself, and afterwards related that a maiden had appeared to her, who touched every part of her broken body and healed it.

Of these martyrs we know practically nothing beyond what is narrated in the *Historia persecutionis provinciae africanae*, written by Victor, Bishop of Vita, who was a contemporary. No very marked *cultus* seems to be traceable. The names as a group do not occur in the Calendar of Carthage or in the *Hieronymianum*.

ST ABRAHAM, BISHOP OF KRATIA   (c. A.D. 558)

THE Lives of the Saints are full of examples of men who had offices of responsibility thrust upon them against their wishes, and in some cases, especially in the East, it is recorded that they subsequently ran away from them in an attempt, usually vain, to find peace and quietness for contemplation. Of these was this St Abraham. He was born at Emesa in Syria in the year 474 and became a monk there. When he was eighteen the community was broken up by raiding nomads, and he fled with his spiritual father to Constantinople. Here they found a home in a monastery of which the older monk became abbot and Abraham procurator. When he was only twenty-six his virtue and ability caused him to be made abbot of Kratia (Flaviopolis, now Geredeh) in Bithynia. At the end of ten years he fled away secretly into Palestine ; but his whereabouts became known and his bishop forced him to return to his duties. Soon after he was himself made bishop of Kratia and he fulfilled that office for thirteen years. Then he again ran away to Palestine and found a refuge in a monastery at the Tower of Eudokia. Here St Abraham led a most mortified life of prayer for over twenty years, and died about 558 without having been recalled to his diocese. He was the most noted of the bishops who occupied the see of Kratia from its beginnings in the third century until its extinction in the twelfth.

The original Greek text of the Life of Abraham by Cyril of Skythopolis, a contemporary, has been edited by H. Grégoire in the *Revue de l'Instruction publique en Belgique*, vol. xlix (1906), pp. 281–296 ; by K. Koikylides in the Greek periodical *Nea Sion*, vol. iv (1906), July, supplement, pp. 1–7 ; and by E. Schwartz in *Kyrillos von Skythopolis* (1939). These editions are founded on a single manuscript in the monastery of Mount Sinai which is unfortunately defective at the end, although an ancient Arabic version has preserved it complete ; on the first two see P. Peeters in the *Analecta Bollandiana*, vol. xxvi (1907), pp. 122–125, who in the same periodical, vol. xxiv (1905), pp. 349–356, had printed a Latin translation from the Arabic. The Arabic journal *Al Mashriq* in which it appeared supplies a curious illustration of the vexatious censorship then exercised in Syria by Moslem authority, for phrases in the ancient text were blacked out because they introduced titles consecrated to the dignity of the Sultan. On the topography, etc., of the Life of St Abraham see especially S. Vailhé in *Échos d'Orient*, vol. viii (1905), pp. 290–294.

BD PETER PASCUAL, Bishop of Jaén, Martyr (A.D. 1300)

THE Valencian family of Pascual or Pascualez (latinized as Paschasius) is said to have given the Church six martyrs under the Moors, of whom Bd Peter was the last. The child received his schooling from a tutor at home, which tutor was a priest of Narbonne, a doctor of divinity of Paris, whom Peter's parents had ransomed from the Moors. Peter went with him to Paris, and having finished his studies there, took the degree of doctor. He then returned to Valencia, and received holy orders at the age of twenty-four. He was a professor of theology at Barcelona until James I of Aragon chose him as tutor to his son, Sancho, who was soon after made archbishop of Toledo. The prince being too young to receive holy orders Bd Peter was appointed administrator of the diocese ; later he was named titular bishop of Granada, which was at that time in the hands of the Moors, but he did not receive episcopal consecration until he was appointed bishop of Jaén in 1296, when it was still under Moorish domination. In spite of all dangers he not only ransomed captives and instructed and comforted the Christians, but also preached to the infidels and reconciled to the Church several apostates, renegades and others. On this account he was seized while on a visitation, carried to Granada, and shut up in a dungeon, with orders that no one should be allowed to speak to him. He received money for his ransom, but with it bought the freedom of some who, he feared, were in danger of apostasy. In spite of solitary confinement he found means to write a treatise against Islam and its prophet, which was circulated among the people and stirred up the authorities to order his death. The night before he suffered he was afflicted with great fear, and was comforted by a vision of our Lord. The next morning whilst he was at prayer he was murdered, receiving stabs in his body, after which his head was struck off. He was seventy-three years old. This is the common tradition, but it appears that he died from the hardships of his captivity.

In 1673 Pope Clement X confirmed the *cultus* of Bd Peter Pascual, and his name was also inserted in the Roman Martyrology, where he is referred to as *Beatus*, though commonly called Saint.

The older lives, such as that of B. Amento y Peligero in folio (1676), are by no means reliable. The best materials are those published by Fr Fidel Fita in the *Boletin* of the

Historical Academy of Madrid, vol. xx (1892), pp. 32–61 ; cf. vol. xli (1902), pp. 345–347. For the general reader of Spanish the most thorough discussion of the problems involved is that of R. Rodriguez de Galvez, *San Pedro Pascual obispo de Jaén y martir* (1900), and see also the *Estudios Criticos* (1903) of the same author.   In these it is satisfactorily proved that Bd Peter was not a member of the Mercedarian Order, and it is shown that he most probably died of the hardships of his captivity, not stabbed or decapitated.   A bulky work has been published on the Mercedarian side by P. Armengol Valenzuela, *Vida de San Pedro Pascual* (1901), but the Bollandist reviewers consider it unconvincing.

7 : ST AMBROSE, Bishop of Milan, Doctor of the Church   (A.D. 397)

COURAGE and constancy in resisting evil is a necessary part of virtue, especially in a bishop, and in this quality St Ambrose was one of the most admirable among all the great pastors of God's Church since the Apostles, while his learning made him one of the four great doctors of the Western church. At the time of his birth at Trier, probably in 340, his father, whose name also was Ambrose, was prefect of Gaul.   Ambrose, senior, died while his youngest child was still young, and his widow returned with her family to Rome.   She took great care in the upbringing of her children, and Ambrose owed much both to her and to his sister, St Marcellina.   He learned Greek, became a good poet and orator, went to the bar, and was soon taken notice of, particularly by Anicius Probus and Symmachus, the last-named being prefect of Rome and still a pagan.   The other was praetorian prefect of Italy,' and in his court St Ambrose pleaded causes with so much success that Probus made choice of him to be his assessor.   Then the emperor Valentinian made him governor of Liguria and Aemilia, with his residence at Milan.   His patron, Probus, with unconscious suitability, said to him at parting : " Go ; and govern more like a bishop than a judge."   The office to which he had been promoted, with full consular rank, was one of the most respon- sible and important in the Western empire, and Ambrose was not yet forty.   With what success he administered his charge for some two years the sequel shows.

Auxentius, an Arian, who had held the see of Milan for almost twenty years, died in 374.   The city was distracted by party strife about the election of a new bishop, some demanding an Arian, others a Catholic.   To prevent, if possible, too outrageous a disorder St Ambrose went to the church in which the assembly was held.   There he made a speech to the people, exhorting them to proceed in their choice in the spirit of peace and without tumult.   While he was speaking a voice cried out : " Ambrose, bishop ! "   The whole assembly took up the cry with enthusiasm, and Catholics and Arians unanimously proclaimed him bishop of Milan.   This unexpected choice astounded Ambrose, the more that, though professedly a Christian, he was still unbaptized.   But in face of the popular clamour the bishops of the province ratified the election, whereupon the bishop elect remarked caustically that " Emotion had overruled canon law ", and tried to escape from Milan.   A relation of all that had passed was sent to the emperor, and Ambrose wrote also on his own behalf, asking that he might be excused.   Valen- tinian answered that it gave him the greatest pleasure that he had chosen governors who were fit for the episcopal office ; and at the same time sent an order to the *vicarius* of the province to see that the election took place.   In the meantime Ambrose once more tried to escape, and hid himself in the house of the senator Leontius, who, when he heard the imperial decision, gave him up, and Ambrose at last yielded.   He therefore was baptized, and received episcopal consecration a week later, on December 7, 374.   He was about thirty-five years old.

Considering that he was no longer a man of this world and resolving to break all ties which could hold him to it, he gave his movables to the poor and his lands and estates to the Church, reserving only an income for the use of his sister, St Marcellina.   The care of his temporalities he committed to his brother, St Satyrus, that he might be free to give himself up wholly to his ministry.   Soon after his ordination he wrote to Valentinian a severe complaint against some of the imperial magistrates.   To which the emperor replied : " I was long since acquainted with your freedom of speech, which did not hinder me from consenting to your election. Continue to apply to our sins the remedies prescribed by the divine law."   St Basil also wrote to congratulate him, or rather the Church, upon his promotion and to exhort him vigorously to oppose the Arians.   St Ambrose was acutely conscious of his ignorance of theological science, and at once applied himself to study the Holy Scriptures and the works of religious writers, particularly Origen and St Basil. For these studies he put himself under the instruction of St Simplician, a learned Roman priest, whom he loved as a friend, honoured as a father and reverenced as a master.   He purged the diocese of the Arian heresy with such success that in ten years there was not one citizen of Milan infected with it, except a few Goths and some of those belonging to the imperial household.*   His personal life was one of simplicity and hard work ; he dined only on Sundays, the feasts of certain famous martyrs, and all Saturdays, on which it was the custom at Milan never to fast (but when he was at Rome he fasted on Saturdays) ; he excused himself from going to banquets, and entertained others with decent frugality.   Every day he offered the Holy Sacrifice for his people, and devoted himself entirely to the service of his flock, any member of which could see and speak with him at any time, so that his people loved and admired him.   It was his rule never to have any hand in making matches, never to persuade anyone to serve in the army, and never recommend to places at court.   St Augustine, when he came to visit him, sometimes found him so overwhelmed with callers, or so busy in the few moments he was able to get to himself, that he went into his room and after some stay came out again, without being noticed by the bishop.   Ambrose in his discourses frequently spoke in praise of the state and virtue of virginity undertaken for God's sake, and he had many consecrated virgins under his direction.   At the request of his sister, St Marcellina, he collected his sermons on this subject, making thereby a famous treatise.   Mothers tried to keep their daughters away from his sermons, and he was charged with trying to depopulate the empire.   " What man, I want to know, ever wanted to marry and could not find a wife ? " he retorted, and maintained that the population is highest where maidenhood is most esteemed.   Wars, he said, and not maidens, are the destroyers of the human race.

The Goths having invaded Roman territories in the East, the Emperor Gratian determined to lead an army to the succour of his uncle, Valens.   But in order to guard himself against Arianism, of which Valens was the protector, he asked St Ambrose for instruction against that heresy.   He accordingly wrote in 377 the work entitled *To Gratian, concerning the Faith*, which he afterwards expanded. The Goths had extended their ravages from Thrace to Illyricum, and St Ambrose, not content to lay out all the money he could raise in redeeming captives, employed

* Milan was in fact the administrative capital of the West at this time.   The imperial court had been moved thither in 303, under Maximian.

gold vessels belonging to the Church, which he had melted down. The Arians reproached him for this, alleging sacrilege. He answered that he thought it more expedient to save the souls of men than gold ; ransom is the significance of the pouring of the blood of Jesus into golden vessels ; and " If the Church possesses gold it is in order to use it for the needy, not to keep it ". After the murder of Gratian in 383 the Empress Justina implored St Ambrose to treat with the usurper Maximus lest he attack her son, Valentinian II. He went and induced Maximus at Trier to confine himself to Gaul, Spain and Britain. This is said to have been the first occasion on which a minister of the gospel was called on to interfere in matters of high politics : and it was to vindicate right and order against a usurper in arms.

At this time certain senators at Rome attempted to restore the cult of the goddess of Victory. At their head appeared Quintus Aurelius Symmachus, son and successor of that prefect of the city who had patronized the young Ambrose, and an admirable scholar, statesman and orator. This man presented a request to Valentinian begging that the altar of Victory might be re-established in the senate-house ; to it he ascribed the victories and prosperity of ancient Rome. It was a skilfully drawn and in some respects moving document, and made use of several arguments that are still familiar in the mouths of non-Catholics. " What does it matter ", for example, " the way in which each seeks for truth ? There must be more than one road to the great mystery." The petition was particularly a covert attack on St Ambrose, and he, having privately received notice of it, wrote to Valentinian demanding that a copy of Symmachus's petition should be communicated to him. He remonstrated at the same time with the emperor for not having at once consulted him, since it was a matter of religion. He then drew up a reply whose eloquence surpassed that of Symmachus, traversing him at every point. From ridiculing the suggestion that what was achieved by military valour was due to the entrails of sacrificed cattle he rose to heights of rhetoric, speaking as by the mouth of Rome herself, who bewails the errors of her past but is not ashamed in her old age to change with a changing world. He appeals to Symmachus and his friends to learn the mysteries of nature from God who created it, and, instead of asking the emperors to give their gods peace, to ask God to give the emperors peace ; and ends with a parable of progress and development in the world. " Through justice truth has prevailed on the ruins of opinions that once ruled the earth." Both documents, that of Symmachus and that of Ambrose, were read before Valentinian in council. There was no discussion. Then the emperor spoke : " My father did not take away the altar. Nor was he asked to put it back. I therefore follow him in changing nothing that was done before my time."

The Empress Justina dared not openly espouse the interests of the Arians during the lives of her husband and of Gratian, but when the peace which St Ambrose arranged between Maximus and her son gave her an opportunity to oppose the Catholic bishop, she forgot the obligations which she had to him. When Easter was near, in 385, she induced Valentinian to demand the Portian basilica, now called St Victor's, outside Milan, for the use of the Arians, herself and many officers of the court. The saint replied that he could never give up the temple of God. By messengers Valentinian then demanded the new basilica of the Apostles ; but the bishop was inflexible. Officers of the court were sent to take possession of the basilica, and the citizens, enraged at these proceedings, seized an Arian priest in the street. St Ambrose, informed of this, prayed that God would suffer no blood to be shed, and sent out priests and deacons who delivered the Arian from the mob. Throughout these troubles, when St Ambrose had the bulk of the excited people and even of the army on his side, he was studiously careful to say or do nothing that would precipitate violence or endanger the position of the emperor and his mother. He was resolute in his refusal to give up the churches, but would not himself officiate in either for fear of creating disturbance. Every effort was made by his adversaries to provoke him, and they commonly referred to him as " the Tyrant ".* " How am I a tyrant ? " he asked. " When I was told the church was surrounded with soldiers, I said : ' I cannot give it up, but I must not fight.' Maximus, whom I stopped from marching into Italy, does not say that I am the tyrant over Valentinian." While he was expounding a passage of Job to the people in a chapel, a party of soldiers, who had been sent to take charge of the larger basilica, came in. They had refused to obey orders and wished to pray with the Catholics. At once the people surged into the adjoining basilica, and tore down the decorations put up for the emperor's visit, giving them to the children to play with. But Ambrose refused a triumph, and did not enter the church himself until Easter day, when Valentinian had ordered the guards to be removed, upon which all joined in joy and thanksgiving. St Ambrose gave an account of these events to Marcellina, who was then at Rome, and adds that he foresees greater commotions. " The eunuch, Calligone," he writes, " an imperial chamberlain, said to me : ' You despise Valentinian. I will cut off your head.' To which I replied : ' May God permit it. Then I shall suffer as a bishop should, and you will act according to your kind ! ' "

In January of the following year Justina persuaded her son to make a law authorizing the religious assemblies of the Arians and, in effect, proscribing those of the Catholics. It forbade anyone, under pain of death, to oppose Arian assemblies, and no one could so much as present a petition against a church being yielded up to them without danger of being proscribed. St Ambrose disregarded the law, would not give up a single church, and no one dare touch him. " I have said what a bishop ought to say ; let the emperor do what an emperor ought to do. Naboth would not give up the inheritance of his ancestors, and shall I give up that of Jesus Christ ? " On Palm Sunday he preached on not giving up their churches, and then, fears being entertained for his life, the people barricaded themselves in the basilica with their pastor. The imperial troops surrounded the place to starve them out, but on Easter Sunday they were still there. To occupy their time Ambrose taught the people psalms and hymns composed by himself, which they sang at his direction divided into two choirs singing alternate stanzas. Then Dalmatius, a tribune, came to St Ambrose from the emperor, with an order that he should choose judges, as the Arian bishop, Auxentius, had done on his side, that his and Auxentius's cause might be tried before them ; if he refused, he was forthwith to retire and yield his see to Auxentius. Ambrose wrote asking to be excused and forcibly reminding Valentinian that laymen (lay-judges had been stipulated) could not judge bishops or make ecclesiastical laws. Then he occupied his episcopal *cathedra* and related to the people all that had passed between him and Valentinian during the previous year. And in a memorable sentence he summed up the principle at stake : " The emperor is in the Church, not over it."

In the meanwhile it became known that Maximus, using Valentinian's persecution of Catholics and alleged frontier irregularities as pretexts, was preparing

* Not in the modern sense, but meaning one who had seized power by force.

to invade Italy. Valentinian and Justina were panic-stricken, and asked St Ambrose to venture on a second embassy to stop the march of a usurper. Burying the memory both of public and private injuries he undertook the journey. At Trier Maximus refused to admit him to audience except in public consistory, though he was both bishop and imperial ambassador. When, therefore, he was introduced into the consistory and Maximus rose to give him a kiss, Ambrose stood still and refused to approach to receive it. And there, publicly, he demonstrated to Maximus that his projected offensive was unjustifiable and a breach of faith, and ended up by asking him to send the remains of Gratian to his brother as pledge of peace. Already on his arrival St Ambrose had refused to hold communion with the court prelates who had connived at the execution of the heretic Priscillian, which meant with Maximus himself, and the next day he was ordered to leave Trier. He therefore returned to Milan, writing in advance to Valentinian an account of events and advising him to be cautious how he treated with Maximus, a concealed enemy who pretended peace but intended war. Then Maximus suddenly and without opposition marched into Italy. Leaving St Ambrose alone to meet the storm at Milan, Justina and Valentinian fled to Greece and threw themselves on the mercy of the Eastern emperor, Theodosius. He declared war on Maximus, defeated and executed him in Pannonia, and restored Valentinian to his own territories and to those of the dead usurper. But from henceforward Theodosius was the real ruler of the whole empire.

He stayed for a time at Milan, inducing Valentinian to abandon Arianism and to have respect for St Ambrose as a true Catholic bishop. But, as was almost inevitable, conflicts arose between Theodosius himself and Ambrose, in the first of which right does not seem to have been wholly on the side of the bishop. At Kallinikum, in Mesopotamia, certain Christians pulled down the Jewish synagogue. Theodosius when informed of the affair ordered the bishop (who was alleged to be directly implicated) to rebuild the synagogue. St Ambrose was appealed to, and he wrote a letter to Theodosius in which he based his protest, not on the uncertainty of the actual circumstances, but on the excessive statement that no Christian bishop could in any conditions pay for the erection of a building to be used for false worship. Theodosius disregarded the protest, and Ambrose preached against him to his face; whereupon a discussion took place between them in the church, and he would not go up to the altar to sing Mass till he had procured a promise of the revocation of the order.

In the year 390 news of a dreadful massacre committed at Thessalonica was brought to Milan. Butheric, the governor, had a charioteer put in prison for having seduced a servant in his family, and refused to release him when his appearance in the circus was demanded by the public. The people were so enraged that some officers were stoned to death and Butheric himself was slain. Theodosius ordered reprisals of unbelievable savagery. While the people were assembled in the circus, soldiers surrounded it and rushed in on them. The slaughter continued for hours and seven thousand were massacred, without distinguishing age or sex or the innocent from the guilty. The world was aghast and all eyes were turned on Ambrose, who took counsel with his fellow bishops. Then he wrote Theodosius a noble letter, exhorting him to penance,* and declaring that he neither could nor would receive his offering at the altar or celebrate the Divine Mysteries before him

---

* *I.e.* not only interior penitence, but also the public canonical penance which the Church then imposed on open and notorious evil-doers.

till that obligation was satisfied. " What has been done at Thessalonica is unparalleled in the memory of man. . . . You are human, and temptation has overtaken you. Overcome it. I counsel, I beseech, I implore you to penance. You, who have so often been merciful and pardoned the guilty, have now caused many innocent to perish. The devil wished to wrest from you the crown of piety which was your chiefest glory. Drive him from you while you can. . . . I write this to you with my own hand that you also may read it alone."

The upshot of this appeal to a man who can hardly have been other than conscience-stricken has unfortunately been obscured by a picturesque and melodramatic story that Theodosius refused to do penance, and that St Ambrose met him in the narthex of the church when he came to Mass with his court, publicly rebuked him, and refused him admittance ; and that the emperor remained excommunicate for eight months until he made a complete submission. This legend has been demolished by Father Van Ortroy, S.J., and the simple words in which St Augustine (who had received baptism from St Ambrose three years before) refers to the emperor's " religious humility " tell us all we really need to know. " Being laid hold of by the discipline of the Church, he did penance in such a way that the sight of the abasement of his imperial dignity made those who were interceding for him weep more than consciousness of offence had ever made them fear his anger." In the funeral oration over Theodosius, St Ambrose himself says simply that : " He stripped himself of every sign of royalty and bewailed his sin openly in church. He, an emperor, was not ashamed to do the public penance which lesser individuals shrink from, and to the end of his life he never ceased to grieve for his error." By this triumph of grace in Theodosius and of pastoral duty in Ambrose Christianity was vindicated to the world as being no respecter of persons, its moral law was shown to bind all equally. And the emperor himself testified to the personal influence of St Ambrose in it ; he was, he said, the only bishop he knew who was worthy of the name.

Theodoret mentions another example of humility and religion on the part of Theodosius whilst he was at Milan. During Mass on a festival, having brought his offering to the altar, he remained within the rails of the sanctuary. St Ambrose asked if he wanted anything. The emperor said that he stayed to assist at the Holy Mysteries and to communicate. Thereupon Ambrose sent his deacon to tell him, " My lord, it is lawful for none but the sacred ministers to remain within the sanctuary. Be pleased therefore to go out and stand with the rest. The purple robe makes princes, but not priests." Theodosius apologized and answered that he thought the custom was the same at Milan as at Constantinople, where his place was in the sanctuary ; and after having thanked the bishop for his instruction he went and took his place among the laity.*

In 393 occurred the pathetic death of the young Valentinian, murdered by Arbogastes while alone among his enemies in Gaul. St Ambrose had set out to succour him, but met his funeral procession before he had crossed the Alps. Arbogastes manoeuvred for the support of Ambrose for his ambitions (he had been told that the bishop was a " man who says to the sun ' Stop ! ' and it stops "). But Ambrose had made it clear, without any personal denunciation, in his funeral

---

* Later it became part of the plan of every Byzantine church to have the representation of a two-headed eagle on the floor outside the sanctuary. This was the place of the imperial throne. Such eagles may still be seen in the East. The Latin direction *ad aquilam chori* has nothing to do with this, but refers to the lectern with its eagle-shaped desk.

sermon what he thought of the death of Valentinian, and he left Milan before the arrival of Eugenius, the imperial nominee of Arbogastes, who now openly boasted the approaching overthrow of Christianity. St Ambrose meanwhile went from city to city, strengthening the people against the invaders. Then he returned to his see and there received the letter of Theodosius announcing his victory over Arbogastes at Aquileia, the final blow to the old paganism within the empire. A few months later Theodosius himself died, in the arms of St Ambrose, who in a funeral oration spoke eloquently of his love for the dead emperor and of the high obligations of his two sons in the control of an empire which was now held together by Christianity itself. Those two sons were the feeble creatures Arcadius and Honorius. And there was perhaps present in the church a certain young Goth, a cavalry officer in the imperial army. His name was Alaric.

St Ambrose survived Theodosius the Great by only two years, and one of his last treatises was on the " Goodness of Death ". His written works, mostly homiletical in origin, exegetical, theological, ascetical and poetical,* were numerous; as the Roman empire declined in the West he inaugurated a new lease of life for its language, and in the service of Christianity. When he fell sick he foretold his death, but said he should live till Easter. He continued his usual studies, and expounded the forty-third psalm. Whilst he dictated, Paulinus, who was his secretary and afterwards his biographer, saw as it were a flame in the form of a small shield covering his head and by degrees passing into his mouth, and his face became white as snow. " I was so frightened ", says Paulinus, " that I remained motionless and could not write. And on that day he left off both writing and dictating, so that he did not finish the psalm". We have this exposition of St Ambrose upon the forty-third psalm, and it ends with the twenty-fourth verse. After having ordained a bishop for Pavia, he was so ill that he took to his bed. At this news Count Stilicho, the guardian of Honorius, was much troubled, and said publicly, " The day that this man dies, destruction hangs over Italy". And he sent messengers to persuade Ambrose to pray for greater length of days. He replied to them, " I have not so behaved myself among you that I should be ashamed to live longer ; nor am I afraid to die, for we have a good Master ". On the day of his death he lay with his hands extended in the form of a cross for several hours, moving his lips in constant prayer. St Honoratus of Vercelli was there, resting in another room, when he seemed to hear a voice crying three times to him, " Arise ! Make haste ! He is going". He went down and gave him the Body of the Lord, and soon after St Ambrose was dead. It was Good Friday, April 4, 397, and he was about fifty-seven years old. He was buried on Easter day, and his relics rest under the high altar of his basilica, where they were buried in 835. The day of his feast is the anniversary of his episcopal consecration, on which date it is also kept in the Eastern church ; and he is named daily in the canon of the Mass of the Milanese province.

Two highly important works dealing with the life and writings of St Ambrose are the book of J. R. Palanque, *Saint Ambroise et l'Empire romain* (1933), regarding which consult the review by Fr Halkin in the *Analecta Bollandiana*, vol. lii (1934), pp. 395–401 ; and an Anglican biography by Canon F. Homes Dudden, *The Life and Times of St Ambrose* (1935) in two volumes. Both these works discuss the career of the saint from many points of view and with a competent knowledge both of the sources and of modern contributions to the subject. The main sources are the holy doctor's own writings and the life by Paulinus ;

* The Breviary hymn *Aeterne rerum conditor* is certainly St Ambrose's, and others are ascribed to him with greater or less degrees of probability.

but there is, of course, much material to be gleaned from St Augustine and other contemporaries, as well as from what Fr Van Ortroy has called " les vies grecques de S. Ambroise " : his important essay forms part of a valuable collection of studies published in 1897 to do honour to the fifteenth centenary of the death of the saint. Here, under the name *Ambrosiana*, we have contributions from many scholars, including one from Dr Achille Ratti (later Pope Pius XI) and others from Marucchi, Savio, Schenkl, Mocquereau, etc. See further R. Wirtz, *Ambrosius und seine Zeit* (1924) ; M. R. McGuire in *Catholic Historical Review*, vol. xxii (1936), pp. 304–318 ; W. Wilbrand in *Historisches Jahrbuch*, vol. xli (1921), pp. 1–19 ; L. T. Lefort in *Le Muséon*, vol. xlviii (1935), pp. 55–73 ; Fliche et Martin, *Histoire de l'Église*, vol. iii (1936), etc. A short *Life of St Ambrose* (Eng. trans.) by the Duc de Broglie, in the series " Les Saints ", though not in all respects up to date, gives a good impression of the saint and his times. A fuller bibliography may be found in Palanque and Dudden as well as in the last edition of Bardenhewer, *Geschichte der altkirchlichen Literatur*, vol. iii. The contemporary life of St Ambrose by the deacon Paulinus is translated by F. R. Hoare in *The Western Fathers* (1954).

ST EUTYCHIAN, POPE   (A.D. 283)

OF this pope practically nothing is known. Though called a martyr in the Roman Martyrology, this is unlikely, as is the statement that he buried 342 martyrs with his own hands, for there was no persecution of Christians in his time ; moreover, he is listed among the bishops, not among the martyrs, in the fourth-century Liberian catalogue. The attribution to him of blessing fruits of the earth in church is an anachronism—this did not come till later ; and the decretals which bear his name are spurious.

St Eutychian died on December 7, 283, and was buried in the catacomb of Callistus. Fragments of his epitaph were found by De Rossi : they contained in Greek letters the words EUTUKHIANOS EPIS[KOPOS].

See Duchesne, *Liber Pontificalis*, vol. i, p. 159.

ST JOSEPHA ROSSELLO, VIRGIN, FOUNDRESS OF THE DAUGHTERS OF OUR LADY OF MERCY   (A.D. 1880)

IT has often been said of wonder-working saints that no miracles of which they were the agents were more remarkable than their own lives. A writer about Sister Mary Josepha Rossello, Dr P. D. Sessa, points out that her life (so far as is known) was not marked by visions, heavenly voices, or other marvels ; but there was the no less striking fact that the three sisters with which her congregation began increased in a few years to over a hundred, and that the first little house became the mother of sixty-eight affiliations during her lifetime.

St Josepha was born in 1811 at Albisola Marina, a pleasant little town on the Ligurian coast of Italy. She was the fourth of the nine children of Bartholomew Rossello and his wife Mary Dedone, Bartholomew being a potter by trade, and they named her Benedetta, a choice of good augury. Benedetta was a lively and intelligent child, and Dr Sessa refers to her in her early years as *piccola condottiera*, " little leader ". But the word *condottiere* has in history another meaning, " freebooter ", and indeed there seems to have been an element of dashing enterprise, such as one associates with, *e.g.* Sir John Hawkwood, in Benedetta's make-up. It was illustrated in her childhood by the incident of the pilgrimage. A visit of the people of Albisola was organized to the shrine of our Lady of Mercy at Savona, and because of the distance all children were left at home. In their parents' absence Benedetta Rossello got up a pilgrimage of her own among her playmates, both girls and boys ; headed by a banner—an apron on a broomstick—they went in procession to pray at the little local sanctuary of our Lady of Mercy. On the way back they sang hymns and, hearing them, the sacristan thought it was the Savona pilgrims returning and gave the signal for the church bells to be rung. So the children's crusade had a triumphal return, as was only right and proper. Benedetta seems to have been about nine at the time of this performance.

She was always sensitive to the beauty of created things, especially of the sea and at certain times of the day, when it would arouse in her sudden unexpected bursts of gaiety. Naturally then she had a fellow-feeling for St Francis of Assisi, and when she was sixteen she was received into his third order and came under the spiritual guidance of a Capuchin friar, Father Angelo of Savona. For a time she wished to become a solitary, but her director dissuaded her, and when she was nineteen she took service with the Monleone family in Savona. " The hands are made for work, and the heart for God ", she said, and her work for the next seven years was to look after Mr Monleone, who was an invalid. The money she earned she sent home, for her family had got rather badly off. She could have stayed in the comfortable home of the Monleones for the rest of her life, but when her patient died her desire to " leave the world " revived more strongly than ever.

At this time the bishop of Savona was Mgr Augustine de Mari ; he was very perturbed by the dangers and dissolute life that beset many girls and young women in the city, and wanted to initiate work on their behalf. This came to the ears of Benedetta Rossello. She had already been refused by one convent for lack of a dowry, so she called on the bishop and offered her services. He was impressed by her appearance and manner, and accepted her offer. On August 10, 1837, Benedetta, her cousins Angela and Dominica Pescio, and a fourth, named Pauline Barla, took up their residence in a shabby house called the Commenda in Windy Street at Savona. They called themselves the Daughters of our Lady of Mercy, and Benedetta took the names Mary Josepha. Their endowment was a very little furniture, a straw mattress each on the floor, a sack of potatoes and four shillings and twopence ; there was also a crucifix and a statue of our Lady. Their work was to instruct poor girls, especially in the things that pertain to God, and later on to open hostels, schools and hospitals—in fact, to do works of mercy under the inspiration of divine compassion.

The congregation was formally inaugurated in October of the same year. The first canonical superioress was Sister Angela, Sister Josepha being mistress of novices and almoner ; in 1840 she was elected to the first place, and remained there for the rest of her life. The community outgrew its first quarters, and moved into a rented mansion that became the mother house, the core of the huge group of buildings that forms the *casa generalizia* in Savona today. One of Mother Josepha's early trials was the death of the good and generous Mgr de Mari, especially as the vicar capitular was hostile to her community ; but the new bishop, when he was appointed after considerable delay, proved to be of Mgr de Mari's mind. It was he who approved the rule of the congregation in 1846, when it numbered thirty-five members; it had already, under difficulties, sent out its first colony, to work in the municipal schools and hospital at Varazze. From then on it spread to many other places in northern Italy. Not, of course, without its troubles. Sometimes there was opposition ; Mother Josepha's health broke down, and the bishop had to insist that she should go away for a rest ; and there were money difficulties. These last were partly met by two unexpected legacies, one being from Mother Josepha's old friend and employer, Mrs Monleone.

It had always been a project of Mgr de Mari that there should be rescue-homes for young women who had gone astray, and Mother Josepha had not forgotten it. In spite of a discouraging first experiment at Genoa, she eventually succeeded in establishing three such homes, which she called Houses of Divine Providence ; one of them was in her own birthplace, Albisola, where it was housed in the building that had been the home of Ferdinand Isola, a Franciscan slain out of hatred of the faith by the Turks at Skutari in 1648.   It was said of Mother Josepha that whenever she had five pounds to spare she always wanted to found something new.   One of these new enterprises was a House of Clerics to foster and help on vocations to the priesthood.   Mother Josepha's energy and foresight were too much for many of the clergy, who strongly opposed this innovation ; but she succeeded in winning over the bishop, Mgr Cerruti.   Not only did he allow the House of Clerics to remain open, but his successor, Mgr Boraggini, actively encouraged it.   Then, in 1875, came the first foundation in America, when a company of the Daughters of Our Lady of Mercy, with the blessing and recommendation of St. John Bosco, left for Buenos Aires ;   soon their schools, hospitals, rescue-homes and other works were flourishing in the New World.

The portrait of St Josepha in her later years shows a firmly moulded face, full of energy, but calm, with just a touch of obstinacy—a characteristic type of " Victorian " old lady.   In fact, those of the present writer's generation might well say on seeing it, " She looks like my old grandmother ".   She was one of those saints whose grandeur of soul was joined to a complete simplicity of outlook. The foundress of numerous convents and their charitable establishments was never more herself than when she was sweeping the floors, polishing the tables or doing the washing-up.   When she was sixty-four the effects of her unremitting toil began seriously to tell ;   she developed a weakness of the heart and lost the use of her legs, so that she could only oversee the work of others and no longer take an active part in it herself.   This depressed her sadly.   " I'm a useless burden ", she said, " always getting in people's way ".   And together with this trial she was visited with a " dark night of the spirit ", beset by numberless scruples and convinced that she was fit only for eternal reprobation.   But her faith was equal to her apparent forsakenness.   " Cling to Jesus ", she repeated over and over again to her community.   " There are God, the soul, eternity ; the rest is nothing ".   Josepha Rossella went to her reward, peacefully and with humble confidence, on December 7, 1880.   She was sixty-nine years old.   Her canonization took place in 1949.

A life of St Josepha by Katherine Burton was published privately.   Her collaborator Francis Martinengo wrote her life in Italian, and a useful sketch by Dr Piera Delfino Sessa was published at Turin in 1938.   As a tertiary of their order, Josepha is included among the Franciscan saints.

8 : THE IMMACULATE CONCEPTION OF THE BLESSED VIRGIN MARY

BY the bull *Ineffabilis Deus* of December 8, 1854, Pope Pius IX, by an exercise of his supreme pontifical power of infallible teaching, pronounced and defined it to be " a doctrine revealed by God and therefore to be believed firmly and constantly by all the faithful that the Blessed Virgin Mary in the first instant of her conception was, by an unique grace and privilege of Almighty God in view of the merits of Jesus Christ the Saviour of the human race, preserved exempt from all stain of original sin." That is to say that her soul at the first moment of its creation and infusion into her body was clothed in sanctifying grace, which to every other child of Adam is only given in the first instance after birth and, since Christ, at baptism (though it is generally held that Jeremias and St John Baptist received it before birth, but not at conception); the stain of original sin was not removed but excluded from her soul. For two hundred and fifty years before this solemn definition the doctrine of the Immaculate Conception had been universally believed in the Church (it was, of course, implicit in the deposit of faith from the beginning) and public teaching to the contrary was forbidden; but it was not " of faith " (it had somewhat the same position as the doctrine of the Assumption of our Lady held until 1950). It is therefore found that Alban Butler writes on this day under the heading simply of the " Conception of the Blessed Virgin Mary ", and says that " it is the most generally received belief, though not defined as an article of faith, that in her very conception she was immaculate. Many prelates and a great number of Catholic universities have declared themselves in strong terms in favour of this doctrine; and several popes have severely forbidden any one to impugn or to dispute or write against it. Nevertheless, it is forbidden to rank it among articles of faith defined by the Church, or to censure those who ' *privately* hold the contrary '." But, he goes on, it is sufficient for us, who desire as dutiful sons of the Church to follow her direction in all such points, that she manifestly favours this opinion. . . . " The very respect which we owe to the Mother of God and the honour due to her divine Son incline us to believe this privilege most suitable to her state of spotless holiness." Since Pius IX spoke in 1854 the reservations mentioned by Butler have ceased to exist and every Catholic is bound to believe by divine faith that the doctrine of the Immaculate Conception is true.

A liturgical feast commemorating the conception of our Lady by the power of her father in the womb of her mother (without any reference to Mary's sinlessness) seems to have been originally celebrated in Palestine; and there is much reason to believe that the idea of this conception feast for our Lady was suggested by the earlier existence of a conception feast for St John Baptist, which is found at the beginning of the seventh century. For a long time the expression Conception of Mary was taken to mean the conception of our incarnate Lord within her womb by the power of the Holy Ghost (which we celebrate on the feast of the Annunciation), and consequently the new feast referred to was called the Conception of (or by) St Anne.* In the ninth century it was imported to southern Italy and Sicily from Constantinople, still called the Conception of St Anne† and with no idea of the *immaculate* conception. The first clear evidences of a feast of the

* It is a quite understandable error among non-Catholics not informed on the matter that the expression Immaculate Conception refers to the virginal conception of our Lord.

† The feast has maintained this name in the East and even the Catholic Byzantines call it officially the " Child-begetting of the holy Anne, mother of the Mother of God ", and keep it on December 9, the original Eastern date. But, of course, it is for them now the same feast as our Immaculate Conception. The dissident Eastern churches have no official teaching about the doctrine: some theologians have repudiated it, others have taught it. The people probably believe it, at least implicitly. The original Russian sect of Old Believers is said to have professed it formally. The calendar of the Anglican Book of Common Prayer still has the " Conception of the Virgin Mary " on December 8.

Conception of our Lady, and under that name, in the West come from England, at Winchester, Canterbury and Exeter just before the Norman Conquest. This was identified with December 8 ;* and when we remember that in Jerusalem and Constantinople, and also in Naples, December 9 was the day assigned for this observance it seems probable that the determining influence came from the East.

In England, again as in the East, the observance began in the monasteries, and its first two mentions are found in calendars of the abbey called the New Minster, at Winchester. It met with opposition as an innovation. But a disciple of St Anselm, the monk Eadmer, wrote an important treatise on our Lady's conception, and the archbishop's nephew, another Anselm, introduced the feast of the Conception into his own abbey at Bury St Edmunds. It was soon taken up by Saint Albans, Reading, Gloucester and others. Some monks of Westminster, where the prior, Osbert of Clare, favoured the feast, challenged its lawfulness, but it was approved by a synod in London in 1129. At the same time the feast began to spread in Normandy, though whether it was first brought there from England or from southern Italy, then in Norman occupation, is not clear.

The adoption of the feast in the cathedral church of Lyons, about the year 1140, was the occasion of a protest by St Bernard which precipitated a theological controversy that was to last for three hundred years, the point at issue being the moment at which the sanctification of Mary took place. But however the controversy fluctuated from one to another of its several sides, the observance of the feast of the Conception of our Lady steadily progressed. In 1263 it was adopted by the whole Order of Friars Minor, who became the great defenders of the Immaculate Conception, whereas the Dominican theologians generally opposed it. But in spite of its popularity in England, Canterbury did not adopt the feast until 1328, and it was not till 1476 that the Franciscan pope, Sixtus IV, officially adopted it for the Roman church. The feast was still of the Conception of the Immaculate One rather than of the Immaculate Conception as we understand it, though, as Butler pertinently notes, the sanctification of our Lady rather than her bare conception is the object of the Church's devotion. But in 1661 Pope Alexander VII declared that the feast celebrated the immunity of our Lady from original sin in the first moment of the creation of her soul and its infusion into her body, *i.e.* the moment of " passive conception " in the sense of the Catholic doctrine. In 1708 Pope Clement XI imposed the festival on the whole Western church as a feast of precept.

After the solemn definition of the dogma in 1854 the name of the feast was altered to the Immaculate Conception of the Blessed Virgin Mary, and nine years later a new Mass and Office in accordance therewith was prescribed. Since then, and indeed for some time before, the veneration of our Lady as immaculately conceived has become one of the most popular aspects of Marian devotion. Of the eighteen dioceses of England and Wales, ten have our Lady as conceived sinless for their principal patron, and she was declared patroness of the United States under this title by the first Council of Baltimore eight years before the definition. Hundreds of churches throughout the world are dedicated to God in honour of our Lady so regarded.

There is, of course, an immense literature connected with the doctrine of the Immaculate Conception and with its liturgical celebration. Perhaps the fullest account is furnished in

* The date was fixed by the feast of the Birthday of our Lady, nine months before September 8. Why this date was selected for the birthday is not known.

the article by Fathers Le Bachelet and Jugie in DTC., vol. vii, which runs to over three hundred and fifty columns. See also on the feast Fr Thurston in *The Month*, 1904, May, June, July and December, with E. Bishop's criticisms in the *Bosworth Psalter*, pp. 43–51, and *Liturgica historica*, pp. 238–259 ; and on the entry in early Irish calendars, Fr Grosjean's very important " note " in *Analecta Bollandiana*, vol. lxi (1943), pp. 91–95, where he shows that these entries got into certain manuscripts " par une bévue de copiste ". There are two valuable articles on the feast in the Byzantine church in *Bessarione*, September and December 1904. The first well-considered theological treatise arguing soberly that our Lady's conception was immaculate is that of Eadmer, the devoted adherent and biographer of St Anselm, though in this he departs from the view held by the saint himself. The text with other matter was critically edited in Slater and Thurston, *Eadmeri Tractatus de Conceptione Sanctae Mariae* (1904). It has been translated into French by H. del Marmol (1923). For many centuries after Eadmer's day the discussion went on, but for this see the bibliography of Fr Le Bachelet and the article of A. W. Burridge in the *Revue d'histoire ecclésiastique*. vol. xxxii (1936), pp. 570–597, entitled " L'Immaculée Conception dans la théologie de l'Angleterre médiévale ". There is a recent work by M. Jugie, *L'Immaculée Conception dans l'Écriture sainte* (1952). For the origin of the Western feast, see Fr. S. J. P. van Dijk in the *Dublin Review*, 3rd and 4th qrs., 1954 ; and for the devotion, Mgr H. F. Davis in the latter issue of the same.

ST ROMARIC, ABBOT (A.D. 653)

IN the account of St Amatus of Remiremont given herein under September 13 it is related how he brought about the conversion to God of a Merovingian nobleman named Romaric, who became a monk at Luxeuil ; and how they afterwards went together to the estate of Romaric at Habendum in the Vosges, and established the monastery which was later known as Remiremont (*Romarici Mons*). The father of Romaric had lost his life and his lands at the hands of Queen Brunehilda, and his young son became a homeless wanderer ; but at the time of his meeting St Amatus, Romaric was a person of distinction at the court of Clotaire II, with considerable property and a number of serfs. These he enfranchised, and it is said that when he was tonsured at Luxeuil several of these newly freed men presented themselves to the abbot for the same purpose. Remiremont was founded in 620 and St Amatus was its first abbot, but his duties soon devolved upon St Romaric, who at the time of his death had governed for thirty years. The size of the communities enabled the *laus perennis* to be established, the Divine Office being sung without intermission by seven alternating choirs, a practice which St Amatus had learned when he was at Agaunum. Among the early recruits was the friend of Romaric, St Arnulfus of Metz, who about 629 came to end his days in a near-by hermitage. Shortly before his death St Romaric was disturbed by the news that Grimoald, the son of another old friend, Bd Pepin of Landen, was plotting to exclude the young prince Dagobert from the Austrasian throne. The aged abbot made his way to Metz, where he remonstrated with Grimoald and warned the nobles who supported him. They heard him quietly, treated him with courtesy, and sent him back to his monastery. Three days later St Romaric died. In 1051 a solemn enshrining of his relics was authorized by Pope St Leo IX, who was a benefactor of Remiremont. The present town of that name marks the site to which the nuns' monastery was removed at the beginning of the tenth century ; the monks' monastery continued on the hill above till the Revolution.

There are two biographical texts, the first of which has been printed by Mabillon, and edited more critically in modern times by B. Krusch in MGH., *Scriptores Merov.*, vol. iv, pp. 221–225 ; see also G. Kurth, *Dissertations académiques*, vol. i (1888).

9 : SS. HIPPARCHUS AND HIS COMPANIONS, THE SEVEN MARTYRS OF SAMOSATA   (A.D. 297 OR *c.* 308 ?)

WHEN the *caesar* Galerius returned from his campaign against the Persians (or when Maximinus was ruling in Syria), he celebrated a festival at Samosata upon the banks of the Euphrates, and commanded all to assist at the sacrifices which were to be made to the gods. Hipparchus and Philotheus, magistrates of the city, had some time before received the Christian faith, and in the house of Hipparchus they made an image of the cross, before which they worshipped the Lord Christ. Five friends, young men, named James, Paregrus, Abibus, Romanus and Lollian, coming to visit them, found them in this room praying before the cross ; and they asked them why they prayed at home at a time when by the emperor's orders all were assembled in the temple of Fortune. They answered that they worshipped the Maker of the world. " Do you take that cross for the maker of the world ? " they asked, and Hipparchus answered, " We worship Him who hung upon the cross. We confess Him to be God, and the Son of God. It is now the third year since we were baptized by James, a priest of the true faith, who now gives us the body and blood of Christ. We therefore find it unlawful to stir out of doors during these three days, for we abhor the smell of the offerings with which the whole city reeks." After much discussion the five young men declared that they also desired to be baptized, and Hipparchus sent a messenger to the priest James with a letter. James forthwith covered the sacred vessels with his cloak, and coming to the house found the seven men. Saluting them he said, " Peace be with you, servants of Jesus Christ, who was crucified for His creatures ". James and his fellows fell at his feet and said, " Have pity on us and give us the mark of Christ, whom we worship ". When they had prayed together the priest, saluting them, said, " The grace of our Lord Jesus Christ be with you all ". When they had made a confession of their faith and abjured idolatry he baptized them, and immediately gave them the sacred Body and Blood. This being done, he took up the holy vessels and, again covering them with his cloak, made haste home, fearing lest the pagans should discover them together ; for the priest was an old man in ragged garments, while Hipparchus and Philotheus were men of rank and the other five also of good birth.

On the third day of the festival the emperor inquired whether the magistrates had all performed the duty of sacrificing on this public occasion. He was told that Hipparchus and Philotheus had for three years past constantly absented themselves from public worship. Thereupon the emperor gave orders that they should be led to the temple and compelled to sacrifice. The messengers, coming to the house of Hipparchus, found the seven above-mentioned together, but at first took only Hipparchus and Philotheus. The emperor asked them why they scorned both him and the gods, to which Hipparchus replied that he blushed to hear wood and stone called gods. The emperor commanded that he should receive fifty stripes, and promised to make Philotheus *praetor* if he complied. The confessor replied that honours upon such terms would be ignominy. He then began to explain the creation of the world with great eloquence, but the emperor interrupted him, saying he saw that he was a man of learning and that he would not put him to the torture, hoping that his own reason would convince him of his errors. He gave orders that he should be put in irons, and confined in a separate dungeon from Hipparchus. In the meantime an officer was sent to seize the five that were found with them. When they also refused to sacrifice the emperor urged on them that they were young, and threatened that if they persisted in their obstinacy they should be beaten and then crucified like their Master. Their answer was that they were not frightened of torture, so they were chained and kept in separate cells, without meat or drink, till the festival should be over.

The solemnity in honour of the gods being concluded, a tribune was erected in a meadow near the banks of the Euphrates, and the emperor having taken his seat the confessors were brought before him. The two old magistrates were led first by chains about their necks, and the others followed with their hands tied. Upon their refusal to sacrifice they were all stretched upon the rack and each received twenty stripes. Then they were carried back to their prison, with orders that no one should be allowed to see or help them and that they should be given just enough bread to keep them alive. They were left thus for over two months, when they were again brought before the emperor, looking more like corpses than living men. When again invited to sacrifice, they asked him not to seek to draw them from the way which Jesus Christ had opened to them. The emperor replied with fury, " You seek death ! Your desire is granted, that you may cease to insult the gods. " He then commanded that gags should be put in their mouths, and that they should be crucified. They were being hurried towards the place of execution when several magistrates represented that Hipparchus and Philotheus were their colleagues in the magistracy, who ought to settle their accounts and the public affairs which had been left in their hands, and that the others were patricians who ought to be allowed at least to make their wills : they therefore begged that some respite might be granted them. The emperor assented and gave the condemned into the hands of the magistrates for the stated purposes. They led them into the porch of the circus and, having taken the gags from their mouths, said to them privately, " We obtained this liberty under pretence of settling public business with you, but in reality to have the chance of speaking to you in private to beg your intercession with God and to ask your blessing for this city and ourselves. " The martyrs gave their blessing and addressed the people that were assembled. The emperor was informed and sent a reprimand to the magistrates for letting criminals speak to the people. Their excuse was that they dare not forbid it for fear of a tumult.

The emperor ordered seven crosses to be set up near the gate of the city, and again ordered Hipparchus to obey. The old man, laying his hand upon his bald head, replied, " As this in the course of nature cannot be again covered with hair, so shall I never change and conform to your will ". Whereon the emperor had a goat's skin fastened on his head and then jeeringly said, " Your bald pate is now covered with hair. Sacrifice, therefore, according to your own condition." They were fastened to their crosses ; and at noon several women came out and bribed the guards to let them wipe the faces of the martyrs and sponge away the blood. Hipparchus died on the cross in a short time. James, Romanus and Lollian died the next day, being stabbed by the soldiers as they hung. Philotheus, Abibus and Paregrus were taken down while they were yet alive and their heads pierced with spikes. It was ordered that their bodies should be thrown into the river, but Bassus, a Christian, redeemed them from the guards for money and buried them in the night at his farm in the country.

This Syriac *passio* was first printed, with a Latin translation, by S. E. Assemani in his *Acta sanctorum martyrum orientalium*, vol. ii, pp. 124–147. Another edition of the Syriac text is that of Bedjan in vol. iv of his *Acta martyrum et sanctorum*. A translation of the document in French will be found in H. Leclercq, *Les Martyrs*, vol. ii (1903), pp. 391–403. The name here presented as Hipparchus is also transliterated Hyperechius, or Hypericus. In the Byzantine church these martyrs were commemorated on January 29, and among the Armenians in October. In DCB., vol. iii, p. 85, Dr G. T. Stokes points out that the description of the baptism of the younger disciples contains points of great liturgical interest, and he raises the question of the date and emperor concerned.

ST LEOCADIA, Virgin and Martyr　　(A.D. 304 ?)

THE Spanish poet Prudentius does not mention St Leocadia in his hymns on the martyrs written at the end of the fourth century, but there was a church dedicated in her honour at Toledo at the beginning of the seventh, so her *cultus* has a respectable antiquity. But her *acta* are late, and not reliable. They state that Leocadia was a noble maiden of Toledo, who during the persecution of Diocletian was tortured and remanded to prison by the fierce governor Dacian. While there she heard of the passion of St Eulalia at Mérida and, moved by her example, prayed that she also might be accounted worthy to die for Christ. God granted her prayer, and she succumbed in prison to the sufferings she had undergone. If the reference to St Eulalia be authentic and if that martyr suffered on December 10, then this traditional date of Leocadia's feast cannot be the day of her death, unless we are to suppose that she lingered for twelve months (but *cf.* reference below). A well-known legend about St Leocadia is narrated herein in the account of St Ildephonsus (January 23). She is the principal patroness of Toledo, and three old churches there are dedicated under her name, on the alleged sites respectively of her tomb, her prison and her house.

　　The quite untrustworthy *passio* of St Leocadia is printed in H. Florez, *España Sagrada*, vol. vi, pp. 315–317 and in La Fuente, *Hist. eccl. de España*, vol. i (1873), pp. 335–337 ; on which *cf. Analecta Bollandiana*, vol. xvii (1898), p. 119. We have no reason to doubt the fact of the martyrdom. Her name occurs in the *Hieronymianum* on December 13 ; see Delehaye's commentary p. 646, and also his *Origines du Culte des Martyrs*, p. 369, with the references there indicated.

ST GORGONIA, Matron　　(c. A.D. 372)

ST GREGORY NAZIANZEN the Elder and his wife St Nonna had three children, St Gorgonia, St Gregory Nazianzen and St Caesarius, of whom Gorgonia was the eldest. She married and herself had three children, whom she brought up with the same care that she had received herself. Twice she recovered from illness through sheer trust in the will of Almighty God : once after a bad fall, when she would not let a physician see her, and another time when she received holy communion. Her brother also tells us that once during sickness she visited the church at night and searched the altar for any crumbs of the Blessed Sacrament that might have been overlooked there in hope of a cure—in those days the bread used at the Holy Mysteries was like ordinary household bread, as it still is in most of the Eastern churches. Gorgonia always loved the services of the church and to look after its material building, lived in a sober and God-fearing style, and was most generous to the poor ; and yet, in accordance with a common custom of earlier days, she did not receive baptism till she was past middle age. Her husband received it at the same time, together with their children and grandchildren. At her funeral her brother Gregory made a long oration which was a panegyric of her goodness and the source of what little is known of her.

We know little or nothing of St Gorgonia except what we learn from her brother's panegyric. It is printed in Migne, PG., vol. xxxv, pp. 789–817. On the incident of the visit to the altar at night, see H. Thurston in *Journal of Theol. Studies*, vol. xi (1910), pp. 275–279.

ST BUDOC, OR BEUZEC, ABBOT   (SIXTH CENTURY ?)

THE legend of St Budoc is a characteristic example of romantic and extravagant mediÃ¨val Celtic hagiography. It is first found complete only in the late middle ages, in the *Chronicle of Saint-Brieuc*, compiled some time before 1420. Once upon some unspecified time there was a king in Goëllo (Tréguier in Brittany) who married the beautiful daughter of the king of Brest ; her name was Azenor. One day her father while hunting was bitten by a snake, which seized hold of his arm and would not let go. Whereupon Azenor, who was present, smeared her breast with milk and aromatic oil and so enticed the snake off her father on to herself ; but to get rid of it she had to cut away her own breast together with the snake, and throw them into a fire. God recognized her daughterly piety, healed the wound, and gave her a breast of gold. This aggravated the ill-will of her already jealous stepmother, who accused her of being unfaithful to her husband, the king of Goëllo, whereupon Azenor was put into a cask and thrown into the sea. She prayed to God and St Brigid, and an angel came with food for her and when she gave birth to a boy St Brigid herself was the midwife. This child was Budoc, and when his mother had made the sign of the cross over him, he opened his mouth and said, " Do not be afraid, for God is with us ".

After Azenor had thus lived for five months in the cask, it was washed up on the shore of Waterford harbour and found by a peasant. He hoped it was full of wine, and was about to tap it when a child's voice from within warned him to be careful for there was a baby inside who wanted baptism. The frightened fellow ran off to a neighbouring monastery and fetched the abbot, who opened the cask and released Azenor and her child. The next day he was baptized and named, in Brezoneg, Beuzec, because he was saved from drowning. He was educated by the monks and his royal mother took in washing. Meanwhile, the wicked stepmother died, confessing in her last moments that she had falsely accused Azenor, and the distracted king of Goëllo did not rest till he had found his wife and son. But he died in Ireland and Azenor soon followed him to the grave. Budoc, however, grew up to be abbot of the monastery, and the people called him to be both bishop and prince over them. But after two years he tired of his hard task and, not being able to get a boat, he set out for Brittany in a stone trough or coffin. In this he landed safely near Brest, and eventually came to Dol, where he was welcomed by St Maglorius who wanted a bishop to take his own place. Budoc filled that office for twenty years, and died and was buried at Dol : " an angelic minister, very learned, conspicuous for virtue, whom all the people of that time looked on as a support of the faith and a most firm pillar of the Church."

There was a *cultus* of a saint, or saints, named Beuzec (Budoc) in the north and west of Brittany, and there was a St Budoc who was a bishop at Dol ; but he can hardly have been the same who was the master of St Winwaloe on the Isle Lavret near Bréhat. In Britain his *cultus* was found in Devon and Cornwall, and the tradition at Budock, near Falmouth, was that he was a hermit who had come to that parish from Ireland. But his name is not Irish. It is possible that he came from Pembrokeshire, where he was formerly honoured at and around Steynton. There was a church of St Budoc at Oxford at the time of the Conquest. It may be noted that the proximity of the island monasteries of Beuzec and Maudez near Paimpol in Brittany is repeated in the closeness of Budock to Saint Mawes in Cornwall.

It seems to be altogether a matter of speculation whether there were one or several St Budocs. The best attempt to deal with the problem is no doubt that of Canon Doble in his " Cornish Saints " series (no. 3, 2nd ed., 1937). But see also F. Duine, *Memento*, pp. 65–66, and LBS., vol. i, pp. 328–330.

ST PETER FOURIER, Co-Founder of the Augustinian Canonesses Regular of Our Lady   (A.D. 1640)

Peter Fourier was born at Mirecourt, in Lorraine, in 1565, and at the age of fifteen was sent by his father to the university directed by the Jesuits at Pont-à-Mousson, where he must have met Bd William Lacey, the future martyr, then studying there. He completed a very creditable course of studies and opened a school at his home, but he had already decided against a secular career and at the age of twenty joined the Canons Regular of St Augustine at Chaumousey. In 1589 he was ordained priest ; it was not till some months later that his humility and sense of unworthiness would let him celebrate his first Mass, and then his abbot sent him back to the university for further theological study. He remained there for some years, took his doctorate, and displayed an astonishing memory. When he was recalled to his monastery he was appointed procurator and vicar of the abbey parish ; he carried out his duties under most disheartening conditions, for the observance of the abbey was bad and his attempts to improve it were met with ridicule.

In 1597 he was offered the cure of souls in one of the three other parishes served by the canons, and he chose Mattaincourt, as that presented the greatest difficulties. Mattaincourt is a village of the Vosges which at that time was contaminated by Calvinism and rotten with evil living ; St Peter Fourier worked there for thirty years and is to this day remembered in the neighbourhood as " le bon père de Mattaincourt ". He served his flock first by his prayers and by his example ; he never forgot that he was a canon regular, subject to the vows of religion, and always lived with an austerity, poverty and simplicity befitting the monastic life ; he dispensed with a fire, except for the comfort of visitors, and never refused the needy alms or advice whether spiritual or temporal : his pupil and biographer, Father John Bedel, says that he was particularly compassionate towards those who, through bad business or theft, or other causes outside their control, were less well off than they had been. " For the benefit of such he started a fund, called St Evre's Purse, after the patron-saint of the parish, into which he paid all charitable bequests, fines, et cetera. When any parishioner was in real difficulty, a few hundred francs were given him from this fund so that he could carry on his business, the only condition being that if he prospered it should be repaid. This scheme worked so well that it could be carried on with the interest on the fund." St Peter also established three confraternities in his church : of St Sebastian for men, of the Rosary for matrons, and of the Immaculate Conception for maidens ; this last was among the earliest sodalities of " Children of Mary ". The good parish priest was badly faced with what is today called the problem of " leakage ", and after much prayer and consideration he decided that the free education of children was a first necessity.

He first of all tackled the boys. But the time was not yet ; God's chosen tool for this work was John-Baptist de la Salle, not to be born for another half-century. St Peter Fourier saw at once that he had failed, wasted no more time on it, and turned his attention to four women volunteers, Alix Le Clercq, Ganthe André, Joan and Isabel de Louvroir. These he tested, put for training in the house of canonesses of Poussey in 1598, and in due course they opened a free school at Mattaincourt. The saint was a man of ideas in education and himself gave the mistresses a daily lesson in pedágogy. He was one of the first to use what educationists call the " simultaneous method " ; and he required that the older girls should be taught how to draw up invoices and receipts, should be given practice in composition and in writing letters, and should be able to speak correctly " the language of their province " (he knew nothing of an equivalent to " standard English "). He was urgent that for their own good and the welfare of the state poor children as well as others should be educated in the love of God and so much as possible in everything that would help them to live with decency and dignity, and that their schooling was to cost nothing. Knowing the value of the " dramatic method " he wrote some dialogues on the virtues and vices (with a particular eye to the shortcomings of his parishioners), which the children would recite before their elders in the church on Sunday afternoons. St Peter gave particular instructions to his nuns on how Protestant children were to be treated : " . . . kindly and lovingly. Do not let the other children interfere with or tease them. . . . Do not speak harshly of their religion, but when occasion serves show them, when speaking in general terms to all your pupils, how good and reasonable are the precepts and practices of ours." He used similar methods himself when, in 1625, he was commissioned to combat Protestantism in the principality of Salm. He spent as much time in urging Catholics to change their lives as in urging Protestants to change their faith, and would not provoke them by calling them heretics but referred to them as " strangers ". With Father Bedel and another Jesuit he had more success in six months than his predecessors in thirty years. The new institute of nuns in 1616 received papal approval under the title of Canonesses Regular of St Augustine of the Congregation of Our Lady, and soon spread throughout France ; it is now established as well in England and other countries. In 1628 Pope Urban VIII allowed the nuns to take a fourth vow binding themselves to the *free* education of children. Father Fourier's chief partner, Alix Le Clercq, was beatified as co-foundress in 1947.

St Peter Fourier having been so successful in the reformation of a country parish, he was directed to undertake a less localized and no less difficult task. Monastic life was at a low ebb in Lorraine at that time, and in 1622, having had him appointed visitor to the canons regular by the Holy See, Mgr John de Porcelets de Maillane, Bishop of Toul, called on him to re-establish discipline in the houses of his order and to unite them all into one reformed congregation. His mission was not enthusiastically received, but in the following year the abbot of Lunéville handed over his monastery to St Peter Fourier and a handful of reformed canons. By 1629 the work was done, observance was re-established, and the canons regular of Lorraine formed into the Congregation of Our Saviour. St Peter, much against his wish, was elected their superior general in 1632, saying when he entered into office, " As Jesus Christ gives Himself to men in the Blessed Sacrament, looking for no return but the good they shall receive in communion, so do I give myself to you this day : not for the sake of any honour or advantage I may receive thereby, but only for the salvation of your souls ". It had been his hope all along that the reformed canons would undertake that work of educating boys which he had failed to establish in Mattaincourt, and they were quite willing to take it on. When therefore he sent representatives to Rome in 1627 to see about the recognition of the Congregation of Our Saviour, he told them to bring this matter up : " With regard to the schools that we want, it will be well to show that as boys who do not wish to learn Latin, and others before they enter college, have no religious order to take charge of them, at least in these parts, it looks as if there were a vacant benefice in the Church of God. Let us, then, humbly ask for it." Ask they did, and were refused—in Rome in the seventeenth century it had been forgotten that there was nothing inconsistent with the dignity of the priesthood in teaching in " elementary schools ". But they did in fact do some educational work and had several colleges ; and when the Jesuits were suppressed in the eighteenth century, those of Lorraine handed their colleges over to the canons regular.

St Peter Fourier was greatly attached to the house of Lorraine and Duke Charles IV, so that when in 1636 he was tendered the oath of allegiance to King Louis XIII he refused it and fled to Gray in Franche-Comté. Here in exile he spent the last four years of his life, as chaplain of a convent and teaching in the free school which he caused to be opened. He died on December 9, 1640, and was canonized in 1897. His shrine at Mattaincourt is the resort of numerous pilgrims.

The saint's first biographer was Father Bedel, who had been his disciple and companion. Of the many lives which have since been written it will be sufficient to note those of Father Rogie, Dom Vuillemin, and the Abbé Pingaud. This last has been translated into English. A volume by Father Chérot makes excellent use of the saint's letters, and a new life by B. Bontoux, *St Pierre Fourier*, was published in 1949. See also under Bd Alix Le Clercq (January 9).

10 : ST MILTIADES, POPE AND MARTYR (A.D. 314)

SO little is known about St Miltiades (sometimes written Melchiades) that he is now chiefly remembered on account of its having been during his pontificate that the era of the general persecutions came to an end and the Emperor Constantine gave peace to the Church. He was said to be a native of Africa and was elected to the papacy on July 2, probably in 311. After the battle at the Milvian Bridge, where Constantine defeated Maxentius on October 28, 312, the victorious emperor marched into Rome, and early in 313 toleration was granted to Christians (and to other religions) throughout the empire ; this was followed by the bestowal of privileges on the Church and the removal of legal disabilities.* Christian captives were released from the prisons and mines, and all celebrated the victory of Christ with hymns of praise, honouring God day and night with prayer that the peace which had been granted after ten years of violent persecution might not be taken away.

But amidst these rejoicings the Church was disturbed by the beginnings of the Donatist schism in Africa. It arose out of the appointment of Caecilian as bishop

* There has been no little debate among the learned about the circumstances of this victory and what followed it.

of Carthage, whom the party of Donatus alleged to be invalidly consecrated because (as was said) he had delivered up the sacred books under persecution.* At the request of Constantine the pope called a synod of Italian and Gaulish bishops at Rome, which decided that Caecilian's election and consecration were good and valid. St Augustine, speaking of the moderation which the pope used in this connection, calls Miltiades an excellent man, a true son of peace and father of Christians. A commemoration is made of him in the liturgy of December 10 as a martyr, because, says the Roman Martyrology, he suffered many things during the persecution of Maximian (before he was bishop of Rome).

This holy pope saw a door opened by the peace of the Church to the conversion of many, and he rejoiced at the triumph of the cross of Christ. But with worldly prosperity a worldly spirit too often broke into the sanctuary itself; insomuch that there was sometimes reason to complain with Isaias, " Thou hast multiplied the nation, and hast not increased the joy ". Under the pressure of persecution the true spirit of religion was maintained in many during the first ages; yet, amidst the most holy examples and under the influence of strong motives and helps, sin corrupted the hearts of some, who by abuse of grace became abandoned to wickedness. With temporal honours and security love of the world gained the hearts of many more, and they were by ignorance persuaded that they could serve both God and mammon. Though material goods and prosperity are a blessing, they are also a danger.

There is a short account of Pope Miltiades in the *Liber Pontificalis*, but it tells us little that is trustworthy. A letter of the Emperor Constantine to the pope as well as two other letters connected with the trouble of Bishop Caecilian are preserved by Eusebius, *Eccles. Hist.* bk x, ch. 5. But the beginnings of the Donatist schism belong rather to general church history. It may suffice here to recommend the treatment of the subject by J. R. Palanque in vol. iii of the *Histoire de l'Église*, ed. Fliche et Martin. St Miltiades' true date is January 10: *cf*. CMH., pp. 34 and 428. On the pope's alleged burial place in the cemetery of Callistus, see Leclercq in DAC., vol. xi, cc. 1199–1203; and on the Roman synod, E. Caspar in the *Zeitschrift für Kirchengeschichte*, vol. xlvi (1927), pp. 333–346. For the Constantinian problems see N. H. Baynes, *Constantine the Great and the Christian Church* (1929).

SS. MENNAS, HERMOGENES, AND EUGRAPHUS, MARTYRS (DATE UNKNOWN)

MENNAS (Menas), an Athenian, called " of the beautiful voice ", was sent by the Emperor Galerius to Alexandria to use his learning and eloquence for the pacification of troubles among the citizens. Having carried out his commission he publicly declared himself a Christian, and together with his subordinate, Eugraphus, began to make many converts. The judge, Hermogenes, who on his way to Alexandria had been assured in a vision that the voyage would turn out for his own benefit, summoned the offenders before his tribunal; whereupon, as the worthless *passio* of these martyrs, falsely ascribed to St Athanasius, informs us, Mennas used his beautiful voice to make an address to the court which lasted for four hours. Although this oration made a great impression, it was ordered that his eyes and tongue should be plucked out and his feet flayed. But the next day he was found fully recovered from these outrages, at which miracle Hermogenes himself and many others were converted. Galerius ordered that further tortures should be inflicted

---

* The Donatists held the erroneous doctrines that sacraments given by an unworthy minister are invalid and that sinners cannot be members of the Church.

on them, from all of which they immediately recovered, and all three were eventually beheaded.

This hagiographical fiction is printed in Migne, PG., vol. cxv, pp. 368–416, and there is at least one other redaction of the same story still unpublished. Delehaye inclines to the belief that the whole is a pure invention founded on the popularity of the authentic St Mennas (November 11). The names of the two companions, Hermogenes and Eugraphus, oddly enough, recur at Salona in Dalmatia, a place which was especially connected with the veneration of the Egyptian St Mennas. See the *Analecta Bollandiana*, vol. xviii (1899), pp. 406–407 ; vol. xxiii (1904), pp. 14–15 ; vol. xxix (1910), pp. 144–145. There is a summary of the same legend in the Constantinople Synaxary, December 10, cc. 293–294.

ST EULALIA OF MÉRIDA, Virgin and Martyr   (A.D. 304 ?)

FOR particulars of the passion of St Eulalia, the most celebrated virgin martyr of Spain, we have a hymn written in her honour by Prudentius* at the end of the fourth century and her *passio* of a much later date. She was only twelve years old when the edicts of Diocletian were issued by which it was ordered that all should offer sacrifice to the gods of the empire. Eulalia's mother, observing her ardour for martyrdom, took her into the country. But she found means to make her escape by night, and arrived at Mérida before daybreak. As soon as the court sat the same morning she presented herself before the judge, Dacian, and reproached him with attempting to destroy souls by compelling them to renounce the only true God. Dacian at first tried to flatter and bribe her into withdrawing her words and observing the edicts. Then he threatened and showed the instruments of torture, saying, " These you shall escape if you will but touch a little salt and incense with the tip of your finger ". But she trampled on the cake which was laid for the sacrifice, and spat at the judge. Thereupon two executioners began to tear her body with iron hooks, and lighted torches were applied to the wounds. The fire then caught her hair, and Eulalia was stifled by the smoke and flame. Prudentius tells us that a white dove seemed to come out of her mouth and fly away upward, at which the executioners were so terrified that they fled. Snow fell and covered the body and the whole forum where it lay, till her relics were entombed by the Christians near the place of her martyrdom. A church was built on the spot and the altar raised over them before Prudentius wrote his hymn ; he says that " pilgrims come to venerate her bones, and she, near the throne of God, beholds them and protects those that sing hymns to her ".

The veneration of St Eulalia spread to Africa, and there is a homily of St Augustine for her feast-day ; the oldest existing French poem, the " Cantilène de Sainte Eulalie ", of the later ninth century, relates her story ; and she is among the martyrs mentioned by Bede in his hymn in honour of St Etheldreda and by St Aldhelm. St Eulalia of Barcelona, named separately in the Roman Martyrology on February 12, is greatly venerated throughout Catalonia, under the names Aulaire, Aulazie, Olalla and other forms ; but she is now generally recognized as a double of St Eulalia of Mérida. The fact that Prudentius and Venantius pay tribute to the heroism of one Spanish martyr named Eulalia, making especial mention of Mérida, seems to constitute proof of the genuineness of the cult in

* Alban Butler accords two and a half pages of text to St Eulalia and four and a half pages of small-print footnote (including a paragraph on Sedulius) to Prudentius, " the glory of the ancient Christian poets ".

her case, but it constantly happens that fictitious stories are afterwards written which cause a duplication of the subject so honoured.

The *passio* printed by Florez (*España Sagrada*, vol. xiii, pp. 392–398) must be as old as the sixth century because it was known to St Gregory of Tours, but no dependence can be placed upon the story it contains. Even the few details provided in the poem of Prudentius are probably not much more reliable, but he mentions Mérida as also does Fortunatus, though St Augustine in his sermon says nothing more than that she suffered in Spain. Competent opinion is now definitely satisfied that there was only one St Eulalia, the martyr of Mérida. The Barcelona story is a much later development, incorporating many features of the earlier legend. See on this the convincing essay of H. Moretus in the *Revue des questions historiques*, vol. lxxxix (1911), pp. 85–119 ; which investigation is endorsed by Poncelet, Delehaye (CMH., p. 642), and Leclercq, in DAC., vol. v, cc. 705–732. In this last article the greater part of Moretus' essay is reprinted. The attempt of Z. Garcia Villada (*Historia ecclesiastica de España*, vol. i, 1929, pp. 283–300) to vindicate the independent existence of the Barcelona martyr is too plainly biased by patriotic conservatism. The question of the notices of Eulalia in the early martyrologies has been very fully dealt with by Dom Quentin in his *Les martyrologes historiques*, pp. 71, 162–164, etc. See also the *Acta Sanctorum*, February, vol. ii, and BHL., nn. 2693–2698. There was a Eulalia abbess of Shaftesbury *c.* 1074.

ST GREGORY III, POPE   (A.D. 741)

AMONG the clergy at the funeral of Pope St Gregory II, in the year 731, there was a priest of Syrian nationality who was so well known for his holiness, learning and ability that the people spontaneously carried him off from the procession and elected him by acclamation to the vacant see ; he accordingly became pope as Gregory III. He inherited from his predecessor the problem of dealing with the Emperor Leo III the Isaurian, who had begun a campaign against the veneration of holy images, and one of Gregory's first acts was to send a letter of protest. But the bearer, George, a priest, got frightened and returned to Rome without delivering it, to the indignation of the pope, who threatened to degrade him. So George set out again, but was seized by the imperial officers in Sicily and banished. There-upon Gregory summoned a synod at Rome, wherein bishops, lower clergy and lay-people approved the excommunication of any who should condemn the veneration of images or destroy them. Leo retorted as some of his predecessors had done in similar circumstances : he sent ships to bring Gregory to Constantinople ; but they were lost in a storm, so the emperor contented himself with seizing the papal estates in Calabria and Sicily and recognizing the jurisdiction of the patriarch of Constantinople over eastern Illyricum.

After this inauspicious beginning of his pontificate there was a period of peace, during which St Gregory rebuilt and decorated a number of churches ; in particular he set up a row of pillars before the *confessio* of St Peter, with images of our Lord and the saints thereon and lamps burning around them, a mute but solid protest against Iconoclasm. He sent the *pallium* to St Boniface in Germany, and when the English missionary made his third visit to Rome, in 738, Gregory wrote an appeal to the " Old Saxons " : the letter consisted chiefly of quotations from the Bible, which perhaps were not very meaningful to its heathen recipients. It was this pope who sent the English monk St Willibald to help Boniface.

Towards the end of St Gregory's life the Lombards again threatened Rome. The pope sent a famous appeal for help to Charles Martel and the Franks of the West, rather than to the emperor in the East, but it was long before they could be induced to act. To the bishops of Tuscany Gregory wrote urging them to work for the recovery of four cities captured by the Lombards : if they did not, " I myself, ill as I am, will make the journey, and save you from the responsibility of being unfaithful to your duty ".   Then, on October 22, 741, Charles Martel died, and a few weeks later, on December 10, St Gregory III followed him to the grave. " He was ", says the *Liber Pontificalis,* " a man of deep humility and true wisdom. He had a good knowledge of the Sacred Scriptures and their meaning, and knew the psalms by heart.   He was a polished and successful preacher, skilled in both Latin and Greek, and a stout upholder of the Catholic faith ; a lover of poverty and the poor, a protector of the widowed and the orphaned, a friend to monks and nuns."

There is nothing which can be called an early biography of St Gregory III ; the account in the *Liber Pontificalis* is meagre.   What we know of him is gathered from the chroniclers and from the remnants of his correspondence.   See Mann, *History of the Popes,* vol. i, pt 2, pp. 204–224, and Hartmann, *Geschichte Italiens im Mittelalter,* vol. ii, pt 2, pp. 169 *seq.*

THE LONDON MARTYRS OF 1591

ON October 18, 1591, a royal proclamation led to the stricter enforcement of the laws against Catholics in England, the first fruits of which were seven martyrdoms in London on the following December 10.   The principal priest concerned was BD EDMUND GENINGS, who had been born at Lichfield in 1567 and brought up a Protestant.   As a boy he was of a serious turn of mind, much given, as his brother tells us, to star-gazing, both literally and figuratively.   At the age of sixteen he became page to a Catholic gentleman and was soon reconciled to the Church, whereupon he went to the college at Rheims.   It looked as if ill-health would forestall his desires, but he made a marvellous recovery and by dispensation was ordained at the age of twenty-three.   Mr Genings was a confessor of the faith before he ever left France, for on their way to the court, in April 1590, he and his companions were robbed and imprisoned for three days by Huguenots.   They made a dangerous landing near Whitby, and Genings made his way home, only to find all his family dead except his brother John, who was in London.   He looked for him during a month, and had determined to leave town the following day, when he met him on Ludgate Hill.   John was not particularly pleased to see Edmund, whom he strongly suspected of being a priest, and warned him that if he were he would bring death upon himself and discredit on his friends.   Edmund accordingly decided that it was not opportune then to attempt his brother's conversion, and departed into the country.*   He was back in London in the autumn of 1591, and offered Mass at a house in Gray's Inn Lane, the residence of BD SWITHIN WELLS.

Mr Wells was the sixth son of Thomas Wells, a gentleman of Brambridge, near Winchester, and until middle age seems to have led a peaceful country life, varied by travelling abroad and periods of service in noble houses.   " He was a witty man skilled in divers languages . . . something given to honest and innocent diversions, yet always devout in prayer. . . ."   For six years he gave himself " to a more

* John Genings himself confesses that he " rather rejoiced than any way bewailed the untimely and bloody end of his nearest kinsman, hoping thereby to be rid of all persuasions, which he mistrusted he should receive from him touching the Catholic religion ".   But ten days after the martyrdom he underwent a sudden and very remarkable change of heart and mind, as results of which he became a Catholic, a friar minor, and the minister of the English Franciscan province.   The convent of English tertiary sisters formerly at Taunton was founded by Fr John Genings at Brussels in 1619–21.

profitable employment of training up young gentlemen in virtue and learning ", in other words, he kept a boys' school at Monkton Farleigh in Wiltshire, and eventually came with his wife Margaret to live in London in 1585. He was in prison on account of his religion at least twice during the next six years, and several times examined. On the morning of November 8, 1591, Mr Genings celebrated Mass in his house with a small congregation, and during the celebration Topcliffe the priest-catcher arrived with his officers. The men kept them at bay by force and cajolery until Mass was finished, and then Bd Edmund was seized, together with BB. POLYDORE PLASDEN, also a priest, JOHN MASON and SIDNEY HODGSON, laymen, Mrs Wells and others. Mr Wells was not present but was arrested shortly after.

At their trial Edmund Genings and Polydore Plasden were found guilty of being priests coming in to the realm, Wells of harbouring them, and Mrs Wells, Mason and Hodgson of relieving them, contrary to 27 Eliz. c. 2, and sentenced to death.* Bd Edmund was hanged, drawn and quartered, and Bd Swithin hanged, in Gray's Inn Fields, hard by the Wells's house. On the way thither from Newgate Swithin shouted to someone in the crowd, " Farewell, old friend ! Farewell all hawking and hunting and old pastimes—I am now going a better way ! " Edmund was still fully conscious when the butchery began and cried out in his agony, to whom his companion responded, " Alas, sweet soul ! your pain is great, but it is almost past. Pray for me now, good saint, that mine may come." The hangmen and others reported that he invoked St Gregory when his heart and *viscera* were out of his body. Swithin complained of their keeping him, an old man, standing about in his shirt on a cold day while the noose was arranged, and said to the hangman, " I pray God make of you, a Saul, a Paul ". When Topcliffe said to him, " See what your priests have brought you to, Mr Wells ", he replied, " I am happy and thank God to have been allowed to have so many and such saint-like priests under my roof ". The other three, BB. Polydore, John and Sidney, were executed on the same day, December 10, at Tyburn. With them suffered BD EUSTACE WHITE and BD BRIAN LACEY.

Lacey, a Yorkshire gentleman, was a cousin and assistant of the Ven. Montford Scott and after torture was condemned to be hanged for aiding and abetting this priest. Bd Brian's own brother had informed against them. Eustace White came from Louth, and was a priest ordained in Rome. His parents were Protestants and at his conversion his father had deliberately cursed him. He laboured on the mission in the west of England for three years, until he was betrayed at Blandford by a lawyer with whom he had talked too freely of religion. During his detention in Blandford he made so strong an impression on the local Protestants that it was openly advocated that a petition should be sent to the queen for his release. He was, however, taken to London and treated with extreme barbarity in Bridewell : left closely chained for over six weeks, insufficiently fed, and tortured by Topcliffe seven times, all in a vain hope of making him divulge the names of those who had helped him or in whose houses he had celebrated Mass. He was condemned for his priesthood, and the brutal details of his martyrdom at Tyburn reproduce those of Bd Edmund Genings elsewhere on the same day, whereas his fellow priest, Bd Polydore Plasden, was allowed to hang till he was dead.

A life of Edmund Genings, *alias* Ironmonger, was written by his brother John Genings and printed at St Omers in 1614. Further sources throwing light upon all this group of

* Mrs Wells was reprieved and died in prison eleven years later. Her cause is postponed for further evidence.

martyrs will be found in the publications of the Catholic Record Society, vol. v (1908) ; see especially pp. 204 *seq.*, 131 *seq.* and *passim.* Consult also the full account in MMP., pp. 169–185 ; B. Camm, *Tyburn and the English Martyrs* (1904), pp. 60–72 ; and J. H. Pollen, *Acts of English Martyrs*, pp. 98–127.

BB. JOHN ROBERTS AND THOMAS SOMERS, MARTYRS
(A.D. 1610)

SOME miles north by west of the Merionethshire town of Dolgelley, at the top of the valley between the Rhinogs and the Arenigs, lies the village of Trawsfynydd, near which John Roberts was born in 1577. His family and the exact place of his birth are uncertain, but he seems to have been of ancient stock on both sides, and he is one of the most distinguished figures among the hundred and thirty-six martyrs declared blessed by Pope Pius XI on December 15, 1929. He received his early education from an aged priest and, though brought up nominally a Protestant, he was, as he himself said, always a Catholic at heart. When he was nineteen he went to St John's College at Oxford, where William Laud was still in residence, and Roberts shared the rooms of John Jones, Llanfrynach, afterwards well known as Father Leander-of-St-Martin, O.S.B. He did not finish his course at Oxford, but in 1598 entered as a student of law at Furnivall's Inn. He did not stay there long, for early in the same year he went abroad. The only object of his journey was " amusement and recreation ", but in June he was formally reconciled with the Church at Notre-Dame in Paris by Canon Louis Godebert. He at once betook himself to the English College at Valladolid, where he was admitted on October 18 " on account of his burning desire to become a worker in the vineyard of the Lord ". In 1599 John Roberts followed the example of Augustine (John) Bradshaw and, in the face of many difficulties caused by the authorities at the college, received the Benedictine habit at the royal monastery of San Benito at Valladolid. His old friend John Jones soon joined him, and they were professed, together with six others from the English College, before the end of the following year at the monastery of St Martin at Compostela, Roberts being known in religion as Brother John of Merioneth (Meirion ; *de Mervinia*).

It seemed at the time that the young Welshmen and Englishmen who took this step endangered their call to be missionaries in their own land, for the Spanish Benedictines were bound by perpetual enclosure. But they were justified in listening first to the call of the traditional cloister by subsequent events. On February 27, 1601, Bd Mark Barkworth, who had been the originator and leader of the Benedictine movement among the English students at Valladolid, was martyred at Tyburn. Thereupon petitions were presented to the Holy See that the English monks might be free to go on the mission, and on December 5, 1602, Pope Clement VIII granted this faculty to those of both the Valladolid and Cassinese congregations. Twenty-one days later, on the feast of St Stephen the First Martyr, Father John Roberts set out accompanied by Father Augustine Bradshaw. " Roberts ", says another Welshman, Lewis Owen, a spy from Father John's own neighbourhood and his inveterate enemy, " was the first that had his mission from the pope and his own Spanish prelate to go for England, which made him not a little proud that he should be a second Augustine monk, to convert and reconcile his countrymen to the Roman Antichrist." It took the two monks three months to reach London, and although, unlike their predecessors in 597, they came disguised in plumed hats, doublets and swords, they were soon arrested and deported.

On the testimony of Lewis Owen, Father John did not " neglect his Lord and Master's business, but bestirred himself night and day in negotiating His affairs ". The history of his apostolate is a record of repeated arrest, imprisonment, release and exile ; nevertheless the contemporary Dom Bucelin in his *Benedictus Redivivus* says that : " Amid all the religious who have worked in that island this man may almost be reckoned the chief, both as regards labour and fruitfulness of preaching." In a few weeks he was back in London, succouring the victims of an epidemic so devastating that over 30,000 are said to have died during its first and worst year : all early writers who refer to John Roberts mention his conduct at this time with especial admiration, and he made many converts. In the spring of 1604 he was arrested at some port in the south when about to embark to attend a general chapter of his congregation, accompanied by four postulants. His captors, however, failed to identify him as a priest, and he was released to continue his labours until, during the round-up of Catholics on the day of Gunpowder Plot, November 5, 1605, he was taken at the house of Mr Knight, a scrivener, in Holborn by Chancery Lane, and was committed to the Gatehouse prison at Westminster, within the precincts of the abbey. Here he was kept for eight months and then, at the intervention of the ambassador of France, released and banished. This time Father John remained abroad for over a year, during which time he took a principal part in the foundation, with Father Augustine Bradshaw, of a monastery for English monks of the Valladolid congregation at Douay ; this became the headquarters of the wonderfully preserved English congregation, and is now St Gregory's Abbey at Downside. He returned to England and was arrested for the fourth time at the end of 1607. After an examination at which he refused to take the oath of allegiance in a condensed form (3 Jas. I, cc. 4, 5), Father John escaped from prison, and was at large but in great secrecy till May 1609, when he was first in the Gatehouse, and then Newgate. Again the French ambassador came to the rescue and again John was banished. He went to Spain and then to St Gregory's, Douay, and on a renewed outbreak of plague came back to England for the last time early in 1610. Some Benedictine, perhaps he, was arrested and escaped in July ; but on December 2 he was certainly seized for the last time. It was the first Sunday of Advent, and he was just ending Mass, probably in Mrs Scott's house, when the officers broke in and carried him off, still in his vestments, to Newgate.

Father John Roberts was arraigned, together with Bd Thomas Somers (*alias* Wilson), a secular priest from Westmorland, before Coke, L.C.J., George Abbot, Bishop of London, and others, charged with their priesthood under 27 Eliz. c. 2. They again refused the oath, and Father John admitted under examination that he was a priest and a monk who had come into the country " to work for the salvation of souls, and would continue to do were I to live longer ". Abbot called him a disturber and seducer of the people, to which Father John replied that if he were so " then were our ancestors deceived by blessed St Augustine, the apostle of the English, who was sent here by the pope of Rome, St Gregory the Great. . . . I am sent here by the same Apostolic See that sent him before me." When ordered to be silent, he exclaimed, " I must speak, as my mission is from Heaven. St Matthew says in chapter 28 : ' Go ye and teach all nations, baptizing them and teaching them to observe all things whatsoever I have commanded you.' Your ministers do not do this, because they do not fulfil in their lives and actions the command of Christ. They do not administer the sacrament of penance or of extreme unction. I do. And withal I teach obedience to princes as a matter of conscience, against the false doctrine of Luther and his companions. All this I can prove to you." He rebuked the bishop for sitting with civil judges in the trial of a capital cause, and appealed to the bench to decide the case themselves lest the jury, simple and ignorant men unable to distinguish between a priest as such and a man as a traitor, should incur blood-guiltiness. The appeal was disregarded, the jury found both prisoners guilty, and they were condemned to death.

The next day the Spanish lady Luisa de Carvajal bribed the jailer of Newgate to transfer the two priests from the condemned cell to the company of other Catholic prisoners, and in the evening was enacted a remarkable scene. Twenty confessors of the faith sat down together for supper : at the head of the table was Doña Luisa, to her right and left Father Roberts and Mr Somers. Both martyrs were joyous, and the monk had a scruple of conscience. " Do you not think ", he asked his hostess, " that I may be causing disedification by my great glee ? Had I not better withdraw and give myself to prayer ? " " No, certainly not," she answered. " You cannot be better employed than in letting them all see with what cheerful courage you are about to die for Christ." Before the party broke up Doña Luisa washed the feet of the martyrs, an act of homage which greatly angered the king (James I) when it was reported to him. The next morning they were handed over to the sheriff of Middlesex, drawn on hurdles to Tyburn, and there hanged with sixteen common felons. They were allowed to hang till they were dead, owing to the sympathy and threatening attitude of the crowd. Their heads were then displayed on London Bridge and their bodies buried at Tyburn, from whence they were in great part recovered by Bd Maurus Scott and Doña Luisa. Some relics of Bd Thomas Somers are now at Downside, but the rest have disappeared in revolutionary upheavals. Bd John Roberts was only thirty-three years old, and " the first who out of a monastery, after the suppression of monasteries in England, attacked the gate of Hell and provoked the prince of darkness in his usurped kingdom, which he overcame like his great Master, the prince of martyrs, by losing his life in the conflict."

A full biography of John Roberts was published by Dom Bede Camm in 1897 and this embodies an exhaustive account of the sources. Challoner's narrative (MMP., pp. 317–323) is naturally less complete. On certain subsidiary questions raised in the life consult *The Month*, December 1897, pp. 581–600 ; October 1898, pp. 364–377 ; October 1899, pp. 233–245 ; and November, pp. 348–365. See also T. P. Ellis, *Catholic Martyrs of Wales* (1933), pp. 79–91, and *Welsh Benedictines of the Terror* (1936), pp. 43–54, 76–104 and *passim* ; and *cf.* B. Camm, *Nine Martyr Monks* (1931). For Somers, see MMP., pp. 321–323 ; and for the relics of both martyrs, B. Camm, *Forgotten Shrines* (1910), pp. 355–356, 373, 378.

11 : ST DAMASUS, Pope   (A.D. 384)

POPE DAMASUS is said in the *Liber Pontificalis* to have been a Spaniard, which may be true of his extraction but he seems to have been born at Rome, where his father was a priest. Damasus himself was never married, and he became deacon in the church which his father served. When Pope Liberius died in 366, Damasus, who was then about sixty years old, was chosen bishop of Rome. His accession was far from unopposed, a minority electing another deacon, called Ursicinus or Ursinus, whom they supported with great violence. It appears that the civil power in its maintenance of Damasus used considerable cruelty—Butler's expression, " barbarous proceedings ", is not too strong—from concurrence in which the contemporary Rufinus exonerates him. The adherents of the antipope were not easily quelled, and so late as 378 Damasus had to clear himself both before the Emperor Gratian and a Roman synod of a charge of incontinence maliciously laid against him by his enemies.

Ammianus Marcellinus, the pagan historian of those times, says that the standard of living of the prelates of Rome was a tempting object of ambition, and wishes they would imitate the plainness of the clergy in the provinces. Some show of pomp and state was certainly then made since, as St Jerome reports, a pagan senator of Rome, Praetextatus, said to Pope Damasus, " Make me bishop of Rome, and I will be a Christian to-morrow ". The reflection of this heathen shows how necessary Christian moderation is, if we would properly show in ourselves the spirit of the gospel. Damasus certainly did not deserve to fall under this censure. For St Jerome, who knew him well, being his secretary for a time, severely inveighs against the luxury and state which some ecclesiastics at Rome displayed, and he was not the man to spare their bishop had he deemed him involved. But to such a degree were St Jerome's strictures justified that in 370 Valentinian issued a regulation forbidding clergy to induce orphans and widows to make them any gift or legacy. This edict St Damasus was severe in putting into execution.

Pope St Damasus had to oppose several heresies, but in 380 Theodosius I in the East and Gratian in the West proclaimed Christianity, as professed by the bishops of Rome and Alexandria, to be the religion of the Roman state, and Gratian, on the petition of the Christian senators, supported by St Damasus, removed the altar of Victory from the senate-house and laid aside the title of Pontifex Maximus. In the following year the second oecumenical council was held, the first of Constantinople, at which the pope was represented by legates. But the action of Damasus that was most far-reaching and beneficial down to this day was his patronage of St Jerome and encouragement of his biblical studies, which had their consummation in the Vulgate version of the Bible. Jerome tells us that Damasus himself was learned in the Scriptures, " a virgin doctor of the virgin Church ", and Theodoret says that " He was illustrious for his holy life, and ready to preach and do all things in defence of apostolic doctrine ".

St Damasus is, too, specially remembered for his care for the relics and resting-places of the martyrs and for his work in the draining, opening out and adornment of the sacred catacombs ; and notably—by the ordinary Christian imbued with *pietas* no less than by the historian and archaeologist—for the inscriptions which he set up therein. A large number of his inscriptions and epigrams in verse are extant, either in originals or copies ; one of the best known is that to which we are indebted for all we know about St Tarcisius. St Damasus died on December 11, 384, at the age of about eighty. He had put up in the " papal crypt " of the cemetery of St Callistus a general epitaph which ends :

> I, Damasus, wished to be buried here, but I feared to offend the
> ashes of these holy ones.

He was accordingly laid to rest with his mother and sister at a small church he had built on the Via Ardeatina ; and among his epitaphs which have been preserved in writing is the one which he wrote for himself, an act of faith in Christ's resurrection and his own.

He who walking on the sea could calm the bitter waves, who gives life to the dying seeds of the earth ; He who was able to loose the mortal chains of death, and after three days' darkness could bring again to the upper world the brother for his sister Martha : He, I believe, will make Damasus rise again from the dust.

There is nothing in the nature of an ancient biography of St Damasus which is of any account except the sections devoted to him in the *Liber Pontificalis* (see Duchesne's edition, vol. i, pp. 212 *seq.*, with the valuable notes and preface). For our knowledge of his life we depend mainly upon his correspondence, the epitaphs he composed and scant references in the historians, ecclesiastical and secular. The prologue to the *Libellus Precum* (printed in Migne, PL., vol. xiii, cc. 83–107) is no better than a malicious lampoon composed by his enemies. The standard edition of the epitaphs is that of Ihm (1895) but consult also E. Schäfer, *Die Bedeutung der Epigramme des Papstes Damasus für die Geschichte der Heiligen-verehrung* (1932). Among the more important contributions to the study of the pontificate of St Damasus may be mentioned those of M. Rade, *Damasus Bischof von Rom* (1882) ; J. Wittig, *Papst Damasus I* (1902), as also the same scholar's book *Die Friedenspolitik des Papstes Damasus I* (1912) ; O. Marucchi, *Il Pontificato del Papa Damaso* (1905) ; and J. Vives, *Damasiana* in the collection *Gesammelte Aufsätze zur Kulturgeschichte Spaniens* (1928). See also the account in Duchesne, *History of the Early Church* (1912), vol. ii and the article in DAC., vol. iv, cc. 145–197, which provides a very full bibliography. CMH. (pp. 643–644) contains useful references especially regarding the pope's burial place. There is an exeellent new edition of the epigrams by Fr Antony Ferrua, *Epigrammata Damasiana* (1942).

ST BARSABAS, Martyr   (No Date)

In his fictitious legend Barsabas is called an abbot in Persia, who had under him twelve monks. In the beginning of the persecution by Sapor they were all seized and led in chains to Istachr, a city near the ruins of Persepolis. After vainly trying to make them apostatize by tortures which a human being could hardly survive, the governor condemned them to lose their heads. The martyrs went joyfully to the place of execution, surrounded by soldiers and followed by a mob of people, and the slaughter began. A Mazdean, travelling that way with his wife and children, beheld the venerable abbot singing praises to God, and taking each monk by the hand in turn, as if to deliver him to the executioner ; he saw too a fiery cross shining above the bodies of the slain. The man was so impressed that he got off his horse and whispered to Barsabas, asking to be admitted into his holy company. The abbot assenting, he passed through his hands after the ninth monk, and was beheaded, the executioner not knowing him. Last of all the venerable Barsabas presented his neck to the sword. The example of her husband moved his wife and family to become Christians.

It is difficult to understand what induced Baronius to include this alleged Persian martyr in the Roman Martyrology. He is wholly unknown in the West, and the Constantinople synaxary barely mentions his name under December 11. In the Ethiopic synaxary his story is told in September. Though the story is different, Barsabas seems only a doublet of St Simeon Barsabae, on April 21.

SS. FUSCIAN, VICTORICUS, and GENTIAN, Martyrs   (Date Unknown)

The legend of these martyrs tells us that Fuscian and Victoricus were Roman missionaries who came into Gaul at the same time as St Quintinus, and set themselves the task of evangelizing the Morini. Victoricus established his headquarters at Boulogne and Fuscian at Thérouanne, or rather near by at the village of Helfaut, where he built a small church.   Both of them met with opposition from the pagan Gauls and Romans, but made a number of conversions.   After a time they went together to visit St Quintinus, but when they reached Amiens they found persecution raging against Christians ;   they therefore passed on to Sains, and there lodged with an old man named Gentian.   He was a heathen, but well disposed towards Christianity, and in talking to him of the faith the two missionaries learned of the martyrdom of St Quintinus six weeks before.   When he heard that two Christian priests were at Sains, the governor Rictiovarus arrived there with a troop of soldiers.   He was met by Gentian with a drawn sword, threatening him because he was a persecutor and declaring that he was ready to die for the true God. Rictiovarus accordingly had him beheaded on the spot.   Fuscian and Victoricus were then taken in chains to Amiens, and as they would not renounce their faith after divers tortures they were beheaded, at Saint-Fuscien-aux-Bois.   Among the embroideries of the story of SS. Fuscian and Victoricus is that they rose up and walked away with their severed heads after execution ;   Rictiovarus was driven mad.

The extravagant *passio* of these martyrs is preserved in varying forms.   The text is printed in the *Mémoires de la Société des antiquaires de Picardie*, vol. xviii (1861), pp. 23–43. Although the story is plainly fabulous and has been framed in dependence upon the not less incredible legend of St Quintinus (October 31), still the occurrence of the names of SS. Fuscian and companions in the *Hieronymianum* is some guarantee of the fact that a martyrdom took place in the locality indicated.   The question has been discussed by Duchesne, *Fastes Episcopaux*, vol. iii, pp. 141–152.

ST DANIEL THE STYLITE   (A.D. 493)

AFTER St Simeon the Elder, the first and greatest of them, this Daniel is the best known among the *stylites* or pillar-saints.   He was a child of promise, dedicated to God from before his birth, and a native of the town of Maratha, near Samosata. At twelve years of age he was received at a neighbouring monastery, where some years after he became a monk.   His abbot going on a journey to Antioch took Daniel with him and passing by Telanissae they went to see St Simeon on his pillar.   He let Daniel come up to him, gave him his blessing, and foretold that he would suffer much for Jesus Christ.   The abbot died soon after and the monks would have put Daniel in his place, but he declined and went again to see St Simeon, spending fourteen days in the monastic settlement which was near his pillar.   He afterwards undertook a journey to the Holy Land, but finding the way stopped by war went instead to Constantinople.   Here he passed seven days in the church of St Michael outside the walls, and then made a hermitage for himself at Philempora in an abandoned temple.   He remained there for nine years, under the protection of the patriarch St Anatolius.

After this time he resolved to imitate the manner of life of St Simeon, whose cloak he had obtained after his death in 459.   Simeon had bequeathed this garment to the Emperor Leo I, but his disciple Sergius had been unable to get admittance to the imperial presence to deliver it and so had given it to Daniel.   He selected a spot some miles from the city, overlooking the Bosphorus, and ascended the broad-topped pillar which had been provided by a friend.   Later, having been nearly frozen to death one night, the emperor built him a higher and better home ; it consisted of two pillars fastened together with iron bars, whereon masonry was placed, on the top of which was fixed a covered-in shelter and a balustrade.   The country was subject to high winds, and very severe frosts, but this did not oblige him to leave his pillar, where he lived till he was eighty-four years old. Without descending from it, he was ordained priest by St Gennadius, Patriarch of Constantinople, who, having read the prayers at the bottom of the pillar, went up to the top of it presumably to impose his hands on Daniel, though this is not stated, but only that he gave him holy communion. Daniel did not want to be ordained and accordingly refused to come down. In 465 a fire happened at Constantinople, which consumed eight of its regions. St Daniel had foretold it and advised the patriarch and the emperor to order public prayers to be said twice a week ; but no credit was given to him. The event made them remember, and the people ran in crowds to his pillar where the saint, stretching out his hands to Heaven, prayed for them. The Emperor Leo frequently visited and greatly respected him ; when the king of the Lazi in Colchis came to renew his alliance with the Romans, Leo took him to see St Daniel, as a wonder of his empire. The barbarian king prostrated himself before the pillar, and the holy man was witness of the treaty between the two princes. The sick, who were often allowed to come up his pillar, were frequently cured by Daniel laying his hands upon them or by anointing them with the " oil of the saints ", as it is called in his life ; by which we are to understand the oil which burnt before the relics or images of the saints.* But not all respected the holy man, and early on a plot was laid, by " those who hunted after women of her sort ", to seduce him by means of a well-known harlot named Basiane. When it failed, she asserted that it had in fact succeeded, till her nerve failed and she publicly disclosed the names of those who had egged her on.

A pillar-saint is an unfamiliar, rather frightening and perhaps repellent figure. But the narrative of the life of St Daniel is a fascinating one, and in character he is found to be as simple and practical as his way of life was bizarre : when he taught the crowds that flocked to him, he said nothing " rhetorical or philosophical " but spoke about " the love of God and the care of the poor and almsgiving and brotherly love and of the everlasting condemnation which is the lot of sinners ". There is a pleasant ironical touch here and there, as when Daniel prophesied sore difficulties for Zeno going on a military expedition into Thrace. " Is it possible, I beg you ", asked the Emperor Leo, " for anyone to survive a war without some labour and trouble ? "

Leo I died in 474 and Zeno succeeded in the same year and put an equal trust in the wisdom and virtue of St Daniel. Then Basiliscus, brother to the dowager-empress Verina, usurped the throne and declared himself the protector of the Eutychian heretics. The patriarch of Constantinople, Acacius, sent to St Daniel to acquaint him with what the usurper had done. Basiliscus on his side sent to him to complain of Acacius, whom he accused of raising rebellion against him. St Daniel replied that God would overthrow his government, and added such reproaches that the messenger dared not report them, but besought the saint to write them down and to seal the letter. The patriarch sent twice urgently to entreat Daniel to come to the succour of the Church. At length, with reluctance, he came down from his pillar—" with difficulty, because of the pain in his feet"— and was received with joy and excitement. Basiliscus, frightened at the uproar, retired to his country place, whither Daniel followed him. Not being able to walk for lack of practice, he was carried shoulder-high in a chair, surrounded by the

---

* The custom of anointing both the sick and the healthy with oil from the church lamps is still known in the East.

people as though he were, as was said by one in derision, a new consul. At the
palace the guards would not allow St Daniel to enter, so he shook off its dust from
his feet as a testimony against Basiliscus, and returned to the city. Basiliscus at
length went himself to the saint and promised to annul his orders in favour of
heresy—he pleaded that he was a " simple soldier-man ". Daniel rebuked him
severely for stirring up such trouble, and returned to the top of his pillar where he
lived many years longer, watching over all that went on in the world at his feet, a
power in the troubled history of Constantinople at that time. But Zeno after
twenty months returned with an army from Isauria, and Basiliscus fled. One of
the first things the emperor did after his return was to visit St Daniel, who had
foretold both his banishment and his restoration.

When he was eighty-four years old St Daniel gave his testament for his friends
and disciples : a very short document breathing a lovely spirit of charity and
affection and setting out succinctly the whole duty of man. After celebrating
the Holy Mysteries at midnight on his pillar for the last time he knew he was
dying. The Patriarch Euphemius was sent for, and there St Daniel died in the
year 493, and was buried at the foot of the pillar whereon he had lived for
thirty-three years.

The history of all the better-known pillar-saints has been very carefully studied by
Delehaye in his monograph, *Les Saints Stylites* (1923).   In that book will be found a critical
text of the long Greek life of St Daniel (pp. 1–94), as well as that of an early compendium
(pp. 95–103), and of the adaptation of the Metaphrast (pp. 104–147) ; there is also in the
preface (pp. xxxv to lviii) a description of the manuscripts used and a summary of the life
itself.   The main biography was the work of a contemporary who had himself seemingly
been one of the disciples of St Daniel.   It is a hagiographical document of the highest value,
and its general accuracy is confirmed by a study of other sources for the history of the same
period.   The life was published for the first time in the *Analecta Bollandiana*, vol. xxxii
(1913), and there is an excellent English version, with introduction and notes, in E. Dawes
and N. H. Baynes, *Three Byzantine Saints* (1948).   See also H. Lietzmann, *Byzantinische
Legenden* (1911), pp. 1–52.

BD PETER OF SIENA   (A.D. 1289)

PETER TECELANO was a citizen of Siena and a comb-maker by trade. After living
for some years in happiness with his wife, she died, leaving him childless, and he
joined the third order of St Francis, determining to devote to his neighbour the
time and money that was no longer required for his own household. His life was
quite without exterior event, such as might be led by any pious artisan. He worked
hard and for long hours, and at night would go to some church to pray, where
meditating on St Francis's following of our Lord he conceived the desire to be yet
more closely associated with his religious children. The guardian of the Friars
Minor accordingly gave him permission to live in a cell adjoining their infirmary,
where he continued to carry on his business almost to the end of his life. He
used frequently to visit the sick in the hospital of our Lady *della Scala* and he had
a strong sense of his public as well as his private duties as a citizen : once when
he had been deliberately passed over in the collection of a war-tax, he assessed
himself and insisted on paying what seemed to him to be due.

Bd Peter attained to a high degree of contemplative prayer and received spiritual
graces which it was difficult to hide, so that his holiness became known to many.
His opinion and advice were valued by priests and theologians equally with lay-
brothers and fellow workmen, but not at all by himself : " You are raising too

much wind for this poor dust ", he said to one who praised him. Among his chief
faults in his own opinion was talkativeness, and it took him fourteen years of
hard work to reduce it and build up the habit of silence at which he aimed. He
lived to a very advanced age, and as he lay dying foresaw the calamities which
were shortly to fall on Pistoia and Florence as well as on his own city. He
was buried in the Franciscan church and pilgrims came from all over Italy to
pray and be cured of their infirmities at his tomb. This *cultus* was approved in
1802.

This holy tertiary, who is sometimes called Peter Pettinaio (comb-maker), is noticed
by Wadding and other annalists of the Franciscan Order. There is a life by Peter di
Monterone, said to have been a contemporary, which was printed in Italian in 1529. Another
account was based upon a set of breviary lessons compiled in 1333. Further details regarding
sources will be found in the *Archivum Franciscanum Historicum*, vol. xiv (1921), p. 27. See
also *Monumenta Franciscana*, vol. v (1890), pp. 34–52 ; Mazzara, *Leggendario Francescano*,
vol. iii (1680), pp. 618–623, and Léon, *Auréole séraphique* (Eng. trans.), vol. i, pp. 456–463.
It is commonly held that the " Pier Pettingano ", the efficacy of whose prayers is made known
by Dante in the *Purgatorio*, canto xiii, line 128, was no other than this *beatus*.

BD FRANCO OF GROTTI   (A.D. 1291)

FRANCO LIPPI was a native of Grotti, near Siena, and was born in 1211. As a
youth he was violent, insubordinate and lazy, and after the death of his father he
spent all his time and money in gambling and debauchery. To avoid a prosecution
for murder he joined a band of *condottieri* wherein his evil propensities had full
scope, and by middle age his excesses had ruined his health and more than once
brought him nearly to death. When he was fifty he lost his eyesight, and the shock
of this sudden deprivation occasioned a complete change in him. He made a
general confession and set out on a long and painful pilgrimage to the shrine of
St James at Compostela. There his blindness was healed, but his spiritual
sight remained and he made a further pilgrimage, barefooted, from Compostela
to Rome.

While praying in a Carmelite church Franco had a vision of our Lady in which
he was told he must make public reparation for the endless scandals he had caused
in Siena. He accordingly went about the streets clothed in sackcloth and beating
himself with a whip, and eventually asked to be admitted into the Carmelite Order.
But his age—he was now sixty-five—and his appalling reputation made the friars
dubious of such a postulant, and they told him to try again in five years' time.
Franco persisted, and at last he was allowed to join as a lay-brother. He lived for
ten years in Carmel, and not only his brethren but the whole city was amazed and
edified by his fervour and the austerity of his penance. Visions and miracles were
said to be accorded him, and after his death on December 11, 1291, there was a
spontaneous recognition of him as a very holy penitent. This *cultus* was confirmed
in 1670.

No early separate biography seems to be known, but G. Lombardelli published in 1590,
La vita del b. Franco Sanese da Grotti, and another account by S. Grassi appeared in 1680.
For a more modern setting see *Il Monte Carmelo* (1917), pp. 300 *seq.*

BD HUGOLINO MAGALOTTI   (A.D. 1373)

FEW particulars are known of the life of this holy man, whose feast is kept by the
Friars Minor. He was born near Camerino in the early part of the fourteenth

century, and was left an orphan while a young man. Thereupon he gave his patrimony away to the poor, put on the Franciscan tertiary habit, and became a hermit. His life was entirely given to manual work, contemplation and penance, and the fame of his holiness drew many to his lonely cell. God glorified him with the gift of miracles, and numbers of the sick were healed at his intercession. He died on December 11, 1373, and was buried at the parish church of Fiegni. Pope Pius IX confirmed his *cultus* in 1856.

See Léon, *Auréole Séraphique* (Eng. trans.), vol. iv, pp. 177–178, where it is stated that an old manuscript life was in existence at the time of the beatification. We are also told that he is mentioned by Jacobilli in his *Santi e beati dell' Umbria*, and by other writers of that district.

BD JEROME RANUZZI (A.D. 1455)

THERE is a notable contrast between the characters of the two Servite *beati* commemorated this month, both in their youth and their maturity. Bonaventure Buonaccorsi was a preacher and what is called a man of action, Jerome Ranuzzi was a scholar and contemplative ; while the one spent his life in violence and disorder till nearly middle age, the other from his earliest years was noted for his devoutness and studious habits. Ranuzzi was born near the end of the fourteenth century at Sant' Angelo in Vado, a little town near Urbino which was one of the first to have a convent of Servite nuns, and before his twentieth year took the habit of the Servite friars, receiving the name of Jerome. After his profession he was sent to the University of Bologna, where he took his doctorate in theology, and was afterwards ordained priest and employed as professor in various houses-of-studies of his order in Italy. He was thus engaged for some years, till at last he was given permission to retire for a time to the priory in his native town.

Father Jerome became the valued friend of the whole neighbourhood. His solicitude in both temporal and spiritual works of mercy, his wisdom in both temporal and spiritual difficulties, soon made him known as an " angel of good counsel ". His quality was known to Frederick of Montefeltro, Duke of Urbino, who asked the Servite authorities for his services as theologian and personal adviser. This was the last thing that Bd Jerome wanted, but he was constrained by obedience to accept the post. It is not known how long he remained at Frederick's court, but he was as successful there as in a monastery and conducted negotiations with the Holy See and other matters of state to the satisfaction of his prince. He eventually was allowed to go back to Sant' Angelo, where before his death he rebuilt the nuns' convent. Jerome Ranuzzi died rather suddenly on December 11, 1455, and the devotion of the people was so great and miracles so numerous that his body, instead of being buried in the conventual graveyard, was at once enshrined above an altar in the church of the Servites at Sant' Angelo. This *cultus* was confirmed in 1775.

Some account of this *beatus* may be gathered from A. Giani, *Annales Ordinis Servorum*, vol. i, pp. 491–492 ; and some miracles attributed to him are recounted in vol. iii, pp. 599–600. That no very copious information is obtainable may be gathered from the fact that writers of the Servite Order itself (so Giani complains) have confused this Jerome with another Servite named Jerome, who lived some time before him and died in another part of the country.

12 : SS. EPIMACHUS AND ALEXANDER AND OTHER MARTYRS (A.D. 250)

WHILST the persecution set on foot by Decius raged at Alexandria in 250 and the magistrates were active in searching for Christians, Alexander and Epimachus fell into their hands. Upon confessing the name of Jesus Christ they were loaded with chains and suffered a long and rigorous confinement. After this trial of their faith and patience they were beaten, their sides were torn with iron hooks, and they achieved their martyrdom by fire. St Epimachus is the same who is mentioned in the Roman Martyrology, with St Gordian, on May 10 as having had his relics translated from Alexandria to Rome. St Dionysius, Bishop of Alexandria, an eyewitness of part of their sufferings, gives this short account of them, and also mentions four women martyrs who were crowned on the same day, and at the same place. Ammonaria, the first of them, was cruelly tortured, but declared that nothing could make her repeat the blasphemies dictated by the judge, and was at length led to execution, being, as it seems, beheaded. The second was named Mercuria, a woman of considerable age ; the third was Dionysia who, though a mother of children, cheerfully commended them to God and suffered for His love ; the name of the fourth is not recorded. The judge was furious at not being able to break down the resolution of Ammonaria, and to save his face ordered the other three to be executed at once without preliminary torture.

We know no more regarding SS. Epimachus and Alexander than we are told in a long extract which Eusebius (*Eccles. Hist.*, bk vi, ch. 41) makes from a letter of St Dionysius of Alexandria.

ST FINNIAN OF CLONARD, BISHOP (*c.* A.D. 549)

FINNIAN of Clonard was the outstanding figure among the holy men of Ireland in the period following St Patrick, but the accounts of his life contain many inconsistencies and anachronisms. Three hundred years after his death it was believed that, after becoming a monk, he made a long stay in Wales. He is said to have spent some time at St Cadoe's monastery at Nantcarfan and on the island in the Severn estuary now called Flatholm, which he miraculously cleared of vermin. Many other marvels were attributed to him, including the deliverance of his hosts from Saxon marauders by causing the raiders' camp to be swallowed up by an earthquake. Together with St Cadoc he projected a pilgrimage to Rome, but was admonished by an angel not to undertake it, and to return to Ireland instead. The details are quite unreliable, but it seems that Finnian may have come under the influence of St Cadoc, St Gildas and other Britons, with their emphasis on studies and on the superiority of the monastic state.

When he got back to Ireland Finnian founded churches in Leinster, including schools and monasteries at Aghowle and Mugna. At this last he was the object of a conspiracy, the chieftain's son Cormac provoking his elder brother Crimthann to persecute the saint, in the hope that Finnian would bring misfortune on Crimthann. We are told that this amiable plan succeeded. Crimthann tried to expel Finnian by force, and in the struggle got his leg broken, which accident Finnian named as an omen of the young man's future. But his great monastery was on the Boyne, at Clonard in Meath. Soon after he came here he was visited by a pagan elder, named Fraechan, who was reputed a magician. Finnian asked him from whom came his art, whether from God or another. " You ought to be able to find that out for yourself ", replied Fraechan. " Very well," said the saint, " tell me where is the place of my resurrection." " Not on earth, but in Heaven ", was the reply. " Try again." Fraechan answered as before. " Try yet again ", said St Finnian, rising from his seat. Then it dawned on the magician that he was being made fun of : " It is from where you were sitting ! " he exclaimed.

Yet St Finnian had spoken truly in a double sense, for when disciples gathered round him at Clonard there was indeed a resurrection of religion and learning from his teacher's chair. These are said eventually to have numbered three thousand. Finnian was to be known as the " Teacher of the Saints of Ireland " ; he was " The Master " ; and " like the sun in the high heavens he sent forth rays of goodness and holy teaching to give light to the world ". The education of saints who lived long after his time came to be credited to St Finnian. He was famed for his knowledge of the Holy Scriptures, and Clonard for centuries perpetuated the renown of his biblical studies ; but the school suffered much from the Danes and then from the Normans, till in the beginning of the thirteenth century it ceased to be the religious centre of the diocese of Meath, and the foundation of St Finnian became a monastery of Augustinian canons ; this remained till the sixteenth century. Both on his missions and teaching at Clonard many surprising miracles were attributed to Finnian, especially when it was a question of overcoming the hard-heartedness of some chieftain. He died during the epidemic of yellow-plague in the middle of the sixth century, offering his life for his countrymen : " As Paul died in Rome for the sake of the Christian people, lest they should all perish in Hell, so Finnian died at Clonard for the sake of the people of the Gael, that they might not all perish of the yellow-pest ", says his Irish life. The feast of St Finnian of Clonard is kept throughout Ireland ; he is venerated as a bishop, but it is doubtful if he ever was one.

There is a life in Irish which has been edited by Whitley Stokes in his *Lives of Saints from the Book of Lismore* (*Anecdota Oxoniensia*), pp. 75–83 and 222–230. A life in Latin in the Codex Salmanticensis has been printed by De Smedt in *Acta SS. Hiberniae Cod. Sal.*, cc. 189–210. Some portions of these are translated in Wade-Evans, *Life of St David*, pp. 43–46, and other references will be found in R. A. S. Macalister, *The Latin and Irish Lives of Ciaran* (1921), especially pp. 76–79. See also J. Ryan, *Irish Monasticism*, pp. 115–117 and *passim ;* L. Gougaud, *Christianity in Celtic Lands*, pp. 67–70 ; and J. F. Kenney, *Sources for the Early History of Ireland*, vol. i. The Penitential ascribed to " Vinnianus " may possibly be a compilation by St Finnian (or Findan) of Clonard, but *cf.* note under St Finnian of Moville (September 10). The whole subject of Finnian of Clonard has been excellently studied by Miss Kathleen Hughes ; see her paper on the cult in *Irish Historical Studies*, vol. ix (1954), pp. 13 *seq.*, and on the historical value of the Lives in the *English Historical Review*, vol. lxix (1954), pp. 353 *seq.*

ST CORENTIN, OR CURY, Bishop   (Sixth Century ?)

FROM early in the middle ages St Corentin was venerated as the first bishop of Cornouaille, whose see is now at Quimper, and during the seventeenth century his *cultus* became yet more popular owing to the preaching of the great missioner, Bd Julian Maunoir. But nothing can be said with certainty of the life of the saint. A number of legends about him are current in Brittany and are found in his *vita*, which probably was not written before the thirteenth century. It relates that the people of Cornouaille eventually drew him from his hermitage and sent him to Tours to be consecrated as their bishop by St Martin. By the chapel of St Corentin at Plomodiern there is a " holy well ", and in this stream he used to keep a marvellous fish ; he could cut from it every day sufficient for his requirements, return the fish to the water, and next morning it was whole again.* On one occasion he was able from this fish alone to feed the ruler of the neighbourhood, Grallon, and all his attendants. But one of them tried to verify this miracle for himself and so mutilated the fish that St Corentin, having healed it, dismissed it down the stream for ever, lest worse should befall it. This Grallon is supposed to have endowed his host with land, and Plomodiern belonged to the diocese of Cornouaille until the Revolution. During the Norman invasion the relics of St Corentin were taken from Quimper to the abbey of Marmoutier for safety, from whence an arm was brought back early in the seventeenth century. Veneration of St Corentin was known in the west of England, and he is the eponymous patron of Cury in Cornwall. The confusion of Menez Hom in Cornouaille with Menheniot in Cornwall (which is nowhere near Cury) has given rise to a baseless legend that he was once a hermit there.

The Latin life has been printed by Dom Plaine in the *Bulletin de la Société Archéologique du Finistère*, vol. xiii (1886), pp. 118–152. See Duchesne, *Fastes Épiscopaux*, vol. ii, pp. 242 and 371–375 ; LBS., vol. ii, pp. 181–182 ; F. Duine, *Memento* . . ., vol. i, n. 55, 222 ; but especially Canon G. H. Doble, *St Corentin* (1925) ; and also A. Oheix and E. C. Fawtier-Jones, *La Vita ancienne de S. Corentin* (1925) ; and R. Largillière, *S. Corentin et ses Vies latines* (1925).

ST EDBURGA, ABBESS OF MINSTER, VIRGIN (A.D. 751)

THIS Edburga, belonging to the royal family of Kent, was a disciple of St Mildred, whom she succeeded in the abbacy of Minster-in-Thanet. She is chiefly known as a friend and correspondent of St Boniface, who on one of his visits to Rome met her on pilgrimage there ; but her letters are not extant. After the death of Radbod, which enabled him to return to Frisia, Boniface wrote at once to tell Edburga the news, and asked her to send him a copy of the Acts of the Martyrs ; with her reply she sent him fifty pieces of gold and a carpet, and asked him to pray for the souls of her parents. Edburga seems to have had some reputation as a calligrapher, for later on St Boniface writes from Thuringia again asking for books, to be sent by the priest Eoba, this time the epistles of St Peter, which he would have her write out for him in golden letters. " Gifts of books and clothes, tokens of your affection, have often been a consolation to me in my troubles ", he says.

Boniface's companion St Lull, too, included a silver *stilus* for writing on wax among the presents that he sent to St Edburga. Boniface wrote again thanking her for " holy books ", with which and with " spiritual light " she had " comforted his exile in Germany ". " Fully trusting in your love, I implore you to pray for me, for I am shaken by my shortcomings." Once more, in a letter full of quotations from the Scriptures, he urges the abbess to pray for him, some years before the end came in blood and glory at Dokkum. The life of St Edburga was apparently as peaceful as that of St Boniface was eventful. Nothing more is known of her

* Miraculous fish are common in Celtic folklore ; *cf.* the Irish myth of the " salmon of knowledge ". Several holy wells of Wales had eels in them, and two trout were kept in Ffynnon Beris at Llanberis down to our own day. The eponymous saint of this place, Peris, was commemorated on December 11. Nothing whatever is known about him ; in old Welsh references he was commonly called " the Cardinal ".

except that she had a new monastery built on a fresh site, where the present Benedictine convent at Minster stands.

There is a short Latin life, printed in Capgrave's *Nova Legenda Angliae*, on which see T. D. Hardy, *Descriptive Catalogue of Materials* (Rolls Series), vol. i, pp. 475–477. A fragment in Anglo-Saxon referring to St Mildred and St Edburga has also been printed by Cockayne in his *Leechdoms*, vol. iii, pp. 422–433. But these tell us very little. The only reliable material is to be found in the letters of St Boniface and St Lull quoted above. This Edburga is a different person from the Eadburh who is made the subject of a romantic account by Asser : see R. M. Wilson, *Lost Literature of Medieval England* (1952), pp. 36–38.

ST VICELIN, Bishop of Staargard   (A.D. 1154)

VICELIN, who was to be the apostle of the Wends of what is now Holstein and district, was born at Hameln on the Weser about the year 1086. He studied in the cathedral school at Paderborn, and became in due course head of the school at Bremen and a canon of the cathedral there. It is said, but it is not certain, that he studied at Laon in France ; he was ordained priest by St Norbert at Magdeburg, and in 1126 began those missionary labours among the heathen Wends and other Slavonic tribes that lasted for over twenty years.

The first centre of St Vicelin was at Lübeck, that lovely city that was one of the first victims of " saturation-bombing " in the second world-war, on whose site he founded the first church. But his protector died soon after, and Vicelin moved to Wippenthorp, near Bremen. He was a tireless preacher and teacher and a most successful missionary ; but like other missionaries his work was interrupted and undone from time to time by war. To provide a more permanent centre he founded in Holstein a monastery (afterwards called Neumünster) for Augustinian canons, where one of his pupils was the chronicler Helmold ; later he established another at Högersdorf, and began a third at Segeberg. The missionaries made many converts and all seemed going well when a dire catastrophe blighted their efforts. Obotrite pirates descended upon the whole district, devastating the country and burning and sacking the houses. Their fury was especially directed against the Christians, most of whom were killed or driven out. The priests from Lübeck managed to escape and hid in the marshes, with water up to their necks, until at last they reached safety at Bishorst. But at Segeberg Bd Volker, who is described as " a brother of great simplicity ", was killed by the sword, whilst the other monks took to flight, bearing away the books and relics of the monastery which was utterly destroyed.

In spite of opposition from Frederick Barbarossa, St Vicelin was in 1149 made bishop of Staargard (now Oldenburg) in Holstein, but there is some doubt whether he ever took over his see. In any case he was struck down by paralysis three years later, and spent the last two years of his life in sickness and suffering at the abbey of Neumünster, where he died on December 12, 1154. It is rather curious that this missionary should not be mentioned in the Roman Martyrology, but his feast is observed on this day in north-western Germany.

Helmold, mentioned above, gives an account of St Vicelin's missionary work in his *Chronica Slavorum*, which incorporates much other matter that he learned from the saint himself : it is printed in MGH., *Scriptores*, vol. xxi. See also Kreusch, *Kirchengeschichte der Wendenlande* (1902) ; Krimphove, *Die Heiligen und Seligen des Westfalenlandes* ; A. Hauck, *Kirchengeschichte Deutschlands*, vol. iv ; and the *Acta Sanctorum*, March, vol. i (Bd Volker).

BD THOMAS HOLLAND, Martyr   (A.D. 1642)

Thomas Holland was born in 1600 at Sutton, near Prescot in Lancashire, and was educated in the English colleges at Saint-Omer and Valladolid. When in 1623 the Prince of Wales, Charles Stuart, came to Madrid to negotiate for the hand of the Infanta Maria, Mr Holland was chosen to go and welcome him on behalf of the English students, which he did in a Latin address " which is said to have given great satisfaction to his royal highness and his attendants ". Holland was fluent in French, Flemish and Spanish as well as Latin, and for his learning and goodness was dubbed *Bibliotheca pietatis*, " the library of goodness ", by his fellows.

He entered the Society of Jesus, and was sent on the English mission in 1635. He ministered with considerable fruit for seven years, though handicapped by poor health, which was aggravated by the conditions of life of a missionary priest in London in those days. On October 4, 1642, he was arrested on suspicion, and brought to trial at the Old Bailey two months later on the charge of being a priest from overseas. The evidence of four witnesses against him was insufficiently cogent ; but upon his refusing to make oath that he was not a priest the jury found him guilty, a verdict that gave dissatisfaction to the Lord Mayor and others on the bench, so that the Recorder's deputy gave sentence with reluctance.

Many people visited Mr Holland in prison during the two days before his execution, among them the Duke of Vendôme, who offered to intercede on the prisoner's behalf, an offer that was courteously refused. On the Sunday he heard many confessions and was able to celebrate Mass, which he did again the next day, just before he was led off to Tyburn. At the scaffold it was remarked that neither the sheriff of London nor of Middlesex was present, and it was freely canvassed that this was because they were not satisfied with the justice of the proceedings. The martyr now declared openly before the people that he was a Catholic, a priest and a Jesuit, and prayed aloud for the king and his people, " for whose prosperity and conversion to the Catholic faith, if I had as many lives as there are hairs on my head, drops of water in the ocean, or stars in the firmament, I would most willingly sacrifice them all ". " Which last words were received with a shout of the people. . . ." The hangman allowed him to hang till he was dead, before carrying out the rest of the bloody business.

See Challoner in MMP., where he made use of a Latin life published at Antwerp in 1645. Also Pollen, *Acts of English Martyrs*, and Foley, REPSJ., vol. i.

13 : ST LUCY, Virgin and Martyr   (A.D. 304)

THE English bishop St Aldhelm of Sherborne at the end of the seventh century celebrated St Lucy both in prose and verse, but unfortunately the " acts " on which he relied are a worthless compilation. They relate that Lucy was a Sicilian, born of noble and wealthy parents in the city of Syracuse, and brought up in the faith of Christ. She lost her father in infancy, and she was yet young when she offered her virginity to God. This vow, however, she kept a secret, and her mother, Eutychia, pressed her to marry a young man who was a pagan. Eutychia was persuaded by her daughter to go to Catania and offer up prayers to God at the tomb of St Agatha for relief of a haemorrhage from which she suffered. St Lucy accompanied her, and their prayers were answered. Then the saint disclosed her desire of devoting herself to God and bestowing her fortune on the poor, and Eutychia in gratitude left her at liberty to pursue her inclinations. Her suitor was very indignant, and in his anger accused her before the governor as a Christian, the persecution of Diocletian then being at its height. When Lucy remained resolute the judge commanded her to be exposed to prostitution in a brothel ; but God rendered her immovable, so that the guards were not able to carry her thither. Then attempt was made to burn her, but this also was unsuccessful. At length a sword was thrust into her throat.

Though the *acta* of St Lucy, preserved in various recensions both Latin and Greek, are quite unhistorical, her connection with Syracuse and her early *cultus* admit of no question. She was honoured at Rome in the sixth century amongst the most illustrious virgin martyrs whose triumphs the Church celebrates, and her name was inserted in the canon of the Mass both at Rome and Milan. Possibly on account of her name, which is suggestive of light or lucidity, she was invoked during the middle ages by those who suffered from eye-trouble, and various legends grew up, *e.g.* that her eyes were put out by the tyrant, or that she herself tore them out to present them to an unwelcome suitor who was smitten by their beauty. In either case they were miraculously restored to her, more beautiful than before.

In the cemetery of St John at Syracuse an inscription (fourth or early fifth century) referring to St Lucy has been found, upon which see P. Orsi in the *Römische Quartalschrift*, vol. ix (1895), pp. 299–308. A letter of Pope Gregory the Great proves that in his time dedications were made to her in Rome. See also CMH., p. 647 ; DAC., vol. ix, cc. 2616–2618 ; and G. Goyau, *Sainte Lucie* (1921). There were many folk-lore usages connected with her day, December 13, including the saying " Lucy-light, the shortest day and the longest night ". See Bächtold-Stäubli, *Handwörterbuch des deutschen Aberglaubens*, vol. v, cc. 1442–1446. She is often represented carrying her two eyes upon a dish. See Künstle, *Ikonographie*, vol. ii, and Drake, *Saints and their Emblems ;* as also Dunbar, *A Dictionary of Saintly Women*, vol. i, pp. 469–470. The enthusiasm evoked by the story of St Lucy is curiously attested by Sigebert of Gembloux who wrote a Latin poem of 1400 lines in her honour, which was printed by E. Dümmler in 1893. The reference to St Aldhelm is to his *De laudibus virginitatis ;* see *Aldhelmi Opera*, ed. R. Ehwald in MGH., *Auct. antiquiss.*, vol. xv (1919), in prose, pp. 293–294, in verse, lines 1779–1841.

SS. EUSTRATIUS AND HIS COMPANIONS, MARTYRS (DATE UNKNOWN)

" IN Armenia ", says the Roman Martyrology, " the passion of the holy martyrs Eustratius, Auxentius, Eugenius, Mardarius and Orestes, during the persecution under Diocletian. Of these, Eustratius, first of all under Lysias and then at Sebastea under the governor Agricolaus, was together with Orestes subjected to cruel torments, and being cast into a furnace gave up the ghost. Orestes, however, was laid upon a fiery metal plate, and so passed to the Lord. The others, having suffered the cruellest punishments from the governor Lysias at Arabraca, achieved martyrdom in various ways. Their bodies were afterwards translated to Rome and honourably buried in the church of St Apollinaris." St Eustratius was an Armenian of good family, and St Orestes a soldier who was converted by the sight of his fortitude under torture. St Eugenius was his servant, and Mardarius and Auxentius two friends who had interceded for him. Their relics are still venerated in the church of Sant' Apollinare. The *passio* of St Eustratius is a good example of how such documents were interpolated and expanded for didactic and edificatory ends : the martyr is made to argue at great length with the magistrate, discussing passages from Plato and the poets in support of their arguments.

There is a late Greek *passio* which has been printed in Migne, PG., vol. cxvi, pp. 468–505. It has been pointed out that the mention of a will or testament in this account shows a dependence on the story of the forty martyrs of Sebastea (March 10). Consult also Delehaye, *Les passions des martyrs* . . . (1921), pp. 266–268, and *Zeitschrift f. kath. Theologie*, 1894, pp. 291–292. Reference is not infrequently made to this group in Byzantine literature under the name of " the five saints ". Fragments of the *passio* have been found in a ninth-century handwriting, but we have no guarantee that there were five martyrs who bore these names or that they suffered in the persecution of Diocletian. An Armenian version of the *passio* is printed in *Vitae et Passiones Sanctorum*, published at Venice in 1874, vol. i, pp. 435–475.

ST JUDOC, OR JOSSE (A.D. 668)

JUDOC was a son of Juthaël, King of Armorica (Brittany), and brother of that Judicaël who has a *cultus* in the diocese of Quimper. The *Chronicle of Saint-Brieuc* says of Judicaël that " Terror of his name alone was sufficient to keep evil men from violence, for God, who watched over him without ceasing, had made him brave and mighty in battle ; it happened more than once that with the aid of the Almighty he was able to put whole troops of the enemy to flight by the strength of his sword-arm alone ". About this King Dagobert I at Paris had rather different views, and he sent St Eligius to try and restrain his turbulent neighbour, to whom the foundation of the abbey of Paimpont is attributed.

About the year 636 Judoc withdrew from secular life and, it is said, was ordained priest in Ponthieu. After a pilgrimage to Rome he eventually settled as a hermit at Runiacum near the mouth of the Canche, later called after him, Saint-Josse. Here he died about the year 668. We are told that his body was not buried in the earth and that it remained incorrupt ; moreover, the surprising circumstance is added that his hair, beard and nails continued to grow with such luxuriance that his successors in the hermitage had to cut them from time to time,

It is said that Charlemagne gave this hermitage at Saint-Josse-sur-Mer to Alcuin as a hospice for cross-Channel travellers, and that Alcuin sometimes stayed there. According to the tradition of the New Minster (Hyde) at Winchester, St Judoc's relics were brought there, about the year 901, and this translation was commemorated on January 9. The saint's name figures in half-a-dozen old English calendars, and he is mentioned in the Roman Martyrology. Chaucer's *Wife of Bath* swears " by God and by Seint Joce ".

One early Latin life of St Judoc, dating from the beginning of the ninth century, has been printed by Mabillon, vol. ii, pp. 542–547. There are, however, others of later date, notably that of Isembard, a monk of Fleury, and that of Florentius of Saint-Josse-sur-Mer, which have probably contributed more to the relatively wide diffusion of this popular legend. The monograph of J. Trier, *Der hl. Jodocus ; sein Leben und seine Verehrung* (1924) is not exhaustive as regards sources, nor wholly reliable ; see on this the *Analecta Bollandiana*, vol. xliii (1925), pp. 193–194. For a sermon on St Josse by Lupus of Ferrières, see W. Levison, in the *Festschrift Walter Goetz* (1927). The cult of St Judoc was widespread : churches were dedicated in his honour even in the Tirol (Fink, *Kirchenpatrozinien Tirols*, 1928). Consult also Duine, *Memento*, p. 49, and Van der Essen, *Étude critique sur les saints mérovingiens*, pp. 411–413. The treatment of St Judoc in art is discussed by Künstle, *Ikonographie*, vol. ii, pp. 330–331 ; and the folk-lore aspects in Bächtold-Stäubli, *Handwörterbuch des deutschen Aberglaubens*, vol. iv, cc. 701–703. For the resting-place of the saint's relics, see Fr P. Grosjean in *Analecta Bollandiana*, vol. lxx (1952), p. 404.

ST AUBERT, Bishop of Cambrai and Arras   (*c.* A.D. 669)

A LIFE of St Aubert (Autbertus) was written at the beginning of the eleventh century (which is sometimes, but probably wrongly, attributed to St Fulbert of Chartres), but it is so inadequate that the four pages which Alban Butler devotes to the saint are made up chiefly of vague generalities and more or less irrelevant historical notes.   Nothing at all is known of St Aubert until he came to the see of Cambrai in 633 or later.   When about the year 650 the unknown hermit St Gislenus set about establishing a monastery near Mons, attempts were made to prejudice the bishop against him.   St Aubert refused to judge him unseen, and as the result of an interview gave him every encouragement and eventually consecrated his church.   Among those studying for the priesthood at Cambrai was a young man called Landelin, who ran away to live a wild and dissolute life.   He came back penitent, and was so well handled by St Aubert that he became a monk, founded monasteries, and is named as a saint in the Roman Martyrology. The name of St Aubert is associated with the undertaking of the monastic life by a number of distinguished lay-people at this time, such as St Vincent Madelgarius and his family and St Amalburga, the mother of St Gudula.   More certain is his presence at the translation of the relics of St Fursey to Péronne by St Eligius about 650.   Aubert's own burial-place was in St Peter's church at Cambrai, where was afterwards an abbey of canons regular which bore his name.

The Latin life mistakenly ascribed to Fulbert is printed in full by Ghesquière, *Acta Sanctorum Belgii*, vol. iii, pp. 529–564.   A collection of miracles will be found in the *Analecta Bollandiana*, vol. xix (1900), pp. 198–212.   On the confusion which has arisen between Autbert, Bishop of Cambrai, and Audebert, Count of Ostrevant, see the *Analecta Bollandiana*, vol. li (1933), pp. 99–116.

ST ODILIA, OR OTTILIA, Virgin   (*c.* A.D. 720)

THERE lived in the time of King Childeric II a Frankish lord of Alsace named Adalric, married to a lady named Bereswindis.   To them was born, near the end of the seventh century, at Obernheim in the Vosges Mountains, a daughter who was blind from her birth.   This was a matter first of irritation and then of unreasoning fury to Adalric ; he regarded it as a personal affront to himself and a reflection on the honour of his family, in which such a misfortune had never happened before.   In vain did his wife try to persuade him that it was the will of God, decreed in order that His almighty power might be made manifest in the child.   Adalric would have none of it, and insisted that the babe should be slain. Bereswindis was able at length to turn him from this crime, but only on condition that the child should be sent away and nobody told to whom it really belonged. She fulfilled the first part of this condition, but not the second, confiding the baby and its history to a peasant woman who had formerly been in her service.   When this woman's neighbours asked awkward questions, Bereswindis arranged for her and all her family to go away and live at Baume-les-Dames, near Besançon, where there was a nunnery in which the girl in due course could be brought up.   Here she lived until she was twelve years old, without, for reasons not explained, ever having been baptized.   Then St Erhard, a bishop at Regensburg, was warned in a vision that he was to go to the convent at Baume, where he would find a young girl who had been born blind ; her he was to baptize, giving her the name of Odilia, and she would receive her sight. St Erhard thereupon consulted St Hidulf at Moyenmoutier, and together they went to Baume. They found the girl and baptized her, giving her the name of Odilia (Ottilia, Othilia, Odile), and when he had anointed her head St Erhard touched her eyes with the chrism and at once she could see.

Odilia continued to serve God in the convent, but the miracle of which she had been the subject and the progress she now made in studies raised up the jealousy of some of the nuns and they began to indulge in petty persecution. So Odilia sent a letter to her brother Hugh, of whose existence she had been told, asking him to do for her whatever his kind heart should suggest. St Erhard meanwhile had acquainted Adalric with his daughter's recovery, and that unnatural parent was more angry than ever, flatly refusing Hugh's request to have Odilia home and forbidding the mention of her name. Hugh nevertheless sent for her, and it so happened that he was standing with his father on a neighbouring hill when Odilia arrived in a wagon, surrounded by a crowd of people. When Adalric heard who it was and how she came to be there, he raised his heavy staff and with one blow stretched Hugh dead at his feet. In his remorse he turned to his daughter and was as affectionate to her as he had before been cruel. Odilia lived at Obernheim with a few companions who joined her in her devotions and charitable works among the poor. After a time her father wanted to marry her to a German duke, whereupon she fled from home and, when she was closely pursued, a cliff-face at the Schlossberg, near Freiburg in Breisgau, opened to admit and conceal her. To get her home again Adalric promised her his castle of Hohenburg (now called the Odilienberg) to turn into a monastery, and here she became abbess. Finding that the steepness of the mountain was a discouragement and inconvenience to pilgrims she founded an auxiliary convent lower down on the eastern side, called Niedermünster, with a hospice attached.

It is said of the holy foundress that some time after the death of her father she received a supernatural assurance that her prayers and penances had released him from the state of Purgatory, and that St John the Baptist appeared to her and indicated the site and dimensions for a chapel which she wished to build in his honour. Other supernatural visitations and a number of miracles are also attributed to her. After ruling the convent for many years St Odilia died on December 13, about the year 720.

Such, in brief, is the legend of St Odilia about whose life the truth is as elusive as the popular veneration of the saint is definite. Her shrine and her abbey were the objects of a great devotion throughout the middle ages ; they were favoured by the emperors from Charlemagne to Charles IV, and among those who were drawn to Hohenburg by devotion were St Leo IX, while he was still bishop of Toul, and, it is said, King Richard I of England. The pilgrimage was no less popular among the common people, and St Odilia was venerated as the patroness of Alsace before the sixteenth century. Tradition pointed to a spring as having been by her miraculously called from the rock for the convenience of the nuns and their pilgrims, and its waters were (and are) used for bathing unhealthy eyes while invoking the intercession of the once blind saint. The same custom is observed by pilgrims to the Odilienstein in Breisgau, where the rock opened to receive her. After undergoing many vicissitudes the shrine of St Odilia and the remains of her monastery came into the possession of the diocese of Strasburg, and since the middle of last century the Odilienberg has again become a place of pilgrimage. Her relics are preserved in the chapel of St John the Baptist, a medieval building on the site of the one above referred to as built by St Odilia herself : it is now more commonly called by her name.

The text of what has been proved to be a tenth-century Life of St Odilia has been edited by W. Levison in MGH., *Scriptores Merov.*, vol. vi (1913), pp. 24–50 ; and *cf. Analecta Bollandiana*, vol. xiii (1894), pp. 5–32 and 113–121. But even here in the judgement of Levison hardly anything can be accepted as reliable history. At the same time St Odilia continues to be one of the most popular saints not only in Alsace but also in Germany and France. There is a considerable literature concerning her, of which an idea may be formed from the references in Potthast, *Wegweiser*, vol. ii, p. 1498, and in DAC., vol. xii (1936), cc. 1921–1934. Much information may be gleaned from different volumes of the *Archiv f. elsässische Kirchengeschichte*, as for example an article in vol. viii, pp. 287–316 on " Das Odilienlied in Lothringen ". For the most part the devotional lives of St Odilia, such for example as that of H. Welschinger in the series " Les Saints ", are historically unreliable. This last even treats as a serious document the forgery of Jerome Vignier which was exposed by L. Havet in the *Bibliothèque de l'École des Chartes*, for 1885. On St Odilia in art see Künstle, *Ikonographie*, vol. ii, pp. 475–478, and C. Champion, *Ste Odile* (1931). At the time of the battles of Verdun during World War I, St Odilia became very celebrated in France through the attribution to her of a completely apocryphal prophecy. It was again current, though less widely, during 1939–1945.

BD JOHN MARINONI (A.D. 1562)

THIS servant of God is the last in order of date of official veneration to be included in Alban Butler's text and is one of the few *beati* (whether officially or popularly so called) admitted by him into his work. The *cultus* of Bd John was authorized by Pope Clement XIII in 1762, so that Butler must have written the notice of him to be added to the second edition. Francis Marinoni was the third and youngest son of a good family of Bergamo, but was born at Venice in 1490. Having entered the ecclesiastical state, he served among the clergy of St Pantaleon's church ; and when he was ordained priest became chaplain, and afterwards superior, of the hospital for incurables at Venice. He was called thence to be a canon in the church of St Mark, where his life was the edification of his colleagues and of the whole city. Out of a desire of serving God more effectively he resigned his benefice and in 1528 joined the clerks regular called Theatines. He made his profession in 1530, being then forty years of age, under the eyes of their founders, St Cajetan and Mgr Caraffa, and on this occasion changed his first name for John. When St Cajetan was called from Venice to found the house of clerks regular of St Paul at Naples he took Marinoni with him. In that city he never ceased to preach the word of God with admirable simplicity and fruitfulness, and was chosen several times superior of his community, which he maintained in a perfect spirit of apostolic charity and zeal. Both by his prayers and by his exhortations in the pulpit and confessional he was an instrument of salvation to many. When St Cajetan came back to Naples in 1543 Bd John was his right-hand man in the establishment of *montes pietatis*, benevolent pawnshops for the help of the poor, in the city and its neighbourhood. He refused the office of archbishop of Naples, and died there on December 13, 1562, ministered to by St Andrew Avellino, who wrote an account of his former novice-master.

See a biography by J. L. Bianchi, *Ragguaglio della vita del B. Giovanni Marinoni* (1763), and another sketch by J. Silos, republished in view of the beatification in 1762.

BD ANTONY GRASSI   (A.D. 1671)

VINCENT GRASSI, of Fermo in the Italian province of the Marches, was a gentleman of pious life with a great devotion to our Lady of Loreto.   When he died in 1602 his son Antony was ten years old, and the boy inherited his father's devotion while he improved his piety into holiness.   As a schoolboy he got into the habit of frequenting the local church of the Oratorian fathers, and there he met Father Flaminio Ricci, a personal disciple of St Philip Neri, who determined the boy's vocation and encouraged him therein.   Accordingly, in spite of some spirited opposition from his mother, Antony when he was seventeen joined the community at the Oratory.   He was a keen student and entered the congregation bearing the reputation of a " walking dictionary ", and soon acquired the good grasp of scriptural and theological science that he already had of the classics and philosophy. The Oratory at Fermo was the third founded during the lifetime of St Philip Neri, and in the atmosphere of his gracious spirit Bd Antony was formed as a Christian priest.   For some years he was tormented by scruples, but these left him entirely from the hour that he celebrated his first Mass, and thenceforward an imperturbable serenity was his notable characteristic.   " I have never seen him put out ", said Father Mazziotti, s.j., and Cardinal Facchinetti of Spoleto testified to the same effect.

In 1621, when he was twenty-nine and had been some years a priest, a thing happened which left an indelible mark on Father Grassi : a small scar on his body but a profound impression on his soul.   He was kneeling at prayer in the church of the Holy House at Loreto when he was struck by lightning.   Such an experience is of sufficient rarity to make his account of it of great interest.

> I felt shaken and as though I were outside myself ; and it seemed to me that my soul was separated from my body and that I was in a swoon. . . . Then I was roused by a great crash, like thunder, and I opened my eyes and found that I had fallen head-first down the steps.   I saw bits of stone on the floor and the air was filled with a smoke so thick that it seemed like dust. I thought that plaster must have fallen from the ceiling, but on looking up I saw that it was undamaged.   Then I saw that a piece of skin had been ripped off one of my fingers, and I remembered a story I had heard of a priest at Camerino who was killed by lightning, on whose body there was no mark except some skin off his hand.   So when I saw my finger I thought that I too was going to die.   And a sort of heat burning my inside made me feel yet more like it, and when I tried to move my legs there was no feeling in them.   I was afraid that that scorching heat would reach my heart and kill me.   I was helpless, and lay without moving on the steps, thinking that if I could not die in the Oratory I should at any rate do so in a sanctuary of the Mother of God.   Then someone bent over me, and I told him I could not move ; he called for help and a chair was brought and I was put in it, when I fainted again.   But I was conscious that my head and arms and legs were dangling uselessly, and my sight and speech had failed, though my hearing was acute.   I knew someone was suggesting the holy names of Jesus and Mary to me.

When he recovered full consciousness Father Grassi still thought he was going to die, and asked for extreme unction.   The doctor recommended that it should be given, but that Father Grassi be first carried to his lodging. " Then I made the discovery that if we believe death to be close at hand we become quite indifferent to this world and know all earthly things to be emptiness. . . . After this they gave me some soup, and I passed a quiet night." He recovered in a few days, when he found that his underclothes had been scorched : these were given to the Loreto church as a thank-offering. He also states that the shock completely cured him of acute indigestion. A more important result was that henceforward Father Grassi felt that his life belonged to God in a very special manner ; not a day was allowed to pass without his making a special act of thanksgiving for his preservation, and every year he made a pilgrimage to Loreto with the same intention.

Shortly after this happening Bd Antony asked for and received faculties to hear confessions, which for the remainder of his life was one of his most notable activities. He brought to it the same simplicity as to everything else : listening to the penitent's accusation, saying a few words of exhortation, imposing a penance and giving absolution. He preferred not to give direction or to suggest rules of life or to give advice on anything not directly bearing on the matter of the confession. At the process of his beatification convincing testimony was given that he possessed the gift of reading consciences, not merely in generalities but in specific actions of which he could have no natural knowledge. In 1635 Bd Antony was elected superior of the Fermo Oratory, an office which he filled with such satisfaction to his brethren that they re-elected him every three years till the end of his life. He used to say that in forming an estimate of a person care should be taken not to regard a single action or trait alone but the whole of them, in which more good than bad would generally be found. He was, accordingly, a very gentle superior, and when he was asked why he did not show more severity replied, " I do not think I should know how. Is this the way ? " and assumed a sham air of authoritarian pomposity. In the same way he neither practised nor recommended unusual bodily austerities. When some inquisitive person asked him if he wore a hair-shirt he replied that he did not, because he had learnt from St Philip that it is better to begin with spiritual mortification. " Humbling the mind and will ", he said, " is more effective than a hair-shirt between your skin and your clothes."

This did not mean that he was easy-going ; on the contrary, he insisted on the following of the Oratorian constitution *ad litteram* and maintained his community at a very high level of observance and efficiency by his personal example and by quiet encouragement and reproof. His quietness extended to his own voice, and loud speech he would not tolerate. His playful admonition, " If you please, Father, only a few inches of voice ", was quite enough. Bd Antony's influence extended beyond his own house ; Archbishop Gualtieri of Fermo said he could not bear to think of losing him, and Cardinal Facchinetti of Spoleto and Cardinal Emilio Altieri (afterwards Pope Clement X) used frequently to seek his counsel on both spiritual and administrative matters. When food riots took place at Fermo in 1649 it was Father Grassi who tried to mediate between the cardinal-governor and the people, and was nearly shot by the mob for his pains. At all times he had a great concern for the good of his native town and its people : nothing would induce him to make social or ceremonial engagements, but he would go out at any time of the day or night to visit the sick or dying or anyone else who needed his services. As he grew older his prescience, both of the future and of events at a distance, increased, and was frequently used both for consolation and warning in his dealings with the many who came to him.

As he approached his eightieth year Bd Antony had the humiliation of the failure of some of his faculties.   He had to give up preaching because, owing to the loss of teeth, he could not make himself understood, and then to cease hearing confessions.   But he was still as active as ever in intent, especially when there was any chance of reclaiming a sinner.   But after a fall downstairs Bd Antony was confined to his room, and at the end of November 1671 he had to take to his bed. He died a fortnight later, Archbishop Gualtieri having come every day himself to give him holy communion.   Almost his last acts were to reconcile two fiercely-quarrelling brothers and to restore the sight of Father Remigio Leti sufficiently to enable him to celebrate Mass, which he had not been able to do for nine years. Numerous miracles were attributed to the intercession of Antony Grassi, but owing to civil disturbances and other causes his beatification was not achieved until the year 1900.

Father Antony's life was written by his devoted friend and disciple Fr Cristoforo Antici, and very shortly after death an official enquiry into his virtues and reputed miracles was begun by the archbishop of Fermo, Mgr Gualtieri, who knew him well and held him in much veneration.   The printed documents of the process of beatification are still accessible. In 1901 a detailed biography for English readers was publi3hed by Lady Amabel Kerr under the title *A Saint of the Oratory* ; see, too, E. I. Watkin, *Neglected Saints* (1955).

14 : ST SPIRIDION, Bishop of Tremithus   (Fourth Century)

MANY stories are told of this Cypriot saint, who was at the same time a shepherd, married and a bishop.   Sozomen, who wrote in the middle of the fifth century, says that a gang of thieves attempting one night to carry off some of his sheep were stopped by an invisible hand, so that they could neither steal nor make their escape.   Spiridion (or better, Spyridon), finding them thus the next morning, set them at liberty by his prayers and gave them a ram, lest they should have been up all night for nothing.   The same historian says that it was the saint's custom to fast with his family for some days in Lent without eating anything.   Once during this time, when he had no bread in his house, a traveller called to rest and refresh himself on the road.   Spiridion, having nothing else, ordered some salt pork to be boiled, for he saw the traveller was very tired.   Then he invited the stranger to eat.   He excused himself, saying that he was a Christian. Spiridion, himself setting the example by way of courtesy, replied that therefore he was quite free to eat ; thereby reminding the stranger both that ecclesiastical precepts do not bind unreasonably and that to a Christian no food is in itself forbidden.

St Spiridion was chosen bishop of Tremithus, on the sea-coast near Salamis, and thenceforth combined the care of sheep with the care of souls.   His diocese was very small and the inhabitants poor, but the Christians were regular in their lives ; there remained among them some idolaters.   In the persecution of Galerius he made a glorious confession of the faith.   The Roman Martyrology says he was one of those who lost their right eye, had the left leg hamstrung, and in that state were sent to work in the mines, and (mistakenly) that he was among the bishops at the Council of Nicaea in 325.   There is a legend in the East that on the way to the council he fell in with a party of other bishops, who were alarmed lest the rustic simplicity of Spiridion should compromise the cause of orthodoxy.   So they told their servants to cut the heads off the mules of Spiridion and his deacon, which was done. When he prepared to set off before dawn the next day and discovered the crime, Spiridion was not at all discomfited. He told the deacon to put the severed heads upon the bodies, and at once they grew together and the animals lived. But when the sun rose it was found that a mistake had been made in the dark : for the bishop's white mule had a brown head and the deacon's brown mule had a white head. During the council a pagan philosopher named Eulogius made an attack on Christianity, and an aged, one-eyed bishop, unpolished in manner and appearance, got up to reply to the urbane scoffer. He affirmed the omnipotent God and the incarnation of the Son for the redemption of all people as things beyond proof to be held by faith : did Eulogius believe them, or did he not ? After a pause the philosopher was constrained to admit that he did. " Then ", said the bishop, " come with me to the church and receive the sign of faith." And Eulogius did so, for, he said, words and arguments cannot resist virtue, meaning thereby the power of the Holy Ghost manifested in the unlearned bishop. Later writers identify this bishop with St Spiridion, but without authority.

A certain person had deposited for safety in the hands of Spiridion's daughter Irene something of great value. This he demanded of the bishop after her death ; but it was not to be found and nobody knew where it was. Whereupon, it is said, St Spiridion went to the place where his daughter was buried, called her by her name, and asked where she had put the missing article. Then she answered him, giving directions where she had hid it that it might be more safe : and it was found there. Spiridion had very little learning, but he had made the Scriptures his daily study and had learned what respect is due to the word of God. Once when the bishops of Cyprus were assembled together, St Triphyllius, Bishop of Ledra (whom St Jerome commends as the most eloquent man of his time), was preaching a sermon. Mentioning that passage, " Take up thy bed, and walk ", he said "couch" instead of " bed ", thinking that word the more elegant and suitable. St Spiridion objected against this false nicety and attempt to add graces to what was more adorned with simplicity, and asked the preacher whether the word our Lord Himself had used was not good enough for him.* The relics of St Spiridion were translated from Cyprus to Constantinople, and again to Corfu, where they are still venerated. He is the principal patron of the Catholics of Corfu, Zakynthos and Kephalonia.

Besides the relatively early references made to St Spiridion by the historians Socrates and Sozomen, it seems that a life of him was written at the beginning of the seventh century by Leontius of Neapolis. This is preserved to us only in the later adaptation of the Metaphrast (Migne, PG., vol. cxvi, pp. 417–468). There is also a memorial discourse by Theodore of Paphos (printed in part by Usener, *Beiträge zur Geschichte der Legendenliteratur*, pp. 222–232, and edited complete in 1901 by S. Papageorgios), but it proves to be in large part simply a plagiarism from an anonymous Life of Bishops Metrophanes and Alexander of Constantinople (see P. Heseler, *Hagiographica*, 1934). It is also stated that a life of St Spiridion was written in elegiacs by his pupil, Triphyllius of Ledra, but this has not survived. In Byzantine art Spiridion is recognizable by his peculiar shepherd's cap : see, for example, G. de Jerphanion, *Les églises rupestres de Cappadoce* (1932) ; and the *Byzantinische Zeitschrift* for 1910, pp. 29 and 107. See P. Van den Ven, *La Légende de S. Spyridon* (1953), " beau travail d'édition et de critique " (Fr F. Halkin).

---

* The obvious reflection that this rebuke would sometimes apply also to Alban Butler himself is modified by the further reflection that the fashions of the eighteenth century are not ours. But there are not wanting writers and speakers to-day who might with advantage ponder this anecdote.

SS. NICASIUS, Bishop of Rheims, and his Companions, Martyrs (A.D. 451 ?)

An army of barbarians ravaging part of Gaul plundered the city of Rheims. Nicasius, the bishop, had foretold this calamity to his flock in consequence of a vision, and urged them to prepare for the visitation by works of penance. When he saw the enemy at the gates and in the streets, forgetting himself and solicitous only for his spiritual children, he went from door to door encouraging all to patience and constancy. When the people asked him whether they should yield or fight to the end he, knowing that the city must fall, replied, " Let us abide the mercy of God and pray for our enemies. I am ready to give myself for my people." Standing at the door of his church, in endeavouring to save the lives of some, he exposed himself to the swords of the infidels, who cut off his head. St Florentius, his deacon, and St Jucundus, his lector, were massacred by his side. His sister, St Eutropia, seeing herself spared in order that hers might be another fate, threw herself upon her brother's murderer and kicked and scratched him till she too was cut down and killed.

There is a *passio* incorporated in Flodoard, *Historia Remensis ecclesiae*, for which see MGH., *Scriptores*, vol. xiii, pp. 417–420, and other texts in the *Analecta Bollandiana*, vol. i and vol. v. Consult also Duchesne, *Fastes Épiscopaux*, vol. iii, p. 81. It seems probable that Nicasius was martyred by the Huns in 451, rather than by the Vandals in 407.

ST VENANTIUS FORTUNATUS, Bishop of Poitiers   (c. A.D. 605)

Venantius Honorius Clementianus Fortunatus, born near Treviso about 535 and educated at Ravenna, is better known as a poet than as a saint. He was a popular man during his lifetime, admired by King Sigebert and his courtiers as well as by St Radegund and her nuns, and his writings continued to receive increasing appreciation up to the time that a sixteenth-century Italian panegyrist said that his heavenly pindaric hymns were enough to make Horace himself feel humble. After that there was a reaction, which helped the formation of a more just estimate. But it can hardly be denied that the popularity of Fortunatus was in a measure due to an obvious human weakness—his desire to please and to be pleased. St Radegund and Abbess Agnes and Duke Lupus deserved the eulogies he addressed to them ; such people as Charibert and Fredegund did not at their best. Fortunatus left Italy when he was about thirty in order to return thanks at the shrine of St Martin at Tours for his recovery from some eye-trouble. He wrote poems to all the bishops and other distinguished people who entertained him on the road and, his visit to the court of Metz coinciding with the royal wedding, he composed an *epithalamium* for Sigebert and Brunehilda. At Paris he was particularly impressed by the care with which the clergy sang the Divine Office.

From Tours Fortunatus went to Poitiers, where he settled down, was ordained priest, and formed his lifelong friendship with St Radegund, Abbess Agnes, and the nuns of Holy Cross, for whom he became a sort of *factotum* and unofficial steward. A constant exchange of letters went on between him, his " mother " Radegund, and his " sister " Agnes, letters that were often accompanied by poems, most of which are lost. The friendship was intimate enough to be playful, and serious enough to be fruitful.   One Lent Fortunatus wrote Radegund a letter in Latin verse in which he asks her not to shut herself up so closely during the penitential season : " Even though the clouds have gone and the sky is serene, the day is sunless when you are absent."   He tells her to drink wine and to eat more for the sake of her health, and thanks her for the fruit and dishes she had sent him. " You told me to eat two eggs in the evening : to tell the truth I ate four.   I wish I could find my mind always as prepared to submit as my stomach is ready to obey your orders."   And he tells her he sends flowers, roses and lilies, when he can get them.

In 569 the Emperor Justin II sent a relic of the True Cross to the monastery, and we see Fortunatus in another mood.   King Sigebert deputed St Euphronius of Tours solemnly to deposit it in Holy Cross (Meroveus of Poitiers, who was no friend of Fortunatus, having refused), and for that occasion Fortunatus wrote the hymn *Vexilla regis prodeunt,* which we now sing as a Vespers hymn at Passiontide and on feasts of the Cross.   He was at his best as a liturgical poet, and there is another hymn of the Passion of his used in the Roman liturgy, *Pange Lingua gloriosi lauream certaminis;* the Easter *Salve festa dies* is also his.   St Radegund died in 587, and Agnes also dying about that time Fortunatus mixed more in public and ecclesiastical affairs, being a welcome guest on all occasions that could be suitably celebrated in verse.   He associated particularly with three holy bishops, SS. Felix of Nantes, Leontius of Bordeaux and Gregory of Tours, the last of whom encouraged him to collect and publish his poems.   Ten books of them were made public during his life.   His more formal works include Lives of St Martin and St Radegund and of several other saints. Sometime about the year 600 he was elected bishop of Poitiers, but governed the see for only a very short time.

Venantius Fortunatus was peculiarly, almost morbidly, alive to the sufferings and hardships of women, as may be seen in his lines on virginity, addressed to the Abbess Agnes, and elsewhere in his works.   But this sensitiveness of temperament makes him the more valuable as a recorder of the part played by Christian life and thought in Merovingian Gaul, a part which in its finer manifestations was to a very considerable extent in the hands of women.   The usual estimate of Fortunatus personally is that he was " an illustrious personage, a good poet and a great bishop ". Not all judgements have been so kind, and adverse critics have asserted that he pushed tact and prudence beyond the border of mean-spiritedness and flattery, and that his guiding principle was to get as much enjoyment out of life as possible.   It must be admitted that he seems often rather too anxious to please ; but it must also be admitted that, properly understood, to " make the best of both worlds ", is a praiseworthy Christian ambition.   No honest way of life is inconsistent with sanctity, and St Venantius Fortunatus was a cultured Roman gentleman of refined taste and rather fastidious habits.   His name has not been admitted to the Roman Martyrology but his feast is kept by several French and Italian dioceses.

Our knowledge of Fortunatus is mainly derived from Gregory of Tours and from the poet's own writings and correspondence.   The best text of these is that edited by Leo and Krusch in MGH., *Auctores antiquissimi,* vol. iv.   For a literary appreciation of his writings it will be sufficient to refer to M. Manitius, *Geschichte der lateinischen Literatur des Mittelalters,* vol. i, pp. 170–181, with other references in the succeeding volumes.   See also a long article in DAC., vol. v, cc. 1982–1997 ; DTC., col. vi, cc. 611–614 ; and DCB., vol. ii, pp. 552–553, in which last article the shortcomings of Fortunatus are perhaps a little unduly emphasized. Text and translation of five lyrics of Venantius in Helen Waddell, *Mediaeval Latin Lyrics* (1935), pp. 58–67. For the *cultus*, see Fr B. de Gaiffier in *Analecta Bollandiana*, vol. lxx (1952), pp. 262–284.

BD BARTHOLOMEW OF SAN GIMIGNANO   (A.D. 1300)

BARTHOLOMEW BUONPEDONI, commonly called Bartolo, was born at Mucchio, near San Gimignano in Tuscany, during the earlier part of the thirteenth century, and was destined by his father for marriage and a secular avocation. But Bartolo had other ideas, and left home to become a servant in the Benedictine abbey of St Vitus at Pisa. He worked in the infirmary and made so good an impression that it was suggested to him that he should take the habit. While he was considering this our Lord appeared to him in sleep, and told him that he would win his crown by twenty years of physical suffering rather than by becoming a monk. Having received some training at the monastery, Bartolo, when he was thirty, was ordained priest and appointed to the parish of Peccioli. He had become a tertiary of the Order of St Francis, and he lived and fulfilled his pastoral duties in complete accord with the spirit of that saint. He took into his house a youth Vivaldo (Ubald), who after Bartolo's death became a hermit and is venerated for his sanctity to this day.

In 1280 Bd Bartolo was smitten by a disease which was recognized as leprosy, and he remembered what our Lord had told him about twenty years of suffering. Accompanied by the faithful Vivaldo, he retired to the leper-house of Celloli, of which he was made master and chaplain, and though the disease was malignant in him it never incapacitated him from celebrating Mass. He lived thus, in infinite patience and ministering to his fellow sufferers, until December 12, 1300, just twenty years after his leprosy began. He was buried in the Augustinian church of San Gimignano, where towards the end of the century one of the friars wrote an account of his life and miracles. His tomb is still venerated in the same church. He has been called " the Job of Tuscany ", and he is known always in San Gimignano as Santo Bartolo. A local feast was approved in 1499 and the *cultus* was formally confirmed in 1910, the Friars Minor fixing the feast for December 14.

The decree of confirmation of *cultus*, printed in the *Acta Apostolicae Sedis*, vol. ii (1910), pp. 411–414, contains a relatively full summary of the life of this *beatus*, and it mentions that Prosper Lambertini (Benedict XIV) considered that the *cultus* had already been equivalently sanctioned in 1499 in virtue of a papal delegation of Alexander VI. Fuller details of Bartolo's history are given in Wadding, *Annales Ordinis Minorum ;* and in Mazzara, *Leggendario Francescano* (1680), vol. ii, pt 2, pp. 681–684. See also Léon, *Auréole Séraphique* (Eng. ed.), vol. iv, pp. 165–169, who appeals more directly to a life by the Augustinian, Fra Giunta, written, it is said, in the fourteenth century. There is a popular life in Italian by E. Castaldi, *Santo Bartolo* (1928).

BD CONRAD OF OFFIDA   (A.D. 1306)

CONRAD became a friar minor when he was fourteen years old, and was afterwards associated both with the friary founded by St Francis himself at Forano in the Apennines and with the great convent of Alvernia. Before he was ordained priest and became a preacher he was employed for years as cook and questor, and several remarkable stories are told of him. He is said to have had the same guardian angel as St Francis, and to have often conversed with him about the seraphic founder. Throughout his life Conrad had only one religious habit, he always went barefoot, and his love of poverty impelled him to that party in his order which at first was known as the Spirituals or *Zelanti*. He was closely associated with Peter John Olivi, and in sympathy with Angelo Clareno and Fra Liberato, the leaders of the " Celestine " hermits ; Bd Conrad's own ideas were more moderate, though he gave credence and circulation to the legend that St Francis had risen from the dead to encourage the Spirituals, having, it was said, been told it by Brother Leo.

But the chief companion of his life was Bd Peter of Treja, who accompanied him in his preaching journeys and was present in the woods on that Candlemas-day when our Lady appeared to Conrad and laid the Child Jesus in his arms. It was said of these two that they were " two shining stars in the province of the Marches, like dwellers in Heaven ; for between them there was such love as seemed to spring from one and the same heart and soul, so that they bound themselves, each to the other, by an agreement that every consolation that the mercy of God might vouchsafe them they would lovingly reveal the one unto the other ". The author of the *Fioretti* further calls Brother Conrad a " marvellous zealot of gospel poverty and of the Rule of St Francis, of so religious a life and so deserving before God that Christ, the Blessed One, honoured him in life and in death with many miracles ". When he was sixty-five years old Bd Conrad died while preaching at Bastia, near Assisi, and was buried there. Some years later his relics were carried off to Perugia, and they now rest in the cathedral of that city beside those of Brother Giles. His *cultus* was confirmed in 1817.

The main outlines of his life are sketched by Bartholomew (Albizzi) of Pisa and other Franciscan chroniclers. See, for example, Mazzara, *Leggendario Francescano* (1680), vol. ii, pt 2, pp. 678–681. The biography compiled by B. Bartolomasi as far back as 1807 was published by M. Faloci-Pulignani in the *Miscellanea Francescana*, vol. xv–xvii, but it tells us very little of Bd Conrad's relations with the *Zelanti*, the great point of interest. See, however, the *Historisches Jahrbuch* for 1882, pp. 648–659, and for 1929, pp. 77–81, as also the *Archivum Franciscanum historicum*, vol. xi (1918), pp. 366–373. There is an account of Bd Conrad in Léon, *Auréole Séraphique* (Eng. trans.), vol. iv, pp. 174–177.

BD BONAVENTURE BUONACCORSI   (A.D. 1315)

IN the year 1276 St Philip Benizi came to Pistoia to preside at a general chapter of the Servite Order, and took the opportunity to preach to the people of the place, which was torn by factions. Among his hearers was a man, some thirty-six years old, belonging to the noble Buonaccorsi family, who was a leader of the Ghibellines and notorious as a desperate character. This Bonaventure was so moved by St Philip's exhortations to peace and concord that he went to him and accused himself of being a prominent fomenter of disorder and a cause of much misery and injustice. So penitent was he that he asked to be admitted among the Servite friars. St Philip was naturally a little doubtful about so sudden and complete a change, and tested the aspirant by imposing a public penance : Bonaventure had openly to make reparation for his misdeeds and personally ask the pardon of all whom he had wronged or caused to oppose him. This he did with such thoroughness and goodwill that St Philip took him from Pistoia to Monte Senario to make his novitiate at the headquarters of the order. Bonaventure persevered in his good resolutions, and after his profession was joined to St Philip as *socius* and admitted to the priesthood. For the next few years he was constantly with the prior general, who with the papal legate Cardinal Latino was trying to bring peace to Bologna, Florence and other distracted cities. The spectacle of the reformed Ghibelline going about in the habit of a mendicant friar and preaching brotherly love made a deep impression.

In 1282 Bd Bonaventure was made prior at Orvieto, but on the death of St Philip was called to the side of his successor, Father Lottaringo, and was eventually made preacher apostolic, with a commission to preach missions throughout Italy, which he did with great effect.   In 1303 he was made prior at Montepulciano for the second time, and there assisted St Agnes in the foundation of her community of Dominican nuns, whose director he was.   From thence he was moved to his native Pistoia, where civil war had again broken out and the enfeebled city was threatened by the Florentines.   By the diffusion of confraternities and of the Servite third order, called Mantellate, Bd Bartholomew endeavoured to bring back the people to a sense of their responsibilities as Christians, and was tireless in his preaching on behalf of peace and civic unity.   He died at Orvieto on December 14, 1315, and was buried in the Servite church in the chapel of our Lady of Sorrows as a testimony of the respect in which he was held by his brethren.   This was also testified by the fact that even in his lifetime he was known as *il Beato*, and miracles were reported both before and after his death.   The *cultus* of Bd Bonaventure Buonaccorsi was confirmed in 1822.

There seems to be no mention of any separate medieval life of Bd Bonaventure, but Poccianti in his *Chronicon* (1567) provides the outlines of a biography, which is developed by A. Giani, *Annales Ordinis Servorum*, vol. i, pp. 118 *seq.* and *passim*.   See also Sporr, *Lebensbilder aus dem Servitenorden* (1892), p. 621.   Further reference should be made to the early volumes of the *Monumenta Ordinis Servorum B.M.V.*, which began to be published in 1892.

BD NICHOLAS FACTOR   (A.D. 1583)

VINCENT FACTOR was a Sicilian tailor who came to live at Valencia in Spain, where he married a young woman called Ursula, and in 1520 their son, Peter Nicholas, was born.   He was a pious child and quick at school, and when he was fifteen his father wanted him to go into the business, but Nicholas heard a call to the religious life and in 1537 joined the Friars Minor of the Observance in his native town.   He made rapid progress in his order, and many times asked to be sent on foreign missions, but had to content himself with working for the conversion of the Moors in Spain : he is said twice to have offered to throw himself into a furnace if, on his coming out unhurt, his hearers would receive baptism.   But the offer was refused.   During the last year of his life Bd Nicholas migrated to the Capuchin Friars Minor at Barcelona, but returned to his own branch after a few months. " I left those men, who are entirely holy ", he told the Carthusians at La Scala, " to go back to men who are also entirely holy."

The biographers of Bd Nicholas devote most of their space to accounts of his austerities and of the marvels connected with his name.   He used always to take the discipline before celebrating Mass and three times before preaching, and carried his physical mortifications to such a degree that he was delated to the Inquisition for singularity.   His raptures, miracles and visions were so frequent that St Louis Bertrand said he lived more in Heaven than on earth, and among many examples of supernatural knowledge was an announcement of the victory of Lepanto the day after the battle.   He was known and revered by the great ones of Spain from King Philip II downwards, and his personal friends included St Paschal Baylon, St Louis Bertrand and Bd John de Ribera, all of whom gave evidence for his beatification. Among the characteristic stories told of Nicholas, in which there would seem to be a considerable degree of exaggeration or misunderstanding, are that our Lady through the mouth of a statue once told him to go and celebrate Mass, whereupon he was assisted in vesting by St Francis and St Dominic ; that divine love so warmed his heart that cold water into which he plunged became heated almost to boiling-point ; and that Satan frequently attacked him in the form of a lion, a bear, a snake and the like. Bd Nicholas Factor died at Valencia on December 23, 1583, and was beatified in 1786.

Long accounts of Bd Nicholas may be found in all the Franciscan chroniclers. For example, in Mazzara's *Leggendario Francescano* (1680), he fills pages 718 to 749 in vol. ii, pt 2 ; and in the *Croniche* of Leonardo da Napoli, pt 4, vol. ii, more than 120 closely printed pages are devoted to him. The best biography is probably that of G. Alapont, *Compendio della Vita del B. Niccolò Fattore*, which claims to be based upon the process of beatification and was printed in 1786. A short life in English was included in the Oratorian Series in the middle of the last century, and see also Léon, *Auréole Séraphique* (Eng. trans.), vol. iv, pp. 178–191.

15 : ST NINO, Virgin   (Fourth Century)

U NCERTAINTY surrounds the beginnings of Christianity in the former kingdom of Georgia (Iberia), but the story of the beginning of its evangel-ization told by Rufinus is accepted—and improved on—by the Georgians themselves and generally in the East. He tells us that early in the fourth century an unnamed maiden (whom the Georgians call Nino and the Roman Martyrology, not knowing her name, " Christiana "), carried off captive into the country, made a great impression on the people by the sobriety and chastity of her life and the long time, by day and night, that she gave to prayer. When questioned, she simply told them that she worshipped Christ as God. One day a mother brought her sick child to Nino, asking her how it ought to be treated. Nino told her that Jesus Christ was able to heal the most desperate cases and, wrapping the child in her rough mantle, called on the name of the Lord, and gave the baby back in perfect health to its mother. Rumours of this cure came to the queen of Iberia, who was herself ill, and she sent for Nino ; when Nino declined to come, the queen had herself carried to her, and she also was cured. When she would thank and reward her benefactress she was told that, " It is not my work, but Christ's ; and He is the Son of God who made the world ". She reported these words to the king who, when he soon after got lost in a mist while hunting, swore that if this Christ was God and would show him his way home he would believe in Him. Instantly the mist cleared ; and the king kept his word. He and his wife were instructed by St Nino, he announced his change of religion to the people, gave licence to the slave-girl to preach and teach, and began to build a church. In the course of its building God worked another miracle at the word of His servant, for a huge pillar, which neither men nor oxen had been able to move, turned itself on to its base and, after remaining suspended in the air, transported itself to its right place, before the eyes of a large crowd. The king sent an embassy to the Emperor Constantine, telling him what had happened and asking that bishops and priests might be sent to Iberia, which was duly done.

Rufinus learned this story from an Iberian prince, Bakur, whom he met in Palestine before the beginning of the fifth century, and it may well be believed that the conversion of Georgia was begun in the reign of Constantine and that a woman had a prominent part in it. The narrative of Rufinus has been translated —and amplified—into Greek, Syriac, Armenian, Coptic, Arabic and Ethiopic, while in Georgian literature there is a whole cycle of Nino legends, which are utterly worthless. Rufinus gives no localities for his events, or the name of the king and queen concerned, or even the name of the saint—much less her nationality or place of origin. Later versions supply these omissions several times over. Nino (sometimes said to have been not a captive slave but a voluntary fugitive from the persecution of Diocletian) came from Cappadocia—and also from Rome, Jerusalem and the Franks : the Armenians make her an Armenian and associate her with St Hripsime. After seeing Christianity firmly established in the land she is said to have retired to a cell on a mountain at Bodbe in Kakheti. Here she died and was buried ; later the place was made an episcopal see and her tomb is still shown in the cathedral. It is also interesting to note that from time immemorial the cathedral of Mtzkheta has been known as the church of the Living Pillar. It is certain that Georgia was largely Christian at the time Rufinus wrote, but what was the truth behind the story he heard from the Georgian prince (and even what exactly that story itself was) it is now impossible to say.

The passage of Rufinus, regarding the provenance of which there has been much discussion, may be best consulted in Mommsen's text as published in the Berlin Academy's edition of Eusebius. But the whole question has been greatly elucidated by Fr Paul Peeters in his article " Les Débuts du Christianisme en Géorgie " (*Analecta Bollandiana*, vol. l, 1932, pp. 5–58). The elements which have contributed to the development of the fantastic story of St Nino in its various forms are too complicated to be discussed here. The legend does not appear in its best known shape before 973, and the texts written in Georgian are still later in date. In the Oxford *Studia Biblica et Ecclesiastica*, vol. v, a life of St Nino has been translated into English from the Georgian by M. and J. Wardrop, and a somewhat cognate Armenian text is made accessible in the version of F. C. Conybeare, but the early dates there assigned to these documents are quite unwarranted. In German an essay by M. Kekelidze, *Die Bekehrung Georgiens zum Christentum* (1928) may be read with advantage. On the miraculous cross of St Nino see also Peeters in the *Analecta Bollandiana*, vol. liii (1935), pp. 305–306. In Egypt, St Nino was sometimes known as " Theognosta ", a name which seems to have arisen out of a misunderstanding of the Greek version or text of Rufinus, who does not give any name to the maiden apostle.

## SS. VALERIAN AND OTHER MARTYRS IN AFRICA	(A.D. 457 AND 482)

IN addition to St Dionysia and those mentioned with her on the sixth, other victims of the Vandal persecutions are commemorated this month. Under King Genseric took place the martyrdom of the bishop St Valerian " who, when more than eighty years old, was told to give up the sacred vessels of his church. On his constant refusal so to do it was commanded that he be driven out of the city by himself and that no one be allowed to receive him in his house or on his land ; wherefore he remained for a long time in the public street, uncared for, under the open sky, and in this confession and defence of Catholic truth he ended the course of his blessed life." On the morrow, likewise, is kept the feast of the many consecrated virgins who suffered under Huneric. They were hung up by the arms and jerked up and down, branded with hot irons, sold into slavery, driven into the desert and in other ways harried and killed for Christ's name's sake.

We know nothing of these martyrs beyond what we learn from the *Historia Wandalicae Persecutionis* (bk i, c. 39) by Victor of Vita. See also Quentin, *Martyrologes historiques*, p. 353.

ST STEPHEN, Bishop of Surosh   (*c.* A.D. 760)

ACCORDING to his Greek *vita* this Stephen was a native of Cappadocia in Asia Minor, who became bishop of Surosh (now Sudak) in the Crimea on the coast of the Black Sea. During the Iconoclast persecution under the Emperor Leo III he was exiled for his defence of the veneration of images, but was restored to his see on the accession of Constantine V to the imperial throne in 740. In his later years St Stephen was outstanding for his preaching of the gospel among the neighbouring Slavs and Khazars and even, it is said, among the Varangians. The very late (fifteenth century) Russian version of his life narrates that a band of Varango-Russians marauding in the Crimea was dispersed by the sudden appearance of the bishop ; the conversion of their leader, Yury, said to be from Novgorod, followed. The feast of St Stephen of Surosh is kept by the Russians, and there has been a revived interest in the saint among the learned in recent times together with St George of Amastris (February 21), because of their significance for the early history of the Varangians and of Christianity in Russia.

See Baumgarten, *Aux origines de la Russie*, cap. ii (1939) ; Taube, *Rome et la Russie*, t. i, *passim* (1947) ; Maltzev's *Menologium* (1900). Father Martynov, in *Annus ecclesiasticus Graeco-Slavicus* (*Acta sanctorum*, October, vol. xi), in his *observanda* on the calendar for December 15 gives a number of references of value to students.

ST PAUL OF LATROS   (A.D. 956)

THE father of this hermit was an ófficer in the imperial army who was slain in an engagement with the Saracens. His mother then retired from Pergamos, which was the place of his birth, to Bithynia, taking her two sons with her. Basil, the elder, took the monastic habit upon Mount Olympus in that country, but soon for the sake of greater solitude retired to Mount Latros (Latmus). When their mother was dead he induced his brother to embrace the same state of life. Though young, Paul had experienced the world sufficiently to understand the emptiness and dangers of what it has to offer. Basil recommended him to the care and instruction of the abbot of Karia. St Paul desired for the sake of greater solitude and austerity to lead an eremitical life ; but his abbot, thinking him too young, refused him leave so long as he lived. After his death Paul's first cell was a cave on the highest part of Mount Latros, where for some weeks he had no other food than green acorns, which at first made him very sick. After eight months he was called back to Karia. It is said that when he worked in the kitchen the sight of the fire so forcibly reminded him of Hell that he burst into tears every time he looked at it.

When he was allowed to pursue his vocation Paul chose a new habitation on the most rocky part of the mountain, where for the first three years he suffered grievous temptations. A peasant sometimes brought him a little food, but he mostly lived on what grew wild. The reputation of his holiness spreading through the province, several men chose to live near him and built there a *laura* of cells. Paul, who had been careless about all corporal necessaries, was much concerned lest anything should be wanting to those that lived under his direction. After twelve years his solitude was so much broken into that he withdrew to another part of the mountains, whence he visited his brethren from time to time to cheer and encourage them ; he sometimes took them into the forest to sing the Divine Office together in the open air. When asked why he appeared sometimes so joyful, at other times so sad, he answered, " When nothing diverts my thoughts from God, my heart overflows with joy, so much that I often forget my food and everything else ; and when there are distractions, I am upset ". Occasionally he disclosed something of the wonderful communications which passed between his soul and God and of the heavenly graces which he received in contemplation.

But St Paul wished for yet closer retirement, so he passed over to the isle of Samos, and there concealed himself in a cave. But he was soon discovered and so many flocked to him that he re-established three *lauras* which had been ruined by the Saracens. The entreaties of the monks at Latros induced him to return to his former cell there. The Emperor Constantine Porphyrogenitus wrote frequently to him asking his advice, and often had reason to repent when he did not follow it. Paul had a great tenderness for the poor and he gave them more of his food and clothes than he could properly spare. Once he would have sold himself for a slave to help some people in distress had he not been stopped. On December 6 in 956, foreseeing that his death drew near, he came down from his cell to the church, celebrated the Holy Mysteries more early than usual and then took to his bed. He spent his time in prayer and instructing his monks till his death, which fell on December 15, on which day he is commemorated by the Greeks. He is sometimes referred to as St Paul the Younger.

After having been printed for the first time in the *Analecta Bollandiana*, vol. xi (1892), a still more carefully revised text was edited by Delehaye in the volume *Der Latmos*, issued in 1913 by T. Wiegand and other scholars, with abundant illustrations and archaeological comments. The Life of St Paul, written by an anonymous disciple, is one of the most trustworthy of Byzantine biographies. In Wiegand's volume it is supplemented by a panegyric from MS. Vatican 704 previously unprinted. See also the *Zeitschrift f. kath. Theologie*, vol. xviii (1894), pp. 365 *seq.*, and the *Revue des quest. histor.*, vol. x (1893), pp. 49–85.

ST MARY DI ROSA, Virgin, Foundress of the Handmaids of Charity of Brescia   (A.D. 1855)

THREE and a quarter centuries after Savonarola had foretold woe on the wickedness of the city of Brescia (prophecy that was fulfilled when the French seized and sacked the city in 1512), there was born there the third of the holy ones who, in the first half of the nineteenth century, were the contemporary glories of its citizens ; the other two were Bd Ludovic Pavoni and Bd Teresa Verzeri. Mary di Rosa (called Paula or Pauline at home), born in 1813, was sixth of the nine children of Clement di Rosa, and his wife, Countess Camilla Albani. Her childhood was uneventful, but saddened by the death of her deeply loved mother when Paula was eleven. When she was seventeen Paula left school to look after the household for her father, and he began to look around for a suitable husband for her. When he had found one, Paula was rather startled, and took her difficulties to the archpriest of the cathedral, Mgr Faustino Pinzoni, a sagacious priest who had already dealt prudently with her spiritual problems. He decided himself to see Clement di Rosa, and explained gently to him that his daughter had decided that she would never marry. At a time when it was common, especially at the higher social levels, for fathers to pay little attention to the likes and dislikes of their children, notably in the matter of daughters' marriages, it speaks well for Cav. Clement that he agreed to respect Paula's resolution almost without demur, and throughout his life he seems to have supported her in what may have appeared to him as wild schemes.

During the next ten years Paula continued to live at home, but engaging herself more and more in social good works, in which she had the worthy example of her father before her eyes. Among his properties was a textile mill at Acquafredda where a number of girls worked, and one of Paula's first undertakings was to look after the spiritual welfare of these young women; this solicitude she extended to those of Capriano, where the Rosas had a country house. Here, with the co-operation of the parish priest, she established a women's guild and arranged retreats and special missions in the parish, with such good results that the rector hardly knew his own flock. Reference has already been made, in speaking of Bd Ludovic Pavoni and Bd Teresa Verzeri, to the cholera epidemics that devastated northern Italy at this time, and the outbreak at Brescia in 1836 gave Paula di Rosa another opportunity. She asked her father's permission to work among the stricken in the hospital, and after some doubt and with considerable trepidation he agreed. The hospital welcomed Paula, who was accompanied by a widow, Gabriela Echenos-Bornati, who had already had some experience of nursing the sick, and they set an example of selfless hard work and gentle care that made a very deep impression on everybody.*

In consequence Paula was asked to undertake the supervision of an institution which was a sort of workhouse for penniless and abandoned girls—a delicate and difficult post for a young woman of only twenty-four. She filled it successfully for two years, but then resigned in consequence of a difference with the trustees, who did not want the girls to lodge in the house at night. Paula herself then established a small lodging-house with room for a dozen girls to sleep, and at the same time gave her attention to a work that had been projected by her brother Philip and Mgr Pinzoni, namely, a school for deaf-and-dumb girls, on the lines of what Ludovic Pavoni was doing for boys. This school was still in its infancy when Paula handed it over to the Canossian sisters, who wished to do the same work in Brescia on a bigger scale.

All this was a really extraordinary ten-year record for a woman still under thirty and of delicate health and physique. But there was a certain virile quality in Paula di Rosa, and she had a physical energy and courage hardly to be expected —she once rescued somebody from a bolting horse and carriage in very dangerous circumstances. And her mind was to match, quick, acute and steady, so that, while living with heroic virtue, she was not content that intellectually and psychologically her religion should remain at the level of the " penny catechism ". She acquired an unusual knowledge of theology, and brought to her reading the same liveliness of spirit and delicacy of perception that informed her dealings with practical affairs. Her mental ability was particularly noted when she became involved in the complexities inseparable from the establishment of a religious congregation, and she was further helped by a remarkably good memory for people and things, large and small.

This congregation began to take shape in 1840, first in the form of a religious society of which Paula was appointed superioress by the Archpriest Pinzoni. With her was associated Mrs Bornati (who indeed may be called co-foundress), and the object of the society was to look after the sick in hospitals, not simply as nurses but as giving the whole of their time and interest unreservedly to the sick and suffering. They took the name of Handmaids of Charity, and the first four

* Manzoni's description in *The Betrothed* (*I Promessi Sposi*) of the isolation-hospital in Milan gives an idea of the conditions in which they worked.

members took up their residence in an inconvenient and dilapidated house near the hospital ; these were soon joined by fifteen Tirolese, who had heard about the undertaking from a visiting missioner, and before long the community numbered thirty-two. Their work aroused admiration that was publicly expressed in the press by a local doctor, who underlined the spiritual as well as the physical activities of the handmaids ; but at the same time there was serious unfavourable criticism. Some people resented their presence as intruders, and tried to discredit them. This did not prevent an invitation, within three months of their foundation, to undertake similar work at Cremona, and this invitation was accepted. Of the difficulties at Brescia, " I hope that is not our last cross ", wrote Paula to the Cremona house, " because to tell the truth I should have been sorry had we not been persecuted ".

Before long a new and more commodious house in Brescia was given to the handmaids by Clement di Rosa, and their provisional rule of life was approved by the bishop in 1843 ; but there was a counter-balance to these causes for rejoicing a few months later, when Gabriela Bornati died. Paula was thus deprived of her chief lieutenant, but she still had Mgr Pinzoni to advise and guide her, and the society continued to grow and to undertake the direction of new hospitals. But in the summer of 1848 death took the archpriest too, and that at a time when political upheaval was convulsing Europe and war had come to northern Italy. Paula's first response to new opportunities was to staff St Luke's military hospital, where again the handmaids had to meet the opposition of doctors who preferred secular nurses and military orderlies. Civilian victims of war and prisoners were succoured and, anticipating Florence Nightingale by several years, the Handmaids of Charity ministered to the souls and bodies of the wounded on the battlefields. In the following year came the terrible " Ten Days of Brescia ". Paula and her sisters were at the disposal of all sufferers without distinction, but some disorderly troops made an attempt on the hospital. Paula, supported by half-a-dozen sisters, went to the front door to meet them : they carried a great crucifix, with a lighted candle on either side. The soldiers wavered, halted, and slunk away. And the crucifix (still preserved at Brescia) was carried from sick-bed to sick-bed that each occupant might give it a grateful kiss.

Paula aimed at a body of sisters who should combine spiritual with temporal care, lives of prayer and work, active but not " activist " or busybodies, " rushing about the streets with bowls of soup ", as St Louisa de Marillac put it ; and there was wide scope for such organizations in Italy at that time. So in the autumn of 1850 she set out for Rome ; on October 24 she was received by the pope, Pius IX ; and two months later, with most remarkable speed for Rome, the constitutions of the congregation of Handmaids of Charity of Brescia were approved. The approval of the civil power was less speedy, and it was not till the summer of 1852 that the first twenty-five sisters and their foundress made their vows, and Paula took the name of Maria Crocifissa, " Mary of the Crucified ". The canonical erection of the congregation was the signal for its quick extension, but for Mother Mary the end was at hand, so far as this world was concerned. She was only forty-two, but she had taken every ounce out of her slight and delicate frame, and her recovery from illness on Good Friday 1855 looked miraculous. There was still work to be done—a threat of cholera at Brescia, convents to be opened at Spalato in Dalmatia and near Verona. Then at Mantua she collapsed, and reached home only to say, " Thank God He has let me get home to Brescia to die ". And die she did, very peacefully and quietly, three weeks later, on December 15, 1855.

Mgr Pinzoni, who knew her so well, said of St Mary di Rosa that " her life is a marvel that astonishes everybody who sees it " ; and the spirit of it all was confided to one of her sisters when she told her that " I can't go to bed with a quiet conscience if during the day I've missed any chance, however slight, of preventing wrong-doing or of helping to bring about some good ". She would go out at a moment's notice by day or night to look after somebody ill, to sit at the bedside of a dying sinner, to settle a quarrel, to comfort someone in distress. And the people of Brescia acknowledged this when they flocked to her funeral. She was canonized in 1954.

There is a full life in Italian by V. Bartoccetti, *Beata Maria Crocifissa di Rosa* (1940) ; a very adequate ninety-page summary, under the same title, by a member of the congregation ; and another life by Dr L. Fossati. There seems to be nothing about her in any other language, perhaps because all the houses of the Handmaids of Brescia are in Italy or near by.

16 : ST EUSEBIUS, Bishop of Vercelli   (A.D. 371)

S T EUSEBIUS was born in the isle of Sardinia, where his father is said to have died in chains for the faith. His mother, when left a widow, took him and a daughter, both in their infancy, to Rome, where Eusebius was brought up and ordained lector. He was called to Vercelli, in Piedmont, and served that church with such distinction that he was chosen to govern it by the clergy and people. He is the first bishop of Vercelli whose name we know. St Ambrose assures us that he was the first who in the West united the monastic discipline with the clerical, living himself with some of his clergy a common life in community. For this reason St Eusebius of Vercelli is specially venerated by the canons regular. He saw that the best and first means to labour effectually for the sanctification of his people was to form under his own eyes a clergy on whose virtue, piety and zeal he could depend.   In this he succeeded so well that other churches demanded his disciples for their bishops, and a number of prelates came out of his school who were shining lamps in the Church of God.   He was at the same time very careful personally to instruct his flock, and, moved by the force of the truth which he preached and persuaded by the sweetness and charity of his conduct, many sinners were encouraged to change their lives.   But in 354 he was called to the public work of the Church at large, and for ten years following was a distinguished and persecuted confessor of the faith.

In that year Pope Liberius deputed St Eusebius, with Lucifer of Cagliari, to beg the Emperor Constantius to assemble a council to try and end the trouble between Catholics and Arians. Constantius agreed, and a council met at Milan in 355. Eusebius, seeing things would be carried by force through the power of the Arians, though the Catholic prelates were more numerous, refused to go to it till he was pressed by Constantius himself. When the bishops were called on to sign a condemnation of St Athanasius that had been drawn up, Eusebius refused, and instead laid the Nicene creed on the table and insisted on all signing that before the case of St Athanasius should be considered. Great tumult and confusion followed. Eventually the emperor sent for St Eusebius, St Dionysius of Milan and Lucifer of Cagliari, and pressed them to condemn Athanasius. They insisted upon his innocence and that he could not be condemned without being heard, and urged that secular force might not be used to influence ecclesiastical decisions. The emperor stormed and threatened to put them to death, but was content to banish them.   The first place of exile of St Eusebius was Scythopolis (Beisan) in Palestine, where he was put in charge of the Arian bishop, Patrophilus.

He was lodged at first with St Joseph of Palestine (the only orthodox household in the town), and was comforted by the visits of St Epiphanius and others, and by the arrival of the deputies of his church of Vercelli with money for his subsistence. But his patience was to be exercised by great trials.   Count Joseph died, and the Arians insulted the bishop, dragged him through the streets half naked, and shut him up in a little room, where he was pestered for four days with all manner of annoyances to make him conform.   They forbade his deacons and other fellow confessors to be admitted to see him, so he sent a letter to Bishop Patrophilus addressed, " Eusebius, the servant of God, with the other servants of God who suffer with him for the faith, to Patrophilus the jailer, and to his officers ".   After a short account of what he had suffered, he asked that his deacons might be allowed to come to him.   Eusebius undertook a sort of " hunger-strike ", and after he had remained four days without food the Arians sent him back to his lodging.   Three weeks afterwards they came again, broke into the house, and dragged him away. They rifled his goods, plundered his provisions, and drove away his attendants. St Eusebius found means to write a letter to his flock, in which he mentions these particulars.   Later he was removed from Scythopolis into Cappadocia, and some time afterwards into the Upper Thebaid in Egypt.   We have a letter which he wrote from this place to Gregory, Bishop of Elvira, praising him for his constancy against those who had forsaken the faith of the Church.   The undaunted confessor expresses a desire to end his life in suffering for the kingdom of God.

When Constantius died towards the end of the year 361, Julian gave leave to the banished prelates to return to their sees, and St Eusebius came to Alexandria to concert measures with St Athanasius for applying proper remedies to the evils of the Church.   He took part in a council there, and then went on to Antioch to put into effect the wish of the council that St Meletius should there be recognized as bishop and the Eustathian schism healed.   But he found it widened by Lucifer of Cagliari, who had blown on the coals afresh by ordaining Paulinus bishop for the Eustathians.   Eusebius remonstrated with him for this rash act ; but the hasty Lucifer resented this, and broke off communion with him and with all who, with the Council of Alexandria, received the ex-Arian bishops.   This was the origin of the schism of Lucifer, who by pride lost the fruit of his former zeal and sufferings.

Unable to do any good at Antioch, St Eusebius travelled over the East and through Illyricum, confirming in the faith those who were wavering and bringing back many that were gone astray.   In Italy St Hilary of Poitiers and St Eusebius met, and were employed together in opposing the arianizing Auxentius of Milan. Vercelli, on the return of its bishop after so long an absence, " laid aside her garments of mourning ", as St Jerome puts it, but of the last years of St Eusebius nothing is known.   He died on August 1, on which day his eulogy occurs in the Roman Martyrology.   He is therein referred to as a martyr, but the Breviary makes it clear that he was so by his sufferings and not by his death.   In the cathedral of Vercelli is shown a manuscript copy of the gospels said to be written by St Eusebius : it was almost worn out with age nearly a thousand years ago when King Berengarius caused it to be covered with plates of silver. This manuscript is the earliest *codex* of the Old Latin version in existence. St Eusebius is among the several persons to whom the composition of the " Athanasian Creed " has been attributed.

The fathers who by their zeal and learning maintained the true faith made humility the foundation of their labours. Conscious that they were liable to be mistaken, they said with St Augustine, " I may err, but I will never be a heretic ". This humility and caution is necessary in profane no less than in religious studies. Many pursue their speculations so far as to lose touch with common sense, and by too close an application to things beyond their abilities spoil their own understanding. Cicero justly remarks that nothing can be invented so absurd that some philosopher has not said it. So true it is, as the Apostle tells us, that " knowledge puffeth up " : not of itself, but through the propensity of the human heart to pride ; the most ignorant are usually the more apt to overrate their knowledge and abilities.

In the absence of any proper biography of St Eusebius—that printed by Ughelli is of late date and little value—we are dependent upon the bishop's own letters, upon a notice in the *Viri illustres* of St Jerome, and upon the controversial literature of the times. But the main incidents of his life have to do with general ecclesiastical history. See, for example, Hefele-Leclercq, *Histoire des Conciles*, vol. i, pp. 872 *seq.* and 961 *seq.* ; Duchesne, *Hist. ancienne de l'Eglise*, vol. ii, pp. 341–350 ; Bardenhewer, *Geschichte der altkirchlichen Literatur*, vol. iii, pp. 486–487 ; and especially Savio, *Gli antichi vescovi d'Italia*, vol. i, pp. 412–420, and 514–544.

BD ADO, Archbishop of Vienne   (A.D. 875)

ADO came of a good family of the Gâtinais and was educated in the abbey of Ferrières, near Sens, under the celebrated Lupus Servatus. Refusing all inducements to return to the world he became a monk there, and soon had an established reputation for holiness and learning. He was still young when Markward, abbot of Prüm, begged of Abbot Sigulf that Ado might teach the sacred sciences in his monastery, and the request was not refused. Ado so taught as to make all that were under his care truly servants of God ; but difficulties and disagreements arose, and he had to leave Prüm. Eventually he came to Lyons, and St Remigius, archbishop of the city, kept him there and gave him charge of the parish church of St Romanus. His former master, Lupus, who had been chosen abbot of Ferrières, became his advocate, and, the see of Vienne falling vacant, Ado was chosen archbishop and consecrated in 859. He was indefatigable in preaching the truths of salvation. He usually began his sermons with the words : " Hear the eternal truth which speaks to you in the gospel ", or " Hear Jesus Christ, who says to you ", or a similar expression. He was an altogether admirable bishop, and an implacable opponent of Lothair II of Lorraine in the matrimonial affairs that came before Pope St Nicholas I. King Charles the Bald sent him to Rome to present the case of the wronged Theutberga, and he was the legate sent by the pope with letters imperatively annulling the infamous proceedings of the Synod of Metz.

Bd Ado was the author of several written works, of which the best known is the martyrology that bears his name, of which the first version was prepared at Saint-Romain between 855 and 860. Dom Leclercq says of it that " It has contributed in a considerable measure to mislead the traditions of martyrologists and its unfortunate influence is found at work in almost all [pertinent] questions that have embarrassed historians ". Through the Martyrology of Usuard, which was an abridgement of it, and its use in later revisions, it has had a strong and regrettable influence on the official Roman Martyrology.   Among the works which Ado used in its preparation was one known as the *Martyrologium Romanum Parvum*, purporting to be an ancient martyrology of the Roman church.   He tells us that when he was at Ravenna he saw a manuscript of this, which had been sent by one of the popes to Aquileia, and he accordingly made a copy of it for his own use.   It is now known that the *Parvum* was spurious, a document contemporary with Ado himself.   It has even been suggested that it was Ado who fabricated it.   This need cause no surprise, for it was not till long after his time that the forgery or " doctoring " of documents began to be seen as a practice deserving the reprobation that is now properly given to it.   Even in our own time it is not uncommon to find continued currency given to pious legends and hagiological stories, without expressed advertence to their being only doubtfully true or even certainly false as records of historical fact.

Bd Ado also wrote Lives of St Desiderius (Didier) and St Theuderius (Chef), and a Universal Chronicle of the Six Ages of the World, from the Creation to A.D. 869.   It was considered desirable that Vienne, like other episcopal cities in southern Gaul (see, *e.g.* Arles, under St Trophimus on the 29th of this month, and Lazarus at Marseilles on the 17th), should have had an apostolic origin ; and it seems that Ado was responsible for the tradition that Crescens was sent by St Paul not into Galatia but into Gaul (2 Timothy iv 10) : his solemn commemoration at Vienne as its first bishop is still recorded in the Roman Martyrology on December 29, and referred to in the entry of his martyrdom in Galatia on June 27.   Ado died at Vienne on December 16, 875.   He is often accorded the title of Saint, but the Roman Martyrology refers to him as *Beatus* only.

There is a life of Ado printed in Mabillon, vol. iv, pt 2, pp. 262–275, but its value as an historical source is questionable.   Ado's connection with the see of Vienne is discussed by Duchesne, *Fastes Épiscopaux*, vol. i, pp. 147, 162, 210.   The whole matter of his relation to the martyrology called by his name has been very thoroughly investigated by Dom Quentin in his *Martyrologes historiques* (1908).   See also DAC., vol. i, cc. 535–539 ; and DHG., vol. i, cc. 585–586.

ST ADELAIDE, WIDOW   (A.D. 999)

WHEN in the year 933 Rudolf II of Upper Burgundy concluded a treaty with Hugh of Provence in their struggle for the crown of Italy (Lombardy), one of the terms was that Rudolf's daughter, Adelaide, then a baby of two, should marry Hugh's son, Lothair.   Fourteen years later her brother, Conrad of Burgundy, saw to the fulfilling of this contract, Lothair being by then nominally king of Italy, but actually in the power of Berengarius of Ivrea.   One child was born of the marriage, Emma (she eventually married Lothair II of France), and in 950 Lothair of Italy died, not without strong suspicion of having been poisoned by Berengarius, who succeeded him.   Berengarius then tried to make Adelaide marry his son, and on her refusal treated her with brutality and indignity, and shut her up in a castle on Lake Garda.   At this time the German king, Otto the Great, was leading an army into Italy to try to reduce the north to order.   He defeated Berengarius and released Adelaide ; or, as it is said, she escaped from her prison and joined him.   To consolidate his authority in Italy, Otto married Adelaide, who was twenty years his junior, on Christmas day 951, at Pavia.   Of this union five children were born.   Ludolf, Otto's son by his first wife (sister of Athelstan of England), was jealous of the influence of his stepmother and her children and became a centre of discontent and rebellion, but to the German people the gentle and gracious Adelaide soon endeared herself. In 962 Otto was crowned emperor at Rome. Nothing is heard of Adelaide for the next ten years, till in 973 her husband died and their eldest son succeeded.

Otto II was a good and spirited prince, but hasty and self-sufficient, and on his accession to power he soon estranged his mother and allowed himself to be turned against her by his wife, the Byzantine Theophano, and other counsellors. Adelaide left the court and went to her brother, Conrad, at Vienne. She appealed to St Majolus, abbot of Cluny, whom she had wanted to see made pope when Benedict VI was murdered in 974, and he eventually succeeded in bringing about a reconciliation ; mother and son met at Pavia, and Otto asked pardon on his knees for his unkindness. She sent gifts to the shrine of St Martin at Tours, including Otto's best cloak, and asking for her son the saint's prayers—" you who had the glory of covering with your own cloak Christ the Lord in the person of a beggar ".

But similar trouble came when Otto died in 983. Otto III was a baby and his mother, Theophano, became regent. She had the flair for politics of the great Byzantine princesses and in this respect was more capable than her mother-in-law. Adelaide again left the court, but Theophano died suddenly in 991 and the old empress came back to be herself regent, a task now beyond her strength and peace-loving nature, though she had the assistance of St Willigis of Mainz. Throughout her life she had shown herself generous and forgiving to enemies, and amenable to the wise guidance in turn of St Adalbert of Magdeburg, St Majolus and St Odilo of Cluny, who called her " a marvel of beauty and grace ". She founded and restored monasteries of monks and nuns, and was urgent for the conversion of the Slavs, whose movements on the eastern frontier troubled her closing years before she finally returned to Burgundy. Death overtook her at a monastery of her foundation at Seltz, on the Rhine near Strasburg, on December 16, 999. St Adelaide was canonized c. 1097.

The most reliable source of information regarding St Adelaide is the " Epitaphium " of St Odilo of Cluny. It is printed in MGH., *Scriptores*, vol. iv, pp. 635–649, and in Migne, PL., vol. cxlii, cc. 967–992. But a good deal may also be gleaned from the chroniclers of the period. There is a German life by F. P. Wimmer, *Kaiserin Adelheid* (1897). See also DHG., vol. i, cc. 516–517.

BD SEBASTIAN OF BRESCIA   (A.D. 1496)

DURING the thirteenth century the family of the Maggi was one of the most powerful in Brescia and at the head of the party of the Guelfs ; at the time of the birth of Bd Sebastian, early in the fifteenth century, it had declined from its former estate, but the name was still held in honour. Sebastian entered the Order of Preachers when he was fifteen, and his ministry was attended with much success : large numbers were brought to repentance, quarrelling families and communes were reconciled, and the work of his order strengthened ; but few particulars are known of his busy life. He was a powerful preacher and an admirable superior in the many friaries that he governed. He recognized the genius and virtues of Jerome Savonarola, whose confessor for a time he was, and at the age of twenty-nine, when Father Jerome had been professed only six years, he made him master of the novices at Bologna. Bd Sebastian was a strict upholder of monastic observance, and worked doggedly at the reform of several houses, especially that of Lodi, where he set the example

of begging from door to door for the support of the community.   As a superior
he wished to be treated with the openness of a father, and was then gentle and
indulgent ; but when his brethren regarded him merely as a master, he was
accordingly severe.   When suffering from sickness Bd Sebastian insisted on carrying out a visitation of his province, but when he reached the priory of Santa Maria
di Castello at Genoa he could go no further ; this, he said to his companions, was
to be the place of his rest for ever.   He died there on December 16, 1496, and all
Genoa came to his tomb, whereat many miracles were reported.   The *cultus* of
Bd Sebastian Maggi was confirmed in 1760.

   Mortier in his *Histoire des maîtres généraux O.P.*, vol. iv, pp. 548–550, speaks in some
detail of Bd Sebastian, and he figures in nearly all the lives of Savonarola : see, for example,
Herbert Lucas, *Fra Girolamo Savonarola* (1906), pp. 10, 191 *seq.*, etc.   A short account is
also given by Procter, *Lives of Dominican Saints*, pp. 339–342.   For a fuller bibliography
see Taurisano, *Catalogus hagiographicus O.P.*

BD MARY OF TURIN, Virgin   (A.D. 1717)

THERE lived at Turin during the seventeenth century a count of Santena named
John Donato Fontanella.   He was a religious and well-loved man and married an
equally good wife, Mary Tana, whose father was cousin-german to St Aloysius
Gonzaga.   They had eleven children, of whom the ninth, Marianna, was a girl
of particular intelligence and promise.   When a child of six, emulating St Teresa,
she concocted a scheme with her little brother to run away and live " in the desert " ;
but they spoiled it by oversleeping on the morning intended for their departure.
Two years later, when making recovery from a serious illness, she experienced her
first vision, and from that time began to show a strongly ascetic disposition ; in
the following year she made her first communion.   A deep impression had been
made on her mind by contemplation of the blow in the face given to our Lord by
the servant of Caiaphas, and a strange incident is related in that connection.   One
evening, when Marianna was kneeling at Benediction with one of her sisters, a
strange man on her other side turned suddenly and violently slapped her cheek.
The man escaped in the ensuing confusion and was never seen again.   When she
was something over twelve, Marianna, by a not very creditable ruse in concert with
the nuns to evade her mother, joined the Cistercians at Saluzzo to live among their
alumnae ; but she was not happy there and, on the death of her father, went home
to keep house for her mother.   She became ever more drawn to the religious life
and in 1676, after some difficulties with her family, was admitted in her sixteenth
year to the Carmel of Santa Cristina.   Here her first experience was one of great
home-sickness ; following that, an intense distaste for her new life and dislike
of the novice-mistress.   But she persevered and was in due course professed.
   After seven years in the convent Sister Mary-of-the-Angels, as she was now
called, was visited by a long and severe " dark night ", during which she was
tormented by numerous diabolical assaults and manifestations.   She was guided
through this by a very able director, Father Laurence-Mary, O.C.D., and at the end
of three years began to come into more peaceful ways and to attain higher states
of prayer.   In 1690 she wrote to Father Laurence an account of a mystical experience which marked the end of her violent struggles.   That Sister Mary herself
was of a vehement disposition her own physical penances show.   At one time she
was scourging herself to blood daily, compressing her tongue with an iron ring,

dropping molten wax on her skin, even suspending herself cross-wise by ropes from a beam in her cell. Of such practices we may borrow from the words of Father George O'Neill, S.J., her Irish biographer : " No one is asked to imitate, no one is bound to admire them." When she was thirty she was appointed novice-mistress, and three years later prioress, offices which she took up with deep reluctance and discharged with an equally marked ability. At the suggestion of Bd Sebastian Valfré she undertook a new foundation with a small house and inadequate endowment at Moncaglieri ; and having overcome opposition from both ecclesiastical and civil authorities she was able to establish the nucleus of a community there in 1703, and the convent is still in being. Sister Mary herself wished to go there, but the people of Turin would not suffer it ; all, from the members of the ducal family of Savoy downwards, were accustomed to go and ask the advice and prayers of the prioress of Santa Cristina, especially during the war with the French.

During the last twenty years of her life Bd Mary continued to have remarkable experiences and gifts, among them what appeared to be a literal " odour of sanctity ". This scent emanated from her person, and was communicated to her clothes and even to things that she touched, from which it was sometimes difficult to eradicate. From about 1702 this phenomenon was permanent, and among the witnesses to it was Father Costanzo, afterwards archbishop of Sassari in Sardinia. He characterized it as " neither natural nor artificial, nor like flowers or aromatic drugs or any mixture of perfumes, but only to be called an ' odour of sanctity ' ". It is stated that certain secondary relics of the *beata* at Moncaglieri still retain this fragrance. At the same time Bd Mary, like so many other mystics, was also notably proficient and careful in the practical matters, keeping accounts, looking after workmen, and so on, which fell to her lot as prioress. At the end of the priorate of Mother Teresa-Felix in 1717 the nuns of Santa Cristina wished to elect Bd Mary for a fifth term of office. She thought that her physical weakness would prevent her from giving a proper example of observance, and appealed to her confessor and to the prior provincial, but they both refused to interfere. Whereupon she set herself to pray that, if it were God's will, she might shortly die ; and within three weeks she was very ill. Punctilious obedience to superiors had been so marked in her life that the nuns now implored them to " give her an obedience " to recover. They demurred, and Mary said, " Obedience wills what God wills, and therefore I will what obedience wills. Were the impossible possible I would do as you ask ; but I have so stormed the heart of Jesus to get my desire that He has granted it. It cannot be changed now." She blessed all her sisters, and Father Costanzo asked, without saying who she was, for a last word for " another daughter ", who was in fact the young Princess di Carignano who had hurried to the convent when she heard that Mother Mary was dying. " May our Lord bless her ", she murmured, " and give her real detachment from the world—for everything here comes to an end." Bd Mary-of-the-Angels died on December 16, 1717, and seven years later her cause was introduced at the instance of Victor Amadeus II of Savoy ; but she was not officially declared blessed until 1865.

A full account of this Carmelite mystic will be found in the book of Father G. O'Neill, *Bd Mary of the Angels* (1909). It is based upon a life written in Italian by Father Elias-of-St-Teresa who had known the *beata* personally and was able to utilize what survived of an autobiography which she wrote by command of her superiors. A later Italian account is by Father Benedetto (1934).

17 : ST LAZARUS　　(First Century)

IN the eleventh chapter of his gospel St John gives a full account of the raising from the dead by our Lord of Lazarus of Bethany, the brother of Martha and Mary and the much-loved friend of Jesus ; but the Bible tells us nothing of the subsequent life of this man called back from the dead. Nor is anything really known. The pseudo-Clementine writings say he followed St Peter into Syria, but according to the tradition received in the East he, with his sisters and others, was put into a leaking boat by the Jews at Jaffa, and by a supernatural interposition of providence landed safely on the island of Cyprus. He was, they say, made bishop at Kition (Larnaka), and died there in peace after thirty years. In 890 the Emperor Leo VI built a church and monastery in his honour at Constantinople, and translated some of the reputed relics from Cyprus.

The presence of St Lazarus in the West is first heard of in the eleventh century, in connection with the legend of St Mary Magdalen in Provence. In a letter written by Pope Benedict IX on the occasion of the consecration of the abbey church of St Victor at Marseilles reference is made to its possessing the relics of St Lazarus of Bethany, but nothing is said of his having been bishop there or preaching in Provence as the medieval legends assert. According to these Lazarus was put into the oarless and rudderless boat with the others (Mary Magdalen, Martha, Maximinus, etc.) and landed with them in the south-east of Gaul. He made a number of converts at Marseilles, became their bishop, and was martyred under Domitian on the site of the Saint-Lazare prison. He was buried in a cave, over which the abbey of St Victor was subsequently built. From there his relics are supposed to have been taken to Autun, where some human remains were enshrined in the new cathedral in 1146. The existence in the crypt of St Victor's at Marseilles of the epitaph of a fifth-century bishop of Aix named Lazarus, who had to resign his see and visited Palestine before dying at Marseilles and being buried there, may throw light on the origin of these curious legends about St Lazarus of Bethany ; and also the bringing of relics of St Nazarius from Milan to Autun in 542.

There is abundant evidence that the memory of Lazarus was devotionally honoured both in early days at Jerusalem and later throughout the Church. The pilgrim lady Etheria (*c.* 390), tells us of the procession which took place to the *Lazarium* (where Lazarus had been raised from the dead) on the Saturday before Palm Sunday. Etheria was much impressed by the enormous crowd which packed the whole vicinity. But we also find some similar celebration, nearly always connected with Lent, in the Western church. At Milan, Passion Sunday was called *Dominica de Lazaro*, and in Africa, as we learn from St Augustine, the gospel of the restoring to life of Lazarus was read at the night office before the dawn of Palm Sunday.

See DAC., vol. viii, cc. 2009–2086, and the references already given under St Mary Magdalen (July 22). Mention may also be made of the article " Lazarus " by L. Clugnet in the *Catholic Encyclopedia* (vol. ix, p. 98), and of a contribution of Father Thurston to the Irish quarterly, *Studies*, vol. xxiii (1934), pp. 110–123. No heed can be paid to the supposed presence of relics of St Lazarus at Autun ; there is much better ground for crediting the oriental tradition that his body reposes at Kition in Cyprus. See the *Lexikon f. Theologie und Kirche*, vol. vi, c. 432. For the liturgical observances, see Abbot Cabrol in DAC., vol. viii, cc. 2086–2088.   In the later middle ages St Lazarus was credited with having left an account of what he had seen in the next world before he was recalled to life : see Max Voigt, *Beiträge zur Geschichte der Visionenliteratur im M.A.*, vol. ii (1924).   The military order of hospitaller-knights of St Lazarus of Jerusalem (still existing in the form of two separate orders, of merit and knighthood, in Italy and France) did not take its name from this St Lazarus but from the fictitious Lazarus, " full of sores ", of our Lord's parable.

ST OLYMPIAS, Widow   (*c.* A.D. 408)

St Olympias, called by St Gregory Nazianzen " the glory of the widows in the Eastern church ", was to St John Chrysostom something of what St Paula was to St Jerome.   Her family belonged to Constantinople, and was one of distinction and wealth.   She was born about the year 361, and left an orphan under the care of the prefect Procopius, her uncle ; it was her happiness to be entrusted by him to Theodosia, sister to St Amphilochius, a woman who, St Gregory told her, was a pattern of goodness in whose life she might see as in a glass all excellences. Olympias had inherited a large fortune and was attractive in person and character, so that her uncle had no difficulty in arranging a marriage that was acceptable to him and to her, namely with Nebridius, for some time prefect of Constantinople. St Gregory wrote apologizing because age and bad health kept him from attending the wedding, and enclosing a poem of good advice for the bride.   The husband appears to have been an exacting man, but within a very short time Nebridius was dead, and the hand of Olympias was being sought by several of the most consider-able men of the court.   The Emperor Theodosius was very pressing with her to accept Elpidius, a Spaniard and his near relation.   She declared her resolution of remaining single the rest of her days :   " Had God wished me to remain a wife ", she said, " He would not have taken Nebridius away."   Theodosius persisted, and as her refusal continued, he put her fortune in the hands of the urban prefect with orders to act as her guardian till she was thirty years old.   The prefect even hindered her from seeing the bishop or going to church.   She wrote to the emperor, somewhat acidly perhaps, that she was obliged to him for easing her of the burden of managing and disposing of her money, and that the favour would be complete if he would order it all to be divided between the poor and the Church.   Theodosius, struck with her letter, made an inquiry into her manner of living, and restored to her the administration of her estate in 391.

St Olympias thereupon offered herself to St Nectarius, Bishop of Constantinople, for consecration as a deaconess, and established herself in a large house with a number of maidens who wished to devote themselves to the service of God.   Her dress was plain, her furniture simple, her prayers assiduous, and her charities without bounds, so that St John Chrysostom found it necessary to tell her some-times to moderate her alms, or rather to be more cautious in bestowing them, that she might be able to succour those whose distress deserved preference :   " You must not encourage the laziness of those who live upon you without necessity.   It is like throwing your money into the sea."   In 398 Chrysostom succeeded Nec-tarius in the see of Constantinople, and he took St Olympias and her disciples under his protection, and guided by him her benefactions were spread abroad ;   an orphanage and a hospital were attached to their house, and when the expelled monks came from Nitria to appeal against Theophilus of Alexandria they were fed and sheltered at the expense of Olympias. St Amphilochius, St Epiphanius, St Peter of Sebaste and St Gregory of Nyssa were among her friends, and Palladius of Helenopolis refers to her as " a wonderful woman . . . like a precious vase filled with the Holy Spirit " ; but it was with her own bishop that friendship was most mutually affectionate and trusting, and she was one of the last persons whom Chrysostom took leave of when he went into banishment in 404. It was necessary to tear her from his feet by violence.

After his departure, Olympias shared the persecution in which all his friends were involved. She was brought before Optatus, the prefect of the city, who was a heathen, on a charge of having set fire to the cathedral, but really that she might be persuaded to hold communion with Arsacius, the usurper of the bishopric. But Olympias was more than a match for Optatus, and was dismissed for that time. She was very ill all the winter, and in the spring was exiled, and wandered from place to place. About midsummer in 405 she was brought back to Constantinople and again presented before Optatus, who sentenced her to pay a heavy fine because she refused to communicate with Arsacius. Atticus, successor of Arsacius, dispersed the community of widows and maidens which she directed, and put an end to all their charitable works. Frequent sicknesses, outrageous slanders and persecutions succeeded one another. St John Chrysostom comforted and encouraged her from his places of exile by letters, of which seventeen have come down to us and give an idea not only of his misfortunes but of hers as well. " As you are well acquainted with suffering you have reason to rejoice, inasmuch as by having lived constantly in tribulation you have walked in the road of crowns and laurels. All manner of corporal diseases have been yours, often more cruel and harder to be endured than many deaths ; you have never been free from sickness.* You have been overwhelmed with slanders, insults, and injuries and never been free from some new tribulation ; tears have always been familiar to you. Among all these, one single affliction is enough to fill your soul with spiritual riches." In another letter he writes : " I cannot cease to call you blessed. The patience and dignity with which you have borne your sorrows, the prudence and wisdom with which you have managed delicate affairs, and the charity which has made you throw a veil over the malice of your persecutors have won a glory and reward which hereafter will make all your sufferings seem light and passing in the presence of eternal joy." We know also from these letters that St John entrusted Olympias with the execution of important commissions for him.

It is not known where St Olympias was when she heard of St John Chrysostom's death in Pontus on September 14, 407 ; she herself died at Nicomedia on July 25 in the following year, not much more than forty years old. Her body was taken to Constantinople, where " she had become so celebrated for her great goodness that her very name was considered worthy of imitation, parents hoping that their children would be built on a like model ".

Our knowledge of this holy widow is derived partly from Palladius, the letters of Chrysostom and the writings of other contemporaries, but also from a Greek Life which was printed

---

* Elsewhere he writes to her : " Much patience is needed to see oneself unjustly deprived of wealth, driven from home and country to exile in an unhealthy climate, chained and imprisoned, loaded with insults, railing and contempt. Even the calmness of Jeremias could not resist such trials. Yet not even these or the loss of children dear as our very heart's blood or death itself, the most terrible of evils in human estimation, are so trying to bear as bad health."

for the first time in the *Analecta Bollandiana*, vol. xv (1896), pp. 400–423, together with an account of the translation of her remains (*ibid.*, vol. xvi, pp. 44–51) written much later by the superioress (*Ama*) Sergia. See also the article of J. Bousquet, " Vie d'Olympias la diaconesse ", contributed to the *Revue de l'Orient chrétien*, second series, vol. i (1906), pp. 225–250, and vol. ii (1907), pp. 255–268. The life seems to have been composed in the middle of the fifth century and is clearly posterior to Palladius, as is proved by quotations made from this source. One chapter, the eleventh, seems to be a later interpolation by another hand. The letters of St John Chrysostom to St Olympias have been translated into French by P. Legrand, *Exhortations à Théodore ; Lettres à Olympias* (1933). See also H. Leclercq in DAC., vol. xii, cc. 2064–2071.

ST BEGGA, Widow   (A.D. 693)

PEPIN of Landen, mayor of the palace to three Frankish kings, and himself commonly called Blessed, was married to a saint, Bd Itta or Ida, and two of their three children figure in the Roman Martyrology : St Gertrude of Nivelles and her elder sister, St Begga. Gertrude refused to marry and was an abbess soon after she was twenty, but Begga married Ansegisilus, son of St Arnulf of Metz, and spent practically the whole of her long life as a nobleman's wife " in the world ". Of this union was born Pepin of Herstal, the founder of the Carlovingian dynasty in France. After the death of her husband, St Begga in 691 built at Andenne on the Meuse seven chapels representing the Seven Churches of Rome, around a central church, and in connection therewith she established a convent and colonized it with nuns from her long-dead sister's abbey at Nivelles. It afterwards became a house of canonesses and the Lateran canons regular commemorate St Begga as belonging to their order. She is also venerated by the *Béguines* of Belgium as their patroness, but the common statement that she founded them is a mistake due to the similarity of the names. St Begga died abbess of Andenne and was buried there.

A life of St Begga, together with some collections of miracles, has been printed in Ghesquière, *Acta Sanctorum Belgii*, vol. v (1789), pp. 70–125 ; it is of little historical value. See also Berlière, *Monasticon Belge*, vol. i, pp. 61–63 ; and DHG., vol. ii, cc. 1559–1560. There can be little doubt that the word *beguinae*, which we first meet about the year 1200 and which, as stated above, has nothing to do with St Begga, was originally a term of reproach used of the Albigensians : see the *Dictionnaire de Spiritualité*, vol. i, cc. 1341–1342.

ST STURMI, Abbot   (A.D. 779)

STURMI, the son of Christian parents in Bavaria, was entrusted to the care of St Boniface who left him to be educated under St Wigbert in his abbey of Fritzlar. He was there in due course ordained priest and did mission work in Westphalia for three years, after which he was allowed with two companions to lead an eremitical life in the forest at Hersfeld. This place was unprotected from the marauding Saxons, and was otherwise unsuited to them, and was soon abandoned. St Boniface had found a district further south more suitable for a monastery from which the Saxons could be evangelized, and St Sturmi rode down into it on his donkey and selected a site at the junction of the Greizbach and the Fulda. In 744 the monastery of Fulda was founded, St Boniface appointing St Sturmi its first abbot. It was the favourite foundation of St Boniface, who intended it to be what in fact it became under the fostering care of Sturmi, the pattern monastery and seminary of priests for all Germany ; he used frequently to visit it to superintend its progress, and his body was buried in the abbey church. Soon after its foundation St Sturmi went into Italy to study Benedictine observance at its fountain-head at Monte Cassino, and it seems that Pope St Zachary gave his monastery complete autonomy by withdrawing it from episcopal jurisdiction and subjecting it directly to the Holy See. The abbey of Fulda continued to prosper under St Sturmi, but he. was involved in serious difficulties after the martyrdom of St Boniface, for the attitude of his successor at Mainz, St Lull, towards the monastery was very different. Lull claimed that it should be subject to him as bishop, and the ensuing struggle was long and bitter. In 763 an order was obtained from Pepin for the banishment of Sturmi, and Lull nominated a superior in his place, but the monks of Fulda refused to accept him and expelled him from the house, threatening that they would go in a body and appeal to the king. To pacify them Lull told them to choose a superior of their own, whereupon they elected a life-long disciple of Sturmi. He took a deputation of monks to court, and they were successful in inducing Pepin to recall their beloved abbot, who returned to Fulda amid great rejoicing after two years of exile.

The efforts of St Sturmi and his monks to convert the Saxons did not meet with much external success, and the wars of Pepin and Charlemagne, first punitive and then of conquest, were not calculated to recommend his religion to the heathen. St Sturmi, like many missionaries before and since, was working under the greatest handicaps furnished by the civil power : it seemed to the Saxons that the faith of Christ was preached to them " with an iron tongue by their bitterest enemies ". When Charlemagne was recalled from Paderborn to attack the Moors in Spain, the Saxons at once rose and drove out the monks ; Fulda itself was threatened. In 779 Charlemagne returned and St Sturmi accompanied him to the mobilization at Düren which preceded fresh military success against the Saxons, but he did not live to recommence his missions. He was taken ill at Fulda and, in spite of the efforts of the physician sent by Charlemagne, died on December 17, 779. The name of St Sturmi, called by the Roman Martyrology the Apostle of the Saxons, was added to the roll of saints in 1139 ; he is apparently the first German known to have become a Benedictine monk.

The *Vita S. Sturmii* belongs to the best class of early medieval biographies. It was written by Eigil, himself also abbot of Fulda, about fifty years after the founder's death. It has been many times printed, *e.g.* in Migne, PL., vol. cv, cc. 423–444, and in MGH., *Scriptores*, vol. ii, pp. 366–377. See also the sketch of Sturmi's activities given by H. Timerding in *Die Christliche Frühzeit Deutschlands ; zweite Gruppe* (1929) ; and M. Tangl, *Leben des hl. Bonifazius, der hl. Leoba und des Abtes Sturmi* (1920), Introduction. The life by Eigil is translated by C. H. Talbot in *Anglo-Saxon Missionaries in Germany* (1954).

ST WIVINA, Virgin　　(A.D. 1170 ?)

LITTLE is related of the life of St Wivina that is not common to many other holy nuns of the middle ages. She was a Fleming, well brought up, and by the time she was fifteen had made up her mind to " leave the world " and her father's house. She was, however, sought in marriage by a number of suitors—foremost among whom was a young nobleman named Richard, who had the approval of her parents. This young man was very much in love with her, and when she made it clear to him that she would accept no earthly husband he took it so hardly that he became ill and his life even was in danger. Feeling herself responsible for his unhappy state, Wivina prayed and fasted for him until he was restored to health, as it were miraculously. When she was twenty-three she left her father's house secretly, taking only a psalter with her, and with one companion made a hermitage of branches in a wood near Brussels, at a place called Grand-Bigard. Here her solitude was much disturbed by people who came from the city to see her out of curiosity. Count Godfrey of Brabant offered her the land and an endowment wherewith to build a monastery on it, which she gladly accepted. She put herself and her community under the direction of the abbot of Afflighem, a monastery near Alost (it is still in being) which at that time, according to the testimony of St Bernard, was peopled by angels rather than men. Under such auspices the nunnery of Grand-Bigard prospered, though not without grave difficulties for the abbess ; some of her subjects found her lacking in discretion, especially in the matter of austerities, and did not keep their opinions to themselves. St Wivina pointed out to them that they were being led away by Satan, but it required a miracle to persuade them that their abbess was in the right. After her death the abbey became a place of pilgrimage, and many miracles of healing took place at her tomb. The relics of St Wivina are now in Notre-Dame-du-Sablon at Brussels.

There is a legendary account of her which has been printed by the Bollandists in the volume *Anecdota J. Gielemans* (1895), pp. 57–79. Her psalter, written in the early twelfth century, is still preserved at Orbais in Brabant. See also Van Ballaer, *Officium cum Missa* (1903).

18 : SS. RUFUS AND ZOSIMUS, MARTYRS   (*c.* A.D. 107)

WHEN St Ignatius of Antioch was at Philippi in Macedonia, on his way to martyrdom in Rome, he had with him SS. Rufus and Zosimus, citizens of Antioch or of Philippi itself. On the instruction of Ignatius, the Philippian Christians wrote a fraternal letter to their fellows at Antioch, and were answered by St Polycarp of Smyrna, to whom St Ignatius had commended the care of his church. In his letter, which during the fourth century was read publicly in the churches of Asia, he refers to Rufus and Zosimus, who had the happiness to share in Ignatius's chains and sufferings for Christ, and likewise glorified God by martyrdom under Trajan about the year 107. St Polycarp says of them : " They have not run in vain but in faith and righteousness, and they are gone to the place that was due to them from the Lord, with whom they also suffered. For they loved not the present world, but Him who died and was raised again by God for us. . . . Wherefore I exhort all of you that you obey the word of righteousness and exercise all patience, which you have seen set forth before your eyes, not only in the blessed Ignatius and Zosimus and Rufus, but in others that have been among you and in Paul himself and the rest of the apostles."

Nothing more is known of these martyrs than is contained in St Polycarp's letter. There is no indication of an early *cultus* of any kind.

ST GATIAN, BISHOP OF TOURS   (A.D. 301 ?)

ACCORDING to St Gregory of Tours St Gatian was one of the six missionary bishops who came to Gaul from Rome with St Dionysius of Paris about the middle of the third century. He preached the faith principally at Tours, of which church he is venerated as the founder and the first bishop. Having continued his labours with unwearied zeal amid many dangers for fifty years he died in peace. His memory was held in veneration, but it appears that much of his work was undone. A medieval legend says that St Gatian was one of the seventy-two disciples and was sent to Gaul by St Peter himself. This is certainly a fiction.

St Gregory of Tours mentions St Gatian in his *Historia Francorum*, bk i, ch. 10, and bk x, ch. 31, as also in his *Gloria confessorum*, bk iv, ch. 39. The fact that Gatian is not commemorated in the *Hieronymianum* suggests there was no very active *cultus*, but we are told that St Martin of Tours enshrined his relics with honour. Duchesne discusses the case of Gatian in his *Fastes Épiscopaux*, vol. ii, pp. 286, 302.

ST FLANNAN, BISHOP   (SEVENTH CENTURY ?)

ST FLANNAN, whose feast is kept throughout Ireland, is venerated as the first bishop of Killaloe, a diocese nearly conterminous with the district of Thomond, of which his father, Turlough, was chieftain. Flannan was educated by a monk, who taught him not only letters but also " to plow, sow, reap, grind, winnow and bake for the monks ". According to his very late life, Flannan determined, in spite of the opposition of his friends and relatives, to make a pilgrimage to Rome, and he achieved the voyage in the miraculous manner common in Celtic hagiology, namely, on a floating stone. While there he was consecrated bishop by Pope John IV (*d.* 642), and on his return to Killaloe all the people assembled to hear the instructions and messages of the Holy Roman See. The exhortations and teaching of St Flannan caused his father in his old age to become a monk under St Colman at Lismore. Three of his sons having been killed, Turlough asked Colman for a special blessing on his family. Whereupon Colman made seven strides and said, " From you shall seven kings spring " : and so it was, all of them called Brian. Flannan was afraid that the kingship would descend to him, and that he might be ineligible for it he prayed that he should be visited with a physical deformity. Accordingly, says his biographer, " scars and rashes and boils began to appear on his face so that it became most dreadful and repulsive ". St Flannan is supposed to have preached as well in the Western Isles : a small group off the west coast of Lewis, the Seven Hunters, is also known by his name. Several great marvels are attributed to him, as well as such Celtic practices as reciting his office immersed in icy water.

There is a Latin life of St Flannan in the Codex Salmanticensis (defective in one leaf). It has been printed in the Bollandist edition of the *Acta Sanctorum Hiberniae ex Codice Salmanticensi*, pp. 643–680. Another text has been edited by Fr Paul Grosjean, from a Bodleian manuscript, in the *Analecta Bollandiana*, vol. xlvi (1928), pp. 124–141, and with this also a third fragment in the library of Trinity College, Dublin. " Flannan, prince of gentleness " is a phrase which occurs in some manuscripts of the *Félire* of Oengus on December 18. The life of St Flannan seems to be rather exceptionally late and extravagant. See also KSS., p. 350.

ST WINEBALD, ABBOT   (A.D. 761)

IT has been related herein under the date February 7 that a certain West Saxon, St Richard, set out on a pilgrimage to Rome with his two sons, SS. Willibald and Winebald, and died at Lucca. The young men went on to their destination, whence Willibald undertook a further pilgrimage to the Holy Land ; but Winebald (or Wynbald), who had been delicate from his childhood and was ill, remained at Rome, where he studied for seven years and devoted himself with his whole heart to the divine service. Then, returning to England, he engaged several among his kindred and acquaintances to accompany him back to Rome, and there he dedicated himself to God in a religious state. St Boniface came on his third visit to Rome in 739 and enlisted Winebald to help in the founding of the Church in Germany. Winebald followed him into Thuringia and, being ordained priest there, received the care of seven churches, which he ministered to from Sulzenbrücken, near Erfurt. Being harried by the Saxons, he extended his labours into Bavaria, and after some years of strenuous missionary work returned to St Boniface at Mainz. But he could not settle down there, and went to his brother St Willibald, who was now bishop of Eichstätt. Willibald wanted to found a double monastery which might be a pattern and seminary of piety and learning to the numerous churches which he had planted, and he asked Winebald and his sister St Walburga to undertake it.

Winebald therefore went to Heidenheim in Württemberg, where he cleared a wild spot of ground of trees and bushes and built first little cells for himself and his monks and shortly afterwards a monastery. A nunnery was set up adjoining, which St Walburga governed. The idolaters attempted the life of St Winebald because of his unflinching efforts to impose Christian morality, but he escaped these dangers and continued to enlarge Christ's fold, maintaining in his religious community the spirit of their holy state, teaching them above all things to persevere in prayer and to keep inviolably in mind the life of our Lord, as the standard from which they were never to waver and never to cease to hold up to the pagans around them. He established the Rule of St Benedict in both the monasteries, which formed an important centre of English learning. St Winebald was afflicted for many years with sickness (he had an altar in his own cell at which he offered Mass when he was not able to go to the church) and this much hampered his missionary work for he could undertake only short journeys. For this reason he was unable to end his days at Monte Cassino as he wished to do. Once he set out on a visit to Würzburg and on the way was brought almost to the point of death at the shrine of St Boniface at Fulda ; after three weeks he was better, but at the next town had a relapse and was in bed for another week. The end came after three years of nearly continual illness, and after a tender exhortation to his monks he died in the arms of his brother and sister on December 18, 761. Hugeburc, the nun who wrote the Life of St Winebald, assures us that miraculous cures took place at his tomb, and St Ludger writes in the Life of St Gregory of Utrecht that, " Winebald was very dear to my master Gregory, and shows by great miracles since his death what he did whilst living ".

The trustworthy biography of St Winebald was written by a nun of Heidenheim, Hugeburc ; the best text is that of Holder-Egger in MGH., *Scriptores*, vol. xv, pp. 106–117. Some further information is furnished in the *Hodoeporicon* of St Willibald, written by the same Hugeburc, which is translated in C. H. Talbot, *Anglo-Saxon Missionaries in Germany* (1954), and also for the Palestine Pilgrims Text Society by Bishop Brownlow in 1891. Other details may be gathered from the correspondence of St Boniface, from the Life òf St Walburga and from the earlier portion of F. Heldingsfelder's *Die Regesten der Bischöfe von Eichstätt* (1915). See also *Analecta Bollandiana*, vol. xlix (1931), pp. 353–397 ; and W. Levison, *England and the Continent . . .* (1946) ; see therein for Hugeberc, p. 294.

19 : SS. NEMESIUS AND OTHER MARTYRS   (A.D. 250)

DURING the persecution of Decius, Nemesius, an Egyptian, was apprehended at Alexandria upon a charge of theft. He cleared himself of that,
but was immediately accused of being a Christian. Thereupon he was
sent to the prefect of Egypt and, confessing his faith, he was ordered to be scourged
doubly more grievously than the thieves. Afterwards he was condemned to be
burnt in company with robbers and other malefactors ; whereby, as the Roman
Martyrology says, he had the honour and happiness more perfectly to imitate the
death of our divine Redeemer.

ARSENIUS, HERON and ISIDORE, with DIOSCORUS, a youth only fifteen years old,
were committed at Alexandria in the same persecution. First of all the judge
took the boy in hand and began to cajole him with fair speeches ; then he assailed
him with various tortures, but Dioscorus could be overcome in neither way. The
rest, after enduring like torments, were burnt alive. But the judge discharged
Dioscorus, on account of his years, saying he allowed him time to repent ; and he
departed free, " for the consolation of the faithful ". In the Roman Martyrology
St Nemesius is commemorated on December 19, the rest of these martyrs on the
14th. On the 8th is mentioned the finding of the relics at Rome of another ST
NEMESIUS and other martyrs. They have two other entries in the Martyrology—
their martyrdom on August 25 and translation of relics on October 31—though
they are known only from the spurious *passio* of Pope St Stephen.

Alban Butler also mentions in this place SS. MEURIS and THEA, two women at
Gaza in Palestine, who when persecution raged under the successors of Diocletian
bore bravely the cruelty of men and malice of the devil, and triumphed over both.
Meuris died at the hands of the persecutors ; but Thea lived some time after she
had passed through dreadful torments, as we learn from the Life of St Porphyrius
of Gaza.

Of Nemesius we know nothing but the few sentences which Eusebius (*Eccl. Hist.*, bk vi,
ch. 41) has extracted from St. Dionysius of Alexandria. Similarly Meuris and Thea are
mentioned only in the Life of Porphyrius by Mark the Deacon.

ST ANASTASIUS I, POPE   (A.D. 401)

ST ANASTASIUS was a Roman and the successor of St Siricius in the year 399 ;
among his friends and admirers were St Jerome, St Augustine and St Paulinus of
Nola. The first named wrote of him that he was a distinguished man, of blameless
life and apostolic solicitude, whom Rome did not deserve to possess long lest the
world's head be cut off while ruled by such a bishop (referring to the subsequent
invasion by Alaric the Goth). St Jerome was as kind in speaking of his friends as
he was merciless to his opponents, and Anastasius earned his gratitude by condemning certain writings of Origen (*d.* 254), about which Jerome was having a
fierce controversy with Rufinus.

Besides the account in the *Liber Pontificalis* (for which see the text and notes of Duchesne's
edition, vol. i, pp. 218 *seq.*), we have a few authentic papal letters, as well as references in
St Jerome, St Paulinus of Nola, and St Augustine. Consult further E. Caspar, *Geschichte
des Papsttums*, vol. i (1930), pp. 280–294, and Hefele-Leclercq, *Histoire des Conciles*, vol. ii,
pp. 126–135.

BD WILLIAM OF FENOLI   (*c*. A.D. 1205)

INFORMATION is lacking about this holy Carthusian lay-brother, whose *cultus* was confirmed by Pope Pius IX in 1860.   It is known that he belonged to the charter-house *Casularum* in Lombardy and as he was in charge of the external business of the monastery his sanctity was a matter of more public knowledge than is usually the case among Carthusian monks.   " He was untutored in theology, in philosophy and in worldly knowledge, but in spiritual life and good works he was most learned. His holiness was made known by very many miracles both during his life and after his death."   Accounts of some of the miracles attributed to him have been pre-served.   One preposterous marvel is stated to have happened during his lifetime. When returning from his field work leading a mule William was attacked by robbers.   Having no weapon to defend himself, he seized the leg of the mule, pulled it out of its socket, and brandishing it against his assailants, put them all to flight.   This done he restored the leg to its place and the mule went on uninjured. It seems to be certain that in still existing paintings Bd William is represented with the leg of a mule or donkey in his hand.

An account of this good brother is given both in Le Couteulx, *Annales Ordinis Cartusiensis* vol. iii, pp. 293–302 ; and in the *Analecta Juris Pontificii*, vol. v, 1861, cc. 129–134.   In both, the greater part of the space is taken up with attestations of miracles alleged to have been worked at the intercession of Bd William many centuries after his death.

BD URBAN V, POPE   (A.D. 1370)

WILLIAM DE GRIMOARD was born at Grisac in Languedoc in 1310, his father being a local nobleman and his mother a sister of St Elzear de Sabran.   He was educated in the universities of Montpellier and Toulouse and became a Benedictine ; after his ordination he returned to his old universities and then went on to Paris and Avignon to study for his doctor's degree.   He taught in those places, and was appointed abbot of St Germain's at Auxerre in 1352.   At this time the popes were residing at Avignon and for the next ten years Abbot William was constantly called on to undertake diplomatic missions for Pope Innocent VI, who in 1361 made him abbot of St Victor's at Marseilles and sent him to Naples as legate to Queen Joanna.   While he was there he heard that Innocent was dead and that he had been elected in his place.   He returned at once to Avignon, where he was consecrated and crowned, and took the name of Urban because " all the popes called Urban had been saints ".   He was the best of the Avignon popes, though like most of them he was too much of a " nationalist " (as we should say now) to be a really satisfactory pontiff of the Universal Church, and the abuses by which he was surrounded were beyond his strength to eradicate.

The great event of his pontificate was his attempt, abortive though it was, to restore the papacy to Rome.   In 1366, ignoring the opposition of the French king and the French cardinals, he informed the emperor of his intention to return to the City, and in April of the following year he set out.   At Carneto he was met by a host of envoys, ecclesiastical and lay, by a Roman embassy bearing the keys of Sant' Angelo, and by Bd John Columbini and his Gesuati waving palms and singing hymns.   Four months later he entered Rome in state, the first pope it had seen for over half a century, and when he looked upon the state of the City he wept.

The great churches, even the Lateran, St Peter's and St Paul's, were almost in ruins, and he at once set to work to restore them and to make the papal residences habitable. Immediate steps were taken to revive the discipline of the clergy and the fervour of the people, work was soon found for all, and food was distributed freely to the destitute.

In the following year Urban met the Emperor Charles IV, a new alliance was made between the empire and the Church, and Charles entered Rome leading the mule on which the pope rode. Twelve months later the emperor of the East, John V Palaeologus, also came, disclaiming schism and seeking help against the Turks. Urban received him on the steps of St Peter's, but he could give him no help : it was more than he could do to maintain his own position. He had failed to crush the *condottieri*, Perugia had revolted, France was at war with England, his French court was restless and discontented, his health was failing : Urban prepared to go back to France. The Romans implored him to stay, Petrarch made himself the mouthpiece of Italy to keep him in Rome, St Bridget of Sweden rode out to Montefiascone on her white mule to warn him that if he left Italy his death would swiftly follow. But it was all to no purpose. In June 1370 he declared to the Romans that he was leaving them for the good of the Church and to help France ; on September 5, " sorrowful, suffering and deeply moved ", he embarked at Carneto ; and on December 19 he was dead. Petrarch wrote : " Urban would have been reckoned among the most glorious of men if he had caused his dying bed to be laid before the altar of St Peter's and had there fallen asleep with a good conscience, calling God and the world to witness that if ever the pope had left this spot it was not his fault but that of the originators of so shameful a flight." But this one weakness was forgiven him, and a chronicler of Mainz sums up contemporary opinion : " He was a light of the world and a way of truth ; a lover of righteousness, flying from wickedness and fearing God."

Urban V was entirely free from the prevailing vices of his age and worked hard for the reform of the clergy, beginning with his own court, where the venality of the officials was notorious.* He maintained many poor students and encouraged learning by his support of universities, *e.g.* Oxford, and his encouragement of the foundation of new ones, *e.g.* at Cracow and Vienna. He awarded the custody of the relics of St Thomas Aquinas to the Dominicans of Toulouse, and instructed the university of that city that : " We will and enjoin on you that you follow the teaching of the blessed Thomas as true and Catholic teaching, and promote it to the utmost of your power." Pilgrims came to Urban's tomb in the abbey church of St Victor at Marseilles, his canonization was asked for and Pope Gregory XI promised the King of Denmark that it should be undertaken. The times were too troubled ; but the *cultus* continued, and in 1870 it was confirmed by Pope Pius IX, the feast of Bd Urban being added to the calendar of Rome and of several French dioceses.

From the point of view of this pontiff's personal holiness the most important sources will be found collected in the volume of J. H. Albanès and U. Chevalier, *Actes anciens et documents concernant le B. Urbain V* (1897). This includes the ancient lives, of which there are several, and the evidence, reports of miracles, etc., presented in view of his canonization

* Among the cardinals he made was Simon Langham, Archbishop of Canterbury, who was promptly turned out of his see by King Edward III because he had not asked the king's leave to accept the honour.

as early as 1390. There is besides this a very considerable literature, of which an excellent bibliography is provided in G. Mollat, *Les papes d'Avignon* (1912), pp. 102–103. See further G. Schmidt in Sdralek's *Kirchengeschichtliche Abhandlungen*, vol. iii, pp. 157–173, and E. Hocedez in the *Analecta Bollandiana*, vol. xxvi (1907), pp. 305–316. There is a life by L. Chaillan (1911) in the series " Les Saints ", but the best account is that of G. Mollat in his work mentioned above.

20 : SS. AMMON AND HIS COMPANIONS, MARTYRS   (A.D. 250)

ST DIONYSIUS, Bishop of Alexandria during the persecution under the Emperor Decius, wrote to Fabian, Bishop of Antioch, an account of the sufferings, heroism and failures of the Egyptian Christians, which has been preserved for us in the *Ecclesiastical History* of Eusebius. In the course of it he mentions a certain Christian who, when he was brought to trial, began to fear and to waver. Some Christian soldiers who were among the guards, fearing that the man would deny his faith, made signs to him by looks, gestures, and nods to stand firm. The magistrate noticed this, made an inquiry, and amid the clamour of the onlookers five soldiers broke from the ranks and declared themselves Christians. The magistrates were extremely disturbed and the prisoners correspondingly encouraged by the profession of the soldiers, who duly suffered with the rest ; " and by their victory Christ, who had given them this firmness of mind, gloriously triumphed ". Their names were Ammon, Zeno, Ptolemy, Ingenes and an older man, Theophilus.

As in the case of St Nemesius we know nothing of these martyrs but what St Dionysius of Alexandria reports in a passage cited by Eusebius, *Eccles. Hist.*, bk vi, ch. 41.

ST PHILOGONIUS, BISHOP OF ANTIOCH   (A.D. 324)

ST PHILOGONIUS was brought up to the law, and made a considerable name at the bar for his eloquence, integrity and ability to make " the wronged stronger than the wronger ". While still a layman, with a wife and daughter, he was in 319 placed in the see of Antioch upon the death of Vitalis ; and St John Chrysostom mentions the flourishing state of that church in his time as proof of his zeal and excellent administration. In the storms which were raised against the Church by Maximinus and Licinius, St Philogonius confessed his faith and was imprisoned. His festival was celebrated at Antioch on December 20 in the year 386, at which Chrysostom pronounced his panegyric, touching lightly on his virtues because, as he says, he left the detail of them to the bishop Flavian, who was to speak after him.

Chrysostom speaks in moving terms of the peace which this saint now enjoys in a state where there are no conflicts, no insurgent passions, no more of " those icy words, ' mine ' and ' yours '," which fill the world with wars, families with quarrels, and individuals with disquiet, envy and malice. St Philogonius had so renounced the world that he received in this life the earnest of Christ's spirit in its fullest degree. A soul must here learn that spirit and state of the blessed if she hopes to reign with them hereafter : she must have some acquaintance beforehand with the mysteries of grace and the works of love and praise. People are not invited to consort even with a temporal king, as St Macarius says, until they have been instructed in the manners and customs of a court, so that they may not come to it in complete ignorance of its ways.

Here again all the information we possess comes from a single source, a sermon of St John Chrysostom. The text is printed in Migne, PG., vol. xlviii, pp. 747–756. On the degree of credit which attaches to the evidence of such panegyrics see the warnings given by Delehaye in his book *Les Passions des Martyrs et les Genres littéraires* (1921), ch. ii, pp. 183–235.

ST URSICINUS, ABBOT   (*c.* A.D. 625)

THE Swiss town of Saint-Ursanne, on the Doubs at the foot of Mont Terrible, has its name from Ursicinus (or Ursinus), a disciple of St Columban. He was one of the monks who left Luxeuil and joined their abbot at Metz after he had been driven from his monastery. Like St Gall and others, St Ursicinus settled down in what is now Switzerland, formed a small community which he governed according to the Rule of St Columban followed at Luxeuil, and preached the gospel to the pagans of the neighbourhood. St Ursicinus died some time before the middle of the seventh century, revered for his holiness and miracles. Two other saints of this name are commemorated this month. On the 1st the Roman Martyrology has a bishop of Brescia, of whom nothing is known except that he took part in the Council of Sardica in 347 ; and on the 14th a sixth-century bishop is venerated at Cahors.

Not much that is certain is known of St Ursicinus. The short text printed in Trouillat, *Monuments de l'évêché de Bâle*, vol. i, pp. 40–44, is only a compendium of an eleventh-century life and quite unreliable. See, however, Chèvre, *Histoire de Saint-Ursanne* (1891). The cult of St Ursicinus is attested by some early church dedications. In DCB. vol., iv, p. 1070, he is described as an " Irish monk ", but Dom Gougaud does not mention him in his *Saints irlandais hors d'Irlande* (1937). On the other hand the mention of a bell which purports to be a relic of St Ursicinus, see Stückelberg, *Geschichte der Reliquien in der Schweiz* (1908) is perhaps suggestive of an Irish origin. See also the brief mention of St Ursanne in Mgr Besson, *Nos origines chrétiennes : Étude sur la Suisse romande* (1921).

ST DOMINIC OF SILOS, ABBOT   (A.D. 1073)

THIS Dominic was born at the beginning of the eleventh century at Cañas in Navarre, on the Spanish side of the Pyrenees. His people were peasants, and for a time he followed their way of life, looking after his father's flocks among the foothills of the mountains. This work encouraged his taste for solitude and quietness, and he soon became a monk at the monastery of San Millán de la Cogolla. He made great progress in his new state, was entrusted with works of reform, and became prior of his monastery. In this office he came into conflict with his sovereign, Garcia III of Navarre, because he refused to give up some possessions of the monastery which were claimed by the king. Garcia at length drove Dominic and two other monks away, and they were welcomed by Ferdinand I of Old Castile, who sent them to the monastery of St Sebastian at Silos, of which Dominic was appointed abbot. The monastery was in a remote and sterile part of the diocese of Burgos, and was in a state of extreme decay, both materially and spiritually. Under the government of St Dominic this decay was arrested, then the house began to progress, and eventually he made it one of the most famous in Spain. Many miracles were recorded of Dominic in the course of his work, and it was said that there were no diseases known to man which had not been cured by his prayers.

The Roman Martyrology refers to the belief that Christian slaves among the Moors, to the number of three hundred, were liberated when they called upon God in his name. Dominic died on December 20, 1073.

St Dominic of Silos is especially venerated in the order of Friars Preachers, because a century less four years after his death, he appeared, according to the tradition, to Bd Joan of Aza who had made a pilgrimage from Calaroga to his shrine, and promised her that she should bear another son. That son was the founder of the Preachers, and he was named Dominic after the holy abbot of Silos. Until the revolution of 1931 it was the custom for the abbot of Silos to bring the staff of St Dominic to the royal palace whenever a queen of Spain was in labour and to leave it by her bedside until the birth had taken place.

There is a life by a monk, Grimaldus, who purports to be a contemporary. This has been printed, with a few slight omissions, in Mabillon, vol. vi, pp. 299–320. A metrical life by Gonzalo de Berceo (edited by J. D. Fitzgerald in 1904), which was written about 1240, adds little to our historical knowledge but is perhaps the earliest verse composition in Castilian speech. Much interest has been taken in St Dominic since the treasures of the library of Silos have become known : see, for example, M. Férotin, *Histoire de l'Abbaye de Silos* (1897) ; A. Andrés in the *Boletin de la real Academia Española*, vol. iv (1917), pp. 172–194 and 445–458 ; L. Serrano, *El Obispado de Burgos y Castilla primitiva* (1935), vol. ii ; and a short life by R. Alcocer (1925).

21 : ST THOMAS, APOSTLE   (FIRST CENTURY)

S T THOMAS was a Jew and probably a Galilean of humble birth, but we are not told that he was a fisherman or the circumstances in which our Lord made him an apostle. His name is Syriac, and means the " twin " ; Didymus, as we know he was also called, is the Greek equivalent. When Jesus was going up to the neighbourhood of Jerusalem in order to raise Lazarus to life the rest of the disciples endeavoured to dissuade Him, saying, " Rabbi, the Jews but now sought to stone thee ; and goest thou thither again ? " But St Thomas said, " Let us also go, that we may die with Him ", so ardent was his love of his Master. At the last supper, when our Lord said, " Whither I go you know, and the way you know ", it was Thomas who asked, " Lord, we know not whither thou goest, and how can we know the way ? " and so drew from Him those words in which are contained the whole Christian faith, " I am the Way and the Truth and the Life. No man cometh to the Father but by me." But this apostle is especially remembered for his incredulity after our Lord had suffered, risen from the dead, and on the same day appeared to His disciples to convince them of the truth of His resurrection. Thomas was not then with them and refused to believe their report that He was truly risen : " Except I shall see in His hands the print of the nails, and put my finger in the place of the nails, and put my hand into His side, I will not believe." Eight days later, when they were all together and the doors shut, the risen Christ was suddenly in the midst of them, greeting them : " Peace be to you." Then He turned to Thomas and said," Put in thy finger hither, and see my hands ; and bring hither thy hand and put it into my side. And be not faithless, but believing." And Thomas fell at His feet, exclaiming, " My Lord and my God ! " Jesus answered, " Because thou hast seen me, Thomas, thou hast believed. Blessed are they that have not seen, and have believed."

This is all that we are told of St Thomas in the New Testament, but, as with the other apostles, there are traditions, of great unreliability, about his missionary activities after the descent of the Holy Ghost at Pentecost. Eusebius states that he sent St Thaddeus (Addai ; August 5) to Edessa to baptize King Abgar, and the field of his own ministry is assigned to Parthia and " the Medes, Persians, Carmanians, Hyrcanians, Bactrians and other nations in those parts ". But the most persistent tradition is that which says that he preached the gospel in India. This is supported from several seemingly independent sources, of which the chief is the *Acta Thomae*, a document dating apparently from the first quarter of the third century. The story told by these *acta* is as follows : When the Apostles at Jerusalem divided the countries of the world for their labours, India fell to the lot of Judas Thomas (so he is often called in Syriac legends). He was unwilling to go, pleading lack of strength and that a Hebrew could not teach Indians, and even a vision of our Lord could not alter his resolution. Thereupon Christ appeared to a merchant named Abban, the representative of Gundafor, a Parthian king who ruled over part of India, and sold Thomas to him as a slave for his master. When he understood what had taken place, Thomas said, " As thou wilt, Lord, so be it ", and embarked with Abban, having only his purchase price, twenty pieces of silver, which Christ had given to him. During the voyage they landed at a port and were present at the wedding festivities of the ruler's daughter. At the playing of a Hebrew flute-girl Thomas was moved to sing, and he sang of the beauty of the Church under the figure of·a bride. But as he sang in his own tongue nobody but the flute-girl understood him ; and she loved him, but he sat with his eyes on the ground and would not raise them to her. That night Jesus Christ, having the appearance of Thomas, appeared to the bridal pair and persuaded them to a life of complete continence. When the ruler heard of this he was indignant and sent for the stranger, but Abban and Thomas were gone, and only the flute-girl remained, weeping because she had not been taken with them. But when they told her what had befallen the young couple she put away her grief, and went to wait upon them.

Meanwhile Abban and Thomas continued their journey and came to Gundafor's court in India, and when the king asked the apostle's trade he replied, " I am a carpenter and builder. I can make yokes and ploughs and ox-goads, oars for boats and masts for ships ; and I can build in stone, tombs and monuments and palaces for kings." So Gundafor ordered him to build a palace, and Thomas laid out the plans, with " doors towards the east for light, windows towards the west for air, a bake-house on the south, and water-pipes for the service of the house on the north ". Gundafor went on a journey, and in his absence Thomas did no building but spent all the money given him for the work on the poor, saying, " That which is the king's to the kings shall be given ". And he went about the land preaching and healing and driving out evil spirits. On his return Gundafor asked to be shown his new palace. " You cannot see it now, but only when you have left this world ", replied Thomas. Whereupon the king cast him into prison and purposed to flay him alive. But just then Gundafor's brother died, and being shown in Heaven the palace that Thomas's good works had prepared for Gundafor, he was allowed to come back to earth and offer to buy it from the king for himself. Gundafor declined to sell, and in admiration released Thomas and received baptism together with his brother and many of his subjects. " And at dawn he broke the Eucharist and let them partake at the table of the Messias ; and they rejoiced and were glad."

Afterwards Thomas was preaching and doing marvels throughout India, until he got into trouble with a King Mazdai for converting ("bewitching") his wife, his son and other important people. Eventually Thomas was led to the top of a hill where, having had orders from the king, "soldiers came and struck him all together, and he fell down and died". He was buried in a royal sepulchre, but afterwards some of the brethren carried away his relics to the West.

It is now commonly agreed that there is no truth behind the extravagant but interesting story just outlined, though there was undoubtedly a king named Gondophernes or Guduphara, whose dominions about the year A.D. 46 included the territory of Peshawar; and attempts have been made to identify King Mazdai (whose name might be traced to a Hindu original) with the contemporary King Vasudeva of Mathura. Unfortunately, speculation about St Thomas cannot be left there. At the other end of India from the Punjab, along what is known as the Malabar Coast, particularly in the states of Cochin and Travancore, there is a large population of native Christians who call themselves "the Christians of St Thomas". Their history is known in detail since the sixteenth century, but their origin has not yet been indisputably determined—though theories are far from wanting. There have certainly been Christians there since very early times, and in their liturgy they use forms and a language (Syriac) that undoubtedly were derived from Mesopotamia and Persia.* They claim, as their name indicates, to have been originally evangelized by St Thomas in person. They have an ancient oral tradition that he landed at Cranganore on the west coast and established seven churches in Malabar; then passed eastward to the Coromandel Coast, where he was martyred, by spearing, on the "Big Hill", eight miles from Madras; and was buried at Mylapore, now a suburb of that city. There are several medieval references to the tomb of St Thomas in India, some of which name Mylapore;† and in 1522 the Portuguese discovered the alleged tomb there, with certain small relics now preserved in the cathedral of St Thomas at Mylapore. But the bulk of his reputed relics were certainly at Edessa in the fourth century, and the *Acta Thomae* relate that they were taken from India to Mesopotamia. They were later translated from Edessa to the island of Khios in the Aegean, and from thence to Ortona in the Abruzzi, where they are still venerated.

The Roman Martyrology combines several legends and adopts the view that St Thomas preached the gospel to the Parthians, Medes, Persians and Hyrcanians, passed into India, and was there martyred at "Calamina". This name occurs only in later writings and nobody has yet succeeded in identifying the place; upholders of the Malabar tradition have of course endeavoured to connect it with the neighbourhood of Mylapore. The Martyrology mentions the translation of his relics to Edessa on July 3, but in Malabar, and indeed throughout the Syrian

* In addition to other native Christians there are over 1½ million Christians of St Thomas, of whom more than a half are Catholics (called "of the Syro-Malabar rite"). Also, since 1930, the small body of the Syro-Malankara rite). Most of the remainder are now Jacobites, but there is a considerable number of "Reformed Syrians" (who particularly arrogate to themselves the name of St Thomas Christians : *Mar Thomakkar*) and some Protestants, as well as a tiny group of Nestorians. All these divisions have happened since 1653.

† It is stated in the *Anglo-Saxon Chronicle* that King Alfred in 883 sent Sighelm, Bishop of Sherborne, with offerings to Rome and to SS. Bartholomew and Thomas in India, in fulfilment of a vow.

churches, this date is the principal feast of St Thomas, commemorating his martyr-dom " in the year 72 A.D."

The apocryphal Acts of St Thomas may be most conveniently consulted in the edition of Max Bonnet (1883). It is generally agreed that the original text has not been preserved in its primitive shape but that the Greek form in which it has come down to us does not very materially depart from its first conception. The Syriac version has undergone much more substantial revision and interpolation. Although the strong gnostic colouring of these acts has been exaggerated (see on this Harnack, *Die Chronologie der altchristlichen Litteratur*, vol. i, pp. 545–549) still it cannot be mistaken, and, as Fr P. Peeters rightly insists, the apocryphal character of the document was patent to all orthodox teachers in the early Church. It is denounced by St Epiphanius, by St Augustine, by St Turibius of Astorga, by Pope St Innocent I and in the decree of Pseudo-Gelasius. The Syrian Greek who was probably the fabricator of the story would have been well able to learn from traders and travellers such details as the name Gondophernes with other topical matter, and this colouring does not warrant us in supposing that any germ of historical truth forms the basis of the *Acta Thomae*. See on all this Peeters in the *Analecta Bollandiana*, vol. xviii (1899), pp. 275–279 ; vol. xxv (1906), pp. 196–200 ; vol. xxxii (1913), pp. 75–77 ; vol. xliv (1926), pp. 402–403. These notices all deal with books which propound theories from divergent points of view founded on the contents of the apocryphal acts. A few may be mentioned as roughly representative of the considerable literature of the subject. A. von Gutschmid (*Kleine Schriften*, ii, pp. 332–394) was dominated by the idea that the acts represent a Christianized version of Buddhist legends. Sylvain Lévi in the *Journal Asiatique* for 1897 strove to elucidate names and incidents as if he were dealing with an historic document ; W. R. Philipps in *The Indian Antiquary* for 1903, and J. F. Fleet in the *Journal of the Royal Asiatic Society* for 1905 brought criticism to bear on the identifications of Lévi ; Bishop Medlycott in his uncritical book, *India and the Apostle Thomas* (1905), sought to find confirmation in the acts for the tradition that St Thomas died at Mylapore ; Fr J. Dahlmann, *Die Thomas-Legende* (*cf.* Fr Thurston in *The Month* for August 1912, pp. 153–163), attached great importance to the historic data of the story but did not attempt to reconcile it with Mylapore, while Father A. Väth in a booklet, *Der hl. Thomas, der Apostel Indiens* (1925), follows circumspectly in the same course. At the same time the defenders of the southern India tradition have not been silent. Among many brochures printed in support of the claims of Mylapore, the book of F. A. D'Cruz, *St Thomas the Apostle in India* (1929), deserves notice. It takes account of such later literature as the articles of Dr A. Mingana and D. J. N. Farquhar in the *Bulletin* of the John Rylands Library, Manchester (1925). Beyond doubt a few Pahlavi (*i.e.* Parthian) inscriptions, seemingly Christian in character, engraved round crosses, exist at Mylapore and in Travancore. It is likely enough that the Malabar coast was evangelized from Edessa at a later date, and that in the course of time a confused tradition connected this with the Apostle St Thomas himself. Father Thurston summarizes the question in the *Catholic Encyclopedia*, vol. xiv, pp. 658–659. *The Apostles in India* (Patna, 1953), by A. C. Perumalil, is a useful popular summary.

ST ANASTASIUS II, Patriarch of Antioch, Martyr   (A.D. 609)

The intrepid defender of orthodoxy, St Anastasius I of Antioch, was succeeded in that see in 599 by another Anastasius. He at once sent a profession of faith and notice of his election to Pope St Gregory the Great, who in his reply approved the orthodoxy of Anastasius and urged him, as the first fruits of his episcopate, to purge the Antiochene churches of simony. In the year 609 the Syrian Jews broke out into riots, provoked by the forced " conversions " among them of the Emperor Phocas, and among their Christian victims was the patriarch. After treating him with great indignity they put him to death, mutilated his corpse, and burned it. This crime was punished by the imperial officers with a severity and injustice no less criminal. Anastasius was looked on as a martyr and his name has been inserted in the Roman Martyrology, but he receives no *cultus* in the East. The translation into Greek of St Gregory's *De cura pastorali* is due to St Anastasius II, though some have assigned it to his predecessor and identified the two bishops as one. Nevertheless, St Anastasius I was a separate person, who was exiled from his see for twenty-three years for having opposed the amateur theologizing of the Emperor Justinian ; he is commemorated on April 21.

Apart from two letters of Pope St Gregory I, we know nothing of St Anastasius but what we learn from Theophanes, *Chronographia*, in Migne, P.G., vol. cviii, p. 624. See also DHG., vol. ii, c. 1460.

22 : ST FRANCES XAVIER CABRINI, Virgin, Foundress of the Missionary Sisters of the Sacred Heart (A.D. 1917)

In a Motu Proprio of John XXIII dated 25 July, 1960, this feast was transferred to 3 January. In the United States this feast is celebrated on 13 November.

AUGUSTINE CABRINI appears to have been what in England of the past was called a very substantial yeoman, who owned and farmed land around Sant' Angelo Lodigiano, between Pavia and Lodi ; his wife, Stella Oldini, was a Milanese ; and they had thirteen children, of whom the youngest was born on July 15, 1850, and christened Maria Francesca (later she was to add Saverio to the second name, which is what Xavier becomes in Italian).

The Cabrini were a solidly religious family—everything about them was solid —and little Frances came particularly under the strict care of her sister Rosa, who had been a school-teacher and had not escaped all the dangers of that profession. But the child profited by Rosa's teaching, and suffered no harm from her unbending discipline. There was perhaps a certain precocity about the child's religion, but it was none the less real. Family reading aloud from the " Annals of the Propagation of the Faith " inspired her with an early determination to go to the foreign missions—China was the country of her predilection. She dressed her dolls as nuns ; she made paper boats and floated them down the river manned with violets to represent the missionaries going to foreign parts ; and she gave up sweets, for in China there would be no sweets so she had better get used to it. Her parents, however, had decided on Frances being a school-teacher, and when old enough she was sent to a convent boarding-school at Arluno. She duly passed her examinations when she was eighteen, but then came a great blow : in 1870 she lost both her parents.

During the two years that followed she lived on quietly with Rosa, her unassuming goodness making a deep impression on all who knew her. Then she sought admittance to the religious congregation at whose school she had been, and was refused on the ground of poor health ; she tried another—with the same result. But the priest in whose school she was teaching at Vidardo had got his eye on her. In 1874 this Don Serrati was appointed provost of the collegiate church at Codogno, and found in his new parish a small orphanage, called the House of Providence, whose state left much to be desired. It was managed, or rather mismanaged, by its eccentric foundress, Antonia Tondini, and two other women. The Bishop of Lodi and Mgr Serrati invited Frances Cabrini to help in this institution and to try to turn its staff into a religious community, and with considerable unwillingness she agreed.

Thus she entered upon what a Benedictine nun has called " a novitiate of sorts, compared to which one in a regular convent would have been child's play ". Antonia Tondini had consented to her coming, but instead of co-operation gave her only obstruction and abuse. Frances stuck to it, however, obtained several recruits, and with seven of them in 1877 took her first vows. At the same time the bishop put her in charge as superioress. This made matters much worse. Sister Tondini's behaviour was such that it became an open scandal—indeed, she seems to have become somewhat insane. But for another three years Sister Cabrini and her faithful followers persevered in their efforts to build up the House of Providence, patiently hoping for better times, till the bishop himself gave up hope and ordered the place to be closed. He sent for Sister Cabrini and said to her, " You want to be a missionary sister. Now is the time. I don't know any institute of missionary sisters, so found one yourself." And quite simply she went out to do so.

There was an old, disused and forgotten Franciscan friary at Codogno, and into this Mother Cabrini and her seven faithful followers moved, and as soon as they were fairly settled in she set herself to draw up a rule for the community. Its work was to be principally the Christian education of girls, and its name The Missionary Sisters of the Sacred Heart. During the same year these constitutions were approved by the bishop of Lodi ; within two years the first daughter house was opened, at Grumello, and soon there was another, at Milan.

The above few sentences are easily written ; the actuality was rather different. There were such tiresome obstructions as objection to the word " Missionary " in the sisters' title (" Inappropriate to women "), and the mother who invoked the law because of the " enticement " of her daughter. But the general progress of the congregation and the trust of Mother Cabrini were such that in 1887 she went to Rome to ask the Holy See's approbation of her little congregation and permission to open a house in Rome. Influential efforts were made to dissuade her from this enterprise—seven years' trial was far too little : and the first interview with the cardinal vicar of the City, Parocchi, confirmed the prudence of her advisers. But only the first. The cardinal was won over ; Mother Cabrini was asked to open not one but two houses in Rome, a free school and a children's home, and the decree of first approval of the Missionary Sisters of the Sacred Heart was issued within a few months.

We have seen that from early days Frances Cabrini's eyes had been turned towards China. But now people were trying to make her look the other way. The bishop of Piacenza, Mgr Scalabrini, who had established the Society of St Charles to work among Italian immigrants in America, suggested she should go out there to help the work of those priests. She would not entertain the idea. The archbishop of New York, Mgr Corrigan, sent her a formal invitation. She was worried : everyone—except her old friend Mgr Serrati—was pointing in the same direction. Then she had a very impressive dream, and she determined to consult the pope himself. And Leo XIII said, " Not to the East, but to the West ". When a child Frances Cabrini once fell into a river, and ever afterwards she had a fear of water. She now, with six of her sisters, set out on the first of many voyages across the Atlantic ; and on March 31, 1889, they landed in New York.

Everybody knows the huge numbers of Italians, Poles, Ukrainians, Czechs, Croats, Slovaks and others that have emigrated to the United States in relatively recent times. The religious history of these immigrations has yet to be properly written. It is enough to say here that at that time there were 50,000 Italians in and around New York City alone. The majority of them seem never to have learned the elements of Christian doctrine ; not more than 1200 of them ever assisted at Mass ; ten of the twelve priests of their own nationality had left Italy

on account of misbehaviour.   It was much the same in north-western Pennsylvania.
For most of them their economic and social conditions were to match.   No wonder
that the third plenary council of Baltimore and Archbishop Corrigan and Pope
Leo XIII were very perturbed.

Nor was the sisters' reception in New York much more encouraging.   They
had been asked to organize an orphanage for Italian children and to take charge
of an elementary school : but on arrival, though warmly welcomed, they found no
home ready for them, and had to spend the first night at least in lodgings that were
filthy and verminous.   And when Mother Cabrini met Archbishop Corrigan she
learned that, owing to disagreements between himself and the benefactress concerned, the orphanage scheme had fallen through, and the school consisted of
pupils but no habitable building.   The archbishop wound up by telling her that
he could see nothing for it but that the sisters should go back to Italy.   To which
St Frances replied with characteristic firmness and definiteness, " No, Monsignor,
not that.   The pope sent me here, and here I must stay ".   The archbishop was
impressed by this straightforward little woman from Lombardy, and also by her
credentials from Rome ; moreover, it must be admitted he was a man of no great
firmness of policy, liable to change his mind quickly and often.   He now raised no
objection to their staying, and arranged for them to be temporarily accommodated
by the Sisters of Charity.   Within a few weeks St Frances Cabrini had made
friends with the benefactress, Countess Cesnola, reconciled her with Mgr Corrigan,
found a house for the sisters, and made a start with the orphanage on a modest
scale.   By July 1889 she was able to revisit Italy, taking with her the first two
Italo-American recruits to her congregation.

Nine months later she returned to America with reinforcements to take over
West Park, on the Hudson river, from the Society of Jesus.   The growing orphanage was transferred to this house, which also became the mother house and novitiate
of the congregation in the United States.   Its work was prospering, both among
immigrants in North America and among the people at home in Italy, and soon
Mother Cabrini had to make a trying journey to Managua in Nicaragua where, in
difficult and sometimes dangerous circumstances, she took over an orphanage and
opened a boarding-school.   On her way back she visited New Orleans at the
request of its archbishop, the revered Francis Janssens.   Here the scattered
Italians, mostly from the south and Sicily, were in a specially sad state : they
included some wild, lawless elements, and only a little time before eleven of them
had been lynched by infuriated but no less lawless Americans.   The upshot of
St Frances's visit was that she was able to make a foundation in New Orleans.

That Frances Cabrini was an extraordinarily able woman needs no demonstra-
tion : her works speak for her.   Like Bd Philippine Duchesne before her, she was
slow in learning English and never lost her strong accent ; but this apparently was
no handicap in successful dealings with people of all kinds, and those with whom
she had financial business (necessarily many and important) were particularly
impressed.   In only one direction did her tact fail, and that was in relation to
non-Catholic Christians.   She met such in America for the first time in her life—
and that was the root of the trouble : it took her a long time to recognize their
good faith and to appreciate their good lives.   Her rather shocking remarks in this
connection in earlier days were the fruit of ignorance and consequent lack of
understanding.   But she was far-seeing and ready to learn, and did not reject
things simply because they were new, as her ideas about children's education show.

It is obvious that Mother Cabrini was a born ruler, and she was as strict as she was just. Sometimes she seems to have been too strict, and not to have seen where her inflexibility was leading. It is not clear, for instance, how she thought she was upholding sexual morality when she refused to take illegitimate children in her fee-paying schools : it would appear to be a gesture that penalized only the innocent. But love ruled all, and her strictness was no deterrent to the affection she gave and received. " Love one another ", she urged her religious. " Sacrifice yourselves for your sisters, readily and always. Be kind to them, and never sharp or harsh. Don't nurse resentment, but be meek and peaceable."

The year 1892, fourth centenary of the discovery of the New World, was also marked by the birth of one of the best-known of St Frances's undertakings, the Columbus Hospital in New York. Actually it had been begun in a small way by the Society of St Charles a little before, and the " take-over " was attended by difficulties that left with some a legacy of resentment against Mother Cabrini. Then, after a visit to Italy, where she saw the start of a " summer house " near Rome and a students' hostel at Genoa,* she had to go to Costa Rica, Panama, Chile, across the Andes into Brazil, and so to Buenos Aires—a very different journey in 1895 from what it is today, though Mother Cabrini's love of natural scenery did much to compensate for its rigours. In Buenos Aires she opened a high-school for girls : and of those who pointed out the difficulties and hazards of what she was doing, she enquired, " Are we doing this ?—or is our Lord ? " After another voyage to Italy, where she had to cope with a long lawsuit in the ecclesiastical courts and face riots in Milan, she went to France and made there her first European foundations outside Italy ; and the autumn of 1898 saw her in England. Mgr (later cardinal) Bourne, then bishop of Southwark, had already met St Frances at Codogno and asked her to open a convent in his diocese, but no foundation was made at this time.

And so it went on for another dozen years. Surely were a patron saint more recent and less nebulous than St Christopher required for travellers, St Frances Cabrini would be first on the short list. Her love for all the children of God took her back and forth over the western hemisphere from Rio to Rome, from Sydenham to Seattle ; by the time the constitutions of the Missionary Sisters of the Sacred Heart were finally approved in 1907 the eight members of 1880 had increased to over a thousand, in eight countries ; St Frances had made more than fifty foundations, responsible for free-schools and high-schools and hospitals and other establishments, no longer working in America for Italian immigrants alone—did not the prisoners in Sing-Sing send her an illuminated address at the congregation's jubilee ? Of the later foundations only two can be named here : the great Columbus Hospital at Chicago and, in 1902, the school at Brockley, now at Honor Oak. Nor can the attendant trials and troubles be dwelt on, such as the difficulties caused by the Bishop of Vitoria (St Frances was first invited to Spain by Queen Maria Christina) or the opposition of factions in Chicago, Seattle and New Orleans, which last the sisters later repaid with their heroic work during the yellow-fever epidemic of 1905.

From 1911 Mother Cabrini's health was failing : she was then sixty-one and physically worn out. But it was not till six years later that she was seen to be failing alarmingly. And then the end came with extreme suddenness. No human

---

* On the way back Mother Cabrini went ashore at Gibraltar and recorded seeing the " English canon of incredible size ". Undoubtedly a " big gun ".

person was present when St Frances Xavier Cabrini died in the convent at Chicago on December 22, 1917. Mother Cabrini was canonized in 1946; her body is enshrined in the chapel of the Cabrini Memorial School at Fort Washington, N.Y. No doubt there were many saints in the United States before her, no doubt there have been, and will be, many after. But she was the first citizen of that country to be canonized, to have her sanctity publicly recognized by the Church of Christ. Her glory belongs to Italy and to America, to the Church and to mankind. It is hardly conceivable that anybody should do what she did, in the way she did it, without having been a saint, one who lived with heroic goodness : Pope Leo XIII saw this, and more, nearly fifty years before her canonization, when he said, " Mother Cabrini is a woman of fine understanding and great holiness . . .' she is a saint ".

The first standard life of Mother Cabrini was *La Madre Francesca Saverio Cabrini*, written by one of her congregation (Mother Xavier de Maria) and published in 1928. Ten years later appeared *La Beata Francesca Saverio Cabrini* by Emilie de Sânctis Rosmini, and there are other biographies in Italian. *Viaggi della Madre Cabrini, narrati in varie sue lettere* has been translated into English. A short and characteristic study by Father Martindale was published in 1931, and a life by the Rev. E. J. McCarthy at Chicago in 1937. *Frances Xavier Cabrini: the Saint of the Emigrants* (1944), by a Benedictine dame of Stanbrook, is a model of excellence as a life of a saint intended for general readers. For a short and unambiguous reference to the state of Italian immigrants in U.S.A., see Zwierlein, *Life and Letters of Bishop McQuaid*, vol. ii, pp. 333–335, and for their statistics, etc., the *Catholic Encyclopedia*, vol. viii, pp. 202–206. Another American biography is *Too Small a World*, by Theodore Maynard (1948).

SS. CHAEREMON, ISCHYRION AND OTHER MARTYRS (A.D. 250)

ST DIONYSIUS OF ALEXANDRIA in his letter to Fabian of Antioch, speaking of the Egyptian Christians who suffered in the persecution under Decius, refers to the many who were driven or fled into the desert, where they perished from hunger, thirst and exposure, by wild beasts and by men as wild ; many also were seized and sold into slavery, of which only some had been ransomed at the time he wrote. He singles out for mention by name Chaeremon, a very old man and bishop of Nilopolis, who with one companion had taken refuge in the mountains of Arabia and had never been seen or heard of again ; search was made by the brethren but not even their bodies were found. St Dionysius also mentions Ischyrion, who was the procurator of a magistrate in some city of Egypt, traditionally Alexandria. His master ordered him to sacrifice to the gods, but he refused and neither abuse nor threats could move him. So the enraged magistrate had him mutilated and impaled. Both these martyrs are named in the Roman Martyrology today.

These again are martyrs whose names are only rescued from oblivion by an extract which Eusebius (bk vi, ch. 42) has made from a letter of St Dionysius of Alexandria.

BD JUTTA OF DIESSENBERG, VIRGIN (A.D. 1136)

BD JUTTA was sister to Count Meginhard of Spanheim, and she led the life of a recluse in a small house next to the monastery founded by St Disibod on the Diessenberg. She was the " noble woman " to whom was confided the care of St Hildegard, when she was a child, and it was Jutta who first taught her Latin, to read and to sing. Other disciples came to her, and these were formed into a community over which she presided as prioress for some twenty years. " This woman ", says St Hildegard, " overflowed with the grace of God like a river fed by many streams. Watching, fasting, and other works of penance gave no rest to her body till the day that a happy death set her free from this mortal life. God has given testimony to her holiness by many startling miracles." The relics of Bd Jutta drew crowds of pilgrims to the Diessenberg, and their forthcoming removal was one of the grounds of the opposition of the monks to St Hildegard's transference of her community to Bingen.

No life of Bd Jutta seems to have been printed, but a manuscript account is in existence copied from the great *legendarium* of the Augustinian canons of Bödeken. See the *Analecta Bollandiana*, vol. xxvii (1908), p. 341 ; and also J. May, *Die hl. Hildegard* (1911).

BD ADAM OF LOCCUM   (*c.* A.D. 1210)

THIS monk, with others of the name, is called Blessed in menologies of the Cistercian Order ; the little that is known of him is derived from the *Dialogue of Visions and Miracles* of his fellow Cistercian, Caesarius of Heisterbach. Adam was priest and sacristan of the abbey of Loccum in Hanover, and while still a schoolboy was twice miraculously delivered from ill-health, as he related to Caesarius. While he was at Loccum the church of the monastery was being repaired, and Adam began to carve a piece of the stone that was lying among the builder's materials. His schoolmaster saw him and, after the manner of many of his kind, peremptorily told him to put the stone down or he would be excommunicated. Young Adam was so frightened by this threat that he was taken ill, and even believed to be dying. However, he saw in a vision St Nicholas and St Paternian, who decided that he should not die just then, and he was well in the same hour. Another time he was at school at Münster in Westphalia and got up one morning to go to church, when he found he had made a mistake in the time and the church was not yet open. He therefore knelt down and said the Angelical Salutation thrice according to his custom when entering a church, and upon looking up saw that the door was open and seven beautiful women sitting therein. Adam was at that time suffering from eczema, and one of them asked him why he didn't look after his head. He replied that he did but the physicians had not done it any good. Then the lady told him that she was the Mother of Christ and that she knew his devotion to her, and commanded him to approach. He was to wash his head in a decoction of the wood of the spindle-tree three times before Mass, in the name of the Holy Trinity. She laid her hand on his head, and when he had done as he was told his complaint was cured never to return.

" It is clear that there is nothing more efficacious and no remedy more sure than the medicine of the Blessed Virgin ", observes the novice in the *Dialogue*. To which the monk replies : " And no wonder. For it was she who brought to us the medicine of the whole human race, as it is written, ' Let the earth bring forth the living creature ', that is to say, let Mary bring forth the man Christ."

Bd Adam told other marvels to Caesarius, but these were not written down for our delectation and improvement.

This holy Cistercian is spoken of by Caesarius in his *Dialogus de Miraculis* in bk vii, chs. 17 and 25, as well as in bk viii, ch. 74. Nothing more seems to be known of Bd Adam than Caesarius tells us. There is an English translation of the *Dialogus* (2 vols., 1929). The monastic buildings at Loccum are now a Protestant seminary, and the Lutheran land-bishop of Hanover has the official title " Abbot of Loccum ".

23 : THE TEN MARTYRS OF CRETE   (A.D. 250)

UPON the publication of the edict against Christians under Decius the activity of a barbarous governor soon made victims in the isle of Crete. Among the martyrs who there triumphed none were more conspicuous than Theodulus, Saturninus, Euporus, Gelasius, Eunician, Zoticus, Cleomenes, Agathopus, Basilides and Evaristus, commonly called the Ten Martyrs of Crete. The three first were citizens of Gortyna, the capital.   United in their confession of Christ, they were arrested, dragged along the ground to prison, beaten, stoned by the mob, and at length presented to the governor at Gortyna.   As soon as they appeared in court they were ordered to sacrifice to Jupiter, because on that very day their countrymen celebrated a festival in his honour.   They answered that they would never sacrifice to idols.   The president said, " You shall know the power of the gods ; you show no respect to this great assembly, which worships the omnipotent Jupiter, Juno, Rhea and the rest ".   The martyrs replied that they were only too well acquainted with the history of the life and actions of Jupiter, and that those who look upon him as a god must look upon it as a divine thing to imitate his wickedness.

The people were ready to tear them to pieces on the spot if the governor had not restrained them and commanded the martyrs to be tortured.   They endured all with joy, and answered to the cries of the mob, who pressed them to spare themselves by obeying and sacrificing to their gods, " We are Christians and would rather die a thousand times ".   The governor at length, seeing himself vanquished, condemned them to die by the sword.   They went forth triumphantly to the place of execution, praying that God would have mercy on them and on all mankind, and would deliver their countrymen from the blindness of idolatry.   When their heads were struck off, and the crowds dispersed, other Christians buried their bodies, which were afterwards taken to Rome.   The fathers who composed the Council of Crete in 458, writing to the Emperor Leo I, claimed that through the intercession of these martyrs their island had been till that time preserved from heresy.

The Greek *passio* of these martyrs is preserved in two forms.   The more trustworthy is that edited by A. Papadopoulos-Kerameus in his *Analecta*, vol. iv, pp. 224–237.   The second belongs to the class usually attributed to the Metaphrast and it is printed in Migne, PG., vol. cxvi, pp. 565–573.   The tradition of their martyrdom still seems very strong in the neighbourhood of Gortyna.   The village in which they actually suffered bears the name Hagioi Deka (Ten Saints) : a broken slab is shown with ten hollow depressions which is said to mark the places where they knelt to receive the fatal stroke.   See the *Analecta Bollandiana*, vol. xviii (1899), p. 280.

SS. VICTORIA AND ANATOLIA, VIRGINS AND MARTYRS   (DATE UNKNOWN)

THE valueless *passio* of St Anatolia relates that when she refused, in consequence of a vision, to accept her suitor Aurelius he went to her sister, Victoria, and asked her to persuade Anatolia to marry him. Victoria's efforts were not only unsuccessful, but she herself was converted to her sister's views and broke off her own betrothal with one Eugenius. The young men then removed the maidens from Rome to their respective country villas and tried to starve them into a different frame of mind. Anatolia was denounced as a Christian, and her end is thus summarized in the Roman Martyrology on July 9 : " After she had healed many throughout the province of Picenum who were suffering from various diseases and had brought them to believe in Christ, she was afflicted with several punishments by order of the judge Faustinian ; and after she had been freed from a serpent that was set upon her and had converted [the executioner] Audax to the faith, lifting up her hands in prayer, she was pierced with a sword." Victoria met with a similar fate, perhaps at Tribulano in the Sabine hills. " She refused either to marry Eugenius or to sacrifice and, after working many miracles whereby numerous maidens were gathered to God, she was smitten to the heart by the executioner's sword at the request of her betrothed ".

Both St Anatolia and St Victoria had a *cultus* in various parts of Italy, but the real circumstances of their martyrdom are not known. The sentiments regarding marriage expressed in their *passio* are of the exaggerated and unguarded kind which, though often found in Christian documents, approximate more to the heretical doctrines of Encratism than to the teaching of the Catholic Church. Like the *passio* of St Lucy, that of St Victoria was utilized by St Aldhelm of Sherborne in his works *De laudibus virginitatis*.

Although the *passio* of these martyrs, preserved to us in varying and inconsistent texts (see BHL., nn. 417–420 and 8591–8593), is historically valueless, still there are grounds for believing in their real existence. See P. Paschini, *La passio delle martire Sabine Vittoria ed Anatolia* (1919) ; Lanzoni, *Le diocesi d'Italia*, pp. 347–350 ; Schuster, *Bolletino diocesano per Sabina*, etc. (1917), pp. 163–167 ; and especially Delehaye's CMH., pp. 364 and 654, with his *Étude sur le Légendier romain* (1936), pp. 59–60.

ST SERVULUS (*c.* A.D. 590)

IN this holy man was exemplified what our divine Redeemer taught of Lazarus, the poor man full of sores who lay at the gate of the rich man's house. Servulus was a beggar, afflicted with the palsy from his infancy, so that he had never been able to stand, sit upright, lift his hand to his mouth, or turn himself from one side to another. His mother and brother carried him to the porch of St Clement's church at Rome, where he lived on the alms of those that passed by, and whatever was left over he distributed among other needy persons. And for all that he was able to save enough to buy some books of Holy Scripture which, as he could not read himself, he got others to read to him ; and he listened with such attention as to learn them by heart. Much time he passed singing hymns of praise and thanksgiving to God in spite of continual pain. After years thus spent he felt his end draw near, and in his last moments he asked the poor and pilgrims who had often shared his charity to sing hymns and psalms by his bed. Whilst he joined his voice with theirs he on a sudden cried out, " Do you hear the great and wonderful music in heaven ? " When he had spoken these words he died, and his soul was carried by angels into everlasting bliss. The body of Servulus was buried in St Clement's church, and his feast is annually celebrated in that church on the Coelian Hill outside of which he was wont to lay.

St Gregory the Great concludes the account he gives of Servulus, in a sermon to his people, by observing that the behaviour of this poor sick beggar loudly condemns those who, when blessed with good health and fortune, neither do good works nor suffer the least cross with tolerable patience.   He speaks of him as one who was well known both to himself and his hearers, and says that one of his monks, who was present at his death, used to speak of the fragrant smell which came from the dead beggar's body.   Servulus was a true lover of God, not careful and troubled about his own life, but solicitous that God be honoured, and all that he could suffer for this end he looked upon as reward.   By his constancy and fidelity he overcame the world and all bodily afflictions.

We know nothing about Servulus but what we learn from St Gregory the Great.   See his *Dialogues*, bk iv, ch. 14, and also one of his homilies, printed in Migne, PL., vol. lxxvi, c. 1133.

ST DAGOBERT II OF AUSTRASIA   (A.D. 679)

Two French dioceses keep the feast of King Dagobert II, who was the son of another sainted king, Sigebert III ; but there seems no particular reason except popular tradition why he should be regarded as a saint, much less as a martyr.   He was still a child when he succeeded to the throne of Austrasia in 656, and he was exiled by his guardian, Grimoald, the unworthy son of Bd Pepin of Landen, who gave the crown to his own son, Childebert.   Dagobert was taken to Ireland by Dido, Bishop of Poitiers.   We learn from Eddi's Life of St Wilfrid of York that that saint befriended Dagobert, who in 675, on the murder of Childeric II, was repatriated by the good offices—and " in style "—of St. Wilfrid and recovered his kingdom.   When Wilfrid was on his way to Rome to appeal against St Theodore of Canterbury and King Egfrid, he came to the court at Metz and the king wished to reward his services by bestowing on him the vacant see of Strasburg ; but Wilfrid refused it.   When Dagobert met his death on December 23, 679, while hunting in the forest of Woëvre in Lorraine, it was attributed to " the treachery of dukes with the consent of bishops ".   He was buried near by at Stenay.   As in the several other similar instances, *e.g.* St Sigismund of Burgundy, the circumstances of his death caused Dagobert to be regarded as a martyr and this led to his *cultus* as a saint.

The tenth-century Life of Dagobert (best edited by B. Krusch in MGH., *Scriptores Merov.*, vol. ii, pp. 511–524) is of little value, but see Krusch's supplement in vol. vii, pp. 474 and 494.   Eddi's references to Dagobert are of great interest.   They may conveniently be consulted in Colgrave's edition of the Life of St Wilfrid (1927), and *cf.* Vacandard, *Vie de St Ouen*, pp. 283–286.   See further Bede's *Eccles. Hist.*, in Plummer's edition, vol. ii, pp. 318 and 325 ; F. Lot, *Histoire du moyen âge* (1928), vol. i, pp. 282 and 286 ; B. Krusch in *Historische Aufsätze K. Zeumer gewidmet* (1910), pp. 411–438 ; and Gougaud, *Christianity in Celtic Lands*, p. 153.   Referring to the many years Dagobert is said to have spent in Ireland, Gougaud remarks : " No doubt this fact accounts for the presence of these Irishmen in Aquitaine at a later time."   *Cf.* also W. Levison, *England and the Continent* . . . (1946), pp. 49–51.

BD HARTMAN, BISHOP OF BRIXEN   (A.D. 1164)

HARTMAN was born at Polling and educated at the Augustinian monastery of St Nicholas at Passau, wherein he eventually became a canon.   His virtues and talents were unusual, and when Conrad, archbishop of Salzburg, wished to introduce regular discipline and the common life among his clergy he invited Hartman to

become dean of the metropolitan chapter. This was in 1122. When Hartman
had formed these canons to the regular life, Conrad transferred him to the provostship of the monastery of Herrenchiemsee in order that it might be reformed, and
from there he was called by St Leopold, Margrave of Austria, to the house of
canons he had founded at Klosterneuburg. When the see of Brixen in Tirol
became vacant in 1140, Bd Hartman was called to be its bishop, and two years
later he founded the regular chapter of Neustift in his cathedral city and liberally
endowed it. Shortly after, with one of his cathedral canons, he established the
hospice of the Holy Cross for poor pilgrims in Brixen. Bd Hartman was highly
respected by the Emperors Conrad III and Frederick I. He was involved in the
troubles between the last-named and Pope Alexander III, but neither threats nor
promises could alienate him from the Holy See. After governing his church most
holily for twenty-four years he died—in a bath—on December 23, 1164. In 1784
the *cultus* of Bd Hartman was confirmed by Pope Pius VI.

There is a medieval Latin Life of Bd Hartman which is printed in Pez, *Scriptores rerum
austriacarum*, vol. i, and which was also edited by H. Zeibig, *Vita b. Hartmanni* (1846).
See upon this H. R. von Zeissberg in the *Archiv f. österreich. Geschichte*, vol. lvi (1878),
pp. 447–464. A more modern biography, in German, is that of A. Sparber (1910).

ST THORLAC, BISHOP OF SKALHOLT   (A.D. 1193)

CHRISTIANITY was planted in Iceland at the end of the tenth and the beginning
of the eleventh century, and made such progress that the island was soon divided
into two dioceses, Skalholt and Holar, which in 1152 were made suffragans of
Nidaros (Trondhjem) : Iceland had been colonized and evangelized from Norway.
During the twelfth century two bishops, one from each see, were venerated as saints
locally and in Norway, namely, John of Holar and Thorlac of Skalholt. The life
of the last-named is narrated in the *Thorlakssaga* by a cleric of Skalholt. We are
told that Thorlac Thorhallsson was a deacon when he was fifteen and a priest three
years later, and then, being a promising young man, was sent abroad to study :
he is said to have visited Lincoln. After ten years, in 1161, Thorlac returned to
Iceland full of reforming zeal. He was joyfully received by his mother and sisters,
who expected him to settle down to the semi-secular life led by most of the clergy
there in those days, but instead he devoted himself to study and the ministry. His
biographer gives an account of Thorlac's daily rule of life, which began with the
singing of the *Credo, Pater noster*, and a hymn directly he awoke ; he recited a
third of the psalter every day, and had an especial devotion to the titular saints of
the churches in which he ministered. Some years later an heirless farmer died,
leaving his land and house to the Church with instructions that Thorlac should
establish a monastery there, and he accordingly formed a community of canons
regular, of which he was abbot. We are told that Thorlac's mother went with him
to Thykkviboer to be cook and housekeeper for the new community. In 1178 he
became bishop of Skalholt, and was consecrated by Archbishop St Eystein in
Nidaros.

The way was now clear for Thorlac to introduce and promote the higher
spiritual standards and improved ecclesiastical discipline which he knew that the
good of souls required and the Church demanded. On the side of discipline this
resolved itself chiefly into endeavours to impose the observance of clerical celibacy·
and to abolish lay patronage and impropriation, with their associated abuse of
simony, and his episcopal career is a record of his efforts in these directions and the

successes, difficulties and checks with which he met. He received far more opposition than encouragement, often from men of goodwill or from those to whom he could reasonably look for support, but to the end he did not withdraw from the struggle or modify his policy. He had the encouragement of his metropolitan, the forceful St Eystein, who was fighting a similar battle in Norway, and with his approval used the weapon of excommunication for the first time in Iceland. In his sixtieth year Thorlac determined to resign his see and retire to the abbey of Thykkviboer, but death overtook him before he could put this resolution into effect, on December 23, 1193. Five years later he was canonized by the *althing* (assembly) of Iceland. This proceeding of course had no valid ecclesiastical effect, but it encouraged the popular and liturgical *cultus* that was undoubtedly accorded to Thorlac until the change of religion. This *cultus* has not been confirmed by the Holy See. Two books of the miracles of Thorlac Thorhallsson were written down within a few years of his death.

There are certain fragments of Latin lives or breviary lessons relating to St Thorlac, which have been printed by Langebek in his *Scriptores rerum Danicarum*, vol. iv, pp. 624–630, as well as the *Thorlakssaga*.   A pretty full notice is devoted to him by Gley in the *Biographie universelle*, but otherwise it seems difficult for any who are not specialists in the Scandinavian languages to learn much about Bishop Thorlac that is reliable.   *Cf.* also Baumgartner in *Kirchenlexikon, s.v.* Island.   The Saga of Thorlac may be read in a German translation by W. Baetke, *Islands Besiedlung und älteste Geschichte* (1928).

BD MARGARET OF SAVOY, Widow   (A.D. 1464)

BD MARGARET was allied in blood to the principal royal houses of Europe, her father being Amadeus of Savoy and her mother a sister of the Clement VII who claimed to be pope at Avignon during the " great schism ".   In 1403 she made a marriage befitting this high rank, with Theodore Palaeologus, Marquis of Montferrat, a widower with two children, a headstrong soldier but a good Christian at heart.   Margaret herself had no children but was devoted to those of her husband, and soon endeared herself on all hands, working selflessly for the people during a plague and the famine which followed it in Genoa.   In 1418 the Marquis of Montferrat died.   Margaret, after endeavouring for a time to bring the unhappy marital affairs of her step-daughter to a successful issue, went to live on her estate at Alba in Piedmont, where she bound herself by vow to widowhood and a life of good works.   But she was still young, thirty-six at the most, and politically a most desirable match, and Philip Visconti of Milan wanted to marry her.   He was an old enemy of the Montferrats and a man of deplorable character, and Margaret refused him, pleading her vow.   So Visconti went off to Pope Martin V and came back with a dispensation for her, but she remained firm in her determination not again to change her state.

In her youth she had been friendly with St Vincent Ferrer, and to strengthen her position she took the habit of the third order of St Dominic and with other ladies formed a community at Alba.   This retired life of prayer, study and charitable works lasted for some twenty-five years ; there is in the royal library at Turin a volume of the letters of St Catherine of Siena and other matters copied and bound " by order of the illustrious lady, Margaret of Savoy, Marchioness of Montferrat " during this time.   Then Pope Eugenius IV gave permission for the tertiary sisters to become nuns, in the same place and under the rule of Bd Margaret.   During the last sixteen years of her life ecstasies and miracles are alleged in abundance, among them a vision of our Lord offering her three arrows, labelled respectively Sickness, Slander and Persecution. Certainly Margaret suffered from all three. She was accused of hypocrisy, of tyrannizing over her nuns, and her ill-health was attributed to self-indulgence, and Philip Visconti spread the rumour that the convent was a centre of the Waldensian heresy. This was a peculiarly shocking charge to bring against children of St Dominic, and the innocent friar who was their confessor and director found himself in prison. Margaret went to demand his release, but only had her hand brutally crushed between the heavy doors of the castle for her pains, and it was some time before the man was vindicated from the malicious accusation of having corrupted both the faith and morals of his charges.

Bd Margaret of Savoy died on November 23, 1464, strengthened by a vision, seen by others besides herself, of St Catherine of Siena. Her *cultus* was confirmed in 1669.

Four or five lives of Bd Margaret seem to have been published in the seventeenth century, that by G. Baresiano appearing in 1638. In more modern times we have an Italian biography by F. G. Allaria (1877), another without the author's name (Torino, 1883), and a shorter notice included in M. C. de Ganay's book, *Les Bienheureuses Dominicaines* (1914), pp. 251–277. See also Procter, *Lives of Dominican Saints*, pp. 334–337.

24 : ST GREGORY OF SPOLETO, Martyr　　(A.D. 304 ?)

THIS Gregory is said to have been a priest and martyr at Spoleto, but apparently there is doubt whether he ever existed outside the pages of his fictitious *passio*. This tells us that when Flaccus, the governor of Umbria, arrived at that city with an order from the Emperor Maximian to punish all Christians, its inhabitants were gathered into the *forum* and Flaccus asked whether they had all abandoned worship of the gods. The chief magistrate said that they had not, but that a man called Gregory was very active among them and had thrown down images. Soldiers were immediately despatched to bring him before the tribunal. When he appeared Flaccus asked, " Who is your God ? " Gregory replied, " He who made man to His own image and likeness, who is all-powerful and immortal and who will render to all men according to their works." Flaccus told him not to talk so much and to do as he was told, to which Gregory answered, " I know not what your command implies, but I do what I am bound to do ". " If you want to save yourself ", said the governor, " go to the temple, and sacrifice to Jove and Minerva and Aesculapius. Then you shall be our friend and receive favour from our most invincible emperors." St Gregory retorted, " I desire no such friendship, nor do I sacrifice to devils but only to my God, Jesus Christ ". The judge commanded him to be hit in the face for his blasphemies and to be roasted to death. But from this he was saved by an earthquake which destroyed a quarter of the city. The next day, after further torture, he was beheaded.

The *passio* of this martyr, which survives in many manuscript copies, has been printed by Surius, and, subject to a curious transformation by which it has been converted into a story of the martyrdom of St George, by Father Delehaye in the *Analecta Bollandiana*, vol. xxvii (1908), pp. 373–383. Delehaye points out that the *passio* is a mere work of fiction, and that there is no independent evidence that any such martyr as Gregory was honoured at Spoleto in the early centuries. A copy of this fabrication was in the hands of Ado and through him the notice has passed into the Roman Martyrology. Some comments on the *passio* will be found in Dufourcq, *Étude sur les Gesta Martyrum romains*, vol. iii, pp. 98–100.

ST DELPHINUS, Bishop of Bordeaux   (A.D. 403)

The first mention of this, the second bishop of Bordeaux, is his presence at the Synod of Saragossa in the year 380, when the Priscillianists and other heretics were condemned.   The greatness and holiness attaching to the name of Delphinus are chiefly a matter of inference from the facts that he was a valued correspondent of St Ambrose and had strong influence with Pontius Meropius Anicius Paulinus, better known as St Paulinus of Nola.   The conversion of the last-named was principally the work of his wife and St Delphinus, who eventually baptized him. Five of the letters of Paulinus to his spiritual benefactor have been preserved and witness to the respect in which he held St Delphinus.

Besides St Ambrose and St Paulinus (the latter is best consulted in the Vienna *Corpus Scriptorum*, vol. xxix, nn. 10, 14, 19, 20 and 35), Sulpicius Severus also makes mention of Delphinus in his *Chronicle* (bk ii, ch. 48).   A *Vie de St Delphin* was published by Fr Moniquet in 1893, but it is severely criticized in the *Analecta Bollandiana*, vol. xii, pp. 460–462.

SS. THARSILLA and EMILIANA, Virgins   (*c.* A.D. 550)

St Gregory the Great had three aunts, sisters to his father, Gordian the *regionarius*, who led an ascetic religious life in their father's house.   Their names were Tharsilla, who was the eldest, Emiliana and Gordiana.   Tharsilla and Emiliana were even more united by the fervour of their hearts and the bond of charity than by blood. They lived in their father's house on the Clivus Scauri as in a monastery and, encouraging one another to virtue by discourse and example, made great progress in spiritual life.   Gordiana joined them, but she was often impatient of silence and retirement and, being called to another way of living, married her guardian. Tharsilla and Emiliana persevered in the path they had chosen, enjoying divine peace and love until they were called to receive the recompense of their fidelity. St Gregory tells us that Tharsilla was visited one night with a vision of her great-grandfather, Pope St Felix II (III), who showed a place prepared for her in Heaven, saying, " Come ; I will receive you into this habitation of light ".   She fell sick soon after, and as her friends were crowding round her bed she cried out, " Away ! Away !   My saviour Jesus is coming ! "   After these words she breathed out her soul into the hands of God on the vigil of Christmas.   The skin of her knees and elbows was found to be hardened, " like the hide of a camel ", by her continual prayer.   A few days later she appeared to Emiliana, and called her to celebrate the Epiphany in Heaven.   Emiliana in fact died on January 5 following.   Both are named, on the respective days of their death, in the Roman Martyrology.

St Gregory the Great speaks of these aunts not only in his *Dialogues* (bk iv, ch. 16), but also in a homily (see Migne, PL., vol. lxxvi, c. 1291).   *Cf.* Dudden, *St Gregory the Great*, vol. i, pp. 10–11, and Dunbar, *Dict. of Saintly Women*, vol. ii, p. 242.

SS. IRMINA, Virgin, and ADELA, Widow   (*c.* A.D. 710 AND *c.* 734)

According to the tradition the Princess Irmina, called a daughter of St Dagobert II, was to have been married to a Count Herman.   All preparations had been made for the wedding at Trier when one of the princess's officers, who was himself in love with her, inveigled Herman to a steep cliff outside the town and there threw his rival and himself over the edge.   After this tragic end to her hopes Irmina obtained her father's permission to become a nun.   Dagobert founded or restored for her a convent near Trier.   St Irmina was a zealous supporter of the missionary labours of St Willibrord, and in 698 gave him the manor on which he founded his famous monastery of Echternach.   This gift is said to have been in recognition of his having miraculously stayed an epidemic that was devastating her nunnery, and is about the only thing that seems certain concerning Irmina.

St Adela, another daughter of Dagobert II, became a nun after the death of her husband, Alberic.   She is probably the widow Adula, who about 691–692 was living at Nivelles with her little son, the future father of St Gregory of Utrecht. She founded a monastery at Palatiolum, now Pfalzel, near Trier ; she became its first abbess and governed it in holiness for many years.   Adela seems to have been among the disciples of St Boniface, and a letter in his correspondence from Abbess Aelffled of Whitby to an Abbess Adola is addressed to her.   St Irmina is mentioned in the Roman Martyrology, but the *cultus* accorded popularly to St Adela has not been confirmed and she is not venerated liturgically.

The story of Irmina's early life, recounted only by the monk Thiofrid nearly 400 years after her death, is probably quite fabulous.   There is evidence that part of it is based upon a forged charter.   The Latin Life of St Irmina, edited by Weiland in MGH., *Scriptores*, vol. xxiii, pp. 48–50, is, however, the work of Thiofrid, and not of Theodoric nearly a century later.   See for all this the *Analecta Bollandiana*, vol. viii (1889), pp. 285–286 ; and also C. Wampach, *Grundherrschaft Echternach*, vol. i, pt i (1929), pp. 113–135, and *cf.* the documents printed in pt ii (1930).   On Adela consult DHG., vol. i, c. 525.   See further, E. Ewig in *St Bonifatius* (1954), p. 418 ; and C. Wampach, " Irmina von Oeren und ihre Familie " in *Trierer Zeitschrift*, vol. iii (1928), pp. 144–154.

BD PAULA CERIOLI, Widow, Foundress of the Institute of the Holy Family of Bergamo   (A.D. 1865)

Constance Cerioli was born at Soncino, near Bergamo, in 1816, the last of the sixteen children of Don Francis Cerioli and his wife Countess Frances Corniani, and was educated by the Visitation nuns.   At the age of nineteen she was married to a wealthy widower of sixty, Gaetano Buzecchi-Tassis.   He was a worthy man but misanthropic and unattractive, and in any case Constance's agreement to the marriage was only passive.   The match was made by the parents in accordance with the custom of the time and place, of which custom her biographer, Father Federici, says, " It is not so much illogical . . . as a usurpation ".   The results in this case were certainly painful, but not tragic, for from very early years Constance was drawn to God and sincerely relied upon His grace.   The marriage subsisted for nineteen years, and three children were born.   Two died in infancy ; the eldest, Charles, lived to be only sixteen, and his memory was an important influence throughout his mother's life.

Gaetano Buzecchi died in 1854, leaving his widow extremely well off.   That the orphans of the countryside should be the real heirs of this fortune was finally decided by a chance word of her parish priest.   Constance at once took two motherless children into her mansion of Comonte, at Seriate in Lombardy ; and she determined to devote herself and her estate to the welfare of orphans, boys and girls, specifically the children of peasants, who should be brought up and trained with the life of the land in view.

Her first helper and always her right-hand was Louisa Corti.   Her advisers and faithful friends were Canon Valsecchi and the bishop of Bergamo, Mgr

Speranza. On the other side were those who said she was "cracked", as the bishop reported to her. "So I am", she replied, "by the lunacy of the Cross". Other helpers soon joined, and in 1857 Constance Cerioli made her religious vows, taking the names Paula Elizabeth ; a few months later the Sisters of the Holy Family came officially into being. They increased and prospered, and in another five years the second part of Sister Paula's project was born ; a brothers' branch of the congregation, to look after male orphans, was established at Villa Campagna, near Soncino, in the care of John Capponi, a hospital official from Leffe.

Sister Paula always resolutely confined her work to the preparation of children and young people for *rural* life. In those days agriculture and its workers were not the public concern that they are today, and Italy owes not a little in this matter to the Institute of the Holy Family, notably to the agricultural training given at the boys' establishments. It is appropriate that this work should have been begun not a great way from Virgil's Mantua. *O fortunatos nimium, sua si bona norint, agricolas* : "How blest indeed are husbandmen, did they but know their happiness ! " It was part of Bd Paula's vocation to help them to know it, in spite of the atrocious poverty of Italian peasant life.

She did not long survive the foundation at Villa Campagna. She had always been delicate, with a slight spinal deformity, and her heart became increasingly troublesome. She died in her sleep at Comonte in the early hours of Christmas eve, 1865. She had named her foundation after the Holy Family, her devotion to St Joseph was outstanding : the day could not have been better. And the quietness of her passing was of a piece with a life that, for all its activities, was always marked by interior peace and devotion to Jesus Christ. Bd Paula Cerioli was beatified in 1950.

In addition to the documents of the beatification process there are the memoirs of Mother Corti and the writings of the *beata*. A biography by Mgr P. Merati was published in 1899. These were all fully used by the Rev. E. Federici in his official life of Bd Paula (1950).

25 : THE BIRTHDAY OF OUR LORD JESUS CHRIST, COMMONLY CALLED CHRISTMAS DAY

WHEN all things were accomplished which according to the ancient prophets were to precede the coming of the Messias, Jesus Christ, the eternal Son of God, having taken human flesh in the womb of the Virgin Mary and being made man, was born of her for the redemption of mankind. The all-wise and all-merciful providence of God had, from the fall of our first parents, gradually disposed all things for the fulfilling of His promises and the accomplishing of the greatest of His mysteries, the incarnation of His divine Son. A decree had been issued by the Emperor Augustus ordaining that all persons should be registered at certain places, according to their respective provinces, cities and families. This decree was an occasion for the manifestation to the whole world that Christ was a descendant of the house of David and tribe of Juda. For those of that family were ordered to be registered at Bethlehem, a small town in the tribe of Juda, six miles from Jerusalem to the south. It had been David's home, and Joseph and Mary had come thither from Nazareth, fifty-six miles almost north from Jerusalem. Micheas had foretold that Bethlehem-Ephrata (*i.e.* house of bread : fruitful) should be ennobled by the birth of " the ruler in Israel ", Christ. Mary therefore undertook this tedious journey with her husband, in obedience to the emperor's order for their enrolment in that city.   After a slow journey through mountainous country they arrived at Bethlehem, and there found the public inns already full ; nor were they able to get any lodgings at all.   In this distress they at last went into a cavern in the side of the ridge whereon Bethlehem is built, which was used as a stable.   It is a common tradition that an ox and an ass were in it at the time.*

In this place the mother when her time was come brought forth her divine Son, wrapped Him in swaddling clothes and laid Him in the manger.†   God was pleased that His Son, though born on earth in obscurity and poverty, should be at once acknowledged by men and receive the first fruits of their homage and devotion.   But the great ones of the world, the wise among the Jews and Gentiles, the elders and princes, who seemed raised above the level of their fellows, are passed over.   Certain shepherds were at the time keeping the watches of the night over their flock.   To them an angel appeared, they saw themselves surrounded with a great light, and they were suddenly seized with fear.   But the angel said to them, " Fear not !   For behold I bring you good tidings of great joy, that shall be to all the people.   For this day is born to you a Saviour, who is Christ the Lord, in the city of David.   And this shall be a sign unto you : you shall find the infant wrapped in swaddling clothes and laid in a manger."   And there appeared with the angel a multitude of heavenly spirits, praising God and saying, " Glory to God in the highest, and on earth peace to men of good will ! "   Then the wondering shepherds said to one another, " Let us go over to Bethlehem, and let us see this word that is come to pass, which the Lord hath shewed to us ".   They hastened thither, and found Mary and Joseph, and the infant lying in the manger.   " And, seeing, they understood of the word that had been spoken to them concerning this child.   And all that heard wondered at those things that were told them by the shepherds (but Mary kept all these words, pondering them in her heart)."   Then they did homage to the Messias as to the spiritual king of men, and returned to their flocks glorifying and praising God.

The message delivered by the angel to those shepherds is addressed also to us, " to all the people ".   By them we are invited to worship our new-born Saviour ; and our hearts must be insensible to all spiritual things if they are not filled with joy at the consideration of the divine goodness and mercy manifested in the Incarnation, the coming of the promised Messias.   The thought and foreknowledge of this mystery comforted Adam in his banishment ; the promise of it sweetened the pilgrimage of Abraham ; it encouraged Jacob to dread no adversity and Moses to brave all dangers and conquer all difficulties in delivering the Israelites from Egyptian slavery.   All the prophets saw it in spirit with Abraham, and they rejoiced.   If the expectation gave the patriarchs such joy, how much more ought the accomplishment to give to us.   " The letter of a friend ", says St Peter Chrysologus, " is comforting, but his presence is much more welcome ; a bond is useful, but the payment more so ; blossoms are pleasing, but only till the fruit appears. The ancient fathers received God's letters, we enjoy His presence ; they had the

* It was current in the fifth century.   Such a tradition is a very natural one to arise, and Isaias i 3 could be quoted in support of it (by, of course, an accommodation) : " The ox knoweth his owner and the ass his master's crib. . . ."

† The cave beneath the basilica of the Nativity at Bethlehem has an unbroken tradition of authenticity of very great antiquity.   In its floor is set a silver star, around which is the inscription : *Hic de Virgine Maria Jesus Christus natus est* ;   Here Jesus Christ was born of the Virgin Mary.

promise, we the accomplishment ; they the bond, we the payment." Love is the tribute which God asks of us in a particular manner in this mystery ; this is the return for all He has done and suffered for us. He says to us, " Son, give me thy heart ". To love Him is our sovereign happiness and the highest dignity of a human creature.

Christ's life is the gospel reduced to practice. He instructs us at His very birth, beginning first to practise, then to preach. The manger was His first pulpit, and from it He teaches us the cure of our spiritual maladies. He came among us to seek our miseries, our poverty, our humiliation, to repair the dishonour our pride had offered to the Godhead, and to apply a remedy to our souls. And He chose a poor mother, a little town, a stable. He who adorns the world and clothes the lilies of the field beyond the majesty of Solomon is wrapped in clouts and laid in a manger. This He chose to be the very sign of His identity. " This shall be a sign to you ", said the angel to the shepherds, " you shall find the child wrapped in swaddling clothes and laid in a manger." It is a powerful instruction. " The grace of God our Saviour hath appeared to all men, instructing us ", says the Apostle, all men, the rich and the poor, the great and the small, all who desire to share His grace and His kingdom, instructing us in the first place in humility. What is the whole mystery of the Incarnation but the most astonishing humbling of the Deity ? To expiate *our* pride the eternal Son of God divests Himself of His glory and takes the form of man in his every circumstance—save sin. Who would not think that the whole creation would be overwhelmed with the glory of His presence and tremble before Him ? But nothing of this was seen. " He came not ", says St John Chrysostom, " so as 'o shake the world at the presence of majesty ; not in thunder and lightning as on Sinai : but He came quietly, no man knowing it."

In the 5199th year of the creation of the world, from the time when God in the beginning made out of nothing the heavens and the earth ; the 2957th year after the flood ; the 2015th year from the birth of Abraham ; the 1510th year from Moses and the going-out of the people of Israel from Egypt ; the 1032nd year from the anointing of David king ; in the 65th week according to the prophecy of Daniel ; in the 194th olympiad ; the 752nd year from the foundation of the city of Rome ; the 42nd year of the rule of Octavian Augustus, all the earth being at peace, in the sixth age of the world : Jesus Christ, the eternal God and Son of the eternal Father, willing to consecrate the world by His most merciful coming, being conceived by the Holy Ghost and nine months having passed since His conception, was born in Bethlehem of Juda of the Virgin Mary, being made man. The birthday of our Lord Jesus Christ according to the flesh.

No other celebration of the Christian year, not even Easter itself, does the Roman Martyrology announce in so solemn a fashion. But for all that—and it seems especially strange to English-speaking people for whom in practice Christmas is the great religious festival of the year—this feast is not among the most primitive in the Church, and, liturgically considered, ranks not only below Easter, but also below Pentecost and the Epiphany. The commemoration of the birth of our Lord by a separate feast began only in the fourth century (before 336), and at Rome, from whence it soon spread to the East, where hitherto the birth had been commemorated as a lesser aspect of the feast of the Epiphany.

The dates or reckonings in the quotation from the Roman Martyrology given above are of course not all historically correct or verifiable : for example, we know now that the creation of the world took place many more than 5199 years before the birth of our Lord, and it is likely that that birth was earlier than in the year 752 after the founding of the city. But if the year of the birth of Christ is uncertain, its day is even more so, and there is hardly a month of the twelve to which respectable authorities have not assigned it. How December 25 came to be pitched on for the commemoration is not known, and has been the subject of lively discussions. The notion of an origin in the Roman *Saturnalia* of December can be safely disregarded ; but there is some likelihood that the solar feast of *natalis Invicti* (the Birthday of the Unconquered [Sun]), itself observed at the winter solstice about December 25, helped to determine the date. In any case the Roman custom of commemorating the birthday by a special feast on that date became general, and has so remained throughout Christendom, with a few isolated exceptions. The Nestorians are said not to have adopted the separate feast until the fourteenth century ; the dissident Armenians never have done so. They continue the primitive usage of commemorating our Lord's birth and baptism together on the Epiphany ("shewing forth"), and so are the only Christians in the world who have no Christmas day.*

Father Delehaye in his commentary on the *Hieronymianum* lays stress upon the reluctance of the church of Jerusalem to admit what they regarded as this new feast of the birth of our Lord, though a sermon of St John Chrysostom makes it clear that it had been adopted in the Syrian city of Antioch as early as 376. In the sixth century Cosmas Indicopleustes apparently considered it something of a scandal that in Jerusalem no celebration of the Nativity as such had yet been introduced ; but before the death of the Patriarch St Sophronius, which occurred about 638, it is plain from one of his sermons that Jerusalem had conformed to that usage of the rest of Christendom. Since Father Delehaye wrote, a thoroughly systematic, and, one may say, exhaustive discussion of the origin of the Christmas festival has been published by Dom B. Botte, who thinks that the evidence constrains us to admit that the assignment of the birth of our Lord to December 25 was due to the occurrence on that day of the pagan celebration of the *natalis Invicti*. It must be remembered that as long as paganism was dominant or widely prevalent, the Christians, a *gens lucifuga*, had much reason to mask their own distinctive beliefs and practices under observances or symbols which attracted no attention. On the other hand, Mgr Duchesne holds that the birth of Christ was identified with December 25 because His conception was supposed to have occurred on the day on which He also died, both coinciding with the (official) spring equinox, March 25. The same was the day, according to a widespread belief, on which the world was created. It may well be held, with Abbé Michel Andrieu, that these theories are not irreconcilable and that there is truth in both. The little tractate of the fourth century, *De solstitiis et aequinoctiis*, of which Dom Botte has published a critical text, does not conflict with the suggestion. Dom Botte has

* Among the stricter sort of Protestant dissenter in England and, especially, Wales, there is, or was till recently, an interesting survival of Puritan tradition. These, when Christmas falls on a Sunday, observe it in the penitential manner proper to their conception of what is due to the Lord's Day (or, as they put it, "the Sabbath is more important than Christmas"). The usual Christmas rejoicings and observances are deferred till Monday. Some Scottish Presbyterians apparently ignore Christmas altogether.

also collected a number of testimonies regarding the pagan celebration in oriental lands of the birth of an " aeon ", some greater divinity, on January 6. This being associated with a Dionysus festival, in which wine replaced water in the fountains, may possibly have found expression in the curiously mixed character of the Epiphany feast, combining as it did the homage of the Magi, the baptism of our Lord, and the miracle of Cana.

When the pilgrim lady Etheria visited Jerusalem near the end of the fourth century the Nativity was still observed there as part of the Epiphany on January 6, but the birthday aspect was very much to the fore. She describes how on the vigil the bishop, clergy, monks and people of Jerusalem went to Bethlehem and made a solemn station at the cave of the Nativity. At midnight a procession was formed, they returned to Jerusalem, and sang the morning office just before dawn. Then in the morning they assembled again for a solemn celebration of the Holy Eucharist, which was begun in the great basilica of Constantine (the *Martyrion*) and consummated in the chapel of the Resurrection (the *Anastasis*). In the sixth century these Jerusalem observances were duplicated or imitated at Rome. At cockcrow the pope celebrated Mass at the Liberian basilica (St Mary Major), to which the reputed relics of the wooden crib were brought during the seventh century ; then, later in the day, a procession was made to St Peter's, where he sang Mass again. In between these two celebrations came another, which took place at the church of (St) Anastasia below the Palatine (see notice below). By the middle of the twelfth century the third Mass also was being sung at St Mary Major, because of the distance of St Peter's from the Lateran, where the popes then lived. Thus is seen the origin of the three Masses which every priest may celebrate on Christmas Day ; and these Masses are still labelled in the Missal with the name of the respective stations : " at the Crib at St Mary Major ", " at St Anastasia ", " at St Mary Major ". Later, the observance was given a mystical significance, the Masses representing the aboriginal, the Judaic and the Christian dispensations, or the " triple birth " of our Lord, by which He proceeds from the Father before all time, was born of the Virgin Mary, and is spiritually reborn in our souls, by faith and charity. Or they may be regarded in this way : The midnight Mass celebrates the eternal birth of Jesus the divine Word. " The Lord said to me : Thou art my Son. . . . With thee is the principality in the day of thy strength . . . from the womb before the day-star I begot thee." The Mass at dawn sees Jesus as the true light, the spiritual sun. " A light shall shine upon us this day. . . . We are bathed in the new light of thy incarnate Word." And in the third Mass the Babe of Bethlehem is honoured as Christ the King, God and man. " A child is born to us . . . whose government is upon his shoulder. . . . All the ends of the earth have seen the salvation of our God. . . . Come, ye nations, and worship the Lord . . . justice and judgement are the preparation of thy throne."

There is, of course, an immense literature dealing with the birth of our Lord from every point of view, devotional, chronological and liturgical. In addition to the references giv en herein on January 6 under the Epiphany, attention must be specially called to what is noted by Fr Delehaye in CMH., pp. 7-8, and to Dom B. Botte's *Les origines de la Noël et de l'Epiphanie* (1932). See also L. Duchesne, *Christian Worship* (1931), pp. 257-265 ; M. Andrieu, in the *Revue des sciences religieuses*, vol. xiv (1934), p. 624 ; and what is said herein on March 25 under the Annunciation. For other points of view see H. Usener, *Das Weih-nachtsfest* (1911) ; A. Baumstark in *Oriens Christianus*, 1902, pp. 441-446, and 1927, pp. 310-333 ; Cabrol in DAC., vol. v, cc. 1412-1414 ; Kellner, *Heortology*, pp. 127-157 ; Schuster, *The Sacramentary*, vol. i, pp. 361-377 ; O. Cullman, *Weihnachten in der alten*

Kirche (1947 ; French trans., 1949) ; and studies by FF. Frank and Engberding in the *Maria Laach Archiv für Liturgiewissenschaft*, vol. ii (1950). For a good summary of the development of the feast, see A. A. McArthur, *The Evolution of the Christian Year* (1953), pp. 31 *seq.*

ST EUGENIA, Virgin and Martyr   (Date Unknown)

THE legend of St Eugenia, like that of St Marina, St Reparata and others, is the tale of a woman disguised as a monk and accused of a crime she could not commit. For variety it may here be told in the words of the *Golden Legend*.

> Eugenia, the noble virgin, which was daughter to Philip, duke of Alexandria, which for the emperor of Rome governed all the land of Egypt. Eugenia issued privily out of her father's palace with two servants [called SS. Protus and Hyacinth], and she went into an abbey in the habit and array of a man, in which abbey she led so holy a life that at the last she was made abbot of the same. It happed so that no man knew that she was a woman, yet there was a lady accused her of adultery tofore the judge, which was her own father. Eugenia was put in prison for to be judged to death. At the last she said to her father much thing for to draw him to the faith of Jesus Christ. She rent her coat and showed to him that she was a woman and daughter of him that held her in prison, and so she converted her father unto the Christian faith. And he was after an holy bishop, and at the hour that he sang his Mass he was beheaded for the faith of Jesus Christ ; and the lady that had falsely accused Eugenia was burnt with fire of Hell with all her party. And after that Claudia [the mother of Eugenia] and all her children came to Rome, and much people were by them converted, and many virgins by Eugenia. Which Eugenia was much tormented in divers manners and at the last by the sword accomplished her martyrdom, and thus made the offering of her proper body to our Lord Jesus Christ, qui est benedictus in saecula saeculorum, Amen.

Eugenia was sent to join the monks in the first place by Helenus, Bishop of Heliopolis, who had met and baptized her when she had fled from her father's house in male clothes ; and the false accusation was prompted by her repelling the advances of a woman whom she had miraculously cured of sickness.

The romantic particulars of her masquerading as a young man seem to have been arbitrarily attributed to St Eugenia, a Roman martyr who was buried in the cemetery of Apronian on the Via Latina, where afterwards a basilica was built in her honour, which was restored during the eighth century.

Two Latin texts of this legend have attracted attention. The older is that printed in the *Sanctuarium* of Mombritius, but from this a very much revised version was constructed at an early date and has acquired wider publicity. It is printed in Rosweyde, *Vitae Patrum*, pp. 340–349, and is also to be found twice over in Migne, PL., vols. xxi and lxxiii. Two or three different Greek adaptations are also known in manuscript, and that of the Metaphrast is printed in Migne, PG., vol. cxvi, pp. 609–652. Besides these there is a Syriac version, published with an English translation by Mrs A. Smith-Lewis in *Studia Sinaitica*, vols. ix and x ; and another in Armenian which F. C. Conybeare edited and translated in *The Armenian Apology of Apollonius*, though the early date he assigns to this text is quite unwarranted. Finally, the earlier portion of the story exists in an Ethiopic text, which has been printed and rendered into English by E. J. Goodspeed. Delehaye in his *Étude sur le légendier romain* (1936), pp. 171–186, has commented upon the legend exhaustively, and both here and in his CMH. he shows that there is solid ground for believing that St Eugenia was an authentic Roman martyr.

MANY MARTYRS AT NICOMEDIA   (A.D. 303)

THE martyrdom of, according to the Greeks, 20,000 Christians at Nicomedia on Christmas day in the year 303 is thus recorded by the Roman Martyrology : " At Nicomedia the passion of many thousands of martyrs, who came together for the Lord's service on Christ's birthday. The Emperor Diocletian ordered the doors of the church to be shut and fire to be made ready round about it and a tripod with incense to be set before the door : and then that a herald should proclaim so that he could be heard that they who wished to escape the fire should come outside and offer incense to Jupiter. And when they all with one voice declared that they were ready to die for Christ's sake, the fire was kindled and they were consumed therein. And so they merited to be born in Heaven on that very day whereon Christ for the world's salvation was pleased to be born on earth."

There is historical record of the church at Nicomedia being wrecked—not burned—on February 23, 303, by order of Diocletian, but nothing is said of people being killed ; on the other hand, there was no feast of Christmas kept there so early as the beginning of the fourth century.

This has been taken over into the Roman Martyrology from a Greek source. The Synaxary of Constantinople, as edited for the *Acta Sanctorum*, commemorates on December 28 (cc. 349–352) 20,000 martyrs burned to death at Nicomedia, adding details corresponding to the above. The number is, of course, wildly exaggerated, but there is much evidence both in Eusebius (bk vi, chs. 5–8) and in the Syriac *breviarium* that Nicomedia was a hotbed of persecution in the year 303.

ST ANASTASIA, MARTYR   (A.D. 304 ?)

THE *passio* of St Anastasia relates that she was the daughter of a noble Roman named Praetextatus and had St Chrysogonus for her adviser. She married a pagan, Publius, and during the persecution of Diocletian cared for the confessors of the faith in prison, whereupon her husband forbade her to leave the house. Chrysogonus having gone to Aquileia, she kept up a correspondence with him and, when Publius died on an embassy to Persia, went to Aquileia herself to succour the Christians there. After the martyrdom of SS. Agape, Chionia and Irene, Anastasia herself was arrested and brought before the prefect of Illyricum at Sirmium, being visited in prison and fed by the dead St Theodota. Then with another Christian and a number of pagan criminals she was put aboard a vessel and abandoned at sea ; but Theodota appeared again and piloted it to land, and the pagans were all converted. Anastasia was taken to the island of Palmaria and put to death by being burned alive, staked to the ground with her arms and legs outstretched and the fire kindled about her ; two hundred men and seventy women were martyred in various ways at the same time.

These stories are entirely apocryphal. St Anastasia has been venerated at Rome since the late fifth century, when her name was put in the canon of the Mass, but so far as is known she had nothing to do with the City. Her *cultus* originated at Sirmium in Pannonia, where she was perhaps martyred under Diocletian, but no authentic particulars of her life and passion have come down to us. While St Gennadius was patriarch of Constantinople, during the second half of the fifth century, the relics of St Anastasia were translated from Sirmium to that city, and a considerable *cultus* of the saint followed. The special interest of St Anastasia is in the historico-liturgical fact that she has the distinction of being commemorated at the second Mass on Christmas day.

There was in Rome, at the foot of the Palatine Hill near the Circus Maximus, a church called the *titulus Anastasiae*; it had been built in the fourth century and had its name from a foundress called Anastasia. It was an important church, and it soon came to be called the church of St Anastasia—as it is to this day. It was at this church that the pope sang the second Mass on Christmas day and, during the sixth century and for some time after, this Mass was proper to St Anastasia. This adventitious liturgical importance of the martyr, due to local conditions at Rome in the fifth-sixth century, is now reduced to the familiar commemoration at the Mass of the Dawn. It does not even seem that there was any tradition of St Anastasia having been put to death on December 25 : the Greeks now keep her feast on the twenty-second, venerating her as a *megalomartyr* and " the Poison-healer ".

The long document which may be called the " Acts of St Anastasia " has never been printed as a whole, though the several episodes of which it is made up have most of them been edited separately under the names of the martyrs respectively concerned, *e.g. Passio S. Chrysogoni, Passio S. Theodotae*, etc. There is also a Greek version which only exists in manuscript. A very full discussion of this strange medley will be found in Delehaye's *Étude sur le légendier romain*, pp. 151–171. As he shows, the purpose with which this hagiographical fiction was compiled was to claim Anastasia as a Roman saint, seeing that she was now honoured there as patron of the *titulus Anastasiae*. It is possible that Arnobius the Younger, who lived in the middle of the fifth century, was already acquainted with the story of St Anastasia (see Dom Morin, *Études, textes, découvertes*, 1913, pp. 328, 391–392), but the matter is not clear. Consult further Duchesne in *Mélanges d'archéologie et d'histoire*, vol. vii (1887), pp. 387–413 ; J. P. Kirsch, *Die römischen Titelkirchen* (1918), pp. 18–23 ; Lanzoni, *Titoli presbiterali* (1925), pp. 11–12 and 58–59.

BD JACOPONE OF TODI   (A.D. 1306)

JACOPONE, baptized Jacopo, was born of the good family of Benedetti at Todi in Umbria about the year 1230. He read law at Bologna, where he probably took his doctorate, and began to practise in his native town. He seems to have been known neither for virtue nor evil-living, and certainly showed no signs in his earlier years of his later religious fervour. About 1267 he married Vanna di Guidone, a young woman beautiful both in person and character, who, for all their married life lasted only a year, proved to be his good angel. Vanna was tragically killed at a wedding *festa*, when a balcony upon which she and other guests were standing collapsed. She was the only one to lose her life, and the shock of this sudden deprivation, coupled with the vivid realization of his wife's goodness (he is said, for example, to have discovered an unsuspected hair-shirt on her dead body, which he supposed to be worn in penance for his sins), wrought a remarkable change in Jacopo. Indeed, it would be not unreasonable to conclude that for a time his mind was unhinged. He threw up his profession, put on the habit of the Franciscan tertiaries, and became, as it has been put, " a sort of Christian Diogenes " ; his eccentricities were so absurd and so public that the children in the streets of Todi looked on him as a harmless show and familiarly called him Jacopone : the name stuck. On one occasion he crawled on hands and knees across the main square, wearing the harness of a donkey ; on another, he turned up among a wedding party at his brother's house tarred and feathered all over. He lived thus as a sort of public penitent for ten years.

In 1278, after some natural hesitation on the part of the friars, Jacopone was admitted among the Franciscans of San Fortunato at Todi as a lay-brother. He is said to have chosen this state out of humility. He may well have done so. But the fact that his sympathies were with the more strict party among the Franciscans, the Spirituals, may have had something to do with it, for they considered that St Francis had intended his followers to be priests only exceptionally. For a dozen years or so Brother Jacopone remained at Todi, and as he gradually attained a more stable state of equilibrium he began to produce more and more lyric poems and songs in the Umbrian dialect, which were very popular. They were deeply religious and mystical verses, these *laude*, and were adopted by the Flagellants and other zealots for public singing and reciting ; both words and cadence lent themselves aptly to that Franciscan *jubilus* whose manifestations seem to have been remarkably like those of the Welsh preachers' *hwyl*. But Jacopone was candid and outspoken, and San Fortunato was a Conventual house. He was involved in difficulties with his brethren there, and became a more and more prominent figure among the Spirituals, of whom Bd Conrad of Offida and Bd John of Alvernia were his close personal friends. Jacopone was among those friars who in 1294 petitioned Pope St Celestine V for permission to live apart from the order, but in a few weeks Celestine had resigned and Cardinal Gaetani, the opponent of the Spirituals, was pope as Boniface VIII. When in 1297 there was an open rupture between the two Colonna cardinals and the pope, Jacopone was one of the three Franciscans who helped in the drawing-up of the manifesto which claimed that Boniface had been invalidly elected ; he became a literary propagandist for the Colonna party and produced a savage attack on the pope, beginning : " O papa Bonifatio molt ay jocato al mondo." Without subscribing to the extravagant opinion that " to have had [Boniface] for an adversary was itself an honour ", it may well be held that Friar Jacopone opposed the pope in perfect good faith : partisans were not the only people at the time who held the view that Pope Celestine's abdication was uncanonical. When the papal forces captured Palestrina, the Colonna stronghold, Jacopone was seized and imprisoned in a horrid dungeon there for five years. Not even the jubilee year of 1300 saw his release. During this time he composed some of the most beautiful of his poems, and also some of the most aggressive, satirical and trenchant pieces in curious contrast with the touching devotion and searching mysticism of the others.

Jacopone is best known as the putative author of the hymn *Stabat Mater dolorosa*, but there is no certainty as to who in fact wrote it. He is also credited with the companion hymn, or as some stern critics say the parody, the less well-known *Stabat Mater speciosa* (for Christmas). The *Dolorosa* is said to have been ascribed to him in a manuscript of the fourteenth century, and both appear in an edition of his *laude* printed at Brescia in 1495. The *Speciosa* was rescued from oblivion by Frederick Ozanam, who reprinted it for the first time in his *Poètes franciscains en Italie au XIIIᵉ siècle* in 1852. The English hymnologist Mearns inclined to the view that Jacopone wrote the *Speciosa* but not the *Dolorosa* ; but there is no certain proof that he wrote any Latin poems at all.

On the death of Boniface VIII at the end of 1303 Friar Jacopone was set at liberty, and he went to live first at a hermitage near Orvieto and then at a Poor Clare convent at Collazzone, between Todi and Perugia. Here he died on Christmas day, 1306(?). He received the last sacraments from Bd John of Alvernia and there are moving, but conflicting, accounts of his last moments. In 1433 his relics were translated to the church of San Fortunato at Todi, and how he was regarded there can be read upon his tomb : " The bones of Blessed Jacopone dei Benedetti of Todi, of the Order of Friars Minor. He became a fool for Christ's sake and, having deceived the world by a new artifice, took Heaven by storm. He fell asleep in the Lord on March 25, A.D. 1296 [*sic*]. This monument was put up by Angelo Cesi, Bishop of Todi, in the year 1596."

Much has been written about Fra Jacopone. In the *Bollettino Francescano storico-bibliografico*, vol. ii (1931), pp. 81–118 and 201–223, no less than 994 books and articles are enumerated which are in one way or another concerned with him. Apart from what can be gathered from his poems, we learn curiously little of his life except for the sketch in the *Franceschina* of Jacopo Oddi (fifteenth century) ; most of our information is late and unreliable. In a short but valuable review of the centenary literature in the *Analecta Bollandiana*, vol. xxviii (1909), pp. 231–234, Fr Van Ortroy states that the cult was confirmed by the Holy See in 1868, and he points out that further support has been found for Ozanam's contention that the famous satire " O papa Bonifatio " has been interpolated. The specialist, A. Tenneroni, in the *Nuova Antologia*, 1906, pp. 623–636, has satisfied himself that the most bitter passages were added subsequently by another hand ; and see his work on the poet published in 1939. For English readers there is an excellent article on Fra Jacopone by Father L. Oliger in the *Catholic Encyclopedia*, vol. viii, pp. 363–365 ; a sympathetic study by Edmund Gardner in *The Constructive Quarterly*, vol. ii (1912), pp. 446–460, and such books as those of Evelyn Underhill, *Jacopone da Todi* (1919), and A. Macdonnell, *Sons of St Francis* (1902). See also J. Pacheu, *Jacopone de Todi, Frère Mineur* (1914) ; C. Cadomo, *Il Cantore della Povertà* (1923) ; N. Sapegno, *Frate Jacopone* (1923) ; P. Barbet, *B. Jacopone de Todi, l'auteur du Stabat* (1943) ; and I. Steiger, *Jacopone da Todi, Welthass und Gottesliebe* (1945). The text of the " Laude " may be conveniently consulted in vol. vi of the series *I Libri della Fede*, edited by G. Papini (1922). It is interesting to find that St Bernardino of Siena made long extracts from Jacopone's writings. Some of these are still preserved in the saint's own handwriting with this heading : " Here begin certain canticles or *laude* of our holy modern David, Fra Jacopone da Todi." See *Archivum Franciscanum Historicum*, vol. xxix (1937), p. 237.

26 : ST STEPHEN, THE FIRST MARTYR (*c.* A.D. 34)

THAT St Stephen was a Jew is unquestionable, and he probably was a Hellenist of the Dispersion, who spoke Greek. The name Stephen is Greek, Stephanos, and signifies " crown ". The circumstances of his conversion to Christianity are not known. St Epiphanius says he was one of the seventy disciples of our Lord, but this is unlikely. We are told of him in the book of the Acts of the Apostles when, there being numerous converts, the Hellenists murmured against the Hebrews, complaining that their widows were neglected in the daily ministration. The Apostles assembled the faithful and told them that they could not relinquish the duties of preaching and prayer to attend to the care of tables ; and recommended them to choose seven men of good character, full of the Holy Ghost and wisdom, who might superintend that business. The suggestion was approved, and the people chose Stephen, " a man full of faith and of the Holy Ghost ", and Philip, Prochorus, Nicanor, Timon, Parmenas and Nicholas a proselyte of Antioch. These seven were presented to the Apostles, who praying, imposed hands upon them, and so ordained them the first deacons.

" And the word of the Lord increased, and the number of the disciples was multiplied in Jerusalem exceedingly ; a great number also of the priests obeyed the faith. And Stephen, full of grace and fortitude, did great wonders and signs among the people." He spoke with such wisdom and spirit that his hearers were unable to resist him, and a plot was laid by the elders of certain synagogues in Jerusalem. At first they undertook to dispute with Stephen ; but finding themselves unequal to the task they suborned false witnesses to charge him with blasphemy against Moses and against God. The indictment was laid in the Sanhedrin, and he was dragged thither. The main point urged against him was that he affirmed that the temple would be destroyed, that the Mosaic traditions were but shadows and types no longer acceptable to God, Jesus of Nazareth having put an end to them. " And all that sat in the council, looking on him, saw his face as if it had been the face of an angel." Then leave was given him to speak, and in a long defence, set out in Acts vii 2-53, he showed that Abraham, the father and founder of their nation, was justified and received the greatest favours of God in a foreign land ; that Moses was commanded to set up a tabernacle, but foretold a new law and the Messias ; that Solomon built the Temple, but it was not to be imagined that God was confined in houses made by hands : the temple and the Mosaic law were temporary, and were to give place when God introduced more excellent institutions by sending the Messias himself. He ended with a stinging rebuke : " You stiff-necked and uncircumcised in hearts and ears, you always resist the Holy Ghost ; as your fathers did, so do you also. Which of the prophets have not your fathers persecuted ? And they have slain them who foretold of the coming of the Just One, of whom you have been now the betrayers and murderers : who have received the law by the disposition of angels, and have not kept it."

The whole assembly raged at Stephen, but he, being full of the Holy Ghost and looking up steadfastly to the heavens, saw them opened and beheld the glory of God and the Saviour standing at the right hand of the Father. And he said, " Behold, I see the heavens opened, and the Son of man standing on the right hand of God ". " And they, crying out with a loud voice, stopped their ears and with one accord ran violently upon him. And, casting him forth without the city, they stoned him ; and the witnesses laid down their garments at the feet of a young man whose name was Saul. And they stoned Stephen, invoking and saying, ' Lord Jesus, receive my spirit '. And falling on his knees, he cried with a loud voice, saying, ' Lord, lay not this sin to their charge '. And when he had said this he fell asleep in the Lord." The reference to the witnesses required by the law of Moses, and the whole circumstances, suggest that this was not an act of mob violence, but a judicial execution. And of those that were " consenting to his death " one, Saul, the future apostle of the Gentiles, was the first and greatest fruit of the seed of the blood of the first martyr of Christ. " Devout men took order for Stephen's funeral, and made great mourning over him " ; the finding of his relics by the priest Lucian in the fifth century is referred to herein under August 3.

We have, of course, no knowledge of the life of St Stephen outside the pages of the New Testament. But with regard to the festival and the *cultus* of the protomartyr the reader may consult with advantage the CMH., and Duchesne's *Christian Worship*, pp. 265–268. From before the close of the fourth century both in the East (as the *Apostolic Constitutions*, viii, 33, show even for Syria) and in the West, St Stephen was commemorated on December 26. There seems to be nothing to tell us why at so early a period this particular day should have been pitched upon. The early *cultus* of Stephen in Jerusalem has been discussed very fully by Cardinal Rampolla, *S. Melania Giuniore*, pp. 271–280. On the representations of St Stephen in art, and on popular beliefs and practices associated with his day, see Künstle, *Ikonographie*, vol. ii, pp. 544–547 ; *Lexikon für Theologie und Kirche*, vol. ix, cc. 796–799 ; and Leclercq in DAC., vol. v, cc. 624–671.

ST ARCHELAUS, Bishop of Kashkar   (No Date ?)

THE Roman Martyrology signalizes the death on this day in Mesopotamia of St Archelaus the bishop, famous for his learning and holiness. St Jerome says in his *De viris illustribus* that : " Archelaus, a Mesopotamian bishop, composed a book in Syriac about the discussion that he had carried on with Manes, who came from Persia. This book has been translated into Greek and is known to many. Archelaus lived in the time of the Emperor Probus, the successor of Aurelian and of Tacitus." The story is that a Syrian named Marcellus had brought about the release of a number of Christian slaves, and was congratulated on his charitable action by the heresiarch Manes, who took the opportunity to inculcate his teaching. Marcellus reported the matter to his bishop, Archelaus, who undertook disputations with Manes. These " acts " are an interesting document in the history of Manichaeism, but it was not written in Syriac or by Archelaus. Photius, in recommending his brother to read the book against the manichaeans of Heraclian of Chalcedon (whose style, he says, " combines atticism with ordinary language, like a schoolmaster entering into a contest of superatticism "), quotes Heraclian as saying that the disputation of Archelaus was written by one Hegemonius. Research has shown that the disputation was only a literary device, and that it was composed years after Manes was dead. It therefore seems that St Archelaus, of whom nothing else is recorded, was as fictitious as his dispute, invented for the occasion by Hegemonius.

The whole matter of the *Acta Archelai* is very obscure ; but see Bardenhewer, *Geschichte der altkirchlichen Literatur*, vol. iii, pp. 265–269 ; DCB., vol. i, pp. 152–153 ; and P. Alfaric, *Les écritures manichéenes* (1918), pp. 55 *seq.*

ST DIONYSIUS, Pope   (A.D. 269)

BECAUSE of persecution the Roman see was vacant for nearly a year after the martyrdom of St Sixtus II. It was then filled in the person of the presbyter Dionysius—perhaps a Greek—who was described by his namesake of Alexandria as an admirable and learned man. By a synod convened by the pope this same St Dionysius in Egypt was required to give an account of views expressed by him when writing against Sabellianism, which he did at considerable length. Like Stephen I and others of his predecessors, Pope St Dionysius sent alms to Christians in distant lands, especially to the church of Caesarea in Cappadocia, which had been ravaged by the Goths. The edict of tolerance of the Emperor Gallienus enabled Dionysius to restore order in ecclesiastical administration and forward the works of religion after a period of persecution ; though not the first pope to die in peace, he is the first to whom the title of martyr is not accorded liturgically.

As in the case of all the early popes, there is nothing corresponding to a biography. We depend upon a few sentences in the *Liber Pontificalis* (Duchesne, vol. i, p. 157) and upon scattered references to his activities in Eusebius (bk vii, chs. 7 and 30) and in St Athanasius, St Basil, etc. See E. Caspar, *Geschichte des Papsttums*, vol. i (1930), pp. 92 *seq.* ; F. X. Seppelt, *Der Aufstieg des Papsttums* ; Leclercq in DAC., vol. xiii, cc. 1186–1188. It is astonishing to find that Pope St Dionysius is venerated as a member of the Carmelite Order —a claim which it would be difficult to substantiate.

ST ZOSIMUS, Pope   (A.D. 418)

ST Zosimus is said by the *Liber Pontificalis* to have been a Greek by birth, son of the presbyter Abram, and he succeeded Pope St Innocent I. Nothing is known of his previous career or personal life, but his pontificate of under two years was a busy one, chiefly due to the appeal of the Pelagian Caelestius from his condemnation by the bishops of Africa. Zosimus was constrained to modify his first judgement in this matter ; and he had further difficult relations with the African bishops, arising out of an irregular appeal to Rome made by a priest and the erroneous ascription by the pope of a canon, quoted in justification of the priest, to the Council of Nicaea. During his last illness St Zosimus had several cataleptic seizures which so much resembled death that he was several times supposed to be dead before he was. He died on December 26, 418.

The notice of Pope Zosimus in the second edition of the *Liber Pontificalis* (Duchesne, vol. i, p. 225), differs somewhat from the first. See also E. Caspar, *Geschichte des Papsttums*, vol. i, pp. 344 *seq.* ; Seppelt, *Der Aufstieg des Papsttums*, pp. 158 *seq.* ; DAC., vol. xiii, c. 1263.

BD VINCENTIA LOPEZ Y VICUÑA, Virgin, Foundress of the Daughters of Mary Immaculate   (A.D. 1890)

This *beata* was born in 1847, daughter of a well-to-do lawyer at Cascante in Navarre, and from her earliest years her father gave careful attention to her religious upbringing. The decisive point of her life was when she went to Madrid in order to go to school there, and came under the strict but beneficent influence of an aunt who had founded a home for orphans and domestic servants. At the age of nineteen Vincentia made a vow of celibacy, and was soon convinced that she had a call to the religious life, though not to an enclosed congregation. In particular she was concerned about what would happen to the work for girls when her aunt was no longer alive. In her uncertainty she received no help from her parents who, since she rejected both marriage and a Visitation convent, could see no alternative to her going on living at home. However, an illness of their daughter alarmed them, and she was allowed to return to her aunt, Doña Eulalia, in Madrid.

Here, under the supervision of Father Hidalgo, s.j., plans were drawn up to form the staff of the servants' home into a religious community, and in 1876 Vincentia and two others were clothed in the religious habit by Bishop Sancha of Madrid. Mother Vincentia's intense spiritual life was combined with a very practical and far-seeing charity ; she did not make the mistake of expecting too much from people borne down by the difficulty of keeping body and soul together, and her work at the home bore good fruit. Vocations were plentiful, half a dozen similar establishments were opened in other cities, and in 1888 the Holy See issued the decree of praise of the institute of Daughters of Mary Immaculate for the Protection of Working Girls. Mother Vincentia refused to finance the work by conducting schools : instead she chose the hard way of begging, and insisted to her nuns that those who would help the poor must be prepared to be poor themselves. Doña Eulalia, who had learned the practical needs of such an undertaking, gave herself and her whole fortune to it ; and homes, hostels, technical-training schools, canteens and the like for domestic and other workers were brought within the orbit of the congregation's activities. It was soon realized how true is the proverb that " The Devil finds work for idle hands to do ", and that religion is bound up with social questions, " politics " : it became a sort of slogan with Mother Vincentia's daughters that " Steady employment is the safeguard of virtue ".

At her clothing Bd Vincentia declared that the work she was undertaking " so completely satisfies my heart's desire that, should it cost me suffering or death, I here and now offer God that sacrifice. I count myself happier in the service of these my sisters than the great ones of this world in the service of their lords and kings. May our Lord give me grace to fulfil my undertaking ". That grace she received abundantly and used abundantly; and in the event the sacrifice of death was early called for. She was not yet forty-four when she died on December 26, 1890. Afterwards her congregation spread to South Africa and other lands (including England), and the foundress was solemnly beatified in 1950.

Among Bd Vincentia's works was the formation of a " triple alliance " between the houses of her congregation and the convents of Carmel and the Visitation in Spain to make reparation for the indifference shown by so many to the love of the Sacred Heart and especially for the carelessness and tepidity of some of those vowed to perfection in the religious life.

See J. Artero, *Vida de la V. Madre Vicenta Maria* ; A. Romano, *La Beata Vincenza M. Lopez Vicuña* (1950). A C.T.S. pamphlet seems to be the only item in English.

27 : ST JOHN THE EVANGELIST, Apostle (c. A.D. 100)

ST JOHN THE EVANGELIST, distinguished as the " disciple whom Jesus loved " and often called in England, as by the Greeks, " the Divine " (*i.e.* the Theologian), was a Galilean, the son of Zebedee and brother of St James the Greater with whom he was brought up to the trade of fishing. He was called to be an apostle with his brother, as they were mending their nets on the sea of Galilee, soon after Jesus had called Peter and Andrew. Christ gave them the nick-name of Boanerges, " sons of thunder ", whether as commendation or on account of some violence of temperament (*cf.* Luke ix 54) is not clear. St John is said to have been the youngest of all the apostles, and outlived the others, being the only one of whom it is sure that he did not die a martyr. In the gospel which he wrote he refers to himself with a proud humility as " the disciple whom Jesus loved ", and it is clear he was one of those who had a privileged position. Our Lord would have him present with Peter and James at His transfiguration and at His agony in the garden ; and He showed St John other instances of kindness and affection above the rest, so that it was not without human occasion that the wife of Zebedee asked the Lord that her two sons might sit the one on His right hand and the other on His left in His kingdom. John was chosen to go with Peter into the city to prepare the last supper, and at that supper he leaned on the breast of Jesus and elicited from Him, at St Peter's prompting, who it was should betray Him. It is generally believed that he was that " other disciple " who was known to the high priest and went in with Jesus to the court of Caiaphas, leaving St Peter at the outer door. He alone of the apostles stood at the foot of the cross with Mary and the other faithful women, and received the sublime charge to care for the mother of his Redeemer. " ' Woman, behold thy son.' ' Behold thy mother.' And from that hour the disciple took her to his own." Our Lord calls us all brethren, and He recommends us all as such to the loving care of His own mother : but amongst these adoptive sons St John is the first-born. To him alone was it given to be treated by her as if she had been his natural mother, and to treat her as such by honouring, serving and assisting her in person.

When Mary Magdalen brought word that Christ's sepulchre was open, Peter and John ran there immediately, and John, who was younger and ran faster, arrived first. But he waited for St Peter to come up, and followed him in : " and he saw and believed " that Christ was indeed risen. A few days later Jesus manifested Himself for the third time, by the sea of Galilee, and He walked along the shore questioning Peter about the sincerity of his love, gave him the charge of His Church, and foretold his martyrdom. St Peter, seeing St John walk behind and being solicitous for his friend, asked Jesus, " Lord, what shall this man do ? " And Jesus replied, " If I will have him to remain till I come, what is it to thee ? Follow thou me." It is therefore not surprising that it was rumoured among the brethren that John should not die, a rumour which he himself disposes of by pointing out that our Lord did not say, " He shall not die ". After Christ's ascension we find these two same apostles going up to the Temple and miraculously healing a cripple. They were imprisoned, but released again with an order no more to preach Christ, to which they answered, " If it be just in the sight of God to hear you rather than God, judge ye. For we cannot but speak the things we have seen and heard." Then they were sent by the other apostles to confirm the converts which the deacon Philip had made in Samaria. When St Paul went up to Jerusalem after his conversion he addressed himself to those who " seemed to be pillars " of the Church, chiefly James, Peter and John, who confirmed his mission among the Gentiles, and about that time St John assisted at the council which the apostles held at Jerusalem. Perhaps it was soon after this that John left Palestine for Asia Minor. No doubt he was present at the passing of our Lady, whether that took place at Jerusalem or Ephesus ; St Irenaeus says that he settled at the last-named city after the martyrdom of SS. Peter and Paul, but how soon after it is impossible to tell. There is a tradition that during the reign of Domitian he was taken to Rome, where an attempt to put him to death was miraculously frustrated (see May 6) ; and that he was then banished to the island of Patmos, where he received those revelations from Heaven which he wrote down in his book called the Apocalypse.

After the death of Domitian in the year 96 St John could return to Ephesus, and many believe that he wrote his gospel at this time. His object in writing it he tells us himself : " These things are written that you may believe that Jesus is the Christ, the Son of God ; and that, believing, you may have life in His name." It is entirely different in character from the other three gospels, and a work of such theological sublimity that, as Theodoret says, it " is beyond human understanding ever fully to penetrate and comprehend ". His soaring thought is aptly represented by the eagle which is his symbol. St John also wrote three epistles. The first is called catholic, as addressed to all Christians, especially his converts, whom he urges to purity and holiness of life and cautions against the craft of seducers. The other two are short, and directed to particular persons : the one probably to a local church ; the other to Gaius, a courteous entertainer of Christians. The same inimitable spirit of charity reigns throughout all his writings. This is not the place to refer to the objections that have been raised against St John's authorship of the Fourth Gospel.

Early writers speak of St John's determined opposition to the heresies of the Ebionites and of the followers of the gnostic Cerinthus. On one occasion he was going to the baths when, learning that Cerinthus was within, he started back and said to some friends that were with him, " Let us, brethren, make haste and be gone, lest the bath wherein is Cerinthus, the enemy of truth, should fall upon our heads ". St Irenaeus tells us he received this from the mouth of St Polycarp, St John's personal disciple. Clement of Alexandria relates that in a certain city St John saw a young man of attractive appearance in the congregation, and being much taken with him he presented him to the bishop whom he had ordained there, saying, " In the presence of Christ and before this congregation I commend this young man to your care ". The young man was accordingly lodged in the bishop's house, instructed, kept to good discipline, and at length baptized and confirmed. But the bishop's attention then slackened, the neophyte got into bad company, and became a highway robber. Some time after St John was again in that city, and said to the bishop, " Restore to me the trust which Jesus Christ and I committed to you in presence of your church ". The bishop was surprised, imagining he meant some trust of money. But when John explained that he spoke of the young man, he replied, " Alas ! he is dead ". " What did he die of ? " asked St John. " He is dead to God and is turned robber ", was the reply. Thereupon the aged apostle called for a horse and a guide, and rode away to the mountain where the robber and his gang lived. Being made prisoner he cried out, " It is for this that I am come : lead me to such an one ". When the youth saw it was St John he began to make off with shame. But John cried out after him, " Child, why do you run from me, your father, unarmed, and an old man ? There is time for repentance. I will answer for you to Jesus Christ. I am ready to lay down my life for you. I am sent by Christ." At these words the young man stood still and burst into tears, tears wherein, as Clement says, he sought to find a second baptism. Nor would St John leave that place until he had reconciled the sinner to the Church. This charity which he had so conspicuously himself he constantly and affectionately urged in others. St Jerome writes that when age and weakness grew upon him at Ephesus so that he was no longer able to preach to the people, he used to be carried to the assembly of the faithful, and every time said to his flock only these words : " My little children, love one another." When they asked him why he always repeated the same words, he replied, " Because it is the word of the Lord, and if you keep it you do enough ". St John died in peace at Ephesus about the third year of Trajan, that is, the hundredth of the Christian era, being then about ninety-four years old according to St Epiphanius.

As we may learn from St Gregory of Nyssa, from the Syriac *breviarium* of the early fifth century, and from the Carthaginian Calendar, the practice of celebrating the feast of St John immediately after that of St Stephen is of very ancient date. In the original text of the *Hieronymianum* (about A.D. 600) the commemoration seems to have been thus entered : " The Assumption of St John the Evangelist at Ephesus and the ordination to the episcopate of St James, our Lord's brother, who was the first of the Jews to be ordained by the apostles bishop of Jerusalem and gained the crown of martyrdom at the time of the pasch." One might have expected John and James, the sons of Zebedee, to be coupled in such a notice, but this is clearly the other James, the son of Alpheus, who is now honoured with St Philip on May 1. The phrase " Assumption of St John " is notable, containing as it does a clear reference to the last portion of the apocryphal " Acts of St John ". In this widely circulated fiction, dating from the late second century, it was represented (evidently in view of the saying that this particular disciple "should not die",

John xxi, 23) that St John at the end of his days in Ephesus simply disappeared : his body was never found.   On the other hand, according to the Greeks his resting-place at Ephesus was well known, and famed for marvels.   The *Acta Johannis*, though preserved to us only imperfectly and condemned for heretical tendencies by many early authorities, *e.g.* Eusebius, Epiphanius, Augustine and Turibius of Astorga, seems to have done much to create a traditional legend.   From this source, or in any case from pseudo-Abdias, comes the story which was the basis of the frequently recurring representation of St John with a chalice and a viper. The apostle was challenged by Aristodemus, the high priest of Diana at Ephesus, to drink of a poisoned cup.   He did so without sustaining any harm and thereby converted the high-priest himself.   Upon this incident seems to be founded the folk-custom, prevalent especially in Germany, of the " *Johannis-Minne* ", the loving-cup or *poculum charitatis*, which was drunk in honour of St John.   In medieval *ritualia* a number of forms of blessing are preserved which were supposed to render such a draught efficacious against dangers to health and helpful to the attaining of Heaven.

The literature about St John and his writings is of course extremely extensive and need not be gone into here.   On the more general historical question consult Fouard, *St John* (Eng. trans.) ; Fillion, *St Jean l'Evangéliste* (1907) ; C. C. Martindale, *Princes of his People*, vol. i (1920) ; J. Chapman, *John the Presbyter* (1911) ; and on the liturgical aspects, Duchesne, *Christian Worship*, pp. 265–268 ; and Kneller in *Stimmen aus Maria Laach*, vol. lxvii (1904), pp. 538–556.   The apocryphal literature is very fully discussed in Hennecke, *Neutestamentliche Apokryphen* (1904), especially pp. 423–459 ; and its sequel, *Handbuch zu den neutestamentlichen Apokryphen* (1904), pp. 492–543.   The best edition of the *Acta Johannis* is that of Max Bonnet (1898).   For special points see Delehaye's CMH., and *Synaxarium Cp.*, c. 665 ; A. Franz, *Die Kirchlichen Benediktionen in Mittelalters* (1909), vol. i, pp. 294–334 ; Bächtold-Stäubli, *Handwörterbuch des deutschen Aberglaubens*, vol. iv, cc. 745–757 ; and Künstle, *Ikonographie*, vol. ii, pp. 341–347.

ST FABIOLA, Matron   (A.D. 399)

Fabiola, of the *gens Fabia*, was one of the patrician Roman ladies who entered the path of holiness and renunciation under the influence of St Jerome, but her life was for the most part very different from that of St Marcella or St Paula or St Eustochium, and she was not a member of the circle that gathered round Jerome while he was living in Rome.   Or at least a coolness sprang up between them, for Fabiola was of a lively, passionate and headstrong disposition, and when the dissolute courses of her husband made married life impossible she obtained a civil divorce and, her husband yet living, united herself with another man. Upon the death of her second consort Fabiola submitted to the canons of the Church, presenting herself for public penance at the Lateran basilica, and was readmitted to communion with the faithful by Pope St Siricius.   She now devoted her great wealth to works of charity, gave large sums to churches, and communities in Italy and the adjoining islands, and founded a hospital for the sick whom she gathered from the streets and alleys of Rome, waiting on them in person.   It was a great moment in the history of our civilization, for this was the first Christian public hospital in the West of which there is record.

In the year 395 Fabiola went to visit St Jerome at Bethlehem, in company with a relative named Oceanus, and stayed there with SS. Paula and Eustochium. Jerome was on bad terms with the bishop of Jerusalem, John, on account of the controversy with Rufinus about the teaching of Origen, and attempts were made, even fraudulently, to enlist the sympathy and influence of Fabiola on the side of the bishop, but they failed to shake her loyalty to her teacher. Fabiola wanted to spend the rest of her days at Bethlehem, but the life of the consecrated women was not suited to her : she needed company and activity, and St Jerome remarks that her idea of the solitude of the stable of Bethlehem was that it should not be cut off from the crowded inn. A threatened incursion of the Huns finally determined her to quit Palestine. They had overrun Syria, and Jerusalem itself seemed in danger, so St Jerome retreated with his followers to the coast for a while. When the peril was past and they returned to Bethlehem, Fabiola went back to Rome.

At this time a priest named Amandus put a *dubium* to St Jerome : Might a woman, who by force had been made to take another man while her dissolute husband was still living, be received to the communion of the Church without doing canonical penance ? This question ostensibly referred to the sister of Amandus, but is generally supposed to have been put on behalf of Fabiola as a " feeler " before taking a third partner. St Jerome made no mention of her in his reply, but was contemptuous of the " force " alleged in the case : " If your sister wishes to receive Christ's body and not to be accounted an adulteress, she must do penance ", he answered. Anyway, for the remaining three years of her life Fabiola continued her works of public and private charity, notably being associated with St Pammachius in the foundation at Porto of a large hospice for poor and sick pilgrims. It was the first of its kind and within a year of its opening " became known ", says St Jerome, " from Parthia to Britain ". But Fabiola continued to be restless, and was on the point of setting out on another long journey when death overtook her. The whole of Rome attended the funeral of their beloved bene-factress. St Jerome was in touch with St Fabiola till the end, and wrote two treatises for her : one, on the priesthood of Aaron and the mystical significance of the sacerdotal vestments, he completed while her ship was being got ready to sail from Jaffa ; the other, on the " stations " of the Israelites in the wilderness, was not finished till after her death. It was eventually sent to Oceanus together with an account of Fabiola's life and death, the one wandering journey being a type or image of the other.

What we know of St Fabiola is mainly from St Jerome, *Epist.*, 77, which is printed in Migne, PL. vol. xxii, cc. 690–698. See also A. Thierry, *Saint Jérôme,* vol. ii, and F. Cavallera, *S. Jérôme, sa vie et son œuvre,* vol. ii, with Leclercq in DAC., vol. vii, cc. 2274–2275 ; and DCB., vol. ii, pp. 442–443.

ST NICARETE, Virgin   (*c.* A.D. 410)

THE Roman Martyrology mentions today St Nicarete, an oldish woman of Con-stantinople who " flourished in holiness during the reign of the Emperor Arcadius ". She belonged to a good family of Nicomedia and left home to live in Constantinople, where she devoted herself to good works. She is said to have successfully treated St John Chrysostom when he was ill, and he wished her to become a deaconess and supervise the unattached consecrated virgins of the city ; but St Nicarete would undertake neither office. She was a steadfast upholder of the bishop against his adversaries, and in consequence suffered persecution with St Olympias and other faithful ones, and like them chose to go into exile. It is not known whither she went or when or where she died, but it was probably her native Nicomedia.

The church-historian Sozomen speaks of Nicarete (bk viii, ch. 3), who is believed to be the lady skilful in the healing art to whom Chrysostom refers in his fourth letter to Olympias. There seems, however, to be no evidence of *cultus* even among the Greeks. See further Tillemont, *Mémoires*, vol. xi, pp. 133–134.

SS. THEODORE AND THEOPHANES   (*c.* A.D. 841 AND 845)

THESE brothers were natives of Kerak, across the Dead Sea, formerly the land of the Moabites, from whence their parents went and settled at Jerusalem. They both in their youth became monks in the monastery of St Sabas, and by their progress in learning and virtue acquired a high reputation. The patriarch of Jerusalem obliged Theodore to receive priestly orders, and when Leo the Armenian waged war against holy images sent him to exhort the emperor not to disturb the peace of the Church. Leo had Theodore scourged, and banished him with Theophanes to an island at the mouth of the Black Sea, where they suffered much from hunger and cold. But they were not long there before Leo died, when they returned to their monastery at Constantinople. The Emperor Theophilus, a violent iconoclast who ascended the throne in 829, caused the two brothers to be whipped and banished once more.

Two years later they were brought back to Constantinople, and when they still persisted in their refusal to communicate with the iconoclasts, Theophilus commanded twelve lines of iambic verse, composed for that purpose by a courtier, to be inscribed on their foreheads. The sense of the verses was as follows : " These men have appeared at Jerusalem as vessels full of the iniquity of superstitious error, and were driven thence for their crimes. Having fled to Constantinople, they forsook not their impiety. Wherefore they have been banished from thence and thus stigmatized on their faces." They were laid upon benches and the letters cut or pricked upon their skin. This barbarity took a long time and was interrupted by the coming on of night, so the torture was completed the next day. Then they were again banished, this time to Apamea in Bithynia, where St Theodore died. Theophilus died about the same time, and St Methodius was made patriarch and restored holy images in 842. St Theophanes was then honoured for his confession of the faith and made bishop of Nicaea, that he might more effectually concur in overthrowing a heresy over which he had already triumphed. He wrote a number of hymns, including one on St Theodore, and died on October 11, 845. He is distinguished by the Greeks as " the Poet ", but both brothers are commonly surnamed " Graptoi ", that is, " the Written-on ". They are named together in the Roman Martyrology today.

In this case we have a Greek life of Theodore attributed to the Metaphrast. It is printed in Migne, PG., vol. cxvi, pp. 653–684. These confessors are also spoken of by such later historians as Cedrenus and Zonaras in their account of the reign of the Emperor Theophilus. Some measure of *cultus* seems to be attested by the fact that a notice of Theodore and Theophanes appears in the Constantinople Synaxary (ed. Delehaye, pp. 130–131), but the day there assigned to their memory is October 11, though in other texts a mention occurs on December 28.

28 : THE HOLY INNOCENTS   (*c.* A.U.C. 750)

HEROD, called " the Great ", who governed Jewry under the Romans at the time of the birth of our Lord, was an Idumaean ; not a Jew of the house of David or of Aaron, but the descendant of people forcibly judaized by John Hyrcanus and himself exalted by the favour of imperial Rome.   From the moment, therefore, that he heard that there was One " born king of the Jews ", and that already wise men came from the East to worship Him, Herod was troubled for his throne.   He called together the chief priests and scribes, and asked them where it was that the expected Messias should be born ; and they told him, " In Bethlehem of Juda ".   Then he sent for the Magi secretly, and cross-examined them about their movements and their expectations, and finally dismissed them to Bethlehem, saying, " Go and find out all about this child.   And when you know where he is, come and tell me—that I too may go and worship him."   But the Magi were warned in their sleep not to return to Herod, and they went back to their own country by another way.   And God by an angel warned Joseph to take his wife Mary and her child Jesus and fly into Egypt, " for it will come to pass that Herod will seek the child to destroy him ".

" Then Herod, perceiving that he was deluded by the wise men, was exceeding angry.   And sending killed all the men children that were in Bethlehem and in all the borders thereof, from two years old and under, according to the time which he had diligently inquired of the wise men.   Then was fulfilled that which was spoken by Jeremias the prophet, saying : A voice in Rama was heard, lamentation and great mourning ; Rachel bewailing her children and would not be comforted, because they were not " (Matt. ii).

Josephus says of Herod that " he was a man of great barbarity towards everybody ", and narrates a number of his crimes, crimes so shocking that the slaughter of a few young Jewish babies becomes insignificant among them, and Josephus does not mention it.   The number of Herod's victims is popularly supposed to have been great : the Byzantine liturgy speaks of 14,000, the Syrian menologies 64,000, and by an accommodation of Apocalypse xiv 1–5, it has even been put at 144,000.   Of the lowest of these figures Alban Butler justly remarks that it " exceeds all bounds, nor is it confirmed by any authority of weight ".   Bethlehem was a small place and, even including the environs, could not at one time have had more than twenty-five boy-babies under two, at the very most ; some inquirers would put the number so low as about half a dozen.   There is an oft-repeated story told by Macrobius, a heathen writer of the fifth century, that the Emperor Augustus, when he heard that among the children under two which Herod had commanded to be slain his own son had been massacred, said, " It is better to be Herod's hog (*hus*) than his son (*huios*) ", alluding to the Jewish law of not eating, and consequently not killing, swine.   But in fact the son referred to was an adult, Antipater, put to death by order of his dying father.

The feast of these Holy Innocents (who in the East are called simply the Holy Children) has been kept in the Church since the fifth century, and she venerates them as martyrs, who died not only for Christ but actually instead of Christ : " flores martyrum ", she calls them ; buds, as St Augustine says, killed by the frost of persecution the moment they showed themselves.   Nevertheless they are not treated liturgically as ordinary martyrs.   The colour of the vestments at Mass is purple and the *Gloria* and Alleluia are not sung ; but on the octave-day, and when the feast falls on a Sunday, red vestments are worn and *Gloria* and Alleluia sung as usual. This feast was formerly called Childermas in England, and St Bede wrote a long hymn in honour of the Innocents. They are naturally specially venerated at Bethlehem ; their feast is there a holiday of obligation, and every afternoon of the year the Franciscan friars and children of the choir visit their altar under the basilica of the Nativity and sing the hymn from Lauds of the feast, " *Salvete, flores martyrum* ".

It may be sufficient here to note that throughout the Western church, excepting apparently in the Mozarabic ritual, the Holy Innocents from the sixth century onwards have been commemorated on this day, December 28. In the *Hieronymianum*, however, the phrase used is *natale sanctorum infantium et lactantium* (the birthday of the holy babes and sucklings), and the still earlier calendar of Carthage also speaks of *infantes*, not *innocentes*. On the other hand, in certain sermons of St Augustine where " the octave day of the infants " is mentioned, the context makes it plain that he is not thinking of the children of Bethlehem, but of those who were " infants " because they were recently baptized. See CMH., p. 13 ; Duchesne, *Christian Worship*, p. 268 ; and Kneller in *Stimmen aus Maria Laach*, vol. lxvii (1904), pp. 538–556.

ST THEODORE THE SANCTIFIED, ABBOT (A.D. 368)

SUCH was the glory which the Church received in the fourth and fifth centuries from the light of the monastic order which then shone in the deserts of Egypt that Theodoret and Procopius apply to the state of these holy recluses those passages of the prophets in which it is said of the age of the new law of grace that, " The wilderness shall rejoice and shall flourish like the lily ; it shall bud forth and blossom, and shall rejoice with joy and praise " (Isaias xxxv 1, 2, etc.). One of the most eminent among these saints was the abbot Theodore, disciple of St Pachomius. He was born in the Upper Thebaid about the year 314, of wealthy parents, and when he was between eleven and twelve years of age, on the feast of the Epiphany, he gave himself to God with precocious fervour, determining that he would never prefer anything to the divine love and service. Eventually the reputation of St Pachomius drew him to Tabenna, where he appeared among the foremost in promise of his followers, and Pachomius made him his companion when he made the visitation of his monasteries. Pachomius had him promoted to the priesthood and committed to him the government of Tabenna, shutting himself up in the little monastery of Pabau.

St Pachomius died in 346, and Petronius, whom he had declared his successor, died thirteen days after him. St Orsisius was then chosen abbot, but finding the burden too heavy for his shoulders and the group of monasteries threatened with rising factions, he placed St Theodore in charge. He assembled the monks, exhorted them to unanimity, inquired into the cause of the divisions and applied effectual remedies. By his prayers and endeavours union and charity was restored. St Theodore visited the monasteries one after the other, and instructed, comforted and encouraged every monk in particular, correcting faults with a sweetness which gained the heart. He wrought several miracles, and foretold things to come. Being one day in a boat on the Nile with St Athanasius, he assured him that his persecutor, Julian the Apostate, was that moment dead in Persia and that his successor would restore peace to him and the Church : both of which were soon confirmed. One of St Theodore's miracles provides an early example of the use of blessed water as a sacramental for the healing of body and soul. The story is told by a contemporary—St Ammon. A man came to the monastery at Tabenna, asking St Theodore to come and pray over his daughter, who was sick. Theodore was not able to go, but reminded the man that God could hear his prayers wherever they were offered. To which the man replied that he had not a great faith, and brought a silver vessel of water, asking the monk that he would at least invoke the name of God upon that so it might be as a medicine for her. Then Theodore prayed and made the sign of the cross over the water, and the man took it home. He found his daughter unconscious, so he forced open her mouth and poured some of it down her throat. And by virtue of the prayer of St Theodore the girl was saved and recovered her health.

It is related that once while St Theodore was giving a conference to his monks, who were working at the same time making mats, two vipers crawled about his feet from under a stone. So as not to interrupt himself or disturb his audience he set his foot upon them till he had finished his discourse. Then taking away his foot he let them be killed, having received no harm. One of his monks happening to die on Holy Saturday in 368, Theodore went to assist him in his last moments, and said to those that were present, " This death will shortly be followed by another which is little expected ". At the close of the week St Theodore made a customary discourse to his monks, for it was their custom to meet all together in the monastery of Pabau for the celebration of Easter, and had no sooner dismissed them to their own monasteries than he was taken ill, and died peacefully on April 27. His body was carried to the top of the mountain, and buried in the cemetery of the monks there, but it was soon removed and laid with that of St Pachomius. St Athanasius wrote to the monks of Tabenna to comfort them for the loss of their abbot, and bids them have before their eyes the glory of which he was then possessed.

Such information as was available in the seventeenth century concerning the history of St Theodore will be found collected in the account of St Pachomius which was published in the *Acta Sanctorum*, May, vol. iii. A number of new texts have come to light, mostly in Coptic, or in translations from Coptic sources : see the bibliography given herein under St Pachomius (May 9). But for the life of St Theodore the *Epistola Ammonis* is especially important : it is printed in the *Acta Sanctorum*, May, vol. iii, pp. 63–71. For English readers much may be learnt from H. G. Evelyn White, *The Monasteries of the Wadi n'Natrun*, pt ii, but heed must be paid also to the criticisms published thereon by P. Peeters in the *Analecta Bollandiana*, vol. li (1933), pp. 152–157. The Greeks commemorate this saint in May, and the Roman Martyrology formerly on December 28, but in the latest editions he is named on the date of his death, April 27.

ST ANTONY OF LÉRINS   (*c.* A.D. 520)

HE was born at Valeria in Lower Pannonia during the time of the barbarian invasions, and his father dying when he was eight years old he was entrusted to the care of St Severinus, the intrepid apostle of Noricum. Antony probably lived with him in the monastery he had founded at Faviana, and as a boy saw Odoacer go by on his triumphant march to Rome. Severinus died about 482 and Antony was then taken charge of by his uncle Constantius, Bishop of Lorch in Bavaria. He became a monk, and withdrew from Noricum into Italy with the other Romans in 488. He was then about twenty. He made his way to the neighbourhood of Lake Como, and there attached himself to a priest named Marius, who directed a number of disciples there. Marius conceived a great admiration for Antony and wanted him to be ordained priest and share in his work ; but Antony's vocation was for the solitary life and, leaving Marius, he joined two hermits near the tomb of St Felix at the other end of the lake. Here he lived in a cave, spending his time in prayer, study and cultivating his garden, but he was distracted by frequent visitors. A murderer, hiding from justice, simulated devotion and attached himself to Antony as a disciple, but the saint " read his soul ", exposed his imposture, and the man fled. Antony had to go also, for this incident made him better known than ever. At last, despairing of finding complete solitude and fearing the respect he received would make him vain, he passed over the Alps into southern Gaul and became a monk at Lérins. St Antony died there revered for his virtues and miracles. His life was written by St Ennodius of Pavia.

Little is known to us of this Antony beyond what Ennodius has recorded in the life referred to. It has been edited in the Vienna *Corpus Scriptorum ecclesiasticorum latinorum*, vol. vi, pp. 383–393 ; in MGH., *Auctores antiquissimi*, vol. vii, pp. 185–190 ; and in Migne, PL., vol. lxiii, cc. 239–246. See also DHG., vol. iii, c. 739.

29 : ST THOMAS BECKET, ARCHBISHOP OF CANTERBURY, MARTYR
(A.D. 1170)

THERE is a well-known story that the mother of St Thomas Becket was a Saracen princess who followed his father, a pilgrim or crusader, from the Holy Land and wandered about Europe uttering her sole words of English, " London " and " Becket ", till she found him ; whereupon she became a Christian and married him. There is no foundation in fact for this legend. Several contemporaries speak of the saint's parentage. FitzStephen, a cleric in his household, says, " His father was Gilbert, sheriff of London, and his mother's name was Matilda. Both were citizens of burgess stock, who neither made money by usury nor followed any trade, but lived respectably on their income."* Others say that her name was Rohesia ; she was a Norman like her husband. Their son was born on St Thomas's day 1118, in the city, and he was sent to school with the canons regular at Merton in Surrey. When he was twenty-one he lost his mother, and soon after his father. Gilbert's means had been seriously diminished, and Thomas " went into the office " of a relative in London, one Osbert Eightpence (*Huit-deniers*). He was also employed by Richer de l'Aigle, who used to take him out hawking and hunting and encouraged in Thomas the love of field-sports that never left him. One day when he was in pursuit of game his hawk made a stoop at a duck and dived after it into a river. Thomas, fearing to lose his hawk, leaped into the water and the rapid stream carried him down to a mill, where he was saved only by the sudden stopping of the wheel, which appeared miraculous. This incident is characteristic of Thomas's impetuosity, rather than a cause of his " taking life more seriously ".† When he was about twenty-four he obtained a post in the household of Theobald, archbishop of Canterbury. He received minor orders and was greatly favoured by Theobald, who saw to it that Thomas was provided with a number of benefices, from Beverley to Shoreham. In 1154 he was ordained deacon and the archbishop nominated him archdeacon of Canterbury,

* Typical examples, no doubt, of those worthy folk of whom FitzStephen himself speaks : " The citizens of London are notable before all other citizens in civility of manners, attire, table and talk. The matrons of this city are perfect Sabines."

† It is traditionally located at a place called Wade's Mill in Hertfordshire, on the Rib between Ware and St Edmund's College, a spot better known for its association with another Thomas, *viz.* Clarkson, the slavery abolitionist.

which was then the first ecclesiastical dignity in England after the bishoprics
and abbacies.　Theobald committed to him the management of delicate affairs,
seldom did anything without his advice, and sent him several times to Rome on
important missions; nor had he ever reason to repent of the choice he had made
or of the confidence he reposed in Thomas of London, as he was commonly called.

In the Norse *Thomas Saga Erkibyskups* the brilliant young ecclesiastic is
described as, " slim of growth and pale of hue, with dark hair, a long nose and
straightly-featured face.　Blithe of countenance was he, winning and loveable in
his conversation, frank of speech but slightly stuttering in his talk, so keen of
discernment and understanding that he could always make difficult questions plain
after a wise manner."　It is such men that monarchs like to have around them.
Moreover, it was the diplomacy of Thomas of London that had obtained from the
pope, Bd Eugenius III, discouragement of the succession to the throne of Stephen's
son Eustace, thus making the crown secure to Henry of Anjou.　Accordingly we
find him in 1155, at the age of thirty-six, appointed chancellor by King Henry II.
" Thomas now ", says his secretary, Herbert of Bosham, " as it were laid aside the
archdeacon and took on the duties of chancellor, which he discharged with enthusiasm and ability ", and his talents had full scope, for the importance of the
chancellor was equalled only by that of the justiciar.　As a later chancellor and
martyr named Thomas was the personal friend as well as the servant of his sovereign, Henry VIII, so Becket was a friend of Henry II—but with a yet greater
degree of intimacy.　It was said that they had but one heart and one mind, and
this being so it can hardly be questioned that to Becket's influence were partly
due those reforms for which Henry is justly praised, *e.g.* his measures to secure
justice and equitable dealing by a more uniform system of law.　But their friendship
was not confined to a common interest in affairs of state, and their personal relations
at times of relaxation have been aptly described as " frolicsome ".

One of the outstanding virtues of Thomas the Chancellor was unquestionably
magnificence—but it is to be feared that he erred by excess of it.　His household
compared with that of the king, and when he was sent into France to negotiate a
royal marriage his personal retinue numbered two hundred men; there were
several hundred more, knights and esquires, clerics and servants, in the column,
eight wagon-loads of presents, music and singers, hawks and hounds, monkeys
and mastiffs.*　The French gaped and asked, " If this is the chancellor's state,
what can the king's be like ? "　His entertainments were on a correspondingly
generous scale, and his liberality to the poor proportionate.　In 1159 Henry raised
an army of mercenaries in France to recover his wife's county of Toulouse.　In
the resulting war Becket served, followed by seven hundred of his own knights,
and showed himself not only a good general, but a good fighting-man as well.
Clad in armour he led assaults and even, cleric though he was, engaged in hand-to-
hand encounters.　It is not surprising that the prior of Leicester, meeting him
at Rouen, exclaimed, " What do you mean by dressing like that ?　You look more
like a falconer than a cleric.　Yet you are a cleric in person, and many times over
in office : archdeacon of Canterbury, dean of Hastings, provost of Beverley, canon
of this church and that, procurator of the archbishopric—and likely to be archbishop too, the rumour goes ! "　Thomas took the reproach in good part, and said

---

* Two wagons, FitzStephen tells us, were laden with beer in iron-bound casks, to be
given to the French, " who like that kind of drink ; for it is wholesome, clear, wine-coloured
and of a better taste."

he knew three poor priests in England any one of whom he would rather see archbishop than himself, for he would inevitably have to choose between the royal favour and God's. Though immersion in public affairs and a secular grandeur of state was the predominating aspect of Becket's life as chancellor, it was not the only one. He was proud, irascible, violent and remained so all his life ; but we also hear of " retreats " at Merton, of taking the discipline and of prayer in the nightwatches ; and his confessor during the first part of his career testified to the blamelessness of his private life under conditions of extreme danger and temptation. And if he sometimes co-operated too far in schemes of his royal master that infringed the rights of the Church, he was not afraid to withstand him in such matters as the marriage of the abbess of Romsey.

Theobald, archbishop of Canterbury, died in 1161. King Henry was then in Normandy with his chancellor, whom he had resolved to raise to that dignity. Thomas flatly told the king, " Should God permit me to be archbishop of Canterbury I should soon lose your Majesty's favour, and the affection with which you honour me would be changed into hatred. For several things you do in prejudice of the rights of the Church make me fear you would require of me what I could not agree to ; and envious persons would not fail to make this the occasion of endless strife between us." The king paid no regard to his remonstrance ; and Thomas refused to acquiesce in accepting the dignity till Cardinal Henry of Pisa, legate from the Holy See, overruled his scruples. The election was made in May 1162 ; Prince Henry, then in London, gave his consent in his father's name ; and Becket set out immediately from London to Canterbury. On the road he gave private charge to several clergy of his church to warn him of the faults which they should observe in his conduct, " for four eyes see more clearly than two ". On Saturday in Whit-week he was ordained priest by Walter, bishop of Rochester, and on the octave of Pentecost was consecrated by Henry of Blois, bishop of Winchester.*

Soon after he received the *pallium* from Pope Alexander III, and by the end of the year there was a notable change in his manner of life. Next his skin he wore a hair-shirt, and his ordinary dress was a black cassock and linen surplice, with the sacerdotal stole about his neck. By the rule of life which he laid down for himself he rose early to read the Holy Scriptures, keeping Herbert of Bosham by him that they might discuss the meaning of passages together. At nine o'clock he sang Mass, or was present when he did not celebrate himself. At ten a daily alms was distributed, and he doubled all the ordinary alms of his predecessor. He took a siesta in the afternoon, and dined at three o'clock among the guests and household in the great hall, and, instead of music, a book was read. He kept a notably good table, decently served for the sake of others, but was himself now very temperate and moderate. He visited the infirmary and the monks working in the cloister nearly every day, and sought to establish a certain monastic regularity in his own household. He took an especial care for the selection of candidates for holy orders, examining them personally, and in his judicial capacity exerted a rigorously even-handed justice : " the letters and requests of the king himself were of no use to a man who had not right on his side ".

Although the archbishop had resigned the chancellorship contrary to the wish

* St Thomas decreed that this anniversary should be observed throughout his province as a feast of the Most Holy Trinity, over a hundred and fifty years before the feast was made general in the West.

of the king, the relations between them remained for some time pretty much as before. In spite of some differences Henry still showed him great marks of favour and seemed still to love him as he had done from their first acquaintance. The first serious sign of displeasure happened at Woodstock, when the king was holding his court there. It was customary to pay two shillings a year upon every hide of land to the sheriffs of the counties, who in return protected the contributors against the rapacity of minor officials (it apparently was " graft " of the worst kind). This sum the king ordered to be paid into his exchequer. The archbishop remonstrated that it was a voluntary payment which could not be exacted as a revenue of the crown, adding, " If the sheriffs, their sergeants and officers defend the people, we shall pay ; otherwise, not ". The king replied with an oath, " By God's eyes, this shall be paid ! " " By the reverence of those eyes, my lord king ", answered Thomas, " not a penny shall be paid from my lands." Henry said no more at that time, but his resentment was roused. Then came the affair of Philip de Brois, a canon who was accused of murder. According to the law of those times he was tried in the ecclesiastical court, and was acquitted by the bishop of Lincoln ; but a king's justice-*in-eyre*, Simon Fitzpeter, then tried to bring him before his own court ; Philip refused to plead, and addressed Fitzpeter in insulting terms. Thereupon Henry ordered him to be tried both for the former murder and the later misdemeanour. Thomas pressed for the case to come before his own court, and the king reluctantly agreed. Philip's plea of previous acquittal was accepted for the murder, but for the contempt of court he was sentenced to be flogged and suspended for a time from his benefice. The king thought the sentence too mild, and said to the assessors, " By God's eyes, you shall swear that you did not spare him because he was a cleric ". They offered to swear it ; but Henry was not satisfied.

Accumulation of conflicts of these kinds provoked him in October 1163 to call the bishops to a council at Westminster, at which he demanded the handing over of criminal clergy to the civil power for punishment. The bishops wavered, but St Thomas stiffened them. Then Henry required a promise of observance of his (unspecified) royal customs. St Thomas and the council agreed, but " saving their order ". So far as the king's object was concerned this was equivalent to a refusal, and the next day he ordered Thomas to give up certain castles and honours which he had held since he was chancellor. In a stormy interview at Northampton the king in vain tried to make his old friend modify his attitude, and the trouble came to a head at the Council of Clarendon, near Salisbury, at the beginning of 1164. For a brief space St Thomas, having received little encouragement from Pope Alexander III, was very conciliatory and promised to accept the customs ; but when he saw the constitutions in which were expressed the royal customs which he was to uphold, he exclaimed, " By the Lord Almighty, no seal of mine shall be put to them ! " They provided *inter alia* that no prelate should leave the kingdom without the royal licence or appeal to Rome without the king's consent ; no tenant-in-chief was to be excommunicated against the royal will (this had been claimed from the time of William I, but was a clear infringement of spiritual jurisdiction) ; the custody of vacant benefices and their revenues was to be held by the king (this abuse had been recognized during the reign of Henry I) ; and—what proved to be the critical point—that clerics convicted and sentenced in ecclesiastical courts should be at the disposition of the royal officers (involving a possibility of double punishment).

The archbishop was bitterly remorseful for having weakened in his opposition to the king and setting an example which the other bishops were too ready to follow. " I am a proud, vain man, a feeder of birds and follower of hounds ", he said, " and I have been made a shepherd of sheep. I am fit only to be cast out of the see which I fill." For forty days and more, while awaiting absolution and permission from the pope, he would not celebrate Mass. He tried assiduously to heal the breach, but Henry now pursued him with persecution which culminated in a suit for 30,000 marks alleged to be owing from the time when he was chancellor (although he had received a clear discharge on becoming archbishop). At Woodstock the king refused him audience, and Thomas twice made vain attempts to cross the Channel to put his case before the pope. Then Henry summoned a council at Northampton. It resolved itself into a concerted attack on the archbishop, in which the prelates followed in the wake of the lords. First he was condemned to a fine for contempt in not appearing at a case in the king's court when summoned ; then various monetary causes were brought against him, and finally the demand to produce certain chancery-accounts. Bishop Henry of Winchester pleaded the chancellor's discharge ; it was disallowed. Then he offered an *ex gratia* payment of 2000 marks of his own money ; it was refused. On Tuesday, October 13, 1164, St Thomas celebrated a votive Mass of St Stephen the Protomartyr. Then, without mitre or *pallium*, but bearing his metropolitan's cross in his own hand, he went to the council-hall. The king and the barons were deliberating in an inner room. After a long delay the Earl of Leicester came out and addressed the archbishop. " The king commands you to render your accounts. Otherwise you must hear judgement." " Judgement ? " exclaimed St Thomas, " I was given the church of Canterbury free from temporal obligations. I am therefore not liable and will not plead concerning them." As Leicester turned to report this to the king, Thomas stopped him. " Son and earl, listen : You are bound to obey God and me before your earthly king. Neither law nor reason allows children to judge their father and condemn him. Wherefore I refuse the king's judgement and yours and everybody's ; under God, I will be judged by the pope alone. You, my fellow bishops, who have served man rather than God, I summon to the presence of the pope. And so, guarded by the authority of the Catholic Church and the Holy See, I go hence." Cries of " Traitor ! " followed him as he left the hall. That night St Thomas fled from Northampton* through the rain, and three weeks later secretly embarked at Sandwich.

St Thomas and his few followers landed in Flanders and, arriving at the abbey of St Bertin at Saint-Omer, sent deputies to Louis VII, King of France, who received them graciously and invited the archbishop into his dominions. The pope, Alexander III, was then at Sens. The bishops and others from King Henry arrived there and accused St Thomas before him,† but left again before the archbishop reached the city. Thomas showed the pope the sixteen Constitutions of Clarendon, of which some were pronounced intolerable, and he was rebuked for ever having considered their acceptance. On the day following he confessed that he had received the see of Canterbury, though against his will, yet by an election

---

* St Thomas of Canterbury is a principal patron of the present diocese and cathedral of Northampton.

† His chief clerical enemy, Gilbert Foliot, bishop of London, began to harangue with great vehemence. The pope interrupted him : " Spare, brother." " Shall I spare him, my lord ? " asked Gilbert. " Brother, I did not say spare him, but spare yourself."

perhaps uncanonical, and that he had acquitted himself ill in it. Wherefore he resigned his dignity into the hands of his Holiness and, taking the ring off his finger, delivered it to him and withdrew. The pope called him again and reinstated him in his dignity, with an order not to abandon it for that would be visibly to abandon the cause of God. Then Alexander recommended the exiled prelate to the abbot of Pontigny, to be entertained by him.

St Thomas regarded this monastery of the Cistercian Order as a religious retreat and school of penance for the expiation of his sins; he submitted himself to the rules of the house and was unwilling to allow any distinction in his favour. His time he passed in study, but also in writing both to his supporters and opponents letters which were increasingly unlikely to help on a peaceful settlement. King Henry meanwhile confiscated the goods of all the friends, relations and domestics of Thomas, banished them, and obliged all who were adults to go to the archbishop that the sight of their distress might move him. These exiles arrived in troops at Pontigny. When the general chapter of the Cistercians met at Cîteaux it received an intimation from the King of England that if they continued to harbour his enemy he would sequestrate their houses throughout his dominions. The abbot of Cîteaux can hardly be blamed for hinting to St Thomas that he should leave Pontigny, which he did, and was received at the abbey of St Columba, near Sens, as the guest of King Louis. Negotiations between the pope, the archbishop, and the king dragged on for nearly six years. St Thomas was named legate *a latere* for all England except York, excommunicated several of his adversaries, and was menacing as well as conciliatory, so that Pope Alexander saw fit to annul some of his sentences. King Louis of France was drawn into the struggle. In January 1169 the two kings had a conference with the archbishop at Montmirail, whereat Thomas refused to yield on two points; a similar conference in the autumn at Montmartre failed through Henry's last-minute intransigence. St Thomas prepared letters for the bishops ordering the publication of a sentence of interdict on the kingdom of England; and then suddenly, in July 1170, king and archbishop met again in Normandy and a reconciliation was at last patched up, apparently without any overt reference to the matters in dispute.

On December 1 St Thomas landed at Sandwich, and though the sheriff of Kent had tried to impede him the short journey from there to Canterbury was a triumphal progress: the way was lined with cheering people and every bell of the primatial city was ringing. But it was not peace.* Those in authority were glowering, and Thomas was faced with the task of dealing with Roger de Pont-l'Evêque, archbishop of York, and the bishops who had assisted him at the coronation of Henry's son, in defiance of the right of Canterbury and perhaps of the instructions of the pope. St Thomas had sent in advance the letters of suspension of Roger and others and of excommunication of the bishops of London and Salisbury, and the three bishops together had gone over to appeal to King Henry in France; while in Kent Thomas was being subjected to insult and annoyance at the hands of Ranulf de Broc, from whom the archbishop had recently (and rather tactlessly at such a time) again demanded the restoration of Saltwood castle, a manor belonging to the see. After a week at Canterbury St Thomas visited London, where he was joyfully received, except by Henry's son, " the young King ", who refused to see

---

* In the previous March St Godric had sent St Thomas a message foretelling that he would return to England and die soon after. His farewell words to the bishop of Paris were, " I am going to England to die ".

him ; after visiting several friends he arrived back in Canterbury on or about his fifty-second birthday. Meanwhile the three bishops had laid their complaints before the king at Bur, near Bayeux, and somebody declared aloud that there would be no peace for the realm while Becket lived. And Henry, in one of his fits of ungovernable rage, pronounced the fatal words which were interpreted by some of his hearers as a rebuke for allowing this pestilent clerk to continue to live and disturb him. At once four knights set off for England, where they made their way to the infuriated Brocs at Saltwood. Their names were Reginald Fitzurse, William de Tracy, Hugh de Morville, and Richard le Breton.

On St John's day the archbishop received a letter warning him of his danger, and all south-east Kent was in a state of suppressed ferment and ominous expectation. In the afternoon of December 29* the knights from France came to him. There was an interview, in which several demands were made, particularly that St Thomas should remove the censures on the three bishops ; it began quietly and ended angrily, the knights departing with threats and oaths. A few minutes later, shouting, breaking of doors and clangour of arms was heard, and St Thomas, urged and hustled by his attendants, began to move slowly towards the church, his cross carried before him. Vespers was being sung, and at the door of the north transept he was met by a crowd of terrified monks. " Get back to choir ! " he exclaimed, " I will not come in all the time you are standing there." They drew back a little, and as he entered the church armed men were seen behind in the dim light of the cloister (it was nearly dark). Monks slammed the door and bolted it, shutting out some of their brethren in the confusion. These beat loudly at the door. Becket turned round. " Away, you cowards ! " he cried, " a church is not a castle ", and re-opened the door himself. Then he went up the steps towards the choir. Only three were left with him, Robert, prior of Merton, William FitzStephen, and Edward Grim ;† the rest had fled to the crypt and elsewhere, and soon Grim alone remained. The knights, who had been joined by a subdeacon named Hugh of Horsea, ran in, shouting, " Where is Thomas the traitor ? " " Where is the archbishop ? " " Here I am ", he replied, " no traitor, but archbishop and priest of God ", and came back down the steps, standing between the altars of our Lady and St Benedict.

They shouted at him to absolve the bishops. " I cannot do other than I have done ", he answered. " Reginald ! you have received many favours from me. Why do you come into my church armed ? " Fitzurse's reply was to threaten him with an axe. " I am ready to die ", said St Thomas, " but God's curse be on you if you harm my people." Fitzurse seized his cloak and pulled him towards the door. Becket snatched himself clear. Then they tried to carry him outside bodily, and he threw one of them to the ground. Fitzurse flung away his axe and drew his sword. " You pander ! " exclaimed the archbishop, " you owe me fealty and submission ! " " I owe no fealty contrary to the king ", Fitzurse shouted back. " Strike ! " And he knocked off his cap. St Thomas covered his face and called aloud on God and his saints. Tracy struck a blow, which Grim intercepted

---

* It was a Tuesday. Becket was born and baptized on a Tuesday ; his flight from Northampton, his leaving England, a vision of martyrdom he had at Pontigny, his return from exile, his death, all took place on Tuesday. Henry II was buried and the martyr's relics were translated on Tuesdays.

† Respectively, his aged adviser and confessor, a cleric of his household, and an English monk.

with his own arm, but it grazed Thomas's head and blood ran down into his eyes. He wiped it away, and when he saw the crimson stain cried, " Into thy hands, O Lord, I commend my spirit ! " Another blow from Tracy beat him to his knees, and murmuring, " For the name of Jesus and in defence of the Church I am willing to die ", he pitched forward on to his face. Le Breton with a tremendous stroke severed his scalp, breaking his sword against the pavement, and Hugh of Horsea scattered the brains out of the skull with his sword-point. Hugh de Morville alone struck no blow. Then, shouting " The king's men ! The king's men ! " the murderers dashed away through the cloisters—the whole thing was over in ten minutes—while the great church filled with people and a thunderstorm broke overhead. The archbishop's body lay alone, stretched in the middle of the transept, and for long no one dared to touch or even go near it.

Even after making full allowance for the universal horror which such a deed of sacrilege—the murder of a metropolitan in his own cathedral—was bound to excite in the twelfth century, the indignation and excitement which soon spread throughout Europe and the spontaneous canonization of Thomas Becket by the common voice testify to the fact that the inner significance of his death was realized on all hands : that a necessary vindication had been made of the rights of the Church against an aggressive state and that the archbishop of Canterbury, in some ways an unsympathetic character, whose methods were not beyond reasonable criticism,* was a martyr and worthy to be venerated as a saint. The discovery of his hair-shirt and other evidences of an austere private life, and the miracles which from the very first were reported in large numbers at his tomb, added fuel to this fire of devotion. It is very doubtful how far Henry II can be held directly and deliberately responsible for the murder ; but the public conscience could not be satisfied by anything less than that the most powerful sovereign in Europe should undergo a public penance of a most humiliating kind. This he did in July, 1174,† eighteen months after the solemn canonization of St Thomas as a martyr by Pope Alexander at Segni.‡ On July 7, 1220, the body of St Thomas was solemnly

---

* Even in the moment of his death Grim overheard a monk declare that it was the deserved penalty for his obstinacy, and at the University of Paris and elsewhere could be found some who maintained that it was a just execution of one who " wished to be more than king ".

† When news of the murder was brought to him he shut himself up lamenting, and fasted alone for forty days. He narrowly escaped an interdict, which, indeed, his French dominions were put under for a short time. His first penance, when he received absolution from the papal legates, was at Avranches in May 1172. A pillar still marks the spot, at the site of the old cathedral.

‡ In his interesting and valuable *Historical Memorials of Canterbury* Dean Stanley discusses the subsequent careers of the murderers. In reference to the legend that three of them went to Palestine, died there, and were buried in Jerusalem " *ante ostium templi* ", he adds a footnote : " The front of the church of the Holy Sepulchre is, and always must have been, a square of public resort to all the pilgrims of the world, where no tombs either of murderer or saint could ever have been placed. The church of the Templars was the Mosque of the Rock, and the front was the sacred platform of the sanctuary—a less impossible place, but still very improbable. Nothing of the kind now exists on either spot." The learned dean was here mistaken on both points. In the square before the Holy Sepulchre church there is the tomb of an Anglo-Norman knight, one Philip d'Aubigny—not one of Becket's murderers. On the south side of the platform of the Dome of the Rock is the mosque called al-Aksa, formerly a church. Herein, some thirty years ago, the present writer was shown by the *imam* the place where tradition says the three knights were buried. It was then covered with matting, but I was assured there was no trace of the inscription which Roger Hoveden mentions. But the place is also called the tomb of the sons of Aaron.

translated from its tomb in the crypt to a shrine behind the high altar by the archbishop, Cardinal Stephen Langton, in the presence of King Henry III, Cardinal Pandulf, the papal legate, the archbishop of Rheims, and a vast gathering.   From that day until September 1538 the shrine of St Thomas was one of the half-dozen most favoured places of pilgrimage in Christendom, famous as a spiritual sanctuary, for its material beauty and for its wealth.   No authentic record of its destruction and spoliation by Henry VIII remains ; even the fate of the relics is a matter of uncertainty, though they were probably destroyed at that time when his memory was, naturally enough, particularly execrated by the king (but that he held a form of trial at which " Thomas, sometime archbishop of Canterbury ", was convicted of treason and his bodily remains ordered to be publicly burnt, is almost certainly apocryphal).   The feast of St Thomas of Canterbury is kept throughout the Western church, and in England he is venerated as protector of the secular clergy ; the city of Portsmouth has the privilege of observing as well the anniversary of the translation.

There is probably no other medieval saint of whom so many biographies were written by contemporaries as St Thomas of Canterbury.   A list of the Latin lives will be found in BHL., nn. 8170–8248, and all the more important of these, together with the collections of miracles, have been printed in the seven volumes of *Materials for the History of Thomas Becket*, edited for the Rolls Series by Canon J. C. Robertson and Dr J. B. Sheppard.   Further, there are several lives in French or Anglo-Norman, of which the most noteworthy is that by Guernes de Pont-Sainte-Maxence, as well as others in Icelandic, more particularly one which seems to have used contemporary materials now no longer in existence.   This was edited for the Rolls Series by E. Magnusson, under the title, *Thomas Saga Erkibyskups*. Of some of the lives the authorship is known, as, for example, that by William FitzStephen and that by John of Salisbury, but there are others in which identification of the writer is not so easy.   A discussion of this problem and of that of the priority or interdependence of these biographical materials would be out of place here.   The critics who have undertaken the task, such as Louis Halphen (in the *Revue Historique*, vol. cii, 1909, pp. 35–45), and E. Walberg (*La Tradition historique de St Thomas Becket avant la fin du XIIe siècle*, 1929) are by no means in agreement.   See on this the *Analecta Bollandiana*, vol. xl (1922), pp. 432–436, and vol. xli, pp. 454–456.   *The Life of St Thomas Becket* by John Morris (1885), still retains its value, and that of L'Huillier, *St Thomas de Cantorbéry* (2 vols., 1891), is also full and fairly reliable ; the shorter sketch by M. Demimuid in the series " Les Saints " is not so satisfactory, but that of Robert Speaight (1938) may be recommended.   For the history of the conflict between Thomas and Henry, see D. Knowles, *The Episcopal Colleagues of . . . Becket* (1951) ; and see the same writer's Raleigh lecture, *Archbishop Thomas Becket* (1949) ; and R. Foreville, *L'Église et la royauté en Angleterre sous Henri II* (1943). Several Anglican contributions to the subject may also be recommended as making faithful and on the whole sympathetic use of the historical materials.   For example, the essay of Professor Tout, *The Place of St Thomas of Canterbury in History* (1921), is an excellent publication of the Rylands Library, Manchester.   The same may be said of the pages referring to the martyr in Z. N. Brooke's *The English Church and the Papacy* (1931), as also of W. H. Hutton's *Thomas Becket* (1926), and of Miss Norgate's article in the DNB.   On the other hand, *The Development of the Legend of Thomas Becket* (1930), by P. A. Brown, and E. A. Abbott's *St Thomas, his Death and Miracles* (1898) are notably censorious and rationalistic.   The contention supported by Canon A. J. Mason (in his book, *What became of the Bones of St Thomas ?*, 1920), that a skeleton brought to light in the crypt of Canterbury cathedral in 1888 was that of the martyr, has been answered by Fathers Morris and Pollen (see *The Month*, March 1888, January 1908, and May 1920), and this negative conclusion is supported by such Anglican authorities as Dean Hutton and Professor Tout.   A surprising feature regarding the martyrdom is the rapidity and world-wide range of the *cultus* which followed.   Barely ten years later we find St Thomas depicted in the mosaics of the cathedral of Monreale in Sicily, and at the end of little more than a century he is inscribed on December 29 in an Armenian synaxary.   For the pictorial representations of St Thomas of Canterbury, see especially the monograph of Tancred Borenius, *St Thomas Becket in Art* (1932).

ST TROPHIMUS, Bishop of Arles　　(Third Century ?)

AMONG those who accompanied St Paul on his third missionary journey was a Gentile from Ephesus called Trophimus, the same whose presence with him later in Jerusalem was the occasion of the uproar against the Apostle. He " hath brought in Gentiles into the Temple and hath violated this holy place ! For they had seen Trophimus the Ephesian in the city with him, whom they supposed that Paul had brought into the Temple." He is mentioned again in the second epistle to Timothy as having been left at Malta, sick.

When Pope St Zosimus wrote to the bishops of Gaul in 417, he refers to the Holy See having sent a Trophimus into Gaul, whose preaching at Arles was the source from which the waters of the faith spread over all the land. One hundred and fifty years later St Gregory of Tours says that St Trophimus of Arles, its first bishop, was one of the six bishops who came from Rome with St Dionysius of Paris in the middle of the third century. Nothing at all is known of Trophimus of Arles except the statement of Pope Zosimus, but he came to be identified with his namesake of Ephesus.

There is of course nothing in the nature of a life, though St Trophimus, in view of the dedication of the cathedral of Arles, the words of Pope Zosimus, and other references, must be accounted an authentic historical personage. The statement that he was identical with the Trophimus mentioned by St Paul in 2 Tim. iv 20, is a characteristically wild invention of the martyrologist Ado. See Quentin, *Martyrologes historiques*, pp. 303 and 603 ; Duchesne, *Fastes Épiscopaux*, vol. i, pp. 253–254 ; and DCB., vol. iv, p. 1055.

ST MARCELLUS AKIMETES, Abbot　　(*c.* A.D. 485)

THE Akoimetoi differed from other Eastern monks only by this particular rule, that the monastery was divided into several choirs which, succeeding one another, continued the Divine Office day and night without interruption ; whence was derived their name of the " not-resters ". This institution was set on foot by a Syrian, St Alexander, who founded a monastery at Gomon on the Black Sea. His successor John removed his community to a monastery which he built at the Eirenaion, a pleasant place on the opposite shore of the Bosphorus to Constantinople. St Marcellus, who was chosen third abbot of this house, raised its reputation to the highest pitch, and he was himself the most distinguished of the Akoimetoi monks. He was born at Apamea in Syria, and by the death of his parents was left master of a large fortune. He conceived a distaste for secular pursuits and, repairing to Antioch, made sacred studies his whole employment. He then went to Ephesus, and there put himself under the direction of certain men of God, and what time was not spent in prayer he employed in copying books. Soon the reputation of the austerity and solitude of the Akoimetoi drew him thither, and he made such progress that John, when he was chosen abbot, compelled him to be his assistant ; and upon his death Marcellus was elected in his place.

When the opposition of the Emperor Theodosius II and some of the ecclesias-tical authorities had died down, the monastery flourished exceedingly under his prudent and saintly administration ; and when he was at a loss how sufficiently to enlarge his buildings, he was abundantly supplied with means by a rich man, who took the habit with all his sons on the same day. St Marcellus himself when he became a monk had insisted on giving away every penny he had left ; he was most insistent on the observance of poverty and would allow no hoarding or investment of any sort : he thought a ten-days' supply of food in hand too much. The Akoimetoi had been hitherto rather contemptuous of manual work, and this also he insisted that they should all undertake, whether they liked it or not. The community numbered three hundred members, and from all parts of the East applications were made to St Marcellus for individual monks to be made abbots, or groups to form *nuclei* of new establishments. The most famous of these was the monastery in Constantinople founded with some Akoimetoi by the ex-consul Studius in 463.

Apostolic work that could be conducted from their monastery was included in the activities of these monks, and St Marcellus was an outstanding figure in all contemporary movements against heresy at Constantinople ; he was one of the twenty-three archimandrites who signed the condemnation of Eutyches in the synod held by St Flavian in 448, and he assisted at the Council of Chalcedon. When the Emperor Leo I proposed to raise the Goth consul Patricius to the dignity of *caesar*, Marcellus protested against such power being given to an Arian, and correctly foretold the approaching ruin of the family of Patricius. In 465 a great fire took place in Constantinople, eight of the sixteen quarters of the city being destroyed. The people testified to the holy reputation of St Marcellus by attributing the staying of the disaster to his intercession. He governed his monastery for some forty-five years and died on December 29, 485.

Our information comes from a detailed Greek biography attributed to the Metaphrast and printed in Migne, PG., vol. cxvi, pp. 705–745. See also *Synax. Const.* (ed. Delehaye), cc. 353–354 ; Pargoire in DAC., vol. i, cc. 315–318, and *Échos d'Orient*, vol. ii, pp. 305–308 and 365–372 ; and *Revue des questions historiques*, January 1899, pp.69–79.

ST EBRULF, or EVROULT, Abbot   (A.D. 596)

EBRULF was brought up at the court of King Childebert I. Here he married but after a time the pair agreed to separation ; the lady took the veil in a nunnery, whilst he distributed his goods among the poor. It was, however, a considerable time before he was able to obtain the leave of Clotaire I to go from court. At length, he was enabled to go to a monastery in the diocese of Bayeux, where his virtues gained him the esteem and veneration of his fellow monks. But the respect which he met with was a temptation, and to avoid it he withdrew, with three others, and hid in a remote part of the forest of Ouche in Normandy. These new hermits had taken no proper measures for their support, but they settled near a spring of water, made an inclosure with a hedge, and built themselves wattle huts. A peasant discovered them, to his great astonishment, and warned them that the wood was a haunt of outlaws. " We have come here ", replied Ebrulf, " to weep for our sins. We put our confidence in the mercy of God, who feeds the birds of the air. We fear no one." The countryman brought them the next morning loaves and some honey, and soon after joined them. One of the thieves happened upon them, and he too endeavoured to persuade them that their lives would be in danger. St Ebrulf answered him as he had answered the peasant. The robber himself was converted and brought many of his companions, like-minded with himself, to the saint, by whose advice they betook themselves to work for an honest living. The hermits tried to cultivate the land, but it was too barren to yield sufficient, even for their abstemious way of living. So the inhabitants of the country brought them in little provisions, which St Ebrulf accepted as alms.

The advantages and consolations of uninterrupted contemplation made Ebrulf desire to live always as an anchorite, without being burdened with the care of others. But he could not be indifferent to the salvation of his neighbours. He therefore received those who desired to live under his direction, and for them he was obliged to build a monastery which afterwards bore his name. His community increasing and many offering him land, he built other monasteries of men or women. He used to exhort his religious particularly to manual labour, telling them that they would gain their bread by their work and Heaven by serving God in it. St Ebrulf died in 596 in his eightieth year after, it is said, living for over six weeks without being able to swallow anything except the Sacred Host and a little water.

There is a rather full life compiled by an anonymous ninth-century writer. It has been printed by Surius with his usual emendations of the Latin phraseology. But the abridged or modified version which will be found in Mabillon, vol. i, pp. 354–361, with supplementary additions from Ordericus Vitalis, may be regarded as reasonably adequate. See also the preface of Leopold Delisle's edition of Ordericus's *Historia ecclesiastica*, pp. lxxix–lxxxiv. In the *Bulletin de la soc. hist. arch. de l'Orne*, vol. vi (1887), pp. 1–83, J. Blin has edited a French poem of the twelfth century recounting the history of St Evroult. There is also a short popular life by H. G. Chenu (1896).

BD PETER THE VENERABLE, ABBOT　　(A.D. 1156)

AT the beginning of the twelfth century the abbacy of Cluny, an office which entailed a headship of hundreds of monasteries and their dependencies throughout Europe, was held by an incompetent and unworthy monk, Pontius, who had been elected when he was too young. In the face of a growing discontent, he resigned in circumstances that amounted to deposition and, his successor having died almost at once, Peter de Montboissier, Prior of Domène, was elected. Peter, of a noble family of Auvergne, had been educated at the Cluniac house of Sauxillanges, and by the time he was twenty he was already prior of Vézelay; when chosen to rule the mother house and federation he was still only thirty. That was in 1122, and during the thirty-four years that he governed Cluny it reached a point of influence and prosperity that it never again touched. But the early days were not auspicious. In 1125 the ex-abbot Pontius came out of Italy with an armed following, threw himself into Cluny when Peter was absent, drove out all who would not accept him, and proceeded to conduct the monastery and its affairs in a most disorderly way. Both parties were summoned to Rome, and Pope Honorius II sentenced Pontius to be degraded and imprisoned. An unhappy controversy sprang up between Cîteaux and Cluny, St Bernard accusing the Cluniacs of being relaxed, and they retorting that Cistercian life was impracticable. The general trend of the controversy showed Abbot Peter as more representative of the tolerant wideness of St Benedict's rule; and in so far as the Cistercian complaints were justified Peter, together with Abbot Suger of Saint-Denis, ultimately met the criticism by inaugurating a reform and tightening up discipline. It was at this time, in 1130, that Abbot Peter visited England, when an attempt was made to bring the abbey of Peterborough under Cluny. In 1139 he journeyed into Spain, where he found two translators who knew Arabic, and for the advancement of learning he paid them well to make for him Latin versions of the Koran and of some astronomical works.

In 1140 Peter Abelard came to Cluny on his way to Rome to appeal against the condemnation of his opinions pronounced at Sens, but while there news was brought that the condemnation had been confirmed by Pope Innocent.   Abbot Peter thereupon offered Abelard a home, obtained a mitigation of his sentence from the Holy See, and brought about a meeting and reconciliation between him and St Bernard.   He showed himself a most generous friend to Abelard, and when he died two years later Abbot Peter sent his body for burial to the Abbess Heloise at the Paraclete, with an assurance that he had died absolved and in communion with the Church.   He also wrote an extravagant epitaph, comparing the dead philosopher with Socrates, Plato and Aristotle.   It was typical of Peter the Venerable that he combined kindness and sympathy for the erring with a just detestation of their errors : he defended the Jews against massacre but admitted that they gave provocation ; he wrote against the Petrobrusian heretics in the south of France ; and he assisted at the synod of Rheims when the teachings of Gilbert de la Porrée, bishop of Poitiers, were impugned.   He was greatly esteemed by his contemporaries and kept up a large correspondence with those who consulted him, as well as writing theological and polemical treatises, sermons and hymns, *e.g.* the Christmas prose " *Caelum, gaude, terra, plaude* ".   It is appropriate that the author of this lovely hymn should have died, according to his wish, on Christmas day, 1156, after having preached about the feast to his monks.

Peter the Venerable was revered as a saint by the faithful at large as well as by his own congregation.   This *cultus* has never been formally approved by the Holy See, but his name was inserted in French martyrologies and his feast is observed in the diocese of Arras on December 29.

Two medieval lives of Peter the Venerable are preserved to us.   The first and more important is by Rodulf, his constant companion ; .the second is not properly a biography but a collection of extracts from the chronicle of Cluny.   Both are printed in Migne, PL., vol. clxxxix, cc. 15–42, and some other materials in the form of poems or panegyrics are added in the same prolegomenon to Peter's own writings and letters.   It is from these last that our knowledge of him and his character is mainly derived.   'An excellent account of the holy abbot and his literary work is furnished by P. Séjourné in DTC., vol. xii (1933), cc. 2065–2082 ; and there is also a good article by G. Grützmacher in the *Realencyklopädie für protestantische Theologie und Kirche*, vol. xv, pp. 222–226.   The bulk of this article may be read in English in the *Expository Times* for 1904 (vol. xv, pp. 536–539).   See further, J. de Ghellinck, *Le mouvement théologique au XIIᵉ Siècle* (1914) ; Manitius, *Geschichte der lateinischen Literatur des Mittelalters*, vol. iii (1931), pp. 136–144 ; and J. Leclercq, *Pierre le Vénérable* (1946), an excellent work.

30 : SS. SABINUS AND HIS COMPANIONS, MARTYRS   (A.D. 303 ?)

ACCORDING to the legend, Sabinus, claimed as a bishop by several Italian cities, and several of his clergy were arrested during the persecution under Diocletian ; Venustian, the governor of Etruria, had them before him and offered for the veneration of Sabinus a small statue of Jupiter.   The bishop threw it contemptuously to the ground and broke it, whereupon Venustian ordered the hands of Sabinus to be cut off.   His two deacons, Marcellus and Exsuperantius, also made a confession of faith, and were scourged and racked, under which torments they both died.   Sabinus was taken back to prison and the bodies of his two deacons were buried at Assisi.   A widow named Serena brought her blind son to Sabinus, who blessed him with his handless arms and the boy was healed. Whereupon a number of the bishop's fellow-prisoners asked for baptism.   This, it is said, led also to the conversion of the governor Venustian, who had an affliction of the eyes, and he with his wife and children gave their lives for Christ. St Sabinus was beaten to death at Spoleto, and buried a mile from that city. St Gregory the Great speaks of a chapel built in his honour near Fermo, for which he asks relics of the martyr from Chrysanthus, bishop of Spoleto. These martyrs are remembered today in the Roman Martyrology, which on December 11 names another ST SABINUS, bishop of Piacenza, during the fourth century. He was a man of so great learning and holiness that St Ambrose used to submit his writing to him for criticism and approval before publication.

The story told above depends upon a worthless *passio* which was fabricated in the fifth or sixth century. There is no evidence that Sabinus was bishop of Assisi or Spoleto or any other place. The *passio* was first published in the *Miscellanea* of Baluze-Mansi, vol. i, pp. 12–14. See further, Delehaye, *Origines du culte des martyrs*, p. 317, who does not dispute that there was, in fact, a martyr of this name who was buried a short distance from Spoleto, though we know nothing of his story. Consult also Lanzoni, *Le diocesi d'Italia*, vol. i, pp. 439–440 and 461–463 ; with G. Cristofani, *Storia di Assisi*, vol. iii, pp. 21–23.

ST ANYSIA, MARTYR   (A.D. 304 ?)

ANYSIA was a Christian girl whose parents had both died, leaving her wealth with which she generously befriended the needy. Whilst the governor Dulcitius carried on a cruel persecution at Thessalonica to deter the Christians from holding religious assemblies, she one day resolved to go to the meeting of the faithful. As she passed the gate of Cassandra, one of the guards happened to see her and stepping in front of her asked where she was going. Anysia started back and, fearing danger, made the sign of the cross on her forehead. The soldier seized hold of her and asked roughly, " Who are you, and where are you going ? " " I am a servant of Jesus Christ ", she replied, " and am going to the Lord's assembly." " I will prevent that ", he said, " and will take you to sacrifice to the gods. Today we worship the sun." As he spoke he tore off her veil to look at her face. Anysia tried to stop him, and struggled with the man, who became so angry that he drew his sword and ran her through the body. She fell in her tracks, and there died, and when peace came to the Church the Christians of Thessalonica built an oratory there. The *acta* say that the murderer acted on the strength of an (entirely mythical) edict of Galerius who, thinking the execution of Christians beneath his dignity, had given permission for them to be killed at sight.

The Greek *passio* of St Anysia, which lacks historical confirmation, was first printed by C. Triantafillis in a miscellany of Greek unpublished texts which he brought out at Venice in 1874. St Anysia was, however, commemorated in countries under Byzantine influence and a short notice of her is found in the Constantinople Synaxary (ed. Delehaye), cc. 355–357. A second text of the *passio* was published by J. Viteau in 1897, but it is very inadequately edited. See the *Byzantinische Zeitschrift*, vol. vii, pp. 480–483.

ST ANYSIUS, BISHOP OF THESSALONICA   (c. A.D. 410)

WHEN Ascholius, bishop of Thessalonica, died in the year 383 and Anysius was put in his place, St Ambrose wrote to the new bishop saying he had heard he was a zealous disciple of Ascholius and expressing the hope that he would prove " another Eliseus to his Elias ". Very few particulars are known of the life of St Anysius, but he is known in church history on account of the action of Pope St

Damasus in making him patriarchal vicar in Illyricum, which was later to become debated ground between Rome and Constantinople ; these powers were renewed and confirmed by St Siricius and St Innocent I.   St Anysius was a strong supporter of St John Chrysostom and went to Constantinople to uphold his cause against Theophilus of Alexandria ; in 404, together with fifteen other Macedonian bishops, he appealed to Pope Innocent to judge the cause on account of which Chrysostom had been exiled from his see, that they might abide by his decision.   Chrysostom wrote a letter thanking Anysius for his efforts.   It was during this saint's episcopate that there took place at Thessalonica the shocking massacre which has been referred to in the account of St Ambrose.   The virtues of St Anysius were highly praised both by St Innocent I and St Leo the Great.

There is no life of St Anysius and our knowledge of him is dependent upon scattered notices, which are discussed, for example, by Tillemont, *Mémoires*, vol. x, pp. 156–158. See also Duchesne, " L'Illyricum ecclésiastique " in the *Byzantinische Zeitschrift*, vol. i (1892), pp. 531–550 ; J. Zeiller, *Les origines chrétiennes dans les provinces danubiennes* i (1918), pp. 310–325 ; and L. Petit, " Les évêques de Thessalonique " in *Échos d'Orient*, vol. iv (1901), pp. 141 *seq.*

ST EGWIN, Bishop of Worcester   (A.D. 717)

EGWIN, said to have been a descendant of the Mercian kings, devoted himself to God in his youth, and succeeded to the episcopal see of Worcester about 692.   By his zeal and severity in reproving vice he incurred the hostility of some of his own flock, which gave him an opportunity of performing a penitential pilgrimage to Rome, to answer before the Holy See complaints that had been made against him. Some legends tell us that before setting out he put on his legs iron shackles, and threw the key into the Avon, but found it in the belly of a fish, some say at Rome, others on his passage from France to England.   After his return, with the assistance of Ethelred, King of Mercia, he founded the famous abbey of Evesham, under the invocation of the Blessed Virgin.   According to the story, a herdsman called Eof had a vision of our Lady, who was then seen by Egwin himself, and at the place of these visions the monastery was established (Evesham = Eof's hamm, or meadow).   Then, probably about 709, the bishop undertook a second journey to Rome, in the company of Kings Cenred of Mercia and Offa of the East Saxons, and we are told he received considerable privileges for his foundation from Pope Constantine ; after the disturbances of the tenth century, Evesham became one of the great Benedictine houses of medieval England. According to Florence of Worcester, St Egwin died on December 30, in 717, and was buried in the monastery of Evesham.   His feast is observed in the archidocese of Birmingham.

There is an eleventh-century life printed by Mabillon (saec. iii, pt 1, pp. 316–324), and see BHL. 2432–2439 ; for the life and miracles in the Gotha MS. I. 81, see *Analecta Bollandiana*, vol. lviii (1940), pp. 95–96 ; and *cf.* T. D. Hardy, *Descriptive Catalogue . . .*, vol. i, pp. 415–420 ; the Evesham Chronicle, ed. W. D. Macray in the Rolls Series (vol. xxix, 1863, Introduction) ; and R. M. Wilson, *Lost Literature of Medieval England* (1952), p. 104. See the *Acta Sanctorum*, January, vol. i ; Stubbs in DCB., vol. ii, pp. 62–63 ; and *St Egwin and his Abbey* . . . (1904), by the Stanbrook nuns. St Egwin's body was translated to a more honourable place in 1183, probably on January 11, on which day many English martyrologies mark his festival. See Stanton, *Menology*, pp. 615 *seq.* It is a very curious thing, as William of Malmesbury long ago pointed out, that Bede makes no mention of Egwin or of Evesham.

31 : ST SILVESTER I, POPE   (A.D. 335)

SILVESTER I, like his predecessor, St Miltiades, is better remembered for the events which took place during his pontificate than for anything we know about his personal life and acts. Living at a time of such importance it was inevitable that many legends should grow up around him, such as those incorporated in the *Vita beati Silvestri*, but they are without value as historical records. The *Liber Pontificalis* states that he was the son of a Roman named Rufinus. He succeeded Miltiades in 314, less than a year after the Edict of Milan had granted freedom to Christianity, and the most significant legends about him are those which bring him into relation with the Emperor Constantine. These represent Constantine as suffering from leprosy, which, upon his conversion to Christianity, was cured by baptism received at the hands of Silvester; whereupon, in gratitude and in recognition of the vicar of Christ on earth, the emperor granted numerous rights to the pope and his successors and endowed the Church with the provinces of Italy. This story of the " Donation of Constantine ", which was embroidered and used for political and ecclesiastical ends during the middle ages, has now long been recognized as a fabrication. But one point in it, the baptism of Constantine by St Silvester, still finds a place in the Roman Martyrology and Breviary.*

A few months after his accession St Silvester was represented at a synod convened at Arles to deal with the Donatist dispute : the bishops there commended the pope for not coming in person but instead remaining in the place " where the Apostles daily sit in judgement ". In June 325 there assembled at Nicaea in Bithynia the first oecumenical or general council of the Church : probably over 220 bishops attended, nearly all orientals, and Silvester of Rome sent legates, two priests : a Western bishop, Hosius of Cordova, presided. The council condemned the heresy of Arius, but this was only the beginning of a devastating struggle within the Church. There is no record that St Silvester formally confirmed the signature of his legates to the acts of the council.

It is probable that it was to Silvester rather than to Miltiades that Constantine gave the palace of the Lateran, and there the pope set up his *cathedra* and established the Lateran basilica as the cathedral church of Rome. During his pontificate the emperor (who in 330 removed his capital from Rome to Byzantium) built also the first churches of St Peter on the Vatican, Holy Cross in the Sessorian palace and St Laurence outside the Walls ; and the pope's name, joined with that of St Martin, is now given to the cardinalitial-titular church founded at this time near the Baths of Diocletian by a priest called Equitius. St Silvester also built a church at the cemetery of Priscilla on the Salarian way : there he was himself buried in 335 ; but in 761 his relics were translated by Pope Paul I to St Silvester *in Capite*, now the national church of English Catholics in Rome. His feast has been general in the Western church since the thirteenth century, on December 31, and it is also observed in the East (January 2), the first pope of Rome after the Church emerged from the catacombs.

In an article entitled " Konstantinische Schenkung und Silvester-Legende " contributed to the *Miscellanea Francesco Ehrle*, vol. ii (1924), pp. 159–247—the thirty-eighth issue of

* In fact the first Christian emperor remained a catechumen till he lay on his death-bed, and then, eighteen months after the death of St Silvester, was baptized by an Arian bishop at Nicomedia.

the series *Studi e Testi*—W. Levison, whose critical competence will be disputed by none, has published a most valuable study of the famous " Donation of Constantine ". Of this spurious document a good account is given by J. P. Kirsch in the *Catholic Encyclopedia* (vol. v, pp. 118-121), but Levison has arrived at a much clearer determination of the various elements which contributed to the fabrication of the forgery in the more developed form. Earliest in date seems to be a story of St Silvester invented for the edification of pious readers in the second half of the fifth century. It includes, for example, an account of a theological discussion between St Silvester and twelve Jewish doctors. There are signs that the *Liber Pontificalis* (see Duchesne's edition, vol. i, pp. cxxxv and 170-201) has borrowed from this in speaking of the " Constitutum Silvestri ". But there was also another redaction of this legend which transposes the incident of the dragon and modifies some other details. In the ninth century we find texts in which these elements were fused together and supplemented. Moreover, as early as the sixth century, Greek versions of the story began to appear (see BHG., nn. 1628-1632). One text of this Greek rendering has been preserved to us in as many as forty existing copies. Levison, however, firmly rejects the theory of A. Gaudenzi that the Greek text of the Donation of Constantine is the source from which the Latin was copied. There were also translations of the " acts " of St Silvester in Syriac and Armenian, and a metrical homily attributed to James of Sarug. In some of these oriental versions St Silvester is represented as accompanying St Helen to Palestine and as having taken part in the discovery of the True Cross. A good idea of the important place occupied by St Silvester in later medieval thought may be obtained from the *Speculum Ecclesiae* of Giraldus Cambrensis and from the *Polychronicon* of Ralph Higden, vol. v. *Cf.* also Döllinger, *Papstfabeln*, pp. 61 *seq.* and Donato, *Un papa legendario* (1908). For the history of the pontificate see E. Caspar, *Geschichte des Papsttums*, vol. i, pp. 115 *seq.*, and Poisnel, " Un concile apocryphe du Pape St Silvestre " in *Mélanges d'archéol. et d'histoire*, 1886, pp. 3-13. For a supplementary note to Levison's article see *Zeitschrift der Savigny . . .*, vol. xlvi (1926), pp. 501-511. *Cf.* N. H. Baynes, *Constantine the Great and the Christian Church* (1929).

ST COLUMBA OF SENS, Virgin and Martyr (Date Unknown)

THIS Columba is traditionally regarded as a native of Spain who, when she was sixteen, came into Gaul, with other Spaniards who were subsequently martyred, and settled at Sens. She is supposed to have been of noble but pagan parents, and, having left them secretly to avoid the worship of false gods, to have been baptized at Vienne. When Aurelian came to Sens he ordered St Columba and her companions to be put to death. Her *passio* tells an extravagant tale of her being defended, first from dishonour and then from the hands of her gaolers, by one of the bears belonging to the amphitheatre. She was beheaded at the fountain of Azon on the road to Meaux, and buried by a man who had recovered his sight upon invoking her.

The *cultus* of St Columba spread over France and Spain, and to Italy, and her feast is still kept in certain dioceses. But an attempt to revive popular devotion towards her in France in the middle of last century was not very successful. The abbey of Sainte-Colombe, which sheltered her relics, was the chief religious house of Sens ; its third church was consecrated by Pope Alexander III in 1164. In the next year St Thomas Becket arrived at the monastery, when he fled from England to appeal to the pope and had had to leave Pontigny, and made it his headquarters till he returned home to martyrdom.

This *passio*, though preserved in varying forms in a good many manuscripts, is historically worthless. It has been printed by Mombritius, and by the Bollandists in their *Catalogus hagiographicus Bruxellensis*, vol. i, pp. 302-306. See further Tillemont, *Mémoires*, vol. iv, p. 347 ; and especially G. Chastel, *Ste Colombe de Sens* (1939), containing a new text of the *passio* and important particulars of the *cultus*.

ST MELANIA THE YOUNGER, WIDOW   (A.D. 439)

MELANIA the Elder was a patrician lady of the *gens Antonia*, who was married to Valerius Maximus, who probably was prefect of Rome in the year 362. At twenty-two she was left a widow and, having put her son, Publicola, in the hands of guardians, she went into Palestine and built a monastery at Jerusalem for fifty maidens. There she settled down herself, living a life of austerity, prayer and good works. Her son meanwhile grew up in Rome, became a senator, and married Albina, the Christian daughter of the pagan priest Albinus. Their daughter was St Melania the Younger, who was brought up a Christian in the luxurious household of her religious but ambitious father.

In order to ensure a male heir to his great wealth and family reputation Publicola affianced his daughter to her kinsman Valerius Pinianus, a son of the prefect Valerius Severus. Melania, however, wished to devote herself entirely to God in a state of maidenhood. But her parents would have none of it and in 397, her fourteenth year, she was married to Pinian, who was then seventeen. It is not surprising that, having been forced into marriage against her will, and deeply shocked by the sensual licence that she saw all around her, Melania asked her husband that they should live together in continence. But Pinian would not, and in due course their first child, a girl, was born. She died in infancy. Melania's inclinations were known to be as strong as ever, and her father took steps to prevent her associating with those religious people who would encourage her discontent with the life which he wished her to lead. On the vigil of the feast of St Laurence in the year 399, her father having forbidden her to watch in the basilica because she was again with child, she spent the whole night on her knees in prayer in her own room. In the morning she assisted at the Holy Mysteries in the church of St Laurence, and on her return home was prematurely brought to bed and, with difficulty and danger, gave birth to a boy. He died the next day. Melania lay between life and death, and Pinian, who was sincerely and devotedly attached to her, swore that if she were spared she should be free to serve God as she wished. Melania recovered and Pinian kept his vow, but Publicola bitterly disapproved and for another five years made her conform exteriorly to the life of her status in every respect. Then he was overtaken by mortal sickness, and as he lay dying he both confirmed to his daughter all his estates and begged her forgiveness because, " fearing the ridicule of evil tongues, I have grieved you by opposing your heavenly vocation ".

Her mother Albina and Pinian became more than reconciled to Melania's new way of life ; they adopted it themselves, and all three left Rome for a villa in the country. Pinian was only gradually won over, and long insisted on wearing the rich dress affected by those of his rank. The biographer gives a touching and convincing account of how his wife persuaded him to lay aside the more for the less expensive clothes, and finally to be content with plain garments made by herself. They took with them many slaves and set an example by their treatment of them, and soon many young girls, widows and over thirty families had joined them. The villa became a centre of hospitality, of charity and of religious life. But St Melania was fabulously wealthy—estates belonging to the Valerii were to be found all over the empire—and she was oppressed by all these possessions ; she knew that the superfluity of the rich belongs to their hungry and naked neighbours, that, as St Ambrose says, the rich man who gives to the poor does not bestow an alms but pays a debt. She therefore asked, and received, the consent of Pinian to the sale of some of her properties for the benefit of the needy.   At once their relatives, who thought them mad, prepared to profit by this latest lunacy.   Severus, the brother of Pinian, for example, bribed the tenants and slaves on his brother's lands to promise that if they were sold they would refuse to recognize any master but himself.   Such difficulties were made that recourse was had to the emperor, Honorius.   St Melania, dressed in plain woollen clothes and veiled, presented herself before Serena, the emperor's mother-in-law, and so impressed her by her bearing and words that she persuaded Honorius to take the equitable sale of the estates under the protection of the state.   The proceeds were as far-flung as the lands themselves : the poor, the sick, captives, bankrupts, pilgrims, churches, monasteries were relieved and endowed in large numbers all over the empire, and in two years Melania gave their freedom to eight thousand slaves.   Palladius, in his contemporary *Lausiac History*, says that the monasteries of Egypt, Syria and Palestine received benefactions from her, and gives a detailed account of her manner of life.

In 406 she, with Pinian and others, was staying with St Paulinus at Nola in Campania.   He would have liked to have had her and her husband as " perpetual guests " : he called her the " blessed little one " and the " joy of Heaven " ; but they returned to the villa near Rome, only to have to flee within a few months before the oncoming invasion of the Goths.   They took refuge in a villa which St Melania had retained at Messina, where they had with them the aged Rufinus.   But inside of two years the Goths had reached Calabria and burned Reggio, and they determined to go to Carthage.   They purposed first to visit St Paulinus in sympathy with his sufferings under the invasion, but they were driven by a storm to shelter at an island, probably Lipari, which was being held to ransom by pirates.   To save the people from catastrophe St Melania bought off the freebooters with a huge sum in gold.   They eventually took up their residence at Tagaste in Numidia.   Pinian made as profound an impression as his wife, and when he visited St Augustine at Hippo (he called them " real lights of the Church ") a riot occurred in a church because the people wanted him to be ordained priest to minister to them and they thought he was being held back by the bishop of Tagaste, St Alipius.   Order was only restored by the promise of Pinian that, were he ever ordained, he would exercise his ministry at Hippo.   While in Africa St Melania established and endowed two new monasteries, one for men and one for women from among those who had been slaves on her land there.   She herself lived with the women, but would not let them try to emulate her own standard of austerity, for she took food only every other day.   Her personal work was the transcription of books, in both Greek and Latin, and five hundred years later manuscripts were still in circulation that were attributed to her hand.

In the year 417, accompanied by her mother and her husband, Melania left Africa for Jerusalem, and lodged in the pilgrims' hospice near the Holy Sepulchre.   From thence she made an expedition with Pinian to visit the monks of the Egyptian deserts, and on her return, fortified by the example of these athletes, she settled at Jerusalem to a life of solitude and contemplation.   Here she met her cousin, Paula, niece of St Eustochium, and was by her introduced to the society of the marvellous group presided over by St Jerome at Bethlehem, whose fast friend she became.   When they first met, Melania, we are told, " went to meet him in her usual recollected and respectful way, and kneeled down at his feet humbly asking his blessing ".   After fourteen years in Palestine Albina died, and in the next year Pinian followed her to the grave : he is named with Melania in the Roman Martyrology. She buried them side by side on the Mount of Olives, and built for herself a cell close by the tombs of her faithful companions. This was the nucleus of a large convent of consecrated virgins, over whom St Melania presided. She was very solicitous for the health of her charges (a bath was provided, for which an ex-prefect of the imperial palace paid) and her rule was remarkable for its mildness at a time when early monasticism sometimes seemed to degenerate into the pursuit of corporal austerity for its own sake. Four years after the death of her husband St Melania heard that her maternal uncle, Volusian, who was still a pagan, had come on an embassy to Constantinople. Several efforts had been made to convert him, and she determined now to try herself to move him in his old age. She therefore set out with her chaplain (and biographer), Gerontius, and after a hard winter journey reached Constantinople in time to forward and witness the conversion of Volusian, who died in her arms the day after receiving baptism. Before he had made up his mind, the enthusiasm of Melania was going to carry the matter to the Emperor Theodosius. We are told that Volusian appealed to her piety and good feeling not to do so : " Do not force the free will which God has given to me. I am ready and anxious to have the stains of my many sins washed away ; but were I to do it at the emperor's order I should be as one constrained and have no merit of voluntary choice."

On Christmas eve, 439, St Melania went to Bethlehem, and after the Mass at dawn told Paula that death was at hand. On St Stephen's day she assisted at Mass in his basilica and then with her sisters read the account of his martyrdom from the Bible. At the end they wished her good health and " many happy returns of the day ". She answered, " Good health to you also. But you will never again hear me read the lessons." Then she made a visit of farewell to the monks, and on her return was seen to be seriously ill. She summoned her sisters and asked their prayers, " for I am going to the Lord ", and saying that if she had sometimes spoken severely it was for love of them : reminding them of her words : " The Lord knows that I am unworthy, and I would not dare compare myself with any good woman, even of those living in the world. Yet I think the Enemy himself will not at the Last Judgement accuse me of ever having gone to sleep with bitterness in my heart." Early on Sunday, December 31, Gerontius celebrated Mass and his voice was so choked with tears that St Melania sent him a message that she could not hear the words. All day long visitors came, until she said, " Now let me rest ". At the ninth hour she grew weaker, and in the evening, repeating the words of Job, " As the Lord willed, so it is done ", she died. She was fifty-six years old.

St Melania has been venerated liturgically from early times in the Byzantine church, but, beyond the insertion of her name in the Roman Martyrology, she has had no *cultus* in the West until our own day. Cardinal Mariano Rampolla published a monumental work on St Melania in 1905. This attracted much attention, and a certain *cultus* ensued. In 1908 Pope Pius X approved the annual observance of her feast by the Italian congregation of clerks regular called the Somaschi, and it has also been adopted by the Latin Catholics of Constantinople and Jerusalem.

Considerable fragments of a Latin life of St Melania had long been known to exist in various libraries, and these were printed in the *Analecta Bollandiana*, vol. viii (1889), pp. 16–63. The Greek text was edited from a manuscript in the Barberini library by Delehaye in the same *Analecta*, vol. xxii (1903), pp. 5–50. In 1905 Cardinal Rampolla, who had discovered a complete copy of the Latin in the Escorial, printed both Latin and Greek in a sumptuous folio volume, *Santa Melania Giuniore Senatrice Romana*, with a long introduction, dissertations and notes. Considerable difference of opinion existed regarding the relations of the Greek and Latin versions, which are far from being concordant in either content or phrasing. In a long contribution to the *Analecta Bollandiana*, vol. xxv (1906), pp. 401–450, Fr Adhémar d'Alès examined their variations in detail, arriving at the conclusion that the life had been compiled by her disciple Gerontius about nine years after her death in a first draft written in Greek, but that the texts in Greek and Latin which we now possess were elaborated independently a few years afterwards from this original. Some centuries later the Metaphrast produced his own sophisticated version of the biography. This has long been in print in Migne, PG., vol. cxvi, pp. 753–794. An admirable résumé of Melania's history was published by G. Goyau in the series " Les Saints " (1908), and in English there is an adaptation of the biographical sketch which Cardinal Rampolla prefixed to his book (1908). See also Leclercq in DAC., vol. xi, cc. 209–230.

BD ISRAEL (A.D. 1014)

THIS holy Augustinian is venerated as a saint by the canons regular of the Lateran and in the diocese of Limoges, but little is recorded of him except vague and edifying generalities : " he gave a good example to all and was assiduous at the Divine Office, careful in attending to the wants of the sick, most careful in celebrating the Holy Mysteries according to the Church's rites. . . ." He became a canon regular at Dorat in the Limousin, and was promoted to the office of precentor, from which he was taken to be official to Aldoin, bishop of Limoges, whom he accompanied to the French court. At the request of the canons he was sent by Pope Silvester II to be provost of the monastery of St Junian, in Haute-Vienne, and he restored this community both temporally and spiritually : destroying factions, reforming observance, and rebuilding their church. Bd Israel then returned to Dorat, where he had the formation of St Walter, afterwards abbot of L'Esterp, and took up again the duties of precentor. He died there on December 31, 1014, and his tomb was made famous by miracles.

A medieval Latin life was printed in 1657 by P. Labbe in his *Nova Bibliotheca manuscriptorum librorum*, vol. ii, pp. 566–567. As he is the presumed author of a poem on our Lord Jesus Christ, a short notice of Bd Israel is also given in the *Histoire littéraire de France*, vol. vii, pp. 229–230.

THE saints and just, from the beginning of time and throughout the world, who have been made perfect, everlasting monuments of God's infinite power and clemency, praise His goodness without ceasing ; casting their crowns before His throne they give to Him all the glory of their triumphs : " His gifts alone in us He crowns." We are called upon with the whole Church militant on earth to join in praising and thanking God for the grace and glory he has bestowed on his saints. At the same time we earnestly implore Him to exert His almighty power and mercy in raising us from our miseries and sins, healing the disorders of our souls and leading us by the path of repentance to the company of His saints, to which He has called us. They were once what we are now, travellers on earth : they had the same weaknesses which we have. We have difficulties to encounter : so had the saints, and many of them far greater than we can meet with ; obstacles from kings and whole nations, sometimes from the prisons, racks and swords of persecutors. Yet they surmounted these difficulties, which they made the very means of their virtue and victories. It was by the strength they received from above, not by their own, that they triumphed. But the blood of Christ was shed for us as it was for them and the grace of our Redeemer is not wanting to us ; if we fail, the failure is in ourselves. The saints are a " cloud of witnesses over our head ", showing us that a life of Christian perfection is not impossible.

APPENDIX I

A MEMOIR OF ALBAN BUTLER

By Herbert Thurston, s.j.

THE completion of this revision of *Butler's Lives of the Saints* seems to provide a suitable occasion for saying a few words about Alban Butler himself. One feels that, even at the distance of nearly two centuries, an apology is due to that venerable scholar for the scant respect with which his great work may seem to have been treated. I must frankly admit that in this new edition little, comparatively speaking, has been retained of the eighteenth-century original. Mr Attwater, in that portion of the undertaking for which he is responsible, has shown rather more deference to the primitive text than is paid in the first six volumes, but I doubt if anywhere in the series half a dozen consecutive sentences of Butler have been retained without alteration. Readers who may compare, for example, the new November entries with the old, will observe that whereas in the latter the notice of St Charles Borromeo occupied fifty pages, only twelve pages are now * devoted to this model of pastors. All this compression is, no doubt, regrettable, but when room has to be found for almost twice the number of entries space must inevitably be economized. Moreover, in the case of such well-known saints as St Charles Borromeo, St Francis of Assisi, St Antony of Padua, St Teresa, etc., a C.T.S. pamphlet can always be purchased for a few pence which will provide more copious detail than can reasonably be looked for in any encyclopedia or general collection of biographies. And Butler's style, it must be confessed, as judged by modern standards, is deplorably stilted and verbose. Indeed, in not a few of his biographical notices and pious moralizings he seems to be deliberately spinning out the slenderest thread of fact or of thought in order to make it cover as many pages as possible.

But Alban Butler as a man, a priest and a scholar, leaves, to my thinking, a far more favourable impression than in his character of a writer of English. Though it may seem to be beginning at the wrong end, I am tempted to quote a passage from a letter of an English lady, Mrs Paston, then resident at St Omer's, written on May 23, 1773, eight days after his death.† The original, still preserved, bears the address :

> A Madame
> Madame Mère Supérieure très
> digne des Dames Chanoinesses
> Anglaises Rue des Carmes
> à Bruges.

* [That is, in the first revised edition.—D. A.]

† I am greatly indebted to the Reverend Mother Prioress of the Canonesses Regular of the Lateran, still occupying the same convent at Bruges, for the communication of this letter and of other documents. Charles Butler, in his Memoir of his uncle, says : " Those who remember him during his residence at St Omer's, will recollect his singular respect for Mrs More, the Superior of the English convent of Austins at Bruges."

There is little punctuation in the document and the spelling and phrasing would even then, I fancy, have been open to criticism. But it would spoil the eighteenth-century flavour of this feminine epistle if I tampered with either. I reproduce the relevant portion exactly as it stands in the accurate copy sent to me :

> I have met with a severe trial which has greatly desordered me by the Death of that great and good Man Dear Mr. Butler he died like a Saint and when his speech failed him ye tears of Devotion streamed down his face with his Eyes Lifted up to Heaven he quited this miserable World, it seems as if he foresaw his Death as he settled all his temporall affairs so short a time before his illness ; he desired to be buired in a Church yard ye nearest any English house where his Death might happen but ye Heads of ye Church here would not consent to that. Ye service and high Mass was first performed at ye Collidge Church after which he was caried to ye Parish Church ye service again performed and his Body brought Back in ye most solemn manner and buired close to his confessional, I was so happy [*sic*] not to be present, such a melancholy sight was never seen here ; their was hundreds of people as at ye Great Procession, and ye tears shed by men and women of all ranks was never seen before. Many I believe was not sensible how much they esteemd him till he was no more. I pitty ye poor Gentlemen of ye Collidge who are quite sensible of their Loss and greatly afflicted.

Mrs Paston was evidently on intimate terms with Alban Butler, then president of the College of St Omer's. Her daughter Harriet, probably under his direction, had shortly before entered the convent at Bruges, and the mother adds in a postscript to her letter :

> Our kind respects waits on Mr. Berington* and all ye good Community please Madam to assure Harriet of all thats kind and tender from us. I received her Letter which I shall not answer till I have ye pleasure of hearing from her how she settles in her new state of life, Mr. James Butler [Alban's brother] told me it ought to be a great satisfaction ; that he saw good Mr. Butler shed tears of tenderness for Harriet after she left his room ; which was a great mark of his friendship for her. Many thanks Dear Madam for yr goodness to my Son, who we expect soon.

At the back of another fold of the letter is written :

> Poor Mr. Butler's picture was drawn after his death ; I have not yet seen it they say it is not so good a likeness as might have been expected as he looked much better after he was dead, I have procured a few locks of his venerable grey hairs which I shall keep with true veneration.†

---

* Mr Thomas Berington was then the convent chaplain and confessor. See the sympathetic references to him in C. S. Durrant, *Flemish Mystics and English Martyrs*, pp. 353–356.

† There can be little doubt that Mrs Paston belonged to the Norfolk Pastons and was a near connection of the Bedingfields of Oxburgh, who were so closely associated with the English nuns at Bruges. It would not, therefore, be extravagant to regard the letter just quoted as a sort of tardy supplement to the famous Paston correspondence of three centuries earlier. This, as is well known, is the most important collection of English letters which has come down to us from the middle ages, throwing as it does a remarkable light upon the religious and social life of the fifteenth century.

Curiously enough, it seems to be stated in the *Laity's Directory* for 1774 that Alban Butler was buried in the chapel of the English Augustinian nuns (*i.e.* the Canonesses of the Lateran) at Bruges ;* but this must certainly be a mistake. It was no doubt caused by the memorial tablet, which, as is duly recorded in the convent " Annals ", was put up outside their chapel at the request of Butler himself, who left them six guineas in his will. The inscription runs as follows :

D. O. M.

O GOD, FATHER OF ALL,
MAY THY NAME BE SANCTIFIED,
BY ALL,
IN ALL THINGS,
ETERNALLY.
MAY THY MOST PERFECT WILL
BE ACCOMPLISHED
BY ALL BEINGS UNIVERSALLY :
AND MAY THE SOULS OF YE FAITHFULL
REST IN PEACE.
AMEN

R.A.D.D. ALBANUS BUTLER
COLLEGII ANGLO-AUDOMAROPOLIT.
PRÆSES PIISSIMUS AC DOCTISSIM :
HUJUS CONVENTUS
AMICUS ET BENEFACTOR,
PONERE JUSSIT.
OBIIT
DIE XV MAII 1773.
R. I. P.

A man who, as these extracts show, was himself capable of so much feeling and of inspiring it in others, is not likely to have been a dried-up pedant or an uncompromisingly stern ascetic. And indeed, whenever we are able to learn anything of the impression made by Alban Butler upon those who were in personal contact with him, we find a note of kindliness, tolerance and understanding which belies the rather grim severity of the reflections scattered throughout the " Lives ". A few extracts illustrating this side of his character will be quoted later on, but we may turn now to the recognized data of his career so far as they are made known to us in published documents.

Alban Butler, the famous hagiographer, was born on October 24, 1710, at Appletree in Northamptonshire. His family had at one time possessed considerable landed property and they seem to have been for the most part faithful to the old religion. A century earlier there had been another Alban Butler at Aston-le-Walls, which is the next parish to Appletree, and this ancestor, who owned a large estate, undoubtedly professed Catholicism even in the days of James I and his son. But Simon, the grandfather of our Alban, seems to have been an unsatisfactory character. He turned Protestant and is said to have squandered the family fortunes in riotous living. Alban's father, however, was a devout Catholic, though, since we are told that he died in 1712, he can have exercised no personal influence upon the religious training of his children. The mother may have lived somewhat

---

* See the Publications of the Catholic Record Society, vol. xii, *Obituaries* (1913), p. 17 ; but as the statement is in square brackets this may be an addition by the editor.

longer, but it is clear from a farewell letter of hers which has been preserved that she was taken from her family while they were still quite young.　Charles Butler in his Memoir of his uncle has printed this letter which certainly shows Alban's mother to have been a model Christian, of that " Garden of the Soul " type which those days of persecution brought forth in wondrous plenty.　She writes :

> MY DEAR CHILDREN,
>
> Since it pleases Almighty God to take me out of this world, as no doubt wisely forseeing I am no longer a useful parent to you (for no person ought to be thought necessary in this world, when God thinks proper to take them out), so, I hope, you will offer the loss of me with a resignation suitable to the religion you are of, and offer yourselves.　He who makes you orphans so young, without a parent to take care of you, will take you into His protection and fatherly care if you do live and serve Him who is the author of all goodness. Above all things prepare yourselves, whilst you are young, to suffer patiently what afflictions He shall think proper to lay upon you, for it is by this He trieth His best servants.　In the first place give Him thanks for your education in the true faith (which many thousands want), and then I beg of you earnestly to petition His direction what state of life you shall undertake, whether it be for religion or to get your livings in the world.　No doubt but you may be saved either way, if you do your duty to God, your neighbour and yourselves. And I beg of you to make constant resolutions rather to die a thousand times, if possible, than quit your faith ; and always have in your thought what you would think of were you as near death as I now think myself.　There is no preparation for a good death but a good life.　Do not omit your prayers, and to make an act of contrition and examen of conscience every night, and frequent the blessed sacraments of the Church.　I am so weak I can say no more to you, but I pray God bless and direct you and your friends to take care of you. Lastly I beg of you never to forget to pray for your poor father and mother when they are not capable of helping themselves.　So I take leave of you, hoping to meet you in heaven to be happy for all eternity.　Your affectionate mother.
>
> ANN BUTLER *

So little of this world's goods had been left to Ann and her husband that the education of the children had to be provided for by friends.　Alban, according to his nephew's Memoir, " was sent to a school in Lancashire at a very early age ". Assuming that this statement is correct, it is quite likely that the school in question was one kept by Dame Alice Harrison at Fernyhalgh, not far from Preston, and the late Mr Joseph Gillow tells us that he had seen a long narrow oak table which was used in Dame Alice's school.　" It was covered ", he says, " with initials cut by the boys, amongst whom were many who subsequently became distinguished ecclesiastics, such as Alban Butler, the writer of the *Lives of the Saints*."† The occurrence of the initials A. B. can hardly of itself be regarded as conclusive evidence,

---

* Her maiden name was Birch ; she was the daughter of Henry Birch, Esq., of Gorscott, Staffordshire.

† See the Publications of the Catholic Record Society, vol. xxiii (*Lancashire Registers, IV*, 1922), p. 130.

and one cannot but suspect that there is some looseness of statement in Charles Butler's references to these early days. On the one hand he appeals to the testimony of a school-fellow of Alban's in the following terms : " A gentleman, lately deceased, mentioned to the editor that he remembered him at this [Lancashire] school, and frequently heard him repeat to a numerous and wondering audience of little boys, the history of the chiefs and saints of the Saxon era of our history, with a surprising minuteness of fact and precision of chronology." On the other hand, Charles Butler in the very next sentence communicates this further information : " About the age of eight (!) years, he was sent to the English college at Douay. It appears from the diary of that college that Mr Holman of Warkworth (whose memory, for his extensive charities, is still in benediction in Oxfordshire and Northamptonshire), became security for the expenses of his education. About this time he lost his father and mother." Now it is quite certain from a series of entries in the Seventh Douay Diary,* that Alban Butler and his brother James first came to Douay on June 14, 1724, and that in the October of the same year Alban was placed in the class of " Grammar ", while James was assigned to " Rudiments ". Alban was then fourteen, not eight, years of age. It is possible, therefore, that the future hagiographer was at school in Lancashire until he was more than thirteen, and this renders the story of the little ones sitting entranced while Alban told them stories of the Anglo-Saxon saints a little less improbable.

In the Douay Diary the steps of Alban Butler's career, first as pupil and then as master, can be traced from year to year. On Easter Sunday, 1734, during his fourth year of theology, he was ordained priest. Subsequently the office was assigned him, first of professor of philosophy, and afterwards of theology. He was also at this period engaged in copying manuscripts connected with the lives and sufferings of the English martyrs for the use of Bishop Challoner, who was then preparing his book, *Memoirs of Missionary Priests*. Butler's transcripts, which include twenty-seven separate pieces written in his own hand, are now at Oscott College. In August 1745 it is recorded in the Douay Diary that John and James Talbot, the brothers of the Earl of Shrewsbury, in company with Butler, went to Dunkirk on a holiday excursion, and the tour seems to have extended even to Italy. Both the two brothers Talbot afterwards became vicars apostolic in England. In 1749 Alban Butler returned to labour in his own country, but his hope of being able to work in London at his great book on the lives of the saints was to some extent shattered by the claim of the vicar apostolic of the Midland district to retain his services for Staffordshire. Later he became chaplain to the Duke of Norfolk and tutor to his nephew and heir, whom he accompanied on tours. Nevertheless, helped by a period of residence in Paris, Butler was able to bring the earlier months of his *Lives of the Saints* to completion before 1756, in which year the first volume was issued. It is commonly stated that at Bishop Challoner's suggestion the footnotes prepared for the work were omitted on account of the cost. This however, is only partially true. Some of the quite disproportionately long notes which appear in the posthumous library edition are not to be found in the book as it was originally printed in 1756–59, but it would be a great mistake to suppose that the first issue is devoid of reasonable annotation. In 1766 he was appointed president of the English College of St Omer which had formerly belonged to the

---

* See the Publications of the Catholic Record Society, vol. xxviii, pp. 117, 121, etc. In this volume the Seventh Douay Diary is printed in full.

Jesuits now expelled from France, and this office he still retained at the time of his death in 1773 *.

From these facts it will be realized that Alban Butler was above all a scholar, not primarily a man of great missionary activities.   At the same time he was always ready to give spiritual help to any who appealed to him, and throughout his life he was most conscientious in the discharge of every religious duty.   Sundry letters quoted in his nephew's published Memoir emphasize these characteristics.   One of these writers, who was with Alban for eight years at Douay College (*i.e.* from October 1741 to October 1749), says for example :

> He opened the college door to me when I came as a boy to Douay and the first sight of him appeared to me then so meek and so amiable that I thought I would choose him for my ghostly Father. . . . As to heroic acts of virtue which strike with admiration all that see or hear of them I cannot recollect more than an uniform constant observance of all the duties of a priest, professor and confessor.   He was always at morning meditations, seldom omitted the celebration of the Holy Sacrifice of the Mass, which he said with a heavenly composure, sweetness and recollection, studying and teaching assiduously, dictating with an unwearied patience so equally and leisurely that everyone could, if he wished to do it, write his dictates in a clear and legible hand ; nor do I remember that he ever sent a substitute to dictate for him, so exact and punctual he was in his duty as a professor.   I never knew one more ready to go to the confession seat, at the first intimation of any, even the least or youngest boy.   He heard his penitents with wonderful meekness, and his penetration, learning, judgement and piety were such as to move them to place in him a singular confidence.

The same writer stresses the zeal with which he lent spiritual and temporal aid to the needs of the Irish soldiers fighting on the French side, and to " the English, wounded and maimed, who were brought prisoners to Douay in 1745 and quartered in barracks, in great numbers, after the battle of Fontenoy ", and he goes on " he also procured for them temporal succour and relief, so beneficently, that the Duke of Cumberland, then *Generalissimo* of the British and allied armies, being informed of it, promised him special protection, whenever he came over into England ".†

Another enthusiastic admirer, this time a Frenchman, the Abbé de la Sêpouze, who was his colleague as vicar general at the time that Alban Butler, in the last years of his life, was president of St Omer's College, speaks of him with not less affection and reverence, and in particular lays stress upon the keenness of his pursuit of learning even to the end of his days.   He writes, for example :

> Every instant that Mr Butler did not dedicate to the government of his College he employed in study ; and, when obliged to go abroad, he would

---

* [When in 1755 there was question of choosing a coadjutor to Bishop York as vicar apostolic of the Western district, Bishop Challoner wrote to Bishop Stonor that Bishop Petre " is more inclined to name Alban Butler (whom he thinks the gentry of that part of the world will be more taken with) than Mr Walton " (quoted by Dom Basil Hemphill in *The Early Vicars Apostolic of England*, 1954, p. 145)].

† Charles Butler, *An Account of the Life and Writings of the Rev. Alban Butler*, pp. 12–14 (1799).

read as he walked along the streets.   I have met him with a book under each arm, and a third in his hands, and have been told that, travelling one day on horseback, he fell a-reading, giving his horse full liberty.   The creature used it to eat a few ears of corn that grew on the roadside.   The owner came in haste, swearing he would be indemnified.   Mr. Butler, who knew nothing of the damage done, no sooner perceived it, than blushing he said to the country-man with his usual mildness that his demand was just; he then draws out a Louis-d'or and gives it to the fellow, who would have been very well satisfied with a few pence, makes repeated apologies to him, easily obtains forgiveness and goes his way.*

Lest it be thought that these favourable appreciations were prompted only by a clannishness which bound together the numerically insignificant band of devotees of the ancient faith, the victims of the drastic penal laws which were still in force, it may be interesting to borrow from the diary of an Anglican clergyman, an antiquary of recognized learning who counted Horace Walpole and the poet Gray with many other distinguished men among his intimate friends.   This was the Rev. William Cole, rector of Bletchley and later vicar of Burnham, Buckingham-shire, to whom a rather lengthy notice is devoted in the *Dictionary of National Biography*.   He is himself the charmingly gossiping writer of a diary which has in great part been published with introductions by Miss Helen Waddell.†   Mr Cole came to make Alban Butler's acquaintance in circumstances which we may leave him to describe later, but meanwhile, an amusing incident, recorded in another of Mr Cole's voluminous manuscripts, may serve to give an idea of the diarist's very friendly attitude towards Catholics.   He had chanced to mention the *Lives of the Saints* which he had purchased, and he then goes on :

> There happened an odd affair relating to the author of this book the Rev. Mr Alban Butler, a secular priest of Doway and chaplain to his Grace the Duke of Norfolk.   I was told it at the time when it happened by his and my friend the Rev. Charles Bedingfield, Recollect and friar of the Franciscan Convent of Doway, of the Suffolk family of that name‡ . . . for the friar was bred a Protestant but was afterwards converted pretty early in life.   He now lives as chaplain to the family of Mrs. Markham, at Somerby Hall, near Grantham in Lincolnshire.   Having received two letters from him since I returned from Paris, I write this Feb. 1, 1766.
>
> This gentleman Mr Alban Butler, going upon a mission to Norwich, had directed his portmanteau by the carrier to be left at the Palace for him in that city.   It seems the Duke of Norfolk's house is called ' the Palace '.   As he was utterly unknown at Norwich, and as there was a Doctor Butler at that time as a visitor with Bishop Hayter, the portmanteau was carried by

* Charles Butler, *An Account of the Life and Writings of the Rev. Alban Butler*, p. 110 (1799).

† *A Journal of my Journey to Paris in* 1765, by William Cole, M.A., F.S.A., edited by F. G. Stokes (1931).   *The Bletcheley Diary of Mr William Cole*, edited by F. G. Stokes (1931).

‡ Mr Cole explains in a parenthesis that " Father Charles Bedingfield was not of the Baronet's family, but of a Protestant family related to it, the head of which I well remember, a fellow-commoner of St John's College, Cambridge ".   All this is in MS. Addit. 5826 (fol. 15vo) in the British Museum.

mistake to the Bishop's Palace, and was opened by Dr Butler, who finding therein a hair-shirt, disciplines, indulgences, missals, etc., the mistake was soon found out, and as soon communicated to the Bishop, who began to make a stir about it.   But by the mediation of the Duke of Norfolk, the affair was hushed up, and Mr Butler had his box or portmanteau restored to him.

It must be remembered that at this date not one of the penal laws against Catholics had yet been repealed.   It was still open to the common informer to denounce any priest for saying Mass, and so when we read that Bishop Hayter " began to make a stir about it ", any action on his part might easily have involved good Mr Butler in consequences even more serious than mere expense and un-pleasantness.   A certain William Payne, known as " the Protestant carpenter ", was as active in those days in conducting a campaign against all that savoured of Popery as the Kensits have been in our own times.   The judges, for the most part, were reluctant to convict, and when, on June 25, 1768, the Rev. Mr Webb was tried in the King's Bench, Lord Mansfield, who presided, pointed out in delivering judgement that " all the twelve judges had been consulted on the point, and that they had all agreed in opinion that the statutes were so worded that, in order to convict a man upon them, it was necessary that he should be first proved to be a priest, and secondly that it should be proved that he had said Mass ".*   But even after this ruling the " Protestant carpenter " did not desist, and as late as 1771 Bishop James Talbot, the coadjutor of Bishop Challoner, was brought to trial at the Old Bailey for " exercising the functions of a popish bishop ".   That such prosecutions most frequently failed was but a poor compensation for the annoyance created ; and they did not always fail.   In 1767 an Irish priest, J. B. Maloney, was convicted of saying Mass and sentenced to perpetual imprisonment.

Mr Cole tells us that he had made a note of the story just recounted on the back of the title-page of one of the volumes of Mr Butler's *Lives of the Saints*, and he adds :

I had bought all his books [4 volumes of the *Lives of the Saints* printed at London in 8vo, the first volume in 1756 and the last in 1759] as they came out and had often read them much to my satisfaction, as he is both a very ingenious and learned man, as his said books very sufficiently evince, and, as I had heard also a very great character of his humanity from several of our common friends, I was determined to call upon him, as well to satisfy my curiosity in viewing the noble college founded by Lewis XIV, or rather rebuilt by him for the English Jesuits in that city, as to see a person whose character and writings had given me much pleasure.

Accordingly, on my arrival at the post-house, a very noble inn, where I ordered my dinner, getting there from Calais about 3 o'clock, while that was preparing, I went to the college and introduced myself to Mr Butler, then President of the same since the expulsion of the Jesuits from France in 1762 and 1763, who received me with great civility, insisted on my sending for my portmanteaux and servant from the inn and my supping and lying at the college.   His manner of pressing me was so insistent and urgent that I could not refuse it ; though it is probable I was the first priest of the Church of England that ever slept within those walls.   Before we went out he showed

* See *The Catholic Magazine*, vol. i, p. 717 (1832).

me every part of that very noble College, which was now converted into a seminary for English secular priests, and for a place of education of Catholic English scholars, over whom Mr Butler was placed as chief with the title of President. I was informed that he was very averse from taking this charge upon him, as it seemed to intrude upon the rights of a Society for whom he had a great regard ; yet being much importuned by the Archbishop of Rheims, the Bishops of Beauvais and Amiens, and well knowing that if he did not accept of it, the whole would have been converted to some other use, and not to the benefit of the English, and that the Society could not be injured by his acceptance of it, he at length yielded to the judgement of his friends, who thought none of his order more capable of discharging so difficult a task as the right education of youth as himself.

Mr Cole goes on to give some description of the building, as he does also in his Paris diary recently printed. From the independent account in MS. Addit. 5826 the following passage may be of some interest :

It is a very large and spacious College with a noble and beautiful front of stone to the street, which is a principal one leading from the cathedral to St Bertin's Abbey. The chapel of the College is but small considering the great number of students it contained during the time the Jesuits had possession of it. There are now not above 30 scholars under Mr Butler's direction, but there can be no doubt that it will increase after a time, as the present governor of it has shown himself to be so able as well as so religious and pious a scholar.

In the printed diary we learn that Mr Butler took Cole for a walk to see the abbey of Saint-Bertin and the cathedral. On their return to the college :

It being a fish day, we had a very elegant supper of fish, omelette, sallads and other things of that sort in the parlour where three young English priests, whose names I don't recollect, Sir Piers Mostyn, Baronet, a young gentleman of about 17 or 18 years of age, thin and seemingly not very healthful, who was there for his education, and a thin tall gentleman of Durham, who had lost one eye, of the age of between 30 and 40, as I judged, and a great talker, but whose name I heard not, supped and spent the evening with us. There was also an Irish priest, who was called in a certificate I saw in his hand, the Abbé Morison, who that day brought from Lisbon a young English merchant's sons, to be put under the care of Mr Butler. I was very hospitably and agreeably entertained, and slept in a very neat and pretty apartment, purposely kept for strangers. My servant also lodged in the College, the servants of which undertook to get me a place in the Lille diligence for the morrow. As it set out by 4 in the morning [the date being October 19th, it must have been completely dark at that hour] I took leave of the President and the other gentlemen by about 10 that evening with many acknowledgements of their kind and civil treatment.*

Trivial as these details may seem they help to fill in the picture we may form of the life led by Alban Butler in the years of his presidency at St Omer's. He was fifty-five at the date of Cole's visit, and died less than eight years later. There

* *The Paris Diary* of William Cole, p. 11.

can be no doubt that our traveller—the friend, let me repeat, of such men as Horace Walpole and the poet Gray—was favourably, even deeply, impressed by his contact with the author of *The Lives of the Saints*.　The references made to Butler in his letters to Father Bedingfield and other friends are always more than civil, and it is clear that the good Franciscan, who was Cole's neighbour in England, knew that the antiquary was greatly interested in the President of St Omer's.　Writing to Cole on August 11, 1767, Bedingfield reports :

> I heard some time ago that the Bishop of St Omer's* was coming to England with his *intimado* Mr Alban Butler.　The latter is grumbled at by his friends on this side for making them wait so long for his " Movable Feasts ". But it seems the nuns of Lisbon have prevailed with him to write the Life of one of their own community, which is just come out, and I propose getting one of my popish bookseller, Coghlan of Duke Street, Grosvenor Square, who sends me down anything I write for.†

To which Cole replies that he " wished he could have seen Mr Butler while he was in England to have returned his civilities to me at St Omer's ".　And he adds that he would be glad to have his book concerning the life of the nun of Lisbon.　Father Bedingfield, no doubt, always hoped that this very tolerant Anglican parson would end by joining the Church, and Cole, in December 1765, mentions having received a letter from him " speaking ", he says, " in a sort of style as if I was going over sea with a full resolution of turning Catholic ; in which he was much mistaken ".‡

Still, it is certain that there were aspects of ecclesiastical life in France which made a great appeal to Cole.　On returning home after his visit to Paris he sent to Butler some notes and emendations, couched in very courteous language, which he had jotted down in reading the latter's valued work on the saints, and he also expressed his grief and alarm at the great wave of irreligion which, as he had himself noted on his journey,§ seemed to be spreading over France.　His letter, perhaps, is worth quoting almost entire as giving an idea of the tone of French society at that date.　This was what Butler would have to encounter, if ever he ventured forth from his retreat to mix with the world around him.

> I found (Cole writes) it would not be easy to find any sympathetic companionship with the natives who do not love us and indeed have no reason to do so ; but the one thing which disgusted me most was the looseness of their principles in point of religion.　I travelled to Paris through Lille and Cambray in their public *voitures* and was greatly scandalized and amazed at their open and unreserved disrespect, both of the trading and military people, for their clergy and religious establishment.　When I got to Paris it was much worse. I had an opportunity, by a friend's being at Paris, with whom I spent most of my afternoons ‖ and where was a great resort of French company of the best sort, as he was a man of fashion and literature, to be further convinced of the

---

* This was Mgr de Conzié who was translated from Arras to the see of Saint-Omer in 1766.　Charles Butler, in his Memoir, speaks of him at some length.
† Addit. MS. 5824, fol. 25vo.
‡ *Paris Diary*, p. 374.
§ Cole speaks feelingly of this in his *Paris Diary*, pp. 25, 218, etc.
‖ This was undoubtedly Sir Horace Walpole.

great prevalency of deism in that kingdom, where if they go on at the rate they have done for these last few years, it is much to be feared that any mode of Christianity, much more the best, will fare but ill with so loose a people. I was shocked at this barefaced infidelity, as well as my friend who is so far from being a bigot to any form of Christianity that we rather looked upon him in England as indifferent to all : so that it was with the greatest pleasure I often heard him engaged very warmly in defence of our common Christianity against these " Philosophers " as the French deists affect to call themselves ; and upon this principle that it was time enough to think of pulling down the present established form of worship when they could agree among themselves to establish a better. The French nobility, ladies as well as men, military, gentry and even tradesmen, etc., are infected with this new philosophy. God alone knows where it will end ; but I fear the worst. I ever thought we were bad in England ; but I never heard so much public infidelity anywhere as while I was in France ; where, however, to its honour be it spoken, they have spewed out Rousseau ; while England, according to custom, has licked up the vomit. I hope you will pardon the indelicacy of the expression, but resentment to see the folly, blindness and ill-judgement of my countrymen, who are now a-madding in caressing a man, whom all good government, Christian or heathen, ought to detest, forced me to make use of it. All our newspapers for this last fortnight have had regularly two or three articles relating to this great Mr Rousseau and his settling in England. If the Emperor had paid us a visit, more noise could not have been made about it ; and we seem to think we have made a great acquisition in a man, who, was it not already in part done to his hands, has it in his heart to unloose all ties, both civil and ecclesiastic. But I will have done with this argument, and will only add that it gave me the most hearty concern to think what was likely to become of the flourishing Gallican Church, if a stop, a providential stop, be not put to this present phrenzy.*

For all that, Cole concludes his letter with the surprising suggestion that he himself would be glad to settle down on the other side of the English Channel. His actual words are these :

> I must own I still long after a retreat somewhere about you, or in Normandy, if a proper place could be found. I lament I had so short a time with you, as I am fearful I shall have no opportunity of talking this and other matters over with you in England. However, if you should have a call here, I should be infinitely happy to see you at this place ; which I might the sooner hope for as you told me the neighbouring county of Northampton was your native one. I assure you a most hearty welcome and shall be glad of every opportunity to approve myself, reverend sir, your much obliged and faithful servant Wm. Cole.
>
> *Bletcheley* Feb. 1, 1766.

Butler returned a very full reply ; and that his correspondent valued it is proved by the fact that he not only kept the original—it may still be found bound up in Addit. MS. 6400—but also made a copy in another of his manuscript books

* Letter of William Cole to Alban Butler, dated January 26, 1766, in MS. Addit. 5826, fols. 18vo to 21vo.

(Addit. MS. 5826). Its main portion is a sympathetic reinforcement of Cole's lament over the spread of infidelity in France, telling him, with a characteristic exuberance of phrase, that his " frightful portraiture of the monstrous growth of libertinism and irreligion alarms and disturbs me beyond expression. A good deal indeed I knew to be true." But the conclusion of the epistle is in a thoroughly practical vein, and was intended no doubt to encourage Cole in the idea of settling abroad.

> The necessaries and conveniencies of life are grown much dearer in France than formerly, but not in the same proportion as in England, where, I much fear, in a few years one-half the people will become beggars, and be maintained by the other half. I have everywhere found amongst the French a sufficient number of friends both obliging and very cordial and agreeable. Should you ever be inclined to try these parts (and the neighbourhood of England I have always found to have very agreeable circumstances) it would make me completely happy, if in my power, to contribute in any thing to make your situation agreeable. The most advantageous way of employing money here is now in the life prents upon the King which yield 10 per cent, or on the clergy for ever 5 per cent.

The final courteous phrases are those of the period :

> I am sorry you should think our poor entertainment to have deserved to be remembered. I shall always think myself much obliged to your goodness in accepting our humble lodging, and shall more so, if you ever find it convenient to favour us with your company for a longer time and as frequently as it shall suit your convenience. In every thing in my power I shall be very happy to obey your orders, execute any commissions, or give any proof of the most sincere respect and esteem with which I am, Hond. revd. Sir,
>
> Your most obliged and devoted humble servant,
>
> A. BUTLER

Alban Butler did not write with the vivacity and point which distinguish the letters of Horace Walpole, Lord Chesterfield or Fanny Burney. His realization of the eternal verities no doubt kept him always far removed from anything like a frivolous tone. But it seems, none the less, to have been the conviction of all with whom he came in contact that he was a friend who inspired trust, a man whose high principles were stimulating to those more worldly or infirm of purpose, a Christian in whom asceticism had not killed human feeling, and a scholar who, in intellectual matters, sought only the truth and never spared himself pains to attain it.

*   *   *

Perhaps a few words may here be added to supplement what has been written in the preface to the first volume of this series on Alban Butler's work as a hagiographer. He was not, of course, the first to produce in English a general collection of saints' lives arranged in the order of the calendar. One of the earliest compilations of this kind was the *Legenda Aurea*, written in the middle of the thirteenth century by the Dominican, Bd James de Voragine, who died archbishop of Genoa (see herein under July 13). This work was translated and printed by William Caxton, the father of English typography. In its English dress the *Golden Legend* proved to be almost the most popular of Caxton's publications. Several editions, reproducing the same version, came from the press in the first thirty years of the sixteenth century, but after the breach with Rome it was not reprinted, and under the repressive influence of Elizabeth's enactments against the introduction of popish books, Catholics for a long time had nothing to take its place. It was only in 1609 that there appeared, probably at Douay, the first part of a work bearing the title :

The Lives of Saints written in Spanish, by the learned and reverend Father Alfonso Villegas, Divine and Preacher ; translated out of Italian into English and conferred with the Spanish. By W. and E. K. B.

The translators are believed to have been two brothers, William and Edward Kinsman, but a certain amount of obscurity surrounds the whole production. The last four months of the year did not appear until 1614, with a rather pathetic preface, of which I quote a few sentences :

We present thee now at length, dear Christian reader, with the four last months of their glorious lives, whose names, as renowned saints of God, are in the Roman calendar. This debt, I must confess, hath been due this long time, but could not be discharged until this present, wherein the grace of God hath freed our passage through a main sea of difficulties. For such is the nature of all Catholic writings in our distressed country. What through penury, pressure, and long imprisonment of their authors at home, ignorance, neglect and carelessness of such as are put in trust abroad, we must wind ourselves out of a labyrinth of crosses, before we can bring to light our labours. And even then must they run so many hard fortunes and have such bad welcome and entertainment, that only this were able to check all endeavours not strengthened by the hand of God.

The welcome, however, does not seem after all to have been so very cold, for several reimpressions followed in the course of the next twenty years, some of them being augmented by additions from Father Ribadeneira and other sources. This bulky work of Father Pedro de Ribadeneira (who, as a lively youth of only thirteen, had been received into the Society of Jesus by St Ignatius Loyola himself as far back as 1540) was entitled *Flos Sanctorum* and was published in Spanish at Madrid. The first volume, a folio of 708 pages, appeared in 1599 ; the second, containing 870 pages, followed in 1601. The work was dedicated to the queen of Spain, Margaret of Austria, and had a great vogue, being translated into many other languages and frequently reprinted, sometimes entire and sometimes in abridgements. So far as devout Catholic readers were interested in hagiography, Father de Ribadeneira's work was probably the main source of information about the saints during the seventeenth century and a great part of the eighteenth, for all but the very scholarly. In 1669 a translation of it appeared in English in a surprisingly sumptuous form with the following title :

The Lives of Saints, with other Feasts of the year, according to the Roman Calendar. Written in Spanish by the Rev. Fr. Peter Ribadeneira, Priest of the Society of Jesus, and translated into English by W. P. Esquire. To which are added all those which have been put into the Calendar since the author's edition until the year 1669 ; besides those Feasts of Spain which the author himself hath inserted. Printed with Licence. St. Omers ; Joachim Cartier. 1669.

The book was a folio of 1036 pages and it contained several full-plate illustrations. A second edition of the same translation, but this time divided into two volumes, was printed in 1730 under the editorship of Father Thomas Coxon, s.j. The " W. P. Esquire " who had made this version, much more, we may assume, as a labour of love than in hope of any financial advantage, was the Hon. William Petre, the son of the second Lord Petre, by Katherine, daughter of Edward Somerset, fourth Earl of Worcester. He had been a student both at Exeter and Wadham Colleges in Oxford and had attended the Inns of Court.

But in the course of the seventeenth century there had come about a great advance in hagiographical studies, especially through the work of the Bollandists, as well as those of Mabillon and Tillemont. Education was spreading, and many devout people, both ecclesiastics and laymen, began to realize that much which was recorded of the more popular saints, especially the stories of martyrdoms in the early centuries and miracles at a later date, was pure legend and quite unworthy of credence. A certain reaction set in against the wholesale and unquestioning reception of the supernatural which prevailed in such books as those of Ribadeneira and Villegas. Writers who took their tone from Launoy or Baillet felt free to ridicule the credulity of the devout, and made it an accusation against the Church that she propagated such fables for her own pecuniary interest. Something of this change of feeling no doubt manifested itself in the book which Dr Charles Fell (a priest whose real name seems to have been Umfreville) began to publish in London in 1729 with the following title :

> Lives of the Saints collected from Authentick Records of Church History, with a full Account of the other Festivals throughout the year. The whole interspersed with suitable Reflections, together with a Treatise on the Moveable Feasts and Fasts of the Church.

It came out, with certain delays, in four volumes, but it seems to have been by no means a financial success. Dr John Kirk, in his *Biographies*, tells us of these Lives that " Dr Robert Witham of Douay wrote observations on them and denounced them at Rome. His principal complaint was that the author had taken them mainly from Baillet and had recorded few miracles."

We cannot doubt that Alban Butler, who knew Robert Witham well, was fully acquainted with the opinions entertained at Douay regarding Dr Fell's *Lives* ; moreover, Baillet's book, *Les Vies des Saints composées sur ce qui nous est resté de plus authentique et de plus assuré dans leur histoire* (Paris, 1701), was at that date a burning topic in ecclesiastical circles throughout France.* It seems to me that anyone who reads attentively Butler's " Introductory Discourse " to his first volume cannot fail to detect a reference to the situation which then existed, and a very clear expression of his determination, while following the sound criticism of Tillemont and the Bollandists, to abstain from anything which might seem like sympathy with Baillet's uncompromising mistrust of the supernatural.

" Certain critics of this age, as they style themselves ", writes Butler, " are displeased with all histories of miracles, not considering that these wonders are,

---

* The greater part of this collection of Lives was delated to Rome and eventually put on the Index.

in a particular manner, the works of God, intended to raise our attention to His holy providence and to awake our souls to praise His goodness and power ; often also to bear testimony to His truth.   Entirely to omit the mention of them would be an infidelity in history, and would tend, in some measure, to obstruct the great and holy purposes for which they were effected.   Yet a detail of all miracles, though authentically attested, is not the design of this work.   Wherefore in such facts it seemed often sufficient to refer the reader to the original records."   Even more significant perhaps is a phrase occurring in a footnote a little further on, in which Butler remarks : " On the other hand, some French critics in sacred biography have tinctured their works with a false and pernicious leaven and under the name of erudition established scepticism."

The *Lives of the Saints*, as sent to the press by Alban Butler in 1756, were at an early date translated into French by a certain Abbé Godescard, possibly with some additions and modifications.   As may be seen from the printed catalogue of the Bibliothèque Nationale, this French translation was often reprinted, but its tone seems to have given great offence to Mgr Paul Guérin, subsequently the editor of a rival and much more voluminous collection of saints' lives, known as *Les Petits Bollandistes*.   On the very first page of his preface Mgr Guérin brackets Godescard (*i.e.* Butler) with Baillet, and declares that the reader of either of these books carries away " the same sort of impression which is given by a beautiful garden which has been blighted by the onset of winter.   The breath of the critic, cold and death-dealing, has swept over it, and has not left a single blossom or a trace of perfume."   Nor is this enough ; a few lines further on he tells his readers :

> Butler is not a faithful mirror of the past.   He is far from transmitting to us the radiance of those saintly characters which the men of their own day beheld in all its splendour.   If he does not cast them down from the pedestal upon which the piety of past ages has grown accustomed to venerate them, he rarely leaves intact that halo of glory with which God encircled their modest heads.   If he does justice to the courage with which they stripped themselves of all earthly attachments, he is careful not to disclose anything of that mantle of glory with which God invested them in exchange.   No doubt, he was afraid of dazzling or shocking eyes which in the bare and arid atmosphere of Protestantism had become atrophied and thus insensible to any gleam of divine light or to the sweet and tender glow in human lives which is a reflection of heaven.

All this is a curious revelation of the mentality which prevailed both among the clergy and the devout laity of France in the middle of the last century.   It is inconceivable that anyone acquainted with the original text of Butler's Lives could look upon the author as hypercritical, or as a *dénicheur des saints*, to use the phrase originally coined, I think, to fit the case of de Launoy.   The entire honesty of Butler and his great personal devotion to the saints is conspicuous in every word of his preface.   His criticism is based entirely upon that of such approved guides as the early Bollandists, who, as their successors in our own day have shown, did not even in many cases push their criticism of sources far enough.   Butler never took the lead in any sort of inconoclastic assault upon tradition.   His own personal attitude, both to the saints and to his readers, was very much that of the William or Edward Kinsman who, in the 1614 preface from which I have previously quoted, concluded with these words :

> Wherefore, dear Christian reader, doubt not to welcome and entertain that guest whose presence with pleasure will afford thee profit. And when thou dost find some few such things as are more to be admired than imitated, pass not thy judgement upon them with passion ; measure not the virtues of God his Saints by thy own feebleness, go not about to weaken or discredit the promises of Christ, nor confine the omnipotence of God within the narrow bounds of human reason ; for the holy God hath already foretold us that God is admirable in His Saints, and Christ did promise that His disciples should work greater wonders than their Master's.

BEATI AND SANCTI

By Herbert Thurston, s.j.

THERE is a popular impression, an impression shared even by some Catholics, that the process followed in the beatification and canonization of saints is analogous to that by which the Sovereign creates a Knight of the Garter or raises a commoner to the peerage. The analogy, if it exists at all, is a very imperfect one, for it suggests that the initiative in this conferring of spiritual dignities comes from the pope and not from the people. The assumption is that the vicar of Christ, having honours to bestow in the Church triumphant as well as in the Church militant, causes search to be made among the available records in order to discover the most worthy recipient of his favour＇ According to this mistaken view the Sovereign Pontiff fixes his choice upon this one or that, who has died in the repute of sanctity and then, after a certain measure of inquiry, declares the servant of God to be " Blessed ". Supposing that this is well received and that further miracles are reported, canonization follows in due time, and the candidate thus approved is proclaimed worthy of universal veneration.

An investigation of past history, or a study of such an essay as that of the Bollandist Father H. Delehaye, entitled *Sanctus*, will show that the idea thus outlined is almost the reverse of what actually happens, and of what in fact has always happened, since the beginning. It is not the pope who is anxious to " make saints ", but the people who have to be restrained from making them too easily. The impulse comes, not from above, but from below. The faithful of some particular locality, impressed by the virtue, the sufferings or the miracles of one who has lived in their midst, are convinced that he must be dear to God and are eager while invoking his intercession to pay him such honour as their devotion suggests. In the earliest centuries it was the martyr who alone evoked this popular enthusiasm, but soon it was realized that a martyrdom which was lifelong and self-imposed might be even more worthy of admiration than that which was terminated by a single blow of the executioner's sword. Thus confessors and virgins took their place among those heavenly patrons in whose honour the holy sacrifice was offered. For many centuries no other sanction was sought than that of the local bishop. With his permission the sacred remains were disinterred and enshrined in some more conspicuous place. Following upon this " elevation ", Mass was celebrated each year upon the anniversary of him or her who was so commemorated, and this *dies natalis* (heavenly birthday) was entered in the calendar or martyrology of the diocese or province.

This was the first step in what we might describe as the evolution of the process of canonization. So far as it went, it really corresponded much more closely to the modern beatification. The holy people who were so honoured were entitled only to a local and restricted veneration, and the recognition of eminent virtue had no binding force for the Church at large. But often the cult, which seemed to be favoured by miraculous answers to prayer, spread to other countries, even those remote from the place of origin. Relics or representative tokens where conveyed to a distance, and in these new shrines they became the nucleus of a fresh manifestation of popular enthusiasm. The local martyr-lists and calendars borrowed from one another, and when a name was famous, such, let us say, as that of St Cyprian, St Basil, St Martin of Tours or St Athanasius, it was ere long adopted everywhere, and the cult was thus ratified by the acceptance of the universal Church. To this day the majority of the feasts which stand in the calendar of the Roman missal commemorate saints who had no other canonization than that which is involved in this general approval. No formal pronouncement of the Holy See has ever proclaimed them holy, and no evidence of miracles performed was deemed necessary for this recognition.

It is, however, obvious enough that any such rough and ready canonization by popular acclaim, subject only to the sanction of the local bishop, was open to grave abuses. The enthusiasm of the crowd is not always discriminating, nor were medieval bishops in all cases sufficiently learned or vigilant to cope with the indiscretions—and not seldom the frauds—of foolish or mercenary promoters of a new cult. In the course of time the Holy See found it necessary to intervene, or, more correctly, the pope began to be appealed to to ratify a decision already arrived at in practice. The first papal canonization is believed to be that of Bishop Ulric of Augsburg, who died in 973 and was formally declared by Pope John XV twenty years later to be entitled to the devout veneration of all the faithful. Then in the latter part of the twelfth century, Alexander III definitely reserved to the Holy See the right to pronounce when the claims of a candidate to saintship were in question, and although for a time local cults still grew up and flourished in many places without much interference, the principle that a valid canonization could only be effected by a papal bull of a very formal kind eventually came to be everywhere recognized.

Down to the beginning of the sixteenth century, or even later, there is little evidence that any significant distinction existed between the terms *beatus* and *sanctus* as applied to holy people, nor does the word " beatification " seem to occur with a technical meaning which opposes it to " canonization ". The early cases quoted by Benedict XIV in his great work on the subject (*De Servorum Dei beatificatione et Beatorum canonizatione*, lib. I, cap. xx, nn. 18–19) are not entirely conclusive. At the same time it may be assumed, as already suggested, that the exhumation (or " elevation ") and enshrining of an ascetic's holy remains did constitute a recognition of his sanctity, roughly equivalent to the later process of beatification. It was in any case accepted as a preliminary step to canonization and a sufficient warrant for local cults. But with the close of the sixteenth century, or possibly earlier, a quite definite distinction was established between the *beatus* and the *sanctus*. By the papal decree of beatification the veneration of a particular servant of God was permitted, but with limitations confining the public expression of the cult to the celebration of Mass in his honour or the exposing of his picture or relics, to certain localities, or to a certain religious order, or to churches to which the privilege was specially granted. Even so, there was for a long time no public solemnity in St Peter's at Rome to celebrate the papal approval of the virtues of the newly beatified. The first public function of this sort, such as now generally takes place even for an *approbatio cultus*, seems to have occurred in 1662, under Alexander VII on the occasion of the beatification of St Francis de Sales. Earlier than this, and notably in the sixteenth century, the pope often deputed the bishop of the diocese or some prelate of distinction to inquire into the case, and by delegated authority to permit the celebration of Mass or other forms of *cultus*, a definite clause being inserted in the instrument to the effect that this concession was not to be understood as constituting a canonization of the holy person in question.   A case in point is preserved in the decree of Hugh, bishop of Constance, who in virtue of powers conferred by Pope Julius II permitted the monastery of St Gall in 1513 to keep the feast of Blessed Notker, the famous writer of sequences, who had been a monk in that abbey.   As Notker Balbulus died in 912, this formal, even if indirect, approval of *cultus* takes us back to a time earlier than that of St Ulric of Augsburg, who, as stated above, passes for the first saint to have been papally canonized.   But there have been many other confirmations of *cultus* since then which approve the liturgical veneration of bishops, abbots, martyrs, etc., still more remote in date.   To take a single example, Pope Leo XIII, on the appeal of the then recently created hierarchy of Scotland, sanctioned the keeping by that country of nineteen separate festivals, amongst which is that of St Palladius who is supposed to have lived in the fifth century.   The claim of most of these celebrations to continued recognition seems to have been mainly based upon the fact of their inclusion in the Aberdeen Breviary, a service book of the late middle ages.*   It is in virture of decrees similar to the one just mentioned that feasts in honour of St Theodore of Canterbury, St Chad, St Oswald, St Winifred, etc., are kept in various English dioceses.

Since the pontificate of Urban VIII the procedure in beatification causes, in spite of some modifications subsequently introduced, has been definitely regulated, and remains quite distinct from the canonization process which may supervene. It consists essentially in a petition addressed to the Holy See by some person of credit, or some corporate body, such as a religious order, that a process of inquiry may be set on foot regarding the sanctity of a particular individual who has died in the repute of holiness.   If the petition is acceded to, a postulator of the cause is appointed, who approaches the bishop of the diocese concerned with a view to the constitution of an " informative process " in which witnesses are interrogated before a court of ecclesiastical judges in accord with a carefully drafted questionnaire, and these depositions are recorded in writing.   The court, composed of a president and at least two assessors, conducts the proceedings in the presence of an official critic, " the promoter of the faith ", who though he cannot himself cross-examine the witnesses, can call upon the judges to put questions which he considers desirable.   All the evidence having been heard, the *procès verbal* is sealed up and despatched to Rome, together with letters from the judges and the promoter of the faith, but these are not opened until after the writings of the servant of God have been read and approved, and the question arises of the formal " introduction of the cause ".   From the materials provided by the " informative process " a summary of the case is printed and distributed to the Congregation of Rites.   To this are commonly added some specimens of the petitions which have been addressed to the Holy See, begging that the matter of the beatification may be taken in hand without delay.   If all is approved by the congregation, the sanction of the Sovereign Pontiff is obtained and the cause is thereby formally introduced, the first stage in the process being thus completed.   The servant of God, however, according to present legislation, is not yet entitled to be styled " Venerable ".

* The decree is dated July 11, 1898, and is printed in the *Analecta Ecclesiastica* for that year, page 403.

There still remains, in fact, very much to be done. Letters are addressed to the Holy See to obtain the signing of *litterae remissoriales* in which a new examination of witnesses in the diocese of origin, called the *processus apostolicus*, is conducted before judges, this time deputed by the Holy See itself. It is only after this evidence has been collected and discussed that the material is again submitted to the Congregation of Rites, who pronounce a series of verdicts, first on the proof of the repute for sanctity in general, then on the validity of the process, then on the heroic character of the candidate's virtues in particular, then on the supernatural origin of the miracles adduced, and finally on the question whether a decree of beatification can safely (*de tuto*) be pronounced. At all these stages, often separated by considerable intervals of time, opportunity is given to the promoter of the faith to expound and print his objections. After a favourable decision has been arrived at as to the heroic character of the virtues, the candidate is entitled to be called " Venerable ", and when the decision *de tuto* has been reached, the papal decree of beatification and the solemn proclamation in the Vatican basilica usually follow without notable delay.

As already stated, the whole process has its starting-point in an appeal made to the Holy See by those who are cognisant of the virtues of the servant of God. Moreover, after the " informative ", or diocesan, process has been completed and sent to Rome, the *Codex Juris Canonici* (canon 2077) suggests that it is desirable that petitions for the expediting of the cause should be addressed to the Holy See by persons of standing, providing only that these petitions be spontaneous and made by those who have knowledge of the facts. A book on the *Canonization of Saints*, by Canon T. F. Macken (1910), goes so far as to say : " The Church rarely takes action until petitioned in this way, and the memorials should give expression to the remarkable reputation for sanctity . . . enjoyed by the deceased servant of God, and the widespread holy desire that the Supreme Pontiff should place him on the venerated roll of the saints." What is made clear in the official *Codex pro postulatoribus* is that these petitions are meant to lay stress upon the continuance and further spread of the repute for sanctity, as well as upon the urgent popular desire that the beatification should be proceeded with. All this bears out the idea that the starting-point in the canonization process is the appeal of some group of the Christian faithful who are eager to pay homage to one of God's servants whom they believe to be especially dear to Him and whose intercession they consequently wish to invoke. But before acceding to this desire the Supreme Pontiff has to be satisfied regarding two points in particular. First of all it must be made clear that the subject who has inspired this devotion has given a worthy example of holiness and in fact has practised virtue in an heroic degree. Secondly, he must be convinced that the desire which prompted the appeal for a declaration of sanctity was not a mere evanescent wave of feeling, but persists.

In the case of martyrs another important point which nowadays has to be rigorously established by evidence, is the fact that the martyr was put to death *in odium fidei*. This is a question which has two aspects. On the one hand it should be shown that the persecutor was animated with malice against the Christian faith or against some feature of the Church's teaching. On the other hand the disposition of the martyr is also in question, and it must be made clear that he faced death not for vainglory or any unworthy motive, but steadfastly in a spirit of loyalty to Christ and His Church. Among those who in earlier ages were venerated as martyrs, there are not a few who seem to have been simply the victims of some brutal assault provoked by personal resentment, greed or frustrated ambition. It may be said that with regard to the whole patristic and early medieval period, the Church, recognizing the impossibility of any adequate historical inquiry after the lapse of so many centuries, is content to abide by the traditions of the past. Those who can be shown by the testimony of martyrologies and calendars to have been honoured then with the veneration of the faithful, are left in possession of their courtesy title. They are in this way honoured with an equipollent canonization, but the infallibility of the Holy See is not in any way involved if subsequent discoveries make it clear that grave misunderstandings have occurred, and that the faith of simple people has in some sense been imposed upon.

With regard, however, to those whose virtuous life and blessed death have been proclaimed to the world in a solemn bull of canonization, it is the more commonly held opinion that such a pronouncement is irreformable, and that the Church cannot have erred in declaring them to be the friends of God and in the enjoyment of bliss everlasting. This does not, of course, apply to statements which may occur in the bull of canonization relating, for example, to past historical facts or to the supernatural character of certain events represented as miraculous. No stigma of heresy attaches to the denial that any particular cure or portent was a true miracle, though it is mainly upon the proof of the occurrence of such reputed miracles, after beatification has taken place, that the resumption of the cause depends and also its successful progress towards the goal of final canonization. The implication undoubtedly is that by the working of fresh miracles the Almighty has set His seal upon the decision arrived at in the beatification decree, and that the Sovereign Pontiff is thereby empowered to declare with full confidence that universal and unrestricted veneration may be paid to the blessed soul whom God has so honoured.

I am not in this brief note attempting any sort of analysis of the modifications which arise from varying circumstances when the case is presented *per viam non cultus*, or as *extraordinaria casus excepti seu cultus*. Neither need anything be said of the special case of martyrs except to note that the same evidence is not required of heroic virtue, and that miracles may here more easily be dispensed with. The feature which I wish particularly to emphasize is the fact that in the equipollent canonizations of those holy men and women who lived before the thirteenth century, and the beatifications which are conceded merely in the form of a *confirmatio cultus*, the Church is committed to little or nothing in the way of a sifting of evidence. Nothing more is affirmed than that the faithful may legitimately continue the practices of devotion which many centuries have made familiar.

[An example of *confirmatio cultus* is provided by the first group of blessed English martyrs. Their so-called beatification in 1886 was in fact a recognition and confirmation by the Holy See of the *cultus* approved by Pope Gregory XIII in 1583 when he allowed their representation as martyrs on the walls of the chapel of the English College in Rome. Since the above appendix was written an important article by S. Kuttner on " La réserve papale du droit du canonisation " has appeared in the *Revue historique de droit francais et étranger*, n.s., vol. xvii, pp. 172–228 ; and in English an Anglican scholar, the Rev. E. W. Kemp, has published a study of *Canonization and Authority in the Western Church* (1948) ; see also Father Delehaye's *Sanctus* (1927), mentioned above. For the general reader there is a good summary by Mgr P. E. Hallett, *The Canonization of Saints* (C.T.S., 1948).—D. A.]

APPENDIX III

RECENT BEATIFICATIONS

During the ten years that have elapsed since this edition of Butler's "Lives" was published there has been a number of new beatifications and canonizations. There have also been considerable changes in the general calendar of the Roman church, on which other calendars in the Western church are based.

Changes have been inserted in many places in these volumes each time the volumes went to press. Notes of beatifications and canonizations are given below where it was impossible to insert the biographies in their proper places. The complete index in volume IV, however, does contain cross references. Changes that have already been noted in the text are not repeated here.

JANUARY

4: Bd Elizabeth Ann Seton (née Bayley). Born in New York City, 1774; married William Seton, 1794; widowed in 1803; received into the Catholic Church in 1805; made religious vows, 1809; died at Emmitsburg in Maryland, 4 January 1821. Mother Seton founded the American Sisters of Charity and was the first native-born American citizen to be beatified, in 1963.

5: Bd John Nepomucen Neumann. Born in Bohemia, 1811; he was ordained priest in New York City in 1836 and joined the Redemptorist congregation; consecrated fourth bishop of Philadelphia in 1852; he died there on 5 January 1860. Bishop Neumann, a naturalized American citizen, organized Catholic schools into a diocesan system. He was beatified in 1963.

FEBRUARY

7: Bd Eugenia Smet (Mother Mary of Providence), foundress of the Helpers of the Holy Souls. Born in Lille in 1825; founded her congregation in 1856 in Paris; died there, 1871. She was beatified in 1957.

MARCH

3: Bd Innocent of Berzo. Born at Berzo in northern Italy, 1844. He was a secular priest from 1867 until 1874, when he joined the Capuchin Friars Minor. He died at Bergamo, 3 March 1890, and was beatified in 1961.

15: Bd Placid Riccardi, Benedictine monk. He was born at Trevi in Umbria, 1844; entered the monastery of St Paul outside the walls at Rome, 1868; died there 15 March 1915. He was beatified in 1954.

APRIL

7: Bd Mary Assunta Pallotta, religious of the Franciscan Missionaries of Mary. Born in Italy in 1878; died in China, 7 April 1905 and beatified in 1954.

11: Bd Helen Guerra, foundress of the Congregation of St Rita, later called the Oblates of the Holy Spirit. She was born at Lucca in 1835, and died there on 11 April 1914. It was through her that Pope Leo XIII wrote the encyclical letter "Divinum illud munus," on devotion to the Holy Spirit. She was beatified in 1959.

MAY

4: Bd John Martin Moye. He was a missionary priest in China and founder of the Sisters of Divine Providence. Born in Lorraine, 1730; died at Trier on 4 May 1793 and beatified in 1954.

JUNE

6: Bd Marcellinus Champagnat, founder of the teaching congregation of Little Brothers of Mary, or Marist Brothers. He was born near Lyon in 1789, died on 6 June 1840, and was beatified in 1955.

15: Bd Aloysius Palazzolo, founder of the Brothers of the Holy Family and the Sisters of the Poor. Born at Bergamo in 1827; ordained priest, 1850. His charitable work was particularly concerned with the reclaiming of prostitutes. He died on 15 June 1886 and was beatified in 1963.

JULY

20: BB. Leo Ignatius Mangin, Ann Wang and their companions, Martyrs. Four French Jesuits and fifty-two Chinese lay people martyred by the Boxers in 1900. Beatified in 1955 (*cf.* herein, vol. iii, pp. 59-62).

AUGUST

11: Bd Innocent XI. Benedict Odescalchi, born at Como, 1611; elected pope, 1676; died in Rome on 11 August 1689. He was beatified in 1956.

20: Bd Teresa Jornet Ibars, foundress of the Little Sisters of the Aged Poor. She was born in Catalonia in 1843, and was a school teacher for a time before making her religious foundation. She died 20 August 1897 and was beatified in 1957.

27: Bd Dominic Barberi. Born near Viterbo in Italy, 1792; ordained priest in the Passionist congregation, 1818; missioner for seven years in England, where he received John Henry Newman into the Church in 1845. He died near Reading in 1849 and was beatified in 1963.

OCTOBER

17: BB. John Baptist Turpin du Cormier, Mary L'Huilier and their companions. Fourteen priests, three nuns and a lay woman martyred at Laval in 1794 during the French Revolution. They were beatified in 1955.

DECEMBER

9: Bd Francis Antony Fasani, priest in the order of Conventual Friars Minor. He was born at Lucera in Apulia in 1681, and died at the friary there in 1742. He was beatified in 1951.

15: Bd Mary Margaret d'Youville (née Dufrost de Lajemmerais). Born at Varennes near Montreal, 1701; left a widow in 1722, she devoted herself to hospital work and in 1738 founded the Grey Nuns of Canada. She died on 23 December 1771 and was beatified in 1959.

*   *   *

Bd Leonard Murialdo. A secular priest, born at Turin in 1828. He devoted his life to the welfare of young people and of manual workers, establishing the first "family house" in Italy for young working men. He founded the Society of St Joseph in Turin, where he died in 1900. He was beatified in 1963.

Bd Nunzio Sulprizio. A layman, born 1817 in the Abruzzi province of Italy. He was a blacksmith by trade, who died in 1836 at the age of nineteen. He was beatified in 1963.

Bd Vincent Romano. Born near Naples, 1751. He was the parish priest of Herculano (possibly the former Herculaneum, near Pompeii). He died in 1831 and was beatified in 1963.

Note.—In an article on the mystic Orsola Benincasa printed in *The Month* for February 1939, Father Herbert Thurston refers to Bd Giovanna Maria Bonomo as "a stigmatica and a mystic whose writings had considerable influence"; and he expresses regret that he omitted an account of her from the revised Butler. This *beata* was born in the diocese of Vicenza in 1606, and became a Benedictine nun at Bassano, where she died in the convent of St Jerome on March 1, 1670. She was beatified in 1783. Father Thurston gives references to a Life in French by Du Bourg ,(1910) and to the *Dictionnaire de Spiritualité*, vol. i, c. 1860. The article referred to above is reprinted in *Surprising Mystics* (1955), a collection of Father Thurston's papers edited by Father J. H. Crehan, s.j.

INDEX

Individual members of groups, e.g., of martyrs, are not entered in this index if they have only a bare mention in the text.

References in this index are given to the dates of feasts under which the names occur in these four volumes; on these dates, see the editor's preface in Volume I, page vi. Names of beati *and* beatae *are so noted ; all the rest are, or are commonly called, Saint. Individual members of groups. e.g. of martyrs, are not entered herein if they have only a bare mention in the text.*

A

Aaron (with Julius)	*July* 3
Abachum	*January* 19
Abbo. *See* Goericus	
Abbo of Fleury	*November* 13
Abdon	*July* 30
Abercius	*October* 22
Abibus (with Gurias)	*November* 15
Abraham Kidunaia	*March* 16
Abraham of Carrhae	*February* 14
Abraham of Kratia	*December* 6
Abraham of Rostov	*October* 29
Abraham of Smolensk	*August* 21
Abundius (with Abundantius)	*September* 16
Acacius (or Achatius)	*March* 31
Acacius (or Agathus)	*May* 8
Acca	*October* 20
Achard. *See* Aichardus	
Achatius. *See* Acacius	
Achilleus (with Felix)	*April* 23
Achilleus (with Nereus)	*May* 12
Acisclus	*November* 17
Adalbald	*February* 2
Adalbert of Egmond	*June* 25
Adalbert of Magdeburg	*June* 20
Adalbert of Prague	*April* 23
Adalhard (or Adelard)	*January* 2
Adam of Loccum, Bd	*December* 22
Adamnan of Coldingham	*January* 31
Adamnan (or Eunan) of Iona	*September* 23
Adauctus (with Felix)	*August* 30
Adaucus	*February* 7
Addai	*August* 5
Adela	*December* 24
Adelaide (empress)	*December* 16
Adelaide of Bellich	*February* 5
Adelard. *See* Adalhard	
Adelelmus (or Aleaume)	*January* 30
Ado, Bd	*December* 16
Adolf of Osnabrück	*February* 14
Adrian (martyr)	*March* 4
Adrian (with Eubulus)	*March* 5
Adrian (with Natalia)	*September* 8
Adrian III	*July* 8
Adrian Fortescue, Bd	*July* 11
Adrian of Canterbury	*January* 9
Adulf	*June* 17
Aedesius. *See* Frumentius	
Aedh Mac Bricc	*November* 10
Aegidius. *See* Giles	
Aelred (or Ailred)	*March* 3
Aengus (or Oengus) the Culdee	*March* 11
Aengus MacNisse. *See* Macanisius	

Aemilius (with Castus)	*May* 22
Afan	*November* 16
Afra	*August* 5
Agape (with Chionia)	*April* 3
Agape of Terni	*February* 15
Agapitus (martyr)	*August* 18
Agapitus (with Sixtus)	*August* 6
Agapitus I	*April* 22
Agapius (with Timothy)	*August* 19
Agatha	*February* 5
Agatha Kim, Bd. *See* Laurence Imbert	
Agathangelo of Vendôme, Bd	*August* 7
Agathangelus (martyr)	*January* 23
Agatho (pope)	*January* 10
Agathonice	*April* 13
Agathopus	*April* 4
Agathus. *See* Acacius	
Agericus (or Airy)	*December* 1
Agilbert	*October* 11
Agnello of Pisa, Bd	*March* 13
Agnes	*January* 21
Agnes of Assisi	*November* 16
Agnes of Bohemia, Bd	*March* 2
Agnes of Montepulciano	*April* 20
Agrecius	*January* 13
Agricola (or Arègle)	*March* 17
Agricola (with Vitalis)	*November* 4
Agricolus	*September* 2
Agrippina	*June* 23
Aichardus (or Achard)	*September* 15
Aidan (or Maedoc) of Ferns	*January* 31
Aidan of Lindisfarne	*August* 31
Aignan. *See* Anianus	
Aigulf (or Ayoul) of Bourges	*May* 22
Aigulf (or Ayoul) of Lérins	*September* 3
Ailbhe	*September* 12
Ailred. *See* Aelred	
Airy. *See* Agericus	
Alban	*June* 21
Alban (or Bartholomew) Roe, Bd	*January* 21
Alban (or Albinus) of Mainz	*June* 21
Alberic (abbot)	*January* 26
Alberic Crescitelli, Bd. *See* the Martyrs of China, II	
Albert the Great	*November* 15
Albert of Bergamo, Bd	*May* 11
Albert of Cashel	*January* 19
Albert of Jerusalem	*September* 25
Albert of Louvain	*November* 21
Albert of Montecorvino	*April* 5
Albert of Trapani	*August* 7
Albinus. *See* Alban of Mainz	
Albinus (or Aubin) of Angers	*March* 1

Alcmund (bishop)	*September* 7	Amand (bishop)	*February* 6
Alcmund (martyr)	*March* 19	Amand of Bordeaux	*June* 18
Alcuin, Bd	*May* 19	Amata, Bd	*June* 9
Alda, (or Aldobrandesca), Bd	*April* 26	Amator. *See* Amadour	
Aldegundis	*January* 30	Amator (or Amatre)	*May* 1
Aldemar	*March* 24	Amatre. *See* Amator	
Aldhelm	*May* 23	Amatus (or Amé), (abbot)	*September* 13
Aldobrandesca. *See* Alda		Amatus (or Amé), (bishop)	*September* 13
Aldric	*January* 7	Ambrose (doctor)	*December* 7
Aleaume. *See* Adelelmus		Ambrose Autpert	*July* 19
Aled (or Almedha)	*August* 1	Ambrose Barlow, Bd	*September* 10
Alexander (with Epimachus)	*December* 12	Ambrose Traversari, Bd	*November* 20
Alexander (with Epipodius)	*April* 22	Ambrose of Siena, Bd	*March* 20
Alexander (with Eventius)	*May* 3	Amé. *See* Amatus	
Alexander (with Sisinnius)	*May* 29	Amicus	*November* 3
Alexander Akimetes	*February* 23	Ammon (abbot)	*October* 4
Alexander Briant', Bd	*December* 1	Ammon (martyr)	*December* 20
Alexander Rawlins, Bd	*April* 7	Amphilochius	*November* 23
Alexander Sauli	*October* 11	Anacletus. *See* Cletus	
Alexander of Alexandria	*February* 26	Anastasia (martyr)	*December* 25
Alexander of Comana	*August* 11	Anastasia (with Basilissa)	*April* 15
Alexander of Constantinople	*August* 28	Anastasia (with Cyril)	*October* 28
Alexander of Jerusalem	*March* 18	Anastasia Patricia	*March* 10
Alexia. *See* Alix		Anastasia (or Astrik)	*November* 12
Alexis	*July* 17	Anastasius I (pope)	*December* 19
Alexis Falconieri. *See* Founders of the		Anastasius I of Antioch	*April* 21
Servites		Anastasius II of Antioch	*December* 21
Aleydis (or Alice)	*June* 15	Anastasius of Cluny	*October* 16
Alferius	*April* 12	Anastasius the Fuller	*September* 7
Alfwold	*March* 25	Anastasius the Persian	*January* 22
Alice. *See* Aleydis		Anatolia (with Victoria)	*December* 23
Alipius	*August* 18	Anatolius of Constantinople	*July* 3
Alix Le Clercq, Bd	*January* 9	Anatolius of Laodicea	*July* 3
All Saints	*November* 1	Andrew (apostle)	*November* 30
All Souls	*November* 2	Andrew Abellon, Bd	*May* 17
Allowin. *See* Bavo		Andrew Avellino	*November* 10
Allucio	*October* 23	Andrew Bobola	*May* 21
Almachius (or Telemachus)	*January* 1	Andrew Corsini	*February* 4
Almedha. *See* Aled		Andrew Dotti, Bd	*September* 4
Alnoth	*February* 27	Andrew Fournet	*May* 13
Alodia	*October* 22	Andrew Hibernon, Bd	*April* 18
Aloysius Gonzaga	*June* 21	Andrew Kagwa, Bd. *See* Charles Lwanga	
Aloysius Palazzolo, Bd Appendix III		Andrew of Anagni, Bd	*February* 17
Aloysius Rabata, Bd	*May* 11	Andrew of Antioch, Bd	*November* 30
Alpais, Bd	*November* 3	Andrew of Crete	*July* 4
Alphaeus	*November* 17	Andrew of Crete (the Calybite)	*October* 20
Alphege (or Elphege) of Canterbury	*April* 19	Andrew of Fiesole	*August* 22
Alphege (or Elphege) bf Winchester		Andrew of Montereale, Bd	*April* 12
	March 12	Andrew of Peschiera, Bd	*January* 19
Alphius	*May* 10	Andrew of Pistoia, Bd	*May* 30
Alphonsus Liguori·	*August* 2	Andrew of Rinn, Bd	*July* 12
Alphonsus Navarette, Bd. *See* Martyrs of		Andrew of Siena, Bd	*March* 19
Japan, II		Andrew of Spello, Bd	*June* 3
Alphonsus de Orozco, Bd	*September* 19	Andrew of Strumi, Bd	*March* 10
Alphonsus Rodriguez	*October* 30	Andrew the Tribune	*August* 19
Alphonsus Rodriguez (martyr), Bd. *See*		Andronicus (with Athanasia)	*October* 9
Roque Gonzalez		Andronicus (with Tarachus)	*October* 11
Altman	*August* 8	Angadrisma	*October* 14
Alto	*February* 9	Angela Merici	*May* 31
Alvarez of Cordova, Bd	*February* 19	Angela of Foligno, Bd	*February* 28
Amadeus Amidei. *See* Founders of the		Angelina of Marsciano, Bd	*July* 21
Servites		Angelo (martyr)	*May* 5
Amadeus of Lausanne	*January* 28	Angelo of Acri, Bd	*October* 30
Amadeus IX of Savoy, Bd	*March* 30	Angelo of Borgo, Bd	*February* 15
Amadour (or Amator)	*August* 20	Angelo of Chivasso, Bd	*April* 12
Amalburga (virgin)	*July* 10	Angelo of Florence, Bd	*August* 18
Amalburga (widow)	*July* 10	Angelo of Foligno, Bd	*August* 27

C

Dionysius, Bd (with Redemptus)
November 29
Dionysius of Alexandria	*November* 17
Dionysius of Corinth	*April* 8
Dionysius of Milan	*May* 25
Dionysius of Paris	*October* 9
Dionysius the Areopagite	*October* 9
Dioscorus. *See* Nemesius of Alexandria
Disibod	*September* 8
Dismas. *See* The Good Thief
Dodo, Bd	*March* 30
Dogmael	*June* 14
Dometius the Persian	*August* 7
Dominic	*August* 4
Dominic, Bd (with Gregory)	*April* 26
Dominic Barberi, Bd	Appendix III
Dominic Loricatus	*October* 14
Dominic Savio	*March* 9
Dominic Spadafora, Bd	*October* 3
Dominic of the Causeway	*May* 12
Dominic of Silos	*December* 20
Dominic of Sora	*January* 22
Dominica (martyr)	*July* 6
Dominica (with Indractus)	*February* 5
Domitian of Maestricht	*May* 7
Domitilla	*May* 12
Domnolus of Le Mans	*May* 16
Donald	*July* 15
Donatian (with Laetus)	*September* 6
Donatian (with Rogatian)	*May* 24
Donatus of Arezzo	*August* 7
Donatus of Fiesole	*October* 22
Donnan	*April* 17
Dorotheus (with Peter)	*March* 12
Dorotheus of Tyre	*June* 5
Dorotheus the Younger	*January* 5
Dorothy	*February* 6
Dorothy of Montau, Bd	*October* 30
Dositheus	*February* 23
Drausin. *See* Drausius
Drausius (or Drausin)	*March* 7
Drithelm	*September* 1
Droctoveus (or Drotté)	*March* 10
Drogo (or Druon)	*April* 16
Drostan	*July* 11
Drotté. *See* Droctoveus
Druon. *See* Drogo
Dubricius (or Dyfrig)	*November* 14
Dulas. *See* Tatian
Dunstan	*May* 19
Duthac	*March* 8
Dyfrig. *See* Dubricius
Dympna	*May* 15

E

Eanswida	*September* 12
Eata	*October* 26
Ebba	*August* 25
Eberhard of Einsiedeln, Bd	*August* 14
Eberhard of Marchthal, Bd	*April* 17
Eberhard of Salzburg	*June* 22
Ebrulf (or Evroult)	*December* 29
Edbert	*May* 6
Edburga of Minster	*December* 12
Edburga of Winchester	*June* 15

Edith of Polesworth	*July* 15
Edith of Wilton	*September* 16
Edmund (martyr)	*November* 20
Edmund Arrowsmith, Bd	*August* 28
Edmund Campion, Bd	*December* 1
Edmund Catherick, Bd	*April* 13
Edmund Genings, Bd. *See* Martyrs of London, 1591
Edmund of Abingdon (or of Canterbury)	*November* 16
Edward Campion, Bd. *See* Martyrs of Canterbury
Edward Coleman, Bd. *See* Martyrs of the Oates Plot
Edward Fulthrop, Bd. *See* William Andleby
Edward James, Bd. *See* Martyrs of Canterbury
Edward Jones, Bd	*May* 6
Edward Oldcorne, Bd	*April* 7
Edward Powell, Bd	*July* 30
Edward Stransham, Bd	*January* 21
Edward Waterson, Bd	*January* 7
Edward the Confessor	*October* 13
Edward the Martyr	*March* 18
Edwin	*October* 12
Egbert	*April* 24
Egwin	*December* 30
Eiluned. *See* Aled
Elesbaan	*October* 24
Eleusippus	*January* 17
Eleutherius (with Dionysius)	*October* 9
Eleutherius (abbot)	*September* 6
Eleutherius (martyr)	*April* 18
Eleutherius (pope)	*May* 30
Eleutherius of Nicomedia	*October* 2
Eleutherius of Tournai	*February* 20
Elfleda	*February* 8
Elias (martyr)	*February* 16
Elias of Jerusalem	*July* 20
Eligius (or Eloi)	*December* 1
Elizabeth (with Zachary)	*November* 5
Elizabeth Ann Seton	Appendix III
Elizabeth Bichier des Ages	*August* 26
Elizabeth of Hungary	*November* 19
Elizabeth of Mantua, Bd	*February* 20
Elizabeth of Portugal	*July* 8
Elizabeth of Schönau	*June* 18
Elizabeth the Good, Bd	*November* 17
Elmo. *See* Erasmus and Peter Gonzalez
Eloi. *See* Eligius
Elphege. *See* Alphege
Elzear of Sabran	*September* 27
Emerentiana	*January* 23
Emeric, Bd	*November* 4
Emeterius	*March* 3
Emilian Cucullatus	*November* 12
Emiliana	*December* 24
Emily de Rodat	*September* 19
Emily de Vialar	*June* 17
Emily of Vercelli, Bd	*August* 19
Emma	*June* 30
Emmanuel Ruiz, Bd	*July* 10
Emmeramus	*September* 22
Emygdius	*August* 9
Encratis	*April* 16
Enda	*March* 21

John (with Paul)	*June* 26	John du Lau, Bd	*September* 2
John I (pope)	*May* 27	John Leonardi	*October* 9
John Almond, Bd	*December* 5	John Liccio, Bd	*November* 14
John Amias, Bd	*March* 16	John Lloyd, Bd	*July* 22
John the Baptist	*June* 24	John Lockwood, Bd	*April* 13
his Beheading	*August* 29	John Marinoni, Bd	*December* 13
John Baptist Machado, Bd. *See* Martyrs		John Martin Moyë Appendix III	
of Japan, II		John Mason, Bd. *See* Martyrs of London,	
John Baptist Rossi	*May* 23	1591	
John Baptist Turpin, Bd. Appendix III		John Massias, Bd	*September* 18
John Baptist de la Salle	*May* 15	John Munden, Bd. *See* Thomas Hemerford	
John Baptist of Almodovar, Bd *February* 14		John Nelson, Bd	*February* 3
John Baptist of Fabriano, Bd	*March* 11	John Nepomucen	*May* 16
John Beche, Bd	*December* 1	John Nepomucen Neumann Appendix III	
John Berchmans	*November* 26	John Nutter, Bd. *See* Thomas Hemerford	
John Bodey, Bd	*November* 2	John Ogilvie, Bd	*March* 10
John Bonnard, Bd. *See* Martyrs of		John della Pace, Bd	*November* 12
Indo-China, II		John Payne, Bd	*April* 2
John Bosco	*January* 31	John Pelingotto, Bd	*June* 1
John Boste, Bd. *See* Martyrs of Durham		John Perboyre, Bd	*September* 11
John de Brébeuf. *See* Martyrs of North		John Pibush, Bd	*February* 18
America		John Plesington, Bd. *See* Martyrs of	
John de Britto	*February* 4	the Oates Plot	
John Buoni, Bd	*October* 23	John Porro, Bd	*October* 24
John Calybites	*January* 15	John Rainuzzi, Bd	*June* 8
John Carey, Bd. *See* John Cornelius		John Regis	*June* 16
John Cassian	*July* 23	John Ri, Bd. *See* Laurence Imbert	
John de Castillo, Bd. *See* Roque Gonzalez		John de Ribera	*January* 6
John Chrysostom	*January* 27	John Rigby, Bd	*June* 21
John Climacus	*March* 30	John Roberts, Bd	*December* 10
John Colombini, Bd	*July* 31	John Robinson, Bd. *See* Martyrs of	
John Cornay, Bd. *See* Martyrs of Indo-		Canterbury	
China, I		John Roche, Bd. *See* Martyrs of London,	
John Cornelius, Bd	*July* 4	1588	
John Damascene	*March* 27	John Rochester, Bd. *See* Martyrs of	
John Dominici, Bd	*June* 10	the Charterhouse	
John Duckett, Bd	*September* 7	John Rugg, Bd. *See* Hugh Faringdon	
John Eudes	*August* 19	John Ruysbroeck, Bd	*December* 2
John Eynon, Bd. *See* Hugh Faringdon		John Sarkander, Bd	*March* 17
John Felton, Bd	*August* 8	John Shert, Bd	*May* 28
John Fenwick, Bd. *See* Martyrs of the		John Slade, Bd	*October* 30
Oates Plot		John Soreth, Bd	*July* 30
John Finch, Bd	*April* 20	John Southworth, Bd	*June* 28
John Fisher	*July* 9	John Speed, Bd. *See* Martyrs of Durham	
John Forest, Bd	*May* 22	John Stone, Bd	*May* 12
John Gavan, Bd. *See* Martyrs of the		John Storey, Bd	*June* 1
Oates Plot		John Thorne, Bd. *See* Richard Whiting	
John Grande, Bd	*June* 3	John Vianney	*August* 8
John Grove, Bd. *See* Martyrs of the		John Wall, Bd	*August* 26
Oates Plot		John Zedazneli	*November* 4
John Gualbert	*July* 12	John of Alvernia, Bd	*August* 13
John Haile, Bd	*May* 11	John of Avila, Bd	*May* 10
John Hewett, Bd. *See* Martyrs of London,		John of Bergamo	*July* 11
1588		John of Beverley	*May* 7
John Houghton, Bd. *See* Martyrs of		John of Bridlington	*October* 21
the Charterhouse		John of Capistrano	*March* 28
John Ingram, Bd. *See* Martyrs of		John of Chinon	*June* 27
Durham		John of Constantinople	*August* 28
John Ireland, Bd	*March* 11	John of Dukla, Bd	*September* 28
John Jones, Bd	*July* 12	John of Egypt	*March* 27
John Joseph (of the Cross)	*March* 5	John of Gorze	*February* 27
John Kemble, Bd	*August* 22	John of the Goths	*June* 26
John Lalande. *See* Martyrs of North		John of Kanti	*October* 20
America		John of Matera (or of Pulsano)	*June* 20
John Lantrua, Bd. *See* Martyrs of		John of Matha	*February* 8
China, I		John of Meda	*September* 26
John Larke, Bd	*March* 11		

Landry. *See* Landericus
Lanfranc of Canterbury, Bd   *May* 24
Lanfranc of Pavia, Bd   *June* 23
Lanvinus, Bd   *April* 14
Largus (with Cyriacus)   *August* 8
Laserian (or Molaisse)   *April* 18
Laurence (martyr)   *August* 10
Laurence Giustiniani   *September* 5
Laurence Humphrey, Bd. *See* Roger
  Dickenson
Laurence Imbert, Bd   *September* 21
Laurence Loricatus, Bd   *August* 16
Laurence Nerucci, Bd   *August* 31
Laurence O'Toole   *November* 14
Laurence Richardson, Bd. *See* Martyrs
  of London, 1582
Laurence of Brindisi   *July* 21
Laurence of Canterbury   *February* 3
Laurence of Rippafratta, Bd   *September* 28
Laurence of Spoleto   *February* 3
Laurence of Villamagna, Bd   *June* 6
Laurentinus (with Pergentinus)   *June* 3
Laurus   *August* 18
Lazarus   *December* 17
Lazarus of Milan   *February* 11
Leander of Seville   *February* 27
Lebuin (or Liafwine)   *November* 12
Leger (or Leodegarius)   *October* 2
Lelia   *August* 11
Leo (with Paregorius)   *February* 18
Leo I   *April* 11
Leo II   *July* 3
Leo III   *June* 12
Leo IV   *July* 17
Leo IX   *April* 19
Leo Mangin, Bd. Appendix III
Leo (or Lyé) of Mantenay   *May* 25
Leo of Saint-Bertin, Bd   *February* 26
Leobinus (or Lubin)   *March* 14
Leocadia   *December* 9
Leocritia. *See* Lucretia
Leodegarius. *See* Leger
Leonard Kimura, Bd. *See* Martyrs of
  Japan, II
Leonard Murialdo, Bd   Appendix III
Leonard of Noblac   *November* 6
Leonard of Port Maurice   *November* 26
Leonard of Vandœuvre   *October* 15
Leonides of Alexandria   *April* 22
Leontius of Rostov   *May* 23
Leopold of Austria   *November* 15
Leopold of Gaiche, Bd   *April* 2
Lésin. *See* Licinius
Lesmes. *See* Adelelmus
Leu. *See* Lupus of Sens
Leufroy. *See* Leutfridus
Leutfridus (or Leufroy)   *June* 21
Lewina   *July* 24
Lewis. *See* Louis
Liafwine. *See* Lebuin
Liberata. *See* Wilgefortis
Liberatus of Capua   *August* 17
Liberatus of Loro, Bd   *September* 7
Libert. *See* Lietbertus
Liborius   *July* 23
Licinius (or Lésin)   *February* 13

Lietbertus (or Libert)   *June* 23
Lifard. *See* Liphardus
Limnaeus   *February* 22
Linus   *September* 23
Lioba   *September* 28
Liphard. *See* Liudhard
Liphardus (or Lifard)   *June* 3
Liudhard   *May* 7
Livinus   *November* 12
Loman   *February* 17
Longinus   *March* 15
Louis of France   *August* 25
Louis Allemand, Bd   *September* 16
Louis Bertrand   *October* 9
Louis Grignion of Montfort   *April* 28
Louis Morbioli, Bd   *November* 16
Louis Sotelo, Bd. *See* Martyrs of
  Japan, II
Louis Taurin-Dufresse, Bd. *See* Martyrs
  of China, I
Louis of Anjou   *August* 19
Louis of Thuringia, Bd   *September* 11
Louisa Albertoni, Bd   *February* 28
Louisa de Marillac   *March* 15
Louisa of Savoy, Bd   *September* 9
Loup. *See* Lupus of Troyes
Luan. *See* Moloc
Lubin. *See* Leobinus
Luchesio, Bd   *April* 28
Lucian (with Marcian)   *October* 26
Lucian of Antioch   *January* 7
Lucian of Beauvais   *January* 8
Lucillian   *June* 3
Lucius (" king ")   *December* 3
Lucius (with Montanus)   *February* 24
Lucius (with Ptolemaeus)   *October* 19
Lucius I (pope)   *March* 4
Lucius of Adrianople   *February* 11
Lucretia (or Leocritia)   *March* 15
Lucy (martyr)   *December* 13
Lucy Filippini   *March* 25
Lucy de Freitas, Bd. *See* Apollinaris
  Franco
Lucy of Amelia, Bd   *July* 27
Lucy of Caltagirone, Bd   *September* 26
Lucy of Narni, Bd   *November* 16
Ludan   *February* 12
Ludger   *March* 26
Ludmila   *September* 16
Ludolf   *March* 30
Ludovic Pavoni, Bd   *April* 1
Ludwig, Bd. *See* Louis of Thuringia
Lufthildis   *January* 23
Lughaidh. *See* Molua
Luke (evangelist)   *October* 18
Luke Belludi, Bd   *February* 17
Luke Kirby, Bd. *See* Martyrs of London,
  1582
Luke the Younger   *February* 7
Lull   *October* 16
Lupicinus (with Romanus)   *February* 28
Lupus (or Leu) of Sens   *September* 1
Lupus (or Loup) of Troyes   *July* 29
Lutgardis   *June* 16
Luxorius   *August* 21
Lydwina of Schiedam, Bd   *April* 14
Lyé. *See* Leo of Mantenay

M

Macanisius	*September* 3
Macarius of Alexandria	*January* 2
Macarius of Ghent	*April* 10
Macarius of Jerusalem	*March* 10
Macarius the Elder	*January* 15
Macarius the Wonderworker	*April* 1
Macartan	*March* 26
Maccul. *See* Maughold	
Macedonius the Barley-eater	*January* 24
Machabees, The Holy	*August* 1
Machar (or Mochumma)	*November* 12
Machutus. *See* Malo	
Macrina the Elder	*January* 14
Macrina the Younger	*June* 19
Madeleine Barat	*May* 25
Madeleine Fontaine, Bd	*June* 27
Madelgaire. *See* Vincent Madelgarius	
Madelgisilus (or Maugeille)	*May* 30
Madern. *See* Madron	
Madron (or Madern)	*May* 17
Maedoc. *See* Aidan of Ferns	
Maelor. *See* Maglorius	
Maelrubha. *See* Malrubius	
Mafalda	*May* 2
Magdalen Albrizzi, Bd	*May* 15
Magdalen di Canossa, Bd	*May* 14
Magdalen Panattieri, Bd	*October* 13
Magenulf (or Meinulf)	*October* 5
Magi, The	*July* 23
Maglorius (or Maelor)	*October* 24
Magnericus	*July* 25
Magnus of Orkney	*April* 16
Maharsapor	*October* 10
Maimbod	*January* 23
Majolus (or Mayeul)	*May* 11
Majoricus	*December* 6
Malachy of Armagh	*November* 3
Malchus	*October* 21
Mallonus. *See* Mellon	
Malo (or Machutus)	*November* 15
Malrubius (or Maelrubha)	*April* 21
Mamas	*August* 17
Mamertus	*May* 11
Mamilian. *See* Maximilian (martyr)	
Manechildis (or Ménéhould)	*October* 14
Manettus. *See* Founders of the Servites	
Mannes, Bd	*July* 30
Mappalicus	*April* 17
Marcella of Rome	*January* 31
Marcellian (with Mark)	*June* 18
Marcellina	*July* 17
Marcellinus (pope)	*April* 26
Marcellinus (with Peter)	*June* 2
Marcellinus Champagnat, Bd.	Appendix III
Marcellinus of Carthage	*April* 6
Marcellinus of Embrun	*April* 20
Marcellus (with Apuleius)	*October* 8
Marcellus (with Valerian)	*September* 4
Marcellus I (pope)	*January* 16
Marcellus of Apamea	*August* 14
Marcellus of Paris	*November* 1
Marcellus of Tomi	*August* 27
Marcellus Akimetes	*December* 29
Marcellus the Centurion	*October* 30

Marchelm	*July* 14
Marcian (or Marian)	*April* 20
Marcian (with Lucian)	*October* 26
Marcian (with Nicander)	*June* 17
Marcian of Constantinople	*January* 10
Marcian of Cyrrhus	*November* 2
Marciana of Rusuccur	*January* 9
Marcolino of Forlì, Bd	*January* 24
Marcoul. *See* Marculf	
Marculf (or Marcoul)	*May* 1
Margaret (or Marina)	*July* 20
Margaret Bourgeoys, Bd	*January* 19
Margaret Clitherow, Bd	*March* 25
Margaret Colonna, Bd	*November* 7
Margaret Mary	*October* 17
Margaret Pole, Bd	*May* 28
Margaret Ward, Bd. *See* Martyrs of London, 1588	
Margaret of Città-di-Castello (or of Metola), Bd	*April* 13
Margaret of Cortona	*February* 22
Margaret " of England "	*February* 3
Margaret of Hungary	*January* 26
Margaret of Lorraine, Bd	*November* 6
Margaret of Louvain, Bd	*September* 2
Margaret of Ravenna, Bd	*January* 23
Margaret of Savoy, Bd	*December* 23
Margaret of Scotland	*June* 10
Margaret the Barefooted	*August* 27
Margaret the Penitent. *See* Pelagia the Penitent	
Mari	*August* 5
Marian. *See* Marcian	
Marian (with James)	*April* 30
Mariana of Quito	*May* 26
Marianus Scotus, Bd	*February* 9
Marina (or Margaret)	*July* 20
Marina (or Pelagia)	*February* 12
Marinus (San Marino)	*September* 4
Marinus (with Astyrius)	*March* 3
Marius (or May)	*January* 27
Marius (with Martha)	*January* 19
Mark (evangelist)	*April* 25
Mark (pope)	*October* 7
Mark (or Martin)	*October* 24
Mark (with Marcellian)	*June* 18
Mark Barkworth, Bd	*February* 27
Mark Crisin, Bd	*September* 7
Mark Fantucci, Bd	*April* 10
Mark of Arethusa	*March* 29
Mark of Modena, Bd	*September* 23
Mark of Montegallo, Bd	*March* 20
Maro	*February* 14
Mars. *See* Martius	
Martha	*July* 29
Martha (with Marius)	*January* 19
Martial (with Faustus)	*October* 13
Martial of Limoges	*June* 30
Martin (or Mark)	*October* 24
Martin I (pope)	*November* 12
Martin de Porres, St.	*November* 5
Martin of Braga	*March* 20
Martin of Tours	*November* 11
Martin of Vertou	*October* 24
Martina	*January* 30
Martinian (with Maxima)	*October* 16
Martinian (with Processus)	*July* 2

697

Martinian the Hermit	*February* 13	her Motherhood	*October* 11
Martius (or Mars)	*April* 13	her Presentation	*November* 21
Martyrius (with Sisinnius)	*May* 29	her Purification	*February* 2
Martyrs of Arras	*June* 27	her Sorrows	*September* 15
Martyrs under the Boxers	*July* 9	her Visit to Elizabeth	*July* 2
and Appendix III		Our Lady of Lourdes	*February* 11
Martyrs of Canterbury and others	*October* 1	Our Lady of Mount Carmel	*July* 16
Martyrs des Carmes. See John du Lau		Our Lady of Ransom	*September* 24
Martyrs of the Charterhouse	*May* 11	Mary, Our Lady " of the Snow "	*August* 5
Martyrs of China, I	*February* 17	the Name of Mary	*September* 12
Martyrs of China, II	*July* 9	the Holy Rosary	*October* 7
Martyrs of Compiègne, Carmelite	*July* 17	Mary (martyr)	*November* 1
Martyrs of Crete, The Ten	*December* 23	Mary (with Flora)	*November* 24
Martyrs of Damascus	*July* 10	Mary Assunta, Bd Appendix III	
Martyrs under the Danes	*April* 10	Mary Bartholomea, Bd	*May* 28
Martyrs of Dorchester	*July* 4	Mary Cleophas	*April* 9
Martyrs of Douay	*October* 29	Mary Desmaisières	*August* 26
Martyrs of Durham	*July* 24	Mary Frances	*October* 6
Martyrs of Ebsdorf	*February* 2	Mary Goretti	*July* 6
Martyrs of England and Wales (general)		Mary L'Huilier, Bd. Appendix III	
	May 4	Mary Magdalen	*July* 22
Martyrs of Gorcum	*July* 9	Mary Magdalen Martinengo, Bd	*July* 27
Martyrs of Indo-China, I	*July* 11	Mary Magdalen dei Pazzi	*May* 29
Martyrs of Indo-China, II	*November* 6	Mary Magdalen Postel	*July* 16
Martyrs of Japan, I	*February* 5	Mary Margaret d'Youville Appendix III	
Martyrs of Japan, II	*June* 1	Mary de Mattias, Bd	*August* 20
Martyrs of Japan, III	*September* 10	Mary Mazzarello	*May* 14
Martyrs of Korea	*September* 21	Mary Pelletier	*April* 24
Martyrs of Laval. Appendix III		Mary di Rosa	*December* 15
Martyrs of Lithuania	*April* 14	Mary Soledad, Bd	*October* 11
Martyrs under the Lombards	*March* 2	Mary de Soubiran, Bd	*October* 20
Martyrs of London, 1582	*May* 28	Mary of Cerevellon	*September* 19
Martyrs of London, 1588	*August* 28	Mary of Egypt	*April* 2
Martyrs of London, 1591	*December* 10	Mary of Oignies, Bd	*June* 23
Martyrs of Lyons	*June* 2	Mary of Pisa, Bd	*January* 28
Martyrs of Mar Saba	*March* 20	Mary of Turin, Bd	*December* 16
Martyrs of Najran	*October* 24	Mary of the Incarnation (Acarie), Bd	
Martyrs under Nero	*June* 24		*April* 18
Martyrs at Nicomedia	*December* 25	Masabkis, The. *See* Emmanuel Ruiz	
Martyrs of North America	*September* 26	Maternus of Cologne	*September* 14
Martyrs of the Oates Plot	*June* 20	Mathurin. *See* Maturinus	
Martyrs of Orange	*July* 9	Matilda. *See* Mechtildis	
Martyrs of Paraguay	*November* 17	Matilda (widow)	*March* 14
Martyrs in Persia, The CXX	*April* 6	Matrona	*March* 15
Martyrs of the Alexandrian Plague		Matthew (evangelist)	*September* 21
	February 28	Matthew of Girgenti, Bd	*October* 21
Martyrs of Prague, Servite	*August* 31	Matthew of Mantua, Bd	*October* 7
Martyrs of Salsette	*July* 27	Matthia of Matelica, Bd	*November* 7
Martyrs of Samosata, The Seven		Matthias (apostle)	*February* 24
	December 9	Matthias Murumba, Bd. *See* Charles	
Martyrs of Scillium	*July* 17	Lwanga	
Martyrs of Sebastea, The Forty	*March* 10	Maturinus (or Mathurin)	*November* 1
Martyrs of September 1792	*September* 2	Maturus. *See* Pothinus	
Martyrs of the Serapeum	*March* 17	Maudez. *See* Mawes	
Martyrs of Sinai	*January* 14	Maughold (or Maccul)	*April* 27
Martyrs of Toulouse	*May* 29	Maugille. *See* Madelgisilus	
Martyrs of Uganda	*June* 3	Maura (with Brigid)	*July* 13
Martyrs of Utica	*August* 24	Maura (with Timothy)	*May* 3
Martyrs of Valenciennes, Ursuline		Maura of Leucadia. *See* Anne (virgin)	
	October 17	Maura of Troyes	*September* 21
Maruthas	*December* 4	Maurice of Agaunum	*September* 22
Mary, The Blessed Virgin	*August* 15	Maurice of Carnoët	*October* 13
the Annunciation	*March* 25	Maurice of Hungary, Bd	*March* 20
her Assumption	*August* 15	Maurilius of Angers	*September* 13
her Birthday	*September* 8	Mauruntius	*May* 5
her Immaculate Conception	*December* 8	Maurus (abbot)	*January* 15
her Immaculate Heart	*August* 22	Mawes (or Maudez)	*November* 18

Nicephorus (martyr) — *February* 9
Nicephorus of Constantinople — *March* 13
Nicetas (abbot) — *April* 3
Nicetas of Constantinople — *October* 6
Nicetas of Novgorod — *January* 31
Nicetas of Pereaslav — *May* 24
Nicetas of Remesiana — *June* 22
Nicetas the Goth — *September* 15
Nicetius (or Nizier) of Besançon — *February* 8
Nicetius (or Nizier) of Lyons — *April* 2
Nicetius of Trier — *December* 5
Nicholas I (pope) — *November* 13
Nicholas Albergati, Bd — *May* 9
Nicholas Factor, Bd — *December* 14
Nicholas von Flüe — *March* 22
Nicholas Owen, Bd — *March* 12
Nicholas Paglia, Bd — *February* 14
Nicholas Pieck — *July* 9
Nicholas Studites — *February* 4
Nicholas of Forca Palena, Bd — *October* 1
Nicholas of Linköping, Bd — *July* 24
Nicholas of Myra (or of Bari) — *December* 6
Nicholas of Sibenik, Bd — *December* 5
Nicholas of Tolentino — *September* 10
Nicholas the Pilgrim — *June* 2
Nicomedes — *September* 15
Nikon " Metanoeite " — *November* 26
Nilus of Rossano — *September* 26
Nilus the Elder — *November* 12
Ninian — *September* 16
Nino — *December* 15
Nizier. *See* Nicetius
Noel Chabanel. *See* Martyrs of North America
Noel Pinot, Bd — *February* 21
Non (or Nonnita) — *March* 3
Nonius (or Nuñes), Bd — *November* 6
Nonna — *August* 5
Nonnita. *See* Non
Norbert — *June* 6
Notburga — *September* 14
Nothelm — *October* 17
Notker Balbulus, Bd — *April* 6
Novellone, Bd — *August* 13
Nuñes, Bd. *See* Nonius
Nunilo — *October* 22
Nunzio Sulprizio, Bd   Appendix III
Nympha — *November* 10
Nymphodora — *September* 10

O

Octave of Christmas — *January* 1
Oddino, Bd — *July* 21
Odhran. *See* Otteran
Odilia (or Ottilia) — *December* 13
Odilo — *January* 1
Odo of Cambrai — *June* 19
Odo of Canterbury — *July* 4
Odo of Cluny — *November* 18
Odo of Novara, Bd — *January* 14
Odoric of Pordenone, Bd — *January* 14
Odulf — *June* 12
Oengus. *See* Aengus
Olaf — *July* 29
Oldegar. *See* Ollegarius
Olga — *July* 11

Olive of Palermo, Bd — *June* 10
Oliver Plunket, Bd — *July* 11
Ollegarius (or Oldegar) — *March* 6
Olympias — *December* 17
Omer (or Audomarus) — *September* 9
Onesimus the Slave — *February* 16
Onuphrius — *June* 12
Opportuna — *April* 22
Optatus of Milevis — *June* 4
Optatus of Saragossa — *April* 16
Oringa, Bd — *January* 4
Orsiesius — *June* 15
Osanna of Cattaro, Bd — *April* 27
Osanna of Mantua, Bd — *June* 20
Osburga — *March* 30
Osmund — *December* 4
Oswald of Northumbria — *August* 9
Oswald of Worcester — *February* 28
Oswin — *August* 20
Osyth — *October* 7
Otger — *May* 8
Otteran (or Odhran) of Iona — *October* 27
Ottilia. *See* Odilia
Otto of Bamberg — *July* 2
Oudoceus. *See* Teilo
Ouen (or Audoenus) — *August* 24
Outril. *See* Austregisilus
Oyend. *See* Eugendus

P

Pachomius — *May* 9
Pacifico of Cerano, Bd — *June* 8
Pacifico of San Severino — *September* 24
Pacian — *March* 9
Padarn (or Patern) — *April* 15
Pair. *See* Paternus of Avranches
Palladius (bishop in Ireland) — *July* 7
Pambo — *July* 18
Pammachius — *August* 30
Pamphilus of Caesarea — *June* 1
Pamphilus of Sulmona — *April* 28
Pancras (martyr) — *May* 12
Pancras of Taormina — *April* 3
Pantaenus — *July* 7
Pantaleon (or Panteleimon) — *July* 27
Panteleimon. *See* Pantaleon
Paphnutius (bishop) — *September* 11
Papylus — *April* 13
Paregorius — *February* 18
Parisio — *June* 11
Parthenius (with Calocerus) — *May* 19
Paschal I (pope) — *February* 11
Paschal Baylon — *May* 17
Paschasius Radbertus — *April* 26
Pastor (with Justus) — *August* 6
Patern of Ceredigion. *See* Padarn
Paternus of Abdinghof — *April* 10
Paternus (or Pair) of Avranches — *April* 16
Patiens of Lyons — *September* 11
Patricia — *August* 25
Patrick — *March* 17
Patrick Salmon, Bd.   *See* John Cornelius
Patroclus of Troyes — *January* 21
Paul (apostle) — *June* 29
  his Conversion — *January* 25

Tigrius — *January* 12
Tilbert — *September* 7
Tillo — *January* 7
Timothy (bishop) — *January* 24
Timothy (with Agapius) — *August* 19
Timothy (with Hippolytus) — *August* 22
Timothy (with Maura) — *May* 3
Timothy of Montecchio, Bd — *August* 26
Titus (bishop) — *February* 6
Torello, Bd — *March* 16
Toribio. *See* Turibius
Torquatus — *May* 15
Transfiguration of Our Lord, The — *August* 6
Triphyllius — *June* 13
Trond. *See* Trudo
Trophimus of Arles — *December* 29
Trudo (or Trond) — *November* 23
Trumwin — *February* 10
Trypho (with Respicius) — *November* 10
Tudwal — *December* 1
Turibius of Astorga — *April* 16
Turibius of Lima — *April* 27
Tutilo — *March* 28
Twelve Brothers, The — *September* 1
Tychon — *June* 16
Tyrannio — *February* 20
Tysilio (or Suliau) — *November* 8

U

Ubald of Florence, Bd — *April* 9
Ubald of Gubbio — *May* 16
Ulphia — *January* 31
Ulric of Augsburg — *July* 4
Ulric of Zell — *July* 14
Ultan of Ardbraccan — *September* 4
Ultan of Fosses — *May* 2
Uncumber. *See* Wilgefortis
Urban I — *May* 25
Urban II, Bd — *July* 29
Urban V, Bd — *December* 19
Urbicius (abbot) — *June* 3
Ursicinus (abbot) — *December* 20
Ursmar — *April* 19
Ursula — *October* 21
Ursulina, Bd — *April* 7

V

Vaast. *See* Vedast
Vaclav. *See* Wenceslaus
Valentina — *July* 25
Valentine (bishop) — *January* 7
Valentine (martyr) — *February* 14
Valentine Berrio-Ochoa, Bd. *See* Martyrs of Indo-China, II
Valeria (with Vitalis) — *April* 28
Valerian (martyr in Africa) — *December* 15
Valerian (with Marcellus) — *September* 4
Valerius (with Rufinus) — *June* 14
Valerius (with Tiburtius) — *April* 14
Valerius of Saragossa. *See* Vincent of Saragossa

Valéry (or Walaricus) — *April* 1
Vaneng. *See* Waningus
Vanne (or Vitonus) — *November* 9
Varus — *October* 19
Vedast (or Vaast) — *February* 6
Venantius Fortunatus — *December* 14
Venantius of Camerino — *May* 18
Venerius of Milan — *May* 4
Verdiana, Bd — *February* 16
Veremund (abbot) — *March* 8
Verena — *September* 1
Veronica — *July* 12
Veronica Giuliani — *July* 9
Veronica of Binasco, Bd — *January* 13
Viator. *See* Justus of Lyons
Vicelin — *December* 12
Victor I — *July* 28
Victor III, Bd — *September* 16
Victor Maurus — *May* 8
Victor of Marseilles — *July* 21
Victor the Hermit — *February* 26
Victoria. *See* Saturninus, with Dativus
Victoria (with Acisclus) — *November* 17
Victoria (with Anatolia) — *December* 23
Victoria Fornari-Strata, Bd — *September* 12
Victorian (abbot) — *January* 12
Victorian (martyr) — *March* 23
Victoricus (with Fuscian) — *December* 11
Victorinus of Corinth — *February* 25
Victorinus of Pettau — *November* 2
Victricius — *August* 7
Vigilius of Trent — *June* 26
Vigor — *November* 1
Villana, Bd — *February* 28
Vincent Ferrer — *April* 5
Vincent Madelgarius — *September* 20
Vincent Pallotti — *January* 22
Vincent de Paul — *July* 19
Vincent Romano, Bd — Appendix III
Vincent Strambi — *September* 25
Vincent of Agen — *June* 9
Vincent of Aquila, Bd. *See* John of Alvernia
Vincent of Cracow, Bd — *March* 8
Vincent of Lérins — *May* 24
Vincent of Saragossa — *January* 22
Vincentia Gerosa — *June* 4
Vincentia Lopez, Bd — *December* 26
Vincentian — *January* 2
Vindician — *March* 11
Virgil of Arles — *March* 5
Virgil (or Feargal) of Salzburg — *November* 27
Vitalian (pope) — *January* 27
Vitalis (with Agricola) — *November* 4
Vitalis (with Valeria) — *April* 28
Vitalis of Savigny, Bd — *September* 16
Vitonus. *See* Vanne
Vitus (with Modestus) — *June* 15
Vivaldo, Bd — *May* 11
Viviana. *See* Bibiana
Vladimir — *July* 15
Vodalus (or Voel) — *February* 5
Voel. *See* Vodalus
Volusian — *January* 18
Vulflagius (or Wulphy) — *June* 7
Vulmar — *July* 20

282.092
B

Butler's lives of the
Saints

$140.00
811075

10/16/1997
9468371

DATE			